Consumption and the World of Goods

Consumption and the World of Goods

Edited by

John Brewer and Roy Porter

London and New York

First published in 1993 by Routledge

First published in paperback in 1994
by Routledge
11 New Fetter Lane, London EC4P 4EE

Simultaneously published in the USA and Canada
by Routledge
29 West 35th Street, New York, NY 10001

Reprinted 1997

This collection © 1993, 1994 Routledge; individual
chapters © 1993, 1994 individual contributors

Typeset in Baskerville No. 2 by Florencetype Ltd,
Kewstoke, Avon
Printed and bound in Great Britain by
T. J. International Ltd.

British Library Cataloguing in Publication Data
A catalogue record for this book is available from the
British Library.

Library of Congress Cataloguing in Publication Data
also available

ISBN 0–415–11478–0

Contents

Figures

Tables

Plates

Notes on contributors

Jean-Christophe Agnew teaches American Studies and History at Yale University and is the author of *Worlds Apart: The Market and the Theater in Anglo-American Thought, 1550–1750* (1986).

Joyce Appleby, who teaches at UCLA, is a historian of early modern England and America. Author of *Economic Thought and Ideology in Seventeenth-Century England* (1978), she has studied the impact of economic change upon social thought. Her most recent book, a collection of essays, is *Liberalism and Republicanism in the Historical Imagination* (1992).

T. H. Breen is the William Smith Mason Professor of American History at Northwestern University. He was formerly the Pitt Professor of American History and Professorial Fellow at Trinity College, Cambridge. His most recent books are *Tobacco Culture: The Great Tidewater Planters on the Eve of the Revolution* (1985) and *Imagining the Past: East Hampton Histories* (1989), which won the 1990 prize for the outstanding book on historic preservation. He is currently working on a volume entitled *The Baubles of Britain: The American and Consumer Revolutions of the Eighteenth Century*.

John Brewer is Professor of History at UCLA. Between 1987 and 1991 he was Director of the Clark Library and the Center for Seventeenth and Eighteenth-Century Studies and principal investigator on the research project 'Culture and consumption in the seventeenth and eighteenth centuries'. His most recent book, *The Sinews of Power*, was published in 1989.

Peter Burke is Reader in Cultural History at the University of Cambridge, and Fellow of Emmanuel College. His recent books include *The Historical Anthropology of Early Modern Italy* (1987) and *The Fabrication of Louis XIV* (1992).

Colin Campbell is Senior Lecturer in Sociology at the University of York and author of *The Romantic Ethic and the Spirit of Modern Consumerism* (1987).

Patricia Cline Cohen is Associate Professor of History at the University of California at Santa Barbara. She is the author of *A Calculating People: The Spread of Numeracy in Early America* (1982).

David Cressy is author of *Literacy and the Social Order: Reading and Writing in Tudor and Stuart England* (1980), *Coming Over: Migration and Communication between England and New England in the Seventeenth Century* (1987) and *Bonfires and Bells: National Memory and the Protestant Calendar in Elizabethan and Stuart England* (1989).

Jan de Vries is Professor of History and Economics at the University of California, Berkeley. He is the author of numerous books and articles on European economy and society in the sixteenth, seventeenth and eighteenth centuries. His publications include *The Dutch Rural Economy in the Golden Age, 1500–1700* (1974), *The Economy of Europe in an Age of Crisis, 1600–1750* (1976) and *European Urbanization, 1500–1800* (1984).

Cissie Fairchilds is a social historian of early modern France. She received her Ph.D. from Johns Hopkins University and is at present Professor of History at Syracuse University. She is the author of *Poverty and Charity in Aix-en-Provence, 1640–1789* (1976) and *Domestic Enemies: Servants and their Masters in Old Regime France* (1984).

C. Y. Ferdinand is Fellow Librarian of Magdalen College, Oxford. She is an associate editor of 'A Biographical Database of Members of the London Book Trades 1555–1830' and was formerly Leverhulme Research Fellow on the History of the Book in Britain project.

Iaroslav Isaievych is Director of the Institute for Ukrainian Studies at the Academy of Sciences of Ukraine. His recent publications include *Greek Culture in the Ukraine: 1550–1650* (1990) and *Between Eastern Tradition and Influences from the West: Confraternities in Early Modern Ukraine and Byelorussia* (1990).

Sidney Mintz is the Wm L. Straus Jr Professor of Anthropology at the Johns Hopkins University. Mintz received his B.A. (Psychology) from Brooklyn (NY) College in 1943 and his Ph.D. (Anthropology) from Columbia in 1951. He has carried out research in Puerto Rico, Jamaica, Haiti and Iran, and specializes in the social history of rural communities. After twenty-four years of teaching at Yale, in 1974 Mintz moved to Johns Hopkins with two colleagues to establish a department of Anthropology there. Mintz's books include *The People of Puerto Rico* (1956), *Worker in the Cane* (1960), *Caribbean Transformations* (1974), *Sweetness and Power* (1985) and (with Richard Price) *The Birth of African–American Culture* (1992).

John Money is Associate Professor of History at the University of Victoria, British Columbia. His publications include *Experience and Identity: Birmingham and the West Midlands, 1700–1800* (1977) and numerous articles on English provincial society during the eighteenth century. His main interest is in the adaptations and transformations which constituted the actual fabric of England's supposed *ancien régime*.

Chandra Mukerji is Professor of Communication and Sociology at the University of California, San Diego. She is author of two books, *From Graven Images* (1983) and *A Fragile Power* (1989), as well as numerous articles on culture and political economy.

Jeremy D. Popkin, Professor of History at the University of Kentucky, has published extensively on the history of the European press before and during the French Revolution. He is the author of *The Right-Wing Press in France, 1792–1800* (1980), *News and Politics in the Age of Revolution: Jean Luzac's 'Gazette de Leyde'* (1989) and *Revolutionary News: The Press in France, 1789–1799* (1990).

Roy Porter is Senior Lecturer in the Social History of Medicine at the Wellcome Institute for the History of Medicine. Recent books include *Mind Forg'd Manacles: Madness in England from the Restoration to the Regency* (1987), *A Social History of Madness* (1987), *In Sickness and in Health: The British Experience, 1650–1850* (1988), *Patient's Progress* (1989) – these last two co-authored with Dorothy Porter – and *Health for Sale: Quackery in England, 1660–1850* (1989).

Simon Schaffer lectures on History and Philosophy of Science at Cambridge University. He is the author (with Steven Shapin) of *Leviathan and the Air Pump: Hobbes, Boyle and Experimental Life* (1985) and editor (with David Gooding and Trevor Pinch) of *The Uses of Experiment* (1989).

Simon Schama is Professor of History, Mellon Professor of the Social Sciences and Senior Associate at the Center for European Studies at Harvard University. He is the author of *Patriots and Liberators: Revolution in the Netherlands 1780–1813* (1977, reissued in paperback 1991), *Two Rothschilds and the Land of Israel* (1979), *The Embarrassment of Riches: An Interpretation of Dutch Culture in the Golden Age* (1970) and most recently of a historical novel, *Dead Certainties (Unwarranted Speculations)* (1991). His work has been translated into ten languages.

Carole Shammas is Professor of History at the University of California-Riverside and the author of *The Pre-Industrial Consumer in England and America* (1990).

Barbara Maria Stafford, Professor of Art History at the University of Chicago, has a longstanding interest in the relationship between art and the sciences. Her book *Voyage into Substance* (1984) represents a particular fascination with natural history during the Enlightenment. The problems binding the history of art with the history of medicine is taken up in *Body Criticism: Imaging the Unseen in Enlightenment Art and Medicine* (1991). Professor Stafford recently received a John Solomon Guggenheim Fellowship and the Senior Humboldt Prize.

John Styles is a member of the Research Department at the Victoria and Albert Museum and is head of the M.A. course in the History of Design run jointly by the Museum and the Royal College of Art. He co-edited, with John Brewer, *An Ungovernable People. The English and their law in the Seventeenth and Eighteenth Centuries* (1980) and is author of numerous articles on manufacturing, law and criminality in eighteenth-century England. He is currently engaged on research into clothes, fashion and English society, 1660–1820.

Amanda Vickery is a lecturer in modern women's history at Royal Holloway and Bedford New College, University of London. Her doctorate was entitled 'Women of the local elite in Lancashire, 1750–*c*. 1825'.

Lorna Weatherill has eclectic interests. She is currently the database applications adviser in the University of Newcastle upon Tyne, England, where she specializes in consultancy for researchers in arts and social sciences. She was formerly a research fellow in the University of St. Andrews, Scotland. Here she worked on consumer industries and consumer behaviour in early modern Britain and has published widely in the field. She is the author of *Consumer Behaviour and Material Culture in Britain, 1660–1760*, (Routledge, 1988) and edited *Richard Letham's Account Book, 1725–1765* (British Academy, 1990).

John E. Wills, Jr is Professor of History and Director of the East Asian Studies Center at the University of Southern California. He is the author of *Pepper, Guns, and Parleys: The Dutch East India Company and China, 1662–1681* (1974) and *Embassies and Illusions: Dutch and Portuguese Envoys to K'ang-hsi* (1984); co-editor with Jonathan D. Spence of *From Ming to Ch'ing: Conquest, Region, and Continuity in Seventeenth-Century China* (1979); and author or co-author of two chapters on Sino-western relations for the *Cambridge History of China*.

Preface

The papers in this volume were part of the three-year research project mounted by the Center for Seventeenth and Eighteenth Century Studies and the Clark Library at UCLA on 'Culture and Consumption in the Seventeenth and Eighteenth Centuries'. This project was partially funded by grant no. RO-21623-88 from the Interpretive Research Division of the National Endowment of the Humanities. Additional resources came from the Dean of the Division of Humanities at UCLA, the Center and the Clark Library.

The project director, John Brewer, would like to thank not only all the scholars who took part as paper-givers and discussants but the staff of the Center and Library whose efforts made the project possible. Roy Porter wishes to thank Frieda Houser, Departmental Secretary at the Wellcome Institute, for her help in processing the contributors' essays.

This volume is the first of three published by Routledge from the Clark Library series. The others are John Brewer and Susan Staves (eds), *Early Modern Conceptions of Property* (1994) and John Brewer and Anne Bermingham (eds), *Word, Image and Object: Culture and Consumption in the Seventeenth and Eighteenth Centuries* (forthcoming).

1
Introduction

John Brewer and Roy Porter

Our lives today are dominated by the material objects that proliferate all around us, and by the prospects and problems they afford. It is peculiar that the history of this 'world of goods' has, at least till very recently, been so little addressed by historians. Economic history has long been entrenched; social and cultural history have vastly expanded their domains in recent years. Yet none of these disciplines has set the history of consumer societies high on its agenda; and, though the opportunities are present, the three have rarely joined forces to tackle what ought to be a fruitful and unifying mutual concern.

As events over the last few years in eastern and central Europe have been suggesting, in the modern world the ultimate test of the viability of regimes rests in their capacity, in the literal sense, to 'deliver the goods'. Today's verdict is that state communism has failed to meet this demand; erstwhile Marxists are now looking to the west for their models of abundance. If, over the long haul, what J. H. Plumb has, in a different context, called the growth of political stability hinges on the ability of politico-economic systems to satisfy expectations of the good life, surely it is high time for 'big history' to address one of the special features of modern western societies: not just industrialization, or economic growth, but the capacity to create and sustain a consumer economy, and the consumers to go with it. Modern western economies have transformed the material world, and thereby, it seems, stabilized the social and the political.

The early history of consumer societies has not been totally neglected. Notable studies have appeared, assessing the transformation of the medieval void into a culture full of objects, not least Chandra Mukerji's wide-ranging *From Graven Images: Patterns of Modern Materialism* and Joan Thirsk's more specialized *Economic Policy and Projects*.[1] A lively scholarship surveys the distinctive forms of consumer-capitalism emerging in the second half of the nineteenth century and flourishing in the twentieth: department stores, international exhibitions, advertising, consumer psychology, industrial design and so forth.[2] And, in some ways, most ambitiously of all, *The Birth of a Consumer Society* (1982), jointly written by Neil McKendrick, John Brewer and J. H. Plumb, addressed head-on the key questions of the roots and rise of consumer-capitalism.[3] Probing the time and place of the 'take-off' into

1

consumerism, that work suggested that it was, in fact, eighteenth-century England that had witnessed the first 'consumer revolution'. Above all, the authorial trio seriously addressed the implications of material plenty from different disciplinary positions. As an economic historian, Neil McKendrick explored the strategies through which entrepreneurs could create, and then cash in upon, a new hunger for belongings and services.[4] From the social-historical angle, J. H. Plumb showed the impact of new gratifications upon cultural horizons and expectations of life in the age of the Enlightenment.[5] And, assessing the political implications, John Brewer showed how the pressures and problems of commercial society helped call into being a new middle-class politics.[6] The volume aimed to demonstrate that analysis of consumer societies must go far beyond mere enumerations of the accelerating rates at which pots and pans, geegaws and jigsaws were acquired. For the concept of consumer society has far wider significations, characterizing social orders whose expectations, whose hopes and fears, whose prospects of integration, harmony or dissolution, increasingly depended upon the smooth operation and continued expansion of the system of goods.

   The Birth of a Consumer Society was a swallow, preceding a summer which has yet to follow. The hope of the authors that the economic, socio-cultural and political dimensions of consumption would be conjointly researched has hardly yet come to fruition in major cross-disciplinary works. It is noteworthy, for instance, that consumerism and the impact of material abundance figure hardly at all in the new three-volume *Cambridge Social History of Britain*.[7] A certain degree of scepticism continues to be bruited about the heuristic value of the concept to historians. Some of this centres on specific questions. Was eighteenth-century England really the site of this happy event? Didn't consumerism emerge earlier, in Renaissance Italy and the Low Countries, and then reveal all its major features in the 'embarrassment of riches' enjoyed by the burghers of the seventeenth-century Dutch Republic?[8] Or, to pose the question differently, wasn't the eighteenth century far too early to expect to find manifestations of *mass* society, *mass* culture and *mass* production? Should we not be looking for those developments in the age not of Josiah Wedgwood but of Henry Ford?[9] Several of the contributors to the present volume – above all, Jean-Christophe Agnew in his survey of methods, approaches and historiographies, and John Styles in his closing essay – think out loud upon these genuinely complex issues of language and categorization.[10]

   But there is a more general scepticism which needs to be identified and addressed, a discomfort with the very concept of the history of consumerism. Not (as might have been suggested a decade or two ago) on the grounds that the study of material culture is a trivial pursuit. We are all semiologists now, convinced by the arguments of such cultural anthropologists as Clifford Geerz and by literary structuralists like Roland Barthes and his successors – to say nothing of *The Psychopathology of Everyday Life* – that every object bears a meaning and tells a story: belongings are good to think with.[11] Rather there is an underlying objection, a fear that to interpret the last few centuries in terms of the rise of consumerism is some kind of ideological ploy, an old progress theory being smuggled back in new clothes. The suspicion has been most directly articulated from the political right: J. C. D. Clark has condemned attempts to identify early consumer societies as Whiggery Redivivus, yet another example of teleologically reading back the present into the past, or of endowing earlier centuries with a spurious modernity.[12] But one senses a no less impassioned, if not so clearly stated, antipathy from leftish historians, evidently fearful that concentration upon the history of the creation and fulfilment of customer demand will, willy-nilly, endorse a panglossian, hidden-hand history, which ratifies the claims of market capitalism to give the people what they want, and thereby obscures the history of poverty, oppression, uprooting, deskilling – in short, of class struggle in industrial capitalism.[13]

There has long been, of course, ideological antipathy from the left to the seductions of capitalist materialism, perhaps summed up most seminally in work by R. H. Tawney such as *The Acquisitive Society* (1923). This distaste for the fruits of capitalism may be regarded as an honourable tradition of idealist dissenting radicalism; alternatively one may see it as displaced Puritanism, latter-day Luddism, elitist snobbery or pseudo-aristocratic prejudice. From Carlyle, Ruskin and the Arts and Crafts movement, through to the Leavisites, the march of material progress has commonly been disparaged by British critics and historians as a source of alienation, selling the birthrights of craft and community for a can of pottage.[14] Such views owe much both to Christian Socialism and to the young Marx's 'anthropological' critique of capitalist reification and the fetishism of goods (the more you have the less you are).[15] Amongst modern Marxist philosophers, Herbert Marcuse has been notable for his exposés of the politically reactionary functions of acquisitiveness ('repressive desublimation').[16] Today, commodity capitalism has become one of the targets of the 'Green' political movement.

Critics red, green, and of many other hues, however, would insinuate that to highlight consumerism as a key tool of historical interpretation is necessarily to underwrite market economics and the politics accompanying it. It means, of course, no such thing – as is surely proved by the uniting of some two dozen distinguished scholars of radically different backgrounds, commitments and beliefs, as contributors to this book. It is, rather, the view of all who have written for this book that our understanding of the development of western societies will remain dramatically impoverished unless we confront the fact that such polities, uniquely in world history, have come to revolve around the mass consumption of goods and services. We need to understand how this system originated and how it has functioned. And to do this, it is imperative that we investigate in the most comprehensive way the links connecting this material culture (one often highly and increasingly inegalitarian) to the political and social systems with which it has become symbiotic.

Various questions suggest themselves. Has the emergent world of goods by some economic–technological necessity precluded the possibility of certain sorts of regimes (the *ancien régime* or brute tyranny), and has it pre-empted certain kinds of political future (for example, proletarian revolution as outlined in the *Communist Manifesto*)? How far should we see consumerism as a *mentalité*, informing attitudes not only towards goods and belongings, but also personal relations and political philosophies?[17] In what ways does history reveal the manipulation of attitudes such as emulativeness by political leaders and dealers, by the psy-professions, by public relations agencies, no less than by manufacturers, marketeers and their publicity machines?[18] Alongside *homo faber*, and *homo economicus* and all the other 'men' inscribed in modern society, we need to assess how far the new world of goods was simultaneously created by, and creating, a new sort of man (and woman): *homo edens*, the consumer, or, even less flatteringly, *homo gulosus*.[19]

In short, the problem with the concept of the history of consumerism is not that it is irredeemably ideologically loaded, but that it has been, till now, historiographically immature. It has not yet been the subject of searching criticism nor have its programmes been fully put into effect. It needs to be broken in and put through its paces. Yet it carries great promise. The point of this volume, and the two planned to follow it, is to explore the notion's value in interpreting the central transformations in the histories of Europe and North

America over the last several centuries, not just in economic history or the history of material culture, but across a far wider spectrum of human affairs.

This volume is divided into six sections, each addressing a particular problem area. The first, 'Problems, methods and concepts', is mainly methodological and historiographical. As a historian, Jean-Christophe Agnew examines recent writings that have argued for the utility of 'consumerism' as an analytic category. He points to some of the difficulties encountered by attempts to translate terms derived from twentieth-century circumstances to earlier eras, and the dangers of circularity; he is also concerned with the reality of the beast: the consumer. Is he who consumes automatically a 'consumer'? Do 'consumers' necessarily possess a consumerist mentality? How can one legitimately infer attitudes and dispositions from behaviour?

These difficulties are further addressed by the sociologist Colin Campbell, who indicts customary explanations of consumer behaviour in terms of 'emulation', 'fashion' and 'demand' for being little better than question-begging, and suggests an alternative reconstruction of the mentality and structure of feeling of consumer man.[20] Avoiding tautology, Campbell aims to reconstruct the precise structures of feeling which gave consumerism a boost in the latter part of the eighteenth century.

It is hardly possible to explore the idea of consumption without running up against a disturbing paradox: the deep ambiguities associated with the very word, 'consume'; it suggests both an enlargement through incorporation and a withering away. Consuming is thus both enrichment and impoverishment. The significance of semantics is central to Porter's paper. For, alongside its politico-economic meanings, 'consumption' had a precise medical connotation: the wasting disease we nowadays call tuberculosis. Porter seeks to uncover the metaphorical and symbolic undertones of consumption through playing on the contemporary doubling of meanings in a society in which extremes of consumption (under- and over-eating and drinking) and a growing abundance of goods were commonly regarded as deleterious to health.[21]

The next section, 'Goods and consumption', situates rising consumption within its wider economic, political and ideological contexts. As Peter Burke emphasizes in his cross-cultural study of Europe and the Orient, it was not only in western societies that massive personal wealth accumulated[22] or the ostentation of possessions became a conspicuous feature of social life and worldly values.[23] Yet, as Jan de Vries's survey of western economic developments makes abundantly clear, it was unique aspects of the development of capitalism, first around the Mediterranean and then on the 'Atlantic rim', and in particular the role played by urbanization[24] and the social and political structures associated with it, which ensured in the Euro-American world an unprecedented proliferation of manufactured articles from the seventeenth century onwards.[25] There is some irony in the fact, noted by John Wills in his account of the overseas, imperial dimension of western economic expansion, that Asiatic producers of tea, sugar, spices and other primary goods found markets in Europe of a magnitude they could never have hoped to achieve in Asia itself.[26]

Along similar lines to Peter Burke, Joyce Appleby reminds us that economic expansion does not occur in an ideological vacuum. The multiplication of goods upset entrenched Christian religio-moral teachings, with their denunciations of Mammon and the love of lucre, and threatened conservative theories of social order, which stipulated (partly through sumptuary laws) that each rank must have, and must remain within, its proper material trappings. One of the historical tasks of what we may loosely call the Enlightenment was to forge new sets of moral values, new models of man, to match and make sense of the opportunities and obligations, the delights and dangers, created by the brave new world of goods.[27]

In the third section, 'Production and the meaning of possessions', the focus narrows to consider the acquisition and use of goods from the viewpoint of providers and buyers. Measuring the profusion of goods in earlier centuries itself poses teasing historical questions. As Lorna Weatherill emphasizes, even such apparently valuable forms of documentation as inventories, taken at death, afford very inadequate (and hence putatively highly misleading) indices of the entire range and quantity of belongings owned during the subject's life-time.[28] Official records, such as trade statistics, may be equally misleading, since (as Carole Shammas demonstrates), in the case of commodities such as tobacco and tea, smuggling accounted for an unknowable percentage of total imports, and hence consumption. Often we need to look, as Cissie Fairchilds suggests, at more impressionistic sources – pamphlets, polemics, legal cases, trade disputes and so forth – to gain a truer indication as to what kinds of commodities were in demand.

Despite such obstacles to the compilation of a full historical inventory of 'the world of goods we have lost', the essays in this section show that belongings resonated with powerful meanings. These were many, were often overlapping and frequently contested. People could value their belongings because they were new, or alternatively because they carried the patina of age; because they were unique or because they were all the rage. As Amanda Vickery argues, in early modern society, women may have derived considerable status from the fact that it was they who, in their role as keeper of the house, endowed belongings with private, family meanings. There may be vital connections between the expanding world of objects and the changing role of women in the eighteenth century which go far beyond the well-worn account of the supposed emergence of 'separate spheres'.[29] The new accent in the eighteenth century upon domesticity, and the emotional intensification of the nuclear family, clearly derive in part from growing opportunities for the cherishing of household 'decencies', comforts and luxuries.[30]

But it would be a mistake to assume that the new world of goods was primarily or overwhelmingly domestic, merely to do with the building of 'home'. As Tim Breen argues, personal accoutrements, perhaps clothes above all, created styles which established public identities, by processes of assimilation and distinction. Small, stable, face-to-face societies perhaps have less need of the kinds of status-symbol identity badges conferred by publicly recognizable standardized belongings and tastes. Arguably, eighteenth-century society – notably in North America – by virtue of becoming increasingly mobile and hence more anonymous, leant more heavily upon the aid of mass-produced symbols of social position and social aspiration. Not least, argues Cissie Fairchilds, a genre of cheap luxury goods (fans and umbrellas, for example) excited a brisk sale in metropolitan centres: the attraction of such 'populuxe' products lay in enabling a wide social cross-section to appear to be in the swim of the latest fashions. Emulation will not explain everything; but it deserves better than to be dismissed as a vacuous category. Yet one-dimensional discussions, as Sidney Mintz stresses in his discussion of changing dietary patterns, will get us nowhere.

Indeed, as an item of consumption, food proves exceptionally complex. This is partly because it is simultaneously necessity and luxury. And partly because of its extreme ephemerality (once consumed, it disappears totally) and the complex signals associated with eating and fatness: it is good to be seen to be able to afford to consume food *ad lib*: it is (or has become) vulgar to be fat. All these ambiguities are well illustrated by the custom of the potlatch.[31]

The modern world of goods is predicated upon information and visibility. Remove knowledge, publicity and advertising, and the itch to consume does not merely subside; as a *mentalité*, it becomes unthinkable. The next two sections of this volume, 'Literacy and numeracy' and 'The consumption of culture: books and newspapers', address the part played by the new communication technologies in the distribution of objects.

Patricia Cline Cohen suggests a scene of uneven numeracy.[32] Not surprisingly, this age of buying and selling was an age which valued arithmetic, encouraging the skill through the spread of mathematical texts; but aspirations perhaps outran achievements. David Cressy's survey of the rise of literacy demonstrates that some of the most notably literate groups in English society – for instance, the urban gentry, and female members of the high bourgeoisie – were precisely those whom contemporaries identified as those at the centre of the networks of fashion.[33]

There is no surprise in this, since one of the major items of polite reading in the eighteenth century was the newspaper, whose *news* focused at least as much upon fashions, happenings and items for sale as upon kings and battles. Even a provincial newspaper such as the *Salisbury Journal*, serving an essentially rural constituency, kept readers in touch with metropolitan tastes and trends – indeed, as Christine Ferdinand shows in her assessment of the newspaper as a dynamo of consumption, increasingly so as the century wore on.[34]

Here certain contrasts suggest themselves between England and other parts of Europe. The English newspaper was financially dependent upon advertising, and gave it many column inches – up to 25 per cent of the total paper. Such was not the case in France, where, as Jeremy Popkin indicates, it was politics that sold newspapers.[35] Advertising was wholly unimportant, and the newspaper played only a minor role in promoting consciousness of economic change.

This applies all the more so in eastern Europe. Iaroslav Isaievych's account of the development of printing in the Ukraine and in Russian- and Polish-speaking parts of eastern Europe shows how the message of the printed word remained a mixture of official propaganda and religious devotion. And even in Britain, it would be unwise to presuppose too close a rapport between 'modernity' in educational skills and 'modernity' in attitudes. John Money's analysis of the early eighteenth-century Somerset journal keeper (and, intriguingly, excise officer) John Cannon, shows that this inveterate, even obsessional, thinker-with-the-pen used his writings to confirm himself in the most traditional religious and moral orthodoxies. No small element in the rise of the consumer society were the anxieties and anger it raised amongst those convinced that the world was running mad after innovation and that all was going to the dogs.[36]

If every object in the world of goods was emblazoned with meanings (many of them multiple), some were more palpably 'heraldic' than others. Objects of conspicuous display, and above all, 'designer' items specifically intended to be visible and admired, overtly played upon, and reflected, the fact that material life formed a stage with its sets, props and actors engaged in the drama of being. New material objects could indeed be highly ostentatious, designed to communicate the emotions appropriate to spectacle. As Simon Schaffer stresses in his account of the consumption of popular science, the experiments and demonstrations of Enlightened natural philosophers aimed to conjure a sense of awe, while at the same time convincing audiences of their veracity by their ocular immediacy. The staging of 'wonder', the creation of conviction, obviously carried critical political (even party-political) overtones in an age when all manner of 'authority' was being questioned and challenged, and when turbulent out-of-doors politics threatened disorder.[37]

Something rather similar may be true of gardening vogues. As Chandra Mukerji emphasizes, each successive individual landscaping style told its own story about nature, about the aesthetics of good taste, about proprietorship and position. In England in particular, the 'private' gardens of grandees' stately homes were designed to be shown to the public, as part of a display of conspicuous swank (and, it might be added, horticulture emerged as one of the thriving new service industries of the consumer society).[38]

Visual images, verbal signs and the world of things formed a triangle whose stresses and strains need to be insisted upon. As Barbara Stafford reminds us, the visual, precisely because it was so tangibly, sensually direct, had been consigned, ever since Plato's cave, to the lowest rung in the traditional intellectual hierarchies of the philosophers. Hence there are philosophical as well as technical reasons why the post-Gutenberg explosion in the printed word may not, perhaps, have produced a fully equivalent revolution in visual image-making. Was a lack of technical skill, and of technological means, also a factor here? That is one of the problems addressed in John Styles's analysis of the communication of design details in industrial production. There certainly appears a paradox. The accelerating demands of fashion meant that manufacturers – of metal goods and textiles, for example – had to produce items precisely matching buyers' visual expectations. Yet little evidence survives of the routine use of design *drawings* to convey this information: verbal descriptions seem to have been far more common. Is this an accident of the survival of sources? Were illustrations genuinely wanting? Were drawings thought to carry less authority, or to be less reliable? Or were merchants and agents genuinely illiterate with the pencil?[39]

The messages conveyed by words and images reinforce the ambivalences contemporaries felt about the new world of goods. Golden Age Dutch still lifes and genre paintings lovingly depict cornucopias of commodities, even as the emblematic meanings of such belongings – candlesticks, lace, tulips – tell the viewer, as Simon Schama argues, that all is vanity.[40]

Schama hereby explicitly raises an issue touched upon by many other contributors, notably Appleby and Money: the strength of contemporary suspicion towards, or outright hostility to emergent consumerism, in the name of traditional religious, moral and socio-political values.[41] This volume stresses the new bubbling atmosphere of excitement in eighteenth-century and early industrial society for the new world of goods; an 'equal but opposite' volume could document, perhaps at greater length, the jeremiads against luxury issuing from press and pulpit against materialism and acquisitiveness, mainly from the spokesmen of the established order, fearful that the spread of belongings would spread subversive ideas and unduly raise expectations. Enlightenment economic and social theory was uncertain whether the surest guarantee of social stability was a poor and ignorant labouring class (roughly, the Mandevillian view) or a prosperous, and thus 'co-opted' working sector.

Schama's reminder about vanity is, in any case, timely. The purpose of this volume is not to pretend that the rise of the consumer society is the key to all modern history. It is, however, to encourage a new way of seeing and interpreting – one which, when properly elaborated, refined and qualified, will, it is hoped, illuminate key aspects of the life of society hitherto obscure or mystified. If it helps to unveil such visions, this book will have served its purposes.

Notes

1   Chandra Mukerji, *From Graven Images: Patterns of Modern Materialism* (New York: Columbia University Press, 1983); Joan Thirsk, *Economic Policy and Projects: The Development of a Consumer Society in Early Modern England* (Oxford: Clarendon Press, 1978).

2   John Brooks, *Showing off in America: From Conspicuous Consumption to Parody Display* (Boston: Little, Brown & Co., 1981); Clifford E. Clark, Jr, *The American Family Home, 1800–1960* (Chapel Hill: University of North Carolina Press, 1986); Ruth Schwartz Cowan, 'The "Industrial Revolution" in the home: household technology and social change in the twentieth century', in Thomas J. Schlereth (ed.), *Material Culture Studies in America* (Nashville, Tenn.: The American Association for State and Local History, 1982), 222–36; W. Hamish Fraser, *The Coming of the Mass Market, 1850–1914* (Hamden, Conn.: Archon Books, 1981); Asa Briggs, *Victorian Things* (London: Batsford, 1988); Paul Greenhalgh, *Ephemeral Vistas: A History of the Expositions Universelles, Great Exhibitions and World Fairs, 1851–1939* (Manchester: Manchester University Press, 1988); Dolores Hayden, *The Grand Domestic Revolution: A History of Feminist Designs for American Homes, Neighborhoods and Cities* (Cambridge, Mass.: MIT Press, 1981); William R. Leach, 'Transformation in a culture of consumption: women and department stores, 1890–1925', *The Journal of American History*, lxxi (1984), 319–42; Roland Marchand, *Advertising the American Dream: Making Way for Modernity, 1920–1940* (Berkeley: University of California Press, 1985); Michael B. Miller, *The Bon Marché: Bourgeois Culture and the Department Store, 1869–1920* (Princeton: Princeton University Press, 1981); Benjamin D. Singer, *Advertising and Society* (Don Mills, Ont.: Addison-Wesley, 1986).

    Useful examples of an older, less theorized, style of scholarship include Alison Adburgham, *Shops and Shopping, 1800–1914* (London: George Allen & Unwin, 1964); David Alexander, *Retailing in England During the Industrial Revolution* (London: Athlone Press, 1970); D. Davis, *A History of Shopping* (London: Routledge & Kegan Paul, 1966); J. H. B. Peel, *An Englishman's Home* (Newton Abbot: David & Charles, 1978).

3   Neil McKendrick, John Brewer and J. H. Plumb, *The Birth of a Consumer Society: The Commercialization of Eighteenth-Century England* (London: Europa, 1982).

4   Neil McKendrick, 'Introduction: the birth of a consumer society: the commercialization of eighteenth-century England', in McKendrick, Brewer and Plumb, *Birth of a Consumer Society*, 1–8; 'The consumer revolution of eighteenth-century England', ibid., 9–33; 'The commercialization of fashion', ibid., 35–99; 'Josiah Wedgwood and the commercialization of the potteries', ibid., 100–45; 'George Packwood and the commercialization of shaving: the art of eighteenth-century advertising, or "The Way to Get Money and be Happy" ', ibid., 146–96. See also Neil McKendrick, 'Home demand and economic growth: a new view of the role of women and children in the Industrial Revolution', in Neil McKendrick (ed.), *Historical Perspectives: Studies in English Thought and Society in Honour of J. H. Plumb* (London: Europa, 1974), 152–210. And for the entrepreneur, Eric Robinson, 'Eighteenth-century commerce and fashion: Matthew Boulton's marketing techniques', *Economic History Review*, 2nd series, xvi (1963–4), 39–60.

5   J. H. Plumb, 'The commercialization of leisure', in McKendrick, Brewer and Plumb, *Birth of a Consumer Society*, 265–86; 'The new world of children', ibid., 286–315; 'The acceptance of modernity', ibid., 316–34.

6   John Brewer, 'Commercialization and politics', in McKendrick, Brewer and Plumb, *Birth of a Consumer Society*, 197–262.

7   F. M. L. Thompson (ed.), *The Cambridge Social History of Britain, 1750–1950*: vol. 1, *Regions and Communities*; vol. 2, *People and their Environment*; vol. 3, *Social Agencies and Institutions* (Cambridge: Cambridge University Press, 1990). See, however, John Brewer, *The Sinews of Power* (London: Unwin Hyman, 1989), which analyses the symbiosis between growing commercial wealth and political power in Georgian England. For background to some of the issues Brewer raises see Peter Clark, *The English Alehouse: A Social History, 1200–1830* (London: Longman, 1983); idem, *Sociability*

and Urbanity: Clubs and Societies in the Eighteenth Century (Leicester: Leicester University Press, 1986).

For scholarship exploring the signs of an eighteenth-century consumer revolution, see Hoh-cheung and L. Mui, *Shops and Shopkeeping in Eighteenth-Century England* (London: Methuen, 1987); Edward Copeland, 'Jane Austen and the consumer revolution', in J. David Grey, A. Walton Litz and Brian Southam (eds), *The Jane Austen Companion* (New York: Macmillan, 1986), 77–92; idem, 'Money talks: Jane Austen and the *Lady's Magazine*', in J. David Grey (ed.), *Jane Austen's Beginnings: The Juvenilia and Lady Susan* with a foreword by Margaret Drabble (Ann Arbor and London: UMI Research Press, 1989), 153–71; James Thompson, 'Jane Austen's clothing: things, property, and materialism in her novels', *Studies in Eighteenth-Century Culture*, xiii (1984), 217–31. There is some interest in consumerism in other periods; see Christopher Dyer, 'The consumer and the market in the later Middle Ages', *Economic History Review*, xlii (1989), 305–27; Robert O. Herrmann, 'The consumer movement in historical perspective', in David A. Aaker and George S. Day (eds), *Consumerism: Search for the Consumer Interest* (New York: Free Press, 1974), 10–18.

8   Simon Schama, *The Embarrassment of Riches: An Interpretation of Dutch Culture in the Golden Age* (London: Fontana, 1988); F. J. Fisher, 'The development of the London food market, 1540–1640', *Economic History Review*, v (1935), 46–64; idem, 'The development of London as a centre of conspicuous consumption in the sixteenth and seventeenth centuries', *Transactions of the Royal Historical Society*, xxx (1948), 35–50; idem, 'The growth of London', in E. W. Ives (ed.), *The English Revolution, 1600–1660* (London: Edward Arnold, 1968), 76–86; idem, 'London as an "engine of economic growth" ', in J. S. Bromley and E. H. Kossmann (eds), *Britain and the Netherlands: Metropolis and Province*, vol. 4 (The Hague: Nijhoff, 1971), 3–16; Margaret Spufford, *The Great Reclothing of Rural England* (London: Hambledon Press, 1984).

9   On mass production and mass markets in the twentieth century see James J. Flink, *The Car Culture* (Cambridge, Mass.: MIT Press, 1975); R. Tamar Horowitz, 'From elite fashion to mass fashion', *Archives Européennes de Sociologie*, xvi (1975), 283–95; John B. Rae, *The Road and Car in American Life* (Cambridge, Mass.: MIT Press, 1971).

10   See also J. -C. Agnew, *Worlds Apart: The Market and the Theater in Anglo-American Thought, 1550–1750* (Cambridge: Cambridge University Press, 1986). Broader anthropological dimensions are broached in Arjun Appadurai (ed.), *The Social Life of Things: Commodities in Cultural Perspective* (Cambridge: Cambridge University Press, 1986).

11   C. Geerz, *The Interpretation of Cultures* (New York: Basic Books, 1973); Roland Barthes, *Elements of Culture* (Cambridge: Polity Press, 1989).

12   J. C. D. Clark, *English Society, 1688–1832: Ideology, Social Structure and Political Practice During the Ancien Régime* (Cambridge: Cambridge University Press, 1985); idem, *Revolution and Rebellion: State and Society in England in the Seventeenth and Eighteenth Centuries* (Cambridge: Cambridge University Press, 1986). The centrality of the growth of material prosperity to nineteenth-century theories of progress, particularly Macaulay's, is well conveyed in David Spadafora, *The Idea of Progress in Eighteenth Century Britain* (New Haven: Yale University Press, 1990).

13   For critiques from the left, see Max Horkheimer and Theodor W. Adorno, *Dialectic of Enlightenment* (New York: Herder & Herder, 1972); Nick Rowling, *Commodities: How the World was Taken to Market* (London: Free Association Books, 1987); E. Yeo and S. Yeo (eds), *Popular Culture and Class Conflict* (Brighton: Harvester, 1981); for a sensible stricture on sentimental views on popular culture, see J. M. Golby and A. W. Purdue, *The Civilization of the Crowd: Popular Culture in England, 1750–1900* (London: Batsford, 1984).

14   R. H. Tawney, *The Acquisitive Society* (London: G. Bell & Sons, 1923). For these traditions of cultural criticism, see E. P. Thompson, *William Morris: Romantic to Revolutionary* (London: Pantheon, 1977); Raymond Williams, *Culture and Society, 1780–1950* (London: Chatto & Windus, 1958); idem, *The Long Revolution* (London: Chatto & Windus, 1961); idem, *The Country and the City* (London: Chatto & Windus, 1973). From its own rather different, lofty, standpoint, Thorstein Veblen's classic *The Theory of the Leisure Class* (New York: Macmillan, 1912) also ultimately declines to treat

the world of goods seriously. Werner Sombart, *Luxury and Capitalism*, tr. W. R. Dittmar (Ann Arbor: University of Michigan Press, 1967) engages more seriously with the problem of the interpretation of abundance. Some of these traditions are dissected in Peter Burke, 'Revolution in popular culture', in Roy Porter and M. Teich (eds), *Revolution in History* (Cambridge: Cambridge University Press, 1986), 206–25.

15   See B. Ollmann, *Alienation* (London: Cambridge University Press, 1971); D. McLellan, *The Young Hegelians and Karl Marx* (London: Macmillan, 1969).

16   Herbert Marcuse, *One-Dimensional Man: Studies in the Ideology of Advanced Industrial Society* (London: Routledge & Kegan Paul, 1964).

17   These are the questions underlying C. B. Macpherson, *The Political Theory of Possessive Individualism: Hobbes to Locke* (Oxford: Oxford University Press, 1964).

18   For the role of the psy-professions in the shaping of the modern self see Nikolas Rose, *Governing the Soul: The Shaping of the Private Self* (London: Routledge, 1990). The older work of Vance Packard helped pioneer inquiries along these lines.

19   Such is, of course, the utilitarian project. See Elie Halévy, *The Growth of Philosophical Radicalism* (London: Faber & Faber, 1924); see also Louis Dumont, *Homo Hierarchicus: The Caste System and its Implications* (London: Paladin, 1972).

20   The article in this volume builds on, and refines, the analysis to be found in C. Campbell, *The Romantic Ethic and the Spirit of Modern Consumerism* (Oxford: Basil Blackwell, 1987). Sociological perspectives are also conveyed in Grant McCracken, *Culture and Consumption: New Approaches to the Symbolic Character of Consumer Goods and Activities* (Bloomington: Indiana University Press, 1988); Alan Macfarlane, *The Culture of Capitalism* (Oxford: Basil Blackwell, 1987); Marcel Mauss, *The Gift* (London: Routledge & Kegan Paul, 1970); Russell W. Belk, 'Gift-giving behavior', in Jagdish N. Sheth (ed.), *Research in Marketing*, vol. 2 (Greenwich, Conn.: JAI Press), 95–126; D. Miller, *Material Culture and Mass Consumption* (Oxford: Basil Blackwell, 1987); Mike Featherstone, *Consumer Culture and Postmodernism* (London: Sage, 1991). There are suggestive accounts of the creation of fantasy expectations in P. Camporesi, *Bread of Dreams: Food and Fantasy in Early Modern Europe* (Cambridge: Polity Press, 1989); and John Carswell, *The South Sea Bubble* (London: Cresset Press, 1960).

        For 'demand', see Elizabeth W. Gilboy, 'Demand as a factor in the Industrial Revolution', in R. M. Hartwell (ed.), *The Causes of the Industrial Revolution in England* (London: Methuen, 1967), 121–38; W. A. Cole, 'Factors in demand, 1700–80', in R. Floud and D. N. McCloskey (eds), *Economic History of Britain since 1700*: vol. 1, *1700–1860* (Cambridge: Cambridge University Press, 1981), 36–65; D. E. C. Eversley, 'The home market and economic growth in England 1750–1800', in E. L. Jones and G. E. Mingay (eds), *Land, Labour and Population in the Industrial Revolution* (London: Edward Arnold, 1967), 206–59; E. L. Jones, 'The fashion manipulators: consumer tastes and British industries, 1660–1800', in L. P. Cain and P. J. Uselding (eds), *Business Enterprise and Economic Change* (Kent State, Ohio: Kent State University Press, 1973), 198–226; B. Lemire, 'Developing consumerism and the ready-made clothing trade in Britain 1750–1800', *Textile History*, xv (1984), 21–44; Charles W. King, 'Fashion adoption: a rebuttal to the "trickle-down" theory', in Stephen A. Greyser (ed.), *Toward Scientific Marketing* (Chicago: American Marketing Association, 1963), 108–25.

21   For further theoretical and practical discussions of interpretations of material culture see Mihaly Csikszentmihalyi and Eugene Rochberg-Halton, *The Meaning of Things: Domestic Symbols and the Self* (New York: Cambridge University Press, 1981); J. Deetz, *In Small Things Forgotten* (New York: Doubleday, 1977); Mary Douglas and Baron Isherwood, *The World of Goods: Towards an Anthropology of Consumption* (New York: Norton, 1978, Harmondsworth: Penguin, 1980); Ian Quimby (ed.), *Material Culture and the Study of Material Life* (New York: Norton, 1978); Daniel D. Reiff, *Small Georgian Houses in England and Virginia* (London and Toronto: University of Delaware Press, 1986); Thomas J. Schlereth, *Material Culture: A Research Guide* (Lawrence, Kansas: University of Kansas Press, 1985); idem, 'Material culture studies in America, 1876–1976', in

Thomas J. Schlereth (ed.), *Material Culture Studies in America* (Nashville, Tenn.: The American Association for State and Local History, 1982), 1–75; idem, 'Material culture studies and social history research', *Journal of Social History*, xvi (1983), 111–43; idem, 'Contemporary collecting for future recollecting', *Museum Studies Journal*, ii (1984), 23–30; idem, 'The material culture of childhood: problems and potential in historical explanation', *Material History Bulletin*, xxi (1985), 1–14. N. J. G. Pounds, *Hearth and Home: A History of Material Culture* (Bloomington: University of Indiana Press, 1989) is an ambitious attempt to create a comprehensive factual history of things.

22 Measuring personal wealth is a deeply vexed issue, which has attracted animated debate. On the 'long eighteenth century' in Britain, see W. D. Rubenstein, *Elites and the Wealthy in Modern British History: Essays in Social and Economic History* (Brighton: Harvester, 1987); R. Grassby, 'The personal wealth of the business community in seventeenth-century England', *Economic History Review*, xxiii (1970), 220–34; idem, 'Social mobility and business enterprise in seventeenth-century England', in D. Pennington and K. Thomas (eds), *Puritans and Revolutionaries* (Oxford: Clarendon Press, 1978), 355–81; L. D. Schwarz, 'Income distribution and social structure in London in the late eighteenth century', *Economic History Review*, xxxii (1979), 250–9; idem, 'Social class and social geography: the middle classes in London at the end of the eighteenth century', *Social History*, vii (1982), 167–85; Donna Andrew, 'Aldermen and big bourgeoisie of London reconsidered', *Social History*, vi (1981), 359–64; H. Horwitz, ' "The mess of the middle class" revisited: the case of the "big bourgeoisie" of Augustan London', *Continuity and Change*, ii (1987), 263–96; Peter Earle, *The World of Defoe* (London: Weidenfeld & Nicolson, 1976); idem, *The Making of the English Middle Class: Business, Society and Family Life in London, 1660–1730* (London: Methuen, 1989); Peter H. Lindert and Jeffrey G. Williamson, 'Revising England's social tables, 1688–1812', *Explorations in Economic History*, xix (1982), 385–408; idem, 'Reinterpreting Britain's social tables, 1688–1913', *Explorations in Economic History*, xx (1983), 94–109. Amongst the lower orders similar disputes characterize the 'standard of living' debate: A. J. Taylor (ed.), *The Standard of Living in Britain in the Industrial Revolution* (London: Methuen, 1975); Elizabeth W. Gilboy, *Wages in Eighteenth Century England* (Cambridge, Mass.: Harvard University Press, 1934).

23 On the interpretation of conspicuous consumption see Peter Burke, *The Historical Anthropology of Early Modern Italy: Essays on Perception and Communication* (Cambridge: Cambridge University Press, 1987); Thorstein Veblen, *The Theory of the Leisure Class* (New York: Macmillan, 1912); Roger S. Mason, *Conspicuous Consumption* (New York: St Martin's Press, 1981); Norbert Elias, *The Civilizing Process*: vol. 1, *The History of Manners*; vol. 2, *Power and Civility*; vol. 3, *The Court Society* (New York: Pantheon, 1978, 1982 and 1983 respectively).

24 Above all, see J. de Vries, *European Urbanization, 1500–1800* (Cambridge, Mass.: Harvard University Press, 1984). Recent work examining urbanization, economic modernization and the role of the town as a centre of consumption and fashion includes Peter Borsay, 'The English urban renaissance: the development of provincial urban culture, c. 1680–1760', *Social History*, v (1977), 581–603; idem, 'Urban development in the age of Defoe', in Clyve Jones (ed.), *Britain in the First Age of Party, 1684–1750* (London: Hambleton, 1987), 195–219; David Cannadine, *Lords and Landlords: The Aristocracy and the Towns, 1774–1967* (Leicester: Leicester University Press, 1980); C. W. Chalklin, *The Provincial Towns of Georgian England* (Montreal: McGill University Press, 1974); P. J. Corfield, *The Impact of English Towns 1700–1800* (Oxford: Oxford University Press, 1982); M. Daunton, 'Towns and economic growth in eighteenth-century England', in P. Abrams and E. A. Wrigley (eds), *Towns in Societies* (Cambridge: Cambridge University Press, 1978), 245–77; J. Walvin, *English Urban Life, 1776–1851* (London: Hutchinson, 1984); E. A. Wrigley, 'A simple model of London's importance in changing English society and economy, 1650–1750', *Past and Present*, xxxvii (1967), 44–70.

25 This is not the place for a comprehensive note on the literature on economic development. Broadly, see F. Braudel, *Civilization and Capitalism, 15th–18th Century*: vol. 1, *The Structures of Everyday Life*; vol. 2, *The Wheels of Commerce*; vol. 3, *The Perspective of the World* (New York: Harper & Row,

1985); Maxine Berg, *The Age of Manufactures, 1700–1820* (London: Fontana, 1985); Maxine Berg, Pat Hudson and Michael Sonenscher (eds), *Manufacture in Town and County before the Factory* (Cambridge: Cambridge University Press, 1983); J. D. Chambers and G. E. Mingay, *The Agricultural Revolution 1750–1880* (London: Batsford, 1966); C. Clay, *Economic Expansion and Social Change in England, 1500–1700*, 2 vols (Cambridge: Cambridge University Press, 1984); E. L. Jones (ed.), *Agriculture and Economic Growth in England, 1600–1815* (London: Methuen, 1967).

On the huge question of the nature of the 'industrial revolution' in eighteenth-century England, see David Cannadine, 'The present and the past in the English Industrial Revolution, 1880–1980', *Past and Present*, ciii (1984), 131–72; M. Fores, 'The myth of a British Industrial Revolution', *History*, lxvi (1981), 181–9; Phyllis Deane, *The First Industrial Revolution* (Cambridge: Cambridge University Press, 1965); idem and W. A. Cole, *British Economic Growth, 1688–1959* (Cambridge: Cambridge University Press, 1969); Peter Mathias, *The Transformation of England* (New York: Columbia University Press, 1979); idem, *The First Industrial Nation: An Economic History of Britain 1700–1914*, 2nd edn (London: Methuen, 1983); David Landes, *The Unbound Prometheus: Technological Change and Industrial Development in Western Europe from 1750 to the Present* (London: Cambridge University Press, 1960); N. F. R. Crafts, 'English economic growth in the eighteenth century: a re-examination of Deane and Cole's estimates', *Economic History Review*, xxix (1976), 226–35; idem, 'Industrial revolution in England and France: some thoughts on the question, "why was England first?" ', *Economic History Review*, xxx (1977), 429–41; idem, *British Economic Growth during the Industrial Revolution* (Oxford: Clarendon Press, 1985); idem, 'British economic growth, 1700–1850: some difficulties of interpretation', *Explorations in Economic History*, xxiv (1987), 245–68; idem, 'British economic growth, 1700–1831: a review of the evidence', *Economic History Review*, xxxiv (1983), 365–73; F. Crouzet, 'England and France in the eighteenth century: a comparative analysis of two economic growths', in R. M. Hartwell (ed.), *The Causes of the Industrial Revolution in England* (London: Methuen, 1967), 139–74; Julian Hoppit, 'Understanding the Industrial Revolution', *Historical Journal*, xxx (1987), 211–24; Peter H. Lindert, 'Remodelling British economic history: a review article', *Journal of Economic History*, xliii (1983), 988–90; E. A. Wrigley, *Continuity, Chance and Change: The Character of the Industrial Revolution in England* (Cambridge: Cambridge University Press, 1988).

26 K. N. Chaudhuri, *The Trading World of Asia and the English East India Company, 1660–1760* (Cambridge: Cambridge University Press, 1978); Noel Deerr, *The History of Sugar*, 2 vols (London: Chapman and Hall, 1949–50); Sidney Mintz, *Sweetness and Power* (New York: Viking, 1985).

27 See also Joyce Appleby, 'Ideology and theory: the tension between political and economic liberalism in seventeenth-century England', *American Historical Review*, lxxxi (1976), 499–515; idem, *Economic Thought in Seventeenth-Century England* (Princeton, NJ: Princeton University Press, 1978); Albert O. Hirschman, *The Passions and the Interests: Political Arguments for Capitalism before its Triumph* (Princeton, NJ: Princeton University Press, 1977).

28 For further discussion see Lorna Weatherill, *Consumer Behaviour and Material Culture, 1660–1760* (London: Routledge, 1988).

29 For the position of women in eighteenth-century society, see Susan D. Amussen, *An Ordered Society: Class and Gender in Early Modern England* (Oxford: Basil Blackwell, 1988); Alice Clark, *Working Life of Women in the Seventeenth Century* (London: Cass, 1968; 1st edn, 1919); Bridget Hill, *Women, Work and Sexual Politics in Eighteenth-Century England* (Oxford: Basil Blackwell, 1989); Mary Prior (ed.), *Women in English Society, 1500–1800* (London: Methuen, 1985); M. Scheuermann, 'Women and money in eighteenth-century fiction', *Studies in the Novel*, xix (1987), 311–22; A. J. Vickery, 'Women of the local elite in Lancashire, *c.* 1760–1828' (University of London, Ph.D. thesis, 1991). For the 'separate spheres' case, see Leonore Davidoff and Catherine Hall, *Family Fortunes: Men and Women of the English Middle Class, 1780–1850* (London: Routledge, 1992). For the legal position of women see Susan Staves, *Married Women's Separate Property 1660–1830* (Cambridge, Mass.: Harvard University Press, 1990).

30   Carole Shammas, 'The domestic environment in early modern England and America', *Journal of Social History*, xiv (1980), 1–24; idem, *The Pre-Industrial Consumer in England and America* (Oxford: Clarendon Press, 1990); Lorna Weatherill, 'Consumer behavior and social status in England', *Continuity and Change*, ii (1986), 191–216; idem, 'A possession of one's own: women and consumer behaviour in England, 1660–1740', *Journal of British Studies*, xxv (1986), 131–56; W. Rybczynski, *Home: A Short History of an Idea* (London: Heinemann, 1988). For growing family intimacy see Lawrence Stone, *The Family, Sex and Marriage in England, 1500–1800* (London: Weidenfeld & Nicolson, 1977); R. Trumbach, *The Rise of the Egalitarian Family: Aristocratic Kinship and Domestic Relations in Eighteenth Century England* (New York: Academic Press, 1978); R. Chartier (ed.), *A History of Private Life*: vol. 3, *Passions of the Renaissance* (Cambridge, Mass.: Belknap Press, 1989); Michell Perrot (ed.), *A History of Private Life*: vol. 4, *From the Fires of Revolution to the Great War* (Cambridge, Mass.: Belknap Press, 1990).

31   See also Tim Breen, 'An empire of goods: the anglicization of colonial America, 1690–1776', *Journal of British Studies*, xxv (1986), 467–99; idem, 'Baubles of Britain: the American and consumer revolutions of the eighteenth century', *Past and Present*, cxix (1988), 73–104; Jack P. Greene, *Pursuits of Happiness: The Social Development of Early Modern British Colonies and the Formation of American Culture* (Chapel Hill: University of North Carolina Press, 1988). For background to Fairchilds's Paris, see Daniel Roche, *The People of Paris: An Essay in Popular Culture in the Eighteenth Century* (Leamington Spa: Berg, 1987). For clothes and status see Alison Lurie, *The Language of Clothes* (New York: Random House, 1981).

    On food and fatness, see Sidney Mintz, *Sweetness and Power* (New York: Viking, 1985); J. J. Brumberg, *Fasting Girls: The Emergence of Anorexia Nervosa as a Modern Disease* (Cambridge, Mass.: Harvard University Press, 1988); Hillel Schwartz, *Never Satisfied: A Cultural History of Diets, Fantasies and Fat* (New York: Free Press, 1986).

32   Patricia Cline Cohen, *A Calculating People: The Spread of Numeracy in Early America* (Chicago: University of Chicago Press, 1982); Keith Thomas, 'Numeracy in early modern England', *Transactions of the Royal Historical Society*, xxxvii (1987), 103–32.

33   David Cressy, *Literacy and the Social Order: Reading and Writing in Tudor and Stuart England* (Cambridge: Cambridge University Press, 1980); idem, 'Books as totems in seventeenth-century England and New England', *Journal of Library History*, xxi (1986), 92–106; R. Houston, 'The development of literacy in northern England, 1640–1750', *Economic History Review*, xxxv (1982), 199–216.

34   Jeremy Black, *The English Press in the Eighteenth Century* (London: Croom Helm, 1986); G. A. Cranfield, *The Development of the Provincial Newspaper 1700–1760* (Oxford: Clarendon Press, 1962); J. J. Looney, 'Advertising and society in England, 1720–1820: a statistical analysis of Yorkshire newspaper advertisements' (Princeton University, Ph.D. thesis, 1983); John Feather, *The Provincial Book Trade in Eighteenth-Century England* (Cambridge: Cambridge University Press, 1985); Isabel Rivers (ed.), *Books and Their Readers in Eighteenth-Century England* (Leicester: Leicester University Press, 1982). Improvements in internal communications are here important. See J. A. Chartres, 'The capital's provincial eyes: London's inns in the early eighteenth century', *London Journal*, iii (1977), 24–39; idem, *Internal Trade in England, 1500–1700* (London: Macmillan, 1977); idem, 'Food consumption and internal trade', in A. L. Beier and R. Finlay (eds), *London 1500–1700: The Making of the Metropolis* (London and New York: Longman, 1986), 168–95; W. Albert, *The Turnpike Road System of England 1663–1840* (Cambridge: Cambridge University Press, 1972).

35   Highly illuminating on the conditions of the Press in France are the writings of Robert Darnton. See *The Business of Enlightenment: A Publishing History of the Encyclopédie, 1775–1800* (Cambridge, Mass.: Harvard University Press, 1979); idem, *The Literary Underground of the Old Regime* (Cambridge, Mass.: Harvard University Press, 1982).

    More broadly, the rise of the consumer society cannot be understood except in context of a wider grasp of the emergence of the commercial writer, i.e., of Grub Street. See A. S. Collins, *Authorship in the Days of Johnson* (London: Routledge & Kegan Paul, 1927); R. L. W. Collison, *The Story of Street Literature: The Forerunner of the Popular Press* (London: Dent, 1973); Pat Rogers, *Grub Street: Studies in a Subculture* (London: Methuen, 1972); idem, 'The writer and society', in Pat Rogers (ed.), *The Context of English Literature: The Eighteenth Century* (London: Methuen, 1978), 1–80; J. W. Saunders, *The Profession of English Letters* (London: Routledge & Kegan Paul, 1964); Margaret Spufford, *Small Books and Pleasant Histories: Popular Fiction and its Readership in Seventeenth-Century England* (Athens, Ga: University of Georgia Press, 1981).

36 John Sekora, *Luxury: The Concept in Western Thought, Eden to Smollett* (Baltimore: Johns Hopkins University Press, 1985). For the uses of literacy see David Vincent, *Literacy and Popular Culture: England 1750–1914* (Cambridge: Cambridge University Press, 1989).

37 For scientific display, see Simon Schaffer, 'Natural philosophy and public spectacle in the eighteenth century', *History of Science*, xxi (1983), 1–43; Ian Inkster, 'Culture, institutions and urbanity: the itinerant science lecturer in Sheffield 1790–1850', in S. Pollard and C. Holmes (eds), *Essays in the Economic and Social History of South Yorkshire* (Barnsley: South Yorkshire County Council, 1976), 218–32; idem, 'The social context of an educational movement: a revisionist approach to the English mechanics' institutes, 1820–1850', *Oxford Review of Education*, ii (1976), 277–307; idem, 'Studies in the social history of science in England during the Industrial Revolution' (University of Sheffield, Ph.D. thesis, 1977); idem, 'Science and society in the metropolis: a preliminary examination of the social and economic context of the Askesian Society of London, 1796–1807', *Annals of Science*, xxxiv (1977), 1–32; idem, 'Marginal men: aspects of the social role of the medical community in Sheffield 1790–1850', in J. Woodward and D. Richards (eds), *Health Care and Popular Medicine in Nineteenth-Century England* (London: Croom Helm, 1977), 128–63; Eric H. Robinson, 'The Lunar Society: its membership and organization', *Transactions of the Newcomen Society*, xxxv (1962–3), 153–77; R. E. Schofield, *The Lunar Society of Birmingham* (Oxford: Oxford University Press, 1963); M. Berman, *Social Change and Scientific Organization: The Royal Institution, 1799–1844* (London: Heinemann Educational, 1978). For more general discussion of the idea of the theatre of life see J.-C. Agnew, *Worlds Apart: The Market and the Theater in Anglo-American Thought, 1550–1750* (Cambridge: Cambridge University Press, 1986); John Brewer, *The Common People and Politics, 1750–1790s* (Cambridge: Chadwyck-Healey, 1986).

38 For the wider world of display see Terry Castle, *Masquerade and Civilization: The Carnivalesque in Eighteenth-Century English Culture and Fiction* (London: Methuen, 1986), and, behind that, Mikhail M. Bakhtin, *Rabelais and his World*, tr. H. Iswolsky (Cambridge, Mass.: MIT Press, 1968); David Cressy, *Bonfires and Bells* (London: Weidenfeld & Nicolson, 1989); H. Cunningham, *Leisure in the Industrial Revolution* (London: Croom Helm, 1980); R. D. Altick, *The Shows of London: A Panoramic History of Exhibitions, 1600–1862* (Cambridge, Mass.: Belknap Press, 1978); the theatricality of art is discussed in John Barrell, *The Political Theory of Painting from Reynolds to Hazlitt* (New Haven: Yale University Press, 1986). For taste and aesthetics, see B. Sprague Allen, *Tides in English Taste (1619–1800)* (New York: Pageant Books, 1969). For the moralization of nature, see John Brewer and Stella Tillyard, 'The moral vision of Thomas Bewick', in E. Hellmuth (ed.), *The Transformation of Political Culture: England and Germany in the Late Eighteenth Century* (Oxford: Oxford University Press, 1990), 375–408.

39 On matters of design see Adrian Forty, *Objects of Desire: Design and Society 1750–1980* (London: Thames & Hudson, 1986); John Gloag, *The Englishman's Chair* (London: Allen & Unwin, 1964); idem, *A Social History of Furniture Design: From BC 1300 to AD 1960* (London: Cassell, 1966). Some of the insights on the relevance of styles to the late twentieth century contained in Peter York, *Style Wars* (London: Sidgwick & Jackson, 1980) apply well to the eighteenth century.

40 On ideology encoded in visual images see Ronald Paulson, *Popular and Polite Art in the Age of Hogarth and Fielding* (Notre Dame: University of Notre Dame Press, 1979); Norman Bryson, *Word and Image: French Painting of the Ancien Régime* (Cambridge: Cambridge University Press, 1983); and at a more popular level, M. Dorothy George, *English Political Caricature 1793–1832* (Oxford: Clarendon

Press, 1959); idem, M. Dorothy George, *Hogarth to Cruikshank: Social Change in Graphic Satire* (London: Allen Lane, 1967); Michael Duffy (ed.), *The English Satirical Print, 1600–1832*, 7 vols (Cambridge: Chadwyck-Healey, 1986); David Kunzle, *The Early Comic Strip: Picture Stories and Narrative Strips in the European Broadsheet ca. 1450–1826* (Berkeley: University of California Press, 1973); idem, *The History of the Comic Strip: The Nineteenth Century* (Berkeley: University of California Press, 1989).

41 See above all John Sekora, *Luxury: The Concept in Western Thought, Eden to Smollett* (Baltimore: Johns Hopkins University Press, 1985). The second volume in this present series (to be edited by John Brewer and Susan Staves), dealing explicitly with attitudes towards possession and property, documents at greater length the debate about the evils of things.

Part I
Problems, methods and concepts

2

Coming up for air: consumer culture in historical perspective

Jean-Christophe Agnew

Then, the mariners were afraid and cried every man unto his god, and cast forth the wares that were in the ship into the sea to lighten it of them.

(Jonah 1: v, 3: vi, vii)

Taking this dramatic passage from the Book of Jonah for his epigraph, the historian Simon Schama opens the second part of his book, *The Embarrassment of Riches*, with a fascinating discussion of 'Feasting, fasting, and timely atonement' among the Dutch of the Golden Age. For Schama the tale of the terrified sailors jettisoning their cargo neatly captures the sense of foreboding that haunted Holland's otherwise complacent bourgeois culture during the sixteenth and seventeenth centuries. Masters of banking and trade and for a time rulers of the sea, the Dutch none the less displayed a nagging ambivalence toward the commodities that served as both the source and signature of their affluence. Was not the very visibility of their wealth, they wondered, an invitation to disaster? Were so many goods not an omen of evils yet to come? This, then, was their 'embarrassment'.

The terms of embarrassment could run both ways, of course. Like the polished, auratic skull of a Dutch vanity painting, such anguished spiritual reflection on the comforts of commerce could just as easily deepen the lustre of the material objects upon which it ostensibly stood in judgement. Nor is Schama the first historian to remark on the material and symbolic density with which the Dutch infused the prints and paintings of their commodity-world. Still, few scholars can rival his own dazzling interpretations of the cultural meanings the Dutch attached to such otherwise prosaic items as pipes, soap and herring. And among Schama's readings, none is more impressive than the extended explication of a series of popular engravings of beached whales with which he begins his analysis of the complex attitudes the Dutch brought to the consumption of their own 'riches'.

Beached whales. An unpromising beginning, one might think, for a discussion of Dutch domestic possessions, but Schama manages to sort out the meanings of these prints in a fashion that gently but firmly leads the reader from the whale-ridden shores of the North Sea into the quiet interiors of the northern Renaissance, which is to say, into the hearts and hearths of the Dutch. In fact, by the time Schama's reading is complete, the prints have been made to yield up almost as much wealth as the whales themselves. We learn, for example, of the Dutch fascination with mapping and measurement and of their hunger for news of the odd and miraculous; we read as well of their commercial interest in beached whales and of their corresponding fear of them as auguries of national misfortune and providential reminders of the vanity of worldly goods.[1]

The surplus of meaning that Schama finds at play in these marine images is truly remarkable; it is almost as if – in contemporary American terms – the *National Geographic*, the *National Review* and the *National Enquirer* were condensed into a single tabloid image. The whales have not just been thought about; they have been thought through and through. 'Metaphorical compression', Schama calls this process and then shows how Dutch engravers used the technique to navigate their own commercial route between the conflicting public demands for allegory, inventory and reportage – demands that were driving 'the first mass consumers' art market in European history'.[2] As to the whales, he writes, 'the great leviathans, their sonar scrambled by the North Sea, were migrating not only from Atlantic to Arctic, but from the realm of myth and morality to that of matter and commodity, sometimes becoming stranded on the submarine slopes of Dutch cultural contradiction'.[3]

Description doesn't get much thicker than this. Between the tactility of the imagery and the surfeit of its significance, Schama's panorama of Dutch culture teems with art and artefacts that are larger, not to say longer, than life. Indeed, so dense and nuanced is Schama's treatment of the Dutch world of goods that one must occasionally remind oneself that his is an interpretation of Dutch culture, not of Dutch *consumer* culture. And the reminder is that much more necessary because of the ease with which one could fit *The Embarrassment of Riches* together with a number of other important recent studies that have challenged virtually every aspect of our understanding of the development of consumer culture in the west. If we cannot now speak about contemporary consumer culture without at least nodding towards sixteenth- and seventeenth-century Europe, then that reflex alone attests to the impact of the new scholarship. It would seem appropriate, then, to offer a preliminary review and assessment of a body of work that has – within a period of a few years – compelled so many historians to revise their familiar notions about culture, commodities, consumers and their historical relationships.

I

Now while there is no single interpretive paradigm or point of departure from which to chart this sea-change in our present thinking about consumer culture, one might for convenience's sake invoke two influential strands of critical thought that have set the boundaries to the debate and, at the same time, defined its moral and political charge. The first strand is English and extends from Thomas Carlyle's caustic denunciations of advertising puffery through George Orwell's even grimmer ruminations, a century later, on the 'sodden' ideological messages of the British boys' weeklies.[4] The second strand of thinking is continental and extends from Marx's discussion of commodity fetishism to the work of Georg Lukács, Walter Benjamin and the Frankfurt School. These two traditions of criticism differ in important respects, but they both picture western history and culture – time and space – as invaded and colonized by commodities and commodity-relations. Orwell epitomizes this state of affairs most vividly and mockingly in the fictional figure of George Bowling, a pitiable, *petit bourgeois* anti-hero who squanders his modest racetrack winnings upon a futile pilgrimage to the lost fishpond of his youth, only to find a rubbish-heap upon which a new housing development is to grow. 'What's the good of trying to revisit the scenes of your boyhood?' the indignant Bowling concludes. 'They don't exist. Coming up for air! But there isn't any air. The dustbin we're in reaches up to the stratosphere.'[5]

This is a familiar refrain. On the other side of the Atlantic, we hear the same plaintive message in Stuart Ewen's recent attack on 'the politics of style in contemporary culture'. Ewen's title, *All Consuming Images*, itself registers the deep, almost platonic distaste he feels for the ubiquitous productions – the modern hoardings – of the culture industry. To him the politics of style means the 'dominance of surface over substance',[6] yet he also discovers, to his dismay, that such surfaces can run disturbingly deep. Having asked his undergraduate students to write on the question of style, for example, Ewen is appalled to discover just how thoroughly the vagaries of fashion have entered into their constructions of self; there, in the memoirs his inner-city students have written, the ordinary and sometimes extraordinary claims of their own lives insert themselves, when they do not actually lose themselves, in the far more insistent and accelerated half-lives of contemporary commodities. It could be said that for these students history also appears as an embarrassment of riches, but if so, it is an embarrassment prompted less by the fear of sudden reversal than by the spectre of imminent obsolescence. Styles may be recycled, but the goods themselves are soon jettisoned; sneakers to die for today become artefacts to reminisce about tomorrow. And 'though the long-term ecological implications of this trajectory may be disastrous', Ewen adds that 'from a strictly merchandising point of view, it is *the air we breathe*'.[7] History has been thus doubly lost, buried under the weight of shoddy goods and repressed beneath the surface of a shopworn consciousness.

Aesthetic revulsion and political despair converge in Ewen's work, but in that respect so too do the Orwellian and Marxian strands of cultural criticism to which I have alluded. To the English concern with the designers of consciousness, Ewen adds the Continental concern with the design itself, with the peculiar ways in which the commodity has captured and colonized American culture in the image of its own relations – in the image, that is, of images. Even more than his earlier book, Stuart Ewen's *All Consuming Images* conjures up the presence of a horizonless ideological flatland, an impoverished consumerist dystopia whose mirage-like surfaces leave the radical political imagination no way out. For all its gestures in the direction of post-modernism, then, Ewen's latest work harks back to an older tradition of criticism – not just to George Orwell's ideas but to Georg Lukács's notion of reification, to Max Horkheimer's and Theodor Adorno's portrait of the culture industry as mass deception, and, not least of all, to Herbert Marcuse's concept of ideological one-dimensionality.[8] In fact, it is this unwaveringly pessimistic view of the massive *totality* of contemporary consumer culture that makes Ewen's work such a convenient signpost (and foil) from which to measure the intellectual and political distance travelled by the most recent generation of writers on consumer culture.

This is not to say that the initial steps away from the pessimistic reading of consumer culture were particularly easy ones. They weren't, and a fair sense of the difficulties encountered along the way may be had by a glance at a collection of essays that appeared in 1983 under the title *The Culture of Consumption*.[9] The contributors to this volume, myself included, advertised their work as attempting to rehistoricize and retheorize American consumer culture. 'Historians have taken the world of goods for granted', I wrote at the time. 'More precisely, they have taken that world as the outcome of other historical developments –

industrial capitalism, for example – that are felt to be more compelling.'[10] Consumer culture deserved a more considered historical treatment, we felt, if not on its own terms then in its own time. This meant, among other things, backdating the emergence of consumer culture in America to the 1880s and linking that birth in turn to the social formation of a professional–managerial class. Not all the authors approached this story in the same way, but whether our frameworks were Weberian, Marxist or Durkheimian, the story we did tell remained in many respects a familiar one, marked by the shift from a producer-ethic to a consumer-ethic, from a salvationist ideal to a therapeutic ideal, and from local performances to mass-mediated spectacles. And though the editors acknowledged that conspiratorial theories of mass deception were inaccurate, people being 'not that passive', the collection itself remained an unashamedly supply-side enterprise: a study of the producers, stylists and critics of a hegemonic consumer ideal and not an inquiry into 'patterns of consumption' or the 'lives of ordinary consumers'.[11] Despite the distance we tried to put between ourselves and the pessimistic critiques of a Ewen or a Marcuse, our contributions were understandably received as revisions and extensions of the Frankfurt School's central insights and assumptions.[12] One-dimensional man, and he was quite plainly a man, had emerged weightless and famished as early as the turn of the century. Or so the collection seemed to suggest.

Of course I caricature *The Culture of Consumption* here, but then I am scarcely the first to do so, and such caricatures can and do serve to inspire corrective impulses among other scholars. And, in that respect, it seems fair to say that we now stand corrected.[13] The narrative, interpretations and methods laid out in our volume – not to mention those laid out in Stuart Ewen's work – have all been challenged in the intervening years. Not only do we now have before us outstanding histories of early modern material culture and promotion, of nineteenth-century popular culture and recreation and of twentieth-century advertising and working-class consumption, but we have as well a variety of intriguing approaches to consumer culture growing out of other disciplines. These would include new sociological and anthropological studies of tastes, goods and their uses; literary studies of reader response and cultural studies of genre formation and of the symbolic or semiotic order of consumption.[14] We have, to borrow again from Simon Schama, an embarrassment of riches, and in accordance with Schama's own formulation of Dutch ambivalence in the Golden Age, I would like to convey some of my excitement and pleasure in this new-found wealth and, at the same time, some of my lingering doubts and questions.

Exciting as this body of work may be, however, it would be tedious to review it all. Instead, I shall select and group works according to the triple challenge I see them posing to the conventional understanding of the history of consumption: first, their challenge to the received narrative of consumption in the Euro-American world; second, their challenge to the perceived causes and conditions of that history; and third, their challenge to the judgements on consumer culture – moral, aesthetic and political – that have for so long underwritten and overdetermined our perspectives on the subject. At the risk of anticipating my argument, let me also summarize briefly what I see as the results of these challenges. First, historians have shifted the birth of western consumer culture to the early modern period and deferred the arrival of mass consumer culture to the mid-twentieth century. Second, they have rejected the Weberian dichotomies between puritanism and romanticism and, correspondingly, between saving and spending and in some instances, they have also abandoned the classic Marxist distinction between use-value and symbolic value. Finally, they have revalued the political and moral dimensions of fantasy, fetishism, dream and wish – the keywords of consumer mystification as it has heretofore been understood. As a result, the productionist, supply-side and hegemonic interpretation of consumer culture has been shaken, if not overthrown, leaving one-dimensional man marooned on a small and ever shrinking island of history.

II

Let me return, then, to the first of the challenges I have enumerated: the challenge to the received narrative or periodization of consumer culture, for the question of narrative entails, as it almost always does, virtually every other question a historian might bring to a subject. As it happens, the recent backdating (as I have called it) of consumer culture to the early modern period is a by-product of a much earlier debate over the origins of industrial capitalism in the west, a debate in which historians tended to divide over the relative roles of commerce and class – or of exchange and production. Yet even within the ranks of those who favoured the market as the prime motor of development, historians fell into two camps: the globalists or world-systems advocates, who looked to the international wheels of commerce as the vehicle of capitalist development and the nationalists, who looked to indigenous demand as the driving force. The world-systems advocates were associated with the work of Fernand Braudel and Immanuel Wallerstein, and it was upon their example and that of John Nef and Werner Sombart, that the historical sociologist, Chandra Mukerji, relocated the origins of 'modern materialism', as she called it, in fifteenth- and sixteenth-century Europe.[15] As the title of her book, *From Graven Images*, suggests, she saw the international commerce in prints, maps and calicoes as both modelling and diffusing a new and intense orientation toward material objects. A 'hedonistic culture of mass consumption' she called this new worldview and contrasted it with the now classic, Weberian portrait of an ascetic, savings-minded Reformation.[16] Mukerji, it should be added, did not so much discard Weber's psycho-historical sequence of savings and spending, asceticism and hedonism, as telescope it in time. As a result, she transformed a story of anguished cultural and temperamental change from one ethic to another into a portrait of complementary and mutually energizing traits. Early modern capitalists saved *and* spent, and, in doing so, ushered in modernity.

Standing not so much against as with the internationalists were the nationalists, historians like Joan Thirsk, D. E. C. Eversley, Jan de Vries and most recently, Simon Schama, all of whom stressed the impact of home demand upon commercial and industrial development.[17] In Holland, for example, where the North Sea appears to have played the role of a merciless Calvinist Providence, Schama painted a complex, Breugelian panorama of a 'perennial combat between acquisitiveness and asceticism' within the society and within the minds of the Dutch.[18] As sceptical of Weber as Mukerji was, Schama likewise found in this internal fusion of opposite impulses a motive force powerful enough to move the Dutch economy ahead of its rivals.[19]

For Braudel, though, the 'right string to pull to start the engine' of capitalism was always demand, and it has been to the demand-side of the capitalist market-place that current revisionists have devoted most of their attention.[20] Among these efforts by far the most influential revisionist manifesto appeared in the essays that Neil McKendrick wrote for the book he co-authored with John Brewer and J. H. Plumb in 1982: *The Birth of a Consumer Society*, subtitled *The Commercialization of Eighteenth-Century England*. Building upon the earlier studies of home demand by Thirsk, Plumb himself and others, McKendrick announced the discovery of 'a consumer revolution in eighteenth-century England'. He agreed with Braudel's belief that 'there is always a potential consumer society ready to be awakened in any society', but insisted that for the eighteenth century, only England presented the right mix of ingredients: a fluid social structure, rising wages, an emulative bourgeoisie and its servants, a showcase capital city and an intellectual environment increasingly hospitable to the public benefits of private vices.[21]

All that seemed missing from this heady stew of latent hedonism was a chef to stir it up, an entrepreneur sufficiently alert to the possibilities before him; thus McKendrick's interest in Josiah Wedgwood, the pottery king. The choice of Wedgwood, however, was not an immediately obvious one, since his historical reputation to that point had been as a pioneer of large-scale craft production, industrial discipline and the division of labour. Indeed, what made McKendrick's argument that much more persuasive was the ease with which he was able to transfer Wedgwood's achievement as an entrepreneur from the supply side to the demand side of England's commercialization. Despite, or more accurately because, of his many aristocratic connections, Josiah Wedgwood had made himself into a promotional wizard, able, as McKendrick put it, to 'milk the effects of social emulation and emulative spending' among England's middling ranks.[22] Economists have traditionally referred to such imitative or bandwagon phenomena as 'Veblen effects', but having described what he considered 'one of the most brilliant and sustained campaigns in the history of consumer exploitation', McKendrick wondered whether such behaviour were not better labelled as 'Wedgwood effects'.[23]

Wedgwood thus stood in for a variety of merchandising pioneers whose bold promotional campaigns released an unprecedented wave of bourgeois spending that spread across the kingdom and, as production and distribution caught up with demand, eventually spilled over into Britain's colonies. In other words, 'by creating new wants and provoking new needs', these orchestrators of desire were able 'to create new demand which would not have become economically operational without the requisite entrepreneurial skills to conjure it into existence'.[24] Imaginative as these businessmen were, though, and bold as McKendrick's view of them may have been, his argument as a whole bore the marks of the original historical debate that had given it birth, namely the argument over the origins of England's industrial revolution. It was Wedgwood – the entrepreneur – and not his consumers who pulled the strings of demand. In fact, had McKendrick not been so visibly impressed by Wedgwood's indisputable brilliance as a promoter, the strikingly magical and manipulative metaphors ('exploiting', 'milking', 'conjuring') with which he formulated his revisionist account could have been as easily assimilated to the kind of conspiratorial or hypodermic theory of mass culture before which even the most devoted hegemonic theorist might balk.[25] To put it another way, McKendrick's story of the birth of a consumer society in eighteenth-century England left us with an unforgettable portrait of its enterprising midwife but with only the faintest sketch of the infant itself. We were still in important respects fixed on the supply side of the ledger, with the mechanics of demand-stimulation now included in the costs of production.

As we shall see, McKendrick's work, like that of his central figure Wedgwood, had important reverberations on the other side of the Atlantic. But perhaps one of the most thoughtful and provocative responses to it came some five years later from within Britain itself and in the form of a book with the deliberately Weberian title, *The Romantic Ethic and the*

Spirit of Modern Consumerism. Written by an historical sociologist, Colin Campbell, *The Romantic Ethic* accepted McKendrick's reperiodization of western consumerism while seeking to remedy its cultural or demand-side shortcomings. Drawing on a number of disciplines, including (interestingly) the philosophy of mind, Campbell dismissed what he called McKendrick's 'instinctivist, manipulationist, Veblenesque' approach to the consumer revolution as an inadequate explanation for a pattern of consumption that eighteenth-century critics themselves labelled as manic and addictive.[26] Purchasing power, he argued, could not of itself generate new propensities to consume, just as marketing brainstorms could not explain the new willingness of entrepreneurs to shift resources toward promotion. Fashion and its democratization were less the answer to the question of consumer culture's birth than the problem to be resolved; the problem, that is, of explaining both the rapid multiplication and the equally rapid extinction of wants. In other words, how might one account for the almost Proustian cycle of anticipatory pleasure and consummatory disappointment upon which the Wedgwoods of the eighteenth century so skilfully played?[27]

Twentieth-century economists, from Werner Sombart to Tibor Scitovsky and Albert O. Hirschman, have long wrestled with the problem of consumer disappointment or 'exit', but it was Campbell's special contribution to imbue this seemingly timeless puzzle of evanescent demand with the kind of historicity – of time-boundedness – that McKendrick's work had conferred upon the strategies of its manipulation.[28] Consumer letdown and the longing that disappointment nourished were indeed consequences of manipulation, but of a manipulation, Campbell insisted, in which consumers pulled their own strings. How and why, then, had England's middling orders learned to do this? This was the question Campbell set for himself, and for us.

Though the argument of *The Romantic Ethic* is far too complex and nuanced to recapitulate adequately here, it may reasonably be said to hang on a distinction Campbell drew between 'traditional' and 'modern' hedonism. Traditional hedonism oriented itself towards the material attributes of objects as means to relieve discomfort, he argued, whereas 'modern, autonomous, and self-illusory hedonism' oriented itself towards the imagined associations of objects as means to cultivate a 'state of enjoyable discomfort'.[29] Modern hedonism operated in a twilight zone of longing best typified in the experience of window-shopping.[30] Its peculiar, daydream-like fusion of the pleasures of fantasy and reality inserted itself into that ever-expanding moment or 'hiatus' between actual production and consumption (or between desire and consummation), which is to say, the moment of circulation or exchange. By Campbell's lights, modern (i.e., eighteenth-century) hedonism collapsed the Weberian dichotomy and sequence between deferred and immediate gratification – savings and spending – into a single, iterable experience of unquenchable desire. Like Veblen and, in a measure, like the anthropologist Mary Douglas, Campbell treated the symbolic values of consumer objects as their use-value, but unlike them he defined those communicative uses as fundamentally private, covert and inconspicuous. Where Veblen and Douglas had treated acquisitions as forms of direct address, Campbell regarded them as – at best – soliloquies. The modern consumer or hedonist, he argued, 'is continually withdrawing from reality as fast as he encounters it, ever-casting his day-dreams forward in time, attaching them to objects of desire, and then subsequently "unhooking" them from these objects as and when they are attained and experienced'.[31] This was the dialectic of demand that Campbell saw entering, 'irreversibly', into eighteenth-century English commercial culture.

But if this was how bourgeois Britons stimulated their own demand, one may still ask why? Here Campbell, who might otherwise have been expected to join Mukerji and Schama in jettisoning once and for all Weber's theoretical legacy, unexpectedly and quite ingeniously proposed (under Weberian auspices) a theory of an 'other Protestant ethic'. Specifically, he located an alternative and, once again, complementary, intellectual tradition within the Reformation, a tradition running parallel to Weber's inner-worldly asceticism but rejecting its emotional economies. Campbell thus traced a genealogy of feeling extending from Dutch Arminian ministers through increasingly secular latitudinarian, sentimentalist and romantic writers of the eighteenth century. Their cumulative impact was to legitimize the kind of affective self-indulgence at play in the new consumerism.[32]

As with Weber's own genealogy of asceticism, Campbell's party of feeling was perhaps the most ideational and therefore least compelling feature of his causal argument. But his case for the 'other Protestant ethic' was not a purely intellectualist one. Much as Caroline Bynum has argued in relation to the fasting practices of Catholic women during the Middle Ages, so Campbell suggested the intimate, if not dialectical, relation between the control and the exploration of appetite and feeling. As he put the relation, 'both the delaying of gratification and the suppression of emotion work together to create a rich and powerful, imaginative inner life within the individual, the necessary prerequisite for a "romantic" personality', and, one need only add, for a modern consumer.[33]

With this move, it is possible to say that Colin Campbell had not so much reconstructed the 'Protestant ethic' as deconstructed it: demonstrating, albeit deductively, how that super-fluity of feeling which asceticism was in earnest to displace could become, by the very power of its own repressive mechanisms, the sentimentality it eventually came to embrace.[34] But to acknowledge, as Campbell did, this 'social irony' is to recognize its familiarity as well. Americanists, for example, will make out in this dialectic of discipline and desire many of the features of Daniel Bell's theory of the cultural contradictions of capitalism, of Ann Douglas's theory of the feminization of American culture and of Jackson Lears's theory of the shift from salvation to self-realization – all of whom critically link the cultural fascination with intense and expressive feeling to the onset of an anti-puritanical consumerism.[35] Unlike Bell, Douglas and Lears, however, Campbell rejected any formulation of these dichotomies as contradictions, much less as a sequence of declension. There was for him no lamentable fall out of Calvinist discipline into the symbolically impoverished world of consumerism. To the contrary, he saw an almost Hegelian leap in the imaginative possibilities – a new emotional 'recipe-knowledge' so to speak – available to the west as a result of the centuries-long 'rationalization of pleasure'. For Campbell, the historical irony of 1960s counter-culture was not its moral sellout to contemporary consumerism but its moral indebtedness to a centuries-old tradition of hedonistic longing – not *Thirtysomething*, in other words, but two-hundred-and-thirtysomething.[36]

III

Already, then, we can see how an historical reperiodization of consumer culture has brought with it a reconceptualization of its causes and a revaluation of its moral and political consequences. Still, to backdate origins in this fashion is to leave out just those men and women whose class, race or religion placed them outside the orbit of Reformation rhetoric and Wedgwood advertisements. What, for example, of the so-called counter-cultures of

America's native and ethnic working classes? If consumer culture as a middle-class phenomenon dates from eighteenth-century England, if not fifteenth-century Florence and sixteenth-century Holland, what of consumer culture as a mass phenomenon? At what point did the 'masses' effectively enter and thereby constitute a recognizable consumer culture? In what way did they do so, and with what consequences?

For a population as heterogeneous and polyglot as America's working men and women, no definitive answer and certainly no definitive point of entry seems possible. But glancing over the extraordinarily rich and detailed studies of working-class leisure that have appeared over the past decade, we are encouraged to look to the 1930s and 1940s as a pivotal historical moment when commodity culture achieved sufficient breadth and density as to define the ground – if not the atmosphere – within which a shaken society was to be restored and reconstructed. Before then it seems more useful to speak of the presence of an urban, commercial culture spanning the century between 1830 and 1930. By that I mean a fully commercialized yet distinctively local or regional network of cultural production and exchange, with goods, services and performances organized in a fashion closer to cottage industry than to mass production.[37] By that I also mean a commercial culture with (at least) two quite distinct dimensions and market orientations. The first dimension would encompass the high-profile, English-speaking forms of amusement – from theatre to vaudeville – that flourished in nineteenth-century America. Until the syndication and eventually the broadcasting of these forms after the turn of the century, these leisure commodities remained typically local, syncretic, male, rowdy and often combative forms of cultural expression. As Lawrence Levine has recently shown, impresarios served up scenes from Shakespeare along with entr'acte gymnastics and farcical finales, all open of course to the vigorous commentary of the audiences.[38] Fragmented and satirical as these performances seem to us, they are none the less distinguishable from our own time's deeply ironic ventures into cultural pastiche. Where a critic like Fredric Jameson regards the plagiarized or cannibalized texts of postmodernism as grim reminders of cultural dispossession, Levine treats the motley offerings of nineteenth-century theatre as evidence of the insistently proprietary claims that urban folk made upon their stage.[39]

The second dimension of working-class consumerism moved in many respects away from this mixed (if still Anglicized) public sphere and towards a realm of ethnic separateness and insularity. As Roy Rosenzweig has shown in relation to leisure goods and services and as Lizabeth Cohen has argued more recently in relation to consumer durables, immigrant workers and their families entered hesitantly, if at all, into the developing infrastructure of bourgeois consumption – the sanitized 'dream worlds' of the movie palace, department and chain stores.[40] And when new goods and services were purchased, they were often incorporated into imported, inherited or in other ways alternative systems of meaning. As a consequence, even imitative or emulative consumption stood at an oblique angle to mainstream consumer culture by virtue of the different reference points of respectability and fashionability to which these Veblen – or Wedgwood – effects were aligned.[41]

Again, the arguments and examples of these studies are too complex to summarize here, but, taken together, they tell a story of a staggered working-class entry into the world of 'rationalized pleasure', an entry delayed and deferred by the constraints of income, race, ethnicity, gender and their corresponding cultural meanings. But as it is also a story retold with every new migration to American shores, the narrative of this encounter with organized leisure bears a striking resemblance to Herbert Gutman's now classic account of immigrant workers' repeated encounters with (and resistance to) the world of rationalized labour.[42] And like Gutman, these historians reject the received image of the blue-collar consumer's passive immersion in a ready-made mass leisure experience; working-class consumption was less a form of cultural suicide than a model of cultural awakening, a case of native and immigrant workers actively appropriating and transforming leisure goods to suit their pleasures and purposes. So active in fact were these working men and women in shaping the conventions and content of urban commercial culture that when television – a truly mass medium – finally did appear, its promoters looked to earlier vernacular forms (from variety to vaude-ville) and to conspicuously blue-collar themes to draw a mass audience. Describing television as the 'central discursive medium in American culture' in the post-World War II period, George Lipsitz has suggested that the industry's dream of entering every household drove the producers of the early family sitcoms to piece together a working-class 'realism' in their shows, a realism whose awkward and refractory social content the industry itself could not fully control.[43] Determined to confer legitimacy and credibility upon the prospect of post-war consumerism, television was compelled to dramatize the very social tensions and contradic-tions for which consumption was being offered up as a resolution. The result of these grudging concessions to the 'real', Lipsitz concludes, was the opening up of these half-hour parables of consumption to the possibility of 'oppositional or negotiated readings' by their blue-collar audiences.[44] Even at the high point of consumerism's Happy Days, then, the culture industry inadvertently infused its products with the same malaise the products were supposed to resolve. If the industry did indeed operate as an ideological hypodermic needle, as some mass culture critics insisted, its solution appeared to carry unanticipated and unwanted antibodies.

As this capsule summary of George Lipsitz's argument indicates, I hope, mass consumer culture has offered scholars an especially fertile field in which to nurture a new and hybrid form of cultural history born of the marriage between American social and labour history on the one hand and literary and cultural theory on the other. Lipsitz himself has acknowledged the intellectual influence of Mikhail Bakhtin's notion of the 'dialogic imagination', Stuart Hall's notion of the 'ideological effect' and Fredric Jameson's notion of reification as models for his own analysis of post-war television, and these same theoretical influences are every-where visible as more and more historians come to look upon the boundaries between high and low cultural commodities as themselves politically contested conventions.[45] Now there have been many interesting developments springing out of this cross-fertilization between history and cultural studies, but one of the most intriguing (and arguable) has been the political redemption of consumer choices once airily dismissed as forms of working-class escapism and wish-fulfilment. This recuperation of blue-collar consumer fantasy proceeds, though, on quite different premises from those upon which Colin Campbell has reinterpreted and reclaimed the bourgeois daydream. Whereas Campbell treats the middle-class longing after goods as a characteristically private, almost Rousseauan reverie that has been wishfully freed of all obstacles and discomforts, the interpreters of working-class consumption have stressed the social dimension of that consumption and the class, gender and generational tensions with which its fantasies are invariably laced.

Perhaps one of the most impressive and innovative instances of such an interpretation is Michael Denning's recent study of the nineteenth-century dime novel, *Mechanic Accents*. There he argues against those literalist and co-optative readings of the novels that take the genre's formulaic happy endings as parables of working-class assimilation and incorporation into an

Algeresque or bourgeois scheme of upward mobility. Instead he argues for a subversive, allegorical reading of the dime novel that takes its seemingly harmonious endings as covert enactments of class expropriation and redistribution.[46] For him, then, class functions less as a set of boundaries structuring the production of cultural commodities than as a set of accents inflecting their consumption. And since those inflections run through and through commodities in a manner that keeps them forever open to political reclamation, commodities thereby become both objects and sites of symbolic struggle; overtly, as in the tradition of working-class dandyism stretching from the Bowery B'hoys and Gals of 1840s New York to the Zoot Suiters of 1940s Los Angeles;[47] but covertly also, in, say, the licensed pleasures that Janice Radway and Anne Snitow see women claiming from Harlequin Romances, or in the more explicit generational and gender negotiation of sexual pleasure and freedom that Kathy Peiss and John Kasson have found at play in turn-of-the-century New York City.[48]

To the extent, then, that pleasures publicly enjoyed, if not flaunted, cease to be a bourgeois, male prerogative and become instead an object of competitive claims, the pleasure principle itself has been politicized. From this perspective a world of increasingly libidinized goods would seem to present as many opportunities for aggressive as for repressive desublimation. The ghost of the Frankfurt School thus returns unbidden to the interpretation of consumer culture, but this time in the guise of Herbert Marcuse's deepest utopian longings.[49] The resemblance is striking. However different may be the starting points of these historical ventures into the alternative dream-worlds of middle-class and working-class consumers, they all seem to converge upon the same end-point: the counter-culture of the 1960s and its ambiguous aftermath. Is that surprising?

Is it really surprising that a generation of scholars raised on mass culture and, many of them, involved in the movements of the 1960s should chafe against a tradition of inquiry into mass consumer culture hobbled between the stark alternatives of celebration and revulsion? And is it any more surprising that the fantasy life long associated with commodity-consumption should at this moment receive another look and, with it, another historical and political valuation? I think not. Recent cultural studies on the left reveal a discernible restlessness with the old categories of consumer culture, a restlessness that springs from something more, I suspect, then the hunger for novelty. Rather, it seems to grow out of the conviction that mass culture, mass consumer culture – whatever its origins – can no longer be discussed as if its presence were still an open question, a matter of choice. One way to dispose of that sense of moral or political option, then, is to push the boundaries of consumer culture backward in time, making the moment of its birth coeval with that of capitalism itself; another strategy is to push its boundaries outward in space so as to encompass all contemporary experience.[50] Consumer culture thus dissolves historically and analytically into the success of its own inexorable proliferation. Under this dispensation, it might be claimed, as an indignant George Bowling did some sixty years ago and as an impatient Michael Denning did only recently, that 'We have come to the end of "mass culture"; the debates and positions which have named "mass culture" as an other have been superseded. There is no mass culture out there; it is the very element in which we all breathe.'[51]

After this long hunt for the leviathan of consumer culture, it is ironic indeed to discover that we are all, like Jonah and Orwell, inside the whale – inside the whale and thus unable in any intelligible sense to take its outward, historical measure.[52] Perhaps that is why one notes a preference within recent cultural studies for metaphors of mapping, as if the task remaining for the historian lay in the careful, detailed charting of this ever-expanding universe of goods

– complete, of course, with its fissures and fault lines of class, race, gender and ethnicity. Obviously, there is a world of political difference between these critics' careful mapping of the 'politics of value' and the glib, zip-code demographics served up in current micro-marketing manuals. But there is at the same time an uncanny structural and figurative resemblance in the world-picture each tendency presents of a totalizing yet reassuringly segmented culture of consumption.[53] Redrawn in this way, the globe appears as a crazy quilt of desire which, depending on one's agenda, may be mobilized to produce a hegemonic bloc or a marketing coup: a Rainbow Coalition or a pot of gold.

Yet another indication of the way in which the world of goods has expanded to fill the available analytical space – to become, as it were, the air we breathe – has been the gradual marginalization of labour and production in many recent cultural studies. What began after 1968 as a legitimate effort to correct the labour metaphysic of classical and Marxist political economy and to restore the symbolic dimension of consumption has given way to a blanket dismissal of such categories as subsistence, use-value and labour.[54] The word 'production' survives largely as a figure of speech, a metaphor used to evoke the active powers at play in the symbolic uses to which a produced and purchased good may be put. Consumers invariably reread, reconfigure and recontextualize their purchases, and, in doing so, reproduce, recreate and refashion themselves. Not surprisingly, terms like 'fashion', 'fiction' and 'fabrication' have all acquired such strong connotations with manual or craft labour – a kind of mental inscription upon the material world – as to displace many of their earlier associations with semblance, illusion and deceit. In this manner consumption becomes 'cultural work', productive of 'cultural capital', and grist for cultural 'resistance'.[55] From the ashes of the dead author (or producer) arises the heroic figure of the restless reader (or consumer), for it is in the sphere of consumption, as the anthropologist Daniel Miller has recently argued, that 'the strategies of recontextualization are at their most advanced'. Consumption, Miller has announced, 'is now at the vanguard of history'.[56] All that remains for this customized Marxism to perform, then, are the last rites on itself.

Daniel Miller's approach, it should be said, is far more Hegelian than Marxist. For him consumption belongs not to the mysteries of commodity fetishism, as Georg Lukács and his followers insisted, but to 'the full project of objectification in which the subject becomes at home with itself in its otherness'.[57] This is a lot to swallow, to be sure, but whatever one's doubts at the prospect of a Hegelian epiphany in the housewares department of K-Mart, it is worth noting how closely Miller's notion of consumption as the act of a home-making (as distinct from a homeless) mind conforms to the arguments of several other sociologists and anthropologists.[58] Even more significantly, for my purposes, Miller's approach to consumption recalls some of the most influential writing in the historiography of consumer culture, namely, Warren Susman's now classic essays on America in the 1930s and 1940s.[59] In those pieces Susman illustrated in brilliantly eclectic fashion the essentially conservative and domesticating role played by consumer culture during those years of crisis. Deliberately ignoring the political and labour history that had dominated the interpretation of the Depression and the wartime homefront, he instead held up every artefact of consumer culture he could lay his eye upon – from Disney films to the 1939 World's Fair – in order to show how variously yet how deeply they all had suggested, not to say constructed, a sense of belonging.[60] In a way, Susman's argument was about mass cultural commodities as belongings, as cultural properties so powerfully and personally evocative as to have invented the 'American Way of Life' in their image.

Susman's interpretation of consumer culture, it is safe to say, has permanently altered our understanding of the larger history of the 1930s and 1940s in America. By showing this mass experience of home-coming to have been achieved in the sphere of consumption, Susman established a turning-point not just in history but for historiography as well. It seems appropriate, then, to close this review and assessment with some further reflections about this 'moment' and its mementos. With luck we might be able to get outside the whale and take stock – in Melvillian, if not Orwellian fashion – of the riches and limits of Warren Susman's legacy.

IV

Susman was interested in what he called 'middle-class America', but many of the recent studies of working-class consumption likewise look to the mass culture of the 1930s and 1940s as a pivotal orientation for the working class as well. By the end of the Depression, historians seem to agree, the insularity and autonomy of urban, commercial culture had greatly diminished. Local groups, according to Lizabeth Cohen, had also 'lost their ability to control the dissemination of mass culture'. Chain stores at last displaced local shops; talkies 'hushed' noisy movie audiences; and radio now broadcast network fare in place of the chaotic local programming that had typified the 1920s.[61] Mass culture had finally arrived, and though the culture industry was prepared to segment its markets, it none the less serviced them out of the same national infrastructure.

Having acknowledged this institutional transformation, however, these same historians have been quick to point out that American working men and women were not thereby incorporated into a system of middle-class values or, for that matter, into a pattern of labour quietism. Quite the reverse in fact. As Roy Rosenzweig suggests towards the end of his study of Worcester's working class and as Ronald Edsforth argues throughout his study of Flint's blue-collar households, the pervasive promise of American consumerism inspired the labour militance of the 1930s and after.[62] Whether it was the car described in Robert and Helen Lynd's study of Middletown or the fully applianced, nuclear household pictured in Thomas Bell's labour novel of 1941, Out of this Furnace, the working-class dream of consumption became, according to this argument, the business class's nightmare of production as pickets and sit-downs spread throughout the industrial heartland. 'Even in the depths of the Great Depression', Edsforth writes, 'most working people did not give up the dream of a new way of life.' 'Instead', he adds, quoting Susman, ' "Many who might have chosen the socialist way went instead with the hope of the culture of abundance" .'[63]

What then is at stake here if consumerism only fuelled the militance it was designed to quench? As I see it, it is not so much the issue of mass absorption into a monolithic consumer culture, for working men and women doubtless continued to dream, to 'think' and to use their goods with different accents. What is at work in this struggle, however, and what deserves further scrutiny is an implicit cultural reformulation of working-class consumer expectations as political or proto-political entitlements. And that is news, for if to this image of depression-born, consumption-fuelled labour militance, we add the thesis – first intimated by Susman but most recently developed by Robert Westbrook – that war mobilization likewise operated on conspicuously private, consumptionist themes, then we may very well be describing a process whereby private desires reconstructed notions of public rights and obligations – reconstructed them, that is, in the image of the objects upon which those desires happened to be cathected.[64] As one wartime GI was reported to have said, 'I am in this damn mess as much to help keep the custom of drinking Cokes as I am to preserve the million other benefits our country blesses its citizens with.'[65]

There is something admittedly disarming about a confession of this sort, but disarming in a more troubling sense than might appear at first. For it is one thing to pursue the politics of consumption, to struggle over and through the meaning of goods; it is quite another thing to pursue the consumption of politics, to form one's political thought and practice upon the model of commodity-exchange. Depressions and wars are by definition moments of crisis, moments when a society is potentially open to radical definitions of its political, social and economic foundations. And what the history of twentieth-century consumption is telling us is that a far-reaching ideological redefinition of polity and society did begin to take hold during the 1930s and 1940s: the promotion of the social contract of cold-war liberalism, which is to say a state-sponsored guarantee of private consumption. But, more importantly, we are also being told that this redefinition of rights and obligations articulated itself in the seemingly innocuous language of soft drinks, cars and household appliances, and that it therefore occurred, as Colin Campbell might put it, privately, imaginatively and inconspicuously – in short, without discussion.

This is not to suggest, however, that Franklin D. Roosevelt was the first political leader to exploit the symbolic dimensions of goods. Embargoes, boycotts and fasts all have long and honorable traditions. We need only think of the courtly endorsement of black cloth during the Middle Ages, or the traditional references to England and roast beef, or, for that matter to the Swadeshi movement in India.[66] Closer to home, one thinks as well of Timothy Breen's innovative study of the non-importation movement before the American Revolution. One thinks of it in particular because in many ways Breen's argument about nation-building in the 1760s and 1770s seems to rehearse Warren Susman's own interpretation of national rebuilding in the 1930s and 1940s.[67] It seems fitting, then, to close this discussion of the historiography of consumer culture by comparing Susman's and Breen's accounts, for by their juxtaposition we are enabled to throw the central questions of periodization, causality and judgement into greatest relief.

The two accounts resemble one another because they both attempt to interpret different, critical moments in the history of American nationalism as structurally and symbolically conditioned by consumer goods. But in other respects, Breen's argument is also an imaginative extension of Neil McKendrick's eighteenth-century consumer revolution to American shores. By 1775, Breen points out, the American colonies were absorbing some nine thou-and different commodities, most of them British, with the result that the colonists were becoming gradually and visibly Anglicized. 'The colonists belonged to an empire of goods', he concludes, and 'loyalty depended on commerce . . . and not upon coercion'.[68] Drawing here on symbolic anthropology rather than Antonio Gramsci, Breen suggests that commodities were the most widely shared 'semiotic order' in the colonies and that the patriots did not hesitate to conscript this system of signs when constitutional crises erupted in the 1760s and 1770s. Without knowing it, then, British parliamentarians effectively 'transformed private consumer acts into public political statements'.[69] Non-importation agreements further politicized these goods, such that the 'artefacts of a consumer culture took on a new symbolic meaning'. In other words, the 'confrontation with British imports was extending the political horizons of ordinary people', extending them in a way that would make it 'possible for the colonists to imagine a new nation'.[70] For the colonists British imports suddenly became, as Mary Douglas might put it, 'good for thinking'.[71]

Perhaps. But one may still wonder about the thought or systems of thought these goods were drafted to express. For it is just as plausible to argue that the rich, differentiated and conspicuously British language of goods was just that which non-importation deliberately and extravagantly negated. And the rhetoric of *that* denial – the rhetoric, that is, of non-importation – operated in considerable measure at a distance from the 'language' of those commodities, for it sprang directly out of the evangelical and republican traditions that the patriots deployed exactly in order to defamiliarize those commodities around which British loyalties were suspected to have formed. Indeed, one could argue that non-importation Anglicized imported goods as never before, stripping them of any domestic cultural accretion that might have adhered to them. Moreover, when one recalls that Americans promptly rushed back to their British goods after the Revolution, one realizes that the co-ordinates of loyalty and citizenship lay not in the sphere of goods – and certainly not in anything that could be called a consumer culture – but rather in other spheres: religion, ideology and so on. As I've already suggested, then, there is an important historical and theoretical distinction to be drawn between the politicization of commodities and the commodification of politics, between a concept of citizenship framed around religion and republicanism and a concept of citizenship framed around an 'American Way of Life', especially when that way of life is defined as a shifting ensemble of cultural and material commodities. Only the latter concept, one would think, indicates the presence of a 'consumer culture'.[72]

Still, when one is told that the colonists' experiences with British goods expanded their political horizons and enabled them to imagine a new polity, it is easy to telescope the historical differences between the 1770s and the 1930s and imagine for oneself a trajectory of consumer culture lofting upwards from Timothy Breen's eighteenth-century colonies through Daniel Boorstin's nineteenth-century 'consumption communities' to Warren Susman's twentieth-century 'Adlerian Age of Adjustment'.[73] More to the point, one is tempted to think of the cognitive effects of consumption in much the same way that Thomas Haskell has elsewhere urged us to think of the cognitive effects of commerce, which is to say as a practice that has historically expanded our perceived horizons of human efficacy and moral responsibility.[74] Now, were goods that good to think?

I don't think so. True, commodities have and will continue to be used to construct and communicate the meaning of social relationships and, if Colin Campbell is right, to order and indulge our affective response to them.[75] But there is nothing in the literature that I have reviewed here to support the view that commodity consumption has enhanced our appreciation of the remote consequences of our acts or has clarified our responsibilities for them. A political unconscious, an allegorized desire, a subversive reverie of plenitude – all may provide the commodified ground for alternative or oppositional readings of consumer culture. But the distance between that ground and the groundwork required to translate such longings into organized practice seems vast indeed. Like Simon Schama's whales, it seems infinitely more likely that in the migration back from matter and commodity to myth and morality, one would find oneself stranded on the 'submarine slope . . . of cultural contradiction'.

Even less charitably, one could argue that it is precisely because the meanings of commodities are so fluid and recontextualizable that questions of responsibility and accountability remain submerged within them. Whatever the personal meanings that the American GI may have attached to the custom of Coke-drinking that he fought for in World War II, they probably did not include the conviction that he was also fighting for the Coca-Cola company. How, then, might it be said that his political horizons were thereby extended and his concept of citizenship thereby clarified by Coke?

And how, finally, might it be said that the soldier's sense of citizenship was thereby intensified? How does brand loyalty mediate civic loyalty? The question arises because, as Ronald Edsforth and others have pointed out, there has been a strong chronological parallel between consumer booms and anti-communist campaigns in this country since the 1920s.[76] To many historians, such a connection merely confirms their suspicion that employers are always ready to promote moral panics in order to defeat the demands of a militant and organized labour force. But the connection between appeals to the Good Life and appeals against the Evil Empire also lends weight to Michael Walzer's thesis that a market-modelled liberalism must of necessity draw on other, non-liberal traditions and fears in order to inspire a loyalty that reaches beyond the market-place.[77] As the GI's invocation of Coke suggests, commodities can be used – ironically, nostalgically, militantly – to put the state in its place; but they are next to useless when deciding what to put in place of the state.

If such reflections seem a trifle abstract, one need only consider the recent turn of events in eastern Europe to see how directly they bear upon the future its citizens are forging for themselves. There, people are being encouraged to treat the language of commodities as the vernacular of civil society and the Esperanto of European unity, so it seems reasonable to wonder what language will be employed to reconceive the polity. No fully-fledged consumer culture exists in eastern Europe, of course, but the images of such a culture are familiar to virtually everyone and have been for some time. They *are* the horizon, and it is easy to imagine that if Hobbes were to rewrite his thoughts on the social contract in such a context, he too would surely recast his infamous cover-portrait of Leviathan as a construct of commodities rather than of people. So much for the 'recipe-knowledge' of consumer culture: whatever else such knowledge may yield up, it seems as likely to obscure as to clarify our social and political consciousness.

And, I might add, historical consciousness as well. The last decade of research has boldly challenged and immeasurably enriched our picture of consumer culture, but the very richness of that work – the thickness of its description and the detail of its maps – has at times submerged important questions of periodization, of power and, if you will, of principle – questions that historians can ill afford to ignore. Some time ago, for example, the National Archives in Washington, DC received $600,000 from the Philip Morris Companies in return for an agreement permitting the firm to stage a two-year, $30 million television and print advertising campaign that invited the public to 'join Philip Morris and the National Archives' in celebrating the bicentennial of the Bill of Rights.[78] Were it not for the awkward spectre of death that presently haunts Marlboro country, one could scarcely imagine an objection being raised to such a quid pro quo. Yet it is precisely the controversy over tobacco, with all of its rich, polysemous and contestatory symbolism, that distracts us from the implications of an arrangement that would further elide the difference between a bill of rights and a bill of goods. The privatization of civil rights and obligations is a problem that reaches far beyond eastern Europe, and neither the history nor the historiography of consumer culture has done much to help us think about it.[79] It is for that reason that I have laid such stress on questions of historicity, causality and politics in my remarks. We need more studies of consumer culture, to be sure, but we need breathing-space as well – a chance to reconnoitre a subject that otherwise threatens to engulf us all: to leave us, that is, inside the whale.

Notes

Earlier versions of this article were presented at the Organization of American Historians Meeting in St Louis and at the Clark Library, Los Angeles, April 1989, as well as at the European University Institute, Florence, November 1989. I am grateful to the participants for their criticism and suggestions, especially to John Brewer, Michael Denning, Roy Porter, Thomas Haskell and Kathy Peiss, and to Roy Rosenzweig and Robert Westbrook. Special thanks too to Cassandra Cleghorn and my students in AmSt.794.

1 Simon Schama, *The Embarrassment of Riches: An Interpretation of Dutch Culture in the Golden Age* (New York: Knopf, 1987), 130–44.
2 ibid., 143, 318.
3 ibid., 140.
4 George Orwell, 'Boys' weeklies', in *A Collection of Essays* (New York: Harcourt Brace Jovanovich, 1981), 308–9.
5 George Orwell, *Coming Up for Air* (London: Secker & Warburg, 1948), 220.
6 Stuart Ewen, *All Consuming Images: The Politics of Style in Contemporary Culture* (New York: Basic Books, 1988), 4–11.
7 'Kids are dying for designer duds', *New Haven Register*, 12 November 1989; 'A growing urban fear: thieves who kill for "cool" clothing', *New York Times*, 6 February 1990; *All Consuming Images*, 271, 52, original emphasis.
8 Georg Lukács, *History and Class Consciousness* (Cambridge, Mass.: MIT Press, 1971); Max Horkheimer and Theodor W. Adorno, 'The culture industry: enlightenment as mass deception', in *Dialectic of Enlightenment*, tr. John Cumming (New York: Seabury Press, 1972), 120–67; Herbert Marcuse, *One-Dimensional Man* (Boston: Beacon Press, 1964).
9 Richard Wightman Fox and T. J. Jackson Lears (eds) *The Culture of Consumption: Critical Essays in American History, 1880–1980* (New York: Pantheon, 1983).
10 Jean-Christophe Agnew, 'The consuming vision of Henry James', in Fox and Lears (eds), *Culture of Consumption*, 68–9; Neil McKendrick had ventured a similar complaint a year before in his introduction to Neil McKendrick, John Brewer and J. H. Plumb, *The Birth of a Consumer Society: The Commercialization of Eighteenth-Century England* (Bloomington: Indiana University Press, 1982), 5–6.
11 Fox and Lears (eds), *Culture of Consumption*, x.
12 The work of William Leiss, a student of Herbert Marcuse (and Herbert Gutman), influenced my essay, for example.
13 It should be said that a few works have kept pretty much to the chronological scheme of *The Culture of Consumption*, among them: Daniel Horowitz, *The Morality of Spending: Attitudes Toward the Consumer Society in America, 1875–1940* (Baltimore: Johns Hopkins University Press, 1985); Simon J. Bronner (ed.), *Consuming Visions: Accumulation and Display of Goods in America, 1880–1920* (New York: Norton, 1989); Susan Strasser, *Satisfaction Guaranteed: The Making of the American Mass Market* (New York: Pantheon, 1989).
14 Some of these works will be discussed in this essay; for a more complete bibliography, see Horowitz, *Morality of Spending*, 187–201, as well as Charles F. McGovern, 'The emergence of consumer history', paper presented at the Organization of American Historians Meeting in Reno, Nevada, March 1988.
15 Chandra Mukerji, *From Graven Images: Patterns of Modern Materialism* (New York: Columbia University Press, 1983), 22–9.

36   Jean-Christophe Agnew

16   ibid., 2; this portrait, it should be said, has been coloured as well by the hand of R. H. Tawney; though Weber's work focused on the Puritan sense of 'calling', his name has come to be associated with anything remotely to do with Protestant asceticism.
17   Joan Thirsk, *Economic Policy and Projects: The Development of a Consumer Society in Early Modern England* (Oxford: Oxford University Press, 1978); D. E. C. Eversley, 'The home market and home demand, 1750–1780', in E. L. Jones and E. E. Mingay (eds), *Land, Labour, and Population in the Industrial Revolution* (London: Edward Arnold, 1967), 206–59; Jan de Vries, 'Peasant demand patterns and economic development: Friesland 1550–1750', in William N. Parker and Eric L. Jones (eds), *European Peasants and their Markets: Essays in Agrarian History* (Princeton: Princeton University Press, 1976), 205–38; Neil McKendrick, 'Home demand and economic growth: a new view of the role of women and children in the Industrial Revolution', in Neil McKendrick (ed.), *Historical Perspectives: Studies in English Thought and Society* (London: Europa, 1974), 152–210.
18   Schama, *Embarrassment of Riches*, 338.
19   ibid., 298.
20   Fernand Braudel, *The Wheels of Commerce*, tr. Siân Reynolds (New York: Harper & Row, 1982), 177.
21   ibid.; both McKendrick and Schama resurrect Mandevillian ideas in their work; see McKendrick, Brewer and Plumb, *Birth of a Consumer Society*, 15–19, 51–3; Schama, *Embarrassment of Riches*, 297, 321, 467–8; Mandeville, it should be noted, was a Dutch *émigré* to England; for a recent critique of this thesis in relation to English industrialization, see Ben Fine and Ellen Leopold, 'Consumerism and the Industrial Revolution', *Social History* xv (May 1990), 151–79.
22   McKendrick, Brewer and Plumb, *Birth of a Consumer Society*, 72.
23   ibid., 103, 140–1.
24   ibid., 71.
25   For such metaphors, see ibid., 13, 42, 43, 71 and *passim*.
26   Colin Campbell, *The Romantic Ethic and the Spirit of Modern Consumerism* (Oxford: Basil Blackwell, 1987), 42–3.
27   ibid., 36–57.
28   Tibor Scitovsky, *The Joyless Economy: An Inquiry into Human Satisfaction and Dissatisfaction* (New York: Oxford University Press, 1976); Albert O. Hirschman, *Shifting Involvements: Private Interests and Public Action* (Princeton: Princeton University Press, 1982).
29   Campbell, *Romantic Ethic*, 77–95, esp. 86.
30   Compare Agnew, 'Consuming vision', 73.
31   Campbell, *Romantic Ethic*, 86–7.
32   ibid., chs 6, 7.
33   ibid., 222; see also Caroline Walker Bynum, *Holy Feast and Holy Fast: The Religious Significance of Food to Medieval Women* (Berkeley: University of California Press, 1987).
34   For a different kind of deconstruction of capitalist asceticism, see Walter Benn Michaels, *The Gold Standard and the Logic of Naturalism* (Berkeley: University of California Press, 1987), ch. 5; see also my discussion of Adam Smith in *Worlds Apart: The Market and the Theater in Anglo-American Thought, 1550–1750* (Cambridge: Cambridge University Press, 1986), 177–88.
35   See Daniel Bell, *The Cultural Contradictions of Capitalism* (New York: Harper & Row, 1978); Ann Douglas, *The Feminization of American Culture* (New York: Avon, 1977); T. J. Jackson Lears, 'From salvation to self-realization: advertising and the therapeutic roots of the consumer culture, 1880–1930', in Fox and Lears (eds), *Culture of Consumption*, 3–38.
36   Campbell, *Romantic Ethic*, 217–18; Bell makes much the same point but with a different judgement, *Cultural Contradictions*, 73–4.
37   I am indebted to Lawrence Senelick for this sense of cottage industry.
38   Lawrence W. Levine, 'William Shakespeare in America', in *Highbrow Lowbrow: The Emergence of Cultural Hierarchy in America* (Cambridge, Mass.: Harvard University Press, 1988), 13–81.

39 Fredric Jameson, 'Postmodernism and consumer society', in Hal Foster (ed.), *The Anti-Aesthetic: Essays in Postmodernist Culture* (Port Townsend, Wash.: Bay Press, 1983), 113–14; still, it could be said that Levine glosses the extent to which nineteenth-century plebeian playfulness towards Shakespeare might have been mocking a campaign for cultural sacralization that was already underway.

40 Roy Rosenzweig, *'Eight Hours for What We Will': Workers and Leisure in an Industrial City, 1870–1920* (Cambridge: Cambridge University Press, 1983); Lizabeth Cohen, 'Encountering mass culture at the grass roots: the experience of Chicago workers in the 1920s', *American Quarterly*, xli (March 1989), 6–33; 'Embellishing a life of labor: an interpretation of the material culture of American working-class homes, 1885–1915', *Journal of American Culture*, iii (Winter 1980), 752–75; *Making a New Deal: Industrial Workers in Chicago, 1919–1939* (Cambridge: Cambridge University Press, 1990); on the limited reach of such new retailing institutions as catalogues and chain stores, see Strasser, *Satisfaction Guaranteed*, 219, 249. Though a good deal has been written on cultural production in black communities, correspondingly little has been done on consumer goods and their consumption.

41 For a theoretical treatment of the ways in which goods may be 'singularized' or 'decommoditized' by their incorporation into other personal, familial or cultural frameworks of meaning, see Igor Kopytoff, 'The cultural biography of things: commoditization as process', in Arjun Appadurai (ed.), *The Social Life of Things: Commodities in Cultural Perspective* (Cambridge: Cambridge University Press, 1986), 64–91.

42 Herbert G. Gutman, 'Work, culture and society in industrializing America, 1815–1919', in *Work, Culture and Society in Industrializing America* (New York: Knopf, 1976), 3–78.

43 See George Lipsitz, 'The meaning of memory: family, class, and ethnicity in early network television' and 'Why remember Mama? The changing face of women's narrative', in *Time Passages: Collective Memory and Popular Culture* (Minneapolis: University of Minnesota Press, 1990), 39–96.

44 ibid., 69.

45 M. M. Bakhtin, *The Dialogic Imagination*, ed. Michael Holquist, tr. Caryl Emerson and Michael Holquist (Austin: University of Texas Press, 1981); Stuart Hall, 'Culture, the media, and the "ideological effect" ', in James Curran, Michael Gurevitch and Janet Woollacott (eds), *Mass Communication and Society* (Beverly Hills: Sage, 1979); idem, 'Notes on deconstructing "the popular" ', in Ralph Samuel (ed.), *People's History and Socialist Theory* (London: Routledge & Kegan Paul, 1981); Fredric Jameson, 'Reification and utopia in mass culture', *Social Text*, i (1979), 130–48; for a more recent formulation of this challenge to cultural boundaries – in relation to the status of middlebrow culture – see Andrew Ross, 'Introduction' and 'Reading the Rosenberg letters', in *No Respect: Intellectuals and Popular Culture* (New York: Routledge, 1989), 1–41.

46 Michael Denning, *Mechanic Accents: Dime Novels and Working-Class Culture in America* (London: Verso, 1987), 200–13.

47 Christine Stansell, *City of Women: Sex and Class in New York, 1789–1860* (New York: Knopf, 1986), 90–100; Mauricio Mazon, *Zoot Suit Riots* (Austin: University of Texas Press, 1984).

48 Janice A. Radway, *Reading the Romance: Women, Patriarchy, and Popular Literature* (Chapel Hill: University of North Carolina Press, 1984); Ann Barr Snitow, 'Mass market romance: pornography for women is different', *Radical History Review*, xx (Spring/Summer 1979), 141–61; Kathy Peiss, *Cheap Amusements: Working Women and Leisure in Turn-of-the-Century New York* (Philadelphia: Temple University Press, 1986); John Kasson, *Amusing the Million: Coney Island at the Turn of the Century* (New York: Hill & Wang, 1978).

49 Herbert Marcuse, *Eros and Civilization: A Philosophical Inquiry into Freud* (Boston: Beacon, 1955); Richard King, *The Party of Eros: Radical Social Thought and the Realm of Freedom* (Chapel Hill: University of North Carolina Press, 1972), ch. 4; see also Fredric Jameson, 'Pleasure: a political issue', in *Formations of Pleasure* (London: Routledge & Kegan Paul, 1983), 1–14; idem, *Powers of Desire: The Politics of Sexuality*, ed. Ann Snitow, Christine Stansell and Sharon Thompson (New

York: Monthly Review Press, 1983).

50 See note 45; both Fredric Jameson and Stuart Hall have challenged the distinction drawn between 'authentic' popular culture and mass consumer culture; James Clifford has made similar arguments to anthropologists in *The Predicament of Culture: Twentieth-Century Ethnography, Literature, and Art* (Cambridge, Mass.: Harvard University Press, 1988); see also the inaugural issue of the journal *Public Culture* (1988).

51 Michael Denning, 'The end of mass culture', *International Labor and Working-Class History*, xxxvii (Spring 1990), 17.

52 George Orwell, 'Inside the whale', in *Collected Essays* (London: Secker & Warburg, 1961), 118–59.

53 See Arjun Appadurai, 'Commodities and the politics of value', in Appadurai (ed.), *Social Life of Things*, 3–63; John Clarke, Stuart Hall, Tony Jefferson and Brian Roberts, 'Subcultures, culture, and class', in Stuart Hall and Tony Jefferson (eds), *Resistance Through Rituals: Youth Cultures in Post-War Britain* (London: Hutchinson, 1976), 9–74; for the family resemblance between the two tendencies, compare Pierre Bourdieu, *Distinction: A Sociological Critique of the Judgment of Taste*, tr. Richard Nice (Cambridge, Mass.: Harvard University Press, 1984) and Michael J. Weiss, *The Clustering of America* (New York: Harper & Row, 1988); for a different criticism of the mapping metaphor, see Janice Radway's comment on Michael Denning's article, 'The end of mass culture', entitled 'Maps and the construction of boundaries', *International Labor and Working-Class Newsletter*, xxxvii (Spring 1990), 19–26.

54 The change can be best appreciated in Jean Baudrillard, *Selected Writings*, ed. Mark Poster (Stanford: Stanford University Press, 1988); but compare as well Marshall Sahlins's *Stone Age Economics* (Chicago: Aldine, 1972) with Sahlins's *Culture and Practical Reason* (Chicago: University of Chicago Press, 1976).

55 On the concept of 'cultural capital', see Bourdieu, *Distinction, passim*; Daniel Miller, *Material Culture and Mass Consumption* (Oxford: Basil Blackwell, 1987), 76, 106.

56 Miller, *Material Culture*, 213.

57 ibid., 192.

58 See, for example, Appadurai (ed.), *Social Life of Things*; Mihaly Csikszentmihalyi and Eugene Rochberg-Halton, *The Meaning of Things: Domestic Symbols and the Self* (Cambridge: Cambridge University Press, 1981); Grant McCracken, *Culture and Consumption: New Approaches to the Symbolic Character of Consumer Goods and Activities* (Bloomington: Indiana University Press, 1988).

59 Warren I. Susman, 'The culture of the thirties', 'Culture and commitment', 'The people's fair: cultural contradictions of a consumer society', in *Culture as History: The Transformation of American Society in the Twentieth Century* (New York: Pantheon, 1984), 151–229.

60 Orwell's 'Inside the whale' runs like a thread through Susman's 'The culture of the thirties'; see also Roland Marchand, *Advertising the American Dream: Making Way for Modernity, 1920–1940* (Berkeley: University of California Press, 1985); Richard Pells, *Radical Visions and American Dreams: Culture and Social Thought in the Depression Years* (New York: Harper & Row, 1973).

61 Cohen, 'Encountering mass culture', 26.

62 Rosenzweig, '*Eight Hours*', 226–8; Ronald Edsforth, *Class Conflict and Cultural Consensus: The Making of a Mass Consumer Society in Flint, Michigan* (New Brunswick: Rutgers University Press, 1987).

63 Edsforth, *Class Conflict*, 224.

64 'Commodities are symbols of belonging', Michael Walzer has written;

> standing and identity are distributed through the market, sold for cash on the line (but available also to speculators who establish credit). On the other hand, in a democratic society, the most basic definitions and self-definitions can't be put up for purchase in this way. For citizenship entails what we might call 'belongingness' – not merely the sense, but the practical reality, of being at home in (this part of) the social world. This is a condition that can be renounced but never traded; it is not alienable in the marketplace.
>
> (*Spheres of Justice: A Defense of Pluralism and Equality* (New York: Basic Books, 1983), 106)

See also Robert Westbrook, ' "I want a girl just like the girl that married Harry James": American women and the problem of political obligation in World War II', *American Quarterly*, xlii (December 1990), 587–614; 'Fighting for the family: private interests and public obligation in World War Two', paper presented at the Organization of American Historians Meeting in St Louis, Missouri, April 1989.

65 Quoted in E. J. Kahn, *The Big Drink: The Story of Coca Cola* (New York: Random House, 1960), 13, and in Richard Kuisel, 'Coca-Cola au pays des buveurs de vin', *L'Histoire*, xciv (November 1986), 24. Such a response can easily be interpreted as a backhanded commentary on the more abstract and pretentious themes of morale-building, but to focus entirely on the symbolism that the response deflates is to ignore that symbolism – namely, Coca-Cola – which is thereby inflated; compare Paul Fussell, *Wartime: Understanding and Behavior in the Second World War* (New York: Oxford University Press, 1989), 90.

66 See Jane Schneider, 'Peacocks and penguins: the political economy of European cloth and colors', *American Ethnologist*, v (August 1978), 413–47; C. A. Bayley, 'The origins of Swadeshi (home industry): cloth and Indian society, 1700–1930', in Appadurai (ed.), *Social Life of Things*, 285–321.

67 T. H. Breen, 'An empire of goods: the Anglicization of colonial America, 1690–1776', *Journal of British Studies*, xxv (October 1986), 467–99; idem, ' "Baubles of Britain": the American and consumer revolutions of the eighteenth century', *Past and Present*, cxix (May 1988), 73–104.

68 Breen, 'Baubles of Britain', 86.

69 ibid., 88.

70 ibid., 93, 104.

71 Mary Douglas and Baron Isherwood, *The World of Goods: Towards an Anthropology of Consumption* (New York: Norton, 1979), 62; the phrase is of course a deliberate echo of earlier structuralist formulations by Claude Lévi-Strauss and Stanley Tambiah.

72 The term is Breen's, 'Baubles of Britain', 91.

73 Daniel Boorstin, *The Democratic Experience* (New York: Random House, 1973), 89–114, but esp. 145–8; Susman, 'Culture and commitment', in *Culture as History*, 202.

74 Thomas Haskell, 'Capitalism and the origins of humanitarian sensibility, parts I and II', *American Historical Review*, xc (April 1985), 339–61; xc (June 1985), 547–66.

75 See, for example, Fred Hirsch's discussion of 'positional goods' in *Social Limits to Growth* (Cambridge, Mass.: Harvard University Press, 1978); Bourdieu, *Distinction*; Roger S. Mason, *Conspicuous Consumption: A Study of Exceptional Consumer Behavior* (Farnborough, Hants: Gower, 1981).

76 Edsforth, *Class Conflict*, 216 and *passim*; see also George Lipsitz, *Class and Culture in Cold War America: 'A Rainbow at Midnight'* (South Hadley: J. F. Bergin, 1982), ch. 8; Paul Boyer, *By the Bomb's Early Light: American Thought and Culture at the Dawn of the Atomic Age* (New York: Pantheon, 1985); Elaine Tyler May, *Homeward Bound: American Families in the Cold War Era* (New York: Basic Books, 1988).

77 See Michael Walzer, *Obligations: Essays on Disobedience, War, and Citizenship* (Cambridge, Mass.: Harvard University Press, 1970).

78 *New Haven Register*, 4 December 1989.

79 On privatization and questions of civic accountability, see Sheldon S. Wolin, *The Presence of the Past: Essays on the State and the Constitution* (Baltimore: Johns Hopkins University Press, 1989), 25–7, and more generally, Alan Wolfe, *Whose Keeper? Social Science and Moral Obligation* (Berkeley: University of California Press, 1989).

3
Understanding traditional and modern patterns of consumption in eighteenth-century England: a character–action approach

Colin Campbell

Introduction

In their attempts to explain the consumer revolution which occurred in England in the eighteenth century, historians have relied heavily on Veblen's theory of conspicuous consumption. Whilst according due significance to facilitating improvements in both the means of production and distribution, there has been a general recognition that any satisfactory overall explanation of the phenomenon must include some reference to changes in the conduct of consumers, and here, by common consent, stress has been placed on emulative motives. That is to say, the prevailing assumption has been that particular sections of the population of England revised their consumption patterns at this time as a consequence of a new willingness to give expression to their desire to be regarded as equal in social standing to those who were their acknowledged social superiors.[1] There are, however, several reasons for regarding this thesis as unproven.

First, evidence concerning the nature and extent of the ownership of goods, as provided for example by analyses of probate inventories, merely shows that a 'trickle-down' process was taking place during this period, something which in itself reveals nothing about the nature of consumer conduct. The first fundamental mistake of interpretation which is made, therefore, is to assume an identity between this 'trickle-down' phenomenon and imitative behaviour. The fact that a merchant or shop-keeper was now both able and willing to purchase a product previously a characteristic of superior aristocratic consumption patterns does not necessarily mean that he sought to imitate an aristocratic way of life. This is to make an assumption concerning the nature of motives and intentions for which no evidence has been presented. It certainly cannot be assumed that all consumption is *ipso facto* emulative in character as some commentators appear to do. Indeed, it is important to stress that many goods are likely to be desired for their own sake rather than for any prestige which may be attached to them (or even, in some cases, despite the connotations of lowly status which they carry); something which is especially likely to be the case with products such as coffee, tea, chocolate and sugar which yield their own immediate and obvious satisfactions.

Second, behaviour which is imitative is not necessarily also emulative. That is to say, an eighteenth-century farmer's wife may copy the style of furnishing seen in a local aristocrat's house without this necessarily implying that she is acting out of any desire to become a lady or to rival or excel her perceived superiors in fashionableness or social standing. Imitation is itself merely an activity, not a motive. Thus, to take another common example, the fact that a lady's maid chooses to do her hair in the same style as her mistress does not necessarily mean that she aims to be taken for a lady herself or that she imagines that the two of them have thereby become social equals. Interestingly, this was an assumption commonly made by commentators at the time, who were quick to presume that imitative conduct revealed the presence of emulative motives. However, like their modern-day proponents of the emulative thesis, they provided little evidence for this assumption. Why then should they have been so quick to jump to this conclusion? What seems more than likely is that since most of these observers of the social scene were themselves either members or representatives of the superior classes, their jealous regard for their own privileges, combined with an intense anxiety about the stability of the social order (especially after 1789), meant that they were prone to see imitative consumption as inherently threatening. In other words their strident condemnation stemmed less from any knowledge that such conduct arose out of emulative desires than fear that it might, with the consequence that they condemned imitation for what it could represent rather than what it was known to be.

Third and finally, it needs to be remembered that emulation is more of an intention than a motive, or more correctly, that it is a goal consistent with many different motives. Thus, even if it is known that the consumption of a new good stems from emulative desires, we may still be left to ponder over the motives involved. To dub an activity 'emulative' is in this sense merely to begin the process of understanding; it remains to establish precisely what is being emulated and why. For example, does the maid's intention to compete with her mistress in the style and opulence of her dress merely imply a desire to rival her in fashionableness or does it stem from a more general ambition to be considered her social equal? Is she seeking, through this emulative conduct, to impress her fellow servants, her family and friends, her mistress, any strangers she meets on the street or indeed herself? Does this striving to impress stem from envy of her mistress, from a need to boost her own feelings of self-esteem, or from naked social ambition? Is the way of life exemplified by social superiors the object of emulation merely because of its association with high status or is it regarded as an ideal in its own right? If we consider the ideal of gentility for instance, does striving to realize this ideal mean that one is endeavouring to improve one's social position or one's character?

It should be clear from this brief discussion that an emulative theory of consumption contains many difficulties which are rarely addressed, the fundamental error arising from a confusion of consequence with intention. The unwarranted and unproved assumption is that since differences in patterns of consumption serve to fulfil the function of delineating boundaries in an hierarchical system of social status, any changes that individuals make in their consumption habits must stem from a desire to alter their own perceived position in that system. In reality, however, as far as emulative conduct is concerned, intention and consequence have a more subtle and complex relationship, with deliberate attempts to improve one's esteem in the eyes of others frequently doomed to failure, whilst those people who do not consciously seek to impress often succeed in making the biggest impression. More generally, the mistake made is the failure to recognize that any one observed pattern of conduct is actually consistent with a variety of subjective meanings, motives and intentions.

In view of these difficulties it is important to realize that there are alternatives to the 'emulative thesis' as well as ways of approaching consumer behaviour which do give due weight to the real motives and intentions of individuals.

It is not merely the Veblenesque tradition which is deficient in this way, as few of the theoretical perspectives commonly employed to study consumer behaviour actually accord a central role to the subjective meanings which, in reality, accompany and inform conduct. Instead such meanings tend to be overlooked in favour of those extrapolated by the analyst from a study of the consequences of action (as is the case with Bourdieu as well as Veblen) imputed on the basis of a priori assumptions concerning human nature (as in the case of classical economics) or discarded in favour of those meanings 'discovered' by the investigator to be associated with consumer artefacts and activities (as is the case with much structuralist and semiotically inspired work).[2] In none of these forms of analysis is the operative subjective meaning, that which actually makes the behaviour in question significant for the actors who embarked on it, ascribed an important role in the explanatory scheme. It should be obvious, however, that such observer-created categories of meaning can rarely be equated with those which initiated and accompanied the action, and hence in so far as such conduct is freely undertaken, cannot be used to explain its occurrence; although they might be added to the operative motives and intentions to create a more adequate level of explanation. Thus, it would seem essential to any proper process of historical explanation to accord a central role to those motives and intentions which actually served to prompt individuals to act.

The recent fashion for semiotically inspired analyses of both contemporary and past human institutions and practices has served the valuable function of shifting the focus of analytic attention from behaviour to meaning. Unfortunately, it has also served to promote the idea that 'meaning' can be the subject of investigation in itself, independent of the purposeful conduct of individuals. Since, in addition, this form of analysis is easy to undertake, many scholars have been tempted to take advantage of the endless scope for the discovery of meaning which each human practice or cultural artefact represents. But human beings do not typically either create or experience meaning for its own sake. On the contrary, meaning is normally a dimension of conduct representing the outcome of the attention paid to objects (including the activities of others) by knowing, aware subjects. It is also crucial to remember that such attention does not normally derive from idle curiosity but arises out of the subject's need to attain some given purpose or goal. Meaning is thus not merely a subjective phenomenon (in the sense of being something possessed by a subject) but an ingredient of action; something which provides it with a historical and socio-cultural specificity. Thus even when researchers do pay attention to the real meanings which objects possess for people they often fail to locate these in the contexts of purposive conduct, leaving the meaning unrelated to the past or present goals and intentions of the individuals concerned.[3]

Of course, not all conduct is 'action' in the sense of being accompanied by a clear and conscious awareness of its nature, purpose and motives. Much of what we do consists of well-established routines and is habitual in character. One of the prime tasks in any historical or social science analyses, therefore, is to establish how far the conduct under examination approximates to 'action' or 'habit', as only the former can sensibly be explored through an interpretative method. Fortunately, one clear indication of action, which can usefully be employed and which is very pertinent in connection with a study of consumption in eighteenth-century England, is that it is clearly marked by controversy. Where conduct is the subject of dispute and debate, and even more, the object of conflicting moral views, then it is extremely unlikely that individuals would be able to engage in it in an unthinking and habitual manner. On the contrary, they are probably only too aware of the need to justify what they are doing. From this it can be seen that the consumption of goods in eighteenth-century England, and especially the consumption of 'luxury' goods, is a highly suitable subject for the interpretative method. The position advocated here is that the actual subjective meanings which prompt and guide action remain an indispensable ingredient in any successful theory of conduct and that the only proper place in which to search for such meaning is in the conscious minds of acting individuals. Hence any successful theory of consumer behaviour requires that one understands the patterns of subjective meaning which actually inform and accompany the action under scrutiny and not those apparently 'objective' meanings, including motives and intentions, which theorists have ascribed to them.

The failure to deal adequately with this dimension of subjective consciousness is particularly obvious when it comes to the complex issue of motivation. All too often motives are presumed and imputed when they need to be established. Frequently this occurs by a process of first naming an activity as 'consumption' and then automatically employing a well-known theory of consumption as an explanation. Thus buying and wearing fashionable clothes is commonly labelled a 'consumption' activity and consequently 'explained' by reference to Veblenesque theories of status-maintenance or status-enhancement. Yet this is a purely external interpretation of the actions concerned and makes no reference to the conscious intentions or stated motives of the people concerned. Did they regard their activity as 'consumption'? Why exactly did they feel that it was important to be 'in fashion'? What motives would they have declared prompted their conduct? Typically these questions remain unasked as the analyst proceeds to explain through presumption what is 'going on'. Frequently these presumptions are so implicit that they are simply woven into the descriptive accounts of historical events. Thus, to take an example at random, Mukerji refers to members of the Burgundian court in the fourteenth century as 'adorning themselves with much more elaborate costumes *to display their growing wealth*' (italics added).[4] Now this may indeed have been an intention of the courtiers in dressing as they did, it may even have been their motive rather than their stated intention, but how do we know? Where is the evidence that 'displaying wealth' was a major component in the conscious reasons for embarking on such conduct? One may not doubt that it was a consequence of such actions (though even here evidence of the reactions of others is needed to establish this), but consequences cannot explain actions unless they also coincide with intentions.

Many other examples could be given of the way that doubtful assumptions concerning motives are built into historical accounts. Not uncommonly they appear in the guise of 'enabling-style' observations, such as 'this increase in wealth *enabled* the trading classes to afford to imitate aristocratic modes of dress', and 'the increase in the supply of market goods *enabled* the middle classes to indulge a whole range of wants and desires which had previously been frustrated' (italics added).[5] This choice of words is interesting for the way in which it allows the difficult issue of motives to be side-stepped. One is not told why the 'trading classes' should want to imitate aristocratic modes of dress or given any evidence that they deliberately used their wealth to achieve this end; and, equally, the suggestion that the middle classes had previously experienced 'frustration' is an assumption, as is the claim that they subsequently consciously set out to 'satisfy new wants'. Such interpretations of conduct as these phrases imply are externally imputed and largely unsubstantiated by any evidence concerning what the people themselves actually thought they were doing. It follows that there is a need for a perspective which does set itself the task of inquiring into such operative meanings and thus which can justifiably be described as a truly historical treatment of motives and meanings. It also means that one must set aside pseudo-actor theories, like those of neo-classical economics, Veblen and Goffman, which purport to account for conduct from the point of view of the individual, but actually only deal with single abstract, postulated notions of subjective meaning and not with the various, discrete, concrete modalities which, in reality, inform conduct.

A character–action approach

Focusing on the discrete and historically specific meanings which inform actions does, however, present the investigator with difficulties. How are these to be discovered, for example, given that the individuals concerned are not available to be questioned? And, in addition, how is the investigator going to construct accounts which transcend mere *ad hoc* redescriptions of the actions concerned, given that over-generalized, imputed theories of motive are to be rejected?

One possible answer is to recognize, first of all, that willed human conduct is verbally constructed and guided, and that 'motives' are largely constructed by individuals out of the 'vocabularies' available to them.[6] It is indeed the concepts and terms existing in such vocabularies which are drawn on by individuals when 'creating' their subjectively mean-ingful actions. This means that although the actual motives and intentions which guided the real historical persons are not directly available for study, the material from which these meanings were constructed is; for it is embodied in the surviving cultural record such as diaries, novels, letters, autobiographies, histories and even dictionaries. Consequently it is possible, at the very least, to plot the range of potential meanings and motives which an individual could have drawn upon at any given period. Second, one can negotiate a position somewhere between that analyst's arrogance, in which diverse social and cultural groups are imputed to have acted out of a single universal (and unconfirmed) motive, and the partici-pant's particularity, in which the conduct of individuals is understood in terms of unique constellations of meaning. This is possible if one approaches the problem of motive in a two-stage manner, viewing conduct as generated by a single, if not simple, motivational principle, but recognizing that this will lead to varying forms of conduct depending on the more specific social, cultural and historical circumstances. This is a possibility if behaviour is recognized as possessing a significant character-relevant dimension.

Briefly stated, this means that to the extent that conduct is conscious and willed it is also perceived by the acting individual as ethical or moral; as, in effect, 'justifiable'. This is indeed a defining characteristic of action with individuals reluctant to engage in acts which they cannot satisfactorily 'justify' to themselves. This stress on justification should not be seen as implying acceptance of the commonly held view that a 'justification' is merely a verbalization which is constructed by an individual in order to render the action in question acceptable to some critical or questioning audience. On the contrary, a justification is here seen as an integral ingredient of action, in practice not fully separable from its motivation.[7]

Now whilst many 'justifications' for conduct are embedded in the statuses and roles which people occupy, a separate dimension relates to their conduct as a 'person' and cross-cuts these situationally specific reasons for acting. These centre instead on the concept of character and the consequent justification of action in terms of specific ideals of character. The value of regarding human conduct as oriented to ideals of character is that it both invokes a general motive principle – that the behaviour of individuals is to be understood in terms of their perceived pattern of character-based justifications – whilst also recognizing that the content of these ideals are socially and historically differentiated such that the precise form of the ensuing conduct will vary with time and place.

By advocating an approach to the study of historical phenomena which concentrates upon understanding the conduct of individuals as guided by character considerations it is not intended to suggest that historians should adopt a 'culture and social character' perspective of the kind which has been developed in both anthropology and sociology,[8] nor to endorse that strange hybrid called 'psycho-history' in which psychological or psychoanalytic theories are overlaid on top of historical data.[9] In contrast to both of these, the perspective proposed involves treating character as the name for that entity which individuals consciously strive to create out of the raw material of their personhood. It is thus not equatable with personality, as that term usually covers the sum total of an individual's psychic and behavioural characteristics, nor is it something which can simply be understood as the unproblematic outcome of dominant cultural patterns and processes of socialization. On the contrary, character covers only that portion of the conduct of individuals which they can be expected to take responsibility for, and is the entity imputed to underlie and explain this willed aspect of their behaviour. As such it has an essentially ethical quality not possessed by the concept of personality. Although in some cultures there is a stress on the given nature of certain qualities of character,[10] there is usually, in addition, clear recognition of the fact that individuals are responsible for making their own character and hence should be rewarded or blamed accordingly. Given that individuals themselves share this view, it becomes possible to regard their behaviour as governed by character considerations and especially a concern to bring their own conduct into line with an ideal.

It is not suggested, however, that ideals primarily exert an influence in a direct didactic fashion, even though some people may no doubt alter their behaviour as a consequence of being told that they should do so. The primary assumption is that individuals desire to exemplify or express these ideals in themselves, or to put it more accurately, they wish to believe that they do. It is assumed that people want to believe they embody the ideal in question and hence do not normally feel the need to undergo any vigorous programme of character development. But, whilst they may not feel that they have to do much in order to become 'refined', 'sensible' or 'possessed of genius', taking it for granted that they already possess these qualities, they will feel the need to convince themselves of this fact. In other words, ideals of character are important because they prescribe admirable qualities which individuals of worth should possess, and, whilst most people will feel inclined to believe that they possess them, they will need reassurance from time to time that this is indeed the case. This reassurance must take the form of conduct; action which unambiguously indicates the quality or qualities concerned, for although individuals may fervently believe that they possess courage, intelligence or taste, their own inner doubts on this score can only be silenced by acts which effectively reveal them. It is therefore less the desire to mould oneself as a person in conformity with whatever ideal of character one subscribes to which is the prime motive, but rather the desire to *confirm* through conduct the fact that one does conform to the ideal.

This is not an endorsement of a Goffmanesque view of conduct as primarily directed at impressing others or 'presenting the self' to best possible advantage on all occasions.[11] There may, of course, be such a concern with impression-management and the good opinion of others present in much conduct, but that is not the assumption made here. Indeed, the widespread view, implicit in such analyses as Goffman's, that the conduct of individuals can be understood as primarily a self-interested attempt to manipulate or impress others is firmly rejected. On the contrary, it is claimed that it is more realistic to see conduct as directed at reassuring oneself of one's moral worth and although this is sometimes achieved by first impressing others, a crucially different motivational structure is involved.

Of more importance is the fact that the dramaturgical metaphor favoured by Goffman and his followers results in conduct being viewed piecemeal in its discrete 'scenic' units or 'acts' and hence does not provide a general integrated perspective from which to understand the behaviour of the individual as a whole. Each item of conduct is examined separately in relation to its particular 'audience' and the 'presentation needs' which are involved. Consequently the person fails to become the principal unit of analysis, being displaced by the actor, an entity whose only motive seems to be a restless desire to impress others. Equally, a Goffmanesque perspective does not help to explain how people conduct themselves when not subject to the scrutiny of others. Once, however, one recognizes that action governed by character considerations is primarily self-directed it becomes possible to include private and covert conduct into the explanatory scheme.

Character ideals specify, in broad terms, what constitutes perfection in a man or a woman. They do not accomplish this, however, by prescribing the detailed nature of conduct in specific circumstances so much as by naming personal qualities possessed by such an individual. These qualities, it is then assumed, will in turn serve to guarantee that impeccable conduct is then forthcoming under all circumstances. The precise nature of these qualities naturally vary from ideal to ideal, but they tend to focus on such questions as whether the suppression or expression of emotion is the more important and, in addition, which emotions it is proper to display. In addition, there is usually some specification of the manner or 'style' in which activities are to be undertaken (for example, with conscientiousness or nonchalance), as well as how prized abilities such as creativity, wit and courage should be ranked. These qualities and abilities are then combined into a meaningful and integrated picture for others to emulate. Such models provide individuals not just with an overall guide to conduct but a complex set of incentives and disincentives for engaging in various actions. In fact the individual is presented with an array of differentially evaluated actions and whilst the performance of some would serve to confirm the ideal self-image, others would not. Generally therefore the assumption one can make is that to the extent that it is possible for an individual to represent a potential action as indicative of an admirable or virtuous character then it is likely to be undertaken.

This is a non-instrumentalist conception of conduct, in which actions are viewed in terms of the intrinsic value placed on them rather than some further, distant end to which they might be directed. Each performance of an action which is recognized as 'indicative' of an admired quality provides its own gratification to the actor in terms of both reassurance (that they possess the desired quality) and self-congratulation. This does not mean that the action in question might not also possess an obvious instrumental dimension – the two possibilities do not exclude each other – but that this instrumentality is overlaid by a set of meanings which are of characterological significance. It is often this second layer of meaning, however, which can provide vital clues to the motivational and justificatory nature of the conduct in question. An example taken from eighteenth-century English drama will be used to illustrate this point and the general style of analysis.

In the mid-eighteenth century there was a marked upsurge in the practice of elopement on the part of young middle-class women. Now it could be said that the 'meaning' of an act of elopement is easy enough to understand. That is to say, one assumes that the purpose behind it is immediately comprehensible. The couple (and perhaps more especially the woman) determine to marry because they are in love and finding themselves thwarted in this aim because of the opposition of her parents, decide to defy them and elope. All of which may, however, be perfectly true without bringing to light the full range of meanings involved. In *Polly Honeycombe* (a farce by George Colman, first produced in 1760), the heroine, an avid novel reader, contemplates the choice between obeying her parents' wishes and marrying Mr Ledger, the successful businessman or eloping with the penniless poet, Mr Scribble. In the course of the stage soliloquy in which she ponders this problem she recalls all the novels she has read in which the heroines do in fact elope, subsequently declaring that she too 'has as much love and as much spirit as the best of them' and hence will act as they did.[12]

Now what is especially interesting about the lines which Polly is given in this (admittedly fictitious) example is that they suggest how the act of elopement is endowed with the capacity to confirm qualities of character. That is to say, by eloping Polly may succeed in proving to herself that she does indeed possess ample love and spirit (a successful outcome is not, of course, guaranteed). In that sense she is attributing a meaning to her decision and the ensuing action which transforms it into a 'test' of character and hence providing herself with a powerful motive for action. To comprehend fully this decision to elope therefore it becomes necessary to understand what exactly terms like 'love' and 'spirit' might have meant at this time and which social groups were in the habit of admiring such personal qualities.

It is not suggested that a determination to manifest 'love' and 'spirit' constitutes a full explanation of Polly's decision to elope or a complete account of her motives for doing so. As noted earlier, such actions have practical outcomes which are clearly intended. Nor, of course, is it suggested that individuals always succeed in realizing their intentions (Polly might well have come to recognize that in the event she failed to act with 'spirit'). What is claimed is that the fact that the conduct also has an important dimension of character significance is important for a proper understanding of the motivational meaning underlying such an action. In the first place, this dimension clearly facilitated its occurrence by assisting Polly in her decision and in developing the determination to carry it out, whilst second, it helped her to 'legitimate' her action in the face of her worries about defying parental authority. That is to say, by representing her elopement to herself as action which displayed her admirable qualities she was able to convince herself of the justifiability or rightness of what she was doing and thereby offset the condemnation of those who upheld a more traditional morality.

It follows, from the approach advocated above, that one begins an analysis of a topic like consumption not by studying behaviour but by outlining the character ideals extant for a particular period under consideration. These ideals are then examined to see what differential pattern of virtues they specify and what implications these might have for conduct in general. One is looking to see not simply what forms of behaviour endow the individual with merit and which bring forth condemnation, but what precisely are the subjective meanings attached to various items of conduct. Only then does it become possible to see what implications these ideals might have for consumer-relevant behaviour, remembering that 'consumption' is not likely to be a particularly salient or meaningful category of action to individuals themselves. In this way the analyst can reconstruct not, of course, a complete picture of the conduct of past groups, but an understanding of their probable sense of 'justifiable' conduct. This is certainly not to suggest that individuals always and everywhere behave in ways which are consonant with their own sense of what is 'just' or 'justifiable'. There will be times when they knowingly act in ways which they represent to themselves as 'wrong' or 'unjustifiable'. What is suggested, however, is that their overall pattern of conduct will none the less tend to conform to their perceived pattern of 'justifications' on the grounds that the likelihood of an individual engaging in a given act corresponds with the extent to which he or she can present it to themselves as 'justifiable'.

Before embarking on a survey of eighteenth-century ideals of character it is necessary to have a clear idea of what might be covered by the term 'consumption', otherwise it will be difficult to perceive the relative significance of the ideals discussed. Whilst one might be tempted to treat this as a common-sense category to cover the selection, purchase and use of goods and services, this approach overlooks the crucial significance during this period of the development of 'modern' consumerism. What precisely characterizes consumer behaviour in its 'modern' form is a subject of debate, but the author has argued at length elsewhere that this should be viewed as a distinctive form of hedonism, one in which the enjoyment of emotions as summoned through imaginary or illusory images is central.[13] The emergence of this autonomous, illusory hedonism, combined with the ranking of pleasure above comfort is seen as the critical defining feature of modern consumerism. The focus in the following discussion is thus less on how different ideals of character might have affected consumer behaviour in general, than how they may have inhibited or facilitated the emergence of these distinctive features of conduct. Three major types of character ideal are considered, ranging over a period from the late seventeenth to the early nineteenth centuries; two of these, that of sensibility and the romantic–bohemian ideal, were primarily endorsed by the middle classes, whilst the third was associated with the aristocracy.

The ideal of sensibility

The eighteenth-century character ideal of sensibility can be seen to centre upon a susceptibility to emotions of particular moral significance. As Vickers expresses it, sensibility meant 'an ideal sensitivity to – and spontaneous display of – virtuous feelings, especially those of pity, sympathy, benevolence, of the open heart as opposed to the prudent mind'.[14] Viewed in this way, it is possible to see sensibility as a charismatic quality akin to the gift of grace itself. Indeed, it would seem that it was not uncommonly regarded in this manner, as evidence of the goodness, if not superiority, of a person's soul. There was certainly a tendency to judge the soul of a man by the degree of emotion he displayed, as Wellek observes.[15] Laurence Sterne, in particular, seems to have held the view that sensibility was a gift from God, regarding the faculty as 'a mixture of the physiological and the spiritual, of those feelings in the human nervous system that correspond to God's contact with mankind, elevating it to the force underlying human love and charity'.[16] In line with this view, Sterne's readers seem to have experienced a degree of self-congratulation for their emotions. 'Like him they easily persuaded themselves that the gift of tears is a proof of the excellence and loftiness of [their] nature, and exclaimed when the tears were over: "I am positive I have a soul".'[17]

Typically, sensibility covered feeling sorry for oneself, feeling sorry for others and being moved by beauty, with, as a result of Shaftesbury's teachings on the identity of ethics and aesthetics, all responses having equal significance as indications of goodness.[18] Responsiveness to beauty thus became a crucial moral quality, such that any deficiency in this respect became a moral lapse, whilst correspondingly virtue became an aesthetic quality, such that, in turn, any moral lapse was 'bad taste'. Consequently 'taste' itself became the most important of an individual's qualities of character.

A person's ethical sensibility was understandably largely judged by their treatment of others, especially such stock symbols of pathos as small children, the poor and animals, and if they did indeed possess a 'true delicacy', then they were expected to experience and display a genuine pity, an emotion which, it was assumed, would lead on to generous, philanthropic actions.[19] A more direct and convenient way of assessing an individual's sensibility, however, especially at first meeting or where the treatment of others could not easily be observed, was through their aesthetic taste or sense of beauty. This could be done directly, by asking someone to demonstrate their sensibility through their own performance on a musical instrument, for example, or by reciting poetry; or, more indirectly, through their response to someone else's performance. Interestingly, Lady Louisa Stuart recalled how, when she first read Henry Mackenzie's *Man of Feeling* at the age of 14, she was 'secretly afraid lest she should not cry enough to gain the credit of proper sensibility'.[20] Alternatively, one could merely inquire of a person's opinions concerning art and artists in general, or perhaps, more commonly, judge their reaction to the beauties of nature, with, in particular, their appreciation of the picturesque serving as the critical test.[21] In any of these instances a failure to express the 'correct' aesthetic judgement would be seen as direct evidence of a lack of virtue.

It can easily be seen how this ideal of character might have had profound implications for consumer behaviour as individuals would be bound to regard all those objects which advertised their taste as also indicative of their moral standing. To manifest sensibility was crucial because it was tantamount to manifesting virtue and hence, as sensibility was increasingly associated with displaying a fashionable sense of 'taste', not to be 'in fashion' was tantamount to being of dubious moral standing. Rather, therefore, than seeing fashion-conscious conduct as evidence of social status-seeking, it would be more accurate to regard it – for those who subscribed to this ideal of character – as an effort to protect one's 'good name'.

The aristocratic ideal of character

The eighteenth-century aristocratic ideal of character ultimately derived from the Renaissance ideal of the gentleman and courtier as one who was an accomplished lover, soldier, wit, man of affairs, musician and poet. Noble birth was assumed, whilst the only truly honourable profession was to bear arms; and although required to be accomplished in many fields, it was important for a gentleman to do them all with nonchalance.[22] As a courtier there was an overriding obligation to please, and to ensure that public occasions were free of all embarrassment. Apart from this, the central feature of the aristocratic ethic was the concept of honour, which usually took precedence over all other values. At the same time, this ideal of a proud, independent and accomplished man, jealous of his honour, was almost entirely secular; religion was not a matter of great concern and there was little attempt to plumb the depths of the soul. Such an ethic appears more favourable to pleasure-seeking and hence modern attitudes towards consumption than the more puritanical outlook of the middle classes and it was clearly anti-ascetic in character; yet, despite this, it cannot be said to have provided a suitable basis for that form of autonomous hedonism which underpins modern consumerism.

The primary reason for this is that no premium is placed on passion. Instead it is an ethic which emphasizes restraint and permits only casual and limited displays of sentiment. Any excess of emotion, whether of anguish or ecstasy, would be unseemly and ungentlemanly, representing bad manners. This absence of passion meant that little interest in the enjoyment of powerful emotional stimulation was likely to emerge from this particular cluster of values. In addition, such an ethic was necessarily other-regarding in orientation, with the courtier required, as noted, to ensure that his behaviour was pleasing to others rather than to himself, and this concern with the effects of action naturally inhibited the degree of interest in self-gratification. But, above all, it was the supreme importance attached to the concept of honour which constrained egoistic hedonism, with, consequently, pride taking precedence over pleasure.

These two features, the avoidance of all emotional excess in the interest of restrained, 'civilized' behaviour, and the competition for honour within a small social elite, comprise the distinctive features of the aristocratic ethic in both the seventeenth and the eighteenth centuries. It was, in effect, a mannered ethic, both in the sense that stress was placed upon the way things were done, and because behaviour was itself stylized, self-conscious and closely governed by convention. Hence even though this ethic was capable of being adapted to suit a modern consumer-oriented culture, in itself it can hardly have brought this about. The negative attitude towards strong emotion carried with it a comparative lack of interest in the thrill of feeling, and although the concern with reputation can be adjusted to aesthetic spheres, there is a lack of that intense introspective imagining which facilitates longing.

One might imagine that the general dissoluteness of the English aristocracy during the eighteenth century was a clear indication of hedonistic motives, but this is not necessarily so, as an apparent excessive indulgence of the appetites is not actually incompatible with a generalized stoicism and a hostility towards emotion. This is because such activities as heavy drinking, gambling, womanizing and engaging in energetic and dangerous sports can often represent attempts to demonstrate heroic or manly qualities. Typically they are communal in nature, taking the form of character contests in which there is a predominant concern to demonstrate strength, stamina, will-power and self-control. Thus, an activity which appears to be motivated by sensory hedonism, like drinking, may well be pursued past the point at which any pleasure is obtained, the object being to maintain the front of sobriety for as long as possible. Pleasure in this example has the same status as pain, both constituting forms of stimulation which have to be overcome if the individual is to ensure or enhance his reputation. Thus, whilst some interest in sensory hedonism may help to influence the choice of activities selected for such contests, it can be seen that a stoical ethic still underlies conduct. A fact which is reinforced by the accompanying tendency to reject sensuousness (mainly because of its feminine associations) together with any suggestions of an alliance between pleasure and spirituality. Most of these features are especially evident in that fascinating variant of the aristocratic ethic which was dandyism.

The dandies

The dandies constituted a small, exclusive social group, mainly, it would appear, of men who had little real claim to aristocratic lineage and yet who had experienced a privileged education.[23] They led the leisured life of gentlemen, often on borrowed money, and typically spent their time gambling, drinking, going to the theatre, doing the 'social round', womanizing or engaging in gentlemanly sports like boxing and tennis. In addition, of course, they devoted a great deal of time and money to their clothes and general appearance.

Refinement, and its expression in elegance, constituted the core of their ideal, whether in dress or deportment. Dress was to be perfect, but understated, as were all gestures and expressions of feeling,[24] whilst an emphasis upon refined and subtle conversation led to a premium being placed upon wit. To attain this ideal of refined behaviour was successfully to display a superiority of self, and hence arrogance was also a defining characteristic of the dandy. Naturally competition between them was intense as each strove by means of dress, gesture, tone of voice, glance and overall manner, coupled of course with wit, to triumph not only over all situational risks to their poise but over each other. It was a measure of Brummell's skill in this respect that he was universally acknowledged, for many years, as being the leading dandy, or in the language of his day, 'top of the male ton'.[25]

To be successful within the terms set by such an artificial and elaborately mannered ethic requires the individual to exercise continuous control over all impulses and emotions. It is not surprising, therefore, to discover that a stoic impassivity and imperturbability were major dandy characteristics, especially in circumstances of great stress. Moers refers to the dandy's need 'to tighten, to control' in order to attain his ideal,[26] whilst Baudelaire (who was actually a later romantic–dandy hybrid) said that 'the dandy doctrine of elegance and originality is as demanding as the most rigorous monastic rule',[27] and that consequently extreme self-control was unavoidable.[28]

This was a psychological necessity in a character ideal which emphasized the achievement of restrained and self-conscious, 'mannered' conduct. What is more, it was a stoical self-control which did not preclude indulgence of the appetites. Although Brummel never married, nor it would appear, had any kind of love-life, this does not seem to have been normal among the dandies,[29] the majority of whom seem to have enjoyed to the full the pleasures afforded by good food, good wine and bad women, in addition to the excitement offered by sport and war. This apparent hedonism was, nevertheless, largely devoid of any emotionality.

The corollary of the dandy's imperturbability when faced with danger or disaster was the treatment of what might normally be regarded as trivial issues as matters of great moment. Thus, the Duke of Wellington's officers, whilst maintaining a commendable sang-froid in the face of danger, even to the extent of being able to react to the loss of a leg as if it were hardly worth mentioning, were so concerned about maintaining their uniforms in immaculate condition as to want to meet the enemy carrying umbrellas.[30] One might be tempted to say that normal emotional concern was displaced, but the truth is that the apparently minor issues of dress and deportment were of crucial importance in the dandy ethic for the same reason that more obviously aesthetic judgements were important in the cult of sensibility: they revealed one's sense of taste, and hence one's essential quality of self. Here too the ever-present danger was the loss of reputation which can follow from any manifestation of 'bad taste', except that the link is less with virtue than honour, whilst there is little room for an inner-directed judgement which was independent of the attitudes of one's peers. At the same time, aesthetic judgements as such hardly mattered, for it was through conduct that taste was principally assessed. The concept of sensibility still played a part in this ethic, for a premium was placed on possession of that faculty which leads to the discernment of good taste. As far as susceptibility to stimuli was concerned, however, this was conceived of in distinctly physiological terms, to produce the strange combination of emotional impassivity with an extraordinary physical sensitivity. As Moers describes the dandy: 'His nerves are set jangling more easily that those of ordinary men, his teeth are more commonly on edge, his skin prickles and his eyes widen upon less provocation – and he boasts of his delicacy.'[31]

It can be seen from this brief summary of the aristocratic ethic that it did not provide a suitable basis for the development of autonomous, self-illusory hedonism, and hence for the spirit of modern consumerism. This is not to say that the aristocracy did not engage in luxury consumption, as their preoccupation with pride ensured that this would indeed be the case; this is reflected to this day in the many magnificent country houses which remain as monuments to their self-glorification. The same motive ensured that they spent lavishly on more perishable products during their lifetimes, whilst like most elites, some of this expenditure was incurred seeking pleasure with which to offset the boredom created by comfort. Critically, however, the dandies did not evaluate pleasure above comfort, nor perceive that it might be necessary to sacrifice some of the latter for gains in the former, nor indeed did the nature of their ethic really allow for the development of a truly rationalized hedonism.

Such an ethic does appear suited to the promotion of the modern fashion pattern, despite the indifference to aesthetics and, of course, fashions did change in dandy circles with interpersonal competition providing an incentive for innovation. There is, however, no real interest in novelty to compare with that displayed by the middle classes, and to this day aristocratic interest in dress tends to centre upon refinement. This, in turn, stems from the comparative lack of any emphasis upon the introspective inner-directedness characteristic of the puritan tradition. The dandy's striving did not derive from an imaginative dwelling upon ideal models, with as a consequence a guilt-driven dynamic, but from the shame-driven one which stems from other-directedness. Such an ethic, with its Veblenesque overtones, facilitated the spread of fashion, but cannot be regarded as providing the intellectual origins of the modern fashion pattern as a whole.

The romantic ideal of character

Romanticism,[32] as it became translated into a theory of art and the artist, led to the creation of a distinctive ideal of character, one which, although most obviously applied to the artist, was also meant to serve for the consumer or 're-creator' of his products. Since the key characteristic of the divine was taken to be creativity, both in the sense of productivity and of originality, imagination became the most significant and prized of personal qualities, with the capacity to manifest this both in works of art and through an ability to enter fully into those created by others acting as unambiguous signs of its presence. Since, in addition, the true and perfect world which imagination revealed was necessarily the realm of beauty, any exercise of this faculty was accompanied by pleasure, such that use of the imagination and the experiencing of pleasure became largely commensurate. Thus the romantic was someone who had an ideal sensitivity to pleasure, and indicated this fact by the spontaneity and intensity of his emotions. By the same token, he was an individual who could give pleasure to others, not so much directly through his person or his actions, but indirectly, through his embodied imaginings, a pleasure which served spiritually to enlighten them, as it had him. In addition, his idealistic determination and sense of obligation towards his personal 'genius' combined to make him feel estranged from an artificial, materialistic and utilitarian society. Consequently, feeling dissatisfied with a routine existence, and drawn to find consolation in 'nature', he attempts to give expression to his 'real self' whilst seeking to convert others to his vision of a more perfect world.

This ideal of character is the only one of the three examined that places a high moral value directly upon the experience of pleasure, whilst actually devaluing a utilitarian preoccupation with comfort. At the same time, it is imaginatively mediated pleasure which is given a privileged position *vis-à-vis* direct sensation, with sound ethical reasons advanced to support the individual's seeking out and displaying enjoyment. Indeed, those individuals needing reassurance that they live up to this ideal will seek to transform their lives into one continuous sequence of pleasing experiences, taking delight in their own ability to enjoy the novel and the strange, as well as their general capacity for daydreaming. They will also endeavour to manifest their hedonistic capacity in apparently uncontrolled outbursts of powerful emotion, together with a more diffuse and melancholic longing for more perfect experiences. Finally, they will attempt to reveal the unique nature of their selves through an egotistical introspection and determined eccentricity, intent on provoking a disapproving reaction from the upholders of a more conventional and 'common-sensical' morality.

This latter point reveals that the creed of the bohemians was, in essence, that of romanticism, with bohemianism itself being the attempt to express romantic ideals in a complete way of life.[33] Central to this creed was the ideal of self-expression, with the aim of realizing individuality through creativity, plus the abolition of all those laws, conventions and rules which prevented this from occurring; the pursuit of pleasure and the importance of developing to the full one's capacity for enjoyment; the idea of genius; the rejection of rational causality; world-weariness and the natural alienation of the truly talented.[34]

A comparison of the bohemians and the dandies is helpful in revealing some of the essential features of this ethic. Like their predecessors, these 'aristocrats of pleasure' adopted some upper-class values.[35] They sought, for example, to lead a leisured life, having a special aversion to work. Only infrequently, however, did they have sufficient money to be able to maintain an even moderately extravagant existence, though like the dandies they borrowed extensively and rarely paid their debts; consequently, at best, they resembled distressed aristocrats with little to their name but pride. But then for the bohemians there was no shame in being poor. They also resembled the dandies in their tendency to congregate in cliques and social circles, competing with each other in word-play and delighting in provoking the bourgeoisie with their conspicuous dissipations. Unlike them, however, honour and reputation did not depend upon impeccable social conduct in the sense of mastery of good form, but on the display of commitment to romantic ideals. This could be confirmed in the company of one's peers through some evidence of a capacity to indulge in pleasure, an indifference to comfort or simply a readiness to taunt the bourgeoisie. But the romantic bohemian's duty to his personal genius meant that a spiritual dimension existed which transcended any mere concern with social image; hence while the dandy only really existed in the eyes of others, the bohemian must answer to a spirit within himself, and to whose realization he is obliged to devote his life.

It can be seen from this analysis how the romantic ideal of character might have functioned to stimulate and legitimate that distinctive form of autonomous, self-illusory hedonism which underlies modern consumer behaviour. It does this by providing the highest possible motives with which to justify daydreaming, longing and the rejection of reality, together with the pursuit of originality in life and art; by so doing it enables pleasure to be ranked above comfort and counteracts both traditionalist and utilitarian restraints on the expression of desire.

This thesis does not claim that there was a direct identity between 'romantics' and 'modern consumers'. As can be seen from the above analysis the true romantic's attachment to pleasure, to the exotic and the new was likely to be expressed in a high-minded spiritual idealism which rejected what were seen as the purely petty and material concerns of the everyday world of commerce. To that extent, the romantics fiercely opposed what today would be labelled 'consumerism'. But this does not mean that individuals possessed of a romantic sensibility would necessarily scorn the acquisition of worldly goods. What it does suggest, however, is something about both the nature of the products which 'romantics' would seek to acquire and about the meanings which they would attach to their possessions. It is worth remembering in this respect that whilst the bohemians (who espoused an especially rigorous form of romantic faith) despised the bourgeoisie for the importance they attached to such material possessions as houses and furniture, they themselves valued books, works of art, music and clothes. Of course, they did not share the same pattern of valuations as the bourgeoisie but the fact remains that their philosophy of life did not involve a simple rejection of goods so much as a distinctive attitude towards their meaning and use. Simply expressed, they valued objects which possessed a high aesthetic significance and they regarded them as important for the quality of the experience which they offered rather than as mere symbols of wealth or status. If, bearing this in mind, we return to a consideration of the consumer revolution in eighteenth-century England, it becomes possible to see how romanticism might be directly relevant to an explanation of this phenomenon.

What, after all, are the established facts about this revolution in demand for goods? First, that the 'middling classes' were disproportionately responsible for the surge in demand,[36] and second, that 'expressive goods' such as pictures, china, mirrors, musical instruments and clothes constituted a significant proportion of this demand;[37] these two facts being closely connected such that, as Weatherill notes, 'tradesmen' typically consumed a higher proportion of such goods than their social superiors, the gentry.[38] This evidence does not suggest that 'emulation' is the key to understanding the consumer revolution. However, when taken in conjunction with such other parallel developments as the rise of the modern western fashion pattern and the modern novel, it does strongly support the claimed connection with romanticism.

What 'expressive goods' have in common is their connection with the world of art and aesthetics, whether this is in the elite sense of such fine arts as music and painting or merely the more popular commercial arts. The purchase and use of these goods therefore necessarily suggests that consumers were concerned with questions of taste and beauty. Not only that, but the fact that this was associated with a new sensitivity to 'fashion' also indicates that novelty was a crucial ingredient in the criteria of beauty which were commonly applied. As

Lemire observes, it was at this time that 'new clothes came to mean "brand new to the buying public, not the newest items added to one's wardrobe" '.[39] It would seem that the most reasonable interpretation of these facts is that consumers were increasingly adopting a 'romantic' sensibility.

Conclusion

This brief discussion of three eighteenth-century character ideals and their implications, via typical patterns of character-confirming conduct, for the emergence of modern consumer attitudes has tried to show how such a 'characterological' approach enables a more sensitive handling of the variability of the subjective meaning accompanying action than more conventional 'mono-motive' perspectives. By first identifying the different character ideals prevalent in a given period and then noting the degree to which they are adopted or endorsed by different sections of the population, it becomes possible to deduce the degree to which various social groups would have been likely to engage in a given activity, or more accurately, would have felt justified in so doing. More specifically, it means that a basis exists for assessing the probable motivational and justificatory meanings which individuals might have attached to their consumption activities, and, in particular, to imaginatively mediated pleasure. In this way, apparently similar activities, such as following fashion and drinking to excess can be shown to possess different meanings for differently situated socio-cultural groups who are prompted to engage in them out of contrasting motives. This demonstrates the error of assuming, not merely that there is a single 'consumption motive' of universal applicability, but also that there is necessarily a one-to-one relationship between an activity and a motive. This is indeed very unlikely to be the case in situations where the conduct is described by an observer whilst the motive is formulated by the actor.

It can be seen that the approach advocated here has an important but perverse methodological implication. It means that one cannot hope to understand consumer conduct by limiting one's sights to activities conventionally understood by that term. Indeed, the reverse is likely to be the case. Only by taking the historical individuals' primary concerns as the focus of attention can one hope first to understand their conduct and second, to perceive its implications for consumption. One should certainly not assume that because an activity involves the selection, purchase or use of goods that its primary meaning to the individual concerned is as an act of 'consumption', or that merely because 'consumption' was an obvious consequence of an activity that the intention lying behind it was 'to consume'. On the contrary, it would probably be more realistic to assume that many 'consumption effects' are largely the unintended or ironic outcomes of conduct engaged in out of quite different motives. What these are thus becomes the proper object of inquiry.

A further implication of the form of analysis essayed here is that it is the justificatory dimension of conduct which becomes the central focus of attention, and consequently that investigation should move away from a concentration upon the material and economic constraints on conduct to consider those which are ethical and moral in nature. Naturally this means a move away from social and economic history towards that which is cultural and intellectual in character, as those beliefs and attitudes which comprise the material of character ideals have a history, and are themselves naturally subject to modification and change.

Notes

1   See, for example, Harold Perkin, *The Origins of Modern English Society* (London: Routledge & Kegan Paul, 1968); Neil McKendrick, John Brewer and J. H. Plumb, *The Birth of a Consumer Society: The Commercialization of Eighteenth-Century England* (London: Europa, 1972) and Lorna Weatherill, chapter 10 in the present volume.

2   Thorstein Veblen, *The Theory of the Leisure Class: An Economic Study of Institutions* (London: George Allen & Unwin, 1925); P. Bourdieu, *Distinction: A Social Critique of the Judgement of Taste* (Cambridge, Mass.: Harvard University Press, 1984). For a useful summary and critique of the 'discovery of meaning' tradition in the study of consumption see Grant McCracken, *Culture and Consumption: New Approaches to the Symbolic Character of Consumer Goods and Activities* (Bloomington: Indiana University Press, 1988), esp. ch. 5.

3   See, as an instance of what is, in other respects, a valuable study, Mihaly Csikszentmihalyi and Eugene Rochberg-Halton, *The Meanings of Things: Domestic Symbols and the Self* (Cambridge: Cambridge University Press, 1981).

4   Chandra Mukerji, *From Graven Images: Patterns of Modern Materialism* (New York: Columbia University Press, 1983), 171.

5   Quentin Bell, *On Human Finery* (New York: Schocken, 1976), 62, 79.

6   See the approach advocated by C. Wright Mills in 'Situated actions and vocabularies of motive', *American Sociological Review*, v (December 1940), 904–13.

7   This conception of action derives from the work of Max Weber. See, in particular, *The Theory of Social and Economic Organization*, tr. A. M. Henderson and Talcott Parsons, ed. and with an introduction by Talcott Parsons (New York: Free Press, 1964).

8   See, for examples, Ruth Benedict, *Patterns of Culture* (London: Routledge & Kegan Paul, 1935) and David Riesman, Nathan Glazer and Reuel Denny, *The Lonely Crowd: A Study in the Changing American Character* (New York: Doubleday Anchor, 1966).

9   As exemplified, for example, by Gordon Ratray Taylor, *The Angel-Makers: A Study in the Psychological Origins of Historical Change 1750–1850* (London: Heinemann, 1958).

10 See Max Weber, *The Sociology of Religion*, tr. Ephraim Fischoff, with an introduction by Talcott Parsons (London: Methuen, 1965), 155f.

11 E. Goffman, *The Presentation of Self in Everyday Life* (Harmondsworth: Penguin, 1971).

12 Richard W. Bevis (ed.), *Eighteenth Century Drama: Afterpieces* (Oxford: Oxford University Press, 1970), 143.

13 Colin Campbell, *The Romantic Ethic and the Spirit of Modern Consumerism* (Oxford: Basil Blackwell, 1987), Part 1.

14 Brian Vickers, Introduction to Henry Mackenzie, *The Man of Feeling* (London: Oxford University Press, 1967).

15 Rene Wellek, *A History of Modern Criticism: 1750–1950*: vol. 1, *The Later Eighteenth Century* (London: Jonathan Cape, 1955), 73.

16 Maximillian E. Novak, *Eighteenth-Century English Literature* (London: Macmillan, 1983), 157.

17 Joseph Texte, *Jean-Jacques Rousseau and the Cosmopolitan Spirit in Literature: A Study of the Literary Relations between France and England during the Eighteenth Century* (New York: Burt Franklin, 1899), 289.

18 See Stanley Grean, *Shaftesbury's Philosophy of Religion and Ethics: A Study in Enthusiasm* (Athens, Ohio: Ohio University Press, 1967); Basil Willey, *The English Moralists* (London: Chatto & Windus, 1964), 216–31; as well as Louis I. Bredvold, *The Natural History of Sensibility* (Detroit: Wayne State University Press, 1962).

19 See, for an example, J. M. S. Tompkins, *The Popular Novel in England 1770–1880* (Lincoln: University of Nebraska Press, 1961), 105–6 and Appendix II.

20 Vickers, Introduction to Mackenzie, *The Man of Feeling*, p. viii.

21 See B. Sprague Allen, *Tides in English Taste 1619–1800: A Background for the Study of Literature*, 2 vols (New York: Rowman & Littlefield, 1969), vol. 2, 228–9.

22 Maria Ossowska, *The Social Determinants of Moral Ideas* (London: Routledge & Kegan Paul, 1971), 141.

23 See Ellen Moers, *The Dandy: Brummell to Beerbohm* (London: Secker & Warburg, 1960); James Lavers, *Dandies* (London: Weidenfeld & Nicolson, 1968); and T. A. J. Burnett, *The Rise and Fall of a Regency Dandy: The Life and Times of Scrope Berdmore Davies* (London: John Murray, 1981).

24 Moers, *The Dandy*, 18.

25 ibid.

26 ibid., 282.

27 ibid., 116.

28 ibid., 20–1.

29 Burnett, *Rise and Fall of a Regency Dandy*, 42–53 *passim*.

30 Moers, *The Dandy*, 116.

31 ibid., 20–1.

32 It is not possible to deal here with the complicated issue of the correct meaning of this term. For a statement of the author's position see Campbell, *The Romantic Ethic*, 179–95.

33 On bohemianism see Cesar Grana, *Bohemian versus Bourgeois: French Society and the French Man of Letters in the Nineteenth Century* (New York: Basic Books, 1964); Henry Murger, *The Latin Quarter* (*Scènes de la vie Bohème*), tr. Ellen Marriage and John Selwyn, with an introduction by Arthur Symonds (London: Greening, 1908).

34 Grana, *Bohemian versus Bourgeois*, 67–8.

35 The phrase is Murger's, *The Latin Quarter*, 42.

36 See Lorna Weatherill, chapter 10 in the present volume.

37 ibid.

38 ibid.

39 Beverly Lemire, 'Consumerism in preindustrial and early industrial England: the trade in second-hand clothes', *Journal of British Studies*, xxvii (Jan. 1988), 23.

4
Consumption: disease of the consumer society?

Roy Porter

> Consumption may be regarded as a vast pit-fall, situated on the high road of life, which we have not sense enough of our common interest to agree to fill up, or fence round. Heedless fathers and mothers are for ever guiding their sons and daughters directly into it.[1]

Attuned to moral and economic discourse, we hear this as a warning against greed. With ears differently primed, it becomes – as it was intended to be – a call to preventive medicine, a prophylactic against 'consumption' in the sense of tuberculosis. I wish to explore the implications of this pun on pathological consumption.

What makes a commonwealth healthy? It was a problem that endlessly vexed early modern politicians and moralists. Obviously, the body politic had to be kept from wasting away: the poverty of nations was symptomatic of broken constitutions, a recipe for internal disorder and dynastic weakness alike. Rather national strength had to be consolidated, through prosperity and populousness. Yet this too held its dangers. Muscle readily ran to fat, and corpulence was all too often maldistributed. It was a time-honoured complaint that the belly or the head – courts and 'corporations' – privileged themselves at the expense of the true sinews of the state (above all, the 'hands'), organs in danger of withering away.[2]

Wealth was the life-blood, the vital spirits, of the incorporated nation. Hence its office was to flow. Seventeenth-century economists rejected old-fashioned 'bullionism' (the miser's dream that treasure lay in hoarding gold and silver), in favour of the more refined view that true wealth sprang from money in motion, stimulating labour, industry and exchange. William Harvey's discovery of the circulation of the blood perhaps underwrote the mercantilist credo that opulence grew out of the velocity of commercial transactions, providing employment and 'exercise' for the members of the social organism.[3]

Even then, prescribing the right regimen for the body politic posed perplexing policy decisions. For one thing, prestigious teachings warned that excessive wealth was the cancer of the commonwealth. Churches preached against the love of lucre and the sin of unbridled appetite, while civic humanism prophesied that private enrichment sapped public liberty and virtue: 'Luxury', warned John Dennis in 1711, is the 'spreading Contagion which is the greatest Corrupter of Publick Manners and the greatest Extinguisher of Publick Spirit'. Mercantilism itself, philosophically inclined to saving rather than spending, feared affluence would be squandered on dross.[4]

Indeed, the dialectics of wealth and waste were worrisome. Buying and selling were vital for life-giving commerce. Yet what was spending, but the dissipation of accumulated resources, leading to economic entropy? Conspicuous consumption was conspicuous waste.[5] Even routine indulgence on perishables – outlays on heating and food – could be represented as money going up in smoke or down the drain, hence the mercantilist directive that manufactures be exported, for that course would at least recuperate non-perishable specie for the kingdom. If production was the *summum bonum* for early wealth theorists, consumption was their headache.[6]

This was, I would suggest, not least because, in an epistemology accustomed to map the body politic upon the body human, finding the high road to health for the human body was itself highly problematic.[7] Traditional understanding of the springs of life – both elite, deriving from Classical humoralism, and popular – likened vitality to a candle or fire. In this decaying, sublunary sphere, the natural tendency of a flame to sink and die could be postponed – though not infinitely – by renewed external stimuli.[8] Eating and drinking fuelled the vital fires.[9]

In a milieu where hunger, dearth and even famine[10] stalked the land, people needed little persuading that hearty eating and drinking provided fortification against disease, debility and death. Pastoral poetry and still-life paintings amongst the elite, and the low-life Rabelaisian release of the carnival gut-bust charged food and drink with a surrogate eroticism, or even a blasphemous sanctity.[11] Haunted by hunger, the poor fantasized about full bellies.[12] Rhythms of work and rituals of sociability centred on celebrations that symbolically linked cheer, conviviality and community, through affording times and sites devoted to bingeing: the flowing bowl of harvest home, *mardis gras*, wassailing, wakes, the gentleman's club and Sam Johnson's favourite 'throne of felicity', the tavern chair. Beefsteak became the national emblem for Englishmen whose manhood seemingly hinged upon being three-bottle fellows.[13] And all was clinched in the custom of toasting 'healths'. If Hogarth caricatured his contemporaries as swinish sots, it was partly because, for a while at least – the early Georgian 'pudding time' – agricultural improvement made produce abundant and gin dead cheap.[14] The creature comforts of cuisine and cellar loomed large in the Georgian pursuit of happiness.[15]

But they also figured in the quest for health; for traditional wisdom regarded 'high living' as a form of preventive medicine. The Englishman's cultic roast beef was not mere chauvinism, gluttony or fantasy, but positively therapeutic. 'He that does not mind his belly will mind nothing', dogmatized Johnson, perhaps hinting at the old proverb, 'The belly carries the legs and not the legs the belly.'[16] 'Man is an eating animal, a drinking animal, and a sleeping animal', defined the extremely corporeal Dr Erasmus Darwin, convinced that enthusiastic trenchermanship rallied resistance. Such was his own sesquipedality of belly that the great inventor ingeniously had a semi-circle sawn out of his dining-table, so that he could station himself within eating distance.[17]

The stomach – that 'grand Monarque of the Constitution', according to Edward Jenner[18] – needed to be active and tonic, to digest the copious quantities of aliment required to concoct the blood, providing the spirits which enlivened the limbs.[19] Hence the ideal victuals were savoury and strong, and the red meat and wine diet of the rich evidently more invigorating than the insipid water-gruel of the poor.[20] 'My Stomach brave today', purred

Parson Woodforde in 1795, 'relished my dinner.'[21] Rarely a day went by without him logging his menus. Indeed, Woodforde's ultimate diary entry before his death culminates in a last supper: 'Very weak this Morning, scarce able to put on my Cloaths and with great difficulty, get down Stairs with help . . . Dinner to day, Rost Beef etc.'[22]

John Locke was told by one of his friends that his wife, 'in order to her health . . . is entered into a course of gluttony, for she is never well but when shee is eating'.[23] The aptly named William Stout trusted in the healing powers of appetizing viands and a gallant stomach. Having long suffered with a 'sore distemper', and been enfeebled by his doctor's blood-letting, he finally rebelled. 'I got some apatite for nurishment', he recorded:

> The doctor said I was feverish and must take weak meat and drinke, but I covited better. My neighbour John Bryer visited me often and once merrily told me I must take better meat and drink, and toud where there was very good ail, and sent for some, and I drank one or two glassess of it, which very much refreshed me. And my apatite increasing, I easily recovered.[24]

This model of the healthy body as a vital economy, demanding energetic stimulus, was widely accepted, as we have seen, by the medical profession itself. The naval physician, Thomas Trotter, endorsed the advice of the famous Venetian longevist, Luigi Cornaro, who prescribed at 40 two cordial glasses of wine a day, four at 50, and six at 60, while Dr Peter Shaw wrote a book in 1724 to prove *Wine Preferable to Water*, indeed *A Grand Preserver of Health*.[25] Alcohol was medicinal. For long Parson Woodforde swigged a glass of port as 'a strengthening Cordial twice a day', while dosing himself with rum when groggy with 'wind cholic'.[26]

One evening, his niece, Nancy, fell sick with vomiting. He blamed this on

> what she eat at Dinner and after . . . some boiled Beef rather fat and salt, a good deal of a nice rost duck, and a plenty of boiled damson pudding. After dinner, by way of desert, she eat some green-gage Plumbs, some Figgs, and Raspberries and Cream.

For remedy, Woodforde got her to swallow half a pint of rum and water; more rum, rhubarb and ginger followed. She recovered so fast that next day she was tucking in to 'rost Neck of Mutton'.[27]

Prophylactic eating and drinking in turn required energetic waste disposal. For putrifying *excrementa* and indurated faeces would, many feared, produce gastric ferments, flatulence and bile, leading to auto-poisoning. Hence popular physiology attended to evacuations no less than to appetites. Purging was the panacea, but sweats and phlebotomy were important auxiliaries, emetics too (only the Irish lacked faith in them, so the story went, for they could never keep them down).[28]

Medical materialism thus conceived the pulsating body as a through-put economy whose efficient functioning depended upon generous input and unimpeded outflow. But how was this need for positive stimulus to be squared with age-old doctrines – both medical and moral – of temperance, moderation and the golden mean? Might not energizing the system precipitate pathological excess?

'I verily beleeve [Dr Baines] will kill himself ere long by his intemperance', bewailed Anne Finch.[29] Such fears were often voiced, in the light of what an early Georgian pamphlet denounced as 'the present luxurious and fantastical manner of Eating'.[30] Notorious for indigestible favourites such as pudding, the English – a nation of 'gullet-fanciers', according to Charles Lamb[31] – were, as the saying went, digging their graves with their teeth. 'The stomach of the Irish went & came', quipped the wits, 'but that of the English came & stayed.'[32] 'Purging and vomiting almost the whole day', lamented Woodforde on 18 July 1786, 'I believe I made too free Yesterday with Currant Tarts and Cream &c.'[33]

It was a common tale, even down to the ominously lethal 'etcetera'. John Carrington learned the hard way when his love of 'Butock of beef' destroyed first his stomach and then his health. At one dinner, his diary reveals, he pigged himself with 'Roasted hear & a hasht hear & boyled Sholdr of Motton & onions, puding etc. . . . Plenty of punch & good company', but justice proved summary: 'Theese fine made dishes did not agree with me, purged me very much all next day, I am for plane food.'[34] Too late, however! Over the next few months, entry after entry reads 'canot eate nor drink', 'no stomake to eat', and so forth. His belly had gone on hunger strike; decay set in and he died.[35]

Multitudes of others, seduced into habits of convivial gourmandizing, rationalized by the ideology of stimulus, abused their stomachs. And if serious eating was parlous, gross drinking proved still more constitutionally lethal. Erasmus Darwin dubbed alcohol 'the greatest curse of the christian world';[36] and no wonder, for oceans were swallowed, and not just during the gin craze. Sylas Neville recorded bottle days as a medical student in Edinburgh:

> Sun. Sep. 17. Dined at the Fox & Goose, Musselburgh. . . . Lucky I did not go yesterday, as a company of only 8 or 10, chiefly Shiel's friends, drank 27 bottles of claret & 12 of port, besides Punch, & were all beastly drunk.[37]

Such drunkards 'died by their own hands', opined the *Tatler*. Intoxication, judged Samuel Richardson, was 'the most destructive of all vices: *asthma's, vertigoes, palsies, apoplexies, gouts, colics, fevers, dropsies, consumptions, stone,* and *hypochondriac diseases,* are naturally introduced'.[38] Such advice was lost on some. The aptly named Vine Hall was frequently dead to the world: 'drunkenness, horrible depravity', he rebukes himself on one occasion, and, some time later, records 'drunkenness, six days drunk'. To rescue himself he converted to Methodism, soon apostatized back into ardent spirits, and was brought to his senses only when his preacher charged him point-blank, 'Do you love porter better than Christ?'[39]

In short, the black humour of toasting was not lost on the Georgians: 'to drink health is to drink sickness'. For, argued Dr George Cheyne, 'The running into *Drams*' was ruinous; 'neither *Laudanum* nor *Arsenick* will kill more certainly, although more quickly'.[40] And who knew by personal experience, better than that Scottish *bon viveur* physician?

Seeking his fortune, Cheyne took the high road south early in the eighteenth century, haunting London coffee houses and taverns, aiming to drink himself into practice. He rapidly established a name as a witty man-about-town[41] with 'Bottle-Companions, the younger Gentry, and Free-Livers',

> nothing being necessary for that Purpose, but to be able to *Eat* lustily, and swallow down much *Liquor*; and being naturally of a large *Size*, a cheerful Temper, and Tolerable lively *Imagination*. . . . I soon became caressed by them, and grew daily in *Bulk* and in Friendship with these gay Gentlemen.[42]

High living eroded his health, however, and he grew 'excessively fat, short-breath'd, Lethargic and Listless'.[43] Fearing for his life, he quit town, imposed an austere diet, and saw his corporation melt away, 'like a Snow-ball in Summer'.[44] Over the years, suffering radical mood-swings, which G. S. Rousseau has plausibly linked to the anxieties of authorship, Cheyne's weight went up and down like a yo-yo.[45] His worst crisis came around 1720, when, experiencing 'a Craving and insufferable Longing for more Solid and Toothsome Food, and for higher and stronger Liquors',[46] he turned a three-bottle man and blew up to 32 stone, eventually needing a servant to walk behind him carrying a stool, on which to rest every few paces. His legs erupted in ulcers; erysipelas and gout followed; and he took refuge in the 'slow poison' of opiates.[47] At his grossest, he confessed, he 'went about like a Malefactor condemn'd', his gluttony producing 'Giddiness, Lowness, Anxiety, Terror', 'perpetual Sickness, *Reaching, Lowness, Watchfulness, Eructation*', and a nervous hypochondria which 'made Life a Burden to myself, and a Pain to my friends'.[48]

Thus early modern medical gastronomics held that appetite was healthy; but excess brought troubles in train – colloquially the 'blue devils', or what Byron dubbed 'the horrors of digestion'.[49] Above all, protracted bingeing led to exhaustion, dyspnoea, dropsy and even the 'tisick' or tuberculosis. Oliver Heywood, the Nonconformist minister who delighted in the demise of delinquents, thus recorded how a rival preacher, 'a babbling, wretched creature', had first become a 'great drinker as its sd', and had 'at last fallen into a consumption'.[50]

In other words, just as, in the kingdom, wealth easily mutated into waste, so in the individual, excessive consumption could, seemingly paradoxically, produce not strength but physical dissolution. Late seventeenth-century medicine was alarmed by the apparently rapid spread of the various cachexies or wasting diseases – scurvy, cancers, scrofula, *tabes dorsalis*, venereal infections, ascites, catarrhs, dropsy, asthmas and that galaxy of 'hysterick' fevers and 'hypochondriack' melancholias so dear to an earlier medical sensibility. Over a generation before George Cheyne identified nervous disorders as *The English Malady*, Gideon Harvey explicitly designated scurvy as the 'disease of London' and consumptions as the '*morbus anglicus*' – they were 'both an English *Endemick* and *Epidemick*', which by 'devouring of parts' culminated in the 'corruption of the essentials'.[51] Benjamin Marten was shortly to pronounce: 'There is no Country in the World more Productive of Consumptions than this our Island.'[52]

All such scurvies and cachexies were diseases of wasting, exhibiting symptoms including general malaise, weight loss, flaccid flesh, poor skin tone, ulcers that refused to heal, and a general 'rottenness' of health, often put down to what Cheyne diagnosed as 'a manifest or latent scrophulous or scorbutick Taint', liable to prove chronic and even ending in dissolution.[53] This congeries of chronic constitutional conditions – collectively known as 'the consumptions', and including, but not exclusively confined to, tuberculosis[54] – was largely blamed upon excess, exacerbated by the irritating effect of England's coal-smoke choked atmosphere.[55] Over-energetic feasting, toasting and 'sporting in the Garden of Venus' were identified as prime causes of 'wasting diseases', resulting in premature enfeeblement and what Thomas Willis called the 'withering away of the whole body', down to a mere anatomy.[56] So precisely how did 'consumption' create 'consumptions'?

On this matter, post-Restoration eminences such as Christopher Bennet, Gideon Harvey, Thomas Willis, Richard Morton and Benjamin Marten were substantially agreed in laying blame at the door of excess. In his monumental *Essay of Consumptions*, Morton ascribed wasting distempers to 'too plentiful and unseasonable gorging of meat and drink and also an imprudent choice of such meats and liquors as abound with excrementatious parts and are not easy to be digested'. When wasting was accompanied by jaundice, Morton believed that 'the evident procarctic causes of this consumption are commonly frequent and long debauches', laced with liquor.[57] Dissolution occurred through various physiological processes. Marten stressed how burdening the guts brought on violent purging, diarrhoeas and defluxions.[58] The liver and kidneys were likewise unable to cope, resulting in 'dropsies'.[59] And above all, gastric overload distorted digestive processes, creating 'acid spittle' and inducing what Bennet called 'erroneous fermentation', thereby filling 'the blood with Corruption', and rendering it 'sharp' and 'incorrigible'.[60] In similar terms, Morton explained how excess provoked the 'Blood's Alienation' – in other words, a 'morbid disposition of the blood'.[61]

Such inflaming fermentations, it was feared, would in turn provoke ulcerations, tumours, tubercles on the lungs, schirrosities and cancers. These would constitute further 'Obstructions' to the vital processes, and, enlarging parasitically, would eat up the vitals. Stoppages of all kinds – for example, amenorrhoea – must thus be heeded, Morton advised, as harbingers of consumptions.[62]

Gluttony and toping were matched by the equal perils of sex. Writing in the 1760s, William Buchan blamed many consumptive disorders on 'excessive venery', and 'frequent and excessive debaucheries'. 'Late watching, and drinking strong liquors, which generally go together', he noted, 'can hardly fail to destroy the lungs. Hence the *bon companion* often falls a sacrifice to this disease.'[63]

The body sometimes grew emaciated, sometimes bloated; but whichever, its vital actions were clearly in decay. What was to be done? Traditional medicine commended the ubiquitous therapeutics of 'evacuation'.[64] Morton prescribed diaphoretics and bleeding, 'repeated according to the strength of the patient and the present effervescence of the blood';[65] Bennet too was a friend to phlebotomy.[66]

In short, medical opinion argued that wasting conditions followed from growing opportunities for self-indulgence and high living. Buchan explained:

> Consumptions prevail more in England than in any other part of the world, owing perhaps to the great use of animal food and strong liquors, the general application to sedentary employments, and the great quantity of pit-coal which is there burnt.

Wealth, ease and urbanism were above all hazardous to 'the rich, who are not under the necessity of labouring for their bread'.[67]

I have argued that the dialectics of wealth and waste perplexed early economists. I have gone on to suggest that they disturbed the doctors no less, for the enthusiastic consumer could himself end up being consumed, the hearty eater eaten, even before the worms did their work. These apparent paradoxes were addressed by George Cheyne, whose writings on chronic disorders proved particularly pivotal, encapsulating past wisdom, while formulating new philosophies for the future.[68]

Cheyne posed the question of the relationship between civilization and health. Did the wealth of nations secure the health of nations? Far from it. As England rose from rags to riches, her people sank in health, suffering uniquely from that clutch of chronic and constitutional conditions – 'nervous disorders' – which he dubbed 'The English Malady'.[69]

Why so? Cheyne's explanation drew upon familiar primitivist tropes: 'when Mankind was simple, plain, honest and frugal, there were few or no diseases. Temperance, Exercise, Hunting, Labour, and Industry kept the Juices Sweet and the Solids brac'd.' All had changed: 'Since our Wealth has increas'd, and our Navigation has been extended, we have ransack'd all the Parts of the *Globe* to bring together its whole Stock of Materials for *Riot, Luxury*, and to provoke *Excess*.'[70] As the nation had grown 'luxurious, rich and wanton', diseases had mushroomed.[71] The *beau monde* pursued opulent life-styles which only wealth would buy: soft beds, late rising, later nights, artificial lighting and heating, tight-lacing and above all elaborate cuisines culled from all corners of the globe, involving dishes typically rich, salted, sauced, smoked and seasoned, all washed down with distilled liquors and ardent spirits.[72] High living in high society carried high health risks.

Cheyne's formulation of the 'English Malady' as a constitutionally crippling yet socially eligible disorder – a badge of gentility – has been widely analysed.[73] Here I wish to highlight just three of its features.

First, Cheyne set himself up as the apostle, if not of dietary abstinence, at least of austerity. Not only did he frequently put himself on strict regimes, sometimes totally abstaining from flesh and alcohol and living on vegetables and water, but he commended 'seed and milk' diets to other sufferers,[74] especially those afflicted with '*a settled* Hectick (*from Ulcers*), *an* Elephantiasis *and* Leprosy, *a humorous* Asthma, *a chronical* Diabetes, *an incurable* Scrophula *and a deep* Scurvy', to say nothing of '*higher and inconquerable hysterick and hypochondriack Disorders*'.[75]

Many latter-day vegetarians and 'low diet' zealots – not least Shelley – looked back to Cheyne's dietaries for inspiration.[76] Yet Cheyne was no dogmatist. 'The great *Rule* of Eating and Drinking for *Health*', he insisted, 'is to adjust the *Quality* and *Quantity* of our Food to our *digestive* Powers.' Though 'Nothing conduces more to *Health* and *Long Life*, than *Abstinence* and *plain Food*',[77] his measure of moderation was not wholly lenten, advising readers to sink no more than a couple of pints of wine a day, and suggesting that two chicken legs and a wing was sufficient meat for a meal. Cheyne's regimes became popular because he did not require readers to be ascetics. 'If in the *Gratifications* of their *Appetites, Passions* and *Desires*' he argued, people

> follow'd the uncorrupted *Dictates* of *Nature*, and neither spurred her on beyond her *Craving*, nor too violently restrained her in her *innocent Biass*; they would enjoy a greater Measure of *Health* than they do; have their *Sensations* more *delicate*, and their *Pleasures* more *exquisite*; live with less *Pain*, and die with less *Horror*.[78]

Addison and Steele taught decorum to the *nouveaux riches*. Cheyne similarly instructed its Tunbelly Clumsies in the art of civilized eating.[79]

Second, as this last quotation suggests, Cheyne challenged the credit of the 'high diet', by mounting a critique of corporeality, and replacing the carnal with an accent on light diet. Indeed, Cheyne formulated his own spiritualist Christian piety, drawing upon Platonic philosophy and Behmenist mystical immaterialism.[80]

In particular – my third point – Cheyne advanced a life-style designed to refine the grossness of affluence into a kind of 'lightness of being'. He invented a new sociology (an aesthetics for elite living), a psychology (heightened sensibility, indeed, *taste*) and predicated them upon a new physiology, which discarded classical humoralism for the iatro-mechanist idiom of the nerves, diverting attention from the traditional through-put economy of the fluids, and identifying the permanent solids, the nerves,[81] as the key to 'the Human *Machin*'.[82]

Health, contended *The English Malady*, depended not upon humoral equipoise but upon nervous tone. Made up of tubes and fibres, nerves were designed to carry stimulus, sensations and information fast and efficiently throughout the body. Being so delicate, their channels and strings were readily clogged by the swill from overloaded guts, rendering them sluggish and 'glewy'. In particular, acidities caused irritations which encouraged ulcerations, inflammations and other obstructions. Weakened, relaxed nerves would finally produce diarrhoeas, phlegm, spitting, rheums, dropsy, diabetes, scrofula and so forth. Excess thus debilitated the nerves, leading to chronic disease.

Fine physical health, it followed, depended upon keeping these vital fibres springy, clean and tonic. All the more so as those required to shine amongst the *bon ton* were blessed with sharp, delicate sensibilities. Fine spirited people, living, as we say today, on their nerves, were particularly prone to nervous debility. Flaccid fibres would dull finer feelings, producing anxiety and depression. In the coming electric ambience of sensibility and refinement, gross over-consumption had to be abandoned as self-destructive and boorish. The tastes of the rich needed refining. These views proved prophetic.

'There was a consumer revolution in eighteenth-century England', Neil McKendrick assures us. This claim is open to dispute, but no one doubts that aggregate consumption of services and material goods – necessities, decencies and luxuries – was rising among an impressive social cross-section. Transformations in shopping, advertising, marketing and so forth were rendering material acquisition and visible consumption highly eligible activities.[83]

Growing opportunities for participation in the commerce of goods put traditional Christian, humanist and mercantilist injunctions against greed, envy and covetousness under grave pressure. One key response was that ideological assimilation of the newly dominant commercialism which we may call the 'English Enlightenment'.[84] Resourceful apologists contended that desire, and its gratification via rising personal consumption, were not, after all, dangers to the soul, self or state; properly understood, they were universally beneficial. Dudley North proclaimed that 'exorbitant Appetites' were the 'main spur to trade',[85] Bernard Mandeville pronounced private vices public virtues; David Hume judged the passions not a threat to morality but its very foundation, and Jeremy Bentham designated personal pleasures the only yardstick of good. Not least, pursuit of profit was legitimated by Adam Smith through an individualist economics which defined 'Consumption' as 'the sole end and purpose of all production'.[86] 'The idea of man as a consuming animal with boundless appetites, capable of driving the economy to new peaks of prosperity arrived with the economic literature of the 1690s', Joyce Appleby tells us. It was a rhetoric which was to root itself in Georgian minds.[87]

If opinion-shapers thus reversed the wisdom of ages by contending that boundless consumption was healthy for society, what impact, if any, did suchlike opinions have upon perceptions of bodily health? Was there a new medical rhetoric – paralleling that of Mandeville, Hume, Bentham and Smith – reassuring people that their consuming passions paved the right royal road to health?[88]

The matter is complex, but the answer, I believe, is precisely the reverse. Doctors judged new consumption patterns a health threat.[89] Not, as I hope to demonstrate, because the new consumer ethos was seen merely as old 'excess' writ large. But rather because consuming drives, arguably responding to the kind of directives being advanced by Cheyne, had degenerated into far more pathological forms. Such developments I shall explore by turning to the critique mounted by Thomas Beddoes, the radical, yet also fashionable, physician, prominent from the late 1780s to his death in 1806, famous for his friendships with Humphry

Davy and the Romantics, and (most germane here) distinguished for his investigations into tuberculosis at the Pneumatic Institution he founded in the Bristol suburb of Clifton.[90]

Georgian doctors were appalled by the advance of chronic diseases, above all, pulmonary tuberculosis. Its symptoms were listed by William Heberden as

> shortness of breath, hoarseness, loss of appetite, wasting of the flesh and strength, pains in the breast, profuse sweats during sleep, spitting of blood and matter, shiverings succeeded by hot fits, with flushings of the face, and burning of the hands and feet, and a pulse constantly above ninety, a swelling of the legs, and an obstruction of the menstrua in women.[91]

It became a veritable 'white plague'.[92] Early in the eighteenth century, one in ten deaths registered by the London Bills of Mortality had been attributed to pulmonary consumption.[93] By its close, the figure was one in four. Tuberculosis was the single largest killer of adults, in Erasmus Darwin's phrase, a 'giant-malady . . . which . . . destroys whole families, and, like war, cuts off the young in their prime, sparing old age and infirmity'.[94]

Why was consumption spreading so catastrophically? For late Georgian doctors, it was not – as Willis, Morton, Bennet, Marten and others had believed a century earlier – because of crass personal indulgence. It was due, rather, to a subtler shift, to what Beddoes called changes 'in almost every circumstance of the manner of living'.[95] As we will see, the factors he isolated are ones central to McKendrick's 'consumer revolution'.

Two cohorts formed its chief victims. On the one hand, parts of the labouring population. Those so poor as to suffer from absolute 'want of food', especially 'pot bellied' youngsters, were desperately susceptible.[96] Hardly less vulnerable, however, were operatives in sedentary, indoor trades, where workshop atmospheres were polluted with irritant fibres, dust and particles: 'carpet-manufacturers, taylors and lace-weavers', 'gilders', 'stone cutters', 'casters of fine brass-work', glovers, painters and (a splendidly Smithian example) 'needle-grinders', to say nothing of spinners and textile hands.[97] All such succumbed not through inherited constitutional weakness, but because of the 'nature of the occupation', with its 'chemical and mechanical irritating substances'.[98] Such workers were thus 'forced into the disease', through their own 'self-neglect' and the 'unconcern' of their masters.[99]

Drawing upon Sir John Sinclair's analyses of Scottish industry, Beddoes singled out further changes imperilling the work-force. Men who abandoned physical hard labour, allured by good money in 'the almost feminine occupations of the cloathing manufacture', became 'frequently consumptive'.[100] Worse still, innumerable working people had been seduced into wearing the new fashionable textiles – 'light cotton dresses, instead of the warmer plaid which was formerly worn'.[101] These new fabrics provided no protection against cold and damp. It is 'not unnatural to suppose that to the modern passion for light, flimsy, airy dress, so prevalent among all ranks', judged Beddoes, 'no small share of the equally common prevalence of colds, fevers, rheumatisms, asthmas, consumptions, is owing'.[102] Thus the producers of the 'consumer revolution' often paid with their health and even their lives.

But the consuming classes were even more consumed by consumption. Here Beddoes arraigned the affluent of pursuing pernicious life-styles, which sacrificed health to the household deities of fashion. Fetishizing belongings and appearances, they neglected well-being. Running after the mode, the rich clad themselves in the 'light dress' which was all the rage in the Revolutionary nineties.[103] To accommodate themselves to this 'injudicious conduct',[104] they resorted to intense domestic heating. But the fug of stuffy rooms merely exacerbated constitutional delicacy; while the inevitable dramatic changes of temperature in moving from room to room, or from indoors to outside lacerated the lungs. It was far better to wrap up in thick woollens, like the Dutch, or to wear flannel.[105]

Frivolous fashions were but the tip of the iceberg. For the modish 'method of education' fostered in polite circles was almost custom-built to turn children into weaklings.[106] Seduced by the new sensibility, parents pushed their infants into study, music and fine accomplishments. Even girls were now packed off to be 'poor prisoners' in draughty boarding schools.[107] Adolescents, 'weak, with excess of sensibility',[108] were then allowed to loaf around on sofas, reading improving literature and 'melting love stories, related in novels'.[109] Diversions designed to 'exercise the sensibility' proved 'highly enervating'.[110] Not surprisingly, thanks to this 'fatal indolence', 'the springs of their constitution have lost their force from disuse'.[111] All such Lydia Languishes live under 'hazard of consumption', triggered by no more than a cold or chlorosis.[112]

Away with these genteel accomplishments born of snobbish aspirations to sensibility, Beddoes begged parents; abandon the itch to turn children into pampered objects of consumption. They needed robust physical exercise. They should pursue 'Botany and gardening abroad, and the use of a lathe, or the study of experimental chemistry at home'.[113]

Beddoes spied a further insidious danger in sedentariness: the solitary vice. Masturbation became the target of Georgian medical writers who exposed it not just as a sin, vice or character weakness, but as ruinous to health, because it allegedly induced wasting conditions. The more semen was conceptualized as a vital fluid, the more its unproductive onanistic waste could be called to account for epidemic adolescent consumptions. A youth who 'was observ'd to Manstrupate very often', shortly 'died of a deep Consumption, having lived till he became like a Ghost, or living Skeleton', reported *Onania*, the most popular of such sensationalist warnings.[114]

Beddoes entirely endorsed such denunciations of masturbation, which he judged the predictable outcome of the absurd mix of pampering and neglect which passed as polite education. Discussing the poetry of the consumptive Keats, Byron once remarked that 'such writing is a sort of mental masturbation, fr–gg—g his Imagination'.[115] Byron's scurrility echoes the mood of Beddoes's exposure of that hot-house over-refinement, which he saw as the seed-bed for consumption.

Worse still, by being associated with modish sensibility, tuberculosis was becoming positively fashionable.

> Writers of romance (whether from ignorance or because it suits the tone of their narrative) exhibit the slow decline of the consumptive, as a state on which the fancy may agreeably repose, and in which not much more misery is felt, than is expressed by a blossom, nipped by untimely frosts.[116]

The preposterous idea had seeded itself that 'consumption must be a flattering complaint', because decline from the 'valetudinary state' was so gradual, initially painless and non-disfiguring. Conferring an intriguing, enticing languor, consumption had become associated with superior imagination, talents and discrimination.

In the process whereby a girl was 'manufactured into a lady',[117] parents positively encouraged delicacy. Because thin was in, such creatures were allowed to become finical eaters. Hoodwinked by pseudo-medical faddery – maybe they even read Cheyne! – many

parents encouraged vegetarianism, convinced it purified the blood and the nerves: 'There are
. . . among the higher classes, some who keep their children to the fifth, or even the seventh
year, upon a strict vegetable and milk diet', revealed the appalled Beddoes, 'believing that
they thus render the constitution a signal service', seduced by the 'false hope of rendering the
blood of their children pure, and their humours mild'.[118]

All such fashionable fastidiousness had to be abandoned. The medievals could serve as
models. These sturdy swain – their giant armour proved their 'Herculean form' – hunted,
fought, hawked and did without 'effeminate' carriages. 'It seems probable, that the general
diet of former centuries was more invigorating', for the 'opulent of both sexes, appear to have
participated rather more largely of animal food',[119] often breakfasting 'upon a fine beef steak
broiled' – excellent for 'resisting cold'.[120] 'It is not, as Addison supposed, among high dishes,
that gout and palsy lurk', the Brunonian Beddoes asserted: far better 'to *use animal food
freely*'.[121]

The potato, he thought, had 'probably contributed to the degradation of the human
species'.[122] By contrast,

> The salutary effect of animal diet in preventing Scrophula is now generally
> known; and the mistakes of those prudent parents who imagined that by confin-
> ing their children to a vegetable diet, they were purifying their blood, while, in
> reality, they were starving them into scrophula, are now generally recognized.[123]

'Consumption' was thus the ailment of the 'puny'.[124] 'Modern usages' had reduced people to
'an ebb of debility',[125] and in the process, 'British fibre' had been sapped. The roast beef of
old England was becoming a thing of the past. It was high time to return to 'animal food'.[126]

Thus the precious life-style of the discriminating left them specially vulnerable: 'it is upon
the lilies of the land, that neither toil nor spin, that the blight of consumption principally
falls.'[127] 'Fixed . . . immoveably upon well-cushioned chairs and sofas, in hot, close apartments', they were too weak to 'receive and digest a proper quantity of aliment'. Far healthier
were labourers who pursued heavy physical exercise, drank with gusto (he denied that
'excess in respect to wine, directly of itself induces consumption, even in the predisposed'),[128]
and above all, were lusty carnivores. 'The persons most free from consumption are precisely
those that consume most animal food.'[129] Who ever saw a consumptive butcher, fishwife or
Jack Tar?

As is obvious, Beddoes's arguments spell a remarkable turnabout from earlier medical
discourse. Late Stuart doctors blamed consumption on excess; Beddoes indicted deficit. It is
intriguing to speculate how far Cheynian arguments against 'high living' had helped induce
the transformation Beddoes supposedly saw and abhorred.

Above all, Beddoes denounced the tendency, particularly amongst parents, to be blasé
about consumption, subscribing to that archetypal consumer society belief that money would
put everything to rights.[130] The foolish idea had grown up that one could buy back health,
by paying for a trip to a spa, the sea-side or the south. Here mercenary doctors were
culpable, for consumption was providing many with a comfortable living. Too many medical
bigwigs prostituted themselves by pandering to the whims of the well, the semi- and pseudo-
sick and valetudinarians, thereby appropriating for themselves the 'lucrative part' of the
'*sick-trade*'.[131] 'Fashionable physicians, from Ascepiades the Bithynian to Warren the Briton',
cashed in on consumptive ladies whose 'comfortless existence renders them in every sense the
best friends of the medical fraternity. . . . To have half a dozen such patronesses has always

been better than to discover a remedy for the most cruel of human diseases.' 'No single cause, perhaps', concludes Beddoes's tirade, 'has so effectually retarded the progress of medicine.'[132]

Bile aside, Beddoes's perception that doctors' services and drugs had become a key consumer item contains substantial truth. The Georgian sick were attending more doctors than ever, and more often, paying them fatter fees, while still consulting quacks and irregulars, and obtaining mountains of medication, stimulants and sedatives, from apothecaries, nostrum-mongering itinerants and druggists.[133] They were also subscribing to a booming health culture, devouring endless books claiming to make every man his own physician, or to be *The Family Physician* (1807), or offering *Physick for Families* (1674); and investing in well-stocked proprietary medicine-chests.[134]

Such developments induced the drug dependency which Beddoes's contemporary, the naval physician Thomas Trotter, diagnosed as a ghastly new evil.[135] High-stress city life weakened the nerves; the constitution then needed the artificial support of drugs and stimulants, in turn creating a downward spiral of deteriorating health.[136] Coffee, tea, tobacco and soda water had first been used as medicines, but had become reduced to 'necessities'. 'Among some well-meaning people, this inordinate desire for medicine has frequently become of itself a disease.'[137] Ironically, Beddoes, while deploring such developments, himself contributed to them, experimenting, with Humphry Davy and Coleridge's circle, with untried narcotics, from nitrous oxide (laughing gas) to opiates, and being partially responsible for the addiction of Tom Wedgwood.[138]

In early, optimistic days, Beddoes felt confident that gases would provide a sure cure for consumption. These failed. He then put his faith in digitalis, or foxglove – perhaps endorsing the old herbal folk cure, recently publicized by William Withering, because it seemed an alternative to standard drugging therapeutics.[139]

Certainly his most touted tuberculosis treatment involved a repudiation of fashionable consumer society, symbolically resonant in a host of ways far too complex to unpack here. This was the 'cow-house method'. Beddoes urged consumptives to live in barns, with cattle for companions, till cured. 'Stabling with cows' is 'not unpromising',[140] Beddoes insisted, while adding, to defend himself against latter-day Swiftians, 'I feel that I am preparing a feast for those who resort to ridicule.'[141]

The philosophy of the cow-house was two-fold. The beasts themselves, and, above all, their stercoraceous ferment, would yield regular, steady warmth, twenty-four hours a day, the best mode of central heating alive. Moreover, the volatile alkali simultaneously exuded would help purify the lungs. Thus, waste products would prove not wasteful at all, but triumphantly integral to the economy of health, in a manner that would surely have given joy not just to Dr Pangloss but to that great Victorian sanitarian campaigner for recycling excrement, Edwin Chadwick.[142]

Beddoes devoted much of his *Observations on the Consumptive* to evaluating this treatment which he had 'long been in the habit of recommending',[143] even though, he confided, 'not unfrequently did I forfeit the good opinion of my patient'.[144] It had enjoyed signal success. He thus presents the 'narrative of Madame —' who, predictably had gadded around as a bright young thing, 'continuing to go out, to keep late hours, and in *every thing* to live in a manner too agitated for [her] state of health', until her consumption worsened, when she opted for the cow-house treatment. So strong was the vapour 'that every thing white which was brought in, became reddish in a very short time', and, worse, she had to endure idling gawpers who 'came to see me as an object of curiosity'. Nevertheless, she recovered.[145] So too did Mrs Finch, none other than Joseph Priestley's daughter, who, in a letter datelined 'Cow-House, *Oct* 8', explains that 'she has found a cow-house a much more comfortable abode than she had formed an idea of', though the stench was 'nauseous' and 'successive gener-ations of flies were a considerable nuisance': 'I am', she concluded, 'more than ever a friend to the cows.'[146]

Consultations were not always so smooth, however, for certain patients 'spoke of the *disgrace* of being in such a situation', a 'fellow-lodger with the cows'.[147] A scaled-down alternative to being physically 'closeted in a cow-house' was, however, available.[148] For, Beddoes explained, 'Vessels containing the fermentable substances could easily be intro-duced into a warm apartment.'[149]

Beddoes anatomized this 'giant-malady' as the product of an economy and a life-style, as a disease of civilization. 'Consumption may be regarded' – and here we return to my opening quotation, now contextualized –

> as a vast pit-fall, situated on the high road of life, which we have not sense enough of our common interest to agree to fill up, or fence round. Heedless fathers and mothers are for ever guiding their sons and daughters directly into it.[150]

Proceeding 'from domestic mismanagement, and not from the inalterable dispositions of nature', it was preventable.[151] The mentality of 'opulent families' must seem 'paradoxical' indeed, to those convinced that 'health is the first of blessings'.[152]

In this age of self-made men, people made their own illnesses: 'our chronic maladies', judged Beddoes, 'are of our own creating.' Obsession with objects and indifference to health multiplied the 'tribute of lives we render to consumption'; for the desire 'of dazzling strangers by the splendour of an equipage or by the lights of the understanding' was 'so prevalent'. And the remedy? 'We must all learn not to bear to have every thing about us – cloaths, tables, chairs, pictures, statues – all exquisite in their kind – except our progeny.'[153]

This chapter has principally been exploratory. It has drawn attention to ways in which models of society and economy traded upon key images: of system, balance, cycles and circulation. Thinking about the human body likewise predicated notions of exchange, trans-formation, process, getting and spending, work and waste. Both involved conceptions of normality and pathology, health and sickness. And both interacted so sympathetically – through language, metaphor and analogy – that one may rarely be able to pin down strictly documentable 'influence'.

I have tried to avoid making too much of the pun on 'consumption'. Yet, provoked by the very obvious rise in wasting diseases in an increasingly commercial society, people were forced to reflect upon the resonances between the active verb 'consuming' – an act of incorporation – and the intransitive 'consuming' or being 'consumed' – the condition of wasting. Consuming was always producing waste. The traditional world – the world of the humours, of Christian asceticism, of the rural, bucolic economy – saw the disease of con-sumption as a disease of excess; whereas for Beddoes, the evil of consumerism was a sort of fetishism of culture, in which the body had been forgotten in the name of fashionable goals.

We must not think of the consumer society simply in terms of the licence to acquire more. It was, perhaps more crucially, the development of new values which helped people to transcend that very licence to acquire more.[154]

Notes

1 T. Beddoes, *Hygeia*, 3 vols (Bristol: Phillips, 1802–3), vol. 2, 100–1.

2 For the organic understanding of society, see W. J. Greenleaf, *Order, Empiricism and Politics* (London: Oxford University Press, 1964); L. Barkan, *Nature's Work of Art: the Human Body as Image of the World* (New Haven: Yale University Press, 1975); J. B. Bambrough, *The Little World of Man* (London: Longman, Green & Co., 1952); E. Tillyard, *The Elizabethan World Picture* (London: Chatto & Windus, 1943); J. Broadbent, 'The image of God or two yards of skin', in J. Benthall and T. Polhemus (eds), *The Body as a Medium of Expression* (London: Allen Lane, 1975), 305–26; F. Barker, *The Tremulous Private Body* (London: Methuen, 1984); and, more conceptually, B. Barnes and S. Shapin (eds), *Natural Order: Historical Studies of Scientific Culture* (London: Sage, 1979); A. Marcovich, 'Concerning the continuity between image of society and the image of the human of the human body: an examination of the work of the English physician J. C. Lettsom (1746–1815)', in P. Wright and A. Treacher (eds), *The Problem of Medical Knowledge* (Edinburgh: Edinburgh University Press, 1982), 69–87.

3 On early modern economic theory, see Joyce Appleby, 'Ideology and theory: the tension between political and economic liberalism in seventeenth century England', *American Historical Review*, lxxxi (1976), 499–515; idem, *Economic Thought in Seventeenth-Century England* (Princeton: Princeton University Press, 1978); Albert O. Hirschman, *The Passions and the Interests: Political Arguments for Capitalism before its Triumph* (Princeton: Princeton University Press, 1977).

4 For attacks on luxury see J. Sekora, *Luxury: The Concept in Western Thought, Eden to Smollett* (Baltimore and London: Johns Hopkins University Press, 1977); J. G. A. Pocock, *Virtue, Commerce and History: Essays on Political Thought and History* (Cambridge: Cambridge University Press, 1985). Dennis is quoted by Neil McKendrick in 'The consumer revolution of eighteenth-century England', in N. McKendrick, J. Brewer and J. H. Plumb, *The Birth of a Consumer Society: The Commercialization of Eighteenth Century England* (London: Europa, 1982), 19.

5 See W. Sombart, *Luxury and Capitalism* (Ann Arbor: University of Michigan Press, 1967); Thorstein Veblen, *The Theory of the Leisure Class* (New York: Macmillan, 1912); Lawrence Stone, *The Crisis of the Aristocracy 1558–1641* (London: Oxford University Press, 1965) has an excellent discussion of Elizabethan and Stuart conspicuous consumption.

6 For early attitudes towards consumption see Joyce Appleby, 'Ideology and theory', 499–515; W. Letwin, *The Origins of Scientific Economics* (London: Methuen, 1963); A. O. Hirschman, *The Passions and the Interests: Political Arguments for Capitalism before its Triumph* (Princeton: Princeton University Press, 1977).

7 For background culture about the status of the body see F. Bottomley, *Attitudes to the Body in Western Christendom* (London: Lepus Books, 1979); J. Benthall and T. Polhemus (eds), *The Body as a Medium of Expression* (London: Allen Lane, 1975); M. Bernard, *Le Corps* (Paris: Editions Universitaires, 1974); J. O'Neill, *Five Bodies: The Human Shape of Modern Society* (Ithaca: Cornell University Press, 1985); J. -P. Peter and J. Revel, 'Le corps: l'homme malade et son histoire', in J. Le Goff and P. Nora (eds), *Faire de l'histoire*, vol. 3 (Paris: Gallimard, 1974), 169–91; R. Cooter, 'The power of the body: the early nineteenth century', in B. Barnes and S. Shapin (eds), *Natural Order: Historical Studies of Scientific Culture* (London and Beverly Hills: Sage, 1979), 73–92; Roy Porter, 'History of the body', in P. Burke (ed.), *Perspectives on Historical Writing* (Cambridge: Polity Press, 1991), 206–32.

8 For traditional medical concepts of the body system, vitality, disease, decay, ageing and dying see

L. M. Beier, *Sufferers and Healers: The Experience of Illness in Seventeenth-Century England* (London: Routledge & Kegan Paul, 1987); O. Temkin, *Galenism: Rise and Decline of Medical Philosophy* (Ithaca: Cornell University Press, 1973); idem, 'Health and disease', *Dictionary of the History of Ideas*, ii (1973), 395–407. Important for the view of life as a flame are G. Rees, *Francis Bacon's Natural Philosophy: A New Source* (Chalfont St Giles: British Society for the History of Science, 1984), and P. Niebyl, 'Old age, fever, and the lamp metaphor', *Journal for the History of Medicine*, xxvi (1971), 351–68.

9 The culture of eating, drinking and 'digestion' are admirably discussed in Francis McKee, 'The earlier works of Bernard Mandeville, 1685–1715' (University of Glasgow, Ph.D. thesis, 1991).

10 On dearth see A. Appleby, 'Nutrition and disease: the case of London, 1550–1750', *Journal of Interdisciplinary History*, vi (1975), 1–22; idem, *Famine in Tudor and Stuart England* (Stanford: Stanford University Press, 1978).

11 Generally see P. Stallybrass and A. White, *The Politics and Poetics of Transgression* (Ithaca: Cornell University Press, 1986); S. Mennell, *All Manner of Foods* (Oxford: Basil Blackwell, 1985); Mikhail M. Bakhtin, *Rabelais and his World*, tr. H. Iswolsky (Cambridge, Mass.: MIT Press, 1968); T. Dunford, 'Consumption of the world: reading, eating and imitation in "Every man out of his humour" ', *English Literary Renaissance*, xiv (1984), 131–47.

12 For food fantasies see P. Camporesi, *Bread of Dreams: Food and Fantasy in Early Modern Europe* (Cambridge: Polity Press, 1988); idem, *The Incorruptible Flesh: Bodily Mutation and Mortification in Religion and Folklore* (Cambridge: Cambridge University Press, 1988); and, more broadly, Robert Darnton, *The Great Cat Massacre and Other Episodes in French Cultural History* (New York: Basic Books, 1984).

13 Peter Clark, *The English Alehouse: A Social History, 1200–1830* (London: Longman, 1983); Roy Porter, 'The drinking man's disease: the prehistory of alcoholism in Georgian Britain', *British Journal of Addiction*, lxxx (1985), 384–96; John Brewer, 'Commercialization and politics', in McKendrick, Brewer and Plumb, *Birth of a Consumer Society*, 197–264.

14 On diets, see D. J. Oddy, *The Making of the Modern British Diet* (London: Croom Helm, 1976); idem, *Diet and Health in Modern Britain* (London: Croom Helm, 1985); S. Mintz, *Sweetness and Power* (New York: Viking, 1985); P. Pullar, *Consuming Passions: Being an Historic Inquiry into Certain English Appetites* (London: Hamish Hamilton, 1970); B. S. Turner, 'The government of the body: medical regimens and the rationalization of diet', *British Journal of Sociology*, xxxiii (1982), 254–69; idem, 'The discourse of diet', *Theory, Culture and Society*, i (1982), 23–32.

15 For instances, see Roy Porter and Dorothy Porter, *In Sickness and in Health: The British Experience, 1650–1850* (London: Fourth Estate, 1988), 47–9, 160–1.

16 J. Boswell, *The Life of Samuel Johnson*, 2 vols (London: J. M. Dent, 1946), vol. 1, 241; M. P. Tilley (ed.), *Dictionary of Proverbs in England* (Ann Arbor: University of Michigan Press, 1950).

17 C. C. Hankin (ed.), *The Life of Mary Anne Schimmelpenninck*, 2 vols (London: Longman, 1858), vol. 1, 241. For Darwin's consuming passions, see D. King-Hele, *Doctor of Revolution: The Life and Genius of Erasmus Darwin* (London: Faber, 1977); idem (ed.), *The Letters of Erasmus Darwin* (Cambridge: Cambridge University Press, 1981).

18 G. Miller (ed.), *Letters of Edward Jenner* (Baltimore: Johns Hopkins University Press, 1983), 7; cf. R. Squirrell, *Maxims of Health or an Abridgement of an Essay on Indigestion* (London: Murray & Highley, 1798); J. Arbuthnot, *An Essay Concerning the Nature of Aliments* (London: J. & R. Tonson, 1731).

19 For spirits and blood see Valerie Grosvenor Myer, 'Tristram and the animal spirits', in idem (ed.), *Laurence Sterne: Riddles and Mysteries* (London: Vision Press, 1984); M. M. Wintrobe, *Blood, Pure and Eloquent. A Story of Discovery of People, and of Ideas* (New York: McGraw-Hill Book Company, 1980).

20 Mennell, *All Manner of Foods*, 182f.

21 J. Beresford (ed.), *The Diary of a Country Parson: the Rev. James Woodforde, 1758–1802*, 5 vols (reprinted Oxford: Oxford University Press, 1978–81), vol. 4, 213. See also N. C. Hultin, 'Medicine and

magic in the eighteenth century: the diaries of James Woodforde', *Journal of the History of Medicine and Allied Sciences*, xxx (1975), 349–66.

22 Beresford (ed.), *Diary of a Country Parson*, vol. 5, 412.

23 E. S. De Beer (ed.), *The Correspondence of John Locke*, 8 vols (Oxford, Clarendon Press, 1976–81), vol. 1, 341.

24 J. D. Marshall (ed.), *The Autobiography of William Stout of Lancaster 1665–1752* (Manchester: Chetham Society Publications, 3rd series, 1967), vol. 4, 91.

25 P. Shaw, *The Juice of the Grape; Or Wine Preferable to Water: A Treatise Wherein Wine is Shewn to be a Grand Preserver of Health* (London: Lewis, 1724); see also Porter, 'Drinking man's disease' for alcohol, medicine and the doctors.

26 Beresford (ed.), *Diary of a Country Parson*, vol. 3, 174, 274.

27 ibid., vol. 2, 217.

28 See Beier, *Sufferers and Healers*, 133f.; Dorothy Porter and Roy Porter, *Patient's Progress: The Doctors and Doctoring in Eighteenth Century England* (Cambridge: Polity Press, 1989), ch. 3; W. Buchan, *Domestic Medicine or a Treatise on the Prevention and Cure of Diseases by Regimen and Simple Medicines* (Edinburgh: Balyou, Auld & Smellie, 1769), 151.

29 M. H. Nicolson (ed.), *The Conway Letters* (New Haven: Yale University Press, 1930), 266.

30 E. W. Marrs, Jr (ed.), *Letters of Charles and Mary Lamb*, 3 vols (Ithaca: Cornell University Press, 1975–8), vol. 2, 155.

31 Anon., *Hell Upon Earth or the Town in an Uproar* (London: Roberts & Dodd, 1729), 28.

32 J. L. Clifford (ed.), *Dr. Campbell's Diary of a Visit to England in 1775* (Cambridge: Cambridge University Press, 1947), 43.

33 Beresford (ed.), *Diary of a Country Parson*, vol. 2, 258.

34 W. Branch Johnson (ed.), *Carrington Diary, 1797–1810* (London: Christopher Johnson, 1956), 171.

35 ibid., 174–6.

36 For his antipathy to strong drink see E. Darwin, *The Temple of Nature or the Origin of Society: A Poem with Philosophical Notes* (London: J. Johnson, 1803), Canto IV, lines 77–84. See also Porter, 'Drinking man's disease'.

37 B. Cozens-Hardy (ed.), *The Diary of Sylas Neville 1767–1788* (London, New York and Toronto: Oxford University Press, 1950), 226.

38 R. Steele, *Tatler*, 24 October 1710; S. Richardson, *Familiar Letters on Important Occasions*, ed. B. W. Downs (London: Routledge, 1928; 1st edn, 1741), 41. Parson Woodforde thus recorded the death of Milly Chiche: 'she was good to everyone, but herself, and I am afraid that drinking was her death': Beresford (ed.), *Diary of a Country Parson*, vol. 1, 40. The Nonconformist Oliver Heywood took great delight in recording how all the drunkards he knew fell sick and died. J. H. Turner (ed.), *The Rev. Oliver Heywood. B. A., 1630–1702: His Autobiographical Diaries, Anecdote and Event Books*, 4 vols (Brighouse and Bingley: T. Harrison, 1881–5), vol. 2, 281, etc.

39 A. Ponsonby (ed.), *More English Diaries* (London: Methuen & Co, 1927), 180–1.

40 G. Cheyne, *An Essay of Health and Long Life*, 8th edn (London: Strahan and Leake, 1734; 1st edn, 1724), 54.

41 For Cheyne's life, see 'The case of the author', in G. Cheyne, *The English Malady; or, A Treatise of Nervous Diseases* (London: G. Strahan, 1733; reprinted, London: Routledge, 1991), 326–64. For modern accounts, see H. R. Viets, 'George Cheyne, 1673–1743', *Bulletin of the Institute for the History of Medicine*, xxiii (1949), 435–52; W. A. Greenhill, *Life of George Cheyne, M.D., with Extracts from his Works and Correspondence* (Oxford: J. H. Parker, 1846); T. McCrae, 'George Cheyne, an old London and Bath physician (1671–1743)', *Johns Hopkins Hospital Bulletin*, xv (1904), 84–94; W. R. Riddell, 'Dr George Cheyne and the "English Malady" ', *Annals of Medical History*, iv (1922), 404–10; R. S. Siddall, 'George Cheyne M.D., eighteenth century clinician and medical author', *Annals of Medical History*, iv (1942), 95–109.

42 Cheyne, *The English Malady*, 326.

43 ibid.

44 ibid.

45 G. S. Rousseau, 'Mysticism and millennialism: "Immortal Dr Cheyne" ', in R. H. Popkin (ed.), *Millenarianism and Messianism in English Literature and Thought 1650–1800* (Leiden: E. J. Brill, 1988), 81–126.

46 Cheyne, *The English Malady*, 342.

47 ibid., 347.

48 ibid., 349.

49 Quoted in Roy Porter and Dorothy Porter, *In Sickness and in Health*, 144.

50 Turner (ed.), *The Rev. Oliver Heywood*, vol. 2, 248.

51 Gideon Harvey, *Morbus Anglicus, or a Theoretick and Practical Discourse of Consumptions and Hypochondriack Melancholy* (London: Thackeray, 1672), 4, 8, 22 and *passim*; see also idem, *The Disease of London, or a New Discovery of the Scorvey* (London: Thackeray, 1675). On scurvy, see K. Carpenter, *The History of Scurvy and Vitamin C* (Cambridge: Cambridge University Press, 1986). Quack doctors in particular made much of it. See Roy Porter, *Health for Sale* (Manchester: Manchester University Press, 1989), ch. 5.

52 Benjamin Marten, *A New Theory of Consumptions, More Especially of a Phthisis, or Consumption of the Lungs* (London: Knaplock, 1720), 10. For historical epidemiology, see M. J. Dobson, 'Population, disease and mortality in southeast England, 1600–1800' (University of Oxford, D.Phil. thesis, 1982); idem, *A Chronology of Epidemic Disease and Mortality in Southeast England, 1601–1800*, Historical Geography Research Series, 19 (London: Historical Geography Research Group, 1987); idem, *From Old England to New England: Changing Patterns of Mortality* (University of Oxford, School of Geography Research Paper 38, 1987); L. Stevenson, ' "New diseases" in the seventeenth century', *Bulletin of the History of Medicine*, xxxix (1965), 1–21.

53 Cheyne, *The English Malady*, 15. Cheyne included wasting disease under his rubric of the 'English malady'.

54 It is important for us in our post-bacteriological age not to assume that a single, fixed, specific 'ontological' disease was meant by the word 'consumption', its synonym, 'phthisick' – or indeed by most other diagnostic labels. Diseases were rather *sui generis*, marking states and symptoms, not things. Tobias Smollett spent his last years in a decline, suffering with his lungs. But, though a professional physician as well as a writer, it is far from clear that he thought of himself as being the victim of one specific disease, 'consumption'. He rather used a variety of 'symptomatic' terms, such as 'asthma' and 'catarrh'. Above all, he acknowledged that his 'constitution' was broken, partly because so many other complaints kept breaking out, such as skin rashes, which he suspected were 'scurvy', i.e., further marks of constitutional decay. L. M. Knapp, *Tobias Smollett: Doctor of Men and Manners* (Princeton: Princeton University Press, 1949), 245ff. Asthma is a term whose meaning has undergone profound changes: see J. Gabbay, 'Asthma attacked? Tactics for the reconstruction of a disease concept', in P. Wright and A. Treacher (eds), *The Problem of Medical Knowledge* (Edinburgh: Edinburgh University Press, 1982), 23–48.

55 Harvey, *Disease of London*, 11. Harvey noted that smoke produced 'vitiated choler': 33. Thomas Sydenham attributed the high incidence of consumption in London to the fact that 'we live here in a perpetual mist': S. L. Cummins, *Tuberculosis in History from the 17th Century to our own Times* (London: Bailliere, Tindall & Cox, 1949), 26; Richard Morton laid much blame on 'a foggy and thick air and that which is filled with the smoke of coals': see *Phthisiologia, or a Treatise of Consumptions, Wherein The Difference, Nature, Causes, Signs and Cure of all Sorts of Consumptions are Explained* (London: Smith & Walford, 1694), quoted in L. F. Flick, *Development of our Knowledge of Tuberculosis* (Philadelphia: the author, 1925), 100. On Morton, see R. Y. Keers, 'Richard Morton (1637–98) and his "Physiologia" ', *Thorax*, xxxvii (1982), 26–31; R. R. Trail, 'Richard Morton (1637–98)', *Medical History*, xiv (1970), 166–74.

56 For Willis, see Cummins, *Tuberculosis in History*, 16.

57 For Morton, see Flick, *Development of our Knowledge of Tuberculosis*, 99, 155.
58 Marten, *New Theory of Consumptions*, 22, 36.
59 Christopher Bennet, *Theatrum Tabidorum, or the Nature and Cure of Consumptions, whether A Phthisick an Atrophy or an Hectick* (London: W. & J. Inny, 1720), 19.
60 Bennet, *Theatrum Tabidorum*, 33–5.
61 See Flick, *Development of our Knowledge of Tuberculosis*, 134.
62 See ibid., 99. See also Bennet, *Theatrum Tabidorum*, 20.
63 Buchan, *Domestic Medicine*, 219–20.
64 Bennet, *Theatrum Tabidorum*, 24.
65 Flick, *Development of our Knowledge of Tuberculosis*, 129.
66 Bennet, *Theatrum Tabidorum*, 22. Consumptions were widely treated by depletive methods through the eighteenth century. When Arthur Young's daughter, 'Bobbin', was failing with consumption, she was subjected to such 'lowering' treatments. Young believed that her physician, Dr John Turton, 'purged and physicked her until she was little more than skin and bone'. The dying Bobbin's letters to her father, complaining of the endless medicines being poured down her throat, make pathetic reading:

> My dear Papa, – I received your letter yesterday. Thank you for your advice; I had taken the *steel* and *draughts* long before I received it, besides which I take some more stuff . . . and ask him likewise how long the steel, etc. must be taken before you feel any effect from it, for one might take physic for ever without receiving any benefit.
> (J. G. Gazley, *The Life of Arthur Young* (Philadelphia: American Philosophical Society, 1973), 365–7)

67 Buchan, *Domestic Medicine*, 218. For the impact of the atmosphere see J. Arbuthnot, *An Essay Concerning the Effects of Air on Human Bodies* (London, J. & R. Tonson & S. Draper, 1733).
68 For Cheyne, see the sources cited in note 41, above.
69 Roy Porter, 'The rage of party: a glorious revolution in English psychiatry?' *Medical History*, xxviii (1983), 35–50; O. Doughty, 'The English malady of the eighteenth century', *Review of English Studies*, ii (1929), 257–69; C. A. Moore, 'The English Malady', in *Backgrounds of English Literature 1700–1760* (Minneapolis: University of Minnesota Press, 1953), 179–235; J. F. Sena, 'The English Malady: the idea of melancholy from 1700 to 1760' (Princeton University, Ph.D. thesis, 1967).
70 Cheyne, *The English Malady*, 174, 49. Such views were often echoed. Robert Campbell claimed, in a global conjectural history of the interplay of civilization, sickness and the medical profession, that:

> In the first Ages of the World, Mankind subsisted without this Species of Men [i.e., doctors]. Their Diseases were few, and Nature taught them the Use of Simples, to assist her when in Extremity: Temperence, Sobriety, and moderate Exercise, supplied the Place of Physicians to the Patriarchal Age, and every Field spontaneously furnished them with Restoratives more potent than are to be found in all our modern Dispensatories, or most celebrated Apothecaries Shops; but as Vice and Immorality gained Ground, as Luxury and Laziness prevailed, and Men became Slaves to their own Appetites, new Affections grew up in their depraved Natures, new Diseases, and till then unheard of Distempers, both chronick and acute, assaulted their vitiated Blood, and baffled the Force of their former natural Catholicons.

Slowly but inexorably all had changed:

> Then Physicians became necessary; Nature grew weak, and sunk under the Load of various Evils, with which Vice, Lust, and Intemperance had loaded her; her Faculties became numbed, the Frame of the Human Constitution was shaken, and her Natural

Powers debilitated: The Stamina Vitae, the first Principles of Life, were infected, and the whole Mass of Fluids contaminated with the deadly poison: This produced new Phaenomena, uncommon Symptoms, and expiring Nature must be helped by Art to recover her lost Tone, and restore her to her former Functions. The most sagacious observed the Struggles of fainting Nature, guessed the Causes by the outward Symptoms, and administered to her Relief with such Remedies as were most likely to effect a Cure by removing the Cause of the Malady.

(See R. Campbell, *The London Tradesman* (Newton Abbot: David & Charles, 1969; 1st edn 1747), 37)

71 Cheyne, *The English Malady*, 174.

72 ibid., 174.

73 See above, note 41.

74 There is a lively, sociologically oriented, discussion of Cheyne's dietary ideas in B. S. Turner, *The Body and Society: Explorations in Social Theory* (Oxford and New York: Basil Blackwell, 1984), 77f., 169f.

75 Cheyne, *The English Malady*, vii.

76 N. Crook and D. Guiton, *Shelley's Venomed Melody* (Cambridge: Cambridge University Press, 1986); G. Smith, 'Thomas Tryon's regimen for women: sectarian health in the seventeenth century', in London Feminist History Group (eds), *The Sexual Dynamics of History* (London: Pluto Press, 1983), 47–65; idem, 'Prescribing the rules of health: self-help and advice in the late eighteenth century', in Roy Porter (ed.), *Patients and Practitioners: Lay Perceptions of Medicine in Pre-industrial Society* (Cambridge and New York: Cambridge University Press, 1985), 249–82.

77 Cheyne, *Essay of Health and Long Life*, 2. Cheyne's other works offer similar advice. See Cheyne, *An Essay on Regimen* (London: C. Rivington, 1740); idem, *The Natural Method of Cureing* (London: G. Strahan, 1742); idem, *The Method of Cureing Diseases of the Body and the Disorders of the Mind* (London: G. Strahan, 1742).

78 Cheyne, *Essay of Health and Long Life*, 2.

79 F. Childs, 'Prescriptions and manners in English courtesy literature, 1690–1760, and their social implications' (University of Oxford, D.Phil. thesis, 1984); Norbert Elias, *The Civilizing Process*: vol. 1, *The History of Manners*; vol. 2, *Power and Civility*; vol. 3, *The Court Society* (New York: Pantheon, 1978, 1982 and 1984 respectively).

80 Extremely perceptive is G. S. Rousseau, 'Mysticism and millennialism: "Immortal Dr Cheyne" ', in R. H. Popkin (ed.), *Millenarianism and Messianism*, 81–126. Rousseau perfectly captures Cheyne's quest for spirituality; I am less sure that Cheyne is helpfully called a 'millennialist'.

81 For nerves, see G. S. Rousseau, 'Nerves, spirits and fibres: towards defining the origins of sensibility; with a Postscript', *The Blue Guitar*, ii (1976), 125–53; idem, 'Science and the discovery of the imagination in Enlightenment England', *Eighteenth-Century Studies*, iii (1969–70), 108–35; idem, 'Psychology', in G. S. Rousseau and Roy Porter (eds), *The Ferment of Knowledge* (Cambridge: Cambridge University Press, 1980), 143–210; J. Spillane, *The Doctrine of the Nerves* (London: Oxford University Press, 1981); C. J. Lawrence, 'The nervous system and society in the Scottish Enlightenment' in B. Barnes and S. Shapin (eds), *Natural Order: Historical Studies of Scientific Culture* (London: Sage, 1979), 19–40; idem, 'Medicine as culture: Edinburgh and the Scottish Enlightenment' (University of London, Ph.D. thesis, 1984); R. French, *Robert Whytt, the Soul and Medicine* (London: Wellcome Institute for the History of Medicine, 1969).

82 Cheyne, *The English Malady*, 14. In a very Cheynesque way Marten noted that 'Consumptive People are . . . generally observ'd to be very quick, full of Spirit, hasty, and of a sharp, ready Wit'. Though he denied that only 'ingenious Men' were seized, 'it is certain that we do not often met with dull heavy Persons, or such as are slow of Speech, afflicted with this Disease': Marten, *New Theory of Consumptions*, 5.

83 Neil McKendrick, 'The birth of a consumer society: the commercialization of eighteenth-century

England', in McKendrick, Brewer and Plumb, *Birth of a Consumer Society*, vii. For some evidence see Maxine Berg, *The Age of Manufactures, 1700–1820* (London: Fontana, 1985); Lorna Weatherill, *Consumer Behaviour and Material Culture, 1660–1760* (London: Routledge, 1988); idem, 'Consumer behavior and social status in England', *Continuity and Change*, ii (1986), 191–216; idem, 'A possession of one's own: women and consumer behaviour in England, 1660–1740', *Journal of British Studies*, xxv (1986), 131–56; D. E. C. Eversley, 'The home market and economic growth in England 1750–1800', in E. L. Jones and C. E. Mingay (eds), *Land, Labour and Population in the Industrial Revolution* (London: Edward Arnold, 1967), 206–59; E. L. Jones, 'The fashion manipulators: consumer tastes and British industries, 1660–1800', in L. P. Cain and P. J. Uselding (eds), *Business Enterprise and Economic Change* (Kent State, Ohio: Kent State University Press, 1973), 198–226.

84 Roy Porter, 'The Enlightenment in England', in Roy Porter and Mikuláš Teich (eds), *The Enlightenment in National Context* (Cambridge: Cambridge University Press, 1981), 1–18; J. Redwood, *Reason, Ridicule and Religion* (London: Thames & Hudson, 1976).

85 Quoted by Neil McKendrick, 'The birth of a consumer society', 15.

86 For the new importance of consumption in liberal political economy see E. Halévy, *The Growth of Philosophical Radicalism* (London: Faber & Faber, 1924).

87 Appleby, 'Ideology and theory', 509.

88 Highly suggestive is P. Gay, 'The Enlightenment as medicine and as cure', in W. H. Barber (ed.), *The Age of the Enlightenment: Studies Presented to Theodore Besterman* (Edinburgh: St Andrews University Publications, 1967), 375–86. See more broadly his *The Enlightenment: An Interpretation*, 2 vols (New York: Knopf, 1967–9). For discussion see Roy Porter, 'Was there a medical Enlightenment in eighteenth-century England?', *British Journal for Eighteenth-Century Studies*, v (1982), 46–63.

89 An important factor here, arguably, was professional self-interest and identity. As professionals, doctors increasingly, especially in the nineteenth century, aimed to set themselves over and against mere 'trade'. See I. Waddington, *The Medical Profession in the Industrial Revolution* (Dublin: Gill & Macmillan, 1985).

90 For Beddoes, see D. A. Stansfield, *Thomas Beddoes M. D. 1760–1808, Chemist, Physician, Democrat* (Dordrecht: Reidel, 1984); M. R. Neve, 'Natural philosophy, medicine and the culture of science in provincial England' (University College London, Ph.D. thesis, 1984) which is particularly good on his Bristol connections; M. S. Jacobs, 'Thomas Beddoes and his contribution to tuberculosis', *Bulletin of the History of Medicine*, iii (1943), 300–12.

91 W. Heberden, *Medical Commentaries* (London: T. Payne, 1802), 371.

92 For histories of tuberculosis, see note 55, above and René Dubos and Jean Dubos, *The White Plague: Tuberculosis, Man and Society* (London: Gollancz, 1953); L. Bryder, *Below the Magic Mountain: A Social History of Tuberculosis in Twentieth-Century Britain* (Oxford: Clarendon Press, 1988); F. B. Smith, *The Retreat of Tuberculosis 1850–1950* (London: Croom Helm, 1988); L. S. King, 'Consumption: the story of a disease', in *Medical Thinking: A Historical Preface* (Princeton: Princeton University Press, 1982), 16–69; R. Y. Keers, *Pulmonary Tuberculosis: A Journey Down the Centuries* (London: Bailliere, Tindall, 1978); H. D. Chalke, 'Some historical aspects of tuberculosis', *Public Health*, lxxiv (1959), 83–95; R. M. Burke, *A Historical Chronology of Tuberculosis* (Springfield, Ill.: Thomas, 1955); G. N. Meachen, *A Short History of Tuberculosis* (London: Bale, 1936); W. Pagel, 'Humoral pathology: a lingering anachronism in the history of tuberculosis', *Bulletin of the History of Medicine*, xxix (1955), 299–308; E. R. Long, 'Tuberculosis in modern society', *Bulletin of the History of Medicine*, xxvii (1953), 301–19; G. A. M. Milkomane, *The Conquest of Tuberculosis* (London: Macdonald, 1946); P. J. Bishop, 'Blackmore on consumption', *Tubercle*, xxxix (1958), 118–21; idem, 'Thomas Young and his "Practical and historical treatise on consumptive disorders"', *Tubercle*, liv (1973), 159–64; Isabelle Grellet and Caroline Kruse, *Histoires de la tuberculose: les fièvres de l'âme, 1800–1940* (Paris: Editions Ramsay, 1983).

93 Buchan, *Domestic Medicine*, 218.

94 Darwin's phrase is to be found in T. Beddoes, *Letter to Erasmus Darwin, M. D., on a New Method of Treating Pulmonary Consumption and Some other Diseases Hitherto Found Incurable* (Bristol: Bulgin & Rosser, 1793), 61.

95 T. Beddoes, *Essay on the Causes, Early Signs, and Prevention of Pulmonary Consumption for the Use of Parents and Preceptors* (Bristol: Biggs & Cottle, 1799), 11.

96 ibid., 178–9.

97 ibid., 62–4; cf. T. Beddoes, *Hygeia*, 3 vols (Bristol: Phillips, 1802–3), vol. 2, 32–3.

98 Beddoes, *Hygeia*, vol. 2, 24–5.

99 ibid.

100 Beddoes, *Essay on . . . Consumption*, 85. Beddoes is quoting Sir John Sinclair.

101 ibid., 87–8.

102 ibid., 89.

103 ibid., 80. On flimsy fashions, see E. Ewing, *Dress and Undress: A History of Women's Underwear* (London: Batsford, 1978).

104 Beddoes, *Essay on . . . Consumption*, 80. Many other commentators argued that the new thin fashions were unhealthy. 'The doctors tell me', wrote Lady Sarah Napier in 1794, 'that the new fashion of being so thinly clothed in our damp climates checks nature by degrees . . . they perceive a great increase of complaints on the breast amongst young women': B. Fitzgerald, *Correspondence of Emily, Duchess of Leinster*, 3 vols (Dublin: Irish Manuscripts Commission, 1949–57), vol. 2, 350–1. 'Formerly youth was seldom ill', Lybbe Powys remarked in 1805, 'now, from thin clothing and late hours, you hardly see a young lady in good health, or not complaining of rheumatism, as much as us old ones!': E. J. Climenson (ed.), *Passages from the Diary of Mrs Philip Lybbe Powys, 1756–1808* (London: Longmans & Co., 1899), 357.

105 'Flannel should be worn': Beddoes, *Essay on . . . Consumption*, 128–9. Beddoes also recommended the use of 'a tin *foot-warmer*', 'manufactured of a convenient form, by Lloyd, near Norfolk Street, Strand, London': ibid., 132–3.

106 ibid., 90. For aspirant, new, middle-class life-styles, see L. Davidoff and C. Hall, *Family Fortunes: Men and Women of the English Middle Classes* (London: Hutchinson, 1987); L. Stone, *The Family, Sex and Marriage in England 1500–1800* (London: Weidenfeld & Nicolson, 1977); R. Trumbach, *The Rise of the Egalitarian Family* (London and New York, Academic Press, 1978); Peter Earle, *The Making of the English Middle Class: Business, Society and Family Life in London, 1660–1730* (London: Methuen, 1989).

107 Beddoes, *Essay on . . . Consumption*, 121. In *Hygeia*, vol. 2, 11f., Beddoes gave the life history of a consumptive young woman, Louisa, in her own words. She had been brought up by parents who avoided gross frivolity and who had been concerned to give her a good modern education: 'the graver part of light reading was our amusement and the lighter parts of science our study.' All the same, vanity was the 'ruling principle' – a vanity 'of loftier pretensions and a more solemn aspect'. 'Health was never a constant, and seldom an occasional concern.' Often, because the family had other preoccupations, she had suffered from 'too long fasting', and was often 'uncomfortable from chill'.

108 Beddoes, *Essay on . . . Consumption*, 219.

109 ibid., 190.

110 ibid., 121.

111 ibid., 190.

112 ibid., 124.

113 T. Beddoes, *Observations on the Medical and Domestic Management of the Consumptive; on the Powers of Digiralis Purpurea; and on the Cure of Scrophula* (London: Longman & Rees, 1801), 185. Cf. K. Figlio, 'Chlorosis and chronic disease in nineteenth-century Britain: the social constitution of somatic illness in a capitalist society', *Social History*, iii (1978), 167–97; I. S. L. Loudon, 'Chlorosis, anaemia and anorexia nervosa', *British Medical Journal*, ii (1980), 1669–87.

114 *Onania; or, the Heinous Sin of Self-Pollution, and All Its Frightful Consequences*, 15th edn (London: J.

Isted, 1730), Supplement, 22. Many other instances of the supposed link between onanism and consumption were chronicled in the book. A letter to the author from 'An Afflicted Onan' (9 June 1722), who claimed to have been masturbating for three months, confessed, 'I am afraid it has brought me into a Consumption, for I am very thin, and I spit up a great deal of hard Stuff' (49). See also *Supplement*, 142. The anonymous author of *Onania* deplored the fashion for late marriage, since, by consequence, young ladies 'give themselves up to Plays, Balls, Mens Company, wanton Discourse, high living and the like, whereby the humours are heated, and the Desire augmented'. They ended up 'easing themselves', thereby causing 'Cachexies, Hysterick Fits, the Green Sickness, or other Maladies not presently to be Remedied' (79).

Various historians have suggested that medical opinion deplored masturbation on the grounds that it represented 'spending' of a kind improper in a capitalist, thrift-oriented ideology. See F. Gosling, *Before Freud: Neurasthenia and the American Medical Community 1870–1910* (Urbana: University of Illinois Press, 1987); F. J. Barker-Benfield, *The Horrors of the Half-Known Life* (New York: Harper & Row, 1976). These precise connotations do not seem present in Beddoes. He certainly regarded masturbation, however, as a dangerous and unproductive waste of vital fluid and vital energy. For discussion of eighteenth-century onanism see P.-G. Boucé, 'Les Jeux interdits de l'imaginaire: onanism et culpabilisation sexuelle au XVIIIe siècle', in J. Céard (ed.), *La Folie et le corps* (Paris: Presses de l'Ecole Normale Supérieure, 1985), 223–43; E. H. Hare, 'Masturbatory insanity: the history of an idea', *Journal of Mental Science*, cviii (1962), 1–25; R. H. MacDonald, 'The frightful consequences of onanism', *Journal of the History of Ideas*, xxviii (1967), 423–41; J. Stengers and A. Van Neck, *Histoire d'une grande peur: la masturbation* (Brussels: University of Brussels Press, 1984). For Tissot, see S.-A.-A.-D. Tissot, *Onanism or a Treatise Upon the Disorders Produced by Masturbation*, tr. A. Hume (London: no publisher, 1766), 20, 70. Tissot noted that with frequent masturbation, 'Our bodies suffer a continual waste, and if we could not repair this waste, we should soon sink into a state of mortal weakness' (1). Cf. L. J. Jordanova, 'The popularisation of medicine: Tissot on onanism', *Textual Practice*, i (1987), 68–80.

115 Byron: Letter to John Murray, 9.10.1820, in Peter Gunn (ed.), *Byron: Selected Prose* (Harmondsworth: Penguin, 1972), 357; cf. D. C. Goellnicht, *The Poet-Physician, Keats and Medical Science* (Pittsburgh: University of Pittsburgh Press, 1984); Sir W. Hale-White, *Keats as Doctor and Patient* (London: Oxford University Press, 1936).

116 Beddoes, *Essay on . . . Consumption*, 6.

117 ibid., 119.

118 ibid., 114. Beddoes cites the case of a 14-year-old girl who 'had little appetite for animal food, always preferring bread, vegetables and fruit': Beddoes, *Hygeia*, vol. 2, 14. Valetudinarianism and food fads were often linked. When Jane Austen wanted to mock valetudinarianism, she showed Mr Woodhouse picking over his food ('an egg boiled very soft is not unwholesome'): Jane Austen, *Emma*, ed. R. Blythe (Harmondsworth: Penguin, 1966), 54. For the wider sensibilities of 'anorexia', see R. M. Bell, *Holy Anorexia* (Chicago: University of Chicago Press, 1985); J. J. Brumberg, *Fasting Girls: The Emergence of Anorexia Nervosa as a Modern Disease* (Cambridge, Mass.: Harvard University Press, 1988); Hillel Schwartz, *Never Satisfied: A Cultural History of Diets, Fantasies and Fat* (New York: Free Press, 1986).

119 Beddoes, *Essay on . . . Consumption*, 162, 167.

120 ibid., 156.

121 ibid., 116. On Beddoes's Brunonianism, see Roy Porter (ed.), *Brunonianism in Britain and Europe*, *Medical History*, Supplement 8 (London: Professional and Scientific Publications, 1989).

122 Beddoes, *Essay on . . . Consumption*, 166.

123 ibid., 166.

124 ibid., 171.

125 ibid., 175, 176, 108.

126 Beddoes, *Hygeia*, vol. 2, 43. See also Beddoes, *Essay on . . . Consumption*, 127:

To me these females have appeared to exist in a constant valetudinary state; dissolved by heat; pinched by cold; harrassed by sleeplessness on going to bed; unrefreshed by their tardy morning nap; faint when empty; oppressed when full; and in the intermediate time suffering under some of the other plagues of indigestion.

127 Beddoes, *Hygeia*, vol. 2, 43, 44, 68.
128 Beddoes, *Essay on . . . Consumption*, 125
129 ibid., 112, 103. Beddoes reported hearing from Dr William Withering that butchers also kept themselves healthy by inhaling the steam of newly slaughtered carcases.
130 Beddoes, *Hygeia*, vol. 2, 89.
131 Beddoes, *Essay on . . . Consumption*, 260.
132 ibid., 127.
133 See the discussion in Dorothy Porter and Roy Porter, *Patient's Progress* (Cambridge: Polity Press, 1989), chs 7–9; for quack medicines, see also Roy Porter, *Health for Sale*.
134 As illustrations of this genre see *The Family Companion for Health* (London: F. Fayram & Leake, 1729); *The Family Guide to Health* (London: J. Fletcher, 1767). See also Roy Porter, 'The patient in England, c. 1660–c. 1800', in A. Wear (ed.), *Medicine in Society* (Cambridge: Cambridge University Press, 1992), 91–118.
135 See Roy Porter, 'Introduction' to Thomas Trotter, *An Essay on Drunkenness*, ed. idem (London: Routledge, 1988; 1st edn, 1804).
136 For discussion see Roy Porter and Dorothy Porter, *In Sickness and in Health*, ch. 12.
137 Thomas Trotter, *A View of the Nervous Temperament* (London: Longman, Hurst, Rees & Owen, 1807), 105.
138 R. B. Litchfield, *Tom Wedgwood, 1771–1805* (London: Duckworth & Co., 1903).
139 Beddoes, *Essay on . . . Consumption*, 55, 264. On foxglove see J. K. Aronson, *An Account of the Foxglove & its Medicinal Uses, 1785–1985* (London: Oxford University Press, 1985).
140 Beddoes, *Observations on the . . . Consumptive*, 22. Beddoes's cow-cure raises issues regarding the juxtaposition of man and beast, and the transgression of their proper 'separate spheres', in a culture increasingly sensitive about man's unique status (highly relevant is the fate of Gulliver, finally returned to England). At almost the same time, Jenner's cowpox 'vaccine' raised profound popular fears. For a broad background see K. V. Thomas, *Man and the Natural World* (Harmondsworth: Penguin, 1984); P. Stallybrass and A. White, *The Politics and Poetics of Transgression* (Ithaca: Cornell University Press, 1986) contains a fascinating discussion of the pig as an intruder into human culture.
141 Beddoes, *Observations on the . . . Consumptive*, 22.
142 S. E. Finer, *The Life and Times of Sir Edwin Chadwick* (London: Methuen, 1952).
143 Beddoes, *Observations on the . . . Consumptive*, 23.
144 ibid.
145 ibid., 28–34.
146 ibid., 50.
147 ibid., 66.
148 ibid., 85.
149 ibid., 86. Beddoes prints a letter from Dr John Barr, Mrs Finch's physician, stating that 'it gives me the sincerest pleasure that the cow-house has so completely suspended the progress' of her disorder (44). Beddoes notes that he had offered Mrs Finch the choice between going on a sea voyage and '(what might appear a very extravagant proposal) constant residence with cows'. Like a good patient, she had deferred the decision to himself. 'I told her, undoubtedly, residence with cows' (48). In a similar way, he had urged a consumptive man 'to try the cow-house, rather than return to Portugal' (48).
150 Beddoes, *Hygeia*, vol. 2, 100–1. For this idea, see B. Inglis, *The Diseases of Civilisation* (London:

Hodder & Stoughton, 1981).
151 Beddoes, *Essay on . . . Consumption*, 120.
152 ibid.
153 Beddoes, *Hygeia*, vol. 2, 98.
154 Grant McCracken, *Culture and Consumption: New Approaches to the Symbolic Character of Consumer Goods and Activities* (Bloomington: Indiana University Press, 1988).

Part II
Goods and consumption

5

Between purchasing power and the world of goods: understanding the household economy in early modern Europe

Jan de Vries

A jibe frequently directed at demographers is that they succeed in turning sex and death into dull subjects. It can now be said of cultural historians that they seek to make the study of commodities fun, liberating the material world of production and consumption from the dead positivist hand of the economic historian. The economist's confining terminology of budget constraints, elasticities of demand and marginal utility is to be superseded by a symbolic and representational vocabulary whereby commodities reveal fantasies, fetishes, masochistic longings, power urges and internalized oppression. Where the terminology of the economist is designed to remind us of that threadbare cliché 'there is no such thing as a free lunch', that of the cultural historian invites us to frolic in the pleasure garden of consumption, where the will of the consumer can triumph over scarcity and the will of the historian can triumph over 'the laws of economics'.

Under circumstances such as these it may not be possible to establish a real dialogue among the varied parties interested in the history of consumption. My aim, therefore, is to construct a 'common house', furnished with discussions of theory, evidence and methodology (sections I and II) and equipped with a new conceptual framework of the household economy (section III) that may someday allow the lion and the lamb to lie together, speaking amicably of demand curves and desire, of tastes and budget constraints.

I Supply and demand

To the social and cultural historian the economists' great fault, in a word, is the privileging of production: making supply the blade of the supply and demand scissors that does all the cutting. If consumption simply shadows production, its explanatory power must be confined to matters of secondary importance; hence, what Neil McKendrick calls the 'shameful' neglect by economic historians of a consumer revolution.[1]

For this neglect we can blame Jean Baptiste Say. This French economist and disciple of Adam Smith demonstrated to the satisfaction of classical economists that 'supply creates its own demand'. Production, in Mark Blaug's words, 'not only increases the supply of goods but, by virtue of the requisite cost payments to the factors of production, also creates the demand to purchase these goods'. Or, as Say put it, 'Products are paid for by products.'[2]

The acts of production that create commodities depend on various combinations of the factors of production – land, labour and capital. These productive factors must be compensated – by rent, wages and profits, respectively – and these payments are received by the owners and sellers of the productive factors. The individuals and households that receive these payments do not spend it all on consumption. Their 'marginal propensity to consume' will determine which portion is saved – for investment in future production growth – and which is retained as disposable personal income. (In addition, the state takes a portion as tax revenue.) The disposable personal income (and that portion of government revenue not used for public investment) should suffice to buy the output that generated these income flows to begin with.

There are, of course, circumstances in which this circular flow of the economic system is disrupted, especially in the short run. John Maynard Keynes focused attention on the depressing effects of a strong demand for money, and a correspondingly low propensity to consume. He demonstrated that in a market economy demand could fall short of supply and force the factors of production into involuntary idleness, but the phenomenon of under-consumption can hardly be a comfort to proponents of demand-led growth. Another departure from Say's Law involves a nation able to borrow from abroad to finance, via imports, a level of domestic demand in excess of domestic production. Neither of these deviations can endure long enough to sustain demand-led growth, or explain a revolution in consumer behaviour.

In the face of this intellectual legacy, where could advocates of demand-initiated growth processes find refuge? In the first instance, abroad. The early modern European economy and, especially, eighteenth-century Britain, were long held to have benefited from the capture of inter-continental markets. Windfall profits and monopolized colonial markets were thought by Marxist historians to breathe life into a fledgling European capitalism. Especially influential has been the 'General Crisis' theory of Eric Hobsbawm, who doubted the possibility of internal demand growth and believed that after 1650 in northwestern Europe 'forced draughts [of foreign demand] fanned the entrepreneurs' cupidity to the point of spontaneous combustion'.[3]

Economists also turned to foreign markets to help explain the phenomenal growth of industrial production in eighteenth-century Britain. Phyllis Deane and W. A. Cole, in *British Economic Growth 1688–1959* emphasized both the strategic role of exports (to specific industries, such as cotton textiles) and its impact on the overall growth of industrial production. By their reckoning home consumption of industrial products tripled over the course of the eighteenth century while industrial exports increased more than sixfold. Correspondingly, the exported share of industrial output rose from one-fifth around 1700 to one-third around 1800.[4]

Since Deane and Cole wrote, new estimates of population growth and industrial production have altered the data with which they worked, and W. A. Cole, in a retrospective on his earlier work, steps back from any strong claims for export-led growth. It is now not obvious that foreign demand grew more rapidly than domestic.

More damaging still is the knowledge that most foreign demand was colonial, and that colonial demand depended largely on the British market's ability to purchase colonial products. To the extent that British mercantilism (codified in the Navigation Acts) fashioned colonial trade into a closed circuit with the home market, the 'forced draughts' are revealed to be the product of a domestic bellow.[5]

The foreign demand arguments obviously can give little comfort to advocates of a consumer revolution. They speak rather to the limitations of domestic markets. A second approach to reviving demand as a factor in economic growth was the identification of changes in the *pattern* of demand that were propitious for the growth of what in retrospect we see as key economic sectors. These arguments do not deny that purchasing power must come from production, but emphasize the importance of the distribution of income among social classes. Social classes vary in their propensity to consume, and specifically in their propensity to consume industrial products. Moreover, changes in relative prices can divert purchasing power from one sector to another.

The most influential work of this genre – articles by A. H. John, D. Eversley and E. L. Jones – emphasized the demand-side impact of the growth of agricultural productivity in England in the century 1650–1750.[6] In this period agricultural prices fell relative to industrial prices. The shift in the terms of trade in favour of industry increased the market for industrial goods in two ways. Townspeople enjoyed lower food prices and, hence, a larger disposable income available for the purchase of industrial goods. Farmers, on the other hand, enjoyed higher productivity which cushioned the depressing effect of falling prices on earnings. A 'middle class' consumer possessed more financial scope to acquire relative luxuries in the golden years of the early eighteenth century. The agricultural revolution, by this argument, helped shape the pattern of demand in a way that encouraged the production of goods for the 'middling sort'.

This benign trend in relative prices was not extreme, and was reversed forcefully after 1750 (see Figure 5.1). All trends then pointed towards a fall in purchasing power and a diversion of expenditure towards the agricultural sector and, specifically, towards the rental income of great landlords. After 1750 the demand-led growth advocate had to find new arguments.[7] Here it must suffice to note the conclusion of the exhaustive analysis of demand-led growth arguments undertaken by Joel Mokyr in 'Demand and supply in the Industrial Revolution'. 'The . . . notion that supply and demand were somehow symmetric in the industrialization is unfounded. The determination of "when," "where," and "how fast" are to be sought first and foremost in supply, not demand-related processes.'[8]

Mokyr's conclusion left little scope for misunderstanding, but it did not still the voices advocating an autonomous role for demand in the pre-industrial economy. The third, and final effort to 'save the phenomenon' throws all caution to the wind and proclaims a new historical 'revolution'. 'There was a consumer revolution in eighteenth-century England.' So reads the opening sentence of *The Birth of a Consumer Society*, penned by one of that volume's co-editors, Neil McKendrick. He goes on to identify this consumer revolution as 'the necessary analogue to the industrial revolution, the necessary convulsion on the demand side of the equation to match the convulsion on the supply side'.[9]

The choice of the words 'analogue' and 'match', and the pairing of a consumer revolution with the Industrial Revolution seem designed to side-step the issue of an autonomous, active role for consumer demand. Elsewhere he argues that changes in attitude and thought were required to unleash the consumer society, and that new commercial techniques and promotional skills were required, presumably, to speed those attitudinal changes.[10] But, a passage

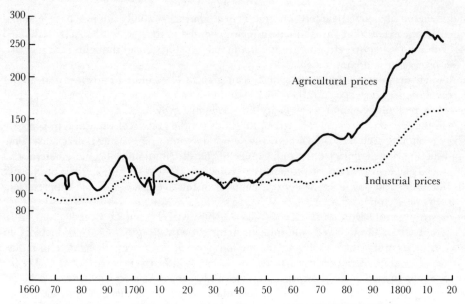

Figure 5.1a Indices of agricultural and industrial prices 1660–1820, smoothed by nine-year moving averages

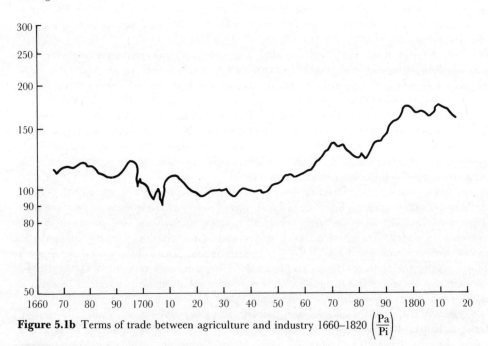

Figure 5.1b Terms of trade between agriculture and industry 1660–1820 $\left(\dfrac{Pa}{Pi}\right)$

Source (for both figures) Patrick O'Brien, 'Agriculture and the home market for English industry, 1660–1820', *English Historical Review*, c (1985), 776.

can also be found where he appears to backtrack, denying 'that the *desire* to consume was an eighteenth-century novelty. It was the *ability* to do so which was new.'[11]

The viability of an eighteenth-century 'consumer revolution' seems to depend on a studied vagueness in definitional statements and a careful removal of most of the concept from the economic to the cultural sphere: desire, attitude, fashion and emulation furnish the vocabulary of this discourse.

II The standard of living and material culture

The argument between economists and social and cultural historians discussed above exists quite independently of any particular historical evidence. But it is intensified by the fundamentally different messages conveyed by the two chief types of documentary evidence available for the historical study of consumption. Depending on the sources he consults, the scholar's gaze is cast either over a sombre scene of limited purchasing power and painful budget constraints or he views an ever-multiplying world of goods, a richly varied and complex material culture.

Evidence from the markets

A major goal of two generations of economic historians has been to chart the long-term course of prices and wages and to compute indexes of real wages. As we shall see, serious methodological problems adhere to these quantitative exercises, but the many real wage indexes that price historians have constructed for various types of labour throughout western and central Europe present a remarkably uniform portrait of the historical course of the purchasing power of labour.[12] The most remarkable of all these time series, and the most frequently cited, was constructed by E. H. Phelps Brown and Sheila Hopkins in 1955. Their time series of daily wage rates for southern English construction labour spanned seven centuries, from 1264 to 1954. They then constructed a cost-of-living index for the same period. Many calculations before and since have simply let the price of wheat stand for the cost of living, supposing that bread so dominated the consumer expenditure of manual labourers that the difficulty of further refinement would not repay the effort. Phelps Brown and Hopkins drew on the rich price histories compiled by Thorold Rogers and William (later Lord) Beveridge to construct a 'basket of consumables' in which four major food groups plus non-food items for fuel, lighting and clothing found representation.

Once they had constructed the two time series it was a simple matter to divide the wage series by the cost of the basket of consumables to arrive at an index of the real wage (see Figure 5.2). Its chief findings, confirmed by many other studies, are a 'golden age of labour' in the post-Black Death fifteenth century followed by a disastrous 'long sixteenth century'. By the early seventeenth century the price inflation had so far outstripped the rise of wages as to reduce labour's purchasing power to less than half of its fifteenth-century level. A combination of periodic wage hikes and gently falling prices gradually restored some – but by no means all – of the fifteenth-century real wage. But this recovery was cut short by 1750, when an accelerating inflation swamped further wage increases. Only the restoration of peace after 1815 brought a new era of real wage recovery which, of course, eventually broke through all previous ceilings.

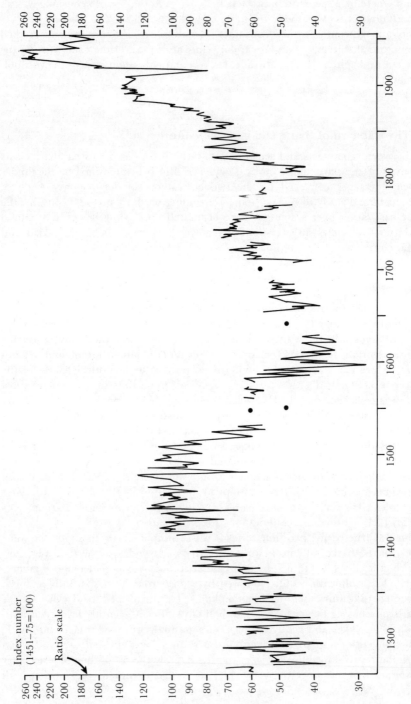

Figure 5.2 Changes in the equivalent of the wage rate of a building craftsman expressed in a composite physical unit of consumables in southern England 1264–1954

Source E. H. Phelps Brown and Sheila Hopkins, 'Seven centuries of the prices of consumables compared with builders' wage-rates', *Economica*, xxiv (1956), 296–314.

This pattern of real wage movements has been shown to stand in an inverse relationship to the course of European population change up to the beginning of the nineteenth century, so that the movements of prices, wages and population appear to form an interlocking Malthusian complex.[13] E. LeRoy Ladurie drew from such data as these the conclusion that French and European society between the fourteenth and eighteenth centuries was immobilized by unyielding technological and biological constraints: 'a peasant population during the course of twelve or thirteen generations, was busy reproducing itself within the limits of certain finite possibilities whose constraints proved inexorable.'[14]

Real wage calculations made for various European locations do not all share precisely the same *rates* of deterioration and improvement. But they do share the same general *timing* and the same direction of *trend*. The reason is not far to seek: nominal wages of the types of labour typically investigated, construction labour, change only infrequently. The stickiness of wages contrasts sharply with the volatility of prices, particularly the food prices that dominate all pre-industrial price indexes. Moreover, the bread grains on which these indexes rely were sufficiently broadly traded to impart a measure of uniformity to almost all time series. The special circumstances of a particular region could change the details but not the broad trends and turning points of the real wage index.[15]

One major exception to these generalizations should be noted. In the later sixteenth and seventeenth centuries, the Low Countries, and especially the Dutch Republic, avoided much of the real wage deterioration suffered by the rest of Europe.[16] A strong demand for labour and productivity improvements pushed wages up sufficiently at least to keep pace with the price inflation. Consequently, while English real wages fell to a historical low point in the forty years after 1580, Dutch labour enjoyed increased purchasing power, regaining much of the ground lost earlier in the sixteenth century. As Figure 5.3 demonstrates, the gap that opened between Dutch and English real wages in the period 1580–1620 was not fully closed until the last decades of the eighteenth century.

This unique case of real wage exceptionality could occur because of the singular concentration of trade and production in 'Golden Age' Holland. Who can doubt that it helps explain the remarkable texture of seventeenth-century Dutch material culture? Yet, all the favourable economic forces at work in the Republic did not succeed in propelling Dutch real wages to a new, demonstrably higher level than had prevailed in the fifteenth and early sixteenth centuries. Had the Dutch escaped from the iron cage that held all of Europe captive, or did they simply occupy a privileged position within it?

Urban and rural wage earners in Holland enjoyed what appear to have been the highest nominal wages (when currencies are compared by market exchange rates or intrinsic silver equivalence) in Europe from around 1600 to some time after 1750. Then London craftsmen caught up with the Dutch standard, and by the end of the century so had wage earners in many other parts of England. Yet, to judge from Phelps Brown and Hopkins, none of this could prevent a sharp fall in real wages during the central decades of the Industrial Revolution.

For obvious reasons, great interest attaches to the standard of living during the Industrial Revolution, and research of much greater sophistication than that of Phelps Brown and Hopkins exists to illuminate the course of real wages. The deep commitment of most participants in these investigations to either the 'optimist' or 'pessimist' camp makes broad generalization very difficult, a difficulty reinforced by the considerable variety of local and sectoral experience uncovered by detailed study. T. S. Ashton long ago argued

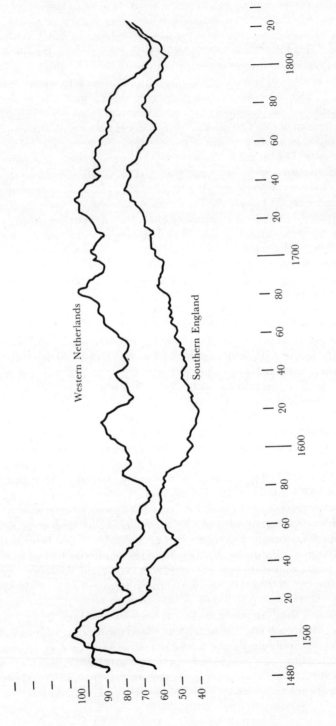

Figure 5.3 Real wages of construction labour in southern England and the western Netherlands 1480–1820, smoothed by thirteen-year moving averages (1451–75=100)

that some groups (those in 'traditional' sectors) lost ground while others (those in the revolutionized sectors) were more likely to have gained higher wages and steadier employment during the Industrial Revolution.[17] Since the latter group represented the future, and felt the impact of the Industrial Revolution, Ashton was an 'optimist', and his view has received strong support in recent investigations. For example, a study of North Staffordshire found the miners and potters there experiencing rising real wages over the period 1750–94, while general labourers and building craftsmen no more than held their own. At the same time, London craftsmen and southern English farm labourers certainly experienced a sharp fall in real wages.[18]

The most telling 'pessimist' criticism focused not so much on the details of calculating real wages as on the assessment of the satisfaction given by the housing, food and drink that could be purchased with those wages. E. P. Thompson offers the classic statement:

> Over the period 1790–1840 there was a slight improvement in average material standards. . . . By 1840 most people were 'better off' than their forerunners had been fifty years before, but they had suffered and continue to suffer this slight improvement as a catastrophic experience.[19]

To the 'pessimists', this was a perverse consumer revolution, and one important reason given for a diminished satisfaction with incomes that they concede may have risen is a growth in the inequality of income distribution.[20]

The most comprehensive study of real English earnings and income distribution, by Lindert and Williamson, reveals a substantial divergence in the fortunes of unskilled, skilled and 'white-collar' workers (see Figure 5.4). The favoured white-collar workers experienced a fourfold increase in real earnings in the century after 1750 while farm labourers advanced by only 50 per cent. Figure 5.4 also reveals that all of this growth in both real income and inequality began with the restoration of peace after 1815. Until then real wages neither rose nor fell by much for any group.[21]

The quantitative investigations of English society conducted by the celebrated 'political arithmetician' Gregory King in 1688 provide estimates of income by occupational and social categories that can serve as the basis for measurements of inequality in the distribution of income. Later efforts to take the measure of English society – by Joseph Massie in 1759, Patrick Colquhoun in 1801 and Dudley Baxter in 1863 – make it possible to track income inequality and measure change over time. Lindert and Williamson's heroic efforts to reduce each of these studies to a consistent form yield results that are as fascinating as they are debatable.[22] England's income distribution becomes much more unequal between 1688 and 1867, they found, but most of the growth in inequality occurred after 1801. Most surprising – and most uncertain – is the finding that the growing inequality occurred because of growth in the income share of the richest 10 per cent (from 42 to 53 per cent of all income) and the stability in the income share of the poorest 40 per cent (about 15 per cent of income). The intermediate 50 per cent, that 'middling sort' one would look to as the vanguard of a consumer revolution, saw its income share fall from 43 per cent in Gregory King's day to 40 or 41 per cent in 1759 and 1801, and finally to 33 per cent in 1867.

The ambiguities of English real wage data and the substantial methodological problems that adhere to all such calculations, to which we shall turn presently, have encouraged a search for alternative quantitative measurements of well-being. From the standard of living

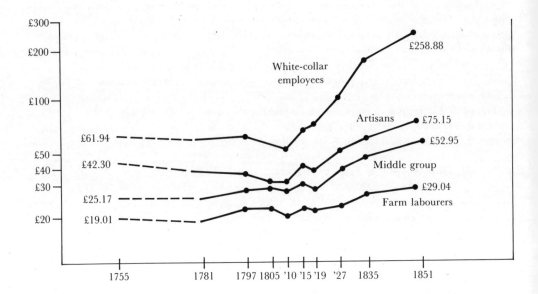

Figure 5.4 Adult male average full-time earnings for selected groups of workers, 1755–1851, at constant prices

Source P. H. Lindert and J. G. Williamson, 'English workers' living standards during the Industrial Revolution: a new look', *Economic History Review*, 2nd series, xxxvi (1983), 12.

attention shifts to the standard of life, as economic historians seek to measure life expectancy, morbidity, nutrition and stature. The average height attained by young adults – when they are measured, typically for military service – appears to reflect a complex of factors strongly related to material well-being.

The height attained by British recruits at age 20 stood at 64.5 inches in 1770 (for those born in 1750). Attained height rose in the next two decades, but then fell. Recruits born in 1790 and raised during the Napoleonic Wars, had fallen back almost to 65 inches. The postwar era saw another advance, but this too was undone, so that recruits born in 1840 were, on average, barely taller than their forerunners born in 1750.[23] These findings do little to strengthen the optimist case, although they do put Britain in the company of Continental countries such as Sweden, Denmark and Hungary, where consequential gains in height occurred only after the mid-nineteenth century.[24]

The best way to summarize recent research on the standard-of-living question is by observing that the question is drifting away from that of the optimist and pessimist – was the Industrial Revolution a 'good thing'? – to a new focus: did the Industrial Revolution occur? Lindert and Williamson concluded that the pessimists only had a case up to 1820, after which real wages rose for all types of labour. This can now be interpreted to mean not that workers until then were denied the fruits of the Industrial Revolution, but that there were few fruits to be denied to the workers. This is not to deny the structural changes afoot or their impact on specific categories of the labour force. My focus here is on the aggregate effect of these dramatic, but localized shocks. It took more time than had previously been thought for them to shape the overall rate of economic growth.

A recent article by Mokyr (unintentionally) makes the same point. He exploits per capita consumption data for tea, coffee, sugar and tobacco to estimate the overall standard of living.[25] Since per capita consumption of three of these commodities barely increases between 1790 and 1840, he concludes that there still may be life in the pessimist case. But since consumption rose rapidly after 1840, and chapters in this volume testify to the rapid growth of per capita consumption of those commodities in the century preceding 1750,[26] the important implications are surely that economic growth began *earlier* than previously thought, that the transforming power of industry was felt *later* than previously thought, and that the century of the Industrial Revolution witnessed no sharp acceleration – not in production, not in consumption.

The European real wage literature identifies a massive erosion of purchasing power for wage earners in the 'long sixteenth century', which the most favoured economy of that era, the Netherlands, was able to resist, but not overcome. It identifies another era of real wage deterioration beginning after 1750 where, once again, the most favoured economy, Britain, was able to limit the damage, but not to achieve uncontroverted material improvement until at least 1820, or perhaps, 1840. Indeed, the single most comprehensive study of this subject, Fernand Braudel and Frank Spooner's contribution to the authoritative *Cambridge Economic History of Europe*, is considerably less nuanced: 'From the late fifteenth century until well into the beginning of the eighteenth century, the standard of living in Europe progressively declined.'[27]

Should we believe these findings? The real wage index is a statistical construction that gives a very precise answer to a very specific question: relative to earlier and/or later periods how much of a specified bundle of goods can be purchased with the daily wage of a particular grade of labour?

Under certain conditions, the answer to this question will approximate a valid answer to the broader question that interests us: what happened to the standard of living of the bulk of the population? But the conditions are exacting, and it would be folly simply to assume that these are fulfilled. To begin with, the index uses a worker's daily wage rate, but it is household earnings, over the course of a full year, that we would prefer to know. The two could, of course, vary in a multitude of ways (more about this below).

Second, wage quotations are most abundant for construction labour and unskilled outdoor labour. The comparability of such occupations over time and across space is a further encouragement to their use. But, the representativeness of such labour for the many other occupations remains an open question. The North Staffordshire study cited above found a substantial divergence between construction labourers and industrial workers, while Lindert and Williamson identified a systematic difference in the post-1820 compensation of different grades of labour.[28]

Their category of 'white-collar employees', who received salaries rather than wages, did especially well after 1820. The same can be said for Dutch salaried employees (such as teachers, clergymen, municipal and institutional employees) in the period 1650 to 1790. In this period, when nominal wages barely changed in Holland, salaried employees experienced, on average, a 33 per cent increase in pay.[29]

Just as the numerator of the real wage index is likely to fall short of being fully representative of household earnings, so the denominator commonly fails to answer to the requirements of a true index of consumer prices. A valid consumer price index (CPI) is an average of the prices of a broad range of items of consumer expenditure, the average being weighted by the importance of each item in the typical consumer's total budget. The index commonly includes expenditures on commodities (such as food, fuel and manufactured products), services, housing and taxes.

Historical approximations of a CPI almost always radically simplify this procedure. In fact, many simplify the CPI to one item – grain, usually wheat.[30] This is justified by the belief that bread was easily the single most important item in most budgets. The more sophisticated early modern price indexes are weighted averages of food and non-food commodity prices. Phelps Brown and Hopkins (for England) and Van der Wee (for Brabant) weigh food at about 80 per cent of total expenditures while fuel takes up nearly half of what remains. This leaves only 10 per cent for all other expenditures, that is, for nearly all the types of purchases that might interest the historian of consumer culture.[31] A further limitation of these and other indexes is their exclusion of non-consumables, such as housing, taxes and services. Years ago T. S. Ashton criticized real wage calculations based on the wholesale price index of N. J. Silberling, by puzzling over the idiosyncratic spending habits of 'Silberling Man', the creature that stood for the representative wage earner in many British real wage studies:

> He did not occupy a house, or at least was not called upon to pay rent. He allowed himself only a moderate amount of bread and very little porridge, and he never touched potatoes or strong drink. On the other hand, he got through quite considerable quantities of beef and mutton and showed a fondness for butter. Perhaps he was a diabetic. The ordinary Englishman of the eighteenth century would have been puzzled by him.[32]

The overwhelming, if not exclusive, emphasis on a few foodstuffs that characterizes the price indexes has two causes. The first is the assumption that food expenditures must have absorbed nearly all of most peoples' budgets. The simple fact that a wage earner's daily pay often could provide little more than a quantity of bread sufficient for the caloric requirements of the 'breadwinner's' household seemed sufficiently compelling to many historians to obviate the need for direct evidence of consumer behaviour. This belief proved convenient because direct evidence of household budgets is exceedingly rare before the mid-nineteenth century.[33]

Besides this lack of budget evidence to guide in assigning weights to consumer prices, there are also shortcomings to the price evidence itself. The many data collections commissioned by the International Price History Commission offer a wealth of price data. But usable time series exist for a surprisingly small number of budget items. The item of consumption must be both widely traded and homogeneous across time and space in order to be taken up in an index. A large number of commodities do not meet this test. Rental housing, for example, is widely traded, but it is not homogeneous. Housing differs from place to place, and the same house may acquire very different qualities with the passage of time. Potatoes, on the other hand, are reasonably homogeneous, but in the eighteenth century they were not widely traded, being produced mainly for home use. Moreover, their great bulk relative to price prevented potatoes from being transported any great distance, which hindered the integration of potato markets.

None of the shortcomings of the available price time series and weights used to form the index would be of much concern if all prices moved in harmony with each other. Then the few available prices would be representative of all other prices, and neither the absence of commodities nor mis-specification of the weights would alter the final outcome. But this is not the case. Moreover, it becomes less the case the more rapid is economic growth and the more we are concerned with changes in consumer behaviour.

Most commodity prices follow a common long-term inflationary or deflationary trend, but each commodity differs in its rate of increase or decrease, and in its short-term variability. The studies of Abel and Slicher van Bath demonstrated how the prices of bread grains were the most volatile, while livestock products generally followed a more muted course.[34] But foodstuffs in general rose and fell much more than the prices of industrial goods, as Figure 5.1 amply demonstrates. Once again, *within* the group of industrial goods, specific changes in production or in markets could generate sharp divergences in price trends.

When the price of each commodity has its own distinct destiny the weighting of a price index is crucial to the outcome. Since we know that the bread grains rise more rapidly than other commodities in inflationary periods (and falls more in periods of deflation) indexes that overweight bread grain (or rely on them exclusively) are destined to distort real wage calculations, overestimating the erosion of real wages as prices rise and overestimating the rise of real wages as prices fall.[35]

These tendencies for real wage calculations alternately to overshoot and undershoot would seem to cancel each other out. In the *very* long run, estimated trends in consumer purchasing power should remain valid. This, too, is definitely not the case. Systematic bias is inherent in the act of constructing a price index, and this bias grows with the span of time covered by the index.

Consider the Phelps Brown and Hopkins real wage index displayed in Figure 5.2. It shows that the purchasing power of builders did not regain its mid-fifteenth-century level until 1880. This certainly represents an underestimate of 1880 purchasing power, and the fault can be ascribed to the price index. Once the commodities and weights to be used in a price index are chosen, the price index will tend to overestimate price increases in later years, and the longer the index runs, the larger the exaggeration of prices becomes. The reason for this is that the consumption mix is constrained to remain the same while relative price changes induce consumers to make substitutions, consuming less of the relatively expensive goods and more of the cheaper. Such changes in demand patterns induced by changes in relative prices (as distinct from changes in tastes) help account for the substitution of potatoes for bread, cotton cloth for linen and tea for beer in the late eighteenth century. Consumers *whose incomes and tastes have not changed* alter the mix of goods they buy – buying more of the goods whose prices are falling – in order thereby to maximize the utility they derive from their expenditures in the face of changes in relative prices.

A price index with weights set at an initial date will overstate price increases since no substitutions are allowed, and also because new goods and improvements in the quality of existing goods must be ignored.

One could, of course, use weights that reflect the consumption pattern at the end of the period under investigation and, literally, construct the price index backwards. Economists call this a Paasche price index, while the more common base-period weighted index is called the Laspeyre price index.[36] The Paasche index has the opposite structural bias as the Laspeyre, understating price increases (since goods whose prices had experienced relative decline are more heavily weighted in the Paasche index). One might regard the use of both indexes as desirable in order to establish upper and lower bounds to the cost-of-living index,[37] but it is precisely in periods of major structural changes in an economy that prices will diverge the most, that substitutions in demand will be greatest and that the two indexes will differ the most. An unresolvable problem – the index number problem – arises, and it is more extreme the more rapid is economic change and the longer the time period under examination.

The real wage indexes that give such a sombre and static portrayal of early modern purchasing power require caution and scepticism of the interpreter: caution because the wage (the numerator) may not be representative of earnings, and the direction of the bias is indeterminate; scepticism because the price index (the denominator) is certain to misrepresent changes in the true cost of living over long time periods. While the direction of the bias is predictable, the extent of the bias is not. This critique of real wage indexes is not intended to dismiss them as useless. On the contrary, they are an indispensable tool – a tool that requires careful use. The chief pitfall to be avoided is the application of its specific answers to broader questions than it is designed to address.

Evidence from the material world

The historian who averts eye contact with the wage and price evidence just discussed and fixes his or her gaze firmly on what I will call 'direct evidence' of the world of goods will gain a very different – a decidedly optimistic – impression of the changing standard of living from the sixteenth to the beginning of the nineteenth century. The impression is more optimistic, but it is less precise: neither the dating of changes in material culture nor the identification of the social or geographical limits to their diffusion can ordinarily be specified with great detail.

We can observe from extant structures and architectural studies a gradual upgrading of housing, as brick replaces wood and lime. In the Dutch cities this *verstening* was concentrated in the fifteenth through early seventeenth centuries, improving physical comfort and reducing the danger of fire.[38] Beginning around 1650 the design of urban dwellings for the well-to-do took a new departure with the introduction of a new division of interior space and a substantial increase in the total amount of space.[39] A century later the new standards of both display and privacy embedded in the new use of space had filtered some distance down the social hierarchy, as special drawing rooms and dining rooms appeared in middle-class homes, and distinct bed chambers came to be identified. The historian seeking the origins of the characteristically nineteenth-century cult of domesticity finds his attention drawn back via English and French intermediaries to the homes of seventeenth-century Dutch burgers.[40]

Paintings and other visual evidence also encourage us to believe in the emergence of a more varied and richer material culture. Seventeenth-century Dutch genre painting may have had no precedent in its celebration of the everyday material world, but it did have followers, so that northern European painting provides an ongoing record of fashion, style and material comfort.

This visual evidence is reinforced by the written word, as novelists, diarists, essayists and journalists provide documentation, often parenthetical and unintentional, of a dynamic material culture. But the evidence is not always parenthetical; from Pepys through Defoe to Arthur Young the concern with material culture is intense if not compulsive.

One aspect of the material world that attracted their attention was trade, the flows of goods that seemed to propel the new material world. The evidence of growing imports of exotic commodities from Asia and the New World together with the dramatic growth of certain domestic industries, such as pottery, distilled spirits and cotton cloth invariably drew the attention of contemporaries to the people who were consuming these commodities: the tea-drinking servant girls, the tobacco-smoking boers, the crockery-buying matrons, the denizens of Gin Lane and the 'bare-faced upstarts' in their 'stock jobber style' parlours. Contemporaries recorded these phenomena out of irritation and puzzlement; they were not inclined to explain such behaviour as a product of the interplay of income, relative prices and utility maximization.

All of these direct sources – physical, visual, literary and archival – encourage us to imagine the gradual and gradually accelerating emergence of a rich and varied consumer culture. But all of these sources are very limited: addressing a restricted range of goods or consumers, or saying nothing about change over time.

In this context one historical source stands out for its potential ability to offer direct evidence on material culture, and to do so systematically and comprehensively over long periods of time and in many western societies. The probate inventory, a legal document ordinarily drawn up upon the death of an adult leaving heirs, especially minor children, was widely employed throughout western and central Europe and in colonial societies. Although the specific form of the probate inventory and its availability varies from place to place, there are probably hundreds of thousands of such documents yet preserved in ecclesiastical, legal and notarial archives.

Probate inventories list the possessions of the deceased and often their monetary value. When complete, they can illuminate the economic activity of the deceased (describing productive capital, financial assets, livestock and farm implements, etc.), the wealth of the deceased (listing assets and outstanding debts) and the material culture of the deceased, recording the physical possessions found in the house, often room by room.[41]

Here our concern is with the third of these issues. A considerable literature is now available addressing questions of *Alltagsgeschichte*, material culture, and consumer demand in pre-industrial society. The present volume introduces the high level of probate inventory-based scholarship focused on England, and the American colonies.[42] Research efforts on the European continent are hardly less numerous, although monographic studies have been slow in coming.[43] The extraordinary richness of the probate inventory – its enumeration of many hundreds of artefacts, assets and liabilities – draws the investigator into an archival abyss from which some never return.

The detail of the inventories plus the substantial variation in the research strategies of investigators makes a summary of findings all but impossible. No equivalent to a Phelps Brown and Hopkins monster time series can reduce this embarrassment of archival riches to its essence. Yet, all of the studies I have examined for colonial New England and the Chesapeake, England and the Netherlands consistently reveal two features. With very few exceptions, each generation of decedents from the mid-seventeenth to the late eighteenth century left behind more and better possessions. However, these growing accumulations of possessions did not come to bulk larger in the total value of estates. Indeed, their relative value fell, and, often enough, their absolute value as well.

To begin in the Dutch Republic, the Friesian peasants whose farm and personal possessions I examined for the period 1550–1750, gradually acquired a variety of 'urban' goods – mirrors, paintings, books, clocks – and gradually upgraded the quality of their home furnishings.[44] Inventories from the mid-seventeenth century began occasionally listing not simply tables, but eight-sided tables, or round tables, and not simply chairs, but chairs with side arms. Simple wooden storage boxes made way for great oak chests; tin and wooden bowls and dishes made way for pottery and delftware. Curtains seemed unnecessary in the sixteenth century; by 1700 they were ubiquitous. These curtains invite the historian's gaze and our eyes are cast on growing collections of silver display objects, from spoons, decanters and bible clasps, to personal adornments for both men and women. These Friesian countrymen and women enjoyed a growing prosperity in the first century, to 1650, but most suffered sharply reduced incomes in the next. Yet, if anything, the pace of material improvement quickened after 1650.

The question of how consumer demand adapts to economic decline is investigated systematically and with great subtlety in a major Dutch probate inventory-based study, Thera Wijsenbeek's *Achter de gevels van Delft: Bezit en bestaan van rijk en arm in een periode van achteruitgang (1700–1800)*. Delft's rich archives permitted her to draw a sample of inventories covering the full socio-economic range of the city's population.[45] The consumer behaviour of the wealthy classes varied considerably, as one would expect, but all placed a clear priority on acquiring, in the face of diminishing income, socially strategic commodities, especially in the realms of clothing, home furnishings and tableware.

To be sure, she could note how some social groups economized in certain areas in order to remain up-to-date in others, but the evidence of a continual movement towards a richer material culture brought her to the conclusion that 'social and cultural developments may take place in relative autonomy, independently of [developments in] the economy'.[46]

In the very different world of colonial America several investigators have charted improvements of the material standard of living and the diffusion of higher material standards into the more remote upland areas in the century preceding the outbreak of the American Revolution.

> Despite their relative poverty and the rustic isolation of a large part of their population, Yankees of the 'middle classes' were participating in what became a transatlantic revolution in consumer tastes and were doing so at the same rate as their counterparts in the wealthier colonies.[47]

Gloria L. Main and Jackson T. Main, noting this of the New Englanders they studied, position their Yankee rustics squarely in a 'transatlantic phenomenon centering on London'.[48]

Peter Earle takes us into the very belly of the whale in *The Making of the English Middle Class*, examining the consumption habits of the business and professional classes – Earle's version of the 'middling sort' – in Augustan London. Predictably enough, he finds that the compulsive urge to accumulate capital that is thought to be lodged in the breasts of such folk did not prevent them from being 'great consumers whose collective expenditure was a major part of the effective demand which kept them all in business'.[49] Basing his analysis on 375 post-mortem inventories spread over the period 1660–1730, Earle documents 'an almost revolutionary change in the type of clothes worn by both sexes' and a major upgrading of domestic interiors, especially among the poorer members of the middle station.[50]

Anyone thinking the altogether exceptional city of London was also altogether exceptional in its consumer behaviour is quickly disabused of this notion by the evidence of English provincial consumer behaviour assembled in Lorna Weatherill's *Consumer Behavior and Material Culture in Britain, 1660–1760*, and presented in her contribution to this volume (chapter 10). She, like Earle, examines 'the middling sort', but hers is a broader band of English society, stretching from the better sort of husbandmen and craftsmen upward to the lesser gentry. Extracting information on twenty 'key' goods from nearly 3,000 inventories in eight regions of England, Weatherill documents 'remarkable instances of rapid growth and change'. While there are differences between town and country, she rejects the notion that their consumer behaviour differed fundamentally (as in the modern city vs traditional countryside); occupation and wealth explains more than location.

'Remorselessly creeping change' is how Eric Jones describes the record of technological change in Europe since the early Middle Ages.[51] In small ways and large, with initiatives taken by thousands of persons in widely scattered locations, the productive powers of European societies improved. The probate inventories seem to reveal an analogous 'material drift' driven by a remorselessly creeping demand for more and better consumer goods of all kinds. 'Consumer revolution' hardly seems to be the right term for such a protracted and broadly based process.

The second basic finding of every study consulted is that this expanding world of goods, filling up the rooms, cupboards and closets of households from Friesland to the Tidewater (and, in truth, considerably beyond) does not register as either a large or as an increasing proportion of the value of probated estates. The world of goods seems oddly disconnected from the world of wealth.

The Friesian peasants accumulated farm capital – livestock, equipment, buildings – throughout the period 1550–1750. Their accumulations of consumer goods did not keep pace in terms of value; they fell steadily as a percentage of total estate value and in many periods even fell in absolute value.[52] The Friesian probate inventories present many problems with respect to valuations. Many inventories could not be used; others had gaps in coverage. These findings must be regarded as provisional, but they conform to more well-based findings in England and colonial America.

Probate inventory valuations are discussed in depth in Carole Shammas's contribution to this volume (chapter 9). I can therefore be brief: Gloria and Jackson Main found that consumption goods declined as a percentage of total probated wealth in southern New England over the period 1640–1774. This they supposed could be explained by the process of investing in farm improvements, which would raise the value of farm assets as frontier settlements aged. '[T]he puzzle lies not in the relative decline of consumption goods. It is, rather, the absolute decline which demands investigation.'[53] The pattern in the Chesapeake did not differ in its essentials. Carr and Walsh show that after an initial rise from the 1650s to the 1670s, the value of consumer durables as a percentage of total estate value fell in every examined county, from 17 to 21 per cent in the period 1678–99, to half the peak level in 1755–77. Here, too, the absolute values often but not always fell.[54]

In England, Peter Earle found that 'there was little change over time [in the value of domestic goods], a rather surprising result since . . . there was a considerable qualitative change in domestic goods'.[55] The Mains' 'puzzle' and Earle's 'surprising result' is, in fact, a basic characteristic of seventeenth- and eighteenth-century probate inventories: the growing prominence of consumer goods was paired with their reduced significance to the total wealth of estate leavers.

In the case of the probate inventory-based studies of consumer demand, the question before us is not 'should we believe these findings?'; rather, it is *what* should we believe about the many findings? These rich sources tend to overwhelm our analytical capacities and to bewilder rather than clarify. The scholars who work with these documents have, of course, devoted a great deal of thought to the problems of data management and interpretation. They had to face any number of often very localized problems in order to make generalizations about hundreds of unique documents. Correspondingly, most studies are accompanied by fat methodological appendices.

Many methodological issues are specific to a particular body of data, but others, especially those involving interpretation, are 'generic'; they involve the very nature of the probate inventory as a source of historical information. I will limit myself here to several methodological issues that bear directly on consumer behaviour.

I have spoken in this essay sometimes of 'material culture' and sometimes of 'consumer demand' and related terms. They certainly should not be used interchangeably. Material culture should refer to that world of goods as it exists, is used and is given meaning by the inhabitants of that world. It is a static concept (no pejorative meaning is intended), one that probate inventories, which give a snapshot of that world at the time of the owner's death, are well suited to address. Consumer demand refers to behaviour that changes, augments, replenishes or diminishes the goods accessible to the individual. It is a dynamic concept, and the probate inventory does not address it directly.

Using the probate inventory to address consumer demand requires that we confront a typical economists' concern: the stock-flow problem. In a simplified, ideal case all the purchases, consumption (i.e., use and deterioration) and sales of goods that occur in a household – the flows – are captured at a moment of time as the stock existing when the inventory is drawn up. These flows vary in their speed – their depreciation rate. The key to interpreting the inventories for purposes of studying consumer behaviour is the proper transformation of stocks into flows, and an important test of the adequacy of an inventory is its inclusion of the less durable items.

The less durable the item the less likely it is to leave a residue in the probate inventories. Obviously, the purchase of services and public goods leaves no trace. The purchase of newspapers will not be revealed in inventories, nor will many of the petty purchases of trinkets, children's toys or other transitory amusements. The inventories are no guide to food consumption since only the most long-lasting of foodstuffs, smoked meat and possibly stores of grain, will be included. When we get to clothing we reach a sufficiently durable category of goods to expect inclusion, but in practice the inventories are often quite imperfect as the clothing of the still-living members of the household is often excluded or the clothing of the deceased is disposed of prior to the inventorization.

As we proceed through the typical durables – kitchenware, tableware, furniture and furnishings – the inventories come into their own. New problems arise at the other end of the spectrum, with those goods that are *so* durable that they function as a store of value.

If some goods are so transitory that they leave no residue, others are misleadingly conspicuous. Goods that are chiefly acquired through inheritance obviously say little about current demand, and they may say little about current fashions and tastes. Moreover, they will surely be more important in a period of population stability or decline than in a period of population growth. In a stationary population, the demand for goods that suffer negligible depreciation must be read from the *rate of change* in the stocks of such goods, not from the *size* of those stocks. In a declining population (such as England from 1680 to 1720 and the Dutch Republic in the same period), even growing stocks of highly durable goods may represent no net additions, and hence no current demand.

This exploration of stock-flow problems prepares us for the seemingly paradoxical finding of so many studies that the diffusion of new goods, the increased quantities of familiar items, the more luxurious character of yet others – all trends now well documented for the late seventeenth and eighteenth centuries – did not express themselves in an enlarged share of total wealth attributable to consumer goods.

First, it is important to recall that a constant stock of consumer durables (as measured in the inventories) does not necessarily imply that the flow of household expenditures on those goods is also constant. The example in Table 5.1 should make this clear:

Table 5.1 Stock and flow: model showing effects of wealth composition and depreciation rates on the flow of consumption expenditures

Year	Total wealth	Consumer durables	Textiles	Tableware	Furniture, silver, etc.
	Stock . . .				
A	100	50	20	10	20
B(1)	100	50	30	10	10
B(2)	200	100	60	20	20
	divided by average lifespan of stock . . .				
Depreciation period		A	10 yrs	30 yrs	30 yrs
		B	5 yrs	15 yrs	30 yrs
			equals flow of expenditures		
		Total			
Annual expenditures					
	A	3.00	2.00	0.33	0.67
	B(1)	7.00	6.00	0.67	0.33
	B(2)	14.00	12.00	1.33	0.67

The example is obviously an exaggeration of what might really have happened but it makes clear that changed depreciation periods (of the sort one might expect when cottons replace woollens and linens, and as glass and pottery replace wooden and pewter tableware) can considerably alter the relationship between stock and flow. This is true whether total wealth increases, B(2), or not, B(1).

Note that this result is independent of price changes for the commodities in question. Shammas and others provide abundant evidence that the prices of clothing and many consumer durables fell substantially in the seventeenth and eighteenth centuries. If a fall in prices to, say, one-half the initial level should be added to the model, it would leave all the numbers unaffected, but the annual expenditures in period B would now suffice to purchase twice as many units of consumer goods. That is, the *quantity* of consumer goods represented by a constant value would double, between A and B, while the speeded depreciation rate would increase the annual expenditure rate needed to maintain the augmented stock of goods.

To put the matter differently and, perhaps, more provocatively, if reduced durability and falling prices were the major factors encouraging increased expenditure on consumer goods, both because the lowered prices increased demand and because reduced durability was associated with the more frequent introduction of attractive new fashions, then it is highly likely that probate inventories would show a *falling* proportion of total value accounted for by consumer goods. Indeed, today most people, after a lifetime of frenetic consumerism and prodigious expenditures, die with personal possessions of inconsequential value, hardly enough to pay for a decent burial. In this respect, the probate inventories surely do reveal the rosy dawn of modern consumerism.

A second interpretive problem concerns representativeness, and this has three major dimensions: the relationship between those deceased persons leaving inventories and all the deceased, the relationship between the deceased and the living and the adequacy of the inventories selected for study to represent the target populations of the deceased. The first of these problems is invariably discussed by researchers, the second is often ignored and the third is always (to my knowledge) passed over in silence.

The simplest and safest way to deal with the first problem is to specify a population for study that corresponds well to the coverage of the inventories. For example, the studies of English middle-class life by Earle and Weatherill deal with the problem of representativeness by selecting a tranche of society known to be well covered by probate inventories. When a more inclusive study is contemplated (such as Wijsenbeek's study of Delft, or my study of rural Friesland) it is wise to follow the same principle of dividing the population into segments (based on some characteristic external to the inventory data, such as occupation or tax status) and selecting inventories for each segment, that is a stratified sample. Appropriately weighted, the findings for each stratum can then yield a comprehensive picture of the society as a whole, or as much of it as can be studied.

Whether one is studying one stratum or several, the boundaries of the strata must be clear and stable. The studies of Earle and Weatherill suggest the possible problems (although they are not themselves guilty of the mis-steps discussed here). By 'middle class' Earle has in mind a stratum consisting of some 20 per cent of adult Londoners; Weatherill has in mind a larger tranche consisting of fully half the population, excluding only the aristocracy at the top and unskilled and semi-skilled labour at the bottom. The type of interpretive pitfalls possible when the boundaries of a stratum vary *within* a single study are obvious.

A related danger of stratified samples is the use of an open-ended category. For example, in her study of Delft, Thera Wijsenbeek sampled the population according to income class as defined by the liability of the deceased to a burial tax. This tax was levied according to one's wealth, rising from no tax for the *Pro Deo* group to successively larger sums in the remaining four categories.[56] But the *Pro Deo* category comprised fully 50 per cent of all the deceased. Since the poorest inhabitants leave few inventories, a random selection from the *Pro Deo* inventories would almost certainly over-represent the upper end of this large and heterogeneous stratum of Delft society. Wijsenbeek sought to avoid this problem by introducing further controls in the selection of inventories to achieve representativeness.[57]

The second type of representativeness problem concerns the relationship between the possessions of the deceased and those of the living. In modern society financial assets are generally thought to vary (among persons of the same social category) by age, according to the life-cycle savings hypothesis of Modigliani. In earlier times the motivation for saving is likely to have differed, but it is unlikely that wealth and the possession of personal property was not strongly correlated with age.[58] It is also well known that household size is correlated with wealth and possessions, and that occupation, holding income and wealth constant, causes the *structure* of personal possessions to vary.

Accurate projection of the material world of the deceased onto that of the living requires that the inventory be linked to other sources that reveal the age, household size, survival of parents and occupation of the deceased. Since inventories are generally made for persons who die leaving minor children, they include persons of all adult ages, but the average age is, of course, far above that of living householders. The efforts taken by Gloria and Jackson Main to ascertain the age of the deceased, requiring the linkage of the New England probate inventories to parish records, are exemplary in this respect. Few probate inventory studies (mine included) have taken this step.

Finally, we come to the technical requirements of the sample itself. How large should the sample of inventories be from which inferences are to be drawn about the population it represents? Statistics textbooks provide guidance on the selection of samples and the determination of sample size. Historians often find the rules of classical statistical sampling less than helpful, and for two reasons, both of which also pertain to the study of probate inventories. First, random sampling of the population is difficult or impossible because of the partial survival of evidence, restricted access to the evidence and/or lack of prior knowledge about the scope of the available evidence. Second, the determination of sample size requires knowledge about the variance in the underlying population. In the formula for determining sample size

$$n = (Z\frac{\sigma}{d})^2$$

the standard deviation of the population (σ) is the critical empirical element. The other elements Z, the standard normal deviate, and d, the confidence interval, are chosen by the investigator and depend on the degree of precision being sought.

Acknowledgement of the obstacles to the application of classical sampling methods does not imply that there is no alternative to the haphazard gathering of arbitrary quantities of inventories. Stratified samples and 'representative' samples can be adequate substitutes for 'random' samples, and the unknown standard deviation of a population can be approximated through the use of pilot samples. A sample of, say, 100 inventories can be taken, and then another sample of 100. The sample means and standard deviations of inventory characteristics can be compared and used to approximate the population parameters.[59]

Researchers using probate inventories never offer formal justifications for the size of the samples they settle on. Historians typically use large samples since their training impresses upon them the need to examine *all* documents (you never know what will turn up!). Sampling is then seen as a regrettable compromise, and by way of compensation the sampling historian collects as much evidence as is humanly possible. This tends to make samples of inadequate size (as opposed to inadequate design) an uncommon problem in historical research.

However, in the case of probate inventories there is some reason for concern. Normally distributed phenomena can usually be accurately inferred from surprisingly small samples. But many of the characteristics being studied in probate inventories have to do with wealth, which is log-normally distributed. For our purposes this simply means that accurate statistics require much larger samples because of the inherently large amount of variance and the importance of outlier observations. (A study of the richest hundred households must take into account that the very richest person is likely to be twice as wealthy as the second richest, and the richest twenty will have about 80 per cent of the wealth of the entire group. The absence of a central tendency requires heavier sampling than would be the case with a normally distributed phenomenon.)

Conflicting stories

The stock-flow problem and the several dimensions of the problem of representativeness make the probate inventory a much more challenging source *for the study of consumer demand* than is generally acknowledged. Nevertheless, the basic finding of long-term growth in the volume and diversity of consumer possessions is so common to all the available studies that it hardly seems possible that it can be placed in jeopardy. It is reassuringly reinforced by other evidence – physical and archival – that speaks to the growing consumer demand for food-stuffs (especially non-European groceries, such as tea, sugar, tobacco), for more durable housing and for increased energy supplies for home heating, cooking and lighting.

How can this diverse but tangible evidence of growing consumption be reconciled with the sombre interpretation of consumer well-being that emerges from the impressively uniform but more highly constructed evidence of wages and prices?

There is no significant conflict in the evidence, and no need for reconciliation, if the 'consumer revolution' were restricted to a small elite. But this is precisely what all scholars deny. They emphasize instead the power of emulation, causing demand to diffuse down-wards from the elites to the middling sorts and from them to their inferiors. McKendrick is most explicit in insisting that 'the market for mass consumer goods reached lower than [the middling groups], it reached as far as the skilled factory worker and the domestic servant class'.[60] The lower boundary of the consumer revolution is by no means settled, but there can be little doubt that the evidence addresses the consumer behaviour of a broad socio-economic band of early modern society.

There is no inconsistency between the material data and the purchasing power measure-ments if the documented growth of consumer demand is confined to specific commodities that have the economic characteristic of being substitutes for items that had earlier been more prominent in the 'basket of consumables'. If growing expenditures for tea were roughly matched by declining expenditures for beer as E. P. Thompson claimed, or if purchases of cotton cloth rose at the expense of linen, or if pottery drove out tin and pewter – then the consumer revolution takes on a different character.[61] Such shifts in consumer behaviour are not without interest, to be sure, but they do not require any increase in purchasing power. They are consistent with shifts in the locus of economic activity, but not directly with any change in the rate of aggregative growth.[62] Probate inventory studies often focus special attention on articles that are new, becoming more common, and more numerous. When less attention is devoted to the articles that are in retreat a bias enters the analysis that exaggerates the growth of demand.

The enormous number of items listed in many probate inventories usually forces the investigator to limit them in some way (Lorna Weatherill confined her attention to twenty 'key' items).[63] This practical step introduces the possibility of a pro-consumption growth bias in the data base if substitutable goods are not included. This issue deserves more attention than it is typically given, but it does not seem likely that all or most of the documented growth of consumption can be explained away as a substitution of new goods for old.

Another way in which the inconsistency between the two bodies of evidence can be removed is if the consumer revolution could be confined to the one period – roughly, the first half of the eighteenth century – when falling prices generate rising real wages to match the growth in consumer demand as revealed by English probate inventories and the importation of sugar, tea and tobacco. But this limitation fails on two counts: most 'consumer revolution' arguments seek to restore demand as a factor in the Industrial Revolution, a post-1760 phenomenon, and the same sources that reveal a growth of demand in the first half of the eighteenth century also reveal such growth in much of the seventeenth. In short, growth in consumer demand is a long-term phenomenon that spans periods defined by price and wage trends in the seventeenth and eighteenth centuries.[64]

III The industrious revolution[65]

The evidence for growth in consumer demand is, I believe, compelling, and it cannot be explained away as a phenomenon restricted to a small social group, a few goods or a brief period of propitious price and wage movements. Nor can it properly be understood with the concept of a 'consumer revolution' defined as the dynamic role of consumers during the British Industrial Revolution. The term 'consumer revolution' should probably be suppressed before frequent repetition secures for it a place in that used-car lot of explanatory vehicles reserved for historical concepts that break down directly after purchase by the passing scholar. The emergence of a consumer society was by no means sudden – certainly not confined to the late eighteenth and early nineteenth century – nor was it limited geographically to Britain.

Any effort to explain this phenomenon, and to reconcile it to the real wage data that seem to deny that it could ever have happened, needs to place it in a broader context than industrializing Britain and needs to penetrate, as it were, behind the interplay of supply and demand curves to examine the institutions that help define the shape and positions of those curves in the first place.

Consumer demand grew, even in the face of contrary real wage trends, because of reallocations of the productive resources of households. A series of household-level decisions altered both the supply of marketed goods and labour and the demand for market-bought products. This complex of changes in household behaviour constitutes an 'industrious revolution', driven by Smithian, or commercial, incentives, that preceded and prepared the way for the Industrial Revolution, which was driven by technology and changes in organization. That is, an industrious revolution, with important demand-side features began in advance of the Industrial Revolution, which was basically a supply-side phenomenon.

At the heart of the concept of an industrious revolution is the household. The pre-industrial household was a unit of reproduction and consumption, functions it still retains (the latter chiefly via the redistribution of income among its individual members), as well as a unit of production. Moreover, a large portion of the household's final consumption was supplied internally, by its own production. In any household where auto-consumption plays a significant role, production decisions are integrally related to consumption decisions. Correspondingly, the increased market orientation of such a household cannot be understood simply as a production response to market opportunities; it is also a response to the household's demand for marketed goods, revealed in a higher demand for the money income necessary to acquire such goods.[66] Under these circumstances, the terms on which the household specializes to produce goods for the market and the terms on which its members' labour is offered to the labour market are partially determined by the household's preferences for market-supplied goods and services (versus home-supplied goods and services) and the perceived relative utility of money income versus leisure.[67]

Note how this argument differs from the Keynesian scenario in which rising demand creates employment for idled productive factors. Until a full employment condition is reached, rising demand can be said to 'cause' the growth of production. The industrious revolution argument does not identify idle resources (committed to the market, but unused), it identifies differently deployed resources (not committed to the market) and specifies the conditions under which the household alters its demand patterns and simultaneously alters its offer curves of marketed output and/or labour.

How did this industrious revolution manifest itself in pre-industrial Europe? The earliest steps occurred in those peasant households that could follow the course of specialization by concentrating household labour in marketed food production. Increased allocational efficiency and the static and dynamic gains from internal trade creation accrue to such a household as it reduces the amount of labour devoted to a wide variety of home handicrafts and services and replaces these activities with market-supplied substitutes.[68] The 'Z goods model' of Hymer and Reznick identifies the formal economic conditions under which a household will be induced to reduce its production of 'Z goods' (non-traded, mainly non-agricultural goods), concentrate productive assets into marketed food production, and substitute purchased manufactures and services (M goods) for the abandoned Z goods.[69] Rising prices for agricultural commodities relative to manufactures obviously encourage this process of resource reallocation, but improvements in the terms of trade for food producers cannot single-handedly bring about full specialization. Rising prices for food cause manufactured goods to become relatively cheaper, to be sure, and this encourages the substitution of M for Z in consumption. But the improving terms of trade for the peasant household also implies rising real income, and this could bring about a growing demand for Z goods. I say 'could', because this income effect depends ultimately on tastes: the perceived superiority of market-supplied goods relative to home-supplied Z goods and leisure. A full redeployment of household labour towards market production is aided by price and technical factors, but it depends on household demand preferences (see Figure 5.5).

The specialization path outlined here was not – could not be – followed everywhere. At a minimum, peasant households needed access to markets and suppliers of incentive goods. Rural households in the maritime regions of the Netherlands achieved substantial market dependence via specialization by the mid-seventeenth century and many parts of England followed suit in the century after 1650.[70] In northern France, George Grantham has

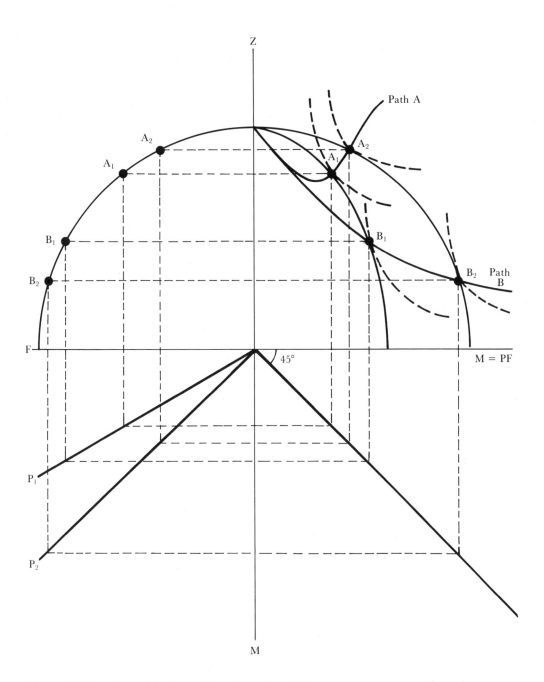

Figure 5.5 Z goods model. (For explanation see note 117)

documented a substantial growth in marketed foodstuffs in the century after 1750 wherever farmers had access to market opportunities offered by urbanization. Using detailed village-level data, Grantham could find little in the way of technological innovation to account for the growth of agricultural output before the late 1840s. Instead, the growth of production proceeded 'along a long-run supply curve whose position was established by the beginning of the eighteenth century, if not before'.[71] Farmers worked harder, shifted their crop mix towards marketable products, and used 'underemployed reserves of child and female labor to expand production for home use of the inferior grains and starches, many of which were grown outside normal crop rotations'.[72] The French peasants studied by Grantham did not abandon altogether self-sufficiency in basic foodstuffs, but they reallocated household labour to increase marketed food output and increase their consumption of manufactured goods. Grantham warns that any measurement of real income that relies on the rising prices of marketed wheat as the cost-of-living deflator would tend to produce an overly pessimistic result. The intensification of production induced by market opportunities had yielded a more elastic supply of foodstuffs than the essentially urban wheat markets could reveal.

A second dimension of the industrious revolution is revealed most clearly by proto-industrial and proletarian households as the underemployed labour on cottar holdings, the voluntary idleness of labour exhibiting a high leisure preference and the low intensity of effort characteristic of most labour gave way to longer and harder work. Truly regular, continuous, supervised labour was with few exceptions a product of the factory system, and was rare before the nineteenth century. A vast and evocative literature chronicles the painful adjustments labourers had to make to satisfy the imperious demands of the factory system.[73] However, it would be a grave error to conclude from this literature that the pace and regularity of employment before the factory reflected an unchanging traditionalism. In fact, a major intensification of labour – measurable in labour force participation rates, days worked per year and effort per unit of labour – occurred in many areas in the course of the early modern era.

Let us begin with the most obvious form of intensification, the reduction of non-working days. The large number of religious and semi-religious feast days honoured by the cessation of labour in the fifteenth century is confirmed by sources in many European countries. Such holidays could exceed 50 per year, limiting the maximum number of days of labour to approximately 250 (a number not reached again in western Europe until after 1960).[74] It is not altogether fair to use this post-plague 'golden age of labour' situation as a benchmark, since the number of workdays had been rather higher in the thirteenth and early fourteenth centuries.[75] But the reduction of free days that began in the sixteenth century, and continued into the eighteenth, brought the maximum number of working days per year to altogether unprecedented levels. This was in part the work of the Reformation, particularly its Calvinist variant. In the Netherlands the forty-seven feast days whose observance was required by guild regulations around 1500 suddenly fell to six with the reform of religion.[76] It is hardly credible that the actual supply of labour suddenly rose by more than 15 per cent. Both economic limitations on the demand for labour and the behavioural constraints on its supply surely made this a gradual adjustment. But by the mid-seventeenth century the 307-day maximal work year was definitely in place.[77]

In England a similar process of intensification can be traced. Builders observed some forty holidays in the late fifteenth century, which an act of Parliament reduced to twenty-seven

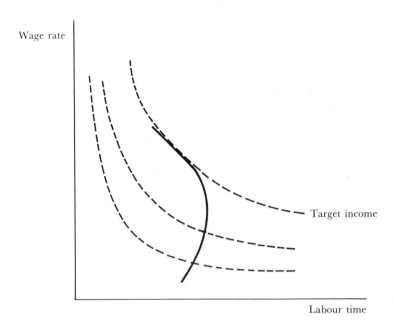

Wage rate

Target income

Labour time

Figure 5.6 The backward-bending supply curve

in 1552. After Cromwell's rule, Restoration governments did nothing to change the Dutch-like practice of observing only a very few holidays around Christmas, Easter and Whitsun.[78]

Protestantism was certainly not the only force pushing towards a longer work year, for the number of observed feast days declined in Catholic countries, too, albeit not so far. By 1600 the number of work days in France reached the 275–85 range.[79]

This opening salvo of labour intensification was permissive rather than compulsory. It increased by some 15 per cent the maximum annual days of work. Is there any reason to believe that the average number of days actually worked increased in like measure? One might also wonder whether any of this had much impact on the work patterns of agricultural households, which surely were influenced more by the seasonal labour requirements of crops and herds than by public policy with respect to saints.

These long-term trends augmented the supply of labour *in theory*; what did so *in practice* was a change in the household evaluation of the marginal utility of money income vs leisure time. Peasant and proletarian households alike appear to have decided in favour of income over leisure. This was certainly no universal phenomenon, for special conditions were necessary to bring such decisions about. But, by the mid-eighteenth century, such behaviour was sufficiently common to have undermined a basic feature of labour market behaviour, the backward-bending labour supply curve.

A backward-bending labour supply curve (see Figure 5.6) occurs when rising wages, after a certain point, cease to elicit more labour supply and give rise instead to a decline in the amount of labour offered. This behaviour is consistent with a desire for a 'target income', that is an income sufficient to secure a 'traditional' or customary standard of living. Income beyond the target level does not possess sufficient utility to justify the necessary reduction of leisure. Consequently, a continued rise of wages, because it permits the target income to be achieved with less labour, causes the supply of labour to decline – to bend backward, as shown in Figure 5.6. Any number of contemporary employers' comments can be found to attest to this behavioural pattern: when real wages were high, 'the labour of the poor is . . . scarce to be had at all (so licentious are they who labour only to eat, or rather to drink)';[80] 'Scarcity', (high food prices), on the other hand,

> promotes industry. . . . [Those] who can subsist on three days' work will be idle and drunken the remainder of the week. . . . The poor in the manufacturing counties will never work any more time than is necessary to live and support their weekly debauches.[81]

The same force that could induce peasant households to shift their labour from 'Z goods', output intended for auto-consumption, to marketed goods, served to induce peasant and proletarian households to substitute labour for leisure. In both cases a rise in the utility of money income stands behind the increased offer of marketed goods and labour, and standing behind the augmented utility of income is a growth in the variety of available consumer goods, and a development of consumer tastes that prefers market-supplied goods to their home-produced substitutes. When these conditions are met a key feature of modern consumer society is put in place: the 'target income' behaviour gives way to a dynamic materialism where desires are insatiable, where, as Sir James Steuart observed, 'Men are forced to labour now because they are slaves to their own wants', and where Adam Smith observed that 'workmen . . . when they are liberally paid by the piece, are very apt to overwork themselves'. In Steuart's eyes the new situation was full of promise: 'wants promote industry, industry gives food, food increases numbers.'[82]

The first stages of this process involved securing employment for under-utilized household labour – labour idle in the slack seasons of the agricultural calendar. Such 'leisure time' is very nearly equal to 'involuntary leisure', the economist's term for unemployment. Since it has a low 'opportunity cost' (the utility of its next best use), such labour time was available in growing amounts for a wide range of by-employments as household demand for money income rose. Utilizing this supply of cheap labour (cheap because of its low opportunity cost) was the challenge before the organizers of what is now called proto-industry.

There is no space available here to survey the now vast literature on the spread through selective regions of Europe of this merchant-organized, mainly rural, system of industrial production.[83] It has medieval antecedents, but its most intensive growth occurred in the seventeenth and eighteenth centuries in northwestern Europe.

Joan Thirsk describes its early development in England, and links it directly to the rise of a consumer society. 'Consumer industries in the sixteenth and seventeenth centuries exploited hitherto underused labour in rural areas as well as absorbing a large share of the extra manpower made available by population increase and immigration.'[84] These consumer industries, she continues, 'dispensed extra cash among wage labourers, cottagers, and small holders, their wives and their children. Purchasing power and productive capacity were thus mutually sustaining.'[85] Thirsk is careful to note, as most investigators of proto-industry must, that 'we cannot speak with certainty of rising *per capita* incomes throughout the population in the seventeenth century', but, she continues,

> we can point to numerous communities in the kingdom, especially in towns and in the pastoral-industrial areas, where the labouring classes found cash to spare for consumer goods in 1700 that had no place in their budgets in 1550 – brass cooking pots, iron frying pans, earthenware dishes, knitted stockings, even a lace frill for a cap or apron.[86]

The land-poor households whose elastic offer curve of labour fuelled these and other consumer industries had their agricultural analogues in those households that offered growing quantities of marketed foodstuffs, and many others, typically with less land, that poured household labour into the production of such labour-intensive and utterly market-oriented crops as tobacco, wine, hops and madder.[87] All of these variants of intensification gave rise to regional specialization and trade, improving the efficiency of the economy as it increased the market orientation of the households.[88]

By the mid-eighteenth century, before the Industrial Revolution, many socio-economic groups in many regions of Europe had redeployed their household labour and reduced their leisure time to increase simultaneously marketed output and money income. The labour of women and children played a prominent role in this process of peasant self-exploitation: the putting-out industries made intensive use of their winter and evening labour while the new, labour-intensive crops typically featured operations – weeding, pruning, plucking, etc. – then deemed well-suited to the abilities of women and children.

When placed in this context, the prominent role played by child and female labour in the leading industries of the British Industrial Revolution is hardly surprising; it is only the continuation and, probably, further intensification of an established trend towards greater paid labour-force participation, but now beyond the confines of the household in the factory and workshop.

Neil McKendrick, in a useful and vigorously argued article, maintained that a consumer revolution, occurring in the second half of the eighteenth century, and reaching lower than the middle classes to the skilled factory worker and the domestic servant class, 'took much of its impetus to consume from the earnings of women and children'. 'In my view', he testified, 'the earnings of women and children and the important contribution they made to the family income can play an important part in providing a more satisfactory explanation [for the consumer revolution].'[89] In fact, he later asserts,

> without the addition of female wages and the earnings of children, it is difficult to explain where a sufficiently large surplus of income over expenditure would have come from, and without a substantial rise in family income it is difficult to see where the increased home demand would come from.[90]

Much of McKendrick's article is devoted to a critique of that vast literature that deplores the participation of women and children in the paid labour force and interprets its incidence during the Industrial Revolution as revelatory of the truly perfidious character of the dark satanic mills. Most of that literature dates from the century after 1850, when both Victorian and reformist opinion held child and female labour to be a proper object of special regulation, and expressed a strong preference for keeping such persons out of the paid labour force altogether.

Viewing the factory labour of women and children from this perspective, McKendrick correctly seeks to supplement the condemnations of the exploitation of women and children with an appreciation of the positive, volitional role played by these workers in the context of the household economy and its consumer aspirations.

However, since McKendrick fails to place the paid labour-force participation of women and children in its *pre*-Industrial Revolution context, he gives the erroneous impression that it was something new with the rise of the factories. Without in any way explaining why women and children should now suddenly enter the paid labour force, he attributes to their new, supplementary earnings a major role in explaining a consumer revolution.

But, if, as I have argued, an 'industrious revolution', featuring the intensified use of women and children in market-oriented production had been gaining momentum for over a century before 1750, then the new, more conspicuous role of women and children as paid labourers is only the extension into new circumstances of an established trend. It cannot support McKendrick's concept of a consumer revolution because it is but one phase of an older, more broadly based process of increasing the rate of paid labour-force participation, and of increasing the intensity of that labour.

This brings us to the third and final dimension of the industrious revolution. Besides the concentration of household labour in marketed production at the expense of auto-consumption (allowing households to capture the static and dynamic gains from trade), and besides the increased paid labour-force participation at the expense of leisure (thereby increasing household income faster than the course of individual wage rates can reveal), there appears to have occurred an increase in the pace or intensity of work in the course of the early modern period, especially in Britain. What I mean here is the achievement of higher labour productivity independent of the rise of more or better capital or land. Gregory Clark, in a series of articles, has identified substantial international differences in the productivity of labour in agriculture and in the textile industry during the nineteenth century.[91] These differences remain large even after the effect of capital, training and natural resources have been taken into account. The performance of British agriculture between 1661 and 1841 offers a particularly striking example: output growth almost kept pace with the rise of population while the number of farm workers grew far less over the interval of nearly two centuries. Consequently output per worker rose by over 50 per cent. Clark found that technical progress could account for but 15 per cent of this; the rest he attributed to more labour per worker (i.e., less leisure) and to more intense work.[92] By the early nineteenth century, when comparative evidence is more plentiful, the differences in the rate at which simple manual tasks were performed by farm workers in various counties are enormous: English farm labourers harvested over four times as much grain per day as Polish peasants (or medieval English peasants), even though the tools and techniques used differed but little.[93] As noted above, Grantham found substantial differences in the pace of work within rural France in the 1840s. The proximity to markets had a strong and direct influence on this pattern of labour intensity.[94] With the right incentives, a large amount of extra output could be squeezed out of the pre-industrial technological complex.

The resolution to the contradiction raised by the wage and probate inventory data is at hand. Households desiring to consume more market-distributed goods and services redeployed their productive assets, offering to the market more goods, more labour and more intensive labour. As a result *annual household money earnings* could grow relative to *individual daily wage rates*, and this could occur independently of technological change or the growth of the capital stock.

The sceptical reader may wonder if the solution to our problem really is at hand. Even if all the outward signs of an industrious revolution are accepted, they could have explanations very different from, even contradictory to, that proffered above.

Price and income effects, independently of any of the changes in tastes that might affect the shape of supply and demand curves, obviously play some role in the processes described above. Just as the rise of post-Black Death real wages influenced the growing number of non-working days, so the sixteenth-century erosion of real wages surely influenced the decline of feast-day observance. Relative price changes (particularly the weakness of grain prices relative to manufactures and specialty crops in the century 1650–1750) undoubtedly encouraged the proto-industrialization process, while large and continuing reductions in the prices of tropical imports – such as tea, coffee and sugar – encouraged their mass consumption independently of any other factors. The analysis presented here does not deny the importance of any of these economic responses, but argues simply that once they are taken into account, a large unexplained residual remains.

A second objection focuses on the explanations given for the reduction of leisure and the increased intensity of work. If a large portion of the pre-industrial population lived at the margin of subsistence, the choice to work more and harder may not have existed. Chronic malnutrition would have imposed a ceiling on productive activity that could only be lifted when classic supply-side factors such as are associated with an agricultural revolution began to be felt. The classic statement of this position, by Freudenberger and Cummins, identifies the formerly abundant leisure time as an involuntary period of

> recuperation necessary to sustain [the worker] for the work he was doing, little as that might have been. The short work week before the Industrial Revolution may have been one aspect of an equilibrium situation determined partly by a high prevalence of debilitating disease and by low and unpredictable supplies of food.[95]

Fogel has interpreted recent studies of stature, mortality and nutrition as consistent with this position. He summarized the provisional findings about caloric intake at the end of the eighteenth century in England and France as follows: in France the bottom 10 per cent of the labour force lacked the energy for regular work and the next 10 per cent had enough energy for less than three hours of light work daily. In England only the bottom 3 per cent lacked the energy for day work, 'but the balance of the bottom 20 per cent had enough energy for about 6 hours of light work (1.09 hours of heavy work) each day'.[96]

An industrious revolution governed by caloric intake instead of a taste for consumer goods is clearly a very different phenomenon than I have developed in this article: it is governed by the supply of food, and cannot have supported a consumer revolution for the non-essential, non-food goods that we know proliferated in the seventeenth and eighteenth centuries. Conceivably, the force of this argument can be deflected by showing that only a small 'lumpenproletariat' faced severe energy constraints, while the rest of the population could make the choices on which the industrious revolution concept depends.[97] My own view is that the estimates of caloric intake are too small, and that a large majority of the north-western European population did not normally face the dismal prospects outlined by

Freudenberger, Cummins and Fogel. Otherwise, this remains an outstanding question in the history of the pre-industrial economy.

It is, in fact, one of a more general class of counter-arguments that have in common an external force coercing household behaviour, and specifically fostering market dependence where the household, if left to its own devices, would prefer to avoid it.

The most important of the coercive forces is poverty. As populations grow the land available per household falls, requiring adjustments in household labour allocation to increase the yields on the available land. This long-term process, as described by Boserup, requires a reduction of leisure time and often conforms outwardly to the specialization and labour-participation augmenting strategies described above.[98] Moreover, the proto-industry phenomenon is thought by most investigators to be a survival strategy employed by impoverished land-poor households. This had been Mendels's view as he developed the concept of proto-industry in studies of the eighteenth-century Flemish countryside.[99] His vision has been contradicted by the Flemish historian Vanderbroeke, who holds that this industrious society enjoyed a prosperous 'golden age' in the eighteenth century.[100] But the dominant position remains that articulated, for all of Europe, by Medick: 'The adult proto-industrial worker was not able to exist as an individual . . . he had to depend to a growing extent upon the "cooperation" of his entire family.'[101] He then quotes a shoemaker from Northampton who reinforces the point:

> No single-handed man can live; he must have a whole family at work, because a single-handed man is so badly paid he can scarce provide the necessaries of life . . . as soon as [the children] are big enough to handle an awl, they are obliged to come downstairs and work.[102]

Moreover, Mendels, Medick, Levine and most other scholars who have developed the concept of proto-industrialization hold that the new earning ability imparted by the spread of rural cottage industry served to increase the size of families rather than the level of consumer demand. Proto-industry, by undermining traditional social controls on demographic behaviour, endowed the Industrial Revolution with its labour force, not its consumers.[103]

Taxes were another external force pushing households into greater market involvement. All western European states greatly increased the real tax burden in the seventeenth century, particularly in its second half when falling commodity prices placed great pressure on agricultural households.[104]

What the long-term effects of population growth, proletarianization and government tax policy could not achieve was more suddenly brought about by the rise of the factory system. By drying up home-based employment possibilities it destroyed any remaining basis for household economic strategies seeking to keep the market at arm's length. By ending the autonomy of the unsupervised worker, it laid the basis for both an extension of the working day and the intensification of work. In short, the supply curves of labour were forcibly shifted to the right by a combination of inexorable demographic and economic processes, social stratification, government policy and technological change. The 'external constraints' school assumes that the households facing all these forces offered, as Levine put it, 'a deep-rooted resistance to the imperatives of capitalist society. . . . [It was an economy] characterized by its "backward-bending supply curve" which means that people worked enough to earn their targeted income and then simply quit'.[105]

Such workers, when forced into the new factories, 'entered a new culture'. As Pollard put it in a pioneering study of early factory management: 'Men who were non-accumulative, non-acquisitive, accustomed to work for subsistence, not for maximization of income, had to be made obedient to the cash stimulus, and obedient in such a way as to react precisely to the stimuli provided.'[106]

No one can doubt that the external constraints listed above were real, and that they contributed substantially to the greater market orientation and paid labour-force participation that is at issue here. In fact, much of what it describes is not inconsistent with the industrious revolution concept. For example, when household labour-force participation, or labour intensity, is increased to prevent the loss of an earlier achieved living standard, it might be interpreted as behaviour coerced by external forces, but action to defend any particular material standard above a physiological minimum is a social decision, and when repeated as higher levels of well-being are reached, a ratchet effect leads the economy towards an industrious revolution. The immediate moments of decision may have been defensive, but the consequences of those decisions led over time to both labour intensification and higher consumption levels.[107]

At bottom there is but one issue distinguishing the industrious revolution concept from the 'external constraint' arguments reviewed above. It does not involve objective matters, but focuses on motivation: did pre-industrial households respond passively or actively to the threats and opportunities presented by the evolving economic environment? More precisely, did they respond, as Levine suggests, by tenaciously seeking to preserve a traditional regime of limited market involvement and target income, or did they act to realize new tastes and preferences of *their own choosing*? This, of course, is simply a restatement of the moral peasant–rational peasant debate, now extended to the pre-industrial labouring population more generally.[108] Adhering to the industrious revolution concept is the belief that acquisitive, or maximizing behaviour, understood in the context of its time, was not alien and 'unnatural', and, hence, was not imposed in the main by political force on a dispossessed and victimized labour force.

There is no space here to elaborate a defence of this much-debated and politically charged proposition. Suffice it to say that no serious argument for the role of broad-based consumer demand in economic development during the seventeenth through nineteenth centuries can be sustained without it. In its absence one must rely on infinitely persuasive tastemakers, trendsetters and fashion manipulators who succeed in forging lower-class emulation out of whole cloth.[109] The ruling class must not only force recalcitrant workers to become a tractable labour force, it must simultaneously force traditional consumers to desire an appropriate array of goods.

Converting the *ability* to buy novelties and luxuries into a *willingness* to do so, as Jones puts it, depended on a shift in tastes. Fashion manipulators such as the now-legendary Josiah Wedgwood could do much to give a specific focus to this process. But they could not bring it into being alone, because, as I have argued here, it also took the *willingness* to shift one's tastes to acquire the *ability* to act on that desire.

One final issue remains to be addressed. Throughout this chapter I have referred to the household as a producing and consuming unit. The 'household' has made decisions about the composition of its production, the relinquishment of leisure and the character of its consumer demand. It is high time we directed a flashlight into this hitherto black box. It is, of course, composed of individuals, differentiated by relationship, age and sex. These individuals did not possess equal power in household decision-making, nor did they benefit or suffer equally from those decisions. These intra-family tensions have been most fully explored with respect to inter-generational distributions of household assets and income. Among property-owning households inheritance at once unites the family in maintaining the health of the household economy and has the potential of dividing members over the transmission of assets.[110] Among proletarian households the sparseness of transmissible assets makes its coherence as a productive unit vulnerable at certain stages of the family cycle, particularly by the early departure of children and their default on the obligation to transfer income to elderly parents.[111]

Our chief concern here is not the comparatively well-explored terrain of income and wealth redistributions across time – where the focus is on the relationship between parents and children – but the veritable *terra incognita* of production and consumption distributions across the members of the family: the distribution of labour and leisure as well as the distribution of consumption, plus the decision-making processes that regulated those distributions. Here the least explored relationship is between the sexes, particularly between husbands and wives.

The decisions of immediate concern to the industrious revolution concept are those to supply more labour – where the market-oriented labour of women and children becomes more prominent as their provision of 'Z goods' diminishes – and the decisions that determine how family income is allocated – where the changing composition of consumer demand might reveal shifts in the relative influence of family members.

Who made the decisions for the household? A 'strict patriarchy' model of the household economy posits a single and self-interested source of decision making: the male head of household disposes of the labour of his wife and children and projects his consumer preference onto the household.

An alternative approach is to define the family as a 'realm of altruism': in economic terms, each family member includes the utility of the other members (as defined by that member) in his or her own utility function. Just how the complicated calculus of joint utility maximization is achieved remains unclear – it invites the application of game-theoretic models of considerable complexity – but this economist's definition of 'the family' has the virtue of focusing attention on a process of negotiation among persons with an affective as well as a material stake in a joint enterprise.[112] This negotiation of utility functions could change the relative influence of family members, especially husbands and wives, without dissolving the essential integrity of the household as an economic unit.

Joan Thirsk alerts us to the possibility of such a shift when she complains that economic historians have paid insignificant attention to the development of English consumer society in the sixteenth and seventeenth centuries. This omission could occur, she argues, because of the criteria of economic importance that

> have been laid down by our menfolk. Starch, needles, pins, cooking pots, kettles, frying pans, lace, soap, vinegar, stockings do not appear on their shopping lists, but they regularly appear on mine. They may ignore them, but could their families manage without them?[113]

Does this inattention of male historians for which Thirsk upbraids them have its parallel in a primarily female origin to the sixteenth- and seventeenth-century consumer demand that buoyed the rural industries chronicled by Thirsk? She does not make this claim explicitly, but McKendrick, addressing the home market during the Industrial Revolution, does. He assumes that the labour of women and children which fuelled industrial production provided them with an income that gave them – the women at any rate – a stronger voice as consumers.

> When a man's wages went up in the eighteenth century the first beneficial effects might be expected to occur in the brewing industry, and in the commercialization of sport and leisure . . . gambling, boxing, horse racing and the like. When a woman's wages went up the first commercial effects would be expected in the clothing industries and those industries which provided consumer goods for the home. Her increased earnings released her desire to compete with her social superiors – a desire pent up for centuries or at least restricted to a very occasional excess.[114]

One need not accede to this Andy Capp-like caricature in its entirety (McKendrick here reduces the [im]moral vs rational peasant debate to a war between the sexes) to appreciate its implications for the industrious revolution concept. The shift from relative self-sufficiency to market-oriented production by all or most household members necessarily involves a reduction of typically female-supplied Z goods and their replacement by commercially produced goods. The role of the wife as a decision maker in consumption was bound to grow, even if her husband was not inclined to frequent bouts of drinking and gambling at the racetrack. The household strategies that fostered the industrious revolution placed the wife in a strategic position, located, as it were, at the intersection of the household's three functions: reproduction, production and consumption.[115]

Even when the household was most implicated in the market economy – with many or all family members working for wages outside the home – it did not dissolve into its constituent individual parts, each with his or her own income and demand pattern. The requirements of reproduction, the crucial importance of income redistribution and the continuing need to provide for inter-generational transfers gave the proletarian family of the Industrial Revolution a surprising resilience.[116] The continued importance of the household as a decision-making unit affecting both supply and demand, is well illustrated by the tendency, beginning after the mid-nineteenth century, for the long-term processes I have called an industrious revolution to be reversed. Although it takes us beyond the period that chiefly concerns us in this chapter, a brief examination of this important phenomenon will help to understand the historical – and contemporary – significance of the industrious revolution.

After the mid-nineteenth century the preference schedule that gave shape to household demand patterns, and simultaneously determined the household's supply of paid labour shifted in favour of Z goods (home produced and consumed goods and services). The reverse process in the seventeenth and eighteenth centuries had redirected the labour of family members – mainly wives and children – from home Z goods activities into market-oriented activities. As real earnings rose in the second half of the nineteenth century (the timing varied by social class and country), a new set of Z goods, associated with the health and training of children and the achievement of new standards of domesticity in the home, came to appear superior to the available range of market-provided goods and services. To acquire these Z goods the labour of wives and children was withdrawn from the labour force as the incomes of adult male workers rose. In the context of Figure 5.5 demand patterns now trace out consumption path A rather than path B, characteristic of the industrious revolution.[117]

The twinned concepts of breadwinners and home-makers came, for the first time, to define the household economy as rising adult male wages were used, in effect, to 'buy back' a portion of the household's labour.

The withdrawal of women from field work in agriculture, the suppression of child labour, the regulation of women's labour in factories – all common to the late nineteenth century – are sometimes interpreted as the imposition of a middle-class image of the family onto the working class. Certainly, for families whose breadwinner earned too little to aspire to the new standards, the imposition of compulsory schooling was resisted and the new models of female propriety resented. But the withdrawal of women and children from the paid labour force was too widespread and voluntary to be generally consistent with this 'external constraint' explanation.[118]

Just as the Industrial Revolution had depended on the buoyant home market supported by households that intensified their labour and strengthened their market orientation, so the Victorian and Edwardian household, for want of a better term, depended on the productivity advances that were the fruit of the Industrial Revolution. Household members could now act to secure a set of consumption goals that previously had been beyond reach for most people and which, ironically, were not provided by the market.

The new home-provided goods and services secured 'respectability', but also lower morbidity and mortality, better nutrition and higher educational levels. They were directly implicated in the process of investing in human capital, which is to say, these Z goods were crucial to the most basic achievements of modern industrial society.[119] These Z goods had few market-supplied substitutes; but they did have market-produced complements (i.e., goods whose demand rose in conjunction with the rise of these home activities). Home furnishings are perhaps the most obvious complement to this 'cult of domesticity'. Carole Shammas observes that

> The emergence of a parlour decorated by women and one which they could properly use for the visits of other women and men was, for all but the elite, a post-1800 development, only discarded in the twentieth century, by which time women had invaded the entire dwelling, pushing men into the basement, den, or garage.[120]

This new household behaviour pattern had profound consequences for the productive system (which became detached from the home, more capital-intensive and more exclusively oriented to the requirements of full-time male workers),[121] the structure of demand (which focused increasingly on 'family' rather than 'individual' goods: consumer durables, housing, home furnishings)[122] and the goals of reproduction (which, to use a crude expression, focused more on 'quality' – the endowment of human capital in children – and less on 'quantity').[123]

By enumerating these most basic characteristics of the 'breadwinner–home-maker household', the distinctiveness of household behaviour in the industrious revolution – and the interdependence of production, consumption and reproduction – becomes apparent. Also apparent is the return, in recent decades, of a new version of an industrious revolution, one in which the massive increase in paid labour-force participation of women (and children) is associated with the rise of market-provided substitutes for the characteristic home-maker Z goods: food preparation, cleaning, child care, health services and even (in still limited quantities) reproduction itself. The new industrious revolution, just as its predecessor, pairs a stagnation or decline of individual wages and salaries with a substantial extension of market-oriented activities. In response, the household releases its last labour reserves to the market, on which it comes to depend utterly. In doing so the modern industrious household loses its last practical functions. Consumer demand becomes more individualized (men, women and children possessing their own purchasing power), expenditures focus increasingly on less durable, immediate-gratification objects, and the reproduction process (i.e., child raising) relies increasingly on market-supplied services.

The new industrious revolution has important features in common with the old one of the seventeenth and eighteenth centuries, but, if my brief characterization has validity, it also differs in an important way. In both the first industrious revolution and its labour-withholding breadwinner–home-maker household successor, the family economy faced the market economy as an autonomous unit, with its own internal functions. Household demand patterns always depended on production and labour allocation decisions internal to the household. In contrast, the new industrious revolution marks the absorption of the remaining substance of the household into the market economy. The last frontier of capitalism is not so much to be found in Third World or other distant markets as it is in the commercialization of the final non-market family labour and production activities.[124]

This excursion into modern times is intended to call attention to the different possible 'modes' of household negotiation with the market economy, and the consequences they can have both for the level of consumer demand and its character. Without wishing to deny the major role that prices and incomes play in determining the position and shape of demand curves in the short run, I have sought to explore how household preferences could help shape the underlying long-run determinants of both supply and demand. In the seventeenth and eighteenth centuries the industrious household helped lay the groundwork for the Industrial Revolution through demand-led changes in its behaviour. It remains to be seen what the current industrious revolution holds in store for us.

Notes

1 Neil McKendrick, 'Introduction', in Neil McKendrick, John Brewer and J. H. Plumb (eds), *The Birth of a Consumer Society: The Commercialization of Eighteenth-Century England* (Bloomington: Indiana University Press, 1982), 5f. McKendrick further develops his criticism of economic historians in 'The consumer revolution of eighteenth-century England', in the same volume, 29–30. The criticism is not new; it was made much earlier, although less stridently, by E. W. Gilboy, 'Demand as a factor in the Industrial Revolution', in A. H. Cole (ed.), *Facts and Factors in Economic History* (Cambridge, Mass.: Harvard University Press, 1932), 620–39; reprinted in R. M. Hartwell (ed.), *The Causes of the Industrial Revolution in England* (London: Methuen, 1967), 121–38.

2 Mark Blaug, *Economic Theory in Retrospect*, 3rd edn (Cambridge: Cambridge University Press, 1978), 153. See also: R. Clower and A. Leijonhufvud, 'Say's Principle: what it means and doesn't mean', in A. Leijonhufvud, *Information and Coordination* (Oxford: Oxford University Press, 1981), 79–101.

3 Eric H. Hobsbawm, 'The general crisis of the European economy in the seventeenth century', *Past and Present*, v (1954), 33–53; vi (1954), 44–65; reprinted in Trevor Aston (ed.), *Crisis in Europe, 1560–1660* (London: Routledge & Kegan Paul, 1965), 47. Another influential study that emphasizes inter-continental and international trade is I. Wallerstein, *The Modern World-System*, vol. 1 (New York: Academic Press, 1974).

4 Phyllis Deane and W. A. Cole, *British Economic Growth, 1688–1959* (Cambridge: Cambridge University Press, 1962), ch. 2.

5 W. A. Cole, 'Factors in demand', in Roderick Floud and Donald McCloskey (eds), *The Economic History of Britain Since 1700*, 2 vols (Cambridge: Cambridge University Press, 1981), vol. 1, 38–9, 43; Donald McCloskey and R P. Thomas, 'Overseas trade and empire, 1700–1860', in Floud and McCloskey (eds), *Economic History of Britain*, vol. 1, 101–2.

6 A. H. John, 'The course of agricultural change, 1660–1760', in Walter Minchinton (ed.), *Essays in Agrarian History*, vol. 1 (Newton Abbot, 1968), 223–53; idem, 'Aspects of economic growth in the eighteenth century', in E. M. Carus-Wilson (ed.), *Essays in Economic History*, vol. 2 (London, 1962), 360–73; and idem, 'Agricultural productivity and economic growth in England', in E. L. Jones (ed.), *Agriculture and Economic Growth in England, 1660–1815* (London: Methuen, 1967), 172–93. E. L. Jones, 'Agricultural productivity and economic growth in England 1660–1750: agricultural change', *Journal of Economic History*, xxv (1965), 1–18.

More recent work emphasizing the growth of agricultural productivity in the period 1650–1750 includes: N. F. R. Crafts, 'Income elasticities of demand and the release of labour by agriculture during the British Industrial Revolution,' *Journal of European Economic History*, ix (1980), 153–68; idem, 'English economic growth in the eighteenth century: a reexamination of Deane and Cole's estimates', *Economic History Review*, 2nd series, xxix (1976), 226–35; and idem, *British Economic Growth during the Industrial Revolution* (Oxford: Oxford University Press, 1985); R. A. C. Allen, 'The growth of labour productivity in early modern English agriculture', *Explorations in Economic History*, xxv (1988), 117–46; and idem, *Enclosure and the Yeoman* (Oxford: Oxford University Press, forthcoming); Patrick O'Brien, 'Agriculture and the home market for English industry, 1660–1820', *English Historical Review*, c (1985), 773–800.

7 A notable effort to identify domestic sources of demand after the mid-eighteenth century is D. E. C. Eversley, 'The home market and economic growth in England, 1750–1780', in E. L. Jones and G. Mingay (eds), *Land, Labour and Population in the Industrial Revolution* (London: Edward Arnold, 1967), 209–52. Recent re-examinations of Eversley's argument have been critical: O'Brien in 'Agriculture and the home market' concludes that

> The slow and faltering development of agriculture [after 1750] did little to extend the home market in manufactures, even if the adverse swing in the terms of trade against industry may have been mitigated to some extent by a recycling of the gains made by landowners and farmers in the form of taxes for central government and as safe investments in the urban economy.
>
> (785)

Joel Mokyr, 'Demand vs. supply in the Industrial Revolution', *Journal of Economic History*, xxxvii (1977), 981–1008, reprinted in Joel Mokyr, *The Economics of the Industrial Revolution* (Totowa, NJ: Rowman & Allanheld, 1985), is similarly negative in his assessment (99).

8 Mokyr, 'Demand vs. supply', 110. Equally decisive and self-confident is Donald McCloskey's assessment. After reviewing possible demand-led accounts of the British Industrial Revolution he concludes 'And so the circle is complete. The pursuit of effects on income related to demand has come back to supply, that extraordinary flowering of ingenuity in many sectors of the British economy known as the industrial revolution.' Donald McCloskey, 'The Industrial Revolution, 1780–1860', in Floud and McCloskey (eds), *Economic History of Britain*, vol. 1, 123.

9 McKendrick, 'Introduction', 1; idem, 'Consumer revolution', 9.

10 McKendrick, 'Consumer revolution', 19–22.

11 McKendrick, 'Introduction', 2. The same point is made in idem, 'Consumer revolution', 23.

12 For a summary of findings see: Fernand Braudel and Frank Spooner, 'Prices in Europe from 1450 to 1750', in E. E. Rich and C. H. Wilson (eds), *The Cambridge Economic History of Europe*, vol. 4 (Cambridge: Cambridge University Press, 1967), 425–30, 482–3; J. Söderberg, 'Real wage trends in urban Europe, 1750–1850', *Social History*, xii (1987), 155–76. Seminal is the work of E. H. Phelps Brown and Sheila Hopkins. Their *Economica* articles published in 1955 through 1957 are brought together in *A Perspective of Wages and Prices* (London: Methuen, 1981).

13 The classic presentations of this 'complex' are found in Wilhelm Abel, *Agrarkrisen und Agrarkonjunktur*, 3rd edn (Hamburg and Berlin: Parey, 1978; 1st edn 1935. Translated as *Agricultural Fluctuations in Europe from the Thirteenth to the Twentieth Centuries*, London: Methuen, 1980); B. H. Slicher van Bath, *De agrarische geschiedenis van west Europa, 500–1850* (Utrecht: H & T Spectrum, 1960. Translated as *Agrarian History of Western Europe, 500–1850*, London: Edward Arnold, 1963); Emmanuel Le Roy Ladurie, *Les Paysans de Languedoc*, 2 vols (Paris: Mouton, 1966. Translated in abridged edition as *The Peasants of Languedoc*, Urbana: University of Illinois Press, 1974), esp. 'Conclusion: a great agrarian cycle', 289–311.

14 Emmanuel Le Roy Ladurie, 'L'Histoire immobile', *Annales E.S.C.*, xxix (1974), 673–82; translated as 'Motionless history', *Social Science History*, i (1977), 122.

15 This is well demonstrated, for the sixteenth century, in Phelps Brown and Hopkins, 'Some further evidence for the eighteenth century', in *Perspective on Wages and Prices*, and for the century after 1750 in Söderberg, 'Real wage trends'.

16 A preliminary presentation of findings of my Dutch labour market project is available in Jan de Vries, 'The population and economy of the preindustrial Netherlands', *Journal of Interdisciplinary History*, xv (1985), 661–82, reprinted in R. I. Rotberg and T. K. Rabb (eds), *Population and Economy: Population and History from the Traditional to the Modern World* (Cambridge: Cambridge University Press, 1986), 101–22. Further discussion of the Dutch departure from the 'European norm' is found in Jan de Vries, 'Welvarend Holland', *Bijdragen en mededelingen betreffende de geschiedenis der Nederlanden*, cii (1987), 229–39.

17 T. S. Ashton, 'The standard of living of the workers in England, 1790–1830', in F. A. Hayek (ed.), *Capitalism and the Historians* (Chicago: University of Chicago Press, 1954), 155.

18 E. H. Hunt and F. W. Botham, 'Wages in Britain during the Industrial Revolution', *Economic History Review*, 2nd series, xl (1987), 380–99.

19 E. P. Thompson, *The Making of the English Working Class* (New York: Vintage, 1966), 212.

20 ibid., 318.

21 Peter H. Lindert and Jeffrey G. Williamson, 'English workers' living standards during the Industrial Revolution: a new look', *Economic History Review*, 2nd series, xxxvi (1983), 1–25.

22 Peter H. Lindert and Jeffrey G. Williamson, 'Revising England's social tables, 1688–1867', *Explorations in Economic History*, xix (1982), 385–408; idem, 'Reinterpreting Britain's social tables, 1688–1913', *Explorations in Economic History*, xx (1983), 94–109. But see the critique of Charles Feinstein, 'The rise and fall of the Williamson curve', *Journal of Economic History*, xlviii (1988), 699–729, especially 720–3.

23 Roderick Floud, Kenneth Wachter and Annabel Gregory, *Height, Health and History: Nutritional Status in the United Kingdom, 1750–1980* (Cambridge: Cambridge University Press, 1990), ch. 4, esp. table 4.1.

24 Robert Fogel, 'Second thoughts on the European escape from hunger: famines, chronic malnutrition and mortality', in S. R. Osmani (ed.), *Nutrition and Poverty* (Oxford: Oxford University Press, forthcoming). Among the countries studied, only France seems to be an exception to the rule. There average final heights of men rose between the last quarter of the eighteenth century and the first quarter of the nineteenth, and remained higher.

25 Joel Mokyr, 'Is there still life in the pessimist case? Consumption during the Industrial Revolution, 1790–1850', *Journal of Economic History*, xlviii (1988), 69–92.

26 Carole Shammas, 'Changes in English and Anglo-American consumption from 1550 to 1800', ch. 9 in the present volume.

27 Braudel and Spooner, 'Prices in Europe', 429.

28 Hunt and Botham, 'Wages in Britain', 395; Lindert and Williamson, 'English workers' living standards', 2–8, 12–13.

29 Jan de Vries, 'The decline and rise of the Dutch economy, 1675–1900', in Gary Saxonhouse and Gavin Wright (eds), *Technique, Spirit, and Form in the Making of the Modern Economies: Essays in Honor*

of William N. Parker (Greenwich, Conn.: JAI Press, 1984), 176.

30 This is the customary method, justified in Abel, *Agrarkrisen und Agrarkonjunktur*, 135, as well as in his *Massenarmut und Hungerkrisen im vorindustriellen Europa: Versuch einer Synopsis* (Hamburg and Berlin: Parey, 1974), 24. Abel's justification is accepted even in recent studies, such as Leo Noordegraaf, *Hollands welvaren? Levensstandaard in Holland 1450–1650* (Bergen, Netherlands: Octavo, 1985). See also W. P. Blokmans and W. Prevenier, 'Armoede in de Nederlanden van de viertiende to het midden van de zestiende eeuw: bronnen en problemen', *Tijdschrift voor geschiedenis*, lxxxviii (1975), 501–38. The authors summarize the literature on late medieval living standards by stating that 70–80 per cent of an average pre-industrial European's budget was devoted to food, 5–15 per cent to housing, and 5–15 per cent to clothing, heating and lighting. Moreover, about half the *total* budget was, on average, spent on bread – that is, 63–70 per cent of all food expenditures were devoted to bread.

31 Phelps Brown and Hopkins constructed a 'basket of consumables' with the following components: meal products (bread grains and legumes), 20 per cent; meat and fish, 25 per cent; butter and cheese, 12.5 per cent; drink, 22.5 per cent; heating and lighting (charcoal, candles, oil), 8.5 per cent; textiles, 12.5 per cent. The commodities used to represent each category varied over time, but the categories *and their weights* remained constant for the entire seven-century period of the study. See Phelps Brown and Hopkins, 'Seven centuries of the prices of consumables compared with builders' wage-rates', *Economica*, xxiii (1956), 296–314. A similar 'basket of essential consumer goods' was constructed for a study of real wages in the southern Netherlands, Herman van der Wee, 'Prijzen en lonen als ontwikkelingsvariabelen: Een vergelijkend onderzoek tussen Engeland en de Zuidelijke Nederlanden, 1400–1700', in *Album offert à Charles Verlinden à l'occasion de ses trente ans de professorat* (Ghent: Universa, 1975), 413–35. Here the weights take the form of fixed quantities of commodities, but non-food items play no larger role than they do in the English study.

The Phelps Brown and Hopkins price index is subjected to detailed criticism in Steve Rappaport, *Worlds within Worlds: Structures of Life in Sixteenth-century London* (Cambridge: Cambridge University Press, 1989), 123–45 and Appendix III. His revised price index for the sixteenth century substantially reduces the rate of inflation of this era of 'price revolution'. He finds fault with the prices used by Phelps Brown and Hopkins (he prefers 'retail' to market, or 'wholesale' prices), but he does not suggest revision of the weights.

32 Ashton, 'Standard of living of the workers in England', 142.

33 For an effort to estimate *total* food expenditures see Carole Shammas, 'Food expenditures and economic well-being in early modern England', *Journal of Economic History*, xxi (1984), 254–69.

34 See Slicher van Bath, *Agrarian History*, 113–15, 209–10, 223–5; Abel, *Agricultural Fluctuations*, 51–2, 116–23, 187–8, 264–7.

35 Shammas argued convincingly that the percentage of total working-class budgets devoted to food expenditures was substantially lower than the often-assumed 80 per cent. Carole Shammas, *The Pre-industrial Consumer in England and America* (Oxford: Oxford University Press, 1990), 123–33. Studies of Amsterdam orphanage expenditures now being carried out by Anne McCants and myself show that bread expenditures rarely exceeded 20 per cent of total food expenditures in the period 1640–1780. Thereafter bread assumed a larger share of the total food budget, but it rarely exceeded 30 per cent.

36 For details see any statistics text, for example, Thomas H. Wonnacott and Ronald J. Wonnacott, *Introductory Statistics for Business and Economics*, 3rd edn (New York: Wiley, 1984), 601–8.

37 This can be done formally by using the Fisher's Ideal Index, which is simply the square root of the Laspeyres index multiplied by the Paasche index. It yields a result intermediate to the two indexes discussed in the text.

38 R. Meischke and H. J. Zantkuijl, *Het Nederlandse woonhuis van 1300–1800* (Haarlem: Tjeenk Willink, 1969). The diffusion of brick construction of farm buildings is followed in J. J. Voskuil, *Van vlechtwerk tot baksteen: geschiedenis van de wanden van het boerenhuis in Nederland* (Arnhem: Stichting

historisch boerderij onderzoek, 1979). For the use of brick in English cities see E. L. Jones and M. E. Falkus, 'Urban improvement and the English economy in the seventeenth and eighteenth centuries', *Research in Economic History*, iv (1979), 193–233.

39 C. W. Fock, 'Wonen aan het Leidse Rapenburg door de eeuwen heen', in P. M. M. Klep, J. Th. Lindblad, A. J. Schuurman, P. Singdenberg and Th. van Tijn, *Wonen in het verleden* (Amsterdam: NEHA, 1987), 189–205; Witold Rybczynski, *Home: A Short History of an Idea* (New York: Viking, 1986), 56.

40 Rybczynski, *Home*, 77 and ch. 3. But see Peter Thornton, *Seventeenth-century Interior Decoration in England, France and Holland* (New Haven: Yale University Press, 1978), 10, where we read that 'true comfort, as we understand it, was invented by the French in the seventeenth century'.

41 Examples of the use of probate inventories for the study of production include: Robert DuPlessis, 'Capital and finance in the early modern Veluwe paper industry', *A. A. G. Bijdragen*, xxviii (1986), 185–97; Jan de Vries, *The Dutch Rural Economy in the Golden Age, 1500–1700* (New Haven: Yale University Press, 1974), 137–53, 215–17; Mark Overton, 'Estimating crop yields from probate inventories: an example from East Anglia, 1585–1735', *Journal of Economic History*, xxxix (1979), 363–78; Robert C. Allen, 'Inferring yields from probate inventories', *Journal of Economic History*, xlviii (1988), 117–25.

On wealth holding see: Alice Hanson Jones, *Wealth of a Nation To Be: The American Colonies on the Eve of the Revolution* (New York: Columbia University Press, 1980); Boudien de Vries, *Electoraat en elite: Sociale structuur en sociale mobiliteit in Amsterdam, 1850–1895* (Amsterdam: De Bataafsche Leeuw, 1986).

Among the many works on material culture see: Thera Wijsenbeek-Olthuis, *Achter de gevels van Delft: Bezit en bestaan van rijk en arm in een periode van achteruitgang (1700–1800)* (Hilversum: Verloren, 1987); A. J. Schuurman, *Materiële cultuur en levensstijl* (Wageningen, A. A. G. Bijdragen no. 30, 1989); J. de Jong, *Een deftig bestaan: Het dagelijks leven van regenten in de 17de en 18de eeuw* (Utrecht: Kosmos, 1987); Lorna Weatherill, *Consumer Behaviour and Material Culture, 1660–1760* (London: Routledge, 1988).

42 See Shammas, 'Changes in English and Anglo-American consumption' and Lorna Weatherill, 'The meaning of consumer behaviour in late seventeenth and early eighteenth-century England', ch. 10 in the present volume. Other important works include: Lois Green Carr and Lorna S. Walsh, 'The standard of living in the colonial Chesapeake', *The William and Mary Quarterly*, vl, 3rd series (1988), 135–59; Gloria L. Main and Jackson T. Main, 'Economic growth and the standard of living in southern New England, 1640–1774', *Journal of Economic History*, xlviii (1988), 27–46; Peter Earle, *The Making of the English Middle Class: Business, Society and Family Life in London, 1660–1730* (Berkeley and Los Angeles: University of California Press, 1989).

43 But, see Daniele Roche, *Le peuple de Paris* (Paris: Aubier Montaigne, 1981); Ruth Mohrmann, *Alltagswelt im Land Braunschweig: Stadt und landliche Wohnkultur vom 16. bis zum frühen 20. Jahrhundert* (Münster: 1990); and a survey of work in progress: Ad van der Woude and Anton Schuurman (eds), *Probate Inventories: A New Source for the Historical Study of Wealth, Material Culture and Agricultural Development* (Wageningen, A. A. G. Bijdragen no. 23, 1980). An important study, although not based on probate inventories, is: Roman Sandgruber, *Die Anfänge der Konsumgesellschaft: Konsumgüterverbrauch, Lebensstandard und Alltagskultur in Österreich im 18. und 19. Jahrhundert* (Vienna: Verlag für Geschichte und Politik, 1982).

44 Jan de Vries, 'Peasant demand patterns and economic development: Friesland, 1550–1750', in William N. Parker and Eric L. Jones (eds), *European Peasants and their Markets: Essays in Agrarian Economic History* (Princeton: Princeton University Press, 1975), 205–65.

45 See note 60.

46 Wijsenbeek, *Achter de gevels*, 335.

47 Main and Main, 'Economic growth', 44.

48 ibid.

49 Earle, *English Middle Class*, 269.

50 ibid., 281, 300. Earle defined the lower boundary of the 'middling sort' as an annual income of £50 and a few hundred pounds of wealth (14).

51 Eric L. Jones, *The European Miracle* (Cambridge: Cambridge University Press, 1981), 63.

52 De Vries, 'Peasant demand patterns', table 6.13.

53 Main and Main, 'Economic growth', 39.

54 Carr and Walsh, 'Standard of living', 142–3 and table IV.

55 Earle, *English Middle Class*, 290–1.

56 The five tax categories, and the percentage of the deceased in each category, were as follows: *Pro Deo*, wealth under 300 gulden, 50–6 per cent; wealth 300–2,000 gulden, 28–31 per cent; wealth 2,000–6,000 gulden, 6–8 per cent; wealth 6,000–12,000 gulden, 2–4 per cent; wealth over 12,000 gulden, 5–7 per cent.

57 Wijsenbeek drew a 'representative-stratified' sample by selecting twenty probate inventories from each tax group in each of the three twenty-five-year time periods chosen for analysis. The twenty inventories in each tax group were constrained to represent equally four different family structures (families with adult children, with minor children, without children and unmarried households), and to be drawn one from each quinquenium of the twenty-five-year period. The selection of each inventory from those eligible (for instance, from the tax class II households with minor children in 1710–14) was done randomly. Wijsenbeek, *Achter de gevels*, 103–10.

58 Further exploration of this issue is certainly warranted. The importance of inheritance in early modern society may be such that household wealth varied more with the survival of parents of the household head than with the age of the household head. In such a case a dichotomous variable, inheritance, could override the continuous variable, age.

59 For an introduction to this very large issue, see: Wonnacott and Wonnacott, *Introductory Statistics*, esp. chs 6 and 23; Roger S. Schofield, 'Sampling in historical research', in E. A. Wrigley (ed.), *Nineteenth-century Society: Essays in the Use of Quantitative Methods for the Study of Social Data* (Cambridge: Cambridge University Press, 1972), 146–90; Melvyn A. Hammarberg, 'Designing a sample from incomplete historical lists', *American Quarterly*, xxiii (1971), 542–61.

60 Neil McKendrick, 'Home demand and economic growth: a new view of the role of women and children in the Industrial Revolution', in Neil McKendrick (ed.), *Historical Perspectives: Studies in English Thought and Society in Honour of J. H. Plumb* (London: Europa, 1974), 172.

61 Thompson, *English Working Class*, ch. 10.

62 In the short run, that is. Although it is hard to demonstrate, the argument that the *pattern* or structure of demand has an independent effect on economic growth is appealing. If purchasing power becomes more concentrated in the hands of a class of persons with a high propensity to consume precisely those industrial products which have the greatest potential for mechanized production, the growing market is likely to encourage such production innovation; such a society is more likely to follow a 'learning curve' of technical change. Identifying the 'correct' commodities and social classes *ex ante* is no easy task. See Albert Fishlow, 'Comparative consumption patterns, the extent of the market and alternative development strategies', in A. Ayel (ed.), *Micro Aspects of Development* (New York: Praeger Publishers, 1974), ch. 3.

63 Weatherill, *Consumer Behaviour*, Appendix I, 203–7.

64 This seems to be the message of work by Thirsk, who emphasizes early seventeenth-century rural industry, Jones, who focuses on rising agricultural productivity and its consequences in the century after 1650 and John and Eversley, who call attention to the rising demand of the first half of the eighteenth century.

65 I first heard this expression used by Professor Akira Hayami in reference to nineteenth-century Japanese economic development. Here I appropriate it to my own uses to signify a household-based intensification of market-directed labour and/or production, related to an increased demand for market-supplied goods and services.

66 The basic argument is made in: De Vries, 'Peasant demand patterns', 206–9. Even though I speak of changes in tastes as motivating 'industrious' conduct (or its opposite, see 119–20, below) the concept is, I believe, broadly consistent with the defence of stable preferences in the classic article

of George J. Stigler and Gary S. Becker, 'De gustibus non est disputandum', *American Economic Review*, lxvii (1977), 76–90. The point of similarity is the common view that a consumer theory based on the family as 'a passive maximizer of the utility from market purchases' should be replaced by the family as 'an active maximizer also engaged in extensive production and investment activities' (77). My position is broadly consistent, but not exactly the same: tastes are not inscrutable and capricious, but the process of 'active maximization' creates new situations, to which people respond creatively.

67 Mokyr, 'Demand vs. supply', acknowledges this as a valid defence of why 'demand factors mattered'. However he doubts that it could 'account for sustained growth' (985). He is right to hold that shifts in the labour supply curve due to a reduced leisure preference are an exhaustible source of growth. This article seeks to demonstrate that the process of household reorganization had many dimensions. Together, and in combination with resulting efficiency gains, they could sustain growth over a considerable time span.

68 De Vries, *Dutch Rural Economy*, 4–17 and Appendix C.

69 Stephen Hymer and Stephen Resnick, 'A model of an agrarian economy with nonagricultural activities', *American Economic Review*, lix (1969), 493–506.

70 De Vries, *Dutch Rural Economy*; Eric L. Jones, 'Agriculture and economic growth in England, 1660–1750: agricultural change', *Journal of Economic History*, xxv (1965), 1–18. Jones's emphasis on the century after 1650 as the temporal locus of England's agricultural revolution is forcefully confirmed in Ann Kussmaul, *A General View of the Rural Economy of England, 1538–1840* (Cambridge: Cambridge University Press, 1990).

71 George Grantham, 'Agricultural supply during the industrial revolution: French evidence and European implications', *Journal of Economic History*, il (1989), 44–5.

72 ibid., 66.

73 See: Sidney Pollard, *The Genesis of Modern Management* (Harmondsworth: Penguin, 1965); and E. P. Thompson, 'Time, work, discipline and industrial capitalism', *Past and Present*, xxxviii (1967), 56–97.

74 K. G. Persson, 'Consumption, labour and leisure in the late Middle Ages', in D. Menjot (ed.), *Manger et boire au Moyen Age* (Nice: Centre d'Etudes Médiévales de Nice, 1984), 219–20; Christopher Dyer, *Standards of Living in the Later Middle Ages* (Cambridge: Cambridge University Press, 1989), 222–3; Abel, *Agricultural Fluctuations*, 59.

75 Persson, 'Consumption, labour and leisure', 218.

76 A. J. M. Brouwer Ancher, *De gilden* (The Hague: Loman en Funke, 1895), 223; Noordegraaf, *Hollands welvaren?*, 57–61.

77 Holidays were limited to Easter, Whitsun, Pentecost, Christmas and New Years, and where these fall on Sundays, the day following. This is evident from wage records of the city of Groningen (Gemeentearchief, Ond archief, 332r bijlagen) and the Hoogheemraadschap van Rijnland (Oud archief, 10905ff.).

78 M. A. Bienefeld, *Working Hours in British Industry: An Economic History* (London: Weidenfeld & Nicolson, 1972), 15–19.

79 Persson, 'Consumption, labour and leisure', 220.

80 'Consideration on taxes' (1764), quoted in Paul Mantoux, *The Industrial Revolution in the Eighteenth Century* (London, 1928; reprinted, New York: Harper & Row, 1961), 62.

81 ibid. A vast body of contemporary commentary on this characteristic is summarized in Edgar Furniss, *The Position of Labour in a System of Nationalism* (New York: Houghton Mifflin, 1919), ch. 6. See also: Peter Mathias, 'Leisure and wages in theory and practice', in idem, *The Transformation of England* (London: Methuen 1979), 148–67; D. C. Coleman, 'Labour in the English economy of the seventeenth century', *Economic History Review*, 2nd series, viii (1956), 280–95. Such commentary cannot always be taken as the product of disinterested observation of actual behaviour. It also functioned as part of an ideology that defined the 'otherness' and incapacity of self-governance of the working population. In addition, it had the practical benefit, as the 'utility of poverty doctine', of justifying

low wages. As such, its frequent repetition, growing more insistent in the retelling, is intended to reinforce the ideology rather than add to the cumulative empirical observations. It is ironic that many historians who regard themselves as champions of the common man appropriate this claim. What had served as a trope justifying the subordination of the 'dependent classes' because of their lack of self-control and spirit of improvement is used by 'moral economy' advocates as evidence of the pre-capitalist natural innocence of common folk. The misunderstanding of liberal political economists is no less a misunderstanding in the hands of their political opponents.

Occasionally, historical evidence penetrates this veil of preconception. W. G. Hoskins, in his classic study *The Midland Peasant* (New York: St Martin's Press, 1965), had to observe that social differentiation was well under way in Wigston Magna long before the village was enclosed and, presumably, subjected to the full onslaught of capitalist farming. 'In a way', he lamented, 'the peasant community was breeding its own downfall, by producing a class of successful landowners . . . whose interests and whole way of thinking gradually became estranged from the peasant system under which their ancestors had lived and prospered in earlier times' (198–9). Similarly, E. P. Thompson followed convention in blaming the lords and gentry for attacking the customary rights of the English peasantry. But he also acknowledged the spread of individualism among the yeomen as contributing to 'the death of the yeomanry as a class': E. P. Thompson, 'The grid of inheritance: a comment', in Jack Goody, Joan Thirsk and E. P. Thompson (eds), *Family and Inheritance* (Cambridge: Cambridge University Press, 1976), 329–33.

82 Adam Smith, *An Inquiry into the Nature and Causes of the Wealth of Nations* (1776); Sir James Steuart, *An Inquiry into the Principles of Political Oeconomy* (London, 1767; reprinted, edited and with an introduction by Andrew S. Skinner, Edinburgh: Oliver & Boyd, 1966), 67. The gradual shift in elite thought with respect to labour-market behaviour is discussed in Joyce Appleby, *Economic Thought and Ideology in Seventeenth-Century England* (Princeton: Princeton University Press, 1978).

83 A 'short course' on this concept might focus on the following: Franklin Mendels, 'Proto-industrialization: the first phase of the industrialization process', *Journal of Economic History*, xxxii (1972), 241–61; Mendels, 'Des industries rurales à la proto-industrialisation: historique d'un changement de perspective', *Annales E.S.C.*, xxxix (1984), 977–1008; Eric L. Jones, 'The agricultural origins of industry', *Past and Present*, xl (1968), 58–71; Hans Medick, 'The proto-industrial family economy during the transition from peasant society to industrial capitalism', *Social History*, i (1976), 291–315; D. C. Coleman, 'Proto-industrialization: a concept too many', *Economic History Review*, 2nd series, xxxvi (1983), 435–48; Peter Kriedte, Hans Medick and Jurgen Schlumbohm, *Industrialization Before Industrialization* (Cambridge: Cambridge University Press, 1981); David Levine, *Family Formation in an Age of Nascent Capitalism* (New York: Academic Press, 1977); Gay L. Gullickson, *Spinners and Weavers of Auffay* (Cambridge: Cambridge University Press, 1986); Maxine Berg, Pat Hudson and Michael Sonenscher (eds), *Manufacture in Town and Country Before the Factory* (Cambridge: Cambridge University Press, 1983).

84 Joan Thirsk, *Economic Policies and Projects: The Development of a Consumer Society in Early Modern England* (Oxford: Oxford University Press, 1978), 169.

85 ibid., 174.

86 ibid., 175.

87 Joan Thirsk, 'New crops and their diffusion: tobacco-growing in seventeenth-century England', in C. W. Chalklin and M. A. Havinden (eds), *Urban Growth and Rural Change 1500–1800: Essays in English Regional History in Honour of W. G. Hoskins* (London, 1974), 76–103; H. K. Roessingh, *Inlandse tabak: expansie en contractie van een handelsgewas in de 17de en 18de eeuw in Nederland* (Wageningen: A. A. G. Bijdragen, 1976); B. H. Slicher van Bath, *Een samenleving onder spanning: geschiedenis van het platteland in Overijssel* (Assen: Van Gorcum, 1957).

88 'Proto-industrialization' as defined by Mendels consists not simply of an expansion of market-oriented rural industry, but of an expansion of market-oriented rural industry taking place in regions experiencing simultaneous commercial agricultural development. Thus, households special-

izing in industrial production were linked, in a complementary regional structure, to households specializing increasingly in food production. Franklin Mendels, 'Les temps de l'industrie et les temps de proto-industrialisation', *Revue du Nord*, lxviii (1981), 21–34.

89 McKendrick, 'Home demand', 172.

90 ibid., 197.

91 Gregory Clark, 'Why isn't the whole world developed? Lessons from the cotton mills', *Journal of Economic History*, xlvii (1987), 141–73; idem, 'Productivity growth without technological change in European agriculture before 1850', *Journal of Economic History*, xlvii (1987), 419–32; idem, 'The costs of capital and medieval agricultural technique', *Explorations in Economic History*, xxv (1988), 265–94.

92 idem, 'Productivity growth', 432.

93 ibid., 425.

94 Grantham, 'Agricultural supply', 70–1.

95 Herman Freudenberger and Gaylord Cummins, 'Health, work, and leisure before the Industrial Revolution', *Explorations in Economic History*, xiii (1976), 1. See also Herman Freudenberger, 'Das Arbeitsjahr', in Ingomar Bog, Günter Franz, Karl-Heinrich Kaufhold, Hermann Kellenbenz and Wolfgang Zorn, *Wirtschaftliche und Soziale Strukturen im saekularen Wandel* (Hanover: Verlag Mund H. Schaper, 1974), 307–20.

96 Fogel, 'Second thoughts on the European escape from hunger', 41.

97 Fogel appears to suggest this possibility in a footnote, where he identifies the malnourished portion of the labour force as the 'lumpenproletariat' and as 'gens de néant'. ibid., 61, note 20.

98 Esther Boserup, *The Conditions of Agricultural Growth* (London: Allen & Unwin, 1965). For explication and discussion of Boserup's concepts see: Jan de Vries, *Dutch Rural Economy*, Appendix A, pp. 17–18; idem, 'Boserup as economics and history', *Peasant Studies Newsletter*, i (1972), 45–50.

99 Franklin Mendels, 'Agriculture and peasant industry in eighteenth-century Flanders', in Parker and Jones, *European Peasants and Their Markets*, 179–204; idem, 'Proto-industrialization', *passim*.

100 Chris Vandenbroeke, *Sociale geschiedenis van het Vlaamse volk* (Beveren: Orion, 1982), esp. Part III, ch. 1.

101 Medick, 'The proto-industrial family', 305.

102 ibid.

103 Levine, *Family Formation*, 9.

104 Key works in a growing literature include: John Brewer, *The Sinews of Power: War, Money and the English State, 1688–1783* (New York: Alfred Knopf, 1989), 88–91; Peter Mathias and Patrick O'Brien, 'Taxation in Britain and France, 1715–1810: a comparison of the social and economic incidence of taxes collected for the central governments', *Journal of European Economic History*, v (1976), 601–90; James Collins, *The Fiscal Limitations of Absolutism: Direct Taxation in Early Seventeenth-Century France* (Berkeley and Los Angeles: University of California Press, 1988); Niels Steensgaard, 'The seventeenth-century crisis', in Geoffrey Parker and Lesley M. Smith (eds), *The General Crisis of the Seventeenth Century* (London: Routledge & Kegan Paul, 1978), 26–56.

105 David Levine, *Reproducing Families: The Political Economy of English Population History* (Cambridge: Cambridge University Press, 1987), 19–21, 39.

106 Pollard, *Genesis of Modern Management*, 190.

107 This process seems to be what Jones has in mind when he speaks of Europeans having been 'K-strategists' and having experienced a 'ratchet effect' whereby numbers were systematically kept below carrying capacity, and the resulting margin of per capita well-being was used to advance the economy. Jones, *European Miracle*, 3, 20, 56. It can also be related to what Persson called 'break out' from the backward-bending labour supply curve. If, referring to Figure 5.6, workers were at the upper left-hand range of the offer curve and experienced a decrease in wage rates, their response might be to preserve the already achieved 'target income' by offering more labour as wages fall. They would 'break out' of the offer curve traced in the figure. If, with a renewed phase of rising wages they did not immediately reduce the supply of labour, they would, by a ratchet

130   Jan de Vries

effect, achieve yet higher income levels. Persson, 'Consumption, labour and leisure', 214.

108 The classic statements of the two positions are found in: James C. Scott, *The Moral Economy of the Peasant* (New Haven: Yale University Press, 1976); Samuel L. Popkin, *The Rational Peasant: The Political Economy of Rural Society in Vietnam* (Berkeley and Los Angeles: University of California Press, 1979); and Alan Macfarlane, *The Origins of English Individualism* (Cambridge: Cambridge University Press, 1979).

109 On the role of emulation and demand manipulation see: Eric L. Jones, 'The fashion manipulators: consumer tastes and British industries, 1660–1800', in Louis P. Cain and Paul J. Uselding (eds), *Business Enterprise and Economic Change: Essays in Honor of Harold F. Williamson* (Kent, Ohio: Kent State University Press, 1973), 198–226; Neil McKendrick, 'The commercialization of fashion', in Brewer and Plumb, *Birth of a Consumer Society*, 34–99. For a critique of these articles, see: Ben Fine and Ellen Leopold, 'Consumerism and the Industrial Revolution', *Social History*, xv (1990), 151–79.

110 Jack Goody, Joan Thirsk and E. P. Thompson (eds), *Family and Inheritance: Rural Society in Western Europe, 1200–1800* (Cambridge: Cambridge University Press, 1978); Lutz K. Berkner, 'The Stem family and the developmental cycle of the peasant household: an eighteenth-century Austrian example', *American Historical Review*, lxxvii (1972), 398–418; Lutz K. Berkner and Franklin F. Mendels, 'Inheritance systems, family stucture, and demographic patterns in western Europe (1700–1900)', in Charles Tilly (ed.), *Historical Studies of Changing Fertility* (Princeton: Princeton University Press, 1978).

111 Child default is a theme of Rudolf Braun, *Industrialisierung und Volksleben: Die Veränderungen der Lebensformen in einem landlichen Industriegebiet vor 1800* (Zurich: E. Rentsch Verlag, 1960) and Michael Anderson, *Family Structure in Nineteenth-Century Lancashire* (Cambridge: Cambridge University Press, 1971), 131–4. For theoretical formulations of the concept see: Paul David and William A. Sundstrom, 'Old-age security motives, labor markets, and farm family fertility in antebellum America', *Explorations in Economic History*, xxv (1988), 164–97 and idem, 'Did rising out-migration cause fertility to decline in antebellum New England? A life-cycle perspective on old-age security motives, child default, and farm-family fertility' (California Institute of Technology, Social Science Working Paper 610, April 1986).

112 Paul A. Samuelson, 'Social indifference curves', *Quarterly Journal of Economics*, lxx (1956), 1–22.

113 Thirsk, *Economic Policies and Projects*, 22–3.

114 McKendrick, 'Home demand', 199–200. His point is developed further by Maxine Berg, *The Age of Manufactures, 1700–1820* (Oxford: Oxford University Press, 1986), 169–72.

115 A masterful account of the growing centrality of wives in the household economy as it becomes more market-oriented is found in David Sabean, *Property, Production, and Family in Neckarhausen, 1700–1870* (Cambridge: Cambridge University Press, 1990), especially ch. 6. On the basis of local court records, Sabean observes 'As women became producers of products which were exchanged for cash, they began to demand considerable say in the disposal of both the products and the proceeds' (174).

116 Michael Anderson, *Approaches to the History of the Western Family, 1500–1914* (London: Macmillan, 1980), 78–9. See also Michael Anderson, *Family Structure in Nineteenth-Century Lancashire* (Cambridge: Cambridge University Press, 1971).

117 In Figure 5.5, quadrant II (upper left) shows a production possibilities curve between Z (non-traded non-agricultural goods) and F (food production), quadrant III (lower left) shows the terms of trade between food and M (manufactures, or non-agricultural goods and services produced outside the household). P_2 represents more favourable terms of trade for the food producer than P_1. Quadrant I (upper right) shows the consumption possibilities curves that correspond to the relative prices represented by P_1 and P_2. Consumption takes place at the tangency of the consumption possibilities curve and the community indifference curves (dashed curves). The successive tangency points derived by shifting the terms of trade trace out the consumption paths A and B, each reflecting a different set of preferences. The 'industrious revolution' is thought to require a

shift from consumption path A to B, as the household devotes more of its resources to the production of the traded good (F) (see quadrant II). As a new set of desirable Z goods (health care, child-training, domestic comfort, etc.) comes within reach, household behaviour can be represented by a shift back from consumption path B to A, although the traded good (F) is now more likely to be wage labour.

118 Anderson, *Western Family*, 83. This interpretation is, I believe, broadly consistent with the analysis of Joan Scott and Louise Tilly in 'Women's work and the family in nineteenth-century Europe', *Comparative Studies in Society and History*, xvii (1975), 36–64. They speak of the 'continuity of traditional values and behaviour' (42) where I invoke the industrious revolution concept; they refer to the 'waning of the family economy' (62) where I speak of the breadwinner-home-maker household, which is, in my view, still very much a family economy, but one with a new emphasis on Z goods.

These claims imply that families pursue 'strategies', not simply for survival, but for the achievement of goals, which, because we observe them changing, cannot simply be treated as implicit or 'inculcated predispositions'. For a lively discussion of the family strategy notion see: Leslie Page Moch, Nancy Folbre, Daniel Scott Smith, Laurel L. Cornell and Louise A. Tilly, 'Family strategy: a dialogue', *Historical Methods*, xx (1987), 113–25. On 'inculcated predispositions' see: Pierre Bourdieu, 'Marriage strategies as strategies of social reproduction', in R. Forster and O. Ranum, (eds), *Family and Society: Selections from the Annales: Economies, Sociétés, Civilisations* (Baltimore: Johns Hopkins University Press, 1976), 117–44.

119 It is worth emphasizing that while the productivity-raising effects of industrialization put these new Z goods 'within reach', they could actually be acquired only through the (re)intensification of a division of labour within the household. A redefinition of gender roles offered major gains from 'increasing returns to investments in sector-specific human capital that raise productivity mainly in either the market or the non-market sphere'. Gary Becker, whose *Treatise on the Family*, 2nd edn (Chicago: University of Chicago Press, 1991) (3) is here quoted, treats this process of sphere definition as an outcome dictated by economic incentives to specialization 'even if a husband and wife are intrinsically identical' (ibid.).

For working-class households desirous of investing in human capital the results of this process (as opposed to its explanation) do not differ in their essentials from the results of Leonore Davidoff and Catherine Hall's study of English middle-class families in the period 1700–1850 (*Family Fortunes* (London: Routledge, 1992), 4) where they sought to show how the economic, social and political aspirations of middle-class men depended crucially on 'networks of familial and female support which underpinned their rise to public prominence'.

120 Shammas, *Pre-industrial Consumer*, 187. The central position of women in this process is also stressed by Rybczynski:

> Ever since the seventeenth century, when privacy was introduced into the home, the role of women in defining comfort has been paramount. The Dutch interior, the Rococo salon, the servantless household — all were the result of women's invention. One could argue, with only slight exaggeration, that the idea of domesticity was principally a feminine idea. So was the idea of efficiency.
>
> (*Home*, 223)

In the new industrious revolution phase, this process could be expected to weaken. Indeed, the modern tendency for electronic devices to constitute the defining items of home furnishing suggests that the historical process sketched by Shammas is now being reversed.

121 Altogether consistent is the observation of Maxine Berg, that, beginning in the second quarter of the nineteenth century, 'not only did workers' organizations become increasingly segmented, but the language of artisan institutions and the perception of skill itself became increasingly identified with masculinity', *The Age of Manufactures*, 160.

122 A statement that well reflects the spirit of an age in which the new Z goods were held up as the highest 'consumer' aspiration of decent folk is made by G. K. Chesterton as part of a social critique based on his observation that (in his day) 'the cultured class is shrieking to be let out of the decent home, just as the working class is shouting to be let into it'.

The key to right thinking, Chesterton asserted, was to have a fixed point, an ideal, from which to analyse conflicting political claims. He found that fixed point 'with a little girl's hair'.

> That I know is a good thing at any rate. Whatever else is evil, the pride of a good mother in the beauty of her daughter is good. It is one of those adamantine tendernesses which are the touchstones of every age and race. If other things are against it, those things must go down. . . . With the red hair of one she-urchin in the gutter I will set fire to all modern civilization. Because a girl should have long hair, she should have clean hair; because she should have clean hair, she should not have an unclean home; because she should not have an unclean home, she should have a free and leisured mother; because she should have a free mother, she should not have an usurious landlord; because there should not be an usurious landlord, there should be a redistribution of property; because there should be a redistribution of property, there shall be a revolution. That little urchin with the gold-red hair, whom I have just watched toddling past my house, she shall not be lopped and lamed and altered; her hair shall not be cut short like a convict's; no, all the kingdoms of the earth shall be hacked about and mutilated to suit her.
>
> (G. K. Chesterton, *What's Wrong With the World* (London: Chatto & Windus, 1910), as quoted in Gilbert Meilaender, 'What families are for', *First Things*, vi (1990), 34)

See also Scott and Tilly's 'Women's work in nineteenth-century Europe', where they call attention to the fact that 'some socialist newspapers described the ideal society as one in which "good socialist wives" would stay at home and care for the health and education of "good socialist children" ' (64).

123 On this concept see: Richard A. Easterlin, 'The economics and sociology of fertility: a synthesis', in Tilly (ed.), *Historical Studies of Changing Fertility*, 57–133.

124 This point is prefigured by Joseph Schumpeter's analysis in *Capitalism, Socialism and Democracy* (New York: Harper & Row, 1942). In ch. 14, 'Decomposition', he writes of the 'disintegration of the bourgeois family'. Although he is chiefly concerned with the 'upper strata of the bourgeoisie' to which the capitalist order 'entrusts [its] long-run interests' he notes that:

> the phenomenon [of decomposition] by now extends, more or less, to all classes.. . . . It is wholly attributable to the rationalization of everything in life, which we have seen is one of the effects of capitalist evolution. . . . The capitalist order rests on props made of extra-capitalist material [and] derives its energy from extra-capitalist patterns of behavior which at the same time it is bound to destroy.
>
> (157–62)

In this context feminism, doing battle against society's last significant extra-capitalist patterns of behaviour, may be seen as establishing the conditions for 'the highest stage of capitalism'.

6

European consumption and Asian production in the seventeenth and eighteenth centuries

John E. Wills, Jr

It is a fine summer morning in 1730. The prosperous London merchant flings back the chintz quilt, very old-fashioned but a beloved family heirloom, straightens his muslin night-shirt and puts on his Chinese silk dressing-gown as the maid enters with the tea, milk and sugar. She trips, and the newly bought matched blue and white china tea service is smashed. There will be a row. It will be worse because his wife has been in a bad mood ever since she learned that her country cousins can buy from peddlers patterns of calico and chintz not yet seen in London, and finer teas. It is a relief to think that he must meet a promising new customer at Garraway's coffee house this afternoon, and that with any luck the meeting will go on late into the evening.

Sugar, tea, coffee, porcelain and Indian and Chinese textiles (silks, chintzes, muslins, calicos and dozens more names) were conspicuous components in the emergence of consumer societies in Europe in the eighteenth century whose centres of production were in Asia and the Americas. The spread of the mass consumption of sugar is discussed by Sidney Mintz in chapter 13 of this volume. In any case, its connections with the African slave trade and with New World settlement set it apart in many ways from the goods of Asian origin discussed in this chapter.[1]

Of course, European consumption of Asian luxury goods was not a new phenomenon in this period; it can be traced back to Roman imports of Chinese silks. Pepper, cinnamon, cloves and nutmeg made their way from their Indian Ocean production areas to the eastern Mediterranean and thence to Europe throughout the Middle Ages; they continued to do so in the seventeenth and eighteenth centuries, but despite all the blood and treasure the Europeans spent in seeking to control their passage to Europe, the quantities sold there did not grow dramatically.

The growth commodities in Asian exports to Europe in the late seventeenth and eighteenth centuries were those for which there was a steadily broadening market at stable or falling prices. In the early stages of the spread of demand for these goods, their exotic associations sometimes spurred demand, and the fact that middling people might own something from India or China contributed to the glamorizing of consumption in the emerging middle-class culture. For some items, especially tea, it seems that exoticism never was very important. For many, it was accompanied or soon followed by more durable sources of demand, as consumers came to appreciate their genuine new utilities: the stimulant value of coffee and tea and their use in preparing warm, nutritious drinks, and the lightness, comfort and workability of cotton cloth. Their wide availability – nearly everyone in England drank tea and wore Indian cottons in the eighteenth century – was a result of their low cost, in turn partly a result of the lower standard of living of the producers, and the more modest needs for housing and clothing of dwellers in the tropics.

Here we may begin to suspect that these boons to European consumers were at least in part at the expense of exploited Asian producers. The history of the contributions of the world economy to consumption in the richer countries is full of West Indian sugar plantations, Indian and Indonesian colonial plantations in the nineteenth and early twentieth centuries, banana republics, cheap labour assembly plants and many more cases of exploitation of non-European producers. However, in each of the case studies below we find that European traders in Asia began to export these goods to Europe when they tapped into an already thriving and sophisticated network of intra-Asian trade. Europeans traded in ports and markets ruled by Asians, where they could not exclude or distort the competition of Asians and other Europeans and prices were set by market forces. Their demand for export goods stimulated economic growth in producing areas. In many cases this situation met the needs of the Europeans remarkably well for many decades. But the Europeans found it hard to accept its uncertainties, and early and late sought ways to exert greater control, exclude competitors and maximize short-run profits. In the cases studied here, they eventually managed to do so for coffee and for some key elements of the Indian textile trades, creating production and trade regimes that were exploitative of Asian producers or destructive of their industries. No such transition was made, however, for the tea and porcelain of China.

The Asian networks of commerce in which the Europeans participated served many kinds of Asian consumers. Some of them, notably southeast Asian consumers of Indian textiles, were a long way from any kind of changeable 'consumer society', demanding exactly the same kinds of fabrics year after year. Elsewhere, we can see quite a few analogues to the consumer society phenomenon in Europe discussed in this and other chapters in this volume. Both China and Japan in the eighteenth century had important urban, commercial sectors in which there was much extravagant dress and rapid change in fashion, wide distribution of specialized food products, and the consumption of food, rice wine and tea in restaurants and tea shops was a vital part of social life. In the Ottoman Empire the coffee house was as important a social institution as it was in London and Paris. India's consumption of its own splendid products probably was more centred on its many opulent courts, less 'urban-bourgeois' than in the cases above. If, despite these important partial analogues, we find nothing in Asia fully comparable to the steady spread of mass consumption and the intercontinental sources of supply seen in the European consumer societies, our efforts to explain this contrast will very quickly entangle us with the whole problem of the emergence of the modern world economy and all the sources of European domination of it: technological advance, American precious metals, the regime of competitive mercantile states, European domination of inter-continental trade and so on.

Maritime Asia

This chapter is a very preliminary exploration of the territory at the intersection of two rapidly developing fields of historical study. One is the history of consumption in early modern Europe which is the focus of this volume. The other is the history of maritime Asia in early modern times. Recent changes in the historiography of the latter field have not been very widely noticed outside the circles of scholars who are making direct contributions. I would suggest the nature and depth of the changes by calling the field the history of maritime Asia instead of the label under which I began studying it around 1960, the history of European expansion in Asia. The European expansion approach directed all attention to the great problem of the long rise of European naval and commercial hegemony in Asian waters, at the expense of any ability to think coherently about the changing political economies and commercial networks of the peoples of Asia themselves. Recent work in Asian maritime history, while still very much interested in the vicissitudes of European trade and power and continuing to make a great deal of use of European-language sources, is much less Eurocentric, much more apt to be the work of historians of one part or another of Asia, frequently themselves Asian. One of its centres of intellectual energy is at the Delhi School of Economics.[2]

As a result of this recent work, we see that participants in the maritime history of every part of Asia included Asian navigators, merchants, pirates, investors, merchant-princes and so on, and that these Asian participants remained effective competitors of the Europeans far longer than earlier scholars had thought. We see not an 'age of Vasco da Gama', but a series of incursions and accommodations to or partial disruptions of established Asian patterns of trade and power. The anomaly to be explained is not the survival of Asian trade and power but the survival of the Europeans as organizationally coherent presences in the Indian Ocean. As a result of their various survivals, they were positioned to pick up the pieces and gain power for themselves as various Asian polities, ranging in size and complexity from the segmented monarchies of Indonesian ports to the Mughal Empire, passed through succession crises or longer declines of political cohesion. Muslim trade in the western Indian Ocean, for example, was highly competitive with European trade until the land routes on which it depended became chronically unsafe as a result of the decline of internal order in the Mughal, Safavid and Ottoman Empires in the late eighteenth century.[3] The European survivals owed much to some distinctive forms of organization, especially the intermingled structures of monarch, nation and cities in the Portuguese Estado da India and the great chartered East India Companies of the English, the Dutch and others. The Europeans also found ready-made roles into which they could fit – in the structures of adjustment and avoidance among multiple communities in India, in the political economy of the Mughal Empire and in the politics of hegemonic interference in coastal small kingdoms in Indonesia.

From the end of the Dutch–Portuguese wars in 1665 to the outbreak of large-scale Anglo-French conflict in India in the 1740s, European power in India and in the Far East made few dramatic changes or advances. The Dutch territorial advances in Java were an important variation from this pattern. Everywhere except in Indonesia the Europeans controlled only enclaves, and had to adjust themselves to Asian political, economic and cultural norms. But it was precisely in these decades that Asian products became part of the consumption revolution in northwestern Europe. The dominant European presence in Asian waters was that of the great Dutch and English East India Companies.[4] The general pattern was one in which the centralized decision-making and ordering systems of the great companies made their Asian agents remarkably sensitive to changing tastes and fashions in Europe, and the dispersed but highly commercialized structures of production in Asia very effectively provided the goods the Europeans wanted to buy. This fit, it now seems to me, was not only an important part of the European consumer revolution but also an important aspect of these long decades when the European presence became so thoroughly accepted and so quietly naturalized in ports from Bombay to Canton.

Indian textiles in Europe

In both India and China, the Europeans encountered highly varied and sophisticated cloth-producing industries.[5] Chinese silk fabrics and raw silk for European looms were luxury products, too expensive to open up any new markets among lesser folk, plagued until 1700 by the shifts and insecurities of Dutch and English connections with China, facing stiff competition thereafter from the cheaper silk products of Bengal. The cotton and silk fabrics of India already had markets all the way from the Middle East to the Spice Islands. They moved via the Red Sea and Persian Gulf throughout the Muslim heartlands. Europeans wanting to buy cloves, nutmeg and pepper in Indonesia found that the islanders would not accept anything in exchange except silver and Indian cloth. Thus the Europeans' first motives for purchase of Indian fabrics were the requirements of Asian markets, especially those of the Spice Islands. An important new market emerged with the growth in the late seventeenth century of the African slave trade and the Caribbean sugar economy; large quantities of cotton fabrics, mostly of low to medium quality, were exported for sale in West Africa or to Caribbean slave-owners. In Europe in the early seventeenth century, the demand for Indian fabrics was not very large and was almost entirely for table and bed linens, wall hangings and other house furnishings, not for clothing. The turning point towards a rapidly growing demand for Indian cottons for clothing seems to have come some time after 1670. J. Cary commented in a pamphlet published in 1699 that

> It was scarce thought about twenty years since that we should ever see Calicoes the ornaments of our greatest Gallants (for such they are whether we call them Muslins, Shades, or anything else) when they were then rarely used . . . but now few think themselves well dresst till they are made up in Calicoes, both men and women, Calico Shirts, Neckcloths, Cuffs, Pocket-handkerchiefs for the former, Head-Dresses, Nightroyls, Hoods, Sleeves, Aprons, Gowns, Petticoats, and what not for the latter, besides India-Stockings for both Sexes.[6]

K. N. Chaudhuri, in the best economic-historical analysis of this trade I have seen, argues that

> Although part of the rising new demand probably came from the substitution of cotton for the traditional non-wool fabrics manufactured in Europe, much of it must have been additional to the existing consumption generated, by the utility and novelty of the Indian products. The lack of definite proof for this statement is tempered by the observable rate of expansion which was much too rapid to have been accounted for by substitution alone.[7]

It will come as no surprise to students of the consumption revolutions of this period that this growth of demand, and the associated growth of demand for silk fabrics of Indian manufacture, did not just happen, but were assiduously promoted by merchants who thoroughly understood the social foundations of European demand. This is especially clear in the 1680s, when the English Company's efforts to find new buyers for its imports were stimulated by formidable competition from the Dutch and from English 'interlopers'. In 1681 the English Company directors wrote to their servants in India,

> Now [Know?] this for a constant and generall Rule, that in all flowered Silks you change ye fashion and flower as much as you can every year, for English Ladies and they say ye French and other Europeans will give twice as much for a new thing not seen in Europe before, though worse, then they will give for a better silk for [of] the same fashion worn ye former years.[8]

In 1683 they ordered the Surat factory to supply chintzes printed on finer cloth that would be found suitable for upper-class women, as they already were in Holland, while in England their use still was confined to 'the meaner sort'. By 1687 they could report that chintzes had become 'the ware of Ladyes of the greatest quality, which they wear on the outside of Gowns and Mantuoes which they line with velvet and Cloth of Gold'. Perhaps most interesting, if we are looking for indications of ways in which a broader market was opened up, is a 1682 letter to Madras ordering the purchase of 200,000 shifts ready-made, in order to 'introduce the using of Callicoe for that purpose in all these Northern parts of the world'. For seamen and other workers, they were to be made from strong blue and white cloth; for middling people, from 'white midling'; for ladies and gentlewomen, of fine white cloth.[9]

Rising prices for Indian fabrics in the 1690s are strong evidence for strengthening demand, but the English Company's figures on its own imports are surprisingly low; this was a time of two rival companies in England and a great deal of authorized and unauthorized private trade. There was much agitation for restriction of Asian cloth imports, culminating in the rioting of the Spitalfields silk weavers in 1697 and the Act of 1700 forbidding the use or wearing of 'all wrought silks, Bengalls, and stuffs mixed with silk or herbs, of the manufacture of Persia, China, or East India, and all calicoes painted, dyed, printed, or stained there'.[10] The English developed very large re-export trades to the continent and imported large quantities of white cloth to be printed and finished in England. Substantial quantities of the 're-exports' to the continent were unloaded at remote spots on the Kent and East Anglian coasts and peddled door to door throughout the country, so that by 1719 the Government admitted that there were 'more Callicoes worn in England that pay no duty than what are painted and worn here that do pay duty'.[11] English Company imports of Asian textiles continued to flourish; they had hit peaks over £400,000 total purchase price in two years in the 1680s but more generally were in the £100,000–200,000 range until after 1710; from 1710 to 1760, thirty-two years were over £400,000.[12] Dutch Company cargoes roughly matched these quantities. In the late eighteenth century English exports continued to grow, especially from Bengal, reaching £800,000 per year in the 1790s.[13]

Europeans in the Indian textile trades

The first major centre of European trade in western India was Surat; for the English it eventually was supplemented and politically superseded by Bombay. Gujarat, for which

Surat was the port, was a major centre of cotton textile production, with long experience in export to the Middle East. Sophisticated networks of trade and procurement of textiles reached far to the north, into the Delhi–Agra area. Political power was Muslim; merchant activity was shared among Muslims, Hindus, Armenians and many others. The Dutch and English East India Companies had no difficulty setting up trading outposts as far inland as Agra. They had no significant political privileges beyond the range of the guns of a few coastal forts. They were simply novices in a sophisticated trading world, trying to learn how to get the goods they wanted by diverting or modifying production for export to the Middle East. Here as elsewhere in India they found the services of Indian brokers indispensable for smooth relations with political authorities. At least as important, textile production every-where in India was divided into many processes, each one undertaken by a different community or caste. These phases were co-ordinated by market transactions, as raw cotton was sold to spinners who sold their product to weavers, who sold theirs to finishers and so on. The complexities of inter-group relations and long-established market practices were simply beyond the comprehension of any outsider. The Europeans always found this dependence on Indian brokers hard to accept. They preferred to deal with reliable independent brokers, but sometimes made them employees of their factories (trading stations) for the sake of more thorough control of their actions. European records are full of complaints of the bad faith of their brokers and of accusations that they cheated the producers and were responsible for their extreme poverty. Modern scholars still have a hard time explaining the inability of the producers to increase their incomes as demand for their products grew, but it is clear that the contemporary complaints against the brokers also reflect the Europeans' constant unease with situations in which they were dependent on Asian merchants or otherwise not fully in control of the situation. Exports from western India dominated the first decades of Dutch and English trade in Indian textiles, but were badly disrupted by a major famine in 1630 and never fully recovered. Thereafter the Europeans carried their experience and their prejudices acquired in this area to production zones of more enduring importance on the east coasts of the Indian peninsula.

The Coromandel coast (the southeast coast of India, with Madras as the leading English port) was the area of greatest expansion in the late seventeenth century, but in the eighteenth century Bengal was the land of opportunity, accounting for over half of all Dutch and English textile cargoes from Asia to Europe. In both, production was dispersed and intrica-tely specialized; different groups of people occupying different niches in local caste systems grew the cotton or raised the silkworms, spun the thread, wove it and dyed it. Surroundings might seem primitive – especially in south India weavers worked outdoors, under trees – but the quality of the best products, like the famous 'flowing water' transparent muslin, was far beyond the competence of European craftsmen. Highly detailed and specific knowledge of procedures for a particular stage of production of a particular kind of goods was passed down in a particular group of families in a particular place. Procedures for the fixing of vegetable dyes through a complex series of chemical treatments were triumphs of folk technology. There were many different names for local types of cloth – Chaudhuri has a list of eighty-five fabric names,[14] and I suspect that just scratches the surface – and many traditional local sizes, weaves and designs, but Indian craftsmen were thoroughly accustomed to market transactions, and agents of the Europeans seem to have had no trouble finding skilled workers who would try new sizes and weaves or would modify their colours and decorations to suit European tastes.

At each connection between two stages of production merchants were involved, and frequently they had to advance money to the producers before they could plant, spin, weave or dye. (In general this was not a 'putting-out' system; the craftsmen owned their means of production and used the advances they received to buy their raw materials.) As the Europeans accumulated experience, including a good many unwelcome instances of bad debts and erratic quality, they occasionally attempted to deal directly with the producers, but for the most part they found it better to leave the intricacies of dealing with producers and political authorities to Indian brokers, for the reasons noted above. In Bengal the great brokers had semi-official status, and by the eighteenth century they sometimes joined in a single contract for a year's trade with a given European company.[15] In Coromandel the Europeans took a more active role in bringing a group of merchants together into a 'joint stock company' in which they pooled their capital and each had a specified share of the trade. Both arrangements helped to keep the trade moving smoothly in the face of individual merchant insolvencies and difficulties in obtaining satisfactory deliveries from the producers. The companies sent detailed orders as to what to purchase to their servants in India, accompanied, especially in the English case, by even more detailed comments on the quality and relative profitability of the goods received. They watched anxiously over purchase prices and hectored their agents in India to keep them low, but in general they were quite capable of providing the capital needed for the maintenance and growth of a profitable line of trade. The Europeans in India could be ruthless in paying lower prices for goods that did not meet their specifications or refusing them altogether, but they were not in control of production or of its co-ordination, they were in competition with each other and with powerful Indian merchants buying for sale in India or elsewhere in Asia and the Middle East, so that in many ways their decisions were shaped not only by their orders from Europe and their own interests but also by the dynamics of Indian commerce. The sophistication of Indian merchants, the highly dispersed organization and superb skills of Indian craftsmen and the centralized communication and ample funds of the great companies, turned out to be a remarkably effective combination for bringing Indian fabrics to very large numbers of European consumers.

The story of the European presence in India in the late eighteenth century is dominated by the complex drama of the English seizure of hegemony in Bengal and the spread of their power across the sub-continent.[16] European private traders, especially Englishmen exploiting their privileged positions in Bengal, became much more important, so that figures for Company trade are a less reliable indication of actual total volumes. In any case, the most important economic changes were in the political economy, as the English Company began to collect the revenues of Bengal and use them to finance its exports, thus ceasing the import of precious metals that previously had been necessary to balance the trade. The Bengal revenues also financed the spread of English power across India and the Indian Ocean phase of the world war against Napoleon. Englishmen repatriating the wealth they had won as soldiers of fortune and privileged traders and monopolists added to the strain on the Bengal economy.

It has long been thought that in the late eighteenth and early nineteenth centuries the hand-loom textile industries of India were victims of the competition of the emerging machine industry of England. This probably was a factor in the situation, but Hameeda Hossain in an important recent book has shown how the policies of the English Company put such severe pressure on the producers of Bengal that many of them were forced to abandon textile production and revert to agriculture.[17] As early as the 1750s the expansion of the cotton-weaving industries of Bengal was beginning to be hampered by the inability of India's cotton-producing areas to keep pace with the expanding demand for raw cotton. The situation was aggravated by growing exports of Indian raw cotton to China and to England in the late eighteenth century. The Bengali producers might have been able to buy more if they could have paid more, but they worked on very small margins of profit, and the Company authorities were completely oriented to maintaining *their* margins of profit, absolutely uninterested in raising the prices they paid for the products of Bengali looms, which might have encouraged increases in production or at least allowed the producers to stay in business. As the producers always depended on advances from the Company, they were perpetually in debt to it and rarely completely caught up on their contract commitments. The Company attempted to deal with the situation by bringing the producers under ever tighter control so that they would have to meet their commitments to the Company and could not get in touch with any other buyers. Many came to live and work in special production centres. By a series of administrative and legal changes culminating in the legal code of 1793, weavers under contract to the Company came to be treated as its employees, not independent contractors. At the same time the Company was becoming less interested in the profits of trade and more in maximizing revenue collections, so that local tax collectors sometimes hounded poor spinners and weavers ruthlessly for tax payments. The result was widespread abandonment of textile production and flight from the Company's villages and work centres. A decline in the quantity and quality of textile production was already apparent in the 1790s and continued thereafter.

Coffee and tea in Europe

Thomas Rugge's *Mercurius Politicus Redivivus* for 14 November 1659 contains the following: 'Theire ware also att this time a Turkish drink to be sould, almost in evry street, called Coffee, and a nother kind of drink called Tee, and also a drink called Chacolate, which was a very hearty drink.'[18]

Coffee was a product of the world of Islam, and there it has retained down to our own times some of the ceremonial and sociable functions associated with alcoholic beverages in Christendom. According to one tradition, in the early 1400s a holy man residing in Mocha discovered its usefulness for keeping awake during all-night religious exercises. Muslim theologians and rulers did not always approve of it, but its use spread fast. By the mid-sixteenth century it was well established in the cities of the Ottoman Empire, and the coffee house as a place of male sociability and discussion had become a basic feature of Muslim urban culture. Europeans lived and traded in these cities – Constantinople, Aleppo, Alexandria, Cairo – and reports on the coffee-drinking habit can be found in many accounts of sixteenth-century European travellers in the Near East. Several decades seem to have passed, however, before these merchants and travellers brought coffee-drinking back with them to Europe. If further investigation sustains the present impression that coffee-drinking came to Venice, the city most deeply involved in eastern Mediterranean trade, fifty years or more after it was well established and conspicuous in Cairo and Aleppo, the contrast with the rapidity of its spread in England after its first introduction may indicate that this great merchant city still lacked in some way the kind of consumer responsiveness to exotic novelties seen in London, Paris and Amsterdam in the middle and late seventeenth century.

The first coffee house in London was opened in 1652. A Levant trade merchant seems to have helped his Greek or Armenian former servant and his former coachman get started in the business. A handbill for it made nothing of its exotic associations but praised the stimulant quality of coffee, and insisted that the steam from a hot cup was good for a headache or a stuffy nose, that it was good for the digestion, and that it helped to prevent miscarriages and cure 'Consumption . . . the Spleen, Hypocondriack Winds, and the like'.[19] These medicinal claims were fiercely disputed, as they had been in the world of Islam and would be in other parts of Europe.

The spread of coffee consumption in England seems to have been more thoroughly studied than for other parts of Europe, partly because of the remarkable role of the coffee house in that crucible of early modernity, that city of writing for money, doubting religion, reading newspapers, arguing about scientific experiments and constitutional principles that was Restoration London. Almost immediately the coffee house became a place to go to read the newspapers, hear the day's rumours and argue. Individual coffee houses soon became known as the meeting places for men with certain kinds of business to transact or certain kinds of opinions to discuss. Pepys and Aubrey participated in the debates at the Turk's Head, which frequently took on a strongly anti-monarchical character and which sometimes were concluded by the passing of a 'ballot box' into which every customer dropped his vote. Dryden, Pope, Addison, all were devotees of the society and conversation of particular coffee houses. Many prosperous middle-class Londoners spent part of every day in a particular coffee house. The institution has been described as midway in function and time between a tavern and a private club.[20]

The exotic Turkish and Levantine associations of coffee were somewhat more conspicuous in its reception in Paris than in London. A Paris coffee house, opened in 1672 by an Armenian, was patronized almost exclusively by Knights of Malta and other foreigners. We also read of a small man with a limp named Candiot who carried a portable brazier through the streets of Paris and sold coffee for two sous per cup, including sugar. By about 1700, there were about 300 coffee houses in Paris, including elegant ones in the Foire Saint Germain that were well-known intellectual meeting places, and some where even ladies of high quality would have their carriages stopped outside and a cup of coffee brought out to them. So coffee consumption in these early years already would seem to have anticipated everything from the appeal of the exotic, to street vending, to drive-ins to the Café des Deux Magots!

Northern Europeans had more limited experience of the Far East than of the world of Islam in the seventeenth century, and the growth of the consumption of tea carried little or no Chinese or Japanese cultural baggage. Some efforts were made to find a medicinal role for it, while other medical men warned of the effects of excessive consumption. It seems to have been occasionally available in the coffee houses of London from the 1660s on; Samuel Pepys recorded his first taste of it in that decade. But the market remained very small; in 1678, imports of under 5,000 pounds were reported to have glutted the London market. In the 1680s neither the Dutch nor the English East India Company had a well-established trade with China. And neither the uncertainties on the China coast nor the limited home market for tea held out any great prospects for expansion of trade.

It seems to have been in the 1690s that tea began to be more widely accepted as a consumer good, being sold by London grocers and served in tea shops frequented by ladies as well as gentlemen. It may be important that it was about this time that alcoholic drinks began to be sold in many coffee houses. Tea, and perhaps also chocolate, became associated with the pleasures of domesticity and respectable family life. Ladies could visit some tea shops without scandal. The ladies' tea party at home became so common as to elicit satirical comment in both England and Holland. In eighteenth-century London there were a number of famous tea gardens, where couples and families might stroll in the open, enjoy the music, have tea and other refreshments, in a pleasant and relatively respectable atmosphere; if the coffee house evolved into the London club, the tea garden sounds like an ancestor of the Tivoli in Copenhagen.[21]

By the 1720s the common black tea called Bohea had declined in price, and some green teas were even less expensive. These low prices were maintained for the rest of the century, even amid the moderate inflation of the last decades, and, along with the general economic growth of these years, facilitated a spread of the tea-drinking habit until it was thought to be nearly universal in England and Scotland. Very soon the English began drinking their black tea with milk and sugar; most early tea services include both sugar bowls and milk jugs. Thus the general popularity of tea can be attributed not just to its flavour and its stimulating qualities but to its convenience as a means of taking a bit of quick warm nourishment, including sugar. Tea also became very popular in the Netherlands, but seems to have been much less commonly used elsewhere in Europe; the British market remained the great magnet that shaped the trade.

This did not lead immediately to English domination of the export of tea from China. Great Britain taxed tea imports at 80–100 per cent of the sale price at the London auctions, making it extremely profitable to smuggle tea into the kingdom. It seems likely that at many times in the eighteenth century half of the tea consumed in Great Britain was illegally imported; even as the quantities consumed grew after 1763, the scope and sophistication of smuggling grew proportionately. The smugglers sometimes provided better qualities and wider assortments than the legal sales of the East India Company, and contributed to the development of a genuinely national market by distributing their imports from all the coasts of England and Scotland rather than just from London.[22] The tea destined to be smuggled into Great Britain was bought in China by the agents of various European East India Companies, and found its way into smuggling channels from their home ports, most importantly Copenhagen, Amsterdam, Ostend and the ports of Normandy and Brittany.

Coffee from Mocha to Java

Coffee was produced on the mountainsides and in the shaded valleys of Yemen, that 'island' of rain-catching mountains between the warm waters of the Red Sea and the Indian Ocean and the wastes of the Empty Quarter. As demand expanded around 1700 this area rather soon ran out of room for expansion of production onto hillsides with the right combination of water, sun and shade. Coffee was carried to India and beyond in the flourishing Muslim trade net; here, as in Indian textiles, the European traders hooked onto a pre-existing trade network, learned from it and remained in competition with it. The coffee trade was dominated by Muslim traders from the north, whose activities in the Red Sea were linked to the great pilgrimage trade to Mecca, which brought a stream of silver from the north into the area, where the silver was used to buy fabrics and spices from the Indian Ocean as well as coffee.[23]

The growth in European demand for coffee led to regular Dutch and English trading at Mocha on the Yemen coast from around 1700,[24] and by about 1715 most purchases were being made at the inland market of Beit el-Fakih (transcribed by the English as 'Beetle-fuckee') near the producing areas. Price-setting in this market was dominated by a few large merchants, but the Europeans also bought quite small quantities from others. Prices changed rapidly with the arrival or non-arrival of ships or caravans or with changing estimates of the quantity of the next crop. It was estimated that sales to the European ships were only one-eighth of the total exports, the rest going north, by caravan (land) or ship (Red Sea), to the Middle East. The great local merchants engaged in a variety of speculative manoeuvres, buying up larger stocks on reports of rising prices at Jedda or Cairo. The Europeans, despite their usual uneasiness among Muslim 'fanatics', were not badly treated, but they were completely at the mercy of market changes in which they were minor factors at best. Worst of all, price increases after 1710 seem to have stimulated only limited increases in production, so that after 1715 there were increasing complaints of shortages in the Yemen markets. The European response to this was the rapid development of coffee plantations in tropical areas under European control, in Jamaica, in Barbados and first and most dramatically in Java.

The Dutch East India Company was able to respond so rapidly to the expanding European demand for coffee because it was not only a great centralized trading company but also the territorial ruler of substantial areas around the Indian Ocean. Thus it could reach directly into the countryside to encourage coffee planting, compel it if necessary, and insist on delivery only to itself at fixed prices. Experiments of this kind on Ceylon (modern Sri Lanka) and Amboina (Ambon, in the Spice Islands) were tentative and short-lived. In the Preanger highlands south of Batavia on Java, the climate was right, there was tropical forest land available for clearing and cultivation, and the local Javanese 'regents', under the Company's suzerainty but more or less autonomous in their small realms, were quite ready to respond to new opportunities for income from their territories. At first the Company set its purchase price high enough that both regents and cultivators were amply motivated, and many peasants migrated into the coffee areas. The results were spectacular; by 1725, the Company was obtaining 4–5,000,000 pounds of coffee a year in Java, probably equal to the exports of all Europeans from Mocha in these peak years. Then it cut the price it paid the regents by 75 per cent. The regents somehow maintained the production, very probably compelling peasants to maintain and harvest the coffee plantations.[25] The record of Dutch plantation production in Indonesia, either on their own or in co-operation with local elites, reaches back to the Banda Islands in the 1620s and down to our own century. The drastic reduction of coffee prices made possible by Dutch–Javanese complicity in exploitation of the peasantry must have contributed to broadening coffee consumption in Europe. The expansion of coffee cultivation in Java is the only one of my cases where Asian production for European consumption did not begin in market-driven 'free choice' by the Asian producers.

The market-driven coffee production of Yemen eventually was reduced to a tiny marginal share of the world market by the great plantation producers. Mocha still had 20,000 people in the early nineteenth century but in 1901 had only about 400. The once-thriving centre of world trade today has only a few buildings standing, and little hope of revival.[26]

Tea and the Canton system

The only maritime exports of tea from China before the late seventeenth century were limited quantities to supply Chinese emigrants in Southeast Asia, but once the Europeans developed a taste for tea they could tap the expertise of an immense network of production and trade for consumption within China. In 1690 the Dutch East India Company abandoned efforts to obtain satisfactory conditions of trade in the ports of the Ch'ing Empire and left trade between Chinese ports and Batavia to Chinese merchants and the Portuguese of Macao. This made excellent sense at the time but later would prove completely inadequate for the quality control and storage necessary for the tea trade, so that the Dutch resumed voyages to Canton in 1728. English trade was already showing considerable energy, but records on it for the 1690s, a time of two rival companies and much private trade, are very meagre. Document-able regular voyages to Canton began in 1699 with one English and one French ship; by 1717 there were twenty. In addition, tea went to Batavia in Chinese and Macao Portuguese shipping for sale to the Dutch and shipment on to Europe; in its best years the volume in this channel equalled that of the direct English and French trade to Canton. In the 1720s and 1730s one phase after another of sharp competition among the European companies led to falling prices, dumping and rapidly increasing shipments to Europe, which seem to have been crucial in broadening the market for tea and in establishing low price levels that remained remarkably constant to the end of the century.[27]

The general picture of the growth of tea exports to Europe is reasonably clear, although much statistical refinement and careful use of all available European archives is still needed. It seems safe to say that between 1720 and 1740 the total doubled from about 30,000 piculs (one picul = 60.5 kg) to about 60,000, doubled again to about 120,000 by 1765, and again to 240,000 by 1795. There also was a shift towards finer and more expensive kinds of tea. It seems likely that the smugglers led this shift and the English Company lagged behind; the continental companies that supplied the smugglers shifted earlier and more rapidly than the English Company.

The system of production and commercial co-ordination that facilitated and sustained this remarkable growth bore some superficial resemblances to the systems that made the Bengal textile exports possible. Production was fragmented, usually into tea gardens cared for by individual families. Stages of processing and transportation to Canton were not vertically integrated but were accomplished by a series of purchases and sales. Powerful brokers were essential both as reliable traders and as political intermediaries. The differences were at least as striking. Foreigners had long been directly involved in production processes in India, relocating producers, having brokers on their payrolls and so on. Indian political culture permitted such involvement, and the great difficulties of ordering and quality control in the textile trades seemed to require it. In China, no foreigner connected with the tea trade ever got beyond the suburbs of Canton. The tea gardens were hundreds of miles away, in the mountains of Fujian and Jiangxi provinces. The great merchants of Canton generally pro-vided adequate quality control on their deliveries, and accepted European rejections of tea of inadequate quality not just at the time of delivery but even when it was sent back from Europe. Three factors may have contributed to this China–India contrast. The problems of quality control probably were intrinsically less intricate for tea than in the Bengal cloth trades. The Chinese merchants may have been more thoroughly committed to good faith in trading. Perhaps also the Europeans were simply making the best of a situation in which the security conscious Ch'ing regime would never allow any more direct interference in production processes.

Ch'ing statecraft was not in principle hostile to commerce, but assumed that as a source of revenue it was less substantial and reliable than the taxation of land. The tax quotas from the Canton trade that supported the regular budget of the Ch'ing state were in fact not large and grew only very slowly as the trade expanded. The officials' primary goal in managing all forms of foreign relations was defensive, keeping foreigners securely isolated and under control so that they could not cause trouble in the interior of the empire. They recognized that this would be much easier to accomplish if the foreigners were content with the way their trade was running. Late in the eighteenth century, for example, they worked very hard to collect the bad debts of the Canton merchants to the English. Also, the Imperial Household developed a financial interest in the trade that was much more substantial than that of the regular bureaucracy. The Court developed a passion for European clocks and clockwork, which were purchased in Canton, largely from English ship officers who brought them in their permitted private trade; a collection of them still can be seen in the Beijing Palaces. Moreover, the proceeds of taxation of trade beyond the statutory quota were delivered to the Imperial Household Department; at the end of the century this was as much as a million taels of silver per year.

The Chinese tradition of government regulation of trade emphasized the delegation of management to substantial merchants who would honour their commitments, pay fair prices, guarantee transactions of others and pay the taxes on the trade. Frequently such delegation was to a group of merchants or firms, a guild or hong (Cantonese pronunciation) collectively responsible for all members' fulfilment of their responsibilities. The Ch'ing authorities began experimenting with such arrangements for foreign trade at Canton in the 1720s. Soon every foreign ship was assigned a 'security merchant' who was responsible for the payment of all taxes and tolls connected with its trade and for the good behaviour of its merchants and crew. Various forms of maintaining supervision of the trade by a direct representative of the Imperial Court were tried. From 1750 on this took the form of the office of Superintendent of the Guangdong Maritime Customs, always filled by a Manchu of the Imperial Household Department. In the 1750s tensions rose as numbers of ships and sailors increased and as fears of Roman Catholic subversion based in Macao were revived. The English were finding it hard to obtain security merchants for their ships, since these merchants were required to buy any fancy clocks, imported mainly by English captains, and sell them to the Superintendent of Maritime Customs, often at a loss. The English responded to these pressures by trying to trade at other ports farther north and to communicate their grievances directly to the Court at Beijing. They succeeded only in reinforcing the defensive orientation of Chinese policy. Europeans had sometimes been allowed to trade at other ports, but in 1760 their trade was definitively confined to Canton. A new set of regulations required them to leave Canton at the end of the trading season and forbade them to send letters into the interior. A monopoly of European trade was granted to ten merchant firms. At first they traded as a unit, with combined capital and a single price agreement with each East India Company. The English allied with two of the most powerful merchants, and in 1771 secured dissolution of the joint trading. The designated firms retained their monopoly, but now traded and made contracts separately.

Late in the century new stresses resulted from the presence of growing numbers of English private traders from India. They frequently lent money to the Chinese merchants, hard-pressed to remain solvent as the scale of the trade grew and official extortion increased. Merchants tried to provide for payment of bad debts through the establishment of a common reserve fund, and officials attempted to enforce collection of debts. The system was remarkably effective in providing the foreigners with high-quality goods and in honouring contracts, but the foreigners, among whom the English now were by far the most important, were never at ease with restrictions imposed by Asians. They grew increasingly restive as debt troubles continued and the number of solvent hong firms declined.

By way of conclusion

Around 1800, the strands of power and production discussed in this chapter were becoming interwoven, and whether viewed from Canton, Batavia, Calcutta or London, one important focus of change was the building of a British state in India. Opium production in Bengal, a major source of revenue for the British, was stimulated by private traders' exports to Dutch possessions and elsewhere in Southeast Asia and to China. Although the commercially driven expansion of the Canton tea trade continued, illegal opium imports and the presence at Canton of men whose expectations of European–Asian relations had been formed in cowed and plundered Bengal made it increasingly unstable and conflict-ridden. Important parts of the Indian hand-weaving industries were undermined by the Company's obsession with revenue and lack of interest in encouraging increased production. Plantation production under the impetus of the colonial state had already moved the centre of the world coffee trade from Mocha to Java; in the nineteenth century it would lead to far more plantation production in the Dutch possessions and to tea plantations in India and Ceylon competing with continued Chinese production.

Asian production for European consumption had begun as Europeans tapped but did not control existing Asian commercial networks, frequently stimulating Asian production and leading to bullion inflows to India and China. From the mid-eighteenth century on, it was transformed step by step by European state-building and coercive intervention. By 1840 forced cultivation was spreading rapidly in the Dutch realms, and Indian Army units were engaged in a war with China brought on by British intransigence and opium imports.

Notes

1 Given the diversity of the phenomena discussed, the many parts of Asia and Europe involved, and the very uneven quantity and quality of the scholarly literature on which I have relied, it should be emphasized that the accounts of the trade in various Asian commodities given here should be taken as first approximations.

2 See John E. Wills, Jr, 'Maritime Asia, 1500–1800: the interactive emergence of European dominance', *American Historical* Review, forthcoming. A broad sampling of the India-centred work can be found in Ashin Das Gupta and M. N. Pearson (eds), *India and the Indian Ocean, 1500–1800* (Calcutta: Oxford University Press, 1987). An outstanding example of the work being done at Delhi is Sanjay Subrahmanyam, *The Political Economy of Commerce: Southern India, 1500–1650* (Cambridge: Cambridge University Press, 1990).

3 Ashin Das Gupta, *Indian Merchants and the Decline of Surat, c. 1700–1750* (Wiesbaden: Steiner, 1979).

4 An excellent survey of the companies is Holden Furber, *Rival Empires of Trade in the Orient,*

1600–1800 (Minneapolis: University of Minnesota Press, 1976). Chapter 5 on 'East India goods' is an important survey of the topic of my paper.

5   This section and the next rely on the classic study by John Irwin and P. R. Schwartz, *Studies in Indo-European Textile History* (Ahmedabad: Calico Museum of Textiles, 1966), and on the analyses of Kristof Glamann, *Dutch–Asiatic Trade, 1620–1740* (Copenhagen: Danish Science Press, and The Hague: Nijhoff, 1958), chs 6, 7, and K. N. Chaudhuri, *The Trading World of Asia and the English East India Company, 1660–1760* (Cambridge: Cambridge University Press, 1978), chs 11, 12.

6   Glamann, *Dutch–Asiatic Trade*, 142.

7   Chaudhuri, *Trading World*, 282–3.

8   Glamann, *Dutch–Asiatic Trade*, 142.

9   Chaudhuri, *Trading World*, 281–7.

10 ibid., 290–1, 294–5, 547.

11 Irwin and Schwartz, *Indo-European Textile History*, 37–8.

12 Chaudhuri, *Trading World*, 547–8.

13 Hameeda Hossain, *The Company Weavers of Bengal: The East India Company and the Organization of Textile Production in Bengal, 1750–1813* (Delhi: Oxford University Press, 1988), 67.

14 Chaudhuri, *Trading World*, 500–5.

15 ibid., 306–8; Om Prakash, *The Dutch East India Company and the Economy of Bengal, 1630–1720* (Princeton: Princeton University Press, 1985), 97–112.

16 For an excellent recent summary see C. A. Bayly, *Indian Society and the Making of the British Empire* (*The New Cambridge History of India*, II, I) (Cambridge and New York: Cambridge University Press, 1988), chs 1–3.

17 Hossain, *The Company Weavers of Bengal*.

18 William H. Ukers, *All About Tea*, New York: Coffee and Tea Trade Journal, (1935), i, 41.

19 William H. Ukers, *All About Coffee*, New York: Coffee and Tea Trade Journal, (1934), i, 50.

20 An excellent collection of lore on the introduction of coffee to Europe and on coffee houses is ibid., i, 21–100; ii, 690–703. See also Glamann, *Dutch–Asiatic Trade*, ch. 10 and Chaudhuri, *Trading World*, ch. 16.

21 Ukers, *Tea*, ii, 389–407. See also Glamann, *Dutch–Asiatic Trade*, ch. 11 and Chaudhuri, *Trading World*, ch. 17.

22 Hoh-cheung Mui and Lorna H. Mui, 'Smuggling and the British tea trade before 1784', *American Historical Review*, lxxiv (1) (Oct. 1968), 44–73.

23 Ukers, *Coffee*, i, 12–19; Ashin Das Gupta, 'Introduction II: the story', in Das Gupta and Pearson, *India*, 25–45, at 30.

24 For the Mocha trade see Hans Becker, Volker Hörfeld and Horst Kopp, *Kaffee aus Arabien: Der Bedeutungswandel eines Weltwirtschaftgutes und seine siedlungsgeographische Konsequenz an der Trockengrenze der Ökumene* (Wiesbaden: Steiner, 1979), chs 1, 2; Chaudhuri, *Trading World*, ch. 16; Glamann, *Dutch–Asiatic Trade*, ch. 10; Furber, *Rival Empires*, 253–5.

25 G. J. Knapp, 'Coffee for cash: the Dutch East India Company and the expansion of coffee cultivation in Java, Ambon, and Ceylon, 1700–1730', in J. van Goor, *Trading Companies in Asia, 1600–1800* (Utrecht: HES, 1986), 33–49.

26 I am grateful to Mohamad and Lucinda Almawada of Sana'a for making it possible for me to visit Mocha and Beit el-Fakih in September 1989.

27 This section is based on J. L. Cranmer-Byng and John E. Wills, Jr, 'Ch'ing trade and diplomacy with maritime Europe, 1644–c. 1800', *Cambridge History of China*, vol. 9 (in press). Other important summaries include Glamann, *Dutch–Asiatic Trade*, ch. 11, Chaudhuri, *Trading World*, ch. 17 and C. J. A. Jörg, *Porcelain and the Dutch China Trade* (The Hague: Nijhoff, 1982), ch. 2. A very rich long study is Louis Dermigny, *La Chine et l'Occident: Le Commerce à Canton au XVIIIe siècle* (Paris: SEVPEN, 1964).

7

Res et verba: conspicuous consumption in the early modern world

Peter Burke

On peut lire tout le style de vie d'un groupe dans le style de son mobilier et de son vêtement.

(Pierre Bourdieu)

The Protestant Ethos is characteristically averse to display.

(Ernest Gellner)[1]

The aim of this chapter is to place a western phenomenon in a global context, to compare and contrast consumption in early modern Europe, more or less from 1500 to 1800, with two other regions, China under the late Ming and early Qing dynasties and Japan under the Tokugawa.[2] I must make it clear at the start that I am a historian of Europe who is unable to read Chinese and Japanese. All the same, I do not apologize for making this attempt at comparison. Historians of Europe will never be able to say what is specifically western unless they look outside the west.[3]

It will be obvious that the strategy of this chapter follows that of Max Weber, and even more closely that of Fernand Braudel in his famous study of capitalism and material culture, which emphasizes parallel trends (like the population explosion of the sixteenth century) in different parts of the globe.[4] In that volume, Braudel has a good deal to say about the world of goods; there are chapters on food and drink, clothes, housing and money. However, his study of material culture has little to say about culture in the sense of mentalities, symbols or values. Consumption, yes. Conspicuous consumption, no.[5]

The focus of this chapter, on the other hand, will be on conspicuous consumption, its symbolism and significance. Although consumption takes many forms – food, clothes, housing, festivals, etc., the analysis will be concerned with only one of them, interior decoration and furnishings. It will also be limited to the consumption of elites – rich merchants and mandarins in China, *daimyo* in Japan and nobles in Europe.

Conspicuous consumption is of course a matter of considerable debate among historians today. It is one of several linked debates about the history of material culture. There is, for example, the commercialization debate, about the rise of consumer society, to which later chapters will be addressed. There is also the privacy debate, in which historians discuss whether the replacement of benches by chairs or the shift from collective bowls to individual plates and cups or the development of specialized bedrooms (all recognizable early modern trends) are expressions of a new individualism or concern for intimacy.[6]

These debates may be new, but concern with some of the issues goes back several generations, at least among sociologists and anthropologists. It was at the end of the last century, for example, that Franz Boas, working among the Kwakiutl Indians in the Vancouver area, noted the significance of the potlatch, the competitive destruction of goods in the struggle for power between chiefs.[7] It was not long before Thorstein Veblen pointed to analogies to the potlatch nearer home. Indeed, it was Veblen who put the term 'conspicuous consumption' into general circulation.[8] It has, for example, been employed by historians of Tudor and Stuart England, notably by the late F. J. Fisher and (with explicit reference to Veblen) by Lawrence Stone.[9]

Today, we are familiar – and even over-familiar – with the idea that people often acquire goods not because they need them or even desire them directly but for other reasons. In the narrow sense of the term 'conspicuous consumption', they acquire goods, like the Kwakiutl chiefs, to compete with others. In a wider, looser, less reductionist sense of the term, the goods are considered to be acquired not for themselves but for what they symbolize, for their associations, for their contribution to a particular image of ourselves.[10]

The case-studies cited so far suggest an extremely general question. Is this indirect use of goods a universal tendency, part of our human nature, or is it simply characteristic of a particular type of social organization, the consumer society? To give a general answer to this question is beyond my power and in any case it is not my purpose. The aim of this chapter is to contribute to a future general answer by looking at conspicuous consumption in a few regions of the world in the sixteenth, seventeenth and eighteenth centuries.

In the course of considering these cases, it may be useful to bear three general problems in mind. The first is conceptual, the second sociological, the third methodological.

As soon as one begins to try to work with a concept, it begins to dissolve, to seem less clear than one had thought. The term 'conspicuous consumption' is no exception. What image does this phrase call up before your inner eye? Is it one of American managers and their families competing for status, like Kwakiutl chiefs, by buying more and more expensive automobiles? Perhaps they do, but all the same it is surely a mistake to follow Veblen and to reduce the meaning or the symbolism of goods in the USA today to status seeking.[11]

Material goods transmit all sorts of messages about their owners, and it is the historian's job to decode these messages.[12] Status seeking is only one example of what it is useful to call, following the sociologist Erving Goffman, 'the presentation of self'.[13] Consumption is often used as a means for presenting the self in a favourable light. In fact, it is not only conspicuous consumption which helps in presenting the self. Inconspicuous consumption transmits its own message and so does conspicuous refraining from consuming. Seventeenth-century examples would include Philip IV of Spain (who adopted the simple collar or *golilla* to discourage splendid ruffs among his courtiers), as well as the French Jansenists, Catholic examples of what Weber called 'the Protestant ethic', a term which Gellner uses still more widely so as to include Islam.[14] In other words, we should avoid identifying conspicuous consumption with magnificence. In a particular social context, simplicity may be the best way of making oneself conspicuous, as later examples will suggest.

A second problem is more sociological: *whose* consumption are we talking about? How widespread was conspicuous consumption in the early modern world? It can hardly have affected everyone equally, since a considerable proportion of the peasantry of early modern Europe were more or less self-sufficient and made little use of cash except to pay the tax-collector. All the same, there is evidence for conspicuous consumption by townspeople and peasantry, especially in the eighteenth century. Even in a village of subsistence farmers, the possession or the use of a chest of embroidered linen or a set of painted plates might have distinguished one family from another. In villages producing goods for the market, in Elizabethan England, for example, the profits were recycled into housing.[15] I have tried to argue elsewhere, with special reference to Scandinavia, that the eighteenth century was a golden age of peasant material culture, the result of the rise of a market in handicrafts. Ironically enough, the same market forces would lead in the long term to a decline in quality and even to the destruction of traditional material culture.[16] In cities, the opportunities for the material expression or construction of an individual or collective identity were obviously even greater. In seventeenth-century Dutch towns, such as Delft, craftsmen and shopkeepers decorated their houses with paintings.[17] In eighteenth-century London, so the German historian Hans Medick has argued, the consumption of gin and other expensive commodities 'functioned as a vehicle of plebeian self-consciousness' and should be interpreted as a claim on the part of plebeians to be as good as their so-called betters.[18]

The third problem is methodological: how can one investigate conspicuous consumption in the early modern world? What are the sources? Some of these sources are extremely well known, inventories, for example. In the case of early modern Europe, many inventories of possessions have survived. These inventories allow precise and revealing comparisons and contrasts to be made between different regions and periods. On this basis, for example, Trajan Stoianovitch has stressed the sheer poverty of goods in the Balkans before 1830, together with the survival of traditional materials such as wood; while Jan de Vries has shown how the profits of an increasingly commercialized agriculture in Friesland between 1550 and 1750 were turned into curtains, clocks, mirrors, silver buttons and spoons, and what contemporaries called 'mantlepiece-covers', *schoorsteenkleeden*.[19]

We should not limit ourselves to inventories, however, but go beyond them in at least two directions. In the first place, towards archaeology. We need an archaeology of early modern Europe, not only in the metaphorical sense associated with Michel Foucault but also in the literal sense. In fact, some archaeologists have become interested in the use of 'precious materials as expressions of status' in early times, while others have moved well beyond prehistory to write books about *The Archaeology of the Consumer Society* or *The Archaeology of Us*.[20] In calling for an archaeological approach to the early modern period, not just to colonial America but more generally, I do not necessarily mean digging. There is fortunately no need to excavate the palace of Versailles (though it might be interesting to dig in the courtyard in search of a midden). The point I want to make is rather different. It is that many historians, whose paradigm of evidence is what they call the 'document', still have to learn how to read other kinds of material object.

However, material objects do not tell us enough about their significance for the people who used them. They do reveal something – marks of wear show the archaeologist whether or not an object was in regular use. Again, paintings and prints of interiors give us valuable information about the arrangement and use of furnishings which no other sources record. To learn more about the meaning of objects, however, and how they were viewed by their users, we must turn to literary sources. A few years ago, one of the leading French exponents of quantitative or serial methods, Michel Vovelle, put forward an eloquent plea for the use of literary evidence in the history of attitudes to death. I should like to enter a similar plea for a literary as well as a quantitative approach to the history of material culture. In the case of the early modern world, the evidence about material objects in poems, stories and plays is a rich vein which has hardly begun to be exploited. One purpose of this chapter is to suggest how this evidence may be used.

I turn to Asia first, as an exercise in defamiliarization, in the hope of avoiding western ethnocentrism. The Chinese case does seem to fit the conspicuous consumption model, and even on occasion the more limited, cynical model of status seeking. Indeed, the evidence takes us back further than it is possible to go in the case of western Europe; as far back as the Han dynasty (*c.* 200 BC–AD 200) there are signs of the appropriation of traditional status symbols by the upwardly mobile.[21] In the fourth century AD, collecting works of art, notably ink-paintings and calligraphy, was already fashionable, and faking was not uncommon. By the ninth century the art market was well developed.[22]

However, the evidence for conspicuous consumption in China is richest for the Ming dynasty, which came to an end in the mid-seventeenth century, and in the Qing dynasty which succeeded it. The rise of a 'new urban mercantile' society in sixteenth-century China was associated with a new wave of art collecting, in which old objects were particularly valued. The rise of the market in antiques led to more digging and more faking.[23]

In the eighteenth century, the signs of conspicuous consumption are even more clear. The obvious case to cite is that of a group of sixty-odd *nouveaux riches* who made their fortune in salt production and salt trading and lived in and around the city of Yangzhou. These entrepreneurs did not accumulate capital, but spent it on eating and drinking, on horses, and on the patronage of scholarship and the arts, more especially on drama and on opera. Again, the Anhui merchants of the Huizhou region tried to 'buy their way' into literati culture by lavish patronage of the arts. They were not allowed to build on a large scale, but their small houses were richly decorated and full of works of art, ancient and modern.[24] These 'salt fools', as contemporaries called them, doubtless with envy as well as malice, were criticized for their extravagant and luxurious way of life. In fact, there was a debate on luxuries in China in the seventeenth and eighteenth centuries, in other words at much the same time as in the west. The emperor Qianlong, for example, complained in 1781 that 'customs daily become more extravagant'.[25] In the Chinese case, however, this debate was a reactivation of a traditional Confucian denunciation of luxury which goes back at least as far as the Han dynasty.

The best evidence for the change in material culture is of course the surviving material objects themselves, to be found in many museums in the west as well as in China. The arts of inlay, enamel and lacquer flourished in this period, and magnificent tables, chairs, sets of writing equipment and so on are not difficult to find (Plate 7.1).[26] Jade 'became available on a new scale'.[27] Porcelain became richer and more colourful, abandoning the simplicity of earlier dynasties.

Were attitudes to material culture essentially the same in China as in the west or did consumption have a different meaning? Let us take a few concrete examples, to see whether or not China diverges from the western model. These examples come from literary sources (inventories do exist in China, but they are much rarer than in early modern Europe). Among the new features of sixteenth-century Chinese culture was the rise of a new literature of leisure for an urban public which lacked the traditional education in the Confucian classics.[28] From about 1600 onwards, it is possible to find guides to elegant living which place more emphasis on material objects than the equivalent literature in the west, in other words the courtesy-books or *livres de civilité* by authors such as Erasmus, Castiglione and Della Casa, discussed by Norbert Elias in his famous study of the process of 'civilization'. Examples of these guides are Gao Lian's *Eight Discourses on the Art of Living*, and the *Treatise on Superfluous Things* by Wen Zhenheng.[29]

The evidence of the guides to elegant living may be supplemented by that of novels, notably the early seventeenth-century *Jin Ping Mei* (*Golden Lotus*), described by the French sinologist Jacques Gernet as 'the first novel of manners', and the mid-eighteenth-century *Hong Lou Meng* or *Dream of the Red Chamber*, otherwise known as *The Story of the Stone*. The *Jin Ping Mei*, for example, which tells the story of a rich merchant from Shandong, Ximen Qing, a connoisseur of *objets d'art* as well as a great drinker and a great womanizer, is a novel absolutely stuffed with descriptions of expensive furnishings. One of Ximen's wives' beds, for example, is ornamented with mother of pearl, while the interior is decorated with 'towers, pavilions, flowers, birds and animals'.[30] Another bed, for use in summer, is made of marble and ornamented with black lacquer and with gold.[31] Ximen and his friends drink from 'goblets of chiselled silver' or from 'little golden cups in the shape of chrysanthemum flowers'.[32] The cane chairs in his library are from Burma, 'with nails of gold and agate from Yunnan'.[33] Ximen's house is also decorated with paintings, examples of calligraphy and antiques, including bronze incense-burners.[34]

Fiction is of course an unreliable source for actual behaviour in the period with which it deals, because the author may have satirical rather than purely descriptive intentions. The *Golden Lotus*, for example, is probably best interpreted as a parody rather than a description of competitive display.[35] Whether it is to be read literally or not, however, literature of this kind remains invaluable as evidence for the history of values, dreams and aspirations.

Even richer descriptions of material culture are to be found in the later and greater novel, Cao Xuequin's *The Story of the Stone*. It is altogether appropriate that the title of the story refers not to a person but to a precious object. I like to think of this novel as a kind of eighteenth-century Chinese *Buddenbrooks*, a nostalgic chronicle of the decline of a great merchant family, the Jias, doomed because, as an outsider puts it, 'Both masters and servants . . . lead lives of luxury and magnificence . . . they can't bring themselves to economise.'[36]

The contents of different rooms in the family mansions are described with loving care, so that the novel sometimes reads like an inventory of *objets d'art*, often antiques: paintings, calligraphic scrolls, mirrors, low tables of coloured lacquer, brocade curtains, yellow cedar-wood armchairs, 'A long high table of carved red sandal-wood ornamented with dragons' and so on. It may be significant that these objects are often, though not exclusively, associated with women; with Phoenix in one novel as with Ximen's wives and mistresses in the other. But this is a problem for sinologists to explore.

These Chinese examples raise an important general question. For whom was this consumption conspicuous? Who was expected to see it? My impression, for what it is worth, is that this Chinese display of wealth was more private than was the norm in Europe, but not so private as to deserve the term 'inconspicuous'. It was not the façade (as in Italy) but the interior of the house which was decorated on a lavish scale. The display was intended for the family and its friends.

In Japan, as in the case of China, examples of conspicuous consumption can be found long before the early modern period. One has only to turn to the masterpiece of Japanese literature *The Tale of Genji*, written in the eleventh century, to note the interest in beautiful material objects at the imperial court. In the fifteenth century, the law-code of the Ashikaga shogunate offers evidence of both conspicuous consumption and attempts to curb it.

> There prevails a love of eccentricity or originality, figured brocades and embroidered silks, of elaborately mounted swords. . . . Those who are rich become more and more filled with pride; and the less wealthy are ashamed of not being able to keep up with them.

In the later sixteenth century, the so-called Momoyama period, the trend towards display is even more apparent. As in Ming China, the arts of enamel and lacquer flourished, and many magnificent examples of tables, trays, book-cases, writing-boxes, reading-stands and so on have survived (Plate 7.3).[37] Folding screens (*byobu*) were gilded and painted at great expense.

The importance of new families in this trend to magnificence is worth underlining. The shogunate forbade merchants to make use of lacquer, but were unable to prevent display on the part of rich sake brewers, moneylenders and China traders in the early sixteenth century. In the second half of the century, Japan's new rulers were deeply involved in conspicuous consumption. Oda Nobunaga, for example, commissioned a magnificent series of large-scale wall-paintings (making considerable use of gold leaf) for Azuchi Castle in 1576, doubtless to impress his followers.[38] His successor Toyotomi Hideyoshi went still further in pursuit of legitimacy, so that his recent biographer speaks of his 'vulgar' display.[39] His new residence at Kyoto was particularly magnificent. Particularly interesting from the point of view of the idea of conspicuous consumption is Hideyoshi's patronage of the tea ceremony. The ceremony developed at this period, thanks to men like Sen no Rikyu (a client of Hideyoshi's). Its stress on purity and simplicity (*sabi* and *wabi*) is in the tradition of Zen 'emptiness', but it can also be seen as a reaction against contemporary magnificence. The preference for rough Korean tea-bowls, for example, was a conspicuous simplicity, and even, perhaps, a protest against the gold-leaf culture of the shoguns. However, the shoguns, Nobunaga and still more Hideyoshi, turned the tables by appropriating the tea ceremony for their own purposes and of course transforming it in the process. Hideyoshi had a golden tea-room built and in 1587 he organized the Grand Kitano Tea Ceremony, a grand public event which was scheduled to last for ten days and was the antithesis of the traditional ritual, which was deliberately private, simple and small in scale.[40]

Hideyoshi's successor Tokugawa Ieyasu founded a dynasty during which conspicuous consumption reached new heights, or at least spread further down the social scale. The early Tokugawa period was a time of peace, agricultural revolution and urban growth, more especially the growth of three large cities, Edo (later Tokyo), Osaka and Kyoto. It was also a time of important changes in the arts and also in art patronage.

Like the absolute monarchs of Europe at this time, the Tokugawa shoguns tried to weaken the aristocracy, or *daimyo*, by forcing them to come to court, cutting them off from their local power bases and encouraging them to spend in a lavish and competitive manner. They were expected to construct great houses in Edo, gilded inside and out.[41] These houses often had grand gateways, some of them built specifically for the entry of the shogun on an official visit.[42] The procession of a *daimyo* from his estate to the court at Edo was also a great occasion for display, with banners, umbrellas, palanquins and so on, as was noted by one of the rare western observers, the German physician Engelbert Kaempfer.[43] Kimonos became richer than before, while lacquer-work continued to be magnificent.[44]

What the shoguns had not expected, and did not approve, was the spread of the habit of conspicuous consumption to other social groups, especially in the so-called 'Genroku Era', the late seventeenth and early eighteenth centuries. At first sight at least, Genroku Japan looks like the example every Marxist historian of early modern Europe would pray for – if they prayed – an unusually clear case of the rise of the bourgeoisie (the local term is *chonin*). Although Tokugawa law placed the merchants at the bottom of the four-rung social ladder (samurai, then peasants, then craftsmen and finally merchants), this legislation was as unworkable as Canute's command to the waves. In the late seventeenth century, the new rich became very rich indeed, especially the rice-brokers, who were the Japanese equivalent of the salt merchants in China.

These new rich turned to the arts, evading the sumptuary laws and turning economic into cultural capital, which can be documented from inventories, wills, tax records and proceedings for bankruptcy as well as from literary or archaeological sources. The reason that I suggested that Tokugawa Japan is the example Marxist historians pray for is that the links between the arts and society were unusually explicit. Merchants were forbidden to construct three-storey houses on the grounds that these were too ostentatious for their officially humble position.[45] Only the upper classes were allowed to see the traditional drama, the Noh plays; and they were forbidden to see the new urban drama of *kabuki* and *joruri*. One leading seventeenth-century painter of fans and screens, Sotatsu, worked in two styles, a traditional style for *daimyo* and monasteries and a new style for the *chonin*.[46] Outside the court, the leaders of fashion were actors and courtesans. A new society was producing a new culture. There was a trend towards the commercialization of leisure, at much the same time as in the great cities of the west, Paris, Rome and Madrid as well as London. In Edo, Kyoto and Osaka it took the form of tea houses rather than coffee houses, sumo wrestling rather than boxing or bull-fights, but the role of courtesans, the theatre and cheap print was remarkably similar in east and west.

In practice, as one might have guessed, the separation between social groups and cultural genres was very much less clearcut than it was in principle. The boundaries were transgressed on both sides. The *daimyo* could not keep away from the pleasure quarters. Lower-status groups also appropriated or imitated high culture. Wood-block prints of kimono patterns associated with noble ladies allowed townswomen to imitate them. There were classes in swordsmanship for townsmen, although they were officially forbidden to wear swords in public.

As in the case of China, contemporary literature offers vivid descriptions of the consumption patterns of the rich at this time. The best examples of such descriptions are surely those to be found in the late seventeenth-century stories of Iharu Saikaku, a writer of merchant background who was a pioneer in the literature of manners. Saikaku loves to give concrete details of material objects and also to tell his readers how expensive they are. Saikaku may be compared with Daniel Defoe in his combination of surface moralizing with a subtext of attraction to the material goods (including sex) and also of making the book attractive by means of these goods.

One of Saikaku's books is particularly informative in this regard, the *Japanese Family Storehouse* or *Millionaire's Gospel Modernised*.[47] This is a collection of stories about men who rise from rags to riches, packed with details about the way in which they make their money and the way in which they show off their wealth afterwards on fashionable pursuits, some of them once reserved for the aristocracy, such as the tea ceremony, perfume appreciation, football (which had courtly associations in Japan), etc.

As the author puts it, 'a rich man who is modest in the display of his wealth is a rare phenomenon . . . those who cut a fine figure on a slender income are more in the fashion of these degenerate times'. But he goes on to describe with apparent zest a rich variety of objects such as palanquins, 'hammer-headed walking-sticks', silk kimonos for both sexes, decorated with 'delicate Ukiyo stencil-patterns, multi-coloured "Imperial" designs, and dappled motifs in wash-graded tints'.[48] A spendthrift young heir is described as remodelling his house according to the Kyoto model, with a waiting-room with hanging scrolls, miniature mountains and lakes in the garden with bridges of Chinese sandalwood, while 'On the face of the tiles lining the overhanging eaves he set his initials in gold relief.'[49]

As in the case of China and Japan, conspicuous consumption in western Europe goes back much further than the sixteenth century, as sumptuary laws as well as surviving material objects show.[50] If one focuses on interior decoration, however, one soon becomes aware that although individual objects might be magnificent in the Middle Ages, the ensemble was relatively sparse, even in a building as outwardly impressive as the Palazzo Strozzi in Florence.[51] It was only in Renaissance Italy that it became fashionable to fill houses with *objets d'art*, and only in the seventeenth and eighteenth centuries that it became customary for private houses in European cities to display a great quantity of magnificent and expensive material objects.[52] The chronology of conspicuous consumption in the case of Europe is therefore remarkably similar to the chronology for China and Japan.

For example, the urban palaces of Italian nobles of the seventeenth and eighteenth centuries were stuffed with precious objects: tapestries, velvet curtains, wall-coverings in tooled leather (sometimes gilt), four-poster beds, vases and bowls, silver or silver-gilt gradually yielding to Chinese porcelain, inlaid tables and cabinets, suits of armour (of less and less practical use as time went by) and so on.[53]

A good many of these objects may still be seen in museums or even *in situ*, but the impression they give is not spectacular enough. The most magnificent furnishings were generally those least likely to survive because, in seventeenth-century Italy and elsewhere, tables, chairs and beds were not infrequently made of solid silver and have subsequently been melted down. If it were not for the evidence of inventories and the testimony of foreign travellers, we would know nothing about them. The English virtuoso John Evelyn, for example, visiting Italy, noted in his journal on a number of occasions that he had seen bedsteads of solid silver set with pearls, onyx, turquoise and other jewels. The publicity of the private rooms is worth noting, an apparent contrast with China.

This publicity suggests that the function of these objects was indeed to be conspicuous. The same message is communicated by the names, initials or coats of arms of the owners still to be seen on the façades of the palaces, and also by inscriptions such as PRO INVIDIA ('in order to be envied').[54] Contemporary literature also reveals something about the uses of these objects and their meaning for their owners. As it happens, and this may be no coincidence, western fiction no less than eastern fiction was increasingly concerned with material objects at this time.

There were of course precedents for this preoccupation in the classical *ekphrasis* (for example, the description of the shields of Achilles and Aeneas by Homer and Vergil). Again, the first novel of manners in the west, the *Satyricon* of Petronius, especially its most famous scene, the feast given by the *nouveau riche* Trimalchio, gives an elaborate description of luxurious tableware, used to characterize the host as a man without taste. The work is of course as satirical as its name and (as in some of the Chinese and Japanese cases already discussed), it would be unwise to trust specific details, such as the silver toothpicks, but as evidence of contemporary attitudes the *Satyricon* is invaluable.

Petronius' text is a relatively isolated example (though there is other evidence of the rise of conspicuous consumption in Rome under the emperors). From the late Renaissance, on the other hand, we begin to find an increasing concern with material objects in works of European literature, from the adventures of Lazarillo de Tormes to Philip Sidney's *Arcadia*, with its elaborate descriptions of houses and their decoration.

In French literature, as in Chinese and Japanese literature, the novel of manners emerges in the seventeenth century. The best French example is probably Antoine Furetière's *Roman bourgeois* (1666), a story about contemporary Paris which is particularly concerned with the use of clothes and language in attempts by the professional bourgeoisie to pass for noble, but also includes some interesting comments on interiors. For example, we are told of an avaricious advocate whose chamber was 'a real room of antiques [*une vraye salle des antiques*]', not in the sense of containing 'fine curiosities [*belles curiositez*]' but rather of old-fashioned furniture, some in the 'Gothic' style, which showed that the owner was not a man of taste.[55] In a similar work by César-François de Prefontaine, first published in 1660, the poverty-stricken hero is taken to a *chambre garnie* with 'a large wooden bed in the old style [*fait à l'antique*]', in a room which is dirty and full of spiders' webs.[56]

Splendid material objects also appear in other types of literature, such as the heroic romances of the seigneur de La Calprenède and Madeleine de Scudéry, notably her *Grand Cyrus* (1649–53), set in classical antiquity but full of contemporary allusions. Again, Mademoiselle de Scudéry's novelesque *Promenade de Versailles*, published in the same decade as Furetière, describes with admiration the interior decoration of the king's grand cabinet, with

> mirrors crowned with golden suns, an infinite number of magnificent and rare things, laid out at different levels on little tables . . . little obelisks of goldsmith's work . . . armchairs covered with cloth of silver over a blue base . . . their cost is sufficient to indicate their beauty.[57] (Plate 7.6)

In the case of Italy, some romances, like the Chinese *The Story of the Stone*, take their titles from material objects which were among the status symbols of the period, such as gondolas and carriages.[58] References to precious material objects are even more common in poems such as Torquato Tasso's epic *Gerusalemme Liberata* (1581), especially the description of the garden of the enchantress Armida, and Marino's *Adone* (1623), particularly the second canto, 'the palace of love', with its descriptions of busts, statues and grottoes.

Some evidence from non-fiction points in the same direction. The British ambassador to France at the beginning of the seventeenth century remarked on the 'magnificences' of the courtiers there:

> on days of parade, they make more shew of riches than we do, in the multitude of their pearls, stones, broderies and suchlike; as also for their household furniture theirs, I take it, exceedeth ours both in richness and commodiousness.[59]

Again, a treatise by the Italian physician Giulio Mancini, discusses the collecting of pictures, and pays attention not only to their form and content but also to their price, to the ways in which to distinguish originals from copies, to the frames, and to the appropriate rooms in which different paintings should be hung – landscapes in the more public galleries, portraits and battle-scenes in antechambers or rooms in which serious negotiations would take place, and sexually provocative pictures (*le lascive*) in inner rooms for the owner and his friends to enjoy in private.[60] In other words, Mancini offers something like a guide to elegant living along the lines of Gao Lian and Wen Zhenheng.

Readers of this chapter will have noticed a certain hesitation between a more modest thesis, which is easier to document, and a more ambitious one, which is more speculative. The modest thesis declares that an increasing concern with material culture can be found in the literature of Europe and Asia, between the late sixteenth and the late eighteenth centuries. The ambitious thesis asserts that this period witnessed an increasing preoccupation, if not obsession, on the part of the upper classes, with material objects, either for themselves or for what they symbolized. I would not care to assume that literary changes necessarily reflect social ones. But if elites were not increasingly concerned with conspicuous consumption, how else can one explain the changes in the literature?

In any case, we have the evidence of the increasing splendour of the objects themselves, so far as they have survived, to combine with the references in the literary sources. Assuming that this combination of testimonies makes the ambitious thesis worth discussing, it is time to discuss possible explanations of these common Eurasian trends. Contact between the cultures is not to be ruled out. After all, Chinese porcelain and lacquer-work was fashionable in eighteenth-century Europe. Some Japanese merchants enriched themselves through the trade with Japan. The rise of conspicuous consumption in Ming China may also have something to do with the influx of American silver from the late sixteenth century onwards, exported to China by Europeans to compensate for their unfavourable balance of trade.

As far as I can see, these connections are less important than two trends which were similar but independent.

In the first place, the increasing influence of courts in late Renaissance Italy (notably the courts of the Medici in Florence and Rome), in the France of the Bourbons and in the Japan of the Tokugawa (the court of the shogun, not that of the emperor). In these cases the contribution of courts to what Norbert Elias calls the 'civilizing process' is particularly evident, though his argument might be given a somewhat more cynical twist.[61] Rulers encouraged or obliged their most powerful nobles to come to court. Attendance at Edo was formally compulsory on the *daimyo*, attendance at Versailles virtually compulsory for *les grands*. For the rulers, the aim was to tame the barons by cutting them off from their local power bases and encouraging them to ruin themselves on competitive conspicuous consumption. Henri IV, for example, as the British ambassador explained, encouraged the great nobles to live at court, where 'by play, and other unthriftiness, they grow poor'.[62] For the barons, who in France and Japan alike had recently emerged from a period of deep involvement in civil conflicts, consumption was a continuation of warfare by other means (as it seems to have been for the Kwakiutl after the Canadian government forced them to live at peace).

In the second place, the rise of cities and of the new rich. Already in the sixteenth century the political theorist Giovanni Botero had observed that living in close proximity in cities made the Italian nobility more prone to competitive display than they had previously been.[63]

This observation is borne out not only by the history of Naples and other Italian cities but also by that of early modern Paris, Madrid, London and (as an earlier section in this chapter suggested), of the new capital of Edo.

The idea that new nobles or new rich are more prone to conspicuous consumption than their established colleagues was and is commonplace. Unlike some other commonplaces, it seems to be supported by concrete evidence. In Venice, for example, it may be illustrated by examples of families who joined the patriciate in the later seventeenth century.[64] In France, obvious examples come from the world of the financiers, most spectacularly of all Nicolas Fouquet, whose more than regal expenditure on a festival in honour of Louis XIV is said to have led to his arrest and disgrace a few days later. The 'salt fools' of China and the rice-brokers of Japan had their equivalents in Europe.

These comparisons are not of course intended to imply that socio-cultural trends were identical in western Europe and east Asia in the early modern period. Some contrasts between China and the west have already been mentioned. Differences in family structure are also likely to have affected both the level and the type of consumption in each society. In any case, socio-cultural trends were far from uniform in each of the countries discussed. Conspicuous consumption in Madrid, the capital of a powerful monarchy, took forms which were different from the merchant republic of Venice or from Rome, where the leading nobles were clerics. In Japan, early modern Edo, the centre of power, had a different socio-cultural profile from Kyoto, the seat of the imperial court, and Osaka, a more purely mercantile city (let alone the smaller castle-towns). Again, it is necessary to distinguish the consumption of Chinese mandarins from that of merchants, even if the behaviour of each group affected that of the other. It is to be hoped that regional specialists will add to these qualifications and refine the generalizations offered in these pages. All the same, the apparent rise of a more conspicuous kind of consumption in different parts of the world at much the same time remains intriguing. Can the comparison be extended to other parts of the world (for example the Ottoman Empire)? How can the timing be explained? How was it possible to break out of the vicious circle of escalating competitive consumption? To take such questions seriously would require a book rather than a chapter and a polyglot interdisciplinary team rather than an individual. I hope at least to have shown that there is still much to be gleaned by following in the footsteps of Fernand Braudel and Max Weber.

Notes

1   P. Bourdieu, *La Distinction* (Paris, 1979); E. Gellner, *Muslim Society* (Cambridge, 1981).

2   This chapter has been delivered in the form of a lecture at the Clark Library, Los Angeles; at Sophia University, Tokyo; at a meeting of the Japanese Economic History Society, also in Tokyo; at the Bocconi University, Milan; and at a conference on comparative history in the Institute of General History, Moscow. I learned a great deal from the discussions on all these occasions.

3   A number of specialists on the history of China and Japan have commented on this work, shown me objects and given me references. In particular I should like to thank Bill Atwood, Craig Clunas, Toshio Kusamitsu, Kazu Kondo, Hideo Kuroda, Kate Nakai and Ronald Toby. They are not of course responsible for any misuse of their advice.

4   F. Braudel, *Civilisation matérielle et capitalisme* (Paris, 1967, revised edn under title *Les Structures du quotidien*, Paris, 1979; published in English as *The Structures of Everyday Life*, tr. S. Reynolds (London, 1981)).

5   A point made by P. Burke, 'Material civilisation in the work of Fernand Braudel', *Itinerario*, v (1981), 37–43, and S. Clark, 'The Annales historians', in Q. Skinner (ed.), *The Return of Grand Theory in the Social Sciences* (Cambridge, 1985), 177–98.

6   D. H. Flaherty, *Privacy in Colonial New England* (Charlottesville, 1972); J. Deetz, *In Small Things Forgotten: The Archaeology of Early American Life* (New York, 1979); W. Rybczynski, *Home* (New York, 1986); A. Pardailhé-Galabrun, *La Naissance de l'intime* (Paris, 1988).

7   F. Boas, *Contributions to the Ethnography of the Kwakiutl* (New York, 1925). Cf. H. Codere, *Fighting with Property* (New York, 1950).

8   T. Veblen, *Theory of the Leisure Class* (New York, 1899).

9   F. J. Fisher, 'The development of London as a centre of conspicuous consumption', *Transactions of the Royal Historical Society*, xxx (1948), 37–50; L. Stone, *The Crisis of the Aristocracy* (Oxford, 1965).

10 M. Douglas and B. Isherwood, *The World of Goods* (London, 1979); M. Csikszentmihaly, *The Meaning of Things* (Cambridge, 1981); C. Campbell, *The Romantic Ethic and the Spirit of Modern Consumerism* (Oxford, 1987).

11 V. Packard, *The Status Seekers* (London, 1960); contrast D. Riesman, *The Lonely Crowd* (New York, 1950).

12 Douglas and Isherwood, *World of Goods*.

13 E. Goffman, *The Presentation of Self in Everyday Life* (New York, 1959).

14 E. Gellner, *Plough, Sword and Book* (London, 1988), 104.

15 W. Hoskins, 'The rebuilding of rural England 1570–1640', reprinted in idem, *Provincial England* (London, 1965), ch. 7.

16 P. Burke, *Popular Culture in Early Modern Europe* (London, 1978), 244ff.

17 J. M. Montias, *Artists and Artisans in Delft* (Princeton, 1982); cf. P. Benedict, 'The ownership of paintings in seventeenth-century Metz', *Past and Present*, cix (1985), 100–17.

18 H. Medick, 'Plebeian culture in the transition to capitalism', in R. Samuel and G. Stedman Jones (eds), *Culture, Ideology and Politics* (London, 1982), 94. Cf. N. McKendrick, J. Brewer and J. H. Plumb, *The Birth of a Consumer Society* (London, 1982). For similar phenomena in eighteenth-century Austria, cf. R. Sandgruber, *Die Anfänge der Konsumgesellschaft* (Munich, 1982).

19 T. Stoianovich, 'Material foundations of preindustrial civilisation in the Balkans', *Journal of Social History*, iv (1970–1), 205–62; J. de Vries, 'Peasant demand patterns and economic development: Friesland 1550–1750', in W. N. Parker and E. L. Jones (eds), *European Peasants and their Markets* (New Haven, Conn., 1975), 205–36.

20 G. Clark, *Symbols of Excellence* (Cambridge, 1981); R. A. Gould and M. B. Schiffer (eds), *Modern Material Culture: The Archaeology of Us* (New York, 1981); K. Hudson, *The Archaeology of the Consumer Society* (London, 1983).

21 M. J. Powers, 'Artistic taste, the economy and the social order in former Han China', *Art History*, ix (1986), 285–305.

22 J. Alsop, *The Rare Art Traditions* (New York, 1982), 241ff.

23 ibid., 249ff.; C. Clunas, *Superfluous Things: Material Culture and Social Status in Early Modern China* (Cambridge, 1991), 91–115; J. Gernet, *History of Chinese Civilisation* (Cambridge, 1982; 1st edn, 1972), 429ff.

24 P.-T. Ho, 'The salt merchants of Yang-Chou', *Harvard Journal of Asiatic Studies*, xvii (1954), 130–68; cf. Sandi Chin and Cheng-chi Hsü, 'Anhui merchant culture and patronage', in J. Cahill (ed.), *Shadows of Mount Huang* (Berkeley, 1981), 19–24; C. Mackerras, *The Rise of the Peking Opera 1770–1870* (Oxford, 1972).

25 S. Naquin and E. Rawski, *China in the Eighteenth Century* (New Haven, Conn., 1987), 63.

26 Examples and illustrations in C. Clunas, *Chinese Furniture* (London, 1988).

27 Naquin and Rawski, *China in the Eighteenth Century*, 76.

28 Gernet, *Chinese Civilisation*, 446f.

29 N. Elias, *The Process of Civilisation*, tr. E. Jephcott (London, 1981; 1st edn, 1939); C. Clunas, 'Books

and things: Ming literary culture and material culture', in F. Wood (ed.), *Chinese Studies* (London, 1988), 136–41.

30   A. Lévy, *Fleur en fiole d'or* (Paris, 1985), ch. 29, 598.

31   ibid., ch. 34, 692.

32   ibid., ch. 14, 289; ch. 34, 698.

33   ibid., ch. 34, 692.

34   ibid., ch. 20, 411; ch. 34, 692.

35   Clunas, personal communication, 1988. K. Carlitz, *The Rhetoric of Chin P'ing Mei* (Bloomington, 1986) does not discuss this problem.

36   Cao Xuequin, *The Story of the Stone*, 5 vols (Harmondsworth, 1973–86), vol. 1, 74.

37   Kazuko Koizumi, *Traditional Japanese Furniture* (Tokyo, 1986), 62, 63, 68, etc.

38   C. Wheelwright, 'A visualization of Eitoku's lost paintings at Azuchi Castle', in G. Elison and B. L. Smith (eds), *Warlords, Artists and Commoners* (Honolulu, 1981), 87–105.

39   M. E. Berry, *Hideyoshi* (Cambridge, Mass., 1982), 189.

40   H. P. Varley and G. Elison, 'The culture of tea', in Elison and Smith, *Warlords*, 187–222; G. Elison, 'Hideyoshi, the bountiful minister', in ibid., 223–44.

41   A gilt-edged tile from a *daimyo* residence is displayed in the Faculty Club of its successor, the University of Tokyo at Hongo.

42   W. H. Coaldrake, 'Edo architecture and Tokugawa law', *Monumenta Nipponica*, xxxvi (1981), 235–84. Cf. E. Kaempfer, *The History of Japan*, 3 vols (Glasgow, 1906; 1st edn, London, 1727), vol. 3, 75–6, on the 'stately palaces' and their 'stately gates'.

43   Kaempfer, *History of Japan*, vol. 2, 331f.

44   B. von Ragué, *A History of Japanese Lacquerwork* (Toronto and Buffalo, 1976; 1st edn, 1967), 202f.

45   T. Yazaki, *Social Change and the City in Japan* (San Francisco, 1968), 160.

46   Akiyama Terukazu, *Japanese Painting* (Geneva, 1961), 141f.; Hiroshi Mizuo, *Edo Painting: Sotatsu and Korin* (Tokyo, 1972).

47   Iharu Saikaku, *The Japanese Family Storehouse*, tr. G. Sargent (Cambridge, 1958).

48   ibid., 23, 26.

49   ibid., 65–7.

50   L. C. Eisenbart, *Kleiderordnungen der deutschen Städte zwischen 1350 und 1700* (Göttingen, 1962); D. Hughes, 'Sumptuary law and social relations in Renaissance Italy', in J. Bossy (ed.), *Disputes and Settlements* (Cambridge, 1983), 69–100.

51   R. Goldthwaite, *The Building of Renaissance Florence* (Baltimore, 1981).

52   For England, France and the Netherlands, see P. Thornton, *Seventeenth-Century Interior Decoration* (New Haven, Conn., 1978).

53   Details and references in P. Burke, 'Conspicuous consumption in early modern Italy', *Kwartalnik Historyczny Kultury Materialnej*, xxx (1982), 43–56, reprinted in Burke, *Historical Anthropology of Early Modern Italy* (Cambridge, 1987), ch. 10.

54   M. Bogucka, 'Le bourgeois et les investissements culturels', in A. Guarducci (ed.), *Investimenti e civiltà urbana, secoli xiii–xviii* (Florence, 1989), 571–84, the quotation on 571.

55   A. Adam (ed.), *Romanciers du 17e siècle* (Paris, 1958), 954.

56   C.-F. de Prefontaine, *Les Aventures tragicomiques du Chevalier de la Gaillardise* (Paris, 1662 edn), 20.

57   M. de Scudéry, *La Promenade de Versailles* (Geneva, 1979; 1st edn, 1669), 47–9, my translation.

58   G. Brusoni, *La gondola a tre remi* (Venice, 1657); idem, *Il carrozzino alla moda* (Venice, 1658).

59   G. Carew, 'A relation of the State of France', c. 1609, first printed in T. Birch (ed.), *An Historical View* (London, 1749), 435.

60   G. Mancini, *Considerazioni sulla pittura*, ed. A. Marucchi (Rome, 1956), esp. 143–5. Cf. Sabba da Castiglione, *Ricordi* (Venice, 1560; 1st edn, 1549), no. 109.

61   Elias (1939); idem, *The Court Society*, tr. E. Jephcott (Oxford, 1983; 1st edn, 1969).

62   Carew 'A relation of the State of France', 453.

63   G. Botero, *Grandezza delle città* (1589: published in English as *Greatness of Cities*, London, 1956; 1st edn, 1606), 260.

64   P. Burke, *Venice and Amsterdam* (London, 1974), 84ff.

8
Consumption in early modern social thought

Joyce Appleby

My subject is consumption – the desiring, acquiring and enjoying of goods and services which one has purchased – and I will concentrate upon my historical predecessors' investigation of consumption, examining what they have said about these activities, but especially what they failed to say, for my search of relevant texts took me to a void, an emptiness – at best, a hiatus or lacuna. I can pose the puzzle of this silence in several ways: why is it that consumption has rarely been examined thoroughly or dispassionately despite its centrality to economic life? Why is consumption uniformly construed negatively even though there is abounding evidence that consuming is pleasurable and popular and brings rare moments of satisfaction? Why, in the floodtide of Enlightenment enthusiasms for freedom – free speech, free inquiry, free labour, free trade, free contract – was free consumption never articulated as a social goal? Or put another way, why has the opportunity to consume been made dependent morally upon the opportunity to produce, but functionally upon the opportunity to purchase? I can think of no other human predisposition so essential to economic growth which has been so perversely treated. Why is it, to put the question in more total terms, that consumption, which is the linchpin of our modern social system, has never been the linchpin of our theories explaining modernity?

These questions take us back to the initial efforts to understand the emerging commercial economy. English men and women in the middle of the seventeenth century did not know that they had crossed a barrier which divided them from their own past and from every other contemporary society. Yet they had. Somewhere around 1650 the English moved beyond the threat of famine. It is true that chronic malnutrition lingered on for the bottom 20 per cent of the population, not completely disappearing for another century, but famine was gone. In the future there would be food shortages, skyrocketing grain prices, distress and dearth, but never again would elevated grain prices go hand in hand with rising mortality rates. Agricultural productivity combined with the purchasing power to bring food from other places in times of shortage had eliminated one of the four horses of the apocalypse from England's shores. A powerful reason for maintaining strict social order had unobtrusively disappeared, leaving behind a set of social prescriptions whose obsolescence had to be discovered one by one in the course of the next two centuries. It would be hard to exaggerate the importance of freedom from famine just as it is exceedingly difficult to follow all of the ways this material circumstance influenced behaviour and belief.

A second feature I would draw your attention to was the population growth which started again in Europe in the middle decades of the eighteenth century. The world's population had expanded and contracted over three millennia, but with eighteenth-century population growth a vital revolution was in the making. Unlike the old accordian-like pattern that had characterized previous European population fluctuations, the increase in people this time laid a new basis for future growth with each augmented cohort forming a kind of springboard from which world population still continues to soar. Food supplies were to be severely strained but instead of shrinking they expanded to sustain new levels of population. The twenty million Frenchmen Louis XIV ruled in 1700 became the forty million Frenchmen who couldn't be wrong in 1914. English population grew at an even faster clip. And in England's North American colonies – that catch basin of surplus people from northwestern Europe – the number of people doubled every twenty-five to twenty-six years.

Even more remarkable, the goods that people wanted grew apace – grew even faster than the number of people. A peculiar dynamic of the emerging world commerce had revealed itself most strikingly in England's first colony, that fragile outpost of European life established by the Virginia Company on the far side of the Atlantic. This settlement was explicitly tied to plans for extracting and producing vendible commodities. In 1617 John Rolfe successfully hybridized a tobacco strain which could compete with the much-esteemed Spanish orinoco. His leaf triggered a boom. Throughout the 1620s tobacco fetched between $1^1/_2$ and 3 shillings a pound, a price high enough to encourage Virginia Company shareholders to pour money and men (and a few women) into their plantations. Cultivation spread along the tidal rivers emptying into the Chesapeake Bay. The volume of exports surged. When the inevitable bust of oversupply followed this boom of demand-driven expansion, prices dropped to as low as a penny a pound – a twenty-fourth of the price of good Virginia tobacco in the 1620s. However, at this cheap price a whole new crowd of consumers could and did begin to buy tobacco, or as we would say metaphorically, entered the market. Their demand in turn created an incentive to cut production costs in order to supply this larger body of consumers with cheap tobacco at a profit. Success at this endeavour sustained a slower expansion of tobacco cultivation for two centuries. A similar thing happened in 1634 with Dutch bulbs, only to be repeated over and over again with cutlery, calicos, printed pictures, blankets, pottery, pewter and pepper.[1]

When ordinary people joined their social superiors in the pursuit of the pleasures of consumption, their numbers changed the character of the enterprise. Retrospectively we can see that this boom and bust cycle unintentionally widened the market for new goods. Investors responded to the profits of the boom; ordinary people to the opportunity of the bust. This dynamic enabled commerce – a feature of human society as old as the Bible – to move out of the interstices of a traditional social order and impose its imperatives upon the culture as a whole. The enormous augmentation in the volume of goods when ordinary people became consumers meant enormous augmentations in the wealth and power of those nations and persons who participated successfully in supplying the new tastes.

We are of course used to hearing the litany of new products entering European markets from the sixteenth century onwards – first from the fabled East India trade, then from the homely shops of ingenious artisans, finally to be overtaken by the prodigious outputs of the marvellous machines of the factory age. Rattling off the names of new condiments, textiles and inventions has served as the incantation for summoning the spirits that presided over the rise of the west. These details of early modern enterprise have supplied the factual grist for the mill of material progress.

Told within the familiar narrative of the liberation of *homo faber*, man the maker, modern history presents no problems. There are no ruptures in the telling, if not the living, of this age so long as the stunning and devastating transformation of the world wrought by the cumulative revolutions of technology and human adaptations appear as the end-point of a plan which has design and meaning. But we, alas, live in a post-industrial era. We can't conceive of our own time as a mere coda. We've known civilization and its discontents too long to subscribe to the notion that the discontents are epiphenomenal. We have even begun to entertain doubts about the inevitability of the events in our past. We've lost faith that these transformations were either natural or evolutionary. Significantly, these doubts have enabled us to hear other voices from the past – the crazies who preferred occult mysteries to the plain and simple truths of nature; the atavists who harkened back to ancient prudence. Tuning into these alternative voices has unchained our imagination. We can begin to see that our history told as the history of progress might have served as the intellectual equivalent of whistling through the graveyard.

What was profoundly unsettling, even shattering about the cumulative gains in material culture which became manifest by the eighteenth century was that they made it evident that human beings were the makers of their world. There is no way to underestimate the reverberations of such a discovery; they resonate through every modern discourse. And if we are post-modern it is because we can now reflect upon these discourses in science, politics and literature from a perspective standing outside the engagement itself. We see how Hobbes's irreverences become the ingenious truths of Scottish moral philosophers, to be transmogrified once more into the social science disciplines of the first half of the twentieth century.

Here I am reminded of a passage in Louis Dumont's *From Mandeville to Marx*. After detailing the western conception of society as the interactions of rational, utility-maximizing, self-improving, materialistic individuals, Dumont commented that this was a radically aberrant world view shared by no other culture. Rather than ask why other people were taking so long to become like us, he suggested, we should turn our curiosity around and ask how 'this unique development that we call modern occurred at all'.[2] There has been a punitive arrogance in the west's refusal to see its cultural differences as differences and to characterize them instead as the end-point in a universal process. This grand explanation robbed the events of the indeterminacy essential to historical narrative and hence obscured the dynamics of change at work.

A peculiarly intense form of curiosity in western culture drew the countries of western Europe along the path of innovation which grew ever wider as the pathbreakers pushed against a comparatively weak attachment to customary practices. On this broad avenue of human inventiveness Europeans encountered themselves as the creators of their own social universe. But this discovery took place while the actual social arrangements of their world reflected traditional assumptions about divine punishments, fallen human nature and the inherent frailty of civil society. How was social order to be maintained when collective understandings were being undermined by the new Promethean powers at large in the world?

Consumption – the active seeking of personal gratification through material goods – was the force that had to be reckoned with. Like other social activities, consumption had first to be named before it could be discussed. I want to look at four responses to this new phenomenon, four sequential engagements with the idea of abundance and its social consequences: the Restoration pamphleteers on trade who first took note of new patterns of spending; the Augustans' revival of classical wisdom about luxury; the Scottish intellectuals' reaction to the classically inspired laments about corruption and finally Malthus's mordant rebuff to the enthusiasts of the French Revolution.

The first observers of England's material abundance had no trouble discerning the human impulse animating the lively round of goods that encompassed Europe and its colonies in a new trade system. I'll quote from a few:

> The Wants of the Mind are infinite, Man naturally Aspires, and as his Mind is elevated, his Senses grow more refined, and more capable of Delight; his Desires are inlarged, and his Wants increase with his Wishes, which is for everything that is rare, can gratifie his Senses, adorn his Body and promote the Ease, Pleasure and Pomp of Life.

From another

> the main spur to Trade, or rather to Industry and Ingenuity, is the exorbitant Appetites of Men which they will take pains to gratifie, and so be disposed to work, when nothing else will incline them to it; for did Men content themselves with bare Necessaries, we should have a poor World.[3]

Research done within the last two decades has confirmed the assertions of contemporaries that it was domestic consumption, not foreign trade, that sustained England's manufacturing expansion in the eighteenth century.[4] Simon Schama has made a similar case for Dutch economic development in his *The Embarrassment of Riches*.[5] However, these early investigators of consumption, writing in the 1680s and 1690s, did not lay the foundation for a theory of commercial sociability. Rather, it was the critics of material abundance who seized the discursive high ground in England, appealing to classical republican texts to stigmatize novelty as the harbinger of social unrest. Using the essay form to inveigh against the new consuming tastes, these Augustan moralists read the goods they saw in haberdashery shops and food stalls as dangerous signs of corruption and degeneration. Against the delights of consumption, they pitted predictions of social disintegration. The only antidote: frugality and simple living for the people, austere civic virtue in their leaders. These alone could provide the social underpinnings for the Constitution, itself England's sole preserver from the terrors of history, that zone of irrational behaviour which made up the realm of *fortuna*.[6]

Consumption, as I have described it, figured in the political discourse of eighteenth-century England under the rubric of luxury. Luxury was not a thing, but a concept. As John Sekora has pointed out, the Greek view of luxury was a secular and rational complement to the Hebrew view. Luxury for the Hebrews represented a complex of evils moving from the personal and inveterate propensities of man to the ethical tendencies of the nation which collectively succumbs to temptation. The gravest feature of the repeated lapses recorded in the Old Testament was the evidence of disobedience. When a people ignore the law of necessity they undermine the established hierarchy between law-giver and subject. Necessity sets limits and happiness consists in having the rational capacity to abide by those restraints.

Luxury brings disorder because it destroys harmony and prevents the human being from fulfilling his or her nature.

In both Christian and classical thought the central unworthiness of human beings stemmed from their desiring things that were unnecessary, that is from their desire to consume. The control of this endemic envy, vanity, gluttony and lust required draconian laws and God's redeeming grace. Essayists, political figures, novelists, journalists – all contributed to an unrelenting, unrelieved depiction of the horrors awaiting England if the nation did not mend its luxurious ways. Luxury was not a personal indulgence; it was a national calamity, as the account of the ravages of luxury offered in the books of Samuel and Kings so powerfully demonstrated.

Hebraic tradition, which gave English Puritans so rich a rhetorical resource for vivifying sin, identified luxury with desire and desire with disobedience. Eve indulged in luxury when she unnecessarily ate the fruit of the tree of knowledge. The Israelites persisted in the most serious of human errors in their yearnings for things that they did not need nor had the right to claim. If represented graphically luxury, of course, is a woman – sometimes a powerful evoker of desire carrying the comb and mirror of cupidity and self-love; at other times an abject naked woman under attack from toads and snakes.

Depicted as a constant psychological drive, the attraction to luxury can never be more than suppressed, and the act of suppressing it constitutes the reason and justification for the minute control of the status, duties and privileges of all members of society. When in the *Republic*, Glaucon asked why the state should not provide for the citizens' wants as well as their needs, Socrates describes the inevitable engorgement of people that would follow this abandonment of the limits of necessity:

> Now will the city have to fill and swell with a multitude of callings which are not required by any natural want; such as the whole tribe of actors, of whom one large class have to do with forms and colours; another will be votaries of music – poets and their attendant trains of rhapsodists, players, dancers, contactors; also makers of diverse kinds of articles, including women's dresses. And we shall want more servants. Will not tutors be also in request, and nurses wet and dry, tirewomen and barbers, as well as confectioners and cooks; and swineherds too.[7]

In other words Athens will be visited by economic development.

It fell to Aristotle to explain how authority and necessity were linked. I must say it's ingenious. As nature shows that the household is subject to the father so most persons must be subject to the dominion of the legislator. The rulers embody reason which teaches restraint and it is a sign of luxury for slaves, women, servants, tradesmen, artisans, mechanics, the immature, the illiterate and the weak to want what they do not need. In restraining them, the male leaders are demonstrating reason for the whole. From such an Aristotelian conception of order came the sumptuary laws common in Europe which elaborated specific standards of decorum and decoration under the doctrine of 'consumption by estates'. It was their obligation to maintain order among the predictably disorderly that saved the landowning elite of England from the sting of the criticism about its luxurious consumption. While technically as prone to sin as others, the elite supplied security to the whole society through its vigilance in controlling servants, young people and women – that trilogy of categorical unfitness. To incriminate the guardians was to weaken the only dyke against the floodtide of riotous consumption.

Both the sentiment and the metaphor are reflected in Henry Fielding's reference to a 'vast torrent of Luxury which of late Years hath poured itself into the nation . . . almost totally changed the Manners, Customs, and Habits of the People, more especially of the lower Sort'. A political evil, luxury has inspired in the poor, he went on to explain, a desire for things they may not and cannot have, hence their wickedness, profligacy, idleness and dishonesty. Daniel Defoe less dramatically spoke of the decline of the Great Law of Subordination.[8] Shops bulging with cheeses, sweetmeats, coffee, tea, table linens, dry goods, gadgets, pictures and prints gave the lie to Fielding's assertion that the lower sort desired things they could not have. It was exactly their increasing ability to buy what was being made available in ever cheaper forms that created the crisis of social leadership.

What Sekora so nicely captures is the way that the human desire for the sensual pleasures of eating, entertainment, adornment and comfort, made manifest in actual consumption, became evidence for the need for strictly enforced hierarchies of authority in the home, the shop, the street, the town hall and the church. However, the disjuncture between the jeremiads on luxury and the actually visible, even conspicuous, behaviour of ordinary people cried out for clarification. As Bernard de Mandeville had earlier pointed out, English moralists were not confronting the fact that they were preaching truths which, if followed, would bankrupt the nation and undermine its greatness. The private vices of personal indulgence, Mandeville warned, amounted to the public benefit of national prosperity. Vice, not virtue, stoked the engine of commerce. Mandeville's goal, however, was to point up the hypocrisy in the outcry against luxury, not to endorse the abandonment of society to the consuming impulses of the least discerning members of society.

Roy Porter, writing on the English Enlightenment, has pointed to the strain of eudemonism running through the century's public commentary. Indeed he has characterized the English Enlightenment by its mildness. Not forced to overthrow an oppressive old regime like their neighbours across the Channel, prosperous Englishmen settled down to enjoying the affability afforded them by urban life. Sipping coffee, displaying new forms of politeness, relishing the wit of Addison and Steele, Porter's 'affluent, articulate and ambitious' Londoners, along with their provincial imitators, bent their minds to considering ways to make the world safe for egoism. Because the English had dealt with political tyranny in a previous century, they could address the more fundamental modern problem – the one connected with a recognition that society is a human product – of how individuals could pursue life, liberty, wealth and happiness while maintaining the social solidarity and order agreed upon by all as essential.[9]

If the optimistic men of Porter's English Enlightenment preferred *belles lettres* to compre-hensive philosophies, the same cannot be said for the Scotsmen – Adam Ferguson, Thomas Reid, John Millar, Dugald Stewart, David Hume and Adam Smith – who moved the discussions about luxury and egoism onto an entirely different plane.[10] Classical republica-nism had taught that men – and it was just men and only men of independent means – realized their full human potential when they participated in civic affairs. Supported by a substructure of labouring men and all women, this idealized citizen realized moral autonomy because of his independence from the necessities imposed by nature and through the inter-action of a community of peers. A highly artificial construct, classical citizenship elevated the citizen above the crass, mundane, earthy and vulgar, and tested his fitness by his capacity to be virtuous. Commerce reeked of all the proscribed qualities, linking men and women together in new systems of interdependence while trading on physical needs, worldly tastes, undisciplined wants and preposterous yearnings. Where classical republican thought utterly failed was in explaining the economic changes transforming society. Without abandoning a concern with the moral dimension of the new market society, the Scots directed their attention to analysing the new forces at work.

Following Hume, Smith saw that in the esteemed primitive societies where men and women retained the whole of their produce, there was material equality, but lives of misery and want. In commercial societies with their flagrantly unequal distribution of wealth, the labouring poor prospered as well. This apparent paradox led Smith to examine the secret spring of British abundance – the organization of labour through the division of productive tasks. Fed with ever-renewed freshets of capital, the modern commercial system would escape the cycle of luxury, corruption and decline, because it had enlisted the self-improving energies of most members of society.

Of course Smith's description of how nations grow wealthy through commerce – ingeniously detailed as it was – would not have answered the moral question posed by republicanism had he and Hume before him not considered human morality from a new perspective, that of the great sympathies and sociability enlisted in commercial society. Smith gave to all human beings the propensity to truck and barter, as well as the incessant drive to improve their condition. From these promptings men were drawn to each other's company. Here in the market place, not the political assembly of classical times, modern men developed the capacity to reflect upon themselves in society, to excel by emulating virtue and shunning dishonour. In the concourses of commerce, men acquired their notion of probity and justice. As Thomas Paine wrote in *The Rights of Man*, economic life drew upon the naturally sociable and co-operative aspects of human nature. Commerce works 'to cordialize mankind', Paine wrote, 'by rendering nations, as well as individuals, useful to each other'.[11]

It was also a feature of modern life that ordinary labourers were independent, feeding themselves through their wages and thereby participating in the system of natural liberty. By shifting investigations of human character from politics to economics, the Scots were including labouring people in their conceptual universe. Modern commerce had made it possible for all to be independent and thus cut the critical link in classical theory between independent citizens and the dependent, disenfranchised workers, leaving those categories to be redrawn on the basis of gender and race. Within the realm of independent men – wage-labourers, merchants, manufacturers and landlords – the natural operation of the invisible hand of the market could regulate affairs better than the legislator, thus adding to the freedom from servile dependency a freedom from overweening political authority. If commercial exchanges rather than government authority unified the nation, the talented few – the men of extraordinary virtue and rectitude – had no function which could justify their privileges. Indeed the whole concept of justification of privilege made its way into social discourse through the door marked utility.

Although it took him until Book IV to say it, Smith placed consumption at the heart of modern market society.

> Consumption is the sole end and purpose of all production and the interest of the producer ought to be attended to, only so far as it may be necessary for promoting that of the consumer. The maxim is so perfectly self-evident, that it would be absurd to attempt to prove it.[12]

Yet Smith was far from happy with the human propensity to consume, characterizing it variously as a fascination for 'baubles and trinkets', a passion for accumulating objects of 'frivolous utility' and, worse, a vehicle for deception with the false promise that wealth will bring happiness. Money will at best 'keep off the summer shower', he said, 'but not the winter storm', thus leaving humans more exposed than before to anxiety, fear and sorrow, disease, danger and death.[13]

Probing for the causes of the avidity so evident in his society in the last months before his death, Smith concluded that it was envy and admiration for the rich and powerful and fearful contempt of the poor that drove men to seek wealth. And since in modern society with its striking inequality of condition the prods from above and beneath were omnipresent, the material wants of man would be insatiable. In reasoning thus, Adam Smith anticipated at least a part of Max Weber's celebrated line that 'A man does not "by nature" wish to earn more and more money, but simply to live as he is accustomed to live and to earn as much as is necessary for that purpose.'[14]

It was one of the strengths of the Scottish moral philosophers to build upon human nature as they found it and to discern the springs of moral action from the close observation of men in their own society. In the 'uniform, constant and uninterrupted effort of every man to better his condition' Smith found the greatest grounds for hope.[15] For this was the human disposition that prompted men to defer pleasure, to save, to compete and to shun prodigality.

Here the middle-class character of the Scottish ideal shows itself, but in fact no rigorous analysis of consumption was carried out. Rather it was sentimentalized. From the middle of the eighteenth century through to our own time a particular kind of consumption has been approved, that which was associated with respectable family life. In the eighteenth century the word 'comfort' began to figure as the happy mean between biting necessity and indulgent luxury. Working over a draft treaty sent to him from John Adams in 1787, Thomas Jefferson replaced the word 'necessities' with that of 'comforts'. The new American nation would establish commercial treaties on the basis of exchanging comforts, not necessities.[16] Mary Wollstonecraft elaborated the concept in her *Historical and Moral View of the Origin and Progress of the French Revolution* when she explained that the French people had never acquired an idea of that independent, comfortable situation in which contentment is sought rather than happiness, because the slaves of pleasure or power can be roused only by lively emotions and extravagant hopes. In fact she goes on to observe the French don't even have a word in their vocabulary to express comfort, 'that state of existence, in which reason renders serene and useful the days which passion would only cheat with flying dreams of happiness'.[17]

The urban conviviality which commercial prosperity introduced into the eighteenth-century Anglo-American world had narrowed to a family-based respectability in the nine-teenth century. Increasingly the desire to better oneself became associated with the motive of providing for one's family. Novelists gave respectability a distinctly material embodiment in the cleanliness and cut of clothes, the privacy afforded in the home and the accoutrements required to support the round of domestic rituals. It is tempting to claim that the family was sentimentalized in order to supply the safe avenues for what otherwise might be riotous broadways of spending.

The passions which the French Revolution evoked challenged the benign optimism of those making their peace with Adam Smith's market society. Across the Channel it became apparent that competitive self-interest could translate quickly into violent clashes of interest. The discreet scepticism of David Hume flowered into the open irreverence of Thomas Paine, promulgated to ordinary people through mass printings. By making the economy rather than the polity the basic institution of the society, the Scots had left politics in something of a conceptual limbo. If labour created value instead of being God's curse on Adam, what was the position of the labourer? Even liberty and equality looked different when the economy rather than the polity became the pre-eminent social system. What need was there of the talented few whose extraordinary virtue and rectitude alone preserved the constitution if it was the economy that provided stability? And how firm was that stability? Commerce as the principal socializer lacked a certain disciplinary rigour.

These discursive speculations were shunted aside when economic commentators began groping for the certainties of science. The most striking reworking of consumption in modern social thought came from Thomas Malthus. Writing in the closing years of the eighteenth century, Malthus put forward a population theory which interpreted abundance as spurious and pernicious. He sidestepped the debate about human predispositions and socializing influences, arguing instead that human beings were ruled by a set of inexorable equations. Consumption was at the centre of his theory. Abundance created cheap food. In good times, men and women married early and had lots of children. Without the positive checks of war and disease (construed negatively in other discourses), human population would grow geometrically, swiftly outpacing the incremental increases of harvests which brought forth the surplus births. Would these unequal potentialities come into actual collision? Malthus was unequivocal about the immediate relevance of his mathematical discovery. 'The period when the number of men surpass their means of subsistence has long since arrived, has existed ever since we have had any histories of mankind, does exist at present, and will for ever continue to exist', he wrote in the first essay which appeared in 1798.[18] Nor could deferred marriage and family limitations relieve this parlous human condition.

Malthus forestalled further speculation about the theoretical effects of material progress by consigning human beings to a new determinism, the one inflicted by nature. A proper understanding of the dynamics behind human procreation eliminated the troubling question of how to render social justice in an age of increasing abundance. Utopian dreamers like Condorcet and William Godwin could say that perverse social institutions accounted for the persistence of human misery in the presence of unparalleled wealth – Godwin had argued just this in his celebrated essay, *An Enquiry Concerning Political Justice* – but Malthus permanently reordered the debate. The crucial issue became whether men and women could regulate their numbers and thereby avoid the evils of population pressure. Malthus said, 'no', and for the next thirty-eight years he refined his explanation of Nature's great catch-22 about plenty and poverty.

The possibility of easy living demonstrated to Malthus that it was only biting necessity that got human beings to exert themselves. Thus while the fear of famine was evil, it was only a partial evil, because it acted for a greater good. And, he stressed, not enough people knew about it. Instead of forming correspondence clubs to circulate radical tracts, working men should be taught their true situation. Malthus's words bear quoting:

> the mere knowledge of these truths, even if they didn't operate sufficiently to produce any marked change in the prudential habits of the poor with regard to marriage, would still have a most beneficial effect on their conduct in a political light, making them on all occasions less disposed to insubordination and turbulence.

Although the lower classes were clearly the focus of Malthus's attention, his principle was universal: 'Want has not infrequently given wings to the imagination of the poet, pointed the flowing periods of the historian, and added acuteness to the researches of the philosopher.'[19]

Malthus's sober strictures on the inevitable tendency of abundance (that is, more food) gave economics its label as the dismal science. In the hands of Ricardo the dreadful implications of omnipresent scarcity were worked out in the famous iron law of rents and declining rate of profits. Much that had remained open-ended in Smith was now closed. Demand, the activity closest to consumption, re-entered the picture as marginal utility, a concept which permitted all the passions of motivation from frivolity, vanity and boredom to ambition, avarice and need to be weighed on the same scale.

In ensuing decades the Malthusian principle of scarcity moved from economics to biology and then returned to sociology with powerful reverberations through all educated discourses in the nineteenth century. Human beings were folded back into nature. Physiology replaced original sin as the source of suffering. A uniform human nature and the stinginess of the physical environment controlled human destiny. Only familiarity keeps us from enjoying the irony that at a time when human productive powers were about to explode, competition for scarce resources became the centrepiece of theorizing in both biology and economics. The range of choices open to people had never been greater and yet it was positivism not poetry that dominated social thought. Variety and abundance became a permanent feature of western society, revealing the fecundity of human inventiveness, the insatiability of human curiosity, the splendour of human talents and the inaccuracy of aristocratic assumptions about ordinary peoples' abilities. Yet the reigning social theories assumed that human beings invariably sought gain through the equally invariant invisible hand of the market. Scholarly light narrowed to a laser beam directed at the workings of rational choice, utility maximization and competition for scarce resources while the rich diversity of human personality found no place in social theory.

The most consequential intellectual response to abundance was the awareness that human society was the product of human effort. To a large extent this is what is meant by secularization. Enveloped within the story of progress, this fact holds no terrors and few problems. Our proleptic histories assume that people want to rush into the future to enjoy their share of progressive improvement. In reality this encounter with unmitigated social responsibility was very troubling because it threw into high relief the issue of social justice, or more simply, how abundance was to be distributed. The classical discourse on luxury held the ground for a while, but it offered no intellectual tools for analysing economic developments. One of the responses to dramatic changes in the material world was the desire to explore the dynamic behind economic development. As William Reddy has noted, this extraordinary effort to understand the exchange economy ended up with a doctrine of indifference.[20] The existence of system was perceived – no mean feat – but once perceived it was declared best left alone. Those who spoke of the delights of the new material culture and the prospect of a more just distribution of them were drowned out by the new social scientists who gave human beings a nature so invariant that its inexorable workings determined social existence.

In this essay I have made consumption a generous concept, one that connects the social world of invention, taste and production with the personal world of sociability, experimentation and enjoyment. Why burden the concept of consumption with all this? Because in a commercial society consumption registers the range of human satisfactions; it leads to the creation of group affinities; it reveals the shifting patterns of human intentionality. What facets of human experience could be incorporated in a theory generous to consumption? I can think of three: self-indulgence, personal identity and privacy. Through consumption people indulge themselves, seeking gratification immediately and tangibly. Self-indulgence is a *terra incognita* in our social knowledge. Like sex in the nineteenth century, self-indulgence is so overly condemned that we can only approach it obliquely. We say that ordinary people – the masses – consume because they have been infected with artificial wants dreamed up by the international league of producers, or we treat it as a residual category – what people do when they are blocked from nobler activities like philanthropy, meaningful politics and becoming mature.

In addition to giving us access to the meaning of self-indulgence the study of consumption gives us a window on the elaboration of personal identity. Consumption offers people objects to incorporate into their lives and their presentation of self. This is as true of reading material as clothes and furnishings – purchasing and enjoying artefacts of material culture involves a constant expression of self. For this reason consumption opened up new avenues for rebellion. What were all those young women in the early nineteenth century doing when they eagerly consumed the literature of romance? They were seeking pleasure, learning about the world, finding models and exerting their own desires in the face of a clerical offensive against the reading of novels. Fashions set norms, but like statements, fashions point the way to their subversion. In every elaboration of a fresh style there is simultaneously created an armoury of defiant gestures. Perhaps not the grand stuff of revolutions, but splendidly innovative in the minor skirmishes of everyday insubordination.

Finally, consumption is instructive because the expanded world of goods enabled people to create privacy and embellish intimacy. Nothing so marked the eighteenth century as the building and refurbishing of residential space. And men and women seized this opportunity to shelter their informal, personal acts from outside scrutiny, first by simply adding partitions to close off rooms and subsequently by incorporating into their notion of privacy the daily acts of sleeping, eating, bathing, entertaining and reading, with appropriate rooms for each.

The novelty in consumption in the early modern period came from the inclusion of more and more people in the spending spree. Elite groups had always consumed and used consumption for self-gratification, establishing identity and creating privacy. Mass consumption was the driving force behind the new productive systems. Coming to terms with this reality impinged upon every social and political relation. Ordinary people had to brave the ridicule of others and buy beyond their station. Members of the elite had to give up many of the visual cues of their superiority. More important, they had to accept – however grudgingly – that ordinary people were self-activating agents, masters of their own dollars and shillings, if not their destiny. This dialectic of assertion, condemnation, indulgence, lamentation, insubordination and indignation remains an unexplored side of the democratization of society. Insisting upon the universality of the motive of gain has obscured the variety of human satisfactions sought through the market. It's not that our humanity requires commerce for its fulfilment, but rather that in a commercial society, a whole battery of new cultural means has been created to articulate a broader range of human intentions.

The economic development and social transformation which characterized the modern era depended upon changes in attitudes, habits and levels of consumption, and yet our social theorists from Smith through Malthus, Ricardo, Marx, Weber and Arthur Lafer have concentrated upon production. Their vocabulary has been drawn from the forbidding lexicon of control, discipline, struggle and competition. Through the course of two centuries, economic thought itself moved from the rhapsodizing of promoters through the moral outrage of Augustan classicism to the quantifiable factors of invariant responses and predictable outcomes.

Meanwhile back at the peddler's cart, the fair, the haberdashery, the milliners, the greengrocers, the market stall, the department store, the boutique, the discount house, the merchandise mart and the suburban mall, grown men and women, little children and their grandparents, have continued to consume, checked only by the limits of credit.

Notes

This chapter was originally delivered as a lecture at the Clark Library on 21 October 1988.

1   Sidney Mintz explores the complicated response to the popular consumption of New World commodities in *Sweetness and Power: The Place of Sugar in Modern History* (New York, 1985).

2   Louis Dumont, *From Mandeville to Marx* (Chicago, 1977), 6–7.

3   [Nicholas Barbon], *A Discourse of Trade* (London, 1690); [Dudley North], *Discourses upon Trade* (London, 1691), 14.

4   Neil McKendrick, 'Home demand and economic growth: a new view of the role of women and children in the Industrial Revolution', in idem (ed.), *Historical Perspectives: Studies in English Thought and Society in Honour of J. H. Plumb* (London, 1974).

5   Simon Schama, *The Embarrassment of Riches* (New York, 1987), 298–335.

6   I am indebted to John Sekora, *Luxury: The Concept in Western Thought, Eden to Smollet* (Baltimore, 1977) for this discussion of consumption considered under the rubric of luxury. See also J. G. A. Pocock, *The Machiavellian Moment: Florentine Political Thought and the Atlantic Republican Tradition* (Princeton, 1975).

7   Sekora, *Luxury*, 44.

8   ibid., 5, 299.

9   Roy Porter, 'The English Enlightenment', in Roy Porter and Mikuláš Teich (eds), *The Enlightenment in National Context* (Cambridge, 1981), 1–18.

10   For a particularly insightful discussion of the Smithian tradition see Keith Tribe, 'The "histories" of economic discourse', *Economy and Society*, vi (1977), 314–44. See also Isvan Hont and Michael Ignatieff, 'Needs and justice in the *Wealth of Nations*: an introductory essay' and Nicholas Phillipson, 'Adam Smith as civic moralist', in *Wealth and Virtue* (Cambridge, 1983). I am also indebted to the unpublished writing of Charles Nathanson.

11   Thomas Paine, *The Rights of Man* (London, 1791–2), 99.

12   Adam Smith, *An Inquiry into the Nature and Causes of the Wealth of Nations* (New York, 1937), 625.

13   Hont and Ignatieff, 'Needs and justice', 10.

14   Max Weber, *The Protestant Ethic and the Spirit of Capitalism* (New York, 1958), 60.

15   Smith, *Wealth of Nations*, 324–5.

16   Thomas Jefferson to John Adams, 27 November 1785, in Lester J. Cappon (ed.), *The Adams–Jefferson Letters: The Complete Correspondence between Thomas Jefferson and Abigail and John Adams*, vol. 1 (Chapel Hill, 1959), 103.

17   Mary Wollstonecraft, *An Historical and Moral View of the Origin and Progress of the French Revolution and the Effect it has Produced in Europe* (London, 1795), 511. I am indebted to Anne Mellor for this reference.

18   Thomas Robert Malthus, *An Essay on Population* (London, 1798), 54, as cited in Thomas Sowell, 'Malthus and the utilitarians', *Canadian Journal of Economics and Political Science*, xxviii (1962), 272.

19   Malthus, *Essay*, 2nd edn, vol. 2 (London, 1803), 200.

20   William Reddy, *Money and Liberty in Modern Europe: A Critique of Historical Understanding* (Cambridge, 1987), 78–82.

Part III
Production and the meaning of possessions

9

Changes in English and Anglo-American consumption from 1550 to 1800

Carole Shammas

To economic historians concerned with growth and development – which is to say almost all economic historians – interest in studying production has, traditionally, far exceeded interest in studying consumption. Theoretical predilections have been aided by empirical realities: records of past production decisions have survived in much greater number than records of past household expenditure decisions. Consequently it has been possible to argue quite persuasively that all important demand factors could ultimately be traced to changes in production.[1]

If there has been one group that has consistently challenged, whether explicitly or implicitly, the supply-side orthodoxy, it has been historians of the early modern period, those working on the sixteenth, seventeenth and eighteenth centuries, when the household was the site of both production and consumption. For example, Jan de Vries in his study of the Dutch household economy has theorized that early modern households might have specialized in production out of a desire for market goods that were different or superior to the goods they produced at home. In other words, changes in demand resulted in changes in production, rather than vice versa.[2] The moral to be drawn from this argument is not that a demand *primum mobile* be substituted for a supply one, but that the reason *why* people make economic development decisions may not be knowable, because it requires information about motivation. One cannot automatically assume that price and income changes have their origin in new production strategies. And one ignores at one's peril demand factors and questions such as *who* consumed *what* and *when*, just the kind of question that early modern social and economic historians, many using probate inventories, have been asking over the past ten to fifteen years, as they describe trends in the consumption of specific goods and services.

Where neo-classical economics is most helpful is in furnishing methods for analysing the immediate (as opposed to the initial and probably unknowable) sources for change in consumption. Did income rise, did prices fall, or did the proportion of expenditures going towards particular goods and services shift? Economists distinguish between absolute changes and elasticities (proportional changes), savings and expenditures, non-durable and durable expenditures. This type of categorization is quite useful. Where, once again, historians of early modern consumption have made a contribution, however, is in their willingness to study shifts *within* standard household expenditure categories. These shifts are as important as shifts between expenditure categories because of their impact on the standard of living, or to put it in terms of human capital theory, labour productivity, and because of their influence on production.

What I want to investigate here are changes in consumer demand for two types of goods – groceries and consumer durables – for which it is generally conceded some change occurred during the early modern period. The magnitude of the change and how one explains it, though, are open questions that are best answered, in my opinion, by combining certain modes of analysis favoured by economists with the historian's interest in the substance rather than the form of consumer demand. We want to know if rising incomes, falling prices or a switch in the way the household budgetary pie was divided accompanied new demand for a category of expenditure, but we also need to know, specifically, *who* consumed *what* particular good and *when* in order to know what exact change we are explaining and what its implications are for the standard of living.

Sugar products, caffeine drinks and tobacco became objects of mass consumption long before 1800, over the objections of contemporary social critics who considered labouring-class consumption of products formerly classified as luxuries a shameful waste of money. Because most groceries were imports, it is possible to consult trade statistics, which exist from the late seventeenth century on, about the growth in the popularity of these commodities in both England and the thirteen colonies. Consumer durables, however, were more often manufactured within the country and so probate inventories, the sources used to study household production, provide the best information. Such goods were, of course, not new in the early modern period, but a certain subgroup of durables, according to available research, did first enjoy a mass market during this time.[3] Interestingly enough, the majority of these goods might be classified as semi-durable in the sense that, if routinely used, they would require early replacement. Pottery, glassware, paper products and, in clothing, cheaper linens, cottons and thin woollen weaves were less likely to last as long as items made of wood, iron, brass, pewter, skins, fine linens and heavy woollens. Ironically, as housing, if we are to believe scholars who have looked at vernacular building in this period,[4] grew more sturdy and permanent, furnishings may have become more disposable. What will be focused upon here are the long-term trends in grocery and durables consumption, and, also, in the case of the latter, the nature of the change in expenditures for durables and the characteristics of those households that altered their demand for that category of good. Did the availability of the new products result in a structural change in expenditures, cutting into spending for production goods or savings? Or did changes in prices and real wages as well as substitution of cheaper commodities for dearer ones account for the difference? If there was a structural change, what can we find out about the household characteristics associated with it?

The consumption of groceries in England and America

Probably the most striking development in consumer buying during the early modern period was the mass adoption by the English and the colonials of certain non-European groceries.

Table 9.1 documents the growth in the importation of these commodities into England and Wales between the 1550s and 1800. In 1559 groceries constituted less than 10 per cent of the value of all imports. Pepper was the major mass-consumed grocery. The value of imported dried fruits exceeded that for sugar. No tobacco, tea, coffee or chocolate came into London at all. In the later 1600s the percentage increased to 16.6 per cent and by the 1770s it came to one-third. This gain is particularly impressive when it is realized that the prices of the main groceries – tobacco, sugar products and caffeine drinks – all fell sharply during the period. In fact, the temporary absence of any gain between 1663–9 and 1700 can probably be explained by the big drop in the cost of sugar and tobacco.

Table 9.1 The percentage of the total value of imports in groceries: England and Wales 1559–1800

Year	% in groceries
1559*	8.9
1663–9*	16.6
1700	16.9
1750	27.6
1772	35.8
1790	28.9
1800	34.9

*Calculated from Port of London figures, assuming that London's imports represented 80 per cent of total for the country and that 5 per cent of the value of imports in the outports were groceries in 1559 and that 10 per cent were in 1663–9.

Sources Joan Thirsk, *Economic Policy and Projects* (Oxford, 1978), Appendix 1; Ralph Davis, 'English foreign trade 1660–1700', *Economic History Review*, 2nd series, xvii (1954), Appendix; Elizabeth Boody Schumpeter, *English Overseas Trade Statistics, 1697–1808* (Oxford, 1960), 11.

Literary evidence about courtiers and London trend-setters smoking tobacco and drinking tea abound. The question is, when did usage of the various grocery products spread beyond the elite and the citizens of the metropolis and how sustained was the growth over the three centuries? For a good to be considered a mass-consumed commodity in any given place, two things must happen. It must be bought by people of varied income levels and they must be buying it on a more or less regular basis. Here a grocery item will be considered to be mass consumed if enough was imported to allow a quarter of the adult population to use it at least once daily.[5] In most cases, of course, more than 25 per cent probably used the item but not every day.

The best place to begin is with tobacco, because chronologically it was the first of the new mass-consumed groceries. As it was a crop grown primarily in the thirteen colonies, no accurate records of consumption exist for America, although all evidence points to it becoming a mass-consumption item almost immediately after becoming a staple. Colonial consumption of the product, it is believed, averaged between 2 pounds and 5 pounds per capita per annum during the eighteenth century.[6]

Large-scale shipments of the plant into England began with the settlement of the Chesapeake. It was also grown, of course, in many other colonies and, despite government

Table 9.2 Tobacco imported for home consumption:* England and Wales 1620–1799

Years	Legal imports: lbs per capita (annual average)	Years	Estimated total of legal and illegal: lbs per capita (annual average)
1620–9	0.01		
1630–1	0.02		
1669	0.93		
1672	1.10		
1682, 1686–8	1.64		
1693–9	2.21	1698–1702	2.30
		1703–7	1.56
1700–9	2.23	1708–12	2.23
1710–19	1.57	1713–17	1.80
		1718–22	2.62
1720–9	1.83	1723–7	2.13
		1728–32	2.23
1730–9	1.00	1733–7	2.00
		1738–42	1.65
1740–9	0.96	1743–7	1.56
		1748–52	1.94
1750–9	1.65		
1760–9	1.37		
1770–9	0.65		
1780–9	1.43		
1790–9	0.87		

*For years 1620–94, when only total imports without indication of amount re-exported are available, it was assumed that one-third of total retained.

Sources US Bureau of the Census, *Historical Statistics of the United States, Colonial Times to 1970* (Washington DC, 1975), 1190–1, Schumpeter, *English Overseas Trade*, 61–2, and Robert C. Nash, 'The English and Scottish tobacco trades in the seventeenth and eighteenth centuries: legal and illegal trade', *Economic History Review*, 2nd series, xxxv (1982), 367.

laws to the contrary, in England itself until the end of the seventeenth century.[7] The first column in Table 9.2 reports the annual average of pounds per capita of legal imported tobacco retained for home consumption. The figures suggest that sometime in the mid-seventeenth century, tobacco, by the standard described above, became a mass consumption item. *Circa* 1670 per capita consumption reached one pound. Two pounds of tobacco a year would probably allow enough for a pipeful a day, and so total imports could furnish 2,700,000 or 50 per cent of the total populace with that ration. The actual number of regular smokers fell far below that, yet there was too much tobacco around in 1670 for it to have been all consumed by an elite group. For either the wealthiest 5 per cent of the population or the adult population of London to have been the only consumers, each person would have had to smoke 20 pounds a year, about three times the amount consumed by Britons in the mid-twentieth century.

If full information on imports and domestic production were available, it might actually turn out that mass consumption began prior to 1650, in the 1630s or 1640s when producer prices dropped to one-fourth or less of the original selling price. During the late 1630s, London alone received an average of 1.8 million pounds legally, enough for one quarter of the adult population to smoke 2 pounds annually; much of that was exported, however. Still, with outport totals and domestic production, which was at its height, the total could conceivably have come near to mass consumption levels. The Stuart government, always on the lookout for a new revenue source, slapped a licensing fee on retailers in 1633, indicating the existence of a nationwide trade.[8]

While tobacco enjoyed the most rapid diffusion of any commodity being studied here, desire for the weed seemed to wane in the next century. From the figures in column 1 of Table 9.2, the reader might well conclude that tobacco usage peaked at the beginning of the eighteenth century at around 2 pounds per capita and turned sharply downward thereafter. Before jumping to that conclusion, however, smuggling must be considered.

The import duties on tobacco were very high in England, exceeding the initial cost of the commodity. After a sizeable customs hike in 1685, it became particularly worth the while of English traders to evade the tariffs.[9] According to contemporary accounts, they bribed customs officers to declare merchantable tobacco 'damaged' or to enter the weights of hogsheads below their true poundage. Scotland, it appears, engaged in more than its fair share of this type of manoevring and surreptitiously exported much of the contraband into England. Finally there was the re-exporting of American tobacco to off-shore islands or abroad and then smuggling it back for duty-free sale. Relanding, frequently done via the coast of France, proved difficult during the wartime years 1689–1713, which may explain why the drop in legal imports retained for home consumption did not occur earlier. In the 1730s, the British government considered tobacco smuggling to be such a problem that they sent out troops to deal with those in the trade and proposed changing the import duty to an excise. Public outcry, however, was so enormous that the politicians backed off from making the substitution.[10]

The effects of smuggling and other fraud on the per capita consumption figures have been estimated by Robert Nash for the period 1698–1752 and appear in the last column of Table 9.2. His corrections suggest neither a big drop nor an increase during the first half of the eighteenth century but rather a rate of consumption fluctuating around 2 pounds per capita.

The trend that needs explaining, then, instead of decline, is one of no growth in per capita consumption during the 1700s or at least up to the American Revolution. Without data on individual consumption patterns, however, explanations are not that easy to give. Demographic changes, especially an increase in the proportion of the population under 15, would depress per capita figures, but that development would have had little effect until the last few decades of the eighteenth century.

The fact, though, that smoking remained largely the preserve of adult males certainly put limitations on its continued growth. In addition, pipe smoking, the primary means of taking tobacco in early modern England, was closely associated with the alehouse. Almost from the beginning, publicans had been the main retailers of both tobacco and the pipes, and they offered easy access to affordable amounts of the narcotic. The pipeful became another of the refreshments connected with alehouse social life. When in the later eighteenth century the alehouse fell into decline,[11] it is hard to believe it did not affect smoking habits as well. It is interesting to note that British tobacco consumption only began to rise above early modern levels in the twentieth century with the marketing of the cigarette, a product that attracted many new customers, especially among the female population.

The first of the new mass-consumed groceries, then, gained acceptance almost immediately, but also soon reached a plateau. Sugar, on the other hand, had a slower start, yet once

Table 9.3 Sugar and rum imports for home consumption: England and Wales 1663–1799

Years	Sugar: lbs per capita (annual average)	Rum: gallons per capita (annual average)
1663, 1669	2.13	n.a.
1690, 1698–99	4.01	n.a.
1700–09	5.81	<0.01
1710–19	8.23	<0.01
1720–9	12.02	0.02
1730–9	14.90	0.06
1740–9	12.73	0.08
1750–9	16.94	0.14
1760–9	20.20	0.15
1770–9	23.02	0.22
1780–9	21.14	0.17
1790–9	24.16	0.24

Sources: Richard B. Sheridan, *Sugar and Slavery: An Economic History of the British West Indies 1623–1775* (Baltimore, 1974), 22, 404, 493, and Schumpeter, *English Overseas Trade*, 60–2.

it took off demand continued to grow right into the modern age. The English population was quite familiar with the sweetener long before the sixteenth century. Their acquaintanceship, however, took the form of small lumps received as gifts or as special treats. High prices, reflecting limited supplies, kept sugar out of the daily life of most people. Even in the sixteenth century when New World sources caused the real price of the product to drop by two-thirds, a pound of sugar still cost over a shilling, as much as a labourer's wage for two days' work. Over the course of the seventeenth century, the price dropped by half, and between 1700 and 1750 the price went down another one-third.[12] Although sugar never became cheap, it eventually furnished nearly as many calories per penny as did meat or beer.

Table 9.3 gives an indication of the trend in sugar consumption. The earliest figures are for the 1660s and they show annual consumption at about 2 pounds per capita. Probably for a person to be regularly sweetening food or drink with sugar required about 24 pounds a year. *Per capita* consumption actually reached those levels by the third quarter of the eighteenth century. It is not necessary for per capita figures to be that high, however, to consider sugar mass consumed. By the end of the seventeenth century sugar imports per head were at 4 pounds, which would furnish nearly 900,000 people, about a quarter of the adult population, with 24 pounds. Again, in reality, probably a small group consumed more than 24 pounds, and most consumed less. Still, the amounts present seem to indicate it was a constant presence in the lives of a significant number of English men and women before 1700. Decadal growth rates during the eighteenth century were over 40 per cent before 1730, spurts that are often attributed to the rising popularity of tea (see below), although tea clearly needed sugar more than vice versa and if tea and other caffeine drinks had not been available probably the sweetener would have been combined with some other substance.

Much of the sugar imports listed in Table 9.3 were actually consumed in a form other than brown sugar. Some was refined, during which process not only whitened sugar emerged but also molasses, which in turn could be consumed, often by those unable to afford sugar, or made into rum. Then there were the West Indian imports. Apparently little molasses was brought into England after 1720; instead English refiners manufactured it. But rum was another matter. Increasingly large quantities were shipped over the course of the eighteenth century and traders smuggled in additional amounts to avoid the paying of duties.[13] The liquor was very popular with sailors and rum punch enjoyed great popularity among the general population. The second column in Table 9.3 indicates the volume of *legal imports* consumed. By the end of the century it amounted to almost a quart per capita, and that was not counting the rum made from sugar imports or entering as contraband.

The year-by-year trend in the consumption of sugar products by Americans is not known. Aside from the record of refined sugar imported from England, series on West Indian sugar, molasses and rum importation are not available for the thirteen colonies, and even if they were, the considerable smuggling of sugar and molasses from non-British areas of the Caribbean would have to be taken into account. What can be done is to compare the 1770 consumption of sugar products in England (including Wales) with the intake in the thirteen colonies, because there are estimates of American consumption for that year. As it turned out, the English imported more sugar per capita, 23.7 pounds to America's 14.2, but the latter's much greater intake of rum, as measured by imports of rum and molasses, made the per capita consumption of the thirteen colonies much higher than that of the mother country. Americans brought in an estimated 1.7 gallons of rum and 3 gallons of molasses per capita. Meanwhile the per capita drinking of rum by the English, even if they smuggled in an amount of rum equal to the 0.2 gallons they legally imported and imported as much as 0.2 gallons of molasses, was less than one-quarter of that of the colonists, and their consumption of molasses one-fifteenth. If all of the sugar products consumed by both are converted into calories, the estimated imports of England yielded 140 calories per capita daily while those of the thirteen colonies totalled 260, almost double the English figure.[14]

Finally there is tea, the most popular of the caffeine drinks among the English in the early modern period. The East India Company began importing Chinese tea in the 1660s, but shipments were sporadic and often of relatively small amounts, because the Company had no direct access to China. Then, in 1713, they established trade with Canton, and imports became more regular and voluminous.[15] Of course at no time prior to 1784 did English men and women depend solely on legally imported tea. With duties on the average doubling the net cost of the drink, alternative vendors, mainly the trading companies of other European countries, found a ready market. In some years the tea of the East India Company may have represented as little as one-quarter of the total imported. The colonies had even less compunction about evading the duties, particularly after the tea duty became embroiled in the general rebellion against British commercial regulation and taxation.[16]

Table 9.4 displays what is known about the amount of tea legally imported into England and America for consumption. The trend in both places is onward and upward, except for the war years in the 1770s. The amounts for most of the years, however, are below what would be expected if tea was being mass consumed. Thus the need to make some estimate of the level of smuggling.

There were substantial numbers of Londoners consuming tea by 1700, but, given the uncertain supply of even legal tea prior to 1713, the 1720s was probably the first decade in which mass consumption nationwide could have taken place. If it took 2 pounds of tea annually per capita to have a cup a day and an average of 580,800 pounds of tea were imported each year legally, then less than 300,000 people were supplied. For there to be enough tea to meet the standard of 25 per cent of the adult population being constant consumers then over three times that number, or 951,000 people needed a total of 1,902,000

Table 9.4   Tea imports for home consumption: 1700–99 (annual average)

Years	England and Wales		Thirteen colonies	
	Legal lbs per capita	Estimated legal and illegal lbs per capita	Legal lbs per capita	Estimated legal and illegal lbs per capita
1700–9	0.01	n.a.	n.a.	n.a.
1710–19	0.05	n.a.	n.a.	n.a.
1720–9	0.10	n.a.	n.a.	n.a.
1730–9	0.17	0.50	n.a.	n.a.
1740–9	0.29	1.00	n.a.	n.a.
1750–9	0.49	1.10	0.11	0.43
1760–9	0.81	1.60	0.19	0.80
1770–9	0.70	1.40	0.13	n.a.
1780–9	1.26	2.00	n.a.	n.a.
1790–9	2.00	2.10	n.a.	n.a.

Sources Schumpeter, *English Overseas Trade*, 60–1, W. A. Cole, 'Trends in eighteenth-century smuggling', *Economic History Review*, 2nd series, x (1958), 395–409, Hoh-Cheung Mui and Lorna H. Mui, *The Management of Monopoly* (Vancouver, 1984), 12–14 and Benjamin Woods Labaree, *The Boston Tea Party* (New York, 1964), 331 and *passim.*

pounds of tea, and around two-thirds would have had to have been smuggled in. During 1720–3, the authorities believed that much of the smuggling involved relanding of exported cargo. East India Company tea was sold and re-exported to get the customs duty refund and then secretly brought back in. In 1724, the government changed the customs duty to an excise or sales tax to thwart this scheme, and sure enough re-exports plunged. In that year the English retained about 1,200,000 pounds. After that, foreign companies mobilized to supply duty-free tea to the English. It seems likely that in this decade total imports for consumption were in the area of 1–1.5 million or 0.2 pounds per capita annually. All classes in London and surrounding counties and in major provincial centres may have been regular consumers. It seems, though, for there to have been a more generally diffused mass consumption throughout England, smuggling in the last five years of the decade would have had to have been on a scale only associated with the 1730s and 1740s, when it appears mass consumption certainly had taken hold throughout much of the country.[17]

In 1745 the government, again reassessing its duties on tea in the light of rampant smuggling, concluded that in the period 1742–5 about three million pounds of the leaves had been smuggled in. At that point, legal tea may have represented only a quarter of the whole and per capita consumption may have been near 1 pound.

Some hint of what it would have been possible to smuggle in comes from the statistics on what the European companies imported: 8.7 million pounds in 1749–55, 6.8 million during the Seven Years War, 10.3 million in 1763–9 and 13.4 million in 1770–84.[18] It is believed that most of this tea went to consumers in the British Isles and in America. These amounts probably pushed English consumption per capita up to 2 pounds before the British government removed most of the duty from tea in 1784. Although they reintroduced taxes step-by-step as the conflict with France developed in the late 1780s and 1790s, by then the high price of foreign tea and wartime conditions made smuggling of little consequence.

In the 1750s, per capita legal imports of tea into the thirteen colonies resembled those of England in the 1720s, but because of a higher ratio of illegal to legal tea, the actual levels may have been nearer to the total illegal and legal consumption in England during the 1730s,

0.5 pounds, and high enough for the colonists to be considered mass consumers of the product. What seems to indicate that substantial smuggling was being carried out was the suspiciously small amount of tea imported into New York and Pennsylvania ports. One Philadelphia merchant even admitted that, as long as Great Britain imported so little Pennsylvania wheat, the colonists would continue to seek out Dutch and other European markets and smuggle in foreign supplies of tea on return voyages.[19] The New Englanders having no such commodity to trade relied more heavily on the East India Company for supplies. Coffee of course was more popular than tea on the Continent and it is not difficult to see how after the break with Great Britain, coffee may have become more accessible than tea, especially after 1784 when the English market for smuggled tea collapsed.

Behind the story of rising consumption of both legal and illegal tea during the eighteenth century was a falling real price for the commodity. At the time of the American Revolution, English consumers spent half of what they would have in the 1720s for legally imported tea, despite higher duties. After the removal of the tariffs in 1784, the price was halved again. As with sugar, consumers seemed to react to lower prices, although once tea was firmly entrenched in the diet, they did not cut back when prices rose.

The new groceries – tobacco, sugar, caffeine drinks – seemed to offer something for everyone. Big profits for planters and merchants, relatively light weight for shippers, and cheap energy and relaxation for consumers.

Consumer durables in England and America

Most of those who write of a revolution in consumption during the early modern period have been more interested in consumer durables than in groceries. Their eye has been caught by the proliferation of small haberdashery items, clothing accessories such as caps and stockings, linens and cottons, and tableware of various sorts in customs records, shopkeepers' accounts and probate inventories.[20] One has the sense that there must have been a continual increase in spending for these items. It is a little disappointing, therefore, to look at the pound sterling amounts and percentages in Table 9.5 and discover that the trends are not quite as clear-cut as might be desired.

The table shows the percentage of total personal wealth in consumer goods and their mean and median value as revealed in probate inventories from the Midlands and London in England and from the Chesapeake and Massachusetts in America. Both the unadjusted means and those after correction for inflation over time or in colonial currency are given. Total personal wealth is all wealth except realty. Livestock, crops, merchant stock, financial assets and equipment are considered producer goods. Consumer goods are primarily housewares, furniture and apparel. Transportation vehicles such as carriages and even a horse are counted if the horse seemed solely for the conveyance of people. Small stocks of food and pocket money are occasionally included because some inventories simply say 'all the stuff in the kitchen' or 'in the parlour' or 'apparel and purse'. Primarily, though, consumer goods comprised bedding, apparel, linens, brass and pewter and plate and jewellery. These goods (as Table 9.6 shows below) made up from one-half to three-quarters of the total value of consumer goods.

The first measure of consumer demand given in Table 9.5 is that of the percentage of total aggregate personal wealth in consumer goods. As quickly becomes apparent, there is really

Table 9.5 Inventoried wealth in consumer goods: England and the colonies 1551–1774

Place and years	N	Mean wealth: constant £*	% Wealth in consumer goods	Consumer goods mean: current £*	Consumer goods mean: constant £*	Consumer goods median: constant £*
Oxfordshire 1551–90	254	67.2	28.0	9.4	18.8	10.4
South Worcs. 1669–70	275	103.8	28.0	29.1	29.1	17.0
South Worcs. 1720–1	305	153.4	19.9	30.5	30.5	17.0
East London 1661–4	129	72.0	33.6	24.2	24.2	14.0
East London 1720–9	177	1293.1	5.6	72.0	72.0	32.0
Virginia 1660–76	134	139.4	18.7	26.1	26.1	14.3
Virginia 1724–9	299	104.3	27.1	28.3	28.3	18.3
Virginia and Maryland 1774	141	310.0	10.7	33.3	25.0	15.0
Essex County, Mass. 1660–73	300	105.2	33.0	34.7	34.7	27.5
Massachusetts 1774	299	142.8	21.4	39.6	29.8	17.3

*All constant and current values are in pounds sterling. The base years for the constant values are 1660–74 (England). For method of adjustment see Carole Shammas, *The Preindustrial Consumer in England and America* (Oxford, 1990), Appendix I.

Sources Oxfordshire 1550–90 – inventories printed in Michael Ashley Havinden (ed.), *Household and Farm Inventories in Oxfordshire, 1550–1590* (London, 1965); Southern Worcestershire 1669–70 and 1720–1 – probate files in Worcestershire Consistory Court, County of Hereford and Worcestershire Record Office, St Helens, Worcester and in the Prerogative Court of Canterbury, Public Record Office, London; East End of London 1661–4 and 1720–9 – probate files for the parishes of Stepney, Whitechapel, Stratford-le-Bow and St Leonard Bromley filed in the Commissary Court, London Guildhall, in the Consistory Court, Greater London Record Office, London, and in the Prerogative Court of Canterbury, Public Record Office, London; Virginia 1660–77 and 1724–9 – probate files from the county courts of York, Isle of Wight, Westmorland, Northumberland (1660–77 only), and Henrico, Virginia State Library, Richmond; Essex County, Massachusetts 1660–73 – inventories printed in *The Probate Records of Essex County, Massachusetts*, I and II (Salem, 1916–17); Virginia and Maryland, 1774 and Massachusetts 1774 – inventories printed in Alice Hanson Jones (ed.), *American Colonial Wealth*, 3 vols (New York, 1977).

Table 9.6 The value of major categories of inventoried consumer goods:* England and the colonies 1551–1774

Place and years	Bedding			Linen			Apparel			Pewter and brass			Plate and jewellery			Total of means for five categories	% five categories constitute of consumer goods: mean
	N	mean	median	N	mean	median	N	mean	median	N	mean	median	N	mean	median		
Oxfordshire 1551–90	254	4.8	2.4	253	2.8	2.4	196	2.4	1.4	252	2.2	1.4	252	0.8	0.0	13.0	69.1
South Worcs. 1669–70	267	6.9	5.0	265	2.3	1.0		2.8	2.0	266	2.4	2.0	270	1.3	0.3	15.7	54.0
South Worcs. 1720–1	260	6.8	4.0	262	2.8	1.0	31	3.2	2.0	253	2.4	1.6	260	1.1	0.0	16.3	53.4
East London 1661–4	123	5.5	3.0	123	2.1	1.0	87	3.6	1.9	123	2.5	1.0	124	2.5	0.3	16.2	66.9
East London 1720–9	61	8.2	4.0	94	5.3	1.0	71	6.6	3.0	87	1.6	1.0	145	23.8	1.0	45.5	63.2
Virginia 1660–76	128	7.5	5.1	132	1.2	1.0	94	3.2	2.0	133	1.6	1.0	132	0.9	0.1	14.4	55.1
Virginia 1724–9	298	7.9	5.8	297	0.8	0.0	297	1.9	0.8	295	2.4	1.7	296	1.7	0.0	14.7	51.9
Virginia 1774	138	9.8	7.5	138	1.0	0.0	94	5.2	2.3	139	1.0	0.8	141	1.7	0.0	18.7	74.8
Essex County Mass. 1660–73	285	9.2	7.5	291	3.9	2.5	276	5.8	5.0	292	2.1	1.7	300	0.4	0.0	21.4	61.7
Massachusetts 1774	290	6.3	4.5	290	2.0	0.8	282	5.0	3.0	293	1.4	0.8	295	4.4	0.0	19.1	64.1

*All values are in constant pounds sterling, base years 1660–74.

Source see Table 9.5.

not a consistently upward trend. First of all, those areas which had a group of very wealthy people – the rich industrialists and financial magnates of East London 1720–9 and the slave-holders of the Chesapeake in 1774 – show a small percentage of wealth in consumer goods, not because they did not have a lot of consumer durables but because their producer wealth was so great. Cities such as London always produce peculiar results unless wealth is controlled, due to the high concentrations of poor and rich in urban environments and lower per capita rates of leaving probate records. For example in the 1660s, East London (i.e. the East End) appears very poor, and indeed it still was in the 1720s. The only difference was that there were some very rich people living in the area and they were better represented in the 1720s sample than in the 1660s group of inventories. If any generalization can be made about this column, it is that probated decedents in most places held about a quarter of inventoried wealth in consumer goods. Before 1700 the proportions tended to be somewhat higher than that, and after 1700 they were somewhat lower. Because the post-1700 samples were wealthier than the earlier samples, this trend is not too surprising. All modern consumption studies show richer households spending a smaller proportion of their income on consumption and more on savings. Whether the increase in wealth was real or an artefact of who left an inventory and who moved in or out of an area requires a separate study. Suffice it to say that much of the difference in means can be attributed to such factors.

Comparing the changes in wealth with the changes in the proportion in consumer goods within each area indicates that only in the Midlands between the late sixteenth and the late seventeenth century does a rise in mean wealth result in no drop in the proportion in consumer goods. Everywhere else a drop occurred, although in some areas the decline was not as great as the rise in wealth. All in all, however, there is little confirmation of the theory that the supposed transformation of many producers to consumers led to a dramatic increase in the proportion of wealth devoted to consumer goods. The best that can be inferred is that in the first three-quarters of the seventeenth century, English households kept up the proportion 'invested' in durables when their wealth increased; afterwards it fell. It is interesting to compare the proportions with current data. In a 1979 survey of household wealth in America, survey researchers found 12.3 per cent of wealth devoted to household goods and vehicles. If real estate is subtracted from total wealth in order to make the data comparable to the inventories, the percentage doubles, making it about one-quarter and very similar to early modern figures on consumer goods.[21]

In some ways, the means and medians, despite the inflation problem, are a more reliable guide to how accumulation of consumer goods was progressing. The means are reported in both current pounds sterling and in constant terms, after adjustments for inflation. There appears to have been a considerable increase in the real amount spent on consumer goods between the late sixteenth and the late seventeenth century, although that is based on only one sixteenth-century sample. In Oxfordshire in the 1551–90 period, the mean adjusted amount spent on consumer goods was £18.8, whereas in Worcestershire and elsewhere in the period *circa* 1670 it rose to between £24.2 and £34. But there it stayed during the eighteenth century, aside from the idiosyncratic figure for East London. Because, as in that case, a few high values often distort means, it seemed advisable to look at medians as well. The trend, though, is essentially the same. The sixteenth-century median is still noticeably lower, while there is little difference between the late seventeenth and the eighteenth centuries. The median falls between £14 and £18 in seven of the samples. East London is higher (£32) but not as spectacularly so as when means are used. The median for the 1660s–70s

Massachusetts inventories (£27.5) also exceeds that range. This Essex County sample is a great deal more homogeneous than the rest. Among the Puritan immigrants there were few poor, not many rich, nor many single decedents. They had quite substantial holdings of household wares (one-third of their wealth was in consumer goods), perhaps as a protection against uncertain supply. Another study of consumption patterns in colonial Massachusetts also finds that in this period the amount was greater than in subsequent decades.[22]

A glance at the amounts invested in the main categories of commodities comprising consumer goods (Table 9.6) provides some insight into the reason the total failed to increase during the late seventeenth and the eighteenth centuries. The adjusted means and medians suggest that although the money put into bedding (mattress, pillows, curtains, blankets and coverlets as well as the bed frame) and apparel may have been increasing, the other goods, bed and table linen, brass and pewter and plate and jewellery show no positive movement, particularly in the eighteenth century. The decline in brass and pewter is quite marked. With plate and jewellery the means hold up but the medians fall. With bed and table linen the median amounts spent by Oxfordshire decedents in the late sixteenth century were not surpassed except by seventeenth-century Essex County, Massachusetts wealth-holders and, in most cases, the medians and the means moved lower. Some appraisers lumped bed linen in with bedding, but this was done throughout the period under study, so it should not affect the trend.

There are several possible explanations for the pattern of durables spending found in the last two tables. One is that there is something the matter with the data. American probate records do not begin until the mid-seventeenth century and the English inventories become scarce by the 1730s. A lot of different places are used in charting the trend. Also errors could creep into the adjustments for inflation and different currencies.

The trouble with that explanation is that most of the other researchers who have used inventories to analyse trends in the consumption of durables have come up with similar findings. A study of rural Pennsylvania from 1690 to 1735 reports that the average proportion of wealth in consumer goods during this period varied between 25 per cent and 30 per cent with little clear direction up or down. Lois Green Carr and Lorena Walsh report a continual rise in the number of Chesapeake consumer goods that could be called amenities, yet no increase, after accounting for inflation, in the amount devoted to consumer durables. Table 9.7 shows the mean amount invested in consumer goods in three colonial areas – rural Pennsylvania, Massachusetts and Maryland – and they also parallel the results obtained here. In both the northern colonies, where in the beginning religious dissenters of middling-class background constituted a large portion of the population and family migration generally prevailed, the value of consumer goods started out very high. In the 1690s, a decade after the founding of Pennsylvania, decedents held an average of £29.9 in consumer goods and in Massachusetts in the 1656–75 period the mean reached £33, actually the same as reported in Table 9.5 for Essex County, Massachusetts alone. In contrast, inventories from a plantation colony such as Maryland, like those from Virginia, started out with a low amount, not quite £19. In the following decades there is a rise, just as there is a fall in the amounts registered in Pennsylvania and Massachusetts, until there is something of a convergence. The trend over time in the eighteenth century, however, is not clear at all. Nor do deflated series for Massachusetts and Maryland that stretch into the middle and late eighteenth century give any firmer indication of direction.[23]

There are no comparable studies for England in the early modern period that follow the

Table 9.7 Other studies of mean inventoried wealth in consumer goods: the colonies 1650–1753

	Rural Pennsylvania		Massachusetts: Estates of Young Fathers		
Years	N	Mean*	Years	N	Mean*
1690–9	64	29.9	1650–66	33	31.3
1700–4	73	20.8	1667–75	33	35.5
1705–9	70	25.1	1676	31	25.9
1710–14	82	24.2	1677–82	32	29.8
1715–19	124	23.2	1683–9	35	24.8
1720–4	91	19.1	1690–2	32	42.9
1725–9	122	22.6	1693–6	38	28.3
1730–4	157	21.0	1697–1702	30	30.4
			1703–8	33	26.5
	Massachusetts†	Maryland†	1715–18	33	29.7
Years	Mean	Mean	1719–24	38	46.6
			1725–8	34	37.2
1656–75	33.0	18.8	1729–32	33	37.9
1676–96	27.5	23.2	1733–5	34	34.8
1697–1702	28.5	26.6	1736–40	35	27.4
1703–12	33.3	28.4	1741–5	34	21.1
1713–19	22.7	26.7	1746–50	33	35.1
			1751–3	41	43.8

*Means are in pounds sterling.
†Weighted to approximate wealth-holding population.

Sources Jack Michel, 'In a manner and fashion suitable to their degree': a preliminary investigation of the material culture of early rural Pennsylvania', *Working Papers from the Regional Economic History Research Center*, v (1981), 11; Gloria L. Main, 'The standard of living in colonial Massachusetts', *Journal of Economic History*, xliii (1983), 105, and idem, 'The standard of living in Maryland and Massachusetts, 1656–1719', Tables 2 and 3, unpublished paper.

trend in the mean amount devoted to consumer goods from the sixteenth to the eighteenth centuries in the same area. One study covering four villages in north Warwickshire during the seventeenth century furnishes the percentage of wealth devoted to consumer goods in various decades. In contrast to what has been found in colonial America, this study supports the hypothesis that the percentage of wealth in consumer goods rose sharply over the 100-year period. There, consumer goods constituted 27 per cent of wealth at the beginning of the period and a surprisingly high 48 per cent at the end. A study of the domestic goods of peasant labourers found a smaller rise, 10 per cent, between 1560 and 1640.[24] Also, the mean amount of wealth in domestic goods increased slightly over what can be attributed to inflation for this impoverished group. The poor are under-represented in these proportions and means for consumer goods. Consequently, we may assume that the mean amount was actually lower in all periods and the proportions actually higher. In order for this under-representation to have affected the trend, however, one would have to assume that the poor were better represented in certain years than others, a hypothesis for which little evidence exists. One might speculate that the increase in the percentage of wealth devoted to consumer goods in peasant labourers' inventories reflects the reduction in livestock, which made producer goods a smaller proportion of total wealth and thus consumer goods a greater part.

The problem is that the wage work that replaced livestock holding and agricultural production generated credits that could compensate for the absence of animals in the inventory. Credits were very poorly reported in comparison to other assets, however. The slightly higher figures, therefore, could be a result of a shift from producer to consumer or simply an artefact of the measurement error in the financial assets component of total wealth.

If one looks at the means found in other inventory studies of particular areas and/or more limited periods of time where all inventoried decedents were included, they are more in keeping with those found in the English Midlands areas I sampled. In Bedfordshire during the second decade of the seventeenth century, the unadjusted mean was £14.9, right between the mean for Elizabethan Oxfordshire (£9.4) and that of Worcestershire in 1669–70 (£28.0). Samples from all over England in the period 1675–1725 give a mean for household goods of £23. The amount does not, it seems, include apparel. If £5 were added to compensate for the omission of clothing, then the mean would be £28, very near the figures in Table 9.5 for rural areas in the 1660s–70s and the 1720s.[25]

So, although it is always possible that the data for one reason or another are distorted, the weight of the evidence from other studies tends to buttress the arguments that the proportion of wealth in consumer goods did not move steadily upward during the early modern period, and that after some rise in the sixteenth and early seventeenth centuries, the mean amount in consumer goods did not show much upward movement either and in some areas might even have turned downward a bit.

A second possibility is that there was in fact no boom in consumer durables as there was in groceries. Again, though, the sheer number of studies of English and American inventories that show higher consumption after 1660 of a whole array of textile, paper, metal and pottery products, not to mention the work on the growth of rural manufacturing, makes it hard to believe.

Two other possible and not mutually exclusive explanations are left. One is that inventories are a poor source for discovering growth in many of the new durables because of their semi-durable nature. They only catch goods still owned by the person at death. They cannot measure the rate of turnover in goods over the lifespan. Yet many of the new consumer goods were of a more ephemeral nature. The textiles were lighter, whether made of the new draperies, linen or cotton. Chapbooks and other paper products might not make it through the years. Pottery could be destroyed much more readily than wood or brass and pewter. Also, small items such as needles, combs and the like might be too insignificant to inventory and were easily lost. There is a tendency to think of the twentieth century as being the beginning of the disposable products but the early modern population may have experienced as big or an even bigger shift to impermanent objects. The problem with this line of argument is that it is not easily provable with the materials at hand. None the less it has to be mentioned as a hypothesis meriting further examination.

A final explanation that *can* be investigated is the possibility that the cost of goods declined, enabling consumers to buy more and yet invest no more, or in some cases less, in durables or semi-durables. There are two ways that this could have happened, and again, they are not mutually exclusive. The first is that the price of the same manufactured good dropped over the course of the early modern period just as we know some groceries did, and the second is that consumers substituted new cheaper goods for the products they had formerly used.

To try to understand what might have been going on with prices, let us look at the

Table 9.8   Average prices of select textiles in merchandisers' inventories: England 1578–1738

| Type of cloth | Constant prices (base 1660–99) in pence per yard* | | | |
	late 16th century	early 17th century	late 17th century	early 18th century
Woollens				
Broadcloths	138	72	56	54
Kerseys	55	41	21	25
Frieze	17	15	22	21
Serge	41	24	24	19
Baize	36	34	18	10
Flannel	17	11	10	15
Stuffs	n.a.	13	9	9
Linens etc.				
Fine Holland	83	46	41	32
Linen	24	22	11	13
Blue linen	n.a.	13	10	10
Osnaburg	10	10	8	8
Fustian	31	13	8	10
Calico	28	13	12	24
Scotch cloth	n.a.	17	13	10

*To obtain current prices for textiles in the late sixteenth century (1560–99) divide constant price by 1.72, for the early seventeenth century (1600–59) divide by 1.1. Average of Phelps-Brown and Hopkins price index for early eighteenth century (1700–39) is nearly identical to average for the late seventeenth century (1660–99), so no correction is made to that column to obtain constant prices. There are 12 pence to a shilling, 20 shillings to a pound.

Sources Merchandisers' inventories in William Greenwell (comp.), *Durham Wills and Inventories*, part II Surtees Society, xxxviii (1860); James Raine (comp.), *Wills and Inventories from the Archdeaconry of Richmond*, Surtees Society, xxvi (1854); Margaret Spufford, *The Great Reclothing of Rural England* (London, 1984); J. M. Bestall and D. V. Fowkes (eds), *Chesterfield Wills and Inventories 1521–1603 Derbyshire Record Society*, vol. 1 (1977); C. B. Phillips and J. H. Smith, *Stockport Probate Records 1578–1619* (Gloucester, 1985); J. J. Bagley, 'Matthew Markland, a Wigan mercer: the manufacture and sale of Lancashire textiles in the reigns of Elizabeth I and James I', *Lancashire and Cheshire Antiquarian Society*, lxviii (1958), 45–68; D. G. Vaisey, 'A Charlbury mercer's shop, 1623', *Oxoniensia*, xxxi (1966), 107–16; D. G. Vaisey (ed.), *Probate Inventories of Lichfield and District 1568–1680* (Stafford, 1969); John S. Roper (ed.), *Sedgley Probate Inventories 1614–1787* (Dudley, n.d. mimeo); Peter C. D. Brears (ed.), *Yorkshire Probate Inventories 1542–1689*, Yorkshire Archaeological Society, cxxxiv (1972), Kendal, 1972; Peter May (ed.), *Newmarket Inventories 1662–1715* (Newmarket, 1976); Barrie Trinder and Jeff Cox (eds), *Yeomen and Colliers in Telford: Probate Inventories for Dawley, Lilleshall, Wellington, and Wrockwardine 1660–1750* (London, 1980); Francis W. Steer (ed.), *Farm and Cottage Inventories of Mid-Essex 1635–1749* (Chelmsford, 1950); Margaret Cash (ed.), *Devon Inventories of the Sixteenth and Seventeenth Centuries*, Devon and Cornwall Record Society, n.s., xi (1966).

appraisals of the most important semi-durable, cloth, in the inventories of merchandisers (shopkeepers and peddlers) during the early modern period.[26] Table 9.8 shows both current prices (the actual prices appearing on the inventory at the time) and constant prices (the deflated prices) in England from the late sixteenth century to the early eighteenth for wools, linens, cottons and blends. The woollens are of two basic types the older heavier draperies – broadcloth, kerseys and friezes – and the lighter woollens, the new draperies, serge, baize, flannels and stuffs, that also tended to be less expensive. Very limited kinds of linen or linen-like materials (whether made from flax, cotton, nettles or the result of some blend) were available in the sixteenth century, but the varieties, particularly of cheaper grades, greatly increased thereafter. As Table 9.8 indicates, neither blue linen nor Scotch cloth, both very inexpensive fabrics, show up in sixteenth-century merchandisers' inventories but constantly appear in the subsequent periods.

In England, all fabrics, according to the table, dropped in price between the late sixteenth and the late seventeenth centuries with the sole exception of frieze. Even if one converted back to current prices, very few of the textiles cost as much in the late seventeenth century as they had at the end of the sixteenth. Most of the declines were quite dramatic: broadcloth fell about 50 per cent between the first two periods and then another 20 per cent by the late seventeenth century; baize was down 50 per cent by the late seventeenth century and flannel fell only a little less sharply. The non-woollens behaved similarly. The price of fustian (a linen and cotton blend) plummeted to 75 per cent of the sixteenth-century value in constant terms and calico declined by 57 per cent. Considering that we know the amount of money invested in consumer goods also rose considerably during the same 100-year period, most households would have had no trouble greatly increasing their consumption of textile products.

What happened in England between the late seventeenth and early eighteenth centuries is less clear. A few of the fabrics continued to drop: serge, baize and Scotch cloth plus fine Holland linen. Calico, because of British policy limiting the importation of printed cotton cloth, soared in price while the cost of the remainder of the textiles stayed constant or rose only slightly. The biggest development in the English textile trade as the seventeenth century came to a close and the eighteenth century began was the appearance of ready-made garments in the stock-in-trade of merchandisers.[27] Prior to 1700, finished textile goods were limited to accessories such as stockings and handkerchiefs. Few shopkeepers' inventories listed coats, suits, breeches, shirts, petticoats, gowns and so forth. After 1700 they become more common, however, at least in the inventories of English retailers in the south of England, and they are priced generally cheaper than the same articles listed under apparel in personal inventories from earlier periods. The appearance of these finished goods and the fact that there seem to be more retailers stocking the budget materials leads one to suspect that these developments resulted in still further accumulations of textile products by individuals in the first quarter of the eighteenth century.

Because English inventories more or less cease after the 1730s the estate records of later merchandisers are not available. The situation in the colonies can throw some light on what may have occurred, however. Table 9.9 compares prices in Essex County, Massachusetts inventories in 1660–73 and inventories from the same county in Massachusetts in 1774. Because of distance from markets and primitive mercantile links, many seventeenth-century Massachusetts families stockpiled a variety of cloth, something that occurred much less often in England. Consequently the prices for 1660–73 come from inventories of both mer- chandisers and ordinary citizens. For the 1774 prices, though, only the inventories of the former are used. The drop in prices between the two periods is even more dramatic among the colonials. Obviously some of the high cost of cloth in the late seventeenth century can be attributed to Massachusetts being on the fringe of the commercial world. Still, home-made cloth in current as well as constant prices was also high compared to 1774. Furthermore, the extent of the drop suggests more was at work than simply better trade networks and lower transactions costs. The lower prices of many fabrics in 1774 compared to English prices in the early eighteenth century indicate prices may have fallen further in the mid-1700s.

Clearly, the evidence on prices of textile products in these two tables suggests that at least part of the reason consumers could own more new goods, without raising the percentage of wealth in consumer goods nor the amount of real pounds sterling invested in them, is that they had to pay less for them. Prices declined, and the popularity of thinner, less expensive fabrics – lighter wools, linens and cottons – and in the eighteenth century ready-made

Table 9.9 Average prices of select textiles in colonial inventories: Essex County, Massachusetts, inventories 1660–73 and 1774

| Type of cloth | Constant prices (base 1660–9) in pence per yard* | |
	1660–73	1774
Woollens		
Broadcloths	133	109
Kerseys	58	27
Serge	55	27
Baize	45	12
Penistone	38	12
Flannel	28	10
Stuffs	25	11
Linens etc.		
Linen	20	14
Osnaburg	16	5
Fustian (all cotton/linens)	25	8
Calico	18	15
Homemade	28	8

*Values in English pence as in Table 9.7. Base years in that table cover more of the later seventeenth century because prices go up to 1699. To obtain current Massachusetts prices multiply 1660–73 prices by 1.2, and multiply 1774 prices by 1.33 to get current pound sterling prices and by 1.33 again to obtain Massachusetts current prices.

Source see Table 9.5.

garments, also brought the costs down. What remains to be investigated is the extent to which other commodities shared this price history. It is known that the glass and pottery tableware substituted for heavy metals such as pewter cost much less per piece, anywhere from one-half to one-twelfth less, and therefore the value in the inventories would be substantially lower, even if the cost over the life-cycle of the individual was actually the same or higher.[28]

The economic and social characteristics of early modern consumers

Up to this point I have considered trends in consumption, but I have not paid much attention to the characteristics of those doing the consuming. What made some people spend more on consumer goods than others? Because probate records contain a lot of information about those leaving estates, it is possible to evaluate the role of a number of economic and social factors affecting the consumption of durables by individuals.

When economists look at current consumer demand on the individual or micro level, they usually focus in on the relationship between income or total expenditures on the one hand and spending on consumer goods on the other. They measure the rate at which consumer expenditure goes up or down as family income varies. This figure is known as the 'income elasticity of demand'. An elasticity of 1.00 (unity) implies both income and consumer expenditures are rising/falling at the same rate; elasticities over 1.00 denote consumer demand increasing/decreasing at a faster rate; and elasticities under 1.00 indicate increases/decreases in consumer demand at a slower rate. Because over the long run, it is impossible for households to spend more than they make, the income elasticity of total consumer expenditure is under 1.00, although certain categories of goods might exceed unity.[29]

Inventories, because they measure wealth rather than expenditures, cannot furnish figures that are directly comparable to income elasticities. They list stocks rather than flows and perishable goods, most notably food, are generally excluded.[30] Still, this source can tell us some important things about the demand for consumer durables. First, inventories can reveal the degree to which wealth determined the level of consumption, and to what extent other variables came into play. Besides just measuring the effect of wealth, though, something also can be learned about the form the relationship took. The notion – that the pre-industrial consumer was not much of a consumer at all, that the peasantry had a 'traditional' outlook on expenditures and after basic needs were met showed very little proclivity towards further investment in consumer durables – can be expressed in diagrammatic form and tested with the inventory data.

Figure 9.1 displays the three possible forms – horizontal, linear and proportional – that the wealth-consumer durables relationship could take. The top diagram corresponds to the putative behaviour of the 'traditional consumer'. At a certain point, additional wealth stops raising the value of consumer goods. The middle diagram shows a linear relationship: with each increment in wealth, the value of consumer goods rises by the same amount as it rose from the previous increment. Not even modern consumers are believed to indulge in that much consumption because it would violate the notion that the affluent put a higher percentage of their wealth into investment.

The third relationship that might exist is one in which the value of goods continues to climb with increasing wealth but with the rate of growth lower than that for wealth. Progressively, more additional dollars go for producer goods or savings as wealth levels climb. For example a family with total wealth of $10,000 might have $9,000 in consumer goods, but if suddenly wealth shot up to $20,000 through a big salary increase or a legacy, the amount of that increment devoted to consumer goods might not reach $18,000 or 90 per cent of total wealth. A greater proportion of the increment might go to savings. What might stay constant, however, is the percentage increase in the value of consumer goods. So the $9,000 devoted to consumer goods might increase by 90 per cent making the value of consumer goods go up to $17,100 or 85.5 per cent of total wealth. Further increments would keep the value of consumer goods increasing by 90 per cent, but the proportion of wealth devoted to consumer goods would progressively shrink. Such a relationship can be expressed as the curved line in the third diagram (c), and it is assumed to be the modern form. Empirical tests of this modern relationship, of course, have been made with income and expenditure data, not stocks of wealth.

In order to see which of the models best describes the relationship between the value of consumer goods and wealth in the English and colonial inventories, three bivariate regressions must be run for each sample. The first is a simple linear regression of the two variables, diagram (b) in Figure 9.1. The second is what is known as a semi-log transformation, where wealth is logged and, if the data actually resemble diagram (a), the transformation should provide the best fit. If instead the relationship in the data is that of diagram (c) then a double log transformation where both variables are logged should conform best to the contours of the data.

Table 9.10 gives the R^2 values, the measure of goodness of fit, for the three forms of the regression.[31] None of the samples shows the semi-log form of the traditional consumer to give

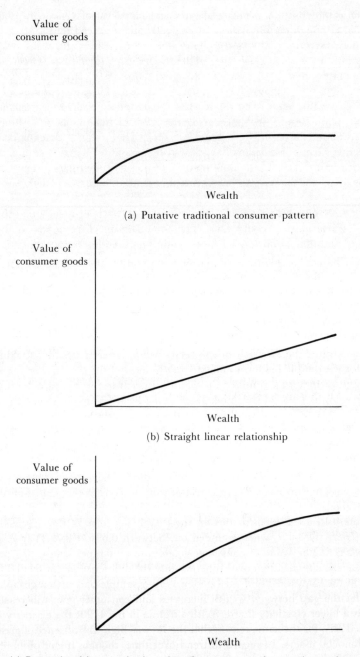

(a) Putative traditional consumer pattern

(b) Straight linear relationship

(c) Proportional increase in the value of consumer goods: putative modern consumer pattern

Figure 9.1 Possible relationships between wealth and value of consumer goods

Table 9.10 A comparison of three forms of the regression of wealth on the value of consumer goods

| Place and years | N | R² | | Elasticities | |
		Linear	Semi-log	Double log	Double log
Oxfordshire 1551–90	254	0.816	0.333	0.601	0.68
South Worcs. 1669–70	275	0.566	0.398	0.624	0.66
South Worcs. 1720–1	305	0.582	0.334	0.571	0.62
East London 1661–4	129	0.895	0.454	0.575	0.67
East London 1720–9	177	0.451	0.334	0.587	0.56
Virginia 1660–76	134	0.450	0.582	0.680	0.73
Virginia 1724–9	299	0.629	0.528	0.793	0.82
Virginia and Maryland 1774	141	0.481	0.411	0.618	0.59
Essex County, Mass. 1660–73	300	0.262	0.508	0.665	0.71
Massachusetts 1774	299	0.214	0.383	0.667	0.62

Source see Table 9.5.

the best fit. The highest values are, with a couple of exceptions,[32] the double log form, meaning that consumer durables tended to keep increasing as people got wealthier but the percentage of their wealth devoted to consumer goods tended to be less. What in modern studies of consumer behaviour tends to be the relationship between income and consumer expenditures also turns out to describe best the relationship between wealth and consumer goods in the early modern period.

Table 9.10 also demonstrates the strength of the relationship between wealth and consumer goods. The R^2s for the double log form indicate that in most of the places, whether in the colonies or in England or in Tudor times or the eighteenth century, from 60 per cent to two-thirds of the variation in the value of consumer goods could be attributed to wealth. This might seem like common sense, except it would not be the case if the traditional consumer model was the true one. In fact, the R^2s for all the samples are so similar to one another that only the Virginia 1724–9 statistic, 0.793 or 79.3 per cent of the variation explained requires any special discussion. Probably the reason that even more variation in consumer goods can be accounted for by wealth in that sample is that those inventories have poor coverage of financial assets which seem often to have less of a relationship to consumer goods than do other kinds of producer goods.[33]

Also included in Table 9.10 are the elasticities for the double log form of the regression equation. For the most part they fall, when rounded off, between 0.6 and 0.7. That is as wealth went up by 1 per cent, the value of consumer goods rose by 0.6 per cent or 0.7 per cent.[34] There is not any clear-cut variation over time. Mainly the differences seem related to the wealth distribution in the samples. The East London 1720–9 sample had such a group of wealthy estates in it that the gap between wealth increases and consumer goods increases was wider. The result is a lower elasticity figure. With Virginia in the 1720s the elasticity is high (0.82 or 0.8 rounded off), for the same reason that the R^2 was high, the absence of great amounts of wealth in financial assets. In regard to trend over time, though, it can probably be said that there is no indication of a rise in the elasticity.

While it is clear that wealth is by far the most important determinant of the value of consumer durables, modern theories of consumption, historical descriptions of economic behaviour and the R^2s of the bivariate regressions themselves suggest that other factors may have been involved as well. Between 30 and 40 per cent of the variation was not explained. What else might have increased the amount people spent on consumer goods in the early modern period?

In the budget studies done by economists, household size is usually the most important variable after income in predicting consumer behaviour. In the expenditure studies it tends to have a positive effect on food expenditures and a negative effect on spending for some durables.[35] With the inventory data on wealth stocks, however, the choice is not between food or durable expenditures but between investing in producer or consumer goods. Consequently, one would expect an increase in family size to raise the amount in consumer durables because more household goods would be required to meet the needs of additional children, servants and relatives.

Market accessibility – whether a person lived in a frontier area or a remote country village as opposed to a market town or city – is believed by many historians and development economists to have had a big effect on consumer expenditures.[36] Households in the former would be less tied to market commodities and more self-sufficient, which would have the effect of boosting their stocks of producer goods and lowering the value of consumer goods. Scholars have sometimes overestimated the self-sufficiency of rural householders. None the less household production in village and town did take different forms.

Related to these theories, but not identical to them, are ideas about the role of social class and occupational status. Sociologists and social historians have been more inclined to posit an effect for social class beyond that caused by income or wealth differences, although they unfortunately do not always hold the latter constant before making claims for the former. Economists tend to be less enamoured of social class explanations and look more exclusively to income. Still, one finding regarding occupation has consistently emerged out of economic research: the comparatively small percentage of income devoted to consumption by contemporary farmers.[37] Occupation, therefore, cannot be dismissed without being tested.

Finally there is the question of the impact of education on consumption. Current research argues that education makes for more efficient consumers and that implies, other things equal, that the variable should decrease the amount spent on consumer goods.[38] On the other hand, it might well be argued that in the early modern period education aided people in market transactions and whetted the appetite for consumer goods.

Tables 9.11 and 9.12 present the results of the multiple regressions run on the English and colonial data, respectively, to test these various theories. The coefficients, significance levels and the R^2 change for all the variables in all the samples are shown. Proxies for certain of the variables had to be used. Number of beds was multiplied by two, after counting zero beds as 0.5, in order to get household size, and then it was logged. As is the case with household size and income in modern consumer expenditure studies, wealth and number of beds are positively correlated. The levels, however, were not so high as to make it impossible to run them both in the equations.[39] Book ownership was used as a proxy for education. The other variables are more straightforward representatives of the factors discussed above.

Among areas and over time periods the similarities are on the whole more striking than the differences, and wealth clearly drowned out most of the other variables. Explained variation fell between about 70 per cent and 80 per cent (except for the London 1661–4 sample where it came out to 62.6 per cent), and of that variation, about 90 per cent can be attributed to wealth and most of the remainder to the proxy for household size. Accessibility to markets as measured by town residency or, in the case of the 1774 Chesapeake sample, coastal county residency was not significant in any sample except that for late eighteenth-century Massachusetts.[40] In most cases, town residency was positively correlated with the amount in consumer goods, but once wealth (probated decedents from towns tended to be wealthier than those in rural areas) and occupational variables were accounted for, the effect disappeared. In the English Midlands, for example, no significant urban effect from living in a provincial town remained after controlling for other variables. Nor did a difference show up in the 1774 Chesapeake sample. However, using larger samples with more urban observations, Lois Green Carr and Lorena Walsh found significant urban/rural contrasts in York County, Virginia, and Ann Arundel County, Maryland.[41] The implication of the contrast between the Midlands results and those of my Massachusetts data and Carr and Walsh's Chesapeake inventories is the none too surprising one that access to consumer durables was a larger problem in the colonies than in provincial England.

Occupational status did not have a very big impact on the amount given over to consumer goods once wealth was held constant. Farmers consistently invested less in durables than did other groups, although only in Worcestershire, not Oxfordshire nor the colonies, was the difference significant at an acceptable level. Did a gap between the durables consumption of farmers and non-farmers emerge in the Midlands during the early modern period? If so, it appears less due to those in trades and crafts, whose coefficients were nearer to those of farmers than to other groups: namely, labourers (who along with some missing cases made up the reference category for occupational status), the elite (those with an honorific title or professionals) and women (who were included as a separate group under occupational status because in inventories they were designated by their marital status not their job). Part of the reason farmers and tradesmen appear so similar in terms of consumption of durables is that the trades category included dual occupation decedents who confuse the results. Still, the contrast between those in agriculture and those who are not seems less pronounced than it is in modern data.[42]

The theory that literacy or education promotes consumption seems to work better for the colonies than England, although the distribution of books was so limited in sixteenth-century Oxfordshire that it is not much of a test there, and lower levels of ownership in Worcestershire during the 1720s than in 1669–70 suggest that the less detailed 1720s inventories may have buried books under general rubrics such as 'household stuff' or 'lumber'. The fact, therefore, that only in the East London sample for the 1720s does English book ownership show up as significant should not be made too much of until further research is carried out.

Evaluating consumer demand in the early modern period

During the early modern period, the demonstrable changes that occurred in consumer demand transpired within each of the two major consumer categories, perishables and durables, rather than between them. That is, the evidence available offers no support for arguing that a long-term change occurred in the proportion of household income or wealth going to either. Instead, within the perishable or food category, a whole group of new commodities appeared with a presumed impact on diet. Between about 1650 and 1750, tobacco, sugar products and caffeine drinks became items of mass consumption, meaning 25 per cent or more of the adult population regularly used them. Because, as demand for these groceries grew the price also fell, and because for a good part of the later seventeenth and

Table 9.11 Determinants of the amount of inventoried wealth in consumer goods* for England

	OLS regression coefficients†				
	Oxfordshire 1550–90	*South Worcs. 1669–70*	*South Worcs. 1720–1*	*East London 1661–4*	*East London 1720–9*
N =	247	217	219	120	161
Variables‡					
Wealth (ln)	0.490	0.517	0.483	0.548	0.378
	(0.000)	(0.000)	(0.000)	(0.000)	(0.000)
Household size (ln)	0.606	0.472	0.610	0.381	0.592
	(0.000)	(0.000)	(0.000)	(0.000)	(0.000)
Town residency	0.072	0.083	0.084	n.a.	n.a.
	(0.401)	(0.426)	(0.358)		
Occupational status					
Elite	n.a.	0.123	0.196	0.036	0.752
		(0.413)	(0.337)	(0.889)	(0.002)
Farmer	–0.074	–0.382	–0.291	n.a.	n.a.
	(0.530)	(0.000)	(0.030)		
Tradesman	0.087	–0.241	–0.208	0.149	0.232
	(0.494)	(0.066)	(0.089)	(0.328)	(0.105)
Widow	0.112	–0.157	–0.153	0.085	0.246
	(0.382)	(0.182)	(0.186)	(0.623)	(0.144)
Book owner	0.503	0.029	0.026	0.149	0.332
	(0.119)	(0.576)	(0.807)	(0.096)	(0.014)
Constant	0.871	0.237	0.047	0.099	0.066
Adjusted R^2	0.753	0.722	0.731	0.626	0.705

*The dependent variable, the pound sterling amount in consumer goods, is in natural log (ln) form.
†The numbers in parentheses are significance levels (t test).
‡The independent variables town residency and book owner are dummy variables coded 1 and 0. The categories of the variable occupational status also are dummied with 1, 0 codes and with labourers and those whose status was missing constituting the reference category.

Source see Table 9.5.

eighteenth centuries the cost of other foodstuffs declined as well, the percentage of a budget taken up by diet need not have increased.

Likewise, inventory evidence does not indicate that the growth in ownership of semi-durables – lighter fabrics, paper products, glassware and pottery – increased the proportion of wealth in all consumer goods (durables and semi-durables) at the expense of producer goods or savings. Rather, the proportion stayed the same or fell because of substitutions of cheaper goods for more expensive ones, falling prices and perhaps in some periods increased wealth. There seems to have been a sharp rise in the real amount of wealth put into consumer goods between the end of the sixteenth century and the later seventeenth century, but the mean and median values in consumer goods stayed fairly constant thereafter. A combination of falling prices and substitutions of less permanent goods for more durable ones probably account for most of the increased accumulation of consumer goods in the eighteenth century. There is a problem, of course, in that inventories only measure stocks of wealth at

Table 9.12 Determinants of the amount of inventoried wealth in consumer goods* for the colonies

	OLS regression coefficients†				
	Virginia 1660–76	Virginia 1724–9	Virginia and Maryland 1774	Essex County, Mass. 1660–73	Massachussetts 1774
N =	129	299	139	263	269
Variables‡					
Wealth (ln)	0.548	0.713	0.438	0.587	0.450
	(0.000)	(0.000)	(0.000)	(0.000)	(0.000)
Household size (ln)	0.392	0.298	0.329	0.393	0.506
	(0.000)	(0.000)	(0.000)	(0.000)	(0.000)
Town residency	n.a.	n.a.	–0.000	0.015	0.433
			(0.853)	(0.811)	(0.000)
Occupational status					
Elite	n.a.	–0.194	0.608	–0.041	0.089
		(0.248)	(0.038)	(0.846)	(0.458)
Farmer	–0.010	–0.130	0.142	–0.161	–0.138
	(0.748)	(0.279)	(0.544)	(0.089)	(0.175)
Tradesman	–0.159	0.041	0.598	–0.210	–0.054
	(0.322)	(0.756)	(0.019)	(0.089)	(0.556)
Widow	n.a.	0.109	0.543	–0.122	0.258
		(0.412)	(0.041)	(0.291)	(0.045)
Book owner	0.174	0.114	0.336	0.142	0.174
	(0.000)	(0.071)	(0.009)	(0.023)	(0.009)
Constant	–0.186	–0.348	–0.185	0.526	0.211
Adjusted R^2	0.793	0.821	0.693	0.725	0.799

*The dependent variable, the pound sterling amount in consumer goods, is in natural log (ln) form.
†The numbers in parentheses are significance levels (t test).
‡The independent variables town residency and book owner are dummy variables coded 1 and 0. The categories of the variable occupational status also are dummied with 1, 0 codes and with labourers and those whose status was missing constituting the reference category.

Source see Table 9.5.

death. If less durable goods replaced articles with more permanence, then outlays of consumer products over the life-cycle could have been greater.

Nor, in looking at the determinants of money 'invested' in consumer goods does one see a very clear, consistent role for variables such as occupational status, education or market accessibility over time.[43] Once wealth and household size are entered into the analysis, these other factors tend to wash out or show relatively minor effects. Of course, once the value of different types of goods are analysed, the results might be different.

A dramatic change in budget proportions has distinguished consumer demand in many western societies at the end of the nineteenth and in the earlier twentieth centuries: a sharp drop in the percentage families spent on food and a notable rise in consumer durables expenditures beginning in the 1920–40 period.[44] These are not the changes perceived in early modern consumer demand. From the evidence presented here, increases in wealth, substitutions and price drops may have kept proportions more or less the same despite major changes in diet and in material possessions. There are demand shifts to explain, but they are *within* the traditional consumption categories of food and durables. Just what those changes meant nutritionally and in terms of domestic well-being will have to be examined elsewhere.

Notes

1 For an articulate expression of this view, see Joel Mokyr, 'Demand vs. supply in the Industrial Revolution', *Journal of Economic History*, xxxvii (1977), 1005.

2 Jan de Vries, *The Dutch Rural Economy in the Golden Age* (New Haven, Conn., 1974).

3 Joan Thirsk, *Economic Policy and Projects: The Development of a Consumer Society in Early Modern England* (Oxford, 1978); Margaret Spufford, *Small Books and Pleasant Histories* (London, 1981); idem, *The Great Reclothing of Rural England* (London, 1984); Lorna Weatherill, 'The growth of the pottery industry in England, 1660–1815' (University of London, Ph.D. thesis, 1981); and Lois Green Carr and Lorena S. Walsh, 'Inventories and the analysis of wealth and consumption patterns in St Mary's County, Maryland, 1658–1777', *Historical Methods*, xiii (1980), 81–104.

4 W. G. Hoskins, 'The re-building of rural England, 1570–1640', *Past and Present*, iv (1953), 44–59, and R. Machin, 'The great rebuilding: a reassessment', *Past and Present*, lxxvii (1977), 33–56.

5 Twenty-five per cent of the adult population means that more than just adults in London and among the elite would have to be consuming an item for it to be counted as a mass consumption good. For consumer durables, the family is a better unit to count than individuals. Unfortunately, most of the data available count individuals or the property of wealth-holders rather than households. Some inventoried decedents do not have their own households. Thus using inventories to indicate the percentage of people having access to a particular household good underestimates its availability, just as the greater wealth of inventoried decedents overestimates the possession of most articles. Specifying adult (i.e. 15 years or over) exerts some control over the variation over time in the proportion of children. During the early modern period, the percentage ranged from 28 per cent to 37 per cent; E. A. Wrigley and R. S. Schofield, *The Population History of England 1541–1871* (London, 1981), 528–9. In the first third of the nineteenth century, it reached 40 per cent. Some of the stagnation in per capita consumption figures in groceries that one sees from 1770 to 1840 may be partially due to the youthfulness of the population. There is very little historical research on the rate of diffusion of consumer goods. See D. S. Ironmonger, *New Commodities and Consumer Behavior* (Cambridge, Mass., 1972), 131–44.

6 US Bureau of the Census, *Historical Statistics of the United States from Colonial Times to 1970* (Washington, DC, 1976), 1162.

7 Joan Thirsk, 'New crops and their diffusion: tobacco-growing in seventeenth-century England', in C. W. Chalklin and M. A. Havinden (eds), *Rural Change and Urban Growth, 1500–1800* (London, 1974), 76ff.

8 On prices in the Chesapeake for tobacco see *Historical Statistics*, 1198. For the 1633 tax on tobacco retailers, see Peter Clark, *The English Alehouse: A Social History 1200–1830* (London, 1983), 134. He writes, 'the lists of licensees confirm our picture of a nation-wide trade, though with some bias towards London and the West Country'.

9 Robert C. Nash, 'The English and Scottish tobacco trades in the seventeenth and eighteenth centuries: legal and illegal trade', *Economic History Review*, 2nd series, xxxv (1982), 354–72. On the average, Chesapeake planters in the late seventeenth century received a penny a pound for their tobacco (*Historical Statistics*, 1198), but the duty came to be four times that amount (Nash, 'English and Scottish tobacco trades', 369).

10 On the excise, see Paul Langford, *The Excise Crisis: Society and Politics in the Age of Walpole* (Oxford, 1975), 26–7.

11 Clark, *English Alehouse*, ch. 11. Nash, 'English and Scottish tobacco trades', 355–6 discusses the theories put forward by Jacob Price and others as to why the tobacco market failed to expand. The fact that, as Price points out, the rise of gin and the fall of tobacco are inversely correlated gives added credence to the notion that the retailing of tobacco and beer were intertwined.

12 In the early seventeenth century brown sugar sold at 13–14d. per pound and white at 20d. or so. At the end of the century, brown could be purchased for 6–7d. and white at 10–12d. By the mid-

eighteenth century the prices had fallen to 5d. and 8–9d. respectively. See Noel Deerr, *The History of Sugar*, vol. 2 (London, 1950), 528–9; G. N. Johnstone, 'The growth of the sugar trade and refining industry', in Derek Oddy and Derek Miller (eds), *The Making of the Modern British Diet* (London, 1976), 62; and Barrie Trinder and Jeff Cox (eds), *Yeomen and Colliers in Telford* (London, 1980), 42.

13　Sheridan, *Sugar and Slavery*, 344–9.

14　ibid.; Elizabeth Boody Schumpeter, *English Overseas Trade Statistics 1697–1808* (Oxford, 1960), 60–2; and John James McCusker Jr, 'The rum trade and the balance of payments of the thirteen continental colonies 1650–1775' (University of Pittsburgh, unpublished dissertation, 1970), *passim*.

15　K. N. Chaudhuri, *The Trading World of Asia and the English East India Company 1660–1760* (Cambridge, 1978), 385–406.

16　Benjamin Woods Labaree, *The Boston Tea Party* (New York, 1968), chs 1–3, and Samuel Wharton, 'Observations upon the consumption of teas in North America, 1773', *Pennsylvania Magazine of History and Biography*, xxv (1901), 139–41.

17　W. A. Cole, 'Trends in eighteenth-century smuggling', *Economic History Review*, 2nd series, x (1958), 395–409.

18　Hoh-Cheung Mui and Lorna H. Mui, *The Management of Monopoly: A Study of the East India Company's Conduct of its Tea Trade 1784–1833* (Vancouver, 1984), 12.

19　Wharton, 'Observations', 140–1.

20　Thirsk, *Economic Policy*; Lois Green Carr and Lorena S. Walsh, 'Inventories'; Carole Shammas, 'The domestic environment in early modern England and America', *Journal of Social History*, xiv (1980), 1–24; Spufford, *Great Reclothing*; and Lorna Weatherill, 'Consumer behavior and social status in England', *Continuity and Change*; i (1986), 191–216.

21　Robert B. Pearl and Matilda Frankel, 'Composition of the personal wealth of American households at the start of the eighties', in Seymour Sudman and Mary A. Spaeth (eds), *The Collection and Analysis of Economic and Consumer Behavior Data* (Urbana, 1984), 24.

22　Gloria L. Main, 'The standard of living in Maryland and Massachusetts, 1656–1719', paper presented at the Conference on the Chesapeake, St Mary's College, St Mary's, Maryland, May 1984, Table 3. She also finds that the Massachusetts means exceeded those of Maryland partially because the former did a better job of including apparel than did the latter.

23　Jack Michel, ' "In a manner and fashion suitable to their degree": a preliminary investigation of the material culture of early rural Pennsylvania', *Working Papers from the Regional Economic History Research Center*, v (1981), 11; Gloria Main, 'The standard of living in colonial Massachusetts', *Journal of Economic History*, xliii (1983), 105; Lois Green Carr and Lorena S. Walsh, 'Inventories', Fig. 4, 89 and 91; Carter Hudgins, 'Exactly as the gentry do in England: culture, aspirations, and material things in the eighteenth century Chesapeake' (unpublished paper, 1984), Table 6; and Lois Green Carr and Lorena S. Walsh, 'Changing lifestyles and consumer behavior in the colonial Chesapeake', in Cary Carson, Ronald Hoffman and Peter Albert (eds), *Of Consuming Interests: The Style of Life in the Eighteenth Century* (Charlottesville, forthcoming 1992). The lack of direction pertains to rural areas. Lorena Walsh finds that investment in consumer goods in Chesapeake towns did rise after 1730, although it is not clear whether that was due to an increase in wealth or whether an increase in the percentage of wealth devoted to consumer goods also occurred; 'Urban amenities and rural sufficiency: living standards and consumer behavior in the colonial Chesapeake, 1643–1777', *The Journal of Economic History*, xlvii (1983), 112–13.

24　Christopher Husbands, 'Standards of living in north Warwickshire in the seventeenth century', *Warwickshire History*, iv (1981), 211. On peasant labourers see Alan Everitt, 'Farm labourers', in Joan Thirsk (ed.), *The Agrarian History of England and Wales 1500–1640* (Cambridge, 1967), 421. The unadjusted mean amount for England 1560–1600 was £2.25 and for 1601–40 £4.5.

25　Bedfordshire mean calculated from data in F. G. Emmison, 'Jacobean household inventories', *The Bedfordshire Historical Record Society*, xx (1938), 45–6. Samples from various areas in England in

Lorna Weatherill, 'A possession of one's own: women and consumer behavior in England, 1660–1740', *Journal of British Studies*, xxv (1986), 134–5.

26 Carr and Walsh ('Inventories', 91–4, 100) have been the only ones to examine price trends of manufactured goods in inventories. Based on their analysis of the Maryland data in 1980 they concluded that 'explanations [for the stagnation in investment in consumer goods] which hinge on . . . a general fall in the price of European imports clearly will not do'. Since then they have found a decline in the prices of manufactured goods up to 1740 in Maryland and 1760 in Virginia (personal communication from Lois Green Carr, January 30 1989). These declines, however, do not explain how the amount of consumer goods owned could have continued to increase after 1760 when the amount expended for them did not. There are several possible explanations. One has to do with the commodities used for the index of consumer manufactures. Carr and Walsh used the prices of two metals, pewter and silver plate, for half of the index and, for the other half, the prices of three linens – osnaburg, canvas and dowlas. Only osnaburg was used after 1721. It is very difficult to find commodities that continue to be listed in over two centuries and also have both price and quantity attached to them. The metals were probably chosen because their valuation by the pound and the ounce allowed some standard of measurement from one inventory to the next. But from what was reported in Table 9.6, plate and pewter expenditures were declining in the eighteenth century. Although traditionally they had been the commodities consumers had stocked up as almost a form of savings, they were not what was stimulating the consumer buying of the 1700s. One wonders if it was the price behaviour of these metals, which were of declining importance and may have been somewhat idiosyncratic, that kept the index from registering a decline. The price of linens, at least osnaburg and dowlas, seemed to have gone down in the English and Massachusetts inventories examined for this study.

27 Spufford, *The Great Reclothing*, 123–5.

28 On the change-over from the older to the new draperies, and the rise of linens and calicos or cottons see G. D. Ramsay, *The English Woollen Industry, 1500–1750* (London, 1982), Spufford, *The Great Reclothing* and Chandra Mukerji, *From Graven Images: Patterns of Modern Materialism* (New York, 1983), chs 5 and 6. Tables 9.7 and 9.8 show how much more expensive broadcloth and even kersey remained in comparison with most lighter fabrics. Weatherill, 'Growth of the pottery industry', ch. 3, compares the prices of pewter and pottery tableware.

29 Total consumer expenditure always has an income elasticity under 1 because savings are much more likely to be affected by changes in income than are consumer expenditures. Often though in consumption studies savings are removed and total expenditures replaces income. In that case certain consumer durables expenditures frequently rise above unity because they are more elastic than most expenditures for food. This is known as Engel's Law and has been modified over the years by contemporary and historical studies of household expenditure. See Daniel B. Suits, 'The determinants of consumer expenditure: a review of present knowledge', in Daniel B. Suits *et al.* (eds), *Impacts of Monetary Policy* (Englewood Cliffs, NJ, 1963), 1–57; H. S. Houthakker, 'An international comparison of household expenditure patterns, commemorating the centenary of Engel's Law', *Econometrica*, xxvi (1957), 532–51; Jeffrey G. Williamson, 'Consumer behavior in the nineteenth century: Carroll D. Wright's Massachusetts workers in 1875', *Explorations in Entrepreneurial History*, iv (1967), 98–135; and Trevor J. O. Dick, 'Consumer behavior in the nineteenth century and Ontario workers, 1885–1889', *Journal of Economic History*, xlvi (1986), 477–88.

30 See Carole Shammas, *The Preindustrial Consumer in England and America* (Oxford, 1990), Appendix I, for a discussion of the limitations of probate inventories as a source and the particular characteristics of each of the data sets used here.

31 R^2 records the amount of variation in the dependent variable (in this case the natural log of the £ amount in consumer goods) 'explained' by the independent variable or variables (wealth, occupational status and so forth). R^2 is measured on a scale of 0 to 1.00; the higher the score, theoretically, the more the behaviour of the dependent variable is influenced by the independent

variables. The size of the R^2, however, can be affected by a number of factors including outliers and errors of measurement. Consequently, it is important to look at the behaviour of the dependent variable and independent variable in a scatterplot. See Shammas, 'Consumer behavior in colonial America', *Social Science History*, vi (1982), Fig. 2.

32 As mentioned above, R^2 of a linear regression is influenced by outliers. In Table 9.9 the linear form in several of the samples is so much higher than the logged form because of a few very large probated estates. Logging has the effect of turning skewed wealth or income distributions into more normal distributions and thus moderating the influence of outliers.

33 In the Virginia samples one of the biggest categories of producer 'goods' were slaves. Financial assets were always under-valued in Virginia because a certain amount of investment and credits were with overseas merchants. Most of that never got counted. Reporting, however, was particularly bad in the 1720s sample.

34 A fuller explanation of elasticities is in Shammas, 'Consumer behavior in colonial America', 74. There is a typographical error in the second paragraph, however: 4.25% should read .425%.

35 Williamson, 'Consumer behavior in the nineteenth century', 118–19.

36 For example, Dorothy Brady in 'Consumption and the style of life', in Lance E. Davis *et al.*, *American Economic Growth: An Economist's History of the United States* (New York, 1972), 61–89, centres her analysis around the differences among farm, village and city families.

37 See, for example W. Lloyd Warner, *Yankee City*, abridged edn (New Haven, 1963), 90–104; and Sandra J. Coyner, 'Class consciousness and consumption: the new middle-class during the Weimar Republic', *Journal of Social History*, x (1977), 310–31.

38 Robert T. Michael, 'Education and consumption', in F. Thomas Juster (ed.), *Education, Income, and Human Behavior* (New York, 1975), 239–40.

39 The correlations between the natural log of wealth and the natural log of household size (as measured by number of beds times 2, with zero beds recoded as 1) ranged between an R of 0.444 to 0.620.

40 I used towns rather than coastal counties for the 1774 Massachusetts regression because the Essex County 1660–73 regression used towns. In Shammas, 'Consumer behavior in colonial America', 76, I used county-level proxies. The coastal counties of Suffolk, Essex and Plymouth, in that order, had a higher £ value in consumer goods than did the inland counties of Hampshire and Worcester.

41 Carr and Walsh, 'Changing lifestyles and consumer behavior', Tables A1 and A4.

42 The results for occupational status in the 1774 Virginia and Maryland sample is rather confusing because 'farmer' is not significant and the other categories are. This happened because both labourers and farmers, other variables held constant, had similar amounts of pounds sterling in consumer goods, while the elite, tradesmen and women all had significantly more. So actually, the pattern for farmers is the same as in the other colonial samples, except that the labourer category in this instance had a little less than the farmers. That is why the farmer category has a positive coefficient, though an insignificant one. For a discussion of all the measurement error that exists in early modern occupational categories see Keith Wrightson, *English Society 1580–1680* (London, 1982), ch. 1.

43 For an articulation of the theory that over time, as people have more discretionary income, taste (e.g. changes in values due to differences in class, education, urban living, etc.) should play a larger role in determining consumer behaviour, see Ruth P. Mack, 'The conference on household production and consumption: a general comment', in Nestor E. Terleckyj (ed.), *Household Production and Consumption* (New York, 1975), 647–51.

44 See Carole Shammas, *The Preindustrial Consumer*, ch. 5 for information on modern food expenditures. On changes in the percentage spent on consumer durables in the first half of the twentieth century see Martha Olney, 'Consumer credit availability and changes in the demand for consumer durable goods, 1900–1940', paper delivered at the 1986 Social Science History Association Meeting, St Louis.

10
The meaning of consumer behaviour in late seventeenth- and early eighteenth-century England

Lorna Weatherill

Introduction

The main argument of this chapter is that the material culture of domestic life was closely associated with the social and practical lives of households and it was in their everyday activities and experiences that the meaning of consumption is to be found. This is a different perspective from those who recognize that increasing demand for a wide range of goods and clothing was important in industrialization and discuss it alongside production, for it focuses on consumers, and their needs, rather than producers and the whole economy.

The meaning of consumption also interested people at the time for they commented on consumer spending, sometimes condemning it, sometimes justifying new habits and new goods, sometimes merely referring to established patterns. They were aware that social life could be linked to consumption patterns, as these comments about the different experiences of the lower, middle and upper classes of the early part of the eighteenth century illustrate:

> the middle state . . . was the best state in the world, the most suited to human happiness; not exposed to the miseries and hardships, the labour and sufferings of the mechanic part of mankind and not embarrassed with the pride, luxury, ambition and envy of the upper part of mankind.[1]

The research upon which this chapter is based was done in order to establish a new factual framework for discussing patterns of consumption.[2] This framework, presented here as a series of tables recording presence or absence of goods in people's homes at their death, is more complicated than it at first appeared. This led me to think about the roles of household goods in people's social and economic lives, leading to the need to explore the 'meanings' that goods seem to have in a variety of respects. These are difficult problems because we are not talking about one 'world of goods' but many, not one pattern of consumption, but many; and they warn against taking any single set of ideas as a single explanation. At the beginning of this chapter three ideas that have appeared and reappeared in writing on consumption are critically examined in the light of what they reveal about consumer behaviour. The factual evidence drawn from probate inventories is then listed and briefly discussed. A discussion of how this can be drawn together to increase understanding of the social and economic meaning of consumption completes the picture.

Some ideas to criticize: luxury, consumerism and emulation

The distinction between expenditure that was (in some sense) essential to maintain physical life, and expenditure that was not essential seems attractive, but is deeply misleading, especially when we are considering people of middle rank. What were basic necessities? Did people die without them or were they just uncomfortable? It is hard to know the meaning of these terms in our own culture, for they vary with circumstances, now as they did in the past. The word 'luxury', for instance is elusive, although it is used to convey the idea of consumption of costly and high-quality goods, food or services; it also carries some implicit judgement that luxuries are immoral. There is also an implied contrast with 'necessity', so that 'luxury' can also contain the meaning that 'If it had been done without by an earlier age, it was unnecessary and therefore a luxury.'[3] The word has also commonly meant something that is desirable but not indispensable, but possibly of higher quality and price than other goods of a similar nature: 'all that assemblage which is rather intended to please the fancy, than obviate the real wants, and which is rather ornamental than useful.'[4] The cultural aspect of luxuries is also recognized by their ability to mark the rank of the owner and thus communicate social position in a non-verbal way.[5] So the word is a shorthand for a number of social and economic ideas but it does not provide a firm basis for examining the meaning of consumer behaviour; although consumption cannot be understood without reference to contemporary ideas on the subject.

It is even more difficult to pinpoint a 'necessity'. In the late seventeenth century most household goods did not 'obviate the real wants' in the sense that some form of physical life could have been uncomfortably maintained without them. Whilst it is amusing to speculate on the minimal food, clothing and utensils needed to survive, it does not make sense to interpret the behaviour of most people in the middle ranks in Britain in these terms, for people did expect to have a selection of domestic goods, although their homes seem sparsely furnished to modern eyes. So whilst 'necessity' could be defined as those things necessary to maintain life, this is an abstract definition and not a meaningful starting point for discussing consumption. Furthermore life was not just physical; the non-material side of life, such as reading, religion, family life, friends, gossip and games were deeply valued, and thus, in some sense, necessary.[6]

What people as individuals, or together as a society, felt was 'necessary' has also to be taken into account and can only be understood by observing their behaviour and priorities, as well as what they chose to own; an argument developed later in the chapter. The idea that there were classes of goods between 'luxuries' and 'necessities', usually referred to as 'decencies', modifies the stark contrasts in the vocabulary but does not remove the need to take account of the priorities shown within a society and these terms should be as carefully used as words about class.

Equally misleading are attempts to link consumption and society in the eighteenth century in terms of 'consumerism'. Amusing anecdotes about the consumerist pleasures of the wealthy, the excesses of those who strived to be fashionably dressed and the attempts of tradesmen to satisfy this kind of demand make compulsive reading, but this social history of consumerism is confined to the wealthier tradesmen and the gentry, who had the time and resources for an increasing range of goods and services by the later eighteenth century. It is hard to see from this what other consumers, whose behaviour is difficult to dramatize, but whose experience was that of a larger proportion of the middle ranking population, were doing. Excitement about new goods and services became much greater towards the end of the eighteenth century and, although fashion and enjoyment were clearly experienced in the late seventeenth century, the 'consumerist' approach to writing about it is not appropriately applied either to the earlier period or to the bulk of the middle ranks.[7]

Social behaviour and consumption have also been linked through saying that the main motivation for owning many goods was a desire to emulate those of higher social rank, in order to keep up appearances. This led, it is argued, to penetration down the social scale in the ownership of various goods, especially if there were price reductions or cheaper versions of the same goods. This is based on a certain amount of polemical contemporary commentary, mostly about the lower orders copying their 'betters', especially in dress, and is clearly only a partial account of social processes. This explanation for changing consumer behaviour does not make sense if looked at closely. If we say that the *main* motive for people's acquisition of new goods was to emulate those of higher social rank, we are already making assumptions about motivation and meaning whilst ignoring particular situations and needs. There is no evidence that most people of middle rank wanted to be like the gentry, although they may have wanted some of the new goods for their own purposes. For example, the first entry in a notebook of sayings kept by a well-to-do Kentish yeoman, Lee Warley, states a balanced position: 'In our Expenses we should neither ape those that are placed in a more exalted sphere, nor sink beneath our proper station.'[8] In the upper ranks advertising and fashion in the eighteenth century played a part in fostering the image of a society falling over itself to consume clothes, furniture, houses, possessions and leisure. Emulation undoubtedly happened but it is not the sole meaning of increasing consumption amongst the bulk of the middling ranks.

Ownership patterns of common domestic goods

A body of factual evidence is needed to enhance existing ideas. To do this, devious means are needed to tease information from primary source material, in this case probate inventories. Even when this one group of documents is as fully exploited as it is in the work reported in this volume, some important questions remain unanswered. For example, we know virtually nothing about consumption by different family members and especially what part was played by women. Likewise, we know little about the lower ranks, who did not leave probate papers, and we continue to know little in detail about the income levels of individuals and households.

Probate inventories are lists of movable goods made by neighbours shortly after a person's death. They are common throughout the seventeenth century but became rare in England after the 1720s; Scottish testaments contain only partial listings of goods and cannot be sampled in the same ways as those from England. Considerable detail is sometimes given of the farming, trade and household goods of the deceased person, together with cash and debts due. They do not record debts owed or any real estate, so they do not give a complete account of the person's wealth. They also record other information, notably the date, the parish of residence and occupation or status, but not the age at death or details about the size and structure of the household. They have been much used in studies of economic and social life of Europe and North America but this is not the place to discuss their limitations and how they can be sampled; there is already a large body of writing on the subject.

The method used for this study was to take an unsophisticated sample from eight parts of England to give a broad geographical coverage; these are listed with Table 10.1. Samples of the same size (sixty-five) were taken from each diocese from the middle year of each decade from 1675 to 1725. Many goods were listed in the documents and about twenty items were selected for special attention on the basis of consistent listing and general interest for domestic behaviour. They range from basic furniture and utensils (tables, pewter and cooking pots) to newly available things like china. Many of them, like knives and forks or utensils for hot drinks, point towards gradual changes in eating and drinking habits. Some, such as books and clocks, show something of a household's cultural interests and point towards contacts with a wider world. These meanings are discussed again at the end of this chapter because their patterns of ownership show notable differences.

Some of the goods were much more common in some places than others (see Table 10.1), especially china, window curtains, looking-glasses and pictures. The places where new goods were important (apart from London) were north-east England, Kent and Cambridgeshire; all in the east of England. Places where domestic goods were more sparse were in the north and west, with a few exceptions, like earthenware and clocks in Lancashire. Hampshire inventories, although sometimes of high value, did not record small durables so frequently. There is no single explanation for these patterns although one important practical factor was ease of supply, and especially ease of trade with London. For example, there was a substantial trade in 'merchant goods' from London to the north-east of England as exchange cargoes for coal.

Towns, and especially London, are often portrayed as playing a crucial role in changing consumer behaviour in the pre-industrial era. Evidence from the inventory sample (see Table 10.2) does not entirely fit with this, for the towns were not 'islands' of active consumption surrounded by 'traditional' values in the countryside. On the other hand, goods were often more frequently recorded in urban inventories, although there were distinctions between different types of goods. The urban inventories were drawn into the sample at random and the proportions found (18 per cent) were roughly in keeping with the proportion of people living in all kinds of urban communities at the time. There were few differences between town and country in ownership of goods like pewter, books and clocks. On the other hand, new and decorative goods were more common in towns and a few were virtually confined there. Pictures and window curtains were scarce in rural areas but quite common in London; looking-glasses were twice as likely in towns as in rural areas. London dominated for some of the indicators of new modes of eating and drinking, like utensils for hot drinks.

Table 10.3 shows that both occupation and locality were important, with tradesmen in towns more likely to own goods than tradesmen in the countryside. This raises questions about the everyday experiences that led to ownership which will be explored in due course. Table 10.4 suggests that there was some diffusion from town to country, and this is clear for utensils for hot drinks, but less so for clocks and books.

There are some remarkable instances of rapid growth and change, shown in Table 10.5, although the years from 1670–1730 are often presented as economically inactive. In some cases goods were already in use in the 1670s and there were only slight changes by 1725. These include well-known things like tables, pewter and books. Second, there were some goods that were already used in a few households in 1675, but by 1725 there had been considerable increases; these include pictures, looking-glasses, curtains and clocks. Third, there were a few new goods, such as china and utensils for hot drinks, where change was rapid and many households recorded these totally new things by the 1720s. Change was also concentrated more in some areas than others. There are many details here, and these add to the patterns already looked at. For example, utensils for hot drinks appeared in Kent, London and the north-east at much the same time but, whilst they were recorded in all areas by 1715, they increased rapidly in London at this time. Earthenware expanded rapidly in some places, but in others there was little change, and even a decline in Lancashire. The differences between the north-west and north-east in book ownership is notable.

There is no single perspective on the relationship between social status, social objectives, behaviour and consumption, due to the complexity of social stratification at this time. Table 10.7 shows ownership of the goods selected by social status and Table 10.8 shows ownership by some individual trades. The middle ranks were people who were neither at the bottom (servants, labourers and wage-earners) or at the top (county gentry and aristocracy) of the social hierarchy as outlined by King and Massie.[9] They therefore include the lesser gentry, professions, merchants, shopkeepers, farmers, yeomen, husbandmen and craftsmen. About half the households in the country fell into these groups in the late seventeenth century (about 700,000 out of 1,400,000) and by the mid-eighteenth century rather over half of the households were in the middle ranks as defined here. The boundaries between the middle and lower ranks were very unclear; husbandmen, for instance, were sometimes barely able to maintain themselves and were quite unlike the better-off farmers or craftsmen. There were differences within occupations, especially where it would be possible to confuse a master craftsman and a wage-earner. The middle ranks were economically, socially and politically important. Even in the seventeenth century the largest market for new and imported goods was amongst these consumers and the wealthiest had an impressive range of household goods. They also made up the local social and political elites in villages and towns and some of them were enfranchised. The professions were of increasing importance, as were merchants and shopkeepers. Many were the forerunners of the 'middle classes' of the nineteenth century and this term was already in use in the later eighteenth century. Some in the middle ranks had distinctly consumerist tastes and a need to assert their position in society through ownership of goods. There were many of modest means whose aim was to live between the excesses of the rich and the deprivation of the poor.

When Tables 10.7 and 10.8 are examined with this in mind, it is apparent that there were differences according to social rank, although these are sometimes unexpected. The gentry, for example, did not predominate, and many expressive goods, such as pictures or china, and even earthenware, were less frequently recorded in their inventories than in those of some of the tradesmen. This is unexpected and illustrates the complexity of the term 'gent', and warns against jumping to conclusions about social processes. It also suggests that ideas about social emulation as a motivation for consumption do need to be re-evaluated. There was a lower ownership of household goods amongst yeomen farmers than amongst tradesmen, even those of lesser rank. They less often owned newer, decorative things, although they were often well equipped with ordinary goods, like pewter and tables. The higher status tradesmen tended most often to have decorative and new items and a large number of active consumers were to be found amongst these occupational groups. By contrast, those of lesser status, such as husbandmen, rarely owned any of the new and decorative goods. From this it is clear that the limit to the markets for household goods lay somewhere between master craftsmen and husbandmen and did not extend to the lower ranks as some writers have suggested. There were too few labourers in the sample to make valid deductions about their behaviour.

In British society it is a mistake to take wealth as a proxy for social position, although this approach may be valid for the North American colonies. For this reason Tables 10.9 and 10.10 are of lesser significance than they might appear from the substantial variations between groups. Furthermore the figures derived from totals in the inventories are not a valid proxy for income, partly because sources of income (and especially whether payments were received in cash) were important and partly because even the valuations of inventories are a misleading measure of wealth.

Tables 10.11 and 10.12 compare men and women, not so much because they explain anything about consumption but because they present interesting insights into social processes. There were 430 women's inventories (15 per cent) in the sample, which is in keeping with the proportions of households headed by women in England at this time (16 per cent). They represent women from the same areas of the country as men, and from the same economic/social groups; they do not represent married women. Some of the women were actively engaged in a trade or farming and this gives some basis for comparisons with men in the same occupations. The striking thing about the tables is that there were any differences at all between households headed by men and those headed by women, for men could have lived in some of them and most had had a man in them formerly. Could this reveal different attitudes towards material life or specific goods on the part of men and women? Did women own different things because their tastes were allowed a free hand in the absence of a male head of household? It is in the things that were different that the answers might be revealed. A higher proportion of men owned clocks than women, reflecting their need to co-ordinate with people beyond the household, whereas women's time scheduling was often more 'task-orientated'. On the other hand, women were traditionally responsible for the household linen, and it is recorded more often in their inventories. Looking-glasses indicate self-awareness and a concern with individual appearance, as well as a concern for decoration; these too appear more often in women's inventories. Pictures are decorative and were more frequent in women's inventories. There is evidence in the higher proportions of tradeswomen with some of the goods that some households headed by women behaved differently from those headed by men. Was this because in these cases, women were able to have a little more freedom about how they spent the resources?

Meanings and material culture

Interpretations of consumer behaviour in the early modern period cannot draw upon accepted concepts to analyse the material side of people's lives. One starting point, implicit in the thought processes behind this work, is that material goods themselves contain implicit meanings and are therefore indicative of attitudes. Through understanding the non-material attributes of goods it is possible to move to the meaning of ownership in social and other terms. For instance, inventories often list cooking equipment in great detail, including all the fire tools, jacks, pots, pans and roasting tools, which in itself suggests the importance that food had in people's lives. Cooking pots represent 'traditional' goods and they were often singled out, as in 'brass pot and all the other brass and ironware'. (There is internal evidence in three dioceses (Carlisle, Lancashire and Lichfield) that these were not consistently listed, for they could have been included in entries like 'all the brass' that were common in these areas.) On the other hand, saucepans represent new cooking methods and were suited to enclosed ranges rather than open fires. Many of the most interesting goods in households were associated with meals and drinking. Wooden utensils, especially trenchers and bowls, were cheap and practical for everyday use but they were not consistently listed and are not therefore included in the tables. Pewter dishes represent well-established eating habits, whilst plates were associated with new ways of eating and new table layouts. Earthenware (including stoneware from the 1680s, white ware and Delft ware) had many different household and dairy functions and therefore represents both traditional and new goods. Knives and forks, on the other hand, were new goods, for they were not fully used at table until the mid-eighteenth century and later. They seem to have been consistently listed, and listed separately from knifes and 'flesh forks' used in cookery. Chinaware was also a new domestic item and was imported in large quantities after about 1700; it was not made in England until the 1740s. It was lighter in shape and usually white with blue or coloured decoration, so it was valued for being pretty. References to utensils that could have been used for hot drinks, such as teapots, tea kettles, coffeepots, teacups and teaspoons, indicate the spread of this new habit with its associated social occasions. Cushions and upholstered furniture would have been interesting as indicators of comfort, but neither are well listed, the former hardly mentioned after 1690, although becoming more common before that. Window curtains indicate a desire for domestic comfort, decoration, warmth and privacy and were relatively unusual in most places.

Other household goods, notably looking-glasses, pictures, books, clocks and silver, indicate different aspects of domestic life. Looking-glasses are good examples of possessions with several possible meanings, for they were decorative and made houses look nicer; they also have an implication that people wanted to look at themselves and ownership indicates a degree of self-awareness, or even vanity. Pictures too have several levels of significance; they are decorative but they could indicate a desire to look beyond the immediate household or location to other people and places. Detail is rare, but where a title is given, they are landscapes or portraits. Likewise, books open the minds of household members to ideas beyond their immediate experience. Clocks were harder to overlook than many things because of their high value and they indicate that people were aware of the time and were able to co-ordinate their daily lives with others outside the home. Silver was valuable and could represent a 'traditional' consumption pattern where silver was accumulated in large amounts instead of other goods and services; there is no evidence that this was done in England.

A further step can be taken by looking at the organization of day-to-day life in households. In doing this the practical and social situations in which goods were used can be understood and some insights into their meanings can be gleaned. This leads to discussion based on the perspectives of the lives of the consumers themselves and the rest of the chapter summarizes some ideas on these subjects. It focuses, as the section on inventories has done, on the 'middle' ranks of British society, namely those between the ranks of labourer and cottager on the one hand and the gentry and aristocracy on the other. This must again be emphasized because many accounts of early modern households are based on evidence from large establishments and much discussion of consumption is non-specific as to social rank. The households of the middle ranks were organized on a relatively small scale; most had between four and seven people in them and houses had three to seven rooms. There were no massive feasts, no accommodation problems for large numbers of servants and no need for formal rules for good behaviour.[10] The implications for domestic goods is that a small number of people chose and used them in the informal environment of the home, but within that environment there were certain accepted standards. All the furnishings of people's houses, as well as the buildings themselves, made physical and visible statements about accepted values and they were used to draw lines in social relationships and to stand as social markers.

At a domestic level the impact of a place or interior was subtle and meanings achieved subconsciously. This impact partly arose (as it still does) from shared expectations and culture which were not clearly documented at the time and therefore obscured from the later investigations of historians. The idea that the man-made environment had social meanings and that use of domestic space is worth exploring has been effectively used by historians of nineteenth-century housing but has been less in evidence in the work of historians of the early modern period. Likewise, those studying buildings have made more use of these ideas than historians of their contents.[11] The main problems with an approach that looks at the meaning of the whole environment is that it was not documented at the time and indirect methods are needed to probe non-verbal meanings. One idea that developed during the research for this project was that it was worth looking at how people fostered images of themselves and their households. I then took ideas and vocabulary based on the work of Goffman and others as a heuristic device to see if it would be meaningful to distinguish between the use of space in different parts of the living area; perhaps some parts would be more valued than others and furnished with more decorative or expensive things.[12] Goffman argued that when people are actively fostering their image their behaviour is different from when people are not showing themselves or are doing essentially private things. Thus there are 'front stages' which are the settings of activities in which people present themselves to others, and can be likened to a theatrical stage. The appearance and ambience of the 'front stage' affects the way that individuals or households can present themselves. Likewise, the 'back stage' is analogous to the backstage of a theatre. Social roles of possessions can be interpreted partly by observing where they were to be found and how space was used.

Space was indeed used in early modern houses in coherent and socially meaningful ways. Inventories show that most households of middle rank had houses with between three and six rooms, although some of the farmhouses were very much larger.[13] There were outhouses for working tools and farming equipment and in all there were enough rooms for activities to be separated. Rooms were used for different purposes and different values could thus be attached to different parts of the living space. In both England and Scotland households had a general living room, which in England was variously called the houseplace, house or hall. In the smaller houses this contained furniture and equipment for many household activities, like tables, seating, cooking equipment, storage space, pewter and miscellaneous other goods associated with daytime living. In England it was virtually unknown to have a bed in the main living room, although in Scotland enclosed and folding beds were normally found in the main living area, which illustrates that room use was socially determined. In England the main room sometimes had decorative things like pictures, a looking-glass or the clock or books. Larger houses had more specialized rooms and many inventories show that there were service areas, such as a kitchen, a dairy or a buttery, for some of the messier activities. Here the household goods were functional but not decorative. Chambers were common in all houses in England, where they were used for sleeping and all kinds of storage; furniture in them varied considerably.

That the use of space in houses served social functions can be seen from changes in room use. The most interesting change in England in the late seventeenth century was that the parlour, formerly a best bedroom with some seating and storage, became a best living room, containing decorative things and new types of furniture. These contrasting parlours of urban tradesmen illustrate the change; the first dates from 1674–5.[14]

> In the Parlour
> A fether bedd bedsted and Furniture a Truckle bedd
> with Furniture a Chest Three Trunckes one Shelfe an old
> 4 0 0
> viol & a little range

The second illustrates how the parlour could be used in new ways, in this case as a room for meals, although sometimes they were furnished as sitting rooms.[15]

> In the Parlour
> 6 cane chaires 2 Elbow chaires One ovell Table
> 25 picktures great and small One tea Tabble 6 sawcers
> 6 cupps, two slopp basons one Tea pott One dish
> 3 3 6
> one cannister and stand one glass lanthorne 2 bird
> cages Window curtains and vallence one
> house Cloath

The advantage of using concepts about how people present themselves to others was that it forced me to look more carefully at how rooms were furnished and what they were used for. Domestic space was used consistently and goods which were decorative or new were often found in parts of the house that would be seen by other people. I now feel that looking at the distinction between 'back' and 'front' provides a way of thinking about the problem without necessarily providing answers. In particular it too is a partial account of social meaning, just as the ideas about consumerism and emulation are only partial. It does lead to my main argument, which is that the material culture of domestic life was associated with the practical and social purposes of households and in this the meaning of consumption can be found. Relationships between ordinary activities and social mores influenced ownership of household goods. This makes a further difficulty for the historian in trying to understand consumer behaviour, for it necessitates an in-depth study of the trivia of domestic life in order to understand the dynamics of household organization and the meanings attached to it. The numerous, time-consuming and arduous activities necessarily undertaken in all households were central to the organization of space and goods within the house and only the larger houses had space devoted exclusively to things other than cookery, eating, clearing up, sleeping and resting. If ownership patterns and consumer behaviour are to be understood in a social context, then patterns of household activities and their meanings need to be described in more detail than a chapter allows.

Cookery, for example, had a central role in domestic life.[16] People of middle rank expected to have food that had been well, if simply, cooked. Part of the social meaning can be seen from the fact that food preparation was generally the responsibility of the wife or housekeeper, rather than servants; even women of gentry status were expected to be able to cook and it was later in the eighteenth century that cookery was normally done by servants. This confirmed the central role of women in giving nurture to household members and, at the same time, indicates that cookery was itself practically and symbolically important. It was normally done in general living rooms but in some places there were separate kitchens; in Norwich (at this time the second-largest town in England) they became common and living rooms and parlours were no longer used for cookery by the early eighteenth century. In rural areas kitchens were less common and cookery was done in the general living room. This enlightens understanding of the meaning of the material culture associated with cookery because basic cooking utensils, such as the ubiquitous pot, were simple and functional. There was little decoration of cooking utensils, suggesting that it was regarded as an activity to be kept out of sight (even in a common living area); the household did not project its image through its cooking equipment.

By contrast a different material culture existed for eating meals, which were important social events at which people sat down together, ate and talked; they were served in accepted ways and people were sensitive to their atmosphere.[17] These daily gatherings were the responsibility of women and the serving of meals was of social significance, although the decisions about what utensils to use and how to present the food were largely subconscious. Dinner was the main meal, eaten at midday by virtually everyone in the seventeenth century, but there were some changes in the half-century before 1750 that have a bearing on social meanings. The exact manner of serving varied from one family to another, as we might expect. Hannah Glasse said, in writing about the layout of the table, that it was up to each household to set its meal as it thought fit:

> Nor shall I take it upon me to direct to a Lady how to set out her Table. . . . Nor indeed do I think it would be pretty to see a Lady's Table set out after the Directions of a Book.[18]

By this time old and new ways existed alongside each other at the upper levels in society addressed by her and she was evidently unwilling to be directive about which was correct, but the implication is that it was important for the occasion to be properly laid out and organized.

The 'traditional' way of serving any meal was that all dishes of food were placed on the table at once and this persisted well into the eighteenth century. The division of a meal into courses was a novelty in the later seventeenth century, confined at that time to the households of some of the fashionable elite in London; for instance, Pepys reports such a dinner in 1669 with Lord Sandwich and others, 'dinner was brought up, one dish after another, but a dish at the time'.[19] At home, Pepys's meals were served in the traditional way, with numerous dishes if he had company and a couple of simpler dishes if he did not.[20] The main dishes were placed on the table and each person had their own plate or trencher onto which they carved or helped themselves from the serving dishes. Food was eaten with a knife or fingers, except for pottage, which was eaten with a spoon. With some food, and in some households, it was taken directly from a large vessel and not served onto a person's own plate at all. Of mid-eighteenth-century Scotland, one observer recalled later that 'it was the custom with the gentry, as it still is with our substantial tenants, for the whole company to eat broth out of one large plate'.[21] Conduct books, aimed at the gentry and aspiring gentry, suggest a number of ways of being polite; that you accept what is offered to you or that you do not take the best pieces but carve or serve yourself from the bit closest to you. It is unlikely that such formality was to be found in smaller family meals, but even here the ideal was for mannerly behaviour. This kind of eating did not result in revolting behaviour at the table, although many contemporary accounts give the impression that it did, especially those from conduct books, which anxiously warn the young and unwary against all sorts of rather nasty-sounding things, like wiping of hands on the hair or putting scraps on the floor.[22] We must not assume that shared utensils and the lack of cutlery as we know it necessarily resulted in indelicate and unmannerly behaviour. Even eating from a common dish with a spoon and pieces of bread could be done neatly, although later changes in behaviour at table led many of the old mores to be associated with poor manners and the lowest ranks in society.[23]

Such meals required simple utensils and layouts, but new ways of serving and cooking meant that there were more courses to serve at the table and more utensils. Knives and forks, for instance, were rare in the first quarter of the eighteenth century, but they gradually spread and by 1750 were much more common. Likewise, simple table layouts, with wooden or pewter dishes or plates, gradually gave way to decorated pottery and porcelain dinner services, especially after 1760.

Associations between drinking and decorated goods can similarly be established. Drinking had very strong social purposes and was often undertaken in public places, such as inns, alehouses or coffee houses.[24] Drinking at home with friends and family was important and many of the visits reported in diaries refer to drinking of some kind. There was a very close association between visiting and refreshments and large amounts of ale and wine were consumed in some households, often from decorated or special vessels of some kind. From the late seventeenth century tea and coffee gradually became more frequent, with massive increases in imports of both after the 1710s. Tea was already familiar to many people of middle rank in the late seventeenth century, and by the mid-eighteenth century to drink tea was an expected part of the behaviour of people of middle rank. The circumstances of tea drinking were different from alcohol and it appealed to people, especially women, who wanted light refreshment during the day or in the evening. In some households drinking tea became something of a ceremony, with appropriate, and expensive, equipment associated with it. Thomlinson, reporting on a clergyman's family near Durham, commented 'Aunt would have 50£ to furnish her drawing room. ie, 20£ for silver tea-kettle, lamp and table'.[25] Not everyone had utensils which cost as much as this and tea was usually made in a more modest way, but the new tea wares were certainly more decorative than anything previously used as household utensils.

Consumption can be viewed from any one of a number of directions: it changed; it was related to urban life; there were social constraints; there were economic constraints; where you lived mattered; how you behaved mattered. Any one of these can be described and gives some account of the changing experience of consumers in the early modern period. How much further we are towards the 'meaning' of consumer behaviour is an unanswered question. We have shown, for example, that there were groups of people owning clocks; we have shown that there were groups of tradesmen. How far these (and many other groups) overlapped gives contingency tables such as those at the end of the chapter. These are at the same time satisfyingly precise and annoyingly imprecise; they invite explanation at the same time as they confound it. The truth never seems within grasp. This is because the groups that we are dealing with (owners or tradesmen in the example) are themselves imprecise and their characteristics variable. Measurement gives the illusion of precision and thus of the possibility of firm conclusions. In other words we can never draw firm conclusions about the meaning of domestic goods due to the very nature of the problem. Nor should we try to do so, for the meaning resides, not in the conclusions but in the search for meaning itself.

Tables

Note on the tables

The tables all show the percentages of probate inventories in which selected goods were recorded. With the exception of Tables 10.11 and 10.12 they are taken from Lorna Weatherill, *Consumer Behaviour and Material Culture, 1660–1760* (New York and London, 1988).

Areas from which the sample was taken

Diocese of Durham, 1675–1715: Department of Palaeography and Diplomatic, University of Durham. This covers County Durham, Northumberland and Berwick-on-Tweed. The inventories for the coastal plain are fuller than those from the Pennine areas, so the coverage is biased towards the more economically developed areas. There were too few inventories for 1725 to take a sample.

Diocese of Carlisle, 1675–1725: Cumbria Record Office, Carlisle. This covers the northern part of Cumbria, Carlisle and the Eden valley, but it does not include Whitehaven.

Diocese of London, 1675 and 1695–1725 from the City division of the Consistory Court of the Diocese, which covered the eastern parishes of the city and some places, notably Whitechapel, outside. These are kept in the Guildhall Library, London. The sample for 1685 was taken from the Middlesex division because records of this date were missing in the Guildhall. These are kept in the Greater London Record Office.

Diocese of Winchester, 1675–1705: Hampshire Record Office, Winchester. These cover Hampshire and the Isle of Wight, and the sample is from both archdeaconry and consistory courts. There are too few inventories to sample after 1705.

Diocese of Chester, South Lancashire division, 1675–1725: Lancashire Record Office, Preston. The sample covers Lancashire south of the River Ribble.

Diocese of Canterbury, 1675–1725: Kent Record Office, Maidstone. These cover the eastern part of Kent only.

Diocese of Ely, 1675–1725: Cambridge University Library, archive department. The sample is from the county of Cambridgeshire.

Diocese of Lichfield, 1675–1725: Lichfield Joint Record Office, Lichfield Public Library. The diocese covers a very large part of the Midlands, including Derbyshire, Staffordshire, northern Shropshire and parts of Warwickshire and Nottinghamshire. The sample was confined to Staffordshire and North Shropshire.

218

Table 10.1 Ownership of goods by region

	No. of inventories	Tables	Cooking pots	Sauce-pans	Pewter	Pewter dishes	Pewter plates	Earthen-ware	Books	Clocks	Pictures	Looking-glasses	Table linen	Window curtains	Knives and forks	China	Utensils for hot drinks	Silver
		%	%	%	%	%	%	%	%	%	%	%	%	%	%	%	%	%
London area	367	92	80	43	91	59	53	41	30	29	37	74	67	40	13	12	15	44
North-east England†	325	93	76	2	95	77	37	26	10	15	25	44	55	14	3	10	3	34
East Kent	390	97	89	11	95	59	39	58	26	36	16	47	81	19	7	3	6	41
Cambridgeshire	390	96	86	6*	93	72	33	32	12	14	9	27	44	9	2	3	2	15
North-west England‡	390	83	57*	5*	92	17*	11*	75	20	33	9	31	15*	8	2	1	1	13
Hampshire§	260	93	73	3	97	50	20	13	24	7	3	19	35	7	2	0§	0§	27
North-west Midlands	390	87	62	13*	94	42	21	17	15	7	4	14	28	3	1	0	1	8
Cumbria‡	390	75	43*	1*	88	11*	4*	23	17	7	3	6	13*	1	1	2	0	10

See also Table 10.6.
†1725 missing.
‡Some goods (marked*) seem to have been badly listed in these areas.
§1715 and 1725 missing.

Table 10.2 Ownership of goods in town and country

	No. of inventories	Mean value of inventory £	Tables %	Cooking pots %	Sauce-pans %	Pewter dishes %	Pewter plates %	Earthen-ware %	Books %	Clocks %	Pictures %	Looking-glasses %	Table linen %	Window curtains %	Knives and forks %	China %	Utensils for hot drinks %	Silver %
London	319	153	92	81	46	92	58	54	42	31	29	41	77	66	43	14	13	16	46
Major town	217	97	91	72	11	93	67	46	45	21	18	41	58	55	27	6	8	6	44
Other town	291	135	92	70	10	94	56	37	39	23	20	23	50	55	15	4	7	3	37
Villages and rural	2,075	126	88	69	5	93	43	20	35	17	17	5	21	35	6	2	1	2	16
All	2,902	128	89	70	11	93	48	27	37	19	19	37	33	42	13	4	4	4	23

The major towns included are: Durham, Newcastle, Berwick, Carlisle, Southampton, Winchester, Canterbury, Cambridge, Shrewsbury, Liverpool and Manchester.

Table 10.3 Ownership of goods by farmers and tradesmen in town and country

	Occupation	No. of inventories	Mean value of inventory £	Tables %	Cooking pots %	Sauce-pans %	Pewter dishes %	Pewter plates %	Earthen-ware %	Books %	Clocks %	Pictures %	Looking-glasses %	Table linen %	Window curtains %	Knives and forks %	China %	Utensils for hot drinks %	Silver or gold %
London	All trades	199	177	93	80	45	91	61	58	48	31	30	43	78	68	44	16	14	17	42
	Farmers	7	103	100	86	57	100	100	100	43	14	43	43	86	71	43	0	14	14	43
Major town	All trades	125	109	94	70	14	95	72	49	51	22	20	43	63	58	30	7	10	9	46
	Farmers	10	106	80	90	0	100	70	40	30	0	20	30	40	40	10	0	10	0	40
Other town	All trades	144	137	97	74	9	97	62	42	39	19	20	26	53	65	14	3	8	3	40
	Farmers	43	118	93	65	9	95	33	23	37	12	16	5	30	35	7	2	5	0	9
Rural or village	All trades	443	109	93	74	8	96	52	28	46	19	22	9	29	46	9	3	3	3	22
	Farmers	1,224	132	89	66	3	94	38	16	31	14	15	2	17	30	4	1	1	1	10
All	All trades	911	128	92	75	17	95	58	40	46	22	23	24	48	55	21	6	7	7	3
	Farmers	1,284	131	89	66	4	94	47	17	32	14	15	3	18	30	4	1	1	1	10

Table 10.4 Changing ownership of goods in town and country

	Saucepans (%)						Clocks (%)						Window curtains (%)					
	1675	1685	1695	1705	1715	1725	1675	1685	1695	1705	1715	1725	1675	1685	1695	1705	1715	1725
London	11	36	43	57	55	73	11	15	19	24	52	51	23	30	43	39	60	62
Major town	3	3	8	10	13	35	7	3	8	28	33	26	20	20	13	31	33	52
Other town	2	7	5	8	31	37	17	16	19	15	31	43	6	13	17	11	29	26
Rural/village	1	2	5	5	9	12	8	8	13	19	29	31	4	5	5	6	7	10

	Earthenware (%)						Pictures (%)						China (%)					
	1675	1685	1695	1705	1715	1725	1675	1685	1695	1705	1715	1725	1675	1685	1695	1705	1715	1725
London	14	19	33	52	59	75	9	26	21	57	60	60	0	0	0	7	33	35
Major town	37	26	39	44	54	74	30	20	32	49	60	48	0	0	11	13	13	9
Other town	36	38	35	26	54	74	21	24	21	6	43	47	0	7	8	8	17	11
Rural/village	26	26	34	34	43	51	2	3	3	5	9	10	0	1	1	2	2	4

	Books (%)						Looking-glasses (%)						Utensils for hot drinks (%)					
	1675	1685	1695	1705	1715	1725	1675	1685	1695	1705	1715	1725	1675	1685	1695	1705	1715	1725
London	18	17	19	41	34	56	58	74	79	81	91	80	0	0	2	7	22	60
Major town	23	23	16	13	23	30	50	59	47	67	62	61	0	0	3	3	12	22
Other town	18	22	24	23	23	42	36	45	49	51	69	74	0	0	2	0	17	16
Rural/village	18	18	16	16	17	13	11	16	20	25	30	28	0	0	0	1	3	6

Table 10.5 Changing ownership of goods

	No. of inventories	Tables	Cooking pots	Sauce-pans	Pewter	Pewter dishes	Pewter plates	Earthen-ware	Books	Clocks	Pictures	Looking-glasses	Table linen	Window curtains	Knives and forks	China	Utensils for hot drinks	Silver or gold
		%	%	%	%	%	%	%	%	%	%	%	%	%	%	%	%	%
1675	520	87	66	2	94	39	9	27	18	9	7	22	43	7	1	0	0	23
1685	520	88	68	6	93	46	18	27	18	9	8	28	45	10	1	1	0	21
1695	497	89	69	8	93	44	21	34	18	14	9	31	41	11	3	2	1	24
1705	520	90	71	11	93	47	34	36	19	20	14	36	41	12	4	4	2	23
1715	455	91	74	17	95	56	42	47	21	33	24	44	44	19	6	8	7	29
1725	390	91	76	23	91	55	45	57	22	34	21	40	37	21	10	9	15	21
All	2,902	89	70	11	93	48	27	37	19	19	13	33	42	13	4	4	4	23

Table 10.6 Regional change in ownership of goods

	Books (%)						Earthenware (%)					
	1675	1685	1695	1705	1715	1725	1675	1685	1695	1705	1715	1725
London area	18	15	19	38	31	52	15	18	33	46	57	74
North-east England	9	9	12	8	14	–	23	18	22	28	38	–
East Kent	28	25	29	25	23	28	38	49	62	52	62	88
Cambridgeshire	11	12	6	18	14	9	11	14	28	42	43	55
North-west England	17	26	20	18	25	15	82	74	82	69	80	65
Hampshire	29	26	23	18	–	–	14	8	14	15	–	–
North-west Midlands	22	15	15	11	17	9	20	12	15	14	18	20
Cumbria	14	17	15	17	22	15	11	18	18	22	29	38

	Pictures (%)						Utensils for hot drinks (%)					
	1675	1685	1695	1705	1715	1725	1675	1685	1695	1705	1715	1725
London area	54	69	79	77	89	78	0	0	2	6	22	57
North-east England	26	45	42	48	58	–	0	0	5	2	9	–
East Kent	37	31	48	48	52	68	0	2	0	3	16	15
Cambridgeshire	6	18	18	42	34	45	0	0	0	2	0	12
North-west England	20	28	35	32	38	34	0	0	0	2	2	3
Hampshire	18	15	20	23	–	–	0	0	0	0	–	–
North-west Midlands	11	8	14	14	29	11	0	0	0	0	2	3
Cumbria	3	6	6	8	9	3	0	0	0	0	2	0

Table 10.7 Social position and ownership of goods

Social status	No. of inven- tories	Total inven- tory £	Mean value House- hold goods £	Tables %	Cooking pots %	Sauce- pans %	Pewter %	Pewter dishes %	Pewter plates %	Earthen- ware %	Books %	Clocks %	Pictures %	Looking- glasses %	Table linen %	Window curtains %	Knives and forks %	China %	Utensils for hot drinks %	Silver %
Gentry	122	320	55	93	84	13	93	55	43	39	39	51	33	62	60	26	11	6	7	61
Trades of high status; clergy; professions	152	193	39	97	75	11	95	54	40	53	45	34	35	62	63	21	7	11	7	51
Trades of interme- diate status	344	157	32	93	77	25	94	62	50	49	24	25	29	56	58	29	11	9	10	38
Yeomen; large farmers	952	165	23	91	69	5	95	41	20	33	18	19	4	21	35	5	1	1	1	13
Trades of low status	435	92	19	92	74	12	96	56	31	42	17	18	15	37	50	12	3	3	4	23
Husbandmen; small farmers	332	32	8	83	57	2	89	33	9	28	4	4	0	9	16	2	0	0	1	2
Labourers	28	16	5	79	79	11	89	57	14	43	4	0	4	4	18	4	0	4	0	0
Widows and spinsters	217	82	18	77	66	12	89	47	22	33	18	13	12	36	46	17	4	4	2	37
Tradesmen; trade unknown	56	115	31	98	82	27	88	55	32	50	32	29	32	57	61	38	9	11	13	46
Occupation or status unknown	264	62	17	83	70	16	88	48	31	27	17	14	18	36	40	16	5	5	6	23
Total	2,902	128	23	89	70	11	93	48	27	37	19	19	13	33	42	13	4	4	4	23

Notes on Table 10.7: criteria for social status

The groups analysed in the table and in the chapter are based on the results of research done by Dr Vivien Brodsky Elliott, 'Mobility and marriage in pre-industrial England' (Cambridge University, Ph.D. thesis, 1978), in which she ordered about fifty occupations and status designations according to the observed trade to which sons were apprenticed and according to the occupations and status of marriage partners. I have used her results, as well as other commentary about status, to place the occupations of the inventoried population into groupings which give an indication of status. The table shows seven groups, ranging from those of gentry status to labourers, together with three others which could not be positioned in the hierarchy because there was too little information about them. In effect this places the trades alongside the well-known groups of gentry, yeomen, husbandmen and labourers. The groups are not inflexible and there was a great deal of diversity, as we would expect in a complex society. The advantage of this way of doing it is that it allows us to examine the impact of social status on behaviour. There are other ways of grouping the occupations given in inventories and these are dealt with in Weatherill, *Consumer Behaviour*, Appendix 3.

Table 10.8 Ownership of goods by selected occupation

Occupation	No. of inventories	Mean value Total inventory £	House-hold goods £	Tables %	Cooking pots %	Sauce-pans %	Pewter dishes %	Pewter dishes %	Pewter plates %	Earthen-ware %	Books %	Clocks %	Pictures %	Looking-glasses %	Table linen %	Window curtains %	Knives and forks %	China %	Utensils for hot drinks %	Silver %
Shoemakers	45	63	17	91	64	8	93	58	33	51	16	8	8	38	47	2	2	4	2	16
Tailors	32	56	16	91	78	16	100	69	41	44	22	16	16	34	44	6	0	0	13	17
Carpenters	32	70	18	90	81	6	97	56	22	38	9	16	3	22	56	13	0	0	0	19
Weavers	48	85	13	88	67	8	96	48	19	44	15	17	2	27	29	4	0	0	2	8
Blacksmiths	49	56	15	82	63	14	90	41	18	35	10	22	8	33	39	12	0	4	0	8
Butchers	37	129	24	97	76	8	97	59	41	32	16	19	19	46	59	11	0	3	3	43
Shopkeepers	87	124	29	98	86	25	95	64	53	48	37	25	34	67	68	40	15	13	11	45
Innkeepers and victuallers	101	151	43	99	81	37	98	72	67	57	19	30	39	70	65	40	21	9	17	46
Mariners	40	85	30	98	70	8	98	68	45	60	18	25	48	70	73	20	3	23	25	60
Merchants	16*	223	46	100	75	6	81	44	38	56	50	38	44	75	56	38	19	25	19	75
Drapers and mercers	21*	303	34	95	81	19	95	43	38	48	43	24	43	67	43	24	5	5	10	43

*Sample too small to be meaningful.

Table 10.9 Ownership of goods by the valuation of the whole inventory

Total inventory valuation £	No. of inventories	Tables %	Cooking pots %	Sauce-pans %	Pewter dishes %	Pewter plates %	Earthen-ware %	Books %	Clocks %	Pictures %	Looking-glasses %	Table li-nen %	Window curtains %	Knives and forks %	China %	Utensils for hot drinks %	Silver %
1–5	84	80	52	7	76	50	20	17	6	0	5	14	19	0	2	1	1	0
6–10	150	81	67	7	86	50	17	28	7	4	9	20	28	6	1	3	3	5
11–25	500	86	67	7	89	48	22	31	11	6	9	27	35	8	1	2	1	11
26–50	552	87	64	10	93	47	23	34	12	11	12	28	39	10	3	3	3	19
51–100	628	90	69	9	93	43	24	39	19	18	11	28	40	11	3	3	4	21
101–250	627	93	78	13	97	49	34	43	26	28	14	41	48	17	5	6	5	31
251–500	234	94	81	15	97	53	38	42	33	44	23	50	60	21	9	7	6	44
Over 500	127	95	85	18	98	50	45	44	46	51	39	61	65	29	15	9	10	67

Table 10.10 Ownership of goods by value of the household goods

Value of household goods £	No. of inventories	Tables %	Cooking pots %	Sauce-pans %	Pewter %	Pewter dishes %	Pewter plates %	Earthen-ware %	Books %	Clocks %	Pictures %	Looking-glasses %	Table linen %	Window curtains %	Knives and forks %	China %	Utensils for hot drinks %	Silver %
1–2	107	61	54	0	66	28	6	23	3	0	0	5	7	0	0	1	0	0
3–5	343	76	56	5	83	38	11	22	7	1	3	10	15	1	1	1	1	2
6–10	598	85	63	5	94	47	18	28	8	6	7	16	29	5	1	2	1	6
11–15	435	92	68	9	94	46	25	38	14	13	7	29	40	9	2	1	1	13
16–25	571	94	73	10	95	50	28	36	18	20	12	31	46	9	2	2	2	23
26–100	772	97	82	18	98	53	42	50	35	39	26	58	64	26	9	8	8	50
Over 100	76	100	91	33	99	59	63	59	3	67	50	84	74	57	29	26	22	84

Table 10.11 Women and men

	No. of inventories	Tables %	Cooking pots %	Saucepans %	Pewter %	Earthen-ware %	Books %	Clocks %	Pictures %	Looking-glasses %	Table linen %	Window curtains %	Knives and forks %	China %	Utensils for hot drinks %	Silver %
Women	430	80	68	13	91	34	19	16	16	36	45	17	4	4	3	34
Men	2472	91	71	10	93	37	19	20	13	32	41	12	4	4	4	22
All	2902	89	70	11	93	37	19	19	13	33	42	13	4	4	4	23

Table 10.12 Women and men in the same occupations

	No. of inventories	Tables %	Cooking pots %	Sauce-pans %	Pewter %	Earth-enware %	Books %	Clocks %	Pictures %	Looking-glasses %	Table linen %	Window curtains %	Knives and forks %	China %	Utensils for hot drinks %	Silver %
Retail trades																
women	31	97	65	32	93	61	32	19	39	58	77	32	13	6	3	48
men	113	93	81	19	94	39	32	25	29	61	63	35	11	8	8	38
Drink trades																
women	9	100	89	33	100	44	11	44	33	89	67	56	22	0	0	56
men	92	98	79	37	97	58	20	28	39	67	64	38	20	10	18	45
Dealers																
women	4	100	75	25	100	50	50	50	75	100	25	25	25	25	25	100
men	39	97	72	8	97	62	18	26	46	69	74	21	3	23	5	56
Services																
women	4	100	100	50	100	100	25	50	75	100	50	100	0	25	25	25
men	12	92	67	33	92	58	17	17	50	58	42	17	0	8	8	42
Crafts																
women	9	89	78	10	100	56	22	22	33	67	78	44	11	22	11	56
men	91	87	71	10	92	34	8	22	7	33	45	12	1	2	1	14
Trade not known																
women	6	83	100	50	83	33	50	33	50	67	50	83	0	0	17	50
men	32	100	88	19	84	50	31	16	25	53	56	28	6	13	13	41
Totals																
women	63	95	79	32	95	57	30	29	43	70	71	46	13	10	8	54
men	379	94	77	20	94	46	21	24	28	56	59	27	9	9	9	39
All	2902	89	70	11	93	37	19	19	13	33	13	42	4	4	4	23

Notes

1 Daniel Defoe, *Robinson Crusoe* (London, 1719).
2 The research upon which this chapter was based was funded by the Economic and Social Research Council of Great Britain from 1981 to 1985. Results are published in: Lorna Weatherill, 'A possession of one's own: women and consumer behaviour in England, 1669–1740', *Journal of British Studies*, xxv (April 1986), 131–56. Tables 10.11 and 10.12 are derived from this article; 'Consumer behaviour and social status in England, 1660–1750', *Continuity and Change*, ii (1986), 191–216; *Consumer Behaviour and Material Culture, 1660–1760* (London and New York, 1988); the twelve tables are taken from this book.
3 These concepts are most fully discussed in D. E. C. Eversley, *Social Theories of Fertility and the Malthusian Debate* (Oxford, 1959); Joyce Appleby, 'Ideology and theory: the tension between political and economic liberalism in seventeenth-century England', *American Historical Review*, lxxxi (1976), 499–515.
4 Adam Ferguson, *An Essay on the History of Civil Society*, 4th edn (London, 1773; 1st edn, 1767), part vi, sect. 2, 375; quoted in Eversley, *Social Theories of Fertility*, 24.
5 Mary Douglas and B. Isherwood, *The World of Goods: Towards an Anthropology of Consumption* (Harmondsworth, 1980), 112, 118.
6 Examples of diaries that give interesting and sometimes moving accounts of domestic life are: J. D. Marshall (ed.), 'The autobiography of William Stout of Lancaster', *Chetham Society*, 3rd series, xiv (1967); C. Jackson (ed.), 'A family history begun by James Fretwell', *Surtees Society*, lxv (1875), 163–244; idem (ed.), 'The autobiography of Alice Thornton, 1627–1707', *Surtees Society*, lxii (1875); W. Brockbank and the Revd F. Kenworthy (eds), 'The diary of Richard Kay, 1716–1751: a Lancashire doctor', *Chetham Society*, 3rd series, xvi (1968).
7 For examples, see N. McKendrick, J. Brewer and J. H. Plumb, *Birth of a Consumer Society: The Commercialization of Eighteenth-Century England* (London, 1982).
8 Lee Warley, 'Accounts and memos', Reading University Library, ms. no. KEN 14.2/1.
9 The best introduction to social position is K. Wrightson, *English Society, 1580–1680* (London, 1982); see also L. Bonfield, R. Smith and K. Wrightson (eds), *The World We Have Gained* (Oxford, 1986). For Scotland there is a brief comparative survey in R. Houston, *Scottish Literacy and the Scottish Identity, 1660–1800* (Cambridge, 1985), 22–37.
10 Mean household size in the English listings was 4.8; P. Laslett, 'Size and structure of the household in England over three centuries', *Population Studies*, xxiii (1969), 199–223. In Scotland the hearth tax records suggest a mean size of around 5; D. Adamson, 'The hearth tax', *Transcript of the Dunfermline and Galloway Natural Historians and Antiquaries Society*, xlvii (1970), 147–58; M. Flinn *et al.*, *Scottish Population History* (Cambridge, 1977), 194–8. Some idea of the houses they used can be gained from numerous studies of buildings, although care is needed to make sure that the particular building was one that might have been used by the middle ranks. See E. Mercer, *English Vernacular Houses: A Study of Traditional Farmhouses and Cottages* (London, 1975); Linda J. Hall, *The Rural Houses of North Avon and South Gloucestershire, 1400–1720* (Bristol, 1983).
11 I was encouraged to think about the subject in this way by reading Douglas and Isherwood, *The World of Goods*; and Mary Douglas, *Implicit Meanings: Essays in Anthropology* (London, 1975). See also A. Rapoport, *The Meaning of the Built Environment: A Nonverbal Communication Approach* (London and California, 1982); *The Mutual Interaction of People and their Built Environment* (The Hague, 1976); N. W. Jerome, R. F. Kandel and Gretel H. Pelto (eds), *Nutritional Anthropology: Contemporary Diet and Culture* (New York, 1980).
12 I have used the ideas and vocabulary in E. Goffman, *The Presentation of Self in Everyday Life* (Harmondsworth, 1969; first published in the USA in 1959); R. A. Gould and M. B. Schiffer (eds), *Modern Material Culture: The Archaeology of Us* (London and New York, 1981).
13 Evidence for room use is drawn from inventories; the generalizations are based on the published

collections. For a list see Weatherill, *Consumer Behaviour*, 243. For a very useful summary of room use in an advanced urban area, see Penelope Corfield and Ursula Priestley, 'Rooms and room use in Norwich housing, 1580–1730', *Post Medieval Archaeology*, xvi (1982), 93–123.

14 John Webster of Doncaster, 14 January 1674–5, in P. C. D. Brears (ed.), 'Yorkshire probate inventories, 1542–1689', *Yorkshire Archaeological Society*, Record Series, no. 134 (1972).

15 Edward Sackley of Rochester, Kent, 'saylesman', 1 September 1717, in Spufford, *Great Reclothing*, 222.

16 Cookery in households of middle rank in the late seventeenth century is not well documented and collections of 'traditional' recipes tend to have a nineteenth-century origin. See Dorothy Hartley, *Food in England* (London, 1954); more concern with change and social context can be found in C. Anne Wilson, *Food and Drink in Britain* (Harmondsworth, 1976). I used two printed collections of recipes kept by women running gentry households; Bette Stitt (ed.), 'Diana Astry's recipe book c.1700', *Publication of the Bedfordshire Historical Society*, xxxvii (1957); M. Masson (ed.), *The Compleat Cook or the Secrets of a Seventeenth Century Housewife by Rebecca Price* (London, 1974). The most useful contemporary cookery book referring to the middling ranks is Mrs Hannah Glasse, *The ART of COOKERY made Plain and Easy*, 1st edn (London, 1747).

17 For general commentary on the meaning of meals, see Mary Douglas, *Implicit Meanings*.

18 Glasse, *The ART of COOKERY*.

19 R. Latham and W. Matthews (eds), *The Diary of Samuel Pepys*, vol. 9 (23–1–1669/70), 423. The diary contains some evocative descriptions of large dinners with family and friends, as opposed to feasts, as well as the amount of work that went into preparing a special meal. See index in vol. 9.

20 Pepys, *Diary*, vol. 1, 26–1–1660/1 and vol. 4, 13–1–1663/4, 13–14.

21 A. Allardyce, *Scotland and Scotsmen in the Eighteenth Century: From the Mss of John Ramsay of Ochtertyre* (London, 1888), 180.

22 There are extracts from these aimed largely at the gentry, in N. Elias, *The Civilizing Process* (Oxford, 1978; 1st edn, 1939). There are good descriptions of the conventions, again aimed at those of the upper ranks, in Hannah Woolley, *The Gentlewomen's Companion* (London, 1675).

23 Most diaries before 1740 record dinner in the middle of the day. Later commentary suggests that some people took to having dinner later in the day from the mid-eighteenth century, and this then served to distinguish working people from those of higher status, but this seems to have happened only at the very end of the period covered by this study.

24 Henri Misson, *Memoirs and Observations in his Travels over England*, tr. Ozell (London, 1719). He visited in 1685, under the heading of visits; E. Hobhouse (ed.), *Diary of a West Country Physician, 1709–1726* (London, 1934); C. Morris (ed.), *The Journeys of Celia Fiennes* (London, 1983),Tunbridge (153) and Lichfield (194), Bath (41), Epsom (379 and 391); P. Clark, *The English Alehouse: A Social History, 1200–1830* (London, 1983), 195–242. Inns had always catered for wealthier clients; inventories show that they were often well furnished.

25 J. C. Hodges (ed.), 'The diary of the Rev John Thomlinson', *Surtees Society*, cxviii (1910), 16 October 1717, 85.

11

The production and marketing of populuxe goods in eighteenth-century Paris

Cissie Fairchilds

To the historians who pioneered the concept of a consumer revolution in the eighteenth century,[1] it was a uniquely *English* phenomenon, something that, as with those other English inventions, industrialization and parliamentary democracy, Continental European countries copied only belatedly and imperfectly in the nineteenth century. This was thought especially true of France, whose eighteenth-century consumer market was characterized by Harold Perkin as 'a small class of luxury consumers' and 'a large mass of consumption-resisting peasants'.[2] French economic historians have generally agreed with this assessment; indeed, the supposed persistence of aristocratic luxury consumption and the lack of a mass consumer market are often cited as major factors retarding France's industrialization in the nineteenth century.[3]

Yet to those who lived through the consumer revolution, France, not England, was its homeland. Paris, not London, set the fashions in consumption for Europe. It was to Paris, not London, that tourists flocked to savour the pleasures of shopping in elegantly decorated stores and equipping themselves with gowns, walking sticks and porcelain of *le dernier cri*. And it was in Paris, not London, that travellers found a lower class prosperous enough to own a few luxuries and eager to follow the latest vagaries of fashion. English tourists in Paris were astonished at the propensity of the Parisian lower classes to spend on fashionable luxuries. In 1775, Dr Johnson's friend, Mrs Hester Thrale, described the streets of Paris as thronged with 'Wenches with umbrellas and Workmen with Muffs'. She saw a stonecutter divest himself of a fashionable coat, muff and snuffbox, all given to his dog to guard, before he set to work on a piece of marble.[4] In 1784, Mrs Fanny Cradock saw similar sights. She once ran into her milkman out for an evening's stroll, 'dressed in a fashionable suit, with an embroidered waistcoat, silk knee-breeches and lace cuffs'.[5]

In this chapter I will argue that these sharp-eyed Englishwomen were right: that urban France *did* experience a consumer revolution in the eighteenth century, and that its salient characteristic was the penchant of the lower classes for what I term 'populuxe' goods, that is, cheap copies of aristocratic luxury items.[6] I will further argue that it was the systems of production and marketing these goods entailed, rather than the persistence of traditional consumption patterns, that were the prime shapers of the French economy in the late eighteenth and early nineteenth centuries.

Our best source for consumption patterns in eighteenth-century France is the *inventaires après décès*, the inventories taken by notaries of the possessions of the recently deceased. Required by law throughout France for the estates of those who died intestate, in Paris and its surrounding regions inventories were also routinely made of the estates of decedents who had been married under the community property provisions of the *coutume de Paris*.[7] Since most Parisians married this way, samples of inventories include a large proportion of all adults who died in Paris at any given time, although they are of course biased not only towards the married but also towards the prosperous – those who left estates large enough to entice relatives to have them inventoried and divided. These inventories are remarkably detailed. They include everything from empty wine bottles in the cellar to bags of rags in the attic, and they contain careful lengthy descriptions of the furniture, clothing and linens forming the bulk of most estates.

To trace the spread of populuxe goods among the Parisian lower classes, I have analysed all the inventories from the years 1725 and 1785 of lower middle- and lower-class decedents – small shopkeepers, master artisans, journeymen, day labourers, domestic servants and the like – found in the surviving records of notaries who practised on the rue St Honoré, now housed in the Minutier Centrale of the Archives Nationales. From 1725 to 1785 the rue St Honoré was transformed from a street of small grocery shops (it was near Les Halles, Paris's major food market) to the most fashionable shopping district of the city, lined with the elegant emporia of jewellers, glovers and *modistes*. Yet its surrounding neighbourhood continued to house a large, poor transient population, and this helps prevent the 'gentrification' of the street from biasing my group of inventories towards the upper levels of the working class – towards artisans and shopkeepers in the luxury trades who might be more likely than other members of the lower classes to emulate the consumption habits of their social superiors.[8] In fact, the inventories from 1785 include more estates of journeymen and day labourers (they form 27 per cent of the lower-class inventories) and fewer of those of shopkeepers and master artisans (58 per cent of the lower-class inventories) than does the sample from 1725, for which the figures are 21 per cent and 67 per cent respectively.[9]

This makes the changes in consumption patterns revealed in the inventories all the more striking (see Table 11.1). My data suggests, first of all, that in the sixty years from 1725 to 1785, France saw the same sorts of changes in consumption patterns that England had experienced during its consumer revolution from 1665 to 1725.[10] In France as in England, the total value of the inventoried estates did not increase substantially from the earlier to the later period; their average worth was 1286 *livres* in 1725 and 1565 *livres* in 1785, a negligible rise when adjusted for inflation.[11] Yet because prices for many items favoured by consumers fell, the later inventories show more goods in greater variety than ever before. As in England, inventories from the later period show that bookcases, chests of drawers, secretaries, writing tables, tea tables, gaming tables and the like joined the standard bed, table and cane-seated chairs to brighten even modest apartments, and the invention of lighter, cheaper textiles allowed even the lower classes to add cloaks, shirts, caps, muffs, fichus, underwear and nightclothes to their wardrobes. Again as in England, inventories show that by the later period cheap and abundant earthenware had replaced scarce and costly tinware in kitchens, and silver was more likely to take the form of decorative table settings than of easily pawnable beakers and cups, which had served as family savings banks in earlier periods.

Table 11.1 Percentages of lower-class inventories containing selected items, 1725 and 1785

	1725	1785
Furniture novelties*	20.3	79.7
Earthenware†	44.1	77.6
Silver	74.6	56.3
'Populuxe' items		
Jewellery	49.2	78.1
Silver and pinchbeck watches	27.1	17.2
Gold watches	5.1	54.7
Stockings	64.4	96.9
Umbrellas	10.2	31.3
Canes	13.6	18.8
Fans	5.1	34.4
Snuff boxes	6.8	32.8
Tea and coffee accessories‡	18.6	45.3
Games	5.1	21.9
Pets§	1.7	6.3
Books	28.8	43.8
N	59	64

*Includes chests of drawers, bookcases, tea tables, writing tables, secretaries.
†Indicates ten or more pieces of earthenware dishes and/or kitchen accessories (mantel decorations, common in 1725, are not included).
‡Includes tea and coffee pots, spoons and sets and tea caddies and *cafetières*.
§Includes birdcages, dog beds, etc. – not the animals themselves.

Source see Appendix.

Perhaps the most striking change revealed in the inventories, and the one that I have highlighted in Table 11.1, is the increasing presence of populuxe items – inexpensive versions of aristocratic luxuries like fans, snuff boxes and umbrellas which added a touch of class to the life of a journeyman or domestic servant. That populuxe goods were desired as symbols of an aristocratic life-style rather than for their own usefulness is, I think, indicated by the figures for silver and gold watches in the table.[12] Had they wanted watches only for their usefulness as timepieces, lower-class Parisians should have been content with cheap pinchbeck or silver ones. Gold watches were a symbol of aristocracy; no *petit maître* aping the *gens de mode* would have considered his ensemble complete without one. As the table shows, cheap watches almost disappeared from lower-class inventories over the course of the eighteenth century, while gold watches show a spectacular rise.

This penchant for populuxe goods which allowed them to ape the aristocracy seems to have been unique to France. English inventories suggest that when the English lower classes acquired extra disposable income they spent it on useful household goods, not populuxe items.[13] It also seems to have been of long standing; complaints that the lower classes attempted to emulate the dress and life-style of their betters date back at least to the early seventeenth century.[14] But before the late eighteenth century the lower classes had been inhibited from buying luxury goods not only by their cost but also by sumptuary laws and by their own acceptance of a hierarchical social order that reserved to the elite certain prerogatives of dress. By the 1780s these barriers to populuxe consumption had fallen. France had

had no new sumptuary laws since the 1720s, and its social order, still dominated by the aristocracy yet displaying increasing possibilities for social mobility and a growing contempt for traditional aristocratic values, was ideal to foster populuxe consumption.[15]

The final ingredient necessary for the growth of populuxe consumption was a system of production and distribution which could furnish a large market cheaply and efficiently. Probably the best such system was that which underlay the English consumer revolution. As Joan Thirsk and Margaret Spufford have shown, the goods which fuelled England's consumer revolution were, until the English Revolution, often produced under royal mono-poly patents granted to entrepreneurs; after 1660 they were manufactured freely by the putting-out system all over the countryside. And they were sold freely in both country and town by wandering chapmen, peddlers unfettered by local restrictions on shops and market days.[16] This system was ideal for fostering a consumer revolution. It was flexible enough to accommodate new products and markets, and the cheap rural labour and low-overhead operations of the chapmen kept costs low and goods therefore within reach of lower-class consumers.

In France, by contrast, many of the goods which fostered populuxe consumption were produced and marketed under guild regulation. In England, guilds were almost moribund by the late seventeenth century because both the courts and the royal government had failed to uphold their monopolies and privileges.[17] But in France, the royal government maintained and extended guild privileges because the guilds performed functions it deemed vital. Through their regulation of apprenticeship and journeymen they disciplined the labour force and thus promoted public order, and through their vigilance over production standards they protected consumers against fraud and maintained France's reputation for high-quality exports, supposedly the backbone of the French economy. Guilds were also a useful source of royal revenue, easily milked by special fees and taxes and by the creation of new masterships which the guilds would have to buy up at inflated prices to maintain their monopolies. Therefore in 1581, when the English government was firmly supporting 'projectors', the French king Henri III issued an edict requiring that all major trades in Paris and most other French cities be organized into guilds and that all craftsmen join them.[18]

The essence of the French guild system was restriction of production.[19] In theory each guild had the exclusive right to make and/or sell a single product, a right protected by its ability to search for and seize illegally made goods. To guarantee each master his fair share of the market, most guilds limited the number of shops a master could own and the number of apprentices and journeymen he could employ (usually to one of each), and forbade masters to sell goods made by others. Even in 1581 it was obvious that with such restrictions guild production could never furnish the needs of a city like Paris, and therefore guild production was supplemented in a number of ways, both legal and illegal. Legal supplements included the manufacture and sale of goods by holders of royal patents and privileges, for the government realized that such patents might encourage innovation and improve France's competitive position in world markets.[20] Also, goods manufactured elsewhere could be marketed in Paris by 'foreign' (non-Parisian) merchants during fairs, and throughout the year by the city's *merciers* (mercers), who numbered around 4,000 on the eve of the French Revolution and sold everything from furniture and fine art through clothing and dry goods to kitchen utensils and pins. Their crowded shops were the remote ancestors of the modern department store.[21] Further, some guilds allowed masters to import and sell goods manufac-tured abroad or in rural cottage industry so long as they paid customs duties on them and had them inspected to see that they conformed to guild production standards. Finally, Parisians could buy goods made by non-guild craftsmen working in the so-called 'privileged areas' of the city, places like the faubourg St Antoine, which, because they were under the jurisdiction of churches, hospitals and the like, were exempt from guild regulations. Customers had to go to these places to make their purchases, however, for craftsmen from the privileged areas were forbidden to sell their goods within Paris itself.[22]

In addition to these legal supplements to guild production, Paris's consumers were also supplied illegally. The city was infested with *chambrelans*, journeymen with no hope of ever gaining a mastership who made and sold goods illegally in their lodgings (hence their name).[23] And merchandise of all sorts was routinely smuggled into the city and sold illegally by the smugglers in inns and cabarets and by *colporteurs* (peddlers) on street corners and bridges.[24]

With these supplements the guild system was not so inflexible or restrictive as it might first appear. This has led some recent historians to propound a revisionist version of guild history which rejects the traditional notion that guild regulations were a brake on French economic development. The revisionists argue that our standard image of guild production as that of a lone master toiling away in a small shop aided only by his faithful apprentice and journeyman is wrong; that, instead, by the mid-eighteenth century many guilds were subcontracting systems in disguise or marketing monopolies for goods produced by rural industry, and that therefore the guild system was not necessarily incompatible with either commercial capitalism or economic expansion.[25] The first of these propositions, that production under the guild system was not confined solely to lone artisans in tiny workshops, is undoubtedly true; for example, Michael Sonenscher has shown that the Parisian luxury trades were organized in elaborate subcontracting systems that allowed the employment of many specialized artisans and the mobilization of large amounts of capital for the production of luxury objects.[26] But I do not think that the second proposition, that the guild system therefore did not restrict French economic development, necessarily follows from it. Instead I believe that the very existence of guild regulations made it difficult for manufacturers and retailers to respond adequately to the new consumer demand of the eighteenth century.

We can see this, I think, when we examine how the populuxe goods newly popular in the period were made and marketed. Let us begin with the stocking, something so cheap and so widely available that by the end of the eighteenth century it had ceased to be a populuxe good coveted for its aristocratic associations and became instead a mass-consumption item valued for its own usefulness. Even in 1725 over 60 per cent of the inventories in my sample contained stockings; by 1785 virtually all of them (97 per cent) did so. Not only did more people own stockings by the end of the century, they also owned more of them. In 1725, the average number of pairs of stockings per inventory was 2.5; by 1785 the figure had risen to 13.5 pairs.

How was this truly massive market supplied? From the start of its career as a desirable consumer item, the stocking was made and sold under the system which the English experience had shown best suited for supplying a large consumer market: the putting-out system. The career of the stocking as a necessary item of wearing apparel began with the invention of the knitted stocking early in the sixteenth century. Because knitting was a traditional craft already familiar to peasant women, the stocking industry from its inception took the form in both England and France of a rural cottage industry unregulated by guilds.[27] In France the only guild to become involved in stocking-making at this early stage was the guild of *bonnetiers* (bonnet-makers) in Paris, which in 1527 claimed the exclusive right to manufacture and distribute silk stockings for the luxury market in the city. The *bonnetiers* were not a craft guild but instead a guild of merchant-manufactures. They organized the production of stockings but did not make them themselves.[28]

Around 1600 the stocking industry was revolutionized by the invention of a machine to knit stockings, the stocking frame or *métier* (see Plate 11.1). The *métier* speeded up production and therefore cut costs; it also produced a more even and therefore more desirable product than hand-knitting.

In eighteenth-century France it was widely believed that a Frenchman had invented the *métier*. What supposedly befell him when he sought a royal *privilège* for it was thought to epitomize the harmful effects of guild exclusiveness on French commerce. Rebuffed in his quest for a royal monopoly because of pressure from the Parisian *bonnetiers*, who were said to have bribed Colbert's valet to obtain a favourable ruling from the royal Council of Commerce, the inventor supposedly sold his secret to the English and died in poverty.[29]

What actually happened illustrates not guild exclusiveness but rather the reluctance of the French government to sanction production outside the guild system. The stocking frame was in fact invented around 1589 by an Englishman, William Lee, who was granted monopoly privileges by the English crown.[30] The machine was brought to France in 1656 by Jean Hindret, a Protestant stockinger from Nîmes who had worked with one in London. He was rewarded by the French government with an exclusive right to use the invention, and he founded a factory in the Château Madrid outside Paris to manufacture stockings on the *métier*. Far from opposing this, the Parisian *bonnetiers* negotiated successfully with Hindret for a monopoly on marketing his wares. In 1666 Hindret's enterprise became a *société de commerce* and obtained a twenty-year monopoly patent from the crown.[31]

Just six years later, however, this patent was revoked. It seems that Colbert and the Council of Commerce had never been enthusiastic about Hindret's monopoly. They realized that one factory could not produce enough machine-knit stockings to satisfy French demand, but they were reluctant to sanction free exploitation of the *métier* for fear that it would ruin the hand-knit stocking industry, mainstay of so many rural families.[32] The ideal solution seemed to be a limited expansion of mechanized stocking production under guild control. In 1672 the government bought out Hindret's patent for 20,000 *livres* and bestowed the right of manufacturing machine-knit stockings on eighteen towns including Paris, where it was given to a new guild of *faiseurs de bas au métier*.[33] Existing Parisian guilds were placated by being given a share of the production process. The *faiseurs de bas* were to knit the stockings on *métiers* in their large workshops. The goods were then sent to the *bonnetiers* of Paris's faubourgs and privileged places to be hand-finished and dyed. Then they were brought back to the city and sold by the Parisian *bonnetiers*. Thus stocking production reverted back to something like its original form of a putting-out system: a system of subcontracting now under guild control, with different guilds responsible for different parts of the production process.

This system never worked as it was supposed to, however. From the first, the potential profits of so lucrative an industry tempted the corporations to trespass on each other's privileges. The *bonnetiers* of the faubourgs illegally acquired *métiers* and manufactured as well as finished stockings; they also illegally sold them in Paris.[34] Meanwhile the Parisian *bonnetiers* also illegally made stockings on *métiers*, and they illegally sold them through street-corner peddling and by opening second shops, both practices forbidden to them by guild statutes.[35] And the *faiseurs de bas* illegally expanded production by renting out *métiers* to artisans in the privileged areas; the latter of course began producing stockings for themselves as well as for their principals and smuggling the illegally made goods into Paris to sell.[36] The government reacted to all this with its usual response to guild conflicts and illegalities: it tried to rationalize the system by uniting the battling guilds and legalizing the illegal practices. In 1716 the *bonnetiers* of Paris and those of the faubourgs were united into one guild. Four years later the *faiseurs de bas au métier* were given permission to farm out work in the privileged areas. And finally, in 1723, this guild was united with the newly enlarged *bonnetiers*.[37] Thus from 1723 until the restructuring of the Parisian guilds after their attempted abolition in 1776, the corporation of *bonnetiers* formed an umbrella organization which enjoyed, in theory at least, a monopoly of the production and marketing of stockings in Paris. The typical Parisian *bonnetier* of the period was a merchant manufacturer who not only organized the production of stockings in a subcontracting system, but also sold both those and others produced elsewhere at wholesale and retail. This should have been very lucrative, and in fact the *bonnetiers* were probably the fastest-growing guild in eighteenth-century Paris, increasing their membership from eighty-eight masters in 1715 to between five and six hundred in 1776.[38] Unfortunately the *bonnetiers* also enjoyed one of the highest rates of bankruptcy of all the Parisian guilds.[39] For in practice their theoretical monopoly of the stocking industry amounted to little, and it was very difficult to succeed as a *bonnetier*.

On the production side, costs were high. *Métiers* were expensive; one bankrupt stockinger, Jean François Tulout, had over 2,000 *livres* invested in them.[40] Labour was also costly. Workers in the stocking industry were among the best organized and highest paid in Paris. They struck for higher wages in 1724 and 1736, and for years they maintained an illegal journeyman's association disguised as a confraternity attached to the Church of St Paul on the rue St Antoine.[41] The *bonnetiers* were at the mercy of their labour force because it was so easy for Parisian stocking-makers to leave their employers, move to the privileged areas, and establish workshops of their own, producing stockings both for their former employers on account and for themselves. The latter, which they sold openly in the privileged areas and clandestinely in the rest of Paris, cut deeply into the market for the *bonnetiers*' legally produced wares. This market was further reduced when, in 1754, the royal government, in the first of a series of free trade edicts which would culminate in the attempted abolition of the guilds in 1776, legalized the production of stockings on *métiers* throughout France.[42] The *bonnetiers*' guild saw a rash of bankruptcies in the late 1750s as its members tried to adjust to the new market conditions.[43]

Many did so by abandoning stocking production and concentrating on retailing. Here, too, however, the *bonnetiers*' supposed monopoly was less useful than it looked. Paris was honey-combed with a vast distribution network which facilitated the illegal sale of stockings. As a royal edict of 1730 noted, cheap stockings were commonly peddled in cafes, cabarets, inns and other public places, by *chambrelans*, workers from the privileged areas, smugglers who brought stockings into Paris without paying the custom duties and professional *colporteurs* like 21-year-old Jean Baptiste Ribotte, who supported himself and his widowed mother by selling not only stockings but also pinchbeck buckles, cheap swords and clandestine literature.[44] Probably most of Paris's lower-class consumers bought their stockings from such sources, for illegally sold stockings were cheaper than the cheapest hose from Nîmes and other mass production centres sold in *bonnetiers*' shops, because the *bonnetiers* had to pay custom duties on their goods. Thus the *bonnetiers* had trouble retaining the lower-class stocking market. They also found it difficult to sell to the upper-class consumer. To retain upscale customers once stockings were no longer status symbols, *bonnetiers* had to develop new marketing techniques to lure elite consumers for whom shopping was becoming an enjoyable leisure-time activity. This meant that a *bonnetier* needed an elegantly and therefore expensively appointed shop, a huge inventory (Pierre Garnier, a *bonnetier* on the rue St Honoré in 1771, stocked 5,871 items, including 3,994 pairs of hose) and even a budget for advertising in the new merchants' almanacs and periodical press.[45] None the less, this seems to have been the direction in which most successful *bonnetiers* were moving. This is shown by the corporation's reaction to the restructuring of the guilds in 1776. Most Parisian guilds protested vehemently when the royal government tried to abolish them in February 1776, and demanded not just their traditional monopolies and privileges but new ones as well when the corporate system was restored and restructured in August of the same year.[46] The *bonnetiers* did not. Instead, they protested when, in the August edict, they were joined with the furriers and hatters: they said they had no desire to master the complicated production processes that furs, and especially hats, entailed.[47] What they wanted was rather to be allowed to get out of manufacturing altogether and become exclusively merchants, and they demanded the right, like that of the *merciers*, to sell almost anything in their shops.[48] In effect, they opted for a free trade economy.

Of all of Paris's populuxe industries, the stocking industry comes closest to supporting the revisionist version of guild history. The *bonnetiers* were indeed, as the revisionists would have it, merchant manufacturers presiding over a subcontracting system of production, not lone artisans painstakingly crafting a product from start to finish in their workshops. 'Guild control' over the industry indeed involved nothing more than the *bonnetiers*' supposed monopoly over the production and sale of stockings in the city. And because of its relatively simple and flexible organization, the industry was able to respond adequately to the vast increase in consumer demand for stockings in the last half of the eighteenth century. Yet even in the stocking industry there are indications that the revisionist view is wrong. After all, the French government sanctioned the relatively simple and flexible organization of the industry only after a more complex system, conforming much more closely to its notion of what guild-controlled production should be, had been tried and had failed, giving rise to numerous conflicts and illegalities. Further, these illegalities persisted even after the system was simplified. Indeed, the stocking industry could respond to the new consumer demand only because illegal production and marketing networks were there to service the lower-class consumer. Finally, by the 1770s, even the chief beneficiaries of guild control of the industry, the *bonnetiers*, seem to have been dissatisfied with it and willing to chance the hazards of a free trade economy. So even this most favourable example points up the inadequacies of the revisionist view of the guilds.

These inadequacies become more apparent when we examine other populuxe industries more firmly under guild control. Take for example that humble rainy-day necessity, the umbrella. The umbrella's career as an item of populuxe consumption began in 1705, when the modern small and lightweight folding umbrella was invented by one Marius, a *maître boursier* (master purse-maker) with a shop in the faubourg St Honoré.[49] Umbrellas and parasols had of course existed for centuries before this, but not as common consumer goods. Apparently originating in China, the parasol had been imported to France and had become fashionable at court by the early seventeenth century. As was usual with new products, several guilds competed for the rights to it. The *tourneurs* (turners) claimed it on the grounds that umbrella handles had to be turned on a lathe like the other things they made, while the *boursiers* argued that they should have it because attaching the fabric of the umbrella to its frame was similar to their lining of purses. The *peigneurs-tabletiers* (comb-makers and inlayers) also put in a claim, although they could not argue that the umbrellas resembled anything they made.[50] None of these guilds vigorously pressed its claim, however, for in the seventeenth century the commercial prospects of the umbrella were not inviting. Permanently open umbrellas and parasols were heavy and clumsy to carry; both a parasol and its bearer might be blown away in a high wind. And even folding umbrellas were large and heavy. Therefore they were purchased only by those with servants to carry them. Their major function was that of status symbol.

All this changed with Marius's invention of the small, lightweight folding umbrella. As Marius shrewdly advertised, his umbrellas 'weigh only 5 or 6 ounces' ('ne pesent que 5 à 6 onces') and 'take up no more space than a small pen-case' ('ne tiennent pas plus de place qu'une petite Escritoire') (see Plate 11.3). Thus their potential market was virtually unlimited. To exploit it, Marius obtained a royal patent for the exclusive right to manufacture folding umbrellas in 1710.[51] But when this expired in 1715, the government, always anxious to bring all manufacturing under guild control, refused to renew it. Therefore the right to make folding umbrellas reverted to the three guilds with previous claims on the parasol. These corporations fought over the new product in competing lawsuits stretching over decades. When these were finally settled in the 1760s, the *tourneurs* had gained the rights to make umbrella frames and to sell finished umbrellas, while the *boursiers* could attach the fabric covering and also sell the finished product.[52] Thus umbrellas were to be produced by a rather simple subcontracting system, with the *boursiers* buying frames from the *tourneurs*, attaching fabric to them, and selling the finished product both back to the *tourneurs* and to the public.

The real victor in the legal battles over the umbrella, however, was the guild whose claim to it was the most doubtful, the *peigneurs-tabletiers*. They won the rights both to make umbrella frames and to attach the fabric, as well as the right to sell the finished product.[53] Almost ruined when cheap English combs had swept the market for their primary product early in the sixteenth century, the comb-makers had long been conscious of the potential of the new consumer market. During the eighteenth century they laid claim to almost every new populuxe item that caught the public fancy: umbrellas, canes, snuffboxes, fans, game boards, cheap crucifixes and rosaries and musical instruments.[54] They pressed these claims in lawsuits opposing the often more legitimate pretensions of other guilds. As Michael Sonenscher has recently pointed out, courts with jurisdiction over the crafts were the favoured arena for trade disputes during the Old Regime. As Sonenscher put it, for journeymen 'the "typical form of protest" . . . was neither the food riot nor the strike, but . . . the lawsuit'.[55] For master craftsmen too, lawsuits were the instrument of choice in trade disputes. The classic tactic of aggressive guilds like the comb-makers was to lay claim to a desirable product in their guild statutes and then to go to court to defend this 'right' against rival guilds. In 1739 the *peigneurs-tabletiers* produced new statutes embodying their claims to the populuxe items listed above. They then successfully defended these claims against challenges from no less than eleven other Parisian corporations.[56]

Apart from their judicial skills, the *peigneurs-tabletiers*, who numbered about 300 in the 1760s,[57] owed their success in the populuxe market to their production and sales methods.

Like the *bonnetiers*, they were in essence a subcontracting system in guild disguise. Because the guild claimed so many different goods, no one master had the skills necessary to make them all. Therefore master *peigneurs-tabletiers* tended to specialize in one product – snuff-boxes, umbrellas or whatever – which they sold both wholesale to *merciers* and to their fellow master comb-makers and retail to the public at large. For example, Julien Augustin Guillot seems to have specialized in umbrella making. The records of his bankruptcy in 1787 reveal that he was owed money for his goods by *merciers* in Orléans, Angers and Douay, as well as by various fellow comb-makers in Paris. They also show that in his own shop he stocked, besides umbrellas, canes, fans and snuffboxes which he had purchased from his fellow guild-masters.[58] These goods had been produced in a subcontracting system. Most master *peigneurs* made as well as sold their specialty product. For example, Jean Antoine Bonhomme, a comb-maker who seems to have actually specialized in combs, had almost 8,000 *livres* worth of tools and unfinished merchandise in his shop when he declared bankruptcy in 1748.[59] Such masters found it difficult to expand production because the statutes of their guild forbade them to employ more than one apprentice or journeyman.[60] Therefore they often put out work on consignment with *chambrelans* and artisans in the privileged areas and even with their fellow masters. When his business failed in 1785, *maître et marchand tabletier* Jean-Baptiste Aubin had over 900 *livres* worth of goods out on consignment with 'Srs. Fortin, Renard and other workers'.[61] *Maître-tabletier* Delavigne housed a fellow master, Sr François Bourette, who worked on consignment for him and six other master comb-makers.[62]

As with the stocking industry, this legal subcontracting system spawned an illegal one as well, for the *chambrelans* and artisans in the privileged areas could not resist producing goods for themselves as well as for the masters who hired them. Often they also illegally sold the goods they made. In 1776, for example, the *chambrelan compagnon-tabletier* Pavant Millerot was arrested while trying to sell twenty-two dozen papier-maché snuffboxes on the rue du Temple, and in the same year Mathieu Joseph Colin, a *tabletier* from the privileged faubourg St Martin, was caught illegally peddling canes and rolling pins within Paris itself.[63] If they did not sell their goods themselves, the *chambrelans* and artisans of the privileged areas often disposed of them to professional *colporteurs* like Jean Fort, nicknamed 'L'Article', described by the police who arrested him in 1774 as 'a notorious peddler of parasols'.[64] Populuxe goods like umbrellas and snuffboxes were ideal stock for peddlers: they were small, lightweight, cheap and coveted. In fact, records of arrests for illegal peddling show that populuxe items like parasols came right behind cheap tinware and cloth as the favourite stock of Paris's illegal *colporteurs*.[65] As with stockings, these illegal sources probably supplied most of the lower-class consumer market for populuxe goods like umbrellas in eighteenth-century Paris, severely restricting the market for goods legally produced and sold by the *peigneurs* and other guildsmen. In 1761 the *peigneurs* complained bitterly to the police: how could they, hampered by guild restrictions on the production and sale of their products, possibly compete with the workshops in the privileged areas, which could expand production as they pleased (the guild stated that the thirty-eight shops making their goods in the faubourg St Antoine employed over 200 workers) and sell what they made throughout the city with impunity?[66]

As had happened with the stocking, once the umbrella ceased to be a status symbol and became a populuxe good widely owned by the lower classes, those who sold it had to lure elite consumers with modern advertising and luxuriously decorated shops. Many of these were owned by *boursiers*, who appear often in the 1770s and 1780s to have abandoned their traditional specialization in purses, and indeed their productive functions in general, and begun calling themselves *marchands de parasols* (parasol-sellers) and concentrating on selling umbrellas, canes and other accessories of the fashionable life in well-appointed shops. An example is M. Fermin Jerôme Chanet, whose shop in 1772 had over 1,200 *livres* worth of parasols and 500 *livres* worth of perfumes, but only 200 *livres* worth of purses.[67] Another is Etienne Gabriel Noguette, who numbered the Duc de Lauzun, the Prince de Conti and the Comte de Boufflers among the customers of his store on the fashionable rue Dauphine, on which he had lavished 5,000 *livres* worth of elegant fittings plus a 2,000 *livre* bribe to the landlord to renew his lease.[68]

Fashionable customers might also buy umbrellas in the shops of *marchands de modes*, the most innovative retailers of eighteenth-century Paris. *Marchands de modes* were originally *merciers* – or often their wives – who sold laces, ribbons and other trimming for clothes.[69] (See Plate 11.7 for the interior of a shop of a *marchand de modes* in the 1730s.) By the last decades of the Old Regime, however, they had evolved in two different directions. Some *marchands de modes* had begun attaching to gowns the trimming they sold, and thereby became the ancestors of the famous French *couturiers* (dress designers) of the nineteenth and twentieth centuries. For in a period when basic dress silhouettes changed only slowly, a gown's trimming rather than its cut made it fashionable and distinctive. Rose Bertin, Marie Antoinette's famous dressmaker, was a *marchande de modes*, not a *couturière*.[70] Paris had a guild of *couturières* (one of the few all female guilds), which had the right to cut and sew women's clothes. But its members catered to the middle and lower classes and were much less fashionable and prosperous than the *marchands de modes*.[71]

Not all *marchands de modes* became dress designers, however. Some concentrated on retailing, adding umbrellas, snuffboxes and other fashionable accessories to their traditional stock of ribbons and laces. The best-known of this type of *marchand de modes* was the proprietor of Le Petit Dunkerque, a shop on the itinerary of every well-heeled tourist in Paris in the 1780s. A visiting Englishwoman, Hester Lynch Piozzi, described it as 'a Great Toy Shop' for adults.[72] It was famous for its elegant décor; one enterprising perfumer advertised that his shop was 'as extravagantly decorated as Le Petit Dunkerque and should be seen by visitors'. The store's immense inventory and its policy of selling at fixed prices clearly marked on the merchandise rather than the traditional haggling made it a precursor of the retailing revolution of the nineteenth century.[73] The proprietor of Le Petit Dunkerque also pioneered even more modern retailing methods. He illegally owned a chain of stores, and he managed to convince the fashionable public that it was so important to own something from his shops that, as with today's designer jeans, the label on his goods was more important to his customers than the products themselves.

The history of the production and marketing of the umbrella in eighteenth-century Paris shows striking parallels to that of the stocking. Like stockings, umbrellas were manufactured in a subcontracting system. And as with stockings, the legal production network spawned an illegal one as well, and the latter probably produced most of the goods for the new populuxe market. Again like stockings, umbrellas were sold through a two-tiered system of marketing, with the populuxe consumer probably buying from illegal peddlers while upmarket customers made their purchases in elegantly appointed shops which were evolving towards stocking a variety of goods. But because umbrellas were more firmly under guild control for a longer period of time than stockings, their production and marketing systems were necessarily more complex. Umbrellas were produced by two parallel legal subcontracting systems (that of turners plus the purse-makers and that of the *peigneurs*), not one like the stocking, and they were sold in two different kinds of shops, those of the *boursiers* and those of the *marchands de modes*. Umbrella production also entailed more conflicts between guilds than did stocking production; few guilds spent as much time or money in court as the *peigneurs*. All this, I would argue, prevented the umbrella industry from responding as effectively as the stocking industry to the new consumer demand of the late eighteenth century. Admittedly umbrellas are more complicated and costly to make than stockings, and admittedly even today they are less a necessity of daily life. Yet I would suggest that at least part of the reason why umbrellas showed up in only 31 per cent of my inventories while stockings were present in 97 per cent is that the guild regulation of the umbrella industry inhibited its expansion.

That guild regulation could restrict an industry's ability to respond to consumer demand is further illustrated by the history of the final populuxe good we will examine, the fan. Unlike stockings and umbrellas, fans were never made and sold under a monopoly patent; instead they were always under guild control. That worked well when fans were luxury items, but when they became populuxe goods guild control gave them production and marketing systems truly Byzantine in complexity and so riddled with illegalities that whole neighbourhoods in Paris where fans were made and sold lived outside the law.

Like the umbrella, the fan seems to have been a Chinese invention, first imported into France in the fifteenth century. Mention of fans in Parisian guild statutes dates from 1511, when the right to make frames for fans was claimed by the *peigneurs-tabletiers*, always alert for new and potentially popular consumer goods.[74] In 1594 the right to make the fan's fabric mounting and attach it to the frame was claimed by the corporation of leather gilders, for in the sixteenth century leather was often used as a mounting for fans.[75]

This rather simple division of labour prevailed until the 1670s, when fans became very fashionable at court. Their new popularity prompted sixty master leather-gilders to break away from the old corporation and found a new guild of 'maîtres éventaillistes, faiseurs et compositeurs d'éventails' ('master fan-makers, manufacturers and assemblers of fans'). In its original statutes of 1677 the new guild claimed the sole right to 'make and attach all the parts necessary for fans, and to sell and market the finished fans in their shops'.[76] Of course this attempted monopoly did not go unchallenged. The *peigneurs-tabletiers* went to court to defend their traditional right to make fan frames, the guild of master painters and sculptors claimed the exclusive right to decorate fans and the *merciers* sought a monopoly on their sale.[77] The glove-makers–perfumers also tried to get a piece of the action, arguing that they had always made items associated with the hand, and adding plaintively that they needed a new product because their traditional goods, gloves and perfumes, were no longer selling well. Cloth gloves were displacing the leather ones they made and sold, and the market for perfume was shrinking as the habit of frequent bathing spread.[78] These conflicting claims gave rise to the usual interminable rounds of lawsuits, and the royal government reacted in its usual fashion: it urged the battling corporations to merge. The union of the *peigneurs-tabletiers* with the fan-makers was proposed in 1727 but did not come about, apparently because the *peigneurs* feared they would have to stop making all their other goods if they merged with the fan-makers.[79]

When all the lawsuits were finally settled in the 1730s, the *peigneurs-tabletiers* emerged with their traditional monopoly on the manufacture of fan frames, the painters gained a monopoly on the painting of fan mountings, the *éventaillistes* had the privilege of manufacturing the mountings and attaching them to their frames, while the *merciers* (or, more specifically, the *marchands de modes*) monopolized the sale of the finished product. The claims of the glove-makers were rejected.[80] This division of labour among the competing guilds meant that fans, like stockings and umbrellas, were manufactured in a guild-controlled subcontracting system, in this case organized by the master fan-makers. In theory, they bought fan frames from the *peigneurs* and placed the mounting on them. Then they sent them to the master painters to be decorated. When that was done, they sold the finished fans wholesale to the *marchands de modes*, who sold them retail to the public.

But this was only in theory. In practice all the guilds involved in fan-making routinely trespassed on each other's prerogatives. In court cases from the mid-eighteenth century we find *éventaillistes* illegally manufacturing fan frames, *peigneurs-tabletiers* illegally painting, mounting and assembling fans, *merciers* illegally making fans and *peintres* (painters) illegally mounting them.[81] We also find masters of all these guilds employing *chambrelans* to increase both their legal and illegal production in every step of the process. In fact, the use of *chambrelans* (or rather *chambrelanes*, for most workers in the fan trade were women) was so widespread that whole areas of the city, like the neighbourhood around the rue Quincampoix where the *éventaillistes'* guild had its headquarters, were dominated by colonies of fan-makers with their own unique subculture. In the 1770s, for example, twenty-four male and female fan-makers lived together on the rue Quincampoix and practised free love in a sort of commune headed by a Freemason.[82] Naturally these *chambrelans* produced for themselves as well as for the masters who hired them, and, equally naturally, the illegally produced items were illegally peddled to a public hungry for populuxe goods. Unlike stockings and umbrellas, fans were usually sold by women, often the wives of the artisans involved in the various steps of the production process. An example is the wife of M. Dourdilly, a master painter, who was arrested in 1739 with forty-two finished fans and three fan frames that she was trying to sell on the Pont-au-Change.[83] M. Dourdilly obviously had been illegally making fan frames and fans as well as legally painting them, and his wife was disposing of the illicit goods. Fans were often peddled outside churches, ideal locations to exploit a largely female market.[84] As with stockings and umbrellas, illegal peddling probably supplied most of the populuxe market for fans, while upmarket consumers made their purchases in shops like Le Petit Dunkerque or, if they wanted something truly unique, ordered custom-made fans. In 1786 the Baronne d'Oberkirch was given a gift by her childhood friend, the Grand Duchess Marie of Russia. It was a custom-made fan of mother of pearl encrusted with gold and enamel and decorated with an exquisitely painted scene of a *fête* at the court of Louis XIV. The two ladies had quite an adventure visiting the 'hovel' where the fan's maker, a man named Méré, lived, to place the order. The Baronne was amazed that Méré refused to sign the fan, for she thought him as talented a painter as Boucher or Watteau. We, who suspect that Méré was a *chambrelan* painter illegally making and selling fans, need not be so surprised.[85]

We can catch further glimpses of the shadowy world of illegal fan production through the police records on *maître éventailliste* Jean Baptiste Batouflet, preserved among the archives of the Bastille in the Bibliothèque d'Arsenal.[86] In 1741 Batouflet was denounced to the police by his wife for carrying on a 'criminal' and 'ruinous' affair with one of his employees, the 24-year-old widow of Charles Antoine Godet, a master painter. Mme Batouflet herself had brought the pair together. Like many wives of master artisans, she ran her own business in a separate but related branch of her husband's trade: she was a fan painter. But she did not have a mastership in the *peintre*'s guild. Therefore she invited the widow Godet, who had inherited her husband's mastership, to live with her; this would legalize her position. Both women worked for various master fan-makers including M. Batouflet, who was very impressed with Mme Godet's talents. According to his wife, M. Batouflet often 'shut himself up alone with Mme Godet, under the pretext of instructing her in work of a new fashion of which he was the inventor and which he wanted to keep secret'. (M. Batouflet obviously was interested in exploiting the new consumer market.) The jealous Mme Batouflet soon sent the young widow away, refusing to pay her for her work. M. Batouflet then took to wife-beating. He also set up his mistress in a series of apartments and lavished all his profits on her.

This, at any rate, was what Mme Batouflet told the police. Her husband and the widow Godet told different stories. Batouflet produced a series of testimonials from *maîtres peigneurs*, *maîtres peintres* and fellow *maîtres éventaillistes* stating that he was a 'perfect *honnête homme* of irreproachable and very regular conduct'. (Mme Batouflet dismissed these as lies by 'workers who dare not defend her because they work for him'.) Mme Godet also produced testimonials from the many landlords, neighbours and employers (master *éventaillistes*, *peigneurs*, *peintres* and even another *peintresse sans qualité* who, like Mme Batouflet, hired the widow to legalize her position) she had encountered since Mme Batouflet turned her out. These paint a grim picture of the life of a *chambrelane* fan worker. Godet's landlords, who frequently invaded her room looking for illegal lodgers (one stated that his wife did that 'two or three times a day') always found her not entertaining a rich lover but instead 'alone at her work'. Neighbours testified that she worked 'from morning to night' but still remained in 'misery'. When work was lacking they loaned her money; when it was plentiful, they helped her do it. (One neighbour, a button-maker, stated that her sister often 'worked with Mme Godet in her room'.) All agreed that the widow was an 'honest, hard-working woman'.

Faced with these contradictory stories, police *commissaire* Ginestre sent agents to check up on the testimony for both sides 'under the pretext of looking for fans to buy'. Their findings supported M. Batouflet and Mme Godet. The former indeed appeared to be an '*honnête homme*' and the latter a '*femme très sage et rangée*, who works very hard'. Therefore Ginestre ordered M. Batouflet to stop beating his wife and Mme Batouflet to stop impugning the honour of the widow Godet.

This episode sheds much light on the manufacture of fans and its attendant illegalities. It shows, for example, the subcontracting organization of the industry: Mme Batouflet described the various master *peigneurs* and *peintres* who testified for her husband as his workers and dependents. It shows, too, how widespread illegal putting-out with *chambrelans* was: Mme Godet worked for master *peigneurs* and *peintres*, who legally could not hire her, as well as for the master fan-makers who legally could, and she in turn subcontracted work out to others, for example when she hired the button-maker's sister to help her finish an order. It shows, too, that masterships were often illegally 'borrowed', and that fans were illegally sold at every step of the production process. Police spies approached both the guildsmen who testified for Batouflet and Mme Godet's neighbours under the pretext of looking for fans to buy. This story also shows that public officials often ignored such illegalities, for nothing in the records indicates that any of the unlawful acts uncovered during the Batouflet investigation was ever prosecuted. Such illegalities were so widespread that the government could scarcely begin to stamp them out.

This was a major reason why the royal government tried to abolish the guilds in 1776. In preparation for their abolition, the finance minister, Turgot, asked his protégé, Albert, the Lieutenant-General of Police for Paris, to write a *mémoire* that could be shown to the king.[87] In it, Albert made the usual free-trade arguments: guild monopolies meant time and money wasted in lawsuits (he estimated that the guilds spent over 400,000 *livres* per year in attorneys' fees[88]), and kept prices high and therefore limited the market for French goods.

But as a policeman he also pointed out the dangers to the state when guild regulations were routinely flouted. Was it not harmful to public order that a poor woman trying to support herself as a *chambrelane* embroiderer could do so only illegally, and that a poor man trying to clothe his family found the cheapest stockings only on the black market? Would not such widespread lawbreaking make people contemptuous of their government?[89] We might wonder if he didn't underestimate the danger, for might not the lack of respect Parisians showed for their government in the early days of the Revolution be due at least in part to the fact that for decades before 1789 they had often been forced to break the law and patronize illegal outlets for the new consumer goods they increasingly craved?

What had caused this deplorable situation? Albert traced the difficulties of the guild system to the new rise in consumer demand in the eighteenth century. 'The taste of the consumer', he wrote, is 'the first law' of commerce. 'To sell goods one must conform to it; and it does not pay attention to guild regulations.' The dynamic, ever-expanding, ever-changing consumer market, with its 'new fashions, new manufacturing processes, new tastes', could be satisfied only by illegal production and sale outside guild regulation.[90]

In his recognition of both the new consumer market of the eighteenth century and the pressures this placed on a guild-regulated economy, Albert was wiser than those later historians who deny that France had a consumer revolution in the eighteenth century and that guild regulations restricted French production. Here I have tried to show, first, that eighteenth-century France saw, at least in Paris, a new middle and lower-class market for consumer goods, especially populuxe items; and second, that these goods were produced and marketed similarly, that is, they were manufactured in subcontracting systems of varying complexity and sold in two-tiered marketing systems, with the populuxe market furnished by peddling and the upper-class market by luxuriously appointed shops carrying a variety of goods; and, third, that because of guild regulations, this system was riddled with distortions, conflicts and illegalities that probably restricted its expansion. When goods like the fan became populuxe instead of luxury items, the elaborate guild-controlled subcontracting systems which had facilitated the efficient production and marketing of luxury objects hindered entrepreneurs from responding to the demand of the new populuxe market. This was an important factor behind the attempted abolition of the guilds in 1776.

Although the royal government was forced to restore the guilds later in the same year, that was not a simple return to the *status quo ante*.[91] Instead, production and marketing of populuxe goods was simplified and clarified. The number of guilds in Paris was reduced from over 200 to 44, usually by combining those which had before competed in producing the same product. For example, in 1776 the *peigneurs* were finally merged with the fan-makers. The servicing of the populuxe market was furthered by allowing the artisans of the privileged areas to sell their goods freely in Paris, and by the protection of peddling against a determined effort by shopkeepers to eradicate it.[92] And the evolution of the luxury shop for the upscale market was hastened when the *marchands de mode* were made into a separate guild and encouraged to continue their innovations in retailing.[93] The system was further clarified and simplified when the guilds were finally abolished completely, to general public acclaim, in 1791.[94] But it remained unchanged in its essentials until the spread of factory production and the rise of the department store began to transform the French economy in the 1850s. Therefore I would argue that the century from approximately 1750 to 1850 should be seen as a distinct period in French economic history – a period when the French economy was largely shaped by a new consumer demand, much of it centred in the populuxe market.

Notes

1   Neil McKendrick, John Brewer and J. H. Plumb, *The Birth of a Consumer Society: The Commercialization of Eighteenth-Century England* (Bloomington and London, 1982).

2   Harold Perkin, *The Origins of Modern English Society* (London, 1969), 91.

3   The argument that the persistence of luxury consumption prolonged the existence of small-scale handicraft production in France and retarded the spread of the factory system is made explicitly in Whitney Walton, 'To triumph before feminine taste: bourgeois women's consumption and hand methods of production in mid-nineteenth century Paris', *Business History Review*, lx (winter 1986), 541–63, and it is implicit in such standard works on nineteenth-century French economic history as Patrick O'Brien and Caglar Keyder, *Economic Growth in Britain and France 1780–1914: Two Paths to the Twentieth Century* (London, 1978), and in works on consumption in nineteenth-century France like Rosalind H. Williams, *Dream Worlds: Mass Consumption in Late Nineteenth-Century France* (Berkeley, 1982); Michael Miller, *The Bon Marché: Bourgeois Culture and the Department Store, 1869–1920* (Princeton, 1981); and Philip G. Nord, *Paris Shopkeepers and the Politics of Resentment* (Princeton, 1986).

4   *The French Journals of Mrs. Thrale and Dr. Johnson*, ed. Moses Tyson and Henry Guppy (Manchester, 1932), 148.

5   *Le Journal de Mme. Cradock: Voyage en France (1783–1786)*, tr. O. Delphin Balleyguier (Paris, 1896), 21.

6   I have borrowed the word 'populuxe' from Thomas Hine, *Populuxe* (New York, 1986), a study of consumption patterns in America in the 1950s. My use of the term differs slightly from his. Hine coined the word to refer to the modern American consumer's desire for 'opulent options added to utilitarian objects', while I use it to refer to a simple desire for cheap copies of luxury goods.

7   The *coutume de Paris* specified that when one of the spouses died, the couple's property was to be inventoried and divided. The surviving spouse was entitled to half of it; the other half went to the heirs of the deceased. The clearest explanation of the provisions of the *coutume de Paris* is in Barbara Diefendorf, *Paris City Councillors in the Sixteenth Century* (Princeton, 1983), 222–5.

8   For the social composition of the neighbourhood of the rue St Honoré see David Garrioch, *Neighbourhood and Community in Paris, 1740–1790* (Cambridge, 1986), 232–6; 253–4.

9   Another factor working against the biasing of my group of inventories is the fact that, although the majority of the clients of my notaries lived in the immediate vicinity of the rue St Honoré, not all did. In fact, my group includes inventories from all areas of the city. And my findings roughly parallel those of Daniel Roche, who with a far larger sample of inventories drawn from all districts of the city also found drastic changes in the consumption habits of the lower classes. See Daniel Roche, *The People of Paris*, tr. Marie Evans (Berkeley, 1987), 127–94.

10 Whether England did indeed experience its consumer revolution sixty years before one occurred in France deserves further investigation. Current research suggests that this is so. (Carole Shammas, 'The domestic environment in early modern England and America', *Journal of Social History*, xiv (1980), 1–24; Margaret Spufford, *The Great Reclothing of Rural England: Petty Chapmen and Their Wares in the Seventeenth Century* (London, 1984); Lorna Weatherill, *Consumer Behaviour and Material Culture in Britain, 1660–1760* (London and New York, 1988), and idem, 'Patterns of consumption in Britain, c. 1660–1760: problems and sources', unpublished paper, Clark Library Seminars, Oct. 1988; Peter Earle, 'The domestic possessions of the London middle classes, 1665–1720', unpublished paper, Clark Library Seminars, Oct. 1988.) But this may simply reflect the fact that historians working with English inventories tend to stop their researches before the middle of the eighteenth century because the quality of the inventories deteriorates after that date (Carole Shammas, personal communication, May 1986). Certainly the evidence about marketing techniques for consumer goods gathered by the authors of *The Birth of a Consumer Society* suggests that the late eighteenth century saw further drastic changes in English consumption patterns. On the other hand, research

into French inventories has been largely confined to the eighteenth century, but current investigations of sixteenth- and seventeenth-century inventories by *maîtrise* students under the direction of Micheline Baulant and Françoise Piponier might reveal important changes in French consumption patterns in earlier periods. None the less, it does seem likely that the English pioneered the consumer society in the late seventeenth century, and that it appeared in France about fifty years later.

11   These totals include only clothing, household goods and other personal possessions, not landed property, *rentes* or other types of financial holdings.

12   Lorna Weatherill has recently rightly cautioned against taking the presence of aristocratic luxuries in middle- and lower-class inventories as a sign that these classes desired to emulate their social betters. 'There is no evidence that most people of middle rank wanted to be like the gentry, although they may have wanted the goods for their own purposes' (Weatherill, 'Patterns of consumption', 20). For an opposing argument see Daniel Roche, *La Culture des apparenies: une histoire du vêtement, XVIIe–XVIIIe sièctes* (Paris, 1989), 87–118.

13   This may not be true. To my knowledge no one has actually looked for populuxe items in English inventories.

14   Louise Godard de Donville, *Signification de la mode sous Louis XIII* (Aix-en-Provence, 1976), 55–8.

15   For sumptuary legislation in France see Philippe Perrot, *Les Dessus et les dessous de la bourgeoisie: une histoire du vêtement au XIXe siècle* (Paris, 1981), 35, n. 14; and Johanna Moyer, 'The call of a return to sumptuary legislation during the French Revolution', unpublished paper, Western Society for French History, 1989.

16   Joan Thirsk, *Economic Policy and Projects: The Development of a Consumer Society in Early Modern England* (Oxford, 1978); Spufford, *Great Reclothing*.

17   Further research on English guilds is badly needed. At present J. R. Kellett, 'The breakdown of guild and corporation control over the handicraft and retail trade in London', *Economic History Review*, x, 3 (April 1958), 381–94, remains the most useful and suggestive work.

18   For the text of the edict see Bibliothèque Nationale (hereafter B.N.) 8° Z Le Senne 4240, *Statuts de la communauté des marchands Gantiers et Poudriers* (Paris, 1772), 67ff.

19   The classic description of the guild system is Emile Coornaert, *Les Corporations en France avant 1789* (Paris, 1968). See also Etienne Martin Saint-Leon, *Histoire des corporations de métiers depuis leurs origines jusqu'à leur suppression en 1791* (Paris, 1922); François Olivier-Martin, *L'Organization corporative de la France d'Ancien Régime* (Paris, 1939); and William H. Sewell, *Work and Revolution in France* (Cambridge, 1980).

20   For government policy on the granting of patents see Thomas J. Schaeper, *The French Council of Commerce, 1700–1715: A Study in Mercantilism after Colbert* (Columbus, 1983), 168–73.

21   The estimate of the number of *merciers* comes from B.N., Collection Joly de Fleury 1728, Communautés des arts et metiers, fol. 135, Estat des differens négoces qui composent le corps de la mercerie. For what they sold see B.N. 4° Z Le Senne 974, *Statuts, ordonnances et règlements des corps des Marchands Merciers . . .* (Paris, 1694). *Merciers* were supposedly only retailers. To protect guild monopolies they were forbidden to manufacture what they sold, although they were allowed to 'refresh' and trim items before sale, rights they often used to cover illicit manufacturing.

22   Other privileged areas included the Louvre, the Gobelins, La Trinité, the Temple, St Jean de Latran, St Germain des Près, St Denis de la Chartre, the faubourg St Martin and the Quinze-Vingts. (B. N. Joly de Fleury 2542, Papiers d'Espagnac, II, fol. 154, Mémoire concernant les lieux privilégiés de Paris.) For descriptions of the organization of work in the privileged areas see Steven Kaplan, 'Les corporations, les "faux ouvriers" et le faubourg St. Antoine au XVIII siècle', *Annales E.S.C.*, xliii, 2 (mars–avril 1988), 353–78; and Raymonde Monnier, *Le faubourg Saint Antoine (1789–1817)* (Paris, 1981), 49–81.

23   Further research on *chambrelans* is badly needed. Currently the best work is Steven L. Kaplan, 'Les "faux ouvriers" de Paris au 18e siècle', in *La France d'ancien régime: Etudes réunies en l'honneur de Pierre*

24 B.N. Recueil Z Le Senne 135 (1), Ordonnance de Police concernant l'étalage et le Colportage des Marchandises (juin 1768).

25 See for examples the works of Michael Sonenscher cited elsewhere, and also Gail Bossenga, 'Protecting merchants: guilds and commercial capitalism in 18th-century France', *French Historical Studies* (Fall 1988), 693–703; and idem, 'La Revolution française et les corporations: trois exemples lillois', *Annales E.S.C.*, xliii, 2 (mars–avril 1988), 405–26; and Simona Cerutti, 'Du corps au metier: la corporation des tailleurs à Turin entre les 17e et 18e siècles', *Annales E.S.C.*, xliii, 2 (mars–avril 1988), 323–52.

26 Sonenscher, *Work and Wages*, 210–43.

27 So argues Joan Thirsk in 'The fantastical folly of fashion: the English stocking knitting industry, 1500–1700', in N. B. Harte and K. G. Pouting (eds), *Textile History and Economic History* (Manchester, 1973), 53–6.

28 Abbé Jaubert, *Dictionnaire raisonné universal des arts et métiers*, vol. 1 (Paris, 1773), 212.

29 This story can be found in Jaubert's *Dictionnaire des arts et métiers*, vol. 1, 212. The great *Encyclopédie* was sceptical about it, however. (*Encyclopédie, ou Dictionnaire raisonné des Sciences, des arts, et des métiers*, vol. 2 (Paris, 1751), 99.)

30 Thirsk, 'Fantastical folly', 68–9.

31 B. N. Joly de Fleury 1732, Lettres patentes portants privilèges accordés à Jean Hindret d'establier dans le château de Madrid une manufacture de bas au métier (juin 1656), fol. 73; ibid., Autres portant l'abrogation au profit de François Estienne du privilège de Hindret . . . (jul. 1666), fol. 75

32 Schaeper, *Council of Commerce*, 174.

33 Archives Nationales (hereafter A.N.) A.D. XI 13, Arrest du Conseil d'Etat . . . Portant Règlement pour les Maîtres Ouvriers et Faiseurs de Bas au Métier . . . (30 mars 1700).

34 See the complaints against the *bonnetiers* of the faubourgs in B.N. Joly de Fleury 1732, Arrest du Conseil d'État du Roy, intrepretation de celuy du 30 mars 1700 . . ., fols 93–8.

35 A.N. A.D. XI 13, Sentence de police . . . qui déffend d'avoir 2 boutiques ou magasins, et de porter ou faire porter aucunes Marchandises de Bonneterie en lieux publics . . . (1718).

36 ibid., Arrest du Conseil d'Etat . . . Portant Règlement pour les Maîtres Ouvriers et Faiseurs de Bas au Métier . . . (30 mars 1700); B.N. Joly de Fleury 1732, Arrest du Conseil d'état . . . du 1 août 1713; fol. 128–9; ibid., lawsuit of the Maîtres Ouvriers en bas au métier against François La Rivière, (20 août 1708), fols 103–5.

37 A.N. A.D. XI 13, Arrest du Conseil d'État, du 23 février 1716, portant réunion de la Communauté des Maîtres Bonnetiers Ouvriers . . . au Corps des Marchands Bonnetiers de Paris; ibid., Déclaration du Roy, concernant les Marchands Fabriquants des ouvrages de Bas au Métier . . . (18 fév. 1720); ibid., Arrest . . . portant réunion de la Communanté des Maîtres Fabriquants de Bas . . . au Corps du Marchands Bonnetiers . . . (12 avril 1723).

38 Bibliothèque de l'Arsenal (hereafter Arsenal), MS Bastille 10321, Etat des maîtres qui composent la communauté des maîtres bonnetiers . . .; B.N. Joly de Fleury 2542, Affaires de Paris, vol. 2, *Observations en forme de Mémoire Pour le Corps des Marchands Bonnetiers de la Ville de Paris . . .* (1776), fol. 177.

39 This is based on an admittedly impressionistic survey of the bankruptcy records of eighteenth-century Parisian firms in Series D 4 B^6 of the Archives de Paris (hereafter A.P.). Eventually I hope to do a systematic analysis of this material.

40 A.P. D 4 B^6 carton 20, dossier 966, Faillite de Jean François Tulout (3 avril 1759).

41 B.N. Joly de Fleury 1732, Sentence de Police . . . contre les Ouvriers et Compagnons de la Fabrique des bas . . . (24 mars 1724), fols 170–1; A.N. A.D. XI 13, Ordonnance de Police, portant règlement pour ce qui doit être observé par les Marchands et Fabriquants de bas au Métier . . .

Above, continuing from previous page:
Goubert, vol. 1 (Toulouse, 1984), 325–31, which is suggestive but far too brief. See also Michael Sonenscher, *Work and Wages* (Cambridge, 1989).

246   Cissie Fairchilds

(23 août 1736); Arsenal MS Bastille 11321, dossier of Medard Fournier, compagnon bonnetier, 1736.

42   A.N. A.D. XI 13, Arrest qui permit d'établir des métiers . . . (1754).

43   Again, this is based on an impressionistic survey of bankruptcy records.

44   For the edit see B.N. Joly de Fleury 1732, Arrest du Conseil d'Etat . . . du 28 mars 1730 . . . qui déffend le Colportage des bas . . ., fols 203–4. For Ribotte see A.N. Series Y 9526, Procès faite après informations en la Chambre de police, contre des compagnons . . . 1766–70, dossier of Jean Baptiste Ribotte (17 juin 1769).

45   For Garnier see A.P. D 4 B^6 carton 43, dossier 2450, Faillite de Pierre Garnier (5 fév. 1772); for bonnetiers' advertising in merchants' almanacs see M. Thomas, *Almanac des marchands, négociants, et commerçants de la France et du reste de l'Europe* (Paris, 1770), *passim*.

46   The best analysis of the guilds' reaction to the attempted abolition is Steven Lawrence Kaplan, 'Social classification and representation in the corporate world of eighteenth-century France: Turgot's "Carnival" ', in Steven Lawrence Kaplan and Cynthia J. Koepp (eds), *Work in France* (Ithaca, 1986), 176–228.

47   For hat manufacturing see Michael Sonenscher, *The Hatters of Eighteenth-Century France* (Berkeley, 1987).

48   B.N. Joly de Fleury 2542, *Mémoire Pour le Corps des Marchands Bonnetiers* . . ., fols 176–9.

49   Alfred Franklin, *La Vie privée d'autrefois: Les magasins de nouveautés*, vol. 4 (Paris, 1898), 318.

50   A.N. A.D. XI 27, Nouveau Recueil des Statuts et Règlements . . . des Maîtres Marchands Tapisseurs . . . (1756), 371–9; B.N. 8° Z Le Senne 11532, Statuts, arrêts . . . pour des Maîtres et Marchands Peigneurs-Tabletiers . . . (1760), 254, 256.

51   B.N. 8° Z Le Senne 11532, Statuts of Peigneurs-Tabletiers, 262.

52   ibid., 35, 268.

53   ibid., 95.

54   ibid., 19–21.

55   Michael Sonenscher, 'Journeymen, the courts, and the French trades, 1781–1791,' *Past and Present* cxiv (Feb. 1987), 90.

56   Both the statutes and their challenges can be found in B.N. 8° Z Le Senne 11532. The *peigneurs* were not the only guild to use such tactics. The *merciers* also frequently claimed rights over new products and pressed these claims in lawsuits. See Steve L. Kaplan, 'The luxury guilds in Paris in the eighteenth century', *Francia*, ix (1981), 273–5.

57   B.N. 8° Z Le Senne 11532, Statuts . . . des maîtres et marchands Peigneurs-Tabletiers, 94.

58   A.P. D 4 B^6 carton 98, dossier 6890, Faillite de Julien Augustin Guillot (27 avril 1787). Perhaps a word should be said here in defence of the use of bankruptcy records for studying business practices during the Old Regime. Such records include lists of creditors and debtors of the bankrupt and therefore allow the historian to reconstruct the suppliers and customers of the business in question. Often they also include account books and inventories of the contents of shops and workshops. Because these are by and large the only business records surviving from the Old Regime, the temptation to use them is very great, although obviously it is dangerous to assume that the business practices of bankrupts were identical to those of the successful and therefore typical of their trade or craft. But the records suggest that many tradesmen went bankrupt because of personal disasters (they fell ill; their wife died), rather than any lack of business acumen. Therefore their commercial practices need not have differed substantially from those of the successful in their field. For further discussion of these issues see Alain Faure, 'The grocery trade in nineteenth-century Paris', in Geoffrey Crossick and Heinz-Gerhard Haupt, (eds), *Shopkeepers and Master Artisans in Nineteenth-Century Europe* (London and New York, 1984), 164–5.

59   A.P. D B^6, carton 7, dossier 363, Faillite de Jean Antoine Bonhomme (28 août 1748).

60   B.N. 8° Z Le Senne 11532, 94.

61 A.P. D 4 B^6 carton 94, dossier 6572, Faillite de Anne Morton, Veuve de Jean-Baptiste Aubin (28 nov. 1785).

62 A.P. D 4 B^6, carton 43, dossier 2427, Faillite de François Bourette (15 jan. 1772).

63 Both cases can be found among the papers of the *peigneurs-tabletiers'* guild seized by the police when the guilds were abolished in 1776. (A.N., Series Y, 11964, Fonds Commissaire Bourgeois, 1776)

64 A.N. Y 9528, Procès faits . . . contre des compagnons menuisiers, carrossiers . . . (1773–4).

65 This assertion is based on an analysis of the items sold by the peddlers arrested in sweeps undertaken by the police at the behest of the *merciers'* guild in 1769, the records of which are in A.N. Y 11956, Fonds Commissaire Bourgeois, 1769.

66 B.N. 8° Z Le Senne 11532, 94–5.

67 A.P. D 4 B^6 carton 46, dossier 2701, Faillite de Sr Fermin Jerôme Charet (16 nov. 1772).

68 A.P. D 4 B^6 carton 83, dossier 5620, Faillite d'Etienne Gabriel Noguette (21 fév. 1782).

69 Jaubert, *Dictionnaire des arts et métiers*, vol. 3, 90. For more on the *marchands de modes* see Roche, *La Culture des apparences*, 308–10.

70 For Rose Bertin see the Baronne d'Oberkirch, *Mémoires*, ed. Comte de Montbrison, vol. 1 (Paris, 1853), 181.

71 For the guild's statutes see B.N. 4° Z Le Senne 969, *Statuts, ordonnances . . . pour la communauté des Couturières . . .* (Paris, 1761). Roche, *La Culture des apparences*, 286–9, discusses conflicts between *couturières* and *modistes*.

72 Quoted in *The French Journals of Mrs. Thrale and Dr. Johnson*, ed. Tyson and Guppy, 143. For other descriptions see J. C. Nemeitz, *Séjour de Paris, c'est-à-dire, Instructions fidèles pour les Voyageurs de Condition*, vol. 2 (Leyden, 1727), 598; and Louis Sebastien Mercier, *Tableau de Paris*, vol. 7 (Amsterdam, 1783), 81–6. For the perfumer's ad see Franklin, *La Vie privée d'autrefois*, vol. 2, 119.

73 Le Petit Dunkerque was almost the only shop in pre-revolutionary Paris to use fixed prices. The only other example I have found is a second-hand store in the Palais-Royal where goods were left on consignment by their owners. For this see M. Thiery, *Guide des amateurs et des étrangers voyageurs à Paris*, vol. 1 (Paris, 1786), 273–4.

74 B.N. 8° Z Le Senne 11532.

75 A.N. A.D. XI 27, Recueil des Statuts et Règlements . . . rendus en faveur des Maîtres Mirotiers, Lunetiers et Bimbelotiers Doreurs sur Cuir, Garnisseurs et Enjoliveurs . . ., 20.

76 A.N. A.D. IX 26, *Lettres, Statuts et Arrests . . . en faveur du Maîtres Evantaillistes, Faiseurs et Compositeurs d'Evantails . . .* (Paris, 1739), 7.

77 For these claims see B.N. 8° Z Le Senne 11532, 30–40, and A.N. A.D. XI 26, 9. The guild of master painters and sculptors did decorative painting on walls and furniture, and its members should not be confused with easel painters, who were not under guild control but instead organized into academies, the Royal Academy of Painting and the Academy of St Luke. See Thomas E. Crow, *Painters and Public Life in Eighteenth-Century Paris* (New Haven, 1985), 23–9.

78 A.N. A.D. XI 26, 69–71.

79 B.N. 8° Z Le Senne 11532, 34.

80 ibid., 86–91.

81 ibid.; A.N. A.D. XI 26, 36–41, 23–5, 32–4.

82 Erica-Marie Benabou, *La Prostitution et la police des moeurs au dix-huitième siècle* (Paris, 1987), 40–1.

83 A.N. A.D. XI 26, 67.

84 For examples see ibid., 60, 65–6.

85 Baronne d'Oberkirch, *Mémoires*, vol. 2, 318–19.

86 Arsenal, MS Bastille 10023, dossier of Jean Baptiste Batouflet.

87 The text of the *mémoire* can be found in B.N. Joly de Fleury 1729, fols 121–42. The document is unsigned, but is convincingly attributed to Albert by Edgar Faure in *La Disgrace de Turgot* (Paris, 1961), 429.

88 B.N. Joly de Fleury 1729, fol. 133.

89   ibid., fol. 137.
90   ibid., fol. 123.
91   The edict abolishing the guilds can be found in B.N. Recueil Z Le Senne 10 (25), *Edit du roi, portant suppression des jurandes et communautés de commerce, arts et métiers* (février 1776); that re-establishing them is in B.N. Recueil Z Le Senne 10 (26), *Edit . . . portant nouvelle création de six Corps de Marchands et de 44 Communautés d'Arts et Métiers* (août 1776). For interpretations of these edicts see Douglas Dakin, *Turgot and the Ancien Régime in France* (New York, 1965), 231–52; Coornaert, *Les Corporations*, 69–71; Faure, *La Disgrace de Turgot*, 424–36; Harold T. Parker, *The Bureau of Commerce in 1781 and its Policies With Respect to French Industry* (Durham, 1979), 20–8; and Eric Agostini, 'Turgot Legislateur, (août 1774–mai 1776)', in Christian Bordes and Jean Morange (eds), *Turgot: économiste et administrateur* (Limoges, 1982), 147–59.
92   For the privileged areas see B.N. Recueil Z Le Senne 10 (16), Déclaration . . . portant règlement en faveur des Ouvriers et Artisans de faubourg St Antoine (déc. 1776), and Kaplan, 'Faux ouvriers', 368. The battle over peddling occurred in Lyon in 1777. A major theme of the pamphlet war it produced was that 'peddling was advantageous to the public, and particularly to bourgeois, workers, and artisans . . . because it enables them to provide themselves at the cheapest possible prices with necessary merchandise without having to go out or lose working time' (A.N. A.D. XI 22, Observations pour les Colporteurs établis et domiciliés à Lyon . . ., 28).
93   A.N. A.D. XI II, Arrêt . . . qui ordonne les Ancien marchands et leurs Veuves . . . faisant le Commerce des Modes . . . (août 1777).
94   See Lianna Vardi, 'The abolition of the guilds during the French Revolution', *French Historical Studies* (Fall 1988), 704–17.

Appendix

The inventories for the year 1725 were drawn from: Archives Nationales, Minutier Centrale, XLII 341–3; XLV 394–7; LIII 230–5; LX 232–3; LXXXIII 306–7; CXIII 308–11; CXVII 341–6.

The inventories for the year 1785 were drawn from: Archives Nationales, Minutier Centrale, IX 787–802; CVIII 710–15; CXIII 554–62; CXVII 918–23; LIII 598–606; LX 454–9; LXXIX 257–63.

12

The meanings of things: interpreting the consumer economy in the eighteenth century

T. H. Breen

The search for the 'meanings of things' – a marvellous phrase suggested by a recent book of similar title – begins at Curtis's, a small tavern located in rural Pennsylvania.[1] It was here in Newcastle – at 'the sign of the Indian King' – that Dr Alexander Hamilton took his breakfast on the morning of 5 June 1744. The Scottish physician was just setting out on a long journey that before the summer's end would take him from Baltimore to New England and back again. Hamilton had no doubts that he was a proper gentleman – at least, by colonial American standards – and as he made his way from village to village, he greeted social peers with easy affability, inferiors with studied condescension. Hamilton recorded the more curious, witty exchanges in a journal published later as *Hamilton's Itinerarium*.

William Morison, a fellow traveller and land speculator returning to Philadelphia, would just as soon have avoided breakfast that morning. Hamilton described the curious scene. Morison, he observed, was 'a very rough-spun, forward, clownish blade, much addicted to swearing, [and] at the same time desirous to pass for a gentleman'. The doctor humoured Morison's pretensions. Not so the woman who ran Curtis's Tavern. Seeing a stranger 'in a greasy jacket and breeches, and a dirty worsted cap, and withal a heavy forward, clownish air and behaviour', she assumed Morison must be 'some ploughman or carman, and so presented him with some scraps of cold veal' and a cup of 'damned washy tea'.

The provocation proved too much for Morison to bear, especially since it occurred in front of the polished Dr Hamilton. ' "Damn him",' Morison spluttered, 'if it wa'n't [*sic*] out of respect to the gentleman in company . . . he would throw her cold scraps out at [of?] the window and break her table all to pieces, should it cost him 100 pounds for damages." ' Morison pulled off the offending 'worsted cap', clapped a 'linen' one on his head, and announced defiantly, ' "Now . . . I'm upon the borders of Pennsylvania and must look like a gentleman".'

After departing the tavern, Morison remained defensive, and in a final attempt to impress the Scotsman, he announced that

> tho' he seemed to be but a plain, homely fellow, yet he would have us know that
> he was able to afford better than many that went finer; he had good linen in his

bags, a pair of silver buckles, silver clasps, and gold sleeve buttons, two Holland shirts and some neat nightcaps, and that his little woman at home drank tea twice a day.[2]

As told by Hamilton, Morison's tale illustrates aspects of the social and cultural history of eighteenth-century consumption that historians all too frequently take for granted. Morison's humiliation reminds us that consumer goods possessed no intrinsic meanings. Things, in this case buttons and caps, shirts and tea, acquired significance only as they were woven into a complex cultural conversation about the structure of colonial society. They were the stuff of claims and counter-claims, of self-representation among people who understood the language of Holland shirts and neat nightcaps.[3]

What we are witnessing in the tavern is the generation of cultural meanings. Consumers like Morison were also producers. The two activities – consuming and producing – were inevitably linked, aspects of a single cultural process, for as soon as a consumer acquired an object, he or she immediately produced an interpretation of that object, a story that gave it special significance.

It is misleading, therefore, to portray eighteenth-century consumers as passive beings. To be sure, the historical literature sometimes gives the impression that colonial Americans were self-sufficient agrarians, people of a pre-capitalist turn of mind who despite heroic efforts found themselves overwhelmed by the intrusive forces of a commercial economy. From this perspective the colonial American consumer becomes a victim, an unwilling or unenthusiastic participant in an expanding Atlantic market.[4]

This familiar interpretation rests, I believe, on a fundamental misunderstanding of the relation between consumption and production. It privileges the work place as the ultimate source of values, of social attitudes and of interests and passions. But surely consumption – the very act of appropriating the goods of the market place – generates meanings as central to the constitution of social reality as are those customarily associated with labour. This is what Roger Chartier, the French cultural historian, seems to have suggested when he wrote – alas, in awkward prose –

> Defined as 'another production,' cultural consumption . . . can thus escape the passivity traditionally attributed to it. Reading, viewing and listening are . . . so many intellectual attitudes which, far from subjecting consumers to the omnipotence of the ideological or aesthetic message that supposedly conditions them, make possible reappropriation, redirection, defiance, or resistance.[5]

In a word, Chartier compels us to reject the notion that early modern consumers were merely soft wax tablets upon which a dominant or hegemonic culture, however defined, freely inscribed its own ideology.

The conversation at Curtis's Tavern raises – for me, at least – a second significant issue. The event involved strangers. Indeed, two of the central figures in this exchange were travellers, men on the move in a society that at mid-century was just beginning to open out, to extend its imaginative horizons beyond the traditional, narrowly bounded communities of an earlier period and to consider the possibility of forming new, larger collectivities, communities of persons who had experienced the 'new birth', who had served in the armies that fought the wars of empire, and who had participated in an exciting Anglo-American market.

The roads of eighteenth-century America carried peddlers, itinerants and soldiers, all representatives of an increasingly fluid society that was in the process of radical reorganization.[6]

My point is that consumer historians should situate Morison's Holland shirts and silver buckles in their proper historical context. We are searching for eighteenth-century meanings, and although it has sometimes been tempting to regard 'consumption' as a general, essentially timeless category of analysis, in other words, as a ubiquitous and unfortunate aspect of modern capitalism, this anachronistic perspective misses the creative specificity of particular societies. The challenge of an eighteenth-century world of goods was its unprecedented size and fluidity, its openness, its myriad opportunities for individual choice that subverted traditional assumptions and problematized customary social relations.[7]

In making these general remarks I am not denigrating a growing body of scholarship that analyses consumer behaviour in early modern America. Much of this work is of high quality. It helps us map out a world of goods and to state with increasing confidence what sorts of colonial Americans were most likely to have purchased various British manufactures.[8]

Still, at the risk of sounding unappreciative, I confess certain uneasiness about the current direction of the field. Closely argued studies seldom rise above the particular. They reveal to us objects that happened to have been listed in probate inventories; in other words, they show us decontextualized things that have lost their meanings, that no longer tell us stories about the creative possibilities of possession, about the process of self-fashioning, or about the personal joys and disappointments that we sense must also have been a product of that eighteenth-century commercial world.[9]

To ask so much from the artefacts of another age is perhaps unreasonable. In all but a few cases, the private associations that gave particular objects special meanings have been lost. Nevertheless, while accepting such constraints, I want to explore the relation between consumer behaviour in eighteenth-century America and the development of larger systems of meanings, to connect market experiences to political ideology and to analyse more fully how ordinary men and women crafted social identities within a rapidly expanding consumer economy.[10] Considerations of this sort raise challenging questions about representations of power and gender.

From this essentially hermeneutic perspective, the study of early modern consumption focuses properly on the intersection of the social and intellectual. The current literature has not systematically explored these connections because, as I have already suggested, it operates largely within an analytic framework that privileges production over consumption, exports over imports and that seems uncomfortable with the notion that broad popular participation in a consumer market could possibly have helped generate radical political ideology.

I

A study linking consumer experience to political ideology begins appropriately with the market itself. Although much about consumer behaviour in eighteenth-century America remains obscure, one can with reasonable confidence hazard several generalizations. First, while the consumption of British goods rose steadily over the course of the entire century, the pace picked up dramatically after 1740. It is the *speed* of the transformation that immediately catches our eye. British Customs Office records – a complete listing of all goods exported from Great Britain to the American colonies during the eighteenth century – reveal that the per capita consumption of British manufactures actually grew at a faster rate than did the population itself. This was an impressive achievement since the American population was doubling every twenty-five years.[11]

In other words, consumer goods flooded the American market. The pace of economic life seemed to be accelerating. Men and women alive at mid-century enjoyed access to a range of goods that their fathers and mothers could not possibly have possessed, and it is not surprising to discover eighteenth-century observers commenting directly on this extraordinary commercial activity. Contemporaries were clearly conscious of a rapidly changing material culture. A Virginian like John Wayles recounted in 1766 that only a generation earlier the planters had lived modestly, spending only a few pounds on imported manufactures. But now, he explained, 'nothing are so common as Turkey or Wilton Carpetts'.[12] And William Eddis, an Englishman who resided briefly in Baltimore, concluded that consumer demand explained the highly visible transformation of the American frontier. 'To supply the real and imaginary necessities' of those who had transformed 'uncultivated tracts' into 'flourishing establishments', Eddis explained,

> store keepers ... were encouraged. ... Warehouses were accordingly erected and woolens, linens, and implements of husbandry were first presented to the view of a laborious planter. As wealth and population increased, wants were created, and many considerable demands, in consequence, took place for the various elegancies as well as the necessaries of life.[13]

The quickening of the consumer market touched the lives of quite ordinary men and women. To be sure, wealthy colonists purchased finer goods than did their less affluent neighbours. But more significant was the fact that almost everyone could – and did – acquire British manufactures. It was a market from which few were excluded. All one needed was money, and sometimes not even that. Easy credit offered throughout the colonies allowed rural farmers and urban artisans to obtain a few yards of coloured cloth, a piece of ribbon, a teapot, little metal items; in other words, one of the tantalizingly small objects included in what eighteenth-century shippers labelled simply as 'parcels of sundries'. After examining hundreds of Massachusetts inventories, Gloria Main claimed to have found persuasive evidence of 'a radically altered life-style among the modestly propertied'.[14] Research carried out in other colonies points to the same conclusion. Even native Americans were caught up in the sudden swirl of fashion. Dr Alexander Hamilton, who as we have already seen, possessed a sharp eye for dress, reported that the Mohawk sachems in Boston 'had all laced hats, and some of them laced matchcoats and ruffled shirts'. These splendid Indians, he thought, appeared 'à la mode François'.[15]

And to all this widespread consumer activity – people of various classes and backgrounds, women as well as men, purchasing ever more goods after 1740 – we must add a third element, choice. Each year the market presented people with more possibilities. Individuals were encouraged to select from among different grades and colours. The language of consumption became increasingly complex, forcing everyone to distinguish with ever greater precision exactly what they wanted.[16] Again, many examples of this explosion of consumer choice could be offered. Let me cite a single case. In 1758 Mary Alexander, a leading New York merchant, ordered from her British supplier David Barclay and Sons eighteen cups and saucers, fourteen coffee cups and ninety-six salad dishes. Alexander soon received a letter from Barclay's begging her to provide more detail. She should describe what she desired 'by round or long common Dishes for Meat, Soup Dishes, or deep Sallad or Pudding Dishes, [for] otherwise [we are] at a Loss to know what' to ship to America.[17] It is clear from the advertising of the eighteenth century that consumers learned quickly. They made demands upon merchants, merchants upon wholesalers, and wholesalers upon British suppliers. Americans wanted the latest styles, and not as an angry George Washington complained in a note sent to his London merchant in 1760, '[of] Articles . . . that could [only] have been used by our Forefathers in the days of yore'.[18]

Even what might be labelled the criminal element of colonial America developed a discerning eye for new British imports. In 1750 John Morrison – no relation to the William Morison who we encountered at Curtis's Tavern – organized a gang of thieves that terrorized Philadelphia. Morrison, a 24-year-old Irishman who had originally migrated to Pennsylvania as an indentured servant, peddled 'Limes and Onions from House to House', and he used his conversations with customers to observe 'how the Windows and Doors were fastened'. Morrison and his accomplices burgled homes and shops, stealing from 'Mr. R—d's House . . . two Silk Gowns, two other Gowns, three fine Aprons, a Tea Chest, some Cambrick Hankerchiefs and other Things, which one of his Companions carried to New York for Sale'. An anonymous pamphlet listed in the manner of a contemporary journal advertisement the other goods that the gang had robbed – a lexicon whose very complexity reveals a growing sensitivity to the possibilities of an expanding consumer market – tea kettles, wearing linen, silver spoons, coats and hats, table cloths, iron boxes, a coffee mill, a pewter basin, a pair of stays, a calico gown, a necklace, a silk waistcoat, a scarlet long cloak, a camblet cloak, a blue cloth jacket, a pair of black silk stockings and two pairs of pumps. The consumer market had created its own criminal class. 'For what Trifles', the author of this piece lectured, 'did this poor Wretch continually hazard his Life!'[19]

By mid-century these 'trifles' had thus become part of a new visual landscape.[20] Colonists could view the imported manufactures on display in urban stores and in rural shops; they purchased them in the countryside from peddlers and factors. Indeed, they could hardly control their curiosity about a range of goods that allowed them to present themselves as more beautiful, as more important or as more cosmopolitan. A single example of consumer eagerness must suffice. Dr Hamilton noted in his journal that he and his slave reached Newport, Rhode Island

> betwixt seven and eight at night, a thick fog having risen, so that I could scarce find the town. When within a quarter of a mile of it my man, upon account of the portmanteau, was in the dark taken for a peddler by some people in the street, whom I heard coming about him and inquiring what he had got to sell.[21]

These particular consumers anticipated perhaps that Hamilton's 'man' was carrying the kinds of goods that they had seen advertised in colonial newspapers in an increasingly elaborate language of textures, brands and colours. What we are witnessing here is the sudden incorporation into a colonial imagination of an unprecedented quantity of consumer goods. Their very presence in daily life compelled creative responses and active appropriations.

Ordinary Americans suddenly found themselves able to shape new identities, to fashion themselves in exciting ways. That was certainly the message of a pamphlet published in

Philadelphia in 1772 under the title *The Miraculous Power of Clothes and the Dignity of Tailors, being an Essay on the Words, Clothes Makes Men*. 'Dunces', the author instructed, 'are they who persuade themselves and others, that nothing but true merit, the love of country, honesty, and, in short, nothing but virtue, can make us happy and truly famous.' But such a view was naive. Imported cloth obviously held the key to success in this consumer society. As the essay explained, 'Clothes alone effect that which virtue, honesty, merit, and love for our country, in vain try to perform.' If the world was a stage, then the 'simple good man' had better acquire the latest styles. There were many choices, of course. The narrator discovered the splendid possibilities while visiting a local tailor's shop, where he 'found [the craftsman] amidst a chaos of velvet, brocade, and other rich stuffs, out of which he created illustrious personages, graces, honours, and other worthies'. The tailor had just cut out a divine and 'was not a little vexed that the velvet would not reach to form completely the right reverend belly'. Workers busily shaped other social identities. 'Over the chair hung two excellencies without sleeves. . . . On the bench lay a great many young beaux, most amiable young gentlemen and sighing lovers, who seemed to wait impatiently for their formation and the evolution of their beings.' The tour of the shop concluded at the door where the author encountered 'two apprentices who had not yet capacity for other work, [and therefore] sat . . . exercising themselves upon the suit of a poet'.[22]

II

No one would treat descriptions of this sort as objective accounts. We are dealing here with perceptions, with cultural readings, with attempts by people of different background and experience not only to interpret the eighteenth-century consumer economy, but also their place within it. This is the point at which social and intellectual history intersect. Real experiences as consumers sparked the production of meanings. These meanings were, of course, highly charged with political implications, for it was through the contest over the meanings of consumption that colonists challenged or defended the traditional social order. For almost everyone the meanings of things raised perplexing questions about gender and equality.

Historians have generally concentrated upon the critique of consumption. It is true that unprecedented consumer activity sparked a shrill, highly moralistic response. By the middle of the eighteenth century that discourse could claim an impressive genealogy. Some statements that appeared in colonial American newspapers and pamphlets sounded as if they had been lifted directly from religious and republican sources that Europeans had been reading for a very long time. But borrowing in itself does not tell us much about the production of meanings. To draw again on Chartier: 'The ways in which an individual or a group appropriates an intellectual theme or a cultural form are more important than the statistical distribution of that theme or form.'[23] The history of the meanings of consumption moves properly from the sociological to the intellectual, from the experiential to the ideological.[24]

With such stipulations in mind, we might pay closer attention to what colonial writers were actually saying about whom. They began predictably enough by describing consumption as addictive, dangerous and volatile. Small, seemingly innocent purchases, they warned, could lead to the destruction of the consumer. Behind every transaction hovered the spectre of luxury. In a typical admonition from this period, Philopatriae reminded the readers of the

Boston Gazette, 'Luxury makes her Appearance in a Manner so engaging, so easily she deceives us under the show of Politeness and Generosity, that we are not aware of Danger, 'till we feel the fatal Poison.'[25] According to another American writer, 'Thus luxury proceeds from one to another; and the baneful contagion spreads at last to the very dregs of the people.'[26]

Because of their high visibility, clothes presented the most troubling challenge to traditional hierarchy. Cloth was the major British import for the entire eighteenth century, and the bright stripes and colourful prints, especially the lighter weight textiles, were quickly transformed into garments. Indeed, dress was the most sensitive index to fashion.[27] 'We run into ... Extremes as to Dress', complained the *Boston Gazette*, 'so that there is scarce any Distinction between Persons of great Fortune and People of ordinary rank.' Another writer insisted in an essay on the merits of setting up a central market in Boston that

> They that are poorer . . . should and must give way to the Rich. Who but they ordinarily should buy the dearest and best of the kind? . . . Now and then we that are poorer may taste of the best too and be thankful. But we should be willing to live low, where God has set us, and having food and raiment (tho' not so much of it as some, nor of so fine a sort), let us be therewith content.[28]

This observer was whistling in the dark. The poor and the middling sorts did in fact purchase fine raiment. And their failure to stay in their proper place nearly drove the Reverend Jonathan Mayhew to distraction. Mayhew, of course, usually appears in colonial histories as a spokesman for radical country politics. He created a minor controversy by celebrating the anniversary of the execution of Charles I. But when he commented on dress, Mayhew fervently defended a divinely sanctioned social order. He pointed out in his *Christian Sobriety* that 'not only the custom of all civilized nations in all ages, but [also] the holy scriptures themselves, warrant some distinctions of dress in persons, answerable to the differences in their stations and circumstances in life'.

The young people of Boston, however, challenged these social and moral conventions, for 'instead of being content with such clothing as is suitable to their degree and circumstances, to their own or to their parents' worldly estate, they aspire after what is far beyond either'. Their clothing, thought Mayhew, was 'wholly disproportionate to their rank and circumstance'. And he concluded – as did many of his contemporaries –

> By this means those good ends which might otherwise be answered in society, by the distinction of dress, are in a great measure defeated; for this confounds all ranks, destroys due subordination, and even inverts the natural order of things, by settling poor people of low degree above the rich, and those that are on high.[29]

During the seventeenth century, Governor John Winthrop had grumbled about 'due subordination'. The legislature of the Puritan commonwealth had even enacted sumptuary laws to make certain that the poor would not confound the social order.[30] It is not clear whether such statutes ever had much effect on actual behaviour, but in Mayhew's time sumptuary laws were out of the question. There were too many consumers purchasing too many yards of brightly coloured cloth. William Tennent, a revivalist not usually regarded an historian of popular manners, understood better than did Mayhew the egalitarian thrust of the consumer economy. 'Formerly Vices were described by the Classes of Mankind to which they belonged', explained the famed evangelist, 'but we find they have spread themselves so universally among all Ranks in the British Empire, that we can no longer describe them in that manner.' Vices, Tennent readily admitted, prevailed

> in a great Degree, in the dissolute Reign of *Charles* the Second, but they were confined chiefly to the Channel of the Court. The middle and lower Classes of People, and the Inhabitants of Villages and Country Places continued Strangers to them. But this cannot be said of the present Generation. Our common and Country People seem to vie with the first Classes of Mankind in Vices, which were formerly peculiar to them alone.

Although Tennent may have been correct about the democratization of sin, neither he nor Mayhew – no, not even the entire American clergy – could turn back the consumer clock.[31]

Within this particular moral critique, women did not fare very well, and colonial writers – almost all of them anonymous scribblers – regularly blamed women for consumer excess. They became symbols of threatening enconomic change. The association of women with luxury, of course, had a long history, and as we have already observed, colonial American commentators certainly borrowed from this heavily engendered moral rhetoric. Indeed, 'luxury' was usually described as a 'she', as effeminate, soft and weak.

Even as we pick up echoes of an older moral tradition, however, we still must account for the extraordinary shrillness of the attack on these particular women. Their acquisition of British imports, their inability to resist the temptations of the market place and their selfish unconcern for hard-working husbands became nearly obsessional themes in the colonial press. 'Are there not too many Wives', one writer asked the readers of the *Boston Gazette* in 1747,

> even among our lower Sort of People, so nice & delicate that they cannot think of any Thing but Velvet & Scarlet to guard them from the Inclemencies of the Winter Air? – Look into the Families of some of these vain Things, and you shall see Poverty enough – Let these precious Help-mates seriously reflect on their Husbands' Conditions – their business failing – their Credit sinking – their little Estates (if any is left) reduced almost to nothing thro' their Extravagancies – When will they leave their Scarlet Cloaks – their Velvet Hoods – their foreign gaudy Dress, and put on humble Homespun, which best becomes them![32]

What soon becomes clear from these diatribes is that colonial writers had in mind *real* women, wives and mothers, female merchants and peddlers, women who welcomed British imports because they knew all too well how difficult and tedious the production of 'home-spun' goods actually was. This writing also suggests that the consumer market may have been a source of female empowerment. Some women certainly rejected a moralistic, usually republican discourse that described them as inherently weaker than men.[33] On 24 July 1732 the *Pennsylvania Gazette* published 'Celia Single's' sarcastic observation: 'I have several times in your Paper seen severe Reflections upon us Women, for Idleness and Extravagance, but I do not remember to have once seen any such Animadversions upon the Men.' And 'Senex' noted in the *Pennsylvania Packet*,

> If the fair sex are thought worthy of blame for their extravagancies in dress, what shall we say to our young gentlemen in their Macaroni coats, hats and shoes. . . .
> I doubt whether a woman would not have thought it less punishment to suffer

death, than to be exposed to the multitude in the ridiculous dress of a modern beau.[34]

The acquisition of goods by women in this economy was an assertive act, a declaration of agency, and male writers found these aggressive expressions of personal independence intimidating. 'Simplicius Honestus' confessed to the readers of a Philadelphia journal that his 'lady friend' had been acting very strangely:

> I lately saw her hair raised up into a fantastic pyramid, which, instead of giving majesty to her charms (as I suppose some mischievous body had persuaded her) disfigured them by a certain air of fierceness, unnatural to her gentle countenance. I would advise her, then, to throw off this whimsical conceit, or I shall conclude that she is giving up the possession of a sincere heart . . . for the vain, coquettish pleasures of making conquests.[35]

Another Philadelphia suitor claimed to have broken off his courtship because the lady's 'absurdity in dress . . . [had] so metamorphosed [her], so horribly disfigured [her], that I am very glad I had not proceeded so far as to declare myself to her'.[36]

The liberal interpretation that I am developing is most emphatically not a form of consumer reductionism. Major social transformations seldom have single causes, and that which occurred in eighteenth-century America does not appear an exception. In politics as well as religion, ordinary men and women were encouraged to make choices from among contending possibilities, to break out of traditional communities and patterns of behaviour, to rely upon their own reason in making decisions, in a word, to reconceptualize the entire social order. Isaac Backus, the famous Baptist leader, stated the general point succinctly in 1768, 'The common people claim as good right to judge and act for themselves in matters of religion as civil rulers or the learned clergy.'[37] So too did the author of an anti-excise pamphlet published in Boston in 1754. He reminded 'Men of common Capacity' that if they did not find the behaviour of their elected representatives acceptable, they now 'have an Opportunity of chuse better Men'.[38] Popular participation in these various activities created reinforcing expectations. If change was indeed inverting 'the natural order of things', then the offenders were 'fanatics' and 'enthusiasts' in religion, demanding freemen in politics and of course, aggressive consumers, both men and women, in the market place.

All these unprecedented and unsettling activities were related to what Jürgen Habermas has labelled the 'bourgeois public sphere'. By that he referred to the creation in the eighteenth century of an imagined public space, a new collectivity of reasoning individuals who spoke in a powerful, critical voice known as public opinion. Those who claimed to speak for the 'public' and who appealed to the public judgement through pamphlets and newspapers challenged the exercise of arbitrary authority. In the name of the 'public', they demanded rights. Habermas was centrally concerned with politics, but it seems to me that his insights could be extended to a 'bourgeois public sphere' that included a broader public, one that imagined that it shared the experience of the 'new birth', that assumed that it had the right to select political representatives and that came to believe that it had as good a claim on the goods of the market place as did any group, no matter how privileged by tradition.[39]

In other words, returning to the focus of this chapter, the meanings of things in eighteenth-century America were bound up with a new, aggressive sense of individual rights based on informed choice. Situated in this manner, consumption was – as I have argued with reference to women – a source of empowerment. The very act of appropriating goods generated meanings. This is what the author of a 1754 pamphlet entitled *The Good of the Community Impartially Considered* reminded his readers during the so-called Excise Controversy:

> Every Man has a *natural Right* to enjoy the fruit of his own Labour, both as to the *Conveniencies*, and *Comforts*, as well as *Necessaries* of Life, *natural Liberty* is the same with one Man, as another; and unless in the Enjoyment of these Things they hurt the Community, the Poor ought to be *allow'd* to use them as freely as the Rich. – But such is the Perversity of human Nature, that when a Man arises to any tolerable Degree of Fortune, he begins to think all below him were made for his Service, and that they have no Right to any Thing, but what is despised & refused by him. We could very well be contented with this, if these Gentlemen would but let us enjoy such Things as we were able to purchase, *freely*; or with the same Freedom they are allow'd to do it: I am sure we Work as hard as they do for it; therefore, I cannot see why we have not as good a *natural Right* to them as they have.[40]

What we are hearing here owed almost nothing to a classic republican discourse which until very recently has dominated our understanding of political ideology in eighteenth-century America. Thanks largely to the work of Joyce Appleby, we have grown suspicious of the hegemonic claims that historians have made for civic humanism.[41] There is no doubt that the members of an educated colonial elite found the classic rhetoric of civic humanism congenial; it was a discourse that helped them situate themselves within an expanding commercial empire. But for all its shrill warnings about power and corruption, its distrust of the market place, its demands for heroic self-sacrifice and Roman simplicity, its insistence on a form of virtue that only propertied freemen could possibly possess and its appeal to 'manly' values, republicanism remained an exclusive, backward-looking ideology that bore only a tenuous relation to the social and economic experience of those consumers who in the market place had found a source of independence, rights and dignity. Republicanism and liberalism were rival representations, locked in a struggle to control and to channel eighteenth-century capitalism. We should see them as different modes of accommodation to economic change, and although these two discourses briefly came together on the eve of the revolution, American consumers continued to consume, to make choices and to resist any group or institution that challenged their right to do so. It is to this powerful discourse – and not to republicanism – that we should look for the sources of a radical, egalitarian tradition.

Let me close with a quotation from a dialogue that that 'forward, clownish blade' William Morison would undoubtedly have appreciated. It originally appeared in 1736 in the *South-Carolina Gazette*. A woman has entered a small shop, and every time she inquires about the cost of a certain object, the proprietor delivers a gratuitous sermon about the vanity of such goods. Finally, a little out of patience, the woman declares, 'Yes, Sir, but I did not ask you the Virtues of it, I ask'd you the Price.'[42]

Notes

1   See Mihaly Czikszentmihalyi and Eugene Rochberg-Halton, *The Meaning of Things: Domestic Symbols and the Self* (Cambridge, 1981). The essay that I prepared for the William Andrews Clark

Memorial Library Lecture Series is part of a larger study that will explore the relation between an expanding eighteenth-century Anglo-American consumer economy and the development of various political ideologies, particularly republicanism and liberalism. Sections of this project which have been published or presented as conference papers provide full bibliographic references to a huge secondary literature and are cited in the notes below.

2   Alexander Hamilton, *Itinerarium. Being a Narrative of a Journey . . . From May to September, 1744*, ed. Albert Bushnell Hart (St Louis, 1907), 13–17.

3   T. H. Breen, ' "Baubles of Britain": the American and consumer revolutions of the eighteenth century', *Past and Present*, cxix (1988), 73–104; idem, 'The meaning of "likeness": American portrait painting in an eighteenth-century consumer society', *Word and Image*, vi (Oct.–Dec. 1990), 325–50.

4   T. H. Breen, 'An empire of goods: the Anglicization of colonial America, 1690–1776', *Journal of British Studies*, xxv (1986), 467–99.

5   Roger Chartier, *Cultural History: Between Practices and Representation*, tr. Lydia G. Cochrane (Ithaca, 1988), 41.

6   Breen, 'Preliminary thoughts on writing a history of choice in eighteenth-century America', paper presented at 'Eighteenth-century politics and culture' conference, Göttingen University, 20 May 1988. Also see Frank Lambert, 'Pedlar in divinity: George Whitefield and the Great Awakening, 1737–1745', *Journal of American History*, lxxvii (Dec. 1990), 812–37.

7   The best general discussion of these topics remains Neil McKendrick, John Brewer and J. H. Plumb, *The Birth of a Consumer Society: The Commercialization of Eighteenth-Century England* (Bloomington, 1982).

8   A useful introduction to the recent literature can be found in 'Forum: toward a history of the standard of living in British North America', *William and Mary Quarterly*, 3rd series, xlv (1988), 116–70. Also Winifred B. Rothenberg, 'The bound Prometheus', *Reviews in American History*, xv (1987), 628–37.

9   See Albert O. Hirschman, *Shifting Involvements: Private Interest and Public Action* (Princeton, 1982).

10 The connection between ideology and experience is explored in T. H. Breen, 'Slavery in a polite society: Virginia's colonial planters and the challenge of commercial capitalism', paper presented at 'Recreating the world of the Virginia plantation, 1750–1829' conference, Charlottesville, Virginia, 31 May 1990.

11 Breen, 'Baubles of Britain', 73–87.

12 John Hemphill, 'John Wayles rates his neighbors', *Virginia Magazine of History and Biography*, lxvi (1958), 305.

13 William Eddis, *Letters from America*, ed. Aubrey C. Land (Cambridge, Mass., 1969), 51–2.

14 Gloria L. Main, 'The standard of living in southern New England, 1640–1773', *William and Mary Quarterly*, 3rd series, xlv (1988), 129.

15 Hamilton, *Itinerarium*, 137–8. The fullest discussion of the accommodation and resistance of native American cultures to the European consumer economy is James Axtell, *The Invasion Within: The Contest of Cultures in Colonial North America* (New York, 1985), 131–78.

16 Breen, 'Baubles of Britain', 79–87.

17 Cited in Patricia Cleary, 'She merchants of colonial America: women and commerce on the eve of revolution' (Northwestern University, Ph.D. thesis, 1984), ch. 4.

18 *The Writings of George Washington*, ed. John C. Fitzpatrick, 39 vols (Washington, DC, 1931), vol. 2, 350; George Washington to Robert Cary and Co., 28 Sept. 1760.

19 *Account of the Robberies Committed by John Morrison. And his Accomplices, in and Near Philadelphia, 1750: Together with the Manner of their being discover'd, their Behaviour on their Tryalls, in the Prison after Sentence, and then at the Place of Execution* (Philadelphia, 1751), 2–10.

20 Dell Upton provides a valuable introduction to this topic in 'New views of the Virginia landscape', *Virginia Magazine of History and Biography*, xcvi (1988), 403–70. Also, William M. Kelso and Rachel Most (eds), *Earth Patterns: Essays in Landscape Archaeology* (Charlottesville, 1990).

260   T. H. Breen

21 Hamilton, *Itinerarium*, 184.
22 *The Miraculous Power of Clothes, and Dignity of the Taylors Being an Essay on the Words, Clothes Makes Men* (Philadelphia, 1772), 3–11.
23 Chartier, *Cultural History*, 5. Also see Albert O. Hirschman, *Shifting Involvements: Private Interest and Public Action* (Princeton, 1982), 46–61; and John Sekora, *Luxury: The Concept in Western Thought, from Eden to Smollett* (Baltimore, 1977).
24 Breen, 'Slavery in a polite society'.
25 *Boston Gazette*, 17 November 1747.
26 ibid., 18 January 1773.
27 Breen, 'Meaning of "likeness" '.
28 *Boston Gazette*, 26 February 1733; ibid., 7 January 1765.
29 Jonathan Mayhew, *Christian Sobriety . . . Preached with a Special View to the Benefit of the Young Men* (Boston, 1763), 151–5, 197–9.
30 See Stephen Foster, *Their Solitary Way: The Puritan Social Ethic in the First Century of Settlement in New England* (New Haven, Conn., 1971), 9–64.
31 William Tennent, *An Address, Occasioned by the Late Invasion of the Liberties of the American Colonies by the British Parliament* (Philadelphia, 1774), 13–16.
32 *Boston Gazette*, 17 November 1747.
33 ibid., 24 July 1732.
34 *Pennsylvania Packet*, 23 November 1772.
35 ibid.
36 ibid., 6 November 1772.
37 Cited in William G. McLoughlin, *New England Dissent, 1630–1833: The Baptists and the Separation of Church and State*, 2 vols (Cambridge, Mass., 1971), vol. 1, 327. Also see Breen, 'Thoughts on history of choice'.
38 *The Review* (Boston, 1754), 8.
39 Jürgen Habermas, *The Structural Transformation of the Public Sphere: An Inquiry into a Category of Bourgeois Society*, tr. Thomas Burger (Cambridge, Mass., 1989). Also see T. H. Breen, 'Retrieving common sense: rights, liberties and the religious public sphere in late eighteenth-century America', in Josephine F. Pacheco (ed.), *To Secure the Blessings of Liberty: Rights in American History* (forthcoming).
40 *The Good of the Community Impartially Considered* (Boston, 1754), 18–19.
41 Joyce Appleby, *Capitalism and a New Social Order: The Republican Vision of the 1790s* (New York, 1984); idem, 'Republicanism and ideology', *American Quarterly*, xxxvii (1985), 461–73; James T. Kloppenberg, 'The virtues of liberalism: Christianity, republicanism, and ethics in early American political discourse', *Journal of American History*, lxxiii (1987), 9–33; idem, 'The creation of the American Republic, 1776–1787: a symposium of views and reviews', *William and Mary Quarterly*, 3rd series, xliv (1987), 550–640.
42 *South-Carolina Gazette*, 17 January 1736.

13

The changing roles of food in the study of consumption

Sidney W. Mintz

Introduction

In this chapter three separate but related themes are discussed. All have to do with the growth of a mass market for sugar and the three stimulant beverages (coffee, chocolate and tea) in England, beginning around 1650.

The first theme concerns the distinctive nature of food and eating as a category of consumption. Food's special status as a consumption good is relevant in this case because the growth in the consumption of sucrose and the stimulant beverages among the English people probably marks the first time in history that marketed edible luxuries were turned into everyday necessities.[1]

The second theme has to do with the social circumstances surrounding these changes in consumption patterns. It cannot be said that we know why the English people became such enthusiastic consumers of the new products; but it is possible to say something about how they did so. Though the discussion remains speculative, from it can be developed some lines of historical inquiry that could contribute to explaining why, in addition to explaining how, this fundamental change took place.

The third and final theme is concerned with a general trend towards certain sorts of food consumption in the modern world, a trend that began at the time when sugar and the stimulant beverages became popular. Of course the modern manifestations of this trend differ from what was happening in eighteenth-century England, but there is enough in common to merit reflection. Though these three themes are not closely linked, through their examination together it should become easier to specify some of the conditions under which new food choices change into habitual preferences.

The distinctiveness of food as an item of consumption

No need is more imperious or more constant than hunger. As the British social anthropologist Audrey Richards pointed out long ago, the need for food is far more powerful and insistent than the sex drive.[2] One can hardly imagine a scenario of social improvement for human beings who suffer from material want that did not include, as one of its basic concerns, the supplying of adequate food.

We must eat every day, and we do it daily – if we can – for the whole of our lives. Most of us have strong feelings about what we eat and the conditions under which we eat; but eat we must. Our hunger signals begin at birth. They matter enormously to us, long before we know about signals at all. Even those for whom, once grown, eating appears almost meaningless – who eat anything or almost nothing, like everything equally or like nothing at all – even for them, eating is fraught with special meaning, as those who must feed them or eat with them often tell us. The same is depressingly true for persons who gorge or starve themselves pathologically.

Those rutted habituations that underlie our eating habits are so close to the core of our memories, to the formation of our character and the launching of our conscious experience, that its substances may be said to become part of us. The old saw about being what we eat, which turns up in a dozen different languages and numerous metaphors, impresses by its very banality: anything *that* everyday must be quite special. Our tastes and habits in other spheres of consumption – dress, say, or music – while also important to us and to our self-conceptions, do not approach food in significance.

And yet the experience of food is not quite like the experience of most other materials of consumption. Food is transient. We eat it, wipe our plates, lick our lips, pat our stomachs, belch demurely, experience satiation. When food is consumed – as mothers commonly tell their babies – 'it's all gone'. Many of the imputed subsidiary satisfactions of consumption – attached, let us say, to the possession of a car, a house, a boat, a horse, or even a watch or sunglasses – are of necessity somewhat different in the case of food. Which is not to say that food lacks many subsidiary satisfactions of its own.

This special aspect of food consumption – the hunger for it, the experience of it, the way it vanishes – merits another word. The sensation of hunger, for all its instancy and its transience, remains powerful. Its satiation does not mean that food is therefore less important, when compared to other things to consume. Food has always occupied an important place in the history of consumption, even if people can satisfy the desire for it merely by eating.

Discussions of the role of food in consumption often refer to it in two quite different connections. There is, first, food as rarity, as a special form of luxury, as 'preciosity': the fresh fish reputedly carried by runners from the sea to the Sapa Inca at Cusco; alpine glacial ice for the Caesars; or the swans, dolphins and other oddities reserved for the palate of the English king. But there is, second, food as grim necessity: the coarse and ordinary food of the masses, in contrast to the rich, rare, plentiful and over-refined food of the privileged. While the rich grow fat and pamper their tummies, the poor long for animal protein, gorge themselves on dried legumes, make soup of tree bark, wolf down porridge for want of bread.

This polar contrast has substance. It is often accompanied by an appropriate vocabulary. The food of the poor is known as 'simple and honest fare'. The food of the affluent is instead rich, savoury and often tainted by foreignness. That polarities mark the eating habits of large societies, and that the rich and the poor may be poles apart, are nutritional and social realities that cannot be overlooked. What may also be remarked, however, is how few scholars – even among scholars of food – have dealt with the ways the rare, odd and precious could, under particular circumstances, become everyday. Perhaps the contemplation of contrastive categories is more interesting than looking at the slippage or elevation, over time, of certain foods. But if no food ever moved up or down the ladder of privilege, much of what has made food so attractive as an index of social change for the study of consumption might be missed.

In the history of European standards of living, food certainly figures at least as importantly as anything else.[3] Yet in the work of recent theorists on consumption, food figures hardly at all. In Colin Campbell's book on the Romantic ethic,[4] for instance, food is not listed in the index; there are only three or four mentions of food in the text. It may be that food is bothersome to theorists of consumption precisely because after you eat it, it's gone. Campbell writes: 'some wants are almost immediately created and satisfied: the sweets and chocolates offered for sale at the point of sale in supermarkets are placed there on exactly this premise.'[5] But the swift satisfaction of the want does not reduce its importance since, in the case of food, desire reasserts itself, usually very soon, often imperiously. Grant McCracken's 1988 work, *Culture and Consumption*, does include food in the index; but two of the three citations turn out to be bibliographical notes referring to the work of others, while the third refers to the significance of some 'special foodstuff',[6] one that is similar to a watch, an article of clothing or a perfume. Here the passing comparison is of food with luxury objects, including objects that are not foods. Food as rarity and the foods of the rich take us in one direction, but because it leads away from food becoming necessity, it also leads away from the present argument.

Because the need for food is so fundamental, when it is satisfied widely such satisfaction can help to displace consuming desires to other spheres. This partly explains why, in the study of consumption in the modern world, other consumables are usually considered more interesting than food. In the case of food, more attention may even be paid to the technology of production and the means of stimulating consumption – advertising, packaging, etc. – than to the substantive nature of the foods themselves. But there was a time when the need for food, even in western societies, was widespread and intense; when those who hungered, even in the west, were proportionately much more numerous than now; and when the intrinsic nature of the foods themselves mattered more. Western Europe in the seventeenth century was like that.

The study of the history of modern foods

In a book that appeared some years ago, entitled *Sweetness and Power*, I attempted to open a discussion of a food, the history of which had changed radically. I thought that the changing consumption of one such food, such as sucrose, could serve as an index of a kind for the transformation to modernity. This transformation, as it took place in western Europe in the seventeenth and eighteenth centuries, was probably the first of its kind in world history. It meant the conversion of certain goods, lately the luxuries of the leisured and rich, into the daily necessities of the overworked and poor. Mostly edible substances at first, these goods were produced in areas remote from Europe, then introduced into mass trade. That trade grew in contrast to the trade history of staples such as wheat, say, or other basic foods. To be sure, wheat had been shipped to Imperial Rome from Egypt to supplement Roman production, and no doubt there were other, comparable cases of the bulk movement of one or another food staple before the seventeenth century. But such cases are probably exceptional.

Sugar and the stimulant beverages were not staple foods, and could not become so.

Perhaps this makes them more interesting, not less; by the mid-eighteenth century, the most important beverage in Britain was being brewed from what was referred to angrily by some as an 'oriental vegetable',[7] imported from China, drunk hot and heavily sweetened with British West Indian sugar. The Scottish historian David MacPherson, writing early in the nineteenth century, put it this way:

> Tea has become an economical substitute to the middle and lower classes of society for malt liquor, the price of which renders it impossible for them to procure the quantity sufficient for them as their only drink. . . . In short, we are so situated in our commercial and financial system, that tea brought from the eastern extremity of the world, and sugar brought from the West Indies and both loaded with the expense of freight and insurance . . . compose a drink cheaper than beer.[8]

The English did not democratize the consumption of gold, diamonds, ermine, ivory or frankincense. But they did democratize the consumption of sugar, tobacco and the stimulant beverages. It takes no logician to conclude that the supply of sugar, tobacco and tea must have been somehow easier to enlarge, and/or a greater source of profit, than the supply of gold or diamonds.

There was some spirited resistance to the widening of consumption of these novel commodities. The social reformer Jonas Hanway, to mention only one of a great many, denounced the consumption of tea and sugar by the poor on grounds, *inter alia*, of damage to health, waste of time, the lowering of productivity and harm done to the foreign trade balance.[9] Yet the consumption of no other commodities in the subsequent century grew as swiftly as did the consumption of these very substances. In the case of sugar, so important was the growth in its use that, together with tea and a few other items, it actually came to be used as a diagnostic of the standard of living, its increased consumption translating into a correlate of the better life.[10]

The transformation of such things into much-desired daily foods could occur in Europe because their prices fell quite steadily, because the buying power of large masses of consumers there had begun to rise and because there were growing numbers of producers – in this instance, as it happened, many of them enslaved – and of sellers to address their needs. But that does not explain why these particular substances, rather than others; nor why then, rather than at some other time. The circumstances give rise to a particular question. What happened over time to endow the consumption of rare and costly substances, consumed in particular ways, with such peculiar symbolic weight, such compelling intensity, that soon enough their absence from daily life would become virtually unimaginable?

There are several different answers to that question, none proven. At first the items in question were all novelties. Those noted here are all edible except tobacco: tea, coffee, chocolate and above all, sucrose – or sugar, as it has long been commonly called (and still is, in everyday English). These somewhat unusual substances all became widely known in western Europe, beginning in the second half of the seventeenth century. Before that time, of them only sugar was known there, and that not well. It had served mainly as a medicine and as a spice, rather than as a sweetener; and being costly, it was familiar principally to the wealthy and powerful. These were 'unusual substances' because all of them began as luxuries. But they were also unusual because of their natures.

Tea, coffee and chocolate are beverage bases; tobacco was smoked, sniffed or chewed.[11]

Sugar in different forms can be extracted from most green plants. But as it was known in the west, and until around 1830, it came only from species of sugar cane, a subtropical grass. In Europe sugar gradually changed from a medicine and a spice into a preservative, a beverage sweetener, a pastry ingredient and, finally, a food. By 'food' is meant here a significant source of nutrients – mostly calories in this case – in the everyday diet of masses of people. Though it was not really until after the middle of the nineteenth century that sucrose would come to provide possibly 15–18 per cent of the caloric intake of an entire nation (and hence, even larger percentages for certain classes and age groups within some European populations), its consumption had grown steadily and rapidly from the late seventeenth century onwards. Lord Boyd Orr would conclude, looking back, that the single most important nutritional datum on the British people in the nineteenth century was the *quintupling* of their consumption of sugar.[12] Even that was less than the rate of growth of sugar consumption in preceding centuries. Sheridan estimates that English sugar consumption increased *twentyfold* from 1663 to 1775, while the population only increased from 4.5 to 7 million.[13]

Many factors appear to have played a part in the rapid growth in popularity of sugar, tobacco and the bitter stimulant beverages among working people in England: poor nutrition, a cold and rainy climate, the gradual development of new work patterns as urban life grew and industry spread, the emulation of the consumption habits of the more powerful and privileged and of course the pleasing taste of sweetness. But I think that express efforts by certain groups to enlarge demand may also have played a part. If so, this would probably be the first such campaign in world history. How intentions to spread the consumption of such an imported substance as sucrose – sugar – could mesh with the readiness of people to experiment with edible novelties is among the features of this history that we do not yet wholly understand.

In my argument I used two terms to describe what I saw as different ways in which substances might percolate downwards in English society, as they became less costly and more common, and as their use among the working poor rose. My contention was that this rise in use began *before* the Industrial Revolution – and, indeed, that it may have contributed in a modest way to the rise of industrial society.[14]

The first such term was intensification. 'Intensification' is what happened when particular sorts of usage travelled with the substances to which they were connected. One example might be the downward diffusion of wedding cakes. In these instances, the role of emulation or imitation in the behaviour of the poor seems fairly clear.[15] But sometimes new substances were re-employed by poor people in new ways, on new occasions and under different circumstances. Tea-drinking among the poor, for instance, probably began in connection with work, not with the home; and the ritual for its use at work, so far as I have been able to tell, bore little resemblance to what the tea ritual – 'tea' – was, and became, in higher-class groupings. I would argue that the rituals of tea evolved differently among proletarians, in other words, and that they independently developed their own meanings. These usages exemplify 'extensification'.

I am unable to explain why some usages closely followed the habits of more privileged folk, while others diverged sharply. It seems certain that mere blind imitation does not explain much. But a fuller description of specific practices will have to come from historians of the period – and local historians at that – before we will be able to understand better how things really did happen.

Descriptions of events help little in getting at causes. But descriptions of the actual usages for such things as tea may clarify somewhat how motives worked.[16] In a recent paper, Austen and Smith stress the desire for 'respectability' as the *primum mobile* of expanding consumption among the poor.[17] Their argument is appealing, particularly because they accept the idea that sucrose and the stimulant beverages played a constitutive role in the advent of industrialism, and were not merely one of its minor accompaniments. That is, such commodities probably helped to build the very sort of society in which they would then be increasingly consumed.[18]

But 'respectability' – presumably associated with moral judgements of worth and economic judgements of class – may specify too narrowly the range of motives operative for new users of substances such as tea which, in this writer's view, were accompaniments to work before they became common in the home. My own view is that 'respectability' is an umbrella term, which could cover hospitality, generosity, propriety, sobriety, social rivalry and much else. Until we know more about specific usages, I would incline towards identifying processes of invention or of imitation, more than trying to specify motives. Thus, Hanway's harangues against tea, for instance, describe how day labourers would co-operate to brew their tea out in the open, 'clubbing' the equipment (teapot, cups, tinder, the tea itself) to be able to drink it at work. Hot, heavily sweetened tea could transform a meal of cold bread and cheese; it was probably the first imported 'pause that refreshes' in history. As accompaniment to a hurried lunch, tea probably gained popularity because it was stimulating, hot, sweet and made the rest of the food go down more easily. At this point in its history as a commodity, tea was probably successful for exactly those reasons that those who touted it said it would be. But I think it likely that only later did tea enter the home, where it might then become an integral part of the proletarian social fabric, and could take on subtler significance. At that point, desire for 'respectability' doubtless mattered more:

> In England the several ranks of men slide into each other almost imperceptibly; and a spirit of equality runs through every part of the constitution. Hence arises a strong emulation in all the several stations and conditions to vie with each other; and a perpetual restless ambition in each of the inferior ranks to raise themselves to the level of those immediately above them. In such a state as this fashion must have an uncontrolled sway. And a fashionable luxury must spread through it like a contagion.[19]

At any rate, the consumption by masses of plebeian consumers of foods such as these marked a turning-point in western history. Beginning with tobacco, sugar and the beverage bases in the seventeenth century, the world consumption picture changed irreversibly. Not only were these new consumers' goods somewhat unusual in nature; they were also intended for large – *and poor* – masses of consumers. Both what the things were, and who was to get them – the structure of production, processing, shipping, marketing and consumption, as well as the ways in which markets took shape and were maintained – were innovations in European society. As it turned out, they were wellnigh irreversible innovations.

In *Sweetness and Power* I concluded by suggesting that the consumption of these items by proletarian consumers marked a turning-point in western history. Masses of European working people, none of whom had ever before had access to products coming from more than a few miles away, now became the everyday consumers of what had quite recently been remote and precious luxuries. As they did so, their relationship to their own labour changed.

Without recognizing it, they became dependent upon markets that far exceeded their own visions of the world. In time they came to recognize external, social standards that measured them by the things that they consumed; and they came to measure themselves by the same standards. The meaning of work, the definition of self, the very nature of material things must have seemed to change, as commodities, in the new capitalist sense, became commonplace. What it meant to be a person would now become a different thing, too.

My intention had been to point to the importance of a newly emerging world in which working people produced less and less of what they themselves consumed; in which they filled most of their needs by selling their labour for wages and buying what they consumed in an impersonal market; and in which their purchases became a measure of some kind of their own identities. These are old and familiar ideas. In this instance, they were invoked in regard to a small number of items – a food, three drinks and tobacco – which were among the first modern commodities. To say that these substances became a measure of people's identities is to claim that the people who consumed them somehow changed, in their own eyes or the eyes of others, by buying and consuming them. Part of this assertion is the idea that the newly emerging capitalist world carried within it differing conceptions both of what an individual was, and of what an individual might become.

Some features of modern eating patterns

In dealing with consumption in modern society, the anthropologist Marshall Sahlins has written:

> individual wants, by encompassing an international division of labor, had become permanent and inexhaustible. Felt moreover as physiological pangs, like hunger and thirst, such needs seemed to be the natural dispositions of the body, springing from human nature itself. The bourgeois economy made a fetish of human needs in the sense that needs, which are always social and objective in character, had to be assumed as subjective experiences of bodily affliction. The corollary of Weber's iron cage of rationality is an exquisite sensitivity to pleasure and pain, duly installed as the hegemonic motives of people's actions. . . . Slave thus to his own desires, Western man was condemned to a life of care and labor, only to know true 'rest' and 'deliverance' as synonyms of death.[20]

From this perspective, the explanation of individual lusts for such goods as sugar and tea is to be found in a redefinition of the social context of needs and desires within which the 'individual' – in quotation marks – is behaviourally visible. Here is Sahlins again:

> This is where social science comes in as an academic reflection on the common experience that by satisfying our own individual needs we create society. In people's existential consciousness, cultural forms of every description are produced and reproduced as the objects of their personal desires. These needs to which scarce pecuniary resources are rationally allocated: they are nothing less than the system of society perceived as ends of the individual. Not only kinship or education, but also Beethoven concerts or night baseball games, churches or

suburban homes, hamburgers or nouvelle cuisine, books, the taste of Coke, and the number of children per family, all these and everything else produced by history and the collectivity appear in life as the preferential values of subjective economizing. Their distribution in and as society seem a function of what people want. Moreover, if the 'labor' freely transacted in the market is only another name for sentient man, even as land is empirical nature, the culture-in-general comes down to the sensory process of seeking pleasure and avoiding pain by the rational evaluation of the objective world. In the end the universe, cultural as well as natural, is constituted by our physiological sensitivities.[21]

Though I am certain that Sahlins would agree that this vision is insufficient by itself to explain how modern consumer society works, I think that he points here eloquently to one of its central features: the heightening of individualized want as an invariant feature of the good life. The idea that we create society through our needs – that the world is a *product* of our desires – is seductive, and remarkably convincing. If each of us does see the world this way, then 'you deserve a break today' takes on a prescriptive aura, almost biblical in its gravity.

In the case of seventeenth-century Britain, we speak of a society on the threshold of modernity, in which a new kind of 'individualism of the masses' would play an ever-greater role. As one would expect, this is even truer of contemporary life, where the stress upon personal, or individual, desires emerges as an important aspect of how modern consumption works. It may be helpful to illustrate this by enumerating several features of contemporary American society, in connection with eating patterns. Though some of these features can be corroborated statistically, others are merely intuitive. Each is dealt with in only a sentence or two here.

First, Americans are eating out more and more. This trend was set in motion at the end of World War II and has not declined since. Eating out allows one to choose from menus; but it actually leaves the decisions about the composition of the foods in the hands of the chef.

Second, Americans are eating more and more prepared food at home. This is really two points, not one. We eat more food brought in, especially from so-called 'ethnic' establishments, pizzerias and Chinese and other Asian restaurants; and we eat more packaged foods, usually only heated before eating. Once again – but even more so – such eating leaves the decisions about what the food will contain wholly in the hands of the processors.

Third, the three-meal-per-day pattern, supposedly typical of American life, has certainly been breaking down during the same forty years that these other trends have been on the rise. The 'interval eating' that has increased between meals is marked by certain characteristic foods, especially salt and sweet.[22]

Fourth, together with this decline in three-daily-meal eating has been a decrease in family eating. Families eat together less and less often, with all members present. Family breakfasts are dwindling; lunch is frequently not taken at home. Even dinner has become less a family meal.

Fifth, the consumption of soft drinks, particularly sweetened and carbonated drinks, has been rising during the same period. At present Americans drink more soft drinks than they do water. Along with the extremely high consumption of processed sugars this and other prepared foods represent, there is also growing consumption of non-sucrose sweeteners such as saccharine and phenylalanine (aspartame).

Sixth – despite the current hubbub about cholesterol – per capita consumption of fats has remained high in American society. While awareness of the problem has grown apace, it has not yet been accompanied by any significant cross-class changes in food habits.

All of these assertions are made here without reference to particular regions or classes, and also without reference to race, ethnicity or gender. We do not have the data needed to fill in the picture solidly. While the social assortment of the national population doubtless does express itself in varying consumption of the same product – such as sugar – we are far from knowing how much, or in what specific ways. These features of contemporary American eating are not typical of all sectors of American life. The consumption of soft drinks, of non-sucrose sweeteners, of so-called 'fast foods', for instance, surely varies by socio-economic class, perhaps by region, and probably by what is called 'race' as well. Patterns of family eating must also be highly variable.[23] In short, our knowledge of our national eating habits is incomplete, particularly in regard to class differentials.

At the same time, what should be apparent from this list of features is that they significantly broaden choice for the individual consumer in one way, even while narrowing it in another. In a restaurant, for instance, one's choice is as wide as the menu, even if one has only minimal control over the ingredients in the food. The same is true in another way when consuming prepared food to be heated at home. By breaking down the familial eating habit, maximum choice over eating time is afforded the individual. Nevertheless, what will be available and under what circumstances, when he or she does want to eat, may be quite narrow; variety and sociability are commonly traded off against 'convenience'. It is easy to claim that these new arrangements maximize individual choice. But there are also good grounds for arguing otherwise.

Individual freedom, desire and addiction: conclusions

It might be possible to formulate a historical hypothesis here, combining the emphasis on individual choice in consumption; the plenitude of consumer goods (food, in this case) in modern society; a new conception of need or desire, as embodied in the idea of the individual in capitalist society, as postulated by Sahlins; and a discussion of the concept of addiction. That formulation will have to wait; but I wish to touch on one aspect of it in conclusion.

It is not difficult to contend that contemporary American society, even while consuming material goods at an unprecedented pace, remains noticeably preoccupied by the moral arena in which sin and virtue are inseparable, each finding its reality in the presence of the other. We consume; but we are not, all of us and always, by any means altogether happy about it. The desire to consume, powerful as it is, does not rest easy on the American psyche. The feeling that one must pay for one's excesses is at least as American as the consumption itself. The feeling that in self-denial lies virtue, and in consumption sin, is still powerfully present. That such a perspective enhances sin as well as enhancing virtue should come as no surprise to anyone.

When William Bennett gave up chain-smoking as a precondition for being named 'drug czar', it is likely that most Americans thought it condign. John Tower sought to make himself fit for the post of secretary of Defense by vowing to renounce the drinking of alcohol, in much the same spirit. Senator Gary Hart, whose candidacy for the presidency was wrecked by alleged sexual indiscretion, never offered publicly to make an analogous sacrifice. Had he done so, however, many Americans, including some TV preachers, would have thought it decorous.

It may be worthy of note that these 'problems' with runaway individual consumption are so matter-of-factly regarded; but it is not noteworthy, really, in a society nearly half of whose members are always on a diet. The same ethical polarities that seize the powerful, in other words, appear to possess us ordinary mortals, as we move unquestioningly from the jogging track to the ice-cream parlour and back again. The stakes, of course, are not so high; and most people are not prepared to concede to the inherent properties of candy bars, for example, what they will concede to those of tobacco or alcohol.

But there may be more to be thought about here. The items whose diffusion was considered in *Sweetness and Power* are, as noted earlier, 'curious' substances, when compared to traditional foods. They are also curious in their effects on human beings. Tea, coffee and chocolate contain stimulants. Tobacco has a depressant effect; once habituated, the user plainly derives a powerful gratification from its use and may have difficulty weaning himself from it, *vide* Mr Bennett. Sugar, unlike the bitter beverages and tobacco, is neither a stimulant nor a depressant. It offers the consumer in highly concentrated form two features of what he or she can otherwise get from fruits and from many vegetables: calories on the one hand, and the taste of sweetness on the other. But no one claims that the experiences of eating fruit and eating refined sugar are the same, even if they are similar.

The relationships which develop between substance and user in the case of ingestibles such as tobacco, the bitter beverages and sugar are complex and interesting. In trying to understand those relationships, we know that words such as 'addictive' must be used with care. Yet most students of tobacco use are now prepared to label tobacco addictive. The same word is commonly used to describe the effects of alcohol on users. Both Bennett and Tower were prepared to pay tribute to what seemed to be the near-irresistible power of these substances.

The word 'addictive' is even sometimes used in connection with the long-term, characteristic effects of coffee, tea and chocolate – though with palpably less confidence. No one has made a convincing case that sugar is addictive, nor has the so-called 'twinkie defence' – the idea that the consumption of processed sugar may produce significant changes in mood and even in behaviour – worked in court. All the same, most people know that the way people feel about processed sugar, or about sweet chocolate, is qualitatively different from the way they feel about pears or apples.

Specific substances do make a difference; and as one moves from foods such as sugar through stimulants such as coffee to drugs such as cocaine or crack, the specificity of the substance clearly makes an enormous difference. At the same time, we are developing a more sophisticated understanding of the importance of context in discussing substances and their attractiveness. The social situation matters, in explaining both how substances affect us, and in understanding why they may seem irresistible. To these arguments may be added the importance of a social system within which individuality is touted and emphasized – in which, as Sahlins puts it, individual needs are felt as 'physiological pangs, like hunger and thirst . . . needs [that] seemed to be the natural dispositions of the body, springing from human nature itself'.[24] When we add together the specific nature of substances such as heavily sweetened coffee or tea, the social context in which we learn to appreciate their consumption, the American emphasis on heightened individual realization through consumption and the good-and-evil polarities of contemporary America, the problems faced by Messrs Bennett and Tower – not to mention the rest of us – may seem altogether inevitable.

It is necessary, none the less, to put these arguments in comparative perspective. Drinking coffee, eating chocolate and smoking cigarettes may be pleasurable for persons of all social and economic strata. But how importantly such pleasurable reactions figure in the total range of satisfactions available to the individual is another matter. Unless we wish to think of this only as a matter of good and bad character, we should be prepared to see the pleasure of candy bars – say – in the context of what other pleasures are available. Food *is* different from other kinds of consumption. Hedonistic consumption of *other* kinds is often accompanied by food. Vacation homes and trips to Europe come and go; the desire to eat goes on forever. The pleasures it provides are swift; but the desire returns at regular intervals. If, as Campbell suggests, one's dreams of satisfaction are as important as their realization in the case of vacation homes, trips to Europe, sports cars and hi-fi equipment, then perhaps food is some sort of crutch, by the use of which one may limp toward the fulfilment of those dreams.[25] And what if there *is* no vacation home, no trip to Europe? What ingestible substances may do for people in more straitened circumstances is, perhaps, more important. The place of sweet things in this different setting – alongside, let us say, the TV or the radio – is different because the context of their consumption is different.

This is by no means to suggest that the events surrounding the adoption of sucrose and the stimulant beverages in eighteenth-century Europe simply foreshadowed the unfolding of contemporary patterns of consumption. But it may suggest that we need to take a longer and more imaginative look at the social contexts of consumption. The specific nature of the consumed substances surely matters; but it cannot, by itself, *explain* why such substances may seem irresistible.

In referring to sucrose and the stimulant beverages nearly twenty-five years ago, I referred to them as 'drug-foods'.[26] By this was meant two rather different things. First, these were substances the consumption of small quantities of which might effect significant physiological consequences for the individual (though one cannot make the same sort of case for sugar in this regard that one can make for tobacco, say, or for coffee). Second, while the psychological utility of such ingestibles may be real, one could argue that their unrestricted use could also be harmful. There is an analogy here with sleeping potions, for instance; with alcoholic beverages; and, these days, with a great many other things, including Pertussin DM, a cough medicine which, National Public Radio told us a few months ago, was wreaking havoc among otherwise well-behaved middle-class adolescents in Salt Lake City, Utah. The contemporary tendency to invest specific substances with the devil – as was done with alcohol in this society a few decades ago – is clearly viewed as preferable by most people to a serious examination of the social context of usage and dependency. It appears to promise short-term solutions, and thus to seem cheaper; it is more sanctimonious; and it puts the blame on chemicals and character, rather than on society itself. That it has been repeatedly demonstrated not to solve social problems is apparently beside the point.

What sweetness and power are about changes shape, then, as one moves towards the modern world. My early concern was the way new 'foods' were conjoined to the emergence of an industrial, time-conscious society, both in the West Indian colonies and in the metropolis; and how this went along with the appearance of a new sort of consumer, who came to use what he bought with the earnings of his labour as a way to redefine himself in relation to others. But the place occupied by these foods, no longer new but still very important in the organization of modern life, can now be examined on other terms.

In these other terms, the meaning of sweetness is heightened under particular circumstances, without regard to our favourable predisposition towards it as a species. It may even be worth considering whether the concept of 'addiction' itself deserves more careful thought, so that chemical and social forces may be seen interacting in more nuanced fashion. That the power of sweetness is undergirded by our primate natures seems to be incontestable. That what goes by the name of addiction must now be integrated into our understanding of the social context of consumption seems equally incontestable, at this point in history. The power of sweetness is not absolute. Unless we wed it to the marvellous power of mind and society to create the social realities by which we live, it remains inanimate and only incompletely understood.

Notes

1   Probably the most striking development in consumer buying during the early modern period was the mass adoption by the English and the colonials of certain non-European groceries. . . . In 1559, groceries constituted less than 10 per cent of the value of all imports. Pepper was the major mass-consumed [imported] grocery. The value of imported dried fruits exceeded that for sugar. No tobacco, tea, coffee or chocolate came into London at all. In the later 1600s the percentage increased to 16.6 per cent and by the 1770s it came to one-third. This gain is particularly impressive when it is realized that the prices of the main groceries – tobacco, sugar products and caffeine drinks – all fell sharply during the period. In fact, the temporary absence of any gain between 1663–9 and 1700 can probably be explained by the big drop in the cost of sugar and tobacco.
(C. Shammas, 'Changes in English and Anglo-American consumption from 1550–1800', ch. 9 in this volume, 178–9)

2   Audrey Richards, *Hunger and Work in a Savage Tribe* (London: Geo. Routledge & Sons Ltd, 1932), 1.
3   The collection of essays in Arthur J. Taylor (ed.), *The Standard of Living in Britain in the Industrial Revolution* (London and New York: Methuen, 1980) provides a rich example. Taylor himself calls attention to the use of the consumption of tea, sugar, coffee and beer as evidence in assessing living standards (ibid.: xxx). In effect, consuming these things came to *mean* having a higher standard of living.
4   Colin Campbell, *The Romantic Ethic and the Spirit of Modern Consumerism* (Oxford and New York: Basil Blackwell, 1987).
5   ibid., 94.
6   Grant McCracken, *Culture and Consumption* (Bloomington: Indiana University Press, 1988), 111.
7   William Falconer, in his *Remarks on the Influence of Climate . . . Etc . . . on . . . Mankind* (London, 1781), is rather negative towards tea. Though he admits it is 'very agreeable to the studious, especially those engaged in the composition of works of genius or imagination, and hence it is emphatically styled the poet's friend', he distrusts its use. He does not believe, for instance, that tea-drinking slowed alcoholic consumption, instead 'making way for the use of spiritous liquors which are often taken to relieve the depression which tea occasions' (254). Even more unexpected is his opinion of the long-term consequences of its use: 'Perhaps the diminutive stature, and cowardly, and at the same time acute and tricking disposition of the Chinese, may be owing, in no small degree, to the use of this vegetable' (255).
8   D. MacPherson, *The History of the European Commerce with India* (London: Longman, Hurst, Rees, Orme & Brown, 1812), 132.
9   Jonas Hanway, *Letters on the importance of the rising generation of the labouring part of our fellow-*

subjects, 2 vols (London, 1767). Hanway's harangues against tea are lengthy and many. But he makes insightful remarks. He notes, for instance, that 'sugar of our own [colonial] growth' is a major reason that so much tea is consumed (vol. 2, 184); that emulation may have played a part in tea's success, since 'this custom seems to have been first artfully introduced as a very rare and dear thing' (vol. 2, 178); that tea-drinking among working people is pastime and entertainment (ibid.); that the French, unlike the English, 'sell the greater part of [their] sugars to strangers' (vol. 2, 184) and so on.

10 Taylor, *Standard of Living*, xxx.

11 Solid chocolate – chocolate 'candy' or 'chocolates' – is a late development. Tobacco, ingested in various forms, was primarily medicinal; indeed, all of these substances could be said to have entered Europe as medicines. The relationship between their supposed medicinal attributes and the form of their ingestion deserves further reflection. The various means by which the narcotics and other drugs now in favour can be ingested is, one suspects, an important aspect of their attractiveness. In some odd way it serves to 'sophisticate' their use. It is perhaps also of passing interest that sucrose, after a century or so of neglect, has just been reintroduced by some doctors as a local antiseptic.

12 J. B. Orr, *Food, Health and Income* (London: Macmillan, 1937), 23.

13 R. Sheridan, *Sugar and Slavery* (Eagle Hall, Barbados: Caribbean Universities Press, 1974), 19–21.

14 In 'Changes in English and Anglo-American consumption', Carole Shammas notes that by the 1660s, groceries (particularly tobacco, sugar and the stimulant beverages) made up 16.6 per cent of imports by value, and by the 1770s, were one-third of imports by value. It is possible to argue that these imports were objects of mass consumption long before industrial capitalism could be said to have typified British society. Cf. ibid., 179.

15 Josef Konvitz has pointed out to me (personal communication, 5 Feb. 1990) that the meanings of intensification, as I have defined it, are probably of a sort made more explicit and public through shop displays, magazines, advertisements, etc.; while the meanings of extensification are 'more implicit and contextual'. I find this a very helpful gloss on my own usage. My particular terminology, however – such as 'intensification' and 'extensification' – is meant to help locate and describe change, and has no other purpose.

16 Assuming, of course, that we ever can answer such questions. Carole Shammas, in explaining the view of de Vries and certain other students of consumption, writes that 'the reason *why* people make economic decisions may not be knowable, because it requires information about motivation' ('Changes in English and Anglo-American consumption', 177). The more that we can say of the conditions under which decisions are made, however, the better our guesses about motivation are likely to be.

17 Ralph Austen and Woodruff Smith, 'Private tooth decay as public economic virtue: the slave-sugar triangle, consumerism, and European industrialization', *Social Science History*, xiv, 1 (1990), 95–115.

18 Sidney Mintz, *Sweetness and Power* (New York: Viking-Penguin, 1985), 180.

19 T. Forster, *An enquiry into the present high prices of provisions* (London, 1767), 41, quoted in Mintz, *Sweetness and Power*, 181.

20 Marshall Sahlins, 'Scienza sociale in Occidente e senso tragico dell'imperfettibilita umana' ('Social science: or the tragic western sense of human imperfections'), *Ressegna Italiana di Sociologia*, xxvii, 4 (ott.–dic. 1986), 505–31, 505–6.

21 ibid., 517–18.

22 Sidney Mintz, 'Choice and occasion: sweet moments', in Lewis M. Barker (ed.), *The Psychobiology of Human Food Selection* (Westport, Conn.: Avi Publishing, 1982), 157–69.

23 Such differentiation makes it difficult to see how an undifferentiated 'capitalism', operating on putatively one kind of 'individual', will make him or her fat in one country and keep him or her at normal weights in another. In this regard, Sahlins's argument from a 'generic capitalism' will not work unless it is inflected socially and culturally.

24 Sahlins, 'Scienza sociale', 506.

25 Campbell, *Romantic Ethic*.

26 Sidney Mintz, 'The Caribbean as a socio-cultural area', *Cahiers d'Histoire Mondiale*, ix, 4 (1966), 916–41.

14
Women and the world of goods: a Lancashire consumer and her possessions, 1751–81

Amanda Vickery

The historical prejudices against the female consumer are legion. Social commentators and moralists have long associated men with the spiritual world and women with the material. Reputedly man's inferior in reason and public virtue, women have been relentlessly derided for their petty materialism and love of ostentation. An allied tradition of socialist analysis, imbued with a similar puritanism, has habitually contrasted the cultures of production and consumption: the former characterized as collective, male, creative and useful, the latter individualistic, female, parasitic and pointless. Moreover much feminist scholarship has displayed equal suspicion of the world of commodities, viewing fashion in particularly negative terms as emblematic of a woman's decorative dependence, the gilding on the patriarchal cage. In consequence, the female consumer has long been a target for criticism or pity, rather than the focus of sustained research. She has rarely been considered on her own terms, or at least on terms that she might recognize – a deficiency which this study sets out to rectify. This chapter investigates female consumption and material culture through a study of the values and practices of one Lancashire gentlewoman, Elizabeth Shackleton. It begins by reviewing existing accounts of eighteenth-century consumer behaviour, in particular historians' characterizations of the female consumer, in order to provide a conceptual framework for the case study. The work then proceeds to an examination of the management of daily household consumption, the place of goods in a range of social practices and the diverse meanings ascribed to material things.

I

The eighteenth century has become associated with the growth of domestic consumption. Recent interest in the *way* this consumption was generated is a reflection of the dissatisfaction that historians have felt with the simple maxim that supply creates its own demand. The main intellectual effort then, has been to explain the growth of consumerism and the spread of goods up and down the social hierarchy. This search for a motivating phenomenon accounts for the popularity of 'social emulation' as a conceptual framework, since emulation theory, which assumes envy and wishful thinking are the norm, provides an explanation for *both* accelerating growth in numbers *and* the wide diffusion of consumables in eighteenth-century England. Historians have tried to examine consumption in two principal ways: through the process of marketing, examining the way demand was promoted and manipulated by producers; and through the bare facts of possession, using inventory data, although this dries up after 1730 in most counties and gives little or no insight into attitudes or motivation. The major deficiency here is that few have looked directly at consumer behaviour and attitudes to material things, either in the process of buying or after acquisition. The emulation model and the unimaginative interpretation of human motivation upon which it rests have filled this research vacuum, permeating both social and economic history, and providing a framework for histories of the luxury trades.

Where scholars of consumption and demand have addressed the question of first causes and the historical meanings of things, most of their answers can be traced back to Thorstein Veblen's *Theory of a Leisure Class*.[1] Historians have exploited Veblen's concept of 'social emulation' as the key to the will to consume. Veblen uses the term to mean both the desire to out-do (and therefore out-consume) one's peers and the envious imitation of elite conspicious consumption. Both interpretations of social emulation have been used by social and economic historians. Harold Perkin's work provides an explicit example:

> At bottom the key to the Industrial Revolution was the infinitely elastic home demand for mass consumer goods. And the key to that demand was social emulation, keeping up with the Joneses, the compulsive urge for imitating the spending habits of one's betters.[2]

Neil McKendrick developed Perkin's thesis and went on to conceptualize this late eighteenth-century phenomenon as a consumer revolution. And thus the consumer society was born, with recognizably modern advertising techniques exploiting a new propensity among the populace to consume in a self-consciously emulative fashion.[3]

The emulation model is also implicit in many specialized accounts of eighteenth-century consumer trades. These have been aimed at an art-historical audience and focus narrowly on the consumer items themselves and questions of aesthetic significance and taste. Yet most rest on a traditional interpretation of the transmission of that taste, whereby modes, manners and artistic ideas reached the London court from Paris, filtered out through the gentry to the provinces and trickled down to the lowly via uppity tradespeople and artful servants. Key carriers of the plague of fashion are presented as socially calculating upstarts. The assumed pattern of diffusion of goods and ideas across society mirrors the hierarchy of McKendrick's consumer society. Anne Buck's evocation of the spread of eighteenth-century fashion illustrates the dress history orthodoxy:

> A mobile and fairly fashion conscious gentry, having acquired their own clothes, were the people of fashion for the less mobile, less well informed ranks below them, their neighbours in country-town, village and hamlet. They presented generally the simpler, less ephemeral versions of fashion, which were more easily understood, more practical to achieve. The actual clothes of their everyday wear often became dress wear for those in the ranks below.[4]

However, both the structure and the chronology of the conventional account of unprecedented and unrestrained late eighteenth-century consumerism have been called into question
by Lorna Weatherill's important work on inventory data between 1675 and 1725.
Weatherill's statistics reveal a dramatic expansion in the ownership of goods in these years,
challenging characterizations of the early eighteenth century in terms of sluggish consumerism or pre-revolutionary traditionalism. Weatherill rejects the assertion that fashionable
goods trickled, in a predictable way, down the social hierarchy. The local consumer elite
consisted of superior merchants. Despite their greater influence and prestige, lesser gentry
and professionals owned fewer fashionable commodities than did drapers and mercers.
Indeed, urban craftsmen were more likely to innovate than rural yeomen.[5] Moving from
structure to meaning, Weatherill is suspicious of all-embracing accounts of consumer motivation and in particular explanations for changing consumption patterns in terms of fashion
and social emulation; not least because frenzied emulation and conspicuous consumption fail
to marry 'with the otherwise sober and serious behaviour of the lesser gentry and people of
middle rank'.[6] Nevertheless, Weatherill is unable to refute the emulation model at the level of
meanings and attitudes. Social meaning cannot be read off the bare fact of ownership.
Probate inventories offer little or no insight into motives for acquisition. They record property at death and thus say nothing of the nature of property-holding throughout the life-
cycle, or of the material and social function of the goods acquired. The evidence Weatherill
marshals cannot answer the questions posed by her own statistics. What motivated tradespeople in the purchase of new domestic goods? Why were decorative goods consumed in
Kent and not Hampshire? Why did gentry and professionals value clocks and books, but not
looking-glasses?[7]

The inadequacies of emulation theory as historical explanation have also been emphasized
by Colin Campbell, a historical sociologist. While accepting the notion of a late eighteenth-
century consumer revolution, Campbell rejects the theory that emulation was a central
mechanism accounting for the upsurge in demand, since no good reason has been given to
explain exactly why people should have been more actively emulative at this particular time.
However, given that Campbell is so critical of McKendrick's interpretation, with its 'fundamental weaknesses at the level of theory', it is surprising that he is not more suspicious of
McKendrick's empirical findings.[8] McKendrick's structure and chronology remain central to
Campbell's reinterpretation.

Veblen's damning portrait of the leisured lady consumer has, for most social, economic
and women's historians, adequately delineated the elite woman's role in the world of goods.
The lady of the leisure class played a crucial role in the performance of conspicious leisure.
Innocent of paid employment, she was ultimate testimony to her husband's wealth and
status, the clothes on her back the tangible proof of his purchasing power. Her unpaid work,
the 'painstaking attention to the service of the master' and 'the maintenance and elaboration
of the household paraphernalia' was a category of leisure, since these tasks were 'unproductive'.[9] In short, the leisured lady's economic *raison d'être* was to consume and display what
men produced, thereby driving her less fortunate sisters to new heights of envious imitation.[10] The Veblen legacy is apparent in McKendrick's explanation for expanding home
demand and economic growth in the eighteenth century. Speaking here for every waged
woman he asserts:

Her increased earning released her desire to compete with social superiors, a desire pent up for centuries or at least restricted to a very occasional excess. . . . It was this new consumer demand, the mill girl who wanted to dress like a duchess . . . which helped to create the industrial revolution.[11]

Though women's wages may fluctuate, clearly their wants remain the same. Even Campbell's critique of McKendrick's uses of 'emulation' takes the central role of women and, by implication, their pathological desire to consume as a given. Campbell's own explanation of the advent of McKendrick's consumer revolution is the birth of modern hedonism among the puritan bourgeoisie, which is expressed in and explains pleasurable consumption. Campbell finds the evidence for this in the rise of the novel, romantic love and fashionable leisure. He alerts us to what he calls the common factor: 'the prominent part played by women in all these spheres, something which was also true of the consumer revolution itself.'[12] Campbell reinforces the old notion that women were in the forefront of the alleged consumer revolution, that their desire to consume is somehow greater than men's, but gives little clue as to why that might be the case. Unfortunately, we are left with the assumption that women are simply innately covetous and congenitally wistful about the prospect of upward mobility.

Superficially, female consumers feature prominently in traditional histories of the luxury trades, with their tea sets and silver, high heels and jewellery, resplendent but characterless. Historians of dress pay direct, if cursory, attention to women's wants and strategies, but these are usually reduced to the need to ensnare a male, and the desire to emulate the elite and beat the Joneses.[13] Generalizations about this homogeneously feminine consumer motivation are illustrated by uncritical quotation from eighteenth-century travellers' reports, satirical social commentary and moralists' diatribes. A familiar tale of frivolous craving for elite modes and therefore social cachet emerges, as here where Aileen Ribeiro quotes Mandeville: '[The] poorest labourer's wife . . . who scorns to wear a strong wholesome frize . . . will starve herself and her husband to purchase a second hand gown and petticoat, that cannot do half the service, because forsooth it is more genteel.'[14]

Ancient prejudices have thus been passed off as actual behaviour. Meaningful research on women's consumption and material culture in the eighteenth century is conspicuous by its absence; a suggestive article by Lorna Weatherill stands alone. By comparing the inventories of men and women (spinsters and widows), Weatherill discovered a higher concentration of decorative items among the possessions of single women, but concludes that the gender contrast was too muted to suggest a distinctively feminine material subculture. Yet unfortunately, inventories cannot determine whether men and women attached *different* meanings to the *same* artefacts, something which must be ascertained if we are to answer the question posed by Weatherill herself: did men and women have different material values in the seventeenth and eighteenth centuries?[15] Weatherill apart, historians have dismissed women's dealings with material things as a category of leisure, domestic material culture as an arena of female vanity, not skill, and shopping a degraded female hobby, not unpaid work. Unnecessarily reliant upon Veblen, historians have reproduced an impoverished assessment of material culture; assuming that beyond their material function goods only convey information about competitive status and sexuality and that consumables once possessed carry the same social and personal meanings for all consumers.

Veblen's ideas are so commonplace one might think he had the last word on consumer motivation and the symbolic character of material things, which is demonstrably not the case. The last ten years have witnessed a massive rethinking of consumer behaviour in the fields of sociology, media studies and design history. Pierre Bourdieu has questioned Veblen's bedrock assumption that social competition necessarily inspires imitation, since it could just as easily provoke differentiation. Bourdieu's *Distinction* depicts a system whereby each class is actively distinguishing itself from other classes, in goods and life-style. Dick Hebdige's work on subcultures and style presents evidence of the appropriation rather than the emulation of elite modes and symbols, in the creation of solidarity among subordinate groups. Meanwhile Jean Baudrillard has questioned whether material things have fixed meanings at all.[16] Imaginative discussions of the meanings of material things have long been found in anthropological theory. Building on Marcel Mauss's dissolution of the gift/ commodity distinction, anthropologists have asserted that while consumption is essentially social and relational, an awareness of comparative social status need not be competitive. Indeed having the same consumer items as the Joneses does not necessarily involve beating them, since a shared material culture is often a factor in social solidarity and cohesion. Moreover, Mary Douglas and Baron Isherwood assert that the primary information goods convey is not status but character, stressing the importance of things in the construction of identity. Most recently, Daniel Miller has argued that however oppressed and apparently culturally impoverished, most people nevertheless access the creative potential of the unpromising material goods about them.[17] The impact of this writing is now being felt by historians, exhibiting an increased willingness to view consumption as a positive contribution to the creation of culture and meanings. The general reassessment of consumption paves the way for the historical reclamation of the female consumer in particular, to which project this chapter contributes.[18]

II

The female consumer who is the subject of this study is Elizabeth Shackleton of Alkincoats (1726–81). Elizabeth was born in London, the only daughter of a London linen draper, John Parker. When her widowed father inherited the family estate through a half-brother, Elizabeth became mistress of Browsholme Hall, in the West Riding of Yorkshire, close to the Lancashire border. In 1751, she married her second cousin Robert Parker of Alkincoats, whose Lancashire estate of at least 160 acres yielded roughly £290 p.a. in rent. Robert Parker died in 1758, leaving the 'jolly widow of Alkincoats' alone with three sons under 5. In 1765, she eloped to Gretna Green with John Shackleton (1744–88), a local woollen merchant, seventeen years her junior. She was 38, he was 21. Eventually, her eldest son Thomas Parker inherited the estate and Alkincoats. Her younger sons, Robert and John Parker, after a variety of apprenticeships in textile-related trades in London, set up in partnership as wholesale hosiers, with a Mr Plestow of Bishopsgate.[19]

Alkincoats was one of the many local manors scattered around the Colne and Burnley valleys in east Lancashire. Geography and the Colne worsted industry integrated this area into the West Riding. The Colne piece hall drew custom from the upper reaches of Wharfedale and Craven. The Parkers went more often to Halifax than to Preston, while Yorkshire families were as common as Lancashire gentry in Elizabeth Shackleton's social network. This network incorporated lesser gentry, many of whom held official positions in their county as magistrates and officers of the militia; county gentry such as the Listers of

Gisburn; professionals, particularly doctors, schoolmasters and lawyers; and merchants, with whom she maintained a furious correspondence in her attempts to find suitable apprenticeships for her sons.[20]

This case study draws on a range of source material: family and estate papers, social correspondence and personal manuscripts. The central source consists of Elizabeth Shackleton's thirty-nine diaries covering a nineteen-year period from 1762, when she was a widow of 36, till her death in 1781 at the age of 55.[21] Sometimes maintaining as many as three diaries a year, Elizabeth Shackleton divided her records into 'Letters to Friends and Upon Business', 'Remarkable Occurrences' and 'Daily Occurrences, Memorandums & Accounts'. Unfortunately for the purposes of this chapter, the accounts were not an exercise in double-entry book-keeping, being almost exclusively concerned with expenditure. If Elizabeth Shackleton kept a global account book (which seems likely) then it has not survived. Lost with it, is the possibility of a precise correlation between income and expenditure over the life-cycle.[22] This is not to suggest, however, that Elizabeth Shackleton's accounts of expenditure were imprecise and unsystematic. The accuracy of her record-keeping can be independently confirmed by comparing the purchases of furniture from Gillows of Lancaster listed in the diaries and the relevant ledgers that survive for the firm.[23] Elizabeth Shackleton's furniture accounts were scrupulously exact in specification and accurate down to shillings and pence. In the case of furniture buying, at the very least, the diaries offer an accurate record; a finding which inspires some confidence in Elizabeth Shackleton as a reporter of everyday details.

III

Ultimate control of financial resources in the Shackleton marriage remains opaque. By the terms of her first husband's will, Elizabeth Parker was charged with co-guardianship of the three Parker children, and by her settlement of 1751, entitled to an annuity of £140 a year. After her second marriage, she continued to receive her jointure in her own name and managed the children's trust accounts until they came of age. From 1765, however, the trust accounts bear John Shackleton's signature, alongside those of the other trustees. Occasional remarks indicate that a Parker–Shackleton marriage settlement was drawn up, but it has not survived.[24] In the absence of financial-legal papers, we must rely on the diaries. Apart from brief periods of anxious effort raising apprenticeship fees, there is no evidence that Elizabeth Shackleton felt financially constrained. The Shackleton marriage was riven with emotional strife, yet there is no evidence of conflict over financial priorities, or Elizabeth's independence as a consumer.[25] The Shackleton household sustained only a handful of servants, and certainly was not grand enough to support a house steward, a clerk of the kitchen or an executive housekeeper to manage and monitor family consumption.[26] The sheer quantity of consumer detail in Elizabeth Shackleton's diaries offers powerful evidence to support the widespread historical assumption that outside the households of peers and plutocrats the daily *management* of consumption fell to the mistress and with it control of routine decision-making.[27]

Among many other functions, the diaries served as a reference manual on the business of consumption and servicing a household; they were cross-referenced to receipts and older accounts ('vid my old pocket book') and often subsequently annotated, as if intended to be consulted on a regular basis.[28] Elizabeth Shackleton kept a tally of the provisions, clothes and household goods she ordered from local retailers, usually with a note on their quality or serviceability and price. When commissioning London relatives to purchase goods on her behalf, she sent remarkably detailed orders and specified how the proxy consumer was to be repaid and the means by which the purchases should be conveyed (either by coach, carrier or personally delivered). All this information was duly transcribed into the diaries. When parcels and boxes of metropolitan products arrived, Mrs Shackleton listed their contents, registering how well they had survived the journey and whether they suited her taste. A general interest in the price, specification and availability of consumer goods emerges from her diaries ('Bought a small quantity of Mackrell at 3d a pound, from Preston. I never saw any in Lancashire but once before'), while her correspondence reveals that she exchanged such information with her friends on a regular basis.[29]

As far as Elizabeth and her female circle were concerned, shopping was a form of employment and one which was most effectively administered by women. Note the language Elizabeth Parker used in 1751 to reprove her fiancé Robert Parker when, through careless procrastination, he bungled her commissions. 'You really are a proper person to entrust with business . . . the next time I employ you, you shall be more punctual.'[30] Thereafter, Robert Parker appeared more mindful of his lady's instructions, apologizing from York in 1756 for silver buckles bought 'contrary to orders' and from Skipwith for some fancy hats 'don't scold abt the latter for cd not bear to see the plain'.[31] Occasional marital disagreements over relatively minor consumption decisions illuminate the sexual division of labour as understood by Elizabeth and her two closest friends. The delayed arrival of a hamper of produce from Pontefract in December 1753, prompted the following explanation from solicitor's wife Jane Scrimshire.

> I am sorry to hear your apples were so long travelled . . . but things always happen wrong when husbands will not hearken to their wives for I co'd not persuade Mr Scrimshire to send them to Wakefield, but now as far as the dignity of a husband will allow he acquiesces.[32]

A month later Mrs Scrimshire admitted herself still 'extremely vexed' with Michael Scrimshire about the spoilt produce and presumably the principle. Thereafter she 'wo'd not let him have any management in sending [perishables]' and declared herself 'determined to have my own way this time'.[33] Jane Scrimshire's conviction that the management of consumption was a proper female concern is echoed in letters from Elizabeth's cousin Bessy Ramsden. When despatching a box of elaborately patterned silks from London in 1764, Mrs Ramsden's apprehensions that they were 'too full of work' for her cousin's taste were dismissed by her husband Revd William Ramsden, a Charterhouse schoolmaster. Proved right, Bessy identified unwarranted male intervention as the source of the problem. 'Dear Cuzz, the plot against your peepers was not of *my* laying. The patterns were of my *husband's* chusing to shew (as he says) his taste. I tell him he had sufficiently shewn that before in his choice of a wife.'[34]

Such material suggests that women jealously guarded their role as family consumers. But this is not to argue that, as a result, men were untainted by the world of goods and fashion, rather that they were expected to consume different items and in a different way. When county business or commercial ventures took Lancashire gentlemen to well-supplied or fashionable towns, they fulfilled their wives' commissions by proxy. They rarely returned from such trips without an additional parcel of toys, novelties and souvenirs. Moreover, while Elizabeth Shackleton saw to the purchase of her sons' linens well into their twenties, they preferred to hunt for less mundane items themselves, expending much energy finding the last word in stylish waistcoats.[35] Undoubtedly, men considered themselves skilful consumers of particular types of commodity. When the Ramsdens fulfilled their cousin's commissions in 1765, Bessy Ramsden bought the 'gowns, caps, ruffles and such like female accoutrements', while William was accountable 'for the wafers, paper and pocket book'.[36] Of course, the way spouses carved up their shopping lists must have varied from couple to couple – after all it would be surprising if a schoolmaster had not been able to judge the quality of stationery. Similarly, John Parker's apprenticeship as a linen draper and his subsequent endeavours in hosiery must have equipped him to deal in fashionable textiles and perhaps accounts for his growing importance to his mother as a proxy consumer in the later 1770s. But the particularity of skill notwithstanding, it is surely significant that the remarkably uxorious William Ramsden was the only man in all the Lancashire manuscripts who ever recorded going to market to purchase humdrum groceries. Other gentlemen, however, did occasionally concern themselves with the purchase and donation of higher status provisions, such as snuff, good tea, wine and barrels of oysters. (They were, of course, obsessively involved in the acquisition and distribution of game.)

Although husbands were not expected to interfere with the daily organization of household consumption, none the less it seems likely they retained ultimate sanction over extraordinary purchases requiring the outlay of considerable capital. For instance, in the once-and-for-all furnishing of Pasture House in the 1770s, while Elizabeth Shackleton ordered small pieces of deal furniture from local craftsmen, it was John Shackleton who went to Lancaster to bespeak their mahogany furniture and his name that appeared in the Gillows ledgers. Furthermore, when her newly married son Tom Parker embarked on his first furniture-buying expedition, Elizabeth Shackleton recorded his departure with all the fanfare of a rite of passage. 'Tom going from Newton to Lancaster to buy new mahogany furniture. God bless and prosper with Grace, Goodness and Health all my own dear children.'[37]

However, while men bought luxuries for themselves and certain commodities for the household and the dynasty, it was still women who were principally identified with spending in the eighteenth-century imagination. In all probability, the stereotypical distinction between the producing man and the consuming woman was endorsed by the visibility and regularity of female shopping, whereas the male consumer escaped general notice because his direct engagement with the market was only intermittent. In sum, while substantive research on the differences between men and women's consumption remains to be done, the Lancashire manuscripts suggest the provisional conclusion that while female consumption was repetitive and relatively mundane, male consumption was by contrast occasional and impulsive, or expensive and dynastic.[38]

IV

A genuine effort to explore women's relationship with the world of goods must move beyond the moment of purchase – a mere snapshot in the long life of a commodity. In fact, Elizabeth Shackleton rarely recorded exactly why she purchased an item, but instead chronicled the way domestic goods were used and the multitude of meanings invested in possessions over time. In consequence, this section is devoted to domestic material culture. It also sets bought commodities in the context of artefacts acquired by other means, such as inheritance, home-production and gift-exchange. The discussion examines the roles of artefacts in social practices: the maintenance of property was a constituent of genteel housekeeping; goods served as currency in the mistress–servant relationship; possessions were key props in inconspicuous ceremonies, but they also demonstrated polite conformity and were easy targets for social criticism. The discussion then proceeds to an elaboration of the range of meanings artefacts could embody.

For Elizabeth Shackleton the social and personal life of things *began* once they had been acquired and entered the household. Alkincoats was comprised of fourteen family rooms, six servant and work rooms and five storerooms.[39] Elizabeth Shackleton supervised which household goods went into which rooms, what was to be stored and what was for immediate use. Things out of use (either because the owner was away or because they were reserved for best) were listed and accounted for.[40] Things in use were constantly cleaned and reorganized either by Elizabeth Shackleton herself or under her close supervision. Her diaries are littered with daily entries which specify the room and cupboard where property was to be found:

> I removed the chest out of the red room in the gallery and took all the linnen out of the linnen drawers over the fireplace in the nursery and put the linnen drawers near the fireplace in the red room in the gallery as they stood to damp before.[41]

Mrs Shackleton acted as domestic inspector, monitoring the condition of household artefacts and recording wear and tear. She saw to the servicing of domestic utensils. Scissors were sent to the Clitheroe chandler to be ground, new cooking utensils were boiled and seasoned and broken china was sent by a china woman to be mended or replaced by Colne shopkeepers. Breakages and household accidents were consistently recorded and with particular emphasis when the object was a valued one.

> Molly Vivers broke my own wash hand basons. I had had it 14 or 15 years.

> To my vexation cross and rude Betty broke Mr S.'s pot that he has had for his tea at breakfast for many years. She pour[ed] hot water in it out of the tea kettle and crack'd it all to pieces.[42]

Linens were laboriously maintained and if beyond mending, adapted. Elizabeth Shackleton regularly cut ancient sheets into tea cloths and worn table cloths into china cloths and dusters. Clothing received particular attention. It was mended, made over, retrimmed, redyed, converted into household items or cast off to servants. Favourite dresses turned up in a variety of guises over the years: 'made me a workbag of my old, favourite, pritty, red and white linnen gown.' And three years later: 'Made a cover for the dressing drawers of my pritty red and white linnen gown.'[43] Thus Mrs Shackleton prolonged the life of her semi-durable possessions, taking delight in ingenious adaptation and economy. 'I cut a pair of fine worsted stockings, good legs and bad feet to draw over my stocking to keep my knees warm. Like them much now they are made properly for the use.'[44] Elizabeth Shackleton's was a thrifty regime wherein every last scrap was utilized. She reproved her improvident married son precisely for his failure to conserve fabric pieces.

> I asked [Tom] for a piece of cloth to make me a pincushion on, he told me he had

none. I said he should keep bits. If they had not done so at Newton, how co'd the old lady have made my own dear, nice, little [grandson] a pair of shoes?[45]

The maintenance of all the household goods at Alkincoats and the majority of the personal possessions therein was a function of Elizabeth Shackleton's domestic surveillance, 'in the housekeeping way'.[46] Even after her sons left home, they availed themselves of her services, both managerial and technical: 'I am happy to have [John] here. Mended up slightly some shirts and nightcaps, all his things much out of repair. God knows he will find it a great and an expensive difficulty to renew them.'[47] These skills were not learned overnight. Commenting on the domestic chaos at Tom Parker's house, Elizabeth Shackleton held her new daughter-in-law Betty Parker responsible, 'All in sad confusion. I think Mrs P. should not molest his things and Mrs P. to blame!'[48] Betty Parker also failed to appreciate the wisdom of Mrs Shackleton's disinterested advice and put her mother-in-law into dirty sheets and a damp bed on an overnight visit. Within a year, however, the new Mrs Parker had somehow got to know the ropes and temporarily redeemed herself with dutiful and dignified housekeeping. 'My good daughter is a most exceeding good wife, she ruffled her husband a shirt and always is industrious and manages with prudent economy.'[49]

Above all, Elizabeth Shackleton resented interference in the smooth running of the household. 'Mr S. exceedingly bad . . . as soon as ever he came down this morning he drank white wine. S. threw that bottle down and another of red port and broke them both. Sad, terrible housekeeping indeed!'[50] Evidently, 'housekeeping' constituted a terrain worth defending. The practice of housekeeping provided Elizabeth Shackleton with an esteemed role. Her skills enabled her to remain useful to her sons and afforded a gratifying means of favourable comparison with other women. For all that, housekeeping was a form of work which lacked an obvious and lasting product. Well-serviced clothes, efficient utensils and gleaming tableware were in themselves rare and tangible proof of Elizabeth Shackleton's labours.

In addition to providing the architecture of her material role, goods were part of the currency of the mistress–servant relationship. That which was Elizabeth Shackleton's to give and her servants' to take was subject to negotiation and reinterpretation. The informal contracts Mrs Shackleton recorded, unlike those of many contemporaries, did not include a specific allowance for tea, coffee, sugar and so on.[51] Yet her servants helped themselves to these expensive and highly symbolic provisions without compunction. To Mrs Shackleton's horror, Susy Smith was discovered dispensing fine white sugar for the servants' tea in 1771 and the cook-housekeeper Molly Vivers was surprised drinking full cream milk in 1772.[52] The expropriation of illegitimate perquisites threatened both Elizabeth Shackleton's authority and her good housekeeping, a dual challenge made explicit in a note of 1779: 'Found Betty Crook making coffee and breaking white sugar to drink with it. Servants come to a high hand. What will become of poor housekeepers?'[53]

The amount of clothing a servant might legitimately expect by way of remuneration was also disputed. By the terms of their contracts, male servants were entitled to a suit of clothes to be replaced at regular intervals.[54] Female servants enjoyed no formal entitlement to new clothes as they wore no livery. In fact, the cost of making garments for female staff was often deducted from their pay. However on a casual basis, a maid could, over time, acquire a substantial wardrobe. She might be paid in kind for occasional tasks. Nanny Nutter received a pair of black silk mitts for knitting Mr Shackleton a pair of claret silk and worsted stockings in February 1773.[55] A maid might also receive discarded clothing when her mistress was feeling bountiful, fond or grateful. 'I gave Molly Blakey my old mode silk cloke because I thought she was poor and came to me when I was desolate and quite without help.'[56] In addition, a favoured maid could expect regular gifts and novelties (ribbons, lace, caps, pocket handkerchiefs, silk mitts, pocket scissors, shoe buckles, necklaces and so on) bought specifically for her. Elizabeth Shackleton's commentary suggests that these goods were offered in a spirit of gracious patronage, not in recognition of the legitimacy of a customary perquisite. But if she hoped to foster deferential gratitude in her workforce, Mrs Shackleton was constantly disillusioned. An entire diary is devoted to the career of an adolescent maid, Nanny Nutter. Numerous ribbons and bonnets later, Elizabeth bitterly recorded 'Nanny Nutter run away . . . there may she remain forever . . . went to be a chambermaid at Carr. An ungrateful lying girl.'[57] Unrepentant and ungovernable servants regularly packed up and threatened to be off 'with their wardrobe'. Indeed, Elizabeth found that withholding a servant's belongings could be a useful tactic in delaying their departure.[58]

These domestic servants have left no direct testimony. From their mistress's records it is clear that they accepted new and cast-off clothes and trinkets, which Mrs Shackleton believed them to value. 'Gave Betty [some] old Oratorio gauze that came off a white chip hat, it will make her feel very fine.'[59] Yet for all Mrs Shackleton's assumptions, it is not clear that wearing a Lady's dress made a parlour maid look, feel or get treated like a lady. To presume she wished she was a lady might seem legitimate, but certainly does not follow from evidence that she accepted a second-hand dress. After all, second-hand dresses could be attractive simply because they had a high resale value.[60] Besides, the strenuous efforts ex-servants made to retrieve their wages and wardrobe, including the threat of legal action, suggest that clothing was seen as an important part of their earnings, rather than merely the coveted equipment of social emulation.[61]

One of the striking features of Elizabeth Shackleton's diaries is the way in which she characterized almost all her possessions (clothes, plate, kitchenware and linen) as either 'best' or 'common'. Common goods were those designated indispensable, but best goods were not necessarily new or fashionable. Neither does this best/common dichotomy neatly correspond with a public/private or front/back characterization of eighteenth-century domestic space. Elizabeth Shackleton drew on a conception of the celebrative and the routine to differentiate the ways things were used. An occasion may indeed have involved company and social display, but that did not define the event, since religious and sentimental observance both generated celebration, with or without an audience. Christian feasts called for special clothes, best tableware and thoughtfully arranged furniture.[62] Family anniversaries were commemorated by private rituals involving new clothes and old treasures. On Tom Parker's 24th birthday, though he was absent and there were no visitors, his mother

> put on in honour to this good day my quite new purple cotton night-gown and a new light brown fine cloth pincushion [made of] a piece of coat belonging to my own dear child, my own dear Tom, with a new blue string.

On his 25th birthday, she donned the same pincushion. Congratulating her youngest son on his birthday in 1777, Elizabeth Shackleton wrote 'I wish and better wish you my own dear love was with us. . . . I have your valuable rings on my fingers, John's picture before me and my bracelet on the table I write upon.'[63] These intimate rituals emphasize the talismanic properties of material things and bear witness to the personal significance of *inconspicuous* consumption. Elizabeth Shackleton used material things to honour God and her family, to lend substance to her relationships and ultimately as reassurance in the face of death. Witness her prayers in May 1779, in her 53rd year:

> I have now only five teeth in all in my head. I left off my old stays and put on my best stays for good. I left off my very old green quilted callimanco and put on my new drab callimanco quilted petticoat for good. God grant me my health to wear it and do well.[64]

This is not to say that Elizabeth Shackleton was ignorant of social convention and the necessity for material and sartorial observance. Guests were usually treated to the best china and linen. When surprise visitors arrived at dinner time, Mrs Shackleton 'made all nice as we co'd for our guests. Used my handsome, new, damask table-cloth which looks most beautiful for the first [time]. Good luck to it. Hope it will do well.'[65] When visiting herself, and in particular when attending dinner parties and celebrations, Mrs Shackleton made a conscious and obvious effort: 'dress'd myself in my best, A high head and low heels.'[66] She endeavoured to dress in a manner appropriate to company and context:

> Mrs W. trailed me through nasty, dirty, vile back streets to [York] minster, where we took several turns. . . . Mrs W. *would* have me put on my beautiful flower'd muslin which was entirely soiled by the dust. Little would I have done it had she not told me we were to have call'd upon Mrs Townend, for her to trail me through all those nasty places in York a hop sack wo'd have done.[67]

Both in public and in private, her commitment to sartorial propriety ran deep. Social discomfort is palpable in this terse but revealing aside. 'Tom so cross, wo'd not let me have a cap out of the green room. I sat bare head a long time.'[68] Evidently, Elizabeth Shackleton's pride in wearing clothes appropriate to company, environment and occasion went beyond a simple desire to impress her visitors.

Mrs Shackleton's concern for proper ceremony or informality expressed in things was not confined to herself. Elegant dress in women, if combined with wifely decorum, merited a pleasant reference from Mrs Shackleton. She had nothing but praise for her nephew's wife Beatrix Lister and their neat, tasteful and elegant home 'Chateau Marshfield'.[69] She approved of various mansions she visited – 'made a long stop to reconitre [Mr Lascelle's] fine and elegant building' – and of the taste and civility of their owners – 'Mr Clayton who was as civil as possible showed me his grounds, canals, garden and the house'.[70] Moreover she was not an automatic critic of luxurious display for she had no quarrel with the glorious raiment of a local lawyer and his wife.

> Mr and Mrs Wainman came in good time to dinner. A very agreeable woman elegantly dress'd – diamonds and pearls on her head. She is half gone with child. A very happy couple they are. Had a handsome carriage, handsome horses, handsome liveries – dark blue with silver.[71]

However, she was quick to call into question the sartorial motivation of those she disliked. Things which demonstrated dignity, civility and elegance in her friends, could in others just as easily represent foolish pretension. Fashionable dress worn by women she disliked was immediately taken to be proof of feminine conceit and inconsequence, as was the case with the unfortunate Miss Clough who was airily written off as 'a dressy person. Wears a very great roll.'[72] Nor was her contempt reserved for women. By 1779, Elizabeth Shackleton suspected that a neighbour, Owen Cunliffe of Wycoller, had been gossiping about her. She vented her spleen in a description of his ostentation and pretension.

> I knew that Captain Cunliffe was at church this day in his regimentals, a small captain, no honour to the Royal Lancashire. Bro't his Whiskey to Colne, his new man in his elegant new livery, red hair well powdered, two new hunters. Can have a fortune by a lady of £9,000 but thinks he deserves thrice that sum. Cunliffe is too short too low. Wants inches for a Captain.[73]

When Sergeant Aspinall, a barrister on the northern circuit, acted against the interests of the Parkers of Browsholme and the Listers of Gisburne Park in the disputed Clitheroe election of 1781, Elizabeth Shackleton was furious. In her diary, she linked Aspinall's naked political ambitions with the architectural improvements recently undertaken at his seat, Standen Hall.

> That scrubby, mean, underbred, lowlived, ungrateful, covetous, designing, stupid, proud Aspinall and his large wife may come to repent. . . . He within thirty years would have esteemed it a *Great* honour and been big of the application of being styl'd recorder of Clitheroe. What a wretch to behave so vilely to his most obliging, generous, worthy neighbours, Browsholme and Gisburne park . . . [he] most probably thinks Mr Curzon's purse will enable him to make a portico or add a venetian window to the beauties of Standen. What nonsense is he! Tho' like such a breed as he comes of . . . such little men.[74]

Clearly, Mrs Shackleton did not disapprove of finery and elegant surroundings *per se*, or indeed of social status expressed in things. None the less, accusations of materialism, pretension and covetousness provided useful ammunition for criticism of those who did not know their place, had slighted her in the past, or whom she simply disliked.

When it came to her *own* things, on the other hand, her professions of their personal value and associations were lofty and sentimental, as one might expect. Things for Elizabeth Shackleton were rich with memory.

> Wrote to my own dear Robert Parker, told him I was concerned I had told him I wo'd send the bible I had promised him, but that upon looking for it, found I had given it to my own dear Tom when he went to Winchester. But had sent him a good common prayer book [instead] given to me by Mr Cowgill of Emmanuel College, Cambridge who was there when his own good father was. . . . I told him I would give him a ring that was made for my own dear mother, her hair under a crystal, the star round it all brilliants, worth ten guineas, which I beg'd he'd ever keep and wear for my sake . . . sent a piece of Brussels lace I promised him, desired he'd keep in remembrance of me.[75]

Even intrinsically mundane items testified to past relationships, or commemorated past events. 'My dear John gives me a full account of [Tom's] wedding. Which letter I shall ever keep while I live.'[76] Gifts were valued in themselves and as material proof of the kind thoughts of others. 'I esteem the ruffles very elegant and handsome, but what enhances the value to me is my dear Tom's most obliging remembrance.' Ever-after, a gift prompted pleasant memories of the donor and the moment of giving, 'with his own dear hands'.[77] Home-made gifts were usually offered by women and were seen as time, labour and affection made concrete. 'Rec'd from Miss Parker . . . a pritty green purse with spangles, her own work which I much value.'[78] Elizabeth treasured items which had once belonged to people she loved, recording the wearing and mending her mother's old shifts and the distribution of her first husband's clothing to his sons. Certain possessions literally embodied something of the original owner, like the ring incorporating her dead mother's hair. It was perhaps with one eye on being remembered herself that Elizabeth Shackleton set about creating a new heirloom, making extensive enquiries, five years before she died, for a craftsman 'who could do me an extreme neat landscape in [my own] hair for my new bracelet'. She also had a bracelet made up of hair from the heads of her three sons 'so as to shew all the hair distinctly'.[79]

Occasional references in the diaries make it clear that Elizabeth Shackleton was not alone in ascribing meanings to inanimate objects. She drew on a shared awareness of the extra-material significance of things and in particular gifts. Tom and Betty Parker, for example, exchanged hair rings as love tokens during their courtship.[80] (However, Betty Parker's sins included cutting up the precious lace which had once belonged to Elizabeth's own mother and being insufficiently appreciative of Elizabeth's gifts.) The regular exchange of produce and trinkets was a widely recognized currency in elite sociability. In fact, Elizabeth's estranged brother Edward Parker signalled his forgiveness in a gift and she appreciated the beginning of the thaw when she received: 'a haunch of venison by the keeper of Bowland for which I gave him five shillings. This is the first present or taste I have had from Browsholme since I changed my name [i.e married Shackleton] being six years ago.'[81] Shared awareness of extra-material meaning is most explicit in the case of painted portraits, which obviously carried the most powerful human resonances and demanded remembrance of the sitter. When Elizabeth's sons Tom and John Parker were at odds, Tom's wife removed John Parker's portrait from her drawing room and with indubitable symbolism returned it forth-with to Elizabeth Shackleton. Elizabeth cherished the abandoned portrait and gave it pride of place: 'On this day my own dear John Parker's picture was done up over the fireplace in the parlour. I am truly happy to see it there and think it does great honour to its situation.'[82] This fulsome response to the likeness epitomizes the way Elizabeth Shackleton used material things to bear witness to and reinforce her social and particularly familial relationships.

Things conjured the past and ensured continuity into the future. The completed purchase of large items of furniture, particularly in the last few years of her life, often occasioned a prayer, confided to her diary. 'John Hargreaves of Coln Edge brought my new mahogany square tea table. I like it very well. God grant Mr S. and myself to have good and long use of it.'[83] Evidently, heavy furniture felt reassuringly permanent and substantial, yet its arrival prompted the ailing Elizabeth Shackleton to contemplate her own mortality, perhaps be-cause furnishing a house was characteristically associated with the beginning of married life rather than its end. Note how she recorded a furniture purchase the year before her death.

> [Arrived a] . . . new mahogany table from Messrs Gillows from Lancaster. It came quite safe and well not the least damage or scratch. It is in 3 parts. The middle a square and 2 ends which are half rounds – all put together makes an elegant oval. The wood very handsome. 16 feet all very strong and made neat it cost the table only £5:5s packing 3s6d in all £5:8:6. Good luck to it, good luck using it and hope we shall all have our healths and do well.[84]

The christening of a functional item was a private ritual: 'I wrote this [her diary] upon our new oak table. The very first time I ever did write upon it, or use it. Good luck attend me.'[85] The recording of first usage is consistent with Elizabeth Shackleton's pronounced awareness of the passage of time and the importance of the past and her memories in her everyday life. Her thirty-nine diaries offer an impressive record of her observance of traditional and less conventional anniversaries. 'A most glorious, hot sunny day. I left my old home at Browsholme this day 25 years and came to my good old house at Alkincoats. God prosper both good homes and their owners.'[86]

Elizabeth Shackleton's sense of the family history and the continuity which Alkincoats represented was brought to its fullest expression when Tom reached his majority in 1777 and claimed his inheritance. 'Great alteration in this family. . . . Tom was whole and sole master of Alkincoats.'[87] Quitting her marital home and household pre-eminence proved a drawn-out process. Mrs Shackleton immediately delivered all her diamonds and valuables into her son's hands. A year later she ritually handed over 'the keys of the bureau where he wo'd find *all* the keys', a symbol of her long years of management. Yet the final rupture did not come till 1779, when Tom Parker married. At which point, she definitively removed herself and her chattels to John Shackleton's modest manor, Pasture House: 'They all saw me come off bag and baggage. Am happy to leave my once happy home to my own dear . . . Tom.'[88] This spectacular loss of status was one she was prepared for and rationalized in what historians have often interpreted as stock gentry terms: the continuity of the family and the line, the importance of old traditions and the fundamental stability of the estate itself being of greater significance than any individual tenant. Thus she deferred to and prayed for Tom and his new wife on their wedding day. 'Grant them health and long life, prosperity and comfort. May they enjoy domestick peace . . . may good old *Alkincoats* flourish in every degree. Long may the usual generous hospitality flourish within and without those walls that ever did.'[89] Elizabeth Shackleton observed both the letter and the spirit of Robert Parker's will. Although she was miserable departing her old home and experienced pangs upon its redecoration ('my poor, good, old yellow room. Transmogrified indeed into elegance'[90]), she remained convinced of the importance of inheritance and perceived herself as a guardian of property entrusted to, and on loan from later generations of Parkers:

> On this day I emptied all and everything belonging unto me out of my mahogany bookcase, bureau and drawers given unto me by my own tender, good, most affectionate parent. They were made and finished by Henry Chatburne on Saturday December the eighth one thousand seven hundred and fifty. I value them much but relinquish the valuable loan with great satisfaction to my own dear child Thomas Parker.[91]

V

Elizabeth Shackleton's material values might appear to exemplify the petty, dynastic pretensions of the minor, provincial gentry, yet it would be mistaken to interpret these values as evidence of a traditional *mentalité*, persisting in an obscure Lancashire valley, remote from commerce and fashion. Elizabeth Shackleton was born in London, the daughter of a City linen draper, and remained a 'professed lover of the place'.[92] She had London newspapers sent up and regularly received gossipy letters from her friends and relatives in the capital.

Although forgoing trips to London after 1751, she intermittently visited polite or well-supplied northern towns (Preston, Warrington, Chester, Wrexham, Wakefield, Pontefract and York) throughout her married life. Information she could not gain for herself was supplied by other women; her principal informants being her friend Jane Scrimshire from Pontefract, her cousin Bessy Ramsden of Charterhouse on the edge of the City of London and her maternal Aunt Ann Pellet who lived in Kensington.[93] Her social network was such that, if she chose, she could purchase metropolitan commodities with ease.

In literature and in life, 'fashion' has proved a difficult concept to define. 'Being in fashion' is used both very loosely to indicate a general accordance with the modes and manners of the times and also more specifically to designate the possession of this season's model. If what historians of demand mean by fashion is the close shadowing of metropolitan high style, then Elizabeth Shackleton's engagement with fashion was very uneven. Even if we restrict our attention to those categories of goods which were at the very core of the eighteenth-century fashion system – furniture, tableware and clothing – the extent to which fashion influenced her purchasing decisions was different in every category. Elizabeth Shackleton's diaries are peppered with the particulars of countless purchases, sufficiently detailed to enable the analysis of her purchases by their place of origin.[94] While household utensils, provisions and groceries were almost invariably obtained within the parish, furniture consumption was regional in scope. With the exception of one or two small pieces, all the new Shackleton furniture was purchased in Lancashire from craftsmen in Colne, Manchester and Lancaster. By stark contrast, the purchase of tableware was overwhelmingly biased towards the metropolis.

Elizabeth Shackleton evidently put a premium on polite china and silverware. Precisely why she did so is not made explicit in the diaries, however the pleasure she derived from exquisite tableware (she was devoted to tea parties, enjoyed examining her neighbours' new purchases and even recorded which women snapped up the china at local house sales) may reflect female investment in meal-time ceremony and domestic sociability.[95] But for all that, Elizabeth Shackleton was no leader of fashion. Unlike her gowns, tableware was only infrequently replaced. Few bulk purchases were made and these were prompted by 'necessity' not the dictates of changing fashion – upon first marriage, remarriage, removal to Pasture House and in response to breakages. Furthermore, the letters Mrs Shackleton received from proxy consumers do not suggest a relentless pursuit of ultra-fashionable wares. Relatives made her aware of current modes and sometimes fashion constrained her choices – the tea tray of china she sought in 1754 could not be had anywhere because of the vogue for tea boards. Similarly, in the 1760s, she had to make do with a candelabra decorated with Greek gods, and not the branching flowers she requested, since the rococo had been superseded by neo-classicism in silverware design.[96] Yet fashion also created unexpected opportunities for canny consumers. They had to decide whether 'to pay the fashion', since the preferences of the fashionable elite were seen to inflate the price of some goods and depress the price of others.

> The nanquen sort is much the present taste and consequently the dearest, but as tis only blue and white will not be thought so fine. However you may have a good, genteel, full sett (that is 42 pieces) for about 5 or 6 guineas since the Beau Monde is chiefly for the ornamental china.[97]

From all of which testimony, it appears that the wives of the provincial gentry were satisfied with 'genteel' tableware and flattered themselves that they were too sensible to be buffeted by the ever-changing winds of metropolitan taste.

Commentary on changing furniture design in Elizabeth Shackleton's diaries is conspicuous by its absence. There is no evidence whatsoever that old-fashioned pieces were replaced by modish novelties, in fact it appears that furniture was bought once in a life-time and expected to last for generations. In furnishing Pasture House from scratch, the Shackletons purchased some mahogany pieces from Gillows of Lancaster. The company was patronized by the bulk of Elizabeth Shackleton's genteel acquaintance in Lancashire and Yorkshire, yet stylistically its furniture was characterized by a rather provincial fashionability. Anyone who wanted high design would betake themselves to a London showroom, not a Lancaster workshop.[98] In sum, when periodically restocking Alkincoats and Pasture House with high quality household goods, the Shackletons appear to have purchased commodities which although broadly fashionable in provincial terms were not in the highest style.

When it came to dress, however, Elizabeth Shackleton prided herself on being *au fait* with 'the reigning fashions'. Her strategically located observers kept her posted on the modes and manners of 'the fine folks', 'the people of distinction', 'the better sort'. Their ability to provide this information varied according to season, sociability and the visibility of 'the ladies of quality'. From Pontefract, 'the metropolis of politeness', Jane Scrimshire was best placed to answer Elizabeth's 'import[ant] questions about negligees' when county families were in the town attending the winter assemblies.[99] Similarly in London, Bessy Ramsden had to attend public functions and arenas such as pleasure gardens, theatres and assemblies in order to identify up-to-the-minute modes. 'As for fashions I believe I must postpone them a little longer as it is too early to tell what will be worn. . . . Excepting to the city assembly once this winter I have not been anywhere in publick.'[100] Thus far, a model of the transmission of taste based on emulation theory is confirmed. Bessy Ramsden regarded London as the 'fountainhead' of fashion, exhibited by an elite minority in arenas of social display.[101] And, what is more, Mrs Ramsden was exceedingly eager to observe these glamorous exhibitions. Witness William Ramsden informing Elizabeth Shackleton of his wife's determination to view the Queen's birthday court from the gallery in 1766.

> Possibly you may suspect this to be curiosity to see the fine folks; not a bit on't, but only to enable her [to atone] with your ladyship for her past sins of omission by sending a letter cramm'd full with such glitterings, dazzlings, diamonds and so forth as will almost put out your peepers unless fortified by a pair of spectacles, with the glasses blackened as when we look at the sun in an eclipse.[102]

Bessy Ramsden was gregarious, a gad-about and a lover of spectacle, yet she was not a straightforward emulator of the ladies of quality. She indulged in gentle mockery of those aspirants to the *Beau Monde* who made themselves ridiculous for the sake of fashion, like a Miss Price who spent an afternoon stabbing insects to produce the current 'flea' colour, or a young bride whose ultra-fashionable trimming of wax strawberries melted in front of the fire. She reported the absurdities of high fashion with relish, describing the Duchess of Devonshire's habit of wearing a wax kitchen garden in her hair, the rage for monstrously oversized bonnets and the lamentable vogue for head-dresses built so tall that ladies were obliged to sit on the bottom of their coaches.[103] Such reports satisfied Mrs Shackleton's curiosity and enabled her to feel pleasantly scandalized. 'I recd a long and an entertaining letter from Mrs Ramsden of the present Indecent, Fashionable meetings of the conspicuous,

Great Ladies of this Isle, fie for shame.'[104] Like Mrs Ramsden, Mrs Shackleton contemplated the *Beau Monde* with a mixture of awed fascination and disapproval.

While Elizabeth Shackleton's correspondents satisfied her general interest in fashion and the fashionable, they also answered specific enquiries concerning the making of negligees, nightgowns and sacks for wear in Lancashire. Her informants made suggestions based on a variety of criteria, recommending dresses that would be fashionable but also durable, versatile, attractive and appropriate to Elizabeth's age and modest height. Modes which originated at court might be rejected on aesthetic grounds – 'very ugly for all they are the Queen's', or in the name of modesty – 'It would not be thought decent for a widow with children to show so much nakedness'. Extreme vogues were thought best confined to the peerage, who were accorded a degree of sartorial licence – 'the above is indeed the present taste and I am sorry to say much entered into by people of no rank'.[105] On the other hand, new designs might be more readily adopted if considered 'becoming', 'in character', 'prettiest for us mothers' or 'an easy fashion', while fabrics were chosen according to the time of year, in colours that would last.[106] Efforts were made to match outfit to occasion. In the 1750s, Ann Pellet suggested a long sack with a hoop for a formal wedding visit because although relatively unfashionable it would look 'much more noble'.[107]

Evidently, Elizabeth Shackleton and her friends kept abreast of London fashion *and* exercised considerable discrimination.[108] Engagement with fashion involved complicated decision-making; some designs were accepted *tout court*, some adapted for use in Lancashire and others rejected out of hand. Mrs Shackleton was not a slavish imitator of elite modes, nor a passive victim of the velocity of fashion, not least because passive victims rarely exhibit a capacity for self-mockery. 'In high conceit with myself' she recorded on her first excursion in a new purple cap from Preston.[109] Clearly her sartorial effort was tempered by knowing amusement. Witness a satirical poem she transcribed.

> Shepherds I have lost my waist. Have you seen my body?
> Sacrificed to modern taste, I'm quite a Hoddy Doddy.
> Never shall I see it more, Till common sense returning
> My body to my legs restore, then I shall cease from mourning.
> For Fashion I that part forsook where sages plac'd the belly
> Tis lost and I have not a nook for cheesecakes, tarts or jelly![110]

VI

Elizabeth Shackleton's records reveal the role of material things in a range of social practices. She presided over and performed the bulk of the day-to-day purchasing for her household and the maintenance of the goods therein. By extension, well-chosen and well-maintained possessions testified to her expertise and gratified her self-esteem. Eventually, many of these possessions served as currency in the mistress–servant relationship. Over and above their purely practical function, Elizabeth Shackleton's possessions both acted as crucial props in unobserved, intimate rituals and displayed her social status to the wider public. When slighted, she deployed the rhetoric of luxury and vanity to belittle the motives and material culture of her enemies. By contrast, her own world of goods was rich and complex. When self-consciously writing about her *own* possessions, she dwelt at length on their sentimental and talismanic associations. Growing frail, she contemplated the durability of the material in contrast to transience of flesh, hoping her heirlooms would guarantee remembrance. Ultimately she drew reassurance from her belief in the continuity of the Parker family and estate and the importance of inheritance. However conservative these values and practices might appear, they did not constitute a reactionary alternative to fashionable behaviour, but an adjunct. Elizabeth Shackleton was a privileged consumer. The very mahogany which carried family history down through time was itself an emblem of genteel status. Mrs Shackleton's property proved that she belonged to the local elite and simultaneously distanced her from the likes of Betty Hartley the shopkeeper. But social differentiation through material possessions is a subtly different phenomenon to social emulation.

Elizabeth Shackleton updated her wardrobe for her own pleasure and for social propriety. Some of her gratification may have derived from the display of London modes to Lancashire society, yet only *once* in her entire correspondence was an item recommended on those grounds. In an effort to reconcile her suspicious cousin to some ostentatious fabrics, Bessy Ramsden exploited the language of emulation. '[The Silks] were to be sure vastly pretty and the extraordinary trouble in the working of 'em will be amply repaid you in the envy &c they will excite among the misses of Coln.'[111] Granted, Elizabeth Shackleton adopted some stylish innovations which originated at court, but that did not necessarily mean she admired the Ladies of Quality or wanted to be the Duchess of Devonshire. Moreover, even if an item was originally bought for the express purpose of dazzling east Lancashire, it could in time become a repository of memories or a grateful reward. ('I gave Betty Cooke my strip'd and sprigged muslin apron above thirty years in my possession.'[112])

It is also important to recall that not all categories of goods were equally susceptible to fashion. Metropolitan chic was more highly prized in clothing than in tableware, in tableware than in furniture and in furniture than in kitchenware. Nor did fashion obliterate all other associations. Elizabeth Shackleton's hair jewellery offers an explicit example of the possible co-existence of different systems of meaning. Constituted of human hair, such ornaments were potent extensions of the self. They were bequeathed to loved ones as heirlooms and were exchanged by lovers as tokens of mutuality and romantic esteem. Private associations notwithstanding, they also signalled an engagement with high fashion, enjoying along with other 'love ornaments' a massive vogue in the later eighteenth century.

Even if the new clothes, tableware and furniture consumed by Elizabeth Shackleton were all broadly fashionable in form, their form neither expressed the full range of her motivations nor did it dictate the function these goods performed for her. Elizabeth Shackleton's records testify to the sheer diversity of meanings it was possible to attach to possessions. Of course meanings were not absolutely rigid since objects accrued different connotations according to use and context, yet some general patterns can be observed. Large or expensive items, bought new or inherited, were suggestive of history and lineage. The reassuring permanence associated with substantial pieces of furniture was akin to that conveyed by the built environment: furniture, carriages, roads, bridges and houses were all blessed in similar terms by Elizabeth Shackleton.[113] Unsurprisingly, pieces of clothing and accoutrements expressed individuality, promoting the remembrance of original owner or donor. Kitchen utensils were valued for trusty service, ingenuity and sometimes novelty, while china and tableware signified genteel ceremony and pleasant sociability.

Of course it is possible that Elizabeth Shackleton was an isolated material obsessive, but this seems unlikely given the corroborating references which can be found in other manuscripts. While demonstrating their expertise as fashionable consumers, Elizabeth's friends also sent her sentimental gifts, for as Jane Scrimshire remarked '*small presents* confirm friendship'.[114] Bessy Ramsden used the language of remembrance to recommend her offerings –

> I have taken the liberty to enclose a cap which you will do me great honour to accept. It is by way of your seeing what will be wore in the second mourning. I do desire that you will wear it for my sake and not put it up in lavender.[115]

A preoccupation with family history expressed in things can be found in Ann Pellet's letters. When Elizabeth was pressed to raise an apprenticeship fee, she asked permission to sell the diamond stay buckles given by her Aunt Pellet. Mrs Pellet authorized the sale with the following proviso.

> I . . . only beg you'll never give them out of your family, as I had [them] many years, was your dear Grandmamma's. Mrs Scrimshire seem'd to entertain some hopes of my giving them to her, but I never once design'd it as it wo'd be very unnatural to give them out of my family.[116]

Although the breadth of commentary on consumption and property found in Elizabeth Shackleton's diaries is unparalleled among surviving Lancashire manuscripts, elements of her value system can be found in the records of other women outside her acquaintance.[117] In effect, the diaries constitute that intact Delft platter (to borrow a metaphor) which allows us to identify and make sense of the shattered fragments scattered across other collections and archives.[118] This is not to suggest, however, that Everywoman's relationship with material culture was the same. Elizabeth Shackleton was in her forties and fifties when she wrote the diaries, a younger woman might have privileged the purchase of novelties over the conservation of old treasures. Furthermore, a custodial attitude to property might be peculiar to the experience of widowhood and trusteeship. Not all women had Elizabeth Shackleton's *opportunity* to develop a housekeeping, curatorial ethos in their dealings with things. Sentimental materialism, along with mahogany furniture, may have been a luxury many women simply could not afford.

The diary and letters of Ellen Weeton Stock, a Lancashire governess and near contemporary of Elizabeth Shackleton's, lend themselves to an analysis of consumer motivation in terms of the pursuit of social acceptance, envy and wishful thinking. 'If I were rich enough to buy furniture and take a house and keep a servant, I could have as much society, highly respectable as I could wish.'[119] Nevertheless amongst the palpable social anxiety and preoccupation with respectability, sentiments of striking similarity to Elizabeth Shackleton's are revealed. Ellen Weeton Stock made every effort to pass on domestic expertise to her daughter by letter, urging Mary Stock to practise measurement, cutting out and sewing and sending minute accounts of her purchases 'for you will never be fit to be a housekeeper unless you know the value of most things in daily use'.[120] Concerned to provide her daughter with a sense of family history, Mrs Stock sent a bundle of humble heirlooms, cataloguing their past associations.

> The green ribbon is part of a boxfull my mother once had; they were taken in a prize which my father captured during the American war. . . . The piece of patchwork is of an old quilt, I made it about 20 years ago; the hexagon in the

middle was of our best bed hangings . . . they were chintzs my father brought home with him from one of his voyages. . . . I am thus minute, my Mary, that you might know something of the history of your mother's family.[121]

Even where things were coveted for social status, this does not preclude the simultaneous existence of more complex responses to material things. Social emulation and conspicuous consumption are useful concepts accounting for purchasing motivation under certain circumstances, but as portmanteau descriptions of eighteenth-century consumer behaviour and material culture they are dangerously misleading. Certainly the language of luxury and longing was available to and occasionally deployed by eighteenth-century consumers, yet this was only one vocabulary among many. Wedgwood china figured in genteel material culture, but took its place alongside an assemblage of other artefacts equally important to their owner: inherited cabinets, family portraits, christening cups, favourite old teapots, home-made purses, scraps of faded gowns and locks of hair set in gold.

Ultimately this essay begs as many questions as it resolves. Since this is the first study of its kind, it is impossible to assess the extent to which the attitudes I have outlined are peculiar to the later eighteenth century. Similar research on the personal records of seventeenth- and nineteenth-century consumers might, after all, uncover similar findings.[122] The extent to which my evidence reveals material values that were distinctively female is also a matter for speculation. Only further investigation of male consumption will clarify this. Nevertheless, recent research on the wills of both sexes suggests marked gender differences in attitudes to commodities once possessed. Women's records consistently reveal a more self-conscious, emotional investment in household goods, apparel and personal effects. On the rare occasions when male testators particularized their personal property they usually referred to tools or livestock.[123] Exactly why this should be the case is in question, although possible answers come readily to mind. A gentlewoman was far more likely than her brothers to inherit personal property, while real property (land) tended to be reserved for male beneficiaries. As a result, most women had only movable goods to bestow themselves.[124] Denied access to the professions and public office, women could not pass on the invisible mysteries of institutional power or professional expertise to their descendants. A gentle-woman's skills were characteristically embodied in that 'unskilled' arena, the household.[125] Small wonder if, in consequence, she turned to personal and household artefacts to create a world of meanings and ultimately to transmit her history.

Notes

For references, suggestions and critical readings I should like to thank Susan Amussen, Maxine Berg, Helen Clifford, Penelope Corfield, Jenny Kermode, Christopher Marsh and John Styles. Furthermore, I must acknowledge the kindness of Mrs Parker of Browsholme, who permitted me to use the manuscripts in the Parker of Browsholme deposit in the Lancashire County Record Office at Preston.

 1 T. Veblen, *The Theory of the Leisure Class: An Economic Study of Institutions* (London: George Allen & Unwin, 1925).
 2 H. J. Perkin, 'The social causes of the British Industrial Revolution', *Transactions of the Royal Historical Society*, lxxv (1968), 140.
 3 N. McKendrick, J. Brewer and J. H. Plumb, *The Birth of a Consumer Society: The Commercialization of Eighteenth-Century England* (London: Hutchinson, 1983), 9–194.

4 A. Buck, *Dress in Eighteenth-Century England* (London: B. T. Batsford Ltd, 1979), 210.

5 L. Weatherill, *Consumer Behaviour and Material Culture in Britain 1660–1760* (London: Routledge, 1988), esp. 25–42, 168–89.

6 L. Weatherill, 'Consumer behaviour and social status in England, 1660–1750', *Continuity and Change*, ii (1986), 191.

7 Weatherill, *Material Culture*, 60, 187–9.

8 C. Campbell, *The Romantic Ethic and the Spirit of Modern Consumerism* (Oxford: Basil Blackwell, 1987). For a useful discussion of the limitations of Veblen's theoretical insights, see 49–57.

9 Veblen, *Leisure Class*, 54.

10 Women's historians and feminists have been preoccupied with the question of decorative femininity and idle leisure. The orthodox chronology assumes a lost golden age of rough-and-ready gender equality before the onset of industrial capitalism and modernity. Between *c.* 1600 and 1850, women in commercial, professional and elite circles are believed to have metamorphosed from economic help-meets engaged in the public world to decorative appendages confined to the private. The female transition from respected producer to passive consumer, however, has now been asserted for so many different periods that justifications in terms of 'uneven development' seem no longer sustainable. See, for example, M. George, 'From good wife to mistress: the transformation of the female in bourgeois culture', *Science and Society*, xxxvii (1973), 152–77; A. Clark, *Working Life of Women in the Seventeenth Century* (London: Routledge & Kegan Paul, 1982; 1st edn, 1919); S. Amussen, *An Ordered Society: Class and Gender in Early Modern England* (Oxford: Basil Blackwell, 1988); L. Davidoff and C. Hall, *Family Fortunes: Men and Women of the English Middle Class, 1780–1850* (London: Hutchinson, 1987). Elements of the orthodoxy have been contested. The most telling criticisms can be found in O. Hufton, 'Women in history: early modern Europe', *Past and Present*, ci (1983), 125–41; M. J. Peterson, 'No angels in the house: the Victorian myth and the Paget women', *American Historical Review*, lxxxix (1984), 677–708; and J. Bennet, 'History that stands still: women's work in the European past', *Feminist Studies*, xiv (1988), 269–83.

11 N. McKendrick, 'Home demand and economic growth: a new view of the role of women and children in the Industrial Revolution', in N. McKendrick (ed.), *Historical Perspectives: Studies in English Thought and Society in Honour of J. H. Plumb* (London: Europa Publications, 1974), 200, 209.

12 Campbell, *Romantic Ethic*, 233.

13 Some historians are more explicit than others about the nature of gender costume. Witness the inimitable Cunningtons: 'feminine fashions were less concerned than male fashions to express Class Distinction, being more intent on the display of Sex Attraction', in C. W. and P. Cunnington, *A Handbook of English Costume in the Eighteenth Century* (London: Faber & Faber, 1957), 26. For practical tips, see 'Costume as a direct method of sex attraction' in C. W. Cunnington, *Why Women Wear Clothes* (London: Faber & Faber, 1941), 41–76.

14 A. Ribeiro, *Dress in Eighteenth-Century Europe, 1715–1789* (London: B. T. Batsford Ltd, 1984), 116. A more subtle treatment of contemporary commentary can be found in Buck, *Dress in Eighteenth-Century England*, 103–19.

15 L. Weatherill, 'A possession of one's own: women and consumer behaviour in England, 1660–1740', *Journal of British Studies*, xxv (1986), 131–56.

16 P. Bourdieu, *Distinction: A Social Critique of the Judgement of Taste* (London: Routledge & Kegan Paul, 1984); D. Hebdige, 'Object as image: the Italian scooter cycle', in idem, *Hiding in The Light: On Images and Things* (London: Comedia, 1988), 77–115; M. Poster (ed.), *Jean Baudrillard: Selected Writings* (Cambridge: Polity, 1988), 119–48.

17 M. Mauss, *The Gift* (London: Cohen & West, 1970); A. Appadurai (ed.), *The Social Life of Things: Commodities in Cultural Perspective* (Cambridge: Cambridge University Press, 1986); M. Douglas and B. Isherwood, *The World of Goods: Towards an Anthropology of Consumption* (New York: Basic Books, 1979); D. Miller, 'Appropriating the State on the council estate', *Man*, n.s., xxiii (1988), 353–72.

18 See J. Attfield and P. Kirkham (eds), *A View From the Interior: Feminism, Women and Design*

(London: Virago, 1989) and C. Steedman, *Landscape for a Good Woman: A Story of Two Lives* (London: Virago, 1986).

19 The best Parker pedigree can be found in *Genealogist*, n.s., xxxi (1914–15), 102–5. John Parker's occupation is confirmed in his daughter's baptismal registration, see G. W. G. Leveson Gower (ed.), *A Register of all the Christninges, Burialles and Weddings within the Parish of Saint Peeter's upon Cornhill, 1667–1774* (London: Harleian Society Publications, 1879), 35. The acreage and rental value of the estate have been calculated from information found in the Lancashire County Record Office (hereafter LRO), DDB/76/1 (1745–58), Account book for Robert Parker, and LRO, DDB/78/1 (1751), Marriage Settlement of Elizabeth Parker and Robert Parker. Elizabeth Parker's jolly widowhood and subsequent elopement is discussed in LRO, DDB/72/183, 188 (1765), B. and W. Ramsden, Charterhouse, to E. Parker, Alkincoats. Tom Parker's inheritance and John and Robert Parker's apprenticeships are recorded in LRO, DDB/81/14 (1772), fols 7–11 and LRO, DDB/81/35 (1779), fol. 80–1. For more information about Alkincoats and surrounding manors, consult S. Pearson, *Rural Houses of the Lancashire Pennines, 1560–1760* (London: HMSO, 1985), 38–57, 118–20.

20 For a detailed discussion of polite networks in Pennine Lancashire and Yorkshire, see A. J. Vickery, 'Women of the local elite in Lancashire, 1750–*c*.1825' (University of London, Ph.D. thesis, 1991), 60–79.

21 LRO, DDB/81/1–39 (1762–81), Diaries of Elizabeth Shackleton of Alkincoats and later Pasture House.

22 For an approximate assessment of global accounting, see LRO, DDB/76/4 (1758–75), Trust Account of Thomas Parker. This account book registers income from rents and investment, plus disbursements on the children's upkeep, travel and tuition. However it carries no information about John Shackleton's income, or that of Elizabeth Shackleton beyond her £140 p.a. jointure. Reference to global yearly expenditure is made once only, see LRO, DDB/81/3 (1764), fol. 12: 'Spent including everything in 1762. £292.0.10. Spent including everything in 1763 £316.0.6.' The diaries contain no evidence of financial anxiety, nor extensive saving; the family appear to have covered ordinary expenditure with a modest margin. However Elizabeth Shackleton experienced considerable difficulty raising apprenticeship fees of £300, see LRO, DDB/81/14 (1772), fols 8, 32, 38.

23 Compare Westminster Public Library, Gillows Collection, 344/7, Wastebook 1779–80, fols 639, 649, 720, with LRO, DDB/81/35 (1779), fols 51a, 202.

24 LRO, DDB/80/29 (1757), Will of Robert Parker of Alkincoats; LRO, DDB/78/13 (1751), Marriage Settlement of Elizabeth Parker and Robert Parker; LRO, DDB/76/4 (1758–75), Trust Account of Thomas Parker, see entries for 1765–75. For reference to the existence of a second settlement, see LRO, DDB/81/27 (1776), fols 62–3.

25 The dynamics of the Shackleton marriage are explored in Vickery, 'Women of the local elite', 113–20.

26 Women in lesser gentry, mercantile and professional circles rarely had the means to employ an executive division of upper servants to liberate them from domestic responsibility. For a picture of the platonic servant hierarchy, see J. Hecht, *The Domestic Servant in Eighteenth-Century England* (London: Routledge & Kegan Paul, 1980), 35–70.

27 Women's independence as routine consumers is confirmed by the efforts American patriots made to secure female co-operation in the colonial boycott of British imports, particularly tea, in the 1760s and 1770s. Consult M. B. Norton, *Liberty's Daughters: The Revolutionary Experience of American Women, 1750–1800* (Toronto: Little, Brown & Co., 1980), 157–63. Consumer boycotting proved an ideal female strategy, adopted by associations of British women in the early nineteenth century. See C. Midgeley, 'Women anti-slavery campaigners in Britain, 1787–1868' (University of Kent, Ph.D. thesis, 1989), ch. 2

28 For examples from the 1760s, see LRO, DDB/81/6 (1767), fols 14, 43; LRO, DDB/81/7 (1768), fols 15, 48, 66; and LRO, DDB/81/8 (1769), fol. 95.

29 For the quotation, see LRO, DDB/81/13 (1771), fol. 57. The exchange of information about fashionable commodities is explored in section v.

30 LRO, DDB/72/19 (15.8.1751), R. Parker, Colne, to E. Parker, Browsholme.

31 LRO, DDB/72/43 (c.1756), R. Parker, York, to E. Parker, Alkincoats, and LRO, DDB/72/45 (c.1756), R. Parker, Skipwith, to Same.

32 LRO, DDB/72/125 (3.12.1753), J. Scrimshire, Pontefract, to E. Parker, Alkincoats.

33 LRO, DDB/72/445, 156, 132 (1754–7), J. Scrimshire, Pontefract, to E. Parker, Alkincoats.

34 LRO, DDB/72/177, 179 (1764), W. and B. Ramsden, Charterhouse, to E. Parker, Alkincoats.

35 Men's gifts from Birmingham, Sheffield, Skipwith and Chester are recorded in LRO, DDB/81/14 (1772), fol. 13; LRO, DDB/81/22 (1774), fols 3, 45. Changing fashions in waistcoats and the acquisition thereof are major themes of the following letters: LRO, DDB/72/322, 328, 331 (1773–7), J. Parker, London, to T. Parker, Alkincoats.

36 LRO, DDB/72/185 (30.4.1765), W. and B. Ramsden, Charterhouse, to E. Parker, Alkincoats.

37 LRO, DDB/81/35 (1779), fol. 51a.

38 This impression is confirmed by H. Clifford, 'Parker and Wakelin: the study of an eighteenth-century goldsmithing firm c.1760–76 with particular reference to the Garrard Ledgers' (Royal College of Art, Ph.D. thesis, 1988), 243. Parker and Wakelin's customers between 1766 and 1777 were made up of 257 men and 43 women. The women's purchases were almost invariably confined to the smaller less expensive items, like individual pieces of teaware, snuff boxes and paste and silver jewellery. Only three women made large orders for investment goods such as entire tea services or gold and precious stone jewellery. See also L. Lippincott, *Selling Art in Georgian London: The Rise of Arthur Pond* (New Haven: Yale University Press, 1983), 66–9. Wealthy and noble women made up a quarter of the customers of Arthur Pond, the painter and art dealer. However their average individual expenditure was in most cases lower than men of the same rank; only two women spent more than £50 and none exceeded £100. Eighty-two per cent of these female consumers made only one purchase as opposed to 62 per cent of the men.

39 LRO, DDB/74/14 (1758), Probate inventory of late Robert Parker.

40 Mrs Shackleton drew up stock-lists of the property she stored for her children, see her 'catalogue of the contents of R. P.'s box with a lock and key in the nursery' enclosed in LRO, DDB/72/307 (28.2.1777), E. Shackleton, Alkincoats, to R. Parker, London. She itemized the belongings she took on a trip, see LRO, DDB/81/3 (1764), fol. 11, and recorded all the clothing her second husband brought with him upon their marriage: LRO, DDB/81/4 (1765), fol. 1.

41 LRO, DDB/81/7 (1768), fol. 104. The organization of furniture, utensils and linens by room and by cupboard is discussed in Vickery, 'Women of the local elite', 197–9. Suffice it to say here that Elizabeth Shackleton was a great believer in good storage. When Alkincoats was being renovated in 1751 Elizabeth urged her first husband Robert Parker 'Pray let no conveniency be lost that you can make by way of cupboards and closets for they are useful in a family', see LRO, DDB/72/12 (3.7.1751), E. Parker, Browsholme, to R. Parker, Alkincoats.

42 LRO, DDB/81/17 (1772), fol. 29 and LRO, DDB/81/35 (1779), fol. 17. For further expressions of regret over the breakage of an entire tea board of china, a wine and water glass and a beautiful 'lyon' teapot from Colne, consult LRO, DDB/81/20 (1773), fol. 82; LRO, DDB/81/35 (1779), fol. 122; and LRO, DDB/81/37 (1780), fol. 27.

43 LRO, DDB/81/26 (1775), fol. 106 and LRO, DDB/81/33A (1778), fol. 187.

44 LRO, DDB/81/33A (1778), fol. 53.

45 LRO, DDB/81/37 (1780), fol. 208

46 LRO, DDB/81/33A (1778), fol. 246: 'Tom called, he stayed an hour. . . . He said he should want a number of things in the housekeeping way, particularly linnen. I might advise Miss Parker about things.'

47 LRO, DDB/81/33A (1778), fol. 60.

48 LRO, DDB/81/35 (1779), fol. 225.

49 LRO, DDB/81/37 (1780), fol. 70.

50 LRO, DDB/81/37 (1780), fol. 203.

51 In the same decade, Parson Woodforde's maids were guaranteed daily tea and sugar by contract, J. Beresford (ed.), *The Diary of a Country Parson: The Reverend James Woodforde*, vol. 1 (London: Oxford University Press/Humphrey Milford, 1924–31), 182, 236–7, 271–2.

52 LRO, DDB/81/13 (1771), fol. 15; LRO, DDB/81/17 (1772), fol. 48.

53 LRO, DDB/81/35 (1779), fol. 257–8.

54 Clothing allowances recorded in LRO, DDB/81/3 (1764), fols 2, 27, and LRO, DDB/81/13 (1771), fol. 74.

55 LRO, DDB/81/15 (1772–5), fol. 26.

56 LRO, DDB/81/37 (1780), fol. 191.

57 LRO, DDB/81/15 (1772–5), fols 85, 99. Elizabeth Shackleton's exuberant generosity is catalogued on fols 16, 24, 26, 46, 56, 82, 86, 100.

58 The ritual packing up of 'bag and baggage' is illustrated in LRO, DDB/81/13 (1771), fols 32–3; and LRO, DDB/81/35 (1779), fol. 119. On the use of clothes as a bargaining counter, see LRO, DDB/81/35 (1779), fols 83–4.

59 LRO, DDB/81/37 (1780), fol. 308.

60 The flourishing second-hand clothes business is reconstructed in B. Lemire, 'Consumerism in pre-industrial and early industrial England: the trade in secondhand clothes', *Journal of British Studies*, xxvii (1988), 1–24.

61 For example, LRO, DDB/81/29 (1776), fol. 98.

62 Refer to LRO, DDB/81/35 (1779), fol. 62; LRO, DDB/81/37 (1780), fol. 259; and LRO, DDB/81/39 (1781), fol. 74.

63 See respectively, LRO, DDB/81/33A (1778), fol. 118, and LRO, DDB/72/310 (16.3.1777), E. Shackleton, Alkincoats, to R. Parker, London. See also LRO, DDB/81/35 (1779), fol. 148: 'I am on this day 54 or 55 years old. . . . I put on my new white long lawn mark'd E.2. in honour of this good day.'

64 LRO, DDB/81/35 (1779), fol. 73.

65 LRO, DDB/81/33A (1778), fol. 223. See also LRO, DDB/81/35 (1779), fol. 96, on the first use of 'new Japan night candlesticks upon the good occasion'.

66 LRO, DDB/81/35 (1779), fol. 221. See in addition fol. 39 and LRO, DDB/81/8 (1769), fol. 69.

67 LRO, DDB/81/37 (1780), fols 154–5.

68 LRO, DDB/81/17 (1772), fol. 85.

69 For approving notice of the amiable and accomplished Beatrix Parker (née Lister) and her villa in Settle, see LRO, DDB/81/33A (1778), fol. 68 and LRO, DDB/81/35 (1779), fol. 235.

70 LRO, DDB/81/10 (1770), fol. 66 and LRO, DDB/81/35 (1779), fol. 87.

71 LRO, DDB/81/39 (1781), fol. 16(6).

72 LRO, DDB/81/17 (1772), fol. 34. She could not resist mocking the 'great talker' Mrs Cunliffe for her elaborate coiffure and even her favourite Mrs Walton in a new muslin gown and long train, see LRO, DDB/81/33A (1778), fols 179, 184.

73 LRO, DDB/81/23 (1774), fol. 72. Another spiteful description of Cunliffe's 'parade and high glory' can be found in LRO, DDB/81/22 (1774), fol. 109.

74 LRO, DDB/81/39 (1781), fols 31–2. Affected architectural features were a popular target for satire in this period, see D. Donald, ' "Mr Deputy Dumpling and family": satirical images of the city merchant in eighteenth-century England', *Burlington Magazine*, cxxxi (1989), 755–63.

75 LRO, DDB/81/30 (1777), fols 8–9. See also fols 32–3.

76 LRO, DDB/81/35 (1779), fol. 77.

77 LRO, DDB/81/25 (1775), fol. 107; LRO, DDB/81/35 (1779), fol. 196.

78 LRO, DDB/81/28 (1776), fol. 53. She was similarly gratified by a lace gift from Miss Smith 'her own knitting', LRO, DDB/81/8 (1769), fol. 88.

79 LRO, DDB/81/27 (1776), fols 47, 97–8.

80 LRO, DDB/81/31 (1777), fol. 102.

81 LRO, DDB/81/13 (1771), fol. 63. For a stimulating discussion of the social significance of exchanges of game in landed society, see D. Hay, 'Poaching and the game laws on Cannock Chase', in D. Hay, P. Linebaugh, E. P. Thompson (eds), *Albion's Fatal Tree: Crime and Society in Eighteenth-Century England* (London: Allen Lane, 1975), 244–53.

82 LRO, DDB/81/39 (1781), fol. 166. The painting officially belonged to Elizabeth Shackleton, given by John Parker in 1776, 'A more valuable gift he co'd not have bestowed', see LRO, DDB/81/27 (1776), fol. 18.

83 LRO, DDB/81/33A (1778), fol. 40.

84 LRO, DDB/81/35 (1779), fol. 202.

85 LRO, DDB/81/37 (1780), fol. 261.

86 LRO, DDB/81/33A (1778), fol. 27. See also LRO, DDB/81/35 (1779), fol. 23.

87 LRO, DDB/81/30 (1777), fol. 40.

88 See respectively, LRO, DDB/81/30 (1777), fol. 40; LRO, DDB/81/33A (1778), fol. 15; and LRO, DDB/81/35 (1779), fol. 213.

89 LRO, DDB/81/35 (1779), fol. 74.

90 LRO, DDB/81/37 (1780), fol. 78. Her unhappiness can be judged by the soothing letter she received from a sympathetic Bessy Ramsden, see LRO, DDB/72/291 (10.7.1777), B. Ramsden, Charterhouse, to E. Shackleton, Pasture House.

91 LRO, DDB/81/35 (1779), fol. 209. She was equally punctilious about her Aunt Pellet's bequest of a silver tea table: '[Ann Pellet] bequeaths it to me now for my life afterwards to go to her God son, my own dear child Thomas Parker, which please God the table must.' Refer to LRO, DDB/81/25 (1775), fols 75–80.

92 LRO, DDB/72/195 (25.12.1766), W. Ramsden, Charterhouse, to E. Shackleton, Alkincoats.

93 The diaries record that Elizabeth Shackleton also received information from Southwark from Mrs and Miss Bullcock, but their letters have not survived, see LRO, DDB/81/8 (1769), fol. 58 and LRO, DDB/81/36 (1780), unfoliated, see entry for 30.4.1780. For biographical data on Ann Pellet (née Southouse), Jane Scrimshire (née Pellet) and Elizabeth Ramsden (née Parker), see Essex Record Office D/DC 27/1010, Will of Henry Southouse; Public Record Office, 11/1016, Will of Mrs Ann Pellet; W. Munk (ed.), *The Roll of the Royal College of Physicians of London*, vol. 2 (London: Royal College of Physicians, 1878), 56; R. L. Arrowsmith (ed.), *Charterhouse Register, 1769–1872* (London: Phillimore & Co., 1974), 420. Further details are in Vickery, 'Women of the local elite', 339–43.

94 A complete breakdown of Elizabeth Shackleton's consumption by individual commodity can be found in Vickery, 'Women of the local elite', 264–76.

95 For an elaboration of the female role in domestic sociability, and their devotion to the tea table and its rituals, see Vickery, 'Women of the local elite', 316–30.

96 See LRO, DDB/72/86 (21.3.1754), M. Bowen, London, to E. Parker, Alkincoats (all Ann Pellet's letters were written by her servant and secretary, M. Bowen; hereafter the author will be designated A. Pellet); LRO, DDB/72/74 (n.d.), B. Ramsden, Charterhouse, to E. Parker, Alkincoats.

97 LRO, DDB/72/86 (21.3.1754), A. Pellet, London, to E. Parker, Alkincoats.

98 For an assessment of the fashionability of Gillows stock, consult S. Nichols, 'Gillow and Company of Lancaster, England: an eighteenth-century business history' (University of Delaware, M.A. thesis, 1982), 9.

99 LRO, DDB/72/123, 134, 137 (1753–4), J. Scrimshire, Pontefract, to E. Parker, Alkincoats.

100 LRO, DDB/72/223 (15.3.1768), B. Ramsden, Charterhouse, to E. Shackleton, Alkincoats. By contrast, Ann Pellet who was older and lived a more retired existence, satisfied herself with 'great inquiries' on her niece's behalf, LRO, DDB/72/92 (11.6.1754), A. Pellet, London, to E. Parker, Alkincoats.

101 LRO, DDB/72/257 (18.9.1772), B. Ramsden, Charterhouse, to E. Shackleton, Alkincoats.
102 LRO, DDB/72/192 (31.5.1766), W. Ramsden, Charterhouse, to E. Shackleton, Alkincoats. William Ramsden was equally whimsical when his wife prepared to visit the Pantheon or 'this terrestrial paradise' in 1772, see LRO, DDB/72/251 (30.1.1772), Same to Same.
103 LRO, DDB/72/280, 284 (1775), B. Ramsden, Charterhouse, to E. Shackleton, Alkincoats.
104 LRO, DDB/81/36 (1780), unfoliated, see entry for 21.4.1780.
105 LRO, DDB/72/184, 280 (1765–75), B. Ramsden, Charterhouse, to E. Parker/Shackleton, Alkincoats. The relationship of fashion, age and decorum was hotly debated by Elizabeth's circle. Ann Pellet disapproved of ladies of 90 years of age parading in flounced negligees and Bessy Ramsden thought polonaises and Italian nightgowns inappropriate for matrons. However Jane Scrimshire believed that it was antiquated to expect that married women should not be interested in fashion. The letters of all three women suggest that different fashions were thought appropriate for different age groups, see LRO, DDB/72/91 (1.6.1754), A. Pellet, London, to E. Parker, Alkincoats; LRO, DDB/72/123 (22.10.1753), J. Scrimshire, Pontefract, to E. Parker, Alkincoats; LRO, DDB/72/285 (n.d.), B. Ramsden and W. Ramsden, Charterhouse, to E. Shackleton, Alkincoats; and LRO, DDB/72/288 (12.11.1776), B. Ramsden, Charterhouse, to E. Shackleton, Alkincoats. That women were capable of sustaining an interest in fashion throughout the life-cycle is confirmed by N. Rothstein (ed.), *Barbara Johnson's Album of Fashions and Fabrics* (London: Thames & Hudson, 1987).
106 LRO, DDB/72/92 (11.6.1754), A. Pellet, London, to E. Parker, Alkincoats; LRO, DDB/72/285 (n.d.), B. and W. Ramsden, Charterhouse, to E. Shackleton, Alkincoats; LRO, DDB/72/133, 147 (n.d.), J. Scrimshire, Pontefract, to E. Parker, Alkincoats. On choice of fabric, see LRO, DDB/72/91, 95 (1754), A. Pellet, London, to E. Parker, Alkincoats.
107 LRO, DDB/72/92 (11.6.1754), A. Pellet, London, to E. Parker, Alkincoats. Hoops were still worn at official functions at court, although increasingly outmoded in everyday wear. Jane Scrimshire endorsed Ann Pellet's recommendation, LRO, DDB/72/134 (20.6.n.y.), J. Scrimshire, Pontefract, to E. Parker, Alkincoats: 'Sho'd make it for a hoop for the bride's visit and then only take out some of the fullness at the sides and it is a negligee.'
108 For a comparable account of the proxy consumption of London modes for special occasions, see A. Buck, 'Buying clothes in Bedfordshire: customers, tradesmen and fashion, 1700–1800', paper delivered to the Pasold Conference on the Economic and Social History of Dress, London, 1985.
109 LRO, DDB/81/26 (1775), fol. 61.
110 LRO, DDB/74/6 (n.d.), Poem 'Given Me by Mrs Parker of Marshfield'. Compare with M. D. George, *Catalogue of Political and Personal Satires Preserved in the Department of Prints and Drawings in the British Museum*, vol. 7 (London: British Museum, 1942), 137–8, 599.
111 LRO, DDB/72/179 (15.6.1764), B. Ramsden, Farm Hill, to E. Parker, Alkincoats. Bessy Ramsden was sufficiently versed in the language of envy and emulation to joke about the social impact of the Duchess of Devonshire's wax fruit 'was I in a longing situation I should certainly mark the little one with a bunch of currants which I saw at the milliners', refer to LRO, DDB/72/280 (18.12.1775), B. Ramsden, Charterhouse, to E. Shackleton, Alkincoats.
112 LRO, DDB/81/35 (1779), fol. 116.
113 For example LRO, DDB/81/37 (1780), fol. 263.
114 LRO, DDB/72/132 (16.5.1754), J. Scrimshire, Pontefract, to E. Parker, Alkincoats.
115 LRO, DDB/72/254 (4.5.1772), B. Ramsden, Charterhouse, to E. Shackleton, Alkincoats. For more on wearing presents to honour the donor, consult LRO, DDB/72/290 (13.5.1777), Same to Same.
116 LRO, DDB/72/122 (c.1761), A. Pellet, London, to E. Shackleton, Alkincoats. On the remembrance of 'dead as well as living friends' and Mrs Pellet's ambition to raise a monument on the grave of her father, see LRO, DDB/72/92, 94 (1754), A. Pellet, London, to E. Parker, Alkincoats.
117 Jane Pedder of Lancaster minutely catalogued her son's possessions, enquired after the state of his shirts, promised him 'some little present that you may say this come from London' and charged

him to preserve a book of pressed flowers exactly as his brother had left it, see LRO, DDPd/17/1 (29.2.1786 and 16.4.1786), J. Pedder, Lancaster, to J. Pedder, Blackburn. An admirer of Miss Martha Barcroft's set a lock of her hair into a ring for remembrance and treasured the little box she had donated, see LRO, DDB/72/1407 (29.9.1785), D. Lang, London, to M. Barcroft, Colne. Ellen Parker acknowledged the power of objects to plead remembrance in letters to her Colne aunts, see for example LRO, DDB/72/1194 (21.6.1817), E. Parker, Selby, to E. Moon, Colne, and LRO, DDB/72/1507 (29.5.1821), E. Parker, Selby, to E. Reynolds, Colne.

118 This metaphor was deployed by Ulrich in assessment of Martha Ballard's diary; see L. T. Ulrich, 'Martha Ballard and her girls: women's work in eighteenth-century Maine', in S. Innes (ed.), *Work and Labour in Early America* (Chapel Hill: University of North Carolina Press, 1988), 72.

119 E. Hall (ed.), *Miss Weeton's Journal of a Governess, 1807–1825*, vol. 2 (London: Oxford University Press, 1939), 353.

120 *Miss Weeton*, vol. 2, 331. See also 324, 326.

121 ibid., 325.

122 Gifts for instance were worn for the sake of the donor in the seventeenth century, see P. Crawford, 'Katharine and Philip Henry and their children: a case study in family ideology', *Transactions of the Historic Society of Lancashire and Cheshire*, cxxxiv (1984), 52–3 and V. Sackville-West (ed.), *The Diary of Lady Anne Clifford* (London: Heinemann, 1923), 44. Lady Anne Clifford also recorded rethreading a string of pearls given by her mother, the first day her daughter wore stays and later a coat, the associations of different rooms and inviting a female visitor into her closet to look at her clothes, see 42, 64, 66, 67, 82. Moreover, the evidence of wills suggests the sentimental associations of artefacts as early as the fifteenth century, see Borthwick Institute of Historical Research, Probate Register VI, fols 227, 214, Register III, fol. 523. (I am grateful to Jenny Kermode for this reference.)

123 This emerges from a comparison of men and women's wills from Birmingham, Sheffield and south Lancashire, 1700–1800 (personal communication from Maxine Berg), and from East Anglia in the sixteenth and seventeenth centuries (personal communication from Susan Amussen and Christopher Marsh). This pattern has also been remarked by historians of eighteenth-century America. Gloria Main notes that women's wills often contained loving descriptions of artefacts in contrast to the male focus on land. If men dwelt on their personality at all, their comments were confined to a favourite animal or gun: G. Main, 'Widows in rural Massachusetts on the eve of revolution', in R. Hoffman and P. J. Albert (eds), *Women in the Age of American Revolution* (Charlottesville: University Press of Virginia, 1989), 88–9. The possibility of a distinctively female attachment to household goods has also been raised by novelists, see H. James, *The Spoils of Poynton* (London: Heinemann, 1897), *passim* and G. Eliot, *The Mill on the Floss* (London: Penguin, 1986; 1st edn, 1860), 280–95.

124 This pattern of testamentary behaviour has been widely observed on either side of the Atlantic, see Davidoff and Hall, *Family Fortunes*, 276, 511; S. Lebsock, *The Free Women of Petersburg: Status and Culture in a Southern Town 1784–1860* (New York: W. W. Norton and Co., 1984).

125 For an imaginative discussion of the relationship between household roles and material values, see M. B. Norton, 'Eighteenth-century American women in peace and war: the case of the Loyalists', *William and Mary Quarterly*, 3rd series, xxxiii (1976), 386–409. Norton compared the claims for compensation made by loyalist men and women exiled during the American War of Independence with useful results. Although the men consistently placed a precise valuation on their house and land, very few of the women were able to do so. By contrast, men submitted inadequate inventories of household goods, such as furniture, tableware and kitchen utensils, while the women could produce minute accounts. To Norton the contrasting lists submitted by men and women suggest not only discrete fields of knowledge, but different material priorities.

Part IV
Literacy and numeracy

15

Literacy in context: meaning and measurement in early modern England

David Cressy

Haunting the statistical studies of literacy assembled over the past generation are the vexatious questions, 'what did literacy mean?' and 'how did literacy matter?' Social historians have worked with industry and ingenuity to discover what proportion of the population could read and write at various times, and how those primary skills were distributed among social and occupational groups. Reports have been generated on the incidence, distribution and penetration of literacy, its gradations and margins and how literacy levels changed over time. Tables and graphs present literacy (or illiteracy) percentages in England, Europe and elsewhere in the world. We now know, for example, that almost 70 per cent of English men and 90 per cent of English women of the mid-seventeenth century could not write their own names, and that the proportions had changed to 40 per cent and just over 60 per cent a century later.[1]

But qualitative issues bedevil the quantitative enterprise. Critics have argued, sometimes convincingly, that figures displaying the measurable achievements of particular groups tell only part of the story. Numerical compilations, however worthy, throw little light on the value of literacy, and leave open the question whether literacy was a product to be consumed or a tool for consumption. What difference did it make if literacy grew or contracted, or was confined to a minority of the population? What were the consequences – social and economic, political and religious – of the skewed configuration of literate skills? The present discussion incorporates some of the fruits of quantitative research, including my own, but is more concerned to understand the social and cultural significance of literacy in early modern England.

'Literacy', of course, means different things to different scholars, and has different resonances and different literatures in different academic disciplines. For some it is a matter of choice and sensibility, what people read and what they made of their reading. It touches on vocabulary and phrasing, coding and transcoding, and the complexity of relationships with text. Literacy, for others, involves a package of skills, a matter of technique rather than taste, including the elementary ability to read and write. People exercise this literacy when they read a newspaper or read directions, when they sign their name or fill in a form. Broad comparative discussions of literacy consider the social uses of writing, and the degree to which a particular culture employs print or script. Anthropologists, social psychologists, educational theorists, cultural historians and literary critics have converged in various ways on the topic, and have credited literacy with diverse cultural, economic or cognitive consequences. These include logical thinking and heightened self-consciousness, bureaucratization and the rise of science. In Third-World development, literacy is associated with liberation, modernization and empowerment, and this view has sometimes been reflected back onto pre-industrial England.[2] Literacy is implicated in the making of consumers as well as the making of citizens, but the evidence for this is problematic.

In order to proceed historically we must shed the notion that literacy was necessarily as important in the past as it appears to be in the present. As adepts of literacy ourselves, scholars and teachers, high practitioners of a mystery dependent on reading and writing, we naturally associate literacy with ability, facility, capability and perhaps even virtue. Literacy, for us, is an indispensable skill that connects us to our sources, to our readers, to our students and to each other. As scholars we are more likely to be rewarded for what we write than for what we say. In a modern mass-literate society, where literacy is universally endorsed and encouraged (though not everywhere mastered or respected), our own cultural preferences tend to coincide with those of the apologists and promoters from the Elizabethan and Stuart past who treated literacy with favour or privileged respect. We risk being misled by our own high valuation of literacy into misunderstanding its place, or its absence, in the world we have lost. Enthusiasm or sympathy for the transformative power of literacy becomes an impediment rather than an asset when it comes to historical research.

I will argue here that literacy was not necessarily as valuable or as enlightening as is often claimed, and that low literacy rates in the early modern period should not be taken as indicators of retardation or deprivation, awaiting rectification by progress. Our quest is not for the history of 'literacy' (reified or deified), but rather the history of society and culture, which is only incidentally illuminated by understanding the circumstance and incidence of reading and writing. I will cite some of the well-known historical polemical and promotional literature, but will insist that its authors' enthusiasm for literacy should be set in a broader historical context, a social and cultural setting in which literacy did not necessarily matter. I then turn to means of measurement and the tabulation of literacy rates. For even if literacy proves an ambivalent indicator of cultural attainment, statistics based on the ability to write none the less provide a subtle and sensitive marker of social differentiation. A quantitative approach facilitates discussion of social structure, occupational stratification, gender and the differences between town and country in the seventeenth and early eighteenth centuries, more fruitful topics, it seems to me, than whether literacy promoted godliness or self-consciousness or was good for profits.

I

England, for most of her history, has been a partially literate society, in which the art of writing and record-keeping was confined to a clerical, governmental and commercial elite. Specialized literacy has been practised since the time of the Romans. Anglo-Saxon scribes and Norman clerks used writing to record their history, to conduct their government and to create literature. So too did their medieval and Renaissance successors. Reading and writing have always been important skills, even though no more than a fragment of the population possessed them. Michael Clanchy demonstrates that the use of writing by Angevin and Plantagenet governments expanded the authority of the state and facilitated the integration of the medieval kingdom, and it is notable that such a transformation could happen while some of the kings themselves were illiterate, and while the vast majority of the population lacked any facility with reading or writing.[3] Not until the sixteenth century did basic reading and writing abilities extend much beyond the clerical and gentle elite, and not before the nineteenth century were they found among the majority of the population. Government, society, economy and culture were not necessarily worse off for this restriction.

Beginning in the sixteenth century, under the trifold pressure of Renaissance humanism, reformed Protestant religion and a diversifying capitalist economy, a succession of writers and agitators made high claims for the advancement of literacy. Among churchmen and businessmen, leaders of the spiritual and the secular order, the belief was widespread that reading and writing were vital skills that produced a broad range of benefits. Most writers stressed the religious advantage in being able to engage directly with the written word of God, and some also drew attention to the worldly assets accruing from competence with script and print. And most writers, explicitly or implicitly, associated literacy with a variety of civic and moral benefits, as if it were the indispensable correlate of civilization. The tradition they established continues today among theorists and policy-makers who associate literacy with modernity, rationality and a more deeply satisfying life.

It is likely, however, that the early promoters of literacy exaggerated their case, and paid too little attention to the needs and circumstances of the general population. Literacy was by no means a necessity in early modern England, when its mystery was limited to less than a third of the population. Even today, when literacy is indispensable, reading and writing have not supplanted the pleasures of face-to-face communication.

Elizabethan Protestant reformers commonly urged

> every man to read the Bible in Latin or English, as the very word of God and the spiritual food of man's soul, whereby they may better know their duties to God, to their sovereign lord the king, and their neighbour.

Seventeenth-century puritans often repeated this theme, lamenting, 'alas, the people perish for want of knowledge. And how can they know God's will that cannot read it?'[4] Richard Baxter, one of the most prolific religious writers of the later seventeenth century, admonished parents, 'by all means let children be taught to read, if you are never so poor and whatever shift you make, or else you deprive them of a singular help to their instruction and salvation'. According to Baxter, 'it is a very great mercy to be able to read the holy scriptures for themselves, and a very great misery to know nothing but what they hear from others'.[5]

Active literacy, here meaning the ability to make sense of selected printed texts, was said to foster religious, social and political discipline; illiteracy, on the other hand, instilled dependency, ignorance and error. Without literacy to guide them in godliness, it was feared that children might become 'idle . . . vile and abject persons, liars, thieves, evil beasts, slow bellies and good for nothing'. Those who could not read were exposed to 'rudeness, licentiousness, profaness, superstition, and any wickedness'. In this view literacy could be engaged in the 'reformation of manners', as part of the moral equipment of a Christian.[6]

Reading and writing could also be credited with securing a variety of secular benefits which were equally important for cultural cohesion. Literacy and education could combat 'misorders' and 'disobedience' and could promote 'policy and civility'. To some seventeenth-century minds a paper-wielding magistracy and a literate population were a prescription for public order and social harmony. There was no shortage of authors willing to testify to 'the vast usefulness of reading', and to argue that writing was the key 'to the descrying and finding out of innumerable treasures'. Through writing, according to the London schoolmaster David Brown,

> all high treasures of whatsoever nature or importance are both intended and prosecuted, secret matters are secretly kept, friends that be a thousand miles distant are conferred with and (after a sort) visited; the excellent works of godly men, the grave sentences of wise men, and the profitable arts of learned men, who died a thousand years ago, are yet extant for our daily use and imitation; all the estates, kingdoms, cities and countries of the world are governed, laws and printing maintained, justice and discipline administered, youth bred in piety, virtue, manners and learning at schools and universities, and that which is most and best, all the churches of God from the beginning established and always to this day edified.[7]

This was as noble and eloquent an argument for literacy as could be wished. Reading was regarded as a tool for cultural integration which could keep the literate in touch with people and ideas across space and time. By programming that reading as a corpus of godly texts, a curriculum of select classical learning or a flow of political and administrative instruction, the leaders of society could embrace, and to some extent control, the increasingly literate population.

The practical, day-to-day benefits of literacy could be even more compelling. Those who were indifferent to godliness and civility might none the less be touched by an argument which appealed to pocket and pride. The lack of literacy, it was suggested, could be socially damaging. According to David Brown, 'not to write at all is both shame and scathe'. The embarrassment of illiteracy might prejudice one's business dealings; your scrivener or partner might take advantage of your deficiency and so through illiteracy you might 'lose some good design'. But worse than being tricked by someone with superior technical capability was the insult to one's self-esteem and public reputation.

> It is shame both to employ a notar to subscribe for thee in any security, and to want that good token of education which perhaps thine inferior hath, for wheresoever any man of honest rank resorteth who cannot write, chiefly where he is not known, he is incontinent esteemed either to be base born or to have been basely brought up in a base or moorland desert, that is, far from any city where there be schools of learning, discipline, policy and civility.[8]

This theme was recurrent in the writing of seventeenth-century educators, who insisted that literacy provided a defence against 'the manifold deceits of this world'. Some even urged practical literacy for women as an insurance against the risks of penurious widowhood. Thomas Dilworth in the eighteenth century rehearsed a similar argument, claiming

> that both sexes should be alike ready at their pen. . . . How often do we see women when they are left to shift for themselves in the melancholy state of

widowhood (and what woman knows that she shall not be left in the like state?) obliged to leave their business to the management of others; sometimes to their great loss, and sometimes to their utter ruin; when at the contrary had they been ready at their pen, could spell well and understand figures, they might not only have saved themselves from ruin, but perhaps have been mistresses of good fortunes.[9]

Caution is essential when reading these advertisements by professional educators – the same caution that is required when looking at religious reformers – to separate their attitudes and motivations from the reality of the world they describe. David Brown, for example, was himself newly arrived in London from Scotland and knew how to work on parvenu insecurities. The writing-masters were drumming up business; the preachers were promoting godly reform. Much of what they had to say seems sensible, and examples survive of men and women whose literacy indeed saved them from penury or brought them closer to God. But there is no direct evidence to tell us whether ordinary people in everyday circumstances felt shamed by the limitations of their literacy, or experienced frustration or complication in their designs. In both its religious and its secular strands, the rhetorical stream gave great weight to the value of literacy, but that does not prove that the population at large agreed with its sentiments or experienced the problems or delights to which it referred. The argument relating to widowhood, for example, urging literacy for economic or matrimonial advantages, had no discernible effect in practice. Before agreeing with the historical proponents of literacy, we need to evaluate the context in which they were uttered and the world to which they belonged.

II

It is no doubt true that deficiencies in basic literacy constrained the audience for written work, and limited participation in the literary, political, religious and commercial culture of the past. It also seems plausible (a hypothesis easier to pose than to test) that the expansion of literacy facilitated the rise of consumerism. The quickening and diversifying economy of the late seventeenth century placed a premium on literate skills, and may have rewarded the better educated. Commercial towns and market trades were among the more literate sectors of society at this time, and there was a significant expansion in their numbers. But the cultural and economic changes of the eighteenth century seem not to have been accompanied by an overall surge in basic literacy. In practice, the importance of literacy varied with social, cultural and historical circumstances, and some of those circumstances could restrain literacy as well as advance it.

In early modern England, as in centuries before, a competent and contented life could be lived entirely innocent of literate skills. Traditional rural activities in particular needed no mastery of reading or writing (although the burgeoning urban and commercial environment apparently made different demands). The English countryman, according to one seventeenth-century observer, could perform his seasonal tasks without recourse to reading or writing.

> We can learn to plough and harrow, sow and reap, plant and prune, thresh and fan, winnow and grind, brew and bake, and all without book. These are our chief businesses in the country, except we be jurymen to hang a thief or speak truth in

a man's right, which conscience and experience will teach us with a little learning.

William Cobbett said much the same two hundred years later: 'great numbers of people are very clever at their different trades, and earn a great deal of money, and bring up their families very well, without even knowing how to read.'[10] Why should the countryman send his son to school, at cost of time and money, if the skills he would bring home had no obvious immediate application? Who needed to be able to read or write if he had standing enough with his neighbours, was possessed of an adequate mind and memory and had learned and could pass on his knowledge of animals, the land and the weather through observation and practice? One could grow prosperous, and go to heaven, without being able to write one's name, since neither wealth nor salvation were utterly dependent on literacy.

This last point, which cuts against the grain of most early modern discussions of literacy, requires amplification. Traditionalists had never conceded that Bible literacy was essential in religious devotion. Thomas More had observed during the stormy first decade of the Reformation, 'many . . . shall with God's grace, though they never read a word of scripture, come as well to heaven'.[11] Despite the evangelical insistence on reading, the Protestant church in England continued to stress the oral elements in liturgical worship and catechetical instruction. Psalms could be sung and sermons heard without the complications of print. The Protestant revolution notwithstanding, it was not necessary to be literate to be devout. A country preacher told his congregation after the Restoration,

> though you cannot read a letter in the book, yet you can by true assurance read your name in the Book of Life, your scholarship will serve. . . . If you cannot write a word, yet see you transcribe a fair copy of a godly, righteous and sober life, and you have done well.[12]

This is not to dismiss the importance of literacy for Bible study, tracts or spiritual record-keeping, but rather to emphasize the continuing vitality of the older oral tradition.

In his other roles, too, the ordinary countryman was under no pressure to become literate. As tenant and farmer, subject and householder, the world of print and script made few inroads into his life. If he dealt with the manor court, quarter session or church courts, all courts of record with a high turnover of paper and ink, his participation was oral, interlocutory and required no mastery of reading or writing. The officials, of course, were literate, but the people who came before the courts most often were not. If a signature was needed to authenticate a document, a mark had just as good standing in law.[13]

Illiterate and semi-literate people were not necessarily disadvantaged when they came into contact with the world of writing. Every street or village had its informal scrivener or writing man who met the needs of his illiterate neighbours. Someone could always be found to set one's affairs in the appropriate form if you needed to write a lease, a letter or a will. Illiterate lovers could correspond with each other at a distance, so long as a third party was available to pen the letters. Letters went between Lancashire and Ireland, and between Massachusetts and Devon, linking couples who were technically illiterate but none the less conversant with the literate form.[14] Nor was authorship impossible. A classic work on horsemanship is said to have been written, through dictation, by a groom who could neither read nor write. Christopher Clifford thanks his scribe, who 'stood so many days with me upon the cold stones at maister Throckmorton's stable at Tortworth [Glos.] to draw out the first draught or copy of this my work'.[15]

Multiple paths and bridges linked the literate and illiterate worlds. The possession of literacy did not remove one from the culture of speech and action, nor did illiteracy necessarily bar one from the culture of script and print (any more than modern 'logocentrism' leads to the closing of eyes to visual information). In practice there was feedback and interaction. As students of theatre know well, much of the cultural life of the seventeenth century was neither strictly literate nor oral, but a combination of both. Jests and proverbs that originated in folklore appeared in printed editions. Folksingers from the sixteenth century to the nineteenth could broaden their repertoire by reference to printed ballads, including some that had been collected from illiterate performers. Sermons were crafted on paper in the minister's study, then delivered live from the pulpit; 'this way', said Richard Baxter, 'the milk cometh warmest from the breast'.[16] A sermon that sparked discussion in the church or the tavern (drawing, perhaps, on some parishioner's written notes) might also be polished for further circulation in print. And the printed text might itself spur further oral exchanges, or be overlain with marginalia or other forms of scribal interaction. Modern academic life is much the same, with loops and feedbacks from discussions and lectures to papers and publications.

Important documents in the early modern period were read out loud as well as filed for the record. Proclamations were proclaimed as well as posted. News-sheets and letters could be read to an illiterate audience at the alehouse as well as studied privately at home. English market towns had their town criers, and so did colonial New England. Notices of importance were 'cried' at the meeting house, where presumably those in attendance could read, and then were 'cried' through the streets, where literacy was less firmly established. In addition to these public duties the seventeenth-century Boston town criers were 'to cry lost and found goods' and 'to keep a book of what they cry'. The town crier was a walking, shouting bulletin board, a forerunner of the daily paper. From a text delivered to him in writing he had to cry out public messages, while the classified advertisements, which may have come to him by word of mouth, were to be inscribed in a book of record. Literacy was a prerequisite of the job, along with a lusty voice, although the social standing that went with it is suggested by the additional duties assigned to the Boston crier in 1666, 'to clear the streets of carrion and other offensive matters'.[17]

Instead of a great divide between oral and literate culture there was substantial overlap and interaction, in which visual, verbal, gestural, scribal and print elements intermingled. Historically, instead of a succession of modes and media, there has been a layering, cross-referencing and impaction.

III

Literacy contains many levels and gradations. It can be imagined as a spectrum or curve, in which even the narrow definition as 'reading and writing' shades into an extensive range of competencies. Literacy, in early modern England, involved an ascending order of accomplishments, from the simple ability to recognize the letters of the alphabet to full fluency in handling the most sophisticated texts. Fine penmanship and stylistic ease belonged to the high end of the range, and literacy in Latin and Greek marked the gilded culmination of the most rarefied scholarly elite. In between were many layers and components, all of which have historical and cultural significance, but few of which are susceptible to measurement. The breadth of this range should be borne in mind when evaluating statistics based on the distinction between signatures and marks.

At the lowest level were people who could not read or write anything. These were totally illiterate, though not necessarily totally disadvantaged. Even people for whom the alphabet was a meaningless jumble were exposed to the influence of writing by virtue of belonging to a text-using society. Those who had learned just to read the alphabet, to distinguish the letters and then to make sense of their combination into simple words and phrases, hovered on the threshold of literacy. They could hardly be called 'readers', but with purpose and effort they could make direct connections to the world of print. Next came the ability to read simple passages. Some people cultivated this skill, and became the readers of popular publications. Others forgot what they knew and sank back towards illiteracy through lack of practice. The teaching of reading, as a basic decoding of print, was the core curriculum in elementary schools, and may also have been taught privately in some households. And some people – there is no way to gauge numbers – may have learned to read as young adults from their masters or workmates.

A further hierarchy of skill may have emerged as readers learned to decipher writing in different forms. The easiest to understand, Keith Thomas has suggested, was Black Letter print, the bastard gothic form used in the elementary teaching texts, the ABC horn book, the catechism and much popular literature. Black Letter printing continued throughout the seventeenth century, especially for ballads, almanacs and publications aimed at the less educated reader. More sophisticated publications used Roman type, the dominant form in printing today.[18]

Familiarity with print came before the ability to read handwriting. Only the more experienced or better educated readers could penetrate the mystery of script or 'writ' as it was known. Anecdotes describe people who could spell their way through the Bible, but were completely helpless when faced with a handwritten letter. The different kinds of hand in use – court hand, secretary, italic, etc. – may also have posed different levels of challenge.

Reading, by its nature, leaves no direct record, so there is no reliable guide to the extent of reading ability within the English population. (Estimates based on the history of printing and publishing are particularly problematic, since so many political and technological variables intervene.) It seems certain, however, that more people could read than could write. Just how many more is a matter for speculation, allowing historians to adopt optimistic or pessimistic positions. The statistics based on signature literacy may be 'a fair indication' or 'a spectacular underestimate'[19] of actual fluency in reading, but the matter remains unresolved. And even if we determine that certain people *could* read, there is often no indication that they did.

Reading and writing were separate skills, taught at different stages in the educational process and often by different specialists. If a child was fortunate enough to attend a school in Elizabethan or Stuart England (and most did not), he would learn to read during the first few years and would only move on to writing as a secondary activity. Reading is a passive skill, involving the visual recognition of patterns; writing, by contrast, is an active skill, requiring manual dexterity, the co-ordination of hand, eye and brain and also, before the modern era, initiation into the arts of cutting quills and preparing ink. Only the more privileged or the more determined reached this level.

A few people may have learned the trick of writing their names when they were otherwise unable to read, but there is little evidence on this score. More common were people with some modicum of reading ability who did not know how to write their names. When put into the situation of having to authenticate a document, illiterates and semi-illiterates alike often made crude scrawls with the pen, producing a line or a cross as a mark. More experience taught some of them to draw a pictogram of their occupation, like Shakespeare's father whose mark represented the shape of a glover's compasses.[20]

It was a significant step from being able to read to being able to write. There may have been a further gradation from forming a signature to writing a sentence, but once a person had mastered the pen there was no limit to what he might express in writing. Only at this stage do we see full and free literacy, a skill that belonged to a minority of the population. Only after the crossing of this threshold do considerations of orthography, syntax, voice, style and substance enter the discussion.

Acquisition of full basic literacy was also constrained by gender. Girls and boys might both be exposed to training in reading, but only young ladies of the gentle and commercial elite were expected to learn to write. Educational plans for the charity schools and charity hospitals often specify that the boys are to be taught reading, writing and arithmetic, the girls to learn to read and to sew. This has led some historians to posit a hidden female readership, semi-literate sisters who are invisible to the historical record, who are none the less keepers and transmitters of a crucial skill, and the avid (though undocumented) audience for books.[21] But even if it can be determined which publications were intended for women (not so simple an exercise as it might seem), that tells us little about who the readers actually were.

IV

Unlike reading, the act of writing leaves a traceable historical record. Most historians now accept that one form of writing – the writing of personal signatures as opposed to marks – provides a meaningful measure of the distribution of literacy. The indicator is not without problems, nor free of controversy, but it has the advantage of being universal, standard and direct, allowing comparisons between groups and comparisons over time. Figures so derived may be taken to indicate the minimum number of readers, and the maximum with facility with the pen (provided, of course, that social bias in the sources is recognized or filtered).

If, as I have argued, literacy and illiteracy were part of a spectrum rather than sharply dichotomous, we might set aside the problem of what an individual signature signifies and turn instead to the lessons that can be learned from their aggregation. Over the past two decades a large body of research has produced figures comparing the literacy of men to women, gentlemen to tradesmen, Londoners to countrymen, Frenchmen to Englishmen, one period to another and so on. So robust are the statistics, so clear cut the pattern, that even scholars with a distaste for quantitative social history are generally willing to employ them. The most recent studies of the female labour market in late Stuart London, and of literacy and popular culture between 1750 and 1914, include tabulations of literacy by percentage that are directly comparable to earlier studies of Tudor and Stuart England.[22]

In the middle decades of the sixteenth century, about the time of the accession of Queen Elizabeth and the birth of William Shakespeare, only 20 per cent of the adult males in

England possessed sufficient literacy to write their own names. Male illiteracy, measured by the making of marks rather than signatures, was close to 80 per cent. For women the figures are even worse. No more than 5 per cent of Tudor women were literate, 95 per cent or more being unable to write their names. Almost a century later, after the full course of the celebrated but overrated 'educational revolution', illiteracy among men was reduced to just 70 per cent. At the beginning of the English civil war, more than two-thirds of all Englishmen – contemporaries of Milton and Cromwell – could not write their names. For women at this time the level of illiteracy was still as high as 90 per cent. By the end of the seventeenth century, however, literacy had become more widespread. Close to 50 per cent of the male population could not write, and the figure for women was 75 per cent. The improvement was sluggish rather than spectacular, but it continued into the eighteenth century as English society became more commercial and more complex. By the 1750s, when marriage registers provide a new source, the level of illiteracy among brides was about 62 per cent, among bridegrooms about 38 per cent.[23]

These figures remind us that high literary achievements and a paper-pushing bureaucracy could coexist with popular illiteracy on a vast scale. English society did not have to be broadly literate for its most accomplished members to make subtle and assertive use of literate forms. Early Stuart women who wrote letters were exceptional, but they were not necessarily handicapped by the fact that most of their contemporaries could not read or write at all. The same is true of their eighteenth-century counterparts.

All the evidence points to a popularization of literacy between the sixteenth and the nineteenth centuries. But the growth was irregular and halting, rather than steady and progressive. The summary figures mask periods of acceleration and recession, and obscure important social, occupational and geographical variations. A surge in literacy in the Elizabethan period was not matched in the century that followed; the long eighteenth century saw marginal improvements and some stagnation, the consumer and commercial revolutions notwithstanding. In the early modern period, the improving literacy of trades-men and craftsmen outstripped that of husbandmen and labourers. Pastoral communities remained almost entirely illiterate, while weaving villages often had substantial populations who could read and write. The urban population became increasingly literate, at a time when the rural sectors appear to have regressed. Pre-industrial England had pockets of literacy, concentrations of potential readers and writers, in a society where traditional means of expression and communication coexisted with the most sophisticated employment of literacy for literature and commerce.

One of the most remarkable findings of this research is the precocious literacy of women in later Stuart London. In a sample of female witnesses before the London ecclesiastical courts, 78 per cent could not sign their names in the 1670s, 52 per cent in the 1690s and just 44 per cent in the 1720s. At a time when three-quarters or more of the women in provincial England could not write their own names, illiteracy in the metropolis, so measured, was reduced to around a half. Affected, perhaps, by the quickening commercial environment, the social demands of the city and the expanding availability of print, the women of Mrs Aphra Behn's London were as literate as men in the countryside. The details of this, its causes and consequences, have yet to be worked out. But a recent study by Peter Earle indicates that literacy was higher for City-born women than immigrants, higher for those born after 1660 and higher for those engaged in the needle trades and shopkeeping than as servants, hawkers or washerwomen.[24]

7.1 Eighteenth-century Chinese lacquer armchair. © The Board of Trustees of the Victoria and Albert Museum.

7.2 Chinese table inlaid with mother-of-pearl, *c.* 1860. © The Board of Trustees of the Victoria and Albert Museum.

7.3 Japanese lacquered pedestal *c.* 1800. © The Board of Trustees of the Victoria and Albert Museum.

7.4 Late seventeenth-century, Japanese gold, silver and black inlaid coffer. © The Board of Trustees of the Victoria and Albert Museum.

7.5 Engraving of a French bedroom by Abraham Bosse, *c.* 1630. © The Board of Trustees of the Victoria and Albert Museum.

7.6 Silver table from Versailles – drawing by Claude Ballin, *c.* 1670. *Source* Statens Konstmuseer/The National Swedish Art Museums.

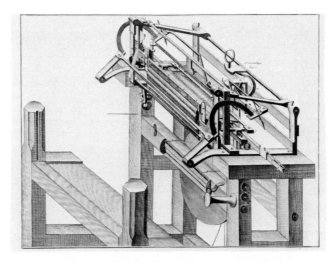

11.1 A *métier* or stocking frame. *Source Encyclopédie.*

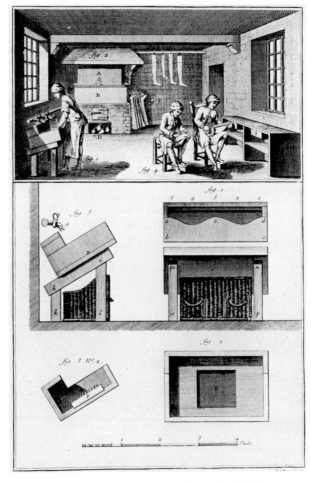

11.2 The manufacture of stockings: fulling and dyeing. *Source Encyclopédie.*

PARAPLUYES
ET PARASOLS
A PORTER DANS LA POCHE.

L ES Parapluyes dont Mr Marius a trouvé le fecret,
ne pefent que 5 à 6 onces: ils ne tiennent pas plus
de place qu'une petite Ecritoire, & n'embaraffent

11.3 Advertising a new product: the pocket-sized folding umbrella. *Source* Musée de la Mode, Paris.

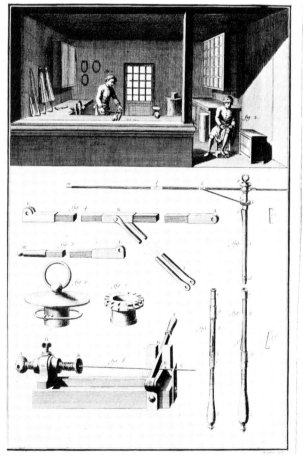

11.4 *Tourneurs* making umbrella frames. *Source Encyclopédie*.

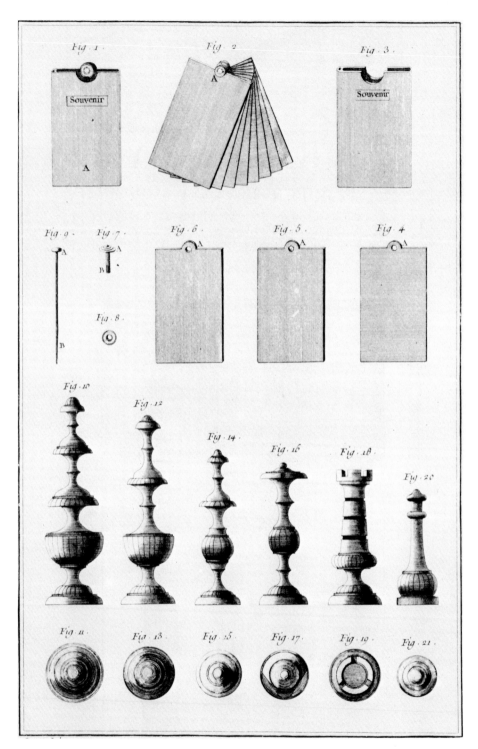

11.5 Some of the many goods made and sold by the *peigneurs-tabletiers*. Shown here: pocket notebooks and chessmen. *Source Encyclopédie.*

Le Marchand de Ruban.
35. *A la flotte, à la flotte mes beaux Rubans.* 6.ᵉ C.

11.6 Selling to the populuxe market: the *colporteur*. *Source* Cabinet des Estampes, Bibliothèque Nationale, Paris.

11.7 Selling to the luxury market: the *marchande de modes*. *Source Encyclopédie*.

The Palais Royal-gallery's Walk.   *Promenade de la gallerie du Palais Royal*

11.8 Shopping as a fashionable pastime: elegantly dressed shoppers in the Palais-Royal, the world's first shopping mall. *Source* Musée de Carnavalet, Paris.

11.9 Women workers mounting fans. *Source Encyclopédie*.

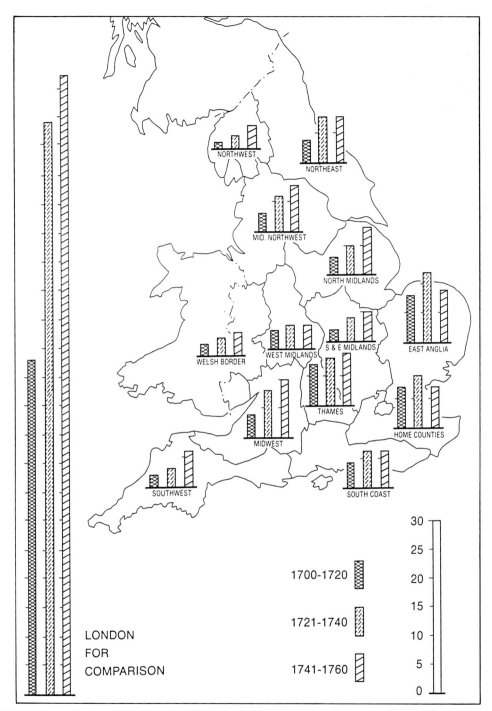

17.1 Mathematical writing in provincial England. Average of decadal totals of entries for three twenty-year periods and thirteen county groups. *Source* J. P. and R. V. Wallis, *Bio-bibliography of British Mathematics and its Applications, Part 2, 1701–1760* (Newcastle-upon-Tyne, 1988). See table 17.1, pp. 366–7.

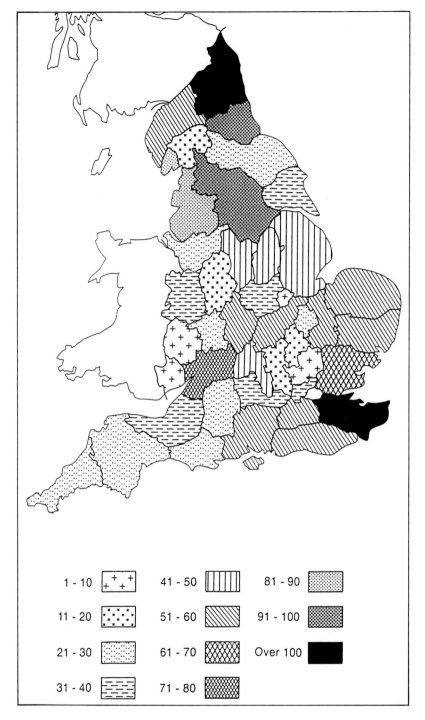

1 - 10		41 - 50		81 - 90
11 - 20		51 - 60		91 - 100
21 - 30		61 - 70		Over 100
31 - 40		71 - 80		

17.2 Mathematical practice in provincial England. *Source* Traceable entries in P. J. Wallis, *Index of British Mathematicians, 1701–60* (Newcastle-upon-Tyne, 1976), shown cumulatively by county. See table 17.2, pp. 367–9.

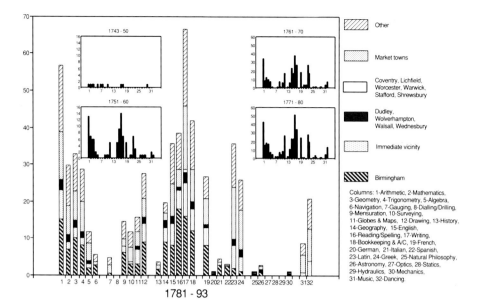

17.3 School advertisements in the *Birmingham Gazette*, 1743–93.

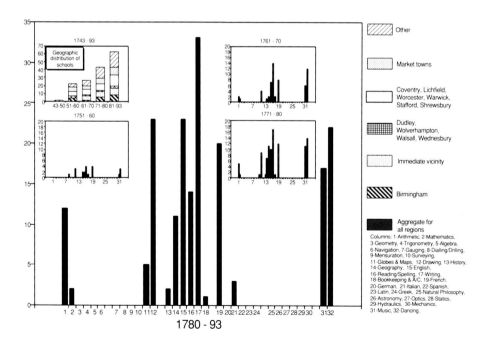

17.4 Girls' school advertisements in the *Birmingham Gazette*, 1743–93.

17.5 Personal emblems.

a) Cannon's cypher, seal and tobacco box (the cypher and seal designed 1725: the tobacco box engraved 1738). The preceding text reads:

'The particulars of which writings & many other matters & things by me done or subscribed to as a witness & was done by others I cannot particularly describe or set forth, nor yet ye time or date & when done or acted, because it was about this time it came in my mind to recollect ye most material part of my past life & actions and to transmit it to ye judicious reader for a caution to him either to avoid such follies as I must confess I precipitately ran into or on ye contrary for an instruction of that part of it wch by God's grace tended to morality, virtue, goodness, duty & good manners, having been so carefull as it behoves every one in this mundane life to keep a just account of all his actions as well knowing he must give an account thereof at the great and tremendous day of ye Lord, when ye secrets of all hearts shall be disclosed & rewards and punishments inflicted according as they shall merit.

'But such as have been overlookt, forgot or neglected (I mean writings) where my hand or seal is set to as a witness or as a principle or suretie are to be distinguished by ye cypher or figure here underneath represented in wch I took particular care to use on such occasions, as also in my letters, that it may be said was very difficult for any one to counterfeit or defeat . . . .

'Cypher for Signing: This was my usuall & common method for signing letters & test[ifying] to all instruments and deeds of whether of mine own doing or calld upon to Test others as by ye figure is shewn.

'Cypher for Sealing: This was my usuall & common seal being of silver or steel & contains all ye letters of my name distinguished [by] 10 balls or spots and cannon dismounted for ye crest as by ye figure is shewn.'

Tobacco box: see p. 365.

b) His guardian angel, 30 November 1742.

'Drew the above Cherub from a copy of Mr. John Willis, sometime writing master at Orchard. Com Dorsett . . . wch he had drawn for one John Brooke his scholar & for whom I had made his will see Novr 5 page 685. Another of ye same I also drew in a page opposite ye Title page.'

17.6 Prudence, providence and the pieties of debt.

a) 'A valuable piece in frame'; 18 June 1737.

The context is typical of Cannon's routine work, and of the ways in which he and his clients became familiar with the intricacies of debt: 'Met old Mr. West of Mere at Mr. Godwin's in Street & there settled ye accounts receipts & disbursements as Trustees for ye children of ye late Mary Smart of Westhay, widow deceased for ye binding out ye said children I drew Indentures & other writings for ye said Trustees and seeing a valuable piece in a frame I thought it proper to oblige my friendly reader with a copy of the words, viz:'

The previous day, Cannon had written a letter 'for Mr. Tho Nicholls in answer to one sent him from one Willm. Marratt at John Greencase's, a Taylor, Leopard's Court, Baldwin's Garden, Leatherlands, London, in wch I set forth ye mean condition of one John Auger (now in Glaston but lately absconded from London), shoemaker & who engaged with ye said Marratt in a note of hand for 5 guineas payable to one Paul Jepson or order, wch is bad, & left him to judge of it. The said Auger dying & ye debt wth him.'

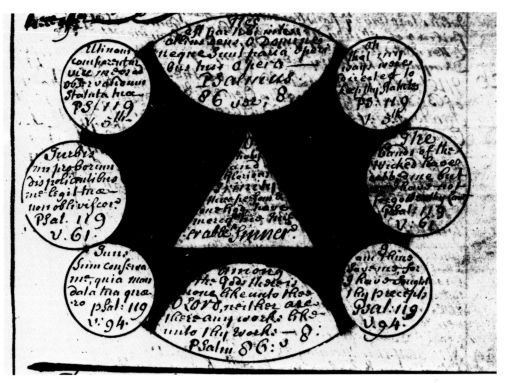

b) Cannon's Cautionary Cosmology, 19 August 1742, the day he finished the rewriting of his memoirs:

'Thus have I by God's Divine permission Transcrib'd and brought down these memoirs from my several & former records, papers and remarks to this Day wth great Labor & toil being almost 2 years since I received this book & which during yt space I was greatly afflicted & in pain from ye threats of many to whom I was Indepted, some of wch I satisfyed & some I still remained ye debtor but wth sincerity to make satisfaction as soon as God shall enable me, and ye assistance of such friends as it pleaseth him to put in yr hearts ye low Ebb and Estate at this time of my circumstances, wch for my sins I confess yt God is just in all his works & righteous in all his ways and therefore thro ye merits of his Dear Son my blessed redeemer I both now and at all times hereafter will magnify his holy name for ever & yt he hath not delivered me to death nor suffered ye crafty wiles of ye devil & man to wreck yr malice & power over me, for wch great mercy of his I have composed the following sentences out of his blessed and most sacred word, Environing ye holy and blessed Trine in wch is all my trust and Confidence whilst on Earth & hopes of a full Enjoyment of Eternal bliss & Joyful resurrection & dwelling among ye Saints in heaven hereafter.'

The biblical texts are all from the Psalms of David. Cannon's Latin was serviceable but rough.

In the middle: 'O holy and glorious Trinity, three persons and one God, have mercy on me
          miserable sinner'

Top and bottom:

(Ps. 86 v 8) 'Nec est par tibi inter allius Deus, O Domine neque sunt paria operibus tuis opera
          Among the Gods there is none like unto thee O LORD, neither are there any works like
          unto thy work.'

Sides:

1 (Ps 119 v 5) 'Utinam comparentur vice meos ad observandum statuta tua
          Oh that my ways were directed to keep thy statutes.'

2 (Ps 119 v 61) 'Turbis improborum dispoliantibus me legit tuae non obliviscor
          The bands of the wicked have robbed me but I have not forgotten thy law.'

3 (Ps 119 v 94) 'Tuus sum conserva me, quia mandata tua quaero
          I am thine save me, for I have sought thy precepts.'

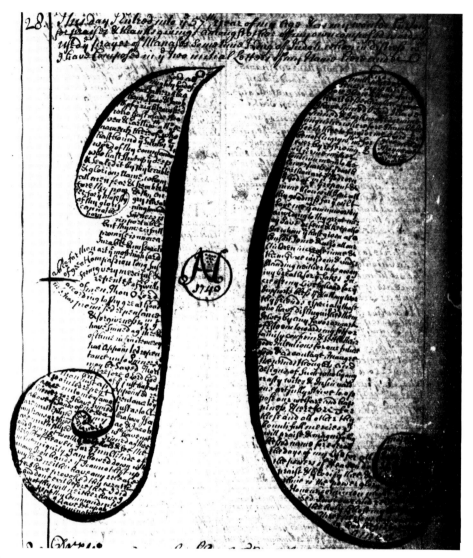

17.7 Monogram and initials, 1740.

A Poem on the year XL

Forty some say will be a year of wonders
Some say a year of Calmness, some of Thunders
What'ere befall us how can wonders cease
War is now as much a wonder as was peace

'This day I entered into ye 57th year of my age & as my wonted custom for praises & thanksgiving amongst others of my own composed words I used ye prayer of Manasses sometime King of Judah when in distress, wch I have composed in ye two initial Letters of my name hereunder'.

Cannon ends this penitential prayer to the God of Abraham, Isaac and Jacob by asking a blessing on 'my worthy friends, especially those who have distinguished themselves by any favor or mark of esteem towards my self or family, & settle their good intentions for our future good & advantage, maugre the minds, thoughts & designs of such who by any crafty wiles & insinuations artfully strive to oppose our welfare and happiness.'

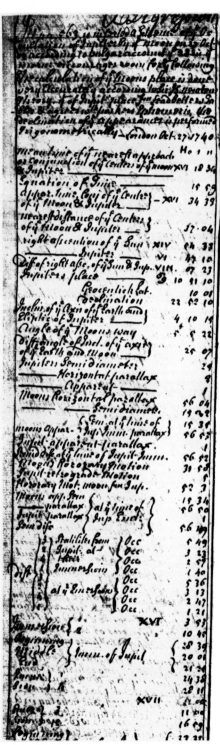
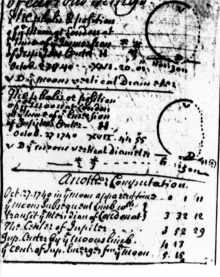

17.8 Astrology.

a) A lunar occultation of Jupiter, 27 October 1740: 'The calculation of ye Moon's place is done very accurately according to Sir Is. Newton's theory; yt of Jupiter's place fm Leadbetter's Tables & agrees wth Parker's Ephemeris. The declination of ye appearances is performed trigonometrically. – London, Oct. 17, 1740.' Part of a comparison of different predictions, by Leadbetter, 'A.B.' of Oxford and Daniel Silk of Birmingham, which had caused controversy in Partridge's Almanac the previous year.

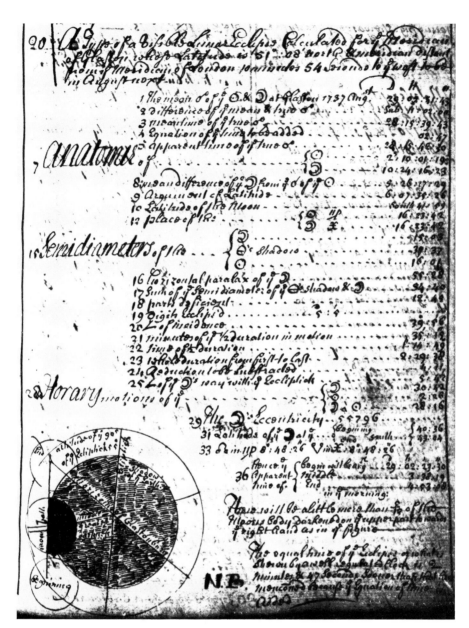

b) 'A type of a visible Lunar Ecclipse Calculated for ye Meridian of Glaston, whose Latitude is 51 deg 08 min north & meridian distant from ye meridian of London 10 min 54 seconds to ye west. To be in August next. 20th July 1737': Cannon's own calculation.

17.9 'Choice observations' and other matters

a) 'The form of ye Execution of a Malefactor at Halifax in ye Wapentake of Morley in ye West Riding of Yorkshire, being yr By law', May 1739.
Cannon cites 'Mag Brit [Magna Britannia] vol. 6, p. 384':
'A felon taken within ye Liberty with goods stolen out of ye liberty or precincts of ye forest of Hardwick shall after 3 markets or meeting days within the town next after his apprehension be taken to ye Gibbet there & have his head bit off from his body, but then ye fact must be certain for he must either be taken Hand Habend viz having his hand in or being in ye very act of stealing, or Backberind, viz having ye thing stolen either upon his back or somewhere abt him without giving any probable account of it.'

b) Admiral Vernon's attack on Porto Bello, drawn from a letter from William Richardson in the *London Evening Post*, 29 March 1740.

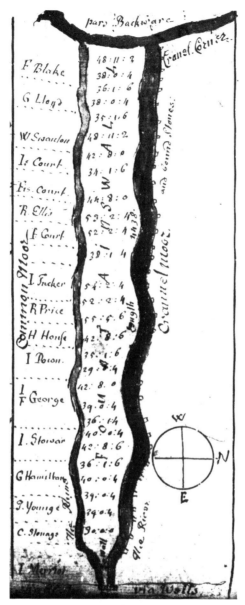

c) Cecilia Stonage's Rhine, 4 September 1736. Four days previously, Cannon and three other men had drained, cleared and surveyed the Rhine and its adjacent land, which lay next to an area recently enclosed by Act of Parliament. On checking his work for fun with a randomly cut length of willow, Cannon was not only pleased with his accuracy, but was also amused to discover that Widow Stonage had got the better of the enclosure commissioners. '. . . and so with the aforesaid stick I found ye content in acres etc of the ropes [used in his previous survey; each rope was 20 ft long] & ye dimensions hereunder. Ye agreement was but 6s per rope, it being honestly worth 9 for which I laughd at them to see how ye widow had bitt them, she being a cunning jilt & talk enough for 10 men. For Mr. Portman told her at Wells at a session of sewers where she freely used her tongue yt if he had been 20 yrs younger he could stop her tail but ye devil could not stop her tongue.'

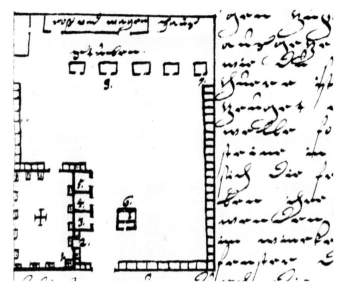

18.1 Plan of the Moscow merchant court from the manuscript of Martin Gruneweg who visited Moscow in 1585. No. 4 on the plan indicates the shop of the Vilnius Byelorussian merchant and printer Mamonich who printed some editions for sale in Russia © Manuscript Division, Biblioteka Gdańska Polskiej Akademii Nauk, Gdańsk, Poland.

18.2 Charter of Jeremiah Tranos, Patriarch of Constantinople, dated 2 December 1587, and containing his approval of the founding of the Dormition Confraternity, its hospital and school in Lviv.

Вечерныѣ. мв҃.

А нашестатокъ оучини покло-

до землѣ, с покорою молачи.

Тебѣ покланаюса едино-

му Бг҃у во Тр҃ци слави-

мому, Оц҃у и Сн҃у, и ст҃му

Дх҃у, и мкса, помл҃уи ма

грѣшнаго .

И тут зарадъ идущи иж

до

18.3 The Saviour on the throne: a woodcut from the prayer-book *Anthologia* (Kiev, 1636).

18.4–5 The title page and an engraving from the book by Joseph Kalymon, *Sol post Occasum oriens* (Kiev, Caves Monastery Printing Press, 1641).

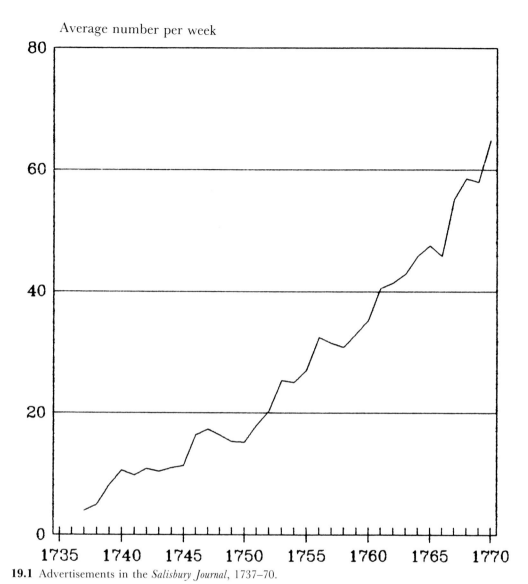

Average number per week

19.1 Advertisements in the *Salisbury Journal*, 1737–70.

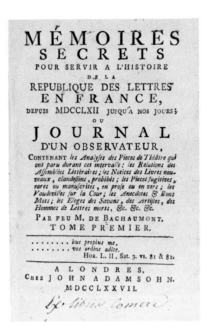

20.1 Title page of a counterfeit edition of the *Mémoires secrets*, one of the 'Mairobert' works issued in the 1770s. The misspelling of the fictitious publisher's name ('Adamsohn' in place of 'Adamson') suggests that this version was put out by a German printer seeking to cash in on the vogue of this kind of unauthorized reporting about pre-revolutionary French politics. *Source* Northwestern University Library, Evanston, Ill.

20.2 *Liberté de la Presse*. This famous engraving from the Directory period telescopes the processes of typesetting, printing and sale of newspapers into a single image that conveys the intensely competitive nature of the press market during the Revolution. *Source* Bibliothèque Nationale, Paris.

20.3 *Père Duchesne*. Three rival versions of the popular pamphlet-journals attributed to the Père Duchesne. Commercial considerations as well as political ones contributed to the multiplication of these publications. *Source* Newberry Library, Chicago, Ill.

21.1 *Plaisirs de l'Ile Enchantée. Première Journée. Festin du Roy et des Reynes.* Reproduced by permission of the Metropolitan Museum, New York.

21.2 Disposition of a magnificent garden. Dezallier d'Argenville, *Theory and Practice of Gardening*. Reproduced by permission of the Clark Library, UCLA.

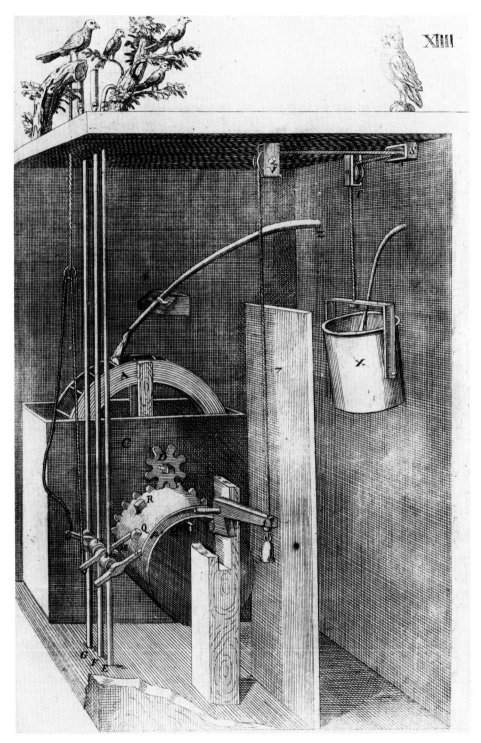

21.3 Design of a hydraulic singing bird for a garden. Salomon de Caus, *New and Rare Inventions*. Reproduced by permission of the Clark Library, UCLA.

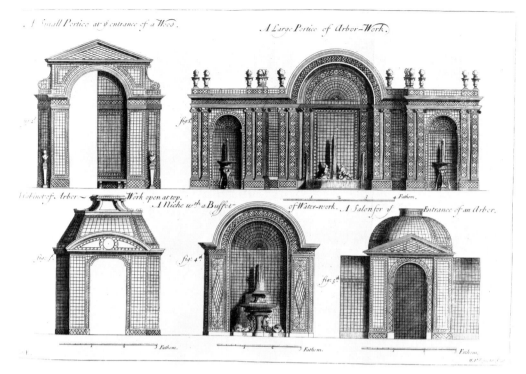

21.4 Classical influence on latticework. A small portico at the entrance of a wood, etc. Dezallier d'Argenville. From the author's collection.

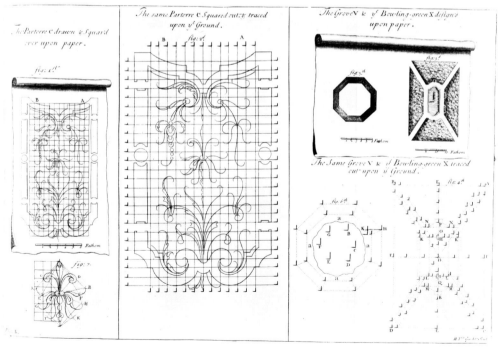

21.5 A parterre drawn and squared, etc. Dezallier D'Argenville. Reproduced by permission of the Clark Library, UCLA.

21.6 *Poliphili Hypnerotomachia*. Reproduced by permission of the Clark Library, UCLA.

21.7 Design for great woods of forest trees. Dezallier d'Argenville. Reproduced by permission of the Clark Library, UCLA.

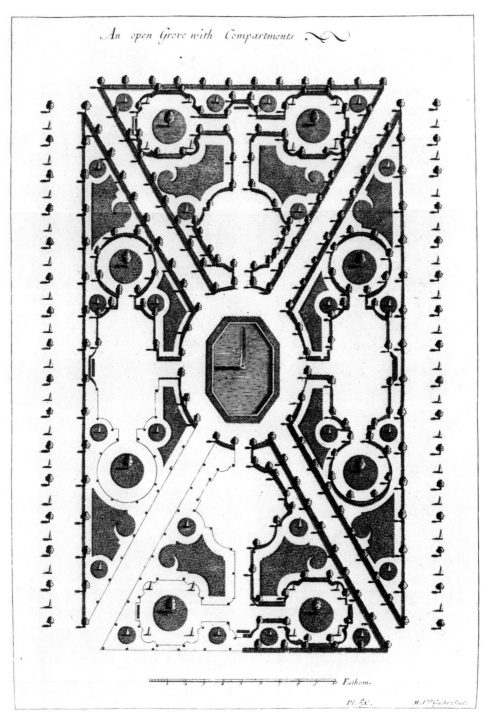

21.8 An open grove with compartments. Dezallier d'Argenville. Reproduced by permission of the Clark Library, UCLA.

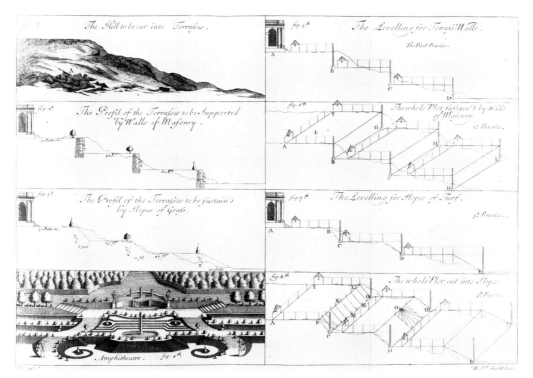

21.9 A hill to be cut into terraces, etc. Dezallier d'Argenville. Reproduced by permission of the Clark Library, UCLA.

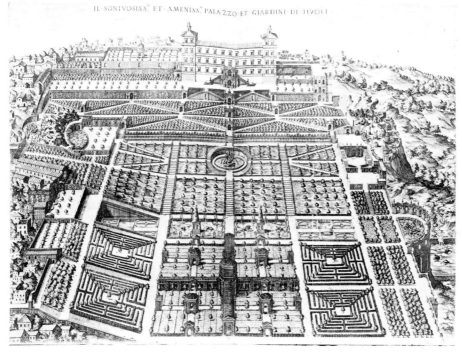

21.10 Villa d'Este at Tivoli. Engraving by Etienne du Perac. Reproduced by permission of the Clark Library, UCLA.

21.11 Looking across the lake at Stourhead, Wiltshire. Reproduced by permission of the Metropolitan Museum of New York.

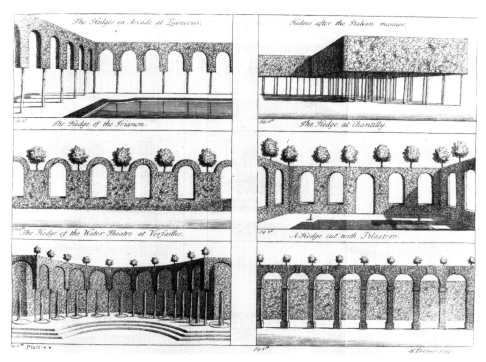

21.12 The hedges in arcade at Liancour, etc. Dezallier d'Argenville. Reproduced by permission of Mark Girouard.

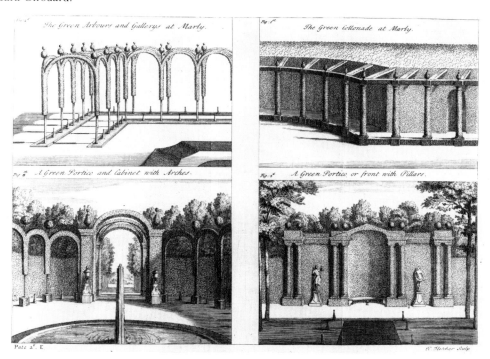

21.13 The green arbours and galleries at Marly, etc. Dezallier d'Argenville. Reproduced by permission of the Clark Library.

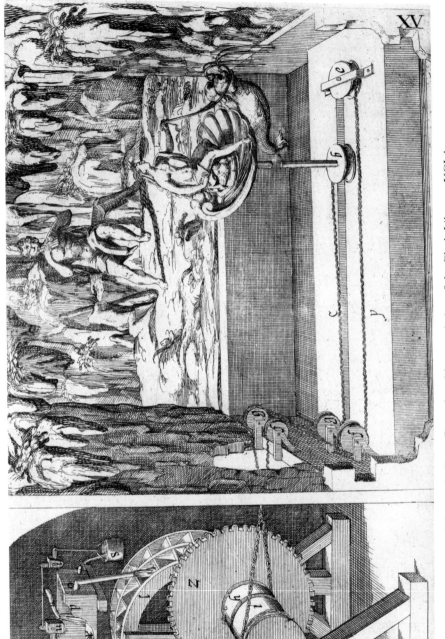

21.14 Mechanisms for a grotto. Salomon de Caus. Reproduced by permission of the Clark Library, UCLA.

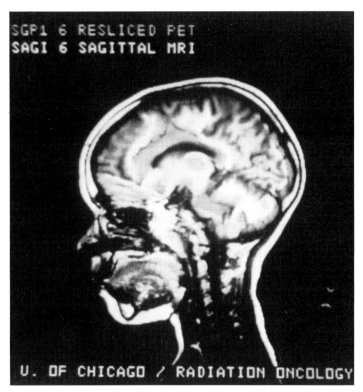

22.1 From David N. Levin, *Superimposed M.R. and PET images*. Photo courtesy of Maurice Goldblatt Magnetic Resonance Imaging Center, Department of Radiology, University of Chicago.

22.2 Giambattista Piranesi, *Appian Way*, etching, from *Le Antichità Romane*, 1756, II, frontispiece. Photo courtesy of Resource Collections of the Getty Center for the History of Art and the Humanities.

22.3 Giambattista Piranesi, *Section of the Tomb of Alessandro Severo*, etching, from *Le Antichità Romane*, 1756, II, pl. XXXII. Photo courtesy of Resource Collections of the Getty Center for the History of Art and the Humanities.

22.4 Giambattista Piranesi, *Pantheon. Interior of the Portico*, etching, from *Vedute di Roma*, 1769, pl. LXXXII. Author's photo.

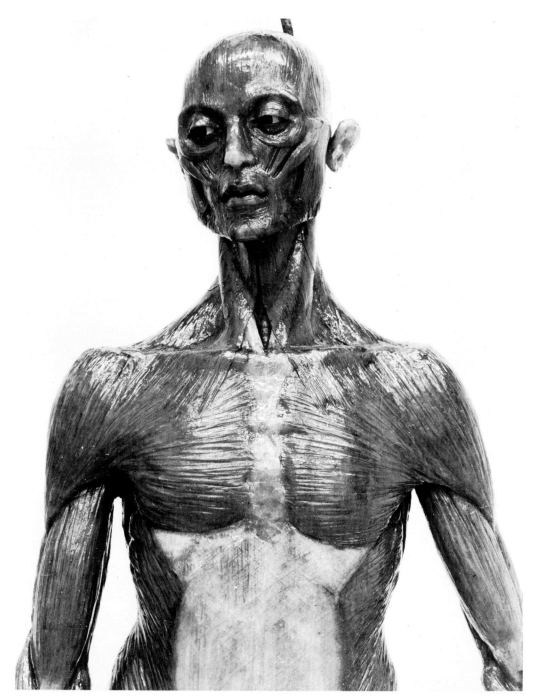

22.5 Felice Fontana ? *Anatomical Figure*, eighteenth-century, wax.
Photo courtesy of Library, Wellcome Institute for the History of Medicine.

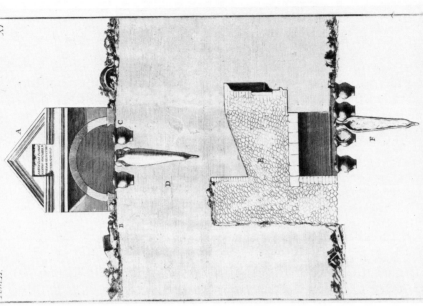

22.7 Giambattista Piranesi, *View and Profile of a Tomb of the Camere de' Liberti, e Servi et di L. Arunzio*, etching, from *Le Antichità Romane*, 1756, II, pl. XI. Photo courtesy of Resource Collections

22.6 Giambattista Piranesi, *Plan and Elevation of the Tomb of Alessandro Severo*, etching, from *Le Antichità Romane*, 1756, II, pl. XXXI. Photo courtesy of Resource Collections of the Getty

22.8 Ferrante Imperatore, *View of Museum*, engraving, from *Historia Naturale*, 2nd edn, 1672, frontispiece. Photo courtesy of Resource Collections of the Getty Center for the History of Art and the Humanities.

22.9 F. Ertinger *View of Library of Sainte-Geneviève*, engraving, from R. P. du Molinet, *Le Cabinet de Sainte-Geneviève*, 1689, frontispiece. Photo courtesy of Resource Collections of the Getty Center for the History of Art and the Humanities.

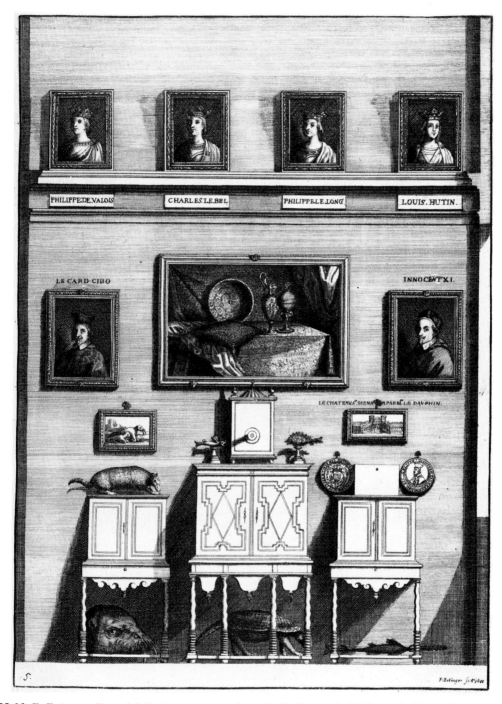

22.10 F. Ertinger, *View of Collection*, engraving, from R. P. Claude du Molinet, *Le Cabinet de Saint-Geneviève*, 1689, pl. V. Photo courtesy of Resource Collections of the Getty Center for the History of Art and the Humanities.

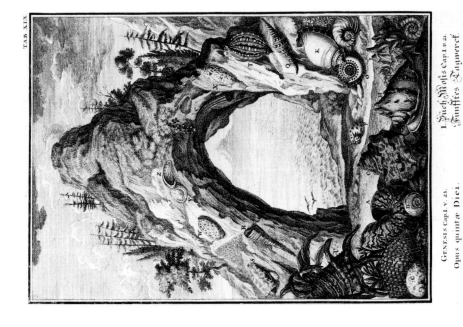

22.12 I. A. Corvinus, *Monuments of the Flood*, engraving, from Jean-Jacques Scheuchzer, *Physique sacrée*, 1732, I, pl. LVII. Photo courtesy of Resource Collections of the Getty Center for the History of Art and the Humanities.

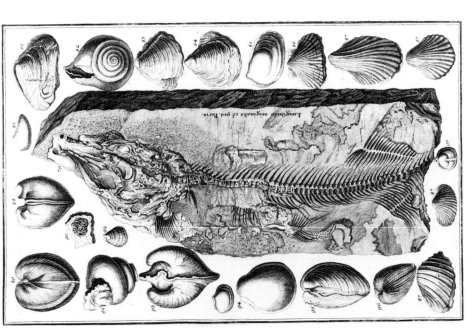

22.11 I. A. Corvinus, *Fossil Remains (Work of the Fifth Day of Creation)*, engraving, from Jean-Jacques Scheuchzer, *Physique sacrée*, 1732, I, pl. XIX. Photo courtesy of Resource Collections of the Getty Center for the History of Art and the Humanities.

22.13 Petrus Camper, *Studies of the Facial Angle: From Ape to Apollo Belvedere*, engraving, from Petrus Camper, *Dissertation physique*, 1791, pl. III. Photo courtesy of National Library of Medicine, Bethesda, MD.

23.1 Willem Kalf, *Still Life with Nautilus Cup*. Reproduced by permission of the Thyssen-Bornemisza Collection, Lugano.

23.2 Dirck van Delen, *Still Life with Tulip in Chinese Vase*. Reproduced by permission of the Museum Boymans-van Beuningen.

23.3 Clara Peeters, *Still Life*. Private Collection.

23.4 Christoffel van den Berghe, *Vanitas with Vase of Flowers*. Reproduced by permission of the Earl of Chichester.

FVI, NON SVM:
ES, NON ERIS.

Et nos floruimus viridante ætate tumentes,
  Nunc præter saniem, putriaq; ossa; nihil.
Tu modò turgescens vernas crispante capillo,
  Mobile labetur tempus, erisq; nihil.

Corpus, quod comis, nihil et, fluitantibus annis,
  Tandem non etiam vile cadauer erit.
Usq; adeo nihil est: virtus manet vna superstes,
  Huius come comas, huius amato decus.   F. Estius

23.5 Jan Saenredam after Hendrick Goltzius, *Allegory on Death*. Reproduced by permission of the British Museum, Department of Prints and Drawings.

23.6 Edwaert Collier, *Vanitas Still Life*. Reproduced by permission of the Museum of Lakenhal, Leiden.

23.7 Pieter Gerritsz van Roestraeten, *Candlestick*. Reproduced by permission of the Museum Boymans-van Beuningen.

23.8 Gerard Dou, *Still Life with Timepiece*. Reproduced by permission of the Staatliche Kunstsammlungen, Dresden.

23.9 Abraham Schoor, *Vanitas Still Life*. Reproduced by permission of the Rijksmuseum Amsterdam.

23.10 Pieter Claesz, *Vanitas Still Life*. Reproduced by permission of the Westfälisches Landesmuseum für Kunst und Kulturgeschichte.

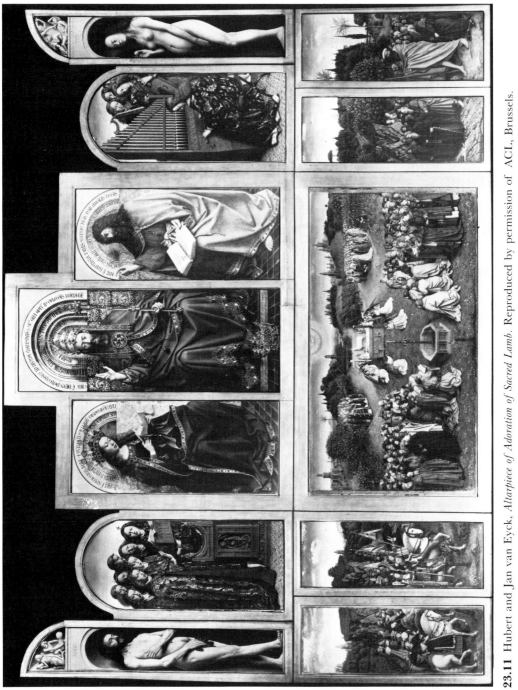

23.11 Hubert and Jan van Eyck, *Altarpiece of Adoration of Sacred Lamb*. Reproduced by permission of ACL, Brussels.

23.12 Quentin Metsys, *The Money Changers*. © The Reunion des Musées Nationaux, Paris.

23.13 Marinus van Reymerswael, *The Tax Gatherers*. Reproduced by permission of the National Gallery, London.

23.14 Govert Flinck, *Roman Consul Marcus Curius Dentatus*. Reproduced by permission of the Stichting Koninkliji Paleis te Amsterdam.

24.1 'The first lecture in experimental philosophy': the properties of fire demonstrated for the London Gentry in the 1740s. *Source The Universal Magazine of Knowledge and Pleasure*, 3 (1748), 49.

24.2 Euphrosyne and her fraternal instructor Cleonicus discuss Benjamin Martin's table electric machine, while their servant, John, works its handle. A Leyden Jar is suspended from the prime conductor, connected to the spinning globe by a chain. *Source* Benjamin Martin, *The Young Gentleman and Lady's Philosophy*, 2nd edn,

24.3 Rackstrow's *Beatification*, displayed in Fleet Street in 1746. An electrified plate above the evacuated crown discharges as a halo. *Source* Benjamin Rackstrow, *Miscellaneous Observations* 1748, frontispiece.

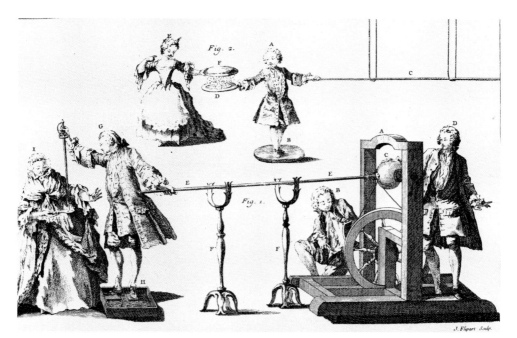

24.4 A French version of Watson's electrical trials in the mid-1740s. The human body becomes a conductor of electrical fluid, children help chaff jump, an insulated gentleman carries a sword which inflames his female companion's spirits of wine, and philosophers and workmen ply their machine. *Source* William Watson, *Expériences et observations pour servir à l'explication de la nature et des propriétés de l'électricité*, 1748, pl. III.

24.5 Benjamin Martin's trade card, featuring his cometary interests of the mid-1750s. *Source* Science Museum Library, 1951–685.

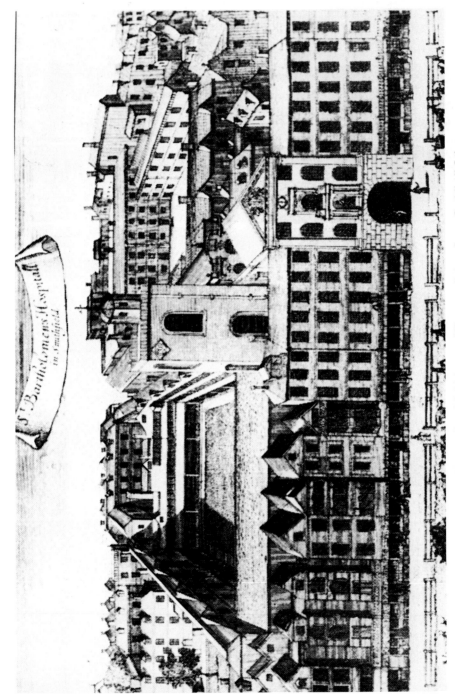

24.6 St Bartholomew's Hospital in the 1720s, the Smithfield home of Tory medicine. *Source* Guildhall Library.

24.7 *Enthusiasm Delineated*, (1739), Hogarth's first (and suppressed) version of his satire of 'litteral and low conceptions of Sacred Beings as also of the idolatrous tendency of pictures in Churches'. *Source* British Library.

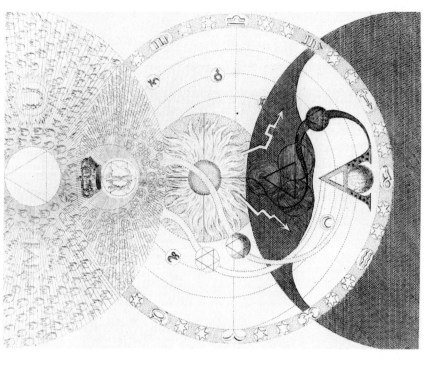

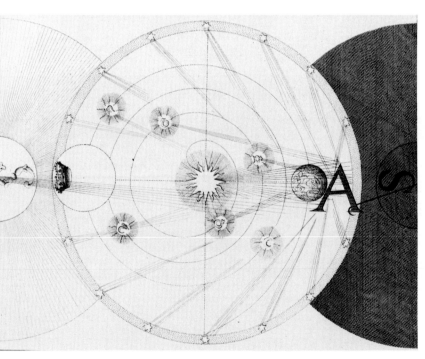

24.8 Behmenist fire sermons: the 1764 edition, prepared by Law's disciples of Andreas Freher's representations of the Fall and Regeneration of man. In (a), Adam (A) falls from his glorious alliance with Sophia/Wisdom (upper S) under the influence of Satan (lower S). This world, under the baleful influence of the planets, appears midway between the realms of blissful and infernal fires. In (b), three paths to bliss. The lowest of humanity (at the base of A) return to infernal fire (the dark triangle). The elevated (the vertex of A) ascend to heaven through the Logos (IC), which has replaced Sophia/Wisdom. The middle rank eventually reach heaven through the realm of fire. M and U are the other two 'flames of fire', Michael and Uriel. *Source* 'Illustration of the deep principles of Jakob Behmen' in Ward and Langcake, *The Works of Jakob Behmen*, 1764, vol. 2, 27–32.

24.9 John Freke presides over the judicial anatomy of Tom Nero in Surgeon's Hall, from Hogarth's 1751 *Reward of Cruelty*: 'Behold the Villain's dire disgrace! / Not Death itself can end'. *Source* British Library.

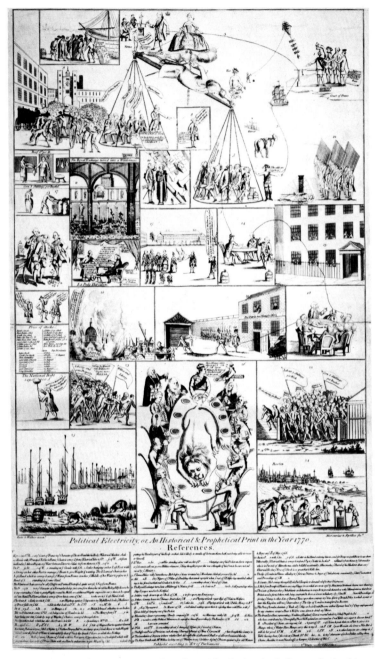

24.10 *Political Electricity* (1770), 'an historical and prophetical print'. Beneath the kite, at top right, 'Lord Bute on the coast of France, in the character of Doctor Franklin, his Body the Electrical Machine', whence a conducting wire links a series of twenty-five tableaux of current discontents. To the left and right of the 'Great Lion Feast', beasts amidst the ruins of London docks and the comparative prosperity of colonial Boston. *Source* British Library.

Every study demonstrates that literacy in pre-industrial England was closely and consistently associated with social and economic position. The ability or inability to write followed the gradient from clean, respectable commercial pursuits, through various types of specialist craft activities, to rough, manual, outdoor occupations. A distinctive hierarchy emerges, in which illiteracy is correlated to status, occupation and wealth. This can be illustrated with figures from the seventeenth century. The percentages varied, of course, from the sixteenth century onwards, but the social pattern remained remarkably coherent over time. The very consistency of these figures, confirmed by every numerical study of literacy, lends confidence to the choice of signatures and marks as an indicator.

Table 15.1 Illiteracy of selected groups in seventeenth-century England

Social group	% illiterate	
	(rural)	(London)
Clergy and professions	0	0
Gentlemen	2	2
Grocers	5	0
Merchants	10	0
Bakers	27	26
Yeomen	33	30
Weavers	49	34
Tailors	51	43
Blacksmiths	56	38
Carpenters	62	40
Husbandmen	79	–*
Shepherds	82	–*
Labourers	85	78
Miners	96	–*
All men	68	45
All women	90	60

*Information not available.

Particular circumstances affected the individual's acquisition of basic literacy. Educational opportunity, religious disposition and family background all played a part, so that men and women of humble origins sometimes went on to become readers and even writers.[25] But overriding these cultural variables was the force of economic and social structure.

The gentle, clerical and professional classes, of course, had full possession of literacy, except for a few who were decrepit or dyslexic. Members of this dominant class, who comprised no more than 5 per cent of the population, were the primary audience for most of the output of the press. Literacy was an attribute of their status and an active element in their lives. Here, and here only, was the seventeenth-century cultivated elite. And among their wives and daughters were the principal female participants in literate culture, a minority within a minority.

Approaching the level of the gentry were city merchants and tradesmen. Country merchants and superior shopkeepers, including drapers and haberdashers, grocers and apothecaries, ranged from 5–15 per cent illiterate. Their London counterparts were fully literate. In the seventeenth century it was still possible to smell a profit without a literate education, but

Table 15.2 Illiteracy in London and East Anglia, 1580–1730

	% illiterate			
	1580–1640	*1660–1700*	*1720–30*	*N*
East Anglia men	70	60	50	>5000
East Anglia women	95	82	74	1122
East Anglia yeomen	40	28	26	635
East Anglia husbandmen	84	79	87	753
East Anglia tradesmen	55	36	34	1494
Norwich tradesmen	32	31	–*	420
London/Middx tradesmen	29	21	8	1568
London/Middx women	90	65	44	1947

*Information not available.

the pressure of shipping news and trade regulations, commercial correspondence and memoranda, made fluency with print and script increasingly important.

Next came a variety of skilled craftsmen and tradesmen of the second rank, men like goldsmiths and clothiers, dyers and leather sellers, who lived by providing specialist services or expensively wrought products. Their literacy reflected their wealth and their social standing. Below them were clustered 'the industrious sort of people', between a third and a half of whom could not write their names. Many were involved in the textile industry, as weavers or fullers, in the processing of agricultural produce, as brewers or maltsters or in manufacturing articles of dress, as tailors or cordwainers. Artisans and craftsmen made little use of literacy in their day-to-day employment, although those who could read became part of the audience for the popular press.

Village artisans, such as blacksmiths and carpenters, millers and butchers, belonged to a less literate cluster in which a half to three-quarters could not sign. Illiteracy was more widespread among bricklayers and thatchers, masons and miners and all-weather outdoor workers like fishermen, shepherds and labourers. Most of their work was heavy and dirty, requiring more brawn than brain. Their employment often isolated these men from regular contact with the rest of society. Paper and writing rarely came their way, so it is not suprising that three-quarters or more were unable to sign; illiteracy among thatchers and miners topped 90 per cent.

Most yeomen could read, and only a third could not write. Literacy was not vital to them, but, as independent farmers involved with leases and land-improvements, it was often useful to be able to read and write. The yeoman's practical literacy included the reading of broadsheets and almanacs, and might extend to works on husbandry and self-improvement.

Table 15.3 Illiteracy in London, 1670–1730

	% illiterate		
	City tradesmen	*Middlesex tradesmen*	*Women*
1670–9	19	24	78
1680–9	23	28	64
1690–1700	7	18	52
1720–9	8	8	44

Some yeomen were also part of the audience for religious chapbooks and editions of merry tales. A few even kept diaries.

Husbandmen, by contrast, were mostly illiterate. These were modest tenant farmers who lacked the yeomen's resources or incentives to acquire education. Four out of five husbandmen could not write their names, and the proportion showed little reduction before the eighteenth century. Their cultural level was similar to that of shepherds and bricklayers. Elizabethan and Stuart poets who idealized the pastoral life must have known that its real practitioners were unlikely ever to read about it. The rural poor were the last to become adept at writing and familiar with print.

This strong social patterning persisted into the eighteenth and nineteenth centuries. In the period 1754–84, for example, illiteracy was 5 per cent among shopkeepers, 19 per cent among yeomen and farmers, 20–30 per cent among various tradesmen, 46 per cent among husbandmen, 51 per cent among building workers and 59 per cent among labourers and servants. Half a century later, in the period 1815–44, the ranking was little changed, although the literacy levels of some groups had actually deteriorated (shopkeepers 5 per cent, yeomen and farmers 17 per cent, tradesmen 15–30 per cent, husbandmen 52 per cent, building workers 38 per cent, labourers and servants 66 per cent). Roger Schofield's figures from marriage registers show that illiteracy had fallen to 40 per cent among men and 60 per cent among women by the accession of George III (from approximately 50 per cent and 70 per cent at the end of the seventeenth century), but the second half of the eighteenth century saw little further movement.[26]

The period between 1720 and 1760 may be one of the most important for the social, cultural and economic history of England, but it is one in which virtually nothing is known about the incidence of literacy. My work, based mainly on ecclesiastical court depositions, draws to a halt around the latter years of George I. Schofield's study depends on the reformed marriage registers, which only required signatures and marks after Hardwicke's Marriage Act of 1754. Nothing is known in detail about the distribution and development of literacy during the age of Walpole and George II, although the summary figures from either end of this period suggest that there were some important changes. Writ large, the evidence points to a general advance in literacy in the first half of the eighteenth century, and overall stagnation in the second half; whether this stands up to detailed scrutiny, and if it does, what accounts for it, is a topic crying out for further research.

At the beginning of the Victorian era more than one in three Englishmen was illiterate, along with half the women. Only with the onset of universal schooling in the late nineteenth century did the situation rapidly change. Illiteracy among young men (bridegrooms) fell below 10 per cent for the first time in the 1880s, and reached its modern level (close to zero) before World War I. Illiteracy among young women (brides) was reduced to 30 per cent by 1870, and then fell rapidly as girls, too, benefited from educational reform. By the end of the nineteenth century young women were more likely to be able to sign than their husbands, especially in southern and southeast England.[27]

These developments call for further analysis and explanation. The impact of industrialization upon literacy rates is still a matter of contention, although on balance it seems that the early factory system was culturally disruptive. The search for a 'threshold' figure, a level of literacy at which industrialization 'takes off' is surely a misguided enterprise, although development economists still look to late eighteenth-century England for a model of economic modernization. The 'industrial revolution', if such a thing existed, owed nothing to a rise in literacy levels, although many of its operatives, and the consumers of its products, could doubtless read and write.

Nineteenth-century figures for the geography of literacy show the new industrial centres lagging behind the rest of the country. In 1856, for example, at a time when national figures show 26 per cent of men and 36 per cent of women unable to sign the marriage register, the boom town of Wigan in Lancashire had illiteracy rates of 50 per cent and 71 per cent. At Exeter, by contrast, a traditional regional centre set well aside from the new industrial mainstream, the figures were 16 per cent and 18 per cent. That such figures do not necessarily point to a cultural revolution is suggested by the mid-Victorian enquiries and surveys which found low levels of practical or functional literacy even among those said to be able to read and write. The eventual achievement of mass literacy cannot be shown to have brought about an increase in godliness, liberality or wisdom.

Notes

1   C. M. Cipolla, *Literacy and Development in the West* (Harmondsworth, 1969); H. J. Graff (ed.), *Literacy and Social Development in the West* (Cambridge, 1981); D. Cressy, 'Levels of illiteracy in England 1530–1730', in Graff, *Literacy*; idem, *Literacy and the Social Order: Reading and Writing in Tudor and Stuart England* (Cambridge, 1980); F. Furet and J. Ozouf, *Reading and Writing: Literacy in France from Calvin to Jules Ferry* (Cambridge, 1982); R. A. Houston, *Scottish Literacy and the Scottish Identity: Illiteracy and Society in Scotland and Northern England 1600–1800* (Cambridge, 1985); idem, *Literacy in Early Modern Europe* (London, 1988); D. P. Resnick (ed.), *Literacy in Historical Perspective* (Washington, DC, 1983); W. B. Stephens, *Education, Literacy and Society, 1830–70: The Geography of Diversity in Provincial England* (Manchester, 1987); D. Vincent, *Literacy and Popular Culture: England 1750–1914* (Cambridge, 1989).

2   W. J. Ong, *Orality and Literacy: The Technologizing of the Word* (London, 1982); G. Baumann (ed.), *The Written Word: Literacy in Transition* (Oxford, 1986); J. Goody, *Literacy in Traditional Societies* (Cambridge, 1968); P. Freire, *Education for Critical Consciousness* (New York, 1980); A. Inkeles and D. H. Smith, *Becoming Modern* (London, 1974); B. V. Street, *Literacy in Theory and Practice* (Cambridge, 1984).

3   M. T. Clanchy, *From Memory to Written Record: England, 1066–1307* (London, 1979).

4   W. H. Frere (ed.), *Visitation Articles and Injunctions of the Period of the Reformation*, vol. 3 (London, 1910), 301; ibid., vol. 2, 20; G. Swinnock, *The Christian Man's Calling* (London, 1663), 22–3.

5   R. Baxter, *A Christian Directory* (London, 1673), 548, 582.

6   Anon., *The Offices of Christian Parents* (London, 1616), 73–4; W. Gouge, *Of Domesticall Duties* (London, 1622), 534, 586; D. Cressy, 'The environment for literacy: accomplishment and context in seventeenth-century England and New England', in Resnick, *Literacy in Historical Perspective*, 23–5.

7   D. Brown, *The Introduction to the True Understanding of the Whole Arte of Expedition in Teaching to Write* (London, 1638), Bv, B4v.

8   D. Brown, *The New Invention Instituted Calligraphia* (St Andrews, 1622), 56–9; Brown, *Introduction*, B3.

9   M. Billingsley, *The Pens Excellencie: or the Secretaries Delighte* (London, 1618), B4, C; T. Dilworth, *The Schoolmasters Assistant*, 17th edn (Philadelphia, 1771), xix.

10 N. Breton, *The Court and Country* (1618), in W. H. Dunham and S. Pargellis (eds), *Complaint and Reform in England 1436–1714* (New York, 1938), 469; W. Cobbett, *A Spelling Book with Appropriate Lessons* (London, 1831), quoted in Vincent, *Literacy and Popular Culture*, 56.

11 T. More, *The Apologye* (London, 1533), 20–20v.

12 R. Steele, *The Husbandman's Calling* (London, 1672), 57.

13 H. Conset, *The Practice of the Spiritual or Ecclesiastical Courts* (London, 1685), 116–17.

14 Cressy, *Literacy and the Social Order*, 16; idem, *Coming Over: Migration and Communication between England and New England in the Seventeenth Century* (Cambridge, 1987), 219–20; idem, 'Environment for literacy', 33.

15 C. Clifford, *The Schoole of Horsemanship* (London, 1585).

16 Baxter, *Christian Directory*, 60.

17 Cressy, 'Environment for literacy', 34.

18 K. Thomas, 'The meaning of literacy in early modern England', in Baumann, *Written Word*.

19 R. Schofield, 'The measurement of literacy in pre-industrial England', in Goody, *Literacy in Traditional Societies*; Thomas, 'The meaning of literacy'; M. Spufford, 'First steps in literacy: the reading and writing experiences of the humblest seventeenth-century spiritual autobiographers', in Graff, *Literacy*.

20 Cressy, *Literacy and the Social Order*, 56–60.

21 E. J. Monaghan, 'Literacy instruction and gender in colonial New England', *American Quarterly*, xl (1988); S. Hull, *Chaste, Silent and Obedient* (San Marino, 1982); E. Hobby, *Virtue of Necessity: English Women's Writing 1649–88* (Ann Arbor, 1988).

22 P. Earle, 'The female labour market in London in the late seventeenth and early eighteenth centuries', *Economic History Review*, 2nd series, xlii (1989); Vincent, *Literacy and Popular Culture*.

23 Cressy, *Literacy and the Social Order*; Houston, *Scottish Literacy*; R. Schofield, 'Dimensions of illiteracy in England 1750–1850' (1973), in Graff, *Literacy*; Stephens, *Education*; Vincent, *Literacy and Popular Culture*.

24 Cressy, *Literacy and the Social Order*, 147–9; Earle, 'The female labour market', 333–6, 343–4.

25 Spufford, 'First steps'.

26 Schofield, 'Dimensions'; Vincent, *Literacy and Popular Culture*.

27 Vincent, *Literacy and Popular Culture*, 24–5.

16
Reckoning with commerce: numeracy in eighteenth-century America

Patricia Cline Cohen

Benjamin Franklin, by all accounts a model Enlightenment man and probably a reasonably clever lad, failed twice in arithmetic, first in the Boston Grammar School he attended and later at a private school run by George Brownell which emphasized commercial training. When Franklin turned 16, in 1722, he was embarrassed by his 'ignorance in figures', so he procured a standard English arithmetic textbook by Edward Cocker and taught himself, 'with ease' he tells us, the whole of arithmetic in short order.[1]

This glimpse of mathematical training in the Boston of the early eighteenth century perfectly captures several curiosities in the history of numeracy in colonial America. The story shows that smart people could stumble and fail at arithmetic. Young Ben was literate, industrious and already obsessive about saving money, and still he failed to make headway in the subject. His experience at school was by no means unusual. The story also demonstrates that a young man could manage to function in an important commercial city, even while claiming not to know much arithmetic. Franklin was not innumerate, of course. Right before the arithmetic confession in his *Autobiography* he describes an early way-to-wealth scheme he had worked out with his brother, who was also his master in a printing establishment. For a short while, Franklin became a vegetarian, and he convinced his brother to pay him half of the standard expense of boarding an apprentice. Young Franklin then spent half again of his food allowance on potatoes, rice, raisins and bread, and pocketed the other half with great satisfaction. Here was a young man who could live on the cheap, buy his own food in the market and cut a financial deal with his master to the benefit of both, and at the same time claim that he was ignorant of figuring. His self-confessed failure in arithmetic clearly did not bar him from simple market transactions and money-saving calculations.

The story also points up one path to success with arithmetic; in this case, Franklin waited until he was older and presumably somewhat more adept in economic transactions, and then he studied a textbook on his own and learned it well, 'with ease' in fact. He felt sufficiently comfortable with math to take up next a book on navigation, which exposed him to simple geometry, and this brought an end to his mathematical education.

Whatever Ben Franklin did not know about arithmetic, his own famous book makes plain that he was numerate as well as literate. The history of literacy has in the last two decades been a major enterprise among historians. Many studies have explored the economic, social, political and cultural consequences of the spread of reading and writing. But the history of numeracy, which the *Oxford English Dictionary* vaguely defines as 'an ability with or knowledge of numbers', has been largely unexamined, and all kinds of interesting questions have only begun to be asked.[2] What skills – or bundles of skills – comprise numeracy? How did people learn to reckon? How much skill did they need to participate in markets? How did people with different levels of skills interact in economic exchanges? What kept men and women from achieving numeracy?

For too long, we have carelessly assumed that low-level numerical skills have been unchanging across the centuries and that the calculations necessary for economic exchange have been essentially the same over time. But in fact, arithmetic education has not been set in concrete, and the acquisition of numerical skills has been unevenly distributed over the Anglo-American population.

Obstacles stand in the way of recovering numeracy's history. In the first place, evidence is fragmentary and hard to come by. By counting the numbers of signed names against x-marks in parish registers and legal documents, historians of literacy claim to know something about literacy rates. (Using writing as a proxy for reading is of course problematic, but it is also very convenient.) However, students of numeracy have no choice but to rely on the kinds of anecdotal and impressionistic evidence that the most rigorous quantitative historians generally distrust. For there never existed a moment, parallel to the signing of a marriage register, when large numbers of people had to step forward and formally demonstrate their ability to add, subtract, multiply or divide. The lack of systematic, serial data for any century but our own makes it impossible to calculate precise rates of numeracy for earlier times.[3]

Second, numeracy is hedged about with difficult questions of definition and meaning, as Ben Franklin's story suggests. What did it mean when people could come out ahead buying and selling potatoes and raisins and yet still claim to be ignorant in figuring? How was it possible to be proficiently numerate while untutored in book-learned arithmetic?

By way of suggesting answers to this and other questions, this chapter explores how arithmetic was taught and what numerical skills were used in commerce in eighteenth-century America, the key century for the spread of numeracy. The steady growth of a commercialized economy in that century spurred and altered the distribution of arithmetical skills, but even more importantly, the political revolution following independence from Britain also had a profound impact on the way arithmetic knowledge was organized and taught.

Untutored numeracy begins with basic language. Ideas about number and the relationship between numbers are inherent in English (as well as most other languages), so to learn a vocabulary of number words is already a small step on the road to numeracy. Just to be able to speak words like three, five and ten implies a concept of greater and smaller quantities. But to say this is not to say very much, for knowing a set of number words implies nothing about actual calculating skills. Most languages have words expressing numbers into the hundreds, thousands and beyond, building the words in various but systematic ways on a base of ten, twelve or twenty. We no longer maintain the old fiction that archaic or non-western peoples counted 'one, two, many'; but in abandoning that fiction, we can see more clearly that counting alone is not the essence of numeracy.[4]

In eighteenth-century America, a child's first introduction to numbers undoubtedly came in the form of number words. In the late twentieth century we often begin to teach the *symbols* for the number words practically simultaneously with the concepts, to very young children. Children's television programming (such as *Sesame Street*) makes the case: arabic numbers are repeatedly presented and associated with a corresponding set of objects which are then counted out, to fix the spoken word, the arabic symbol and the actual quantity of items in the mind. In colonial America, this trio of associations was not the common way to proceed. Illiterate people did not utilize written symbols either for words or for numbers, and even literate people postponed learning arabic notation until a relatively late age, around 10 or 11, long after number words would have entered their active vocabulary. A number word denoted a known quantity; it was a second and separate step to move on to arabic numerals.[5]

If this at first sounds strange, recall that arabic numerals themselves were of relatively recent origin in English culture. For centuries, English men and women had managed to handle counting and simple calculation either in their heads, or by wiggling fingers and maybe toes, or by piling up beans; serious calculation, like that performed by the exchequer or by merchants, required the use of tally sticks (sometimes ingeniously notched, so that small numbers of sticks could stand for large numbers) or counters (a grid painted on a table top, utilizing pebbles in abacus fashion). Written numbers took the form of roman numerals, a kind of condensed version of tally sticks.[6]

Arabic numerals – a new way of writing numbers borrowed from the Babylonians and their Near-Eastern descendants – first filtered into Europe in the tenth century through North Africa and Spain, but they were barely known until the thirteenth century, and only began to come into widespread use in England in the half century between 1500 and 1550. And even after that time, roman numerals remained the preferred symbol system, in titles of kings, in legal documents like wills and contracts, in chapter numbers in books, even in tax lists. The power of the new numbers lay in the place system: a mere nine symbols plus a zero could not only represent any integer, they could also be manipulated to perform actual calculations. In other words, the power of calculation was built into the number symbols themselves (providing one had paper and pen to work with). This advantage was at the same time the chief disadvantage of arabic numerals: they could be easily and damagingly falsified. The simple stroke of a pen could transform a number by a factor of ten; hence the decided preference for roman numerals in legal documents.[7]

The introduction of arabic numerals created a need and opportunity for textbooks to explain the new methods of calculation; the trends in styles of the texts themselves tell us much about the reception and spread of numeracy. The first in English appeared in the 1540s, by Robert Recorde (*The Ground of Artes: Teaching the Worke and Practise of Arithmetike, both in Whole Numbres and Fractions*) and many more (about two dozen titles) followed in the next century.[8] These early texts introduced the symbols and explained their basic operations with the help of examples and problems that used mainly abstract numbers. But by the second half of the 1600s, a very different sort of arithmetic book was dominating the text trade. Arithmetic books from the Restoration period on were clearly targeting a mercantile audience. The examples worked and problems given mainly came from the world of money, goods and exchange. The aim of the newer texts was to transmit problem-solving techniques for specific business situations, not to unfold the whole of fundamental mathematical relations at some deep level. The presumed reader of Edward Cocker's *Arithmetick* or William Leybourne's *Cursus Mathematicus* was a counting-house lad, not a budding university natural philosopher. And there were lots of such lads, to judge by the reissues and new editions; Cocker's book, for example, enjoyed a run of at least 112 editions.[9]

The commercial texts shared a common approach. Arabic symbols were introduced, and the basic operations presented, but with two key differences now. First, because the examples worked in the text were by and large word problems reflecting commercial applications, the cumbersome denominations of British weights and measures had to have a central place in every book. Tables of equivalences filled early pages, differentiating firkins of butter from firkins of soap (56 vs 64 pounds avoirdupois) and multiple meanings of a gallon of ale, depending on whether you were in London or somewhere else. English money with its base-twelve pounds and shillings contributed another dimension to every commercial problem. Addition was not merely simple addition with abstract numbers, it was the art of summing up compound numbers in many denominations. Students had to spend a large chunk of time practising a rule called 'Reduction' – learning to reduce a compound number to its smallest unit to facilitate calculations, as in the problem of how many inches in 3 furlongs and 58 yards?

The horrendous burden of denominate arithmetic – that is, arithmetic that has to pay attention to the denominations of the numbers – apparently led the authors to seek shortcuts somewhere else. What they chose to trim was any form of *proof*, and this was the second key difference between what we might term the earlier pure arithmetic texts and the texts of commercial stripe. The new authors seemed to feel it was a waste of time to try to *explain* the reasons behind every manoeuvre, and so instead they presented arithmetic as a series of *rules*, meant to be learned by heart. Some texts presented the rules in catchy or rhyming phrases, the better to commit them to memory. For each particular situation there was a rule; the trick was to figure out which rule applied to the problem at hand, and then grind out an answer according to the memorized algorithm. This system did not encourage independent thinking. Since rules rather than principles were taught, there had to be a plethora of rules to cover many different situations. Thus there were the rules of simple addition, addition of compound numbers and addition of fractions, often in widely separated chapters of a text, with no clue that they are all variations of the same operation. There was the Rule of Three Direct, the Rule of Three Inverse, the Rule of Fellowship, the Rule of Interest, the Rule of Discount and dozens more. The conception of arithmetic problems as essentially rule-driven formulas spurred the invention of yet more catchy algorithms for use in specific moments of calculation in daily life. One example was the Virgin's Rule, a rule for figuring the bill in a tavern for a group of assorted people including maidens; the apparent assumption that necessitated a special rule was that maidens drank less. None of the standard arithmetic texts of the eighteenth century included the Virgin's Rule, but its perpetuation in folk culture nicely demonstrates the approach to arithmetic encouraged by the standard texts: each act of calculation seemed to be specific to the context in which it occurred.

In place of a universe of specific problems each addressed by a separate rule, modern arithmetic systematizes problems and teaches general approaches. Most likely a modern student would translate a word problem into a simple equation, with x for the unknown and operational signs to signify the calculation to be done. English and Americans in the eighteenth century did not use algebraic notation at all, and neither texts nor, one suspects, teachers, tried to impart knowledge of how to solve word problems logically and systematically.

The famous Rule of Three illustrates this point nicely. The Rule of Three was sometimes called the Golden Rule, and Hodder's text explained why: 'as gold transcends all other Mettals, so doth this rule all others in Arithmetick.'[10] The Rule of Three governed problems dealing with proportions, ratios or costs of multiple units of goods. It is the closest early arithmetic came to a systematic treatment of a class of problems, in this case a class of problems rooted in the common context of economic transactions. A standard curriculum moved from addition to division in whole numbers, through denominate numbers and reduction, and then to the grand finale, the Rule of Three. This was a benchmark Rule; it was the cap to the minimum one could learn and still be considered conversant with figures. Apprenticeship contracts in the eighteenth century often specified that the trainee be taught reading, writing and ciphering to the Rule of Three; it was by far the most common terminal subject in American student-written copybooks. Whether the Rule of Three came last because it was the last easy subject, or whether it came last because it was the corker, the subject that sent students back to the fields or to the workbench, is unclear. But what is clear is that many students' entire arithmetic education ended with the Rule of Three.

Given three parts, to find the fourth, is the way early English and also American texts defined this type of problem. 'If 7 yards of cloth cost 21 Pounds, what will 16 yards cost?' The Rule of Three instructed a student to set down 7:21::16 on paper, and then multiply the middle by the last number and divide the product by the first. Getting the numbers in the wrong order was a major source of grief to students.[11] From the modern standpoint, the real problem with the Rule of Three is that the first step of the solution leads to a meaningless number: 21 pounds times 16 yards equals 336 – what? The calculation makes no sense until the final step, division by the first term, 7 yards. Elementary school students now would be taught to figure what one yard costs, and then go from there. But in the eighteenth century, arithmetic was presented as a heavy memory subject, not a subject that drew on and improved the logical faculties of the mind.

The English arithmetic texts that arrived in America in the late seventeenth and early eighteenth centuries came mostly from this pool of rule-laden, commercial texts. One thorough study of the international flow of books into Philadelphia has concluded that texts by Edmund Wingate, James Hodder, James Cocker and John Ward were in ready supply in bookstores and that such books, along with school books, prayer books and Bibles, were ordered by booksellers by the gross (a nice example of early eighteenth-century reckoning by twelves, for the gross is a measure of twelve dozen, or 144). In contrast, titles in popular literature were ordered in quantities rarely exceeding a half dozen.[12]

Some of the imported arithmetic books found a home in the libraries of leading Philadelphia merchants; it appears they were purchased as reference books, saved on the shelf instead of being passed on to (and used up to tatters by) sons or nephews.[13] This is not surprising in view of the nearly impenetrable prose of arithmetic rules and the lack of careful explanation of even the most basic operations. These were not books to be worked through, studied and comprehended so much as they were books to be consulted.

Even when ordered by the gross, English arithmetic books could not blanket the market in the colonies. American printers saw an opportunity to turn a profit; the chief obstacle to printing an arithmetic text was then – as now – the extra time and expense of setting numerical type. The first pirated edition of an English text was brought out by James Franklin, Benjamin's brother and master, in Boston in 1719.[14] Over the next hundred years, uncounted editions of Cocker, Hodder and Dilworth came forth in America. Only a handful of Americans attempted to bring out original textbooks. There are two plausible hypotheses about the continued reprinting of English texts. One is that perhaps the English texts were entirely satisfactory and there was no room for improvement. But a mere glance at Cocker or Hodder casts doubt on that hypothesis. Who could love a book that defined the zero (cypher) in this fashion: a cypher is 'the beginning of number, or rather the medium between increasing and decreasing numbers, commonly called *absolute* or *whole numbers*, and *negative* or *fractional numbers*'.[15] The default hypothesis is that, difficult as these texts were, there were very few American printers or philomaths competent or ambitious enough to attempt to improve on them.

Indeed, in the entire pre-revolutionary eighteenth century, there were probably fewer than a half dozen indigenous American arithmetics written. The earliest was published in Boston in 1729 and was written by Isaac Greenwood, the first professor of mathematics at Harvard. Greenwood struck a balance between the pure and applied texts, aiming at a broad audience.

> The Language and Manner of Writing [in this book] is such, as the Author hopes will be easily apprehended by those that have not been very much conversant with Books: But it must be acknowledged, He has had his Mind all along upon Persons of some Education and Curiosity. . . . He has not supposed the Reader to be ignorant, of those Principles relating to Numbers, that are of daily Observation in the several Parts of Life. And on this Account, He has thought it improper to go into an elaborate Explanation of the Rules in the lower Parts of Arithmetick, as most Authors have done, seldom to any other Effect than to perplex the Subject, and excite a secret Prejudice.[16]

Greenwood claimed he had sufficiently clear explanations so that his subject would make sense to those of 'the lowest Capacities', but he also made efforts to rope in another group in the social order that he identified as being not usually friendly to arithmetic: 'It cannot be thought an unprofitable task for a Gentleman, especially of Curiosity and Learning, once in his Life to pass through the Rules in this Art.'[17] Greenwood made his living teaching arithmetic at Harvard, a subject which the school had only just begun to offer, and then only in the senior year, so he well knew about the common assumption that arithmetic was a commercial subject, a vulgar subject, one not properly or traditionally offered in a classical education. Notice, too, that Greenwood assumed that everyone would have a passing acquaintance with simple arithmetic, based on 'daily observation' in life, so he could skip over awkward attempts to define zero. But his book really was about simple arithmetic, and his concluding sections of business applications having do to with interest, annuities and percentage loss or gain on sales were really frosting on the cake.

The second American text – entirely in Dutch – appeared in New York in 1730;[18] the third was a Connecticut text of 1748, titled *A Small Tract of Arithmetick, for the Use of Farmers and Country-People*, by Jonathan Burnham. Burnham tried to streamline the subject in helpful ways, as for example his observation that the two rules addition and multiplication were in fact the same thing, just as were subtraction and division, division being, in his words, 'a compendius subtraction'. Burnham hoped that such comments would allay what is now called math anxiety, but a few passages in his book rivalled the traditional English texts for unintelligibility. For example, pursuing the subtraction/division similarity, Burnham cautioned the reader that addition and subtraction required numbers to be in the 'same kind' (that is, addition of pounds to pounds and gallons to gallons), whereas 'Multiplication and Division of Quantities changes the Kind; but in Numbers the same King [kind?] remains'.

Even correcting a possible typo brings no clearer meaning to the sentence.[19] Connecticut farmers and country-people, Burnham's intended audience, probably felt the same helplessness and despair familiar to the studious modern-day reader of a VCR manual who is trying to pre-set the channel selector indicator based on instructions translated from a foreign language.

Burnham had several other genuinely useful tips for country folk. He recommended that anyone who had to measure boards or timber use a 2-foot ruler divided decimally rather than into the standard 12-inch divisions. 'Casting up' multiples of board-feet would then be much easier, allowing one to avoid messy fractions with twelve in the denominator. To measure the volume of irregular solids, Burnham suggested filling a barrel with water, sinking the irregular container in it and noting the displacement of the water. Burnham also had some folksy wisdom on the Rule of Three: 'After a Question is proposed, it is sometimes difficult to set the given Numbers in Due Order', he sympathetically observed.[20] The book included examples in denominate or compound numbers, but its brevity – it was only forty-six pages long – was its real saving grace.

Before the Revolution, none of the few American books supplanted the English texts in popularity. Arithmetic instruction continued to rely on the standard commercial books, or on replicas of those books, in the form of manuscript copybooks. There was no real innovation in the presentation of the material until after the Revolution. Arithmetic was recognized to be a troublesome subject, and the response was not to simplify or change it to make it accessible to reason; instead the response was to delay teaching it until students were older. Children were typically 11 or 12 before embarking on the subject, and then they were rushed through it in one or two years. One striking consequence of delayed teaching is the gender difference in numeracy it produced. For girls were much less likely to be getting any schooling at the age of 11 or 12 than boys were; their education fell off rapidly after age 10, when they had gained minimal reading and writing instruction. Certainly not all boys persevered in school long enough to arrive at instruction in Cocker's text, but for most girls, formal arithmetic was an advanced subject that fell beyond their years of schooling.

The site of arithmetic learning tells us something significant about the place of numeracy in colonial society. In general, American colleges did not require entering students to know any arithmetic until the 1760s; indeed, Harvard did not require it until 1802.[21] Professor Greenwood, who wrote the first American text, taught it at Harvard as a senior subject in the 1720s, and in the 1740s arithmetic became a first-year college subject under later instructors. Most boys who trained for college studied a classical curriculum, and that was not considered compatible with training in the vulgar arts of commercial reckoning. This same dichotomy between classical and practical curricula was maintained in many of the private academies of the late eighteenth century, which offered two separate tracks or programmes for students. One programme emphasized Latin and Greek for the college-bound, and another emphasized writing and arithmetic, for terminal students. Thus arithmetic retained its association with the mercantile rather than the learned life.[22]

Public or district schools were even less likely than academies to offer arithmetic instruction. Students in district schools tended to the young side, so as long as formal arithmetic was thought to be a subject for older minds, these schools could afford to ignore it. Also, the corps of teachers who staffed schools in the north frequently came from the ranks of recent college graduates, who would teach for a few years until an opportunity for a pulpit or a law apprenticeship materialized. Such young men were not often equipped to teach much arithmetic, given the low value placed on the subject in their own training in the academies and colleges. Daniel Webster attended a district school in New Hampshire in the 1780s and came out of it totally ignorant of arithmetic; he learned the subject in the 1790s at Phillips Exeter, and in 1802 was sufficiently comfortable in the English version of arithmetic to crack a joke about non-arabic styles of counting. In a letter to a male friend about the many attractive young ladies in his locale, Webster wrote: 'I forgot to bring a stick to cut a notch, like the Indian, for every one I see.'[23]

District schools, academies and colleges could afford to stint arithmetic because most people – and in America, most people meant farmers – simply did not need to know all those fancy commercial rules to go about their lives. Indeed, a very early example of a rejection of advanced arithmetic can be seen in the inaugural plans for a grammar school in New Haven in 1648, which specifically set out that students should be taught to read, spell, write and 'cypher for numeracion & addicion, and noe further'.[24] Numeration (teaching the meaning of arabic symbols and the concepts of place and zero) was a fit subject, and addition and probably subtraction were also permissible, but few saw need for more.

For city life, with its merchants and captains and seafaring men, more *was* needed, and there were alternatives to public schools and academies to provide instruction. One possibility was on-the-job training, on board a ship (for navigation) or in the back room of the store. But more formal training was offered by individual teachers who hung out a shingle advertising the skills they could teach, in the tradition of the English petty schools. In South Carolina, for example, a Stephen Hartley advertised in 1744 that he could teach reading, writing in several hands (i.e. styles of penmanship) and 'Arithmetick, in all its Parts, Merchant's Accompts, or the Italian Method of Bookkeeping'. Colonial newspapers frequently ran such ads. One talented philomath of the 1750s told about his own training under a private teacher: John Gordon arrived in America around 1714 at age 14 and studied 'in the use of figures' with a Mr Jacob Taylor of Philadelphia; he then became a bricklayer but later moved to Princeton, New Jersey, and set up as a private teacher of navigation and surveying, vulgar and decimal arithmetic and mensuration.[25]

For families outside the ambit of the few colonial cities, yet another possibility was to hire a tutor. The wealthy Carter family of Virginia brought a Princeton student to their plantation for a year in 1773–4 to teach two sons, five daughters and a nephew. The tutor, Philip Fithian, declared the oldest son a 'boy of Genius' and set him to work on Greek and Latin texts; the two other boys, judged to be of lesser talents, were therefore taught English grammar, writing and arithmetic. At the end of June, Fithian assessed their progress in arithmetic: 'Harry begun at Reduction & is now working Fellowship . . . Bob began at Addition and is working Compound Division . . . Priscilla began Addition & is working Division.' These three Carter scholars were 14 and 15 years old. The youngest four daughters apparently were taught no arithmetic at all, just 'writing and English'.[26]

Fithian's diary opens a window on accepted practice in arithmetic training. A boy of genius was spared the vulgar business of arithmetic, and the other boys, teenagers all, stood just at the threshold of learning, at addition and reduction. Only one of the girls ventured to learn any arithmetic at all, probably because she was sufficiently old (15) to cut through those tedious and obscure rules. And finally, Fithian took these relatively innumerate young people and moved them from addition through to division, the Rule of Three and a taste of square roots in about nine months' time. Rapid progress made up for the typically late start in learning arithmetic. Fithian composed a letter of advice to the new tutor for the following year and specifically recommended that he brush up on arithmetic. It may seem simple, he warned, but a review should not be neglected – advice perhaps he wished he had had before embarking on his duties at the Carter plantation.

To summarize, arithmetic beyond the simple addition and subtraction of small numbers was considered a specialized subject, one not routinely taught in institutions of learning like grammar and district schools, academies or colleges. Instead it was seen as a mental skill needed in particular occupations, and the locus of training clustered around the cities where mercantile and seafaring jobs also clustered. Instruction was purchased from specialized teachers; or it was learned on one's own, as Franklin had done in 1722. Years later, when Franklin had his own press in Philadelphia, he brought out an early American text, George Fisher's *American Instructor*, which promised to 'qualify any Person for Business, without the Help of a Master'.[27] That promise probably had a certain appeal for Franklin, in view of his own failure under masters and his faith in self-improvement schemes.

Manuscript arithmetic copybooks exist in surprisingly abundant numbers in many archives now, and they allow a glimpse of the reception of arithmetic by the struggling students. With texts in short supply, and with a mode of instruction that hammered on memory and not understanding, copybooks were an admirably suitable learning tool. Each student purchased a large blank writing-book and essentially copied the instructor's text for him or herself. Rules were stated, one or two examples worked, and then it was on to the next rule. Copybooks might at first seem to be very unrevealing, simply copies of the printed textbook, but in fact they were much more. The students doodled in the margins, or pencilled numerical problems worked in scratch before being entered in ink. Some students wrote their names on the flyleaf and again throughout the book, which provides one way to estimate the ages of the pupils; if handwriting is any index to age, the copybook signatures suggest that rarely did a student start such a book before he or she had a rather adult-like signature; in a few cases, the initial signature is somewhat childish (in cursive but rather large) but by the end the handwriting is quite mature. A few students helpfully provided starting and ending dates, or their own ages, and that evidence corroborates the evidence of the Princeton tutor in Virginia, who moved his teenaged charges along through the basics in one year.

Another revealing clue in the copybooks is that problems were sometimes done wrong; in one case, a comparison of two copybooks at Dartmouth College completed about six years apart shows advanced problems with incorrect answers identical to three decimal places. One suspects that copybooks were often just that – a book to copy in. One early nineteenth-century education reformer confirmed this in his account of copybooks in his own youth, in the 1780s: his teacher could not explain arithmetic and simply took problems out of his own ancient copybook.

> Any boy could copy the work from the manuscript of any other further advanced than himself, and the writer never heard any explanation of any principle of arithmetic while he was at school. Indeed, the pupils believed that the master could not do the sums he set for them.[28]

The survival of arithmetic copybooks over two centuries – in marked contrast to composition notebooks, which are much harder to locate – also indicates something about the use and meaning of such items: students preserved their arithmetics as permanent reference works. No one was expected to learn all the rules of arithmetic and then dispense with the book. Some copybooks even became permanent records of another kind: their owners later used blank pages at the end for keeping commercial accounts, for listing debtors and creditors or for entering the birthdates of their children. One copybook owner even listed the dates on which various cows of his 'went to bull' in the summer of 1775.

What difference did numeracy make in the eighteenth century? Writers of the commercial arithmetic books were clear about the usefulness of their subject matter. Three major purposes were advanced by a knowledge of arithmetic: business, business and business. George Fisher's Philadelphia text, for example, claimed that

> after Writing, the next necessary Step towards qualifying a Person for Business, is Understanding that truly laudable and most excellent Accomplishment, the noble Science of *Arithmetick*; a knowledge so necessary in all the Parts of Life and Business, that scarce any thing is done without it.

Fisher's rule for multiplication of denominate numbers he cleverly called 'Multiplication of Money (what most would learn above any thing)'. His text advanced to bookkeeping, which he called the next skill after arithmetic that a businessman must have.

> It is not without good Reason that most People of Business and Ingenuity, are desirous to be Masters of this Art: for if we consider the Satisfaction that naturally ariseth from an Accompt well kept, the Pleasure that acrues to a Person by seeing what he gains by each Species of Goods he deals in, and his whole Profit by a Year's Trade; and thereby also to know the true State of his Affairs and Circumstances; so that he may according to Discretion, retrench or enlarge his Expences, &c. as he shall think fit.[29]

In other words, advanced levels of numeracy brought satisfaction and pleasure, as well as information necessary for future financial planning. Fisher's bookkeeping instructions were just one of many manuals on bookkeeping available to mid- and late eighteenth-century merchants.

The commercial rules of arithmetic reveal the kinds of business transactions that numeracy facilitated. The Rule of Fellowship explained how to divide profits equitably in a venture where some number of people had risked different initial amounts of capital. A variation was the rule that governed joint ventures when the partners put in or took out money at different times. Loaning money at interest was another major category of problem, as was discounting future prices to present values.

To assume that these exalted levels of computation were normally achieved by eighteenth-century arithmetic users would be wrong, however. Undoubtedly the rules governing division of profit shares were useful, since colonial businesses were often joint ventures, convenient as a way of spreading out risk. But there are no surviving records of much complicated wheeling and dealing. The most extensive study of colonial merchants' accounts has concluded that fancy forms of reckoning hardly ever entered into them. W. T. Baxter studied fifty sets of account books from colonial firms and found that most were very simple entries of credits, debts and trades. End-of-year profit calculations were almost never made, nor was double-entry bookkeeping at all commonplace.[30] The function of account books seems to have been roughly the same, whether kept by the Hancock firm in Boston or by the midwife Martha Ballard in Hallowell, Maine: accounts kept track of complex swaps, of debt and credit relationships, of barter and truck. The midwife Ballard could do it with much less attention to numbers, since she was often trading chickens for midwife services, or a daughter's day labour for sugar, but she and her circle of female traders had worked out a system of value attached to goods and services, and sometimes she noted the value as well as the trade in her diary.[31] The Hancock ledger might look more formal and imposing, but the level of arithmetic skill required to maintain it was hardly greater than Mrs Ballard's.

In their eagerness to impart business skills and avoid mathematical reasoning, the commercial arithmetic texts impeded the progress of arithmetic instruction in the eighteenth century, for they made a newfangled subject even more difficult than it needed to be. So Americans adopted a number of shortcuts to bridge gaps in their figuring skills, shortcuts like the ones Jonathan Burnham of Connecticut recommended – using a decimal foot ruler instead of one with inches, or shortcuts like preferring a neat simple interest rate of 6 per cent on loans, which made a month-by-month calculation of interest a clean $1/2$ per cent. Another very common shortcut to reckoning, used by the numerate and innumerate alike, were *Ready Reckoners*, little books consisting of tables of multiples of various compound measures and prices. No need for the Rule of Three when a *Ready Reckoner* could quickly reveal the price of 21 yards of cloth at any price per yard.[32]

Such shortcuts only worked well in times when the economy was relatively stable; *Ready Reckoners* could anticipate the range of common prices for commodities and provide all the answers, and interest rates could stay at 6 per cent and still be regarded as fair by both debtor and creditor. The American Revolution profoundly upset the relative economic stability of the pre-war years. The financial chaos of the late 1770s and 1780s and in particular the wild depreciation of the new confederation's currency and notes meant that no one could do arithmetic in the market in the old ways. In some places stores posted monthly or even weekly tables of depreciation. States took to issuing their own money or promissory notes (which circulated as a medium of exchange) and that meant that entirely new charts of denominate equivalences had to be considered – equivalences that were changing on a daily basis.

If the war had been short and the monetary chaos confined to the war years, probably no changes in the teaching of arithmetic would have taken place. The less numerate Americans who could not keep mental pace with inflation and competing currencies would have sat on the sidelines, losing out, while crafty and highly numerate businessmen figured out a way to make inflation pay, for them anyway. And that is essentially what happened during the war. But this was not just any war, it was a war for national liberation, and the new government assumed it as axiomatic that the British system of currency would be supplanted by a new, American form of money. So in the 1780s there was much discussion about what kind of monetary system best suited the new Republic.

And as is well known, the new system that finally emerged was a decimal currency, with mills, cents, dimes and dollars. Federal money, as it was called, necessitated new textbooks that could now eliminate large chunks of denominate arithmetic and considerably simplify the need for the rule of Reduction. In *An Introduction to Arithmetic for the Use of Common Schools*, author Erastus Root spelled out the patriotic interconnections between common arithmetic, decimal money and republican government:

> it is expected that before many years, nay, many months, shall elapse, this mode
> of reckoning will become general throughout the United States. . . . Then let us, I
> beg of you, Fellow-Citizens, no longer meanly follow the British intricate mode of

reckoning. – Let them have their own way – and us, ours. – Their mode is suited to the genius of their government, for it seems to be the policy of tyrants, to keep their accounts in as intricate, and perplexing a method as possible; that the smaller number of their subjects may be able to estimate their enormous impositions and exactions. But Republican money ought to be simple, and adapted to the meanest capacity.[33]

Root's text even omitted fractions altogether in favour of decimals, an innovation probably welcomed by schoolchildren but undoubtedly premature.

From the 1790s on, a flood of American arithmetic texts, aimed at 'Traders, Mechanics, and young persons', took up the cause of federal money.[34] But it was not the new decimal money alone that prompted a new look at arithmetic. Equally important was a newly invigorated sense of the importance of widespread education in a republican government. A great question preoccupying Madison, Jefferson and the governing elite at large was how to create citizens for a republican government. How best to assure intelligence, virtue and reason in the citizenry? The key was education, and increasingly mathematics came to be touted as the ultimate form of rational thinking, the school subject that would foster precise and clear thinking. This was not a new idea; quantitative men in seventeenth-century England had claimed the same thing, but their voice had been overpowered by the commercial instructors who were praising arithmetic as the door to economic gain.[35] The idea resurfaced in America in the 1790s, and arithmetic – revised and simplified in new texts – came to be seen as a superb mental discipline rather than as the superb mental torture it had been in colonial days.[36]

And so the arithmetic texts of the new Republic began to alter the old commercial English texts' approach to teaching. The architect Benjamin Latrobe called for new books that would offer proofs and explanations and do away with the 'heavy memory work': 'We do boys from seven to fifteen years old a great injustice in supposing they cannot reason.'[37] Reliance on sheer memory alone gave way to books that attempted rational explanations and fuller demonstrations. A second major innovation was to lower the age at which instruction began: now children of 6 or 7 were thought to be fit pupils for arithmetic and were introduced to arabic numerals and relational concepts. By the 1820s, a third major innovation was under way, eliminating all rules completely and approaching arithmetic as an inductive science, whose principles children themselves could discover as they worked out carefully chosen problems. This last phase of 'new math', of every child struggling to be a tiny mathematician, was very controversial and not very long-lived, but it does mark the end-point of a far-ranging revolution in arithmetic training that had been touched off by the political separation from Britain.

The lens of gender reveals a sharp twist on this seemingly progressive story. Women were less numerate than men in the eighteenth-century world, but relatively few people noticed. Women's deficiencies in numeracy were merely an artefact of the locus of arithmetic training and the assumption that arithmetic was a tool of the world of business. No sex could presume to have a God-given talent for the rule-bound commercial arithmetic of the early modern period. Everyone, including Benjamin Franklin, expected to struggle to make sense of an arcane and obscure subject. The progressive movement of arithmetic after the Revolution – arithmetic taught to children aged 6 and 7, taught in public schools and taught in ways now divorced from commerce and appealing to logic – meant that many more young girls experienced exposure to the subject. In other words, an unintended consequence of redefining arithmetic and putting it in the common schools was to make females far more numerate than they had ever been before.

On the one hand, the spread of female numeracy continues the generally progressive story of the expansion of numerical skills. Like literacy, numeracy allowed women to be less dependent on the protective services of men; it was an opening wedge in the historic emancipation of women that started around the time of the Revolution. On the other hand – and here is the twist – exposing women to arithmetic clashed with the rationale for teaching arithmetic in the schools in the first place, that is the idea that it strengthened the mind and thereby produced more rational citizens to participate in government. Women were citizens, but they did not participate in government. Many educators in the 1820s and 1830s reacted to that paradox by beginning to define mathematics as a quintessentially masculine enterprise, one that women could not hope to master as competently. (Of course, a small band of insistent female educators argued just the opposite, that women could learn it as well, but in trying to prove their point they unwittingly gave wider currency to the stereotype.) Some evidence suggests that young women were in fact not achieving the same level of skill as male students; given the male-oriented contents of nineteenth-century textbooks, the assumption of male superiority in business and the late start that females had in redressing their eighteenth-century relative innumeracy, it would be surprising to find no gender differentials in math attainment in the nineteenth century.[38] Women were becoming more numerate than ever before, but they were accomplishing that feat in the face of stiff competition from men and in an atmosphere that now newly decreed that gender stereotypes were God-ordained differences. The transformation of arithmetic from a narrow commercial skill to an intellectual faculty gave rise to a gender stereotype of lasting duration, from which we still have not managed completely to escape.

Notes

1   *Benjamin Franklin: The Autobiography and Other Writings*, ed. L. Jesse Lemisch (New York: New American Library, 1961), 30.

2   The only historical efforts to explore the extent of numeracy in a manner somewhat parallel to literacy studies are my own book, *A Calculating People: The Spread of Numeracy in Early America* (Chicago: University of Chicago Press, 1982) and Keith Thomas, 'Numeracy in early modern England', *Transactions of the Royal Historical Society*, 5th series, xxxvii (1987), 103–32.

3   For modern times, we have endless amounts of data from standardized mathematical tests given to school children at fixed intervals, so it is quite possible to say some very concrete things about who can divide, who can do word problems, who understands square roots and so on.

4   Claudia Zaslavsky, *Africa Counts: Number and Pattern in African Culture* (Boston: Prindle, Weber & Schmidt, 1973); Karl Menninger, *Number Words and Number Symbols: A Cultural History of Numbers*, tr. Paul Broneer (Cambridge, Mass.: MIT Press, 1969; German edn, 1958).

5   Evidence for these assertions comes from an analysis of about sixty eighteenth-century arithmetic copybooks and from the emphasis placed on learning 'numeration' in seventeenth- and eighteenth-century arithmetic texts aimed at older youth and adult learners. See Cohen, *Calculating People*, ch. 4.

6   Keith Thomas's essay 'Numeracy in early modern England' contains many telling and charming examples of English people operating on the margins of numeracy in the period 1500–1700.

7   Florentine merchants even passed a law in 1299 outlawing the new arabic numbers in business; Florian Cajori, *A History of Elementary Mathematics* (New York: Macmillan, 1917; 1st edn, 1896), 121.

8   Augustus deMorgan, *Arithmetic Books from the Invention of Printing to the Present Time* (London, 1847), a comprehensive bibliography.

9   Edward Cocker, *Arithmetick* (London, 1677); William Leybourne, *Cursus Mathematicus* (London, 1690). Cajori, *History of Elementary Mathematics*, 190–2.

10 James Hodder, *Arithmetick or that Necessary Art Made Most Easy* (London, 1672, 10th edn), 87.

11 I have consulted about seventy student copybooks from the period 1739 to 1825, the bulk of them in Widener Library at Harvard. Time and again, the students get the terms in the wrong order or choose the wrong ones to multiply. For a fuller discussion of one such error, see Cohen, *Calculating People*, 122–3.

12 Edwin Wolf II, *The Book Culture of A Colonial American City: Philadelphia Books, Bookmen, and Booksellers* (Oxford: Clarendon Press, 1988), 60 and *passim* in ch. 2.

13 ibid.

14 The book was Hodder's *Arithmetick*, published for 'the better compleating of Youth, as to Clerkship and Trades', title page.

15 Cocker, 1677 edn, 2.

16 Isaac Greenwood, *Arithmetick Vulgar and Decimal* (Boston, 1729), i–ii.

17 ibid., ii, iv.

18 Peter Venema, *Arithmetica of Cyffer-Konst* (New York: John Peter Zenger, 1730).

19 Jonathan Burnham, *A Small Tract of Arithmetick, for the Use of Farmers and Country-People* (New London, Conn., 1748), 3.

20 Burnham, *Small Tract*, 35.

21 Yale was the exception; President Thomas Clap inaugurated an arithmetic requirement in 1745. Leonard Tucker, 'President Clap of Yale College: another "Founding Father" of American science', *Isis*, lii (1961), 55–77. See also Florian Cajori, *The Teaching and History of Mathematics in the United States* (Washington, DC: Bureau of Education Circular, 1890), 18–35, 55–74.

22 Based on an informal perusal of scores of annual catalogues of New England academies owned by the American Antiquarian Society; see also Robert Middlekauff, *Ancients and Axioms* (New Haven: Yale University Press, 1963); and Harriet Webster Marr, *The Old New England Academies* (New York: Comet Press, 1959), 198–203.

23 'Daniel Webster – autobiography (1829)', *American Journal of Education*, xxvii (1877), 282–3; and D. Webster to Habijah Weld Fuller, 20 Feb. 1802, in *The Papers of Daniel Webster*, ed. Charles M. Wiltse (Ann Arbor: University Microfilms, 1971).

24 Quoted in David Tyack (ed.), *Turning Points in American Education History* (Waltham, Mass.: Blaisdell, 1967), 21.

25 John Gordon, *Mathematical Traverse Tables* (Philadelphia, 1758), preface. This book explained Gordon's invention of a right-angle triangle device that made short work of measurement of boundaries and land areas.

26 'Journal of Philip Vickers Fithian', reprinted in Edgar W. Knight (ed.), *A Documentary History of Education in the South before 1860*, 5 vols (Chapel Hill: University of North Carolina Press, 1949), vol. 1, 578–615.

27 George Fisher, *The American Instructor* (Philadelphia: Franklin & Hall, 1748), title page.

28 'Memoirs of Caleb Bingham', *Barnard's Journal of Education*, v (1855), 336.

29 Fisher, *The American Instructor*, 56, 82, 153.

30 W. T. Baxter, 'Accounting in colonial America', in B. S. Yamey and A. C. Littleton, *Studies in the History of Accounting* (London: Sweet & Maxwell Ltd, 1956), 272–87.

31 Laurel Thatcher Ulrich, 'Martha Ballard and her girls: women's work in eighteenth-century Maine', in Stephen Innes (ed.), *Work and Labor in Early America* (Chapel Hill: University of North

334   Patricia Cline Cohen

Carolina Press, 1988), 70–105; Ulrich, 'Housewife and gadder: themes of self-sufficiency and community in eighteenth-century New England', in Mary Beth Norton and Carol Groneman (eds), *'To Toil the Livelong Day': America's Women at Work, 1780–1980* (Ithaca: Cornell University Press, 1987), 21–34.

32   Daniel Fenning, *The Ready Reckoner, or Trader's Useful Assistant* (Reading, Pa., 1789); other editions of Fenning were issued in Germantown, York, Wilmington (Del.) and Newburyport (Mass.).

33   Erastus Root, *An Introduction to Arithmetic for the Use of Common Schools* (Norwich, Conn., 1796), preface.

34   Josiah Burroughs, *The Assistant, or a Treatise* (Newburyport, Mass., 1796), preface. Other books of the 1790s and the first decade of the 1800s include: Joseph Chaplin, *The Trader's Best Companion* (Newburyport, Mass., 1795); *The American Tutor's Assistant* (Philadelphia, 1797); Daniel Adams, *The Scholar's Arithmetic, or Federal Accountant* (Leominster, Mass., 1801); Caleb Alexander, *New and Complete System of Arithmetic* (Albany, NY, 1802); Osgood Carleton, *Carleton's Compendium of Practical Arithmetic, Applied to the Federal and other Currencies* (Boston, 1810).

35   Keith Thomas finds this same line of thinking in the works of Charles Davenant, Sir William Petty and Sir Josiah Child; 'Numeracy in early modern England', 131.

36   See ch. 4 of my book, *Calculating People*, for an extended discussion of this debate and the role of arithmetic in it.

37   Benjamin Latrobe to Ferdinand Fairfax, 28 May 1798, in Knight, *Documentary History*, vol. 2, 520–1.

38   An extended discussion of nineteenth-century gender differentials in mathematics appears in my book, *Calculating People*, ch. 4 and *passim*.

17
Teaching in the market-place, or 'Caesar adsum jam forte: Pompey aderat': the retailing of knowledge in provincial England during the eighteenth century

John Money

On 25 March 1813, Samuel Pipe-Wolferstan, a gentleman of modest means and liberal views with improving aspirations and a taste for classical letters, who lived near Tamworth in the south-eastern corner of Staffordshire, was thinking of selling a parcel of land called, fittingly for such a tract of Midland clay, Mirey Croft. There was some doubt about its size, so he 'ordered W. Young to measure'. Much to his surprise, however, Young, a local surveyor, had other things on his mind.

> Found him at the unexpected employ of a sort of lexicon of Greek Primaries and Derivatives! 'For Mr. Ward?' [master of Tamworth school] said I in the haste of surprise – 'No' (he seemed not to recognise aught of *him*) 'but for Longman' I think – Greek he could *read* quite readily and Latin he *knew* a little.[1]

In 1813, there were at least 150 years still to pass before the Open University would be any more than a glint in Jennie Lee's eye. Yet like the piece of punning doggerel in the title of this essay, descended from a body of schoolroom lore rooted in the eighteenth century and scrawled countless times since then in the end papers of *Kennedy's Latin Primer* and other such staples of learned pedagogy,[2] the prospect of Mirey Croft's putative surveyor, lexicon in hand, pursuing Greek etymology under the tutelage of one of the country's leading textbook publishers, seems to encapsulate many of the peculiarities of English society, a construct much in the historiographical news at present, and its attitudes to knowledge.

Today, 'knowledge' has become a buzz-word. We are, for instance, told with increasing frequency that our future prosperity depends not on the old constants of material supply and demand, but on the ability to produce, exchange, consume and manipulate 'knowledge'. This, we are to understand, is because to command the form and content of 'knowledge', a term which here conflates information with understanding and tacitly either assumes or ignores value, is to possess the key to all the other springs of prosperity. As the new 'knowledge-based' world of high technology sweeps away the familiar smokestacks of modernity, its advent is conventionally hailed with the same progressive metaphors which once greeted the triumph of its industrial and presumptively obsolescent predecessor. Thus, by a round-about transfer of images, a symposium on 'Consumption and knowledge: education, literacy and numeracy'[3] seems to invite a Whiggish response. In the course of the long eighteenth century, it suggests, knowledge itself was reconstituted. Certain kinds of it which could be empirically verified, and then stored and standardized in print, superseded those in merely oral or traditional forms which could not. To all appearances, such knowledge was not only intrinsically better because more 'objective'. As an asset which could be reliably accumulated and readily exchanged, one for which there was a steady market, it was also more 'useful', both as a form of property and as an object of commerce and consumption. This may suggest that so far as historiography is concerned at least, 'modernity' can be rescued from oblivion on the verge of its own obsolescence by showing that it too was 'knowledge-based' from its infancy. However, it may be that the success of new knowledge, then as now, owed less to its intrinsic superiority than to its greater ability to support such a fiction, and to the consequently greater profitability of its various forms, whether as commodities themselves or as means to manipulate demand for other goods. In this case, it would seem that early capitalist society, for all the progressive appearance of its 'knowledge-base', also shared at its roots the relativism and irony of post-modernism, and therefore the latter's need and nostalgia for tradition.

After surveying very briefly the general history of education in eighteenth-century England as the principal context in which knowledge was purportedly reconstituted, transmitted and consumed, this chapter explores that ambivalence and its implications. It does so, first by setting out one example of the sort of 'knowledge network'[4] through which developments in educational provision in a purely institutional sense became linked to their wider context. It then considers the central, but sparsely documented and therefore too frequently neglected, role of private venture schools and teachers in these developments. This exercise, however, is inherently limited. Conducted at a national or regional level of aggregation, it can establish the outlines of a historical geography for the marketing and thus presumptively for the consumption of knowledge. By their nature, however, the sources on which it is based represent novelty better than continuity, and the situation in the second half of the century, when the salient features of 'modernity' were becoming predominant, better than the first, when those forms were less clear. In addition, they represent only the external aspect of the subject, and for the most part, only one side of that. Though they provide a steadily accumulating mass of evidence about the supply of knowledge, they cannot, by their nature, tell much, except by inference, about the nature of the demand for it, or about what its different kinds actually meant to those who sought and used them. In order to redress these imbalances to some extent by recapturing some of the inward aspects of the subject, the second part of this exploration turns to the particular example of one man who got an obscure living by retailing knowledge in the country during the first half of the century. Though the result does not come close to exhausting the subject, it may perhaps indicate that its dimensions are larger and more varied than is often assumed.

I

In the history of education, as in so many other aspects of the English experience, the long eighteenth century has been more quarried for convenient stereotypes or prototypes than properly studied in its own right. Because education itself has been conventionally defined in terms of institutional systems of provision and the formal ideals, purposes and methods which govern them, it has tended, with some exceptions, to concentrate on the impact of Renaissance, Reformation and the frustrated reforms of the 1650s, to skirt the apparently directionless and fragmented period of *laissez-faire* which followed and to begin again in earnest in the closing decades of the eighteenth century, when religious and intellectual concerns combined with political tensions and socio-economic pressures to provoke once more a concern for systematic innovation and reform.[5] By default, the historiography of education in eighteenth-century England is thus conventionally Whig. Generally, it takes one of two courses. The traditional orthodoxy has been to contrast the increasing laxity and backwardness which beset the 'system' represented by the endowed schools after the Restoration with the vitality of the 'Educational Revolution' of 1560–1640.[6] This decay is attributed to the onset of post-revolutionary cynicism, worldly corruption and Hanoverian torpidity. The keepers of the flame from which the torch of liberal reform would be later rekindled are thus sought elsewhere: in the Dissenting Academies, the Scottish universities and the Weberian pragmatism of middle-class entrepreneurs in the newer industrial areas.[7] More recently a revised version has emerged. This presumes that whatever localized or temporary setbacks occurred thereafter, England had been carried permanently over the basic threshold needed to initiate and sustain the beginning of modernization by 1640.[8] It accepts post-Restoration developments as redirection towards more individualistic and practical purposes rather than absolute neglect. It acknowledges the continuing vitality of the grammar-school tradition well into the eighteenth century,[9] and modifies, if it does not substantially reject, the notion of decline thereafter by recognizing the very significant number of examples of individual change and adaptation which, over the course of the period as a whole, falsify the traditional picture of the eighteenth-century grammar school.[10] What is portrayed is thus not an education system so decayed and corrupt that it had to be rescued and reformed by particular groups and agencies which had escaped its decadence, but rather one which, for all the particular importance of those special elements, had yet sufficient diversity and adaptability within itself to produce and supply the new knowledge which industrialization required.

   This version takes a more catholic view of its subject, and is more disposed to look for 'new trends' within the general corpus of education[11] than to stand on an institutional definition of the subject itself. Thus, it is better able to comprehend related developments which contradict the period's assumed indifference and had a significant influence on education, even though they were not themselves actually part of it. The most direct of these was the recognition that teaching itself, though still far from being distinctly regulated, was becoming a job which required particular knowledge and commitment. As part of the more general emergence of the professions as a new element in the social structure, this was one aspect of larger interlocking processes associated with agrarian change and private commerce, and with the demands and opportunities created by the growth of public credit and the fiscal–military state. An equally important concomitant of these developments was the growth of towns and the appearance, on a scale still small except for London, but formative nevertheless, of a distinctively urban culture. In a number of provincial towns, for example, school facilities were explicitly included in new civic buildings and plans for new public space: in more than one they doubled as assembly rooms. Such incorporation into the stage-set for the 'urban renaissance' does not exactly suggest lack of awareness. Nor, if the concept of a renaissance is rejected as being too general, does the appreciable part which education, especially of the private-venture kind, came to play in the economy of many a 'leisure town' as the century passed.[12]

These changes stimulated, and in large part depended on, a rapid expansion in the production and circulation of books, newspapers and other printed material, especially in cheap serial form. The considerable attention given to this expansion in recent years[13] means that the formal history of eighteenth-century educational supply can now be complemented by an account of wider development and adaptation which leads away from the numerous particular studies of schools themselves, which comprise the normal history of education, to the development of demand. In accord with the desiderata for a mercantile education set out in such well-known and widely circulated treatises as Thomas Campbell's *The London Tradesman* (1747), this was increasingly commercial and practical in nature. The emphasis on utility is supported by the massive, nation-wide growth in the production and circulation of arithmetical and mathematical texts, peaking in the 1740s, which more than doubled during the first half of the century.[14] Equally significant is the evidence of growth in the practical teaching of English, which suggests that it was during the middle decades of the eighteenth century that this was first extensively recognized as a specialty. Charles Ackers printed 265,000 copies of Thomas Dyche's *Guide to the English Tongue* in thirty-three editions between 1733 and 1747.[15] Ian Michael's quinquennial charts of new text publications on English language show the same tendency. After reaching a peak of thirteen (1705–10) during their first period of significant growth, from 1671, spelling and reading texts admittedly fell to a low of two between 1721 and 1725. Thereafter, however, the trend was steadily upwards again, reaching a second peak, of fifteen, in 1745–50, and a third, of twenty-three, in 1785–90. After a brief relapse in the early 1790s, this was regained and remained the minimum level for the next hundred years. Publication of grammar texts also moved upwards from the 1720s, with a sharp peak of thirty-three in the last five years of the century.[16]

To notice only the purely utilitarian aspect of these developments would, however, be to miss at least half their significance. Publication of literary texts, which is probably understated in the available figures because they only include books explicitly intended for school use, also increased at a similar pace from the start of the century, while handbooks of rhetoric and expression, though less numerous, remained at steady levels which also moved higher from the 1750s onwards. This growth in the amount and range of teaching materials was not something that merely testified to scholastic demand and only affected the classroom. Through its effect there, it also acted outwards on attitudes and values to influence the larger dynamics of demand and consumption in society at large. In this sense, it can be linked to the expansion of the new family and recreational market for juvenile literature and educational games exemplified in the success of John Newbery and his fellow explorers of the 'New world of children'.[17]

Similarly, it was the teaching of literary texts in schools, now for the first time explicit and widespread, which surely provided the basic conditions for the popular appropriation of cultural icons, which was one of the least tangible but most pervasive and profound effects of the general increase in publication and print circulation. Of these icons, the most important was certainly Shakespeare. The full story of the ways in which Shakespeare became 'part of an Englishman's constitution' has still to be told. When it is, it will have to embrace not only the various editions of Jacob Tonson, his son's rivalry in the 1730s with the serial publishing empire of Robert Walker and the exploits of Cibber and Garrick on the London stage, but also the provincial stage and the classroom everywhere. John Cannon, whose memoirs of the first forty years of the century provide the second half of this chapter, hardly mentioned Shakespeare. Though he knew many of the poet's own sources at first hand, and was a close student of English history, especially under the Tudors and their predecessors, there was no more Shakespeare in the anthology of 'choice matters and poems' which he compiled in October 1742 than there was elsewhere in his memoirs. A generation later, in the age of Garrick's notorious Jubilee and Thomas Sheridan's elocution lectures, when the beauties of Shakespeare were being extolled to evening classes in the provinces along with 'the glorious art of reading prose', such omission would have been unlikely, to say the least.[18]

Even in the most apparently mundane subjects, use and pleasure combined. Today, for example, writing is conventionally taken for granted as a merely practical necessity with few, if any, obvious cultural connotations of its own, a motor skill whose acquisition is a preliminary chore to be got out of the way before the real business of education begins. Thus, it is easy to overlook the fact that eighteenth-century demand for instruction in good penmanship reflected much more than the practical fact that this was both vital to commerce and government and still comparatively scarce, as anyone who has struggled with the account and minute books of the period's lesser organizations will know.[19] It was also driven by pleasurable curiosity and by aspirations to urbanity. Thus, John Seddon in 1695 offered his readers *The Penman's Paradise* and in 1717, William Brooks promised them *A Delightful Recreation for the Industrious*. *Round Hand* by George Bickham, the leading exponent of the form from 1711 onwards, was ostensibly more utilitarian, but other titles, like Robert More's *New Copy book of English, French and Italian Capital Letters* of 1703, George Shelley's *Natural Writing* (two parts, 1709 and 1714) or his *Penna Volans* (1710) continued to offer the prospect of variety and unforced ease, as well as use.[20] This points to a larger significance, for what lay behind these attractions was an appeal to the social, and ultimately also the political, self-image of the consumer. This had already been expressed as early as 1686, when *The Character of an Honest Merchant* had stipulated that such a person should not only be expert in 'the science of numbers', the procedures and legal instruments of commerce, the price of goods and the art of navigation, but should also have

> the command of his Pen . . . not crampt up to a set Secretary like a Scrivenor's boys nor scrawling long-tails like a Wench at a Boarding-School but a neat, charming mixture of Roman and Italian flowing with a kind of Artificial Negligence.

This polite, but emphatically masculine formula, which was to be frequently repeated, was more than a set of technical specifications. It also described a desirable social type. By the middle of the following century, this had been achieved. In Campbell's *London Tradesman* of 1747, there was no longer any need for artifice. Merchants should be 'of an extensive Genius' and genteel education, and Campbell went on to amplify this. Beyond the need for a 'fair legible Hand', however, he no longer felt any need to emphasize writing as his predecessor had done. There is a political as well as a social message here. *The London Tradesman* appeared in, and itself reflected, the oppositionist context of mid-century commercial patriotism. Three years later, in S. Cook's *Modish Round Hand*, form, function and fashion converged. Thus, even handwriting could become a badge of honour, fit symbol of the reconciliation of virtue and commerce in the public mind.[21]

The growth of mental communications was thus both a response to demand, and a generator and shaper of it which helped to define and legitimate the market-place itself.

Though most of the bookshops, circulating libraries, reading societies and other agencies which ministered to the consumption of knowledge were neither explicitly scholastic nor even necessarily didactic in any sense, they were likely to involve and affect teachers, and they both coexisted and interacted with larger networks which did embody such interests. The extent and character of these can be judged from a consideration of the growth and geography of mathematical writing in England between 1701 and 1760 based on the entries in the second part of Peter Wallis's *Bio-bibliography of British Mathematics and its Applications*.[22] This is represented in Table 17.1a and Plate 17.1 (map), which show its provenance by regional average in three twenty-year periods. Not surprisingly, by far the largest single concentration was in London, but this is offset by the overall predominance of provincial entries. Among the English counties, the highest averages were mostly on the eastern side of the country. Kent, in the Home Counties, and Norfolk, in East Anglia, were especially prominent. The other East Anglian counties were also well represented. Among the latter, however, the Cambridgeshire contribution is less impressive without its University component,[23] and overall numbers in these regions settled back after reaching their peak in the middle twenty years. In the south and east Midlands, on the other hand, there was a gradual increase, attributable to a steady situation in Leicestershire and appreciable growth between 1740 and 1760 in Hertfordshire and Northamptonshire, which offset small declines elsewhere. Further north, the numbers for Nottinghamshire and Derbyshire grew steadily, especially towards the end of the period. So did those for Lincolnshire which, as befitted the home of Sir Isaac Newton, had a strong mathematical tradition and was well represented throughout. In the East and North Ridings of Yorkshire and in the county at large, activity increased between 1700 and 1720 but then stayed level. Rather surprisingly, the situation was similar on Tees and Tyneside, where the importance of North Sea shipping and the development of the north-eastern coalfield might have been expected to produce significant local growth in mathematical writing and publication. However, this region's close links with London through the coastal shipping trade may mean that much of its activity is represented elsewhere. Other indicators, which show much higher levels of activity, suggest that this was indeed the case.[24] Certainly, it was not unusual for teachers of navigation and other mathematical subjects between Tees and Tyne to operate on a seasonal basis, spending part of the year in Newcastle, Gateshead or Sunderland and part in the capital. In more westerly regions, the main trend was growth into the middle of the period which continued through its final third. This was especially so in Lancashire, Cheshire and the West Riding, and in the mid-western counties of the Bristol region; but it also showed in the southwest, particularly in Devon, thanks to Exeter and Plymouth, and even in the far northwest, where it was probably largely attributable to the activities of the Lowther family in the development of Whitehaven and West Cumberland.[25] In the West Midlands, on the other hand, and in the counties of the Welsh Border, there was less interest at this time than perhaps might have been expected. Among the remaining parts of England, the counties of the Thames Valley also showed substantial activity, most of which, however, derived from Oxford and the University,[26] while the south coast showed continuing solidity but no significant development.

Mathematical writing was not only extensively spread; it also involved a wide range of occupations. Table 17.3 sorts these into nine categories according to the descriptions used by the writers themselves. Needless to say, several of the categories overlap, and since many claimed more than one occupation, the totals represent the number of times a description was used, not the total number of writers. This, therefore, is not a census, but it does convey the occupational range of mathematical writers, the connections between different groups and perhaps also an indication of change in the way mathematical writers wished to be perceived towards the middle of the century. The four main categories of contributors were the learned professions, those in 'mathematical vocations', self-styled teachers of various kinds and artisans. Among the first of these, the substantial component from medicine increased steadily until 1750 but then fell slightly.[27] That from the law did the same on a smaller scale. The church's interest, though always large, grew quickly during the first twenty years of the century but levelled off after reaching its maximum between 1721 and 1730. The 'academic' component, on the other hand, grew throughout, despite a declining contribution from those actually resident at Oxford and Cambridge, though the ancient universities continued to account for the lion's share of writers with degrees within the list as a whole.[28]

Among those in 'mathematical vocations', the main self-styled groups were the astronomers, almanac makers, mathematicians *per se* and land surveyors. These all contributed substantially and kept rough pace with each other, but the almanac makers began to drop back somewhat after 1730. Besides these, there were small and stable numbers of cartographers and geographers, a few geologists and a noticeable increase towards the end of the period in those who called themselves architects and electricians. Teachers of various kinds formed the largest of the main groups, and here by far the largest subset were those who explicitly taught mathematics, whose numbers grew very quickly to 1730, more slowly during the next decade and then dropped slightly. Writing masters, schoolmasters and teachers of navigation were all well and steadily represented, the first of these rather better than teachers of accountancy and bookkeeping, though in fact the two descriptions probably overlapped. Though there was an increase in the number who simply called themselves lecturers, relatively few answered to such generic names. Tutor retained some favour, but teacher *tout court* lost much of its limited gain towards 1760.

Turning to the artisans, the main growth was among the opticians and instrument makers. The number of engineers and mechanics also grew, however; and so did those for general craftsmen, farmers and gardeners. Among the lesser categories, accountancy and bookkeeping dominated the contribution from commerce. As they stand, the relatively small numbers here suggest that this was a greater user than producer of mathematical material. The strategic importance of writing on insurance, however, was clearly far greater than its simple quantity would suggest, and any impression of paucity should in any case be modified by the large overlap which certainly existed in practice between commerce and other activities, especially teaching. The same is true of the figures for government. Despite the sharp increase in the 1750s, these almost certainly underestimate the contribution of the customs and excise. Predictably, the navy dominated the explicitly military component. Finally, there was a sizeable and eclectic contribution from literature, journalism and the arts, as well as sustained participation by members of the nobility and gentry who gave no other description of themselves, but clearly belong in association with the elite groups of the learned professions.

To some extent, this account of the writers (and presumptively users) of mathematical material can be extended to the consumers pure and simple by performing a similar exercise on Wallis's earlier *Index of British Mathematicians, 1701–1760*.[29] This presents some difficulties which should be recognized at the outset. Though considerably larger than the writers (4,263 entries compared with 1,090), the group which it seeks to capture is also more difficult to define. Its extent therefore carries a price. Well over a thousand of its entries cannot be specifically placed. In addition, the variable coverage of local and regional sources and reporting on which it is based, in addition to national sources, means that as a measure of distribution, it is much more prone to inconsistency than the list of writers. Nevertheless, nearly three thousand of its entries can be mapped. Table 17.2 and Plate 17.2 (map) do this cumulatively by county.

As with the writers, the country entries in the *Index* far outnumber those from the capital. The other overriding features are the large number of entries which suggest geographic mobility, either by giving more than one place of activity or simply a county at large, and the quantity of lesser market towns and smaller communities which are represented in the country as a whole. The *Index* in fact shows a wide distribution, conforming to the main lines of communication. As might be expected, the university towns are prominent, as are the major regional capitals, such as York and Norwich. County towns and cathedral cities in general are also well represented. On this evidence indeed, the *Index* is a reminder that the cultural profiles of mid- and late eighteenth-century England are by no means the same. At this stage, Birmingham and Manchester were comfortably surpassed by Bristol and Liverpool. Though Birmingham's own total puts it among the best represented inland centres in the *Index*, low entries for its surrounding region, apart from Worcester, which should in any case be associated with the river Severn and the hinterland of Bristol rather than the future Black Country, corroborate the evidence of the writers and suggest that the formal diffusion of mathematical knowledge was relatively slow to reach the West Midlands as a whole.

The *Index* also contains useful information about occupations and this too points to differences between the middle and later years of the century. Of the 106 entries which made Kent the second best represented county in the entire country, 61 were land surveyors, 41 of them working at different times in the county at large and another 20 based on particular towns. Though the number active concurrently did not reach its maximum until the middle decades, surveying was already the principal mathematical occupation in Kent as early as 1710. This predominance applied to the country as a whole, though its actual timing varied from region to region. Several instances, especially among the Yorkshire entries, point also to the existence of partnerships and family businesses extending over two or more generations which not only practised surveying, but also taught it as one of a range of practical and commercial subjects. As with the writers, the *Index* also suggests that mathematical knowledge was more used in the eastern parts of the country during the first half of the century than in the western. What this means is uncertain. On one hand the fact that it echoes the roughly similar predominance in the distribution of new goods revealed by Lorna Weatherill's work on probate inventories[30] points to the familiar Whiggish contrast between progress in the east and backwardness in the west attributable to the influence of London on markets, ideas and the development of provincial culture. On the other hand, it was precisely in parts of eastern England that older mathematical traditions associated with astrology and almanac making remained especially strong. This might suggest some modification to such simple modernization theory: as John Cannon's experience will show, progress and the active retention and propagation of old knowledge were not necessarily incompatible.[31]

Nevertheless, the *Index* does indicate the shape of things to come. Lancashire, South and West Yorkshire and in the north-east, Tees and Tyneside, already stand apart. Sheffield, with seventeen entries including an architect, a mining engineer, two mathematical instrument makers and two *soi-disant* teachers of mathematics as well as the predictable surveyors, conventional schoolmasters and writing masters, was well ahead of Leeds, Rotherham and Doncaster. Mathematical practice in Manchester was likewise already more technical in its stated applications than it was elsewhere in the county, Liverpool included. It was, however, on Tyne and Teesside, thanks to the north-eastern coalfield's direct relationship with London and the area's major involvement in North Sea shipping, that this tendency was most marked. Here, in the densest concentration of mathematical and technical skill outside London, Edinburgh or Dublin, even the ubiquitous land surveyor was eclipsed by the self-avowed teacher and lecturer in mathematical and scientific subjects, able to earn his living directly from the value of his offerings as they stood.

II

The main link between the network of practical knowledge, represented here by the example of mathematics and its applications, and the more formal provision of education was the growing body of private-venture teachers whose activities filled a significant portion of the trades directories which served the main provincial centres from the 1760s onwards. James Sketchley's *Bristol Directory* of 1775, for example, whose proprietor was involved with his brother Samuel in schoolbook publishing and schoolroom leasing in Birmingham as well as Bristol, listed twenty schoolmasters, of whom at least seventeen were private, and seventeen schoolmistresses in the city. Besides these individual listings, there were ten girls', four boys' and four infants' schools, not to mention Bristol's two main endowed schools and the separately listed specialists in writing, accounts, French and other languages, music and dancing who served these various establishments. Twenty years later, the listings in *Matthews' Directory* for 1793–4 were similar, except that the generic 'schoolmaster/mistress' had virtually disappeared, while the list of specialists in writing, accounts and mathematics had lengthened and the number of schools had grown to thirteen for boys and fifteen for girls, of which one in each case was explicitly designated as French. Liverpool, which supported at least thirty-two schoolmasters, ten schoolmistresses and six dancing, fencing and French masters between 1766 and 1774, showed similar characteristics. These two examples, both major ports, both with a significant 'genteel' component in their social structure, especially in Bristol with its own spa and burgeoning residential suburb in Clifton, were perhaps exceptional. Certainly the much shorter list in Elizabeth Raffald's *Manchester Directory* of 1772 or the more modest numbers included among 'Professors of the Polite Arts' in *Sketchley's Birmingham, Walsall and Wolverhampton Directory* of 1767, suggest that among inland manufacturing centres at any rate, such levels could not yet be equalled.[32] A more broadly based enquiry, however, drawing on newspaper advertisements rather than directories, and thus able to take in activity outside the main centres as well as their specific listings, will modify this.

Though they can sometimes be supplemented by linkage to other material such as directories, rate books, membership registers of various kinds, book subscriptions and other lists, the advertisement columns of the newspapers remain the main source of information about private-venture teaching. In a general way, they have already been used to show the extensive presence of private schools in different parts of the country.[33] Plate 17.3 summarizes a rather more detailed analysis of school advertisements from Warwickshire,

Worcestershire, Staffordshire and Shropshire in *Aris's Birmingham Gazette* during its first fifty years, by counting offerings in boys' and mixed schools in the main subject groups through the period, and dividing them into six geographical categories according to their origin: from Birmingham itself, its immediate vicinity, other main manufacturing towns, county towns and cathedral cities, market towns and smaller communities. In addition, a seventh category lists aggregate offerings in girls' schools. For these, curriculum information was too inconsistent to be categorized geographically, though the distribution of the schools themselves is shown.[34] Though they are limited by the idiosyncrasies of newspaper advertisements as a source, the results, especially when combined with other evidence, reflect very clearly the complexities, both of Birmingham itself as a major shopping as well as manufacturing centre,[35] and of its relations with its hinterland.

Besides the presence of a small number of respectable academies and specialist schools of considerable longevity, the main feature in Birmingham itself was the very wide range and flexibility of teaching offered, especially in day and evening classes in the middle and lower price-bracket (the typical range was between three and five shillings per quarter for elementary subjects and from ten to fifteen shillings for languages and mathematics). Many of those involved were immigrants, either from London in the case of a number of teachers of particular trade skills, or from other parts of the country. Charles Martin, for example, a chaser and die-sinker who opened a drawing school on Snow Hill in 1763 and also taught German flute, was a Londoner. So was Thomas Baker, who offered arithmetic, bookkeeping, mensuration, geography, globes and maps, algebra and mathematics when he arrived in Lichfield Street in 1761. His school was still going in the 1780s after at least three changes of ownership. Mr Wheatcroft, on the other hand, had been an assistant master at Nottingham Academy before he opened his own school in St Martin's Court in 1782. Wheatcroft's syllabus, which ranged from the three R's to astronomy, navigation, algebra and fluxions, was strictly businesslike. By this time, however, the demand for civility in Birmingham was at least equal to that in other more obvious places of fashionable resort. Others therefore offered cultivation. At Mr Wood's academy in the Cherry Orchard, entrants who suffered 'the unhappiness of not understanding the meaning of various hard words which daily occur in reading and conversation' were promised, after six months' attendance, an understanding as good for practical purposes as that conferred by a regular classical education. Mr Watson, another Londoner who arrived in 1782, offered both, training his pupils not only in a very full mathematical syllabus, but also, 'the want of an English education' being 'but too visible in the youth of both sexes', in the recital of Milton and Young with proper emphasis and cadence. Similarly Mr Landon taught his pupils the art of reading, like music, by visible signs, so that they learned to express the passions properly. He also tutored adults in 'the glorious art of reading prose'.[36] Many teachers continued to move freely between Birmingham itself and other parts of the region as itinerant specialists serving other establishments. Several were also closely involved in other aspects of business, such as the perennial surveying and accountancy, bookselling or circulating library ownership. Business translation work was another frequent pairing with teaching, especially in the 1780s when the town was rapidly expanding and diversifying its European trade connections. Occasionally, as in the case of Samuel Sketchley, the directory compiler, quondam auctioneer, journalist and educational publisher whose wife ran a girls' boarding school, diversification even ran to leasing rooms to other teachers.

Developments elsewhere in the region were equally important, however, if not more so, because the overall pattern suggests not that new knowledge spread outwards from Birmingham, but that initially at any rate the opposite was the case. The first extensive 'modern' curriculum to be advertised, nearly fifteen years before anything comparable was offered closer to Birmingham, was that of John Ward's Writing and Mathematical School in Leominster, Herefordshire, in 1742, which offered arithmetic, geometry, trigonometry, navigation, gauging, drilling, bookkeeping and the use of globes, sliding rule and other instruments. Similarly Benjamin Talbot, teacher, surveyor and instrument maker, worked between 1758 and 1771 not in Birmingham or Wolverhampton, but in Newport, Shropshire, and later at Cannock, Staffordshire. Indeed, the most notable feature of the entire survey is the prominence not so much of the other main manufacturing centres, nor of the county and cathedral towns, which were conspicuous by their absence from the advertisement columns except as sites for girls' schools, but the number of schools advertising highly developed offerings which were kept successfully, and for considerable periods of time, in lesser market towns and villages, often in close, almost symbiotic relationship with the ancient grammar schools.

Educational relationships between Birmingham and its hinterland were thus both diverse and extensive. A comparable survey of the *Manchester Mercury* between 1752 and 1800 (not shown) reveals both differences and similarities. Overall numbers of offerings advertised were less, though this may simply reflect differences between the two newspapers involved, and growth was concentrated in two periods, 1760–70 and 1785–95, with some decrease in the interval. On the other hand, the Manchester paper carried more advertisements from schools in other leading manufacturing and commercial centres, or situated in other parts of the country altogether, than its Birmingham counterpart. Liverpool was predictably prominent, as was Chester; but Leeds, Sheffield, York and Nottingham were also regular sources. In 1776, a commercial academy in Hamburg was advertised. The same tendency affected girls' schools: though Manchester itself could boast several genteel establishments by the early 1790s, notices were by then appearing from Birmingham, London, Bristol and Bath. In other respects, however, developments were similar. Manchester in the 1780s offered as much diversity as Birmingham, if not more; but again, development was as much distributed through the hinterland as concentrated in the centre itself.

Similar variations certainly existed between other parts of the country, especially when the incidence of particular factors, such as the influence of dissenting academies on other teaching in Northamptonshire or in the northern counties[37] is taken into account. The private-venture teacher was ubiquitous, however. In the northern counties, for example, distance, cost and a lingering sense of regional solidarity may have meant that the ancient grammar schools retained their pre-eminence in the education of the gentry, and thus their cultural hegemony, for longer than they did further south. It was the private teachers in the north, however, who were most closely attuned to changing opportunities and demand, from elementary schooling to adult evening classes and lectures. Consequently, it was they who not only produced, but also consumed (at least subscribed to) the lion's share of the new educational writing over the course of the century. If the old foundations were able to survive and adapt, therefore, it was because of the active interchange, in methods, curriculum, textbook authorship and specialist teaching which developed between themselves and these newer sources.

As was the case further south, one conspicuous result of this was the emergence of education, especially in boarding schools, as a 'cottage industry' appropriate to market towns, particularly those with decent amenities on good lines of communication, but prefer-ably not too closely connected with contagious influences. In the Midlands, for example, Mr Braithwaite's Bowling Green Academy, opened in Bridgnorth in 1783, made much of its 'beautiful, romantic and healthy situation . . . in the midst of that delightful eminence, the Castle Hill', from which his pupils would 'never be permitted to depart . . . without being properly attended'. Seventeen years earlier, in 1766, the master of Uttoxeter School had assured prospective parents that 'the place is rich and plentiful, situation pleasant and air salubrious'. Since he chose 'but a small number in his own house', he took pains to mention that 'there are genteel families in the town ready to receive young gentlemen'.[38] In Northumberland, Alnwick supported no less than fifteen private schools in the second half of the century. In the market towns of the Vale of York, especially Doncaster with its four girls' schools, and in those of Cumbria, boarding-school education with its supporting train of ancillary services was likewise a major factor in local economy and society, not only as a provider of work and an injector of money, but also as a transformer of expectations and consumption patterns. It seems likely, in fact, that the indirect cultural impact of such schools, through their contribution to provincial urban culture itself; through their role in changing the ways in which the relationship between city and country was perceived; and, not least, through the effects of the new social formations and stratifications which they produced, such as the former-pupil societies and reunions which were beginning to be advertised in the papers, far outweighed their direct effects on the development of schooling itself.[39]

In the last analysis, however, all this survey material raises more real questions than it answers. It describes, externally, the kinds of knowledge supplied, when, where and by whom. From this, it may be legitimate to draw some general inferences about demand and consumption, especially in the later decades of the century. Even so, the limits imposed by the nature of the sources are only too apparent. In most cases virtually nothing can be said about the suppliers themselves beyond the record of their advertisements, and inference from these very easily becomes circular and self-defeating. It is at this point, faced with the fact that the sources available so far can say little very specific or direct about the relationship between different kinds of knowledge, or about their real effects on the life and outlook of the prospective consumer, that one confronts once more the incongruous figure of Mr Young, filling his head with the wrong sort of knowledge from the wrong source, when he should have been surveying Mirey Croft. To address fully the problems thus presented – the effects of consumption on knowledge and vice versa; the interaction of literate knowledge as a commodity with other forms and ways of knowing; the reasons why some things, not necessarily those expected, seemed more worth knowing than others, and the paradoxical perpetuation of traditional priorities in the midst of innovation and transformation – would ideally require intensive biographical matching and comparison of suppliers and consumers, teachers and taught, over long periods and extensive areas. In default of this, the second part of this discussion turns to a single example for whom such closer treatment is possible. There are, of course, limits to what can be inferred from one case, especially a relatively early and obscure one. It may, however, serve to capture some aspects of the general process of change which are easily overlooked in its later, more conspicuous stages.

III

Compared with the memoirs and confessions of his fellow countryman James Lackington, that early epitome of enterprise, self-help and self-service in the knowledge business, *Xpovexa seu Annales*, or 'Memoirs of the Birth, Education, Life and Death of Mr. John Cannon, sometime officer of the Excise at Mere, Glastonbury and West Lidford in the County of Somerset', may seem an unlikely test-piece upon which to assess cultural attitudes to knowledge and its consumption in eighteenth-century England.[40] Unlike Lackington, whose book emporium, the Temple of the Muses, with its 140-foot frontage on Finsbury Square, was one of the sights of the town in the century's later years, Cannon never lived in London. There was a time when he had had such hopes. In 1720, as a bright and promising excise officer being vetted for promotion, he seemed about to realize them. Then a year later, professional jealousy, political suspicion, personal extravagance and sheer foolishness brought his discharge from the service. As it was, he hardly left his native county, apart from his posting to Berkshire early in his excise career and a brief visit to the capital at the time of his wedding in 1714. He seldom made it to Bristol, and then on foot, let alone to London. He spiced his memoirs with 'choice Dissertations, Epigrams, Epitaphs, Recipes in Physick and Surgery, Occurrences and brief descriptions of famous men and sayings, with the topography of some cities, towns and places in which he was conversant, very diverting and useful, as also ornamental'.[41] He actually spent his time living in lodgings while eking out the best living he could for the support elsewhere of his wife and family by working as a schoolmaster, accountant and general penman in a minor town, not especially prosperous, in a part of the country whose traditional textile manufactures were gradually declining.

As a 'least-case scenario', there is, however, much to be learned from John Cannon's obscure career: from the kinds of knowledge available to him, the forms in which it reached him and the means by which it did so; from the uses he made of it and the ways in which he conveyed it to others; from his dealings with those around him, and from what these suggest about the relationship between literate and oral forms of knowledge and numeracy. Just as important as these facets of his experience is the way in which they were assembled and what this says about Cannon's view of himself. There is no sign that he ever intended his memoirs for publication: the greater part of his 700 pages consists of a verbatim register of the legal, commercial and personal writings he drew, the measurements and calculations he made and the administrative tasks he performed. He certainly expected his memoirs to be read, however, and they were much more than just a daybook or a correspondence file. Nor were they kept as a confessional diary in the traditional sense. Though they certainly contain frequent passages which are ostensibly 'confessional', most of these read more like retrospective glosses, written at some remove from the actual flux of events and modified by the influence of their author's voracious and eclectic reading, than unmediated response to experience. If anything, John Cannon's memoirs thus represent an intermediate form of production, midway between his own consumption of knowledge, his transmission of it as a teacher and full-blown authorship. Their compilation, from rough notes and at least one previous version, was clearly a sort of hobby, and thus in a cultural sense a form of consumption, celebrating the author's pleasure in his ability to read a book, use a pen and handle a surveyor's rule and his cleverness in using these abilities to get his living. The final version, headed by an emblematic genealogical preface hedged about with biblical talismans, which situated the author and his family in the cosmos, was completed between

1740 and 1742, Cannon's fifty-eighth year. It was clearly meant to be used, if only by his descendants and their acquaintances. These would have found in it not only a remarkable combination of moralistic and picaresque autobiography, often bawdy and on occasion highly explicit.[42] As befitted a work which probably served its writer as a teaching-quarry, they would also have found a carefully referenced and cross-referenced collection of 'general knowledge' which the author had picked up and found useful in the course of a life which, though it never took him very far from home, nevertheless subjected him to a significant series of social and cultural transformations. Cannon's memoirs thus say a good deal about the actualities of education, literacy and numeracy in the eighteenth-century provinces in the half-century which separates the seventeenth-century world of chapmen, small books and pleasant histories depicted by Margaret Spufford[43] from the more conspicuously commercial age of Lackington, Newbery and their like. We have lately been told that this period was primarily characterized by the reinstatement of an *ancien régime*: that it was marked, not by advancing secularism and modernity, but by the search for a moral and political alternative to oligarchy conceived in traditional theological terms, and that the underlying reason why such a recovery of the past was possible was that neither the structure nor the ideology of English society had yet begun to change.[44] If much of what John Cannon thought worth knowing seems to bear that out, the ways in which he came to know it, and the uses which he made of his knowledge to establish the co-ordinates of his world, to create the mental maps which fixed his own place in it and thus to construct his own identity, suggest that things were changing none the less.

He was born in 1684 into solidly respectable circumstances. On both sides of his family, his forbears had, with some exceptions, prospered unspectacularly in central Somerset for most of the previous century. As minor landowners, they had successfully combined husbandry and work 'in a rural way of business', as graziers, butchers, maltsters and fell-mongers. They had also done well from local office-holding and service, such as stewardship, to larger proprietors. On his father's side, Cannon was related to one Lovejoy, 'a cellarer or purveyor in Bloomsbury Square, who was rich . . . and had three sons, all of whom became wealthy and prosperous, being bred to learning', one as a writing master, one as a factor in the Smyrna trade and one as a pewterer. Whether by their own provenance in a region where husbandry and manufacture had long coexisted in the same countryside, or by their London connections, his relations were thus no strangers to commerce and calculation, even when they themselves did not have their letters. Though 'unlearned', his paternal grandfather, whose success as a grazier and butcher was the mainstay of the family's substance, 'yet had a faculty of keeping his accounts by bones, which he carryed to Market always for that purpose, till he had a daughter named Frances who was his bookkeeper, and his sons after her'. Cannon's father, born in 1648, 'being a year remarkable for that bloody and unnatural tragedy acted on the Royal person of His Sacred Majesty King Charles I of blessed memory, whose actors therein has left themselves an indelible stain of shame, reproach and infamy never to be forgotten to the latest posterity by all true loyal hearts', was 'bred up and educated in Good English literature',[45] and assumed the overall management of the family concerns as soon as he was able.

The almost incantatory quality of the passing apostrophe to the royal martyr with which Cannon marked his account of his father, points to one other element which should be added to this introductory sketch. This protestation of unalloyed royalism should probably be taken with a pinch of salt, especially if it is considered in relation to the actual places which he called home. On a map of Somerset drawn according to David Underdown's proposed ecology of seventeenth-century popular culture and allegiance, Mere, Glastonbury and West Lidford would all lie on or close to the hypothetical borderline between 'Chalk' and 'Cheese' countries and their distinguishing cultural and political characteristics. Bridgwater and Taunton apart, the same would be true of most of the other local communities in which Cannon had regular dealings, especially Bruton, Shepton Mallet and Yeovil. A similar ambivalence attends his family's occupations.[46] In the light of this, the fate of the touch-piece, given to his mother when she was taken to be touched by Charles I for the King's Evil during his imprisonment at Carisbrooke Castle, is probably a more reliable guide to the family attitude to monarchy – at least by the time of Cannon's own generation – than his lip-service to the ideology of Divine Right. It was only silver, worth about eight shillings, that being all His Sacred Majesty could afford at the time; but by all accounts it never lost its virtue. It should surely have become a treasured heirloom, and was indeed left as such to Cannon's sister, whose husband sold it.[47] Such an ending suggests, despite Cannon's own silence on the subject, that his family was not only commercially astute, but was also quite prepared to do whatever was necessary to survive in times which were more than usually interesting in Somerset, at no time more so than during Cannon's own infancy.

Apart from his own precocity, there was nothing particularly unusual about Cannon's education. After dame-school, where he 'got pretty well advanced in the bible' he attended two small private-venture schools in Lidford, the first run by the rector's son, who preferred to leave his pupils to their own devices while he went fishing, the second by 'one Humphrey Morris from the Grammar School'. Morris, the son of a surgeon and maltster, was competent and energetic, and Cannon did well under him, being put to Latin and 'some writing at intervals'. However, parental sickness, the forced sale of family property to pay unspecified fines and his master's removal to Yeovil ended his hopes of going on to university. In 1697, when he was thirteen, he was put to the plough. He repined at this blighting of his scholarly promise, but marked it retrospectively in his memoirs by a lengthy dissertation on the superiority of useful knowledge to merely academic learning. Thereafter, he joined his younger brother, working for his father and his uncle as a general farmhand and shepherd. Now, he taught himself as best he could from whatever sources he could lay his hands on, arranging his market-visits so that his brother went to Shepton Mallet while he took advantage of the bookseller at Bruton,

> with which I conversed and bought books and maps, etc. and oftentimes broke
> my market money to compass my ends which I would some way or other excuse
> to my father at night when we were to render an account of my market.

By these means, he progressed from such staples of the chapbook trade as 'The Seven Champions, Fortunatus, Parismus, Dr. Faustus, The Wars of England, Extraordinary Events and the like, in which at the time I greatly delighted',[48] to more weighty matters. Particularly influential was the 'large history of that learned and warlike Jew, Josephus Ben Gorion' owned by one Philip Whitacre, a gardener in Bruton. Whitacre would not let the book out of his hands, but it was his weekly visits to Whitacre's house which created in Cannon

> a fervent desire to reading other authors more authentic and valuable than those
> I had been acquainted with, and was the first foundation of my steady and

> unwearied adherence to English history, with which afterwards my closet plenti-
> fully abounded notwithstanding my several stations or occupations.[49]

He also got hold of *Aristotle's Masterpiece* and Culpeper's *Herbal*. Until confiscated by his mother, these formed the basis of his sexual education. The details of this, which are remarkably frank, may be peripheral to the present discussion, but it deserves to be mentioned, if only in general terms, because, together with his recollection of his various amours, it illuminates his attitudes to basic aspects of his life and career, and these certainly were germane to his views of knowledge and its uses. By his own account, his experience was decidedly voyeuristic, and he recalled it in maturity with appropriate expressions of regret for the sins of his youth. However, he clearly regarded such errors as venial. His experiments, in fact, were probably not more than normally furtive and they had no obviously lasting or detrimental effect. Despite the religious formalism of his repentances, the basic impression left by this aspect of his life is his realistic acceptance of the facts of sexuality in both genders and the balance between his obvious interest in 'carnal relations' and an equally lively awareness of the pitfalls of an imprudent connection. Discounting casual flirtations, he had two serious girlfriends before he met Susannah Deane of West Wycombe, Berkshire, whom he was to marry in 1714:[50] Mary, at home in Somerset, and Joanna, in Berkshire, his first excise posting, who was also probably his first pupil. He 'went steady' simultaneously with both of them for several years, exchanging vows, love tokens and letters, but taking care that while he kept a watchful eye on *their* other affairs, neither of them learnt of the other's existence or interest in him. Despite frequent heavy *tête-à-têtes*, which afforded plenty of opportunity for tempted desire on both sides, he never actually slept with either. He did own up, with some evidence of moral discomfort, to one other intermittent, and consummated, liaison. This was with Anne Heister, named once only in 1707 and thereafter called 'the strumpet Lais', the servant at his digs in Watlington who was only too willing to join him in the mutual loss of their virginities in 1709, two years after his arrival in Berkshire. The circumstances of this lapse seem quite straightforward. As a young and rising exciseman, he did not want to tie himself prematurely to either of his steadies, though he and they clearly enjoyed playing the game of romance for all it was worth. Probably prompted by the loose example of his fellow excise officers, at least one of whom shared his lodgings and quite possibly his mistress too, he tumbled by default into Lais's bed; after which, finding that 'she would use all ways and means with me till she was with child in hopes for me to marry her', and reflecting 'on my past follies and filthy sin of fornication', he looked around for safe haven.[51] Luckily for him, he found it. To call his behaviour 'modern' would be a misnomer. Nevertheless, the pattern of Cannon's dealings with his girlfriends, the predicaments in which he found himself and the conventional sentiments he expressed, will be familiar. The Girl He Left Behind; the First Love of His New Life; Ambition and Desire; the Easy Mistress, and finally, True Love and Happiness Ever After: in fact, if not in fiction, where it is The Girl He Left Behind who ends up in domestic bliss, these surely follow the classic pattern for the attainment of that happy state which was to last in Middle England from Cannon's time until the 1950s. Not that he was ever a paragon of twentieth-century decency and consideration: present sensibility simply boggles at the penchant for lewd, scatological and sometimes brutal horseplay, shared with his male and imposed, with varying degrees of willing collaboration, on his female, acquaintances[52] which he regarded as the *sine qua non* of making 'merry'. Nevertheless, at a time when relations between the sexes below the level of the elite are supposed to have been characterized still by an almost total absence of personal 'affect',[53] Cannon's amours, for all their roughness, suggest a rather different ethos: one in which individual sensibility played a considerable part even when tempered by hard-headedness, and in which the threatened sanctions of religious prohibition were mitigated in practice by a strong sense of present reality. In the final count, he weathered his sexual education and survived his subsequent adventures without any oppressive sense of guilt and with nothing more complicated than a tendency to have vivid erotic dreams featuring his neighbours' wives from time to time, which he recorded and rationalized in unabashed detail.

Though Cannon joined in a normal mixture of popular sports and communal recreations as a young man, and wasted his fair share of time and money on gaming, drinking and other country matters, the account he gave of himself is of one who increasingly defined his existence in terms different from those of his community and used his consumption of knowledge to do so. As the sources of printed material multiplied and the variety of books available to him increased, his obsession with them grew. For a while after he joined the excise service in 1706, it is true that he mentioned them less frequently, no doubt because he had other things on his mind. It would, however, be as serious a mistake to pass lightly over this phase of his life as it would have been to neglect his family background and sexual experience, because it shaped him fundamentally, leaving him with habits of mind and outlook which he retained long after he had left the service, and had ostensibly espoused the 'country' ideas and rhetoric of the patriot opposition in the 1730s. His new work placed him and his colleagues at the point of contact between England's burgeoning 'fiscal–military state'[54] and her growing internal commerce. Now, he was not just a person who could read, write and manage numbers, but one who did these things for a master who brooked no delay and did not tolerate untidiness or error. As Cannon himself found out during his own probation, when a botched entry in his accounts nearly cost him his position,[55] initiation – the word is appropriate – into this world of professional writers, a world empowered by statute which worked according to written rules and exact procedures, was not easy, even after the recruit had passed his entrance exam and obtained his certificate. Cannon's later reminiscences of less diligent or less lucky colleagues, and of the new-entry men he himself trained, show that many did not last the course. Those that did were set apart. When he first met his own tutor and supervisor, Mr Spong, by accident on the Abingdon road in 1707, Spong, who had been taught to use his eyes, recognized Cannon as 'one of the tribe' because he had inadvertently dropped the calibrated ivory tip of his dimension-cane on the roadside.[56]

As a member of 'the tribe', Cannon spent a good deal of his off-duty, as well as his on-duty time, both before and after his marriage, in the company of his fellow officers. This meant that he had to acquire quickly the ability to be at ease in the company of comparative strangers. Such strangers, moreover, included not just his colleagues and superiors in the Excise, but also those in positions of local influence and authority outside it, with whom the service had to be able to co-operate if it was to be effective. This aspect of Cannon's experience points to skills which, though not part of his formal training, were surely among the most important and necessary attributes of a good officer. It is a truism that excisemen were not popular. Besides this, they were not only transferred frequently to prevent frauds, but were also systematically required to check on each other. This points to separateness: the separateness of the service and the separateness of the individual officer within it. This, however, made it all the more important for an exciseman to establish quickly an amicable working relationship with those whom he had to survey, as well as the other agencies with which he had to work, and to be able to penetrate easily the fabric of relationships in the places to which he was posted. He lived and worked, figuratively and literally, in the market-place. To be effective, he needed dependable information about a promiscuous environment: in short, he had to know his way around. Thus, it was essential to establish an acceptable presence in his posting, on which he could base a network of connections and information. To do this, he had to be able to mix easily with other people, especially those with influence.

Cannon took this side of the job seriously, and it is clear that he set out to become good at it. In 1708, 'now being thoroughly acquainted' in the Watlington division, he began to widen his circle beyond the service itself, associating 'myself in all my vacant hours in Innocent games & diversions altho' sometimes expensive & smelt of ye pocket with several young Gentlemen of good reputation whose friends were Clergymen, Gentlemen or Tradesmen'. Later that year, his supervisor, Mr Godfrey, told him 'that it would be more agreeable to him if I would learn to smoak, not failing to set forth that noble qualification in and towards company keeping'. His first heroic attempt ended in spewing failure, but he tried again and 'shortly became a perfect master of ye Art, that in a little time I could vie with Mr. Godfrey or any other person'.[57] Thereafter, even when fully occupied with his work and with alternately courting and fending off either Mary or Joanna, not to mention dallying with Lais, he 'never failed of attending my companions at bowls & other recreations in my vacant hours'. It was not long before this strategy paid dividends. When, in 1710, he prosecuted a drunken assailant for profane swearing, he had to overcome the reluctance of the constable, a tenant of the defendant, to proceed with the charges. It must have helped that the presiding magistrate was 'Mr. Justice Clarke, my good friend'. His personal standing with the county Bench was further enhanced in 1713, when he helped a fellow officer detect and prosecute a large-scale Malt Tax fraud which was being carried on in High Wycombe by the Mayor and his brother. At the same time, he added to his prestige by catching the brothers' tallow chandler uncle, and fellow alderman, red-handed in the use of false weights. These exploits won him not only a commendation and bonus from the Commissioners of the Excise, but also the congratulations of the local butchers who had long been swindled by the tallow chandler.[58]

Not that all his dealings were entirely above-board: as he gained experience, he also learnt how to sail close to the wind without getting caught. The venison pasty feast which he gave in 1709, 'to indulge my fancy and oblige my friends', cost him a pretty penny. It could have cost him his commission, and quite possibly more besides, had one of the guests, Mr Shepard, his landlord, who was also a gamekeeper, realized that the fawn he was eating was the one he and his employer had been missing for the past several days.[59] In 1714, at the behest of his partner in detecting the Malt Tax fraud, who knew him to be a good card player, he got involved in a gaming circle whose other members included the previous year's culprit Mayor of High Wycombe. The circle was run by Captain Cary, the recently returned sub-governor of Barbados, a 'merry facetious man' who had property close by. Since Cary had the accumulated proceeds of seven years' rents and a considerable salary to spend, the stakes grew high, and Cannon and his colleagues found themselves sharply reprimanded by their Collector for their entanglement. Cannon himself, however, had taken care to stay sober while the Captain got drunk. Subsequently, he stayed out of trouble by sending a surrogate. He got to keep his winnings.[60] This ability to look after himself while living just on the right side of the law stayed with him for the rest of his excise career. In 1719, for example, back in Somerset and, as an expert officer, well established on a footwalk in Shepton Mallet,[61] he was treating his friends to samples of a windfall consignment of contraband brandy, rum and black pepper, confiscated by the customs officer at Lyme in Dorset and deposited in his keeping pending condemnation. At the same time, he was ingratiating himself in the town at large by warning its inhabitants of imminent customs searches for additional contraband believed to be hidden there.[62]

Cannon relied on more than an eye for the main chance, hollow legs, a hard head and occasional handiness in a fight, however. What really stood him in good stead was his ability to give a good account of himself if asked to do so. It was to this that he owed the interest of the Hon. John Hunt of Compton Pauncefoot, MP for Milbourn Point, who took his application to the Excise in hand in 1706. Had he not made a good impression on Mr Spong and Mr Parry, the Collector for Berkshire, as a new recruit in 1707, his probation would certainly have ended with the early disaster of his botched accounts. In 1714, on his journey to Taunton after his marriage and transfer from Berkshire, he so impressed his three travelling companions, the Bishop of Winchester's auditor, Denis Bond Esq., MP for Corfe Castle and his clerk, that Bond insisted on his company at dinner and paid his expenses for the two nights they spent on the road together. Similarly, once settled in Somerset and busy getting to know the people on his outride from Taunton, he made a point of cultivating

> the conversation of Mr. Marshall most evenings, he being a great scholar & historian & had recourse to ye coffee-houses every News night & whose memory was so profound that he would relate ye most remarkable passages as Current as if ye paper was before him.[63]

In a job where so much depended on the ability to talk, to listen and to remember, this was the main use of Cannon's knowledge. Carefully collected and arranged under appropriate denominations in the digressions which punctuated his memoirs, it amounted to an exchangeable fund which served as the specie of a commercial sociability. At some point, however, other considerations entered in. Knowledge ceased to be simply a medium of exchange to be used for temporal advantage and became a very personal possession. This is perhaps most evident in the form of Cannon's frequent topographies. These begin with an abridged history usually taken from Speed, Camden or Dugdale, followed by more current information about local economy, government, market times, churches, schools and other charities. They frequently end, however, on a more subjective note which connects such information to incidents in the author's own experience. Thus they act not only like a guidebook, to show the general reader around, but also as a record of Cannon's own mental map of the places where he lived and worked. Later in his life, this combination of public exchangeability and private retention had become one ingredient in the providentialist and rather conservative creed which he found epitomized in the 'valuable piece in a frame I thought it proper to oblige my friendly reader with' in June 1737 (see Plate 17.6a):

Serve God always

Credit		Hearest
Say		Thinkest
Do	Not all that thou	Mayest
Spend		Hast
Desire		Seest

> But in all things take heed to the beginning;
> See the middle & praise the ending;
> Do that is good; say that is true;
> Cherish old friends, change for no new.[64]

Not long after he recorded this caveat against the purchase of wooden nickels, his pursuit of books had transformed the conditions of his life so completely that the sum of his property resided indeed in the cast-off strong box which he had had repaired 'for the better security of my books, writings, papers and apparel, with other of my instruments and things'.[65] The process began soon after his return to Somerset. By 1718, four years married and well established in the Excise, he was buying regularly: not just by weekly or monthly subscription to such projects as 'the Magna Britannia' (*Magnae Britanniae Notitia*), but also a five-volume quarto atlas and other expensive single items 'which laid a foundation for my searching after antiquity'.[66] By this time indeed, the habit was running him into debt, and it was this that proved his undoing in 1721. Already under suspicion for borrowing from tradesmen on his ride in order to service a small mortgage he had contracted with a local attorney the previous year to pay off extravagant housekeeping and clothes bills as well as what he owed for books, he was ostensibly caught returning one maltster on his ride in arrears after collecting duty from him, while allegedly allowing the wettings of others to whom he was known to owe money to go unreported. Truth or falsity was beside the point. His local colleagues, who resented his abilities and his habit of pointing out their own frauds, had already tried twice to frame him for Jacobitism; this time, the circumstantial evidence of malpractice was enough.

From then on, Cannon was seldom, if ever, unencumbered. For the next twenty-two years, debt was one of the main, though unstated, themes of his memoirs, alternately nagging at his conscience and feeding his ego as he juggled his obligations like a modern shopper on the spree shuffling plastic (see Plate 17.6b). 'You might as well take a bear by the tooth as prevail with me to leave off purchasing books' he boasted of his difficulties in 1720–1. A year later, after further borrowing from relatives to stave off other, earlier creditors and liquidating collateral in an unsuccessful attempt to set up as a maltster, he was in still deeper trouble. Yet he was still raising funds to place expensive orders with booksellers in Sherborne and Ilminster. In 1723, things finally caught up with him. To avoid arrest, he had to sell most of his remaining inheritance and household goods, 'so that the proverb was verified in me that "I had nothing left but the dog to hold, or worse, not so much as a hair of his tail" '.[67] After this, his underlying social and economic position was radically different, even though he was able to recover and for the most part maintain external appearances. Hitherto, he had been a landowner, even if only in a small way. Now, his only remaining property and source of credit was what he knew and what he could make of it. This was what turned him into a writing master and accountant. He set up a small school on his own account, and took other paying pupils, young and adult, on an individual basis. He also worked as a clerk for an attorney in Castle Cary, as steward and tutor for a number of local gentry families, more than one of whom turned out to be a bad paymaster, and was taken on as bailiff, rent collector and general agent for the manor of Lidford. By these means, he 'became a tolerable solicitor and undertook conveyances and all sorts of writings and got employment at intervals on my own account, and had my fees, though not as exorbitant as a lawyer'.[68]

By 1732, when he moved to Glastonbury as master of two small privately endowed charity schools, his income from all sources was probably of the order of £60 or £70 a year, slightly better than his excise pay. Though he was now more careful, and could justify his books as essential to his livelihood, there was still a great deal of Mr Micawber in his attitudes. Quite apart from his own experience, his writing work, much of which consisted of small mort-gages, bonds, foreclosure valuations and other instruments, must have made him very familiar with small debt and its ramifications. In the process, it also taught him how it could be managed, and he continued to embrace it cheerfully for the sake of his library. He was in fact now living almost continuously on credit.[69] 'This was a darling fault with me all my life long, and yet I was honest to remit money as I could get it', he recalled of unpaid accounts originally run up in 1725 with a stationer and a mathematical instrument-maker in Bristol.[70] 'Being as to myself honest, sound and just in the censure of these authors', he wrote of his passion for history, 'only this great impediment often retarded my wishes; only the want of monies to buy or furnish myself with such valuable pieces as I often [had] seen in the shops or studies of great and wealthy men.'[71] Even so, he kept up a continuous correspondence during the 1730s and early 1740s with his regular suppliers, the agents of the *Gloucester Journal* and the *Sherborne Mercury*. He was also a regular customer of Mr Mullins and after him his widow in Shepton Mallet, to whom he sent his *Gentleman's Magazines* and his weekly instal-ments of other works to be bound. He got very indignant in April 1738 when a message from Mrs Mullins seemed to suggest that they were not worth the trouble. Between 1740 and 1742, on the lookout as ever for ways to turn a penny, he even got into the business himself in a small way when he agreed to act on commission as an agent for Thomas Warren of Birmingham and Edward Cave of the *Gentleman's Magazine*, distributing *The Rational Farmer* and *The American Traveller*. It was small wonder that in February 1738, he summarized the subjects of his dreams as 'merry passages, rich attire, gold and relations'.[72]

IV

There was nothing obviously 'new' or 'modern' about most of what John Cannon took in, either in form or in content, which is not surprising because his collecting was inspired more by simple emulation than by systematic enquiry. As he reminded his reader in 1732, he 'delighted . . . to peruse the best of authors in diverting histories and other subjects, English Chronicles, Annals and the lives of the eminent fathers of the church in all ages'.[73] Though he seldom mentioned specific titles, when he did, this was what they reflected. In August 1739, he sent seventy-four stitched numbers of Smith's *History of Our Blessed Saviour, Apostles and Primitive Fathers*, which he had been collecting for five years, to be bound by Mrs Mullins. He also collected Rapin's *History*, but did not much like it. Nor did anyone else for that matter: he tried to use two volumes of it as 'debt satisfaction' in 1736 but his Bridgwater creditor would not take them, and though he eventually got rid of one volume in 1738, he had to settle for rather less than he expected in return. Hooper's *History of the Late Rebellion and Civil Wars*, which he began to collect in the summer of 1739, was more to his liking and he persevered with it, as he also did with the *Magnae Britanniae Notitia*, one of his earliest projects. Besides William of Malmesbury and Plutarch's *Lives*, which he tried to get more than once through different agencies, other, similar items included a *Universal History* and Morgan's *Phoenix Britannica*. For more practical matters associated with his writing, accoun-tancy and surveying work, he relied on treatises such as Shaw's *Justice of the Peace* and other reference works which were more frequently lent than returned. When his memoirs ended, he was still trying, as he had been for some time, to get hold of Eaton's *Ecclesiastical Benefices* and Tanner's *Notitiae Parliamentorum*. For recent and current affairs, he relied on Salmon's *Chronology*. For lighter reading, he turned to *The Lives of Highwaymen and Pirates* and *The Secret Trials of the Old Bailey*.[74]

This was the miscellany which fed the digressions and observations with which he punctuated his chronology. Typical of these were his reflections on Useful Knowledge, placed in the account in 1697 but obviously composed much later. These were backed up by thumbnail examples beginning with Alexander the Great and ending with a star-studded, but rather indiscriminate, cast of recent English intellectual champions. 'It would swell these memoirs beyond my design and obstruct the main point I aimed at first', he wrote, reeling off such luminaries as Mead, Sloane, Newton, Whiston, the great protagonists of the Common Law, and all the Archbishops of Canterbury since the Reformation, 'if I should rehearse the great men of this present age famous for law, divinity, physic and mathematic . . . besides others in astronomy, geography and navigation, etc.'[75] 'On mean Beginnings', the rags-to-riches-but-remember-your-origins theme for 1700, did the same thing: here the examples included three popes, the emperors of China, three kings (of Sicily, Poland and Bohemia), an archbishop of Mainz, an Athenian general, Thomas Cromwell and a detailed political and military biographical sketch of the Duke of Marlborough. Another example of the same moralizing from the past was 'Choice Matters from England's Worthies' in 1740, beginning with Constantine the Great and King Arthur. Cannon's other main genre, local history and topography, has already been noticed. Here, he prided himself particularly on his expert knowledge of his own 'country', especially Glastonbury itself and its churches. This, however, led naturally to wider social descriptions, such as his 'Choice Observations' in May 1739 on popular customs, traditions and sayings in different parts of the country, which ended with a detailed drawing of a guillotine, 'the form of the execution of a malefactor at Halifax in the Wapentake of Morley in the West Riding of Yorkshire, being their bylaw'.[76] (See Plate 17.9a)

Other recurring themes were magic and astrology. Throughout his life, and not just in the sense of recording curiosities, Cannon continued to take both of these seriously. He described in detail and with matter-of-fact belief in its efficacy, the sympathetic curing of his brother's rupture by the splitting and rebinding of an ash tree in 1688. In 1703, he gave himself a nasty fright by dabbling in the occult with Thomas Reid, a farm servant, who was an adept in the philosophy of Cornelius Agrippa. It may have been his memory of this, rather than scepticism, which deterred him from enlisting a conjuror to help him find some missing horses in 1723.[77] Portents continued to frighten him: a ghost in 1716; his doppelganger, seen in fact by someone else a year later; the cricket whose chirping, corroborated by a dream, foretold his nephew's death from smallpox in 1736; the raven which circled croaking overhead before flying off in the direction of the church via the house of a sick relative in 1740; or the cormorant which alighted on the tower of St John's two years later. Witchcraft, too, was very much a part of his world, suspected at least three times in the late 1730s, when smallpox was rampant, the weather unnatural and times hard in Glastonbury, of being the direct cause of specific misfortunes.[78]

He devoured almanacs and books of astrology with singular intensity. 'Finished Merlin the British Prophecy, which I transcribed from Geoffrey of Monmouth by Aaron Thompson of Oxford' he wrote on 10 June 1740, 'which I bound or stitched up with Mother Shipton and Nixon's prophecies and titled it Triplex Valicinium.' Not counting the fourteen esoteric sources from Pliny onwards whom he listed as authorities for his digression on augury and astrology in May 1739, he cited three contemporary sources, Middleton's *Practical Astrology*, Woodward's *Astrology* and Saunder's *Astrological Judgement*. Besides the almanacs of Francis Moore, Tycho Wing, John Parker and Charles Leadbetter, the leading titles of the day, at least three other compilers were mentioned as sources for the carefully drawn and dia-grammed data for lunar and solar eclipses, occultations of Aldebaran and other planetary and sidereal phenomena which he painstakingly copied into his text. In 1738, the Aurora Borealis shared space with unexplained aerial phenomena over Bristol and Nottingham and millennial portents in Paris. John Partridges's dire celestial chronology for 1742, extrapolated from the astrological data for every calamity for the previous 760 years, followed hard on the heels of an account of violent weather 'said to be raised by magical act on account of William Daggory's wife, lately dead, and at this time visited him by reason he had not performed her desire on her deathbed'. After this, it is not surprising that the comet which terrified the western counties in March that year and the 'exceeding great light like unto the lightning but more terrible and astonishing' which descended on Glastonbury out of the west in the early morning of 21 December reduced Cannon to near incoherence:

> The effect of these and the like phenomena must be left to God alone although the curiosity of some men who pretend to unriddle such divine mysteries by affixing the cause to planetary motions but if a supernatural cause they are confounded.[79]

So far, then, there is little to distinguish the body of knowledge that Cannon assembled, whether in content, form, organization or use, from the typical categories of the previous 150 years. The only thing which may set him apart is the length to which he was prepared to go to obtain it, and this does not seem to have entailed any systematic change in his definitions of knowledge, whatever it may eventually suggest about his view of himself. The one aspect of his learning which seems to be somewhat different is his attitude to number and its uses. As a young man, the weekly task of accounting for his market-money must have given him some skill with traditional ways of reckoning, and so must his sometimes painful experiences at shacklefarthing, rattlecap and other games of chance. Until 1706, however, when he had to qualify for the Excise, his only formal experience of numbers was what he had been able to pick up on his own from Recorde's *Arithmetic* of 1551. He brought himself up to date with more recent texts, such as Cocker, Ayers and Wingate, who were 'much in request', added practical focus with Lightbody's *Art of Gauging*, and sought help from a tutor whom he soon surpassed.[80] Though he gave no details, he must have learned more, both during his excise apprenticeship and, in his own turn, as an experienced officer teaching new recruits. However good his head for figures, however, his interest in them did not go very far beyond their everyday uses. Most of his regularly copied tabulations and computations remained at the level of routine commercial calculation, occasionally amplified by sketch-maps of survey-ing jobs or the working-out of proportion-problems like that posed by the shared ownership of a load of lumber for repairs to the church roof which occupied him in October 1742.[81] Only rarely is it possible to form an impression of the methods he brought to these tasks, and then they do not convey any highly developed sense of system. In early September 1736, he cleared and surveyed a 'rhine' or rhoyne, one of the large open drains which traverse the Somerset levels, for one of his clients. It must have been quite a big job and he was clearly proud of the achievement, because it was the first which he illustrated: with a map of the drain giving its measurements down to the last fraction of an inch (see Plate 17.9c). Two days later, passing the same way again, he set himself, purely for practice apparently, to measure the land on the adjacent bank, which he did 'with a small stick which I cut from a willow tree, being four feet three and two-tenths part of an inch long'.[82] As for his methods as a teacher, he said nothing about them. The one exception to that, the copybook of numeration, multiplication and questions in vulgar arithmetic which he made up for a pupil in May 1738, says as much about what he taught and how as its dedication does about his skill in verse:

> Within this book if you'd look, you've copies twenty-two.
> Besides the sums as round they comes, full forty-nine I trow;
> Take care to write and cast aright; learn well the numeral table.
> To multiply pray do not fly; do all that you are able.
> Which when well done I shall not disdain to add more to your store;
> And think on me when this you see and time shall be no more.[83]

It would be wrong to expect too much, however. For one in John Cannon's situation, an enthusiasm for figures themselves, for simply counting things properly, performing routine calculations accurately and tabulating the results tidily for later reference and verification, whether the subject was the numbers of Protestants and Papists in Ireland, cost estimates for retiling a roof, property values and rate assessments or schedules of a client's mortgages and other bonds, is probably more significant than his failure to advance to higher or more sophisticated problems. When he measured the riverbank with his willow wand in 1736, he was only half intent on checking his previous work, which he could surely have done much more quickly and easily with the rule he must have used to measure the wand. Really, he was playing a game to test himself, by seeing if he could get the same result by a fortuitous as by a regular yardstick. Besides, Cannon did show some interest in exploring other possible applications for his abilities, like the way of estimating the size of George Whitefield's Moorfields audience from the radius of the space which it occupied which caught his eye in the newspapers in September 1739.[84] Granted, this did not really extend his mathematical ingenuity very far beyond the sort of problem which he would have faced as an exciseman, and his own contribution was confined to correcting the assumed density from nine per square yard to a more realistic four, that being the rate for soldiers standing in close order. Like many others, however, he was much exercised by the Methodist revival, of which he vehemently disapproved, and his reaction does suggest some awareness of the ways in which transferring simple and familiar quantitative procedures to current controversies could reduce them at least to a probable degree of certainty.

Similarly, Cannon's obsession with almanacs and astrology deserves more serious consideration before it is written off as merely benighted. The replacement (or rather adapted co-option) of high, cosmological astrology by Newtonian natural philosophy as the received source of 'authorized prophecy' had still not proceeded far beyond the capital, despite its incipient popularization and its consequent place in the articulation of church and gentry hegemony.[85] During Cannon's lifetime, therefore, popular and judicial astrology (respectively, the use of widely-held astral beliefs in general divination, and the performance of detailed astronomical calculations in order to cast individual horoscopes) still occupied a central place in plebeian and middling mentalities over much of the country beyond London. In this context, Cannon's keen interest in astrology looks rather different. At first sight it seems peculiarly at odds with the worldly and self-centred attitude to knowledge and its uses which he is supposed to have acquired in the Excise as a servant of the new rational state.

However, the fact that attitudes to middling astrology, though they may already have been changing in London, had barely begun to be eroded elsewhere before the 1750s, and that judicial astrology survived as an eminently respectable profession in the provinces until well into the next century, suggests the contrary: that Cannon's interest in the subject, far from being archaic or reactionary, was entirely in keeping with his situation and, in a commercial sense at least, perfectly rational. Certainly, he would have had no difficulty concurring with the opinion of his contemporary, Richard Walton of Warwick, that 'Astrology is a science no way fit or suitable for the study of a poor man; for except he be well accomplished and hath a good collection of Ancient and Modern Authors, he had better sit still'.[86] For John Cannon, who had such a collection, astrology was a proper form of useful knowledge in which he took a proper pride, having been at some pains to acquire it. There is no sign that he ever actually made money from it directly. However, he certainly knew enough both to guide his own actions, and to teach at least the rudiments of the subject.

This raises a second consideration. One important consequence of the provincial survival of popular and judicial astrology, as an examination of Bernard Capp's astrological biographies or Peter Wallis's Mathematical Bio-bibliography will show, was that a very considerable overlap continued to exist between astrology, astronomy and the practice and teaching of mathematics. The continued currency of the first of these was therefore an important vehicle for the reception of the second and third. There is no way of telling how much of the finely tuned astronomical data with which Cannon labelled his frequent celestial diagrams was the result of his own calculation and how much was simply copied. It is difficult to believe, however, that he would have copied it out unthinkingly, simply as a mechanical exercise in penmanship. If he did use his memoir-material as a teaching quarry, as its didactic tone and avowedly 'cautionary' purposes suggest, he must have understood what he was doing. By 1740, when he wrote out a comparison of several different calculations of a lunar occultation of Jupiter on 27 October, including one 'done very accurately according to the theory of Sir Isaac Newton',[87] he must certainly have acquired a good working knowledge of spherical geometry and trigonometry, which he also presumed in his reader (see Plate 17.8). Such an entry would have made little sense to him or to anyone else without it. It should, however, cause some reflection that in this, his only explicit reference to the works of the Scientific Revolution's chief architect, Newtonian theory appears not as the new light of science triumphing over the old darkness of error, but as a superior example of an ancient wisdom.

If this adds substance to Keith Thomas's caution against making easy assumptions about the nature of rationalism and its advance in eighteenth-century England, there is one further twist to be considered. Cannon's preoccupation with astrology also warns against making equally easy assumptions about the uniform continuity of an *ancien régime* mentality that can be simply described as 'traditional'. The provincial survival of popular and judicial astrology certainly argues for the persistence of a number of ideas which had been in circulation for a very long time in one form or another, as does Cannon's own place in that survival. In that sense, certainly, he saw himself, and wanted to be seen, as a supporter of the tried and true: as a trusty servant of the higher powers in church and state who would 'cherish old friends' and 'change for none new'. Yet the past heyday to which many of these ideas looked back had been in the Interregnum, and the writers of at least three of the almanacs which Cannon so industriously excerpted, Salmon, Partridge and Moore, were radical Whigs.[88] The point is somewhat speculative, but at some point this anomaly in the provenance of Cannon's own sense of tradition must have brought him into collision with the received version of

Newtonian cosmology. Having absorbed and then reincarnated in itself the final phase of high philosophical astrology, this newly promulgated orthodoxy, whose 'authorized prophets' were among the most powerful agents of a remodelled gentry cultural hegemony, now regarded what remained of the old tradition as dangerous and uncouth. Faced with such a collision, Cannon would have had either to renounce his former views and interests or resist the new orthodoxy by keeping his distance from it. Despite his own zeal for godliness and good learning and his equal denunciations of Romish superstition and methodistical enthusiasm, his frequent criticisms of modern churchmanship and justificatory expostulations of his own beliefs suggest that he chose the latter course. Certainly, this would help to explain the petty religious and ecclesiastical difficulties which dogged him for much of the time. If he had lived a generation later, one wonders whether he might perhaps have turned Wilkite, like his Wiltshire neighbour, the Chathamite astrologer Henry Season.[89]

On reconsideration, in fact, even the most traditional aspects of Cannon's knowledge and outlook begin to look different. From the little he wrote about it, for example, his school sounds quite conventional. When he first began taking pupils in the 1720s, he 'strictly adhered to the notions of a tolerable writing master and endeavoured to imbibe in youth true Christian morals and virtue'. However, what is important about the hundred Latin and English precepts 'painfully collected' out of the 1726 edition of 'Mr. Garretson's little manual entitled *The School of Manners*', with which he tried to instil these values, is less their derivation from the conduct books of Erasmian humanism, than the fact that such 'little manuals' of the civilizing process had reached rural Somerset in the 1720s.[90] Much the same could be said of the works which fuelled his appetite for topography and his 'steady and unwearied adherence to English history'. What is significant about them is not so much any element of 'new knowledge' in them, but what they suggest about the new availability of existing knowledge, and about the ways in which Cannon's pursuit of it coalesced with his own experience.

Thus, the fact that he could obtain a fair share of the historical scholarship of the previous 150 years in weekly or monthly stitches from the distributors of the country newspapers has implications, not only for his sense of the past, but also for his view of the present.[91] The former, as the copious examples from Greece, Rome, the early Fathers and the medieval church with which he illustrated his periodic moral digressions show, remained grounded in existing traditions of Sacred and Universal History. His examples and accounts of more recent people and events suggest, however, that he was beginning to move beyond this. In 1740, for example, he began his account of England's Worthies with Constantine the Great and King Arthur, and he pestered his bookseller correspondents for the works of William of Malmesbury and Geoffrey of Monmouth. Such evidence of a consuming passion for the so-called 'British' history evokes the 'divers and sundry ancient histories and chronicles' of Thomas Cromwell's preamble to the Act in Restraint of Appeals to Rome of 1534 rather than any more contemporary concern. Cannon clearly did have a special interest in that period, citing Cromwell with evident approval as an example of one who rose from mean beginnings, and on another occasion spending a guinea he could ill afford on a copy of the 1537 Great Bible, which caught his eye in Bristol, where he was supposed to be selling a consignment of books to raise much-needed cash.[92]

The important point, however, is that it was in the first half of the eighteenth century that the political message of Thomas Cromwell's famous preamble and the historical perspective on which it was based began to assume new dimensions, and that this was reflected in

Cannon's own case. Indeed, if this self-taught provincial official and writing master is any guide, the current of nationalism, whose spring Gerald Newman associates with the cultural protest of literati and artist-intellectuals in the 1750s,[93] was already running much more widely than that at least a decade earlier. Apart from the ritual protestations of loyalty with which he introduced his account of himself and his family, and some denials of imputed Jacobitism and Catholicism in the 1720s, Cannon took little notice of politics until the mid-1730s. True, this may be so simply because until then his entries were shorter and more general; but even so, one might have expected at least some reference to the changes which separated the reign of James II from the Excise Crisis, instead of the virtual silence accorded to all of them. From 1735 onwards, however, Cannon's sense of past and present came together, and his historical and topographical digressions were interspersed with political comment in the language of the patriot opposition. By now, he was reading the newspapers closely, culling them every week, not just for crimes, curiosities and sensational trivia, but for the details of foreign and domestic affairs. In July 1739, he exercised his quantitative skills on an analytical comparison of the Commons' behaviour on the Excise Bill and the Convention of Pardo which paid particular attention to the place-vote in each case. Admiral Vernon's triumph at Porto Bello was marked by a detailed sketch-plan of the attack (see Plate 17.9b), while the passing of William Wyndham, Somerset's renowned Tory MP, inspired an elegy on 'The Glory of the West'. It is also notable that more than one entry at this time explains the content of a satirical print, which suggests that the circulation and influence of this material was not confined to London, even at this comparatively early stage in its history.[94]

There are also other more general signs of change in Cannon's underlying attitudes. On 24 May 1736, for example, his impatience with the stupidity of his neighbours led him to a digression on progress which came down squarely on the side of the moderns. 'It was in drowsy times', he complained,

> when learning was at the lowest ebb that Popery and Mohametizing got foot in the world. It was in those days that astronomy, mathematics and curious mathematical performances were slandered with reproachful epithets and all ingenious improvements accounted no less than misprision of treason against the reigning monarchs. . . . The design of this is not so much to expose the ancients and disparage their acquirements as to show that while the world endures there will be occasion for a further progress in all commendable arts and sciences.[95]

A year and a half later, in January 1738, after transcribing an extract from the *Gentleman's Magazine* on smallpox inoculation, he paraphrased the theological arguments for and against it in much the same spirit, concluding after some evident difficulty that those against would, if accepted as valid, apply not only to all medical interventions but to any intentional action whatever, since all of them would have to be construed as interfering with the predestined will of God. Thus the real sin was to deny providence by not adopting a procedure which had been revealed for human use, and by refusing to accept the element of risk inherent in the human condition, in rational submission to the wise dispositions of a hidden but benevolent hand.

> So that he who inoculates for the smallpox does no more than all mankind in some measure every day do. . . . If it be a crime, it is only owing to this: that we do not behold futurity and indeed was never designed we should. But to wait

upon and be submissive in all to the Unerring Wisdom . . . in a sense may be called or accounted, as it were, an inoculation, and every man an inoculator if he projects and acts with good intentions. But the issue does not always answer expectations. It is not fit it always should. He cannot determine what is best, for the lot is cast into the cap. But the whole disposal thereof is done by an invisible hand that can justly determine.[96]

How, finally, did all this affect John Cannon's dealings with those around him, and his view of himself? Certainly he thought of himself, even from an early stage, as different, and expected others to do likewise. Recalling the premature end of his schooling, he wrote, with some exaggeration, that his

aversion to all manner of youthful pastimes and games was apparent to all that knew me, and the constant and firm adherence to books, men of letters and their conversation in those early and forward years and all my life after was a sufficient testimony to what might have been in me.[97]

Equally certainly, those around him could not have cared less most of the time. Even when he was well-established and people were paying for his services, they saw no reason why they should be like him, or emulate his knowledge, however necessary it might sometimes be to them: there was, after all, no point in keeping a dog and barking oneself. Cannon had his uses, up to a point; but beyond that he was a nuisance, especially when he set his pupils to tasks foreign to their parents' understanding, or, as parish clerk, insisted on treating the rate books, not as an alterable means at anyone's beck and call of bringing the past into line with present convenience, but as a strict record to be regularly audited against fraud and embezzlement.

Though he claimed a wide acquaintance, Cannon was thus more often resented for his knowledge than welcomed. 'Such was the hoggish nature and unmannerly behaviour of the natives of Glaston', he complained in September 1738 after a row with the mother of one of his pupils about goings-on in his school, 'that a schoolmaster or a man of letters is set at naught and a pig driver or chimney sweeper or any person resembling their own stamp is more preferable and esteemed by them.'[98] Cannon's favourite epithets for his fellow towns-people were 'illiterate' and 'ungrateful', usually applied in significant conjunction. What they knew and what he knew were clean different things. Of the latter, not even his own brother, still a farmer, wanted any part, as a dispute between them about weights and measures in different markets on 16 May 1740 shows only too clearly:

I used all the learning and skill I could but to no purpose, for he lightly disregarded me, and like an illiterate, or rather conceited and obdurate person, opposed good reason, and in his wonted haughty way flatly bade me depart his house except I would give up every argument and allow him the right, although I demonstrated the matter by the statutes, as also by arithmetical rules.[99]

Even among the other Glastonbury 'notables' – the mayor, churchwardens, other local officials and important citizens among whom he might have been expected to take a respected place – he was never really at home. In 1736 he was recommended to Sir Abraham Elton, the independent Whig MP for Bristol, as

one of the best accountants they had in those parts, that his care and indefatigable pains by his method of bookkeeping and a counterpart from his little book was to satisfy every person who was desirous to know or ask any question in their town affairs.[100]

This, however, did not stop his fellow citizens tampering with his books in order to substantiate complaints against him and justify his replacement two years later. Nor did his official position as master of the Charity School stop them disrupting his classes by setting up a maypole outside his window that spring. In July 1738, an innocent enquiry whether Mr Godwin, sometime mayor, was at the Crown Inn drew from Dr Mortimer, Glastonbury's newly arrived physician, the reply that 'I might go and see, adding [sc. asking] if I busied myself with asking questions of everybody which nettled me so'. Only when Cannon threatened to make the Doctor's 'wig walk another way' did Mortimer climb down, telling him he was 'more fitter to be a devil than a schoolmaster'. Even after this grumbling retreat, Cannon had to invoke the support of the present mayor to defend himself against similar accusations at the Crown the following evening.[101]

By degrees, however, this attitude was beginning to change. As Cannon's reputation grew, he began to be more often consulted as an expert than hired as a servant. When a petition on his behalf for his reinstatement in the Excise was turned down in 1730, he was undismayed. He had been doing some substitute work for the service and continued to do so, but he 'took it not much to heart whether restored or no'.[102] In the political climate of the 1730s, and in his situation, in fact, he was almost certainly better off out of the service than in. In any case, there was some poetic justice in the growing number of requests he was now getting from excisemen in the area who wanted their books independently checked, or the regulations explained, by someone more competent than they were. He was also attracting other clients, not only Sir Abraham Elton and his steward, but also the bailiff of the Duke of Somerset's estate at Mere.

More important than such individual commissions from the gentry and nobility, however, was the cumulative effect of Cannon's continuous involvement in the commercial, legal and personal affairs of his neighbours. They may have resented him, but gradually it dawned on them that many of the jobs for which they used him were not periodic chores which had to be left to someone else even if it was a nuisance, but everyday tasks which they might be better off doing for themselves. This showed in a number of ways. From time to time, he had tried to set up an evening school, but before 1742, there had been no takers. When he tried again, in October that year, he was able to assemble a class of ten or eleven young men who were ready to learn reading and writing for two hours a night during the ensuing winter, even though hard times and smallpox had severely reduced his normal pupils. Similarly, one of his minor jobs from time to time was now ruling and indexing account books for local shopkeepers and tradesmen – and not only preparing them, but also teaching their owners how to use them. On 12 September 1740, he

> posted and settled several bills and a book for that purpose together with an alphabet for Mr. Roger Blake and showed him the necessary use of the method of bookkeeping that way, who before was wholly ignorant of yet a man in business.

Blake, he remarked, 'was not the only dunce in this town that employed me, as instances of that kind in these memoirs manifestly abound'.[103]

However, the passage which captures most succinctly the changes that were taking place, both in John Cannon's world and in his own place in it as a mediator between past and future, is his brief, unobtrusive entry for 26 January 1742:

> Wrote for Eleanor Brook to Mrs. Bourchier at ye boarding school in Taunton whose Daughter Eleanor (sometime my scholar) was under her care, requesting her to get her a pair of Stays for her daughter for which she would content her, & under I wrote to ye maiden to be diligent.[104]

Diligence, even more than his appetite for books, or his sanguine acceptance of debt for their sake, was Cannon's fundamental quality – as much in more weighty matters as in writing out this message from an unlettered mother to the headmistress of her daughter's fashionable boarding school, asking her to get the child a necessary undergarment suitable to her new situation. As Cannon grasped soon after he left the Excise and struck out on his own, it was not necessarily wrong to borrow. What mattered was to maintain his credit by being 'honest to remit money as I could get it',[105] and the key to this was diligence. Diligence made debt manageable, turning it from an agent of corruption to an incentive to virtue. In this, Cannon's example is surely made more significant by its provincialism and smallness of scale, not less. For in such small men, and in their qualities and views, lie the missing links between the ostensibly anti-commercial politics of Neo-Harringtonian virtue espoused by the patriot opposition (to which Cannon himself subscribed), and the formation of values which could support a society which was increasingly dependent for its stability on commerce and credit. It was Frugality, he wrote on 5 July 1738, which was 'the strongest and most efficacious remedy agt. Corruption'.

> A man who knows how to manage his fortune prudently will be Independent tho' ye fortune will be but small, for having once acquired ye Art of governing himself & his affairs there will be no temptation enough strong to induce him to give up ye Liberty which he thereby possesses. Frugality is ye best Engineer for throwing up those works which are intended to keep off misfortune. A small reserve is ye best medicine in ye world. Besides, ye practice of this virtue enables a man to live upon a little if in spight of all honest precaution he should throw ye strokes of fortune and have but little left. – He who by his prudent management has acquired a small bank has it in his power to serve his friends & to do great kindness to others with no inconvenience to himself, which is one of ye highest and most rational pleasures a man can enjoy.[106]

Diligence showed as much in the pains Cannon took over his memoirs as in any of his other acts, and therefore those pains, too, bear witness to his mediation between past and future. To all outward appearances, John Cannon was the very soul of *ancien régime* tradition, a 'true loyal heart'. Nowhere was this more so than in his religion. As a devout son of the church, a strenuous servant of its worldly interests and a teacher of its precepts, he proclaimed at length his belief in its articles, deplored the laxity of its modern clergy, bemoaned the poverty of its curates and wished for the recall of Convocation.[107] He recorded week by week the text of every sermon he heard, in Latin as well as English, and prefaced every New Year (dated by his own birthday, 28 March) with an emblematic prayer of thanksgiving engrossed, as in 1740 when it was inscribed in his own initials, in some personal emblem (see Plate 17.7). Once – and his dreams were frequent, realistic and vivid – he even dreamed that he had been ordained.[108] There is, of course, nothing remarkable in itself about the importance of religion in an early modern diary or autobiography, and its omission from John Cannon's would have been much stranger than its prominence. Cannon's writings on the subject, however, were neither confessional, imaginative nor speculative. What concerned him was dogma and churchmanship: his own. It did so because he needed it to establish and defend his place in the community. For most of his career he was badgered by parish politicians. It began in 1718 when the new rector of St John's, Glastonbury, baulked at burying Cannon's first child in his family's burial ground because he had grown up on friendly terms with members of a Catholic family, though 'I might have been accounted as well of one sect as of another if only bare conversation could prevail'. In 1739, his enemies persuaded the rector to try to deprive him of his clerkship and his family's rights to a pew in St John's on grounds of non-attendance and alleged popery once more. His reply, backed up by legal opinion, was devastating. In nearly ten closely written pages, he pointed out that his wife and children lived elsewhere, which sometimes took him away, as did his work. He reviewed in detail the course of his life and conversation and the religious principles which guided them; and he quoted back at his accusers chapter, verse, text and content not only of every sermon the rector had preached in the previous three years, but also of those which he had heard elsewhere during his absences.[109] In short, his religion, so far as can be judged from his memoirs, sprang not from spiritual conviction, experience or self-examination, or even from theological enquiry. Far from being 'traditional', its orthodoxy was the factitious product of an acquired knowledge, obtained to define and defend a worldly position which was anything but traditional.

Thomas Carlyle would have had a shorter way of putting it: John Cannon's religion was a suit of clothes cut from the knowledge he consumed. Indeed, since the clothes metaphor originated not with *Sartor Resartus* but with John Selden (though he used it differently), and since it is possible that Cannon had read Selden, it is also conceivable that he may himself have had some inkling of this.[110] If so, he would also have recognized an affinity between these mental chattels and the only others, apart from his books, which he valued enough to describe in his memoirs: his cypher-seal, designed about 1725, when he was taking his first independent steps as a writing master and the tobacco box on which he had his cypher engraved thirteen years later (see Plate 17.5a). He described his seal and its authenticating signature, 'very difficult . . . to counterfeit or defeat', so that his writings could be identified by posterity even though he could not list them all himself. It contained all the letters of his name 'distinguished [by] 10 balls or spots & a cannon dismounted for ye crest'. He described the tobacco box because it carried his cypher, but also because smoking, that 'noble qualification in and towards company keeping' which he had learned in his early excise days, played an important part in his life, and the box was thus a treasured possession. Besides his cypher, it carried 'ye motto in latin & place of my nativity & year of ye Lord when I had it done'.

> On ye round of ye Circle were Decorations Such as Network. Doves & heads adorn'd on ye sides. On ye bottom a Scollop with leavidge & foldings. On ye Crest two Tulips, 2 pipes Crosswise & a Black's head with a pipe Smoking. It had a firm Spring & a hing about one Inch & 3 quarters long in wch were above 60 Joynts curiously wrought. Said to be ye Workmanship of a woman at or near Birmingham. Warwickshire, it will hold 4 ounces of Tobacco of an oval form and it cost 12s. 6d. made of Lidiate Steel well polished.[111]

According to Mary Douglas, 'goods . . . are ritual objects' and consumption a 'ritual process whose primary function is to make sense of the inchoate flux of events'. This applies as much to the world of information and knowledge as it does to that of things, since it is through access to these that the individual consumer maximizes his ability 'to construct an intelligible universe with the goods he chooses'.[112] More recently, Jean-Christophe Agnew has proposed that the shared affinities which set market and theatre apart from the common social world are historically more decisive than the difference between them, since it is the theatre which in the Anglo-American world between 1550 and 1750 served as the midwife of a 'new world of "artificial persons" ' capable of bestowing 'an intelligible albeit Protean human shape on the very *form*lessness that money values were introducing into exchange'. This, he says, helped to resolve 'the larger, more refractory questions of personal identity and accountability' raised within 'an increasingly placeless and timeless market process' by the adoption of a sophisticated, but anonymous, body of commercial instruments and contractual law.[113] It was in precisely these conditions that John Cannon got and gave out his knowledge, and from precisely these materials that he got his living and constructed his own identity. As a single and not at all wealthy consumer, his effect on the dynamics of demand was negligible; as a largely self-taught writing master and accountant in a lesser provincial town, his empirical impact on the growth of the knowledge network was probably not a lot greater; so far as one can tell he never read, nor saw a play. If the preceding propositions are true, however, his memoirs of fifty-eight years, forty of them in the market-place, 'from a schoolboy to a ploughboy, and from a ploughboy to an excise man, and from an excise man to a maltster and from a maltster to an almost nothing except a schoolmaster, so that I might be called the tennis ball of fortune', were not just a private stage for himself and his household go(o)ds. Their didactic and 'cautionary' contents, guarded at either end by the cherub (see Plate 17.5b) which he drew for them on 30 November 1742 'from a copy of Mr John Willis, sometime writing master at Orchard, County Dorset, which he had drawn from one John Brooke, his scholar, and for whom I had made his will',[114] epitomize the two-faced traditionalism of English society itself.

Table 17.1a Provenance of mathematical writing in provincial England (cf. Plate 17.1).

	1701–20	1721–40	1741–60
Home counties	7	9	7
South coast	4	6	6
Southwest	2	3	6
Midwest	4	8	10
Thames	7	8	9
South and East Midlands	2	4	5
East Anglia	8	12	9
North Midlands	3	5	8
West Midlands	3	4	4
Welsh Border	2	3	4
Mid-Northwest	3	6	8
Northwest	1	2	4
Northeast	4	8	8

Source J. P. and R. V. Wallis, *Bio-bibliography of British Mathematics and its Applications, Part 2, 1701–1760* (Newcastle-upon-Tyne, 1988).

Home counties	Kent, Middlesex, Surrey
South coast	Sussex, Hampshire and Isle of Wight
Southwest	Dorset, Devon, Cornwall
Midwest	Somerset, Wiltshire, Gloucestershire
Thames	Oxfordshire, Berkshire
South and East Midlands	Buckinghamshire, Bedfordshire, Hertfordshire, Huntingdonshire, Northamptonshire, Leicestershire, Rutland
East Anglia	Essex, Suffolk, Norfolk, Cambridgeshire
North Midlands	Nottinghamshire, Lincolnshire, Derbyshire
West Midlands	Warwickshire, Worcestershire, Staffordshire
Welsh Border	Hereford, Shropshire
Mid-Northwest	Cheshire, Lancashire, West Riding
Northwest	Cumberland, Westmorland
Northeast	Yorkshire (East and North Ridings), Durham, Northumberland

Source Wallis, *Bio-bibliography*.

Entries were originally counted by county and decade. For the sake of simplicity, the results are shown here in thirteen county groups and three periods, 1701–20; 1721–40; 1741–60, based on the average of decadal totals in each period and group. The values produced compare rates and directions of change in different parts of the country; they do not represent actual writings in any direct sense. As averages over space and time, they are of course subject to varying degrees of distortion. For example, the 'Northwest' group pairs Cumberland, which registered a significant local increase in mathematical writing, with Westmorland, remote and sparsely inhabited, where there was as yet little visible sign of it (but see Table 17.2, especially re. Kendal). The values for Cumberland alone would be 1, 3, 7, rather than 1, 2, 4. Provided these limits are borne in mind some further comparisons may be made: Edinburgh, 8, 17, 20; Glasgow, 3, 4, 8; Aberdeen 2, 5, 5; Dublin, 12, 24, 17. Comparison with London and Westminster is difficult without doing still more violence to reality, but rough equivalent values would be 58, 99, 107.

Table 17.1b Provenance of mathematical writing in the American colonies, for comparison

	1701–20	*1721–40*	*1741–60*
Massachusetts	7	11	10
Connecticut	1	2	3
Rhode Island	0	1	2
New York	0	5	5
New Jersey	2	4	1
Pennsylvania	3	12	14
Maryland	1	3	1
Virginia	0	3	1
N. Carolina	0	1	1
S. Carolina	0	2	3
Kentucky	1	1	1
Caribbean	2	4	4

Table 17.2 Mathematical practice in the English counties, cumulatively by county, 1701–60 (cf. Plate 17.2).

Entries		*Particular places named*	*Entries attributed to county at large*
1–10			
Hereford	6	1	6
Huntingdon	9	4	3
Rutland	3	1	0

Table 17.2 continued

Entries		Particular places named	Entries attributed to county at large
11–20			
Bedfordshire	14	6	7
Buckinghamshire	18	9	5
Staffordshire	20	9	5
Westmorland	18	11 (Kendal, 6 entries)	2
21–30			
Cheshire	25	10 (Chester, 10 entries; Warrington, 4)	3
Cornwall	25	11	9
Devon	29	12	0
Dorset	22	13	8
Hertfordshire	27	12	12
Wiltshire	28	11 (Salisbury, 9 entries)	5
Worcestershire	25	8 (Worcester, 15 entries)	3
31–40			
Berkshire	33	12	12
Leicestershire	35	19 (Leicester, 5 entries)	7
Middlesex	36	12 (Hampstead, 9 entries)	8
Shropshire	39	10 (Shrewsbury, 5 entries)	24
Somerset	37	14 (Bath, 11 entries)	9
41–50			
Derbyshire	41	16	21
Lincolnshire	50	19 (Spalding, 9 entries; Stamford 7; Boston 5)	12
Nottinghamshire	41	17 (Nottingham, 15 entries)	7
Oxfordshire	47	10 (Oxford, 36 entries)	2
51–60			
Cambridgeshire	52	8 (Cambridge, 38 entries)	4
Cumberland	51	26 (Whitehaven, 12 entries; Carlisle, 5)	1
Hampshire	52	13 (Portsmouth, 15 entries; Winchester, 7)	15
Norfolk	58	13 (Norwich, 15 entries; King's Lynn, 6)	21
Northamptonshire	55	26 (Northampton, 12 entries)	10
Suffolk	52	10	36
Surrey	51	18 (Richmond, 9 entries; Kingston, 5)	14
Sussex	56	13 (Chichester, 7 entries)	32
Warwickshire	58	18 (Birmingham, 21 entries; Warwick, 8)	11
61–70			
Essex	62	21	32
71–80			
Gloucestershire	77	16 (Bristol, 28 entries; Gloucester, 6)	17

Table 17.2 continued

Entries		Particular places named	Entries attributed to county at large
81–90			
Lancashire	88	21 (Liverpool, 32 entries; Manchester, 15; Lancaster, 8; Preston, 5)	8
91–100			
Durham	93	35 (Sunderland, 10 entries; Darlington, 9; Gateshead, 6)	25
Over 100			
Kent	106	30 (Canterbury, 16 entries)	45
Northumberland	131	21 (Newcastle, 77 entries; Berwick, 13; Alnwick, 9)	5
Yorkshire			
Total	160	55	14
North Riding	18	13	0
East Riding	33	10 (Hull, 12 entries)	0
West Riding	76	31 (Sheffield, 17 entries; Leeds, 9)	
Unassigned	33	1 (York, 19 entries)	14
London and Westminster	432		
Scotland	227	(Edinburgh, 103 entries; Glasgow, 24; Aberdeen, 19)	
Ireland	332	(Dublin, 86 entries; Cork, 24; Limerick, 13; Armagh, 12; Down, 11)	

Source Traceable entries in P. J. Wallis, *Index of British Mathematicians, 1701–1760* (Newcastle-upon-Tyne, 1976).

Table 17.3 Occupational descriptions of mathematical writers, 1701–60

	1701–10	1711–20	1721–30	1731–40	1741–50	1751–60
Learned professions						
Academic	22	44	59	61	70	76
Law	4	8	12	12	13	11
Medicine	23	33	44	52	63	55
Church	34	49	68	68	67	60
Total	83	134	183	193	213	202
Mathematical vocations						
Astronomer	14	18	18	23	31	29
Almanac maker	15	23	27	22	19	21
Mathematician	16	21	23	27	32	34
Cartographer	2	5	5	5	3	3
Land surveyor	18	24	28	34	39	37
Geographer	2	2	4	5	4	4
Electrician	0	0	7	10	13	12
Architect	3	4	10	16	17	17
Geologist	1	1	2	3	3	3
Total	71	98	124	145	161	160

Table 17.3 continued

	1701–10	1711–20	1721–30	1731–40	1741–50	1751–60
Teachers						
Lecturer	8	14	20	20	31	26
Teacher	1	7	12	13	11	6
Writing master	19	22	30	26	35	27
Teacher, maths	31	52	73	79	72	64
Tutor	14	13	12	14	15	10
Schoolmaster	18	16	19	15	30	27
Teacher, navigation	11	16	17	25	20	20
Teacher, accounts	9	12	11	7	11	14
Total	111	152	194	199	225	194
Artisans						
Optician/instrument maker	13	17	28	30	38	37
Engineer/mechanic	7	11	14	18	24	19
Jeweller	0	0	1	1	0	0
Shipwright	2	1	0	1	4	4
Craftsman	4	8	15	16	17	16
Bricklayer/carpenter	2	4	5	6	5	4
Farmer/gardener	5	9	8	13	14	12
Chemist/brewer	0	1	2	4	3	4
Total	33	51	73	89	105	96
Commerce						
Accountant	9	14	21	26	29	24
Merchant	8	8	4	7	10	16
Insurance	1	3	6	6	6	5
Total	18	25	31	39	45	45
Government						
Government	3	5	14	12	15	35
Customs/Excise	3	6	8	14	11	8
Total	6	11	22	26	26	43
Literature/arts						
Writer	5	7	13	15	13	15
Editor	6	8	7	12	12	9
Lexicographer	0	0	1	2	1	2
Printer/publisher	2	5	8	9	13	12
Librarian	1	3	3	3	5	5
Translator	5	7	6	12	10	8
Poet	1	1	1	3	4	5
Painter	1	2	3	2	5	7
Musician	3	2	3	3	3	3
Book trade	4	5	7	8	8	7
Total	28	40	52	69	74	73
Military						
Army	2	3	4	7	10	3
Navy	21	21	18	19	13	18
Total	23	24	22	26	23	21

Table 17.3 continued

	1701–10	*1711–20*	*1721–30*	*1731–40*	*1741–50*	*1751–60*
Other						
MP	1	5	10	7	5	7
Nobility/gentry	11	22	20	20	23	16
Total	12	27	30	27	28	23
Totals						
Learned professions	83	134	183	193	213	202
Mathematical vocations	71	98	124	145	161	160
Teachers	111	152	194	199	225	194
Artisans	33	51	73	89	105	96
Commerce	18	25	31	39	45	45
Government	6	11	22	26	26	43
Literature/art	28	40	52	69	74	73
Military	23	24	22	26	23	21
Other	12	27	30	27	28	23
Totals	385	562	731	813	900	857

Source Wallis, *Bio-bibliography*.

Notes

For Plates 17.5–9, I am grateful to the Somersetshire Archaeological and Natural History Society, who own the Cannon manuscript, and to the Library of HM Customs and Excise, who provided photocopies from their microfilm.

1 The diary of Samuel Pipe-Wolferstan of Statfold, Staffordshire, 1776–1820, is in the William Salt Library, Stafford. I have given an account of it in 'Provincialism and the English "Ancien Régime": Samuel Pipe-Wolferstan and "the Confessional State," 1776–1820', *Albion*, xxi (1989), 389–425.

2 The full couplet is 'Caesar adsum jam forte; Pompey aderat. Caesar sic in omnibus; Pompey in is at'. Besides lesson-notes on stock subjects and various practical jottings, the memorandum book compiled by Thomas White, an itinerant schoolmaster who worked in and around Bristol in the 1740s, contains several contemporary examples (Bristol Archives Office 08158).

3 'Consumption and knowledge: education, literacy and numeracy', workshop in the 'Culture and consumption' programme at the Clark Library, UCLA, 4 March 1989, at which the original version of this essay was presented.

4 Again, the allusion is as much to contemporary jargon as to eighteenth-century circumstance. The educational broadcasting authority of the Province of British Columbia, Canada, for example, which is a frequent user and imitator of Open University materials, uses this as its public name.

5 Cf. the annual list of theses completed for higher degrees in the history of education published by the History of Education Society.

6 Lawrence Stone, 'The educational revolution in England, 1560–1640', *Past and Present*, xxviii (1964), 41–80; Joan Simon, *Education and Society in Tudor England* (Cambridge, 1966); David Cressy, *Education in Tudor and Stuart England* (London and New York, 1976); idem, *Literacy and the Social Order: Reading and Writing in Tudor and Stuart England* (Cambridge, 1980).

7 The main source of this view is A. F. Leach, the Wykehamist school inspector who wrote most of the accounts of eighteenth-century schooling in the original volumes of the *Victorian County History* series, based predominantly on reports to Lord Brougham's Charity Commission between 1819 and 1837.

372   John Money

For literacy during the long eighteenth century, see R. S. Schofield, 'The measurement of literacy in preindustrial England', in Jack Goody and Ian Watt (eds), *Literacy in Traditional Societies* (Cambridge, 1968), 311–25, and 'The dimensions of literacy, 1750–1850', *Explorations in Economic History*, x, 4 (1973), 437–54; also J. M. Sanderson, 'Literacy and social mobility in the Industrial Revolution', *Past and Present*, lvi (1972), 75–104, and debate with T. W. Laqueur, *Past and Present*, lxiv (1974), 96–112. More recently and more generally, see Keith Thomas, 'The meaning of literacy in early modern England', in Gerd Baumann (ed.), *The Written Word, Literacy in Transition* (Oxford, 1986); R. A. Houston, *Scottish Literacy and the Scottish Identity, Illiteracy and Society in Scotland and Northern England, 1600–1800* (Cambridge, 1985); idem, *Literacy in Early Modern Europe: Culture and Education, 1500–1800* (London and New York, 1988).

9 W. A. L. Vincent, *The Grammar Schools: Their Continuing Tradition* (London, 1969).

10 R. S. Tompson, *Classics or Charity? The Dilemma of the Eighteenth-Century Grammar School* (Manchester, 1971).

11 N. Hans, *New Trends in Education in the Eighteenth Century* (London, 1971).

12 Geoffrey Holmes, *Augustan England: Professions, State and Society, 1680–1730* (London and Boston, 1982); John Brewer, *The Sinews of Power: War, Money and the English State, 1688–1783* (London and Boston, 1989); Penelope Corfield, *The Impact of English Towns, 1700–1800* (Oxford, 1982); Peter Borsay, *The English Urban Renaissance: Culture and Society in the Provincial Town, 1660–1770* (Oxford, 1989); Angus McInnes, 'The emergence of a leisure town: Shrewsbury, 1660–1760', *Past and Present*, cxx (1988), 53–89, and debate with Borsay, *Past and Present*, cxxvi (1990), 190–212; and see below, 345–6.

13 G. A. Cranfield, *The Development of the Provincial Newspaper, 1700–1760* (Oxford, 1963); R. M. Wiles, *Serial Publication in England before 1750* (Cambridge, 1957); idem, *Freshest Advices: Early Provincial Newspapers in England* (Columbus, Ohio, 1965); V. E. Neuburg, *Popular Education in Eighteenth Century England* (London, 1971); John Feather, *The Provincial Book Trade in the Eighteenth Century* (Cambridge, 1985).

14 Peter and Ruth Wallis, *Bio-bibliography of British Mathematics and its Applications, Part 2, 1701–60* (Newcastle-upon-Tyne, 1988), and see below, 340–3.

15 Feather, *Provincial Book Trade*, 34.

16 Ian Michael, *The Teaching of English from the Sixteenth Century to 1870* (Cambridge, 1987), 10–13.

17 J. H. Plumb, 'The new world of children in eighteenth-century England' in N. McKendrick, J. Brewer and J. H. Plumb, *The Birth of a Consumer Society: The Commercialization of Eighteenth-Century England* (Bloomington, 1982).

18 Jonathan Bate, *Shakespearian Constitutions: Politics, Theatre, Criticism, 1730–1830* (Oxford, 1989), and cf. Olivia Smith, *The Politics of Language, 1791–1819* (Oxford, 1984).

19 Equally notable is the improvement after *c.* 1750.

20 Cf. Ambrose Heal, *The English Writing Masters and Their Copybooks 1570–1800* (Cambridge, 1931). These particular examples are from a file of unshelved educational material in the Houghton Library, Cambridge, Massachusetts.

21 For *The Character of an Honest Merchant*, see Walter Minchinton, 'The merchants in England in the eighteenth century' in H. G. J. Aitken (ed.), *Explorations in Enterprise* (Cambridge, Mass., 1967), 285, 398. For the problem of reconciling a politics based on classical virtue with the realities of a commercializing society, see John Pocock, 'Authority and property: the question of liberal origins' in idem, *Virtue, Commerce and History* (Cambridge, 1985). The importance which a commercial society has customarily attached to handwriting (especially male) during the past two hundred years, not simply for its legibility, but also for what it is supposed to reveal about character and reliability, needs no particular emphasis. The ways in which 'Character', both in this sense and in its larger Victorian connotations, evolved from earlier ideas of classical virtue as the touchstone of political health and public morality bear thinking about. Cf. Stefan Collini, 'The idea of "Character" in Victorian political thought', *Royal Historical Society Transactions*, 5th series, xxxv (1985), 29–50.

22 My thanks to Neil Hitchin, my research assistant, for helping me in the preparation of the following material.

23 Average of decadal totals in each of the three periods stated, Cambridgeshire.

	Total	Number attributable to the University
1701–20	18	14.5
1721–40	19.5	16
1741–60	14	10

24 See below, 341–3.

25 Cf. J. V. Beckett, *Coal and Tobacco: The Lowthers and the Economic Development of West Cumberland, 1660–1760* (Cambridge, 1981).

26 Average of decadal totals in each of the three periods stated, Oxfordshire.

	Total	Number attributable to the University
1701–20	12.5	11
1721–40	12	8
1741–60	14	9

27 As did the totals in most categories. Whether this reflects a real decline or a peculiarity of the source, in the form of a reduction in the number of separate imprints caused by changes in the structure and dynamics of the book trade, is not clear. Signs of economic stringency during the Seven Years' War, and the increasing pressure put on provincial publishers by consortia of London booksellers who were seeking to maximize their advantage under existing copyright law, point to the latter explanation.

28 Degrees in all categories, where known: Cambridge, 97; Oxford, 81; Leyden, 27; Edinburgh, 24; Aberdeen, 20; Trinity College, Dublin, 15; Glasgow, 12; St Andrews, 12.

29 Peter Wallis, *Index of British Mathematicians, 1701–1760* (Newcastle-upon-Tyne, 1976).

30 Cf. Lorna Weatherill, *Consumer Behaviour and Material Culture, 1660–1760* (London and New York, 1988), and idem, 'The meaning of consumer behaviour in late seventeenth- and early eighteenth-century England', ch. 10 in this volume.

31 See below, 347–66.

32 *Sketchley's Bristol Directory for 1775* (Bath, 1971); *Matthews' New History of Bristol, or Complete Guide and Bristol Directory for 1793–4* (Bristol, 1794); G., T. and I. Shaw, *Liverpool's First Directory: Gore's Liverpool Directory for 1766* (Liverpool, 1907), and idem, subsequent directories for 1767, 1769, 1773 and 1774 (Liverpool, 1928–32); Elizabeth Raffald, *Manchester Directory for 1772* (Manchester, 1889; 1st edn, 1772); *Sketchley's Birmingham, Wolverhampton and Walsall Directory* (Birmingham, 1767).

33 See, for example, Cranfield, *Provincial Newspaper*, 215–16, which uses the Northampton and Norwich papers between 1720–60 and 1749–59 respectively; Plumb, 'New world' (which uses the *Ipswich Journal*, 1743–7, 1783–7); D. M. Harding, 'Mathematics and science education in eighteenth-century Northamptonshire', *History of Education*, i (1972), 139–59 (which uses the *Northampton Mercury*, selectively, 1720–90).

34 This is a condensed representation, by decade, of a longer quinquennial tabulation, for which see J. Money, 'The schoolmasters of Birmingham and the West Midlands, 1750–1790: private education and cultural change in the English provinces during the early Industrial Revolution', *Social History/Histoire Sociale* (Ottawa), xx (1976), 129–53.

35 For Birmingham's prominence as a shopping centre, see Public Record Office, Home Office Papers HO 42/7, 'Calculation of the duty on shops', Sept. 1785. This lists anticipated revenues from London and twenty-nine provincial towns, calculated from rates of between one and two shillings in the pound according to size and rental valued of individual premises. There are

significant omissions, Manchester and Norwich among them, but of the places listed, Birmingham ranks second to Bath and Bristol (combined) in number of shops, and fifth, behind Bath and Bristol, Worcester, Salisbury and Liverpool, in expected yield.

36 Wood, *Aris's Birmingham Gazette*, 26 Nov. 1764; Watson, ibid., 16 Sept. 1782; Landon, ibid., 25 June 1787, 28 Sept. 1788, 31 May 1790.

37 D. M. Harding, 'Mathematics and science education', and idem, 'Some aspects of education in Northamptonshire in the eighteenth century' (University of Newcastle-upon-Tyne, M.Ed. thesis, 1969); Frank Robinson, 'Trends in education in northern England during the eighteenth century, a biographical study' (University of Newcastle-upon-Tyne, Ph.D. thesis, 1973).

38 Bowling Green Academy, *Aris's Birmingham Gazette*, 16 Dec. 1782; Uttoxeter School, ibid., 7 April 1766.

39 Robinson, 'Trends in education'; Borsay, *English Urban Renaissance*; R. W. Unwin, 'Tradition and transition: market towns in the Vale of York, 1660–1830', *Northern History*, xvii (1981), 72–116; J. D. Marshall, 'The rise and transformation of the Cumbrian market town, 1660–1900', *Northern History*, xix (1983), 128–209; McInnes, 'Emergence of a leisure town'. In 1779 Matthew Boulton was strongly advised to send his son to Winson Green Academy near Birmingham as a parlour boarder because as a day-boy he would 'necessarily acquire a vicious pronunciation and a vulgar dialect'. A year later, still aged only 10, Matthew Robinson Boulton was sent right away to Twickenham. The schooling of James Watt Junior followed the same 'liberal and genteel plan': not because the teaching at Winson Green was bad, but because his father, exasperated by the 'insolence, sauciness and disobedience' which he seemed to be learning there, feared for his 'manners and morals'. Cf. A. E. Musson, E. Robinson, *Science and Technology in the Industrial Revolution* (Manchester, 1969), 201–3. In the 1780s, the *Birmingham Gazette* was carrying regular advertisements for several Old Boys' associations, Rugby and Repton among them.

40 Cannon's memoirs are in the Somerset Record Office, Taunton. For James Lackington, 1746–1815, see his *Confessions* and *Memoirs* (New York, 1974); McKendrick, Brewer and Plumb, *Birth of a Consumer Society*; R. G. Landon, 'Small profits do great things: James Lackington and eighteenth-century bookselling', *Studies in Eighteenth Century Culture*, v (1973–4), 387–99. Lackington was born in Wellington, Somerset, four years after Cannon's memoirs ended, and spent his early years in circumstances very similar to Cannon's. The two had much in common, not least their combination of thrusting individualism and caution, and their ambivalence towards Methodism.

41 Cannon, 'Memoirs', fol. 2.

42 Though there are no references to Defoe in the Memoirs, several aspects of them recall Robinson Crusoe and his creator.

43 Margaret Spufford, *Small Books and Pleasant Histories: Popular Fiction and its Readership in Seventeenth Century England* (London, 1981).

44 J. C. D. Clark, *English Society 1688–1832: Ideology, Social Structure and Political Practice during the Ancien Régime* (Cambridge, 1985).

45 Cannon, 'Memoirs', fols 13, 15, 25.

46 David Underdown, 'The problem of popular allegiance in the English Civil War', *Royal Historical Society Transactions*, 5th series, xxxi (1981), 68–94; idem, *Revel, Riot and Rebellion: Popular Politics and Culture in England, 1603–1660* (Oxford, 1985).

47 Cannon was not fond of his sister, whose every whim, as 'her Mother's Minion & Chief favourite, Cabinet Councell, privy purse and Sole Adviser', had, he thought, been indulged to his and his brother's detriment (Cannon, 'Memoirs', fol. 40). Nevertheless, he himself did not hesitate to dispose of a gold signet ring which had come to him from his mother's family when the Excise transferred him back to Somerset from Berkshire in 1714, and he ran out of money in Salisbury on his journey west (fol. 125). It is not clear whether he sold it outright, or merely pawned it, which would have been more consistent with his own professed values. Whatever their intrinsic value as heirlooms, however, rings were clearly regarded as a conveniently portable form of liquifiable asset

and collateral. Like today's gold credit cards, this no doubt enhanced, rather than detracted from their attractiveness as personal ornaments.

48 Cannon, 'Memoirs', fols 30, 41, 42; cf. Spufford, *Small Books*; V. E. Neuburg, *The Penny Histories* (London, 1968); idem, *Popular Education in the Eighteenth Century* (London, 1971).

49 Cannon, 'Memoirs', fol. 42.

50 Susannah, whose parents were dead, had been brought up by her uncle, a Southwark carman. Cannon met her in 1711, when she was 18, and in service at Watlington.

51 For Cannon and his girlfriends, cf. Cannon, 'Memoirs', fols 85–100, *passim*. He had to face down a bastardy suit before he shook Lais off.

52 There are several instances which suggest that this was by no means a male characteristic or preserve.

53 Lawrence Stone, *The Family, Sex and Marriage in England, 1500–1800* (London and New York, 1977).

54 cf. Brewer, *Sinews of Power*.

55 Cannon, 'Memoirs', fols 88–90 and Brewer, *Sinews of Power* 104–5, 109.

56 Cannon, 'Memoirs', fol. 80.

57 ibid., fols 90, 95.

58 ibid., fols 97, 105–9.

59 ibid., fol. 94. One does not know which to admire most: his sharp eyes and ears, which had led him to the fawn on his morning walk three weeks earlier; his ready and observant copying of the keeper's own method of immobilizing the animal so as to fatten it for slaughter; his plausibility in persuading another keeper at the supper to give him an alibi by vouching that the fawn was a lawful gift, or the aplomb with which he stuck to his story and bluffed his way out of trouble.

60 ibid., fols 115, 116.

61 For general conditions of service in the Excise, see Brewer, *Sinews of Power*, 102–10. The 'country excise' was organized in collections, roughly corresponding to the counties, and below that in divisions. Upon posting to a division excisemen were assigned either to a 'footwalk' or to an 'outride'. To prevent fraud, they were regularly 'removed' either to another assignment in the same division, or to another division or collection altogether. Footwalks were generally preferred to outrides, which were apt to entail long days on the road away from home base. Assignments were not supposed to be made by seniority, or to be influenced at all by personal considerations. Nevertheless, Cannon's experience suggests that in some divisions, at any rate, officers with some standing in the service expected informally to have first pick of the footwalk assignments. It is also clear that the favour or disfavour of the divisional supervisor could make the difference between assignments which left a man some time for his own private or domestic concerns and those which did not. Despite the rigorous formal procedures of the service, informal jostling for such favour was part of excise life and of the way in which the service was locally managed.

62 ibid., fol. 148.

63 ibid., fol. 148.

64 ibid., fol. 293.

65 ibid., fol. 414.

66 ibid., fol. 145.

67 ibid., fols 151, 158.

68 ibid., fol. 170.

69 Cf. Julian Hoppit, 'The use and abuse of credit in eighteenth-century England', in N. McKendrick and R. Outhwaite (eds), *Business Life and Public Policy, Essays in Honour of David Coleman* (Cambridge, 1986), 64–78.

70 Cannon, 'Memoirs', fol. 170.

71 ibid., fol. 197.

72 ibid., fol. 343. For Edward Cave's general business activities, cf. Feather, *Provincial Book Trade*. Thomas Warren, proprietor of the shortlived *Birmingham Journal*, was Samuel Johnson's first

employer before he went to London and began writing for Cave. Cave and Warren were also heavily involved in Lewis and Paul's unsuccessful cotton roller spinning venture of 1739. Cf. Peter Mathias, 'Dr. Johnson and the business world', in idem, *The Transformation of England: Essays in the Economic and Social History of England in the Eighteenth Century* (London, 1979), 295–317.

73 Cannon, 'Memoirs', fol. 197.

74 ibid., fol. 202.

75 ibid., fol. 35.

76 ibid., fol. 482. He did not call it that, of course, but what he drew is unmistakably the instrument to which Dr Guillotine was to give his name in 1793.

77 ibid., fols 52–3, 159.

78 ibid., fols 246, 262–3, 555–9, 627, 678.

79 ibid., fols 399, 471–3, 557, 627–33, 696.

80 ibid., fols 64–5. For numeracy and its historical problems, see Keith Thomas, 'Numeracy in early modern England', *Royal Historical Society Transactions*, 5th series, xxxvii (1987), 103–32.

81 Cannon, 'Memoirs', fol. 682.

82 ibid., fols 247–8.

83 ibid., fol. 367.

84 ibid., fol. 513.

85 For the changing status of Astrology, see K. V. Thomas, *Religion and the Decline of Magic* (London, 1971), chs 10–12; Bernard Capp, *Astrology and the Popular Press, English Almanacs, 1500–1800* (London, 1979); Patrick Curry, *Prophecy and Power, Astrology in Early Modern England* (Princeton, NJ, 1989).

86 Quoted in Curry, *Prophecy and Power*, 105.

87 Cannon, 'Memoirs', fol. 581.

88 Curry, *Prophecy and Power*, 79–91.

89 ibid., 126.

90 Cannon, 'Memoirs', fols 162–5; Norbert Elias, *The Civilizing Process*, tr. E. Jephcott (Oxford, 1982).

91 K. V. Thomas, *The Perception of the Past in Early Modern England* (London, 1983).

92 In November 1741, on the credit of a consignment of books which he had catalogued and sent for sale to Felix Farley, the Bristol bookseller and newspaper owner, he borrowed £1–5s. to buy beef and physic for his youngest boy, who was suffering from the itch. Eventually, over Christmas, he had to walk to Bristol to sell the books himself. They fetched eight guineas, one of which he promptly laid out on the Great Bible. Cannon, 'Memoirs', fols 620–30.

93 Gerald R. Newman, *The Rise of English Nationalism, 1740–1830* (London and New York, 1987).

94 Cannon, 'Memoirs', fols 484, 530, 539, 544, 651, 693. Cf. Kathleen Wilson, 'Empire, trade and popular politics in mid-Hanoverian England: the case of Admiral Vernon', *Past and Present*, cxxi (1988), 74–109; Nicholas Rogers, *Whigs and Cities: Popular Politics in the Age of Walpole and Pitt* (Oxford, 1989), ch. 7.

95 Cannon, 'Memoirs', fol. 230.

96 ibid., fol. 324.

97 ibid., fol. 35.

98 ibid., fols 399–400.

99 ibid., fols 553–4.

100 ibid., fol. 240.

101 ibid., fol. 381.

102 ibid., fol. 187.

103 ibid., fol. 577.

104 ibid., fol. 629.

105 ibid., fol. 170.

106 ibid., fol. 377; cf. Pocock, 'Question of liberal origins'.

107 ibid., fol. 264.

108 And that he was besieged in St John's Church (ibid., fols 564 and 569: 12 July, 3 Aug. 1740). Some time later, however, he also dreamed of having 'carnal relations' in the church porch with Jane Bond, in waking life an eminently respectable matron. Not surprisingly, this left him embarrassed and confused (ibid., fol. 629, 26 Jan. 1743).

109 ibid., fols 443ff.

110 'Religion is like the fashion, one man wears his doublet slashed, another laced, another plain, but every man has a doublet. Every man has his religion, we differ about trimming.' *The Table Talk of John Selden*, ed. Sir Frederick Pollock (London, 1927), 117.

111 Cannon, 'Memoirs', fol. 172.

112 Mary Douglas and Baron Isherwood, *The World of Goods: Towards an Anthropology of Consumption* (London, 1978), 65, 95.

113 Jean-Christophe Agnew, *Worlds Apart: The Market and the Theatre in Anglo-American Thought, 1550–1750* (Cambridge, 1986), x, xi and esp. ch. 3.

114 Cannon, 'Memoirs', fols 161, 690.

Part V

The consumption of culture: books and newspapers

18

The book trade in eastern Europe in the seventeenth and early eighteenth centuries

Iaroslav Isaievych

The history of book printing is a well-established scholarly discipline. Much less studied is the history of the book trade, although its importance for both economic and intellectual development can hardly be overestimated. The gradual conversion of books into commodities was always a landmark in the cultural evolution of society. This process was rarely studied in the general European context, and in those cases when it was, eastern European material was not included.

The present chapter is devoted mainly to the history of book publishing and the book trade in three east Slavic countries: Russia, Byelorussia and the Ukraine. For comparison, material related to their eastern European and central European neighbours is also taken into consideration.

The political situation in the region had a tremendous impact on the character of its culture. Only Russian culture developed in the framework of an independent state, which was known in Western and Central Europe as Muscovy. The Ukraine and Byelorussia were included in the political system of the Polish–Lithuanian Commonwealth where Roman Catholicism became a state religion. The Orthodox and even the Uniate churches were discriminated against, which led to the deterioration of the status of Ukrainian and Byelorussian cultures. If in Russia printing was organized by the state, in the Ukraine and Byelorussia it was a part of a cultural activity to which foreign authorities were indifferent and sometimes hostile. In a new polity – the Cossack Hetmanate, which eventually comprised Kiev and the Left-bank part of the country – the position of Ukrainian culture improved in the second half of the seventeenth century.

The initial period of the history of eastern European printing roughly coincides with the so-called greater seventeenth century, including the last decades of the sixteenth century and the early years of the eighteenth century. Only in the last quarters of the sixteenth century was printing firmly established in all parts of the region.[1] We take the beginning of the eighteenth century as the end of the period because of the important changes in book publishing which occurred at that time: the split of Russian printing into 'church' and 'civil-letter' printing, and the introduction by the authorities of the Russian Orthodox Church of the strict censorship on books published in the Ukrainian Hetmanate.

In Russia books were published in Church Slavonic in the Cyrillic alphabet. In Byelorussian and Ukrainian printing, Church Slavonic also prevailed, but Cyrillic books were published in the Ruthenian language as well.[2] There was also printing in the Latin alphabet, predominantly for books in Latin and Polish. The Cyrillic printing of east Slavic peoples had much in common with the printing of the Orthodox South Slavs. On the other hand, the Latin-alphabet book production of the Ukraine and Byelorussia was closely connected with the printing industry of central European countries. It is important to stress that the Latin and Polish languages were used for writing and printing not only by the Polish minority in the Ukraine and Byelorussia but also by Ukrainian and Byelorussian authors who opposed Polish rule in their countries. The Hebrew-language printing in the region did not make its first steps until the end of the seventeenth century.

Before the establishment of indigenous printing there were two major categories of books on the market: manuscript books of local and foreign origin and printed books, all of which were imported from abroad. After the introduction of printing in the east Slavic countries, the competition began between domestic and foreign books, which led to the delineation of their spheres of influence. The patterns of this delineation varied in individual countries according to their cultural traditions and models.

Russian printing during the period under review remained a state monopoly. From the very beginning of printing until 1711 in the vast realm of the tsars, there was only one printing shop of any importance, that of the *Gosudarev pechatnyi dvor* (Tsars' Printing Court) in Moscow, near the Kremlin wall.[3] The attempts to establish printing presses in other places were without any real consequence. The high degree of centralization of book production favoured a great increase of the size of the only publishing enterprise in the country. In 1617–19, the Moscow Printing Court still had a staff of only 15, but by 1624 the figure grew to 98 and by 1642 to 150. In the Ukraine, Byelorussia and Lithuania only the largest printing shops (those of the Kiev Caves Monastery, the Vilnius Jesuit Academy and some others) could afford to have 12–15 workers. For comparison, the following data is useful: in Prague only the famous firm of Melantrich had 25–30 workers and all other printing enterprises maintained staffs of 2–3. In Paris and Lyon printing shops with 15–20 workers were considered large. Froben with 15–20 workers and Plantin with his 150–60 were rare exceptions.[4]

The eminent Soviet Russian scholar N. P. Kiselev characterized the entire Russian printing of the seventeenth century as a 'mere multiplying of traditional liturgical texts', work which according to him was virtually mechanical and did not involve any intellectual activity.[5] This judgement is too severe. It is true that some 95 per cent of all books published were of religious content: liturgical texts, prayer books, later also theological treatises. But in pre-secular society religious texts were used as a means of expressing political, philosophical and sociological concepts. Bitter and sometimes quite sophisticated theological controversies were connected with political and social conflicts and should be considered, contrary to Kiselev's view, as a kind of intellectual activity, even if its forms were extremely archaic. It should be added that most books devoted to religious matters were accompanied by epilogues and sometimes prefaces, some of which were important as an embryonic form of political discourse.[6] A certain movement towards modernization of cultural patterns began when alongside liturgical and prayer books, so-called *chetii knigi*, books designed principally for home reading, began to be printed. The first of such books were a two-volume *Prolog* (abridged biographies of saints) which was published in 1640–3 from an old manuscript and

John Chrysostom's *Margarit* reprinted in 1640–1 from the 1595 edition of the Ukrainian Ostrih press. Soon after that the first truly secular Russian books appeared: *Uchenie i khitrost' ratnogo stroeniia* (translation of Wallhausen's work on military science) in 1647–9, *Ulozhenie* (code of law) in 1649. In the first half of the seventeenth century the Moscow press published twelve non-liturgical titles[7] and in the second half of the century there were thirty-eight of them. So, the trend was in the direction of secularization, but the movement remained very slow.

The clerks of the tsar's 'Department of Book Printing Affairs' (*Prikaz knig pechatnogo dela*) kept very accurate records of all expenditures for the printing of every book as well as a list of buyers. From those records, which are now in the Central State Archives of Ancient Arts in Moscow, it is evident that the cost of book production remained high during all of the seventeenth century. Nearly half of the expenses were used to buy paper, and the salaries of the staff took approximately a third of the enterprise's budget. Although the records are preserved only from 1618, they give us good insight into the changing attitudes of the authorities towards pricing policy.[8] It is certain that Moscow's Printing Court was organized for the interest of the Russian state and church and not for commercial reasons. One of the main motives for establishing printing was to introduce uniformity in the church ritual as a part of centralizing policy of the government.[9] So some quantities of the books printed were sent gratis to monasteries and churches, especially to those in remote provinces. Large consignments of books were dispatched to local authorities for compulsory distribution among parishes which were obliged to pay for them. For several decades most printed books were sold at production cost. After the fire of 1634, the price of most books was increased to finance reconstruction work. But only in the 1640s did the government decide to transform the Printing Court into a commercially oriented and profitable enterprise. The addition to the net cost (*natsenka*) was larger if there was great demand for it.[10] In 1648 the price of Meletii Smotrytskii's grammar (a reimpression of the book first published by a Byelorussian printing shop in 1619) was 50 kopeks per copy, which was one and a half times the net cost of the book. In 1648 the price of the law code was one ruble per copy, that is, 161 per cent of the net cost.

In spite of such high prices the rate of sales was usually high. In 1651 the entire print run of the primer which was 2,394 copies was sold during the very first day of sale. In total, probably more than 300,000 primers printed in Moscow were sold in the second half of the seventeenth century. John Chrysostom's *Margarit* was one of the most expensive books, its selling price being two and a half rubles. Nevertheless on the first day 161 copies were sold and almost as many on the following days. Buyers were people of various stations: burghers, nobles, clergymen and peasants. Many of them were from outside Moscow, sometimes from remote towns and even villages. Some names in the records are accompanied by indications that the purchasers were tradesmen of various specialties: people from 'Clothes Lane', 'Greengrocer's Lane', 'Hardware Lane' and so on. There is no doubt that they, alongside trade with other merchandise, were involved in the resale of books. Towards the end of the seventeenth century, a specialized 'Booksellers Lane' appeared in the centre of Moscow. The booksellers were active also at yearly fairs in various towns and monasteries.

The people who bought books at the Printing Court resold them mostly to those burghers, peasants and communities who purchased the books to donate them to the parish and monastery churches. On many copies of early imprints preserved in libraries, churches and private collections, there are inscriptions of buyers, owners and donors. The most usual was the buying–donation formula, something like the following:

> In the name of the Holy Trinity. I . . . peasant of the village of . . . together with my family bought this sacred book from . . . with my own money . . . rubles and donated this book to the church in the village of. . . . All priests and deacons of this church should pray for the salvation of my and my family's souls. Anyone who dares remove this book from the aforesaid church should be anathemized and excommunicated.

Sometimes there was an addition: 'As I am not literate, the book was inscribed by . . . [usually by a local priest or deacon].' Even non-liturgical books were often donated to churches. Presumably for illiterate buyers, any book in Church Slavonic was associated mainly with religious ritual.

The threat of excommunication could not stop those who wanted to sell books for profit. Liturgical books more often than not are not found in those churches to which they were donated. Many books contain inscriptions about several consecutive sellings and the prices usually rose in rubles from sale to sale. But when we take into account the changing value of money, the conclusion is that the real price of books was falling steadily. The main cause of this was the fact that after most churches were provided with necessary books, the demand significantly dropped. In 1667 some of the printing press employees were dismissed because 25,000 rubles' worth of books in little demand were piled in storage.

In remote areas, especially in Siberia, the prices were initially higher but towards the end of the century, they approached the level of prices in the central part of Russia. This was the result of increased deliveries of books from Moscow to the provinces of the Russian state.

As can be seen, in Russia primary sale of new religious books was monopolized by the state publishing house. Books purchased there were resold further by the wholesale merchants as well as by accidental buyers. Although many restrictions and regulations of the market by authorities remained, the attitude to books as merchandise was firmly established during the seventeenth century.

In his detailed study of eighteenth-century Russian printing, Gary Marker came to the conclusion that the lay publishing activity of the country's rulers was not carried out in response to market conditions or popular demand.[11] Nevertheless, as far as religious book publishing in the seventeenth century is concerned, the widespread dissemination and republication of the same titles in most cases is evidence of the popularity and spontaneous demand for literature of this kind.

The organizational structures of the Ukrainian and Byelorussian printing industries and book trades were much more diversified. There existed at least four main categories of printing enterprises. First of all, there were private presses owned by merchants and printers themselves. Printing presses of Byelorussian merchants Mamonichi in Vilnius, Michael Sl'ozka in Lviv (Lvov) and Maxim Voshchanka in Mahileu (Mogilev) had permanent addresses. But most private printers were travelling craftsmen, *Wanderdrucker*, as the Germans called them. Ivan Fedorov himself, Zaprozhian Cossack Tymofiy Verbyts'kyi, Byelorussian burgher Spiridon Sobol, Orthodox monks Pavlo Domzhyv Lutkovych Telytsia and Sylvestr, the Poles Daniel of Leczyca and Jan Szeliga – all of them were typical itinerant printers. They had to make their enterprises profitable in order to obtain money for further activity. But they were not mere men of business: they certainly connected profit-making with an ideological programme – to preach the 'true faith', to disseminate education and first of all spiritual enlightenment.

The second category is represented by publishing houses owned by magnates: the Ostrih publishing house owned by the most influential Ukrainian noble Prince Constantine Basil Ostrozhskyi and several presses of Lithuanian and Byelorussian Protestant magnates (those in Brest, Nesvizh and others). Only ideological aims were important for their wealthy owners. Most of the printing presses of this type were connected with confessional schools and were administered by the literary–scholarly circles such as the famous Ostrih academy. Professor I. N. Golenishchev-Kutuzov had considered the Ostrih academy to be an ancestor of all east Slavic universities.[12] Perhaps it can also be called the ancestor of all east Slavic scholarly institutions. Thus, the cultural and political interests of the owners and their advisers were reflected in their publishing activity.

The third category is represented by publishing enterprises of the Orthodox confraternities. The most famous and prolific among them were the presses of the Lviv and Vilnius Confraternities. Printing presses were also owned by the Mahileu Epiphany Confraternity and by the Peremyshl' Trinity Confraternity. We do not know of any book published by the latter. Perhaps the Peremyshl' Confraternity press was used for the printing of engraved icons only. The Lviv Confraternity press during the first period of its activity served mainly educational and ideological purposes, publishing textbooks, political pamphlets and literary works. During the second quarter of the seventeenth century the Confraternity press turned into a commercial enterprise and published almost exclusively liturgical texts.

The fourth and the last category was monastery printing presses. For Byelorussian culture, the most important were the press of the Vilnius Holy Spirit Monastery and its branch in Vevis (Evie). In the Ukraine, besides little presses like those in Luts'k and Kremianets' there was one exceptionally large printing house – that of the Kiev Caves Monastery. It published not only liturgical works but also political pamphlets and dramatic and poetic works by teachers and students of the Kiev Mohyla Academy. Pamvo Berynda's Slavic–Ruthenian lexicon, as well as the *Lithos* and *Confession of the Orthodox Faith* by Metropolitan Peter Mohyla were published there.

Today we have evidence about the existence between 1574 and 1648 of not less than twenty-five printing presses in the Ukraine. They were situated in seventeen localities: seven in villages, the rest in cities and towns. Lviv alone had in various times twelve presses. Of twenty-five printing presses, seventeen were owned by Orthodox Ukrainians and produced books mainly in Church Slavonic and Ukrainian (Ruthenian), six enterprises were owned by Polish Roman Catholics, one by Armenians and one by Protestants.[13] In the Grand Duchy of Lithuania, which included Byelorussian and Lithuanian lands, at least twenty-two presses were active in 1569–1648 (eleven Orthodox, one Uniate, four Roman Catholic, three Protestant and three which published both Protestant and Catholic books). Among them eleven were located in Vilnius, the rest divided between fourteen towns.[14] During the second half of the seventeenth century, most printing shops owned by private persons ceased to exist both in the Ukraine and Byelorussia. The leading role was assumed by presses of monasteries and other religious institutions. In the Ukraine they were responsible for more than three-quarters of all titles published from 1651 through 1700. Similar change, quite understandable in the context of the victorious Counter-Reformation, was also characteristic for printing industries of Poland, Bohemia and some other neighbouring countries.

The decentralized structure of Ukrainian and Byelorussian printing largely contributed to the diversity of book production, especially in the early decades of the seventeenth century. But at the same time, most presses, particularly those belonging to the itinerant craftsmen, were very small. The vast majority of books were published by several large enterprises only. For example, in the Ukraine, during the period 1574–1648, 69.9 per cent of the total volume of pages of books was produced by four publishers (29.8 per cent by the Kiev Caves Monastery, 21.7 per cent by the Lviv Confraternity, 12.1 per cent by Prince Constantine Ostroz'kyi and 6.3 per cent by Michael Sl'ozka). In the second half of the seventeenth century 35 per cent of all titles published in the Ukraine came from the Kiev Caves Monastery press, 25 per cent from presses in Chernihiv Orthodox eparchy.

On the Byelorussian territory in the second half of the seventeenth century, only three printing shops were active: those of the Orthodox burgher Maxim Voshchanka in Mahileu (1693–c. 1707), of the Uniate Basilian monastery in Suprasl' (1695–7 and from 1715 on) and of the Radziwiłł family in Sluck (c. 1670–88). In Vilnius only the Jesuit Academy printed books in the second half of the seventeenth century.

Although in Lithuania, Byelorussia and the Ukraine together, print shops were active in thirty-two localities until the middle of the seventeenth century, only the largest cities such as Vilnius,[15] Lviv and Kiev developed into large centres of the book industry and trade. The causes of this were mainly economic: the availability of qualified craftsmen and better market possibilities.

The importance of economic factors was ever increasing during the seventeenth century. Initially, the most important printing presses were organized principally as means of achieving some cultural or ideological goals. For example, the Lviv Confraternity press printed school textbooks, poems by Ukrainian authors and political pamphlets. The Kiev Caves Monastery published a monumental edition of John Chrysostom's commentaries on Acts and Epistles,[16] a book which certainly could not expect commercial success. But when such books did not bring a profit and the initial capital (which often was collected from donations) was exhausted, the publishers had to switch to the more profitable works. In these conditions the only books which could guarantee stable returns were the books for church usage. Due to the scarcity of liturgical books in many churches, the parishioners and donors were willing to pay even very high prices. For example, production costs of Apostol of 1639 from Lviv Sl'ozka's press were 3.5 *zloty*, but the book was sold by the publisher at 12 *zloty* per copy and was resold by secondhand dealers as high as 15–36 *zloty* per copy. The prices of manuscripts of the same book were at this time only 6–10 *zloty*.

The willingness of buyers to pay more for printed books than for manuscripts proves that imprints already were considered more authoritative and prestigious than handwritten volumes. On the other hand, the quite disproportionately high level of selling prices was possible only in conditions of a semi-monopoly of printers related to the vastness of the market. Some church hierarchs, institutions and private printers even tried to turn this semi-monopoly into full monopoly. For example, the Lviv Confraternity, using bribes and 'donations', obtained privileges from the Polish kings and the Orthodox hierarchy in order to eliminate other Ukrainian printers from the city. The Orthodox Metropolitan of Kiev Peter Mohyla excommunicated Sl'ozka for printing the Missal before Mohyla sold out his edition of this book. If eliminating competitors proved impossible, large publishers sometimes concluded agreements on dividing the market.

Only large publishers, such as the Lviv Confraternity and the Kiev Caves Monastery, had regular bookstores attached to their printing shops. Books from those stores were purchased by individual buyers as well as by wholesale merchants who later sold these books at higher prices. For virtually all such merchants, books were only secondary articles sold alongside more profit-making goods. Fairs played an essential role in the book trade as they did in all commerce at that time. Not only liturgical texts but also sermons and religious books used in schools were sold in increasing quantities. Some merchants sold also non-religious books of Ukrainian and Byelorussian publishers, but among them only primers – due to their great print-runs – were of some economical significance.[17] Some non-religious books could be profitable for printers only because authors or their patrons paid for production expenses. Panegyrics and books with panegyrical prefaces often brought reward to authors or publishers from persons to whom these books were dedicated. Sometimes the customers picked up only some of the copies of the book ordered and the rest was sold by the printer. Nevertheless, for most publishers the returns from secular books were minimal in comparison with profits from religious literature.

The profitability of liturgical book printing largely contributed to the changing in the thematic composition of book production. In the Ukraine in 1586–1615, liturgical texts constituted 13 per cent of all titles published and 41 per cent of all printed pages. During the next thirty years, from 1616–45, the proportion of liturgical titles grew to 44 per cent and their page volume reached 66.7 per cent of the total. This occurred mainly at the expense of educational and political literature. Similar trends were characteristic for Byelorussian printing as well. Virtually all books published in Lithuania, Latvia and Estonia were of religious content and were published to propagate the Catholic or Protestant faiths.

Due to the slow rate of sale, even very high prices of liturgical and prayer books could not provide publishers with sufficient returns to buy large stocks of paper for the next editions. This compelled printers to look for additional sources of earnings. For example, Ivan Fedorov was engaged as an administrator of monastery estates in Derman' and tried to make and sell cannons to European monarchs. Michael Sl'ozka traded not only in books but also in cloth and other merchandise. The availability of large reserve funds not affected by market fluctuations eventually helped church institutions to oust burgher-owned enterprises from the scene.

So the concentration of book production which could not be achieved through the orders of the church administration or civil authorities occurred as a result of gradual elimination of small publishers by the largest firms in worsening market conditions. Only initially when the needs of churches for books had not yet been met was there place enough for both large and small enterprises. Once the demand fell, only comparatively large or at least medium-sized printing shops managed to hold their ground. To achieve their goals, the richest and most influential firms used not only economical mechanisms but also non-economical means of pressure. Due to the limited subject-range of printing in Russia, Byelorussia and the Ukraine, the activity of printers could not eliminate hand-copying of books. It is assumed that the total number of copies of books printed in Russia in the seventeenth century exceeded the absolute number of hand-copied ones.[18] But it is quite certain that the number of titles of manuscript books was many times larger than the number of titles of imprints. This applies also to the Ukraine and Byelorussia, although many more titles were published there. In Russia large monastery scriptoria continued to exist not only in the seventeenth century but also in the eighteenth and even the nineteenth centuries. In the Ukraine and Byelorussia most monasteries were small and could not conduct large-scale production of manuscripts. The copying of books was rather decentralized: manuscripts were copied by village priests and deacons, itinerant students and teachers, sometimes also by burghers and even peasants. If in Russia there existed market-oriented scribes, they were not typical for the Ukraine and Byelorussia. In most cases manuscripts were copied for one's own usage or on the orders of persons or congregations. The selling of second-hand manuscripts was much more widespread than the selling of new ones. Not only manuscripts but printed books also served as originals for copying. For example, Cyril Trankvilion-Stavrovets'kyi's *Zertsalo bohoslovii* (*The Mirror of Theology*), which was published in 1618 in Pochaïv and in 1692 in the Univ monastery, was copied through the seventeenth and eighteenth centuries in various parts of the Ukraine and Russia. No less than thirty handwritten copies of this book are known to exist and this figure is only preliminary.[19] This is but one example, but more examples could be cited. Thus it is evident that printers were not willing to print in sufficient quantities even those non-liturgical Cyrillic books which were in high demand. The main reason for this was the absence of a functioning system of selling such books.

Indigenous books, printed and manuscripts, were only a small part of books read. The Cyrillic Church-Slavonic books were used in all countries of the *Slavia Orthodoxa*, which facilitated the influx of such books from one country to another. Books written and printed in the Ukraine and Byelorussia were popular in Russia. The Bible published in 1581 in the Ukrainian town of Ostrih spread widely through the Russian state.[20] In 1584 the Mamonichi, Byelorussian merchants who owned the printing press in Vilnius had a shop in Moscow, where they presumably also sold books. In the 1620s, Moscow Patriarch Filaret banned the 'Lithuanian' (i.e., Ukrainian and Byelorussian) books and some of them were even burned. But such repressive measures could not stop the trade of imported books. In the second half of the seventeenth century, the influx of the books printed in the Ukraine into Russia increased noticeably. On the other hand the liturgical books from the Moscow press were considered very authoritative in the Ukraine and Byelorussia and some of them were even reimpressed there. It is known also that many manuscript books of south Slavic origin continued to circulate in Russia, Byelorussia and the Ukraine during the seventeenth century and even later. The most numerous were liturgical texts, patristic and hagiographic works of Byzantine and south Slavic authors.

Much more diversified were Latin-alphabet books, most of them in the Latin language, which were imported to eastern Europe from the west. After the so-called printing revolution in western Europe, the amount of books available to readers in the Ukraine and Byelorussia increased tremendously. The significance of this fact can hardly be overestimated. Already in the late fifteenth and early sixteenth centuries, imported books were sold at fairs in large cities in the western parts of the Grand Duchy of Lithuania and the Ukraine. Many bookbinders specialized in the foreign book trade. In the second half of the seventeenth century, some twenty bookbinders worked in Vilnius alone. In 1677, they procured a confirmation of their old privileges, according to which heretics and merchants, as well as bookbinders from other towns were forbidden from the book trade. The reinstitution of such restrictive measures proves that bookselling by unauthorized persons continued. In the sixteenth century in Lviv there were already booksellers (*bibliopolae*) who specialized in the book import business: Peter from Poznan (died 1554), Hanus Bricker (died 1573), Balthasar Hybner (died 1591). Inventories of books which remained after their deaths are an important source to the history of the imported book trade. Of great importance are also the inventories of books owned by Lviv burghers, which are preserved in the city archives. Analysis of forty-three known inventories from the years 1560–1653 shows that the most numerous were books published in the Latin language in Cracow, Basel, Frankfurt, Nurnberg, Strasbourg, Paris, Venice and other European cities. Some of those books were bought by Lviv burghers during their travels abroad. Many were ordered through booksellers in Cracow and Gdansk. Among the authors named within the forty-three inventories, the most common are Cicero (eighty-five copies of various editions of his works), Aristotle and Erasmus (fifty-eight copies each), Galen (thirty-seven), Plutarch (thirty-four), Hippocrates (twenty-nine). Greek authors were read mostly in Latin translations. The most popular spheres of interest were classical literature, grammar and rhetorics, medicine and law. The books in the Ukrainian, Church Slavonic and Polish languages were mostly of religious content. Foreign-printed books constituted a majority of books owned by magnate families and Catholic clergy. Many such books were also in the collections of those Orthodox clergymen who were involved in cultural activities. For example, Samuel Dobrians'kyi, hegumen of the Kremianets' Orthodox monastery, to which a print shop was attached, possessed the Kiev edition of *Evanhelie uchytelnoe* (Gospel of Instruction),[21] *The Story of Varlaam and Iosaf* (both in Ruthenian), Aesop's Fables, the works of Cicero, Petrarch, Aldus Manutius (treatise on Latin stylistics) and Erasmus' *Letters of Obscure Men*.

It should be added that the Jewish population of the Ukraine and Byelorussia used Hebrew and Yiddish books published abroad. Only in 1697 did the first Hebrew-language press appear in the small town of Zhovkva, in western Ukraine. During the eighteenth century, several small Jewish presses operated in the Ukraine and Byelorussia. They were able to satisfy only a small part of the demand, thus the majority of Hebrew books continued to be imported.

In the second half of the seventeenth century, the influx of foreign books increased in Russia, especially in the last decades of the century. The famous library of Simeon Polotskii/ Silvestr Medvedev has much in common with private libraries of Ukrainian and Byelorussian educated elites: the interest in classical literature and philology, the presence of books on medicine, jurisprudence, history and the natural sciences. Alongside books from western Europe, they had books from Poland, the Ukraine and Lithuania. But Russian owners obtained foreign books not through booksellers but from visiting foreigners, through acquaintances living or travelling abroad and so forth. There were no booksellers specializing in the foreign book trade in Russia, neither in the seventeenth nor in the early eighteenth centuries.

My final remarks can be only sketchy, not because of the lack of space, but primarily because of the absence of specialized studies on many of the topics involved. But we can be sure that, as a rule, in eastern Europe the initial stages of book printing were conducted more to achieve political and cultural goals rather than for profit-making. Also, in the periods of social and cultural reforms, the reformers were interested more in the social results of book dissemination than in the gains from the sale of them. But practice showed that book publishing could develop or at least achieve stability only if commercial effectiveness could be assured. For the development of publishing, to use the words of Professor Eisenstein, 'the mixture of many motives provided a more powerful impetus than any single motive (whether that of profit-seeking capitalist or Christian evangelist) could have provided by itself'.[22]

In the second quarter of the seventeenth century some Ukrainian publishers, including the Orthodox Metropolitan and bishops, accused each other of greediness. Each printer maintained that he published books to serve people and the church but that his competitor did it out of 'greed for profit'. Some contemporary scholars take such declarations at their face value, but the point is that the possibility of assuring profits through this cultural activity showed that the society was capable of sustaining that kind of activity. The profits from the publishing of literature for which there was a popular demand enabled some publishers to subsidize printing of other books for which demand had not yet ripened.

There were big differences among various countries and their regions. The printing of the Ukraine and Byelorussia achieved some degree of secularization from the very beginning but the process later slowed and in some periods even reversed. Initially Byelorussian printing was concentrated in Vilnius, while Ukrainian publishing developed mostly in the western part of the Ukraine. In the second half of the seventeenth century the centres of publishing activity moved eastwards in both lands. In Russia, noticeable steps towards secularization of the thematic range of printed books as well as towards commercialization of the printing activity began in the 1640s. After that the process continued almost uninterrupted.

The rate of the secularization and the commercialization processes was very slow in all of eastern Europe, which is quite understandable in the given socio-economic and cultural context. Only much later, mainly in the second half of the eighteenth century did changes occur in most eastern European countries that, contrary to Gary Marker's view, are comparable with the western 'printing revolution'.

Perhaps Marker's profound knowledge of the much more sophisticated eighteenth-century printing trade influenced his conclusion that Russian printing in the seventeenth century 'had only episodic impact on Russian culture'.[23] But if we look not from the position of latter development, but from the point of view of the preceding situation, the conclusion can be different. The same is of course true also with the Ukraine, Byelorussia and Lithuania.

It is not easy to make any generalizations about specific forms of influence of the book trade on social change, especially since special studies of the problem are only in the initial stages. Cyrillic book printing certainly contributed to the spread of literacy. Although the vast majority of the population remained illiterate, the number of literate and even well-educated individuals increased slowly but steadily. Buyers and readers of books, mainly of a religious content, existed not only among nobility, clergy and state bureaucracy but also among burghers and peasants and even servants.[24] Of course, educated burghers were not numerous and literate peasants were the exception, but the very fact that such exceptions appeared is notable. The importing of western books was crucial for the functioning of institutions of higher education (the Kiev Mohyla Academy and Catholic colleges in the Ukraine and Byelorussia, the short-lived 'Slavo-Greco-Latin' academy in Moscow) which provided cadres for administrative and cultural activities. It is true that quantities of both domestic and imported books remained insufficient. Still the books which were available on the market had a tremendous impact on those people who were most active in the cultural field and who largely contributed to social changes.

In eastern Europe the initial changes in book production and trade were extremely slow and were confined primarily to the religious sphere. But nevertheless the fact remains that the introduction of printing set in motion significant social and cultural processes while accelerating others.

Notes

The work for this chapter was prepared during my stay at the Harvard Ukrainian Research Institute as a visiting scholar. I would like to express my gratitude to the Institute and the Ukrainian Studies Fund for their generous support.

1   In stating this I do not intend to diminish the importance of printing enterprises which existed in the region earlier. Especially significant were the activities of the first Byelorussian printer Frantsishak Skaryna (Skoryna) in Vilnius in 1523–5. Nevertheless, the fact remains that only from the 1560s and 1570s did printing continue in east Slavic countries without major breaks. See Ia. D. Isaievych, *Pershodrukar Ivan Fedorov i vynyknennia drukarstva na Ukraïni* (*The First-Printer Ivan Fedorov and the Emergence of Printing in the Ukraine*) (Lviv, 1983), 16–30.

2   The so-called 'Ruthenian vernacular' (*prosta rus'ka mova*) was as a matter of fact the common literary language of Ukrainians and Byelorussians. The Church Slavonic was considered by all Orthodox Slavic peoples as the 'highest style' of their written languages. The local variants of the Church Slavonic differed mainly in their pronunciation and accentuation systems. See Ia. Isaievych, 'Der Buchdruck und die Entwicklung der Literatursprachen in der Ukraine (16.–1. Hälfte des 17. Jhdt.)', *Zeitschrift für Slawistik*, xxxvi (1991), 40–52.

3   Several pages printed presumably in Kazan' have been recently found. During the occupation of Moscow by the Poles an edition was produced in Nizhnii Novgorod by Nikita Fofanov, a printer who fled there from Moscow. The printing press of the Iverskii monastery and the 'upper' printing press organized by Simeon Polotskii in the tsar's palace published several books each. See *Chetyresta let russkogo knigopechataniia, 1564–1964* (*Four Hundred Years of Russian Book Printing, 1564–1964*), ed. A. A. Sidorov, vol. 1 (Moscow, 1964), 52–66.

4   For sources of figures given here, as well as later in this chapter, see Ia. D. Isaievych, *Preemniki pervopechatnika* (*Successors of the First-Printer*) (Moscow, 1982), 122–5.

5   N. P. Kiselev, 'O moskovskom knigopechatanii XVII veka' ('On Moscow printing of the seventeenth century'), *Kniga: Issledovaniia i materialy*, ii (1960).

6   A. S. Demin (ed.), *Tematika i stilistiska predislovii i posleslovii* (*Thematics and Stylistics of Prefaces and Afterwords*) (Moscow, 1981); Ia. D. Isaievych, 'Poslesloviia moskovskikh izdanii Ivana Fedorova kak literaturnye pamiatniki' ('Afterwords of Ivan Fedorov's Moscow imprints as works of literature'), in E. L. Nemirovskii (ed.), *Fedorovskie chtenia 1983* (Moscow, 1987), 54–63.

7   Among them five were works by Ukrainian and Byelorussian authors or reimpressions of books previously published in the Ukraine.

8   Tsentranyi Gosudarstvennyi Arkhiv Drevnikh Aktov, fond (record group) 1182. Some examples from these records are given in Ia. D. Isaievych, *Preemniki*, 122, 150–1. Records about book selling at the Moscow Printing Court in 1650–3 and 1663–5 are published in S. P. Luppov, *Chitateli izdanii moskovskoi tipografii v seredine XVII veka* (*Readers of Publications of the Moscow Printing Shop in the Middle of the Seventeenth Century*) (Leningrad, 1973). For a summary of those records with the full list of publications in 1619–52 and data on number of copies, see I. V. Pozdeeva, *Novye materialy dlia opisaniia izdanii moskovskogo Pehatnogo dvora: Pervaia polovina XVII v.* (*New Materials for the Description of the Imprints of the Moscow Printing Court: First Half of the Seventeenth Century*) (Moscow, 1986).

9   E. L. Nemirovskii, *Vozniknovenie knigopechataniia v Moskve: Ivan Fedorov* (*Origin of Printing in Moscow: Ivan Fedorov*) (Moscow, 1964).

10 S. P. Luppov, *Kniga v Rossii v XVII veke* (*The Book in Russia in the Seventeenth Century*) (Leningrad, 1975), 58.

11 Gary Marker, *Publishing, Printing, and the Origins of Intellectual Life in Russia, 1700–1800* (Princeton, 1985), 12–14.

12 I. N. Golenishchev-Kutuzov, *Gumanizm u vostochnykh slavian* (*Humanism among the Eastern Slavs*) (Moscow, 1965).

13 For a list of printing shops in the Ukraine see Ia. P. Zapasko and Ia. D. Isaievych, *Pam"iatky*

knyzhkovoho mystetstva: Kataloh starodrukiv vydanykh na Ukraïni, 1574–1800 (*Monuments of Book Art: Catalogue of Old Imprints Published in the Ukraine, 1574–1800*): vol. 1, *1574–1700* (Lviv, 1981).

14   For a list of printing shops in the Grand Duchy of Lithuania see: A. Kawecka-Gryczowa (ed.), *Drukarze dawnej Polski od XV do XVIII wieku*: Zeszyt 5, *Wielkie Księstwo Litewskie* (*Printers of Old Poland from the Fifteenth through the Eighteenth Century*: part 5, *The Grand Duchy of Lithuania* (Wrocław–Krakow, 1959), 5–6; Ia. Halenchenka, T. V. Neparozhnaia, T. K. Radzevich (eds), *Kniha Belarusi, 1517–1917: Zvodny Kataloh* (*The Books of Byelorussia 1517–1917: Union Catalogue*) (Minsk, 1986), 51–130, 514–18.

15   Books printed in Vilnius constituted 75 per cent of all titles printed in the Grand Duchy of Lithuania in 1553–1660. See M. B. Topolska, *Czytelnik i książka w Wielkim Księswte Litewskim* (*Reader and Book in the Grand Duchy of Lithuania*) (Wrocław, 1984), 119.

16   Ukrainian scholars checked the translation of this book against the Greek original using Sir Henry Savill's edition, published by John Norton in Eton in 1612.

17   At the end of the seventeenth and the early years of the eighteenth centuries, average editions of primers published by the Lviv Brotherhood were 6,000 copies. (See Ia. D. Isaievych, *Bratstva i ïkh rol' v rozvyktu Ukraïnskoï kultury XVI–XVII st.* (*Brotherhoods and their Role in the Development of Ukrainian Culture of the Sixteenth through the Eighteenth Centuries*) (Kiev, 1966), 150.)

18   G. Marker, 'Russia and the "Printing Revolution": notes and observations', *Slavic Review*, xli (1982), 270.

19   Ia. D. Isaievych and I. Z. Myts'ko, 'Zhyttia i vydavnycha diialnist' Kyryla-Trankviliona Stavrovet'skoho' ('The life and publishing activity of Cyril-Trankvilion Stavrovet'slyi'), in *Bibliotekoznavstvo ta bibliohrafiia* (Kiev, 1982), 62–5.

20   E. L. Nemirovskii, *Ivan Fedorov: okolo 1510–1583* (*Ivan Fedorov: c. 1510–1583*) (Moscow, 1984).

21   It was the Byzantine homilary translated into Church Slavonic in the fourteenth century and into Ruthenian by Meletii Smotryts'kyi in the early seventeenth century. Smotryts'kyi's translation was published in Vievis in 1617 and in Kiev in 1637. A facsimile of the Kiev edition was published as the first volume of the Harvard Library of Early Ukrainian Literature: *The Collected Works of Meletii Smotryts'kyi*: vol. 1, *Evanhelie uchytelnoe*, ed. David Frick (Cambridge, Mass., 1987).

22   Elizabeth Eisenstein, *The Printing Press as an Agent of Change*, vol. 1 (Cambridge, 1979), 456.

23   G. Marker, 'Russia and the "Printing Revolution" ', 270.

24   B. V. Sapunov, 'Kniga i chitatel' na Rusi v XVII v.' ('The book and the reader in Russia'), in A. A. Sidorov and S. P. Luppov (eds), *Kniga v Rossii do serediny XIX veka* (Leningrad, 1988), 72.

19

Selling it to the provinces: news and commerce round eighteenth-century Salisbury

C. Y. Ferdinand

In the last printed Newes of September 11, I told you there could be no perfect description of the siege of *Breda* . . . since this, is come ouer a perfect description of the same, the substance whereof is formerly set downe in this Relation. I doe purpose likewise to cut the Map, wherein you may with the eye behold the siege, in a manner, as liuely as if you were an eye-witness: you may not expect this Map this six dayes.[1]

(*The Continuation of the Weekly News*, no. 33, 16 September 1624)

This timely notice of a newly engraved map of Breda is evidently the first advertisement to appear in an English periodical,[2] and appropriately so, for it describes the style and tone of periodical advertising through most of the seventeenth century. Editors of the early newsbooks, like Nathaniel Butter and Nicholas Bourne in 1624, were not slow to understand that these periodicals might economically convey more than news and thereby produce an income beyond that derived from subscription and casual sales, but it was not until the middle of the century that advertising became a regular, substantial section of any London paper.[3] From the appearance of the first newsbook in about 1620 until the 1650s, the emphasis was unquestionably on news and ideas: most periodical advertising was limited to one or two trade notices, that is to the books, pamphlets and medicines sold by the newspaper proprietors and their book-trade colleagues.[4] Notices for lost servants, horses and relatives were in evidence by mid-century, but these, too, were sometimes trade-related since newspaper printers often printed the handbills that were posted round town to advertise such misfortunes. In late May 1657 Marchamont Nedham's eight-page weekly the *Publick Adviser* began publishing. Connected with a number of commercial offices of 'Publick Advice' in London, the *Publick Adviser* carried only advertising. It was evidently discontinued in September of the same year it started,[5] but it was the first of its kind and the first periodical to advertise coffee and chocolate.[6]

In the papers that sold such notices the average number of advertisements per issue increased after the 1650s,[7] but there was little diversification in their content until very late in the century. It is really only in the 1690s that advertisements appeared in any variety –

books, medicines and lost and stolen notices remained in significant numbers, but now individuals outside the book trade began to see the advantages of the newspaper as a uniquely wide-ranging advertising medium: the *London Gazette, Post Boy* and *Flying Post* all promoted lotteries, real estate, numerous auctions and goods for sale in the last few years of the century. This pattern of trade-related advertising with an increasing proportion of more broadly directed notices was one that was to develop in the eighteenth century.

The narrow focus that is characteristic of most seventeenth-century newspaper advertising can be explained in part by the limitations of a pre-consumer-society market: wages were lower than they would be in the eighteenth century; demand was relatively inflexible; luxury commodities went to a small, well-defined group;[8] and other forms of advertising – handbills, word-of-mouth, town criers, shop signs – were evidently adequate to promote local goods and services. But part of the explanation lies in how newspaper proprietors viewed their investments. Before Charles Spens and James Emonson entered into a partnership with the printer William Bowyer, Emonson wrote to Bowyer that within the terms of the new partnership, Spens 'proposes to keep on what he has to do with the News Paper, which will not take up three Hours a Day, as it will be 50L. a year clear Money, and a constant Introduction to the Booksellers'.[9] Emonson was writing in 1754, but there is evidence that successful seventeenth-century newspapers were valued for the same reasons. The 'constant Introduction to the Booksellers' was particularly important, for the booksellers, reinforced by government legislation, became a powerful element in the book trade during the seventeenth century:[10] as copyright owners, booksellers were the ones who employed the printers – including newspaper printers – to print their books and pamphlets, and the trade publishers to distribute them; they could be a dependable source of steady advertising revenue; and newspaper proprietors (frequently booksellers themselves) might find benefits in joining with their colleagues in the purchase of more expensive or riskier copyrights, or in setting up more efficient distribution systems.

London had been the centre of the English book trade from the time Caxton set up shop in Westminster in the late fifteenth century; it was the centre of the newspaper trade too, from its beginnings. In the seventeenth century, this position was reinforced by successive legislation including the Printing Act of 1662, which required the registration of copyright in the Stationers' Company register, in theory limited the number of master printers,[11] and (in fact) allowed them to print only in London, the two university towns and York. The restrictions applied to printing, but not to the sale of books or stationery – these continued selling through the provincial retail outlets that began operation in the fifteenth century. By the time the Printing Act was finally allowed to lapse in 1695, the pattern of centralized book production and ownership, with what amounted to a national distribution system, had been established. The demise of the Printing Act did not significantly alter this pattern, for the London booksellers were well organized by then and had no difficulties maintaining their long-standing monopolies in the rights to the most profitable books. This arrangement benefited both the London and the country book trade, however: the Londoners generally took on the more hazardous, potentially more profitable business of copyright purchase and book production, selling the books in and round the capital, and distributing them through increasingly comprehensive country networks; the provincial booksellers were able to profit from retail sales and local distribution of London imprints, as well as from a complex side trade that might include a variety of goods and services, such as stationery, medicines and bookbinding, some of it deriving from London.

When printers and booksellers began to migrate to the provinces after 1695, they found that book work was practically limited to the occasional edition of a sermon or poem of primarily local appeal. True, the new share-book system, whereby more and smaller shares in copies (that is, copyrights) were offered for sale, made it theoretically easier for the provincial bookseller to establish an interest in important or best-selling books; yet the London establishment, organized more or less in still effective congers, managed to retain its common-law monopoly on the most profitable titles until the mid-eighteenth century. Besides, most established or aspiring authors would naturally seek out a London agent. Job printing of advertisements, notices, warrants and forms was common and meant useful, if irregular, income. The one unrestricted new field in the post-1695 provincial book trade was the country newspaper, which could be developed for steady profits from sales and advertising, and for important contacts with colleagues in the capital. But it was several years before the need for this product was perceived and acted upon.

The London papers, both the printed ones and the handwritten newsletters, had been available to those who could afford them in the provinces from the beginning; indeed their presence may well have inhibited the early growth of the country newspaper, especially just after 1695 when a number of new periodicals sprang up in the capital.[12] It is uncertain who was first to assess and act upon the need for an inexpensive medium for local advertisements and for news extracted from the London papers and, much less often, from regional reports. Most likely it was either the London printer Francis Burges who moved to the country to establish the *Norwich Post*, or another Londoner, William Bonny, with his *Bristol Post-Boy*, both of them in business about 1701.[13] As R. M. Wiles notes, it is significant that Norwich and Bristol were 'progressive cities over a hundred miles from London'.[14] A successful local newspaper brought certain advantages to proprietor and subscriber: the best news culled from a number of London and continental papers for less than the cost of a single London paper; a reliable vehicle for advertisements; steady press work for the printer; and that 'constant Introduction' to booksellers in London and the country. Not all provincial towns provided the progressive market of a Bristol or a Norwich, however, and many were unable to sustain a local newspaper early in the eighteenth century. At least fifteen provincial newspapers were begun before 1712 but only four of those survived the Stamp Act of that year.[15] The commercial incentives to develop a successful newspaper were great though and other proprietors were undeterred: 135 new papers were started between 1713 and 1760. Thirty-nine (a little over 25 per cent) of the total 150 managed to stay in business past 1760.

This then was the economic background to the provincial newspaper advertisement, against which eighteenth-century developments may be measured: a strong London periodical trade that had been operating since the early seventeenth century; London newspapers that were certainly available – but expensive – in the country; a new freedom for printers to set up trade anywhere in the kingdom; a London-based book trade now dominated by the copy-owning booksellers; newspaper advertisements that preferentially included a large proportion of book-trade notices, but were showing increasing evidence of a new consumer orientation; and a postal, commercial and private network, long established but underdeveloped, to distribute London-printed books and newspapers to the major provincial towns. While the country newspaper was in itself innovative, it none the less worked within a traditional framework.

The history of the newspaper in Salisbury demonstrates the precariousness of the early eighteenth-century trade. Samuel Farley[16] believed that the newspaper press had commercial possibilities in Wiltshire in late 1715 when he started up his *Salisbury Post Man*. 'If 200. subscribe' he said, the *Post Man* would be viable.[17] Yet the thrice-weekly paper evidently was too ambitious an enterprise for Salisbury, a town of about 6,600 in 1715,[18] and it failed within a matter of months. There was another attempt to set up a newspaper in Salisbury about fourteen years later, when the brothers William and Benjamin Collins apparently began the *Salisbury Journal*, printed by Charles Hooten.[19] This paper failed too, with Number 58 (6 July 1730). Its last issue, however, carried ten advertisements: three for books; two for real estate; and one each for an apothecary (Charles Hooten evidently), an assembly and concert, a dancing master, a runaway servant and a notice regarding a dispute. Ten is a respectable number, and the variety gives some definition to the market in 1730 Salisbury, but it is significant that the printer of the paper places one of the advertisements, and, more important, that the three book notices are local ones – there is no sign that the proprietors had cultivated the advertising business of London colleagues even after a year in business. This may have been a factor in the first *Journal*'s failure, along with the low subscription numbers implied in Hooten's notice and perhaps a lack of experience in the proprietors (William Collins was 25 years old and Benjamin, probably also his brother's apprentice, was only 15).

When the *Salisbury Journal* resumed publication in 1736, it met with success; indeed it is still running. While the times seemed to favour new papers in general (thirty provincial papers were in business in 1736, six of them established that year[20]), different combinations of factors made some eighteenth-century provincial papers more successful than others. One factor that frequently applied before the mid-century was a simple lack of competition – by 1736 at least some Wiltshire residents must have deplored the absence of a local paper and welcomed the Collins's second attempt to establish one. Then Salisbury and its vicinity had the population to support a newspaper, a fairly stable 6,500–700 inside the town limits during the century. And the greater population within the *Journal*'s catchment area was a diverse one including those connected with the Cathedral and Close, those concerned in local agriculture and those involved with cloth manufacture. Salisbury itself, a regional administrative centre as well as cathedral and market town, falls into the numerous category of 'regional centre' in Peter Borsay's urban hierarchy; his next tier up is 'provincial capital' (the highest level of country town) – all but one of these important cities had newspapers, often competing ones, from early in the century, while regional centres like Salisbury were generally slower to take to the periodical press.[21] Yet the population, diversification and lack of competition had existed before 1736, and much of the *Journal*'s early success must be attributed to Benjamin Collins, who was to demonstrate a solid commercial sense throughout his life.[22] He and his brother William had developed important connections with both the London and the provincial book trade during the years between the first *Salisbury Journal* and this new enterprise. William played an important founding role in this, but his activity was short-lived – he left off business abruptly in mid-1740.[23]

The initial number of the *Salisbury Journal* (27 November 1736) had only one advertisement, for William Salmon's *Builder's Guide*, 'Printed for *James Hodges* at the Lookinglass on *London Bridge*, and Sold by *W. Collins* at *Salisbury*, *J. Gould* Bookseller at *Dorchester*, Mr. *Cook* Bookseller at *Sherborne* and *J. Langford* Bookseller at *Warminster*'. But here were two indicators of the *Journal*'s future success: contacts with London and provincial booksellers and a fledgling provincial distribution network.

A detailed study of this successful newspaper during the years of Benjamin Collins's management from 1736 to 1770 contributes some evidence towards an understanding of the gradual transformation in the mid-eighteenth-century provincial market. In its focus on a single provincial newspaper this case study has a certain amount of cohesion and continuity perhaps missing from broader studies of the provincial press that have drawn on material from multiple eighteenth-century papers.[24] A narrow focus has its own drawbacks, too. One is that similar studies are required to reconstruct the larger context necessary for comparison. J. Jefferson Looney's careful analysis of newspaper advertisements in York and Leeds, although it is based on statistics from sample years, will later provide a point of reference.

Newspaper advertisements can still be read and measured in various ways – in the case of the *Salisbury Journal*, nearly every notice that has appeared in the paper from its beginning up to the present can be consulted. The 50,000 or so advertisements that appeared between 1736 and 1770 are a quantifiable source of information about the eighteenth-century provincial consumer: many of the advertisements – for example those for real property and moveable goods – are represented in this study only by statistics, but those numbers can tell a good deal about selling and buying trends, and about contemporary perception of the overall utility of the newspaper for advertising. Other categories relating to literacy, the history of the book and leisure activities are considered in greater depth; for example, every advertisement for schools of any sort has been transcribed for reference, and any information that can help to describe the growth of the provincial book trade has been noted. In all, ten divisions of advertisement have been recorded: real property; straightforward notices for meetings, of crimes, etc.; medicines; leisure; moveable goods; lost-and-found; services, including professional and transportation; employment; runaways; and book trade. These will be described first in broad statistical outline, and then in greater detail for several categories.

It is important to keep in mind that other advertising media – the town criers, the shop signs, word of mouth, handbills – continued to operate in conjunction with the newspaper; unfortunately their ephemerality (the crier's words transformed within each hearer's memory and then lost, the handbill replaced with a newer notice) makes them practically inaccessible. It is now difficult to gauge with any accuracy their impact on contemporary consumers, their interaction with newspaper advertising, and aspects like numbers, frequency and range; in fact some of the evidence for their effectiveness in the eighteenth century derives from the newspapers themselves.[25]

A measure of developing consumerism, as well as of the commercial health of the *Salisbury Journal*, is in the rapid and sustained growth in the number of advertisements documented here (see Plate 19.1). In 1737, the first complete year of the *Journal*'s life, there were just over 200 advertisements, more than half of them for books. During the 1740s annual totals fluctuated between 550 and about 900, with advertisements for books ranging between 19 and 43 per cent. Benjamin Collins was at his most innovative during this first decade of his proprietorship, experimenting with the typography and placement of notices in his efforts to build up circulation, contacts and advertising revenue. By 1752 there were over 1,000 advertisements carried in the *Journal* each year; nine years later, in 1761, there were over 2,000; in 1768 over 3,000. By 1770, the year Benjamin Collins turned over the management of the newspaper to George Sealy, a former apprentice of his, and John Alexander, a local printer, there were nearly 3,400. It is significant that newspaper advertising increased so dramatically while the population, at least in Salisbury itself, and probably in its area of circulation too, remained stable:[26] a new market for newspapers and the products they advertised was being created, not as a natural development of population growth – a factor in the nineteenth century – but from a reading and buying segment that was expanding rapidly. The idea of the provincial newspaper as an agent for establishing and reaching an extended market had caught on – clearly its readers considered the *Salisbury Journal* an effective advertiser. At the same time the *Journal* was a window onto these very developments.

Who were these reader–consumers and what were they buying and selling? Circulation figures are difficult to come by, but it is reasonable to speculate that about 500 subscribers would have meant a commercially viable provincial newspaper in the 1730s (Farley thought 200 within the Salisbury catchment area were sufficient in 1715).[27] A stable circulation of between 1,500 and 2,000 might have been established in the 1740s, certainly by the 1750s, and Collins was probably not exaggerating much when he described his paper as 'one of the most extensive *Country Papers* in the *Kingdom*, being distributed Weekly in great Numbers thro' the several *Counties* of WILTSHIRE; DORSETSHIRE, SOMERSETSHIRE, GLOUCESTERSHIRE, BERKSHIRE, HAMPSHIRE, and the ISLES OF WIGHT, PURBECK, JERSEY, and GUERNSEY' (*SJ*, 24 September 1745). It is likely that the 1760s saw circulation figures of 2,500 and above. Early in 1770, the editor again described 'The great sale, and very large extent in the circulation of this Journal [that makes] it unnecessary to say any thing in favour of advertising therein' (*SJ*, 8 January 1770), appending a list of thirty-three agents in London and the south-west counties. And by 1780 the paper could claim an extensive circulation of 4,000.[28] Most copies of the paper would have had numerous readers and auditors through the week, primarily in the provinces around Salisbury but also in London, including private subscribers' families and friends, and patrons of the coffee-houses, inns and circulating libraries that took in the *Journal*. This would put readership at the very least above 10,000 in the mid-eighteenth century. In June 1764, a second edition of a particularly popular *Journal* number 'containing some curious and useful instructions concerning cheap fuel, hay-making, and fattening cattle' was issued, because the first, unusually, had sold out. This gives one dimension to the interests – in this case solidly agronomical – of these provincial consumers. The non-commercial content of the paper (the edited news itself, an editorial position that could sometimes be called Tory, a sprinkling of verse, literary and political essays and notices of appointments, bankruptcies and grain prices) adds to the picture of a clientele drawn from the local clothiers, farmers, tradesmen and professional people. Advertisements for the products they bought and sold, most of them locally derived, provide other important evidence.

The most striking difference between the *Salisbury Journal* of the 1730s and of the 1760s is in the *number* of advertisements – from an annual average of 296 in the 1730s, to 675 in the 1740s, 1,350 in the 1750s, to nearly 2,500 in the 1760s and to over 3,300 in 1770. Certainly the newspaper had become by the middle of the century a generally accepted method for promoting local businesses (good news for the newspaper proprietors who derived much of their profit from advertising[29]). The newspaper also became the most effective medium for extending the market for products like boarding schools, real estate and books, as well as for publishing information on highly moveable stolen goods. The new consumer lived anywhere within the broad reach of his country newspaper, for the paper's carrier also undertook to deliver the dyed silks, the hats, the serial books, the tea, the medicines and the silver watches it advertised, as well as the notices for distant services and leisure events, plus the transportation to get there.

If the broad categories of advertisement may now be considered, all ten types are represented in the *Journal* by 1739, when the first employment advertisement appears; all show a gradual increase in numbers; and many reach proportionate stability in the 1740s.

(1) The largest group of advertisements is for books and book-related material in the 1740s and 1750s, with an average of about 30 per cent of the total number; real estate takes the lead in the 1760s when books drop to about 18 per cent.

(2) After 1740 real-estate notices make up about 25 per cent, with highs of 29 per cent in 1763 and 1764, and a low of 20 per cent in 1752.

(3) Advertisements for quack medicines (convenient for the printer because type could be left standing to be reprinted in the following number, but tedious for the reader to see for weeks on end) are popular in the *Journal*'s first decade, at 14 per cent. Thereafter they account for well under 10 per cent of the total – a decrease that was perhaps due to customer complaints.[30]

(4) Sale of moveable goods by newspaper advertisement grows steadily, in numbers *and* proportion, averaging 9 per cent in the 1740s, about 16 per cent in the 1760s.

(5) So too do notices of meetings, robberies, markets and the like, which increase from an average 6 per cent in the 1740s to about 15 per cent later.

(6) Lost-and-found notices remain about 4 per cent of the total through the mid-century.

(7) Notices of fugitive husbands, wives, prisoners and soldiers almost never make up more than 1 per cent.

(8) Advertisements for jobs are relatively rare in the 1740s (some years of that decade saw none at all), averaging less than 0.5 per cent. In 1755 they amounted to 4 per cent, the average through the 1760s.

(9) Leisure activities are promoted in an average 4 per cent of the advertisements throughout this period.

(10) Advertisements for services average 4 per cent in the 1740s; in the 1750s the average doubles and remains at 8 per cent.

In a sense these general statistics rather obscure the developments in eighteenth-century provincial consumer habits, for, aside from the dramatic numerical growth they record, they tend to promote an idea of continuity or very gradual change: there was no exuberant increase in advertisements for leisure activities (in fact that category showed the least proportional change); services averaged about 8 per cent through at least two decades; even for moveable goods, which increased from 9 per cent in the 1740s to 16 per cent in the 1760s, the growth is fairly even. The differences that might be said to signal the changes are to be seen with more clarity in the composition of the individual categories themselves.[31]

Advertisements promoting services are a good example: the first professional service of any kind to be advertised was Philip Davies's new school in Blue Boar Row, Salisbury (5 September 1737, almost a year after the *Journal* began publishing again). The notice is brief and unsophisticated both in approach and typography, describing Mr Davies's credentials (he, like a number of other schoolmasters who looked for customers in the *Salisbury Journal*, had started out as assistant to the famous Mr Willis of Orchard School) and outlining the subjects taught ('*Writing, Arithmetick, Algebra, Geometry, Trigonometry and other useful Learning*'). That the utility of learning is mentioned suggests a newspaper-reading market different from that for the seventeenth-century London papers – Philip Davies directs his notice to the gentleman or tradesman who would ensure his son's practical earning power.

Other early advertisements for services are equally prosaic: the Golden Lyon in Axminster, the Crewkerne-to-London carrier, more schoolmasters, stallions to cover, a hearse 'fit to travel', farriers and so on, with no remarkable changes until the late 1740s. Until then the market for services described in the *Salisbury Journal* was one with a utilitarian bias, taking in a growing literate class that was interested in the cheapest way to convey parcels from Crewkerne to London, or a good farrier or a serviceable education.

The demand for more luxurious services and goods, the lower prices that came with greater production,[32] as well as the opportunity the local newspaper offered for widely promoting such enterprises, introduced new colour to the *Journal*'s growing advertising columns. In 1747 the first advertisements for made-to-order goods appeared, with notices for a whip-maker (11 May), a coat-maker (21 September) and a stay-maker (19 October). The following year more services were offered: brush-making (18 January), coach painting (22 August) and watch-making (14 November). The next twenty years saw advertisements for a whole range of services that traditionally had been offered (and not through newspapers either) only to the wealthier classes – architects, estate surveyors, portrait painters, plumbers, decorative plasterers, gardeners, many of them careful to claim London credentials,[33] all invested in *Salisbury Journal* advertising. This is not to say that any of these skilled services were new ones, rather that for the first time they were being offered to any reader of the *Salisbury Journal* who desired and could afford them. The newspaper was (and is) almost the ideal medium for reaching those who had not yet realized they required the services of, for example, an architect of garden grottoes. If commercialization meant the exploitation of a broader market, then luxury services, promoted through the wide-reaching medium of newspapers, were in the process of commercialization around Wiltshire from the late 1740s.

Education was another area to show the effects of market changes through the eighteenth century. Most of the notices in the *Journal* were for middle-class boarding schools and academies, probably because schools at either end of the scale tended not to advertise in the newspaper: local dame schools drew their recruits from the local population and the top-ranking grammar schools drew on their reputations. The number of educational advertisements in the *Journal* increased at an erratic pace from the 1740s to the 1760s, by when there were usually more than twenty each year. In all, about two hundred teachers or schools in seventy-eight towns bought nearly four hundred advertisements in the *Salisbury Journal* before 1770.[34] A good proportion of the advertisements were for schools that had just opened – evidence for the very existence of some of them, as well as further evidence that literacy was so assisted in the eighteenth-century provinces. In the face of increasing competition educators became remarkably direct in their approach, outlining their curricula, describing accommodation, quoting competitive prices, emphasizing care of morals and behaviour and noting past successes. Most of the advertisements were directed to those parents who were considering honouring one of these educators with 'the tender and important trust of their Children'. But occasionally the approach was to the adult who wanted to cultivate certain skills – for example Mr Edgcombe in Portsmouth usually instructed children for the sea or land; but he also suggested that 'Any Person (that is versed in common Arithmetic, and will omit the projective Part) may be taught to keep an accurate Journal of a Ship's Run at Sea, in a very few Days' and that he could help gentlemen qualify as gunners in the Royal Navy (*SJ*, 29 August 1757). There was nothing revolutionary in the curricula offered – girls were generally taught reading, writing and needlework; boys reading, writing, arithmetic and often Latin, navigation or bookkeeping; many boarding schools offered optional dancing and

French language instruction to their children – but one anonymous 'experienc'd Accomptant from LONDON' took the unusual step of directing the last paragraph of his notice to

> Ladies that would amuse themselves with Business, and at the same Time be truly beneficial to their Families and Children, usefully qualify'd to transact their Husbands Affairs when absent, and consequently in case of Widowhood, be able to manage a Fortune, or carry on Trade, by learning any of the useful Branches of Business aforesaid, may prevent much Expence, and many Inconveniences, that attend to trusting to Servants or others.
>
> (*SJ*, 25 July 1748)

These four hundred advertisements, with their cumulative detail, give us a fairly good idea of the educational options that increasingly became available to middle-class Wiltshire.

The leisure activities that could most effectively be promoted in a country newspaper were the major, increasingly commercial, events – horse races and the entertainments around them, annual musical festivals, the beginning of a series of assemblies, a travelling exhibition – the sort of thing that might attract a public audience from outlying areas. As country people came to have more disposable income, advertisements for out-of-town amusements (and the means of getting to them) increased. No one needed a newspaper to find out about the more ordinary, strictly local events, or even to find information on regular gatherings once the season had started (an assembly that routinely took place in the Vine on Wednesday evenings, say, would usually have only one or two advertisements). And there were always non-commercial gatherings from which the public would have been excluded. This makes leisure advertising a less precise gauge of changes in the market. Still, it is worth looking in greater detail at what the reader of the *Salisbury Journal* might do with his spare time. If he based his leisure plans on what he found in the newspaper, he would have had considerably more to choose from than had his seventeenth-century predecessor.

The coffee-house is one of the very few day-to-day pastimes to be advertised. John Childs's coffee-house took in

> the Votes, King's Speech and Addresses, the Gazette, Daily Advertiser, General Evening-Post, Evening Advertiser and London Chronicle, Salisbury Journal, Monthly Magazines, Sessions Papers and Dying Speeches; the best Coffee, Tea, Chocolate and Capillair, will be constantly provided, with all due and proper Attendance. . . . The Room is conveniently fitted up large, light, and warm, and subject to no Annoyance whatever.[35]
>
> (*SJ*, 28 March 1757)

Francis Collins (Benjamin's brother) ran a coffee-house, the Mitre in Silver Street, for a time. He provided maps to supplement the newspapers, and promised that 'a good Fire will be constantly found at Four o'Clock in the Afternoon, during the Winter Season' (*SJ*, 20 October 1755). A related pastime is to be found in the circulating library: Edward Easton's and Samuel Fancourt's libraries competed for customers in the advertising section of the *Salisbury Journal* in the 1730s and 1740s before Fancourt conceded defeat and moved his library to London.[36] Once a circulating library or reading room was established and known, its proprietor, like the organizer of a series of assemblies, had less need of the newspaper. Advertisements for musical instruments, billiard tables and hunting dogs might also represent leisure possibilities. Otherwise most ordinary folk probably spent their extra time much as Thomas Turner records in his diary – reading, visiting neighbours, dancing, eating and sometimes coming home drunk.[37]

Newspaper advertisements are better at documenting the occasional and annual or semi-annual events, although even then they sometimes give away other forms of advertisement: for example, advertisements for the Salisbury Races usually conclude with a note that there will be balls and assemblies 'as usual', demonstrating a continuing reliance on tradition, word-of-mouth, handbills and perhaps the town crier. There were always clusters of events advertised around race weeks (both in Salisbury and in the surrounding area), assize weeks and, especially in Salisbury, the annual music festival. These inevitably included cock matches, which took place 'as usual' but at different venues advertised from year to year, and often took in various balls, assemblies and ordinaries, as well as the odd wrestling, back-sword or single-stick match. The organizers used the newspaper to promote a broad cultural programme that was designed to appeal to the gentry who might turn up (themselves an attraction at some of these events), to the middling classes with their increasing spending power and even to the contestants who undertook to break so many heads to win the prize at single-stick.[38] Theatre was another activity advertised seasonally, commonly as a 'puff' in the Salisbury news section. A growing interest in the theatre can be detected in the *Journal* from the 1750s in the greater number of advertisements as well as in increased news coverage.

Lower-class blood sports (if such brutal activity can be called sport) like cock throwing were never advertised in the *Salisbury Journal*; in fact, when they are mentioned at all in the news, it is with some distaste. Bull baiting, and the variant badger and stag baiting are advertised a number of times after 1752, but not at all before then. The gentler sport of cricket is noticed only a few times: in the light of its well-documented popularity then,[39] this omission must simply mean that times and locations of cricket matches were easily discovered by other forms of advertisement, and that its commercial potential was not so evident in the eighteenth century. There were also competitions, some of them annual, some occasional, for bell-ringers, florists, marksmen and singers, who were usually required to pay an entry fee.

The itinerant performers, lecturers and showmen who stopped at Salisbury are probably best entertainment value for a twentieth-century audience: for six pence one could view a

> curious little Four Wheel open CHAISE, with the Figure of a Man in it, drawn by a FLEA, which performs all the Offices of a large Chaise, as running of the Wheels, Locking, &c. and all together weighing but one Grain. It has been shown to the Royal Family, and several of the Nobility and Gentry, with great Approbation.

The flea-drawn chaise was part of an exhibition of miniatures, including a working pair of scissors wrapped in a fly's wing (*SJ*, 22 February 1743). A surprising menagerie that included a rhinoceros, a 'surprising Buffalo', a lynx, a 'Man Tyger from Bengal, very surprising' and 'Two surprising Wolfs' toured the Wiltshire area in 1744 (*SJ*, 20 October 1744); a troupe of rope dancers and tumblers was at the Vine in Salisbury early the following year (*SJ*, 15 January 1745). Three mathematical statues spent a week there in 1742. One of them represented 'a Country Lass, with a Pidgeon upon her Head, holding a Glass in her Hand which she lifting up, makes to run out of the Pidgeon's Bill either Red or White Wine, at the Desire of the Spectators' (*SJ*, 4 May 1742). 'Mr. POWELL, The CELEBRATED FIRE-EATER' demonstrated his skills in 1753: his repertoire included eating burning charcoal 'as natural as Bread'; broiling beef in his mouth; and concocting a soup of rosin, pitch, beeswax, sealing wax, brimstone, allum and lead, which he then apparently swallowed 'to the great Surprise of all Spectators' (*SJ*, 14 May 1753).

Trained animals, especially horses, bears and birds, had long been popular entertainment in England. The eighteenth century saw the début of improved performers like the Wonderful Learned Pig, Daniel Wildman's marching bees and Le Chien Savant. Not to be outdone, the English produced their own

> amazing learn'd ENGLISH DOG – This entertaining and sagacious Animal, reads, writes, and casts Accompts by Means of Typographical Cards, in the same Manner that a Printer composes; and by the same Method answers various Questions in Ovid's Metamorphoses, Geography, the Roman, English, and sacred History; knows the Greek Alphabet . . . solves Questions in the four Rules of Arithmetick, tells by looking on any common Watch of the Company what is the Hour and Minute . . . he likewise shews the impenetrable Secret, or tells any Person's Thoughts in Company.
>
> (*SJ*, 23 June 1755)

The 'impenetrable Secret' could in fact be penetrated on purchase of a set of cards from the dog's proprietor after the performance.[40] Compared to the Chien Savant, this was 'a Dog superior in all his Accomplishments to any Thing of the Kind ever yet presented . . . a Dog really vers'd in the History of Nations, Empires, and Kingdoms' (evidently alluding to a deficiency in the French dog). One last performer, Mr Maddox, deserves mention: he worked on the slack wire, mimicked 'the German Flute with his Voice to Admiration' and was accompanied by Signora Catarina from Sadler's Wells who exhibited 'sundry and amazing Postures, never perform'd in England before' (*SJ*, 6 December 1756). He was evidently well received in Salisbury since he returned several times. He was last there near the end of 1756, and we learn from the *Salisbury Journal* that he, along with the comedian Theophilis Cibber and the bookseller James Rudd, perished on the ship *Dublin* two years later when she went down in the Irish Sea (*SJ*, 27 November 1758). These examples can be slightly distracting and it should be stated that the *Journal* advertised a fairly well-balanced programme ranging from the popular to the cultural, from wrestling matches to Handel's oratorios. It should also be remembered that the advertisements are self-selective, in that only those who paid their 2s. 6d. advertised – and by providing wide coverage of certain events, the *Salisbury Journal* played a somewhat prescriptive role, helping to give shape to the body of cultural and leisure activities available to those who read that newspaper.

The development of the provincial book trade is closely related to the home consumer revolution, for it was of course the distribution system developed by the booksellers and newspaper proprietors that systematically brought both news and products to the farthest reaches of every county: a healthy local book trade usually meant a healthy local market. Minor country booksellers played an important role in eighteenth-century trade, acting as paid agents, middlemen and retailers for the big provincial booksellers. Yet frequently the only surviving evidence of such activity is in newspaper advertising. A case in point is Newport, on the Isle of Wight, for which a fairly complete book-trade history can be constructed from advertisements in the *Journal*.

In 1705 John Dunton could write of one Mr Keblewhite, the Isle of Wight's earliest recorded bookseller, that he 'has a good trade, considering the place; but that is not his whole dependence, he has been twice Mayor of the town, and is not only rich, but a grave and discreet churchman'.[41] This Keblewhite seems to have been working in Newport from about 1684 to 1693. The 'place' was probably not much improved in the eighteenth century and F. A. Edwards, writing almost two hundred years after Dunton, was unsuccessful in documenting any real book-trade activity on the island from Keblewhite until the 1790s.[42] To move the investigation up to the present day, a computer-assisted search through the *Eighteenth-Century Short Title Catalogue* (which records books, of course, but also pamphlets and other ephemeral printing) is not much more revealing: only four items falling within the scope of this paper were listed, three sermons and the sensational trial between James Annesley and the Earl of Anglesea.[43] Their imprints discover a total of three booksellers in Newport in the 1740s. Yet the advertisements in the *Salisbury Journal* provide evidence of at least seven booksellers active during those middle years, suggesting a book trade that was a continuing commercial presence throughout much of the century.

Benjamin Collins seems to have employed a bookselling agent on the Isle of Wight from 1740, after he had assumed full control of the *Salisbury Journal*. One incentive for establishing such an outlet was the potential market on the island for books and newspapers – Newport parish alone had a population of something like 3,000 during the mid-century[44] – in addition, Collins possibly had family connections there. Thomas Geare is the first Isle of Wight bookseller to be recorded in the pages of the *Journal*. He may have moved to the island from Yeovil, for a 'T. Geare' was selling Squire's Elixir there in 1737, and he may well have moved specifically to fill the post of off-shore agent for Benjamin Collins. At any rate, an advertisement of 26 August 1740 invites readers to subscribe through Benjamin Collins and Thomas Geare to the *Musical Entertainer*, and in 1742 they are the two local booksellers for the fourth edition of the *London and Country Brewer*. It should be added, as a slight corrective, that Geare was also selling Bolton Simpson's Greek and Latin edition of Xenophon's *Memorials*, so it wasn't all wine and song on the Isle of Wight in those days. By March 1743, Thomas Geare was able to serve islanders from a

> Shop in *Newport*, near the Bugle Inn, facing *St. James*'s Square, [where] Gentlemen may be supply'd with Books in all Languages and Faculties, whether printed at Home, or imported from Abroad. Together with all new Pamphlets, Maps and Prints; and every Thing in the Stationery Way at the lowest Price.
>
> (*SJ*, 1 March 1743)

He also took in books 'to be Bound or Letter'd *firm* and *neat*, . . . on the most reasonable Terms', and of course he sold quack medicines. Quite a reasonable provision for a country town in 1740. In June 1743 Geare is named in the *Journal*'s colophon as an agent for the first and only time; the following week he is replaced by Richard Baldwin, junior, about whom a good deal more is known.[45]

Numerous advertisements in the *Salisbury Journal* attest to the variety of books and pamphlets Baldwin helped market during his three-year term on the island – children's books like *Pretty Book for Children* and *Little Pretty Pocket Book*, Conyers Harrison's *Impartial History of the Life and Reign of Queen Anne* in twenty-two parts, Bishop Berkeley's controversial *Siris*, Dr James's *Medicinal Dictionary*, Sarah Harrison's *House-Keeper's Pocket Book*, *The Universal Library of Trade and Commerce*, local sermons and so on. Besides selling printed material, we find Baldwin advertising to buy any quantity of bees' wax (*SJ*, 14 August 1744); he sold 'All Sorts of Stamp Paper and Parchment, Blank Bonds, and all other Sorts of Blanks' (*SJ*, 27 August

1745), stationery of every variety and, towards the end, Sterrop's True Spectacles, and 'all Manner of Musical Instruments, as Violins, German, and common Flutes, &c. Also, the most curious painted Paper for Rooms' (*SJ*, 24 September 1745).

Baldwin's direct successor was Jonathan Moore, who replaced him in the *Journal*'s colophon from 24 November 1746. Persuading the islanders to buy books was possibly not an easy matter, and business difficulties may have been behind Jonathan Moore's move from the High Street 'to his own House in St. *James's Square*, the Sign of thé Bible' (*SJ*, 25 January 1748). (While he does not seem to have been compelled to sell musical instruments and glasses, he did include bonnet paper among the stock listed at the time of the move.) In August 1749 Jonathan Moore opened a boarding school – 'All Materials [provided] except Printed Books' – where he undertook to instruct in reading, writing and arithmetic, in such a manner that 'Boys of a tolerable Genius' learned 'as much in one Year, as by ordinary Methods in Three', and were thereby 'more expeditiously [fitted] . . . for the public Grammar School, or Business, as their several Circumstances require' (*SJ*, 14 August 1749). The relationship between eighteenth-century provincial booksellers and educators seems to have been an amicable and close one for the most part, and Jonathan Moore is only one *Salisbury Journal* example of the two combined in one man, not only taking advantage of the existing market, but actively creating a new market of readers and buyers. Jonathan Moore's career ended on the Isle of Wight when he died in 1753. He is not to be found in Plomer's *Dictionary of Printers and Booksellers* nor in McKenzie's *Apprentices*.

Neither is Simon Knight 'the Organist' who carried on the business at the Sign of the Bible in St James's Square in hopes that 'such Gentlemen, and others, as were Customers to the deceas'd, will continue their Favours to his Successor'. Like his predecessors, Knight was listed as the Isle of Wight outlet in numerous book advertisements; he also sold stationery goods, patent medicines and those 'Paper Hangings for Rooms'. But he is the first to draw attention to his lending facilities: 'SIMON KNIGHT, BOOKSELLER and STATIONER, . . . lends Books to read either by the single Book or Quarter' (*SJ*, 20 May 1754). And later,

> This is to acquaint all Readers, That Books in all faculties and Parts of Learning, likewise all New NOVELS, HISTORIES, VOYAGES, TRAVELS, &c. are *Lent to Read* by S. KNIGHT, Bookseller in Newport . . . by whom all Kinds of Books are Sold at the lowest Prices, and all Sorts of Almanacks, Baldwin's Daily Journal, Ladies Pocket Book, . . . Wholesale or Retale.
>
> (*SJ*, 23 December 1754)

So by mid-1754 at the latest, residents of Newport could borrow books for a small fee. Simon Knight also provided a bookbinding service. In spite of these innovations, Knight continued his bookselling business only until May 1756 when his stock-in-trade was advertised for sale (*SJ*, 31 May 1756).

Peter Milligan kept the bookshop and house in St James's Square for six years after this, though apparently not without difficulties: less than a year after his arrival, he gave notice that outstanding debts would be placed in an attorney's hands. 'Books, Pamphlets, Weekly Numbers, Monthly Magazines, and Stationary Wares, &c.' were provided as usual until Milligan's stock and household goods were dispersed in a four-day sale in July 1762.

It is useful to have a list of titles that Collins and his local agents believed they could sell from a Newport bookshop, of course, and to monitor trends in local book buying – the weekly delivery of the newspaper clearly encouraged the sale of books in weekly parts, for example. But the advertisements also provide some of the only evidence we have of the developing commercial structure of the provincial book trade: when another country bookseller of comparable standing to the Newport booksellers in the *Salisbury Journal* (William Pitt in Blandford) went out of business in 1749 (*SJ*, 18 December 1749), his stock-in-trade was advertised for sale. His books amounted to about 350 volumes, hardly enough to support the usual provincial dealer's claim that any title published anywhere could be purchased locally as cheap as in London. What the provincial book advertisements suggest is that local booksellers stocked a basic collection made up of one or more copies of those titles actually advertised as available from named retailers. In the case of Thomas Geare and his successors to the Newport bookshop, out-of-stock books would have been ordered through Benjamin Collins in Salisbury, who in turn would have placed orders through his own agents in London. And the carriage from London to Salisbury to the Isle of Wight need not add to the price of a book, since the network of *Salisbury Journal* distributors and newsmen could be employed at no additional expense.

The book advertisements also provide some clues about the different levels of relationship a provincial newspaper proprietor/bookseller like Benjamin Collins might establish with his country colleagues. During the mid-1740s, what seems to be a small consortium consisting of Benjamin Collins in Salisbury (always first named), Richard Baldwin in Newport and Thomas Burrough in Devizes is suggested by the appearance of their three names together in advertisement after advertisement. Other provincial booksellers' names are listed, both in the books ads and in the colophon of the *Journal*, but they do not appear with the same regularity and they are not linked in the same way. This partnership was place-specific, rather than person-specific, for when Richard Baldwin went to London, Jonathan Moore replaces him in that section of the book-trade advertisements, and Simon Knight replaces Moore and so on. The advertisements do not reveal what special arrangements Collins made with his partners on the Isle of Wight and in Devizes – perhaps a higher level of service, including centralized job printing, was involved; and the three could well have invested, as a consortium or provincial conger, in local books. On another level, numerous country booksellers acted as agents for Collins, taking in subscriptions and advertisements for the *Salisbury Journal*, serving as distribution points for the newspaper and selling the products therein advertised. Finally, there was the network of distributors, carriers, newsmen and hawkers, so often mentioned in the pages of local papers. So the advertisements in the *Salisbury Journal* can tell us a good deal about just how books, other goods and services were conveyed and marketed on the Isle of Wight and in almost any provincial town within the *Journal*'s range, starting with the fact that such services existed. The development of the provincial book trade was in effect the development of the mechanism for getting information and goods to the provincial consumer.

It is difficult to draw valid comparisons between what was happening in the newspaper trade in Wessex and in the rest of the provinces. Evidence that the provincial newspaper was employed more and more to circulate news and advertising is to be found in the growing number of titles and subscribers – that seems to be an undisputed national trend, well borne out by the *Salisbury Journal* in the eighteenth century. And more advertising was one general symptom of a growth in consumerism. J. Jefferson Looney's work on Yorkshire newspaper advertisements does, however, offer a few specific points of comparison where this study overlaps with his. Looney finds that newspaper advertising in York, a city he describes as one that attracted wealth, 'a traditional gentry gathering-spot', was somewhat different from newspaper advertising in Leeds, a city that created wealth. This is supported by impressive and detailed statistics compiled for sample years from the *York Courant* and the *Leeds Mercury*.[46] There are similar statistics for the *Salisbury Journal* for two of the sample years (1741 and 1760). The city of Salisbury itself probably attracted more wealth than it created, although within its catchment area there was a good deal of wealth-creating (although not in the increasingly industrial way of Leeds). And indeed a comparison of statistics shows that advertising in Salisbury had more of an affinity with that in York, at least on a rudimentary level.

The year 1760 is especially telling for by then all three newspapers were well-established ones: that year saw a large number of advertisements for books and other printed material in both the York and Salisbury papers (the *York Courant* had 541, the *Salisbury Journal* had 483), while the *Leeds Mercury* had only 88. York and Salisbury advertised more quack medicines (90 and 73 respectively to Leeds's 53); more moveable goods for sale (170 and 221 to 29; more lost-and-found items (77 and 72 to 17); more educational establishments (11 and 20 to 0); more real estate (965 and 421 to 300); and more leisure activities (168 and 64 to 13). It was not simply that the *York Courant* and the *Salisbury Journal* carried more paid notices than the *Leeds Mercury*; the composition of the advertising columns seems to reflect other differences. The three newspapers had in common a high proportion of notices for real estate and books in 1760; but the *York Courant* had a staggering 335 advertisements for stallions to cover – Salisbury had 33, Leeds 8. York's importance as a northern centre for horse racing is further reflected in the similar disproportions for advertisements of race meetings. Salisbury, like York, had a relatively high proportion of advertisements for such cultural activities as lectures, concerts and assemblies in both 1741 and 1760. *Salisbury Journal* advertising, then, describes a market more like that of York than Leeds, a Wessex market that was perhaps, as Looney suggests for York, readier to patronize 'commercialized leisure activity'.

In terms of the *Salisbury Journal* and the market it reached, there is something of a consumer revolution documented in its advertising columns: first, in the record numbers of advertisements; then in the overall greater diversity, most obvious in a comparison with the newspapers of the seventeenth century; and finally in the transitions that took place within each category of advertisement. Services that had been considered luxuries for any but the wealthy were advertised extensively round eighteenth-century Wiltshire; leisure activities were sold to a larger public audience; more and more goods were sold through the newspaper; the system for conveying these goods to customers became more sophisticated; educators pitched their appeals to a broader clientele – the change is noticeable even in the lost-and-founds, where lost anonymous working dogs or hunters with names like Ranger and Smoaker are increasingly replaced with missing Violet, Gregory, Chloe, Fop and (especially) Pompey. In almost every type of advertisement underlying economic change can be discerned: analysis of this one eighteenth-century newspaper describes a lively and changing market in eighteenth-century Wiltshire.

But perhaps the country newspaper should have the last word, at least on the diversity and efficiency of eighteenth-century advertising:

> If any gem'man wants a wife
> (A partner, as 'tis term'd, for life)
> An advertisement does the thing
> And quickly brings the pretty thing.

If you want health, consult our pages,
You shall be well, and live for ages;
Our empirics, to get them bread,
Do every thing – but raise the dead.

Lands may be had, if they are wanted,
Annuities of all sorts granted;
Places, preferments, bought and sold;
Houses to purchase, new and old.
Ships, shops, of every shape and form,
Carriages, horses, servants swarm;
No matter whether good or bad,
We tell you where they may be had.
Our services you can't express,
The good we do you hardly guess;
There's not a want of human kind,
But we a remedy can find.

(Anonymous, *SJ*, 27 December 1784)

Notes

I am, as always, grateful to D. F. McKenzie for his comments on earlier versions of this chapter.

1 Quoted in Folke Dahl, *A Bibliography of English Corantos and Periodical Newsbooks 1620–1642* (London: Bibliographical Society, 1952), 125.

2 Butter and Bourne referred earlier to a book they were about to publish in their *Continuation of Our Weekly Newes*, 21 April 1623, but this notice is more in the way of news than advertisement (see Joseph Frank, *The Beginnings of the English Newspaper 1620–1660* (Cambridge, Mass.: Harvard University Press, 1961), 301 n. 54).

3 See R. B. Walker, 'Advertising in London newspapers, 1650–1750', *Business History*, xvi (1973), 112–30.

4 There was an early link between selling nostrums and selling books, based on their centralized production and national distribution. See John Feather, *A History of British Publishing* (London: Croom Helm, 1988), 118–19, and John Alden, 'Pills and publishing: some notes on the English book trade, 1660–1715', *Library*, 5th series, vii (1952), 21–37.

5 Carolyn Nelson and Matthew Seccombe (comps), *British Newspapers and Periodicals, 1641–1700; a Short-Title Catalogue of Serials Printed in England, Scotland, Ireland, and British America* (New York: Modern Language Association, 1987), Serial 573. Nelson and Seccombe record a complete run of the nineteen numbers in the Thomason Collection, the British Library.

6 Frank, *Beginnings of the English Newspaper*, 258.

7 The *Perfect Diurnall* averaged about six advertisements per number in 1653; Muddiman's *Kingdom's Intelligencer* and *Mercurius Publicus* about five in 1662; L'Estrange's *Newes* and *Intelligencer* about seven in 1665 (Walker, 'Advertising', 113).

8 Aspects discussed in Neil McKendrick, 'The consumer revolution of eighteenth-century England', in Neil McKendrick, John Brewer and J. H. Plumb, *The Birth of a Consumer Society: The Commercialization of Eighteenth-Century England* (Bloomington: Indiana University Press, 1982), 9–33.

9 Bodleian Library, Oxford, MS. Eng. Mis. c. 141, fo. 121.

10 John Feather describes the booksellers' rise to dominance of the Stationers' Company, a process that began early in the seventeenth century, in his *History of British Publishing*, 38–40; enlightening

discussion of the seventeenth-century book trade and its divisions may be found in D. F. McKenzie, *The London Book Trade in the Later Seventeenth Century* (privately published Sandars Lectures, 1976) and in Michael Treadwell, 'London trade publishers, 1675–1750', *Library*, 6th series, iv (1982), 99–134.

11 The number of master printers at work in the seventeenth century usually exceeded the legal limits. See Michael Treadwell, 'Lists of master printers: the size of the London printing trade, 1637–1723', in Robin Myers and Michael Harris (eds), *Aspects of Printing from 1600* (Oxford: Oxford Polytechnic Press, 1987), 141–70.

12 Eleven serial publications were started (or restarted) in 1695, ten in 1696, thirteen in 1697, five in 1698, eleven in 1699, according to a count based on Nelson and Seccombe, *British Newspapers and Periodicals*, 'Chronological index'.

13 Francis Burges, son of a London clerk, was apprenticed to Freeman Collins from July 1692 to December 1699 (D. F. McKenzie, *Stationers' Company Apprentices 1641–1700* (Oxford: Oxford Bibliographical Society, 1974), 35); no record is found of Bonny's apprenticeship. Discussion of the question of priority may be found in R. M. Wiles, *Freshest Advices: Early Provincial Newspapers in England* (Columbus, Ohio: Ohio State University Press, 1965), 14–16 and in G. A. Cranfield, *The Development of the Provincial Newspaper 1700–1760* (Oxford: Oxford University Press, 1962), 13–15.

14 Wiles, *Freshest Advices*, 16.

15 ibid., 17–18 and Appendix B: 'Chronological chart'. The intention of the 1712 Stamp Act and indeed of the other newspaper stamp acts was not primarily oppressive; rather the government hoped to raise revenue by taxing an established and popular commodity. The issue has been widely discussed, but one of the most comprehensive treatments is D. F. Foxon's unpublished Sandars Lectures on the 1712 Stamp Act (University of Cambridge, 1978).

16 A Samuel Farley published *Sam. Farley's Exeter Post-Man* from 1704 until 23 September 1715, the week before the Salisbury paper began. Another of the same name was proprietor of *Sam. Farley's Bristol Post-Man* from about 1713. The name is frequently connected with the eighteenth-century newspaper trade in the south-west of England; Plomer lists a number of related Farleys in his *Dictionary of the Printers and Booksellers Who Were at Work in England, Scotland and Ireland from 1726 to 1775* (Oxford: Oxford Bibliographical Society, 1932), 88–90.

17 The only known copy of the *Salisbury Post Man* is of the first number (27 September 1715), which is in the present office of the *Salisbury Journal*. The *Post Man* continued until at least early 1716: Robert Benson and Henry Hatcher mention the existence of a No. 40 (1 March 1716) in their *Old and New Sarum, or Salisbury* (London: Nichols, 1843), 509.

18 The population of Salisbury in 1695 was probably close to 6,676 (John Chandler, *Endless Street: A History of Salisbury and Its People* (Salisbury: Hobnob Press, 1987; 1st edn, 1983), 35). A parish-by-parish census found a somewhat smaller population – 6,586 – in June 1753 (*Salisbury Journal* (hereafter *SJ*), 2 July 1753).

19 Evidence for both brothers' involvement is in the monogram of their initials (WC/BC) at the head of page one of the *Journal* for 6 July 1730. This is the only number of the first *Salisbury Journal* known to exist, a copy of which is in the present office of the *Salisbury Journal*, Salisbury.

20 Wiles, *Freshest Advices*, Appendix B.

21 Borsay's seven candidates for provincial capital in 1700 are Norwich, Bristol, Newcastle-upon-Tyne, Exeter, York, Chester and Shrewsbury, the last of which had no substantial newspaper until after 1760. While Borsay admits that his urban hierarchy is not a precise measure, it is a useful reference for comparison. See his *The English Urban Renaissance: Culture and Society in the Provincial Town 1660–1770* (Oxford: Clarendon Press, 1989), 4–11.

22 See C. Y. Ferdinand, 'Benjamin Collins, the *Salisbury Journal*, and the provincial booktrade', *Library*, 6th series, xi (June 1989), 116–38.

23 No record of William's death has been discovered and the *Journal* offers no explanation, but death seems the most likely reason for the disappearance of his name from the paper's colophon.

24 G. A. Cranfield's *Development of the Provincial Newspaper* and R. M. Wiles's *Freshest Advices* are both valuable wide-ranging works that allow the newspapers 'to speak for themselves'. Wiles's 'Chronological chart' (Appendix B) and 'Register of English provincial newspapers, 1701–1760' (Appendix C) make his book a particularly useful starting-point for a comparative study. Both have a cut-off date of 1760 however. More recently Jeremy Black has discussed the English newspaper Press in general, starting with the metropolitan Press at the end of the seventeenth century and incorporating material from country papers through the century in his *The English Press in the Eighteenth Century* (Philadelphia: University of Pennsylvania Press, 1987). John Feather's *History of British Publishing* and *The Provincial Book Trade in Eighteenth-Century England* (Cambridge: Cambridge University Press, 1983) help establish the background of the relationship between the provincial trade and the metropolitan trade, again in general terms. Investigations of the newspapers of specific regions have been undertaken by K. G. Burton in his *The Early Newspaper Press in Berkshire (1723–1855)* (Reading: published by the author, 1954), which includes a good history of the *Reading Mercury* and the *Reading Journal*, and J. Jefferson Looney's 'Advertising and society in England 1720–1820: a statistical analysis of Yorkshire newspaper advertisements' (Princeton University, Ph.D. thesis, 1983), and idem, 'Cultural life in the provinces: Leeds and York, 1720–1820', in A. L. Beier, David Cannadine and James Rosenheim (eds), *The First Modern Society: Essays in English History in Honour of Lawrence Stone* (Cambridge: Cambridge University Press, 1989). Looney's work deals specifically with advertising sampled from the papers of two important regional cities.

25 For example, the *Journal* occasionally mentioned an item's discovery after being cried about several towns, and the paper's printers frequently solicited printing jobs, including handbills.

26 In fact the few records available show a slight decrease in Salisbury population from the end of the seventeenth century to the mid-eighteenth (see n. 18 above).

27 R. M. Wiles marshals the circumstantial evidence for provincial newspaper circulation in 'The relish for reading in provincial England two centuries ago', in Paul J. Korshin (ed.), *The Widening Circle: Essays on the Circulation of Literature in Eighteenth-Century Europe* (Philadelphia: University of Pennsylvania Press, 1976), 89. E.g., Isaac Thompson claimed 'nearly two thousand regular purchasers of his *Newcastle Journal*' in 1739; *Whitworth's Manchester Magazine* was printed in 1,200 copies in 1755; Christopher Etherington published a list of 2,260 subscribers to his *York Chronicle* in 1776. Others have made informed speculations about circulation, as J. Jefferson Looney, who plausibly argues that the *York Courant* was distributing about 3,000 copies a week in 1760 while the *Leeds Intelligencer* sold 'a third of that figure' ('Cultural life in the provinces', 487). Until recently no eighteenth-century provincial newspaper account books – that might give true circulation figures – were known to exist. Information provided by the Eighteenth-century Short-title Catalogue project and G. H. Martin, former Keeper of the Public Record Office, led to the discovery in 1988 of the Winchester-based *Hampshire Chronicle*'s records for 1778–83 in the Public Record Office. These give precise figures for printing, circulation and returns for a newspaper that was viewed as a rival of the *Salisbury Journal*: the *Hampshire Chronicle* had an average print run of about 1,500 in the late 1770s and early 1780s (Public Record Office, E. 140/90–1).

28 Mrs Herbert (Norah) Richardson mentions this figure in 'Wiltshire newspapers – past and present. Part III (continued): the newspapers of South Wilts', *Wiltshire Archaeological and Natural History Magazine*, xli (1920), 62. It was evidently derived from a printed receipt for the *Salisbury Journal* now in the Salisbury and South Wiltshire Museum.

29 One newspaper at the end of the century went so far as to claim that 'The Profits of a newspaper arise *only* from Advertisements' (*Reading Mercury*, 10 July 1797; cited in Burton, *Early Newspaper Press in Berkshire*, 45). Subscription revenue probably covered production and distribution costs.

30 No complaints of this sort are recorded in the *Salisbury Journal* – in fact the most frequently printed consumer complaint in the *Journal* is that an advertisement or letter was omitted from an overfull number. However at least one provincial editor incidentally recognized the problem when he defended one of his news items:

supposing the Paragraph alluded to had been a Fiction, we are sanguine enough to hope that it would be more entertaining to our Readers than the whole Column stuffed up with Notices of Quack Medicines, Corn-Salve, Weal Registers, Nun's Drops, etc. etc. etc.

(*Liverpool Chronicle*, 17 March 1758, quoted in
Cranfield, *Development of the Provincial Newspaper*, 222)

31 Categories that were recorded in additional detail for this study are medical advertisements, which include the name of each nostrum; those for leisure activities, which include the activity and location; lost-and-found, which include a description of the missing article; services, which include the type of service – educational advertisements are transcribed in full; employment advertisements, which are broken down by sex when possible; runaways, by type (husband, wife, etc.); and book-trade advertisements, which include details about the book advertised (price, format, method of publication, etc.), as well as a list of the bookdealers involved.

32 Schumpeter-Gilboy price indices, 1696–1823, indicate low consumers' and producers' goods prices from the 1730s, with consumer goods (other than cereals) rising in the 1770s. See Peter Mathias, *The First Industrial Nation: An Economic History of Britain 1700–1914*, 2nd edn (London: Methuen, 1983), Figure 1 and Table 6; 63, 420.

33 Typical is William Biden, a stay-maker who made a point of going 'to London once a Year to have the newest Fashions' (*SJ*, 25 November 1754).

34 The total includes repeat advertisements.

35 Capillair is a drink based in a syrup extracted from maidenhair.

36 For further discussion of Fancourt's unusual career see Monte Little, *Samuel Fancourt, 1678–1768* (Trowbridge: Wiltshire Library and Museum Service, 1984).

37 *The Diary of Thomas Turner, 1754–1765*, ed. David Vaisey (Oxford: Oxford University Press, 1984). There are other published contemporary diaries, but Turner's seems especially relevant – he was a book- and newspaper-reading man, a provincial grocer who used the newspaper to buy some of the goods he retailed.

38 Looney proposes three divisions for leisure activity, which are loosely based on audience: first 'short-term promotions [as lectures, shows, performing animals], which tended to aim at a wide audience, were imported from outside the town and often timed to arrive when the town was packed because of a fair, assize or race meeting'; second 'amateur activities organized from within'; and third, the events organized by and for the 'resident elite' ('Cultural life in the provinces', 489–90). While this structure has not been imposed in this chapter, it might be useful to note that the events described here could fall within Looney's first and third categories.

39 See, for example, David Rayvern Allen, *Early Books on Cricket* (London: Europa Publications, 1987).

40 I am grateful to John Bidwell for revealing the secret: *The Impenetrable Secret Probably Invented by Horace Walpole: An Explanation of the Secret. With a Note on the Original by W. S. Lewis* (Windham, Conn.: Privately printed for W. S. Lewis, 1939).

41 John Dunton, *Life and Errors* (London: S. Malthus, 1705).

42 F. A. Edwards, 'Early Hampshire printers', *Papers and Proceedings of the Hampshire Field Club*, ii (1891), 110–34.

43 ESTC search, April 1988.

44 It was 3,585 in the 1801 census.

45 See C. Y. Ferdinand, 'Richard Baldwin Junior, bookseller', *Studies in Bibliography*, xlii (1989), 254–64.

46 Looney's representative years are 1741, 1760, 1784 and 1807. See 'Advertising and society in England', esp. Appendix D. 'Types of ad: a more detailed breakdown', 299–317.

20

The business of political enlightenment in France, 1770–1800

Jeremy D. Popkin

As the Estates-General began its sessions in Versailles in 1789, Jacques-Pierre Brissot, one of those 'tribunes of the people' Elizabeth Eisenstein refers to in her discussion of the political uses of print in the revolutionary era, published an eloquent demand for freedom of the periodical press. Uncensored newspapers and periodicals, he argued, were the indispensable agents of political enlightenment without which a free constitution could neither be created nor maintained. Only through the press could a large and populous modern country recreate the public forums of the classic city-republics; only through the press could one 'teach the same truth at the same moment to millions of men', and only through the press could they 'discuss it without tumult, decide calmly and give their opinion'.[1] The demand for press freedom, as Brissot articulated it, was an idealistic one: it seemed to have nothing to do with the grubby realities of the publishing trade or of the commercial market for printed goods. As Eisenstein has shown, writers like Brissot called for a free press because only through printed works could leaders reach a national audience in a country as large as eighteenth-century France.

Brissot's call for press freedom was soon answered: the fall of the Bastille enabled him to create his own journal, the *Patriote françois*, and within a few months, dozens of other periodicals had been established in Paris. As Brissot had foreseen, these journals became a forum for the most uninhibited discussion of political issues. But they also constituted something else: the basis of a thriving industry. 'The Revolution, as everyone knows, has ruined the old publishing trade', one journalist wrote in 1790. 'A new kind of publishing trade has replaced it. . . . It is fed exclusively by those frivolous sheets which, like flowers, unfold in the morning and wither by evening, to be replaced by new ones the next day.'[2] Political news and ideas had become commodities to be bought and sold, and the writer who could not put his ideas into marketable form had no chance of being heard above the cacophony of this furiously competitive market-place.

Like many of the changes associated with the French Revolution, this commercialization of political journalism had been foreshadowed under the Old Regime. Periodicals were one of the fastest growing sectors of the eighteenth-century publishing industry. As commodities, these serial works offered publishers many advantages. They had a regular and predictable sale; thanks to the subscription system, the publisher did not have to worry about having a warehouse full of copies that might take years to market. His customers paid in advance for their wares, virtually eliminating any risk. Whereas every book was an individual event, not easily duplicated, a successful periodical came with a built-in sequel, in the form of the next issue.[3] And the periodical seemed ideally suited to the growing reading public of the eighteenth century, which demanded a varied and rapidly changing literary diet. A few 'misanthropic savants' might regret the vogue for journalism, the editors of one mid-century magazine admitted, but 'should one write only for savants, or for those who want to become learned? . . . There is something between total ignorance and profound erudition . . . the multitude is incapable of studying and learning . . . so brochures and periodicals are necessary for our century.'[4] Consequently, the number of periodicals and the variety of subjects represented in them grew steadily throughout the 1700s. Jean Sgard has found 19 French-language periodicals appearing in France during the 1730s, and 65 in all of Europe; by the 1780s, the figures were 73 in France alone and 167 for the entire Continent.[5]

Publishers had long known that there was a strong demand for political news, and that the periodical was a particularly profitable form in which to publish it. The first regularly appearing newspapers had been created in the early 1600s, and there was a steady increase in their numbers throughout the eighteenth century. Successful newspapers were highly profitable: the *Gazette de Leyde*, the most reputable of Europe's news organs in the decades before 1789, earned more than 50,000 *livres* in its best years.[6] But in France, government restrictions severely limited publishers' abilities to enter the market for political news before 1789. A newspaper required a royal *privilège* or permit, and political news was theoretically a monopoly of the official *Gazette de France*. Until the middle of the eighteenth century, the French domestic newspaper industry was limited to that paper and the authorized reprints of it in various provincial cities.[7]

After 1752, the authorities allowed the creation of independent provincial periodicals or *Affiches* in the larger cities, and there were over forty of these by 1789, although their content was strictly commercial and literary.[8] They tended to be smaller and to publish a narrower range of advertisements than the English provincial papers of the period, such as the *Salisbury Journal* discussed in Christine Ferdinand's work (chapter 19 in this volume). In Paris, several other national periodicals were allowed to infringe somewhat on the *Gazette de France*'s monopoly on political news reports. The first daily paper, the *Journal de Paris*, was founded in 1777, and in the 1770s Charles-Joseph Panckoucke built the first French news 'empire', based on his ownership of the privileges for the *Gazette*, the *Journal de Bruxelles* and the *Mercure de France*.[9] But these authorized papers remained censored and confined to the printing of officially approved reports, mostly of foreign news.

For a higher quality of information, French-speaking readers could turn to the long-established extra-territorial gazettes, such as the *Gazette de Leyde* and the *Courrier d'Avignon*. These publications definitely offered fuller news, especially about French domestic affairs, than the domestic papers. But they, too, had their limitations: as John Adams, one of the American colonists' representatives in Europe, complained,

> all these papers . . . discover a perpetual complaisance for the French ministry, because they are always in their power so entirely, that if an offensive paragraph appears, the entrance and distribution of the gazette may be stopped by an order

from court, by which the gazetteer loses the sale of his paper in France, which is a great pecuniary object.[10]

The eighteenth-century French periodical press was thus more extensive and more interesting than the conventional contrast between England's 'libertarian' press system and France's 'authoritarian' one suggests.[11] Nevertheless, the English press was undeniably livelier. The number of periodical publications appearing in England was certainly greater, and their pages were open to a wider range of viewpoints on all subjects; they played a more direct part in both the marketing of goods and the shaping of political opinion. In England, John Brewer has shown that commercially minded printers like John Almon – who, among other things, helped publish the first of Jean-Paul Marat's political writings – were often committed political activists as well.[12] In pre-revolutionary France, the most politically significant publications were frequently printed abroad, by entrepreneurs whose interest in French politics was marginal, or else put out by clandestine operators for whom circulating a polemical message took precedence over running a profit-making enterprise.

Prior to 1789, these French publications were more likely to take the form of pamphlets than periodicals. These topical publications could be much more outspoken than any of the period's journals. From the point of view of publishers, however, pamphlets suffered from an irremediable drawback: they could not be satisfactorily exploited as a profit-making commodity. Normally published clandestinely, they could not be advertised; closely linked to ongoing events, they quickly lost their interest. The pamphlet was above all the weapon of organized political interest groups, such as the Jansenist parlementary magistrates who opposed Louis XV's ministers in a series of well-publicized confrontations from 1750 to 1771, and who could afford to subsidize the publication of propaganda favouring their positions.[13]

It was the last and greatest of these parlementary–ministerial confrontations under Louis XV that seems to have provided the impetus for the conversion of pamphlet journalism into new forms of political publishing that could be effectively commercialized. At the end of 1770, Louis XV, exasperated by twenty years of indecisive conflict with the supporters of the parlements, dismissed his chief minister, Choiseul, and turned the management of the state over to a triumvirate of ambitious and determined officials: the abbé Terray, the duc d'Aiguillon and the Chancellor Maupeou. The latter, in a manoeuvre that has come to be known as the 'Maupeou coup', undertook to cripple the parlementary opposition by replacing the sitting magistrates with a reconstituted court system.[14]

The 'Maupeou coup' inspired the greatest wave of pamphlet literature France had seen since the flood of Mazarinades in the 1640s. The 'Patriots', the supporters of the dismissed parlementary magistrates, generated well over a hundred titles accusing Maupeou of aiming at converting France into a 'ministerial despotism'. The ministers, for their part, engaged in an unprecedented campaign of printed propaganda on their own behalf, resulting in an almost equal number of pamphlets denouncing the magistrates for advocating policies aimed at making France an oligarchical republic. A number of recent studies have shown the role of the 'Maupeou coup' in radicalizing political thinking in France and thus in paving the way for the Revolution of 1789.[15] But the 'coup' also transformed the system by which political affairs were discussed in print.

The underground pamphleteers of 1771–2 demonstrated to one and all that there was a tremendous untapped market for uncensored political literature. In particular, the astounding success of one anti-Maupeou pamphlet series, the *Correspondance secrète et familière de M. de*

Maupeou avec M. de Sor*** Conseiller du nouveau Parlement, must have been an eye-opener for publishers. In time, these pamphlets acquired a quasi-periodical form, with each of the numbered sections giving broad hints of the timing for the next issue, and the Paris bookseller Sébastien Hardy recorded the intense anticipation with which the public waited for these promised sequels. When they did appear, the copies vanished at high prices 'with a speed much like that of a rocket'.[16] Although the work was initially the creation of a well-heeled parlementary agitator, Jacques-Mathieu Augeard, it was reprinted by the Lyon bookseller Joseph Duplain, the cut-throat profiteer who stars in the pages of Robert Darnton's *The Business of Enlightenment*.[17]

Could the popularity of the political discourses contained in the voluminous anti-Maupeou literature be turned into the basis of a continuing publishing enterprise? The answer was yes, and the proof was furnished by a series of publications that began to appear in 1774 and which I will refer to collectively as the 'Mairobert corpus'. Bibliographers, following a tradition dating back to the time of their publication, have attributed these works to one Mathieu-François Pidanzat de Mairobert, and it is indeed tempting to make him the central figure in this story. A retailer of clandestine manuscript *nouvelles* who was also a royal censor and a big-time stock speculator, he is certainly a fascinating figure, who would nicely link the worlds of commerce and politics. Whether he was actually the mastermind behind the 'Mairobert' collection is not clear, and in any event, volumes of the corpus continued to appear long after his death in 1779. But there is no doubt that the works themselves mark a major development in the history of eighteenth-century French journalism, and that their promotion and distribution reveal a keen sense of how to exploit interest in political events for commercial purposes.

Of the works that I include in the 'Mairobert corpus', the best-known is the voluminous *Mémoires secrets*, commonly known as the *Mémoires de Bachaumont*.[18] Literary scholars have mined this thirty-six volume series of gossip and anecdotes about the political and cultural life of Paris from 1762 to the 1780s extensively. The *Mémoires secrets* were the last of the 'Mairobert' works to appear, however. If the bibliographers are correct, Mairobert's first production was a collected edition of the *Correspondance secrète et familière*, published under the title of *Maupeouiana*. The same title was then used for a six-volume collection of anti-Maupeou pamphlet literature, which appeared after the hated minister's dismissal in 1774. But the public was bound to weary of these reprinted pamphlet texts. Successful commercial exploitation of the aftermath of the Maupeou 'coup' required a new approach.

The formula that made the 'Mairobert corpus' into an enterprise that would continue all the way to the Revolution had been found in the midst of the Maupeou crisis, although the results did not appear in print until several years later. According to a subsequent account in the *Mémoires secrets*, in October 1772, the pro-parlementary pamphleteers responsible for the *Correspondance secrète et familière* had decided to change their journalistic tactics. They replaced their satirical pamphlets with a *Journal politique, historique, critique et littéraire des hauts faits de M. de Maupeou*. Their reason was that there was nothing new to say about the political principles at stake in the Maupeou crisis, 'the dogmatics of the matter being exhausted. But new events occur unceasingly and can always busy a historian's pen.'[19] By transforming their work into a day-by-day chronicle, they could keep it going indefinitely.

The first three volumes of the promised *Journal historique* duly appeared in 1774, after Maupeou's dismissal, under the title *Journal historique de la Révolution opérée dans la Constitution de la Monarchie Françoise, par M. de Maupeou, Chancelier de France*. They had the form of a day-by-day account, similar to Pierre L'estoile's celebrated diary of the sixteenth-century wars of religion. The form derived from the manuscript news bulletins or *nouvelles à la main* which wealthy individuals in France and abroad subscribed to in order to obtain news that did not appear even in the extra-territorial gazettes. The compilers of the *Journal historique* made no secret of their indebtedness to such sources, but their printed text was not identical with any known manuscript original.

The *Journal historique* was an immediate success, as the several editions subsequent to the 1774 printing demonstrate. Although it remained banned in France until the Revolution – the French police confiscated a *colporteur*'s copy as late as November 1788[20] – it circulated widely in France and abroad. It could not be advertised openly, but there were other methods of publicity. It was 'puffed', for example, in a set of manuscript *nouvelles* often attributed to the same Pidanzat de Mairobert who supposedly edited the printed work: the manuscript *bulletiniste* expressed the hope that 'the faithful editor of this journal will continue it up to the moment when a new order of things restored the magistrates to all their functions'.[21] If this was in fact Mairobert praising his own work, he certainly knew that a sequel to the *Journal historique* was already in the works. Two additional volumes appeared in 1775, carrying the historical narrative through to the death of Louis XV in 1774, and a further two volumes came out in 1776. In their original form, these were clearly intended to end with the description of Louis XVI's coronation in 1775 and the restoration of the last provincial parlements dismissed by Maupeou. In fact, the edition of the *Journal historique* in the Bibliothèque Nationale in Paris does break off at this point, with the comment, 'This journal would extend indefinitely if we waited until everything had been perfectly restored to its accustomed order to finish it.'[22] But the work's compilers had clearly sensed that they could go on exploiting the formula they had found indefinitely, and indeed other editions of the *Journal historique* contain a breathless description of the *guerre des farines* in Paris in May 1775 that is missing in the Bibliothèque Nationale's version.[23]

If the 'Mairobert' compilers had decided to end the *Journal historique*, it was only in order to launch new projects that would exploit the market they had discovered with their first major venture. The last editions of the *Journal historique* were published in 1776; the following year saw the first volumes of two new series, the *Mémoires secrets* and the *Observateur anglois*. The latter was a direct continuation of the *Journal historique*: it consisted of regular instalments summarizing political events and Court gossip, beginning in December 1775, but heavily padded with older material dating from before the death of Louis XV. The *Mémoires secrets* began somewhat differently: the eight volumes published in 1777 consisted primarily of material from the 1760s. In both cases, one has the impression that the journalistic entrepreneurs behind these ventures, impressed with the success of their *Journal historique*, had decided to exploit their own back files on a much larger scale.

Both the *Observateur anglois* and the *Mémoires secrets* were immediate successes with readers who wanted the inside story on French politics. Horace Walpole's Paris correspondent, Madame du Deffand, begged him to get her a copy of the *Mémoires secrets*: in Paris, 'one can only obtain it with great difficulty'.[24] The manuscript bulletin now in the Bibliothèque Mazarine gave the *Observateur* a negative review, but in terms that probably only whetted subscribers' appetites to see its 'vicious satire of the Court and the city, without restraint or respect even for those who could have expected it'.[25] Two facts attest to the commercial success of both enterprises: first, both were continued steadily for a number of years – the last volumes of the *Observateur*, renamed the *Espion anglois*, appeared in 1785, and the final volumes of the *Mémoires secrets* were still being published at the time of the Revolution – and, second, both inspired numerous reprints and counterfeit editions. There are at least five editions of the early volumes of the *Observateur*, two dated 1777, one from 1780, one from 1782 and one from 1784. The publishing history of the *Mémoires secrets*, which ultimately ran to thirty-six volumes whose original editions were spread out over twelve years, is far more complex, but here again numerous editions of individual volumes can be found. Its compilers complained not only about counterfeit versions of their volumes, but about the numerous abridgements published under such titles as *Chronique scandaleuse*, *Espion des Boulevards*, *Journal des Gens du Monde* and the like.[26]

Over the years, these 'Mairobert' enterprises were transformed from their original highly politicized form into a venture whose aim was clearly to produce a fixed number of marketable volumes per year. The *Journal historique* had begun as a vehemently polemical work devoted entirely to attacking Maupeou's policies. As the political temperature in France declined after the restoration of the parlements in 1774, its successors turned to other fields and often gave the impression of relying on 'filler' to produce the necessary number of pages. The *Espion anglois* chronicled scandalous court cases and its later volumes often included long sections that were frankly pornographic: the *Mémoires secrets*' puff for its companion work's last three volumes drew readers' attention to several chapters on 'modern lesbians', which it hailed as 'spicy and in an absolutely new genre'.[27] Reviewers found the later volumes of the *Mémoires secrets* distinctly inferior to the early sections as well. A German commentator found the continuations 'tamer and more timid: they give us less from the boudoirs and private cabinets of the great, and there is less to satisfy evil-minded readers'.[28] The series had lost the clear political orientation that had dominated the *Journal historique*. Nevertheless, its compilers continued to issue three volumes a year up to the eve of the French Revolution, and booksellers' correspondence shows that the work continued to sell.[29]

The success of the various 'Mairobert' works demonstrates beyond a doubt that uninhibited political news and society gossip had become a highly marketable commodity in French-speaking Europe in the decade and a half before the French Revolution. Clever entrepreneurship had transformed the pamphlet wave of the early 1770s into the basis of a continuing enterprise that outlived its original political impulse and was still churning out profits for printers and booksellers until 1789. The 'Mairobert' entrepreneurs were not the only ones to recognize the tremendous potential for profits in this domain. The year in which their enterprise reached its height, 1777, was also the year in which the most talented of the continent's pre-revolutionary journalists began his most famous enterprise. The author was a figure whose scandalous activities frequently filled the pages of the *Mémoires secrets*: Simon-Nicolas-Henri Linguet.

Linguet was already a celebrity when he undertook the publication of his *Annales politiques, civiles et littéraires* in April 1777. He had made his name in the 1760s as a highly articulate opponent of the *philosophes* and the *Physiocrats*, whose penchant for embracing extreme positions – he considered slavery more humane than wage labour, and despotism a better form of government than limited monarchy – had earned him the status of France's leading *paradoxeur* after Rousseau.[30] Linguet was also a celebrated lawyer with a genius for publicity. At the time of the Maupeou coup, he sided with the unpopular ministers, a move that cost him his legal career when the judges ousted by Maupeou in 1771 reclaimed their seats in 1774. At that point, he turned to journalism, contracting to edit Panckoucke's *Journal de politique et de littérature*, but his attacks on the *philosophes* and his other pet targets led to his dismissal in 1776.

Linguet had earned the handsome sum of 10,000 *livres* a year as Panckoucke's employee, and he consequently had no doubt that the periodical market could be lucrative. Deprived of his post, he decided to create his own journal and market it by himself. Linguet's announced purpose, according to his prospectus, was 'to give a universal and impartial daily history of his century', composed by 'a man whose frankness and inflexible principles are only too well known'.[31] In private, he defined his motives somewhat differently. 'Remember, my friend', he told his Paris distributor, 'that I have only consigned myself to the . . . slavery of this work because of the hope of a quick and solid gain, without which I will break my chains at the end of the year.'[32] No journalist of the period was more determined to profit from his work, and none was to experience and describe the difficulties of exploiting the press market more graphically than Linguet.

Linguet's situation as an independent journal editor was considerably more difficult than his previous post in Paris. There the problems of printing and distribution had been handled by his employer, Panckoucke, one of the canniest and most successful publishers of the day. Linguet, by contrast, had no experience as a publisher, and London was not a major centre of French-language publication; none of the French-language printers there had a major presence on the Continent. Linguet himself complained that 'the workers here are so slow, so careless, that you can't count on them'.[33] In any event, Linguet was determined to avoid falling under the control of a publisher again, and he wanted to keep the profits of his work for himself. To distribute his journal in its main market, France, he employed an amateur agent rather than a professional bookseller, and he specifically instructed would-be subscribers not to follow the normal procedure of placing their order through a regular bookseller, who would take a cut of their payment as a commission and thereby reduce Linguet's income.[34]

The main reason for the success of Linguet's *Annales* was his undeniable talent as a journalist. His powerful writing style was unique and attracted a wide audience. As one recent biographer has put it,

> even if Linguet was not the creator of a genre which already existed, he was certainly the most remarkable and intelligent practitioner of it, the only one capable of making it an effective instrument of political criticism and of the diffusion of ideas.[35]

But Linguet was not naive enough to imagine that his literary skills alone would ensure either the success of his journal or his ability to retain the profits from it. From the outset, he entered into arrangements designed to enlarge the sale of the *Annales* and protect it from counterfeiting. The original edition of the journal would be produced in London and shipped across the Channel, where Linguet's agent Lequesne had managed, in spite of Linguet's repeated provocations of the French government, to obtain a promise that the journal's circulation would be tolerated and that it would in fact be delivered through the royal mails.[36] But Linguet also authorized two reprints of the *Annales*, one in The Hague and one in Lausanne, designed to reach markets in the rest of Europe and to make it unprofitable for unauthorized publishers to copy his work.[37]

Linguet also recognized the value in having journalistic allies, who would praise and publicize his journal in exchange for similar favours in the *Annales politiques*. His involvement in previous controversies deprived him of any chance of such alliances with the journals of the *philosophes*, who had come to dominate the main privileged periodicals in France, particularly the *Mercure de France*, but he found support from the abbé Royou, the successor of the *philosophes'* enemy Fréron as editor of the *Année littéraire* in Paris, and from Jean Manzon, editor of one of the leading international news gazettes, the *Courrier du Bas-Rhin*, as well as from the *Gazette de la Haye*, published by the same Pierre Frédéric Gosse who put out the Dutch edition of the *Annales politiques* in The Hague.[38]

Linguet's various arrangements for publication and publicity certainly paid off. The *Annales politiques* were an immediate success. A Paris manuscript news bulletin reported in early 1778, 'Linguet's journal creates new partisans for its expatriate author every day. Even his enemies cannot help praising this work, which soars gloriously above the thousand and one journals that inundate us.'[39] Linguet, who had cautiously held the press run of the initial issues to 1,500, had to raise it steadily, going as high as 4,000 by the fall of 1779, although he feared that this was 'true folly'.[40] Neither his careful publishing arrangements nor his success were sufficient to protect Linguet from the depredations of the counterfeiters, however. The unauthorized reprinting of periodical publications was a practice that dated back to the seventeenth century, and the counterfeiters were as sure as Linguet was that his new publication would find a wide audience. By the time he was writing the copy for the second trimester of his *Annales*, Linguet claimed to know of six reprints of his journal. At the end of 1777, he wrote to his Paris agent complaining of seven unauthorized editions. 'Voyagers arriving or leaving from Dover are offered a year for 18 *livres*, which makes me suspect they are reprinted here.' When the French entered the American War of Independence and Linguet prudently decided to relocate from London to a neutral country, the number of pirate editions skyrocketed. In mid-1778, he was complaining of fourteen. The journal was interrupted when Linguet was lured to Paris and imprisoned in the Bastille in 1780–2, but when he was able to resume it in 1783, he announced that he now had to deal with nineteen counterfeiters. In 1784, he upped the figure to twenty-two.[41] According to Linguet, there were presses turning out unauthorized copies of his work in almost every printing centre in Europe. Over the years, he mentioned counterfeit editions from Yverdun, Nantes, Bordeaux, Avignon, Bouillon, Brussels, Malines, Liège, Zweibrücken and Cremona. Occasionally, the exasperated Linguet published the prospectuses of these fraudulent editions to document his complaints.[42] Bibliographic research on the copies in present-day libraries amply documents his claims.[43]

The voracity with which publishers all over the European continent battened on Linguet's *Annales* is dramatic evidence of the way in which political periodicals had become hot commodities. The counterfeiters benefited from the difficulty eighteenth-century publishers had in producing large editions of a single work. Beyond a certain limit, the unit costs of publishing with hand-press technology no longer diminished.[44] Furthermore, the cost of delivering copies of a periodical to readers all over the Continent was high – greater than the cost of shipping ordinary books, since each volume of Linguet's journal consisted of eight numbers which had to be mailed separately. Even apart from the fact that Linguet, as he himself admitted, had set the cost of the *Annales* unusually high, there was a clear economic advantage on the side of the counterfeiters, who could turn out a limited edition suited to the needs of their market and distribute it in their own vicinity more cheaply than the distant original. Linguet's complaints indicate that the counterfeit editions normally retailed for only half the price he sought for the original.

Certainly the counterfeiters were not deterred by any moral scruples. Linguet could parody the pirates' prospectuses in the form of an advertisement beginning, 'We will assemble to plunder this house at B. Cartouche's place. . . . The furniture [stolen] will be sold at a third of its true value', and he could argue convincingly that pirate publishers' morals were sure to lead them into reproducing bad books: 'The counterfeiters start by robbing an honest writer or publisher; they wind up by putting out anything that might disturb the public peace, and the general security of society.'[45] But the pirate publishers had their own view of the matter. The German counterfeiter whose response to Linguet is inserted in the Göttingen University copy of the *Annales* argued that his procedure was moral because he was preventing the export of wealth from his state, thereby conforming to its general policy of discouraging costly imports and encouraging local production. Furthermore, he was spreading knowledge of Linguet's ideas to an audience that might not otherwise have had access to them. The audacious pirate implied that Linguet, far from being outraged, ought to be grateful to him for this service.[46]

Unable to bring the counterfeiters to heel, Linguet was left to gnash his teeth over them in repeated complaints in the *Annales*. Their assault on his property was one of the standing themes in almost every volume of the journal. He saw it as evidence of a massive conspiracy against him and lamented the manner in which counterfeiting corrupted the ideal relationship between journalist and reader. In an 'Avis' published in 1783, Linguet charged that 'my shipments are either held up by secret manoeuvres, or intercepted by even more astonishing arrangements. . . . I have sent the previous issues to all the subscribers I know of, but very few have escaped the net drawn around me.' And he rose to a dramatic pitch of paranoia:

> In legends one reads of certain ingenious persecutors who, after having disjointed, torn apart, grilled and boiled certain martyrs, laid them on beds of rose petals, to make them die in circumstances suggesting voluptuousness, or at least dishonesty. The bed prepared for me today is not so soft, but it is the same manoeuvre, and the silence which seeks to smother me is even more clever than the tortures which sought to kill me, for there are men in the world sufficiently unjust to blame me for all these misfortunes.[47]

Linguet's critics continued to charge that there was no conspiracy, and that all his complaints were simply the result of his own avarice. He was widely reported to have made large sums from the *Annales*, as much as 80,000 *livres* a year.[48] Linguet had always argued that an author had every right to calculate on making a living from his work:

> Since from the monarch down to the day-labourer, everyone lives from the income he extracts, whether voluntarily or through compulsion, for his services, the man of letters who does not expect any [reward] from his, would be committing a veritable sin against himself and his heirs.[49]

He maintained that his policy was more honest than that of writers who disdained royalties but accepted pensions: only the self-supporting author could claim to be truly independent.[50] To justify himself, he even provided details of his costs of production, claiming that although printing the journal cost him only a quarter of the sale price, and booksellers' commissions only an eighth, postage and other expenses ate up most of the rest of his income from the work.[51]

Although Linguet stoutly defended his right to make a profit from the *Annales*, he also professed to be particularly outraged by what the existence of pirate editions did to his bond with his readers. The journalist's true reward, Linguet maintained, was his knowledge that he had a devoted audience:

> One of the most cherished compensations for a delicate and sensitive writer in my position, is to know what kind of people esteem him and seek him out; it is to be in a way in daily correspondence with his readers and to be able to go over the [subscription] list and form an impression of where his ideas are destined to go.

This contact with his subscribers was not a crass commercial liaison:

> It is not vanity that is fed by these unsought, uncoordinated and therefore all the more flattering testimonials. It is a sweet, pure joy; it is the refreshing assurance of having devoted friends in all classes and ranks of society.[52]

The counterfeiter's crime was not just material but moral: it disrupted the harmonious communion between writer and reader.

Linguet was aware, however, that the commodity nature of his periodicals also threatened this harmony. After one complaint against the counterfeiters, he lamented,

> The public's coldness and indifference to such matters are extreme, I know. What matters to them is not that the author reaps the fruit of his work, but to have his book cheaply. For a momentary pleasure, and a savings of 20 *sous*, an infinite number of people will unthinkingly make themselves accomplices of a veritable theft.[53]

For him, much was at stake in this matter. His doctrine of intellectual independence required that honest writers 'should not expect or receive anything except from the Public';[54] if the readers allowed themselves to be corrupted, writers would be equally unable to maintain their integrity. But readers were not indifferent to financial considerations when it came to subscribing. The ever-hostile *Mémoires secrets* took pleasure in reporting how Lequesne, Linguet's French agent, was besieged by subscribers demanding refunds when Linguet's imprisonment interrupted the *Annales*'s appearance.[55] Linguet found himself forced to offer material inducements to court those subscribers who were supposed to come to him on the basis of shared feelings and ideas. To entice them, he offered a variety of tangible favours: a free volume, a portrait of the author and an index for each year's collection.[56] When he resumed the *Annales* in 1787, he cut the subscription price from 48 to 33 *livres*.[57]

Despite his repeated complaints, Linguet earned enough from the *Annales* to support himself throughout his years in exile. Indeed, if it was attention he was after, he owed a genuine debt to the counterfeiters: it was their editions that helped elevate the *Annales* to the position of perhaps the most-read journal in Europe. The contemporary observer who put the press run of Linguet's authorized editions of the *Annales* at 6,000 to 7,000, suggested that the counterfeit editions boosted its total circulation to around 20,000.[58] Linguet accused other writers of boasting about the pirating of their works as a way of demonstrating their popularity:[59] perhaps his reiterated complaints served the same function. But the frequency and vehemence with which he returned to the subject, and the elaborate measures he announced to counter the pirates – at one point he decided to have only three of the four sheets composing each issue printed on his own presses in Belgium, with the fourth being printed in Paris so that counterfeiters could not get their hands on a complete copy in time to compete with him[60] – suggest that for Linguet, the piracy issue was more than an advertising come-on. Linguet recorded every iota of his anguish at his inability to control the sale of his own writings, and his experience demonstrated that even the most talented and determined writers were at the mercy of mechanisms they could not control. Not only was political journalism a commodity, but that fact inevitably dominated the life of every writer who engaged in it.

The examples of the 'Mairobert' enterprise and of Linguet's *Annales politiques* demonstrate that political literature was already being tailored to the market before the Revolution, and that the workings of the market-place were in turn having an unmistakable effect on the journalists themselves. Until 1789, however, censorship and the system of booksellers' *privilèges* restricted the growth of the French press market. With the coming of the Revolution, these restrictions collapsed. Journalists were freed to write whatever they pleased, and publishing entrepreneurs were freed to pursue whatever market opportunities they could find. The result was a vast increase in the volume for all kinds of printing with political content. The market was flooded with cheap engravings and caricatures,[61] pamphlets and, above all, periodicals. The number of competing newspapers published in Paris soared: whereas there had been only the four authorized papers in 1788, 140 new titles were started before the end of 1789. It is true that most of these were very short-lived – many never got beyond the circulation of a prospectus – but there is no question that French readers were being offered a far wider range of journalistic products than ever before.[62]

Beyond noting that successful newspapers during the revolutionary decade were highly profitable, the historians of the press during this period have paid little attention to the commercial aspects of these publications.[63] Most have analysed the revolutionary newspapers in purely political terms, and attributed their success or failure to the talent of their most prominent contributors. In fact, however, when the revolutionary-era newsman Pierre-Louis Roederer sought to categorize 'the different means available for the communication of ideas among men in the social state' in 1796, he began his discussion of newspapers with the statement that 'the newspaper is . . . a commodity that is sold'. He mentioned the journalist's role only in passing, and made no mention of the importance of political orientation at all.[64] And there is ample evidence both of the importance of market considerations in shaping the revolutionary press and of the ways in which the commercial free-for-all unleashed by the 1789 'press revolution' affected even the most celebrated writers of the period.

The dozens of competing newspapers in revolutionary Paris were the product of a printing industry that had had to transform itself in a matter of months to meet the French nation's greatly increased demand for news. Prior to 1789, printing and publishing had been tightly controlled by the government and by the printers' guild. The number of printing shops was limited to 36 in the capital and 266 in the French provinces. These licensed printers had every incentive to co-operate with the authorities in preventing the emergence of new competitors, and little reason to question a system which guaranteed them a good living with a minimum of entrepreneurial effort. Printing licences were virtually hereditary, and the vast majority of the compositors and pressmen who worked for these privileged employers knew they had no chance of ever becoming master printers in their own right. Before the Revolution, Paris had been a centre of magazine production, but its newspaper industry had been small; as we have seen, the country's most influential news periodicals, such as the *Gazette de Leyde*, were published outside its borders.

The Revolution shattered the old legal and guild restrictions, and forced printers and publishers to adopt new strategies to make profits.[65] Newspaper publishing was one of the main resources to which they turned. Anyone who wanted to could now open a printing shop or become a publisher, and dozens did. Furthermore, it was mostly these newcomers – former printing-shop workers, printers from the French provinces and even from abroad – who took up the challenge of producing the newspapers that were suddenly so much in demand. M. S. Boulard, one of these new entrepreneurs, sought to cash in on the printing boom by publishing a manual for would-be entrants to the trade: he assured his readers that a decent printing shop could be furnished for little more than 8,000 *livres*, a sum not out of reach even for many members of the petty bourgeoisie, but he was convinced that a newspaper enterprise could be launched for even less. According to his calculations, a single press, a single font of type and the other minimal requirements of the trade should cost only 2,146 *livres*; allowing 1,200 *livres* for advances on wages and rent, he concluded that all it took to become a newspaper publisher was an investment of 3,346 *livres*. Provided the reader of his book kept his advice in mind at all times, Boulard was confident that anyone could get started in publishing without any prior knowledge of the field whatsoever.[66]

Thanks to the fact that subscriptions were paid in advance, 'the journalist has his enterprise assured, he takes no risk, he makes no advances, all his expenses are covered, he has already pocketed all his income before he spends a sou on his subscribers', one writer commented.[67] If a newspaper found readers quickly, the newly fledged publisher had an assured source of regular income; if it flopped, he had at worst a few reams of unsold copies to dispose of, and no matter how few subscribers he had been able to collect, in the furious competition of the revolutionary press market, he could always find a competitor who would pay something to add them to the ranks of his own readers. In 1797, the measly 300 subscribers of the *Déjeuner* struck the owners of the equally shaky *Aurore* as worth a third of the stock in the combined enterprise plus enough money to cover the debts of the failing party of the first part, which amounted to only 300 *livres* in any case.[68]

Boulard's calculations help explain why so many of the newly minted Parisian printers and publishers turned to putting out newspapers, and why it was so difficult for successive revolutionary regimes to discourage this trade. To be sure, many more newspapers failed and quickly disappeared than succeeded, but there were enough dazzling fortunes made in the business to keep attracting new entrants. Poncelin de la Roche-Tilhac had been an anonymous hack-writer before the Revolution. By 1797, he was the publisher of two successful newspapers and owner of one shop worth 40,000 *livres* and a third-interest in another, worth 10,000 *livres*, as part of a total fortune that he estimated at 164,000 *livres*.[69] The publisher Lenormant had been a journeyman printer before 1789; he set up in business for himself, specialized in counter-revolutionary titles and eventually became the printer and part-owner of the immensely successful *Journal des Débats* of the Napoleonic era.[70] And behind every other successful newspaper of the revolutionary era there was an entrepreneur making a healthy profit. Indeed, these largely anonymous figures were the unsung heroes of the press during the revolutionary era: without their enterprise and organizational ability, the flow of political information on which the Revolution depended would have been choked off.

The newspaper publishers who flourished in this politically charged environment needed skill, dedication, tremendous energy and luck. They had to cope with new technical challenges, restless workers, an uncertain legal and institutional environment and the threat of political violence. The most committed and imaginative ones were concerned with every aspect of their publications. Joseph Duplain, an aggressive book publisher under the Old

Regime, was among the most innovative newspaper entrepreneurs of the revolutionary era. To promote his *Courrier extraordinaire, ou le Premier arrivé*, he set up a system of private stagecoaches to deliver his paper ahead of competitors who relied on the regular mails. He also suggested that readers form a network of clubs that would discuss the actions of the National Assembly and exchange their opinions through his paper, and in 1790 he became the first journalist to report regularly on the sessions of the Jacobin club in Paris. When France became involved in war in 1792, he offered substantial sums to soldiers who could 'write legibly' and would send bulletins to his paper. Unlike most revolutionary newspaper publishers, he eagerly, if not very successfully, sought commercial advertising for his paper.[71] Duplain's fate illustrates the special problems of newspaper publishing during the revolutionary era, however: he ran afoul of the revolutionary government and was guillotined in 1794.[72]

Denis-Romain Caillot was another publisher who worried about all aspects of his papers. In his pursuit of profits, he worked all sides of the political fence: in 1791, he was simultaneously printing the pro-revolutionary *Lettres bougrement patriotiques du Père Duchesne* and doing job-printing for the ultra-reactionary abbé Royou, editor of the *Ami du Roi*.[73] In early 1797, Caillot left Paris to try to set up a system of special-delivery coaches like the one Duplain had established in 1790. As he went from town to town making arrangements for this express delivery system, he also took a reading of public opinion and bombarded the editor in Paris with conflicting instructions on how to tailor the paper's content. He kept up with rival papers and chastised his own editor when a competitor scooped him on a major story. Caillot recruited correspondents to expand his paper's news-gathering network, and suggested that his editor steal a march on the other Paris papers by bribing a worker in the government's printing shop to obtain advance copies of new laws, stipulating what should be paid for such service. Even though he had been publishing newspapers for more than six years by the time of this trip, he still found it a full-time job.[74] As if publishing a newspaper was not sufficiently demanding, many entrepreneurs also engaged in other activities. Joseph Fiévée, who printed the successful pro-revolutionary daily *Chronique de Paris* in 1790–3, also published books, pamphlets, plays and a magazine to keep his seven presses occupied, and when the *Chronique* needed additional copy, he sometimes penned it himself.[75]

The busy entrepreneurs of the French press during the Revolution had little time to experiment with new ways of producing their products. They relied on the familiar wooden hand printing press, still basically the same machine that Johannes Gutenberg had invented more than three hundred years earlier: the chaotic conditions of the press market discouraged investments in new technology of the sort that led to the invention of the more efficient Stanhope iron hand-press in England just after 1800. French printers did not even adopt the faster but more complicated and expensive wooden Anisson-Duperron press invented in their own country in the 1780s. To increase production, they simply added more presses: by 1794, Charles-Joseph Panckoucke, publisher of the *Moniteur* and the *Mercure de France*, was presiding over an establishment with twenty-seven presses, employing ninety-one workers.[76] Panckoucke's establishment was a large one for the period, overshadowed only by the gigantic government printing shops, such as the *Imprimerie des administrations nationales*, which had forty presses and several hundred employees in 1794–5, and the even larger *Imprimerie nationale*.[77]

But even the smaller shops which published most of the newspapers during the revolutionary decade needed numerous workers and had to adopt new methods of organizing their printing work. To put out the four separate impressions of the modest *Journal de Perlet* that can be identified by the tiny press numbers in their lower margins would have required a minimum of eight compositors, eight pressmen and a foreman. In fact, considering that the paper appeared seven days a week and that additional workers would have been needed to do tasks such as cleaning and redistributing type that normal printing-shop workers did on slow days when there was no other urgent work to handle, the *Perlet*'s work-force would have had to be even larger, including various less-skilled workers such as the *plieuses* who folded the printed sheets and put pre-printed address labels on copies for the mail. All these workers had to be hurried along on a time schedule very different from that characteristic of work in eighteenth-century book-publishing or job-printing shops. Whereas book printers worked on an erratic schedule suited to the irregular nature of their production, newspaper printers had to achieve regular, dependable output at high speed. To meet the public's demand for the freshest possible information, they had to print at night, which made the work more difficult and forced them to pay higher wages: Boulard indicated that the pressmen, who normally earned 6–8 *livres* for a day's work, expected a premium of 3 *livres* for night work, and 2 *livres* for work on Sundays and holidays.[78] Exactly how work was organized in the crowded Paris printing shops where the 15–30 compositors and printers it took to put out a successful daily paper scrambled about by candlelight to jam hastily set type into printing frames, ink them and manhandle the bulky presses to produce the printed sheets we do not know. But although the owners and workers who rushed about producing the papers of the Revolution used old artisanal methods, they were working under unrelenting time-pressure alien to the pre-industrial world, but only too familiar in the factories that became common in the nineteenth century.

Despite these rigorous working conditions, newspaper publishers had little difficulty luring workers away from more traditional printing enterprises. In 1790, Panckoucke, one of the few Old Regime publishers who was also successful in the revolutionary press market, complained that all workers cared about was the extra money they could earn from night work. 'They have been seduced by the money they can make; but you can be sure that they will soon recognize that this work ruins their health', he warned.[79] But defenders of the new printing shops replied that Panckoucke and his colleagues only raised such arguments because they still believed that 'while making immense fortunes out of the sweat and long hours of their workers, they had the right to treat them with contempt, and subject them to humiliating controls'. But these efforts would not deter workers from abandoning their old employers for new ones whose rates of pay offered 'the hope of putting something aside for their old age'.[80] Newspaper printing workers were loyal to their trade and came to have a strong stake in the survival of the newspaper industry. After the Directory's decree of 18 fructidor V (4 Sept. 1797), which put over thirty counter-revolutionary papers out of business, the police discovered that some of the suddenly unemployed workers from the banned papers' shops had joined together to establish their own paper 'to give themselves a means of making a living'.[81]

Although there were always willing compositors and pressmen to manufacture newspapers, the conditions of haste and unrestrained competition under which they worked meant that the quality of the work they did was often poor. The irascible Jean-Paul Marat took time off from his denunciations of political conspiracies to lament that 'workers without education and civic spirit pitilessly mess up my paper, to save themselves an hour of work'.[82] More familiar with the difficulties of printing at high speed, Joseph Duplain told his readers that the errors in his *Courrier extraordinaire* were inevitable:

> The speed with which I have to write, the lack of time for the workers to make corrections . . . the unavoidable necessity of never reading more than one proof, all that is an invincible obstacle to my goal of putting out work more worthy of you.[83]

Organizing the work process and managing the printing shop were only part of the task of the revolutionary press entrepreneur. He also had to see to the distribution of his paper and collect the money due from its subscribers. In Paris, most papers employed a corps of hawkers who peddled single numbers of each issue in the streets and cafés. Their loyalty and goodwill were essential for the success of any paper; journalist–entrepreneurs like Marat and Jacques-René Hébert, the author of the *Père Duchêne*, went out of their way to cultivate dependable vendors.[84] When the Paris city government tried to limit the number of street-hawkers early in the Revolution, Marat came to their defence, proclaiming that such regulation was 'the cleverest of attacks against the freedom of the press, which becomes meaningless if authors' productions cannot be publicized'.[85]

Provincial subscribers received their copies through the mail or via distributors in the larger towns. Maintaining subscription registers and keeping track of distributors' payments involved considerable clerical work. Caillot's *Courrier extraordinaire* maintained correspondence with distributors in fifty-seven provincial cities in 1797, and the *Journal de la Montagne*, published for little more than a year, accumulated one set of registers listing 5,575 individual subscribers and a second keeping track of the paper's income and outgoings.[86] In 1791, the *Gazette de Paris* employed an officer manager and three to five clerks to cope with this sort of record-keeping.[87] The French press historian Gilles Feyel has suggested that many revolutionary papers disappeared not because of inadequate sales but because their publishers were swamped with subscriptions and lacked the organizational skills to keep up with them.[88] The slowness of mail delivery to the provinces was a constant irritation to newspaper publishers, as Duplain's and Caillot's efforts to set up their own delivery systems indicate. Copies often went astray in the mail, and some papers, like the *Nouvelles politiques* of the Directory era, maintained a regular register of subscribers' complaints.[89]

The newspaper entrepreneurs of the revolutionary decade, harried enough by the difficulties of overseeing the production and distribution of their publications, faced the additional challenge of operating in a viciously competitive market-place without any legal protection, and in a situation where political crises could destroy their enterprises at any time. The demand for political journals was great enough to sustain a large number of titles, but there were always more newspapers trying to carve out niches for themselves than the market could really support. Cut-throat competition was the rule, overriding even political solidarity with like-minded sheets. Under the Directory, when the counter-revolutionary *Précurseur* tried to get copies to its subscribers in southern France faster than its rivals by setting up a satellite printing operation in the Midi, the owners of the equally right-wing *Quotidienne* appealed to the same republican authorities they slandered every day in their columns to punish their rivals for violating the post office's monopoly on delivery.[90]

With the disappearance of the monarchy's system of royal privileges for periodicals, there were no laws defining the property of a newspaper. With such enticing profits at stake, bare-knuckled combat was the rule rather than the exception. Every time a journalist or a publisher came up with a formula that attracted an audience, rival editions, either counter-feits copied verbatim from the original or imitations that used the same techniques and, frequently, the same titles were sure to follow. The weekly *Révolutions de Paris*, one of the instant bestsellers started immediately after the fall of the Bastille, warned readers against unauthorized imitations as early as its eighth issue. In the space of a few months, readers were faced with a rival version of the paper, also titled *Révolutions de Paris*, as well as imitations billing themselves as the *Révolutions nationales* and the *Révolutions de Versailles et de Paris*.[91] The same fate befell the outspokenly counter-revolutionary *Ami du Roi*: it began as a single enterprise in June 1790, but by the following September, there were three rival daily papers claiming the same title, all following more or less the same political line while exchanging scathing insults with one another.[92] The confusion among the half-a-dozen rival publications based on the character of the hot-tempered *Père Duchesne* has bedevilled bibliographers down to the present day, and even the inimitable Marat faced rivals who appropriated his title of *Ami du Peuple*. They 'fight among themselves for my title, my epigraph, my name, my other features', Marat lamented, later remarking of one imitator that 'in a country where justice prevails, he would be condemned . . . to have his hand cut off'.[93] Even assassination did not protect Marat from those who sought to cash in on his journalistic success: after Marat's death, two rivals undertook unauthorized continuations of his paper.

Cases such as the multiple editions of the *Révolutions de Paris* and the *Ami du Roi* demonstrated that the most dangerous rivals a successful newspaper owner faced were his own collaborators. The two competing *Révolutions de Paris* were the result of a split between the author and the publisher of the original work: in this case, Prudhomme, the publisher, triumphed over Tournon, the author. The dispute over the title of the *Ami du Roi* saw the original publisher, Crapart, face off with two of the editorial contributors, the abbé Royou and Montjoye. Combatants in these family feuds knew no restraints. Private contracts among the collaborators in a paper, such as the agreement between the publisher and the printer of the *Miroir* obliging the latter not to undermine the former's right of property in the paper 'directly or indirectly during and after the period of the present agreement either by forming or cooperating on another paper under the same name or by any other act of invasion of the journal and its income'[94] were intended to forestall such civil wars, but their value depended entirely on the good faith of the parties: by the time a court judgement could have been obtained in such a case, it was most likely that either the newspaper-reading public would already have rendered a verdict in favour of one or the other of the disputants, or the paper might well have been suppressed for political reasons.

The newspaper industry none the less never lacked for eager entrepreneurs and willing workers. Despite the political risks, the lure of jobs and profit was simply too great. Even after the Terror and the violent inflation that affected newspapers as it did every other branch of business in France in 1794–5, a journalist–publisher of the period was certain that 'newspapers remain, in spite of their losses, the most lucrative branch of French literature'.[95] The break-even point for a newspaper was low, perhaps as few as 400 to 450 copies per issue,[96] and the rate of profit mounted rapidly after that. Documents from two royalist papers whose records were seized in 1792 indicate that the *Gazette de Paris* earned a clear profit of over 25,000 *livres* on sales of 2,300 copies a day and that Royou's *Ami du Roi* may have brought in as much as 88,000 *livres* in its best year.[97] These high profits resulted from the fact that the revolutionary papers, which competed in every other area, did not challenge each other over prices. Most set their subscription rates close to the 36 *livres* a year that had been standard for the high-quality foreign gazettes before 1789; those that were significantly cheaper, such as the weekly *Feuille villageoise*, delivered many fewer total pages. It is curious at first glance that the newspaper publishers of revolutionary Paris, vigorous risk-taking capitalists in most respects, did not see the reason for sacrificing some of their profit margin to increase their total sales, but there was some logic to their behaviour. Since an increase in sales beyond a certain point meant paying compositors and pressmen to make another impression of the paper, the marginal cost of production did not necessarily drop as sales expanded. Joseph Duplain pointed this out to would-be subscribers in 1792, explaining that he would not be able to accept new requests for copies until he had enough firm orders 'to go on to a new composition'.[98] Furthermore, sticking to the high standard subscription price meant that the paper would cover its costs even if it sold only a few hundred copies, and that profits would be highly satisfactory if it sold a few thousand. The high-price policy was a safe one for all concerned, and it compensated for the extraordinary risks of the revolutionary market. As a result, newspaper publishers could ride out the economic fluctuations of the revolutionary decade without much risk. Even the hyperinflation of 1794–6, which reduced the value of advance subscription payments, does not seem to have bankrupted any but a few marginal papers: most were able to raise their subscription prices fast enough to avoid disaster and, if necessary, they resorted to the legally dubious but pragmatically unavoidable course of simply shortening the length of pre-paid subscriptions.

Behind every newspaper of the revolutionary era there was then an entrepreneur who viewed the publication first and foremost as a profit-making enterprise. But what of the journalists? Were they, like Linguet in the pre-revolutionary years, personally affected by the sordid details of journalistic marketing? Pierre-Louis Roederer, who had defined newspapers as a commodity, attempted to persuade the public that journalists never sullied themselves with such pecuniary matters. 'Most are not the owners of the papers for which they work', he claimed. 'Calculations are exclusively the province of the owners or directors, and ideas are exclusively the authors'.'[99] Even as he wrote these lines, however, Roederer was involved in a lengthy dispute about the division of the profits from his own paper, the *Journal de Paris*.[100] A more honest writer of the Directory period resurrected a famous passage from the pre-revolutionary writings of Linguet to justify the journalists' claim to proper remuneration for their work:

> Why, then, should the writer for a periodical, a writer who devotes his nights and often sacrifices his comfort to instruct his fellow-citizens, why should he not, without ceasing to be honest and scrupulous, figure out the income from his paper, and count on a monetary reward? It is not letting himself be stained by ignominious favours or partialities that he maintains his honesty, and not by refusing a salary he has legitimately earned.[101]

Not many journalists were as open about this aspect of their profession as this man, but even fewer were indifferent to the rewards their efforts could earn them.

Journalism during the Revolution was a profession, and indeed a well-paying one, and the desire to make a living rivalled the urge to make a statement or serve a cause as the principal motive for pursuit of the profession. Jacques-René Hébert, reduced to penury, discovered his journalistic vocation through the accident of a meeting with a publisher willing to pay him to try his hand at writing.[102] Charles Lacretelle earned more than 3,000 *livres* a year for his anonymous reportorial work in the early years of the Revolution,[103] and the stars of the journalistic firmament made far larger sums: 10,000 *livres* a year for Camille Desmoulins, upwards of 12,000 *livres* for Jacques Mallet du Pan as editor of the political section of the

Mercure de France, a reported 25,000 *livres* a year for the young Elysée Loustallot on the *Révolutions de Paris*.[104] These fabulous salaries went to writers who were not even co-owners of their papers: those who were could aspire to even greater revenues. This was a far different world from the one in which Rousseau had sold the rights to the great best-seller of the 1760s, his *Emile*, for 6,000 *livres*. Even though many of the most successful journalists managed to let most of their income slip through their fingers – Marat, Hébert and Desmoulins all died poor – they had earned more with their pens in less time than any other writers before them. The journalists of the French Revolution blazed the way for the writers in other genres who would succeed in tapping the growing mass market for literature in the nineteenth and twentieth centuries.

Those journalists who were in a position to do so drove hard bargains for their services. Isidore Langlois, barely out of his teens when he became a successful right-wing editorialist after thermidor, agreed to write for a daily known as the *Messager du Soir* in 1796 for a guaranteed minimum salary of 3,240 *livres* and a bonus of 1 per cent of the enterprise's gross revenues for every copy sold above 4,000 a day. But the contract also assured him of protection against the hazards of the trade. He was to receive half pay during 'any imprisonment or forced absence caused by the journal'; if he had to emulate Marat and hide in a basement, he would at least have a regular income. A similar provision covered incapacitation due to illness, and another clause specified severance pay. The publisher was also obligated to provide his star employee with a heated and well-lit private office. For a journalist with less than a year's experience, it was a handsome arrangement.[105]

The frequent clashes between journalists and their employers are sufficient testimony to the seriousness with which many writers defended their pecuniary privileges. There was hardly a single prominent journalist of the revolutionary period who did not have to endure an acrimonious quarrel with the publisher of his paper, a dispute usually brought to public attention when both parties began publishing their own versions of the disputed paper. Among the stars of the revolutionary journalistic firmament whose publishers tried to replace them with more pliable or less expensive editorialists were Camille Desmoulins, Jacques-René Hébert and the abbé Royou. Camille Desmoulins spoke for the profession as a whole when he protested against his original publisher's effort to exercise his option to replace the editor of the *Révolutions de France et de Brabant* after its first six months in existence. 'I call [it] my journal, although the publisher claims it is his', Desmoulins wrote. 'I am truly father of my 26 previous issues, since I drew them out of my brain. . . . But this quarrel between the publishers and we unfortunate authors is an old one.'[106] The abbé Royou, opposed to Desmoulins on almost every other issue, agreed with him on this one when he was victimized by the three-way split of the original *Ami du Roi*: 'It is sad indeed . . . that writers are subjected to those who, by the nature of their functions, are not and cannot be anything but their agents.'[107]

Because newspapers were indeed 'hot properties' during the revolutionary decade, even the celebrity journalists found themselves in the condition of wage labourers. Like the American movie stars of the 1920s and 1930s, they enjoyed the prerogatives of fame and fortune, but they were not fully independent unless they could succeed in wresting outright ownership of their titles from their publishers. Marat, the abbé Royou – who had the advantage of a sister who had been the business manager of a well-established journal under the Old Regime – and Hébert were among the minority of journalists who succeeded in doing this, but most lacked either the opportunity or the ability to market their own words.

The commercial nature of the press market thus affected journalists' lives. But did it also leave its mark on the content of their papers? Most of the prominent journalists whose careers we can follow appear to have been more concerned with the success of their chosen political cause than with the market appeal of their words. Those who adopted techniques that have been used to spur sales in other periods of journalistic history had convincing arguments for their behaviour. Jean-Paul Marat, who put screaming summaries at the start of each of his issues, maintained that his sensationalism was a political necessity. It was the patriotic journalist's duty to 'keep [the people] continuously agitated, to keep all minds in ferment, until the government is based on truly just principles'. All journalistic means were legitimate to do this. Marat exalted 'the magic power of a terrible scandal' for protecting the public interest.[108] Political solidarity overrode the competitive instincts normal among journalists propounding the same ideas and seeking the same audience: both patriot and counter-revolutionary writers praised their like-minded colleagues, and the *Révolutions de Paris*'s Elysée Loustallot urged his pro-revolutionary colleagues to contend for the honour of having done the most to bring about the triumph of liberty: 'Patriot writers, let us see which of us will win the palm! how glorious it will be to have been surpassed!'[109] Not until well into the Directory period did the tendency to pad increasingly dull political articles with other kinds of content that had been so clear in the 'Mairobert' volumes of the 1780s begin to show itself in the daily press.

The intensity of the journalists' political commitments and the public's seemingly insatiable appetite for undiluted political news kept the press of the revolutionary years from showing too many visible effects of commercialization. But in a larger sense, the entire shape of the revolutionary press reflected the pressure of a market that demanded something quite different from what political wisdom might have dictated that journalists should provide. The critiques of the daily papers that appeared regularly throughout the Revolution made it clear that their form of journalism was far from satisfying everyone. The distinguished intellectuals who launched the *Chronique du mois* in 1791 argued that their magazine would be indispensable for the political activists 'whose patriotism frequently needs enlightenment from those who have meditated, in their studies, the fundamental bases of public welfare'.[110] Similarly, the entrepreneurs of a *Collection of the Decrees of the National Assembly* complained that the daily papers made it impossible to determine what laws had actually been passed: 'often one doesn't learn whether a decree was passed and signed. . . . To find all the provisions, one has to consult twenty different papers.' But the author of this prospectus admitted that, whatever their defects, the daily papers satisfied 'the public's impatient curiosity'.[111] Alternative ways of commenting on politics in print, whatever their merits, could not compete with the daily political newspaper, devoted to the latest events. It was no accident that when the Committee of Public Safety's spokesman Bertrand Barère made his most vehement attack on this daily press, he used images drawn from the world of commerce and accused the papers of engaging in 'speculation on public opinion. . . . News reports have become, in the hands of these operators of periodicals, commodities that they drive up or down.'[112] The daily newspapers, even if their content was purely informational or ideological, were artefacts of an industry based on the public's demand for the latest, most up-to-date political information, rather than on an interest in thoughtful analysis or government-approved patriotism.

Like the pre-revolutionary political press, the revolutionary news press was thus shaped by the power of the market. Short of time and funds, and wedded to a concept of press freedom that precluded the complete elimination of privately owned newspapers, even the radical Jacobins of 1793–4 stopped short of imposing genuine controls on the press market and moving in the direction of the non-commercial press of modern totalitarian regimes.[113] As a result, the press of the revolutionary period never became a docile instrument of the new ruling elite created by the Revolution. These politicians increasingly freed themselves from any direct control by public opinion: Robespierre's doctrine of revolutionary government justified the rule of an elite, and his post-thermidorian successors increasingly vitiated the election mechanisms that threatened the stability of their grip on power.[114] As a result, the political leaders of the revolutionary period became increasingly hostile towards a press that continued to reflect the disorderly, unregulated force of the market and of public opinion. Even before Napoleon's coup d'état of 18 brumaire VIII, an anonymous bureaucrat had already outlined the solution to the press problem: 'draw up a list of permitted journals, and permit no others to circulate.'[115] As Pierre-Louis Roederer subsequently noted, this meant returning to the conditions of the Old Regime and putting an end to the situation in which newspapers were private properties rather than government-granted privileges.[116] And, of course, such a policy – which the Napoleonic regime promptly adopted by its edict of 27 nivôse VIII, limiting the number of papers in Paris to thirteen – meant curtailing the market's power to influence the content and style of newspapers, since new competitors were excluded.

The newspapers of the Napoleonic period remained, for the most part, profit-making private enterprises; they were still commodities sold for money, rather than given away; and even the drastic Napoleonic censorship did not entirely stifle their ability to reflect public wishes. But the period of unregulated, cut-throat competition in the political press was over, and the most lasting lesson that press entrepreneurs learned from the Napoleonic years was that pure, undiluted politics was less marketable than a mixed diet of political, cultural and literary news, such as the immensely successful *Journal des débats* offered. In retrospect, the period from 1770 to 1800 stands out as one in which politics on paper was saleable in a way that it never was before or afterwards. This period was the one in which modern politics, based on the representation of public opinion, triumphed in France. In contrast to the revolutions of the twentieth century, however, the French Revolution left the distribution of political news and ideas to the market-place. Through their newspapers, private entrepreneurs, some motivated by political conviction and others not, turned political participation into a commodity that could be purchased and consumed, and one that, like such consumer goods as coffee and toiletries, became an integral part of many individuals' daily lives. Whereas late eighteenth-century English political publications were part of a far broader consumer culture, however, French revolutionary periodicals were among the first mass-produced commodities to be marketed throughout the country. In this area, as in many others, the innovations of the French Revolution foreshadowed developments that would only become firmly rooted in French society many decades later.

Notes

I would like to thank Duke University Press for permission to re-use, in modified form, some material that appeared in my book, *Revolutionary News: The Press in France, 1789–1799*, published in 1990. Some of the material on Linguet has appeared in French in Hans Bots (ed.), *La Diffusion et la lecture des journaux de langue française sous l'ancien régime* (Amsterdam and Maarssen: APA-Holland University Press, 1988).

1 Jacques-Pierre Brissot de Warville, *Mémoire aux Etats-généraux: Sur la nécessité de rendre dès ce moment la presse libre, et surtout pour les journaux politiques* (Paris, 1789), 10.

2 *Aux voleurs, aux voleurs*, x (1790).

3 See the insightful analysis in Jean Sgard, 'La multiplication de périodiques', in Roger Chartier, Henri-Jean Martin and Jean-Pierre Vivet (eds), *Histoire de l'édition française*, vol. 2 (Paris: Promodis, 1984), 198–205.

4 'Des feuilles périodiques', in *Ephémerides du citoyen*, i (4 Nov. 1765).

5 Jean Sgard, 'Journale und Journalisten im Zeitalter der Aufklärung', in H.-U. Gumbrecht, R. Reichardt and T. Schleich (eds), *Sozialgeschichte der Aufklärung in Frankreich*, 2 vols (Munich: Oldenbourg, 1981), vol. 2, 32.

6 *Gazette de Leyde*, publisher's papers, in Leiden Gemeente-Archief, Van Heukelom papers, Z(2), no. 119. On the *Gazette de Leyde*, see Jeremy D. Popkin, *News and Politics in the Age of Revolution: Jean Luzac's 'Gazette de Leyde,' 1772–1798* (Ithaca: Cornell University Press, 1989).

7 Gilles Feyel, *La 'Gazette' en province à travers ses réimpressions, 1631–1752* (Amsterdam and Maarssen: APA-Holland University Press, 1982).

8 Jean Sgard *et al.*, *La presse provinciale au XVIIIe siècle* (Grenoble: Centre de recherches sur les Sensibilités, 1983).

9 Suzanne Tucoo-Chala, *Charles-Joseph Panckoucke et la librairie française, 1736–1798* (Pau: Marrimpouey, 1977).

10 Adams to President of Congress, 8 Sept. 1783, in Francis Wharton (ed.), *The Revolutionary Diplomatic Correspondence of the United States* (Washington, DC: Government Printing Office, 1889), vol. 6, 682.

11 For the classic presentation of this contrast, see Fred S. Siebert, Theodore Peterson and Wilbur Schramm, *Four Theories of the Press* (Urbana: University of Illinois Press, 1956).

12 John Brewer, 'Commercialization and politics', in Neil McKendrick, John Brewer and J. H. Plumb, *The Birth of a Consumer Society* (Bloomington: Indiana University Press, 1982), 254–7. Almon is listed as the primary distributor of Marat's anonymous pamphlet, *The Chains of Slavery*, published in English in London in 1774.

13 Jeremy D. Popkin, 'Pamphlet journalism at the end of the Old Regime', in *Eighteenth-Century Studies*, xxii (1989), 351–68.

14 For the most recent account of the 'coup', see Durand Echeverria, *The Maupeou Revolution* (Baton Rouge: Louisiana State University Press, 1985).

15 See especially Keith Baker, 'On the problem of the ideological origins of the French Revolution', in Dominick LaCapra and Steven L. Kaplan (eds), *Modern European Intellectual History* (Ithaca: Cornell University Press, 1982), 197–219, and Dale Van Kley, 'The Jansenist constitutional legacy in the French Prerevolution, 1750–1789', *Historical Reflections/Réflexions historiques*, xiii (1986), 393–453.

16 Hardy, 'Mes Loisirs', BN Ms fr. 6681, entry for 14 Feb. 1772.

17 On the Duplain edition of the *Correspondance*, see the interrogation of Mme Stockdorf, a bookseller, in BN, Anisson-Duperron papers, Ms fr. 22101, 262 (5 April 1773).

18 Louis P. Bachaumont (sic), *Mémoires secrets pour servir à l'histoire de la république des lettres en France, depuis MDCCLXII jusqu'à nos jours* (hereafter *MS*), 36 vols. Several editions exist. On the question of the art critic Bachaumont's contribution to the work, see Louis Olivier, 'Bachaumont the chronicler: a doubtful renown', *Studies on Voltaire and the Eighteenth Century* (hereafter *SVEC*), cxliii (1975), 161–79, a correction to the standard work of Robert Tate, 'Petit de Bachaumont: his circle and the *Mémoires secrets*', *SVEC*, lxvi (1968).

19 *MS*, vol. 24, 207 (26 Oct. 1772).

20 Archives nationales (Paris), V(1) 551, 14 April 1789 (*re* seizure of books from colporteur in Lille, 12 Nov. 1788).

21 Bibliothèque Mazarine, Ms 2398, 23 March 1775.

22 *Journal Historique* (hereafter *JH*), BN edn, vii, 280.
23 'Relation historique de l'Emeute arrivée à Paris, le 3 mai 1775, et de ce qui l'a précédé et suivi', in *JH*, 'Nouvelle édition, revue, corrigée et augmentée', 7 vols (London: 1776; copy in Göttingen University library), 292–334.
24 Madame du Deffand to Walpole, 21 Sept. 1777, in W. S. Lewis (ed.), *Yale Edition of Horace Walpole's Correspondence* (New Haven: Yale University Press, 1960–), vol. 6, 478. It is true that once she had her copy, she told Walpole, 'I find that I truly wasted my money', letter of 12 Oct. 1777, ibid., vol. 6, 483.
25 Bibliothèque Mazarine, Ms 2399, 29 Aug. 1777.
26 *MS*, 'Avertissement des Auteurs', at beginning of vol. 31.
27 *Mémoires secrets*, xxx, 123 (23 Dec. 1785).
28 *Allgemeiner Literatur-Zeitung*, 26 March 1785.
29 See for example the *Société typographique de Cologne*, letter to Société typographique de Neuchâtel (hereafter STN), 7 April 1788, in STN Archives, Bibliothèque publique et universitaire, Neuchâtel, Ms 1219. The STN itself was not involved in the publication of the 'Mairobert' works and stocked only limited numbers of them.
30 On Linguet's ideas, see Darline Gay Levy, *The Ideas and Careers of Simon-Nicolas-Henri Linguet* (Urbana: University of Illinois Press, 1980).
31 *Annales politiques* (hereafter *AP*), i, 4–5.
32 Linguet to Pierre Lequesne, 25 July 1777, in Bibliothèque municipale de Reims (hereafter BMR), Ms 1916.
33 Linguet to Lequesne, 26 Sept. 1777, in BMR, Ms 1916.
34 *Annales*, ix, 196.
35 Ginevia Conti Odorisio, *S. N. H., Linguet, Dall'ancien régime alla rivoluzione* (Rome: Giuffrè, 1976), 201.
36 Levy, *Linguet*, 190–1.
37 *Annales*, ii, 469–73. On the arrangements for the Lausanne edition, see Frances Acomb, *Mallet du Pan* (Durham, NC: Duke University Press, 1973), 107–11, 116–19.
38 *Annales politiques*: iii, 442n.; iv, 293; vi, 50. Manzon's *Courier du Bas-Rhin* published the first summary of Linguet's *Mémoires sur la Bastille* and the first description of the famous engraving of the prison being struck by lightning in its issue of 1 Jan. 1783.
39 F. A. de Lescure (ed.), *Correspondance secrète inédite sur Louis XVI, Marie-Antoinette, la Cour et la Ville de 1777 a 1792*, 2 vols (Paris: Plon, 1866), vol. 1, 133 (1 Feb. 1778).
40 Linguet to Lequesne, letters of 27 June 1777, 17 Nov. 1779 in BMR, Ms 1916.
41 *Annales*: ii, 469–73; iv, 193; x, 161; xii, 319; Linguet to Lequesne, 16 Dec. 1777, in BMR, Ms 1916.
42 *Annales*, vii, 453–55 gives three examples.
43 Jeremy D. Popkin, 'Un journaliste face au marché des périodiques à la fin du dix-huitième siècle: Linguet et ses *Annales politiques*', in Hans Bots (ed.), *La Diffusion et la lecture des journaux de langue française sous l'ancien régime* (Amsterdam and Maarssen: APA-Holland University Press, 1988), 11–19.
44 Paul Gaskell, *A New Introduction to Bibliography* (Oxford: Clarendon Press, 1972), 162.
45 *Annales*, xiii, 15, 20.
46 'A. M. Linguet', tipped in at end of vol. viii, Göttingen University copy of Linguet, *Annales*.
47 *Annales*, x, 161–2.
48 *Politische Journal* (Hamburg, Nov. 1781), 364–5. This figure would not have been implausible had Linguet been able to keep the journal appearing on a regular schedule, which he never managed to do. The *Mémoires secrets* credited him with an annual profit of 50,000 *livres* (entry for 31 Aug. 1778).
49 *Annales*, iii, 18.
50 *Annales*, vii, 461.
51 *Annales*, vii, 468. Linguet's figures include costs for binding, printed address labels and mailing envelopes. Since he provides no figure for the journal's press run, or for the various other costs he

mentions, such as unpaid subscriptions, it is impossible to estimate the real financial situation of the *Annales* during this period.

52 *Annales*, xiii, 10–11.

53 *Annales*, vii, 457.

54 *Annales*, vii, 462.

55 *MS*, 30 Aug. 1782.

56 *Annales*, v, 519–20. At least the latter two promises were kept: the University of Chicago copy has both the portrait and the indexes.

57 Announcement tipped in after p. 36 in vol. xiii of Göttingen copy (Oct. 1787).

58 Levy, *Linguet*, 217n. This suggests the existence of twelve to eighteen counterfeit editions, with press runs of about 1,000 copies, a plausible situation.

59 *Annales*, iii, 13–14.

60 Linguet to Lequesne, letter of 8 Sept. 1778, in BMR, Ms 1916.

61 See Klaus Herding and Rolf Reichardt, *Die Bildpublizistik der französischen Revolution* (Frankfurt: Suhrkamp, 1989), 20–4.

62 For a detailed statistical summary of the 'press revolution', see Claude Labrosse and Pierre Rétat, *Naissance du journal révolutionnaire* (Lyon: Presses Universitaires de Lyon, 1989), 18–25. Two recent overviews of the press during the revolutionary era are Jeremy D. Popkin, *Revolutionary News: The Press in France, 1789–1799* (Durham, NC: Duke University Press, 1990), and Hugh Gough, *The Newspaper Press in the French Revolution* (London: Routledge, 1988).

63 On the profitability of the press, see Jean-Paul Bertaud, *Les Amis du Roi* (Paris: Perrin, 1984), 41–59; William J. Murray, *The Right-Wing Press in the French Revolution* (London: Boydell, 1986), 67–88; and Jeremy D. Popkin, *The Right-Wing Press in France, 1792–1800* (Chapel Hill: University of North Carolina Press, 1980), 54–64.

64 Pierre-Louis Roederer, 'Essai analytique sur les divers moyens établis pour la communication des pensées, entre les hommes en société', *Journal d'économie publique*, 30 brumaire V (Dec. 1796).

65 On the transformation of the publishing industry in Paris, see Carla Hesse, 'Economic upheavals in publishing', in Robert Darnton and Daniel Roche (eds), *Revolution in Print* (Berkeley: University of California Press, 1989), 69–97.

66 M. S. Boulard, *Le Manuel de l'Imprimeur* (Paris: Boulard, 1791), 81–4, 91–2.

67 A. J. Dugour, in *Eclair*, 2 Jan. 1797.

68 Proposed merger contract (never implemented), in Archives nationales (hereafter AN), F 7 3445.

69 Bankruptcy dossier, 10 Feb. 1804, in Archives départementales de la Seine (Paris), D 11 U(3) 24, d. 1638.

70 AN, F 18 25, 'Notes sur les imprimeurs ci-après désignés'.

71 On Duplain's efforts, see André Fribourg, 'Le Club des Jacobins en 1790, d'après de nouveaux documents', *Révolution française*, lviii (1910), 507–54. Duplain's pre-revolutionary publishing career is recounted in Robert Darnton, *The Business of Enlightenment* (Cambridge, Mass.: Harvard University Press, 1979).

72 AN, F 7 4694.

73 On Caillot's work for Royou, see Harvey Chisick, 'Pamphlets and journalism in the early French Revolution', *French Historical Studies*, xv (1988), 630.

74 Caillot letters in AN, F 7 3446.

75 Jeremy D. Popkin, 'Joseph Fiévée, imprimeur, écrivain, journaliste: une carrière dans le monde du livre pendant la Révolution', in Frédéric Barbier *et al.* (eds), *Livre et Révolution* (Paris: Aux Amateurs de livres, 1989), 63–74.

76 Robert Darnton, 'L'Imprimerie de Panckoucke en l'an II', *Revue française d'histoire du livre*, ix (1979), 365. Not all these presses were used for Panckoucke's periodicals: many were employed in producing books such as his mammoth *Encyclopédie méthodique*.

77 On the official printing shops, see August Bernard, *Notice historique sur l'imprimerie nationale* (Paris:

Dumoulin & Bordier, 1848), 67–79. By the end of the Napoleonic period, the *Imprimerie nationale* had grown to 200 presses.

78 Boulard, *Manuel*, 68, 73.

79 Charles-Joseph Panckoucke, 'Sur l'état actuel de l'imprimerie', *Mercure de France*, 6 Mar. 1790.

80 *Ami du peuple* (counterfeit edition attributed to Guignot), 5 March 1790.

81 Van Nussel, publisher of *Diurnal*, to Minister of Police, 6 bru. VI, in AN, F 7 3448B.

82 *Ami du Peuple*, 23 Nov. 1790.

83 *Courrier extraordinaire*, 16 June 1792.

84 Gérard Walter, *Hébert et le 'Père Duchesne'* (Paris: Janin, 1946), 343–4.

85 *Ami du Peuple*, 25 Dec. 1789. On police harassment of colporteurs, see Lise Andries, 'Les imprimeurs-libraires parisiens et la liberté de la presse (1789–1795)', *Dix-huitième siècle*, xxi (1989), 247–61.

86 Caillot, correspondence in AN, F 7 3446; *Journal de la Montagne* registers in AN, T 1495 A and B.

87 William J. Murray, *The Right-Wing Press in the French Revolution: 1789–1792* (London: Royal Historical Society, 1986), 79–80.

88 Gilles Feyel, 'Les frais d'impression et de diffusion de la presse parisienne entre 1789 et 1792', in Pierre Rétat (ed.), *La Révolution du Journal 1788–1794* (Paris: Centre National de la Recherche Scientifique, 1989), 77–99.

89 AN, F 7 3445.

90 Correspondence of *Précurseur*, in AN, F 7 6239A, plaq. 1.

91 Pierre Rétat, 'Forme et discours d'un journal révolutionnaire: les *Révolutions de Paris* en 1789', in Claude Labrosse and Pierre Rétat, *L'Instrument périodique* (Lyon: Presses Universitaires de Lyon, 1985), 173–8.

92 Murray, *Right-Wing Press*, 35.

93 *Ami du Peuple*, 18 May 1790, 18 June 1790.

94 Contract of 13 flor. V. in AN, F 7 3448B.

95 Jean-Pierre Gallais, in *Censeur*, 18 fruc. III (5 Sept. 1795).

96 Feyel, 'Frais'.

97 Bertaud, *Amis du Roi*, 55. These figures agree with estimates made from the more fragmentary records from papers in the Directory period. Popkin, *Right-Wing Press*, 193, n. 27.

98 *Courrier extraordinaire*, 2 May 1792.

99 Pierre-Louis Roederer, 'Examen impartial de cette question: La profession de Journaliste est-elle, de sa nature, un métier vil?', *Journal d'économie publique*, 20 flor. V.

100 See letters in Archives nationales (Paris), 29 AP 91 (Roederer papers).

101 *Censeur des Journaux*, 25 flor. V (14 May 1797). Gallais plagiarized this passage from an article in Linguet's *Annales politiques* of 1777.

102 Louis Jacob, *Hébert. Le Père Duchesne chef des sans-culottes* (Paris: Gallimard, 1960), 37–40.

103 ibid., 57.

104 Figures for Desmoulins and Loustallot in Jean-Paul Bertaud, *Camille et Lucile Desmoulins* (Paris: Presses de la Renaissance, 1986), 90; for Mallet du Pan, Frances Acomb, *Mallet du Pan*, 230–1.

105 Contract in AN, F 7 4281, d. 23.

106 *Révolutions de France et de Brabant*, no. 27.

107 *Ami du Roi* (Royou edition), 'Avis', bound in with vol. 1 of copy in Harvard College Library.

108 *Ami du Peuple*, 8 Nov. 1790, 22 Sept. 1790.

109 *Révolutions de Paris*, 12–19 June 1790.

110 Prospectus, *Chronique du mois*, in *Journal du département de la Vienne*, 7 Nov. 1791.

111 Prospectus, *Recueil des décrets de l'assemblée nationale*, in *Affiches, Annonces et Avis divers du département de l'Yonne*, June 1791.

112 Barère, speech of 22 prair. II, in *Moniteur*, 23 prair. II.

113 For a classic study of the media in a political system where market forces are completely over-

ridden, see the analysis of the Soviet Union under Stalin in Alex Inkeles, *Public Opinion in Soviet Russia* (Cambridge, Mass.: Harvard University Press, 1950).

114 For a particularly lucid analysis of this process, see Werner Giesselmann, *Die brumariansche Elite* (Stuttgart: Klett, 1977), 298–300.

115 'Minute sur journaux', in 14 bru. VIII, in AN, F 7 3452.

116 Roederer to Decazes, letter of 28 March 1816, in AN, 29 AP 91.

Part VI
Consumption, objects and images

21
Reading and writing with nature: a materialist approach to French formal gardens

Chandra Mukerji

In *The Structures of Everyday Life*[1] Fernand Braudel dismisses out of hand Werner Sombart's suggestion[2] that there is a close connection between the ravenous patterns of consumption in early modern court life and the growth of capitalist production. The idea that businesses and trade might have been spawned to fill this demand is not, to Braudel's mind, worthy of serious consideration. Court sumptuousness is a cultural aberration to Braudel, not an essential part of an emerging capitalist economy. There is a tone of deep contempt in this dismissal, presumably because Sombart's approach would lead researchers to sanctify outrageous spending and to study the well-known stock players of elite history, not the equally fascinating but more obscure characters now the major focus of historical research. Sombart violates current norms by thinking and writing about kings and queens. Worse than that, Sombart's approach takes the development of capitalism out of the hands of ordinary entrepreneurs, and puts it squarely into the laps of aristocrats who did little business yet reaped rewards from the economic efforts of others. It seems an insult to those living more modest lives who helped to transform European life through the development of new business practices and a new economic mentality.

However much I might sympathize with Braudel's point of view, I am much taken with Sombart's argument. I am less convinced that the world of court society was so detached from the world of business; the mobility of financiers and other members of the bourgeoisie into noble ranks was dramatic in the French court of the seventeenth century. One can hardly believe seriously that this court's culture was simply furthering traditional noble values, high above the world of commerce. In addition, court cooks, gardeners, midwives, stonemasons and others, although in service to the king, made their livings largely from entrepreneurial activity outside of their court duties. They took their knowledge of court tastes and mores, and used them to provide services to others. What Sombart recognizes quite correctly is that the court cultural system was deeply embedded in capitalist economic development. To understand the culture of capitalism, then, we need to follow Sombart's lead and try to understand in more detail *how* the business culture developing in the early modern period made possible and shaped court life as well as the world of trade.

439

By demonstrating the deep interdependence between seventeenth-century courtly gardens and the capitalist culture of early modern France, I hope to show both the theoretical value and empirical rewards of investigating the material culture at court. One must necessarily start, however, from a much broader and deeper definition of materialism in court culture than the simple demand for luxury that Sombart describes (or the even simpler one Braudel attributes to Sombart). As Braudel points out, life at court may have been glittering, but it was not comfortable, so we should not confuse court sumptuousness with the pursuit of bourgeois comfort or even organized desire for pleasure.[3] What Braudel misses in Sombart is that the latter associates court luxury with social *ambition* and *mobility*, not comfort. At court, luxury was used for making social *claims*, not a comfortable life. The economic system was creating a new financial elite that wanted to realize social aspirations through court society. Sombart demonstrates how much the sumptuousness of court culture was part of a *capitalist* reorganization of culture, spawned by *new* elites to underscore their importance (Plate 21.1).[4]

On the empirical level, it turns out that there is a surprising need for more careful historical study of court consumption because so much of the extant literature on the material life of courts is written in the language of traditional art history, designed more to help connoisseurs understand design traditions than to help historians understand elite culture. The gardens are 'read' as asocial texts, made meaningful through analysis of the rules of their internal orderliness, compared to texts in other media and placed in the history of garden design. It is difficult indeed looking at the symbolism of grottoes or the literary sources of designs for fountains to see patterns of court consumption as having anything more than politically symbolic and aesthetic dimensions.[5] Only the brilliant work by the sociologist Norbert Elias on conspicuous consumption in the French court[6] begins to suggest the potential theoretical rewards of rethinking this history. He argues quite convincingly that developing a highly complex and expensive culture of consumption within the court was not just a way of distracting a bored aristocracy, but a central means by which Louis XIV controlled the French aristocracy. He is concerned more with the political than the economic and cultural consequences of court culture, but he demonstrates definitively that our understanding of the social and cultural complexity of life at court is still rudimentary.

It turns out that the history of French formal gardens is a particularly rich place for seeing the complex culture of court and commerce that appeared in seventeenth-century France (Plate 21.2). Gardens are forms of material culture inscribing affluence and power, legitimating social stations made problematic by economic change. They are places in which statues glorifying Europe's classical heritage and rare imported plants, testifying to the economic reach of the international capitalist trading system, were used to buttress the social claims of their owners and designers. In addition, these gardens were *designed*. They were active means for communicating social location because they were carefully planned and executed, using the rich book culture that was being expanded through capitalist development in the book trade. Finally they were built using exotic flora brought to Europe through the plant trade. From these economic and cultural resources, gardens were constituted as models of the exercise of power over nature, narratives for describing complex social relations and for integrating divergent elements within an organized whole.

While the research I present here on early modern gardens has been focused mainly on the history of French formal gardens, it is impossible to look at these gardens in isolation. They had roots in both Dutch and Italian gardening;[7] they were to influence patterns of garden design throughout Europe; and they can be understood in important ways by comparing them to the English gardens that followed them. Thus the French experience was not simply a local one, and the consequences of the cultural forms nurtured there were not local either. They were deeply entwined in an economic internationalism and cultural cosmopolitanism, helping to define both.[8]

This chapter will focus on four aspects of French formal gardens that demonstrate their ties to the emerging capitalist system and materialist culture: (1) the passion for collection that fuelled elite consumerism and was used to justify economic mobility, including the collection of rare plants in gardens and the collection of sculpture, both antique and new; (2) the new thinking about gardens made possible by the widespread use of writing, drawing and figuring on paper and in books – that material means for intellectual change proliferated by capitalist trade in books; (3) the economic sources and commercial spread of elite design (on the one hand) and trade in plants and seeds (on the other hand), in other words, the connection of garden design to systems of trade; and finally (4) the role of French gardens in the cultural redefinition of nature from a manifestation of God to a kind of secular property to be controlled and used for economic and political power.

Gardens as sites for conspicuous collection

Walk around Versailles, Vaux-le-Vicomte, Chantilly or the Renaissance gardens in Italy, such as Villa d'Este, and you are surrounded with exotic marvels. In Renaissance gardens, you can see the most wonderful sculptures, fountains and grottoes; in French gardens from the seventeenth century, you see both further elaboration of these features (including a dramatic increase in the scale and use of fountains) and a tremendous growth in the variety of vegetation (made possible in part through the design of special buildings and techniques devoted to the propagation and cultivation of rare plants and animals). All these novelties proclaimed the increased power of the French over natural forces and creatures, and the reach of the French trading system that could bring such novelties to France (Plate 21.3).

Collecting exotic objects, including plants and animals, was not new to the early modern period; there were medieval precedents. But collecting a wide range of exotic plants in gardens of the seventeenth century was part of a larger cultural and economic shift that was indeed new. Assembling rare objects from around the world in 'cabinets des nouveautés' became an obsessive preoccupation that engaged large numbers of gentlemen.[9] This newly felt passion for collection was dependent upon a refiguring of the meanings of curiosity and greed in the period that was matched by the growing trading capacities of Europeans that facilitated such collection.[10] The growth of plant collections was often tied to botanical and medical gardens, but it increasingly affected kitchen and pleasure gardens, particularly as more efficient trade in seeds and plants stimulated the growth of market gardening. Once collecting flora and fauna was both sanctified and expedited, collectors' pleasure gardens could become emblems of an impressive global reach that glorified their owners and the social world they lived within. That is why they were such favoured sites for parties, and also why foreign visitors would make special efforts to visit them.[11]

In theoretical terms, one could argue that Bourdieu's system of stratified tastes[12] that people today use to reproduce and make sense of social stratification was brought to life in this period. The disjunction between traditional sources of rank and new sources of economic and political power made social station more problematic, and people used consumption to lay claims to the now less clearly assignable social positions. In this situation, culture became more essential both to mobility and its restriction. If rank was to be determined by wealth in the new set of social relations, and wealth was less directly associated with the economic benefits of landowning, then some system other than inheritance was needed to give children of elites greater chance of achieving high rank in the next generation. Precisely the elaboration of manners and other 'civilized' codes (think of Elias[13]), signs of conspicuous leisure and training (think of Veblen[14]) could give those from elite backgrounds identifying cultural markers that could be inherited and help each new generation to fit into court society. At the same time, those achieving economic success for the first time had identifiable signs of elite cultivation to learn in order to legitimate inclusion in the gentry (at least for their children). So taste became more important as capitalism made social rank more unstable.

The culture of collection was central to this system not just because the ability to collect was dependent on wealth and access to trade, but because it was in accumulating goods that people displayed their tastes. Collectors' items were part of an active communication system of objects just as subtle as written language. With them, people marked their relative social locations, and defined the socio-political universe in which they moved.

Conspicuous consumption was (in contradiction to Veblen[15]) not a waste in this system at all; it was a way to mark ranks where social stratification was unclear. When Louis XIV ascended the throne, the legitimacy of the French monarchy itself was disputed (by the Frondeurs[16]); hence even the monarch himself, at the beginning of his reign, needed to make social claims about his authority. This he did lavishly with his great palaces, their dramatic gardens and the elaborate parties he staged there. Louis XIV used conspicuous display not just to solidify his reign but to elevate his favourites. The multi-day fêtes he organized were dedicated to new mistresses, and the buildings he built for these mistresses were monuments to their power. Other court dignitaries built for themselves – to good and bad effect. Fouquet, Louis XIV's Treasurer, who built the great gardens at Vaux-le-Vicomte, made claims about his power and taste with the chateau and gardens that cost him his position and almost his life.[17]

Saint Simon is eloquently clear about the fluidity of statuses within the court, how they changed from season to season and how much these changes meant.[18] Given the power of subtle moves in and out of favour, one can see how the social instability of the seventeenth century was reproduced within court society and helped to promote the extensive use of material culture for making social claims. In this society, knowing who to imitate in patterns of consumption and how to use prescribed fashions showed political shrewdness and made social life possible. Choosing a certain type of garden design, growing prescribed and exotic fruits and vegetables (particularly out of season) and filling the house with decorative and sweet-smelling plants were salient issues in the finely stratified court world of Louis XIV.[19]

The most developed international plant collections at the beginning of the seventeenth century, not surprisingly, were primarily in botanical and medical gardens, not at court (except for collections of fruit trees, which were developed primarily in royal gardens). The study of natural history had (to that time) been stimulating more of the seed and plant trade, but through the century, elaborate plant collections were increasingly found in the kitchen and pleasure gardens of great houses. More efficient trade in seeds and plants was stimulated first by the European journeys of major gardeners, working for the nobility, who went on voyages (either trading voyages or trips with gentlemen) to survey the decorative or edible plants from other cultures and collect the best of them. Later, collections in pleasure gardens were enhanced by the growth of market gardening that made novel plants available on a commercial basis.[20]

The great seventeenth-century French gardens clearly profited from the plant trade. Colbert wrote on a regular basis (it seems, annually) to the south of France for large quantities of tuberoses, jasmins and jonquils; the king had a particular love of orange trees, based on the lovely scent of the blossoms, the deep green leaves of the plant in winter and the colourful (if not always sweet) fruit, and these too were brought in great quantities to Versailles. Other unusual plants were carried to France from much further. In 1672, Colbert wrote to the director of the West India Company asking for his people to bring back unusual fruits and flowers for the royal gardens; and he regularly asked for plants to be brought from Portugal and the Near and Far East. The plants that he carefully assembled for the royal gardens were not primarily local flora; they were prized and petted exotics from other climates and parts of the world.[21]

The resulting gardens can be seen as living maps, marking the capacity of the French state to control territory and manipulate the natural resources within it; in this way they mapped the political agenda of the state. They also traced the international reach of the trading systems that revolved around the state. They testified to the power of the European politico-economic empire that Louis XIV and Colbert were trying to forge with the offices of the expanding state bureaucracy.

While gardens were central features in the world of courtly consumption and display, and were subject to changes in fashion, their use as sites for collection also gave them a certain conservatism.[22] Gardens might be sites for displaying novelties from the realm of nature (hence linked to the new), but they were equally sites for displaying Europe's classical heritage (hence linked to the past). Statues and buildings in European gardens throughout the early modern period (from the period of Italian Renaissance gardens, through French formal gardens and English landscape gardens) were based on classical models. Like other forms of art and architecture, they were seen as new developments in the Great Tradition, which necessarily had to bow to the classical past. Even as the scientific revolution was restructuring European visions of the natural world and was stimulating new ideas about how to reproduce the natural world in the garden, there remained strong reference to classical work in the built objects in the gardens, reminding viewers that the collector's garden contained the oldest as much as the newest objects of European culture (Plate 21.4).

Unlike the Italians, the French did not have remnants of classical sculpture on hand to place in their gardens, but they could and did follow the Italian model of using extensive statuary in the gardens. Moreover, they imitated sixteenth- and early seventeenth-century Italian sculpture in their gardens, using this more indirect connection to the classical tradition. They even used classical architectural forms in the latticework structures and hedges that were used extensively in *bosques*. Catherine de Medici was instrumental in bringing Italian gardening to France; she was nostalgic for the gardens of her childhood. At the Luxembourg palace and elsewhere, she brought Italian and French gardeners together, and helped to mould Italian garden ideas to local traditions and the local ecosystem. During the seventeenth century, French gardens began to develop a distinctive style, adding Dutch decorative canals and other forms to the Italian model. The gardens spilled out from the walled enclosures typical of Italian gardens, and began to develop new techniques for waterworks. The resulting gardens remained geometrically organized, full of waterworks and dotted with statues from the Great Tradition, but they were no longer Italian or even tied to classical culture in the same way.[23] As French thinkers contemplated the divide between the ancients and moderns and thought about how to improve upon the wisdom of the ancients, French garden designers looked for new ways to use classical style. They used figures from classical mythology, like Latona and Apollo, as subjects for fountains at Versailles, but they reappropriated these figures and their myths to comment on French political culture. Apollo became the Sun King, who represented Louis XIV himself. They also made statues, dressed in classical clothing, to represent such secular and political objects as the major rivers in France. The classical tradition was mobilized in seventeenth-century French gardens to tout the economic success of the region, the technological prowess of its inhabitants, the cultural ingenuity of its artists and artisans and the political ambitions of its court.[24]

The resulting French garden broke the confines of Renaissance walled gardens; it even spread beyond the dreams of the expanded Italian gardens of the Mannerist period. Its sheer size and complexity (based on the difficulties of maintaining diversity and geometrical integration in such a large space) demanded some rethinking of the ideas of geometry and proportions passed down from the ancients. Tradition was reappropriated and placed in the service of a new kind of personal and collective ambition.

French gardens were thus places to collect past and present, plants and statues, fountains, grottoes and orangeries. Garden owners used collection to display a superiority of culture reifying their estimates of their own social standing. Gardens as sites for collection, then, were maps of social ambitions as well as economic reach.

A closer look at the too-familiar story of Vaux-le-Vicomte may be useful for specifying the tie between ambition and conspicuous display in gardens. The story goes that Fouquet, Louis XIV's Treasurer, built this chateau and its beautiful gardens to show his good taste and high standing. The association between high status and collecting artworks was already well set by Mazarin. But Fouquet went a bit further. He made himself into a patron of rising French artists: the architect, Le Brun, the designer, Le Vaux and the garden designer, Le Nôtre. When the work was completed, he had spent enormous sums of money and helped to establish in France a distinctive type of design, particularly garden design. To show off the results, he invited the king to come and visit the new chateau and attend a party in his honour. When the visit was over, Louis had Fouquet imprisoned on charges of graft, and then took Le Brun, Le Vaux and Le Nôtre to build Versailles. Ranum argues that Fouquet was among the new financiers of France who expressed their new elevated social standing through acquisition of property and its lavish development; their ascendency was expressed in novel cultural forms. Fouquet was simply too successful in his cultural innovations and thereby made too grand a claim for his social standing. Although graft was an unspoken tradition in the office of Treasurer, Fouquet was officially accused of that crime. Why was he singled out this way? The simplest answer is that his lavish material display at Vaux made the graft impossible to ignore. As a result of a lack of political discretion in the realm of cultural politics, he lost his office, his property and his role in the development of culture in France.[25]

From this story, we can see how potent gardens could be as a cultural medium in this period. We can see how they were modulated to negotiate rank in a socially unstable environment in seventeenth-century France. And we can see how they did this by functioning as repositories for collections of plants and artefacts that testified to the high taste (and hence high station) of their owners.

Materialist means for making design innovations

Gardens were not just affected by capitalism through social mobility, the plant trade and the culture of collection; they were tied to a new literate view of design that was developing through the book trade. Ideas about what constituted the ancients' views on design came through mass-produced books. Garden designers read books and wrote new ones as treatises on science and art. Garden design in seventeenth-century France was a highly literate activity that developed a high level of reflexivity in design.

This movement in garden design was part of a larger cultural current. The growth of capitalist manufacture and trade in early modern Europe increasingly replaced performative cultural forms with objects. Printed books were only one example. With books, patterns of face-to-face interaction and mutual presentation were replaced with written records.[26] New kinds of thought were then organized around the commercial production and use of these objects, and replaced the more local, oral and performative traditions.

Elizabeth Eisenstein argues that the result of the print revolution was a new reflexivity of thought (and, I would add, design). The reflexivity resulted from exposure to ideas proposed by authors living in other times and places, increasing the self-consciousness and cosmopolitanism of the new literate writer. Authors could both compare their own ideas to those of more people and look at their thoughts with the same detachment they felt towards the work of others.[27] The resulting intellectual shift was clearly tied to capitalist development of the book trade, and garden design was caught up in the movement.

Jack Goody argues, on a more cognitive level, that being able to review thoughts on paper allows people to revise and reorder their thoughts in new ways. When people make lists, for example, they can then look at the list and think about how to order the items on it in some systematic fashion.[28] He presents this argument as a theory of literacy and its cultural consequences, but one can make similar arguments about ciphers and images. Once people look at statistics, they can manipulate them to see what kinds of meanings to derive from them. And once people look at a design on paper, they can play with the geometries without worrying about how they must be applied (Plate 21.5).

As much as French formal gardens were material means for communicating social claims and relations, they were results of this kind of reflexivity of design bred by their origins on pieces of paper. A combination of written words, pictures and numbers were used to formulate French formal gardens, and all were manipulated to enhance their designs. That is why these gardens are properly described as very literate forms. The formality of the gardens testifies to their planning. They are carefully measured and generally bilaterally symmetrical; their measurements are made according to theory and precedent; and their statuary is placed to highlight their references to classical allegories. In all these ways, they were self-consciously ordered and maximized their use of paper-based thought.[29]

In a culture in which the trappings of literacy were signs of high standing, these highly literate gardens were not just interestingly reflexive; they were appropriate means to claiming rank. The orderliness that they conveyed as a result of their careful planning was as much testimony to the power of those who cultivated them as the collection of plants and statues they contained. If the collections demonstrated taste and economic reach, garden designs expressed ambition and the intellectual and organizational capacity to realize ambitions, using the resources of the European cultural heritage.

In their origins on paper, French formal gardens were like their predecessors in Italy. The classical revival in Italy was a major spur to the development of garden design there, just as it was a spur to city planning, design of military equipment, design of hydraulic equipment and architecture. The Romans had been avid planners, and passed this preoccupation through manuscripts to Renaissance Italy along with the traditions of art, science and engineering.

In Italy prior to the Renaissance, there was increased production of manuscript books on natural history and horticulture that also had a role.[30] The smaller and earlier classical revival that accompanied the development of universities and bookselling in Europe had given birth to a literature of herbals and other books like the *Tacuinum Sanitatus* that illustrated plants, their culture and their uses. They are among the first books of practical gardening. Manuscript books from the fourteenth century also demonstrate an early association between the collection of rare flora and fauna and high status. Accurate pictures of plants and animals also filled decorative borders of traditional books like the *Visconti Hours* or the *Hour Book* of Catherine of Cleves; flora and fauna were 'collected' there as rare decorative objects, giving value and honour to the words they surrounded. These images demonstrate how the passion for collecting plants and animals was expressed in book origins before it developed in Renaissance gardens.

Garden designs themselves appear in print with Alberti, using ideas about garden design he absorbed with classical study, namely reading the ideas about the pleasure garden written by Pliny the Younger.[31] The garden was to be enclosed and cool, situated on a hillside and equipped with a table for outside dining. Water was a central feature in the garden, both pools and fountains. And so were topiary bushes, cut in fanciful as well as geometrical patterns. The garden was a place of retreat and fantasy, wish-fulfilment rather than practical activity. It was to be situated by the house so the garden could function as an outdoor living space (Plate 21.6).

The romance that made the fortune of the great humanist publisher Aldus Manutius was also a model for Renaissance gardens.[32] The *Poliphili Hypnerotomachia* not only described in luscious detail great garden delights, but contained delicately beautiful illustrations which depicted garden details that later appeared in Renaissance gardens. The intricate fountains, topiary work and trellises were to become measures of the pleasure garden. So too were the playful surprises like water jets to douse passing visitors. Water-run automata were also described in the book, and helped to stimulate the development of elaborate moving statues in grottoes, and water organs. The garden was also tied to performance and play in a way that fitted the period when performance culture was fed by wealth and literacy, but before it was undermined by them.[33] The tie between texts and gardens in the Renaissance is quite direct and runs through Manutius's great publishing house. The literacy behind these forms is indeed deep.

The stylistic shift towards French formal gardens also had roots in writings and drawings. The garden architect most closely associated with the French formal garden, André Le Nôtre, was not (to the despair of French garden historians) a theorist who wrote down his ideas. But many of the ideas that he moulded into the French style derived from the gardens of earlier French designers who did write and wrote extensively. Bernard Palissy, Salomon De Caus, Charles Estienne, Oliver de Serres, Jacques Boyceau and Claude Mollet[34] were the most notable of them. And Le Nôtre's ideas were put into print in the work of Dezallier d'Argentville.[35] Many of them used their books on gardens mainly to teach bits of practical horticulture or fountain engineering, but they also considered ideas behind the practice of gardening, sometimes philosophical ideas and often design ideas. Geometry was a central concern to most of these writers. The beauty of a garden lay in the geometry of its design, the proportions with which the beds were laid out. The garden was lovely because it revealed the orderliness of God in nature. The geometry of the garden had to be a central abiding concern of designers, for it was here that the value of nature could be expressed.[36] The extent to which the geometry of the garden was a detached system of numerical proportions to be applied to any garden or simply a system to be worked out for each garden site varied from one author to the next. The centrality of science or God as the essential marker of the orderliness of nature might vary from one to the next.[37] The attention to details of design, careful thought about the engineering problems and possibilities of waterworks,[38] or ideas about the shapes of topiary bushes or the lines of alleys varied from one author to the next, but the central issues of geometry and the desire for grounding practice in philosophy remained in most of the writing (Plate 21.7).[39]

This idealist emphasis in gardens might seem to divorce it from the materialist culture of the period, but the irony is that the philosophical debates animating intellectual life were fed by the capitalist book trade and the literate uses of the text that it made possible.[40]

Concern about the geometry of gardens was mirrored in France by the controversies over geometry in architecture that also developed in the seventeenth century. Were the proportions handed down by the ancients absolute forms that determined what was or was not beautiful? To what extent did proportions have to be varied to make up for point of view? To what extent were numerical proportions simply arbitrarily discovered from experience and then codified rather than grounded in some deeper reality? These were larger issues of design that enter into the debates about gardens. What is important about them is less their forms and point of view than the fact that they tied garden design through theory to a highly developed literate elite culture. The powerful members of court society may have been not so bookish themselves (if John Evelyn is to be believed);[41] they left off schooling early to learn riding, dancing and good manners. But the culture that sustained them was organized around literatures that furiously debated issues central to philosophy, and gardens were among them.[42]

By looking a bit more closely at Boyceau's theories, we can begin to get a better sense of how design ideas were connected to larger currents of thought. To Boyceau, nature had two primary characteristics, orderliness and diversity: the two aspects of nature revealed by scientific study. Diversity was revealed to science through empirical observation of particulars. Orderliness was apparent in the mathematical precision of natural laws. The garden, as a representation of the natural, had to display this diversity and mathematical unity of nature. Because they lacked the appropriate complexity, Boyceau argued against the use of square garden plots laid out symmetrically in a walled garden around a central fountain. This had been the typical form for most medieval gardens and was reproduced in many Italian gardens of the early Renaissance. Boyceau liked to have beds of different sizes and shapes in the same garden, not just rectangles either, but circles with four notched beds around them to form a square, lozenge shapes, or rectangles sliced by radiating or other geometrical lines. He also advocated the use of 'embroidery' ('broderie') in parterres, not the geometrical forms for mazes that had been popular in an earlier period. The development of designs in box and flowers which resembled oriental rugs gave the garden bed a better relationship to the complexity of the natural world. This complexity, in turn, had to be harnessed by the use of proportions to lay out the garden beds and their relationships to one another. Although he avoided square beds, he still used geometrical figures for beds, and advocated careful attention to proportions.[43]

Claude Mollet went farther. While Boyceau only included parterre designs in his book, Mollet presented entire garden plans which illustrated the rules of proportion for a formal garden. The gardens were bilaterally symmetrical, and the size of the beds got longer as they moved farther from the house. In this way, the rules of perspective were applied to the design of garden plots. Again diversity and complexity were held tightly within a geometrical system for ordering the garden and making it a whole (Plate 21.8).[44]

In this and many ways, the French formal gardens were deeply literate forms. The use of geometrical beds testified to the numeracy of their designers and the importance of numerical proportions derived from classical sources (Vitruvius in particular).[45] The use of classical allegories in garden architecture, statues and fountains gave the gardens this additional stamp of elevated learning. Even the plant collections had an intellectual edge, since cultivating them was a complicated horticultural experiment that required some botanical knowledge. But the most 'literate' thing about the gardens was the obvious centrality of ideas to their design. The garden to Boyceau was a mirror of nature, but it hardly reflected the look of natural landscapes. Instead, the garden was a realization of the *ideas* of nature current in the period. The land had to undergo extensive changes to fit the images set on paper. And the elaborate plans gave workmen – from engineers building a water system, to masons building walls, to gardeners setting and filling beds – means for co-ordinating their activities. The ordering of the garden and the organization of its construction were both made possible by the use of paper plans (in other words, a rich material culture made possible by trade in books). With these plans the French constructed the elaborately unnatural depictions of 'nature' typical of seventeenth-century formal gardens.

French formal gardens and capitalist enterprise

Small-scale entrepreneurial activity seems so far from the gardens of Versailles that it appears unlikely at first blush that there is any connection between the two, but there are actually a number of clear and some less clear connections. The court life at Versailles was indeed isolated from the day-to-day commerce of urban life in Paris;[46] gardens were often a refuge from the daily intrigues within the chateau.[47] The intellectual richness of the gardens also seemed to remove them from commerce, by setting them free-standing in the Great Tradition. How then could that idyllic world affect or be affected by growing trade and manufactures?

The simple answer is that politics and economics were never clearly distinguished in seventeenth-century France. The state was the primary entrepreneur of the period, developing crown-controlled international trading systems, and crown-sanctioned manufactures. These politico-economic institutions were the ones that supplied most of the luxury goods at Versailles. Gold and silverwork, porcelain, silk and tapestries came to court from French industries some of which were set up by the government or were sponsored by individual members of court to produce the rich luxuries for court life.[48] French mercantilism, developed under the careful scrutiny of Colbert, by making the state the primary economic actor in France, tied economic life in France further to political life. Not only had office-buying brought many members of the bourgeoisie into government, but these new economic institutions brought members of the court into the world of commerce. Given the entrepreneurialism at the top of court life, it should be no surprise that there was also entrepreneurial activity by underlings who served the monarch, his family and his entourage. These were people (from midwives to gardeners) who had appointments at court, but also engaged in business activities related to their position; that is why it is difficult to identify their entrepreneurialism. But they still sold their services (usually in the form of advice) or published books filled with their expertise, taking economic advantage of their position at court.

In a 1692 book for travellers to Paris, Abraham du Pradel[49] repeatedly mentions local artisans (from gardeners to stonemasons) who were in service to the king, but who were also available for private work. Great gardeners like Le Nôtre were routinely 'loaned' by the king to his favourites so they could have a stylish garden. The result was not just a spread of his style of work (the pattern that interests art historians), but economic opportunities for Le Nôtre, who was paid for his services. Those who amassed fortunes at court did not usually gain their fortunes directly from the state treasury, but rather from the business (or graft) opportunities that were opened to them through their offices. They might earn commissions from collecting taxes, or (as in the case of Le Nôtre) from selling their special skills and knowledge of French court tastes. Court appointments, then, can be viewed as partially a system for political distribution of economic opportunities that help to set up a system of private entrepreneurialism.

Although not extremely profitable, books were one of the business opportunities open to those who provided services at court. There seem to have been many readers who wanted to imitate court mores, and would buy books that they could use as a blueprint. These books are among the most obvious records of entrepreneurialism by the 'support personnel' at court, and help to demonstrate how commercially attractive their special knowledge of court culture could be.

Certainly, there were numerous books on gardens written in France in the sixteenth and seventeenth centuries by gardeners with positions at court and reputations based in large part on their elevated status. These gardeners were gentlemen, not labourers, and they were educated because they needed education to provide the kinds of literate touches to the garden for its elite aura. Still, these same gardeners could act as businessmen, periodically designing gardens for other gentlemen for a price. Additionally, when they published books on gardening, they made their ideas about garden design and the cultivation of plants available commercially through text (Plate 21.9).[50]

There were two major kinds of books published on gardens in this period: ones on horticulture alone, and ones that included some ideas about garden design. (There were also specialized books on waterworks and garden engineering, but those were much less typical of the period and not part of this analysis.) The former were by far the most numerous, and they were extremely popular, going through multiple printings.[51] These dealt with how and where to plant fruit trees; how to prune and graft; how to improve soil for making a garden; how to grow plants in pots; how to make hothouses for tender plants; how to design orangeries to suit the trees in them; how and when to plant different kinds of bulbs; and how to lay out a vegetable garden or orchard. Some described different varieties of fruit and how they tasted and lasted on the trees. Others illustrated common gardening tools, pruning and grafting techniques and the flowers of different bulbs so people could know what to expect from them.[52] This kind of information was useful for gardeners of all types, from wealthy gentlemen wanting to put in a new large garden to a literate family with a small piece of land. The fact that it was written by someone with a high position in society gave the words of advice more authority.

The books that contained advice on garden design as well as horticulture may well have had even more authority. Beautiful parterre designs might not have been used by most readers, but they would have made the books even more attractive to gentlemen who were thinking about a well-designed garden. The association with court gardens would have been a commercial asset for many of these authors, since readers of all ranks would tend to trust their judgement. Of course, there were less credentialled gardeners who wrote successful garden books, too. They were often people who wrote on a variety of subjects, including gardens. They were intellectual members of the gentry whose commercial ties came through books.[53]

Court gardeners also were tied to commercial life through the plant trade. Many of the new plants brought to please the court were attractive to other gardeners, and found their way into commercial circles. In the sixteenth century, the international trade in plants was driven by the movements of travellers and exchanges of plants along interpersonal networks. Amateur botanists and their scholarly counterparts maintained this trade. Market gardening and international trade in plants did not grow large and efficient until the seventeenth century. By the beginning of the seventeenth century, much of the trade in plants, not done by botanists, was initiated by aristocratic demand and realized by gardeners who collected plants for the aristocracy (or by ambassadors or pleasure travellers who brought back plants or seeds from their trips).[54] These new plants often found their way into the market-place through grafts, seeds and cuttings. Commercial collectors and cultivators of rare plants had much in common with their counterparts at court, sharing similar interests and expertise. So it should not be surprising that plants would have moved between the two groups, eventually entering the world of market gardeners, where plants as well as fruits and vegetables were brought to market.

I have not found much evidence to link directly court plant collection and the growth of the plant trade in France, but there is ample evidence of it in England, and the English in the seventeenth century are continually lamenting the poor state of the plant trade in England compared to what it was in France.[55] This may mean that market gardeners on the Continent were more active than in England in seeking out new plants and bringing them to market, bypassing the court trade in plants. But there is evidence that by the late seventeenth century gentlemen still coveted any new seeds or seedlings they could acquire, suggesting that the plant trade was still not so organized in France that commercial sources could supply all the plants gardeners desired to use.

The growth of the plant trade, both through court gardens and market gardens, may well have stimulated the demand for the horticultural books mentioned earlier. With the growing range of plants to use in their gardens, gardeners could not depend on traditional horticulture to guide them in the cultivation of their plants. Moreover, when they were faced with new plants to raise that were unknown to them, they were in charge of very precious objects whose death would be sorely felt. So the desire for practical knowledge of plant culture must have been exacerbated by the expanding trade in plants.

One indication of this interaction of commercial forces comes from *The Retir'd Gard'ner*,[56] a book from 1706 containing translations of two French books on horticulture from the seventeenth century. The Englishmen (George London and Henry Wise) who made the translation were from a family of market gardeners who had good reason to want English clients to be able to keep their plants alive, since the death of any plants from their nursery could be blamed on them. They also did a bit of promotion in the book, saying that readers should be sure to get plants and seeds from planter traders of high standing, since even the best care would not keep unhealthy plants alive. (This idea also supports the contention that gardeners with court appointments were likely to be more commercially desirable as consult-ants on gardens or as sources of rare plants, since they were indeed people of high standing in the world of gardens.)

The merging of commercial and court culture affected garden design as well as the distribution of plants and garden books. Just as Michael Baxandall argues that Renaissance painters used commercial values when they placed such emphasis on the mass of objects in their paintings,[57] one can argue that the French garden designers who were so carefully calculating garden geometries were also using the systems of rational calculation associated with the rise of capitalism. The movement towards increasingly dissociating numerical values from some system of absolute value was exactly like the move towards a currency system not based on the value of the metal in the coins but based on abstract attribution of value.[58] The emphasis on a garden design requiring careful measurement of land, taking advantage of surveying techniques and elevating the capacity to measure land exactly into a central element of design, could also be taken as clear evidence of the place of commercially inspired skills in the development of the formal garden. Even the development of rational systems of horticulture, the intellectual rationalization of the gardener's skills, can be taken as a commercially necessary shift in the period when market gardening was growing and agricultural experiments based on science were defined as valuable. The entirety of the designs cannot be explained in these terms, but neither can they be explained solely in terms of the symbolic resources of the Great Tradition. The Great Tradition *and* capitalist enter-prise were continuous parts of the same culture, a materialist culture geared towards appropriation of the natural world.

In these and other ways, the great parks at Versailles, Chantilly and elsewhere were not just refuges for elites to recover from the debilitating aspects of court society and inter-national politics; they were also places where the commercial world entered into the world of the court without any fanfare or recognition. There was nothing to make noise about. After all, the court lived off the success of France's commercial society. Moreover, social mobility at court was mixing the world of commerce with the world of the traditional aristocracy. Hence it could not be so surprising that court gardeners would cultivate ties with the commercial world to enrich their thinking, their gardens and perhaps also their pocketbooks.

The commercial world could enter court culture in this way because it helped to enrich elite consumption. New, highly literate, garden plans realized with exotic plants were easier to construct given expanded trade in plants and garden books. The social claims articulated in parterres and *bosques* could be more grand at the end than at the beginning of the seventeenth century because the commercial resources available to gardeners were simply much more developed.

The meaning of nature in the garden

Expanded commerce and wealth provided European elites with new resources for making claims about their social station and those who provided services at court with new ways to exploit commercially their knowledge of court tastes, but they did not determine what taste would be displayed or what social claims would be appropriately made. Stylistic shifts in garden design during the early modern period not only expressed regional variations in gardening, but also variations in the kinds of messages about taste and social station that elites wanted to convey. So far in this analysis we have treated taste as variant but social claims as uniform across the entire period, but even a brief glance at shifting garden iconography shows this is not the case. We can begin to make sense of the stylistic differences among the gardens of Renaissance Italy, seventeenth-century France and eighteenth-century England by thinking of them as systems for mapping social ambitions on nature. And we can begin to tease out the themes in these three periods by turning to Keith Thomas's writing on the changing meaning of nature in the early modern period.

Thomas argues that there was a fundamental transformation in the meaning of nature during the period, a movement away from seeing nature as creation – as Man's dominion set up by God – and towards a vision of nature as a mechanistic system distinct from the human world, set up by God but working by its own orderly laws.[59] This trajectory takes one from an idealist theology to a materialist science.

The problem is that Thomas's model does not fit the French formal garden very well. His first view of nature maps well onto the Italian Renaissance garden, and the second fits the English landscape garden, but the French formal garden has an ambiguous (and hence very interesting) position in the middle. We can learn something about both the transformation that Thomas tried to explain and the value of French formal gardens to the court by examining these relationships more closely (Plate 21.10).

The Renaissance pleasure garden was very much in tune with the vision of nature as creation. The garden was a kind of Eden, brought to life for the pleasure of human beings. The garden was a playful space, a site for innocent (and not so innocent) delight. Italian Renaissance gardens were full of jokes. They made funny noises, created illusions, sprayed visitors with water and tricked them with mazes. They were alternately enclosed and open, opening up great hillside views and allowing people to hide from one another in trellises and grottoes.[60]

At the same time, Renaissance gardens were spiritual and mysterious. The presence of Greek and Roman gods might make one think that Christian spirituality had no role here, but it was not true because the Renaissance pleasure garden was so clearly an Eden. It was not just that the gardens were idyllic (although they were that); they shut out the world with high walls and tried to fill the inside with perfect beauty in flora and fauna. But they also were designed to exercise God-like control over those who visited them. They were full of tricks (from waterworks to mazes) that disarmed the unwary and demonstrated that a larger power was at work in the garden. Only the designer of the garden (to continue the image of Eden) or his agents were able to anticipate what the automata would do, where the mazes would lead and where the unsuspecting visitor would get wet. The garden, like Eden, was both perfect and treacherous because it was designed and controlled by an impersonal power.

The owners of Italian Renaissance gardens, using their parks as means for conspicuous display, claimed the right to a kind of dominion, a control over part of Eden. To the extent that they connected the design of their gardens to the Great Tradition, they also claimed to be an intellectual elite, better suited to rule than non-elites who lived lives closer to that of animals. Nature was theirs both by spiritual right and because of their special capacity to rule over it. And their social superiority was legitimated by their intellectual and spiritual superiority (Plate 21.11).[61]

In contrast, the English landscape garden was based on a completely different conception of nature and supported a very different vision of the social claims to be made through the garden. The landscape garden was meant to epitomize the natural, as it was available through the senses, providing a model of natural perfectibility. This was not an Eden to reign over or a stage-set for people to perform upon; it was land that had its own contours and qualities, and yet it was also property that people could own and improve. The visitor entering the garden was supposed to enter it alone or in small groups to observe and admire the land's orderly beauty through contemplation. Drawing on ideas from Chinese gardens, English landscape garden designers felt beauty was located in the contour of the land, the shape of a tree, the sudden vista that opened up when rounding a corner of a path, and should be appreciated through thoughtful admiration of its integrity. But the English garden also contained small Greek temples and other icons of the classical tradition that marked them as distinctly European. The resulting English garden was a place of study and contemplation of both a cultural past that valued truth and a natural world that carried it. This garden was a place where individuals learned from nature and were glorified by their association with it as their property.

Perfection and antiquity were here, as they were in the Renaissance garden, but this time, they were connected in a new way to individuals – both individual moral education and private property. The individual in this period of English history was coming to be seen as a kind of property, a responsibility of the person who 'owned' it to cultivate and improve. This improvement came through learning, and nature was one of the primary teachers. Hence the garden was a valuable place in which cultivation of nature (one form of property improvement) could lead to improvement of human beings (another form of property). In this system, the owner of the landscape garden made statements about his responsibility and cultivation through the garden, and simultaneously showed a respect for property. The appearance of classical and poetic references in the garden added to its heuristic value, and hence bestowed greater honour on the owner of the garden.

The landscape garden also gained social value because it was modelled on landscape paintings; the garden was both landed property and a piece of property modelled on a luxury item. While garden flowers were being drawn inside the house on embroidered clothing and furniture upholstery, the image of the land itself that was used to design the gardens was brought indoors through paintings. The results of this exchange were important for the gardens. Garden paths were set up so that those strolling along them would suddenly encounter after turning a corner or passing a clump of trees a view or scene that looked like a landscape painting. In each of these vistas, the proportions of the buildings had to be carefully determined; the views themselves had to be carefully constructed (to draw attention to landscape details and obscure sights beyond the garden). The objects in these scenes had to look natural. Water had to fall and flow, not spray into the air; what animals were in the garden had to roam loose, not show up in unnatural menageries or aviaries; and even garden technology for cutting lawns was replaced by cows and deer, so that the garden would always look entirely natural. The English landscape garden ran to the horizon both because it was continuous with nature itself and because, as property, it needed to be vast to be impressive. There was no boundary; the ha-ha (a deep ditch surrounding the property) was used to keep the cattle and sheep in place without showing the property line. The garden provided a sense of limitless landholdings and so much wealth that vast amounts of the most fertile land could be left unproductive. There was no walled Eden here, just an ideal vision of the country that was simultaneously a representation of nature itself and the fecund property of its owner.

In this garden, the line between wildness and cultivation became increasingly difficult to draw. It was not just that the boundaries of the garden were made obscure; it was that the line between cultivated areas and forests was made problematic. With the decline of stag hunting and the growth of fox hunting, great forested areas were no longer a necessary part of the land around great houses. So trees in the English garden started to be arranged in groves that dotted the countryside. Wildness was encouraged in these groves, and put alongside great green lawns and the house itself. Nature had many faces, just as the garden had many views, and this new image of natural diversity gave the landscape garden a rhythm, in spite of the lack of garden beds or walls to mark bounded garden spaces.

The English who cultivated these gardens on their property often had their portraits painted in their gardens, showing their families in the foreground and their landholdings in the back. These paintings were simultaneously landscape paintings and property inventories. Nature was less a source of pleasure to them than a measure of their worth, their economic value and their social value. In these portraits, land is fertile, but it is also as idle as they are. Yet each is part of an ordered and sensible universe.[62]

What was the role of the French formal garden in relationship to these two visions of the natural? French gardens seem to have had elements of both. They imposed even greater order on the land than Renaissance gardens, and they were clearly pleasure gardens, full of surprises and delights. They made water do tricks; they made garden beds look like rugs rather than patches of wild flowers. At the same time, they were vast and open, moving towards the horizon. They were meant to represent nature as it was understood by science, full of order and diversity. They were designed with long walks that were alternately open and closed, providing lovely views, and quiet places to sit and think.[63]

One could think of the formal garden as a hybrid, holding these contradictory cultural tendencies together (once again making French gardens integrate diversity), but that would not do justice to the innovative character of the style. The garden at Vaux-le-Vicomte was no muddle, forming a bridge between Italy and Britain; the French formal garden presented a distinct vision of nature.

The French neither played with the garden as their dominion the way the Italians did nor contemplated the garden as their property the way the English did. I would argue that they held the garden as a piece of territory, distinct from the forest or fields around it, but extending as far as possible. This garden did not have a God as much as it had a monarch. At Versailles the Greek gods and goddesses were set in the garden as comments on the power of the monarch, not as markers of spirituality or even the classical past. At Vaux-le-Vicomte, there was no monarch, but certainly a territorial claim of grand proportions. At Chantilly, the Grand Condé manipulated his garden, the only territory still left to him after his defeat in Paris.[64] When the designer of the French formal garden organized the garden around the house, pointing to the chateau as the design center, he did this not because he wanted to give the owner a superior view of the garden, but to mark the garden as territory.

This territory was property but not the sort found in the English garden. The English controlled *land*. The land was meant to look like land, something potentially productive, if not in use. The French formal garden was land that was surveyed and measured, stamped as something under human control, not an Eden attributed to God or a fertile field; this land was territory attributable to its ruler.

We can understand what this means a bit better by looking at the land acquisitions of the Parisian financiers who rapidly bought up property around Paris in the seventeenth century. These men were not buying land to work for profit as much as they were seeking territories with which to make social claims. They wanted titles and holdings that would improve their status, not their wealth; the latter they acquired elsewhere. They wanted to translate economic power into political and social power, and for this they needed territories to express their prowess, not land in the English sense.

The glory of the French formal garden was that it integrated such diversity of form and content within its geometrical patterns. One could think of them as models of French government, putting together different departments into a coherent system of order. But that would not quite speak to the garden as a model of nature. To understand that, we need to pay closer attention to the provocative relationship between warfare and gardening in the period which suggests a relationship between territorial acquisition and gardens. Certainly, Louis XIV frequently punctuated periods of fighting with periods of garden-building. As we just saw, the Grand Condé, after his retirement to Chantilly, devoted himself to gardening. One could think of these as rhythms of aggression and retreat, the garden forming the place of retreat, but I think there is more. Expansion of a garden was a way of annexing territory. Finding ways to integrate new areas into a garden was a model of political integration of territory or the rethinking of the shape of a territory.

The territorial character of these gardens was also evidenced in the centrality of borders to the different units of the garden. Unlike the English landscape garden, the French garden was a mass of boundaries, not the walls of the Renaissance garden that closed out ordinary life to create an ideal garden interior, but a plethora of hedges and trees marking the end of one plot of land and the beginning of the next. These lines of demarcation were meant to be seen, but not to impede vision. Moreover, they were meant to help articulate the relationships among the parts of the garden (Plates 21.12 and 21.13).

It is interesting to think about a comment frequently made by garden historians about Le Nôtre's designs. They say that he developed a strong visual rhythm through his arrangement of these borders. The way the hedges around parterres were articulated in relationship to the trees around *bosques* constituted a central visual feature of the designs, simultaneously delineating and separating the garden's parts.[65] The resulting design had the rhythms of a political map in which territorial units and their defined boundaries were the central feature.

Ironically, the seriousness of the garden as a symbol of territory helps to make sense of the garden as a play space. The French court was famous for its playfulness,[66] and gardens were sites for many kinds of sport – from lavish festivals to short hunting parties. If you believe Huizinga and theorists of child's play, playing games can be very serious business. It allows people to transform problematic aspects of their lives into rules of a game that they can manipulate without serious consequence. Children play with their problems to learn to think, act and feel like adults. Adults work out their problems with cultural forms designed in part for that purpose.[67] Take, for example, carnival. It is described by Peter Burke as a 'world turned upside down', one in which people can reverse and make fun of the social control systems which normally repress them. So, too, one can think of the French formal garden, with its organized parcels of land, as a place where political elites could think about the acquisition and management of territory. They could act out dramas of warfare and territorial expansion when they tried to acquire and tear down old villages to enlarge their parks; they could consider ways to integrate diverse territories into a common unit whenever they considered reorganizing the garden; they could play with the development of vast water systems and transportation systems when they considered how to fill their fountains and where to lay their walkways; they could tinker with ways of symbolizing power for political ends when they decided what allegories to refer to in their statues and fountains; and most fundamentally, they could take the organization of diverse land parcels into a whole garden as an aesthetic rather than political issue, defusing but still raising the central territorial problem for the state. It was all very innocent pleasure. If a parterre or *bosque* did not work out, it could be torn down and rebuilt; if a new fountain was desired, the water system would be rethought. The owners of French formal gardens who played with the construction and remodelling of their gardens did not have to think about territory in a conscious fashion. The fact that they did not have to think of the garden as serious allowed them to play with it, and through the play they worked on skills that were actually important to their political lives (Plate 21.14).

These gardens were design triumphs in a period of intense political consolidation and change. Thy were not direct models of the territorial problems of the period to be played with like toy dolls and soldiers, but they were fun precisely because they addressed some of the issues about territorial acquisition and development that accompanied state formation and capitalist development. At the same time, they were reassuring because they displayed an illusion of complete control that generated a deep sense of security and ease. The beauty of Le Nôtre's gardens lay in large part in the tranquillity they maintained in spite of their size and complexity. There was an effortless way in which they integrated the land and house, wood and parterre, grotto and topiary confections. The sense of ease was achieved through excruciatingly careful planning. The control would be impressive in any age, but it meant more perhaps in the seventeenth-century world of shifting social positions and territorial claims. Le Nôtre's gardens were, at least, enormously seductive to people of the seventeenth-century French court who were trying to secure their own positions in society and establish the position of their country in the European political economy.

The image of nature that emerged in the French garden was neither the Christian vision of an Eden for human dominion nor the image of the natural world as a fertile field, simultaneously distinct from and manipulated to enhance human affairs. It was a materialist vision of nature, one equating land with property, but corporate property more than private property. This nature was an expression of a culture of mercantile capitalism, where economic organization was organized around collective control (through guilds or state companies, for example). Land in this system was still an economic resource, but not an individual one, and economic progress was expected to be achieved in large part though large-scale projects to improve transportation and trade. The garden at Versailles was a kind of territory appropriate to this social world. It showed land dominated and delineated, measured and weighed in relation to other bits of territory and put to work for enhancing the prestige and therefore the power of France. This kind of garden was developed through the techniques of rational measurement useful to the political economy; and it was organized in space like the maps of states and plans of estates so frequently drawn from surveys in the late sixteenth and seventeenth centuries. Thus the elaborate garden design of the period was grounded in techniques used to organize a state-based economic and political life.

Early in this paper I emphasized that gardens were used by individuals to claim social status. Now I must add that they were also used as the basis for *collective* claims about the status of France, its economy and the French state. Contemporary commentators from England certainly read them as measures of French economic success, indications of Louis XIV's power and success in inspiring the loyalty of his subjects and markers of the ambitions of the French state. So the communication of political and economic claims for France is clear enough at the time. The fact that the gardens were usually open to the public (from the 1640s), in spite of their being 'private' property, helps to support the idea that they were treated in part as French assets rather than private ones. And certainly, Louis XIV acted as though he designed the garden at Versailles to impress foreigners above all else, to give them a grand impression of the French state in his reign. Ambassadors were the primary audience for the promenade he devised through the park. He made the park more than a stage for displaying his power; he made it an actor in the politico-economic relations among European states. In this way, he made the garden a measured model of territorial control suited to his politico-economic ambitions.

Reading and writing with nature

If I am at all close to the truth with this analysis, then there is much being claimed and done in French formal gardens. These wonderfully elegant and seemingly transcendent creations are deeply caught up in the growth of the modern politico-economic system. They are products of a trade in plants that was piggy-backed on more economically central trading patterns. They are places in which the problems of social mobility and instability generated by capitalist economic activity were played out in claims for social position and importance. They are symbolically transformed maps of territorial hegemony, playful models of control and systematic use of land for power. And they are tributes to the beauties and ambitions fuelled in garden designers by the seductiveness of using pen and paper to think about gardens based on drawings and models of design available in print.

Notes

An earlier version of this paper was first presented at the Clark Library, UCLA, and was published in *Theory and Society*, xix (1990), 651–79.

1 Fernand Braudel, *The Structures of Everyday Life* (New York: Harper & Row, 1979).
2 Werner Sombart, *Luxury and Capitalism* (Ann Arbor: University of Michigan, 1967; 1st edn, 1913).
3 Braudel, *Structures*, 186.
4 Sombart, *Luxury*, chs 1, 4. See also C. Mukerji, *From Graven Images* (New York: Columbia University Press, 1982), particularly chs 1, 5 and 7; and Roy Strong, *Art and Power* (London: Boydell, 1984; 1st edn, 1973).
5 See, for example, William Howard Adams, *The French Garden* (New York: George Braziller, 1979); Derek Clifford, *The History of Garden Design* (New York: Praeger, 1963); Christopher Thacker, *The History of Gardens* (Berkeley: University of California Press, 1979); Naomi Miller, *Heavenly Caves* (New York: George Braziller, 1982); Miles Hadfield, *Topiary and Ornamental Hedges* (London: Adam & Charles Black, 1971); Elizabeth McDougall (ed.), *Fons Sapientiae* (Washington: Dumbarton Oaks, 1978).
6 Norbert Elias, *The Court Society* (New York: Pantheon, 1983; 1st edn, 1969).
7 For the Dutch influence, see Florence Hopper, 'The Dutch classical garden and André Mollet',

Journal of Garden History, ii (1982), 25–40. Italian influence is discussed in every standard history of gardens.

8   I should add that these gardens are both interesting and terribly difficult to study in part because of French attitudes towards them. There is not the kind of extensive French literature on gardens that you find in England (either in the seventeenth century or the present). In the last few years, there has been some renewed interest in the subject in France, but it tends to be very traditional in its admiration for the abstract character of these gardens, its concern for locating the philosophical roots of Le Nôtre's work in Descartes and its notable lack of concern for how or why these gardens were built or maintained. There is also a terrible problem because Le Nôtre did not leave any substantial writings or drawings to use as primary sources for reinterpreting the gardens. One is left with images of his gardens made by engravers, and descriptions of gardens by travellers (mainly English). This is dangerous ground for making historical assertions. But being a sociologist for whom theory-building and modelling history is the primary purpose of looking to the past, I am by definition suspect as an interpreter of historical materials, and I am using that to my advantage. More seriously, I rely heavily in this paper on the more extensive thinking on materialism in the early modern period that I did in previous work.

9   Colbert's famous library was an example of a collection of this sort. See Alfred Neymarck, *Colbert et son temps* (Genève: Slatkine Reprints, 1970; 1st edn, 1877) 178–81.

10 Lorraine Daston, 'Curiosity in early modern science', paper presented at the Colloquium in Science Studies, University of California, San Diego, June 1990.

11 Neymarck, *Colbert*, 258–61. The way Colbert used international trading connections to increase the variety of plants in the royal gardens is documented here. The attraction of these gardens to foreign visitors is obvious in the diaries of visitors like Locke and Ferrier. Ferrier is quoted in John Lough, *France Observed* (Stockfield: Oriel Press, 1985), 147. John Locke, *Locke's Travels in France*, ed. J. Lough (Cambridge: Cambridge University Press, 1953). It is also clear from the itineraries that the king wrote to show the gardens at Versailles to visitors. See Christopher Thacker, 'Manière de montrer les jardins de Versailles', *Journal of Garden History*, i (1972), 49–69.

12 Pierre Bourdieu, *Distinction*, tr. R. Nice (Cambridge, Mass.: Harvard University Press, 1984).

13 Nobert Elias, *The Civilizing Process* (New York: Urizen Books, 1978; 1st edn, 1939).

14 Thorstein Veblen, *The Theory of the Leisure Class* (New York: Mentor Books, 1953; 1st edn, 1899).

15 Veblen, *Leisure Class*.

16 Orest Ranum, *Paris in the Age of Absolutism* (Bloomington: Indiana University Press, 1979).

17 Ranum, *Paris*, 252–9.

18 Saint-Simon, *Saint-Simon at Versailles*, ed. L. Norton (London: Hamish Hamilton, 1958). Saint-Simon, *Historical Memoirs of the Duc de Saint-Simon*, vol. 1, ed. L. Norton (New York: McGraw-Hill, 1967).

19 See also Elizabeth Charlotte, Duchesse d'Orléans, *A Woman's Life in the Court of the Sun King*, tr. E. Foster (Baltimore: Johns Hopkins University Press, 1958).

20 Mukerji, *Graven Images*, ch. 1. Daston, 'Curiosity'.

21 Gardens were extensions of the house in the obsession with collection. Each housed exotic novelties from far away – chinoiserie inside and rare bulbs outside. Images of the same flora and fauna even appeared inside houses embroidered on fabrics for dress, upholstery and draperies (see T. Beck, *Embroidered Gardens* (New York: Viking, 1978)). Petted tender plants were even given their own houses. (Compare this to Veblen's ideas about horses as beloved by elites because they are so expensive to keep, in *Leisure Class*, 143.) Orangeries were built for wintering tender trees. Stoves (or heated glass houses) were developed for growing palms and other large tropical plants as well as medicinal plants (see John Hix, *The Glass House* (Cambridge, Mass.: MIT Press, 1981)). Rare animals were simultaneously sought and placed in specially prepared menageries. (For a description of the collection of rare plants at Versailles, see Ferrier in Lough, *France Observed*, 147. Locke mentions a menagerie at Versailles and another at Chantilly. See Locke, *Travels*, 153, 168–9.)

To understand this from a different point of view, one can draw on Bruno Latour's idea from *Science in Action* (Milton Keynes: Open University Press, 1986), that nature can be recruited as a political ally. He argues that scientists routinely use nature this way when they promote their theories and the power of their institutions by claiming that the *data* from nature tell them what they know. Nature is made to speak on their behalf. In a similar vein, one can argue that nature in early modern gardens was used as an ally to attest to the power and high status of those developing the gardens. An exotic tree was a marker as well as a prize (or prized as a marker), locating its owner in social space at the same time that the owner located the tree in the garden.

22 Gardens had a more limited role in this system than grooming, jewellery, hairdressing and clothing because they were not portable and thus could not be used as continuously for displaying rank. Still, gaining favour from the king was often expressed in such things as the king's gardener designing a favourite's garden. Grand gardens were particularly indicative of high rank because they were only useful socially if others could be brought to see them. Clothes you could take anywhere. This means that not all members of court society were in a position to cultivate and use a great garden. Only those that the court would visit could have the proper communicative effects. Thus having an elite garden at all was from the beginning a way of saying something dramatic about the social centrality of their owners.

23 See Clifford, *Garden Design* and Thacker, *Gardens*. For a brief description of the geography of fashions in dress see Mukerji, *Graven Images*.

24 See Alberto Pérez-Gómez, *Architecture and the Crisis of Modern Science* (Cambridge, Mass.: MIT Press, 1983).

25 Ranum, *Paris*, 252–92. Dent argues that the financiers were not the only group using land for making social claims. People from the high state administration were doing the same thing – albeit with less resistance. He also argues that the financiers were not a particularly capitalist group, in large part because of their importance to state finances, which involved them with the deep irrationality of the state financial system. Still, financiers had a peculiar social position. They were distrusted because of their economic importance. Thus, while their use of land to acquire titles and enter into the nobility was not in itself clear evidence of the entrance of the world of commerce into court life, it was still resented because finance was seen as deeply at odds with nobility. Moreover, Dent argues that the financiers were vulnerable to social distate (and violence) because they were individualistic rather than corporatist. They had no group culture to protect them. In this way, they displayed an individualism that is usually associated with capitalism and commercial culture. They were carriers of a commercial culture that was seen as at odds with court life, but was so essential to it that they were able to experience mobility in spite of the cultural resistance to it. See Julian Dent, *Crisis in Finance: Crown, Financiers and Society in 17th-Century France* (New York: St Martin's Press, 1973), ch. 9 and conclusions, esp. 235–42.

26 As we will see in a later section of the paper, this movement was not a gradual and smooth trend. At first, performance culture was enhanced in early modern Europe by the wealth that could be applied to it. Renaissance processions and festivals are well known. But the materialist culture and capitalist economic development eventually began to undermine these traditional forms and replace them with a more object-oriented culture. See Peter Burke, *Popular Culture in Early Modern Europe* (New York: Harper & Row, 1978), ch. 7.

27 See E. Eisenstein, *The Printing Press as an Agent of Change* (Cambridge: Cambridge University Press, 1979).

28 Jack Goody, 'What's in a list?', in idem, *Domestication of the Savage Mind* (Cambridge: Cambridge University Press, 1977).

29 Historians often say that French formal gardens were designed to be seen from the upper storeys of the buildings around which they were planted. Boyceau wrote about the relationship of the proportions of buildings and the gardens around them. He also talked about how the parterres near the house should look from these windows. (See Adams, *French Garden* and F. Hamilton

Hazelhurst, *Jacques Boyceau and the French Formal Garden* (Athens, Georgia: University of Georgia Press, 1966).) Visitors to French gardens have often marvelled at the views from the house. So there is much to be said for this point of view. The problem is that many French gardens had mounds and balastrades from which to view the beds from above, and although they were secondary to the views from the upper house, they show that the gardens could be seen from above from a variety of perspectives. (See F. Hamilton Hazelhurst, 'Le Nostre at Conflans', in E. MacDougall and F. Hamilton Hazelhurst (eds), *The French Formal Garden* (Washington, DC: Dumbarton Oaks, 1974).) I would argue French formal gardens were really designed to be seen from a bird's-eye view, since they were made first and foremost to look good as a plan on paper. The views from elevated spots like the house were only the best earthly approximations of that heavenly perspective.

I should mention here that the lengthening of the beds as they receded from the house in these plans has been taken as additional evidence that these gardens were meant to be viewed from the house. Although this argument could be made for small gardens, in which the entire garden could be seen from the house, it does not hold for the large gardens typical for the period. These grand gardens were made on such a scale that the view from the house could not encompass the whole vista and viewers could not distinguish all the proportions. This is one bit of evidence that the use of perspective and foreshortening in these plans was not of practical use for viewing the garden, but rather displayed the designer's knowledge of perspective and foreshortening, adding to the literacy of the design and bestowing greater honour on its owner. (Samuel Edgerton discusses perspective as part of a shift in cultural vision, not just a technique for drawing and representing the world. See Edgerton, *The Renaissance Rediscovery of Linear Perspective* (New York: Basic, 1975).)

30   See Lucien Febvre and Henri-Jean Martin, *The Coming of the Book*, tr. D. Gerard (London: NLB, 1976; 1st edn, 1958) on the change in books in this period.

31   Sieveking quotes from Pliny in Albert Forbes Sieveking, *Gardens Ancient and Modern* (London: J. M. Dent, 1899), 15–18; see Thacker, *Gardens*, 95–6 on Alberti.

32   See Martin Lowry, *The World of Aldus Manutius* (Ithaca: Cornell University Press, 1979).

33   Peter Burke, *Popular Culture*.

34   For a description and list of many French garden books from the period, see Phyllis Crumb, *Nature in the Age of Louis XIV* (London: Routledge, 1928), 5. For the texts cited here, see Bernard Palissy, *Recepte véritable*, Edition Critique by K. Cameron (Geneva: Librairie Drozsa, 1988; 1st edn, 1563); Salomon De Caus, *Les raisons des forces mouvantes* (Amsterdam: Frits Knuf, 1973; 1st edn, 1615); Charles Estienne and Jean Liébault, *L'agriculture et la maison rustique* (Lyons: A. Laurens, 1702); Oliver de Serres, *Théâtre de l'agriculture et ménage* (Paris: Michel Vanlochom, 1600); Jacques Boyceau, *Traité du jardinage* (Paris: Michel Vanlochom, 1638); Claude Mollet, *Le jardin de plaisir* (Paris: De Sercy, 1678).

35   Dezallier d'Argentville, *La théorie et la practique de jardinage* (Paris: J. Mariette, 1709).

36   See d'Argentville, *Jardinage*.

37   See Boyceau, *Traité*.

38   See De Caus, *Forces mouvantes*.

39   See Palissy, *Recepte véritable*, Boyceau, *Traité* and Estienne, *L'agriculture* in particular for philosophical speculation.

40   See Mukerji for print and capitalism. See Eisenstein, *Printing Press* for the consequences of books for thought.

41   See Evelyn in Lough, *France Observed*, 1984, 95–6.

42   See Pérez-Gómez, *Architecture*.

43   See Boyceau, *Traité*; Hazelhurst, *Boyceau*, ch. 3.

44   Hazelhurst, *Boyceau* and Mollett, *Le jardin de plaisir*.

45   See Pérez-Gómez, *Architecture*, 166–201; Claude Perrault, *Les dix livres d'architecture de Vitruve* (Paris: J. B. Coignard, 1684).

46   Ranum, *Paris*, ch. 12.

47   Duchesse d'Orléans, *Woman's Life*.
48   For discussion of Colbert and the growth of French industry, see A. J. Sargent, *The Economic Policy of Colbert* (New York: Burt Franklin, 1968), ch. 3. For more extensive discussion of Colbert's policies and their effects on the development of luxuries in France, see Charles W. Cole, *Colbert and a Century of French Mercantilism*, vol. 2 (Hamden, Conn.: Archon Books, 1964), chs 10–12. For descriptions of the support of luxury manufacture by individual members of the court, see W. B. Honey, *French Porcelain* (London: Faber & Faber, 1950).
49   Abraham du Pradel, *Le Livre Commode des Adresses de Paris pour 1692*, ed. Edouard Fournier (Liechtenstein: Kraus Reprint, 1979; 1st edn, Paris, 1878).
50   See for example Mollet, *Le jardin de plaisir*; Boyceau, *Traité*.
51   Crumb, *Nature*.
52   See Estienne and Liébault, *L'agriculture*; Boyceau, *Traité*; Mollet, *Le jardin de plaisir*; De Caus, *Forces mouvantes*; d'Argentville, *Jardinage*; François Gentil, *The Retir'd Gard'ner*, tr. George London and Henry Wise (London: Jacob Tonson, 1706).
53   Locke, *Travels*; Palissy, *Recepte véritable*; Pérez-Gómez, *Architecture*.
54   Ronald Webber, *The Early Horticulturalists* (Plymouth: David & Charles, 1968); Hix, *Glass House*; Hopper, 'Dutch classical garden'.
55   Webber, *Early Horticulturalists*. Locke describes aspects of this trade. See Locke, *Travels*, 216 for the role of correspondents in these exchanges and the mixing of social ranks in this trade.
56   Gentil, *Retir'd Gard'ner*.
57   Michael Baxandall, *Painting and Experience in 15th-Century Italy* (New York: Oxford, 1974).
58   Joyce Appleby, *Economic Thought and Ideology in 17th-Century England* (Princeton: Princeton University Press, 1978).
59   Keith Thomas, *Man and the Natural World* (New York: Pantheon, 1983).
60   See Linda Strauss, 'Automata: a study in the interface of science, technology, and popular culture' (University of California, San Diego, dissertation, 1987).
61   For discussion of this elite sense of superiority and its relationship to Renaissance scholarship, see Lowry, *Manutius*, ch. 1. See also Thomas, *Man*, on the equation of non-elites to animals in the period.
62   Ann Bermingham, *Landscape and Ideology* (Berkeley: University of California Press, 1986).
63   MacDougall and Hazelhurst, *The French Formal Garden*; Thacker, *Gardens*; Clifford, *Garden Design*.
64   G. Macon, *Chantilly* (Paris: H. Laurens, 1929).
65   See Bermingham, *Landscape*; Thacker, *Gardens*; Clifford, *Garden Design*.
66   See, on Versailles, Bernard Champigneulle, *Promenades dans Versailles and ses jardins* (Paris: Club des Libraries de France, 1961), 19–20. On the Luxembourg gardens see Evelyn's account in Sieveking, *Gardens*, 108–9 and another in Lough 1985, p. 114.
67   See Huizinga, *Homo Ludens* (London: Routledge & Kegan Paul, 1949); Barbel Inhelder and Jean Piaget, *The Early Growth of Logic in the Child* (New York: Harper & Row, 1964).

22
Presuming images and consuming words: the visualization of knowledge from the Enlightenment to post-modernism

Barbara Maria Stafford

The production, management and consumption of a flood of bytes spilling out of world-wide databases and computer networks has become a universal obsession. It is not accidental that this overwhelming volume of information – likened to drinking from the proverbial firehose[1] – coincides with a mounting concern for bolstering and maintaining language 'literacy.' Yet the simplistic identification of only verbal skills with a properly 'humanistic' education is profoundly disturbing. It does not take into account the conceptual and perceptual revolution occurring in the presentation of knowledge since the eighteenth century. Equally limited, to my mind, is the notion that educational visualization should use images merely to convey information. This opinion holds that the illustrated data derived from graphics is important, not the image itself.[2] Inscribed into this equally linguistic bias is the false severance of *how* things are presented from what they express. Anyone dismayed by the concealed manipulations often operating in broadcast journalism or political advertisement must see the danger inherent in such a division.

However briefly, I wish to show that present-day written forms of communication were already being challenged, and even swept aside, in an earlier era.[3] My heretical point-of-view is that this turn of events does not necessarily represent cultural decline or a great social evil. In fact, it provides a splendid opportunity for exiting, at last, from Plato's Cave. The new-found power and ubiquity of images calls for teaching innovations and for altering venerable, but unexamined, epistemological models and textual metaphors ('codes', 'alphabets', 'letters', 'spelling', 'grammar'). I believe that only a serious training in visual proficiency will allow us to assimilate, integrate and understand a 'holographic' and multi-disciplinary reality increasingly filtered, transformed and synthesized through three-dimensional imaging. Furthermore, as the battle over the reauthorization of the National Endowment for the Arts and the National Endowment for the Humanities is proving, those of us involved with the visual arts cannot be content simply to champion freedom of speech and to produce or consume innovative artistic works. We are also responsible for articulating to a wider public that understanding the communicative modes and tactics of images is essential to a thorough, humanistic education. We must strive to develop future directions and strategies to prepare broad and informed constituencies for technology's ever-advancing power to make the invisible visible.

If our post-modern times are indeed pre-eminently visual times, they can be set in valuable relief against an earlier chapter in the history of visual communication. For it was precisely in the eighteenth century that the persisting rationalist philosophical attitude towards images hardened into 'systems'. Such theories claimed that pictures and perceptual apprehension, in the words of Baumgarten, were an inferior gnosis.[4] This consumption of presuming and popular images by an official hermeneutic of higher interpretive words was evinced in the academic demotion of pictures to an ornamental, or merely craft, status when bereft of a superior non-visual 'method'.[5] Paradoxically, but not surprisingly, this attempt at textual control occurred in a century unprecedented until then for its sophisticated visual practices, technological inventions and sheer pictorial production. The prejudicial implications of continuing to see images linguistically, that is, as a lesser, transitory and illusory form of written communication, are still playing themselves out.

I

Early twentieth-century modernism was characterized by printed manifestos, by a conceptual abstraction,[6] by painted word games,[7] by alphabetic and numbered collages and calligrams,[8] by what one contemporary architectural critic has termed 'the writing of the walls'.[9] Conversely, the late twentieth century is the media age of vocal, aural and, above all, optical rhetoric:[10] of television cinematics and video spectacles, of interactive computer displays,[11] of performance art, 'procedural' art,[12] fractal and math-art,[13] holography[14] and of that hyper-advertisement, the block-buster exhibition. We are awash in entertainment and information presented sensorially. On the domestic front, it is now possible for the average person to assemble a small-scale television station within his or her four walls. New ultra-stereo wrap-around systems coupled to gigantic screens seem to be fostering a society of Romantic solitaries communicating with other electronically generated spectres. On the biological and cosmic front, the Human Genome Project and the Hubble Space Telescope are on the verge of spewing forth data by the gigabyte. Imaging lies at the heart both of this private creation of evanescent ghosts and the public decipherment and cataloguing of reams of elusive facts and figures that would otherwise remain uninterpretable. Instead of sequencing three billion pieces of DNA, scientists – relying on a visual metaphor – now favour sketching out a 'road atlas' of the genome indicating genetic markers or distinct biochemical features. Yet the overarching human need to find meaningful visual patterns, whether in the living of a life or the conduct of research, has not been seen as a *positive* aspect of the broader drive towards the visualization of knowledge initiated during the Enlightenment. Giving shape to, or mapping, experiential confusion requires learning and special skills. The history of the general move towards visualization thus has broad intellectual and practical implications for the conduct and the theory of the humanities, the physical and biological sciences, the social sciences and, indeed, all forms of education – top to bottom.[15]

The multiple ramifications of this far-ranging aesthetic process of opticalization rest submerged in a culture that, despite its clear reliance on a spate of images, remains ironically mired in a deep logocentrism.[16] By logocentrism I mean that cultural bias, convinced of the superiority of written, or 'propositional', language, that devalues as unknowing sensory, affective and kinetic forms of communication precisely because they often baffle verbal resolution.[17] To produce a new world of perspicuous and informed observers (not just literate readers) will, I believe, require a paradigm shift of Copernican proportions. As more and more people are producing and consuming their own productions, and as cable television and video cassettes further particularize and decentralize messages, the need to suture together a shared culture becomes greater. These marvellous and sophisticated contemporary gadgets for watching belong among the technological apparatus characterizing a long evolution in perception. Knowing something about the common myths surrounding images, their past uses and structures, would help to forge models for future interactive communication as the old linguistic hierarchies fracture. In the era of personal broadcasting and the demassification of visual consumption, perceiving should be given at least as much, if not more, attention than reading. These activities (as we are increasingly learning from the neurosciences)[18] are not merely interchangeable functions or skills. Interconnected (or possibly orchestrated in a network), yes; the image subsumed or generalized to extinction in a number- or text-based logic, no.

Two major periods of production and consumption will be juxtaposed for their mutual illumination. First, I offer a brief overview of the visualization challenge facing us now. Second, I identify telling instances of the idea of communication as informing display developing in the early modern period. Like the twentieth-century electronics revolution, eighteenth-century technology encouraged the privatization of pleasurable beholding. While not yet making it feasible for people to spend more time at home and less time going to their places of work, shops or theatres, it none the less initiated a consumer-driven flexibility in visual communication. New graphic techniques widened the possibilities of articulation within a given medium and provided greater subjective choice in what one was able to see. Eighteenth-century aesthetic and technological innovations, and the visual skills to analyse them, thus have much to teach the twentieth century about the presentation, construction and interpretation of graphical messages of all sorts.

If one were to raise a periscope to survey the contemporary sea of visual information inundating all disciplines, what might one behold? I call attention to a few salient outcrops. Understanding their significance within the current structure of knowledge is enhanced by knowing that they still reverberate with allusions developed in the early modern period. The burgeoning field of neuroscience has led to the 'spatialization' and visibilization of the brain's concealed terrain in a kind of neural photography.[19] Three examples must serve to highlight the 'theatricalization' of mental phenomena into apparitional scenic events. Computer simulations of the brain's interconnected nerve cells provide neuroscientists and cognitive psychologists with literal insights into the dynamic processes by which the mind thinks, senses, feels. Medical imaging devices transparently and non-invasively 'open' opaque surfaces permitting physicians to gaze into formerly hidden depths. X-ray tomography (CT) exposes bone structures. Magnetic resonance imaging (MRI) gives a cross-sectional picture of the architecture of the brain at different levels or 'cuts'. Computers are then used to reconstruct in visual form a three-dimensional translucent display in rotation, or a hovering 'transparent brain'. Its inner parts can be dissected at a touch of the keyboard by stripping away the skull's layers electronically. Difficult craniotomies can thus be 'rehearsed' visually. Positron emission tomographic (PET) scanners provide 'portraits' of the brain as a whole caught in the act of thought. This instrument is a kind of neo-Albertian window on mental operations, and by its means we can view clairvoyantly spatio-temporal patterns of activity arising from neural performances. Mobile chromatic shapes map various cellular and electrochemical properties of the brain involved in diverse sensory and affective processes. Most spectacularly, the superimposition of PET and MRI (Plate 22.1) is leading to the establishment of detailed three-dimensional correlations between specific functions and their location in the brain.[20] As with widespread genetic screening, these imaging breakthroughs are fraught with ethical concerns. The sombre question arises whether insurers, employers and other institutions might be lured by the physiognomic fallacy and try to predict, and exclude, through prognostic tests individuals who carry the 'wrong' genes or mental 'defects'.

Spectacle has also entered the domain of physics. The major American sculptor Kenneth Snelson, in his essay-portrait of the atom, longed for the day when computer graphics might allow us to sit 'in a theater and observe the true wonders of the microphysical world'.[21] In a three decade-long project, which came to fruition only because of computer simulation, Snelson went beyond any currently realizable atomic model. He conjectured about the 'atomic condition' as he saw it, from within, from the electron's perspective, not from the physicist's external and bombarding point-of-view. He thus challenged the thesis held by the founding fathers of quantum theory. These pioneers of the invisible claimed that no pictorial representation could be devised to permit an unmediated description of the quantum world filled with untrackable quarks, interactions among electrons and mysterious quantum exchanges among particles. The mathematical theory which de Broglie, Bohr, Schrödinger and Heisenberg established aimed only to describe systematically the response of apparatus.[22] Yet Snelson's gossamer computer panoramas poignantly harken back to the Enlightenment's desire for diaphaneity. Like Piranesi, and a host of early modern antiquarians, he desired to render perceptible realms declared to be unperceivable directly.

Super-computers thus permit us to see internal and external worlds anew. Again, it is dynamic visualization that can transform an incomprehensible data file into more than a meaningless string of bits and pieces or an infinite series of unrelated fragments. Consequently, many astrophysicists and radiologists, meteorologists and engineers, have begun to decry the widening gap existing between the accumulation of raw numbers and their transformation into a visual format enabling practical analysis.[23] Thunderstorm modelling and the animation of planetary magnetospheres represent only two small instances for making the larger case that visualization of complex data – otherwise literally unimaginable – is now critical to the advancement of many fields of science.[24] In addition, there is a renaissance of widespread serious interest in the use of graphics in the mathematical field of statistics.[25] It seems that the science of the measurement of uncertainty and the calculation of probabilities[26] no longer spurns aesthetic concerns and user-preference evident in well-designed charts and histograms. Moreover, and more importantly, pictorial tools for the discriminant analysis of multivariate data are being created. Chernoff's 'heads', or schematic faces[27] – operating on the principle of much in little advanced by eighteenth-century caricaturists – prove that statisticians, like the rest of us, need succinct images to help them think about multiple and heterogeneous variables.

Legal practice, too, has become increasingly 'cinematic'. Trials are now routinely shaped by reliance on so-called 'demonstrative evidence' in the form of videos. The filming of everything from dramatized mugshots, to 'a day in the life' of a victim, to the re-enactment of crime, gives the old problem of the nature of accurate witnessing and judging a new urgency. The ambiguities surrounding eyewitness testimony, specifically, are set in sharp relief.[28] How does the law establish objective visual criteria for simulating a 'performance' meant to capture 'what really happened' during a transitory event viewed by many subjects, seen from different perspectives, under a variety of emotional conditions, and remembered differently? In short, what constitutes reliable visual evidence? How does the jury member or the trial lawyer, for that matter, recognize distortion, slanting or bias, not only in the verbal account given by witnesses but in the film or representational version of that account? Given the lavish increase in sophisticated court exhibits, in scale models, multicoloured charts, computer simulations and multimedia 'shows', how does a visually naive and unsophisticated jury distinguish responsibly between a message corresponding to the complexities of the actual experience and contrived propaganda advancing a specific, but 'objectively' disguised point-of-view? As G. C. Lichtenberg, the superb eighteenth-century German commentator on Hogarth's graphic works, remarked, the great hermeneutic problem in life lies not in ferreting out truth or lies but in exposing 'very clever false interpretations'.[29]

But the paradigmatic post-modern visual condition – the dissociation of hand from eye, cause from effect, stimulus from response, skill from signal – is to be witnessed in the business world.[30] It is at the site of desktop workstations and farflung databases where the Enlightenment's fundamental contribution to the epistemological structure of the late twentieth century is most evident. In the corporate Platonic cave – a windowless, mirrored or darkly-glazed high rise – smooth and shiny surfaces reflect simulacra. The new workplace is an information-rich organization in which once physical labour and tangible objects related to administrative, productive and personnel activities have become etherealized into chromatic apparitions weightlessly flitting across a computer screen. This 'New Immaterialism' was set in motion by Bishop Berkeley.[31] The production of intangible 'liteness' by the media, and the consumption of the phantasmatic by a broad public, is part of a greater rapid and daily dematerialization. 'Solid' or manufactured objects evaporate into 'unreal' or evanescent appearances through the intervention of circuitry. In a world where information is just *there*, users increasingly neither know nor care where the free-floating and autonomous debris originated.

This present-day sense of the societal ambiguity of technology, accompanied by mixed feelings of excitement and unease, returns us squarely to the Enlightenment. The eighteenth-century preoccupation with visionary territories was linked to an awareness that history had many potential realizations. Eluding the certainty of logical exposition, the total look of a bygone civilization could only be imagined or visualized through chance, partial discoveries. Contingency, variability and fluctuation – the signs of cultural unmooring – were endemic to a period experiencing an explosion of discontinuous and odd finds demanding representation. Optical classification of the strange, the scattered and the singular, in turn, was inseparable from the technological reproductive innovations needed to simulate them.[32] Among the consequences of this dual development were the first sustained reflections on the possibilities, subtleties, power and beauty of visual information and on the importance of visual knowledge of all sorts. The age's chief aesthetic theorists – DuBos, Caylus, Diderot, Falconet, Addison, Shaftesbury, Hogarth, Reynolds, Winckelmann, Lichtenberg – drew an important distinction that is largely forgotten by twentieth-century verbally shaped disciplines. With great sophistication, these thinkers differentiated between imagery *used* as equivalents to discourse, or as illustration, and as an untranslatable constructive form of cognition, or as expression. Broadcast journalism and we who view it, for example, have to come to grips with this distinction in that we must fully understand how to co-ordinate and interpret not only what people say, but *how* they say it, that is, the *style* of what they observably *do*. The art of visual conversation is aided by a format that encourages speakers seated face-to-face to 'perform' their arguments at length. Such communication calls upon the discernment of an audience that, although absent, is urged to participate as if it were present.

Visual knowing entails viewing any problem in three dimensions, at many different levels of detail and from various perspectives. It is the result of an active and constitutive expression that makes visible and intellectually graspable impalpable, ambiguous, mixed, intricate experiences intractable to numerical or linguistic reduction. Conversely, illustration is the didactic pictorial imitation of a preformed, prepackaged simple quantum of verbal information easily ingested by a faceless public. The equally anonymous textual message hides the fact that there is a sender shaping the medium. Expression, on the other hand, as a dynamic, interactive and experimental procedure for the individual re-enactment of an 'authored' perception, brings about enlightenment. Understanding emerges progessively. It is the result of an investigative process as each viewer struggles to relate the medium-suffused message to his or her own experience. Such interactive graphic encounters do not illustrate. Rather, they set before the eyes, or disclose, the complexity and lack of clarity of phenomena that are not yet well understood.

It is on this major, and profoundly educational role of imagery that I wish to linger. Images are not only architectonic, they are iconoclastic in destroying specious certitudes and in revealing ignorance or the limitations of human comprehension. The unique perspective of the eighteenth century on the affective and pleasurable training value of pictures, coupled with the rise of a special technology for visualization, has much to teach the modern viewer (who has forgotten, or is ignorant of, these skills) about the analysis of contemporary visual material. Unlike the intervening age of photography – which unwittingly fostered the illusion of neutral supports for information, the reception of 'reality' without toil and the self-explanatory nature of sight[33] – the eighteenth century, I believe, initiated the pedagogical struggle to comprehend the full power of visual arrays now realized in our twentieth-century culture of pictorial information. Three examples, drawn from the varieties of visual history created during the Enlightenment, must suffice to demonstrate how an understanding of the processes that brought about past visual acuity might contribute to forming more astute observers of the present complexities of life. They are: the reconstruction of past cultures; the exhibition of biodiversity; and the externalization of somatic experience. In each case, the determining desire was to get a glimpse of the unseen. This held whether the goal was to reinstitute a time different from now, long-extinct assemblages of organisms or the hidden shape and patterns of thought.

The desire to attain a visual stratigraphy of the past elicited from the tireless Venetian etcher, Giambattista Piranesi (1720–78), one of the greatest graphic innovations of the age.[34] His radical experimentation with etching, a corrosive chemical procedure for 'biting' a copper plate, was matched only by William Blake's later revision of reproductive engraving. The English poet–illuminator punningly termed his own acid stereotype process the 'infernal' method because it required printing, or exposing to light, what was literally buried beneath an impervious ground, or covered over by drawing.[35] Relying on the same surface and depth analogy implicit in the intaglio procedure, Piranesi performed perceptual rescue work. He systematically unearthed the mutilated *corpus* of Italian antiquity. Unlike modern archaeological restorations, Piranesi's paper excavations in black and white did not despoil eroding monuments of their pathos (Plate 22.2). Thus the 'suffering' surfaces, stuccos, ornament and even aging dirt of the tombs and cinerary urns lining *The Appian Way*, were left

468   Barbara Maria Stafford

intact.[36] From the countless walls, temples, baths and amphitheatres of the *Antichità Romane* (1756), to the Republican and Baroque monuments of the *Delle Magnificenza ed Archittetura de' Romani* (1760), to the subterranean chambers, cisterns and corridors of the *Descrizione e disegno dell'emissario del Lago Albano* (1762), Piranesi uncovered and retrieved the decaying body of Rome. With scalpel-like wielding of the etcher's needle, he applied surgical procedures (learned, I suggest, from medical illustration) to turn the still-living fabric of architecture inside out (Plate 22.3). Furthermore, he appeared to be following Vesalius's lead. The great sixteenth-century anatomist's emotion-laden attitudes had recently received engraved reinterpretation by Jean Wandelaer for B. S. Albinus's (1697–1770) 1725 Leiden edition of the *De Humani Corporis Fabrica*.[37] The anatomist's muscled dead were mobilized by the architect into lithic *écorchés*.[38] Blasted bodies became analogues for hollowed-out ruins, for an eviscerated, but still potent, antiquity. As an intuitive explorer of monuments, he closely resembled the great analyst and extrapolator of the human body. Vesalius was the first to unite the separate functions of lecturer, dissector and practical demonstrator. Similarly, the artist–technologist was the foremost delineator and antiquarian, interpreter and defender of the historically contingent phenomenon that was Rome. As patient *ostensor*, the Venetian etcher invited participation from his audience. His searching fingers of light and dark obliged the viewer's eyes to follow (Plate 22.4). In this visual and manual process of fleshed-out, not simplistic, showing, Piranesi, like the Renaissance anatomist and his important eighteenth-century successors,[39] put his own hand to the business of demonstration, thereby engaging the beholder.

Further, the intaglio process itself allowed him to take 'physiological' soundings. In the *Section of the Tomb of Alessandro Severo*, the superficial or deep registration of various architectural 'tissues' to longer or shorter exposure to acid, to more or less delicate or rough stimulation by the etching needle, clarified the complex vertical structure (Plate 22.3). Piranesi's experimental method for visibilizing the 'irritability' of the ancient fibres on copper plates belonged to the inductive mentality determining the practices of such Hallerian contemporaries as Felice Gaspar Ferdinand Fontana (Plate 22.5) (1730–1805) and Leopoldo MarcAntonio Caldani (1725–1813).[40] Like them, he captured the impalpable passage of time by palpably probing and poking beneath the veneer. Material digs and jabs literally traced the motions of raw muscle as well as the changes occurring within exposed stone and mortar. The actual arduous and lengthy process of physical exploration and visionary recreation was compacted and presented simultaneously, for our re-enactment, on these large and magnificent prints (Plates 22.2 and 22.3). Thus the piecemeal and motley activity of retrieval was experienced corporeally by the viewer in the time spent looking, searching and visually wandering among the *membra disjecta* of ruins.

The power of Piranesi's expressive hieroglyphics lay in abbreviating and synthesizing complex spatio-temporal events without blurring particular divisions (Plate 22.6). The consequences of this interactive approach for visual knowledge was that he broke down longstanding classificatory schemes emphasizing uninterrupted sequence, similarity and homogeneity. The odd, disruptive and heterogeneous appearance of these images suggested that supposedly canonical monuments were simply the accidental results of what had been left over or dug up. Piranesi carefully demonstrated, and asked us to evaluate, how his subjective taxonomy might serve as a guide for ordering a lost world. Yet this vision of totality was always provisional or alterable through the discovery of new remnants.

What Lessing and his followers never understood was that the expressive 'spatial' arts do not seek to represent time. Rather, they prod the observer to experience time by inviting him actively to engage in the construction or deconstruction of the image.[41] From this perspective, Piranesi's 'surgical' methods of demonstration are revealing. These included, first, the use of accidental sections or 'wounds' gaping in deteriorating masonry. Thus the decaying pilasters in the interior of the *Portico of the Pantheon* were made to exhibit the details of their internal structure (Plate 22.4). Like Fontana's anatomical waxes containing nesting parts, the areas for intensive study were controlled and highlighted (Plate 22.5).[42] Second, multiple images were displayed limb-like on the same plate to avoid confusion and to demonstrate conflicting information (Plate 22.7). Third, this candid strategy offered the viewer options through the indication of hypothetical or 'scarred' solutions when a structure was partially buried under accumulated debris. Consequently, Piranesi responsibly sutured the certain to the conjectural, thereby revealing the seamed nature of his vision. He trained the observer, as he trained himself, in the fine art of probability. He taught the viewer – non-didactically and enticingly – to estimate the unknown by knowledgeably judging a maze of seemingly isolated and dispersed remains. In his spatial and temporal series, Piranesi began by anatomizing, or visually separating, parts, and ended by organically synthesizing into a heroic span of views what he dismembered. He thus continues to help the modern beholder to reintegrate and recontextualize historical fragments into the living totality or evolving urban context of Rome.

Piranesi's expansion of the orthodox boundaries of building-type classification resulted from his showing the dramatic effects of contingency operating within material culture. He made manifest, instead of concealing, the alien look of a complex antiquity known only through stray, and even extinct, descendants (Plate 22.2). Displaying the fragments of a broken lineage, of course, had been central to collections of all sorts since the Renaissance (Plate 22.8).[43] The eighteenth-century scientific quest for origins, ancestry and genealogy, however, was permeated by the conviction that images possessed a unique capacity to teach, to uncover the relation of known parts to an unknown whole. The creation of galleries, museums, libraries and natural history cabinets was grounded in a visual encyclopedism persuasively encouraging cross-referencing in a disparate public that strolled and paused before minute details and eye-arresting features (Plate 22.9).[44] Such visual searching and bodily travel, roaming from the insignificant to the significant and back again, prompted mental locomotion. The fluid this's and that's of a rising phenomenal tide were exhibited, and kinetically encountered, as the flotsam and jetsam of an upheaved and changing world that they, in fact, literally were (Plate 22.10).[45]

Mimicking the discontinuous *Wunderkammer*, or magical-display of memory, this pragmatic form of historical reconstruction exposed uncertainty. It disclosed interruptions existing in contemporary systems of categorization.[46] Like Piranesi's etching style, the exhibiting method was juxtapositive. Unlike the false coherence implied by the sequential 'begats' of chronicles, annals or narratives, the multivariate gatherings of *artefacta* and *naturalia* were simultaneously accessible to sight. They thus provoked an immediate awareness of the miscellaneous and chance nature of the act of finding itself. These ill-assorted assemblages demonstrated how we learn painstakingly by gathering and arranging bits and pieces in the dark. There is always more evidence, always another, and better, mode of organization. Stray specimens of cultural and natural debris: portraits of historical figures, *trompe l'œil* still lifes, exotic species, scientific instruments, 'sports' of nature and marvels of metal casting, jostled one another on charged tables. Instead of concealing the absence of connections, the layout or pattern summoned the observer to fill in the gaps.

This combination of recreation and research was intimately tied to the dialogic aspect of visualization. The mix of popular fun and serious scholarship, characterizing the display of collections, was especially in evidence in the spectacle provided by fossils. Their drama consisted in being natural historical 'monuments' left behind by the Flood (Plate 22.12).[47] Significantly, our contemporary non-anthropocentric environmentalist aesthetic[48] originated in the eighteenth century when intrinsic value, and even vitality, was first widely ascribed to non-human natural objects. According to Diderot, Robinet, Delisle de Sales, nature imaged forth the record of its ongoing transformation in pictograms.[49] Graphic granite bore decipherable developmental marks and traces. Dendritic and map agate carried surface landscapes hieroglyphically exhibiting the record of their internal growth and material organization.

Through the broad dissemination of stunningly engraved folios, such as the Swiss Jean-Jacques Scheuchzer's natural-theological Bible, fossil impressions were consumed as instructive visible records of otherwise invisible events (Plate 22.11). Geological concepts such as great age were spatialized as subtly graduated depth. Intangible and imperceptible occurrences, such as the slow passage of time, received tangible and perceptible representation. The team of Augsburg engravers responsible for Scheuchzer's eight-volume work created poignantly veiled prints of fossil fish that obliged the eye to struggle. To discover form, the observer had to excavate it visually from the sediment – a nuanced physical, emotional and intellectual experience that eluded words. The viewer, like the performer, supplemented the *non-finito*. Fragile plaques broken from a primitive ocean floor were vignette performances excerpted from a larger spectacle graspable only in segments. These lithic picture-sculptures offered access to an otherwise unknowable past. As the user's eye 'handled' unfamiliar objects, he or she also learned them.[50] Simultaneously, the intricately organized and labelled plates encouraged diverting interaction. They depended upon the viewer's playful, hide-and-seek engagement with extant and extinct organisms (Plate 22.11).

But the union of laboratory science and diversified aesthetic experimentation was perhaps best served in the great technological innovations of colour printing. This evolution in simulation embraced Jacques Gautier Dagoty's jealously guarded system of the mid-1740s for creating chromatic anatomical reproductions that were 'true to life'. In the opinion of their inventor, these two-dimensional automata surpassed those of his mentor and eventual rival, J. C. Le Blon. The latter's multiple plate mezzotint, or improved three-colour process, led to the manufacture of 'printed paintings'. By mid-century, L. M. Bonnet's production of facsimiles of full-colour pastels[51] finally achieved the difficult co-ordination of Newton's spectrum on eight plates. French science was thus given the technology for visual cognition. By the 1780s, the refined toolwork of Jean-François Janinet's imitation of *manière de lavis*, and Charles Melchior Descourtis's method of superimposing a limited range of colours, provided mineralogy with the means for representing the elusive tints needed to render a convincing transparency revealing inclusions. More importantly, I suggest that it was specifically through these graphic technologies that the fledgling science of crystallography attained the methods to conceptualize, that is, to visualize, and thus actually to lay bare the hidden processes of crystal and mineral formation. Analogously, it is doubtful whether either meteorology or Romantic landscape painting would have flourished at the close of the century without the invention of aquatint. This Anglo-French resin-based chemical process (roughening metal plates directly with acid) made possible not only the convincing representation of wetness but let one contemplate in detail the vagaries of cloudy weather.

For the Enlightenment, powers of discernment, visual acumen and the development of probing habits of sight were requisite skills, and not just in the domain of natural history. Perspicuity was the primary literal and critical tool for delving into the architecture of the body. Art and medicine shared and, indeed, still share somatic metaphors of sign, symptom and hand or touch. Their tangible procedures or material craft interanimated one another on many fronts. None, however, was more central than the need to perceive or make public that most private and most elusive space of all, the human interior. To return to my opening premise I want briefly, and by way of moving towards a conclusion, to develop a contrast in this biological sphere between a verbal and a visual way of knowing.

One strategy for reading hidden terrain (and I intend the linguistic analogy) was derived from rational philosophy (Plate 22.13). Dissection interrogated the inert body by violently laying it bare – much like the deductive dismembering of a coherent thought by a syllogism. The aim of the anatomical method, and I use the term now with its broader epistemological connotation of measured vertical penetration, was to get at a fundamental truth. This important essence lurked beneath a merely visible, unimportant appearance or trivial surface.[52] Such an invisible nugget of transcendent value, it was believed, could be made manifest only through calculation, or the division of the organism into computable parts. The analytical and separating 'knife' of reason successively descended from the epidermal (appearance), to a subcutaneous myology, to attain, finally, the bedrock of bone itself (character). This slicing resembled the parsing of a sentence to arrive at clear meaning or the cutting of a corpse to reach the seat of life. One example, taken from particle physics, will have to stand for the ubiquity of this epistemological method for forcible entry in our contemporary culture. I quote Roy Schwitters, the Harvard physicist, on the importance of the new supercolliders in the search to make apparent the delicate traces of ghostly particles. 'We're going in [to the fundamental particles] with wrecking bars and sledge hammers to try to find the treasure.'[53]

What a contrast this rational–linguistic system of attack makes with visual cognition embodied in non-invasive and non-destructive medical probes (Plate 22.1). Recall that these instruments for the remote 'laying on of hands' transmit ghostly streams of light and dark messages requiring a new science of sensory detection. To make biological knowledge from copious symbolic information, the medical connoisseur of the future, like his artistic counterpart, will have to know how to decode at a distance. He must learn to interpret the infinitely nuanced and ambiguous phantasms emitted by the living human organism as they painlessly float in space. Conversely, the anatomical, lexical and logical mode of knowing tends to render insensate the objects of its scrutiny. By splitting, fragmenting and isolating biota in frozen moments, the procedure is antithetical to the mutable and metamorphic life processes it purports to reveal.[54]

Both methods entailed psychological ramifications. The outer features of the body, especially those located on the face, were used since antiquity to infer an individual's unique, but masked, history. Yet plumbing the character, essence, temperament, spirit, aura or 'inner life' of a person from a marked exterior has proved as difficult as pinning down elusive prions, zoo particles or the Higgs particle. Physiognomy and phrenology involved *reading* the hidden properties of the soul and the intellect. The analysis was anatomical, depending upon the supposed legibility of fixed features and the bony topography of the head. Significantly, mental augury was raised to scientific status in the late eighteenth century through the publications of Johann Caspar Lavater and Petrus Camper.[55] Interpreted as systems of forecasting, such logocentric methods extracted semantic meaning from isolatable looks. Thus they continue to have profound implications evident not only in the screening for genetic predispositions, but in cosmetic surgery.[56] Plastic surgeons use computer modelling in which noses, lips or eyes are so many recombinant spare parts. These biological fragments stock a seemingly infinite database of corporeal 'ready-mades'. This 'physiognomic' application of electronic imagery thus confirms Marcel Duchamp's prediction that the category of 'ready-mades' would eventually embrace the entire universe of objects.[57] Now that the body has become a constructed artefact, the client may select his ideal and ageless persona, frozen in youth, from a repository of reproducible items. Removal is also an option. Wrinkles, creases and folds can be erased, thus further expunging any tell-tale signs of mortality, or of a personal past. Parenthetically, this cosmetic development appears to follow logically from the Leibnizian premise that all discrete data is combinable.[58] When extended to the genetic level, the application of a biological *ars combinatoria* conjures up visions of sperm banks and of decontextualized, faceless couplings occurring in petrie dishes, or otherwise at a remove from particular human bodies.

Similarly, in eighteenth-century physiognomic analysis, the body became any body. This ahistorical abstraction was compounded from excisable qualities. Separable properties or characteristics were thus endowed with a meaning or value irrespective of the individual context in which they inhered. By contrast, the pathognomic theory developed by Georg Lichtenberg[59] disputed the establishment of a presumed correspondence between timeless, buried essence and stilled portions of the anatomy. The German essayist called, instead, for the visualization of mutable chromatic appearances. The full range of human activity was to be captured in expressive gesture, fleeting pantomime and ephemeral emotions. This performative method – enacted with paint and brush on springy and responsive canvas, or fingers pressed in clay or burin and needle exposing metal – aimed to sort out feelingly the transitory and coloured diversity of internal life as lived. This optical auscultation or palpation of a particular body's surface should be seen as analogous to the personal style or expressive handling of artificial materials. Thus the perspicuous artist, like the sensitive physician, could train himself and the willing viewer to perceive and make visible the invisible motions of the heart.

II

In sum, my point has been that we have been moving, from the Enlightenment forward, towards a visual and, now, an electronically generated, culture. Since the time of Plato, however, this visual culture and its magician-creators suffered from a low status.[60] The Platonic analogy is especially apt in view of the contemporary proliferation of technological wizardry and the resulting bodilessness of things. The shadowy video screen and the ghostly computer semblance remind us of the philosopher's consignment of fantastic or sophistic appearances – associated with non-existent or false objects – to the bottom of his divided universe. He deemed such bewitching phantasms, or dim visibles, to be as indeterminate as the chromatic blur hovering in water and as confusingly deceptive as dreams. His Neoplatonic followers, in particular, located these insubstantial and overwhelming 'illusions', along with fluid fictions in general, in a subterranean cavern. That distant sensory darkness was situated at the antipodes from the true and sunlit intellectual verities (*archai*) accessible to rational philosophy.[61] But it is precisely these unseizable images – unlike delusory 'clear and distinct' words or 'reliable' numbers identified with reason – that, paradoxically, do not lie. As kinetic, probable and interactive forms of expression, they openly attest to the conjectural and fluid nature of life lived in the middle zone. They help us to organize and make sense of that floating world, or *milieu*, stretching considerably below certitude and somewhat above ignorance.

I believe, then, as imagists it is time we look to another quarter (the structure and activity of visual cognition itself) both for our praxis and our methods. We must frame a unified theory of imaging from the intersections of the old historical arts with the new optical technologies. True interdisciplinarity would be grounded in the acknowledgement that perception (*aisthesis*) is a significant form of knowledge (*episteme*), perhaps even *the* constitutive form.[62] It is also time to assert that innovative collaboration can occur only in a community of intellectual equals. Moreover, creating such a hybrid or composite art–science of visualization would help to avert a broader social and cultural danger. It offers the model for a concept of learning that challenges our remaining unskilled and naive ingesters of misinformation we did not help to produce.

As we have seen, we possess artistic models and visual methods of analysis – many deriving from the eighteenth century – for not receiving pictures passively but for entering and reassembling them actively. Yet the poverty of our current observational skills is such that the spectre looms of an engulfing, abstract and invisible, technology more sophisticated than its uncomprehending users. The time has also come, then, to cease being disembodied receivers and transmitters of a cynical linguistic propaganda packaged graphically. Educated seeing is precisely about recognizing that information cannot be separated from the manner or style of its display. As Piranesi, Scheuchzer or Lichtenberg demonstrated, the enlightened observer – with the guidance of the artist – patterns and constructs reality through process knowledge.

Let us prepare for this alternative future. In that illuminating image-world, the spatio-visual disciplines would model themselves upon the special characteristics of their 'graphicacy'.[63] I foresee that glad day when feared and despised images, and underrated affective sensory experience in general, are released from their penumbrous prison. The historical process, begun in the eighteenth century, coupling advances in imaging techniques with advances in technology, inevitably leads out of Plato's ill-lit and second-class hotel for experiential transients. No longer defined as subjugated illustrations, or just better conveyors of extant verbal information, images would be recognized as free agents needed to discover that which could not otherwise be known. In that second Enlightenment, our public policy and our pedagogical practice would coincide humanistically. Visual lessons and visual means learned from the past could be applied imaginatively to tackle current problems in imaging.

Notes

1   M. Mitchell Waldrop, 'Learning to drink from a fire hose', *Science*, ccxlviii (1990), 674.
2   For this all-too prevalent view, see Judith R. Brown and Steve Cunningham, 'Visualization in higher education', *Academic Computing* (March 1990), 24.
3   For a full examination of the problem, see my *Body Criticism. Imaging the Unseen in Enlightenment Art and Medicine* (Cambridge, Mass. and London: MIT Press, 1991).

4   I have examined this 'grammatological' aspect of eighteenth-century aesthetics in my *Symbol and Myth: Humbert de Superville's Essay on Absolute Signs in Art* (Cranbury, NJ: Associated University Presses, 1979). See esp. ch. 4, 'Kant, schema, sign'. More recently, I have discussed the resurrection of this word–image polemic in light of post-structuralism's 'theoretical' appropriation of art history. See my 'The eighteenth century: towards an interdisciplinary model', *Art Bulletin*, lxx (March 1988), 6–24. More pointedly, perhaps, the hegemonic aspect of 'literary' control over pictorial hermeneutics has become more insistent as our culture is becoming undeniably ever more visual. The academic economics of this takeover has yet to be 'deconstructed'.

5   For an excellent analysis of the distinction made in mid-century France between *artisans* and *artistes*, that is, between 'decorator' or 'minor art' practitioners of an *art rocaille* and the 'intellectual' painters, sculptors and architects of the *grand goût* (shored up by pro-antique critics) who scorned them, see Marianne Roland-Michel, *La Joüe et l'art rocaille* (Paris: Arthena, 1984). Italy, Germany and England (although to a lesser extent) experienced this reversal when they sent their young artists to study in a now 'classical' Rome under the tutelage of Winckelmann, that lover of ancient allegory and of a 'poetic' art that goes beyond the senses. David Irwin, 'On the imitation of the painting and sculpture of the Greeks (1755)', in idem (ed.), *Winckelmann: Writings on Art* (London: Phaidon, 1972), 61–85.

6   Yve-Alain Bois, 'Malevitch, le carré, le degré zero', *Macula* i (1976), 28–49.

7   Wendy Steiner, *The Colors of Rhetoric: Problems in the Relation between Modern Literature and Painting* (Chicago and London: University of Chicago Press, 1982), 179–81.

8   Benjamin H. D. Buchloh, 'Allegorical procedures: appropriation and montage in contemporary art', *Artforum*, xxi (September 1982), 43–56.

9   Anthony Vidler, *The Writing of the Walls: Architectural Theory in the Late Enlightenment* (Princeton: Princeton Architectural Press, 1987), 43. Vidler connects late eighteenth-century architectural 'physiognomics' to the modern tradition.

10 While post-modernist experience is that of visualization, paradoxically, post-modernist criticism privileges the linguistic signifier as in Althusser's notion of ideology as *langue* or Baudrillard's notion of the fetish as *code*. See Benjamin H. D. Buchloh, 'Ready made, objet trouvé, idée reçue', in *Dissent* (Boston: Institute of Contemporary Art, 1986), 107–22.

11 James Foley and Andries Van Dam, *Fundamentals of Interactive Computer Graphics* (Reading, Mass.: Addison-Wesley, 1982).

12 Michel Bret, 'Procedural art with computer graphics technology', *Leonardo*, xxi, 1 (1988), 3–10.

13 Benoit Mandelbrot, *The Fractal Geometry of Nature* (San Francisco: Freeman, 1982).

14 Otto Mayr *et al.*, *Holographie – Medium für Kunst und Technik*, exhibition catalogue (Munich: Deutsches Museum, 1984).

15 An optimistic sign is the Getty Center for Education in the Arts DBAE Program. See Elliot W. Eisner, *The Role of Discipline-Based Art Education in America's Schools* (Los Angeles: Getty Center for Education in the Arts, 1987).

16 The deep connection between a logocentrism and what might be termed a 'numerocentrism' must also be stressed. Recall the Phoenician origin of numeral letters, their subsequent spread to Greece, Rome, Syria and Arabia, and their ouster of a 'primitive' mode of expressing numbers *orally and through gestures*. See Georges Ifrah, *From One to Zero: A Universal History of Numbers*, tr. Lowell Bair (New York: Viking, 1985), esp. 241–310.

17 To my mind the finest analysis of the metaphor of writing and the book for structuring *all* experience is that of Hans Blumenberg, *Die Lesbarkeit der Welt* (Munich: Suhrkamptaschenbuch Wissenschaft, 1986).

18 See, for example, Stephen M. Kosslyn, 'Aspects of a cognitive neuroscience of mental imagery', *Science*, ccxl (17 June 1988), 1621–6. Also see in the same issue, Michael I. Posner, Steven E. Petersen, Peter T. Fox and Marcus E. Raichle, 'Localization of cognitive operations in the human brain', 1627–31.

19 Eric L. Schwartz, 'Images of the mind', in *Tod Siler: Metaphorms: Forms of Metaphor*, exhibition catalogue (New York: New York Academy of Sciences, 1988), 1–2. In addition to making possible new art forms, neuroscience has begun to change the traditional philosophy of mind. See Patricia Smith Churchland, *Neurophilosophy: Toward a Unified Science of the Mind-Brain* (Cambridge, Mass.: MIT Press, 1986).

20 I am grateful to Robert N. Beck, Director of the University of Chicago's Center for Imaging Science, for demonstrating and explaining the operations of this new technology. The people involved in this forefront work include, in addition to Beck: Chin-Tu Chen, David N. Levin and Charles Pelizzari.

21 Kenneth Snelson, 'An artist's atom' (unpublished paper), 51. Also see my essay, 'The new immaterialism: Kenneth Snelson imagines the atom', in *Kenneth Snelson: The Nature of Structure*, exhibition catalogue (New York: New York Academy of Sciences, 1989), 51–7.

22 J. S. Bell, *Speakable and Unspeakable in Quantum Mechanics: Collected Papers on Quantum Philosophy* (Cambridge: Cambridge University Press, 1987). See esp. the title chapter, 169–72; and 'Bertelmann's socks and the nature of reality', 139–58; and 'Six possible worlds of quantum mechanics', 181–95.

23 Thomas A. DeFanti, 'Cultural roadblocks to visualization', *Computers in Science* (Jan.–Feb. 1988), 5–6.

24 Robert S. Wolff, 'The visualization challenge in the physical sciences', *Computers in Science* (Jan.–Feb. 1988), 16–25.

25 William H. Kruskal, 'Visions of maps and graphs', in *Proceedings of International Symposium on Computer-Assisted Cartography: Auto-Carto II* (1975) (Washington, DC: Bureau of the Census, 1977), 27–36; and idem, 'Criteria for judging statistical graphics', in *Utilitas Mathematica*, xxib (May 1982), 283–310.

26 Stephen M. Stigler, *The History of Statistics: The Measurement of Uncertainty before 1900* (Cambridge, Mass.: Belknap Press of Harvard University Press, 1986).

27 Hermann Chernoff, 'Graphical representations as a discipline', in *Graphical Representation of Multivariate Data* (New York: Academic Press, 1978), 1–11. I am grateful to William H. Kruskal for having drawn my attention to Chernoff's work and, indeed, to the larger problem of representation in statistical analysis.

28 E. F. Loftus, *Eyewitness Testimony* (Cambridge, Mass.: Harvard University Press, 1980).

29 Cited in Frederick Burwick, 'The hermeneutics of Lichtenberg's interpretation of Hogarth', *Lessing Yearbook*, xix (1987), 168. For the proliferation of 'visuals' in the courtroom, note the existence of the Atlanta-based firm Medical Legal Illustrations, Inc., now in its eighth year, and the Chicago-based firm Legal Graphics Inc., currently in its seventh year.

30 Shoshana Zuboff, *In the Age of the Smart Machine* (Cambridge, Mass.: Harvard University Press, 1988).

31 George Berkeley, *A Treatise concerning the Principles of Human Knowledge [1710]*, in idem, *A New Theory of Vision* (New York: E. P. Dutton & Co., 1919), 121, sect. XVIII.

32 The contribution of the phenomenon of travel to the dissemination of a 'pictorialized' experience is studied in my *Voyage into Substance: Art, Science, and the Illustrated Travel Account, 1760–1840* (Cambridge, Mass.: MIT Press, 1984).

33 Vilém Flusser, 'The photograph as post-industrial object: an essay on the ontological status of objects', *Leonardo*, xix, 4 (1986), 329–32.

34 The literature on Piranesi is vast. See esp. Ian Jonathan Scott, *Piranesi* (London and New York: Academy Editions and St Martin's Press, 1975); John Wilton-Ely, *The Mind and Art of Giovanni Battista Piranesi* (London: Thames & Hudson, 1978); Norbert Miller, *Archäologie des Traums* (Munich-Vienna: Hanser Verlag, 1978); *Piranesi e la cultura antiquaria: Gli antecedenti e il contesto: Atti di Convegno* (Rome: Multigrafica Editence, 1983; 1st edn, 1979); Marguerite Yourcenar, *The Dark Brain of Piranesi and Other Essays*, tr. Richard Howard (New York: Farrar, Straus, Giroux, 1984),

476   Barbara Maria Stafford

88–128; Andrew Robison, *Piranesi: Early Architectural Fantasies: A Catalogue Raisonné of the Etchings* (Chicago and London: University of Chicago Press, 1985).

35 David Bindman, *Blake as an Artist* (Oxford: Phaidon, 1977), 38–9.

36 Giambattista Piranesi, *Le Antichità Romane di . . . Architetto veneziano. Tomo secondo. Contenente gli avanzi di Monumenti Sepolcrali di Roma e dell' agro Romano* (Rome: Presso l'Autore, 1756), frontispiece.

37 Charles Singer, *The Evolution of Anatomy: A Short History of Anatomical and Physiological Discovery to Harvey* (New York: Alfred A. Knopf, 1925), 111–35.

38 Zofia Ameisenowa, *The Problem of the écorché and the Three Anatomical Models in the Jagiellonia Library*, tr. Andrzej Potocki (Warsaw: Wydewnictwo Potskiej Akademii Nauk, 1963), 44–6.

39 While Piranesi's graphic innovations have been studied in relation to scenography (see for example *Piranèse et les français, 1740–1790*, exhibition catalogue (Rome: Edizioni dell'Elefante, 1976)), their connection to medical books remains unexplored. One would like to know, for example, what impact Giovanni Maria Lancisi's 1714 edition of the lost plates of Eustachius (1550–74), or Albinus's *Explicatio Tabularum antomicorum Bartholomei Eustachii* (Leiden, 1744), made. On their history and importance, see Howard B. Adelmann, *Marcello Malpighi and the Evolution of Embryology*, vol. 1 (Ithaca: Cornell University Press, 1966), 634–6. More specifically, what did Piranesi learn from that masterpiece of eighteenth-century anatomy, Albinus's *Tabulae sceleti et musculorum corporis humani* (Leiden, 1737), about the analysis of structure and its presentation within an evocative pictorial context? For innovations in eighteenth-century medical books, see: André Hahn, Paule DuMaitre and Janine Samion-Contet, *Histoire de la médecine et du livre médicale à la lumière des collections de la Bibliothèque de la Faculté de Médecine de Paris* (Paris: Olivier Perrin Editeur, 1962), 265ff. Concerning this unexplored connection between anatomy and archaeology in Piranesi's work, it is significant that Robin Middleton, 'G. B. Piranesi (1720–1778): review of recent literature', *Journal of the Society of Architectural Historians*, xl (1982), 333–44, concludes that no fully convincing analysis of his work and its context has yet been made.

40 Mary A. B. Brazier, *A History of Neurophysiology in the Seventeenth and Eighteenth Centuries: From Concept to Experiment* (New York: Raven Press, 1984), 138–43.

41 For G. H. Lessing's attempt to establish laws separating spiritual, temporal poetry from corporeal, spatial painting, see his: *Laocoön: An Essay on the Limits of Painting and Poetry*, tr. Edward Allen McCormick (Baltimore and London: Johns Hopkins University Press, 1984; 1st edn, 1766).

42 For Fontana's silent sanctuary of coloured anatomical waxes, created by his chief worker in wax, Clemente Susini (1754–1814) for Florence's Museo Fisica e Storia Naturale (inaugurated in 1776) and, subsequently, for Vienna's Josephinium, see Mario Bucci, *Anatomia come arte* (Florence: Edizione d'Arte Il Fiorino, 1969), 189–91.

43 See, for example, Ferrante Imperatore, *Historia Naturale di . . . Napolitano. Niella quale ordinatamente si tratta della diversa conditione di minere, pietre pretiose, & altre curiosità. Con varie Historie di piante, & animali, fin hora non date in luce* (Venice: Presso Combi, & La Noù, 1672; 1st edn, 1599), fold-out plate.

44 On the foundation of anatomical museums and natural history collections between 1528 to 1850, see F. J. Cole, *A History of Comparative Anatomy from Aristotle to the Eighteenth Century* (London: Macmillan & Co. Ltd., 1944), 443–63.

45 R. P. Claude du Molinet, *Le Cabinet de la bibliothèque de Sainte Geneviève, divisé en deux parties* (Paris: Chez Antoine Dezallier, 1692), Plate 5.

46 For the growing body of scholarship on the varieties of eighteenth-century collecting, see my 'Eighteenth century', 13, nn. 73–4, 76–7.

47 Jean-Jacques Scheuchzer, *Physique sacrée, ou histoire naturelle de la Bible*, vol. 1 (Amsterdam: Chez Pierre Schenk et Pierre Mortier, 1732), Plate LVII.

48 Bryan G. Norton, *Why Preserve Natural Variety?* (Princeton: Princeton University Press, 1987), 151–6.

49 See my *Voyage into Substance*, 305–20.

50 See my 'Characters in stones, marks on paper: Enlightenment discourse on natural and artificial *taches*', *Art Journal*, xliv (Fall 1984), 233–40.

51 For an excellent recent discussion of the commerce and procedures of print-making, see Victor I. Carlson and John W. Ittmann, *Regency to Empire: French Print-Making 1715–1814*, exhibition catalogue (Minneapolis: Minneapolis Institute of Arts, 1985).

52 William Schupbach, *The Paradox of Rembrandt's 'Anatomy of Dr. Tulp'* (London: Wellcome Institute for the History of Medicine, 1982), 32–4.

53 'Supercollider', *Chicago Tribune* (13 June 1988), 11.

54 M. Ruse, 'Is biology different from physics?' in *Logic, Laws & Life: Some Philosophical Complications*, ed. R. G. Colodny (Pittsburgh: University of Pittsburgh Press, 1977), 91–109. Also see R. J. Faber, *Clockwork Garden: On the Mechanistic Reduction of Living Things* (Amherst: University of Massachusetts Press, 1986), xi.

55 See my ' "Peculiar Marks": Lavater and the countenance of blemished thought', *Art Journal*, xlvi (Fall 1987), 185–92.

56 For some contemporary clinical implications of the physiognomic concept of formal perfection, see: Barbara M. Stafford, John La Puma, M.D. and David L. Schiedermayer, M.D., 'One face of beauty, one picture of health: the hidden aesthetic of medical practice', *Journal of Medicine and Philosophy*, xiv (1989), 213–30.

57 Max Kozloff, 'Johns and Duchamp', *Art International*, viii (20 March 1964), 138–46.

58 G. W. Leibniz's 'elegant artifice' was proposed, first, in the *De Arte Combinatoria* (1666), and again, later, in *Towards a Universal Characteristic* (1677). See *Leibniz Selections*, ed. Philip P. Wiener (New York: Charles Scribner's Sons, 1951), 17–25.

59 G. C. Lichtenberg, *Über Physiognomik wider die Physiognomen. Zur Beförderung der Menschenliebe und Menschenkenntniss*, ed. K. Riha (Steibbach: Anabas Verlag, 1970).

60 Plato, *Republic* 6. 509D–11E; and *Sophist* 235D–6C.

61 For the most thorough analysis of these *chiaroscuro* epistemological metaphors, as they evolved in Platonism and neo-Platonism, see Wesley Trimpi, *Muses of One Mind: The Literary Analysis of Experience and its Continuity* (Princeton: Princeton University Press, 1983), esp. 113–20; 212–16.

62 For the arguments against this claim, see Robert G. Turnbull, 'The role of the "special sensibles" in the perception theories of Plato and Aristotle', in Peter K. Machamer and Robert G. Turnbull (eds), *Studies in Perception: Interrelations in the History of Philosophy and Science* (Columbus, Ohio: Ohio State University Press, 1978), 4–23.

63 For over two decades the British educator, William Baldwin, has argued that school curricula should group geography with English and mathematics as foundation subjects for pre-college education. His argument rests on the thesis that there are four basic types of human intelligence with their respective educational counterparts: literacy, articulacy, numeracy and graphicacy. See Mark Monmonier and George A. Schnell, *Map Appreciation* (Englewood-Cliffs: Prentice Hall, 1988), 4. The irony remains, however, that we have witnessed during this past decade the extinction of geography programmes at the pre-college and college levels. One has to wonder whether, among the several reasons for this demise, there was not the old spectre of logocentrism embodied in the belief that visual media do not sufficiently stimulate the *intellectual* aspects of our mental processes. For early evidence of this conflict between text and image on maps, see Arthur Robinson, *The Look of Maps: An Examination of Cartographic Design* (Madison, Milwaukee, London: University of Wisconsin Press, 1966), 55–7. Significantly, there are no illustrations!

23
Perishable commodities: Dutch still-life painting and the 'empire of things'

Simon Schama

Nothing in the whole tradition of western art so engages with the culture of consumption as a Dutch *pronck* still-life painting. Confronted with the eruption of goods thrown over the canvas the beholder immediately experiences a rush of pleasure, guilt and (for many sensibilities) disgust. It was the 'frugal Dutch' that produced this stupendous celebration of excess, visual hyperbole all the more disconcerting for being elaborately wrought and highly finished representations of objects that are themselves elaborately wrought and highly finished. The lacquer-brilliant paint handling and the unembarrassed, augmented gaudiness of the spectacle makes the painting itself another item in the inventory of luxuries anthologized in the composition.

At their most technically theatrical in the 1660s manner of Willem Kalf or Christian Luycx, *pronck* painting seems to celebrate sensuous pleasure without restraint or inhibition (Plate 23.1). Light glances off polished surfaces or passes through the translucence of glass and wine. The paintings make the eye do the work of the hand, registering the alterations experienced in running fingers over changing surface textures and temperatures: hard crystal, nacreous nautilus cups, shell-smooth porcelain, embossed plate. And it is perhaps this tactile self-indulgence and chromatic glitter that Roland Barthes had in mind when he wrote of Dutch painting as damningly preoccupied with 'matter's most superficial quality: its *sheen*'. Barthes's essay, 'Le monde-objet' ('The world as object'), written in 1953 at the end of what he called his 'first semiological period' remains one of the most psychologically acute and compellingly argued accounts of Dutch art ever articulated.[1] But like much structuralist writing of its time, it is written in blunt attack mode, the enemy being the comfortably upholstered bourgeois culture for whom Barthes, Foucault and Lacan had so much contempt and whose historical sovereignty in this essay was tellingly characterized as 'the empire of things'.

It is, then, as an early form of commodity fetishism that Barthes trained his sights on Dutch still-life painting, that he took to be a paradigm of the moral vacancy he thought distinctive in Netherlandish art and social culture. Its reigning obsession, he thought, was *utilization*, or in our contemporary terminology, consumption, a world of uses and appetites declared by half-eaten turkey-pies and pasties, half-drunk goblets of wine:

478

objects on the tables, the walls, floor, pots, pitchers overturned, a clutter of baskets, bunches of vegetables, a brace of game, oyster shells, pans. . . . All this is man's space; in it he measures himself and determines his humanity, starting from the memory of his gestures, his *chronos* . . . there is no other authority in his life but the one he imprints upon the inert by shaping and manipulating it.[2]

Dutch still-life painting, whether in the more subdued monochromes of Pieter Claesz and Willem Heda, or in the *pronck* glitter of de Heem, Kalf and van Beyeren, signified for Barthes a particular, Faustian moment in the history of western culture, when 'the universe of fabrication has excluded terror':[3] when art dwells on objects for their appearance, for their surface properties; for their advertisement of value. Both shell paintings which gathered items of immense rarity and preciousness (as well as visual flamboyance) and tulip paintings (sometimes actually transferred from auction catalogues) would have testified to what, for Barthes, was a telling equivalence between beauty and costliness. Some of the most stunning examples of this genre, like Dirck van Delen's painting of *a single Generael der Generaelen van Gouda* set in a Chinese *kendi* pot and dated 1637 (Plate 23.2), the year the Dutch 'tulipomania' reached its climax, exemplify not only the entrepreneurial marriage between empirical science and the capitalist market, but also the fateful connection between the 'domestic empire of things' and the global empire of commerce. For Barthes, this Faustian moment coincides precisely and causally with Europe's imperial appropriation of the raw materials and arts of the Oriental and the Atlantic worlds. Dutch culture, peculiarly egregious, naively vulgar in this respect, essentially consisted of what could be classified, inventoried, priced, owned and displayed: coral from the Indies (West and East); Mingware and Japanese lacquer from the China Seas; Turkish and Persian rugs from the Levant; monkeys, parakeets and shells from Coromandel and the Guinea coast and Brazil. The paintings that showed off this booty acted, then, as a form of augmented, or doubly-declared proprietorship, signifying the possession, not just of the expensive painting, but the class of objects it itemized.

For Barthes all these elaborate arrangements of objects, visualized with almost fanatical attention to detail, suggested not just a form of cultural encyclopaedism but an exercise of power: art mobilized to service the appropriation of matter. The 'empire of things' is the reduction of cosmology to catalogue: whatsoever may be measured, enumerated, exchanged, priced, processed and marketed.

Behold then, a real transformation of the object which no longer has an essence, but takes refuge entirely within its attributes. A more complete subservience of things is unimaginable. The entire city of Amsterdam, indeed, seems to have been built with a view to this domestication: few substances here are not annexed to this empire of merchandise.[4]

The materialization of history embodied in the still life is, then, for Barthes the key to all of Dutch painting and by extension the dominant code for the culture that produced it. By the same token its landscapes are seen as places for the exercise of utility, the tempo of busy-ness; the 'inscription of man in space': paths cut through forests, carriages and carts coming and going; waterways depicted less as topography than commercial arteries, a network of trade and communication. Similarly Barthes wittily characterizes group portraits as a variant still life in which human forms are invested with the properties of urban flora and fauna; in Hals's militia paintings, 'fleshy blooms'; faces that belong to some sort of animate taxonomy, a cross between horticultural and zoological production. 'Here the matrix of the human face is not of an ethical order but of a carnal order, not of a community of intentions but of an identity of blood and food, formed after long sedimentation.'[5]

Since what is now known of the subtlety and moral ambiguity of Dutch still-life painting appears to contradict the central assumption of Barthes's essay it should be conceded that there is plenty of evidence in its civic culture to confirm what he intuitively believed to be its deep-dyed materialism. What could be more brashly acquisitive or triumphantly imperialist than Quellijn's sculpture for the roof pediment of the Amsterdam Town Hall featuring the continents of the world bringing their tribute to the sea-goddesses of the rivers Ij and Amstel? The Dutch equivalent of the Italian civic *laudatio* differed from them exactly in paying less attention to a shared body of humanist history and authority and giving a great deal of space to architectural bragging.

Though the form in which Barthes expressed his view of Dutch culture as materially congested and morally empty was radically structuralist, the assumptions on which it rested belonged to a venerable tradition of critical essays. At about the same time in the mid-nineteenth century both John Ruskin and Eugene Fromentin thought the devotion of Dutch art to the rendering of surface, its preoccupation with technically conceived verisimilitude, its greatest flaw, a proof of its ignobility of imagination. Behind them came a whole caravan of travellers from the Republic of Letters – Montesquieu and Voltaire for example – for whom the culture was marked either by cheese-paring parsimony or comical vulgarity or both. What Netherlandish art was good for, and what it was bad for, was perhaps most powerfully suggested by Michelangelo's generalization that its artists 'painted like women'. Though evidently intended as dismissive, the insight that there was something in this northern tradition in which both the objects and the forms of representation approximated to domestic craft or to decorative intricacy, is in fact a challenging clue to its re-evaluation, a way to escape from both materialist and symbolist reductionism. And it is a suggestion to which this chapter will have to return.

There was, in any case, an alternative tradition of French writing about Netherlandish art, one marked first by meditative Catholicism and then by romanticism. Instead of seeing in still-life paintings an insistence on the supremacy of the material world, that tradition supposed it to be something like its exact opposite: the representation of contingency. Surprisingly, such comments can be found even in guidebook literature like that of the prolific Louis Viardot, who in 1860 warned against naive assumptions that such paintings revealed nothing but 'a brutal realism . . . concerned with [only] the surface and the envelope of things and which can never penetrate into interior sentiments, to the soul'.[6] At the end of the century, Paul Claudel, for whom Dutch still-life painting suggested 'a feast for the soul rather than the physical imagination' believed its formal arrangements were meant to suggest not solidity but mutability, not permanence but 'an arrangement in imminent danger of disintegration'.[7] Where Barthes's description of the clutter of objects in these works was skilfully designed to signify the here-and-now factuality, Claudel's ostensibly similar account becomes a kind of meditation on the relationship between the contemporary and the hereafter, the perceived tension between matter and spirit.

> There is a stable motionless background and in the foreground all sorts of objects off balance. They look as though they were about to fall. There is a napkin or a

rug on the point of unrolling . . . an overturned cup, all sorts of vases and fruits tumbled in a heap and overhanging plates. But in the background or rising from the midst of the food like a transparent oblation can be seen some of the beautiful glassware. . . . In my opinion its role here is not only decorative; it does not exist merely for the purpose of catching the inner light . . . it symbolizes something. . . . Why not imagine that this constant relationship between a glass as slender as the flute and a wide goblet often followed by an oval platter is not intentional. . . . Mallarmé would be quite disposed as I do to see (in all this) a kind of dedication to the beyond. It is this almost moral motionlessness in the background, this lining up of semi-airy witnesses in the foreground that gives meaning to all the material crumbling.[8]

Though Claudel's interpretation owed more to his imagination and visual instincts and very little to any familiarity with the rich vernacular of emblem books, his intuitions anticipated the findings of modern scholarship far more closely than Barthes's structuralist positivism. Informed by the congruences between Dutch texts that played obsessively with the metaphorical echoes sounding between physical experience and metaphysical rumination, an art that was once thought to be supremely indifferent to the moral universe is now commonly seen as acutely exercised by ethical accountability. Instances of unmistakable devotional metaphor abound in the formative years of Dutch still-life painting. A *banketje* table-piece by Clara Peeters (Plate 23.3) for example, virtually anthologizes standard allusions to ephemerality (the fly; the burning candle) and eternity (the sprig of rosemary), even if its sweetmeats were not so obviously arranged to suggest the cross and the sacred heart. In 1603, the first known *vanitas* painting by Jacques de Gheyn the Younger (an artist at the heart of Dutch official and even court culture), similarly inaugurated what became a repertoire of stock associations. At their centre was the defining juxtaposition of soap bubble and skull (*homo bulla*); beneath them coins and medals symbolizing, respectively, wealth and worldly renown and, borrowing poetic allusions from the flower's Persian and Turkish origins, the tulip represented as a symbol of death. Other representations, both engraved and painted, emphasized the flower as the essential example of the transient nature of worldly beauty. And in at least one case, a painting of Jan Brueghel the Elder was inscribed with a quatrain spelling out the sombre analogy. The outbreak of moralizing that followed the débâcle of the tulip mania in 1637 only added an extra dimension of contemporary criticism to these standard visual wisdoms. It is possible, in fact, that Van Delen's painting (the more so since he was a painter of churches as well as still lifes) was intended as a morality piece rather than a showpiece.

Is the *vanitas* to be thought of not simply as a sub-genre, but the controlling paradigm of Dutch still-life painting? At any rate, its insistent connections between things of this world and things of the next did not wane as the seventeenth century progressed quite as obviously as some critics and historians argue. On the contrary, as the Dutch Republic became heavily laden with riches and power, so new objects for visual moralizing presented themselves. Leiden painters, from a city that was both strong in its Calvinism and until the last third of the century, a centre of industry, had a conspicuously ambiguous relationship with the representation of wealth. Specializing in high-finish jewel-like works, many of them at the same time continued to gloss their skills in crafting images of luxury with allusions to idolatry and decadence. One of those painters, Edwaert Collier, produced in the 1660s a powerful example of the persistence of these antiphonal themes (Plate 23.6). His *vanitas* is organized around the relationship between the worldly and the eternal, represented in the terrestrial and the celestial globes. At the centre of the composition is another significant juxtaposition: the Dutch translation of Flavius Josephus' *Jewish Wars* with the destruction of the temple engraved as its frontispiece (a reference the Dutch with their strong identification with the history of the Hebrews could not have missed) and at right another translation of the Huguenot pastor De Bartas's *Creation of the World in Seven Days*, a work praised by the poet and dramatist Vondel. Creation and destruction are counter-pointed and surrounded with reinforcing images of passing time and pleasures – a money-bag, an hour-glass (just visible at the back) and one of the most popular song-books, *Cupido's Lusthof*, to suggest the fugitive joys of love and music. And in case the point had not been sufficiently communicated, Collier attached the obvious inscription from Ecclesiastes to the terrestrial sphere.

Even at the very end of the century (when meditative sub-texts are said to have disappeared altogether in favour of decorative ingratiation), a number of Dutch still-life paintings continued to play with the ambiguous relationship between materiality and spirituality, concreteness and insubstantiality. Pieter van Roerstraten's painting of a candlestick made by the London Huguenot silversmith, Antony Nelme (Plate 23.7) is (like many other displays of the products of artistic practice) at once a celebration of the virtuosity and of the limitations of craft. By surmounting a piece of silver worked in the form of a cornucopia with the stock image of a spent candle, an allusion to material abundance is coupled with its opposite.

The same kind of oxymoronic play occurs with paintings of timepieces. Carlo Cipolla and David Landes (among others) have drawn attention to the importance of time measurement in the modernization of European capitalism.[9] By the late Renaissance, clocks had decisively altered a traditional working regime, governed by the seasonal changes in daylight hours, and one in which the domestic or guild artisan could regulate his working hours, in favour of a stricter regulation controlled by the demands of production, exchange and circulation. Trading on the Amsterdam Bourse was regulated by the chiming of the hours on its clock towers and the tempo and intensity of speculation were naturally affected by distance or closeness to the hours of closing. The Dutch were the first commercial culture to produce printed timetables for their enormous network of inter-urban barge traffic and, from available evidence, to succeed in abiding by them. It is no exaggeration, then, to characterize Dutch culture as religiously chronometric. In still-life paintings, however, timepieces, hourglasses, watches and clocks or records of daily activities like the ubiquitous *Groot Comptoir Almanach* (with a portrait of the Bourse printed on the front page), are invariably represented not as auxiliaries of profit but as signals of loss, not of endurance but mortality. In paintings like Gerard Dou's timepiece suspended in its funereal niche (Plate 23.8), worldly time appears less as a capital asset to be 'well-spent' or 'prudently invested' but rather as something merely lived through *en route* to the more meaningful timelessness of eternity.

What is dramatically apparent from such examples (and there are countless more) is that, so far from Barthes's 'universe of fabrication' displaying 'an absence of terror', this particular commercial culture seems almost excessively anxious about both the propriety and durability of wealth. Death's-heads appear in Dutch still-life paintings (and not just in *vanitas* pieces) with extraordinary frequency (see Plates 23.4 and 23.5), whether in startling bravura compositions like Abraham Schoor's symphony of skulls and bones (Plate 23.9), or inserted with elaborate indirectness in paintings like Pieter Claesz's table-piece where the skull serves as a book-rest (Plate 23.10). (As well as any metaphysical poet Claesz understood the dramatic charge he could produce through the surprise effect of macabre incongruousness.)

Death is present at the feast; and these paintings are indeed as much *nature mortes* as *stilleven*. But is death truly the ruler of the 'empire of things'; the indulgence of visual appetite merely the preliminary to a finalizing sense of expiration? Is vitality or mortality the sovereign principle here?

To observe that the genre worked with the tensions between freshness and decay, that it was acutely aware of the sombre aspects of the passing of time is not, however, to demonstrate that *in all cases*, the purpose of Dutch still-life painters was to create a visual sermon out of flowers, wine-glasses and arrangements of fruit. The assumption that a densely symbolic language is necessarily more historically authentic than directly naturalistic representation has often been more reiterated than proved. And the interpretation of Dutch still-life paintings has followed a well-beaten path established for other kinds of seventeenth-century Dutch art. Beginning with the iconographical reinterpretation of genre paintings in the 1960s and moving to still-life art, landscape and now marine painting (can game pieces be far behind?), the methodological history has been the same. A naive realism, said (incorrectly) to be embodied in nineteenth-century critical literature is revised by an iconography, heavily dependent on emblem book engravings and pious poetry, and then is itself corrected by sceptical 'second-generation' iconographical criticism against indiscriminate over-reading.

While this seems to be a perfectly natural intellectual progression, and to have resulted in a healthily complicated respect for the ambiguities of genre paintings, landscapes and still lifes, much of the discussion has proceeded unencumbered by any kind of self-consciously hermeneutic engagement. Not that hermeneutics could possibly adjudicate the endless, usually intuitively determined, questions of the *degree* of symbolic saturation of any of these paintings. But it would, instead, make the whole issue of such adjudication moot. Instead of an insistence that a naturalistic or a symbolic reading must necessarily be mutually exclusive, these qualities might be more persuasively seen in deliberately unstable relation with each other; that in some cases the naturalism of detail was a means by which the whole might be rendered as super-natural; in others the invocation of ephemerality (as in the careful representation of a butterfly) might be the permitting condition for an exercise in visual taxonomy.

What a more hermeneutically informed approach might most usefully challenge is the enduring assumption (across a large body of Dutch art-historical literature) that, surrounded with a notionally sufficient body of historical texts, these representations might be made to yield up some artistic intention that could then be claimed as historically 'correct'. This assumption rests on two claims, dear to traditional art-historical research: first, that there was some sort of unequivocal, unambiguous, monovocal purpose on the part of the artist that, if disclosed, could yield a 'definitive' reading; second, that it is through reconstructing the intellectual, cultural and social world of the artist that we should be able to abolish the historical distance between the moment of creation and our own moment of beholding. At its most ambitious, such a programme even claims to be able to reproduce an accurate *Rezeptionsgeschichte*: the response from patrons and public.

But seventeenth-century Holland is notorious for the absence of precisely the kind of evidence that makes this sort of enterprise feasible: any direct indication from the hand of the artists themselves as to their creative priorities; and a huge void of evidence about the taste of patrons and buyers on the broad art market as to the seriousness or unseriousness with which they took moral commentaries in the art they bought. All we have is the usual stock-in-trade of the social historian of art: inventories, prices, notarial contracts, none of which is any help at all in resolving these issues of interpretation. So that when we are told, in respect of landscapes or still-life art that Dutch sensibility was inescapably religious; that its only historically authentic form of communication was overwhelmingly symbolic and that all naturalistic representation was merely a brilliant subterfuge, the better to intensify these devotional concerns, the response of the cultural historian must inevitably be 'how do you know?', 'what is the status of the evidence produced for such certainty?' In the instance of *vanitas* paintings, the evidence is in fact telling; but the endless invocation of emblem book imagery to set alongside paintings to suggest correspondences does not itself make the case that symbolic communication monopolizes the visual discourse of the time, especially at the expense of habitually painterly practices of spectacle.

Worse, the assumption may actually obscure an understanding of the way in which representation and metaphor are linked together. To read English metaphysical poetry (much translated into Dutch, by Constantijn Huygens among others) is to grasp immediately that one of its signatures was a witty connection between precise close-up description of physical phenomena and the perennial verities they were made to suggest. To work most effectively, the machinery of sensuous perception could not simply be seen to be a pure dependency of moral commentary (as in the most obviously sermonizing specimens of pre-Raphaelite painting for example), but had to operate at a high level of vividness and physical intensity. The risk in this strategy is that the technical means of accomplishing sensuous illusion may actually overwhelm or even obliterate the moral or religious message. In Venice, most notoriously, Paolo Veronese was actually brought before the Inquisition for treating his ostensibly sacred painting of the Last Supper as a pretext for a display of uninhibited epicureanism. And even in the cases of the mid-sixteenth-century work of Pieter Aertsen and Joachim Beuckelaer, usually seen as the starting-point of the Dutch still-life tradition, the division of the composition into immense piles of food in the foreground and the minimal references to the sacred text in the far-recessed background, raise deeply unresolvable issues of the relative weight given to the realms of the holy and the profane.

That these realms are in shifting and underdetermined relationships with each other, but that they necessarily *speak* to each other is all that the hermeneutic circle might offer by way of a covering interpretation. Yet if such an approach delivers the interpreter from the necessity of making some sort of exclusive claim for a naturalist or normative reading, it does not, by the same token surrender to an ahistorical relativism. On the contrary, the subtle and unprescribed relationships between the material and the immaterial in Netherlandish art turn out to have a long and highly suggestive history, one which by turning on its head Michelangelo's unflattering reference to northern artists 'painting like women' may give some sort of sustained pedigree to these creative uncertainties.

From its origins in the late fourteenth century as an autonomous visual culture, Netherlandish painting was distinguished by its emphasis on the detailed rendering of the physical world as a means of dramatizing sacred narrative.[10] It may not be too much to suppose that as a medium, oils were invented by the Van Eyck brothers and their circle not to give natural representations more illusionistic credibility in their own right, but to give the narrative force of the texts new power and immediacy. In crucial details (such as the extraordinary elaboration of the Madonna's headdress and corona in the central panel of the Triptych of the *Adoration of the Sacred Lamb* at Ghent) (Plate 23.11), the transformation of pigment produced unprecedented effects of chromatic saturation and luminosity. With this revolutionary brilliance, the work could itself become akin to the objects of its representation – in this case, jewels. It was a triumph of craft, and akin to other comparable technical achievements in the decorative arts (in tapestry, cloth-weaving, dyeing and glasswork for example) which were at the centre of the Flemish Renaissance. It was these 'womanly' crafts which Michelangelo correctly saw as the guiding paradigms of painting in the Netherlands and which he contrasted invidiously with the classical forms prescribed by sculpture that he took as the highest aspiration for modern practice.

But to equate decorative flair and craftsmanlike fastidiousness with the naive work of imitative naturalism was, as we have seen, a standard mistake made about this type of representation. Almost immediately, Flemish painting in oils used its new techniques to play with the *issue of materiality itself*. That, perhaps, was its most enduring legacy to the art of the Dutch seventeenth century. And nowhere was that play more elaborately exercised than in representations of money. A series of paintings representing bankers (sometimes identified as usurers or tax-collectors) counterpointed, through brilliant effects of detailed visual description the hard-edged accounting and measuring world of money and property with the contemplative spiritual life, conventionally separated in many of these paintings (most famously those of Quentin Metsys – see Plate 23.12) into the worlds of husband and wife. The most startling product of this tradition were the works of the Zeelander, Marinus van Reymerswael (Plate 23.13). He used his stupendous skills of representing the qualities of fabric – its feel, colour, weight and fall – precisely in order to assimilate it to the ugliness of gain and material hubris. In the painting of the two 'moneylenders' for example, the grotesque elaboration of their physiognomies is treated as simply an extension of the correspondingly grotesque extravagance of their head-gear; the folds and piles of the one descending into the wrinkles and crevices of the other; the whole acting as a continuous surface, an excess of fabric turning into a want of humanity. The visual oxymoron only takes on more force on learning that Van Reymerswael, who began his career as a prodigious virtuoso of the craft of naturalistic illusion, ended it as an iconoclast, apprehended for smashing images in his home town of Middelburg. It was, in some sense, a logical outcome for an artist who had created representations that incorporated their own self-criticism.

Northern humanism was much exercised by exactly this kind of dialectical encounter between the sumptuous and the austere. The teaching of More and Erasmus and his pupil Dirk Volkhertszoon Coornhert was neither ascetic nor in the purest sense iconoclast, even when it was fiercely critical of excessive dependence on images for devotional purposes. Erasmus, after all, left the Brothers of the Common Life at Steyn precisely because, in the manner of the stoics, he felt impelled to confront the temptations of the 'empire of things' (government as well as wealth), the better to master and subdue them. Was a similar dilemma the reason why More chose to begin Raphael Hythloday's encounter with Utopia in the great square at Antwerp before the first stock exchange in Europe?

These sort of preoccupations were bound to arise in Antwerp, the imperial city *par excellence*, perhaps (for all the claims of Bruges or Ghent) the *fons et origo* of a true Netherlandish civilization. During the first half of the sixteenth century it was the site not only of a spectacular accumulation of wealth but an equally extraordinary extension of knowledge of the natural world, collected on an appropriately imperial scale. Great cosmographies and *mappae mundi*; collections of flora and fauna; entomological and botanical texts; as well as of oriental ceramics and textiles and paintings, all came to Antwerp in a burst of cultural acquisitiveness.

And though this omnivorous cultural consumption seems to be best described as hungry Aristotelianism, in fact, it was as much coloured by the unifying urges of neo-Platonism. The distinction is less of an arcane quibble than might at first seem to be the case. Thomist scholasticism had accomplished the feat of a divided cosmology that separated into different realms the phenomena of the created world and the sacred mysteries of the Creator. It had enabled the Church to license empirical inquiry on condition that, in the last resort, any acquired knowledge about the physical universe would not trespass on the structure of authority that reserved the dispensation and mediation of sacred mystery to the *ecclesia*. By bringing these two worlds together in a holistically integrated cosmology, neo-Platonism – often a system of signs and clues – threatened this orderly separation, as the doctors of the Church readily understood. For if a careful understanding of the created world could actually be a route (through such signs and signals) towards apprehending the ineffable; if the detail of the Creation was the means through which God made himself manifest, then its accurate and detailed discernment was not merely a permissible but an indispensable instrument of spirituality. This was a line of thought that permitted neo-Platonists like Francis Bacon or Cornelis Drebbel or Huygens to pursue the goals of natural knowledge without ever supposing it conflicted with devotional purity.

There was, then, in the northern Renaissance, a strong cultural predisposition towards seeing the description and representation of natural phenomena as an enrichment of Christian belief. In the Netherlands, because of the ways in which the spectacular effects of a craft-driven art had always served the purposes of sacred narrative, these possibilities surfaced uniquely into the crafty representation of things themselves. The still-life painter could thus use all of his or her skills in the creation of an illusion that would be, at one and the same time, an account of the infinite ingenuity of the Creator and a version of the axiom that the terrestrial world remained but a shadow of the celestial.

This seems to me to belong at the heart of Constantijn Huygens's long poem *Dagh-Werck*,[11] simultaneously a minutely detailed rendering of the animate world and a hymn of praise. Huygens gave further expression to the same sort of sentiment by using the occasion of the completion of the new Amsterdam Town Hall – that most triumphal monument to the empire of things – to write a poem that warned against excessive complacency, and to remind burgomasters of the ephemerality of past empires and the perils as well as the pleasures of riches and power.[12] The burgomasters placed so much store by this kind of sentiment that they actually had the poem incised in marble and set into a plaque in the *burgermeesterskamer* not far from Govert Flinck's equally telling painting of the rejection by the Roman consul Marcus Curius Dentatus of the Samnite gifts of gold in favour of the homely turnip (Plate 23.14).[13]

There were other painterly ways in which Dutch artists responded to the paradoxical requirements of invoking material well-being while at the same time submitting it to the covering regimen of temperance. In one of the most dramatic breaks with past practice, and one precisely contemporaneous with the emergence of the new political nation, a whole generation of painters – landscapists, marine painters and still-life painters – from the late 1620s through to the early 1640s, radically simplified both their subject matter and the chromatic range in which it was described. The result in still-life painting was the extraordinary 'monochrome' pieces of Claesz and the two Hedas that miraculously realized the twin values of simplicity and wholesome sufficiency through which Dutch writers idealized their own shared identity.

That sense of robust beginnings – the breakfast-time of the Dutch Republic – is perfectly balanced by pieces from the end of the century, when, as Huizinga put it, the Republic drowsed in a late sunlit afternoon. One painting in the Hermitage by the little-known Hague artist Martinus Nellius represents a visual anthology of all these themes. An ephemeral butterfly flutters beside a half-peeled lemon placed in a Dutch *roemer* goblet (said to evoke the necessary relationships between sweet and sour; the turning, with time, of sweet wine to acid vinegar); worldly pleasures are concentrated in an over-ripe orange across which a blow-fly crawls. And to the left, holding the tobacco, a vehicle through all of the things of this world, like the days of a life are 'consumed like smoke', is the *Groot Comptoir Almanach*, the gazette of the empire of things, presented as pipe-dream.

Notes

This essay was written before the publication of two critically important discussions of the epistemological and normative issues embodied in Dutch still-life painting; Norman Bryson, *Looking at the Overlooked* (Cambridge, Mass., 1990) and Lawrence Goedde, 'A little world made cunningly: Dutch still life and *ekphrasis*', in Ingvar Bergström, *Still Lifes of the Golden Age: Northern European Paintings from the Heinz Family Collection* (Washington, 1989). Issues of interpretation are directly confronted by E. de Jong, 'The interpretation of still-life paintings: possibilities and limitations' in E. de Jong *et al.*, *Still Life in the Age of Rembrandt* (Auckland, New Zealand, 1982), 27–38. The same catalogue has a helpful history of the critical literature on the genre in Andrea Gasten, 'Dutch still-life painting: judgements and appreciation'. Prior to this recent and reinvigorated interest in the subject, the standard study of Dutch still-life painting was Ingvar Bergstrom, *Dutch Still Life Painting in the Seventeenth Century*, tr. C. Hedstrom and G. Taylor (London, 1956). Sam Segal has recently made an important and thoughtful contribution to the literature in *Een bloemlijke verleden (A Flowery Past)* (Amsterdam and 's Hertogenbosch, 1982) and in William B. Jordan (ed.), *A Prosperous Past: The Sumptuous Still-Life in the Netherlands 1600–1700* (The Hague, 1982), in particular in his essay, 'On meaning and interpretation: the abundance of life and moderation in all things' in the latter catalogue, 29ff. L. J. Bol, *A Modest Message as Intimated by the Painters of the 'Monochrome Banketje'* (Schiedam, 1980) insists on the priority of painterly over iconological concerns in still-life paintings, and demotes iconology to 'an auxiliary field of scholarship' in such discussions.

1   Roland Barthes, 'Le Monde-objet', 21. The essay is available in a translation by Richard Howard in Norman Bryson (ed.), *Calligram: Essays in New Art History from France* (Cambridge and New York, 1988), 107–15, but it is still much better read in the original; Roland Barthes, *Essais critiques* (Paris, 1964), 19–28. References are from this original version.
2   Barthes, 'Monde-objet', 20.
3   ibid., 20.
4   ibid., 22.
5   ibid., 25.
6   Louis Viardot, *Les Musées d'Angleterre, de Belgique, de Hollande et de Russie* (Paris, 1860).
7   Paul Claudel, *The Eye Listens*, tr. Elsie Pell (New York, 1950), 47–8.
8   ibid., 47–8.
9   Carlo Cipolla, *Clocks and Culture: 1300–1700* (London, 1967); David Landes, *Revolution in Time: Clocks and the Making of the Modern World* (Cambridge, Mass., 1983).
10   For a discussion of the Collier (Plate 23.6), see de Jong *et al.*, *Still Life*, 119–203.
11   *Dagh-werck van Constantijn Huygens* ed. F. L. Zwaan (Assen, 1973).

12 The complicated relationship between naturalism, the communication of sacred mystery and formal innovations is, of course, intensively discussed in Erwin Panofsky, *Early Netherlandish Painting, Its Origin and Character*, 2 vols (Cambridge, Mass., 1953) especially on the Van Eyck brothers and the *Adoration of the Sacred Lamb*, 181ff.

13 On the Huygens poem 'Amstelredam' and the Flinck painting, see Lyckle de Vries, *Kunst als Regeringzaak* (Amsterdam, 1975) and Sjoerd Faber, Jacobine Huisken, and Friso Lammertse, *'Van Heeren die hunn' stoel en kussen niet beschaemen': Het stadsbestuur van Amsterdam in de 17de en 18de eeuw* (Amsterdam, 1988), 28, 35.

24

The consuming flame: electrical showmen and Tory mystics in the world of goods

Simon Schaffer

Euphrosyne: But pray, Cleonicus, can you by any Experiments shew me this Matter of Electricity; for otherwise it is talking to me in the Dark?

Cleonicus: Yes, come with me into this Dark Room, and then you will view it in its proper light.

Euphrosyne: Well! It is dark enough sure. What am I to see here?

Cleonicus: You will now see in the Dark what you could not before perceive in the Light.

(Benjamin Martin, *The Young Gentleman and Lady's Philosophy*)[1]

The price of wonderful commodities

In their programme for an anthropology of consumption, Douglas and Isherwood claim that 'underneath any disagreement on tastes, far-reaching metaphysical differences may be revealed'. This suggestion is bolstered by the reflection that values are established as part of the politics of culture. In this process the world of goods reflects and embodies deep metaphysical assumptions about the moral economy.[2] A good case of the interaction between metaphysics, values and taste is provided by Georgian debates on the propriety of the public shows of natural philosophy. For some observers, these shows were a spectacular example of trivialized consumption. It has been customary for historians to endorse this judgement: the tricks of the natural philosophers' trade have been judged to be epiphenomenal distractions from the serious business of science, industry and useful knowledge. The utilitarian message seems more significant than the histrionic medium. Yet both the performers and their critics judged that serious metaphysical issues of wide public import were raised by the showmanship of modish lectures, issues which touched on the relation between theatre, market and divine creation. Especially controversial was the moral ambiguity of the relation between consumer culture and natural philosophy. J. H. Plumb has urged the importance of natural philosophy lectures as part of the eighteenth-century 'acceptance of modernity', and notes that 'perhaps even to the majority the entertainment was of greater importance than the knowledge, but most important of all was the novelty of what was taught'.[3] This relation between entertainment, knowledge and consumption is explored in what follows. A perspective on the market of natural philosophy challenges the received distinction between superficial display and sober application. Lecturers competed with each other for audience and status. Critics sought to subvert the status of the lecturers' enterprise. In these fights systems of values were brought forward for scrutiny, and tacit assumptions about the private vices and public benefits of natural philosophy were rendered explicit.

Recent historiography has helpfully displayed the multivalence of natural philosophical uses. Roy Porter has connected lecturing with 'enlightened' emulation of metropolitan sophistication in provincial milieux; Larry Stewart has emphasized the location of early Georgian lectures amongst the traders and jobbers of the Exchange; and Jan Golinski has shown how these varying utilities were negotiated by promoters of contrasted natural philosophies.[4] So contests about the legitimacy of natural philosophical consumption are good sites for an historical understanding of the emergence of natural knowledge as a commodity. The following discussion delineates the cultural meaning of lecturing on electricity as a key site of fashionable concern. The bulk of the chapter is concerned with a pamphlet war between a peripatetic lecturer, Benjamin Martin, and a London surgeon, the Tory John Freke, who challenged the moral probity of electrical showmanship. Martin has often been treated as the exemplary lecturer, whose cunning entrepreneurship helped spread the gospel of fashionable knowledge through southern Britain. Hence the interest of his metropolitan adversary's pietist critiques of 'novelty' and 'showmanship'. Pietists reckoned that divinely sustained nature should not be used for profit. But they had to construct an appropriate site within commercial culture from which to propagate this gospel. The chapter offers a reconsideration of the notorious coupling of theatre and market and explores the implied audiences for showmanship and for piety. Finally, it is argued that the utility of natural philosophy, as a privileged means of representing nature, depended on complex and fragile boundaries between the world of natural philosophy and those of commercial and theological interest. These boundaries did not make knowledge value-free; they made a new form of value in the command of nature.

In mid-eighteenth-century London, the capital of the so-called 'consumer revolution', command of the most spectacular of natural phenomena became commercial opportunities. After the earthquakes which hit the city in the spring of 1750, a china dealer 'had a jar cracked by the shock. He originally asked ten guineas for the pair: he now asks twenty, because it is the only jar in Europe that has been cracked by an earthquake.' Horace Walpole said the repeated shocks were 'lowering the price of wonderful commodities'; David Hume commented acidly that episcopal 'prescriptions to the multitude' in the earthquake's wake were likely to drive physicians out of business: 'the Bishop of London . . . recommends certain pills, such as fasting, prayer, repentance, mortification and other drugs which are entirely to come from his own shop'.[5] Natural philosophical stories about such events were commodities too. Knowledge was made within the world of goods. Thus Horace Walpole treated the common, electrical, model of seismic action offered in 1750 as 'the fashionable cause, and everything is resolved into electrical appearances, as formerly everything was accounted for by Descartes' vortices, or Sir Isaac's gravitation'.[6]

Electrical fire dominated London natural philosophy in the mid-eighteenth century. Public interest in the new electrical demonstrations was intense. Electricity became a commodity which many could use and which won large markets. As an article of fashion and trade, electricity enrolled the interests of several sections of eighteenth-century society. It was used by natural philosophy lecturers to swell their audiences. 'The ladies and people of quality . . . never regard natural philosophy but when it works miracles': this comment by the Göttingen professor Albrecht von Haller was printed in the appealing *Gentleman's Magazine* in April 1745. Instrument-makers catered for an expanding market with ranges of electrical devices, wares which helped cement English domination of the international market for philosophical instruments. These were accompanied by handbooks containing 'directions for gentlemen who have electrical machines, how to proceed in making their experiments'.[7] A standard repertoire of electrical phenomena was established, relying on the output of the spinning glass globe and the highly popular 'Leyden Jar', a tool developed in the mid-1740s in Germany and the Netherlands involving a glass bottle often lined with metal and filled with water, whose spectacular effects prompted Haller's report. These effects included discharges and shocks around the head, fingers or lips of human victims, the ministration of therapeutic shocks, the ignition of alcohol and the emulation of meteorological effects such as 'Lightning, the Ignis Fatuus, the Shooting Stars, and Aurora Borealis'. At Northampton in February 1747 the audience witnessed 'the motions of the planets and comets shewn by an electrical orrery'; the previous month Birmingham customers were promised a shock from the Leyden Jar 'granted to those that chuse not to feel it who join'd in the same company with those that do'.[8]

Electricity also intersected the concerns of the learned professions. Many writers proposed electrical cures for an extraordinary range of ailments. Cromwell Mortimer, physician and secretary to the Royal Society, speculated in June 1745 that 'future Experiments may evince that Electricity may be used medically, in order to renew and regenerate a proper Quantity of vital Fire, such as is necessary for the conveniently carrying on, and performing the animal Functions'.[9] Lists of electrical cures were printed, electrification of 'bedsteads, bedding, wearing apparel etc.' was commended in the *Gentleman's Magazine*.[10] Electrical fire also raised issues of direct importance for the divines. William Stukeley, chief propagator of the electrical account of earthquakes, insisted that his model allowed the connection between 'earthly wonders' and 'celestial monitions'. The link between electrical and celestial fire was hammered home in the works of visionary and philosophical clergymen such as Richard Lovett of Worcester and Richard Symes at Bristol: 'if you yourselves with the Help of proper Instruments can call forth the Hidden fire and perform wonders with it, what shall he not do with it who is its Creator and who now rules and directs it?'[11] Electrical phenomena could capture an audience, satisfy customers, cure the body and save the soul.

The fashionable career of electricity depended on expensive apparatus, polite customers and big rewards. In his retrospect of the development of electrical philosophy during the century, Joseph Priestley summed up its appeal:

> Electricity has one considerable advantage over most other branches of science, as it both furnishes matter of speculation for philosophers, and of entertainment for all persons promiscuously. . . . Electrical experiments have, in almost every country in Europe, occasionally furnished the means of subsistence to numbers of ingenious and industrious persons, whose circumstances have not been affluent, and who have had the address to turn to their own advantage that passion for the marvellous, which they saw to be so strong in all their fellow-creatures. A man

need not desire a greater income than the sums which have been received in shillings, six-pences, three-pences, and two-pences, for exhibiting the Leyden experiment.[12]

The lecture circuit was the principal means through which expenses could be recouped. The cost of a good lecturing kit was about £300 in the mid-century. Electrical equipment made up a substantial part of this cost. In 1767, when Priestley moved to Leeds, he told the London electrical experimenter and schoolmaster John Canton that devices cheaper than London ones could be made 'under my own inspection'; in the late 1760s Priestley helped design a new machine for which his brother did the turning and Dollond the marketing. Devices were sold to medical users and infirmaries, patronage was won from aristocrats and industrialists alike, published accounts of electricity's progress were tailored to win endorsement and support.[13]

Priestley also knew that 'there are some things that cannot be done in the country',[14] and here the London makers played a crucial role. Priestley's attitude to these workers is examined later in this chapter. Prices could be lowered through skilful marketing and efficient design: in 1762 Martin, one of Priestley's suppliers, issued a catalogue which listed a complete electrical apparatus at prices ranging from 5 to 13 guineas, and portable machines of his own design for as little as 3 guineas. Air pumps, which were needed for the most vivid electrical displays, could cost anything from 4 to 40 guineas for the larger machines complete with accompanying apparatus.[15] Such devices were affordable by a surprisingly wide range of customers. The supply of ready-made machines, accompanied with guidebooks for the virtuosi, helped reproduce standard repertoires of parlour routines, displayed in metropolitan and provincial showrooms and then repeated at home (Plate 24.1). Expenses could be recouped if demonstrators made some machines for use and others for sale: this policy was adopted by Priestley, by French experimenters and commonly in London. The difference between entrepreneur, demonstrator and philosopher was effaced in the market-place, the theatre and the coffee house. In 1746 the celebrated engineer John Smeaton built his own air pumps and electrical globe, 'made of $20\frac{1}{2}$ inches diameter of Green Glass'. The costs were met by showmanship, whose status Smeaton queried but accepted:

> I dont take it yt shewing ye wonders of Electricity for Money is much more commendable . . . than ye shewing any other strange sight or curiosity for ye same end, however if £200 could be got by a worthy employment in yt way I dont see wheres ye harm as there is no fraud or Dishonesty in it.[16]

This was the top of the market, dominated by men such as George Adams, who set up the first large workshop in the mid-1730s, and Jesse Ramsden, who employed as many as fifty hands. Humbler operators, as Henry Baker reported in 1747, charged one shilling per person for their displays; in the early 1750s Canton's school at Spitalfields was visited by the fashionable to see the electrical shows at similar prices.[17]

In the provinces, lecturers such as John Warltire or Benjamin Martin charged subscriptions of a guinea for their travelling courses of twelve or even twenty shows. They worked hard to win respectable clients: between summer 1743 and summer 1748, for example, Martin ran at least nine successive courses in London, Bath and other locations in southern England and the Midlands.[18] The status and manners of the showmen and their audiences were always troubled aspects of this commerce. Martin recalled that even the successful experimenter and entrepreneur J. T. Desaguliers, demonstrator at Oxford and then London, had relied on clerics and gentry to defend him against rural prejudice in the 1730s, while Martin himself remembered

> as my Goods were once carrying into my Lecture-Room, at a certain town, the Rabble crouded about the Door, to know what it was, and one wiser than the Rest immediately cries out, '*Tis a ZHOW come to Town*; and what do we give to zee't? A GUINEA replies the other. Z—nds, says the fellow, this is the D—l of a *Zhow*; why, *Luck-man-zhure*, none but the *Gentle-Vauke* can zee this.[19]

Such responses and criticisms were the penalty of showmanship. Important, too, was the surprise and thus the guarded secrecy of rival electrical display techniques. When a powerful new Leipzig machine reached London in spring 1745, Baker visited Martin Folkes, President of the Royal Society, to view and try the glass barrel before its public display at the Society: 'this must be a secret', he told his correspondent.[20]

Secrecy, surprise, wondermongering and commerce were thus an intimate accompaniment of electrical culture, enabling and yet undermining its philosophical meaning and status. Georgian natural philosophers needed secure private spaces, laboratories, cabinets, gardens, in which to make knowledge, and welcoming public spaces, cafés, theatres, academies, in which to display it. These problems of spatial division and concealed display haunted the development of the natural philosophers' role.[21] The workshop was conventionally a place of suspicious secrecy, fit for delusion or for lowly manual service, not proper to philosophy. The theatre was the space of illusion, an unstable base for the display of realities. Fernand Braudel reminds us that the choice between 'display and discretion' was characteristic of the relationship between government and commerce in the classical age. Nowhere was this truer than in the formation of its natural philosophy. The image of nature as a theatre was an eighteenth-century commonplace. Adam Smith used it to illuminate the natural philosophical task 'to render this lower part of the great theatre of nature a coherent spectacle to the imagination'. The contrast between the private space, behind the scenes, where realities operated, and the realm of mere appearances, on front stage, was used to place the natural philosopher. Fontenelle inaugurated a genre of such contrasts in his best-selling *Conversations on the Plurality of Worlds* (1686): different systems of the world were there accounted as different stories about the way stage-machinery produced its dazzling effects. Smith picked up the reference in the 1750s: the task of natural philosophy was to allay superstitious wonder, and no-one 'wonders at the machinery of the opera house who has once been admitted behind the scenes'.[22]

The interaction between this theatrical project of the Whig natural philosophers and their political culture needs emphasis. Histrionics accounted for social control and for opposition to it. At Tyburn and Newgate, the forces of church and law paraded their authority, while London plebs and their allies developed 'counter-theatres' to parody and resist overweening autocracy or absurd excess.[23] If public theatre were at once the tool of the Whig oligarchy and the chosen means of popular resistance, it is not surprising to find a powerful strand of anti-theatrical polemic amongst Tory critics. A strong high Tory literary tradition emerged, spawned by texts by Collier and Nelson in the 1690s and then sustained by works such as William Law's *Absolute Unlawfulness of the Stage-Entertainment Fully Demonstrated* (London, 1726) and Samuel Richardson's *Seasonable Examination of . . . Playhouses* (London, 1735).[24] The groups which fostered these texts also mounted important attacks on the legitimacy of public lecturing in natural philosophy. In this context, the terminology of 'illusion' and 'enthusiasm' became a key object of inquiry in the search for a new account of legitimate performance, and, significantly, electric fire provided good images of the deceptive relation between audience and performer. One influential French critic observed in 1760 that performers

> must equally trap the public with the force of illusion and make them experience all the movements by which they are animated. This truth, this enthusiasm . . . is, if I may so express myself, the image of the electric shock: it is a fire which is speedily communicated, which instantly embraces the spectators' imagination, which enflames their soul, which forces their heart to sensibility.

The comparison between the real effects of spectacular electrical fire and those of illusory performance was common: David Garrick demanded that performers' genius should, 'like electric fire, shoot through the veins, marrow bones and all of every spectator'. This comparison is immensely important, for electrifying natural philosophical showmanship was the best case in public culture of the claim that artificial phenomena could give its audience access to reality. [25]

An entertainment for angels

Different electrical philosophies acted as varying job descriptions – to describe in lectures or in print the organization of electrical phenomena in the universe was to describe and endorse a specific practice. Such practices defined their moral and philosophical significance and the proper audience at which they aimed. This chapter examines one controversy of the 1740s which centred on the right way of using electricity and highlighted its place in commercial culture. Benjamin Martin was a protagonist in this fight. He argued for the propriety of using electrical performances as part of polite commerce in his public shows at Bath and elsewhere. Electrical fire acquired its rightful place in the emulative culture of Whig provincial life. In his highly successful part-work, *The Young Gentleman and Lady's Philosophy* (first issued in 1755), Martin penned dialogues between a bright young gentlewoman and her learned graduate brother. Their chats helped tout his wares. When Euphrosyne expressed a wish to see 'Fire from Heaven' in trials with lightning rods, Cleonicus promised to take her to 'a Gentleman's house' equipped with the best instruments, amongst which would figure Martin's table electrical machine (Plate 24.2). To which his sister replied:

> Nothing would be so agreeable to me as such a Piece of Scenery as this. How poor and low must all vulgar Amusements be, when compared to this! One would think such a Gentleman would have all the World to visit him; for my own Part, I should think it an Entertainment for Angels, rather than for Men. I am amazed when I think every Gentleman of Fortune has not such an Apparatus in his House.[26]

In a manner which prefigured the advertisements of skilled publicists such as George Packwood later in the century, Martin made his characters condemn the absence of 'a Philosophical Taste' amongst the gentry, 'though the Expence or Trouble of erecting such an Apparatus would be next to Nothing, when compared with the Sums of Money they otherways expend to no Purpose'.[27] Furthermore, following John Wesley's furious assault on medical monopoly in the name of cheap and effective electrotherapy for his Methodist flock, Martin projected a future in which electrical cures would be commonplace, and medical skill levelled: 'there will be a COLLEGE OF ELECTRICIANS; A DOCTOR OF ELEC-TRICITY in every City and Town; and an Electrical Machine and Appratus in every Gentleman's Family.' It might even be possible that 'every man may be his own Electrician and the Diplomatic [i.e. licensed] Gentry quite discarded'.[28]

However, talk of heavenly fire, angelic entertainment and electrical medical degrees was by no means untroubled. Martin's Fleet Street neighbour, the sculptor and electrical performer Benjamin Rackstrow, was well aware of the dangers courted by a mixture of advertising and lecturing: 'Methinks I hear one say, what is this fellow at? Is this a *Preface*? No, 'tis an *Advertisement*! He is puffing about his Company, and tells us of his Business, instead of saying something of his Book.' So Martin's condemnation of corrupted gentlemanly taste and medical licensing was matched by others' condemnation of his own corrupted philosophy. Martin was attacked by John Freke, a surgeon at St Bartholomew's Hospital, a Tory bastion in London. He challenged the facile charlatanry which he alleged characterized electrical displays. Freke reckoned that fire was God's agent, 'the immediate officer of *God Almighty*, which He seems to find in all Things living. Nay, this Power, according to my Conception, seems to be the Cause, under HIM, both of Life and Death.'[29] For Freke, *electrical* fire was this element in its fallen, wrathful state, only visible when humans meddled with nature's balance. He bolstered this claim with a complex spiritualism drawn from the German mystic Jakob Boehme and the non-juring divine William Law. Since electrical fire was the manifestation of God's wrath, its display could have no good moral effects. Nor should it be debased nor used to profit from the rabble or the genteel. In the world of goods, the meaning of electrical fire hinged on control over different parts of nature and the structure of a cosmos. The Martin–Freke debate will be read in terms of rival claims to the ownership of a commodity. The claims of electrical philosophers could be challenged by physicians who wished to monopolize therapy, or by clerics who sought to direct salvation or by enthusiasts who privileged the private experience of spirit. Different social agents had rival investments in a given electrical phenomenon or device.

Developments in the culture of electricity in the 1740s provided these protagonists with some rich interpretative resources. The construction of the Leyden Jar in Germany in 1745 was seen by a large public as a challenging and startling manifestation of electric fire. Haller reported on 'the wonderful discoveries made in Germany': 'ladies of quality' were resorting 'from all parts to the public lectures of natural philosophy, which by that means became brilliant assemblies'. Several key conceptual tools were presented in Haller's review. He mentioned German notions that electricity was 'the same matter which we call *animal spirits*', manifest in living matter. Haller was sceptical: 'are there animal spirits in an iron rod, or a dead carcase?' Haller consistently denied that nervous fluid was electrical, and insisted that nervous action was irreducibly the province of physiology, his own vocation. He referred to an 'electrical atmosphere' surrounding electrified glass globes, providing Franklin with a useful hint. He summarized the wonders which lecturers produced for delighted audiences, including the 'beatification', or fiery halo, which Georg Bose, one of the most successful German lecturers, could make appear around his victim's head.[30]

London performers such as Rackstrow were quick to copy these tricks (Plate 24.3). The leader of London electrical philosophers, the apothecary William Watson, wrote to Bose asking about the secret of this remarkable effect. It emerged that Bose had hidden a studded suit of Leipzig armour beneath his subject's clothes: 'it is true that I have embellished a little my beatification by my style and expressions.'[31] Such embellishment promoted public attention. The *Gentleman's Magazine* and its chief rival the *London Magazine* had circulations of up to 10,000, and both carried numerous comments on electric fire. A correspondent wrote in July 1746 to defend electric animal spirits against Haller. In March and July, the journals summarized stories from the *Philosophical Transactions* about the Leyden Jar in Holland and Paris. Several electrical experiments seemed 'like Magic' or '*Bizarreries*', such as Nollet's notorious demonstration of a shock administered simultaneously to Paris guardsmen, reviewed in John Hinton's lavishly illustrated *Universal Magazine*.[32] When the dispute between Martin and Freke erupted in October 1746, their differences were fully aired in the public sheets. The *Gentleman's Magazine* printed reviews which evaluated the worth of the rivals' views, as did the *London*.[33] Watson's accounts of the new phenomena of the late 1740s were also widely publicized. His work was representative of the debate: he commanded multiple globe devices based on German designs from summer 1745, and he managed to develop increased power from his electric jars by filling them with lead shot.[34] Watson staged extremely striking demonstrations (Plate 24.4). Both Freke and the *Gentleman's Magazine* praised Watson's willingness to admit visiting witnesses at his Aldersgate house.[35] The Royal Society had already awarded him its Copley Medal in November 1745. In summer 1747 he managed trials at Westminster Bridge, Stoke Newington and Highbury Hill, in which electric fire was sent through great distances, across the Thames, and through the experimenters' bodies. 'The Gentlemen present', including the President, Folkes and Watson's colleagues Bevis and Stanhope, were 'much molested in their Operations by a great Concourse of People who many times broke the connecting wire and otherwise greatly incommoded them'.[36]

The principal conceptual tool which Watson and his allies used to interpret these phenomena was the doctrine of active fluids they found in texts by Newton, Homberg and Boerhaave. These fluids were seen as tenuous, elastic and capable of carrying the powers of fermentation, vitality, fire, light and electricity, which powers were ultimately derived from God. In the 1740s natural philosophers reworked Newton's texts to help them describe such fluids. Electrical demonstrations were viewed as powerful evidence for this kind of substance, and hence allegedly provided direct support for Newton's own worldview and thus for an effluvial model of divine power. Watson coined the term 'electrical aether' in autumn 1746. During this decade the Dublin physician Bryan Robinson gave an influential version of 'Sir Isaac Newton's account of the aether'.[37] Benjamin Wilson, a clerk at the Charterhouse and aspiring painter, visited Robinson to discuss the electrical shock in 1746, and prompted the addition of a supplement on electricity to Robinson's book. Robinson told Wilson that 'Sir I. Newton has declared the cause of [Electricity] and I am satisfied your Experiments will fully prove it and Confirm it'.[38] Franklin's friend Patrick Collinson agreed in March 1745 that electricity would prove Newton's aether. Rackstrow reckoned that 'if Sir Isaac were alive to see the experiments we now make of Electricity, he would allow of Elementary Fire himself'. Priestley asked what 'Newton himself [would] have said' about such experiments on 'that tremendous power'.[39] Newton's emblematic status helped electrical philosophers make commerce teach theology.

Because of this status, exchanges between natural philosophers included the establishment of the true ancestry of electrical cosmology. Watson's seminal paper of October 1746 modelled itself on a Newtonian source, and was followed by a set of 'queries' which aped those of the *Opticks*. He claimed that electrical shows displayed the effects of some divinely generated active power, a natural principle of great effect rather than a cunning artifice of crafty human operators and their tricks. But this lesson was taught by Watson alongside very detailed instructions on how the most effective tricks could be performed. He reported that in the Leyden trials 'it seemed to me as though my Arm were struck off at my shoulder, elbow and wrist, and both my legs at the knees and behind the ankles', and also gave the recipe for ways in which 'these phials may be concealed and the shock made more universal'. The combination of natural theology and practical showmanship was invaluable. Watson firmly fixed the image of electrical fire as an active fluid present in all bodies. Electrified bodies would hold surplus fluid as an *atmosphere* on their surface. Glass tubes and generators were so many 'fire pumps', sucking in fluid from 'the floor of the room'; 'the Office of the Globes exactly tallies with that of the Heart in Animals'.[40] Watson shared Haller's worry about an identification of the 'elementary fire' with a 'vital flame', since, he asked, 'do we not find that as much of this fire is producible from a dead animal as a living one?' He cited Boerhaave and 'sGravesande, 'who held fire to be an original, a distinct principle, formed by the Creator himself'. This fire was therefore not inherent in the instruments: they merely served as 'the first movers and determiners of that power', so manifesting its effect to the audience.[41] Watson immediately attracted a number of responses. When Franklin's letters reached London in 1747, Watson claimed that his ideas were the same as those of the Philadelphian. Wilson charged Watson with plagiarism.[42] Freke was prompted to compose his *Essay to Shew the Cause of Electricity* in October 1746 soon after talking with Watson at Child's Coffee House. Lecturers such as Rackstrow and Martin expressed admiration of the 'best' of modern electrical authors, but this was tempered with cautious criticism of the views expressed in the 1746 paper.[43] In October 1746, Martin also produced his own contribution to these commentaries, an *Essay on Electricity*, initiating a violent controversy between the lecturer and the surgeon.

A 'retailer of the sciences' in search of power

Martin's *Essay* was one of a long series of publications accompanying his work as lecturer and instrument maker. Popular dictionaries of arts and sciences were followed by handbooks to instruments. Prices varied from 14 or 18 shillings for versions of *Philosophia Britannica* to 12 shillings for his *Young Gentleman and Lady's Philosophy*, 1 shilling for his remarkable *Panegyrick of the Newtonian Philosophy* and 1s. 6d. for a chart of Comet Halley.[44] John Millburn's recent thorough documentation of Martin's life and works shows how his public life was connected with the development of his natural philosophy. Martin was born into a landed Surrey family in 1704. In the 1730s he set himself up as a schoolmaster in Chichester. In winter 1741–2 he began lecturing on natural philosophy in Reading, Bath, Birmingham and elsewhere. In 1745 he gave courses in London coffee houses, such as George's near the Temple. Customers were to offer 'proposals' for numbers of lectures and convenient times. From the mid-1750s he established a productive instrument-making business in London, dominating sections of the market for microscopes, orreries, electrical machines and air pumps, even attempting to sell a great air pump, 'fitted to adorn the Musaeum of any Nobleman or Gentleman' by subscription in eighty separate half-guinea shares (Plate 24.5).[45] In 1760 he took over the premises in Fleet Street formerly owned by Rackstrow, and business prospered. Martin restocked the Harvard instrument collection after its disastrous fire. Priestley, Tom Paine and Johann Bernoulli were among those who heard him lecture or admired his instruments.[46] But by January 1782, Martin was bankrupt. He attempted suicide, dying of his wounds the following month. His career involved a quest for patronage and status in the market-place of natural philosophy. He sought to show his loyalty to 'true' Newtonianism, his electrical competence, his morality and his close links with the Whig establishment of the Royal Society, in Crane Court round the corner from his shop. Suspicions of itinerant performers and the prolific Grub Street hacks hampered this effort.

Martin's fight with Freke centred on the fraught relationship between patrician patronage and vulgar marketing. A London satire of 1755 described him as a 'self-taught philosopher . . . the great retailer of the sciences', while by the end of the decade, amidst the marked public fascination with the return of Halley's Comet, many tried to portray him as Sidrophel, the astrological charlatan of Butler's *Hudibras*.[47] In his lectures Martin harped on the virtue and propriety of his commercial place. He sought aristocratic Whig patronage, the target of his schemes being the local magnate, Charles Lennox, Duke of Richmond, a Fellow of the Royal Society, companion of Cumberland, patron of Folkes and Watson and according to Horace Walpole, 'the only man who ever loved the Duke of Newcastle'.[48] In November 1741, Martin wrote to him for support for an application to the Royal Society:

> I have no business to maintain my Family by, but a little Shop & my reading Lectures from Town to Town – Hence it is that wherever I come I am continually asked, if I am *Fellow of ye R. Society*, & I have found it as frequent a Disadvantage to say, *No*.[49]

Martin offered the Society his air pump, dedicated tracts to Richmond and his son, but won no help from the Duke, nor the then President, Hans Sloane, nor from his successor, Folkes. His fate was not unique. The eminent hack 'Sir' James Hill, like Martin, was a prolific natural philosopher, journalist and devotee of the stage. He lived at Richmond's mansion at Goodwood, near Chichester, in 1741–3. In 1746, in the midst of the electrical dispute, Hill wrote to Watson and Folkes soliciting support for entry to the Society. It was a humiliating failure. Hill's response was a characteristically blistering attack on the Society, *A Dissertation on Royal Societies*.[50] Martin, however, continued his search for power. He had been tarred with the brush of Duncehood. Such men, Pope sneered in *The Dunciad* (1742–3), always aspired 'to shine in the dignity of F.R.S.'. Fleet Street, bankruptcy and suicide were their common lot, the stage their natural home.[51] Hence it was crucial that Martin defend his vocation and his right to custom against the charge of charlatanry and establish his moral efficacy and social place. His handouts claimed that

> nothing can debase or vilify this noble science but the scandalous management it meets with from quacks and illiterate pretenders. . . . To recover which from such vile prostitution, and give ingenious and generous minds a view of this science in its native worth and excellence, is the principal design of my present proposal.[52]

Martin polished this course from his departure from Chichester in 1741–2 until the early 1750s. Typically, he gave six or twelve lectures, selections from around 300 experiments, exploiting a cabinet valued at 'several hundred pounds'. Handbooks accompanying the courses were distributed through the ingenious Reading businessman John Newbery, who in the 1750s was a notorious campaigner for dubious panaceas, and by 1761 would begin producing the massively successful *Tom Telescope* natural philosophy lectures for children.[53] Martin began adding electricity to his coverage from at least summer 1748. His advertisements stressed instruction and entertainment, fitted to 'the various uses of life and easy to be understood by all capacities', while his course books were themselves laid out like 'scenes in a play: they present the whole most agreeably in parts, which thus immediately affects us and gives us the greatest pleasure and entertainment'.[54] Martin described a world in which it was appropriate and necessary to peddle natural philosophy to polite customers. Martin preferred to ply his trade in a world of active powers sanctioned with Newtonian authority and proved by dramatic experiments. His stock consisted of elegant material devices. So he increasingly stressed the material powers which electrical shows revealed. He drew his audience's attention away from aether towards the matter's powers and their ultimate Newtonian warrant. He reckoned he could extend these powers, and his own command, over swathes of nature and culture: 'as to those we call the *learned professions*, viz. *Law*, *Physic*, and *Divinity*, I appeal to any Man's Judgment if there be any thing in the two last by which they can merit that distinguishing epithet', asked Martin, apart from that power 'wholly due to that Philosophy which is founded on observation, experiment, and mathematical ratiocination?'[55] The market helped propagate Martin's authority, materialize his power and disseminate his cosmology. Ready-made materials would only be desirable commodities if they carried the mantle of settled success. He had to show that his trials and his philosophy were secure. He found it necessary increasingly to poach on the preserves of other disciplines. From the later 1740s he used electrical power as a chief weapon in his fight for the truth and the authority of his own standing as natural philosopher. Since 'the power . . . of Electricity' had 'greatly amused mankind and justly raised their wonder and surprize, it is but natural to expect they should appear very anxious about the . . . manner of accounting for it'.[56]

Martin identified electrical power in matter by differentiating his position from that of Watson. He rejected the received concept of an *elementary* fire and Watson's coinage of the term 'electrical aether'. Instead, he rephrased Watson's claim of early 1746 to suggest that 'electric matter' was held in bodies 'by a very great attracting power'.[57] Forty-two experiments evinced this power in action, including those of lightning and the sensitive plant, with a standard repertoire such as the 'Father Long-Legs' (involving an electrified model insect) and the 'Jet d'eau', in which electrified liquid was forced into a fountain.[58] Martin's claim against the London aetherialist model was that the aether was not a 'principle of the *Newtonian* philosophy', whereas active powers were. Bodies which displayed electrical effects were just those where friction had overcome the strong attracting power between electrical and common matter.[59] The aether was a mark of cheapskate ignorance and catchpenny dispute. 'This fluid . . . is mightily talked of by our Modern Virtuosi and as little understood . . . they have found an easy and cheap Method of being wond'rous wise and doing as much in half a year as Newton himself in half a century.'[60] Martin held that this distracted audiences with vain wrangling and bad business. Instead, his own electrical powers were manifest and demonstrable, the 'best defence against the efforts and assaults of atheists' because displays showed that 'all the Powers of Natural Bodies' were designed by God – and understood by Newton – 'to answer very great purposes'.[61] With his cosmology of materialized powers Martin could offer his audiences a guided tour of the universe: he did so in his remarkable *Panegyrick on the Newtonian Philosophy*. Here the tour began with a vision of the plurality of worlds (each 'immense Fountains of light and heat') and our Sun, whose power was made manifest in hydrostatics, meteorology, vegetation and chemistry. Electrical powers were most vivid:

> we have here open'd to our Minds the *wondrous Laboratory of Nature*, and the stupendous Processes therein carrying on, unheeded and unthought of by the Vulgar. This part of Philosophy is the *Microscope of the Mind*; we hereby view all the small Particles of Matter, endow'd with a *mighty Power of Action*, by which they are constantly actuating each other by ATTRACTION or REPULSION.

Finally, Martin spelt out the links between the action of these fiery powers and the constitution of living bodies. With this cosmology, even medicine and theology could be subjugated by natural philosophy: 'they are without Excuse who pretend to know God, and discourse of his attributes from any other Principles than those of Philosophy.'[62]

A new vocation was offered to Martin's customers – attentive reading of his books, purchase of his equipment and, above all, attendance at his lectures: 'to represent the principal Appearances of Nature to the view of the Audience . . . is in reality . . . of the same use to the Mind, as a Telescope to the Eye.'[63] This career poached upon the concerns of high-status philosophy in astronomy, physiology and physic. For example, Martin helped himself to the work of Stephen Gray to suggest that electricity drove the planets, ignoring metropolitan scepticism of trials in which electrified bodies allegedly orbited a force-centre.[64] These speculations were bolstered by Martin's own influential work on the design of dramatic planetaria, costing as much as 20 guineas, with which he illustrated his lectures from the 1740s.[65] Yet undoubtedly the most polemical of his claims was that directed against priestcraft. Experimental natural philosophy had a theological purpose which might dispossess priests and their allies. 'Those fruitless and perplexing Disputes which have so much and so long distracted the Christian scheme', particularly 'those relating to the Soul', would now apparently 'admit of a thorough decision from the Principles of Philosophy'. Martin allowed himself to lecture in characteristically deist, radical Whig terms against 'the Wizards and Necromancers, the pseudo-Prophets, the Demoniacs, the wonder-working relicts and the group of omnipotent priests that formerly swarm'd in this Island'. Material power in natural philosophy and reformed natural theology in the Church had put them to flight: 'where they bowed, there they fell down dead.'[66] Martin's sneers against enthusiasm and established divinity were matched by his claim that without natural philosophy his betters were 'meer nominal Masters of Art'.[67] These were bold claims to power. By 1755, launching his *General Magazine*, Martin reckoned theology was just 'a *science*' and its practitioners were surrogate experimenters.[68] Martin's anti-clericalism was invaluable in his struggle against supposed rivals and critics. He used the claim that experimental natural philosophy would take over the province of theology to argue that his enemies were morally as well as intellectually reprobate. Writers of the previous century who had proffered speculative sacred histories of the Earth, the staple of orthodox debate, were condemned as fantasists.[69] The right understanding of material power as divine assured the right judgement of the power vested in the lecturers themselves. This is how Martin treated the problem in his dialogues on electricity:

> *Euphrosyne*: On my word, Cleonicus, if you were to shew these Experiments in some Countries with a black Rod in your hand and a three-corner'd Cap, and a rusty furred Gown on, they would certainly take you for a Conjurer and believe you had the Art of dealing with the Devil . . .

Cleonicus: Ignorant people absurdly imagine that some things are above the power of Nature, that is, of God himself.[70]

Martin used his deism to indicate that those who refused to patronize the lecturers' products were no better than '*hominiform animals* or Creatures in the *Shape of Men*'.[71] His critics could easily throw these taunts back at him. They would argue that his lectures were mere accompaniments of corrupted luxury and consumption, and reject the claim to natural philosophical monopoly, and the electrical theories on which these claims rested. For protagonists such as Freke, therefore, the marketing of natural philosophy was itself a moral disaster.

'Plain, calm, business': a pietist form of life

Freke's *Essay on Electricity*, published in October 1746, could perhaps be read as a routine contribution to the London electrical debate. William Stukeley did so, as did the *Gentleman's Magazine*, which praised the *Essay* in fulsome terms.[72] The *Magazine* was less favourable to Martin's pugnacious reply of the following month, his *Remarks on a Rhapsody of Adventures of a Modern Knight-Errant in Philosophy*. Martin had allegedly 'done little more than retail some axioms which he found in Sir *Isaac's* writings. . . . The ungenteel manner in which he has treated Mr. *Freke*, without the least provocation . . . greatly exposes himself.'[73] Martin had 'exposed' himself to the attacks of a leading Tory figure of the London medical and literary scene. In his preface Martin observed satirically that 'when I considered the Force of an Honorary Title . . . I began to think of the hard fate of my Booksellers'. Freke countered that Martin had printed 'what I am sure no Gentleman would have written. . . . If this Person be poor, and did it for Gain, I heartily pity him.'[74] The hint that a vulgar man of trade was abusing his betters, and that an eminent metropolitan savant had here been dragged bathetically into the world of commerce, was central to the controversy. Judged as part of an action of *scandalum magnatum*, Freke's *Essay* would then become an apt target for Whig satire. It was treated thus in *Tom Jones* (1749), two passages of which referred to Freke's account of electrical fire. Fielding wittily contrasted the narrator's proper 'province, to relate facts', with Freke's grandiose scheme, 'of much higher genius', which sought causes in place of 'superstition'. He sniped at Freke's moralizing upon electricity, comparing the communication of fire 'through one person to many others' with the effect of a thorough beating upon domestic peace: 'as they both operate by friction it may be doubted whether there is not something analogous between them, of which Mr Freke would do well to enquire before he publishes the next edition of his book.'[75] The next edition appeared in 1752, the *Treatise on the Nature and Property of Fire*, which also included sections on muscular motion, vitality and magnetism. Both the *Essay* and the *Treatise* made the commercialization of electricity less self-evidently virtuous than it seemed to Martin and his allies. Martin and Freke were separated by a political and professional gulf. Martin depicted Freke as an eccentric Don Quixote, lost in the modern world of natural philosophical marketing. Freke depicted Martin as a 'country showman', crudely exploitative of divine power.[76]

If Freke's *Essay* were read as part of metropolitan electrical culture, his career could be seen as a conventional tale of a provincial surgeon made good. Born the son of a Dorset rector in 1689, Freke reached maturity in the stormy period of the South Sea Bubble and

Walpole's seizure of power. He was apprenticed to the surgeon Richard Blundell, married his master's daughter and inherited his trade.[77] In 1714, the year of Hanoverian succession and the 'providential' Whig triumph, Freke unsuccessfully tried for a surgeon's job at the Whig hospital St Thomas's. It was not until a decade later that he gained the post of assistant surgeon at Tory Bart's (Plate 24.6). The following summer he was made curator of the new museum, began practising lucrative lithotomies and by June 1727 had taken charge of eye operations, earning the not inconsiderable sum of 6s. 8d. for each couching.[78] Freke prospered. He made full surgeon and a Fellowship of the Royal Society in 1729. He discussed pneumatics with Halley, electricity with Watson and unlike Martin, won the patronage of Folkes, to whom he dedicated his *Essay*. He sent notes to the *Philosophical Transactions* on anatomical instruments and observations made at Bart's, and developed an improved obstetric forceps.[79] He attracted some skilful disciples, drew pointed criticism from the apothecaries and published an accessible text for surgical students, which argued for a principled curriculum to displace 'practise by Rote', and was dedicated to the governors of his hospital, which he was wealthy enough to endow in his will.[80] He had a cultivated taste in organ music and maintained an elegant house off Fleet Street at Salisbury Court. He was also one of the leaders of the surgeons' side in the secession from the Barber-Surgeons' Company in 1746–7, a break which led to the establishment of the new Company and the construction of a well-provided theatre near the Old Bailey.[81] Freke's allegiances marked out his status and his politics. His patients included some of the leading Tories and Jacobites of the period, such as the notoriously pro-Stuart MP, Sir Watkin Williams Wynn, head of the secret Cycle of the White Rose. Other contacts included Jacobites such as the surgeon and antiquary Francis Drake and the physician and wit John Byrom. Several members of Bart's were noted supporters of the Pretender.[82] When Freke resigned in 1755, he planned a retirement home at Bath: a 'great man' of Tory London, he marshalled potent resources against his opponent.[83]

Freke reckoned he could clinch the case against the marketing of electricity by bringing into the public domain the private, pietist resources he developed with his spiritual associates in the 1730s and 1740s. These friends included Law, Byrom and the printer and novelist Samuel Richardson. This tightly knit group drew on close readings of a corpus of enthusiast texts, distributed via their contact the fashionable physician George Cheyne. Notable amongst these works were those of Jakob Boehme, or 'Behmen' as he was then known. J. G. A. Pocock has speculated that after the works of Restoration Behmenists such as Samuel Pordage, 'Behmenist ideas persisted and may have been one medium of the underground radical tradition for which we all search hopefully': here, amongst the pietists and non-jurors, Behmenism helped overground Tories diagnose the ills of diseased Whig culture.[84] 'While you dwell in Babylonish state / Your next near neighbour (in the world's account) / May dwell upon thrice sacred Sion's mount', sang Pordage in his Behmenist epic. The key to Freke's position is his devotion to this kind of private *enthusiasm*. This involved the high evaluation of spirit in the moral world, of inner light as the path to salvation, of the private culture of meditation and reflection. Freke sought to expropriate electricity from public lecturers because then he could wed private piety and cultural critique. This alliance of quietism and protest hinged on an ontology of fire and spirit. Thus in his *Essay* he cited Law's important statement made six years earlier that 'all Life . . . is only a kindled Fire of Life in . . . a variety of states: and every dead insensitive Thing is only so because its Fire is quenched'. From the Interregnum onwards, devotees debated these Behmenist doctrines, of the descent of fire as the wrath of God, of the signatures of inner essences in their outward appearances, of the illuminist path. Amongst a polite society of commerce and performance, a form of enthusiasm which distinguished private reality from public illusion could act as a means of expressing 'inner exile', private dissociation from public corruption. Hence the importance of the reading groups and private distribution networks which sustained what Cheyne, in a letter to Richardson, called the 'Relish for spiritual and internal Religion'.[85]

Revulsion against modish natural theology and natural philosophy drew many along this pietist path. Freke's circle adhered to outward conformity and passive obedience to the established power. Three were Fellows of the Royal Society, and Richardson was, for a time, the printer of the *Philosophical Transactions*. Byrom summed up his attitude to the natural philosophers' meetings: 'I entered into the Society chiefly for the sake of meeting with gentlemen, whose company I took delight in. . . . I never so much as put the F.R.S. to my name.' The contrast with Martin's egregious ambitions to join the Society, so as to help his lecturing market, is salutary. But in their private world, the pietists urgently debated mystical religion and drew out its implications for public morals. Their coffee-house talks, devout correspondence and bedside consultations were secretive just because of the subjects they broached and the Behmenist account of proper conduct. Byrom's early *nom de plume* was 'John Shadow': 'I cannot talk of Christianity in a coffee house', he remarked in 1729, soon after meeting Law, 'Mr Law, and Christian religion . . . are mightily out of fashion at present . . . for it is a plain, calm business, and here people are, and love to be, all of a hurry, and to talk their philosophy'. In 1746 he versified his careful friendship: 'With Freedom may I speak? / Yes, to be sure, to R[ichardso]n or F[rek]e!'[86] Cheyne did not write to Law 'on some matters' since 'his letters would fall into the hands of his executors'. He recommended private catalogues of devout books, and told Richardson in 1742 to 'think of it, talk of it among the Brethren, look out proper Persons and let me see the Collections'. In the 1710s and 1720s, Cheyne already acted as a go-between in the chain of book distribution from Amsterdam and Scotland to the Fleet Street booksellers such as Paul Vaillant. In a culture which organized pressure groups and clubs on Masonic lines, it was characteristic that Byrom's campaign for his shorthand should be formed as a pseudo-Masonic society with Byrom as its 'Grand Master'.[87] The Jacobitism of many of this group also prompted secrecy. In August 1739, Byrom and Law talked in Somerset Gardens of their hopes for the current negotiations between Walpole and the Pretender. Law asked Byrom whether he feared the Pretender's coming: 'I said, No, not at all, and [Law] talked in his favour.' Law praised the character of the Old Pretender, but when Byrom revealed he had once met him, while a medical student in France in 1717, Law counselled caution: 'there should not be so much talk about such matters, that the time was not now, that he loved a man of taciturnity.' When Byrom was in Manchester in 1745, he preserved a studied pose in his attitude to the Pretender's arrival, despite (or because of) charges of active support for the rebels.[88]

The pietist group were of the same generation, acquiring place and repute in the 1720s. Law was a noted non-juring polemicist against Hoadly and Mandeville, and a private pietist, studying the *Theologia teutonica*. Byrom, like Law, left a Cambridge fellowship, and on his return from France engineered election to the Royal Society through his friends Jurin and Folkes. He patronized the Tory coffee houses, Child's and the Fountain Tavern. At the same time, Richardson established himself at Salisbury Square, where he was Freke's neighbour, and became known as a 'high flying' supporter of the opposition. He printed, and composed sections of, Wharton's fiercely anti-Walpole *True Briton*, and also published some of Law's early religious tracts.[89] The events of the late 1720s and early 1730s changed these prospects.

Walpole did not fall on George II's accession. A hotly contested election followed Hans Sloane's assumption of the Royal Society's presidency and his attempt to move a loyal address to the monarch. Byrom abandoned a medical career, or 'party slavery', as he called it, and led a campaign against the new President. Hitherto an eccentric protagonist of Newtonian physiology, Cheyne became ever more committed to spiritualist and soteriological natural philosophy, and to its programmatic application in *The English Malady* (1733). The relation between spiritualism and public culture was designedly complex in Cheyne's vision. He damned excessive enthusiasm – the traditional butt of sceptical diagnosis – but also pointed out the ills bred by the consuming passions of high society.[90]

The pietists defined a vulnerable place between raving prophecy and corrupt gentility. The dangers were graphically displayed in Hogarth's *Enthusiasm Delineated* (1739), which posed as a moderate attack on 'the Idolatrous Tendency', was temporarily suppressed for fear of ecclesiastical wrath and appeared two decades later in revised form as *Credulity, Superstition, and Fanaticism* (Plate 24.7). Freke's coterie·tried sympathetically to contrast their quietist devotion with the outward and visible enthusiasms of such public actors as the Camisard refugees, whose startling performances gripped London attention from 1706, or the equally dramatic 'convulsions' of Jansenists in Paris from 1727. 'Enthusiasm' must be mixed with 'temperance': such was Cheyne's prescription and the Behmenist form of life. In 1727, too, the leading Behmenist in England, Richard Roach, produced his messianic text *The Great Crisis*. Roach was the spiritual heir of the Philadelphian Society of the 1690s. Through him, links were forged between Pordage, the prophetess Jane Lead and new interpreters such as the remarkable Andreas Freher, whose wondrous diagrams of the Behmenist cosmos were obtained by Byrom and Law in their spiritual quest, and printed in the 1764–81 Boehme edition produced by Law's followers. This edition was a landmark in the propagation of Behmenist views in Britain; and Freher's diagrams were seen as a triumph of the engraver's art. William Blake, a devotee of the edition, reckoned they were the equal of Michelangelo.[91]

Propagation of these exemplary texts was crucial for the pietists. Law's 1729 *Serious Call to a Devout and Holy Life* distanced him irrevocably from the public Church and drew provisional admiration from Wesley and others. Law's handbook spelt out the social rank he expected of his readership: 'You are no labourer, or tradesman; you are neither merchant nor soldier, consider yourself therefore as placed in a state, in some degree like that of good angels, who are sent into the world as ministring spirits.' Where Martin reckoned electricity was an 'entertainment fit for angels', and thus that his polite audience could purchase enlightenment, Law drew a very different map of the path to celestial bliss. Influential Wesleyan contacts helped the distribution of these handbooks. Byrom also read the work and much of Boehme, and sought out Law at Gibbon's house in Putney.[92] This pietist milieu depended on a literary underground in improving devotional texts. Cheyne gave Law Poiret's visionary assault on John Locke, the *Fides et ratio collectae* (1708), whence Law was driven to study Boehme about 1735: 'he put me in a *perfect sweat*. . . . I followed the impulse with continual aspirations and prayer to God for his help and divine illumination.' Thence Law and Byrom were drawn into public controversy: Law against Tindal and the deists in 1731, Byrom against the Whig clique in Manchester, 'the Gothic enemies of liberty'.[93] Behmenist fervour prompted trouble with the Wesleyans, hitherto passionate admirers. Byrom and Wesley both read Law's first great Behmenist work, *The Grounds and Reasons of Christian Regeneration* (1739), but the latter found it 'philosophical, precarious, Behmenish, void and vain!'[94]

Cheyne, based in Bath, played a key role in this network. Byrom met him there in May 1738. Cheyne and Freke acted as Richardson's medical consultants, while after 1733 Richardson printed the bulk of 'my dear friend' Cheyne's works. Richardson also sent Cheyne books by Boehme and Law, convincing him that Law was 'the greatest, best man, and the most solid and deep of this island'. Cheyne responded with Poiret's works for 'the Brethren'. He reckoned such spiritual catechisms 'will not go far with meer Rationalists'.[95] The key texts of the early 1740s included Law's *Appeal to All that Doubt or Disbelieve the Truths of the Gospel* (1740), which contained his most eloquent exposition of the Behmenist doctrine of fire; Richardson's *Pamela* (1741), which was studied by Byrom and crucially discussed by Cheyne; and Cheyne's own *Natural Method of Curing the Diseases of the Body and the Diseases of the Mind Depending on the Body* (1742), in which it was argued that '*Man* is a diminutive *Angel*, shut up in a Flesh Prison or Vehicle', an image shared by Law and Boehme.[96] Cheyne sent a copy to Richardson, and to Byrom as a man 'conversant in the mysteries of the kingdom of heaven'. Byrom met Freke in summer 1742. Freke had read Law's *Appeal*, and was so impressed by it that he sought out Byrom at Richard's Coffee House in Fleet Street. Byrom reported that 'I took it for granted he came to rally me as a man of wit upon that article', but, to his astonishment, Freke revealed himself as a true disciple of Law. When Byrom asked whether Freke knew others, Freke introduced him at once to Richardson. They talked often of Law's 'admirable and unanswerable' book.[97]

During the 1740s, the regime ran into crisis and the hopes of the opposition rose. London street demonstrations presaged Walpole's fall in early 1742; the *London Magazine* demanded his execution and Tories rallied at the Fountain Tavern. At the Royal Society's favourite haunt, the Mitre in Fleet Street, the pietists now 'talked away upon Mr Law's principles', while Byrom canvassed his own 'natural philosophy that fire was light and spirit', a view drawn from Law's *Appeal*. After a chat with William Watson and Byrom, Freke suggested that Law should be prompted to answer Henry Dodwell's *Christianity Not Founded on Argument* (1742).[98] When Byrom carried this message to Law at King's Cliffe in Northamptonshire the following spring, they also discussed the possibility of versifying the *Appeal*. The traumas of the Old Corps' survival and the '45 disrupted these plans. The suppression of the Jacobite revolt prompted Byrom's verses on the 'Manchester martyrs' and the rebel lords: he tried unsuccessfully to make interest for these victims with contacts he had forged through the Royal Society, Folkes and Richmond amongst them.[99] So after Culloden the pietists worked closely together. In early 1746 Richardson showed drafts of *Clarissa* to Freke, whose *Essay on Electricity* cited Law and Richardson later in the year. Byrom wrote a long poem against the Bishop of London, borrowing heavily from Law's *Spirit of Prayer* (1749). Richardson reprinted it and the Bishop accused Freke of helping write it. In autumn 1751 Byrom finished his versification of Law's Behmenism. This poem, *Enthusiasm*, was planned with Law, printed by Richardson and proof-read by Freke. In spring 1752 Law himself released an open letter on Behmenist natural philosophy, the *Spirit of Love*: Freke published his own *Treatise* a few months later and sent it to Law for his comments.[100]

Law's model of fire was a central topic in the conversations between Freke and the pietists. Even when querying the details of Law's theory, Freke told Byrom that 'I pretend not to contradict him nor J[akob] B[oehme], for whom I feel myself obliged to think with the highest respect'. Law gave his approval of Freke's polemic in full measure:

The world is much obliged to you for that serious and good use which you alone have made of the phenomena of electricity which the wanton philosophy of unblessed erudition was only disposed to turn into show and juggling wonders. Reason and superficial art know no other use of divine discoveries.

Law damned Martin: he soothingly told Freke that 'it is an honour to you that you displease these pygmy philosophers'.[101] Thus while the London electrical community might read Freke's two tracts as contributions to public experimental philosophy, he directed his work at his pietist friends.

The knight errant versus the country showman

Freke's work contrasted with Martin's at every point. Electric fire was not due to active powers placed in matter by God. Instruments were not the key agents in manifesting power. Display was incapable of winning audiences to right religion. Commerce was illegitimate as a means of developing philosophy. Instead, electric fire was an emanation of the *Anima Mundi* and so comprehensible through knowledge of the soul alone.[102] When over-concentrated in any region, it would burst out with the force of God's wrath rather than His benevolence. This dual aspect of fire was a key tenet of Behmenist theory. Law stated in the *Appeal* that since the Fall, the spiritual Trinity had become materialized as fire, light and air (Plate 24.8). Contemplation of nature in its postlapsarian state was virtuous, but such meditation revealed that concealed within this outward and corporeal world was a divine and spiritual one. Fire was virtuous and vital when invisible, malignant when free and visible. Spiritual fire sought to return to its original celestial state. So, according to Law, the pious should attend to the aspect of fire which drew it back towards the divine, and not be distracted by its material form. In this world, 'fire may be separated from love, and then they are become an evil, they are wrath, and darkness, and all mischief'. In his *Spirit of Love* he amplified the argument: 'Fire does two Things; it alters the state of nature, and brings heaven into it.' The dual role of fire as destroyer and ennobler was a laboratory commonplace. It furnished arguments for a startling range of visionary cosmologies in the mid-eighteenth century, some of which developed appealing alternatives to court Whig natural philosophy. Amongst these were Berkeley's Tory account of spiritual fire in *Siris* (1744) and the remarkable *Original Theory of the Universe* (1750) of the Durham lecturer Thomas Wright. In the pietist version this became a warrant for discrimination between impious show and regenerate return to God. Study of nature was crucial, since 'fire has but one nature through the whole Universe'; but this study must be sensitive to the presence of Heaven and Hell in the material world. Freke reckoned Martin had entered an infernal world. Material fire, devoid of grace, was corrupt. When 'more of this fire' was 'crouded together, than was intended by the Authour of all Uniformity', it would be 'no Wonder, in this confined state . . . if that which would be gentle and beneficent, should with all the Power that belongs to it, break out at the first Door which is opened for its Passage from this tortur'd State'. Electrical trials demonstrated Law's claim that 'the same fire which is the majestic glory of Heaven makes the horror of Hell'.[103]

Thus there was no virtue in displaying fire. Freke boasted that 'I profess not to have been engaged in making Electrical Experiments'. The moral basis of electrical shows was removed. Such shows were so many 'Tricks like Ledgerdemain . . . performed by him whose time is little worth'.[104] Freke spelt out the link between the sacred character of hidden fire, 'relieving and comforting', and its corruption when used by lecturers for an audience, 'dividing and tearing things into Pieces'. Law helped sustain the moral message of the attack, because for the Behmenists the soul itself, 'a spark of the Deity', was the most obvious case of fire in its fallen state: 'it is a life that must burn for ever, either as a flame of light and love in the glory of divine majesty, or as a miserable firebrand in that God which is a consuming fire.'[105] The trickery of the electrical lecturers, 'miserable firebrands' to a man, was therefore a betrayal of their divine commission and a subversion of the order of disciplines:

> Is it not a great Disgrace to the Learned to employ this great Secret of Nature, which it pleased God to discover in our Days, to the low purposes of Dancing of Puppets, or beatifying themselves, and with such mean tricks to go on in content-ing themselves rather with the shew of it than seek into the Causes of its amazing Greatness?[106]

Freke matched this attack on the danger of commercial display with an alternative causal story about electrical phenomena. Electrical philosophy was boldly subjected to a vitalist physiology under the mastery of pietist students of the animal economy, not materialist peddlers of electrical machinery. His survey began by scotching the bases of the lecturers' ontology. Fire came from the chemical physicians' *air*, not from the lecturers' vaunted *engines*. To compare these machines with 'fire pumps', as Martin did, was as much as to say that 'Water is caused by Pumping'. By referring electrical fire to the air, Freke made electrical philosophy cognate with traditional pneumatic physiology. He cited the views of 'the most ancient and ablest Philosophers' that just as air was 'esteem'd the *Pabulum Vitae*', so, therefore, it contained fire as the '*Flamma Vitalis*'. Freke needed Behmenist hermeneutics to link his philosophy to this tradition. Boehme had argued that the spiritual world had become material so that 'the inward powers and virtues might have a form and image'. Conventional natural philosophy, which only dealt in outward forms, could therefore be appropriated for spiritual purposes, by abandoning the naturalism of the schools and the absurd empiricism of the moderns. The Lockean vocabulary deployed by Martin and his colleagues to connect low machine-minding with high philosophy was rejected. Behmenists followed their master in dividing outward powers into tendencies away from God, towards Him and an indifferent orbital motion. They used this doctrine of the threefold powers to reinterpret traditional chemistry and natural philosophy. Symes argued that Boehme 'writes in the style in which an electrician would express himself', and that contemplation of the electrical machine was 'only the means of making Visible to us what is hidden in Nature'. Freke, too, used these 'ancient' resources to make his aerial theory of electricity plausible: he reckoned that the powers of attraction and repulsion could be located in the fire held in the atmosphere.[107]

Freke's use of the moderns, especially Newton, was carefully judged. Newton was undenia-bly 'great', and (like Freke) had 'met with Opponents to several of his Theorys'. His admirers, like Watson, were certainly praiseworthy for their 'ingenuity' but their views were philosophically false and theologically unsound.[108] Freke's allies tried to deal with the problem of Newtonian hegemony in their assessment of the authority of the bearer of revealed truth. Freke's comparison of his own travails with those of Newton was designed to point out this trouble.[109] Law used Newton's reputation against Mandeville in 1723 and announced in 1740 that Newton was a secret Behmenist. The non-juror had been branded by the Tory poetaster Joseph Trapp as an enthusiast, who read Boehme 'with almost the same Veneration and implicit Faith that other People read the Scriptures'. Law replied that

Newton was another faithful reader of Boehme, that the basis of Newtonian planetary mechanics lay in Behmenist theories of the contractive, expansive and rotating powers of spirit in matter and that Newton kept all this secret because 'Sir Isaac well knew that Prejudice and Partiality had such Power over many People's Judgments'. Law stated that Trapp's ill-informed assault only proved the wisdom of Newton's caution.[110] In 1742 Cheyne and Byrom discussed Law's claim. Law cited authoritative witnesses that Newton's alchemy was Behmenist, and that Newtonian dynamics was thus confirmed in spiritual theology. He repeated these views in 1752: 'the illustrious Sir Isaac ploughed with Behmen's heifer.' Reaction was hostile: in the 1780s, the *Gentleman's Magazine* carried a debate between Behmenists and rationalists on the plausibility of Newton's involvement in alchemy, the absurd 'avaricious disposition' of such operators and the incredibility of Law's piety: 'Nor would any reasonable person kill a flea on dear Mr Law's word.'[111]

Even more serious than genteel satire was the rejection of Behmenist enthusiasm by many of the High Church, few of whom were likely to be impressed by a pietist Newton. For some, such as the ambitious and frustrated Hutchinsonians, Martin's deism was absurdly gran-diose, but Freke's pietism was dangerously enthusiast.[112] The Oxford young fogey George Horne satirized court Whig Newtonianism in 1751 by tracing its alleged identity with pagan naturalism. He used the arguments of the high Tory Hutchinson to demonstrate the bank-ruptcy of Newtonianism, and he denied that 'anything of Jehovah could appear from natural phenomena'.[113] This cut against lecturers and Behmenists alike. Horne studied Martin and went to Rackstrow's shows. He singled out Martin, 'that hominiform animal', as a 'turnspit' at Desaguliers' 'fine, raree, gallanty show'. He especially condemned Martin's doctrine of light and fire – he suggested that the loss of fire be recouped by taxing the 'self-irradiation' of the enlightened. Even if Freke and Horne agreed on the corruption of Whig philosophers, yet they differed profoundly on whether natural philosophy could ground religion.[114] Horne reckoned not. He read Law closely and decided that 'there seems to be a wonderful affinity between Quakerism and Behmenism'. He would have none of Law's deduction of moral truths from electric fire. He congratulated a colleague for having 'caught Freke tripping and got him in a cleft stick'.[115] Byrom and Richardson reacted in kind, condemning the Hutchinsonians for their extreme rationalism.[116] For the Hutchinsonians the division be-tween divine and mechanical powers was fundamental. The established Church was best defended through superior access to the texts of Scripture, not through an understanding of active principles in nature. 'The Scripture is clear and uniform in its language . . . but how different from all this is the style of J[akob] B[oehme]!' Horace Walpole described the Hutchinsonian strategy as one of 'etymological salvation'.[117] A difference of hermeneutics reflected a difference in Tory politics, between reasoned defence and pietist enthusiasm. Contests between the Hutchinsonians of the Hackney phalanx, and enthusiast Swedenborgians and Methodists, developed from this contrast.[118] These exchanges attested to the doctrines that authoritative spiritual knowledge was best kept secret, that the public sphere was often unworthy of revelation, and that private natural knowledge was best grounded in spiritual meditation. There was no fault in Newton's closet trials, but much danger in the direct communication of his secret discoveries.

Freke recognized that public natural philosophies were inevitably compromised and thus lacked authority. Unlike Watson, he was never 'the Dupe of that philosophical Gibberish of *nervous Fluid, Aether, &c.*'. Instead, he proposed that 'electricity' itself should be replaced by the term '*Vivacity*'.[119] Only with dead bodies, incapable of pulling on fire, could electrical phenomena become visible. Gross electricity was thus entirely due to electrics (insulators) like wax, resin and pitch, 'the excrements only from those Beings that once had life in them'.[120] When fire built up round such bodies breakdown occurred and sparks or forces would be manifest. So in Freke's vitalist 'Fire Statics', a salutary distribution of fire ordained by God could be perturbed by 'the Contrivance of Man . . . or the Disorders in the other Elements'.[121] The great division lay between a pious contemplation of God's occult power, 'a subject which can, with more Nobleness and Dignity employ the Mind of Man, than any I can think of relating to the sublunary Part of this World', and the commerce of the public lecturers who showed 'Bizarreries' drawn from 'excrements' for their own profit, 'to raise the astonishment it is wont to do in uninformed Minds'. In public lectures the powers which 'were intended, when in their due order, to make ev'rything happy and easy, in their disordered state create nothing but confusion'.[122] What Freke shared with Martin was ambition: in the *Essay* and the *Treatise* he extended his vitalist Fire Statics to include problems of life and medicine, meteorology and astronomy. In his surgical textbook Freke extended his vitalism to argue that the theory of air must be made part of the medical curriculum.[123] This effort to grab the territory of conventional electrical and medical philosophy centrally challenged the moral and intellectual propriety of the electrical shows. Martin, for one, took him as a violent, if idiotic, opponent of this commerce. He argued that Freke's performance was a suicidal collection of 'wild reveries' and that the lecturers were more competent, indeed monopolists, in electrical expertise. They, unlike Freke, knew that friction overcame electrical power, that it did not come from the air, and they understood how glass globe generators worked. Freke violated the rules of gentlemanly philosophy conspicuous on the lecture circuit: 'why must he dose other Folks with his Crudities and cram his *Excrements* down their Throats?'[124]

A comparison between the world and the stage

These debates centred on rival codes of piety, gentlemanliness and trade. Freke argued that 'the experimentalists' privileged the bizarre and the incomprehensible because wonders were lucrative, whereas the pious attitude privately searched for causes and related them to God's spirit. In contrast, Martin conceded that 'I should be glad to have a little more Money; yet Thanks to Heaven and Friends, I have no Necessity so great as to be guilty of any *mean or ungenerous Action* for Money'.[125] These alternatives raised the thorny issue of the performers' audience, and the means through which right morality could be communicated. Just as Freke condemned the exploitation of divine fire for gain upon the stage, saw Martin as a trickster and won Law's approval in so doing, so Law himself thundered in his *Unlawfulness of Stage-Entertainment* that plays were worse than idolatrous, and could not be defended as fictions. The theatre was 'a Place where all sorts of People meet to be entertain'd with Discourses, Actions and Representations; which are recommended to the Heart by beautiful Scenes, the Splendour of Lights and the Harmony of Musick'. Law made a political and a hermeneutic point: the genteel were as corrupted by shows as the plebs were by their bestial lives, and the scenes depicted on stage were taken as real and thus equivalent to murder and rape.[126] Law's critique was taken as covert Jacobitism by many of his readers. John Dennis pointed out the link between 'Jacobite Nonjuring Parsons' and the attack on the theatre. He reckoned that Law's overenthusiasm would give Freethinkers grounds for scorn; he charged that 'Mr Law would be very glad to exchange plays for Popery'. Another respondent recommended that Law be sent to Bedlam.[127] Richardson and Byrom also famously sought means of displacing the theatre in public esteem. Richardson penned tracts against the stage, and his *Clarissa*, a tale of redemption and salvation through spiritual and material fires, was touted as 'a dramatic narrative formed on [a] religious plan', and was designed to be consumed amongst the small groups of devout and devoted genteel. Pat Rogers has stressed the importance of the Bluestocking groups who avidly formed Richardson's ideal audience, and the efforts the author made to control the responses of these readers.[128] Richardson's own hostility applied equally to the stage of natural philosophy. In the spa at Tunbridge Wells he described the audience at the lectures of William Whiston, the notorious expositor of Newton's theological and natural philosophical views, as 'gay people, who, if they have white teeth, hear him with open mouths, though perhaps shut hearts'.[129]

This was, ultimately, the crucial lesson which the pietists wished to teach. Public entertainment could not satisfactorily convey moral experience, and the audience's hearts would always be shut. Pious authority was hard to establish. It seemed illusory if kept private, and dangerous if widely displayed. Fielding's brazen assaults on Richardson and Cheyne, and his anti-Jacobite additions to *Tom Jones* in 1747–8, dramatized the vulnerability of this devout pose to the satires of polite culture. The efficacy and propriety of the relation between entertainment and instruction was high on the agenda of the dispute with Fielding. In their discussions on the composition of *Clarissa*, Richardson told Cheyne that 'if we can properly mingle Instruction with Entertainment, so as to make the latter *seemingly* the *View*, while the former is *really* the End, I imagine it will be doing a great deal'.[130] Byrom made just this argument in his satire on Aaron Hill's *Art of Acting*. Hill was a well-known projector and hack, and a close admirer of Richardson, counselling him unsuccessfully to set *Clarissa* for the stage. In his *Art of Acting* (1746) he had briefly outlined a practical physiognomy for those who wished to fabricate emotions. Nothing was better calculated to irk Byrom. He sent Richardson his riposte: where *Clarissa* taught virtue 'without the help' of the theatrical muse, Hill had conjured a mechanics of the artificial soul. Byrom versified the absurd complaints of the theatrical performers against the successes of *Clarissa*'s moral therapy: 'what becomes of us / if prosing Fiction may distribute thus / all that is worth the Notice in a Play?'[131]

Both Richardson and his poetic admirer recognized the hard task in changing an idolatrous enterprise into a moral programme. Byrom's *Enthusiasm*, composed in the 1740s with the aid of Richardson, Law and Freke, sought to distinguish between 'right and wrong Enthusiasm', the former in the meditation of the pious, the latter as common in 'balls and masquerades; / courts, camps and 'changes' as 'cloisters or cells'. Byrom reckoned that 'popular hearsay and wretched compilers' were the enemies of the propagation of truth. But it was unclear that these salesmen could be circumvented. So *Clarissa*, for all its incendiary portrayal of a diabolical Mandevillean, was swiftly to be absorbed in the milieu of the market. Richardson often complained that his books got bought by readers keen to learn as much as they could of Lovelace's exciting deeds. By 1760 Londoners could purchase 'The New Impenetrable Secret; or Young Lady and Gentleman's Polite Puzzle', advertised as 'an entire new set of Entertaining Cards, neatly engraved on Copper-plates, consisting of moral and diverting sentiments', all extracted from Richardson's works. The cards, 'designed to amuse and entertain', sold for 6d., twice the price for a more elegant version, and at a cut-rate for schools. The world of spirit was evidently all too easy to engross amidst the world of goods.[132]

This made it easy for Martin to urge the moral rectitude of his natural philosophy by appealing to the familiar precedent of commercialized preaching, physic and anatomy:

> Who does the Knight mean by *those who shew Experiments for Money*? Do not the *chief Philosophers* in Christendom do this? Do not the *Chemists* and *Anatomists*, the *Physicians*, and *Divines* everywhere, *read lectures for money*? Are they for this reason to be stigmatiz'd with odious names of artful *Tricksters, Cheats*, and *Ledgerdemain-men*? If not then why are those who give *Lectures* in *Electricity* for *Money*?[133]

The barb was well-aimed. Freke's chosen profession of surgery was a spectacular node of the network of money and display. Links between anatomy lectures and public experiment were obvious: in the 1720s, Freke's opposite number at St Thomas's, the Whig surgeon William Cheselden, staged anatomy shows at Crane Court next to the Royal Society with the leading experimenter Francis Hauksbee. Cheselden touted such shows as 'chiefly intended for gentlemen', omitting anything 'neither instructive or entertaining'.[134] The legitimacy crisis of public surgery reached a climax in the later 1740s. Then William Hunter became one of the most celebrated of Freke's colleagues. He won power via relentless entrepreneurship, private enterprise teaching and clever manipulation of corpse supply. From 1747 his private school in the West End was the centre of the medical market-place. In 1756 he left the Company of Surgeons amidst furious controversy. From the 1750s on, with hospital expansion and the demands of war increasing, surgical demonstrations rapidly drew audiences away from the natural philosophers.[135]

Freke's place in this culture was significantly different. He staged the Tyburn anatomy which sparked the riot against the surgeons in 1749, disturbances which also prompted Fielding's magistral recommendation that executions would be more compelling if staged in private. Freke also figures as the presiding surgeon in Hogarth's celebrated *Reward of Cruelty* (1751), a scene set in the new theatre of the Surgeons' Company, where the ambiguities of judicial, theatrical and moral action are strikingly exploited (Plate 24.9). Freke plied his trade within his hospital and the Company, and was rewarded for it. Hogarth, a governor of Bart's, brilliantly hints in his depiction of the surgical execution on Tom Nero that here the brutal realities of surgical display were purportedly transformed into a theatre of moral reward and punishment.[136] Following the Tyburn riots, the establishment of the Surgeons' Company and the Murder Act of 1752, entrepreneurs began to exploit the market for surgery lectures. Publicly distant from this world of the resurrection men, Freke and his colleagues were integrated into the display of justice in exchange for the supply of bodies. The Bart's surgeons hired a house in Cock Lane, near the Hospital, to stage dissections of criminals: 'the executioner, coarsely dressed, entered with the body on his back and let it fall with a thud on the table, after which the President made a small incision over the sternum and bowed to the hangman.'[137] Freke's Hospital sat between Smithfield, an almost unparalleled zone of spectacle and squalor, the home of butchery and Bartholomew Fair, and Newgate, whence the Tyburn march began and where the bodies of the condemned returned.[138] His talk of 'excrements' and 'tricksters' must be put in this setting. The aim was to connect natural philosophical showmanship with the dregs of London culture, to discriminate between the moral theatre of the Surgeons' Hall where divinely validated wrath was visited upon the sinful, and the commercialized tricks of blasphemous lectures. The relation between Fielding and Freke and their work as magistrate and surgeon at Tyburn recalls the former's celebrated stress on the 'comparison between the world and the stage'. Fielding made much of the themes of deception and privacy: 'when we mention transactions behind the curtain, St James's is more likely to occur to our thoughts than Drury-Lane.' His analysis highlights the point that histrionics provided a common model for the interpretation of public commerce, and that this applied especially to the securing of knowledge of reality.[139]

Conclusion: political electricity

Many features of Georgian natural philosophy made its epistemic status dependent on the world of goods. Amongst them were the problems of credit and replicability. These troubles show the link between the knowledge embodied in the geographically separated sites of production and consumption, and the closure of scientific controversies. To secure matters of fact, natural philosophers needed means of assigning credit to controverted testimony. To assess these reports, they insisted upon their capacity adequately to repeat others' experiences. Both trust and replication were contingent on the social order of trade and commerce. Credit crises wracked eighteenth-century Britain, and the development of moveable property seemed to threaten conventions of honour. Thus the obsession with the fragility of trust in Defoe, Fielding and their contemporaries. This problem mattered acutely for a natural philosophy which aimed at communal agreement. Lewis Mumford observes that Baroque metropolitan culture tended 'to discredit local goods and give circulation to those in use at the capital'. Replication of experimental trials hinged on the distribution of standard equipment. Martin's off-the-shelf goods were a key to the reproduction of natural knowledge. Priestley's extensive commentaries on the range of electrical devices were a good way of charting this new world. Lecturers' travels welded local cultures and multiplied the contexts where facts could be made. Even so, individual visits such as that of Nollet to Italy, to scotch electromedical quackery, or Priestley's to Paris, to buy just the same chemicals as those used by his rival Lavoisier, were vital in the course of debate. Experimenters needed to know whom to trust, and they needed access to machines and protocols which were recognizably similar. Priestley often stressed 'the great difference between *seeing* and *reading*. I have not yet found any person, though ever so good a philosopher, and who has read my papers ever so carefully, but is surprised to see me actually make the experiments.' For his community, 'Martin's microscope', 'Smeaton's air pump' or 'Nairne's electrical machine' were terms well-understood by a wide community. Debate was sustainable between Philadelphia, Bath and Leipzig because of these immense and fragile distribution networks.[140] Hence the significance of the controversies between Martin and Freke. The market threatened moral order but helped controversies close by generating a standardized range of instruments, experiments and language with which to describe them. John Money rightly observes that in the natural philosophy lectures 'the distinction between serious instruction and popular entertainment was difficult to maintain'.[141] If this distinction broke down, so did the moral order of natural philosophy. To sustain this order practitioners needed enclosed communities where criteria of reliable credit could be sustained. This often hinged on face-to-face, highly personal encounters, whether in the credit clubs which developed during the radical political strife of the 1760s and 1770s, or the more egregious societies of virtuosi and experimenters, such as Shipley's new Society of Arts or the groups in Birmingham, Derby, Manchester and Newcastle.[142] Yet to make these communities' products matter throughout the world, it was necessary to distribute goods beyond these tight boundaries.

A fine image of the interconnection of these interested coteries within the national culture appeared in 1770, immediately after editions of Priestley's rationalist *History of Electricity* and the inauguration of his emancipatory campaigns, the crisis of Wilkes's Middlesex elections and North's assumption of power. This was a remarkable sheet entitled 'Political electricity'. The loathsome Lord Bute, in the persona of Franklin, was depicted as an electrical machine whence wires carried the active fluid throughout the British body politic. This baleful influence extended to the Cabinet, where ministers dined on the body of the British Lion; to medical consultations, where surgeons probed the corpse of a Wilkesite rioter; and to London docks, where the engines of trade and commerce lay still (Plate 24.10). The link between Bute and electrical machines was just: the King and his minister both evinced major interests in the instrument trade and amassed impressive collections of air pumps, electrical devices and 'philosophical tables'. The previous summer, gathered at Kew to observe the Transit of Venus, the court had entertained leading makers and astronomers. The management of instruments was equivalent to the manipulation of the worlds of politics and goods. Martin's comments about 'seeing in the dark what was invisible in the light' helped make electricity an apt theatrical model of a form of knowledge allegedly public but actually private, where backstage and frontstage became worryingly confused. John Brewer emphasizes that in the transformation of the relationship between state and civil society in the later eighteenth century, labels such as 'public knowledge' reflected 'a widely held desire to push out into the open knowledge and information previously arcane, obscure or private . . . the claim that a specific item of information was *public* knowledge was more often normative than descriptive'.[143] This moral about enclosure and disclosure can be completed by surveying the representation of electricity and commerce in Priestley's influential account of the roles of the natural philosopher, the instrument-maker and the patron.

Priestley redrew the map of electrical philosophy in the *History* which he composed at Warrington Academy in 1766–7 with the encouragement of his London allies, Canton, Watson, Franklin and Richard Price.[144] Good marketing was a key to his literary career. So was political networking: the 'Society of Honest Whigs' at St Paul's Coffee House helped him get access to metropolitan savants. His radical friends engineered election to the Royal Society in 1766 to help sales of the *History*. Priestley also formed a crucial connection with the great radical bookseller Joseph Johnson. The Londoners supplied Priestley with electrical literature, copies of Freke and Martin amongst them.[145] But in Priestley's Franklinist historiography, which displayed the progress of knowledge up to the Philadelphian's great triumph of 1747–50, Freke disappeared and Martin was visible solely as an instrument-maker. 'I made it a rule to myself . . . to take no notice of the mistakes, misapprehensions and altercations of electricians. . . . All the disputes which have no way contributed to the discovery of truth, I would gladly consign to eternal oblivion.'[146] Priestley's highly successful work, which ran to three substantial editions in six years, was accompanied by a cheaper booklet for amateurs, designed effectively to compete with the handbooks of Martin and his colleagues. This *Familiar Introduction to the Study of Electricity* carried advertisements for his own machines: 'he will himself particularly attend to the construction of these machines, and every improvement that hath occurred to him.' His customers were expected to draw the noblest possible conclusions from their homework. The *History* taught that natural philosophy was the truly progressive aspect of civil society, that natural philosophers were of a status higher than priests or magistrates, 'something greater and better than another man', and that philosophical materialism was the key to understanding power.[147]

Priestley described a newly authoritative role for such philosophers: they must be liberated from priestcraft and independent of the interests of commerce. A careful social chart was drawn. Priestley accepted that 'natural philosophy is a science which more especially requires the aid of wealth', but reckoned that 'princes will never do this great business to any purpose' and that 'the spirit of adventure seems to be wholly extinct in the present race of merchants'. So he proposed a series of 'small combinations' of natural philosophers which would be funded by a levy on the metropolitan institutions.[148] The scheme sat well with the contemporary dissenting political formation. By analogy with the Wilkesite and reformist groupings, Priestley's societies sought a new path for natural philosophical culture. Nor could dealers like Martin be relied upon for easy collaboration, even though, as noted above, Priestley was Martin's regular customer and bought a microscope from him in autumn 1767. As a maker himself, Priestley surveyed the current stock of electrical machines, picked fault with most, including those of Martin, and noted that while some 'admit of the experiments being made in a sitting posture, which is a great recommendation . . . to those persons who chuse to do things with little trouble, and who are fond of a studious, sedentary life', most were too fine for philosophy. He alleged that 'I was also instrumental in reviving the use of large electrical machines . . . the generality being little more than play things at the time that I began my experiments'. Makers could produce engines which were 'very elegant and portable', but they were liable to break, 'which electricians in general cannot easily repair, and I would wish philosophers to be as independent as possible of all workmen'.[149]

The thrust of Priestley's campaign was the establishment of an autonomous community of enlightened natural philosophers, 'in the middle ranks of life', capable of mounting an authoritative critique within civil society. Hence his notorious appeal of 1774 that 'the English hierarchy (if there be anything unsound in its constitution) has reason to tremble even at an air pump, or an electrical machine'.[150] Instrument-makers, booksellers and merchants were welcome allies in the cause. They often functioned as sponsors of his work, and that of the societies which he helped promote. But their varying expertise did not entitle them to philosophical status as such:

> The slowness and blunders of mechanics do but ill suit with the ardour of persons engaged in philosophical inquiries. It were much to be wished, that philosophers would attend more than they do to the construction of their own machines. We might then expect to see some real and capital improvements in them; whereas little can be expected from mere mathematical instrument makers; who are seldom men of any science, and whose sole aim is to make their goods elegant and portable.[151]

Doubtless the vocabulary of 'ardour', 'independence' and 'improvement' was integral to the politics of rational dissent. But the criticism of the interested, local concerns of makers and entrepreneurs was to be tempered with the recognition that luxury and commerce were prime movers of natural philosophy. Unsurprisingly, this recognition grew in step with the number of Priestley's patrons from the 1770s. Entrepreneurs, such as Wedgwood, began supplying equipment, finance and philosophical community. In 1776 Wedgwood set out to render 'Doctr. Priestley's very ingenious experiments more extensively useful'. Alongside this balance between commerce and independence, Priestley moved carefully between the argument that experimental philosophy taught piety, because it materialized God's powers, and utility, because his clients could benefit from practical devices. Indeed, he announced his isolation of dephlogisticated air in 1775 as a significant marketing opportunity for aerating rooms and restoring the sick and Wedgwood picked up the hint. Priestley guessed that 'in time, this pure air may become a fashionable article in luxury. Hitherto only two mice and myself have had the privilege of breathing it.'[152]

The controversies described in this chapter brought before the public a fundamental trouble of the relation between the natural world and the world of goods. Natural philosophers were unwilling to credit the knowledge of instrument-makers and showmen, nor were they prepared to submit to the supervision of the pious. Late eighteenth-century proposals aimed to define natural philosophical authority. Some, such as Priestley's radical follower Adam Walker, lectured in London in the 1790s that the natural philosopher 'should shew that the foundation of morality is in the constitution of things'. And things constituted an alternative to culture: the audience 'may judge between Nature's works, and the extraneous systems of art and police'.[153] Doubtless this judgement was accompanied by the rationalization which many have noted in the development of eighteenth-century commercial discourse: consider Simon Schama's comparison of Dutch representations of beached whales, providential emblems in the early 1600s but naturalistic descriptions in the later period, or William Reddy's comparison of virtuoso connoisseurship in early eighteenth-century French trade dictionaries with the reasoned interest in production techniques of post-revolutionary texts.[154] 'Rationalization' carried its own values. The claim that what natural philosophy could represent was uncontaminated by culture was henceforth to be a powerful normative theme. It was bolstered by a division of labour between technicians and philosophers, and a boundary between science and its milieux. Neither of these demarcations was secure. Sceptics remained unconvinced by the natural philosophers' claims that they had escaped from culture to nature. William Blake, a careful reader of Boehme and of Newton, made the point quite brutally. In his annotations on a Tory version of the Lord's Prayer, he observed simply that 'we call nature whatever cannot be taxed'.[155]

Notes

I gratefully acknowledge permission from the British Library to reproduce manuscripts and prints. I have also received very generous help from Adrian Wilson and Tim Underhill.

1 Benjamin Martin, *The Young Gentleman and Lady's Philosophy*, vol. 1 (London, 1759), 301.

2 Mary Douglas and Baron Isherwood, *The World of Goods: Towards an Anthropology of Consumption* (Harmondsworth: Penguin Books, 1980), 73. Compare Fernand Braudel, *Civilization and Capitalism 15th–18th Century*, 3 vols (London: Fontana, 1982), vol. 1, 323–4:

> Can it have been merely by coincidence that the future was to belong to the societies fickle enough to care about changing the colours, materials and shapes of costume, as well as the social order and the map of the world? . . . Fashion is also a search for a new language to discredit the old.

3 J. H. Plumb, 'Commercialization and society', in Neil McKendrick, John Brewer and J. H. Plumb, *The Birth of a Consumer Society: The Commercialization of Eighteenth-Century England* (London: Hutchinson, 1983), 265–334, 329. For public lectures, see Simon Schaffer, 'Natural philosophy and public spectacle in the eighteenth century', *History of Science*, xxi (1983), 1–43. For lectures and utility, Ian Inkster, 'Aspects of the history of science and science culture in Britain, 1780–1850 and

beyond', in Ian Inkster and Jack Morrell (eds), *Metropolis and Province: Science in British Culture 1780–1850* (London: Hutchinson, 1983), 11–54.

4 Roy Porter, 'Science, provincial culture and public opinion in Enlightenment England', *British Journal for Eighteenth-Century Studies*, iii (1980), 20–46; Larry Stewart, 'Public lectures and private patronage in Newtonian England', *Isis*, lxxvii (1986), 47–58; Jan Golinski, 'Utility and audience in eighteenth-century chemistry: case studies of William Cullen and Joseph Priestley', *British Journal for the History of Science*, lxviii (1988), 1–32.

5 Walpole to Mann, 19 May 1750, *Letters of Horace Walpole*, ed. P. Cunningham, 8 vols (London: Richard Bentley, 1857) vol. 2, 207 and idem, 11 March 1750, ibid., 198. For the London earthquakes see T. D. Kendrick, *The Lisbon Earthquake* (London: Methuen, 1956), 20; G. S. Rousseau, 'The London earthquakes of 1750', *Cahiers d'histoire mondiale*, xi (1968), 436–51.

6 Walpole to Mann, 19 May 1750, *Letters*, 207. For electrical models of earthquakes, see Frances Willmoth, 'John Flamsteed's letter concerning the natural causes of earthquakes', *Annals of Science*, xliv (1987), 23–70, 67–9.

7 [Albrecht von Haller], 'An historical account of the wonderful discoveries made in Germany &c. concerning electricity', *Gentleman's Magazine*, xv (April 1745), 193–7, 194. For the attribution of this report, see J. L. Heilbron, 'Franklin, Haller and Franklinist history', *Isis*, lxviii (1977), 539–49. The phrase is from the title of John Neale, *Directions for Gentlemen who have Electrical Machines* (London, 1747). English market leadership is documented in Maurice Daumas, *Scientific Instruments of the 17th and 18th Centuries and their Makers* (London: Portman, 1989), 228–45.

8 Lectures in the Midlands are described in A. E. Musson and E. Robinson, *Science and Technology in the Industrial Revolution* (Manchester: Manchester University Press, 1969), 381–2; J. T. Heilbron, *Electricity in the 17th and 18th Centuries* (Berkeley: University of California Press, 1979), 294; John Money, *Experience and Identity: Birmingham and the West Midlands 1760–1800* (Manchester: Manchester University Press, 1977), 131.

9 Cromwell Mortimer, 'A letter concerning the natural heat of animals', *Philosophical Transactions*, xliii (June 1745), 473–80, 479.

10 Daniel Stephenson, 'Seventeen electrical experiments for a gentleman to perform with plants and animals', *Gentleman's Magazine*, xvii (March 1747), 140–1; compare Henry Baker, 'A letter . . . concerning several medical experiments of electricity', *Philosophical Transactions*, xlv (1748), 270–5.

11 William Stukeley, 'The philosophy of earthquakes', *Philosophical Transactions*, xlvi (1750), 731–50; Richard Lovett, *The Electrical Philosopher* (Worcester, 1774); Richard Symes, *Fire Analysed* (Bristol, 1771), 46. For the pietist milieu of Lovett, Symes and electrical therapists, see Jonathan Barry, 'Piety and the patient: medicine and religion in eighteenth-century Bristol', in Roy Porter (ed.), *Patients and Practitioners: Lay Perceptions of Medicine in Pre-industrial Society* (Cambridge: Cambridge University Press, 1985), 145–75, 154–7.

12 Joseph Priestley, *History of Electricity*, 2 vols, 3rd edn (London, 1775), vol. 2, 134.

13 For Priestley's natural philosophy and commerce, see Simon Schaffer, 'Scientific instruments and their public', in J. A. Bennett (ed.), *Science and Profit in Eighteenth-Century London* (Cambridge: Whipple Museum, 1985), 10–18, 12; Golinski, 'Utility and audience', 17–19.

14 Priestley to John Canton, quoted in Schaffer, 'Scientific instruments', 12.

15 John R. Millburn, *Benjamin Martin: Author, Instrument-maker and 'Country-showman'* (Leyden: Noordhoff, 1976), 219–22, reprints Martin's 1762 catalogue.

16 John Smeaton to Benjamin Wilson, 24 September 1746, British Library MSS ADD 30094 f. 22. For the coffee house and the market see Stewart, 'Public lectures and private patronage'; for the coffee house and politics, see John Money, 'Taverns, coffee-houses and clubs: local politics and popular articulacy in the Birmingham area in the age of the American Revolution', *Historical Journal*, xiv (1971), 15–47; John Brewer, *Party Ideology and Popular Politics at the Accession of George III* (Cambridge: Cambridge University Press, 1976), 148–50.

17 For large workshops see Daumas, *Scientific Instruments*, 237. For Baker and Canton see Baker to Bruni, 31 August 1747, in G. l'E. Turner, 'Henry Baker F.R.S.', *Notes and Records of the Royal Society*, xxix (1974), 53–79, 64; Macclesfield to Canton, 9 July 1751, Royal Society Library MSS Canton II, 19.

18 For Warltire see N. G. Coley, 'John Warltire, itinerant lecturer and chemist', *West Midlands Studies*, iii (1969), 31–44; for Martin see John R. Millburn, *Benjamin Martin: Supplement* (London: Vade-Mecum, 1986), 9–13.

19 Benjamin Martin, *A Supplement Containing Remarks on a Rhapsody of Adventures of a Modern Knight-Errant in Philosophy* (Bath, 1746), 28–9n.

20 Baker to Miles, 29 April 1745, in Willem Hackmann, *Electricity from Glass* (Leyden: Noordhoff, 1978), 104–5.

21 For the natural philosophical place, see Owen Hannaway, 'Laboratory design and the aim of science', *Isis*, lxxvii (1986), 585–610; Steven Shapin, 'The house of experiment in seventeenth-century England', *Isis*, lxxix (1988), 373–404.

22 Adam Smith, *Essays on Philosophical Subjects*, ed. W. P. D. Wightman and J. C. Bryce (Oxford: Clarendon Press, 1980), 107, 42; E. J. Kearns, *Ideas in Seventeenth-Century France* (New York: Columbia University Press, 1979), 161–76. Compare Braudel, *Civilization and Capitalism*, vol. 2, 491–3; Jean-Christophe Agnew, *Worlds Apart: the Market and the Theater in Anglo-American Thought, 1550–1750* (Cambridge: Cambridge University Press, 1986), 177–88.

23 E. P. Thompson, 'Eighteenth-century English society: class struggle without class?', *Social History*, iii (1978), 133–65, 159 and idem, 'Patrician society, plebeian culture', *Journal of Social History*, vii (1974), 382–405; John Brewer, 'Theater and counter-theater in Georgian politics: the mock elections at Garrat', *Radical History Review*, xxii (1979–80), 7–40, 34.

24 For Law's attack, see A. Keith Walker, *William Law: His Life and Thought* (London: SPCK, 1973), 41–6; for Richardson, A. D. Mackillop, 'Richardson's early writings: another pamphlet', *Journal of English and German Philology*, liii (1954), 72–5. Compare Michael Foss: *The Age of Patronage: The Arts in England 1660–1750* (Ithaca: Cornell University Press, 1972), 104–9.

25 Jean-Georges Noverre, *Lettres sur la danse* (1760), 285–6, in Marian Hobson, *The Object of Art: The Theory of Illusion in Eighteenth-Century France* (Cambridge: Cambridge University Press, 1982), 196; Garrick in Earl R. Wasserman, 'The sympathetic imagination in eighteenth-century theories of acting', *Journal of English and Germanic Philology*, xlvi (1947), 265–72, 268.

26 Benjamin Martin, *The Young Gentleman and Lady's Philosophy*, 2 vols, 2nd edn (London, 1772), vol. 1, 319.

27 ibid. Compare Neil McKendrick, 'Commercialization and the economy', in Neil McKendrick, John Brewer and J. H. Plumb, *Birth of a Consumer Society*, 7–194, 146–94.

28 Benjamin Martin, *The Young Gentleman and Lady's Philosophy*, 3 vols, 3rd edn (London, 1781), vol. 3, 261. For Wesleyan electrotherapy and the establishment of a network of London electrical clinics, see John Wesley, *The Journal*, 8 vols, ed. Nehemiah Curnock (London: Charles Kelly, 1909–16), vol. 4, 190 (9 November 1756); A. W. Hill, *John Wesley Among the Physicians* (London: Epworth, 1958); Francis Schiller, 'Wesley, Marat and their electric fire', *Clio medica*, xv (1981), 159–76; John Cule, 'The Rev. John Wesley: "The naked empiricist" and orthodox medicine', *Journal of the History of Medicine*, xlv (1990), 41–63.

29 Benjamin Rackstrow, *Miscellaneous Observations, Together with a Collection of Experiments on Electricity*, (London, 1748), iii; John Freke, *Essay to Shew the Cause of Electricity*, 1st edn (London, 1746), vi.

30 [Haller], 'An historical account', 194–5, 197; R. W. Home, 'Electricity and the nervous fluid', *Journal of the History of Biology*, iii (1970), 235–51.

31 William Watson, 'A letter', *Philosophical Transactions*, xlvi (1749–50), 348–56; Rackstrow, *Miscellaneous Observations*, 49–50.

32 Reports in *Gentleman's Magazine*, xvi (1746), 163, 355–6, 371–4 and 'An abstract of Nollet's Essay

on the Electricity of Bodies', *Universal Magazine*, i (1747), 119–21, 229–30, 265–7. For reports from France see P. Lemonnier, 'Extract of a memoir concerning the communication of electricity', *Philosophical Transactions*, xliv (1746), 290–5, 293–4; J. Turbervill Needham, 'Extract of a letter concerning some new electrical experiments lately made at Paris', ibid., 247–63, 256–8.

33 John Freke, 'Abstract of an essay to shew the cause of electricity', *Gentleman's Magazine*, xvi (October 1746), 521–2; idem, 'Letter on the further discoveries in electricity', *Gentleman's Magazine*, xvi (November 1746), 567–70; idem, 'Substance of an essay to shew the cause of electricity', *London Magazine*, xv (November 1746), 573–6.

34 For Watson's status as electrical philosopher, see Hackmann, *Electricity from Glass*, 109–10; Heilbron, *Electricity*, 296–301; William Watson, 'A sequel to the experiments and observations tending to illustrate the nature and properties of electricity', *Philosophical Transactions*, xliv (1747), 704–49.

35 *Gentleman's Magazine*, xvi (July 1746), 366; Freke, *Essay of Electricity*, 1.

36 William Watson, 'A collection of the electrical experiments communicated to the Royal Society', *Philosophical Transactions*, xlv (1748), 49–92.

37 Bryan Robinson, *Dissertation on the Aether of Sir Isaac Newton* (Dublin, 1743); idem, *Sir Isaac Newton's Account of the Aether* (Dublin, 1745); discussed in R. E. Schofield, *Mechanism and Materialism: British Natural Philosophy in an Age of Reason* (Princeton: Princeton University Press, 1969), 108–14. For Watson's coinage see Watson, 'A sequel', 729.

38 Arnold Thackray, *Atoms and Powers* (Cambridge: Cambridge University Press, 1970), 139; Herbert Randolph, *Life of Sir General Robert Wilson*, 2 vols (London, 1862), vol. 1, 8–10; Robinson to Wilson 1746, British Library MSS ADD 30094 f. 23.

39 Rackstrow, *Miscellaneous Observations*, 56; Priestley, *History of Electricity*, 3rd edn, vol. 2, 136; Collinson to Colden, March 1745, in I. B. Cohen, *Franklin and Newton* (Philadelphia: American Philosophical Society, 1956), 435.

40 Watson, 'A sequel', 706 (globes); 709 (Leyden jar); 716 (floor); 729 (atmosphere); 744 (fire pumps); 728 (heart).

41 Watson, 'A sequel', 745–6, 713.

42 William Watson, 'An account of Mr Benjamin Franklin's Treatise', *Philosophical Transactions*, xlvii (1751–2), 202–11; for Wilson versus Watson see Heilbron, *Electricity*, 299 n.44.

43 Freke, *Essay of Electricity*, 2; Martin, *Supplement on a Rhapsody of Adventures*, 33–8; Rackstrow, *Miscellaneous Observations*, 11–18.

44 For Martin's prices see Millburn, *Martin*, 223 and idem, *Martin: Supplement*, 49–50.

45 Millburn, *Martin: Supplement*, 10–12, 31.

46 Comments on Martin by Paine in Brian Simon, *Radical Tradition in Education in Britain* (London: Lawrence & Wishart, 1972), 50; by Priestley, *History of Electricity*, 2nd edn (London, 1769), 498 and compare Millburn, *Martin: Supplement*, 44–5; by Bernoulli in Daumas, *Scientific Instruments*, 239: 'his shop is one of the best equipped, and his courses are well attended . . . they are made doubly interesting by the beautiful instruments.'

47 For satires see Millburn, *Martin: Supplement*, 27–9; Craig B. Waff, 'Comet Halley's first expected return: English public apprehensions, 1755–58', *Journal for the History of Astronomy*, xvii (1986), 1–37, 25.

48 [Thomas Seccombe], 'Charles Lennox, second Duke of Richmond', *Dictionary of National Biography*, vol. 11, 922; John Millburn, 'Benjamin Martin and the Royal Society', *Notes and Records of the Royal Society*, xxviii (1979), 15–23.

49 Millburn, 'Martin and the Royal Society', 17–18.

50 For Hill, see G. S. Rousseau, 'John Hill: universal genius manqué', in J. A. Leo Lemay and G. S. Rousseau, *The Renaissance Man in the Eighteenth Century* (Los Angeles: William Andrews Clark Library, 1978); Hill to Watson 27 October 1746 in G. S. Rousseau (ed.), *Letters and Papers of Sir John Hill* (New York: AMS Press, 1982), 28–31.

51 Alexander Pope, *The Dunciad in Four Books* (London, 1742–3), book IV 1. 570; for Fleet Street and the hacks see Pat Rogers, *Grub Street: Studies in a Subculture* (London: Methuen, 1972), 153–4.

52 Benjamin Martin, *A New and Compleat Course of Experimental Philosophy* (1743/6 ?), cited in Millburn, *Martin*, 47–8.

53 On Martin and Newbery see Millburn, *Martin*, 40, 45–7; idem, *Martin: Supplement*, 13; William Noblett, 'John Newbery: publisher extraordinary', *History Today*, xxii (1972), 265–71; J. H. Plumb, 'Commercialization in society', in McKendrick, Brewer and Plumb, *Birth of Consumer Society*, 272–3, 301–3; James A. Secord, 'Newton in the nursery: Tom Telescope and the philosophy of tops and balls, 1761–1838', *History of Science*, xxiii (1985), 127–51.

54 Martin's advertisement at Bath, 1744, in Millburn, *Martin*, 51; Benjamin Martin, *Philosophia Britannica*, 2 vols (Reading, 1747), vol. 1, preface, sig. 4ʳ.

55 Benjamin Martin, *A Panegyrick on the Newtonian Philosophy* (London, 1749), 54.

56 Benjamin Martin, *An Essay on Electricity* (Bath, 1746), 5.

57 Martin, *Supplement on a Rhapsody of Adventures*, 35–7, cf. Martin, *Essay on Electricity*, 9.

58 Martin, *Essay on Electricity*, 22–9.

59 Martin, *Philosophia Britannica*, preface, vol. 1, sig. a2ᵛ; Martin, *Supplement on a Rhapsody of Adventures*, 37.

60 Martin, *Young Gentleman and Lady's Philosophy*, 1st edn, vol. 1 (1759), 326.

61 Martin, *Philosophia Britannica*, vol. 1, preface, sig. a4ᵛ; Martin, *Essay on Electricity*, 19.

62 Martin, *A Panegyrick*, 14–15, 20–2, 25, 35.

63 ibid., 46–8.

64 Martin, *Philosophia Britannica*, vol. 1, 34 n.3. For electric astronomy, see Stephen Gray, 'Letter concerning the Revolutions which small pendulous bodies will by electricity make round larger ones', *Philosophical Transactions*, xxxix (1736), 220; 'Account of some electrical experiments intended to be communicated to the Royal Society by Stephen Gray', ibid., 400–3; idem, 'Account of some of the electrical experiments made by Granvil Wheler at the Royal Society's house', *Philosophical Transactions*, xli (1739–41), 112–17; Granvil Wheler, 'Remarks on the late Stephen Gray his electrical circular experiment', ibid., 118–25.

65 For planetaria see Millburn, *Martin*, 96–8: Bernoulli saw Martin's vast 'celestial panorama' of the transits of Venus (Daumas, *Scientific Instruments*, 239).

66 Martin, *A Panegyrick*, 51–2.

67 ibid., 55.

68 Millburn discusses Martin's treatment 'Of Theology as a Science' in *Martin*, 77–8. Martin's *Philosophical Grammar* (London, 1735) was attacked as irreligious by the Somerset divine John Boswell, *A Method of Study* (London, 1738), 320–34: 'the Author has gone out of his way to corrupt the Principles of his Readers [and] to disparage the Authority of the Sacred History' (333).

69 Martin, *A Panegyrick*, 61, 58; idem, *Philosophical Grammar*, 21.

70 Martin, *Young Gentleman and Lady's Philosophy*, vol. 1, 2nd edn, 311.

71 Martin, *A Panegyrick*, 11–12.

72 'An abstract of an essay to shew the cause of electricity', *Gentleman's Magazine*, xvi (October 1746), 521–2; William Stukeley, *Family memoirs*, ed. W. C. Lukis, vol. 2, Publications of the Surtees Society, lxxvi (1883), 378 (December 1752). Wesley also knew of Freke: see Robert E. Schofield, 'John Wesley and science in eighteenth-century England,' *Isis*, xliv (1953), 331–40, 335.

73 'Letter on the further discoveries in electricity', *Gentleman's Magazine*, xvi (November 1746), 557–68, 567.

74 Martin, *Essay on Electricity*, preface, 3–4; John Freke, *Treatise on the Nature and Property of Fire* (London, 1752), 140.

75 For *scandalum magnatum* (legal recourse by nobles in defence of their honour against inferiors'

slander) and its relation with epistemology, see Michael McKeon, *The Origins of the English Novel* (London: Radius Hutchinson, 1988), 151–2. Fielding names Freke in *Tom Jones* (Harmondsworth: Penguin Books, 1966), book 2, ch. 4, 95 and book 4, ch. 9, 179.

76 Freke, *Treatise*, 140–2.

77 John Freke, *Essay on the Art of Healing* (London, 1748), viii; Norman Moore, *The History of St Bartholomew's Hospital*, 2 vols (Pearson: London, 1918), vol. 2, 633–6.

78 Zachary Cope, *William Cheselden* (Edinburgh: Livingstone, 1953), 9; Moore, *History of St Bartholomew's*, vol. 2, 361; V. C. Medvei and J. L. Thornton, *The Royal Hospital of St. Bartholomew* (London: St Bartholomew's, 1974), 210; 'Petition to perform lithotomies', British Library MSS Sloane 4076 f. 171.

79 Freke, *Essay of Electricity*, iv, 2, 21; Freke, 'A case of extraordinary exostoses on the back of a boy', *Philosophical Transactions*, xli (1736), 369–70, and 'Description of an instrument for reducing a dislocated shoulder', *Philosophical Transactions*, xlii (1743), 556–9.

80 Freke, *Art of Healing*, vii; Moore, *History of St Bartholomew's*, vol. 2, 636, 367. For the apothecaries, see *A letter from an apothecary in London to his friend in the country concerning the present practice of physick . . . with remarks on Dr Mead's, Mr Freke's and Mr Cheselden's method of cure for the itch, by externals only* (London, 1752).

81 Sidney Young, *Annals of the Barber Surgeons of London* (London: Blades, East & Blades, 1890), 155; Jessie Dobson and R. Milnes Walker, *Barbers and Barber Surgeons of London* (Oxford: Blackwell, 1979), 59.

82 John Byrom, *Private Journal and Literary Remains*, ed. R. Parkinson, 2 vols in 4 parts, *Chetham Society Remains*, vols 32, 34, 40, 44 (Manchester: Chetham Society, 1854–7), vol. 2, 442, 453. Freke subscribed to Drake's *Eboracum* (1736). For Wynn's Jacobitism see Eveline Cruickshanks, *Political Untouchables: The Tories and the '45* (London: Duckworth, 1979), 19–20; Linda Colley, *In Defiance of Oligarchy: The Tory Party 1714–60* (Cambridge: Cambridge University Press, 1982), 76–7.

83 Freke is described (ironically) as 'a great man' in Byrom, *Journal and Remains*, vol. 2, 559.

84 J. G. A. Pocock, 'No room for the righteous', *Times Literary Supplement* (28 December 1984), 1494, on Christopher Hill, *The Experience of Defeat: Milton and Some Contemporaries* (Harmondsworth: Penguin Books, 1985), 227–42. For the Behmenist tradition in England, see S. Hutin, *Les Disciples anglais de Jacob Boehme aux xviie et xviiie siècles* (Paris, 1960), 39; J. F. C. Harrison, *The Second Coming: Popular Millenarianism 1780–1850* (London: Routledge, 1979), 19–23; Keith Thomas, *Religion and the Decline of Magic* (Harmondsworth: Penguin Books, 1971), 446–8; Christopher Hill, *Milton and the English Revolution* (London: Faber & Faber, 1977), 328–30.

85 Samuel Pordage, *Mundorum explicatio* (London, 1661), 30, in Hill, *Experience of Defeat*, 229. William Law, 'Appeal to all who doubt the Truths of the Gospel', in idem, *Works*, ed. G. Moreton, 9 vols (privately reprinted: Brockenhurst and Canterbury, 1892–3), vol. 4, 132 is cited in Freke, *Essay of Electricity*, 14 and also in Symes, *Fire Analysed*, 26. Law's flint image is from ibid., vol. 6, 89. For spiritual religion, see Cheyne to Richardson, 30 June 1742, in Charles F. Mullett (ed.), *Letters of George Cheyne to Samuel Richardson 1733–1743* (Columbia: University of Missouri, 1943), 102.

86 For Richardson as the Royal Society's printer, see William M. Sale, *Samuel Richardson: Master Printer* (Ithaca: Cornell University Press, 1950), 73. For Byrom and the Royal Society, see Byrom, *Journal and Remains*, vol. 2, 307–8; T. E. Allibone, 'The diaries of John Byrom and their relation to the prehistory of the Royal Society Club', *Notes and Records of the Royal Society*, xx (1965), 162–83. Byrom's pseudonym is discussed in Henri Talon, *John Byrom: Selections* (London: Rockliff, 1950), 3; coffee-house Christianity in Byrom, *Journal and Remains*, vol. 1, 329; reference to 'Richardson and Freke', in Byrom, 'The art of acting', in *Poems*, ed. A. W. Ward, 2 vols in 4 parts, *Chetham Society Remains*, vols 29, 30, 34, 35 (Manchester: Chetham Society, 1894–6), vol. 1, 260.

87 Cheyne and Law, 30 May 1743, in Byrom, *Journal and Remains*, vol. 2, 363; Cheyne to Richardson, 17 September 1742, in Mullett, *Letters*, 112. For the pietist book network, see G. D. Henderson, *Mystics of the North-east* (Aberdeen: Third Spalding Club, 1934), 60–1, and James Keith to Lord

Deskford, 1 May 1722, 177; Stephen Hobhouse, *Selected Mystical Writings of William Law* (London: Rockliff, 1948), 382; G. S. Rousseau, 'Mysticism and millenarianism: "Immortal Dr Cheyne"', in Ingrid Merkel and Allen G. Debus (eds), *Hermeticism and the Renaissance* (Washington, DC: Folger Books, 1988), 192–230, 205, 225 n.63. For Byrom's shorthand, see Talon, *Byrom*, 7–10, 84–92. In May 1727, Byrom wrote that 'If Liberty leave the Royal Society, 'tis confidently asserted that she will retire to the Shorthand one': *Journal and Remains*, vol. 1, 260. For clubs, see John Brewer, 'Commercialization in politics', in McKendrick, Brewer and Plumb, *Birth of a Consumer Society*, 197–262, 217–29; for Masons and the Royal Society, see M. C. Jacob, *The Radical Enlightenment* (London: Allen & Unwin, 1981), 112–13; Brewer, *Party Ideology and Popular Politics*, 149.

88 For Law's Toryism, see Colley, *In Defiance of Oligarchy*, 113; talk of the Pretender, in Byrom, *Journal and Remains*, vol. 2, 259; for Byrom in Montpellier and Avignon, see Byrom to Edward Byrom, 19 September 1717, in W. Thomson, *Previously Unpublished Byromiana* (Manchester: privately published, 1954), 15; for Byrom's Jacobite career in Manchester, see Talon, *Byrom*, 224–42; Byrom, *Journal and Remains*, vol. 2, 385–414; for Mancunian Jacobitism, see Bruce Lenman, *The Jacobite Risings in Britain 1689–1746* (London: Methuen, 1980), 123–4, 258.

89 C. Walton, *Notes and Materials for an Adequate Biography of William Law* (London: privately printed, 1854); Hobhouse, *Law*. For Law against Hoadly and Mandeville, see Walker, *Law*, 19–21, 33–7; for resignation of fellowship see Walton, *Law*, 344 and Byrom, *Journal and Remains*, vol. 1, 20–1. For Richardson as Law's printer, Sale, *Richardson: Master Printer*, 126–7; for his high-flying politics, see T. C. Duncan Eaves and B. D. Kimpel, *Samuel Richardson: A Biography* (Oxford: Clarendon, 1971), 21.

90 For the crisis of the late 1720s, see Bertrand Goldgar, *Walpole and the Wits* (Lincoln: University of Nebraska Press, 1976), 48–9, 64; J. A. Downie, 'Walpole, the poet's foe', in Jeremy Black (ed.), *Britain in the Age of Walpole* (London: Macmillan, 1984), 171–88. For Byrom and Sloane see J. L. Heilbron, *Physics at the Royal Society during Newton's Presidency* (Los Angeles: William Andrews Clark Library, 1983), 35–40; Byrom, *Journal and Remains*, vol. 1, 252–8, 274–5 and ibid., 262 for party slavery. For Cheyne's alleged 'spiritual conversion', see George Cheyne, 'The case of the author', in idem, *The English Malady* (London, 1733), 325–52; I follow Anita Guerrini, 'Isaac Newton, George Cheyne and the "Principia medicinae"', in R. French and A. Wear (eds), *The Medical Revolution of the Seventeenth Century* (Cambridge: Cambridge University Press, 1988), 222–45, 235, 244; see also Geoffrey Bowles, 'Physical, human and divine attraction in the life and thought of George Cheyne', *Annals of Science*, xxxi (1974), 473–88; Rousseau, 'Mysticism and millenarianism', 206–7. For Cheyne on melancholy and luxury, see Roy Porter, 'The rage of party: a Glorious Revolution in English psychiatry?', *Medical History*, xxvii (1983), 35–50, 43–6; for Cheyne's exclusion of religious enthusiasm, see Roy Porter, *Mind-forg'd Manacles: A History of Madness in England from the Restoration to the Regency* (Harmondsworth: Penguin Books, 1990), 80–1.

91 On public enthusiasts, see Ronald Knox, *Enthusiasm* (Oxford: Oxford University Press, 1950), 356–88; Hillel Schwartz, *The French Prophets* (Berkeley and Los Angeles: California University Press, 1980), 191–2; B. Robert Kreiser, *Miracles, Convulsions and Ecclesiastical Politics in Early 18th Century France* (Princeton: Princeton University Press, 1978); for Cheyne's temperance and enthusiasm, George Cheyne, *Essay on Health and Long Life*, 6th edn (London, 1726), 83 and *The English Malady*, ii; Guerrini, 'Newton, Cheyne', 240; Rousseau, 'Mysticism and millenarianism', 208–9; Bowles, 'Physical, human and divine attraction', 479. For Roach and the Philadelphians, see Hutin, *Les Disciples anglais de Boehme*, 81–123; Schwartz, *French Prophets*, 45–51, 195–6; Nils Thune, *The Behmenists and the Philadelphians* (Uppsala: Uppsala University, 1948); Harrison, *Second Coming*, 23. For Freher, Charles Arthur Muses, *Illumination on Jakob Boehme* (Columbia: King's Crown, 1951), 44–72. For the Boehme edition, idem, *Illumination on Boehme*, 69–71; Hutin, *Les Disciples anglais de Boehme*, 161; and Freher's remarkable figures in British Library MSS ADD 5786–8, 5790, published in George Ward and Thomas Langcake (eds), *The Works of Jakob Behmen*, 4 vols (London, 1764–81), 'Illustration of the deep principles of Jacob Behmen', in 'The clavis', vol. 2,

27–32; and ibid., 'Four tables of divine revelation', vol. 3, 23–35 (separate paginations). Blake's praise of Freher is in David Erdman, *Blake: Prophet Against Empire*, 3rd edn (Princeton: Princeton University Press, 1977) 11 n.19.

92 Wesley and Law, in Walker, *Law*, 69; Byrom, *Journal and Remains*, vol. 1, 337 and vol. 2, 216. For Law's readership, see *A Serious Call to a Devout and Holy Life* (1729), 69, cited in Isabel Rivers, 'Dissenting and methodist books of practical divinity', in idem (ed.), *Books and their Readers in Eighteenth-Century England* (London: Leicester University Press, 1982), 127–64, 157.

93 For Law and Poiret, see Hobhouse, *Law*, 381–3. For Law and Boehme, see Byrom, *Journal and Remains*, vol. 2, 363; Walton, *Law*, 26n. For Law versus the deists, G. R. Cragg, *Reason and Authority in the Eighteenth Century* (Cambridge: Cambridge University Press, 1964), 93–8. For Byrom and the Whigs, Byrom, *Journal and Remains*, vol. 1, 440, 468; Byrom, 'On the Whig workhouse bill', in *Poems*, vol. 1, 220–1.

94 Byrom, *Journal and Remains*, vol. 2, 268–73; Wesley, *Journal*, vol. 2, 297; see A. J. Kuhn, 'Nature spiritualized: aspects of anti-Newtonianism', *English Literary History*, xli (1974), 410–11.

95 Byrom and Cheyne in Byrom, *Journal and Remains*, vol. 2, 202; Freke and Richardson, Cheyne to Richardson, 26 October 1739, in Mullett, *Letters*, 58; Richardson prints Cheyne, in Sale, *Richardson*, 157–60; Richardson sends books, see Cheyne to Richardson, 17 May, 29 August and 17 September 1742, in Mullett, *Letters*, 99, 107, 111; for Cheyne versus rationalists, see Cheyne to Richardson, 10 Feb. 1738, ibid., 36. For Cheyne on Law, see Cheyne to Richardson, 26 April 1742, ibid., 25; see also Cheyne to Law, in Walton, *Law*, 370.

96 Byrom on *Pamela*, see *Journal and Remains*, vol. 2, 304; Cheyne on *Pamela*, see Arturi Cattaneo, 'Cheyne and Richardson, epistolary friendship and scientific advice', in Sergio Rossi (ed.), *Science and Imagination in 18th Century British Culture* (Milan: Università degli studi di Milano, 1987), 113–32, 123; Cheyne to Richardson, 24 August 1741, in Mullett, *Letters*, 69; Cheyne on angels, in idem, *Natural Method* (London, 1742), 79.

97 Cheyne sends *Natural Method*, in Byrom, *Journal and Remains*, vol. 2, 308–10; Byrom meets Freke, *Journal and Remains*, vol. 2, 320, 591–2; Law is judged 'unanswerable', Cheyne to Richardson, 9 May 1742, in Mullett, *Letters*, 88.

98 For Walpole's fall and the popular opposition, see Colley, *In Defiance of Oligarchy*, 237; Cruickshanks, *Political Untouchables*, 30, for the Fountain Tavern meeting. For Freke and Byrom, see Byrom, *Journal and Remains*, vol. 2, 328–9. Freke's role is complicated by references to his cousin, William Freke, an Augustan visionary and (from 1720) a Dorset JP. But Byrom normally refers to John as 'surgeon', and William died in 1744. See William Wadd, *Nugae chirurgicae* (London: Nichols, 1824), 208.

99 Byrom, *Journal and Remains*, vol. 2, 365; Talon, *Byrom*, 249; for martyrdom see Daniel Szechi, 'The Jacobite theatre of death', in Eveline Cruickshanks and Jeremy Black, *Jacobite Challenge* (Edinburgh: John Donald, 1988), 57–73, 61.

100 Freke and *Clarissa*, in Richardson to Aaron Hill, 20 January 1746, in John Carroll, *Selected Letters of Samuel Richardson* (Oxford: Clarendon, 1964), 63; for Freke's connections with *Clarissa*, see Rosemary Bechler, ' "Trial by what is contrary": Samuel Richardson and Christian dialectic', in Valerie Grosvenor Myer (ed.), *Samuel Richardson: Passion and Prudence* (Totowa, NJ: Barnes & Noble, 1986), 93–113, 95; Byrom, 'An epistle to a gentleman of the Temple' (1749) in *Poems*, vol. 2, 138–66; *Journal and Remains*, vol. 2, 519–21; Byrom, 'Enthusiasm' (1751), in *Poems*, vol. 2, 167–97, and *Journal and Remains*, vol. 2, 521. For Freke's *Treatise* and Law's *Spirit of Love* see Walker, *Law*, 200–1.

101 Freke to Byrom, 20 May 1754, in Byrom, *Journal and Remains*, vol. 2, 558; Law to Freke, 11 November 1752, in Walton, *Law*, 406.

102 Freke, *Essay of Electricity*, 38.

103 ibid., 26–7; Law, 'Appeal' (1740), in *Works*, vol. 6, 67–8, 136; 'Spirit of Love' (1754), in *Works*, vol. 7, 24–5. For Berkeley and Law on spirit and fire, see Donald Davie, *The Language of Science and the*

Language of Literature 1700–1740 (London: Sheed & Ward, 1963), 58–62; for Berkeley, see G. N. Cantor, 'The theological significance of ethers', in idem and M. J. S. Hodge (eds), *Conceptions of Ether* (Cambridge: Cambridge University Press, 1981), 135–56, 147–8; for Wright see Simon Schaffer, 'The phoenix of nature: fire and evolutionary cosmology in Wright and Kant', *Journal for the History of Astronomy*, ix (1978), 180–200.

104 Freke, *Treatise*, 137–9.

105 ibid., 26; Law, 'Appeal', in *Works*, vol. 6, 65.

106 Freke, *Treatise*, 29.

107 Freke, *Essay of Electricity*, 8, 3–4; Law, 'Appeal', in *Works*, vol. 6, 115; 'The clavis', in Langcake and Ward (eds), *Works of Jacob Behmen*, vol. 2, 21 (separate pagination); Symes, *Fire Analysed*, 17, 12–13. For Behmenist electricity, see Barry, 'Piety and the patient', 154–7; for Behmenist hermeneutics, see Geoffrey Cantor, 'Light and Enlightenment: an exploration of mid-eighteenth century modes of discourse', in David C. Lindberg and Geoffrey Cantor, *The Discourse of Light from the Middle Ages to the Enlightenment* (Los Angeles: William Andrews Clark Library, 1985), 69–106, 76–83.

108 Freke, *Essay of Electricity*, viii, 1.

109 ibid., vii–viii.

110 Law, 'Remarks upon *The Fable of the Bees*' (1723), in *Works*, vol. 2, 4; and 'Animadversions upon Dr Trapp's late Reply' (1740), in *Works*, vol. 6, 201–2. For Trapp as Tory dunce, see Rogers, *Grub Street*, 58.

111 Law to Cheyne, 31 March 1742, in Walton, *Law*, 46; Byrom, *Journal and Remains*, vol. 2, 364; Law, 'Spirit of love' (1754), in *Works*, vol. 8, 19; *Gentleman's Magazine*, lii (1782), 227–8, 329–30, 575–6. See Karl Popp, *Jakob Böhme und Isaac Newton* (Leipzig: Hirzel, 1935), 59–64; Arthur Wormhoudt, 'Newton's natural philosophy in the Behmenistic works of William Law', *Journal of the History of Ideas*, x (1949), 411–29, 426–8.

112 C. B. Wilde, 'Hutchinsonianism, natural philosophy and religious controversy in eighteenth-century Britain', *History of Science*, xviii (1980), 1–24; for Hutchinsonian ambitions, see Colley, *In Defiance of Oligarchy*, 105–6.

113 George Horne, *The Theology and Philosophy in Cicero's Somnium Scipionis Explained* (Oxford, 1751), 10; William Jones, 'Memoirs of the life and writings of Dr Horne' (1799), in Jones (ed.), *Works of George Horne*, 2nd edn, 4 vols (London, 1818), vol. 1, 1–197, 27–8.

114 Horne on Martin, in idem, *Somnium Scipionis Explained*, 23, 37–9; on Rackstrow, in Horne, 'A fair, candid, and impartial state of the case between Sir Isaac Newton and Mr Hutchinson' (1753), *Works*, vol. 1, 441–505, 493n. and Commonplace Book, Cambridge University Library MSS ADD 8134/B.1, 46. The phrase 'hominiform animal' is from Martin: see his *Course of Lectures in Natural and Experimental Philosophy* (London, 1743), 1–3 and *A Panegyrick*, 11–12. The link with Desaguliers is unlikely: see Millburn, *Martin*, 46–7.

115 Horne, Commonplace Book, 'Queries to Mr Law', 99; on Freke, in Horne to Browning, ibid., 44. Compare Horne, 'Cautions to the readers of Mr Law', *Works*, vol. 1, 209–15, 210–11.

116 Byrom against William Jones in Byrom, *Journal and Remains*, vol. 2, 593 (August 1757); Richardson against Hutchinson in Richardson to Loftus, 13 December 1756, in Anna Laetitia Barbauld, *Correspondence of Samuel Richardson*, 6 vols (London: Richard Phillips, 1804), vol. 5, 160–2.

117 For Hutchinson's hermeneutics, see G. N. Cantor, 'Revelation and the cyclical cosmos of John Hutchinson', in R. S. Porter and L. J. Jordanova (eds), *Images of the Earth* (Chalfont St Giles: British Society for the History of Science, 1979), 3–22; Horne, 'A letter to a lady on the subject of Jakob Behmen's writings' (1758), *Works*, vol. 1, 216–32, 222–3; Walpole to Bentley, September 1753, in *Letters*, ed. P. Cunningham, vol. 3, 357.

118 For Hackney phalanx, Pietro Corsi, *Science and Religion: Baden Powell and the Anglican Debate 1800–1860* (Cambridge: Cambridge University Press, 1988), 9–20; for Swedenborgians, see Harrison, *Second Coming*, 72–4; Erdman, *Blake*, 175–7.

119 Freke, *Treatise*, v–vi, 137.

120 Freke, *Essay of Electricity*, 16–17.

121 Freke, *Treatise*, 50; idem, *Essay of Electricity*, 26–7.

122 Freke, *Treatise*, iv, 30; idem, *Essay of Electricity*, v, 12.

123 Freke, *Art of Healing*, 122.

124 Martin, *Essay on Electricity*, preface, 4; Martin, *Supplement on a Rhapsody of Adventures*, 12, 30. There are similar comments on Freke in marginalia to the British Library copy of *Essay of Electricity*, BL 1608/5024.

125 Freke, *Treatise*, iii, 141; Martin, *Supplement on a Rhapsody of Adventures*, 27–8.

126 Law, 'Unlawfulness of stage-entertainments' (1726), in *Works*, vol. 2, 158.

127 John Dennis, *The Stage Defended* (London, 1726), 34, 12–13, 24; idem, 'Mrs. S. O.', *Law Outlaw'd* (London, 1726), 14.

128 Samuel Richardson, *Clarissa*, ed. Angus Ross (Harmondsworth: Penguin Books, 1985), 1495 ('Postscript'); McKillop, 'Richardson's early writings'; Pat Rogers, 'Richardson and the bluestockings', in Myer, *Richardson*, 147–64.

129 Barbauld, *Correspondence of Richardson*, vol. 2, 318–19.

130 For Fielding versus Richardson on authenticity, see McKeon, *Origins of the English Novel*, 382–4, 410–12. For his anti-Jacobitism, see Martin C. Battestin, '*Tom Jones* and "his Egyptian Majesty": Fielding's parable of government', *Proceedings of the Modern Language Association*, lxxxii (1967), 68–77; Thomas Cleary, 'Jacobitism in *Tom Jones*', *Philological Quarterly*, lii (1973), 239–51. Fielding's satire on Cheyne is in *The Tryal of Colley Cibber . . . and the Arraignment of George Cheyne* (London, 1740), 34–5 and is attributed in Martin C. Battestin, *Henry Fielding: A Life* (London: Routledge, 1989), 275. For 'instruction', see Richardson to Cheyne, 31 August 1741, in Carroll, *Selected Letters*, 46–7.

131 Hill to Richardson, 29 November 1748, in Aaron Hill, *Works of the Late Aaron Hill*, 4 vols (London, 1753), vol. 2, 168; for Hill and Richardson see Leo Hughes, 'Theatrical conventions in Richardson' in Caroll Camden (ed.), *Restoration and Eighteenth-Century Literature* (Chicago: Chicago University Press, 1963), 211–35; for Byrom's answer see Byrom, 'Art of acting', in *Poems*, vol. 1, 255–63, 263. Richardson's copy of this is Victoria and Albert Museum, MSS Forster XVI, 2 f.55.

132 John Byrom, 'Enthusiasm', in *Poems*, vol. 2, 167–97, 168, 190; for the Richardsonian cards, see W. M. Sale, *Samuel Richardson: A Bibliographical Record* (New Haven: Yale University Press, 1936), 96–7. For Richardson against Mandeville, see Richardson, *Clarissa*, 847 ('Letter 246'); Christopher Hill, 'Clarissa Harlowe and her times', in idem, *Puritanism and Revolution* (Harmondsworth: Penguin Books, 1986), 351–76, 360. Compare Law, 'Remarks upon *The Fable of the Bees*' (1723), in *Works*, vol. 2, 46–7.

133 Martin, *Supplement on a Rhapsody of Adventures*, 27–8.

134 For Cheselden's lectures see Cope, *Cheselden*, 5. For the connections with public relations ventures, see Geoffrey Holmes, *Augustan England: Professions, State and Society 1680–1730* (London: Allen & Unwin, 1982), 234.

135 For Hunter and commercialization see Susan C. Lawrence, 'Entrepreneurs and private enterprise: the development of medical lecturing in London 1775–1820', *Bulletin of the History of Medicine*, lxii (1988), 171–92; R. S. Porter, 'William Hunter: a surgeon and a gentleman', in W. F. Bynum and Roy Porter (eds), *William Hunter and the Eighteenth-Century Medical World* (Cambridge: Cambridge University Press, 1986), 7–34.

136 Freke is identified as the president in John Ireland, *Hogarth Illustrated*, 2 vols (London: Boydell, 1791), vol. 2, 326n.; his role in the riot is noted in Ronald Paulson, *Popular and Polite Art in the Age of Hogarth and Fielding* (Notre Dame: University of Notre Dame, 1979), 8. Freke was certainly known to Hogarth: see Moore, *History of St Bartholomew's*, vol. 2, 849. For the riot see P. Linebaugh, 'The Tyburn Riot against the surgeons', in D. Hay, P. Linebaugh and E. P. Thompson (eds), *Albion's Fatal Tree* (Harmondsworth: Peregrine Books, 1977), 65–117. For Fielding's role see Battestin, *Fielding*, 480–93; Hélène Desfond, 'Tyburn chez Mandeville et Fielding, ou le corps exemplaire du

pendu', in Paul-Gabriel Boucé and Suzy Halimi (eds), *Le Corps et l'âme en Grande-Bretagne au XVIIIe siècle* (Paris: Sorbonne, 1986), 61–70.

137 For the entrepreneurs, the Company and the role of Hunter and Cheselden, see Zachary Cope, *The Royal College of Surgeons of England* (London: Blond, 1959), 5–11; Cecil Wall, *The History of the Surgeons' Company* (London: Hutchinson, 1937), 60. Toby Gelfand, ' "Invite the philosopher, as well as the charitable": hospital teaching as private enterprise in Hunterian London', in Bynum and Porter, *William Hunter*, 129–51, 143–4, notes the importance of the Barber-Surgeons' split and that hospital teaching at Bart's does not significantly predate the 1760s. On Bart's and the theatre of execution, see Medvei and Thornton, *St Bartholomew's*, 210.

138 For Smithfield and Newgate, see Rogers, *Grub Sreet*, 37–8, 233, 253.

139 For Fielding and the theatre, see idem, *Tom Jones*, book 7, ch. 1, 299; Richard Sennett, *The Fall of Public Man* (London: Faber & Faber, 1986), 109–10; Agnew, *Worlds Apart*, 158–61.

140 For knowledge and commercial geographies, see Arjun Appadurai, 'Commodities and the politics of value' in idem (ed.), *The Social Life of Things* (Cambridge: Cambridge University Press, 1986), 3–63, 41; Braudel, *Civilization and Capitalism*, vol. 2, 408–12. See Lewis Mumford, *The Culture of Cities* (London: Secker & Warburg, 1940), 103 on discrediting localities; for credit crises and public persona, see Norbert Elias, *The Court Society* (Oxford: Blackwell, 1983), 96; for influence in natural philosophy, see Stewart, 'Public lectures and private patronage', 58; Pat Rogers, 'Gulliver and the engineers', in *Literature and Popular Culture in Eighteenth-Century England* (Brighton: Harvester Press, 1985), 11–28. For contemporary cases of replication, see Steven Shapin and Simon Schaffer, *Leviathan and the Air Pump* (Princeton: Princeton University Press, 1985) and Simon Schaffer, 'Glass works', in David Gooding, Trevor Pinch and Simon Schaffer (eds), *The Uses of Experiment* (Cambridge: Cambridge University Press, 1989), 67–104. For Nollet in Italy, see Heilbron, *Electricity*, 353–4; for Priestley in France, see A. J. Ihde, 'Priestley and Lavoisier', in L. Kieft and B. R. Willeford (eds), *Joseph Priestley* (Lewisburg, Penn.: Bucknell University Press, 1980), 62–91, 63–4; for 'seeing and reading', Priestley to Rotheram, 31 May 1774, in Robert E. Schofield (ed.), *Scientific Autobiography of Joseph Priestley* (Cambridge, Mass.: MIT Press, 1966), 146.

141 Money, *Experience and Identity*, p. 131.

142 For the Society of Arts, see D. G. C. Allan, *William Shipley* (London: Scolar, 1968), 50–7; D. G. C. Allan and R. E. Schofield, *Stephen Hales* (London: Scolar, 1980), 100–7. For new societies, see Arnold Thackray, 'Natural knowledge in cultural context: the Manchester model', *American Historical Review*, lxxix (1974), 672–709. For credit clubs and Wilkesite politics, see Brewer, 'Commercialization and politics', in McKendrick, Brewer and Plumb, *Birth of a Consumer Society*, 217–30. For Enlightenment and sociability, see Reinhard Koselleck, *Critique and Crisis* (Oxford: Berg, 1988), 62–75.

143 For 'Political electricity', see F. G. Stephens and E. Hawkins, *Catalogue of Prints and Drawings in the British Museum I: Political and Personal Satires*, vol. 4 (1761–70) (London: British Library, 1883), no. 4422, 649–60. For courtly instrumentation, see R. S. Whipple, 'An old catalogue and what it tells us of the scientific instruments and curios collected by Queen Charlotte and King George III', *Proceedings of the Optical Convention* (London, 1926), part 2, 1–27; G. l'E. Turner, 'The auction sales of the Earl of Bute's instruments, 1793', *Annals of Science*, xxiii (1967), 213–41. See John Brewer, *The Sinews of Power* (London: Unwin Hyman, 1989), 230.

144 Schofield, *Scientific Autobiography of Priestley*, 12–49.

145 For patronage of the *History*, see Golinski, 'Utility and audience', pp. 18–21; Priestley to Canton, 14 February 1766, in Schofield, *Scientific Autobiography of Priestley*, 15–16; Priestley, 'A catalogue of books', in *History of Electricity*, 3rd edn, vol. 2, sig. Cc1; V. W. Crane, 'The club of honest Whigs', *William and Mary Quarterly*, xxiii (1966), 210–33; L. F. Chard, 'Joseph Johnson, father of the book trade', *Bulletin of the New York Public Library*, lxxix (1975), 51–82.

146 Priestley, *History of Electricity*, 3rd edn, vol. 1, xi; for its Franklinism, see Heilbron, 'Franklin, Haller and Franklinist history'; Martin is cited in Priestley, *History of Electricity*, 2nd edn (London, 1769), 498–9.

147 The advertisement is reprinted in Schofield, *Scientific Autobiography of Priestley*, 60. For the character of the philosopher, see Priestley, *History of Electricity*, 3rd edn, vol. 1, xxiii; J. G. McEvoy, 'Electricity, knowledge and the nature of progress in Priestley's thought', *British Journal for the History of Science*, xii (1979), 1–30.

148 Priestley, *History of Electricity*, 3rd edn, vol. 1, xvii–xx.

149 ibid., vol. 2, 109–10. For large machines see Schofield, *Scientific Autobiography of Priestley*, 52–3; for Priestley's custom with Martin, see Millburn, *Martin: Supplement*, 44; Douglas McKie, 'Priestley's laboratory and library and other of his effects', *Notes and Records of the Royal Society*, xii (1956), 114–36, 116 (air pump and orrery), 121 (hydrostatic balance). In 1792 Priestley's own electrical machine was valued at 7 guineas, and his specimen of Nairne's great machine at more than £24, ibid., 117.

150 Priestley, *Experiments and Observations on Different Kinds of Air* (London, 1774), xvi ('middle ranks'), xiv ('English hierarchy').

151 Priestley, *History of Electricity*, 3rd edn, vol. 2, 83.

152 Priestley, *Experiments and Observations on Different Kinds of Air* (London, 1775–7), 2nd edn, 3 vols, vol. 2 (1776), 98 (ventilation), 102 (mice). For Wedgwood, see Schofield, *Scientific Autobiography of Priestley*, 141; Wedgwood to Bentley, 9 October 1776, and Commonplace Book, in Neil McKendrick, 'The rôle of science in the Industrial Revolution: a study of Josiah Wedgwood as a scientist and industrial chemist', in M. Teich and R. M. Young (eds), *Changing Perspectives in the History of Science* (London: Heinemann, 1973), 274–319, 297. For Priestley's politics see D. O. Thomas, 'Progress, liberty and utility: the political philosophy of Joseph Priestley', in R. G. W. Anderson and Christopher Lawrence, *Science, Medicine and Dissent: Joseph Priestley (1733–1804)* (London: Wellcome Trust, 1987), 73–80. For Priestley and commercial interest see Jan Golinski, *Science as Public Culture* (Cambridge: Cambridge University Press, 1992), 69–76.

153 Adam Walker, *A System of Familiar Philosophy* (London, 1799), viii.

154 Simon Schama, *The Embarrassment of Riches* (London: Collins, 1987), 136–7; William Reddy, 'The structure of a cultural crisis: thinking about cloth in France before and after the Revolution', in Appadurai, *Social Life of Things*, 261–84.

155 William Blake, 'Annotations to Dr Thornton's New Translation of the Lord's Prayer' (1827), in *Complete Writings*, ed. Geoffrey Keynes (Oxford: Oxford University Press, 1972), 788; Erdman, *Blake*, 492.

25
Manufacturing, consumption and design in eighteenth-century England

John Styles

Introduction: designing for the 'Empire of Goods'

In a telling phrase, T. H. Breen has recently characterized the Anglo-American Empire that straddled the Atlantic during the eighteenth century as an 'Empire of Goods'.[1] The eighteenth-century British Atlantic world was bound together, he points out, not simply by ties of language or administration, but also by a shared material culture which was constantly nourished by flows of commodities. These commodities circulated both *within* the constituent units of the British Atlantic Empire – England, Scotland, Ireland, the North American and the West Indian colonies – and *between* those units, but it is the flow westward of manufactured consumer products from Great Britain to the North American mainland that most effectively illustrates the themes I want to develop in this essay.

The burgeoning population of colonial British North America (over two million people on the eve of the Revolution, approaching a third of the size of the population of England) was dominated by relatively prosperous, small-scale commercial farmers. The mid-eighteenth-century description of Pennsylvania as 'the best poor man's country in the world' was applicable to many of the other mainland colonies, at least as far as the bulk of the white population was concerned.[2] Like English farmers at the same period, their appetite for consumer goods was more restrained than that of independent craftsmen and tradesmen of a similar level of wealth, but these small colonial farmers were far from being the self-sufficient 'peasants' of colonial mythology.[3] A large proportion of the commodities that flowed westwards across the Atlantic were manufactured consumer products intended for this market; products made principally in England, which was already, at the start of the eighteenth century, probably the most industrialized of the major European states. Breen notes that as early as the 1740s, an upcountry Connecticut shopkeeper's ledger books reveal stocks of gloves, pots, pans, cords, knives, earthenware, thimbles, buckles, buttons, combs, spectacles, nails, silk, wire, tape, pewter dishes and cloth, almost all imported from England. 'Already', said an astonished German clergyman in the 1750s 'it is really possible to obtain all the things one can get in Europe in Pennsylvania, since so many merchant ships arrive there every year.'[4] Yet few of these products were manufactured in the colonies themselves.

527

In other words, North America provided a large market of prosperous primary agricultural producers, with a healthy appetite for finished and semi-finished consumer products, few of which were produced locally in the quantities and qualities desired. Some of these imported products sold, at least in part, on their appearance.[5] A significant and possibly growing proportion of them (though by no means all) were fashion products, in the sense that their successful sale depended on repeated changes in their visual appearance in accordance with changing metropolitan notions of what was fashionable.[6] Yet producer and consumer were separated by thousands of miles of ocean. Although almost all the goods concerned were made by hand, we are often talking about the manufacture of large batches of hundreds or thousands or tens of thousands of individual items to uniform specifications, but specifications that nevertheless changed, often quite frequently, in some cases from year to year. The specifications were set predominantly by the merchants and manufacturers who controlled the various trades, in accordance with their assessment of changes in fashion and in the other influences on demand. The production and supply of a wide range of eighteenth-century manufactured goods was organized along these lines. The processes at work are especially clear in the case of the American market, because of its size and appetite, the distances involved and the relative weakness of manufacturing in eighteenth-century North America, but the production and supply of similar goods in eighteenth-century England was not very different.

Many of these points are familiar enough to economic historians. They are worth re-emphasizing here because historians concerned with the design of manufactured goods have tended to ignore non-luxury products in the period before the entrenchment of factory production in certain limited sectors of British manufacturing between 1760 and 1850. Design historians have failed to think through the implications of the geographical separation of manufacture and consumption in the eighteenth century and before for the design and manufacture of the more mundane consumer products. They have failed, in particular, to explore the ways that information about fashion and design changes was communicated, the capacity of manufacturers and merchants to control and adjust those specifications and the processes by which large quantities of hand-made goods were actually manufactured to fixed (but regularly changing) visual specifications.

Because they assume that the production of large numbers of objects made to fixed specifications was chiefly a consequence of factory mechanization, historians of design have tended to assume that before the coming of the factory and machinofacture, objects were usually made from start to finish by a single craftsman and that such craftsmen determined the look of the product, usually in such a way that every object was unique. Even the most recent general surveys of the history of design, which do recognize the extent of the division of labour before the nineteenth century, locate its roots only in the previous century. For example, in his book *Objects of Desire*, Adrian Forty asserts that 'in the history of every industry, design has become necessary as a separate activity in production once a single craftsman ceases to be responsible for every stage of manufacture from conception to sale. In many industries, this organisational change took place in the eighteenth century.'[7] Before 1700, it is assumed, the craftsman (in the sense used above) was unchallenged.

This was patently not the case. Production of large numbers of objects made to fixed specifications had been widespread in the English woollen textile industry since at least the fifteenth century. In other parts of Europe it had even earlier roots. By the start of the eighteenth century, production of this sort for distant markets was common in a wide variety of English industries, including the manufacture of textiles, metalware, clothing and ceramics. It is important to note, however, that, as in the nineteenth century, in any particular sector of manufacturing, production of large volumes of products to fixed specifications went on side by side with various kinds of bespoke and non-standardized output. Between the sixteenth and the nineteenth centuries there does appear to have been a long-term trend in more and more English industries towards the production of large volumes of products to relatively fixed specifications for distant markets by medium to large firms. Nevertheless, other kinds of production flourished and indeed multiplied, and not simply at the top of the market.

It is with the production in eighteenth-century England of finished or semi-finished consumer goods in large volumes to fixed specifications that this paper is principally concerned. The English appear to have been particularly successful in producing and selling this sort of product in the eighteenth century. The paper considers the character of the industries concerned, the nature of their markets, the ways design decisions were made and implemented and some of the implications of design practice for an understanding of eighteenth-century debates about design.

Mass production?

Historical enquiry into eighteenth-century patterns of consumption has grown apace during the last twenty years. In order to recapture the novelty and distinctiveness of eighteenth-century English consumer behaviour, historians have made lavish use of terms like 'a consumer society', 'a consumer revolution' and 'mass consumption'. To describe the goods that were acquired by these new consumers, they have employed related phrases like 'mass produced' and 'mass consumer products'.[8] Indeed, it appears it is only by using a vocabulary whose origins lie in the very different context of the first half of the twentieth century that historians feel able to express the significance of a Josiah Wedgwood or a Matthew Boulton to a modern audience. There are, however, considerable dangers in the indiscriminate application of these terms to eighteenth-century England. Often it can pre-empt rigorous analysis of the organization of production, the character of the market and the design of the objects produced.

Let us consider the phrase 'mass production' first. The phrase originated in the practice of the production system developed by Henry Ford in his Highland Park plant in Detroit in the 1910s to make the Model T automobile. In this, its purest sense, it involved the production, in huge volume but a very limited number of varieties, of what were by the standards of the day extremely complex mechanical objects. These objects were composed of exceptionally standardized components (to ensure interchangeability and thereby assembly by cheap, unskilled labour), manufactured by means of an intensely dedicated production technology, integrated to achieve high throughputs and low unit costs. The key elements here are the narrowness of the product range, the standardization of the components, the corresponding specialization of the machinery and the low unit cost.[9]

In this pure sense, mass production flourished only briefly, but the phrase has subsequently been loosely attached to production systems embodying elements of the original Fordist formula: large throughput, limited product range, automated production lines, dedicated (as opposed to flexible) machine tools, interchangeable mechanical parts, unskilled labour. Historians of earlier periods have, however, been more profligate in their use of the phrase. For some, it simply means the production of objects in very large numbers. David Graysmith, discussing the making of printed fabrics in the early nineteenth century, comments that 'mass production, defined quantitatively, existed even with old hand-crafted methods'.[10] Neil McKendrick seems to be using the phrase in the same way when he refers to the availability of 'mass-produced cheap clothes' in the later eighteenth century.[11] Others have used it as an appropriate way of capturing the distinctiveness of factory industry as opposed to handicrafts. In discussing the industrial innovations of the late eighteenth century, Peter Mathias refers to 'the conversion of a single industry on to a mass-production basis with large plants driven by more than human power'.[12]

If mass production is simply a matter of the sheer quantity of output generated by an industry or a firm, then its usefulness as a category of historical analysis is limited. Many humble consumer products were produced in hundreds of thousands or even millions each year in the eighteenth century, but often, like the ubiquitous clay pipe, in tiny workshops serving mainly local markets.[13] The last three hundred years has unquestionably witnessed a vast increase in the quantitative capacity of individual production units, associated with the use of increasingly sophisticated machinery and the application of inanimate power. But indiscriminately to label this development mass production is to lose much of the analytical precision the phrase derives from its Fordist origins. A more tightly specified use of the phrase draws attention to the important question of whether quantitative increases in output have necessitated standardization of product type, restriction of product diversity and intensely specialized and dedicated plant.

It is significant in this regard that, outside the literature on consumption, the phrase mass production has been very little employed in discussions of the classic Industrial Revolution of the period between 1760 and 1850.[14] At first sight this may seem surprising, because at the heart of the Industrial Revolution, as conventionally portrayed, was a new kind of production system – specialized machinery, driven by inanimate power and located in the factory – which generated a dramatic increase in the quantity of goods produced and a dramatic fall in their unit cost. However, the introduction of powered machines did not necessarily inaugurate mass production. Closer examination of the products of the new factories makes intelligible the reluctance of historians of the Industrial Revolution to use the phrase to describe these developments.

When we talk about factory mechanization in the period of the classic Industrial Revolution, we are talking principally about textiles – semi-finished consumer goods. In contrast to the Ford production system of the early twentieth century, factory production of textiles in England between 1760 and 1850 was associated with an increasingly diverse range of final products, often customized for particular markets and subject to frequent changes in character according to constant and rapid changes in clothing and furnishing fashions. Henry Ford considered 'the way to make automobiles is to make one automobile like another automobile, to make them all alike, to make them all come from the factory just alike'.[15] Consequently, when General Motors' policy of styling and rapid model change forced him to abandon the Model T, Ford grumbled 'we are no longer in the automobile but in the millinery business'.[16] Textile manufacturers of the classic Industrial Revolution had no such ground for complaint. Their activities often shared many features with the millinery business and, indeed, were intimately linked to it. During the later years of the eighteenth century, for example, the range of pure cotton fabrics expanded dramatically. Similarly, in the second quarter of the nineteenth century, cheap cotton yarn and changes in women's fashion encouraged the creation of a whole new range of mixed worsted and cotton fabrics, as well as the use of new animal fibres like alpaca wool.[17] Moreover, variety in the appearance of the final product was further increased by the enormous expansion of textile printing, particularly on cotton. The new powered machinery may have been specialized, but it was rarely so dedicated to particular product lines that it inhibited constant and rapid changes in the specification of the final product.

This trend towards greater product diversity and variability did not, of course, begin with the introduction of the first powered spinning machines in the 1760s. It was already well-entrenched in the English textile industries by the early eighteenth century. Within the long-established woollen textile industries, the rise of the 'new draperies' in the sixteenth and seventeenth centuries brought about a diversification of product types. At the same time, the process of import substitution, so characteristic of English manufacturing between the mid-sixteenth century and the mid-eighteenth century, involved the establishment, virtually from scratch, of whole new categories of textile manufacture, whether based on European models (like the Spitalfields silk industry), or eastern ones (like cotton printing).[18]

It should be apparent, therefore, that, in anything like its modern sense, the phrase 'mass production' is not generally appropriate to eighteenth-century manufacturing of textiles or, for that matter, to the making of other finished and semi-finished consumer goods in the period. It is possible to distinguish in many industries elements of what later became the fully-fledged mass-production strategy: for example, cost cutting by means of mechanical devices (like metal stamps) and increases in the division of tasks to permit more use of cheap (often female or provincial) labour. But relatively few complex mechanical objects were produced; throughputs were small by twentieth-century standards even in the largest manufacturing enterprises; single-purpose production machinery of the intensely dedicated kind associated with Fordism was rare; interchangeability of mechanical parts was almost entirely absent. It remains a useful exercise, however, to assess eighteenth-century industry in terms of the sort of criteria which have been used here in defining mass production. Such an assessment enables us to specify what was distinctive about eighteenth-century manufacturing enterprises, especially those that served large, distant markets, and what was distinctive about their products.

Although the lack of national economic statistics makes accurate counting difficult, it is clear enough that it was far from unusual in eighteenth-century England for finished or semi-finished consumer goods to be produced in long runs by large, capitalist enterprises for sale in distant markets. Take, for example, the woollen textile industries. In the 1740s Samuel Hill of Soyland, near Halifax, was reputed to be the largest manufacturer in the Yorkshire kersey and worsted industries. He enjoyed an annual turnover of approximately £30,000 (at eighteenth-century values). A turnover of this size would have involved the manufacture of approximately 20,000 pieces of cloth per year, employing perhaps 1,500 workers, overwhelmingly in their own homes for a wage under the putting-out system.[19] Hill was, of course, one of the country's very biggest producers. Most manufacturers operated on a smaller scale, but one that was, nevertheless, significant. More typical of the Yorkshire worsted industry, distinctive for its large number of medium-sized employers, were Robert Heaton of Howarth, who in 1778 made 793 pieces of cloth worth £1,373, and John Sutcliffe of Ovenden, who made 842 pieces of cloth worth £2,035 in 1791, each employing approximately 60 workers.[20] It has been estimated that in the early eighteenth-century Essex worsted industry the average labour force of the larger manufacturers at Colchester was about 200 people.[21]

Even by the standards of the mid-nineteenth century, these were fairly large enterprises in terms of the numbers employed, although the quantity of goods produced was small by comparison with later mechanized worsted production. Manufacturers of this sort were prepared to adjust their products to the requirements of particular wholesale customers, and were often adventurous and innovative in adopting new products, but these firms were not engaged in anything that can meaningfully be termed bespoke manufacturing.[22] Their businesses revolved around the production of a limited, but changing range of product types to set specifications for distant, often export markets (approximately 70 per cent of the production of the Yorkshire worsted industry went abroad, mainly to North America, in the 1770s). In kerseys, for example, Samuel Hill during the 1730s offered eight basic types of cloth of different qualities and at different prices. These he sold by sample. Pattern cards were sent out to wholesale customers in Britain and overseas, and production schedules set up according to the orders received.[23] A flavour of the conventional practice is captured in a letter Samuel Hill sent to a Dutch firm in 1737: 'Most gentlemen that I serve have agreed to take a certain quantity every year and they fix the months wherein they desire them and then they are seldom if ever disappointed.'[24] The smaller Yorkshire firms dealt more narrowly through local merchants, particularly in Halifax and Leeds, but these merchants themselves offered a limited core range of goods, which were sold at home and overseas by samples, pattern cards and sometimes travelling salesmen.[25]

It is worth re-emphasizing that these were enterprises in which a master manufacturer owned the raw materials and specified how they should be worked up by a waged workforce. Production was organized mainly under the putting-out system, with the workers undertaking the work to the master manufacturer's specification in their own homes, using equipment like spinning wheels and looms, which were sometimes owned by the manufacturer and sometimes by the worker. This form of organization, or something like it, was widespread in the production of woollen textiles (the largest single industry producing for distant markets in eighteenth-century England), in the other textile industries (cotton, linen, silk, hosiery, lace), in the manufacture of ready-made clothing (shoes, hats, gloves and, to some extent, garments) and in many aspects of metalworking (watches, locks, buttons, buckles, domestic utensils).

Production of relatively uniform consumer products in large numbers was not, however, restricted to the putting-out form of industrial organization. In some branches of light metalworking, production was physically concentrated in large units. Matthew Boulton's Soho works, which employed 800 to 1,000 people by 1770, was only one of a number of large workshops established in the Birmingham area in the second and third quarters of the eighteenth century to make buttons, japanned wares and associated products.[26] These were trades which often had to cope with rapid changes in fashion. Much less sensitive to fashion was the manufacture of glass bottles, which were hand-blown in huge numbers in coal-fired bottle houses. The Royal Northumberland Bottle Works at Hartley near Newcastle upon Tyne, which in 1788 was said to be the largest bottle works in Britain, produced between a million and two million bottles a year in the 1770s and 1780s. In the 1780s the works combined a small, specialist, almost bespoke trade in apothecaries' bottles and chemistry equipment, with the production of vast quantities of a very limited range of wine bottles to a fixed contract with a London agent.[27] Indeed, so concentrated was the Royal Northumberland Bottle Works' output in the early 1780s that one type of wine bottle accounted for three-quarters of all the items produced.[28]

The manufacture of relatively uniform consumer products was also undertaken by independent small producers, who bought their raw materials, worked them up in their own households and sold the finished product to the dealers who co-ordinated production. This form of organization was characteristic of the Yorkshire woollen (as opposed to worsted) industry, where independent small clothiers predominated, of some of the metal trades in the West Midlands and of the cutlery industry of south Yorkshire. Moreover, there was a variety of organizational forms between the 'pure' independent producer, the large putting-out enterprise and the centralized manufactory, because complex networks of subcontracting proliferated in many of the trades producing batches of consumer products to uniform specifications.

So far the products that are the subject of this chapter have been described as finished or semi-finished consumer goods, manufactured in large volumes to fixed, uniform specifications. The term 'standardized', often associated with the use of interchangeable parts in manufacturing and with the visual regimentation of twentieth-century, mass-produced artefacts, has been deliberately avoided. Can the eighteenth-century products dealt with in this chapter usefully be described as standardized? There are two senses in which one might describe some eighteenth-century products in this way, but they both need to be carefully distinguished from the twentieth-century uses of the term.

First, it is clear that in the eighteenth century it was not unusual for the component parts of consumer products – the intermediate goods of which they were composed – to be manufactured to standard dimensions. Standardization in this sense was particularly widespread in textiles, where yarn counts and cloth dimensions had been established, sometimes by law, since at least the sixteenth century.[29] In the eighteenth century, such standards were not uniform across the different textile fibres, they were not immutable, and they were not usually national in scope. Nevertheless, at any particular period they were effective within each regional industry and they were widely-enough recognized to facilitate inter-regional and international trade in yarn as well as in cloth. Parallel to the standardization of intermediate goods, and similar to it, were the systems of sizing for ready-made clothing, especially shoes and hats, that were in existence by the eighteenth century.[30] This kind of standardization did not inhibit the growth of product diversity; on the contrary, it probably facilitated it. In this respect it differed from some of the effects of twentieth-century standardization, at least as far as mass-produced, mechanical products are concerned. The Ford experience between the 1910s and the 1930s suggests that, in the technological environment of the first half of the twentieth century, the more intense the drive towards standardized, interchangeable mechanical parts, the more restricted were manufacturing flexibility and product diversity.[31]

The second sense in which the term standardization can be applied to eighteenth-century products concerns the way products were defined. Much eighteenth-century manufacturing of consumer goods for distant markets was standardized, in the sense that products were produced in large batches to a range of standard or consistent specifications, determined in advance by a master manufacturer or merchant. These runs or batches were usually made to order, as in the case of Samuel Hill, the Yorkshire textile manufacturer. There was always a good deal of customizing the standard specifications sent out in pattern books and samples to the requirements of clients, but as far as production for distant markets is concerned, unique objects bespoke for individual clients were relatively unimportant in volume terms (although, towards the top of the market, business with a considerable turnover might sometimes operate in this way, for example in silk weaving or silversmithing).[32]

Standardization of consumer products found its most extreme eighteenth-century expression in industries such as the glass bottle manufacture, where some firms supplied a very limited range of goods in huge numbers on fixed, long-term contracts. Other similar examples might be the manufacture of plain linen sheeting, or cheap shoes for American and West Indian slaves. It was in such industries that eighteenth-century manufacturing came closest to modern mass production. But even here there is little evidence that manufacturers were radically reconstituting product definitions primarily to facilitate low cost, capital-intensive, deskilled production methods, in the way that has become familiar in twentieth-century consumer industries like cutlery and furniture.[33] In most of the industries discussed in this chapter, tight definition of individual product types was associated with wide (and widening) product ranges and with frequent changes in and additions to those ranges.

Production was therefore organized and undertaken in such a way that it was possible to alter product specifications. Indeed, where fashionability and novelty played any part in selling the product, it was essential that this should be the case. That does not mean it was always easy. The problems were summed up by Samuel Hill in 1737: 'going from one sort to another spoils all the weavers, as I have experienced all my life in what manufactories I have been concerned in.'[34] Yet 'going from one sort to another' was necessary on a more or less regular basis for the continued prosperity of a vast range of eighteenth-century manufacturing businesses. Meeting specifications depended on the knowledge, dexterity and co-operation of the various workpeople involved, but the specification itself was rarely under their control. It was determined for them either by their employer, or, in the case of independent small producers, by the merchant or the factor who co-ordinated production through numerous market transactions. Arthur Young made plain what he regarded as the normal arrangements in English manufactures when he criticized the attempts of the Dublin Society to promote the Irish industries.

> Where are the men of taste who are to invent? Where the quickness and sagacity to mark and follow the caprice of fashion? Are these to come from weavers? Absurd the idea! It is the active and intelligent master that is to do all this. Go to the weavers of Spitalfields, and see them mere tools directed by their masters.[35]

Young, of course, exaggerated in order to make his point. It would be wrong to suggest that there was *no* room for innovation or initiative regarding the character of the product on the part of the people who actually worked up the materials. Developing specialized mechanical devices that would eliminate variability in products became an important preoccupation of eighteenth-century inventors.[36] Nevertheless, it was rarely possible to make consumer goods with special-purpose machinery contrived to remove as much control from the operative as the devices Henry Ford's production engineers called 'farmer tools', because with them a farmboy could turn out work as good as a first-class mechanic.[37] The division of labour was often very extensive in eighteenth-century manufactures, but tools were rarely dedicated to a single product line. Workers could adjust to new specifications. Hence spinners and their wheels could spin to a variety of counts, weavers and their looms could produce various types and patterns of cloth and even those highly specialized workers who manufactured one part of a watch movement with dedicated tools could produce that part in different sizes and to different standards. But the fact remains that setting those standards, in other words the design of the product, was not the responsibility of the workers who actually made it. Design for much eighteenth-century manufacturing was a specialist process, far removed from the vague notions of artisanal control often associated with the terms handicraft and craftsmanship.[38]

Consumer society, mass consumption, consumer revolution?

Once it was industrial revolutions that were being discovered in almost every century of the modern era. Now it is their demand-side equivalents: consumer revolutions, consumer societies and scenes of mass consumption. The proliferating use of these labels, like the earlier proliferation of the term industrial revolution, poses major problems of periodization for historians. These phrases have been used by historians of eighteenth-century England to suggest that during that century, and especially towards its close, the country saw an unprecedented increase in the consumption of goods, based on a marked intensification of commercial activity and a new and distinctive spirit of fashion-driven acquisitiveness. This growth, it has been argued, underpinned the innovations in productive capacity associated with the classic industrial revolution. But is it really possible to sustain an argument that it was during the eighteenth century, rather than the sixteenth, the seventeenth, the nineteenth or the twentieth, that Britain witnessed the consumer revolution that brought about the emergence of a consumer society and mass consumption? Are we victims of yet another case of taxonomic entrepreneurship run riot?

To an even greater extent than the term mass production, the phrases consumer society and mass consumption have been used by eighteenth-century historians (unlike those who have studied the nineteenth and twentieth centuries[39]) without much effort to specify their meaning precisely, or much concern for their provenance. Neil McKendrick, although never defining them, presents a consumer society as one in which material abundance is aligned with a general, emulative acquisitiveness by means of commercialized sales promotion and marketing techniques. Mass consumption is simply a high *per capita* level of consumption which is not restricted to the very wealthy. The eighteenth century witnessed a consumer revolution because these phenomena emerged then on a significant scale for the first time.

The major difficulty here is that the eighteenth century is presented as an embryonic form of something we all experience today, the bottom rung on a one-way ladder to uniform, modern patterns of consumption. This does little justice to variegated history of consumption in the intervening period, or to the diversity of modern consumption: the different balances in different countries between socialized and market provision, the international differences in receptiveness to standardized as opposed to speciality products, the variety of meanings that artefacts embody (few of them simply emulative). There is little doubt that the range and quantity of goods consumed in England and in its North American colonies did expand in the course of the eighteenth century, but it is much more questionable whether that expansion was so fast and so all-transforming as to constitute in any meaningful sense a revolution. Recent work on the classic Industrial Revolution has emphasized the slowness of the rate of change. If change was far from revolutionary on the supply side, the need to identify a demand-side revolution becomes less pressing.

It is not possible to get round these difficulties simply by postulating an ever-rising tide of something called commercialization, an elastic concept which is used to mean everything from the advent of shops and advertisements to the establishment of market relationships *de novo*. Most historical societies have had some form of commerce. The real challenge for historians, as Richard Johnson has pointed out, is to establish what was *distinctive* about eighteenth-century patterns of consumption, compared with the expansion of consumer choice in the sixteenth and seventeenth centuries, or the 'mass' market growth of the 1880s, or the uneven consumerism of the 1930s or the consumer boom of the 1950s and 1960s.[40]

Unfortunately, the more conceptually rigorous modern literature on mass consumption and consumer societies is not very helpful here. In intellectual disciplines other than history these phrases have been employed (more often than not) as terms of social criticism and moral disapproval. For the mass culture and similar theorists of the inter-war and post-war years, the phrases mass consumption and consumer society were associated with a morally and intellectually barren mass culture, in which the media systematically conditioned the masses into regimented patterns of consumption. From this perspective, mass consumption amounted to a collective delusion characteristic of 'modern' societies, a product of the magic power of capitalism to create endless false needs by means of artificially stimulated fantasies. The consumer society offered only an illusion of choice. Needs were contrived in such a way that they could be satisfied by standardized, mass-produced products whose primary characteristic was a built-in obsolescence necessary for the continuing growth and profitability of big business. Individuals were reduced to passive spectators, alienated from their real selves, without any capacity for creativity or originality.[41] Such views (which continue to enjoy widespread currency, although often in a reworked 'post-modern' guise) have often been grounded in a set of linked conceptual polarities, themselves underpinned by assumptions about the broad sweep of historical change: the assumptions that *gemeinschaft* has been succeeded by *gesellschaft*; real needs by false needs; users by consumers.

Yet these grand evolutionary polarities prove distinctly unhelpful when called upon to assist in the historian's mundane task of periodization. It is extremely difficult to trace in the eighteenth (or any other) century the moment at which the mass media transformed honest English users of 'real' things into deluded consumers of standardized, throw-away commodities, fulfilling inauthentic and illegitimate desires. Simply to itemize the energetic promotional activities of a handful of entrepreneurs, *à la* McKendrick, cannot establish a loss of innocence of such Biblical proportions. Nor can it be unequivocally established by demonstrating an increase in the quantity of goods consumed, or even some general shift in people's propensity (as opposed to their ability) to acquire material goods. The usually unfavourable remarks of contemporary commentators about changing attitudes to consumption, so widely employed by historians in this context, are equally suspect. Many eighteenth-century observers expressed anxiety about the morally debilitating effects of what they perceived to be a rising tide of luxury among the population at large. However, such remarks should be treated more as testimony to the pervasiveness of a certain kind of social discourse than as conclusive evidence of changing patterns of consumer behaviour. The fundamental problem here is conceptual: the shortcomings of those ways of thinking about modern consumption for which the notions of mass consumption and consumer society have been central. The crude division of consumption into the authentic and the manipulated, and the unilinear vision of historical evolution on which that division is founded do no more justice to the complexity and diversity of consumer behaviour, either today or in the past, than McKendrick's conceptually less rigorous formulations.[42]

What can be salvaged from this deeply flawed conceptual legacy for the eighteenth-century historian, and in particular the historian of eighteenth-century design? An understanding of consumption remains essential for an understanding of design, because the way objects look is so intimately tied up with the ways they are consumed, particularly if some notion of consumer manipulation is in play. It is not appropriate here to embark on a wholesale recharacterization of eighteenth-century consumption, but a clearer sense of what was distinctive about the eighteenth century can be arrived at by addressing two issues which originate loosely in the mass culture approach outlined above.

The first of these issues is the social shape of the market for traded consumer goods. Who were the consumers and what did they buy? This is an issue which has occasioned considerable historical dispute, but no very firm conclusions. Given the extreme weakness of the available aggregate data for eighteenth-century England, it has proved difficult to achieve any resolution in either the debate on the demand for manufactured goods in the first half of the eighteenth century, or the debate on the standard of living in the early years of the classic Industrial Revolution.[43] There is general agreement that the English were already relatively wealthy at the beginning of the eighteenth century and that aggregate real incomes underwent a rise in the course of the century, but it remains extremely difficult to establish which sections of the population benefited and to what extent increased income was used to acquire manufactured consumer durables and semi-durables, as opposed to food and other non-durables, or leisure.

One way to get at the behaviour of consumers is through probate inventories. As evidence for consumer behaviour they have many shortcomings: they record stocks rather than flows of commodities; they survive in barely usable numbers for the labouring poor; they are largely unavailable in bulk after 1730 (except for Yorkshire); and what they record is mainly restricted to durable consumer goods. Nevertheless they do demonstrate that during the seventeenth and early eighteenth centuries the groups with middling wealth in English society – farmers, husbandmen, tradesmen and artisan-retailers – became wealthier, lived in more rooms per household and owned an increasing range and quantity of consumer durables. There is every reason to believe that through the rest of the eighteenth century this trend continued, and indeed intensified, not least because of the growth of towns and the rising proportion in the rural population of tradesmen and artisan-retailers.[44] Non-agriculturalists were the most adventurous middling group consumers.

In the present state of inventory research it is hard to perceive a decisive break in these trends between the seventeenth and the eighteenth centuries. What does stand out is the spread among these middling groups from the late seventeenth century of a block of what were often entirely new household goods, consisting most obviously of clocks, prints, earthenware, cutlery, equipment for drinking tea and coffee and window curtains.[45] We should not imagine, however, that a taste for entirely new products was unprecedented. After all, the big initial rise in tobacco consumption, much of which must have been used by this middling group, was over by the end of the seventeenth century and consumption of tobacco stagnated during the eighteenth century.[46] What the inventories suggest is a reorientation from the late seventeenth century of the consumption of the middling sort, especially those who were not farmers. A block of new household products was added to an already well-established, growing market for domestic comfort, previously satisfied by the accumulation of increasingly elaborate furniture, soft furnishings and bedding.[47] This reorientation was probably facilitated by significant (although far from universal) reductions in unit prices. Wooden furniture underwent a substantial fall in price from the 1660s to at least the 1720s, probably as a result of the increased use of imported softwood, while a number of the new household products also became cheaper, most strikingly clocks.[48]

As far as the labouring poor are concerned, the situation is even more murky. Like the middling group, there was probably an extension of consumption, and one that was already well-established in the seventeenth century, although the volume and range of consumer durables and semi-durables owned by the poor was much more restricted.[49] In the absence of substantial inventory evidence, it is difficult to isolate a distinctive eighteenth-century trajectory for this group. Nevertheless, it is clear that ownership of certain types of new consumer durables and semi-durables had become widespread among the labouring poor by the last two decades of the eighteenth century. Cotton gowns and breeches were commonly owned by working people at this period. Earthenware teapots were familiar adornments of their dressers and mantelpieces, and teatime was a conventional way for them to refer to the late afternoon. Labouring men comprised more than half the owners of stolen watches who brought prosecutions for watch theft at the assizes in the north of England in these years.[50] None of these goods had been generally accessible to the labouring poor a hundred years earlier.

How did this change come about? Falling prices played a part, but there is also good reason to believe that family incomes increased, especially because there was more waged work available for women and children.[51] Moreover, the scope of market relationships expanded, although this was not a new phenomenon. At the start of the eighteenth century, poor consumers were already strikingly dependent on money wages, market transactions and national and international as well as local circuits of commodities. However, these forms of market engagement intensified and colonized new sites as the century progressed, and not simply because of the dramatic improvements in communications. In the later eighteenth century, for example, day labour increasingly superseded farm service in the south, and with it came a greater direct reliance for provisions on retail suppliers rather than employers.[52] Local and household manufacture of some basic commodities, such as cheap, coarse linen cloth, tended to be replaced with finished or semi-finished products sourced at a distance.[53] Unfortunately, it is not clear whether greater reliance by working people on retail transactions was associated with increased access to credit and therefore more spending power. We know very little about the shop credit, pawnbroking and petty money-lending that were an inescapable component of the lives of many eighteenth-century working people, although new devices to facilitate the purchase of the more expensive consumer goods did emerge in the eighteenth century, for example the cloth clubs and clock and watch clubs which provided them with the advantages of co-operative purchasing.[54]

What is especially striking about the consumption habits of the eighteenth-century labouring poor is their capacity to respond to accessible innovations. The penetration of this market by gin in the first half of the eighteenth century and by increasingly cheap cotton clothing in the 1780s and 1790s demonstrates the willingness of poor consumers to substitute new commodities for old – gin for beer, breeches made of fustian for those made of leather.[55] Their receptiveness to novelties that were not in any straightforward sense substitutes for existing products is indicated by the spread among significant numbers of poor consumers of wigs, tea and watches. The chronology of innovation – wigs appear to have been adopted by substantial numbers of labouring men early in the eighteenth century and were largely dispensed with after the 1770s – suggests that an interest in fashion and novelty was not something that developed only during the later years of the century, even at this level of the market.[56]

Despite the shortcomings of the available quantitative data, an outline can, therefore, be drawn of the social shape of the eighteenth-century English market for consumer goods and a measure taken of its implications for manufacturers. In many respects trends already established in the seventeenth century were reinforced. The middle and lower levels of the market were strong and expanding. Customers of this sort were crucially important for manufacturers. The rich had far greater individual spending power, but they were numerically insignificant. The orientation of British manufacturers to the middle and lower levels of society was further encouraged by the extremely rapid growth of the largely captive American market, in which people with middling wealth were so prominent. The targeting of British products at these customers and the success of British manufacturers in generating an appropriate mix of quality and price was a matter of general comment in Britain and overseas.[57]

It must be stressed, however, that despite the proliferation of goods amongst the middling sort and especially the labouring poor, for much of the eighteenth century the bulk of their expenditure continued to be on food, and a higher proportion of expenditure went on clothing than on domestic furnishings and other manufactures. Lorna Weatherill has noted how bare by modern standards the domestic interiors of the middling sort could be in the opening decades of the eighteenth century.[58] The same probably remained true, though to a markedly lesser extent, at its close. We are not talking here about the kind of saturation with objects characteristic of many modern western households. Objects were fewer and their range narrower.

Increasingly, middling and labouring consumers were purchasers of goods, and an increasing proportion of what they bought was produced, in part or in whole, by distant manufacturers in long runs. This was a feature of early eighteenth-century English consumption emphasized by Daniel Defoe.

> Suppose the poorest countryman wants to be clothed, or suppose it be a gentleman wants to clothe one of his servants, whether a footman in a livery or suppose it be any servant in ordinary apparel, yet he shall, in some part, employ almost every one of the manufacturing counties of England, for making up one ordinary suit of clothes. . . . Come next to the furniture of [a country grocer's] house; it is scarce credible to how many counties of England, and how remote, the furniture of but a mean house must send them; and how many people are everywhere employed about it; nay, and the meaner the furniture, the more people and places employed.[59]

This is not to suggest, however, that local processing ceased to be important for either perishable or non-perishable commodities. The neighbourhood baker, tailor and shoemaker retained an important manufacturing role, but such local processing became embedded in ever more complex and extensive flows of raw, semi-finished and finished materials. Nor is it to suggest that these developments were uncontentious, as the eighteenth-century history of grain riots, market regulation, retailing guilds and itinerant trading demonstrates.[60] Moreover, we should remember that significant groups in English and North American society, such as slaves, farm and domestic servants, apprentices and paupers in receipt of relief, engaged in relationships of buying and selling indirectly, intermittently or for only a small proportion of what they consumed.

In a purely numerical sense, none the less, there was in the eighteenth century a kind of mass market. Hundreds of thousands of humble consumers bought a wide range of goods from distant producers with some regularity. But caution needs to be exercised regarding the implications of a mass market in this limited sense for product design and particularly product differentiation. Not all mass markets have resembled that which sustained the extraordinary success of the ultra-standardized Model T Ford in early twentieth-century America; a market consisting of a huge, egalitarian, socially homogeneous population in moderately well-off, rural America, where purchasers were hungry for cheap mass motor transport, but shared common tastes and were relatively unconcerned with the potential for social self-differentiation offered by the competitive acquisition of cars as luxury, fashion objects.[61] The social shape of the eighteenth-century English market for consumer goods was probably closer to the mid-Victorian England described by Raphael Samuel, where the middle classes were obsessed with securing household products that expressed individuality, self-differentiation and luxury by means of visual diversity.[62] The kind of receptiveness to visual novelty and differentiation normally associated with the Victorian middle classes was already present at relatively humble levels of the domestic market from the late seventeenth century. The diffusion of the new household comforts, the multiplication of dress and furnishing fabrics and the spread of oriental and classical decoration – what Michael Sonenscher has termed the extraordinary 'ethnicization' of European design[63] – all indicate a tendency for colour and new forms of ornament to proliferate. A taste for visual novelty is also implicit in the shift to lighter, less durable products, especially in textiles. However, these forms of product differentiation did not require the bespoke manufacturing convention- ally associated with speciality craft or luxury production. As has already been pointed out, frequently it was possible to manufacture relatively cheap goods incorporating these charac- teristics in batches to a range of standard or consistent specifications.

The second issue that needs to be addressed in establishing what was distinctive about eighteenth-century consumption is that of consumer manipulation. The eighteenth century saw a new stress on colour and novel forms of ornament in goods acquired by humble purchasers. Does this indicate the emergence of those kinds of consumer manipulation by means of design, marketing and advertising which the mass culture theorists identified as the defining characteristics of consumer societies? It has certainly been the view of historians of eighteenth-century consumption that the manipulation of fashion by means of advertising and other marketing techniques was crucial to its expansion.[64] Considerable caution, how- ever, needs to be exercised here. The eighteenth century did witness the first large-scale use of impersonal, widely broadcast advertising, employing the medium of print. Handbills, trade cards and newspaper and magazine advertisements, which had all been used on a very limited scale in the later seventeenth century, became ubiquitous in the course of the eighteenth century, following the removal of official restrictions on printing in 1695. During the eighteenth century, the numbers of individual advertisements printed in the newspapers alone almost certainly ran into millions. They supplemented, although they by no means entirely replaced, pre-existing, more limited modes of disseminating commercial information, such as the crying of goods and shop signs. These new forms of advertising could be effective well down the social scale.[65] Their creators were extraordinarily precocious in inventing techniques for the new medium. Just as the early film makers of the silent era experimented with almost all the visual techniques that have subsequently been used in the cinema, so eighteenth-century advertisers tried out many of the devices employed in modern advertising copy.[66]

The insinuation of printed advertising into many aspects of eighteenth-century life was a new and highly visible development. But the triumph of the printed advertisement was a strictly limited one. In the absence of representative collections of handbills, an estimate of the total volume of eighteenth-century printed advertising is difficult and any evaluation of its character has to rely disproportionately on the newspaper and the periodical press.[67] Their evidence suggests that the use of the more sophisticated techniques like endorsements, testimonials, special offers and guarantees was restricted to a narrow range of advertisements, especially those for books, proprietary medicines, shoe polish, showmen and travelling salesmen. Very limited use was made of visual devices, and the texts of most advertisements, especially those in the provincial press for manufactured goods other than books and medicines, were pedestrian. They simply listed the goods available and sometimes asserted their quality, cheapness, variety, novelty or metropolitan origin, while flattering customers by referring to them as gentlemen or ladies.[68] Indeed, what these advertisements sometimes suggest is a sellers' market in which considerable difficulty could face the consumer in gaining physical access to goods of the required specification. We are a long way here from the extensive advertising of branded products characteristic of the end of the nineteenth century, or the concern with the mental processes of the consumer, with empathy and therapy, that had become widespread in advertisements by the mid-twentieth century.[69]

In other words, the intensity of printed advertising was relatively low by subsequent standards, much of it made little effort to enhance the image of the product and it was only one of a battery of eighteenth-century techniques whereby the sale of commodities was promoted to the public, many of which operated through the individual retailer. In these circumstances, it is difficult to imagine that eighteenth-century advertising produced the general saturation in product images or the wholesale transfiguration of products into psychological props which the mass culture theorists dubiously claim modern advertisements have engendered. This is not to suggest that a capacity for goods to acquire (or to be endowed with) diverse images and associations was lacking in the eighteenth century, or unknown before it. Such images and associations were not necessarily aspects of sales promotion. For instance, goods had long served as potent symbols of national identity: the roast beef of old England; leather as opposed to wooden shoes; sturdy English woollen cloth as opposed to effeminate French silk.[70] Other images and associations – aristocratic and metropolitan, for example – were prominently employed in the marketing of commodities. It was possible to use them in this way because so many English people were already accustomed to accord considerable (although by no means exclusive) significance to considerations of novelty, fashion and the taste of the metropolitan elite in their dealings with goods.

Advertisements for manufactured goods, other than books and medicines, accounted for only a small proportion of the total volume of advertising. Moreover, with the exception of the well-known examples like proprietary medicines and shoe polish, most advertisements for manufactured goods did not promote a particular branded product or manufacturer, but rather a particular retailer or wholesaler.[71] This is not surprising, because of all the many developments in eighteenth-century marketing, it was the increase in the number of shops that probably had the biggest direct impact on the individual consumer of manufactures. The shops concerned were mainly independent, relatively small retailers, not the chain or department stores of the later nineteenth century with their own heavily promoted brand identities. Nevertheless, it has been calculated that by the 1750s London had achieved a ratio of shops to population that would not be surpassed during the remainder of the eighteenth century or the nineteenth century, and the rest of the country was fast catching up.[72]

The paucity of advertisements by manufacturers calls into question historians' obsession with the exertions made by Josiah Wedgwood in pottery and Matthew Boulton in the button and ornament trade to mount brand-name promotional campaigns directed at the individual consumer. Particular emphasis has been placed on the way they initiated new designs in accordance with or in advance of changes in fashionable taste in order to secure a privileged place in the market, and the way they promoted those designs, by the use of advertising and showrooms, and especially by providing individual luxury products for noble and royal patrons in order to promote the wider fashionability of their less expensive lines. These activities have been interpreted as a precocious form of strategic market management, directly manipulating the consumer in order to sustain production, in the manner of General Motors' styling policy of the mid-1920s.[73]

In fact, brand-name marketing directed at the individual consumer by careful manipulation of design and advertising was rare among those large-scale eighteenth-century manufacturers of consumer durables and semi-durables who produced for the middle and lower sections of the market. However, the activities of Boulton and Wedgwood did have parallels among those producing exclusively for the top of the market. Thomas Chippendale's innovatory designs printed in *The Gentleman and Cabinet Maker's Director* in 1754 served as much as an advertisement for his cabinet-making business to potential wealthy customers as a source of designs for other cabinet makers.[74] Such parallels are not surprising, given Boulton and Wedgwood were also concerned to secure aristocratic custom, although in their cases in order to forge an explicit association in public thinking between their cheaper products and the fashionable elite. Manufacturers of humbler consumer products did not generally make much use of these high-profile techniques of salesmanship, but that is not to say design and marketing were unimportant to them. Their domestic marketing was focused not on promoting their brand names to final customers, but on selling to retailers and wholesalers.[75] As communications improved, information flows intensified, the visual diversity of goods increased and the retail network became more dense, many manufacturers improved their marketing to retailers and wholesalers by making more use of techniques like travelling salesmen, showrooms and pattern books and cards, or by using dealers and agents who employed these techniques.[76] Careful attention by manufacturers to design could be crucially important here. As wholesalers and retailers (who, after all, were specialists in marketing) were well aware, the meanings which accrue to objects are intimately associated with the way they look. Design can therefore sell goods. It was not essential to court the patronage of the aristocratic 'legislators of taste' to endow products with associations of fashionability and exclusiveness. Men like Wedgwood clearly believed it was best to make the aristocratic link explicit to final customers, but it was possible to evoke these and other attractive associations in the minds of consumers simply by ensuring that the product embodied the right visual messages.

The dictates of the market and the implementation of design

Eighteenth-century manufacturers of batch-produced consumer goods faced markets that were often keenly attuned to the visual appearance of their products. Novelty and fashion could be important, although not necessarily dominant, at every level in the market. In some markets, goods that missed the latest fashion trend could not be easily sold. On receipt of a consignment of hats from Stockport, Cheshire that had to be returned for reworking because they were damaged, a London hatmaker commented in 1784, 'they will be good for little; they certainly will look like old hats; let them be done as soon as possible'.[77] The imperatives of constantly changing fashion were particularly pressing on those like the Spitalfields manufacturers of fine patterned silks who supplied dress materials to the extremely wealthy and fashionable, but they also extended to the makers of more modest buttons, buckles, hats, handkerchiefs and other patterned cloths.

As we have seen, the manufacturers of products such as these were often geographically distant from the final consumer. Moreover, they were, more often than not, distant from the metropolitan high society which was so influential on eighteenth-century fashionable taste. Two questions arise regarding the design of their products. First, how did such manufacturers determine the way their products should look in order to enjoy success in a variety of markets? Second, how did they ensure that their workers, often using hand techniques in their own homes, produced goods that accorded with the desired and often very precise visual specifications?

Most existing work on these subjects has focused either on the activities of those producing high design goods for the elite market, or on the distinctive ways design was exploited by Josiah Wedgwood and Matthew Boulton. Particular emphasis has been placed on the latter's initiation of new designs (both in the sense of new products and new forms of decoration) in accordance with or in advance of changes in fashionable taste, in order to secure a privileged place in the market. By making products to original designs, Boulton and Wedgwood were simply doing what had long been established practice in the London luxury trades. Not all metropolitan producers of luxury goods developed new designs, but it could be an important element in the success of such a business. In his discussion of cabinetmaking in *The London Tradesman* of 1747, Campbell emphasized that

> A youth who designs to make a Figure in this Branch must learn to Draw; for upon this depends the Invention of new Fashions, and on that the Success of his Business: He who first hits upon any new Whim is sure to make by the Invention before it becomes common in the Trade; but he that must always wait for a new Fashion till it comes from *Paris*, or is hit upon by his Neighbour, is never likely to grow rich or eminent in his Way.[78]

The fruits of innovation were similar in many of the other luxury trades. The Spitalfields silkmakers, for example, systematically commissioned novel designs in order to pre-empt changes in fashion.[79]

Producers of more modest consumer goods did not generally exercise the same degree of initiative in staying ahead of fashion. They simply adapted the broad trend of prevailing London high fashion to the prejudices and pockets of their intended customers. As in many aspects of eighteenth-century industrial innovation, a process of copying combined with small incremental adjustments was the norm. Stanley Chapman has pointed out the importance of systematic piracy of expensive London designs by Lancashire cotton printers producing for the lower end of the market in the 1780s.[80] During the same decade, the Leeds merchant house of Horner and Turner often arranged for their manufacturing suppliers to imitate woollen and worsted cloths sold by their competitors in continental Europe.[81] Manufacturers were often secretive, but successful copying and adaptation required information about what other producers, and particularly fashion leaders, were doing, as well as information about what different markets were anxious or prepared to accept.[82] Hence the constant monitoring by manufacturers of what producers of similar goods were up to, hence the desperate efforts to secure information on changes in London taste, hence the voluminous advice from agents and wholesale customers on market trends.

If design depended for most producers on copying and adaptation, precisely how was visual information on what was to be copied communicated? One way was simply to acquire an example of the product to be pirated. This was common. In textiles, for example, it was fairly easy to secure a small piece of a competitor's fabric. A 1787 parliamentary committee was informed that a print of a new design from a Surrey printworks had been sent by a London warehouseman to the Peel printworks in Lancashire to be copied. Within a fortnight it was on sale in London at two-thirds of the price of the original.[83]

Another means of communicating visual information was to use two-dimensional depictions of an object or its ornament. One of the most striking new features of late seventeenth- and eighteenth-century manufacturing in England was a dramatic increase in the use of two-dimensional paper plans for subsequent three-dimensional execution. Designs on paper had been employed long before the mid-seventeenth century, by architects and goldsmiths for example, but over the next century and a half there was a massive expansion, at first concentrated in London, but later more extensive, of activities reliant on sophisticated design and ornament, such as cabinetmaking, coachmaking, cotton printing, silkweaving and the manufacture of decorative metalware. At the same time, there were important technical innovations in two-dimensional and low relief ornament: for example, copper plate printing on fabrics, stamping on the softer metals, the use of transfers on ceramics. The consequence was a vastly increased use of both printed and hand-drawn two-dimensional designs in the manufacturing of consumer goods, for a variety of purposes. They were used as sources of visual ideas, as instructions for the execution of the work, for recording information about products and as a means of visualizing products for customers.

As two-dimensional design became more important, designer and pattern drawer emerged as distinct occupational designations. The term designer was first used early in the eighteenth century to describe those who performed the highly specialized task of providing new designs for fine patterned textiles, often on a freelance basis, but by mid-century it was being used more extensively.[84] The demand for drawing and associated skills like engraving grew apace. By the middle years of the eighteenth century there was much complaint about skill shortages in this area. Some of the deficiency had to be made up from overseas and considerable efforts were mounted to provide training. In 1759 it was claimed 'that there are two or three drawing schools established at Birmingham, for the instruction of youth in the arts of designing and drawing, and 30 or 40 Frenchmen and Germans are constantly employed in drawing and designing'.[85]

From the later seventeenth century, the London book and print trade catered to the expanding industrial market for two-dimensional designs with prints and subsequently illustrated source books. As early as the 1660s, the London bookseller and print dealer

Robert Walton stocked prints which he advertised as 'extraordinarily useful for goldsmiths, jewellers, chafers, gravers, painters, carvers, drawers, needlewomen and all handicrafts'.[86] In the eighteenth century, design source books were often targeted at particular trades, like Smith and Linnell's *A New Book of Ornaments Useful for Silver-Smith's Etc.* of 1755 or Chippendale's *The Gentleman and Cabinet Maker's Director* of 1754, although designs for one material could be transferred to another, given the ubiquity of certain types of classical and rococo ornament within elite material culture.[87] From mid-century, if not before, printed designs also circulated in the illustrated trade catalogues issued by some manufacturers of ceramics, light consumer metalwares and even tools.[88] These were unabashed marketing devices, for use in showrooms, by travelling salesmen and by wholesale customers, similar in purpose to the pattern cards and books which were widely employed by textile manufacturers and merchants to circulate samples of fabric.

Clearly the increasing availability of drawing and design skills and the growing circulation in various guises of design illustrations facilitated the acquisition of design information by manufacturers and its adaptation for use in their products (legitimately or otherwise).[89] It is therefore surprising to realize the extent to which manufacturers in many eighteenth-century industries producing batches of relatively modest products on a large scale secured design information by means of the written or spoken word. This was partly because in these industries the crucial design changes were often quite simple – a new range of colours here, a different width of stripe there. In textiles, for example, weaving simple patterned cloths did not necessarily require the painstakingly prepared patterns on point paper used in weaving elaborate designs on unwieldy draw looms in the Spitalfields silk industry. One should not, however, underestimate the richness of the information that could be communicated by means of the written word. The degree of complexity is indicated in a letter that Matthew Boulton wrote to his London buckle agent in 1793 on the need to settle on a terminology for describing changes in fashion: 'As you and I shall often have occasion to speak of forms and proportions of buckles, it is necessary we should settle a distinct language that our definitions may be precise.'[90] In most trades, however, an appropriate language of visual description already existed. Indeed, it was a fundamental aspect of that elusive but much prized knowledge of the trade which was essential to participation in it.[91] But it was also possible for non-specialists to use a verbal language of visual description in the same way. For example, information about new fashions in clothes sufficiently precise to instruct a local mantua maker was sent to a Lancashire gentlewoman from a London relative mainly through the medium of words, not drawings or illustrations.[92]

The importance of a verbal language of visual description was not confined to the process whereby manufacturers secured information about design innovation. It was also central to their ability to adapt that information to their own advantage; to get their workers successfully to produce goods which incorporated those innovations. In other words, it was crucial to communication within the firm. For example, the late eighteenth-century London hatmaker Thomas Davies was accustomed to communicate the design of new hats to the manager of his manufacturing operation in Stockport, Cheshire by letter along the following lines: 'a short napp, almost like a French hat but not so bare, pleasant stiffen'd, rather smart, by no means raggy and not a heavy hat; they are to be from $7^{1}/_{4}$ to $7^{1}/_{2}$, $3^{1}/_{4}$ to $3^{3}/_{4}$ high, not quite upright, a little taper.'[93] Here we observe the use of a specialist vocabulary in combination with a system of standard sizes to communicate precise specifications for a batch of goods.

This kind of verbal communication to specify the intended look of a product was common in other industries. Sometimes words were used in conjunction with three-dimensional devices for communicating visual information, like moulds or sample objects. In the 1770s and 1780s, the London agent for the Royal Northumberland Bottle Works sent his orders to the works manager by letter in the following manner:

> Be so good to send me by first opportunity 6 doz. bottles to the pattern sent, which holds near 2 gallons, must be imitated both in strength and shape as near as possible. 7 doz. parting glasses to 3 patterns sent. 4 doz. 4 gallon bottles, exact to the size of the pattern sent, the neck straight up, the mouth 2½ inch diameter and no less. 100 3 gallon bottles to pattern, no larger in size with good stopper mouths.[94]

The patterns mentioned here were sample bottles.

Even when two-dimensional information was transmitted, words were often an essential accompaniment, because manufacturers did not simply want their workers to copy, but to adapt, adjust and elaborate in ways appropriate to their markets, their materials and their skills. The partners in one Lancashire cotton printing firm at the beginning of the nineteenth century sent samples of other firms' prints to their pattern drawer with accompanying verbal instructions, usually to vary the ground or the motifs, or to change the direction, the emphasis or the size of the pattern. For example, 'Enclosed you have a pattern of one of the Bury House's plate furnitures. Joseph Peel desires you will draw up and engrave two or three patterns similar, they must be showey and full of work.'[95]

Success in the consumer industries depended not only on the products being of a market-able and therefore often a fashionable design, but also on each individual item conforming strictly to a precise visual specification embodying that marketability. Distant wholesale customers who bought on the basis of samples and illustrated trade catalogues expected the goods delivered to them to conform to the look of the sample or the illustration. Uniformity was crucial, but was often extremely difficult to achieve, especially when making adaptations of more expensive products in large batches using inferior materials and cheaper, less skilled and more pressured labour.[96] Consequently manufacturers, agents, wholesalers and retailers were constantly monitoring the appearance of batch-produced goods and chiding their workers and suppliers about visual deficiencies. This kind of visual policing was conducted mainly in words.

In 1781 the London agent for the Royal Northumberland Bottle Works complained to the works manager,

> I have returned you by Dawson some of the [bottles] which are of a very bad quality . . . half the cargoe is such, some of the bottles have necks ¾ of an inch too long, flat shoulders and blown in different moulds. I beg you will take care not to send me any more of those blown in that narrow mould, but let it be destroyed as I cannot sell them on any account.[97]

Davies the London hatmaker commented to his Stockport manager in 1783:

> We have received a little order from Vau as under which beg your attention to; he complains that our hats are not so good as those from other houses, which

occasions our having so few of his orders and that we never send them exact to the sizes he orders them at.[98]

The same problem obliged a Cumbrian glovemaker to offer the following tortuous excuse to a London wholesale customer in 1733: 'The leather is as good as . . . our country affords, not but that there may [be] some of them not so good as other some, for 'tis impossible to have all equally alike.'[99]

Implementing design in large-batch manufacturing of consumer goods in the eighteenth century depended on the dexterity and adaptability of the individual worker, and on the employer's capacity to direct and instruct a workforce. The initiative in specifying design flowed predominantly from master manufacturer to worker, but the ability of workers autonomously to interpret and adapt the manufacturer's instructions was also essential. Much turned on the capacity of employees, frequently working in their own homes within an intense division of labour, to use what were often general purpose tools to produce the required specification uniformly across hundreds or thousands of objects. Much also turned on the ability of the employer to communicate his requirements to such employees with sufficient precision. All sorts of devices for specifying, transmitting and reproducing visual information could play a part here, including moulds, models, dies, transfers, scale patterns and paper designs. In the course of the eighteenth century the use of two-dimensional designs probably increased, but their importance should not be overestimated. In many of these industries a specialized and sophisticated verbal language of visual description remained crucial.[100]

Conclusion: design practice and design training

Eighteenth-century England witnessed considerable efforts to improve the quality of design in manufacturing. As Charles Saumarez Smith has demonstrated, the central thrust of these efforts was to teach drawing and other artistic skills to workpeople.[101] If, as has been argued in this chapter, two-dimensional designs were of restricted importance in many of the industries producing humble consumer goods, why was there such concern to promote drawing?

Part of the answer lies in the rapid expansion during the late seventeenth and eighteenth centuries of those forms of production which relied on the most sophisticated ornament and design, especially for the luxury market. The consequence of this expansion and the technical innovations of the same period in two-dimensional and low relief ornament was a real increase in the need for drawing and engraving skills, a need that sometimes had to be supplied by foreign immigrants. The design debate was conducted principally in London. The metropolitan area was by far the largest manufacturing centre in the country, and it was distinguished by a disproportionately large luxury sector, which made heavy use of both printed and hand-drawn two-dimensional designs.

Another important consideration behind the promotion of drawing skills was the persistent eighteenth-century English obsession with French competition. This was made clear in 1756 by one of the protagonists of design training, William Shipley, the founder of the Society of Arts and owner of a drawing school.

The money given for the encouragement of boys and girls to apply themselves to drawing has not, 'tis hoped, been misemployed, since drawing is necessary in so many trades, that the general knowledge of it must conduce greatly to the improvement of our manufactures, and give them an elegance of air and figure, which a rival nation (where drawing is much encouraged) has found, to its great advantage, capable of setting off even indifferent workmanship and mean materials.[102]

The English worried throughout the eighteenth century about French superiority in the manufacture of luxury goods. Efforts to improve design reached their height in the middle decades of the century, when such anxieties were at their most intense. In the second quarter of the century, before the rapid pre-revolutionary expansion of the North American colonial market, foreign markets for the humble products in which the English excelled (especially woollen textiles) appeared to stagnate.[103] Worries about England being priced out of these markets by its high wage costs prompted the belief that it was necessary for English manufacturing to compete more effectively at the top of the market, a belief reinforced by the perceived buoyancy of luxury imports from France, despite heavy duties and prohibitions. French success in the manufacture of luxury goods seemed to owe everything to the quality of French design.

Such fears receded later in the eighteenth century, as doubts about the success of English products in the middle and lower levels of the markets for consumer goods waned. In the aftermath of the commercial treaty of 1786, which reduced trade restrictions between Britain and France, it was the British who appeared to benefit and the French who complained.[104] What happened to the promotion of drawing skills for manufacturing is less clear. There is no doubt that at the middle and lower levels of the market drawing skills could be very important. The Birmingham toy makers and the Lancashire cotton printers, for example, depended on specialist engravers and draughtsmen. As we have seen, however, such expertise was mainly required for copying and adapting designs to be implemented in large volume by other workers within an intense division of labour, rather than for initiating original designs to be produced in very small numbers. Copying and adaptation did not necessarily entail a high degree of proficiency in drawing and, on the evidence of the early years of Sir Robert Peel's Bury printworks, it required only very small numbers of workers with the appropriate skills. There was no drawing shop at Bury and only one draughtsman employed there.[105] It is therefore questionable how relevant schemes for the encouragement of formal drawing skills, like those promoted in mid-century London, were to manufacturing of this sort, compared with on-the-job training involving some sort of apprenticeship.[106]

In so far as the process of design in the eighteenth century has been explored in detail by historians, the focus has usually been on the part played by the compilers of pattern books in the making of extremely expensive and often bespoke products. The precise role of visual design in the making of many humble consumer goods remains obscure. Understanding it will demand a great deal more attention to the mundane drawing skills required for successful industrial piracy, but a narrow focus on drawing will not suffice if what is to be explained is the changes in appearance of the consumer products discussed in this chapter. That will also require study of the specialized languages of visual description used in the various manufacturing trades; indeed it will require investigation of all aspects of what might loosely be termed their and their customers' visual culture. The history of eighteenth-century design in this wider sense has yet to be written.

Notes

I would like to thank Helen Clifford, Craig Clunas, Bill Doyle, Andrew Federer, Paul Glennie, Fiona Hackney, Julian Hoppit, Joanna Innes, Catherine Ross, Charles Saumarez Smith, Michael Sonenscher, Amanda Vickery, Tim Wales and Jonathan Zeitlin for references and suggestions. Some of the ideas in this essay were first aired in John Styles, 'Design for large-scale production in eighteenth-century Britain', *Oxford Art Journal*, xi (1988), 10–16. Parts of the research were funded by the Pasold Research Fund; I would like to express my gratitude to its Governors.

1 T. H. Breen, 'An empire of goods: the Anglicization of colonial America, 1690–1776', *Journal of British Studies*, xxv (1986), 467–99.

2 J. T. Lemon, *The Best Poor Man's Country: A Geographical Study of Early Southeastern Pennsylvania* (New York, 1976), xiii, n. 1, 5, n. 4.

3 For occupationally specific consumption patterns, see L. Weatherill, *Consumer Behaviour and Material Culture in England, 1660–1760* (London, 1988), ch. 8, and C. Shammas, 'Consumer behaviour in colonial America', *Social Science History*, vi (1982), 77–8. Shammas demonstrates that American farmers owned significantly fewer consumer goods than craftsmen and tradesmen; Weatherill stresses the conservatism of English farmers' patterns of ownership of consumer goods and her figures too suggest lower levels of ownership. The extent of self-sufficiency among eighteenth-century American farmers has been much debated, but recent work suggests that self-sufficient households were atypical. See C. Shammas, 'How self-sufficient was early America?', *Journal of Interdisciplinary History*, xiii (1982), 247–72. Also see J. J. McCusker and R. R. Menard, *The Economy of British America, 1607–1789* (Chapel Hill, 1985), ch. 13.

4 Breen, 'Empire of goods', 493, 489.

5 McCusker and Menard argue that, in the course of the eighteenth century, American production of low quality manufactures grew and imports became increasingly concentrated at the quality and fashionable end of the market; see McCusker and Menard, *The Economy of British America*, 287.

6 The term 'fashion' is an ambiguous one. It has been used by economic historians to mean everything from a visual novelty of almost any kind to the very precise seasonal shifts associated with metropolitan high style in clothes. In this essay, which is concerned mainly with goods destined for non-elite consumers, I use the word to refer to changes in the appearance of products which loosely followed the trend, if not every detail, of metropolitan elite taste.

7 A. Forty, *Objects of Desire: Design and Society, 1750–1980* (London, 1986), 29 and see 42–7. Also see John Heskett, *Industrial Design* (London, 1980), introduction and ch. 1. For a similar view from a social historian, see R. Porter, *English Society in the Eighteenth Century* (London, 1982), 243.

8 All these phrases are used, particularly by Neil McKendrick, in the most influential single work on the subject, N. McKendrick, J. Brewer and J. H. Plumb, *The Birth of a Consumer Society* (London, 1982). For specific instances, see title and 9, 53, 98.

9 For a sustained analysis of these issues see D. Hounshell, *From the American System to Mass Production, 1800–1932* (Baltimore, 1985), especially introduction and chs 6, 7. Hounshell discusses the origins of the phrase 'mass production' at 1–2 and 303.

10 D. Graysmith, 'The impact of technology on printed textiles in the early-nineteenth century', in Design Council, *Design and Industry: The Effects of Industrialisation and Technical Change on Design* (London, 1980), 62.

11 N. McKendrick, 'The commercialization of fashion', in McKendrick, Brewer and Plumb, *The Birth of a Consumer Society*, 53. Clothes were not machine cut or sewn at this period. Elsewhere in the same book (75–6), McKendrick uses the phrase 'assembly line production' to describe the manufacturing system at Josiah Wedgwood's Etruria pottery. This is curious, not simply because there was no mechanical assembly line at Etruria, but because it was not until the installation of tunnel kilns from the 1930s that the use of a continuous process technology became widespread in the British pottery industry.

550   John Styles

12 Peter Mathias, *The First Industrial Nation* (London, 1969), 1.
13 See I. C. Walker, 'Aspects of the clay tobacco pipe industry from the point of view of the manufacturing techniques and of the changing patterns of trade and smoking, and with particular reference to the industry in Bristol' (University of Bath, Ph.D. thesis, 1973), 193–4, 250–5, 272–3.
14 The Peter Mathias quotation above is an unusual exception.
15 Quoted in W. I. Susman, *Culture as History: The Transformation of American Society in the Twentieth Century* (New York, 1984), 136.
16 R. Marchand, *Advertising the American Dream* (Berkeley, 1985), 158.
17 See M. M. Edwards, *The Growth of the British Cotton Trade, 1780–1815* (Manchester, 1967), chs 3 and 4 and Figure B/1, 247; J. James, *History of the Worsted Manufacture in England* (London, 1857), ch. 12 and D. T. Jenkins and K. G. Ponting (eds), *The British Wool Textile Industry, 1770–1914* (London, 1982), ch. 6.
18 This process of product innovation and diversification, before and after the Industrial Revolution, is emphasized in D. C. Coleman, 'Textile growth', in N. B. Harte and K. G. Ponting (eds), *Textile History and Economic History* (Manchester, 1973).
19 F. Atkinson, *Some Aspects of the Eighteenth-Century Woollen and Worsted Trade in Halifax* (Halifax, 1956), 1. The estimates of the size of the labour force are my own, based on eighteenth-century computations. It is not clear whether Hill employed all these workers directly.
20 A letter in the *Leeds Intelligencer*, 24 September 1776 commented on the 'great number of the master manufacturers' in the industry; E. M. Sigsworth, 'William Greenwood and Robert Heaton: two eighteenth-century worsted manufacturers', *Journal of the Bradford Textile Society* (1951–2), 72; Atkinson, *Woollen and Worsted Trade in Halifax*, 65.
21 K. H. Burley, 'The economic development of Essex in the later seventeenth and early eighteenth centuries' (University of London, Ph.D. thesis, 1957), 125–6.
22 Samuel Hill and Robert Heaton both made major innovations in their product ranges, Hill by expanding into bays and serges in the 1730s, Heaton by moving in the early 1780s out of shalloons and into figured worsted cloths.
23 This was also the way scheduling was arranged in the Birmingham toy trade:

> the custom of the trade is to work from orders taken from patterns; that the patterns sent to correspondents abroad, are from 6 to 12 months before they are returned; but the patterns for home trade are generally returned in a month or less.
>
> (*Journal of the House of Commons*, vol. 28 (1757–61), 496–7)

24 Atkinson, *Woollen and Worsted Trade in Halifax*, 2–4.
25 See, for examples, West Yorkshire County Record Office, Calderdale, HAS:307: John Firth, Halifax, letter book, 1739–40, and Public Record Office, C108/101: Horner and Turner merchants of Leeds, letter book, 1787–90.
26 M. Berg, *The Age of Manufactures, 1700–1820* (London, 1985), 290, and M. B. Rowlands, *Masters and Men* (Manchester, 1975), 155–6.
27 Catherine Ross, *The Development of the Glass Industry in the Rivers Tyne and Wear, 1700–1900* (University of Newcastle-upon-Tyne, Ph.D. thesis, 1982), ch. 3.
28 Calculated on the basis of six weeks' production recorded in Northumberland R. O., Delaval Mss., 2/DE.11.5: Day book of bottle and glassware production in the Second and Third glasshouses, 1781–2. Output was recorded in dozens, a term which meant different amounts in different industries, but internal evidence suggests that the dozen used in the Hartley work's accounts was twelve.
29 For example, for yarn standards in the worsted industries see the following acts of parliament: 7 Jac. I, c. 7 (1609), 13 and 14 Car. II, c. 5 (1662), 17 Geo. III, c. 11 (1777), 24 Geo. III, St. 3, c. 3 (1784), 25 Geo. III, c. 40 (1785), 31 Geo. III, c. 56 (1791).
30 For shoes see Randle Holme, *The Academy of Armory* (Chester, 1688), Book 3, 99; for hats see Public

Record Office, C107/104: Chancery Masters' Exhibits, Letter book of Thomas Davies, hatter.

31 Hounshell, *American System to Mass Production*, chs 6, 7.

32 See N. K. A. Rothstein, 'The silk industry in London, 1702–1766' (University of London, M.A. thesis, 1961), 171–2, 218–22 and Helen Clifford, 'Parker and Wakelin: a Westminster firm of goldsmiths in the later-eighteenth century' (Royal College of Art, Ph.D. thesis, 1989), *passim*.

33 I am not convinced by the particular emphasis Adrian Forty places on Wedgwood's desire to facilitate large-scale, serial production in explaining his adoption of neo-classicism. See Forty, *Objects of Desire*, 37–9.

34 Atkinson, *Woollen and Worsted Trade in Halifax*, 14.

35 A. Young, *Arthur Young's Tour in Ireland*, vol. 2 (London, 1892), 133–4. I would like to thank Joanna Innes for bringing this quotation to my attention.

36 C. MacLeod, *Inventing the Industrial Revolution: The English Patent System, 1660–1800* (Cambridge, 1988), 177–8.

37 Hounshell, *American System to Mass Production*, 221.

38 Clifford, 'Parker and Wakelin', demonstrates that even in a supposedly 'craft' trade, like the manufacture of expensive silverware, the making of a piece was rarely undertaken by a single master craftsman, and much of the work was subcontracted outside the workshop, either in whole or in part. Standardized components, such as handles, were sometimes used.

39 See, for example, Rosalind H. Williams, *Dreamworlds: Mass Consumption in Late Nineteenth-Century France* (Berkeley, 1982) and Elizabeth Ewen, *Channels of Desire: Mass Images and the Shaping of American Consciousness* (New York, 1982).

40 Richard Johnson, review of McKendrick, Brewer and Plumb, *The Birth of a Consumer Society* in *Theory, Culture and Society*, ii (1984), 138–9. This section owes a great deal to Johnson's brief, but very perceptive comments.

41 See, for key examples, H. Marcuse, *One-Dimensional Man* (Boston, 1964) and M. Horkheimer and T. W. Adorno, *Dialectic of Enlightenment* (New York, 1972).

42 For an excellent critical discussion of many of these issues, see D. Miller, *Material Culture and Mass Consumption* (London, 1987), chs 8, 9.

43 See W. A. Cole, 'Factors in demand, 1700–1800', in R. Floud and D. McCloskey (eds), *The Economic History of Britain since 1700* (Cambridge, 1981), vol. 1, 36–65 for an overview of the debates and another reworking of the data, and J. Hoppit, 'Income, welfare and the Industrial Revolution in Britain', *Historical Journal*, xxxi, 3 (1988), 721–31 for some important critical comments.

44 E. A. Wrigley, 'Urban growth and agricultural change: England and the Continent in the early modern period', *Journal of Interdisciplinary History*, xv, 4 (1985), 695–8.

45 Weatherill, *Consumer Behaviour and Material Culture in England, 1660–1760*, ch. 2.

46 J. M. Price, 'The transatlantic economy', in J. P. Greene and J. R. Pole (eds), *Colonial British America* (Baltimore, 1984), 32.

47 See, for example, C. Husbands, 'Standards of living in north Warwickshire in the seventeenth century', *Warwickshire History*, iv, 6 (1980–1), 203–15.

48 Information on wooden furniture from Mark Overton of the University of Newcastle, based on Hertfordshire, Worcestershire, Lincolnshire and Durham inventories. For clocks see B. Trinder and J. Cox, *Yeomen and Colliers in Telford* (London, 1980), 101.

49 M. Spufford, *The Great Reclothing of Rural England* (London, 1984), 117–18.

50 Based on criminal depositions for Cumberland, Northumberland, Westmorland and Yorkshire in Public Record Office, ASSI 45/34/1 to 40/1: Northern Circuit depositions, 1780–99. For the use of 'teatime' by a York saddler's wife, see ASSI 45/36/2/63–5. In the fifty-six cases of watch theft for which depositions survive from the 1780s and 1790s in ASSI 45, more than half the owners of the stolen watches were labouring men. Also see B. Lemire, ' "A good stock of clothes": growing consumption of cotton clothing in the last half of the eighteenth century', paper presented to the Pasold Conference on the Economic and Social History of Dress, 1985.

51 I disagree with Hugh Cunningham's comments about the limited extent of children's work during the eighteenth century in 'The employment and unemployment of children in England, c. 1680–1851', *Past and Present*, cxxvi (1990), esp. 121–3. He fails to recognize that in most of the hand textile industries the labour demand for spinning was vastly greater than that for weaving, and that therefore spinning work spread geographically far beyond the core weaving districts. Arthur Young in *A Six Months Tour through the North of England* (London, 1771) gives an excellent sense of just how common textile by-employment was for poor women and children in the 1760s, at least in the north.

52 K. Snell, *Annals of the Labouring Poor* (Cambridge, 1985), ch. 2; H. Mui and L. H. Mui, *Shops and Shopkeeping in Eighteenth-Century England* (London, 1989), 42.

53 N. B. Harte, 'Protection and the English linen trade', in N. B. Harte and K. G. Ponting (eds), *Textile History and Economic History* (Manchester, 1973), 102; N. Evans, *The East Anglian Linen Industry* (Aldershot, 1985), ch. 5. This process was, of course, already well under way in the seventeenth century; see B. Jennings (ed.), *A History of Nidderdale* (Huddersfield, 1967), 171–6.

54 For a watch club near Sheffield in 1782, see Public Record Office, ASSI 45/34/3/48–50; for a Newcastle cloth club in 1788 see ASSI 45/36/2/178–81. For eighteenth-century clubs in general, see J. Brewer, 'Commercialisation and politics', in McKendrick, Brewer and Plumb, *The Birth of a Consumer Society*.

55 For gin see P. Clarke, 'The "Mother Gin" controversy in the early eighteenth century', *Transactions of the Royal Historical Society*, 5th series, xxxviii (1988), 64–5 and 72; for clothing see B. Lemire, 'Consumerism in preindustrial and early industrial England: the trade in secondhand clothes', *Journal of British Studies*, xxvii (1988), 17–18.

56 Based on advertisements describing runaways in the *Worcester Journal*, 1713–1800 and *Jackson's Oxford Journal*, 1753–1800.

57 See, for examples, the comments in 1759 of Sheffield cutlery manufacturers in the *Journal of the House of Commons*, xxviii (1757–61), 497, report from the committee hearing petitions from merchants and manufacturers of Birmingham and Sheffield, and the remarks about British goods by French consuls in the newly independent United States, quoted in P. P. Hill, *French Perceptions of the Early American Republic, 1783–1793* (Philadelphia, 1988), 49, 60.

58 Weatherill, *Consumer Behaviour and Material Culture in England, 1660–1760*, 6–7.

59 D. Defoe, *The Complete English Tradesman*, vol. 1 (London, 1745), 263, 266.

60 E. P. Thompson, 'The moral economy of the English crowd in the eighteenth century', *Past and Present*, 1 (1971); A. D. Leadley, 'Some villains of the eighteenth-century marketplace', in J. Rule (ed.), *Outside the Law: Studies in Crime and Order, 1650–1850* (Exeter, 1982); M. J. Walker, 'The extent of guild control of trades in England, c. 1660–1820: a study based on a sample of provincial towns and London Companies' (University of Cambridge, Ph.D. thesis, 1986); Mui and Mui, *Shops and Shopkeeping*, ch. 4.

61 S. Tolliday, 'Management and labour in Britain, 1896–1939', in S. Tolliday and J. Zeitlin (eds), *The Automobile Industry and its Workers: Between Fordism and Flexibility* (Cambridge, 1986), 30.

62 R. Samuel, 'Workshop of the world: steam power and hand technology in mid-Victorian Britain', *History Workshop*, iii (1977), 56–7. It is of course possible that the extremely rapid growth in the eighteenth century of a North American market that was even then more egalitarian than the British may have had important implications for eighteenth-century British product design.

63 M. Sonenscher, 'Markets, flexible specialisation and the trades of eighteenth-century Paris', paper presented to the International Working Group on Historical Alternatives to Mass Production, Lyons, 1988, 9–10.

64 McKendrick, Brewer and Plumb, *The Birth of a Consumer Society*, 13, 23, 63, 188; E. Jones, 'The fashion manipulators: consumer tastes and British industries, 1660–1800', in L. P. Cain and P. J. Uselding (eds), *Business Enterprise and Economic Change* (Ohio, 1973).

65 For the potential effectiveness of printed advertisements see J. Styles, 'Print and policing: crime advertising in eighteenth-century provincial England', in D. Hay and F. Snyder (eds), *Police and Prosecution in Britain in the Eighteenth and Nineteenth Centuries* (Oxford, 1989), esp. 71, 92, 111.

66 N. McKendrick, 'George Packwood and the commercialisation of shaving: the art of eighteenth-century advertising', in McKendrick, Brewer and Plumb, *The Birth of a Consumer Society*, esp. 182–3.

67 For these issues see, in particular, R. B. Walker, 'Advertising in London newspapers, 1650–1750', *Business History*, xv (1973), 112–30 and J. J. Looney, 'Advertising and society in England, 1720–1820: a statistical analysis of Yorkshire newspaper advertisements' (Princeton University, Ph.D. thesis, 1983), esp. ch. 6.

68 See, for examples, *The Norwich Mercury*, 27 January 1753, advertisement of John White, haberdasher of hats and hosier; *The Norwich Mercury*, 22 August 1752, advertisement of Robinson Farrow, grocer; *The Norwich Mercury*, 25 July 1752, advertisement of Chancellor and company, lacemen.

69 W. Hamish Fraser, *The Coming of the Mass Market, 1850–1914* (London, 1981), ch. 10 and Marchand, *Advertising the American Dream*, 9–10.

70 For similar phenomena in pre-revolutionary America, see T. H. Breen, '"Baubles of Britain": the American and consumer revolutions of the eighteenth century', *Past and Present*, cxix (1988) and idem, 'Empire of goods'.

71 Alfred Chandler points out that before the 1870s manufacturers in the United States generally left advertising to the wholesalers who marketed their goods. The only important exceptions were the makers of books, journals and patent medicines. A. Chandler, *The Visible Hand: The Managerial Revolution in American Business* (Cambridge, Mass., 1977), 290.

72 Mui and Mui, *Shops and Shopkeeping*, chs 1, 2, esp. 44–5.

73 N. McKendrick, 'Josiah Wedgwood and the commercialisation of the potteries', in McKendrick, Brewer and Plumb, *The Birth of a Consumer Society*; Jones, 'The fashion manipulators'; E. Robinson, 'Eighteenth-century commerce and fashion: Matthew Boulton's marketing techniques', *Economic History Review*, xvi (1963–4), 39–60.

74 S. Lambert (ed.), *Pattern and Design: Designs for the Decorative Arts, 1480–1980* (London, 1983), 24.

75 This was, of course, also true of much of Boulton and Wedgwood's marketing.

76 See, for examples, Edwards, *The Growth of the British Cotton Trade*, ch. 8; J. de L. Mann, *The Cloth Industry in the West of England from 1640–1880* (Oxford, 1971), 84–6; Rowlands, *Masters and Men*, 152–4; T. S. Ashton, *An Eighteenth-Century Industrialist: Peter Stubbs of Warrington, 1756–1806* (Manchester, 1939), ch. 5.

77 Public Record Office, C107/104: Davies letter book, undated letter (summer 1784?).

78 R. Campbell, *The London Tradesman* (London, 1747), 171.

79 Rothstein, 'The silk industry in London', *passim*.

80 S. D. Chapman and S. Chassagne, *European Textile Printers of the Eighteenth Century* (London, 1981), 78–81.

81 For example, Public Record Office, C108/101: letter books of Horner and Turner, merchants, of Leeds; letter to Mr George Darby, merchant in Naples, 30 December 1789.

82 For secrecy see Berg, *Age of Manufactures*, 296. For similar practices in the nineteenth century see Toshio Kusamitsu, '"Novelty, give us novelty", London agents and northern manufacturers', in M. Bery (ed.), *Markets and Manufacture in Early Industrial Europe* (London, 1991).

83 Referred to in Chapman and Chassagne, *European Textile Printers*, 81, from *Journal of the House of Commons*, xlii (1787), 584–5; see Public Record Office, C108/101: letter books of Horner and Turner, merchants, of Leeds for similar activities.

84 Information from Charles Saumarez Smith. See his 'Design and economy in mid-eighteenth-century England', paper presented at Oxford University, 1987, and 'Eighteenth-century man', *Designer* (March 1987), 19–21. For designers in the Spitalfields silk industry, see Rothstein, 'The silk industry in London', *passim*.

85 *Journal of the House of Commons*, xxviii (1757–61), 496–7. For a discussion of the whole issue of skill shortages and training, see Saumarez Smith, 'Eighteenth-century man'.

86 Quoted in Leona Rostenberg, *English Publishers in the Graphic Arts* (New York, 1963), 45.

87 Lambert, *Pattern and Design*, sect. 2.

88 See D. Towner, *Creamware* (London, 1978), Appendix 2; Rowlands, *Masters and Men*, 152–3; N. Goodison, 'The Victoria and Albert Museum's collection of metal-work pattern books', *Furniture History*, xi (1975), 1–30; Ashton, *An Eighteenth-Century Industrialist*, 60.

89 The law on design copyright was extremely weak at this period.

90 Quoted in Robinson, 'Eighteenth-century commerce and fashion', 49.

91 See D. Defoe, *The Complete English Tradesman*, vol. 1 (London, 1745), 19–23.

92 Elizabeth Shackleton of Alkincoats, Colne, who is discussed at length in chapter 14 of this volume. I would like to thank Amanda Vickery for this information.

93 Public Record Office, C107/104: Davies letter book, letter dated 3 February 1785.

94 Northumberland Record Office, Delaval Mss., 2/DE.11.11/72; correspondence with Broughton and Harrison, London, bottle traders, 1769–1807: Harrison to Brotherick, 1 September 1781.

95 Letter of 1807, quoted in Chapman and Chassagne, *European Textile Printers*, 84. Also see H. Clark, 'The anonymous designer', in Design Council, *Design and Industry*, 33–8 and idem, 'The design and designing of Lancashire printed calicoes during the first half of the 19th century', *Textile History*, xv (1984), 109–10.

96 A witness before a 1787 parliamentary committee claimed that the Lancashire cotton printers who copied southern firms' designs executed 'them in a much inferior style, and consequently are not at the same expense in cutting their blocks', as well as using cheap colours that ran; *Journal of the House of Commons*, xlii (1787), 584.

97 Northumberland Record Office, Delaval Mss., 2/DE.11.11/76; Correspondence with Broughton and Harrison, London, bottle traders, 1769–1807; Harrison to Brotherick, 9 October 1781.

98 Public Record Office, C107/104: Davies letter book, letter dated 26 July 1783.

99 Public Record Office, C105/15: letters received by James Hudson, linen draper, London, 1731–4; Anthony Wilson, Broughton, Cumberland to James Hudson at his warehouse in Three King Court, Lambert Street, London, 24 March 1733.

100 This calls into question the extent of the contrast identified by Craig Clunas between the 'visual' design practice of Europe and the 'verbal' design practice of China during the seventeenth and eighteenth centuries; C. Clunas, 'Design and cultural frontiers: English shapes and Chinese furniture workshops, 1700–90', *Apollo*, cxxvi (October 1987), 259.

101 Saumarez Smith, 'Design and economy in mid-eighteenth-century England' and 'Eighteenth-century man'.

102 *Gentleman's Magazine* (February 1756), quoted in Saumarez Smith, 'Design and economy'. For the Society of Arts, see D. G. C. Allen, *William Shipley: Founder of the Royal Society of Arts* (London, 1979), chs 3, 4.

103 M. Jupp, 'Economic policy and economic development', in J. Black (ed.), *Britain in the Age of Walpole* (London, 1984), 124–5.

104 J. Black, *Natural and Necessary Enemies: Anglo-French Relations in the Eighteenth Century* (London, 1986), 152.

105 Chapman and Chassagne, *European Textile Printers*, 79. Also see Clark, 'The anonymous designer' and 'Design and designing of Lancashire printed calicoes'.

106 We have here, in an incipient form, the disjuncture that dogged design education in nineteenth-century Britain between fine art sensibilities and the limited skill requirements of manufacturers producing for the middle and lower sections of the market.

Index

stockings, as populuxe goods **230**, 232–5, 238–9
Stoianovitch, Trajan 150
Stone, Lawrence 149
Story of the Stone, The 152
Stout, William 60
Stuart, Lady Louisa 49
Stukeley, William 491, 501
style, politics of 21
Styles, John 2, 7, 527–48
subcontracting system 232–3, 235, 236–42, 532
sugar: increased imports 95, 107, 115, 133, 179, **182**; mass consumption 181–3, 185, 199, 261, 270; as necessity and luxury 261–72; and slave trade 136
supply: democratization of 264; and Industrial Revolution 107, 535; labour 110–13, **111**, 114–19; and privileging of production 22–3, 85–9, 177
Susman, Warren 30–2
Sydenham, Thomas 74 n.55
Symes, Richard 491, 507

tables, inventory evidence 100, 210, **218–25**
taste: changes in 117, 275, 289–90; and character 7, 49, 52, 54, 65; and design 543–4; and garden design 441–2, 444, 452; and values 489–90
Tawney, R. H. 3, 36 n.16
taxation: effect on households 116; on imports 181, 183
Taylor, Arthur J. 272 n.3
tea: accessories 216, **230**, 277, 537; Canton system 144–6, 183; critics of 264, 266; as domestic beverage 266; growing demand for 95, 106, 115, 133–4, 141–2, 178, 179, 216, 261; mass consumption 182, 183–4, 199, 263–8, 270, 538; as necessity and luxury 69; as work beverage 265–6
tea ceremony, and conspicuous consumption 153, 154
technology, changes 101, 107, 116, 126 n.62
television, as mass medium 28
Tennent, William 255–6
textiles: and changing tastes 530–1, 540; durability 191, 200; exports to colonial America 255, 531–2; increased imports 133–4, 136–40, 146; mass production 530–1; prices 192–4, **192**; *see also* putting out system

theatre, and marketplace 27, 366, 489–90, 509–12, 513
Thirsk, Joan 1, 23–4, 112–13, 118, 126 n.64, 231
Thomas, Keith 312, 332 n.6, 359, 452
Thomlinson, John 216
Thompson, E. P. 93, 106, 127 n.81
Thrale, Hesther 228
Tilly, Louise 131 n.118
tin: increased imports 107; reduced demand for 106
tobacco: increased imports 95, 107, 178, 265; mass consumption 179–81, **180**, 199, 264, 266, 270–1, 365, 537; as necessity and luxury 69
Tories, and natural philosophy 493–4, 495, 501–8
towns *see* urbanization
trade: Asian 135–6, 183–4; colonial 86–7, in plants 450–1, 457; *see also* gardens; statistics 5, 99
tradesmen: literacy 314, 315–17, **315**, **316**; and ownership patterns 54, **200**, **201**, 210–11, 214, 216, **219**, **221**, **225**, 537; and transmission of taste 275–6
tradeswomen, and ownership patterns 211, **225**
Trotter, Thomas 60, 69
tuberculosis *see* consumption, pathological

Ukraine, book printing 6, 381–2, 384–90
umbrellas, as populuxe goods 230, **230**, 235–9
Underdown, David 349
urbanization 4, 63, 110; and conspicuous consumption 157–8; and consumption changes 209, 216, **219**, **220**; and household expenditure 198–9, 537
utensils: inventory evidence 209–10, 212, 216, **218–25**; meanings 292

values: female 294; and taste 489–90; use/symbolic 22, 25, 30
Van Bath, Slicher 97
Van Delen, Dirck 479, 481
Van der Wee, Herman 96
Van Eyck brothers 484–5
Van Reymerswael, Marinus 485
Van Roerstraten, Pieter 482
Vanderbroeke, Chris 116

Vaux-le-Vicomte gardens 441, 442, 444, 454
Veblen, Thorstein 24–5, 27, 40, 42, 44, 149, 275–6, 277–8, 442
Versailles, gardens 441, 443, 444, 454, 456–7
Vesalius, Andreas 468
Viardot, Louis 480
Vickers, Brian 48
Vickery, Amanda 5, 274–94
visualization: in Enlightenment thought 466–73; in modern world 462–6
Vovelle, Michel 151

wage rates 89–98, **90**, **92**, **94**, 106–7; and household earnings 114–15, 119–20, 538; pressure to raise 234
Walker, Adam 515
Wallerstein, Immanuel 23
Wallis, Peter 340, 341, 359
Walpole, Horace 416, 490, 498, 508
Walsh, Lorena S. 101, 189, 199, 204 n.26
Walton, Richard 359
Walzer, Michael 34, 38 n.64
Warley, Lee 208
Warwickshire, inventory evidence 190–1
Washington, George 253
waste, and wealth 58–9, 62–3, 70, 442
watches 230, **230**, 538
Watson, William 495–7, 499, 502, 505, 507, 508, 513
Wayles, John 252
wealth: circulation 58; and consumer durables 185–93, **186**, **187**, 195–9, **196**, **197**; durability 481–2; and excess 64; motivation to acquire 169; and ownership of goods 4, 100–5, 200, **200**; and savings 188, 195; and social status 211
Weatherill, Lorna 5, 54, 101, 104, 107, 206–25, 244 n.12, 276, 277, 342, 539
Weber, Max: on action 56 n.7; on capitalism 148, 158; on saving and spending 23, 26, 149, 169, 172
Webster, Daniel 327
Wedgwood, Josiah 24, 117, 514–15, 529, 542, 543, 549 n.11, 551 n.33
Wellek, Rene 48
Wesley, John 495, 504
Westbrook, Robert 31
Whigs, and natural philosophy